REFORMED
DOGMATICS

Herman Bavinck (1854–1921)
Graphite Sketch by Erik G. Lubbers

REFORMED DOGMATICS

Volume 3: Sin and Salvation in Christ

Herman Bavinck

John Bolt, General Editor
John Vriend, Translator

Baker Academic
Grand Rapids, Michigan

© 2006 by the Dutch Reformed Translation Society
P.O. Box 7083, Grand Rapids, MI 49510

Published by Baker Academic
a division of Baker Publishing Group
P.O. Box 6287, Grand Rapids, MI 49516-6287
www.bakeracademic.com

Fourth printing, November 2009

Printed in the United States of America

Library of Congress Cataloging-in-Publication Data
Bavinck, Herman, 1854–1921.
    [Gereformeerde dogmatiek. English]
    Reformed dogmatics / Herman Bavinck ; John Bolt, general editor ; John Vriend, translator.
        p.   cm.
    Contents: v. 1. Prolegomena ; v. 2. God and creation ; v. 3. Sin and salvation in Christ
    Includes bibliographical references and indexes.
    ISBN 10: 0-8010-2632-6 (cloth : v. 1)
    ISBN 978-0-8010-2632-4 (cloth : v. 1)

    ISBN 10: 0-8010-2655-5 (cloth : v. 2)
    ISBN 978-0-8010-2655-3 (cloth : v. 2)

    ISBN 10: 0-8010-2656-3 (cloth : v. 3)
    ISBN 978-0-8010-2656-0 (cloth : v. 3)
    1. Christelijke Gereformeerde Kerk (Netherlands)—Doctrines. 2. Reformed Church—Doctrines.
3. Theology, Doctrinal. I. Bolt, John, 1947– II. Vriend, John, d. 2002. III. Title.
BX9474.3.B38 2003
230′.42—dc21
        2003001037

CONTENTS

5

DUTCH REFORMED
TRANSLATION SOCIETY

"The Heritage of the Ages for Today"
P.O. Box 7083
Grand Rapids, MI 49510

BOARD OF DIRECTORS

Dr. Adriaan Neele
church history department
University of Pretoria
Pretoria, South Africa

Dr. Carl Schroeder
calling pastor for senior citizens
Central Reformed Church
Grand Rapids, Michigan

Mr. Gise Van Baren
businessman
Crete, Illinois

Mr. Henry I. Witte
president
Witte Travel
consul of the government of the
Netherlands
Grand Rapids, Michigan

PREFACE

The Dutch Reformed Translation Society (DRTS) was formed in 1994 by a group of businesspeople and professionals, pastors, and seminary professors, representing five different Reformed denominations, to sponsor the translation and facilitate the publication in English of classic Reformed theological and religious literature published in the Dutch language. It is incorporated as a nonprofit corporation in the State of Michigan and governed by a board of directors.

Believing that the Dutch Reformed tradition has many valuable works that deserve wider distribution than the limited accessibility the Dutch language allows, society members seek to spread and strengthen the Reformed faith. The first project of the DRTS is the definitive translation of Herman Bavinck's complete four-volume *Gereformeerde Dogmatiek* (*Reformed Dogmatics*). The society invites those who share its commitment to, and vision for, spreading the Reformed faith to write for additional information.

Editor's
Introduction

This is the third full volume of Herman Bavinck's *Reformed Dogmatics* prepared by the Dutch Reformed Translation Society as part of its decade-long project to publish the complete English translation from Dutch of Bavinck's classic four-volume work. Prior to the first volume, on prolegomena, published by Baker Academic in 2003[1] and the second volume in 2004,[2] two half-volume works—one on the eschatology section[3] and the other on the creation section[4]—were published. The present volume, on Christ and salvation, contains material never before available in the English language and provides additional insight into the genius of Bavinck's theology. Later in this introduction, we will briefly consider these new dimensions and their contemporary relevance, but first, a few words about the author of *Reformed Dogmatics*. Who was Herman Bavinck, and why is this work of theology so important?

Herman Bavinck's *Gereformeerde Dogmatiek*, first published one hundred years ago, represents the concluding high point of some four centuries of remarkably productive Dutch Reformed theological reflection. From Bavinck's numerous citations of key Dutch Reformed theologians such as Voetius, Moor, Vitringa, van

1. Herman Bavinck, *Reformed Dogmatics*, vol. 1, *Prolegomena*, ed. John Bolt, trans. John Vriend (Grand Rapids: Baker, 2003).

2. Herman Bavinck, *Reformed Dogmatics*, vol. 2, *God and Creation*, ed. John Bolt, trans. John Vriend (Grand Rapids: Baker, 2004).

3. Herman Bavinck, *The Last Things: Hope for This World and the Next*, ed. John Bolt, trans. John Vriend (Grand Rapids: Baker, 1996). This volume presents the second half of volume 4 of the *Gereformeerde Dogmatiek* and will be included in volume 4 of the *Reformed Dogmatics*.

4. Herman Bavinck, *In the Beginning: Foundations of Creation Theology*, ed. John Bolt, trans. John Vriend (Grand Rapids: Baker, 1999). This volume presents the second half of volume 2 of the *Gereformeerde Dogmatiek* and was included in volume 2 of the *Reformed Dogmatics*.

Mastricht, Witsius, and Walaeus (as well as the important Leiden *Synopsis purioris theologiae*),[5] it is clear he knew that tradition well and claimed it as his own. At the same time, it also must be noted that Bavinck was not simply a chronicler of his own church's past teaching. He seriously engaged other theological traditions, notably the Roman Catholic and the modern liberal Protestant, effectively mined the church fathers and great medieval thinkers, and placed his own distinct neo-Calvinist stamp on the *Reformed Dogmatics*.

KAMPEN AND LEIDEN

To understand the distinct Bavinck flavor, a brief historical orientation is necessary. Herman Bavinck was born on December 13, 1854. His father was an influential minister in the Dutch Christian Reformed Church (Christelijke Gereformeerde Kerk), which had seceded from the National Reformed Church in the Netherlands twenty years earlier.[6] The secession of 1834 was, in the first place, a protest against the state control of the Dutch Reformed Church; it also tapped into a long and rich tradition of ecclesiastical dissent on matters of doctrine, liturgy, and spirituality as well as polity. In particular, mention needs to be made here of the Dutch equivalent to English Puritanism, the so-called Second Reformation (*Nadere Reformatie*),[7] the influential seventeenth- and early-eighteenth-century movement of experiential Reformed theology and spirituality,[8] as well as an early-nineteenth-century international, aristocratic, evangelical revival movement known as the *Réveil*.[9] Bavinck's church, his family, and his own spirituality were thus definitively shaped by strong patterns of deep pietistic Reformed spirituality. It is also important to note that though the earlier phases of Dutch pietism affirmed orthodox Reformed theology and were also nonseparatist in

5. The Leiden *Synopsis*, first published in 1625, is a large manual of Reformed doctrine as it was defined by the Synod of Dort. Well into the twentieth century it served as a standard reference textbook for the study of Reformed theology. (It is even cited by Karl Barth in his *Church Dogmatics*.) As an original-source reference work of classic Dutch Reformed theology, it is comparable to Heinrich Heppe's nineteenth-century, more broadly Continental anthology *Reformed Dogmatics: Set Out and Illustrated from the Sources*, rev. and ed. Ernst Bizer, trans. G. T. Thomson (London: Allen & Unwin, 1950; reprinted, Grand Rapids: Baker, 1978). While serving as the minister of a Christian Reformed church in Franeker, Friesland, Bavinck edited the sixth and final edition of this handbook, which was published in 1881.

6. For a brief description of the background and character of the Secession church, see James D. Bratt, *Dutch Calvinism in Modern America* (Grand Rapids: Eerdmans, 1984), ch. 1: "Secession and Its Tangents."

7. See Joel R. Beeke, "The Dutch Second Reformation (*Nadere Reformatie*)," *Calvin Theological Journal* 28 (1993): 298–327.

8. The crowning theological achievement of the *Nadere Reformatie* is the devout and theologically rich work of Wilhelmus à Brakel, *Redelijke Godsdienst*, first published in 1700 and frequently thereafter (including twenty Dutch editions in the eighteenth century alone!). This work is now available in English translation (ET): *The Christian's Reasonable Service*, trans. Bartel Elshout, 4 vols. (Ligonier, PA: Soli Deo Gloria, 1992–95).

9. The standard work on the *Réveil* is M. Elisabeth Kluit, *Het Protestantse Réveil in Nederland en Daarbuiten, 1815–1865* (Amsterdam: Paris, 1970). Bratt also gives a brief summary in *Dutch Calvinism in Modern America*, 10–13.

their ecclesiology, by the mid–nineteenth century the Seceder group had become significantly separatist and sectarian in outlook.[10]

The second major influence on Bavinck's thought comes from the period of his theological training at the University of Leiden. The Christian Reformed Church had its own theological seminary, the Kampen Theological School, established in 1854. Bavinck, after studying at Kampen for one year (1873–74), indicated his desire to study with the University of Leiden's theological faculty, a faculty renowned for its aggressively modernist, "scientific" approach to theology.[11] His church community, including his parents, was stunned by this decision, which Bavinck explained as a desire "to become acquainted with modern theology first-hand" and to receive "a more scientific training than the Theological School is presently able to provide."[12] The Leiden experience gave rise to what Bavinck per-ceived as the tension in his life between his commitment to orthodox theology and spirituality and his desire to understand and appreciate what he could about the modern world, including its worldview and culture. A telling and poignant entry in his personal journal at the beginning of his study period at Leiden (September 23, 1874) indicates his concern about being faithful to the faith he had publicly professed in the Christian Reformed church of Zwolle in March of that same year: "Will I remain standing [in the faith]? God grant it."[13] Upon completion of his doctoral work at Leiden in 1880, Bavinck candidly acknowledged the spiritual impoverishment that Leiden had cost him: "Leiden has benefited me in many ways: I hope always to acknowledge that gratefully. But it has also greatly impoverished me, robbed me, not only of much ballast (for which I am happy), but also of much that I recently, especially when I preach, recognize as vital for my own spiritual life."[14]

It is thus not unfair to characterize Bavinck as a man between two worlds. One of his contemporaries once described Bavinck as "a Secession preacher and a representative of modern culture," concluding: "That was a striking characteristic.

10. Bavinck himself called attention to this in his Kampen rectoral oration of 1888, when he complained that the Seceder emigration to America was a spiritual withdrawal and abandonment of "the Fatherland as lost to unbelief" ("The Catholicity of Christianity and the Church," trans. John Bolt, *Calvin Theological Journal* 27 [1992]: 246). Recent historical scholarship, however, suggests that this note of separatism and cultural alienation must not be exaggerated. Though clearly a marginalized community in the Netherlands, the Seceders were not indifferent to educational, social, and political responsibilities. See John Bolt, "Nineteenth- and Twentieth-Century Dutch Reformed Church and Theology: A Review Article," *Calvin Theological Journal* 28 (1993): 434–42.

11. For an overview of the major schools of Dutch Reformed theology in the nineteenth century, see James Hutton MacKay, *Religious Thought in Holland during the Nineteenth Century* (London: Hodder & Stoughton, 1911). For more detailed discussion of the "modernist" school, see K. H. Roessingh, *De Moderne Theologie in Nederland: Hare Voorbereiding en Eerste Periode* (Groningen: Van der Kamp, 1915); Eldred C. Vanderlaan, *Protestant Modernism in Holland* (London and New York: Oxford University Press, 1924).

12. R. H. Bremmer, *Herman Bavinck en Zijn Tijdgenoten* (Kampen: Kok, 1966), 20; cf. V. Hepp, *Dr. Herman Bavinck* (Amsterdam: W. Ten Have, 1921), 30.

13. Bremmer, *Herman Bavinck en Zijn Tijdgenoten,* 19.

14. Hepp, *Dr. Herman Bavinck,* 84.

In that duality is found Bavinck's significance. That duality is also a reflection of the tension—at times crisis—in Bavinck's life. In many respects it is a simple matter to be a preacher in the Secession Church, and, in a certain sense, it is also not that difficult to be a modern person. But in no way is it a simple matter to be the one as well as the other."[15] However, it is not necessary to rely only on the testimony of others. Bavinck summarizes this tension in his own thought clearly in an essay on the great nineteenth-century liberal Protestant theologian Albrecht Ritschl:

> Therefore, whereas salvation in Christ was formerly considered primarily a means to separate man from sin and the world, to prepare him for heavenly blessedness and to cause him to enjoy undisturbed fellowship with God there, Ritschl posits the very opposite relationship: the purpose of salvation is precisely to enable a person, once he is freed from the oppressive feeling of sin and lives in the awareness of being a child of God, to exercise his earthly vocation and fulfill his moral purpose in this world. The antithesis, therefore, is fairly sharp: on the one side, a Christian life that considers the highest goal, now and hereafter, to be the contemplation of God and fellowship with him, and for that reason (always being more or less hostile to the riches of an earthly life) is in danger of falling into monasticism and asceticism, pietism and mysticism; but on the side of Ritschl, a Christian life that considers its highest goal to be the kingdom of God, that is, the moral obligation of mankind, and for that reason (always being more or less adverse to the withdrawal into solitude and quiet communion with God), is in danger of degenerating into a cold Pelagianism and an unfeeling moralism. *Personally, I do not yet see any way of combining the two points of view, but I do know that there is much that is excellent in both, and that both contain undeniable truth.*[16]

A certain tension in Bavinck's thought between the claims of modernity, particularly its this-worldly, scientific orientation, and Reformed pietist orthodoxy's tendency to stand aloof from modern culture, continues to play a role even in his mature theology expressed in the *Reformed Dogmatics*. In his eschatology Bavinck in a highly nuanced way still continues to speak favorably of certain emphases in a Ritschlian this-worldly perspective.[17]

15. Cited by Jan Veenhof, *Revelatie en Inspiratie* (Amsterdam: Buijten & Schipperheijn, 1968), 108. The contemporary cited is the Reformed jurist A. Anema, who was a colleague of Bavinck at the Free University of Amsterdam. A similar assessment of Bavinck as a man between two poles is given by F. H. von Meyenfeldt, "Prof. Dr. Herman Bavinck: 1854–1954, 'Christus en de Cultuur,'" *Polemios* 9 (October 15, 1954); and G. W. Brillenburg-Wurth, "Bavincks Levenstrijd," *Gereformeerde Weekblad* 10.25 (December 17, 1954).

16. Herman Bavinck, "De Theologie van Albrecht Ritschl," *Theologische Studiën* 6 (1888): 397; cited by Veenhof, *Revelatie en Inspiratie*, 346–47, emphasis added by Veenhof. Kenneth Kirk contends that this tension, which he characterizes as one between "rigorism" and "humanism," is a fundamental conflict in the history of Christian ethics from the outset. See K. Kirk, *The Vision of God* (London: Longmans, Green, 1931), 7–8.

17. Bavinck, *Last Things*, 161 (= *Reformed Dogmatics*, IV, #578). According to Bavinck, Ritschl's this-worldliness "stands for an important truth" over against what he calls the "abstract supernaturalism of the Greek Orthodox and Roman Catholic Church."

In the section on the doctrine of creation (see *Reformed Dogmatics,* II, chs. 8–14), we see this tension repeatedly in Bavinck's relentless efforts to understand and, where he finds appropriate, to either affirm, correct, or repudiate modern scientific claims in light of scriptural and Christian teaching.[18] Bavinck takes modern philosophy (Kant, Schelling, Hegel), Darwin, and the claims of geological and biological science seriously but never uncritically. His willingness as a theologian to engage modern thought and science seriously is a hallmark of his exemplary work. It goes without saying that though Bavinck's theological framework remains a valuable guide for contemporary readers, many of the specific scientific issues he addresses in this volume are dated by his own late-nineteenth-century context. As Bavinck's own work illustrates so well, today's Reformed theologians and scientists learn from his example not by repristination but by fresh address to new and contemporary challenges.

GRACE AND NATURE

It is therefore too simple merely to characterize Bavinck as a man trapped between two apparently incommensurate tugs at his soul, that of other-worldly pietism and this-worldly modernism. His heart and mind sought a trinitarian synthesis of Christianity and culture, a Christian worldview that incorporated what was best and true in both pietism and modernism, while above all honoring the theological and confessional richness of the Reformed tradition dating from Calvin. After commenting on the breakdown of the great medieval synthesis and the need for contemporary Christians to acquiesce in that breakdown, Bavinck expressed his hope for a new and better synthesis: "In this situation, the hope is not unfounded that a synthesis is possible between Christianity and culture, however antagonistic they may presently stand over against each other. If God has truly come to us in Christ, and is, in this age too, the Preserver and Ruler of all things, such a synthesis is not only possible but also necessary and shall surely be effected in its own time."[19] Bavinck found the vehicle for such an attempted synthesis in the trinitarian worldview of Dutch neo-Calvinism and became, along with neo-Calvinism's visionary pioneer Abraham Kuyper,[20] one of its chief and most respected spokesmen as well as its premier theologian.

Unlike Bavinck, Abraham Kuyper grew up in the National Reformed Church of the Netherlands in a congenially moderate-modernist context. Kuyper's student years, also at Leiden, confirmed him in his modernist orientation until a series of experiences, especially during his years as a parish minister, brought about a

---

18. Bavinck, *In the Beginning,* passim (= *Reformed Dogmatics,* II, 407–619 [##250–306]). See "Editor's Introduction," in Bavinck, *Reformed Dogmatics,* II, 19–21.

19. Herman Bavinck, *Het Christendom,* Groote Godsdiensten 2.7 (Baarn: Hollandia, 1912), 60.

20. For a brief overview, see J. Bratt, *Dutch Calvinism in Modern America,* ch. 2: "Abraham Kuyper and Neo-Calvinism."

dramatic conversion to Reformed, Calvinist orthodoxy.[21] From that time Kuyper became a vigorous opponent of the modern spirit in church and society[22]—which he characterized by the siren call of the French Revolution, "Ni Dieu! Ni maître!"[23]—seeking every avenue to oppose it with an alternative worldview, or as he called it, the "life-system" of Calvinism:

> From the first, therefore, I have always said to myself, "If the battle is to be fought with honor and with a hope of victory, then principle must be arrayed against principle; then it must be felt that in Modernism the vast energy of an all-embracing life-system assails us, then also it must be understood that we have to take our stand in a life-system of equally comprehensive and far-reaching power.... When thus taken, I found and confessed and I still hold, that this manifestation of the Christian principle is given us in Calvinism. In Calvinism my heart has found rest. From Calvinism have I drawn the inspiration firmly and resolutely to take my stand in the thick of this great conflict of principles."[24]

Kuyper's aggressive, this-worldly form of Calvinism was rooted in a trinitarian theological vision. The "dominating principle" of Calvinism, he contended, "was not soteriologically, justification by faith, but in the widest sense cosmologically, the Sovereignty of the Triune God over the whole Cosmos, in all its spheres and kingdoms, visible and invisible."[25]

For Kuyper, this fundamental principle of divine sovereignty led to four important derivatory and related doctrines or principles: common grace, antithesis, sphere sovereignty, and the distinction between the church as institute and the church as organism. The doctrine of common grace[26] is based on the conviction that prior to

21. Kuyper chronicles these experiences in a revealing autobiographical work titled *Confidentie* (Amsterdam: Höveker, 1873). A rich portrait of the young Abraham Kuyper is given by G. Puchinger, *Abraham Kuyper: De Jonge Kuyper (1837–1867)* (Franeker: T. Wever, 1987). See also the somewhat hagiographic biography by Frank Vandenberg, *Abraham Kuyper* (Grand Rapids: Eerdmans, 1960); and the more theologically and historically substantive one by Louis Praamsma, *Let Christ Be King: Reflection on the Times and Life of Abraham Kuyper* (Jordan Station, ON: Paideia, 1985). Brief accounts can also be found in Benjamin B. Warfield's introduction to Abraham Kuyper, *Encyclopedia of Sacred Theology: Its Principles,* trans. J. H. De Vries (New York: Charles Scribner's, 1898); and in the translator's biographical note in Abraham Kuyper, *To Be Near to God,* trans. J. H. De Vries (Grand Rapids: Eerdmans, 1925).

22. See especially his famous address *Het Modernisme, een Fata Morgana op Christelijke Gebied* (Amsterdam: De Hoogh, 1871). On page 52 of this work he acknowledges that he, too, once dreamed the dreams of modernism. This important essay is now available in J. Bratt, ed., *Abraham Kuyper: A Centennial Reader* (Grand Rapids: Eerdmans, 1998), 87–124.

23. Abraham Kuyper, *Lectures on Calvinism* (Grand Rapids: Eerdmans, 1931), 10.

24. Ibid., 11–12.

25. Ibid., 79.

26. Kuyper's own position is developed in his *De Gemeene Gratie,* 3 vols. (Amsterdam and Pretoria: Höveker & Wormser, 1902). A thorough examination of Kuyper's views can be found in S. U. Zuidema, "Common Grace and Christian Action in Abraham Kuyper," in *Communication and Confrontation* (Toronto: Wedge, 1971), 52–105. Cf. J. Ridderbos, *De Theologische Cultuurbeschouwing van Abraham Kuyper* (Kampen: Kok, 1947). The doctrine of common grace has been much debated among conservative Dutch Reformed folk in the Netherlands

and, to a certain extent, independent of the particular sovereignty of divine grace in redemption, there is a universal divine sovereignty in creation and providence, restraining the effects of sin and bestowing general gifts on all people, thus making human society and culture possible even among the unredeemed. Cultural life is rooted in creation and common grace and thus has a life of its own apart from the church.

This same insight is expressed more directly via the notion of sphere sovereignty. Kuyper was opposed to all Anabaptist and ascetic Christian versions of world flight but was also equally opposed to the medieval Roman Catholic synthesis of culture and church. The various spheres of human activity—family, education, business, science, art—do not derive their raison d'être and the shape of their life from redemption or from the church, but from the law of God the Creator. They are thus relatively autonomous—also from the interference of the state—and are directly responsible to God.[27] In this regard Kuyper clearly distinguished two different understandings of the church—the church as institute gathered around the Word and sacraments and the church as organism diversely spread out in the manifold vocations of life. It is not explicitly as members of the institutional church but as members of the body of Christ, organized in Christian communal activity (schools, political parties, labor unions, institutions of mercy) that believers live out their earthly vocations. Though aggressively this-worldly, Kuyper was an avowed and articulate opponent of the *volkskerk* tradition, which tended to merge national sociocultural identity with that of a theocratic church ideal.[28]

To state this differently: Kuyper's emphasis on common grace, used polemically to motivate pious, orthodox Dutch Reformed Christians to Christian social, political, and cultural activity, must never be seen in isolation from his equally strong emphasis on the spiritual antithesis. The regenerating work of the Holy Spirit breaks humanity in two and creates, according to Kuyper, "two kinds of consciousness, that of the regenerate and the unregenerate; and these two cannot be identical." Furthermore, these "two kinds of people" will develop "two kinds of science." The conflict in the scientific enterprise is not between science and faith but between "two scientific systems . . . each having its own faith."[29]

It is here in this trinitarian, world-affirming, but nonetheless resolutely antithetical Calvinism that Bavinck found the resources to bring some unity to his

---

and the United States, tragically leading to church divisions. For an overview of the doctrine in the Reformed tradition, see H. Kuiper, *Calvin on Common Grace* (Goes: Oostebaan & Le Cointre, 1928).

27. "In this independent character a special *higher authority* is of necessity involved and this highest authority we intentionally call *sovereignty in the individual social sphere,* in order that it may be sharply and decidedly expressed that these different developments of social life have *nothing above themselves but God,* and that the state cannot intrude here, and has nothing to command in their domain" (*Lectures on Calvinism,* 91).

28. On Kuyper's ecclesiology, see H. Zwaanstra, "Abraham Kuyper's Conception of the Church," *Calvin Theological Journal* 9 (1974): 149–81; on his attitude toward the *volkskerk* tradition, see H. J. Langman, *Kuyper en de Volkskerk* (Kampen: Kok, 1950).

29. Kuyper, *Lectures on Calvinism,* 133; cf. *Encyclopedia of Sacred Theology,* 150–82. A helpful discussion of Kuyper's view of science is given by Del Ratzsch, "Abraham Kuyper's Philosophy of Science," *Calvin Theological Journal* 27 (1992): 277–303.

thought.[30] "The thoughtful person," he notes, "places the doctrine of the trinity in the very center of the full-orbed life of nature and mankind. . . . The mind of the Christian is not satisfied until every form of existence has been referred to the triune God and until the confession of the trinity has received the place of prominence in our thought and life."[31] Repeatedly in his writings Bavinck defines the essence of the Christian religion in a trinitarian, creation-affirming way. A typical formulation: "The essence of the Christian religion consists in this, that the creation of the Father, devastated by sin, is restored in the death of the Son of God, and re-created by the Holy Spirit into a kingdom of God."[32] Put more simply, the fundamental theme that shapes Bavinck's entire theology is the trinitarian idea that grace restores nature.[33]

The evidence for "grace restores nature" being the fundamental defining and shaping theme of Bavinck's theology is not hard to find. In an important address on common grace given in 1888 at the Kampen Theological School, Bavinck sought to impress on his Christian Reformed audience the importance of Christian sociocultural activity. He appealed to the doctrine of creation, insisting that its diversity is not removed by redemption but cleansed. "Grace does not remain outside or above or beside nature but rather permeates and wholly renews it. And thus nature, reborn by grace, will be brought to its highest revelation. That situation will again return in which we serve God freely and happily, without compulsion or fear, simply out of love, and in harmony with our true nature. That is the genuine religio naturalis." In other words: "Christianity does not introduce a single substantial foreign element into the creation. It creates no new cosmos but rather makes the cosmos new. It restores what was corrupted by sin. It atones the guilty and cures what is sick; the wounded it heals."[34]

CHRIST'S WORK OF SALVATION AS HUMAN RESTORATION

In the creation section of volume 2 (chs. 8–14), we see how Bavinck's doctrine of creation serves as a key starting place for his theology.[35] It does this because Bavinck is convinced that the doctrine of creation is the starting point

30. The relation between Bavinck and Kuyper, including differences as well as commonalities, is discussed in greater detail in John Bolt, "The Imitation of Christ Theme in the Cultural-Ethical Ideal of Herman Bavinck" (Ph.D. diss., University of St. Michael's College, Toronto, ON, 1982), especially ch. 3: "Herman Bavinck as a Neo-Calvinist Thinker."

31. Herman Bavinck, *The Doctrine of God,* trans. W. Hendriksen (Grand Rapids: Eerdmans, 1951), 329 (= *Reformed Dogmatics,* II, 329–34 [#231]).

32. Bavinck, *Reformed Dogmatics,* I, 112 (#35).

33. This is the conclusion of Veenhof, *Revelatie en Inspiratie,* 346; and Eugene Heideman, *The Relation of Revelation and Reason in E. Brunner and H. Bavinck* (Assen: Van Gorcum, 1959), 191, 195. See Bavinck, *Last Things,* 200n4 (= *Reformed Dogmatics,* IV, #572).

34. Herman Bavinck, "Common Grace," trans. Raymond Van Leeuwen, *Calvin Theological Journal* 24 (1989): 59–60, 61.

35. See "Editor's Introduction," in Bavinck, *Reformed Dogmatics,* II, 19–21.

and distinguishing characteristic of true religion. Creation is the formulation of human dependence on a God who is distinct from the creature but who nonetheless in a loving, fatherly way preserves it. Creation is a distinct emphasis of the Reformed tradition according to Bavinck, a way of affirming that God's will is its origin and God's glory its goal. Creation thus is the presupposition of all religion and morality, especially Christian teaching about the image of God in all human beings.

Yet, of course, the full truth of the Christian religion cannot be known through creation. A special revelation of God's grace is essential for knowing what our dilemma is and what our misery consists of as human beings (our sin), and how we are to be delivered from it (salvation). So then, one would expect, the two topics of this volume—sin, and salvation in Christ—should be a matter of strictly biblical theology, a matter of listening carefully to the key themes of the revealed word of God in Holy Scripture alone. Indeed, Bavinck reveals himself to be a careful student of Holy Scripture, one whose very thought patterns are shaped by those of the Bible. However, as he often does, Bavinck surprises us with the wide range of his knowledge by framing even the particular, redemptive work of Christ within the framework of the triune God's purposes in creation. In addition to Scripture, the results of cultural anthropology and especially the new science of religious psychology enter into his discussion.

The particular redemptive work of Christ, so Bavinck insists, must be related to general, universal human need and experience, and all of this seen in the larger perspective of God's creation covenant with humanity. After dealing with the universal reality of sin and misery in biblical perspective (chs. 1–4), Bavinck reiterates this anthropological truth at the beginning of his chapter on the covenant of grace (ch. 5). It is, he says, the awful and universal fact of misery that evokes among all people a sense that they need deliverance from sin. God's covenant with Israel is a new beginning and a pure gift of grace. However, the covenant idea is also found among other peoples of the ancient world, and the scriptural language "borrows" from its surroundings, though its content is uniquely gracious. The historical covenant of grace is, nonetheless, rooted in the prior and eternal counsel of peace, the mutual undertaking of the one triune God, Father, Son, and Holy Spirit. Not only does this comfort believers that their salvation is rooted in God's eternal purpose, but it also ties God's redemptive work in Christ to the original good creation and consummated new creation. God's purpose is one and it is universal, directed not to every single individual person but to the whole human race. Finally, in this regard, Bavinck also points out that the application of Christ's work by the Holy Spirit does not abolish human willing and acting but allows them to come fully into their own. Christ sends his Spirit to instruct and enable his own so that they consciously and voluntarily consent to the covenant. God himself supplies what he demands, yet in the covenant of grace God's honor is not at the expense of but for the benefit of human persons by renewing the whole person and restoring personal freedom and dignity.

The person of Christ the mediator (ch. 6), too, is not to be understood apart from the universally expressed need and desire for a mediator found in all religions. The ideas of incarnation and apotheosis occur in virtually all religions, a fact that has led many to conclude erroneously that Israel's messianic expectation is simply borrowed from its neighbors. But Christ is not merely an instance of a genotype; he is known only through mediated special revelation. Jesus is not an idea; he is the unique Son of God who became flesh and dwelt among us. The incarnation of Christ is related to creation; the very possibility of incarnation is built into creation. Adam was a type of Christ; the world was so created that when it fell, it could again be restored. The history of redemption is lengthy and progressive; here, too, God honors humanity's condition. Over against all forms of Gnosticism and Apollinarianism, the church steadfastly maintained the full humanity of Christ. "What is not assumed is not saved."

Similarly, as we move into the work of Christ in his humiliation (ch. 7), Bavinck begins by calling attention to the virtually universal practice of sacrifice in all religions as well as some sort of priestly mediation to perform the sacrifices. What is distinctive about the atoning death of Christ is that he is both priest and sacrifice, the one who mediates by himself, making full atonement. Only a doctrine of full vicarious sacrifice does justice to the truly human nature of Jesus and to genuine human responsibility and culpability. This volume concludes (in ch. 9, #427a) with what may be one of the most remarkable sections in all four volumes of the *Reformed Dogmatics*, an appreciative extended discussion of the new (for Bavinck's time) field of study, the psychology of religion. Bavinck insists that religious experience cannot serve as the foundation for faith or for theology but that, nonetheless, no serious theological study can do without such reflection.

In all this, notably in his appreciation and critique of the psychology of religion studies, Bavinck shows himself to be a biblical and confessional theologian—faithful, pastorally sensitive, challenging, and at the same time open to the modern world and its challenges. It is for this reason that the *Reformed Dogmatics* remains relevant today. Bavinck's life and thought reflect a serious effort to be pious, orthodox, and thoroughly contemporary. To pietists fearful of the modern world, on the one hand, and to critics of orthodoxy skeptical about its continuing relevance, on the other, Bavinck's example suggests a model answer: an engaging trinitarian vision of Christian discipleship in God's world.

In conclusion, a few words about the editing decisions that govern this translated volume, which is based on the second, expanded edition of the *Gereformeerde Dogmatiek*.[36] The nine chapters of this volume correspond exactly to those of the

36. The four volumes of the first edition of *Gereformeerde Dogmatiek* were published in the years 1895 through 1901. The second revised and expanded edition appeared between 1906 and 1911; the third edition, unaltered from the second, in 1918; the fourth, unaltered except for different pagination, in 1928.

original, even though their length is daunting. All attempts to divide the material in a different way seemed artificial and arbitrary. Whereas the original consisted of three main parts ("The Fallen World," "The Person and Work of Christ," and "The Benefits of the Covenant"), we chose to divide the second major section into its two constitutive parts ("Christ the Redeemer" and "The Work of Christ") and added a fourth part ("Salvation in Christ"). In this way, the strong christological concentration of this volume becomes more clear. Strictly speaking, the soteriological (and thus pneumatological) material that begins in chapter 9 continues into the fourth volume. In addition, all subdivisions and headings are new. The latter, along with the chapter synopses, which are also not in the original, have been supplied by the editor. Bavinck's original footnotes have all been retained and brought up to contemporary bibliographic standards. Additional notes added by the editor are clearly marked. Works from the nineteenth century to the present are noted, usually with full bibliographic information given on first occurrence in each chapter and with subsequent references abbreviated. Classic works produced prior to the nineteenth century (the church fathers, Aquinas's *Summa*, Calvin's *Institutes,* post-Reformation Protestant and Catholic works), for which there are often numerous editions, are cited only by author, title, and standard notation of sections. More complete information for the originals, or accessible editions, is given in the bibliography appearing at the end of this volume. Where English translations (ET) of foreign titles were available and could be consulted, they have been used rather than the originals. Unless indicated in the note by direct reference to a specific translation, renderings of Latin, Greek, German, and French material are those of the translator, working from Bavinck's original text. References in the notes and bibliography that are incomplete or could not be confirmed are marked with an asterisk (*). To facilitate comparison with the Dutch original, this English edition retains the subparagraph numbers (##307–432 in square brackets in the text) used in the second and subsequent Dutch editions. Cross references to volumes 1–3 of *Gereformeerde Dogmatiek* cite the page numbers of the already-released volumes of *Reformed Dogmatics*. Subparagraph numbers (marked with #) accompany these references to facilitate cross-reference to the Dutch editions. Cross references to volume 4 of *Gereformeerde Dogmatiek* cite only the subparagraph number (marked with #).

A word is also in order here about the Scripture references. Since the verse numbering in the Dutch Authorized Version (*Statenvertaling*) differs from that of modern English versions, the original references were adjusted for contemporary English Bible readers. In the course of checking and adjusting these references, it was discovered that many of Bavinck's "proof texts" do not transparently provide proof for the claim being made. The recognition that Bavinck may have had reasons unknown to us for citing a particular passage and the desire to preserve the integrity of the original work led to the conservative editorial strategy of leaving passages unaltered unless they were very clearly in error. Some references were correctible (e.g., verses in an adjoining passage were determined to be the ones intended, or digits had obviously been inadvertently transposed); a very few were deleted.

The editor here gratefully acknowledges the assistance of Calvin Theological Seminary students Courtney Hoekstra and Joel Vande Werken, who did an enormous amount of legwork in tracking down bibliographic items and helping with the footnotes and bibliography.

PART I

THE FALLEN WORLD

1

THE ORIGIN OF SIN

The fallen world in which we live rests on the foundations of a creation that was good. Yet, it had scarcely been created before sin crept into it. The origin of sin is a mystery; it is not from God, and at the same time it is not excluded from his counsel. God decided to take humanity on the perilous path of covenantal freedom rather than elevating it by a single act of power over the possibility of sin and death.

Genesis 2:9 speaks of two trees, the tree of life and the tree of the knowledge of good and evil. Both are integral to the Genesis narrative, and attempts to discount one or the other destroy narrative meaning. Similarly, efforts to explain the meaning of either of the trees in terms of progress and development (tree of life as awakening of sexuality) ignore the plain reading of prohibition and punishment associated with eating the trees' fruit. No, the story is a unity, and it is about the fall of humanity and the origin of sin. Genesis 3 is not a step of human progress but a fall.

This fall, however, is not simply human effort to achieve cultural power as a means of becoming independent from God. The Bible does not portray human cultural formation as an evil in itself so that rural simplicity is preferable to a world-dominating culture. The point of the "fall" narrative in Genesis is to point to the human desire for autonomy from God. To "know good and evil" is to become the determiner of good and evil; it is to decide for oneself what is right and wrong and not submit to any external law. In short, to seek the knowledge of good and evil is to desire emancipation from God; it is to want to be "like God."

The entry into sin comes by way of the serpent's lie. The serpent's speaking has often been mistakenly considered an allegory for lust, sexual desire, or errant reason. The various mythical interpretations and even attempts to explain the narrative in terms of animal capacity for speech before the fall all fail to meet the intent of the passage and the teaching of Scripture as a whole. The only appropriate explanation is to recognize, with ancient exegesis, the entrance of a spiritual superterrestrial power. The rest of the Bible, however, is relatively silent about this, though its entire narrative rests on this spiritual conflict between the two kingdoms. Sin did not start on earth but in heaven with a revolt of spiritual

25

beings. In the case of humanity, the temptation by Satan resulted in the fall. Scripture looks for the origin of sin solely in the will of rational creatures.

The Christian church has always insisted on the historical character of the fall. In our day this is challenged by historical criticism as well as evolutionary dogma. Those who would challenge this notion attempt instead to accommodate it by demonstrating the reality of the fall from experience, thus validating Genesis 3 as a description of reality rather than as history. This rests on a misunderstanding; it ignores the fact that we need the testimony of Scripture in order to "read" our experience aright. Neither the Genesis account nor its historical character can be dispensed with. In fact, objections to the reality of the fall are themselves increasingly under review by more recent trends in the biblical and archeological/ anthropological sciences. The Genesis account, especially of the unity of the human race, speaks positively to our conscience and our experience.

Though no true parallel to the biblical account has been found, it is clear from the myths of other ancients that underlying the religious and moral convictions of the human race are common beliefs in the divine origin and destiny of humanity, in a golden age and decline, in the conflict of good and evil, and in the wrath and appeasement of the deity. The origin and essence of sin, however, remain unknown to them. The origin of sin is sometimes found in the essence of things, its existence even denied by moralists and rationalists, treated as illusion or desire as in Buddhism, or dualistically traced to an ultimately evil power. Philosophers have treated sin as hubris that can be overcome by human will, as ignorance to be overcome by education in virtue, or even as a fall of preexistent souls. However, outside of special revelation sin is either treated deistically in terms of human will alone or derived pantheistically from the very necessary nature of things.

Both views also found their way into Christianity. The British monk Pelagius rejected all notions of original sin and considered every person as having Adam's full moral choice of will. The fall did not happen at the beginning but is repeated in every human sin. Though the church rejected Pelagianism in its extreme form, Roman Catholicism maintained the notion of a less than completely fallen will, limiting the fall to the loss of the donum superadditum, *which can only be restored by sacramental grace.*

When the Reformation rejected Roman Catholic dualism, streams within Protestantism, notable rationalist groups such as the Socinians as well as the Remonstrants robbed Christianity of its absolute character by dispensing with the need for grace in some measure. The image of God is regarded as the fully free will, which, like that of the pre-fall Adam, remains intact. While we are born with an inclination to sin, this inclination is not itself culpable; atonement is needed only for actual sin. Suffering is not necessarily linked to sin; it is simply part of our human condition.

Interesting attempts have been made to reconcile Pelagius with Augustine. Ritschl agrees with Pelagius that the human will and actual sin precede the sinful state or condition. But he also then insists that these singular sinful acts mutually reinforce each other and create a collective realm of sin that exerts influence on us, a reinforcing reciprocity that enslaves all people. Others combine Ritschl's approach with evolutionary theory. When this is envisioned in strictly materialistic and mechanistic terms, all notions of good and evil, the possibility of a moral life, vanish behind physical and chemical processes. A more acceptable route is to see the evolution of moral life as one in which human beings rise above their primitive animal nature as they become more humanized, more civilized. From this evolutionary viewpoint, sin is the survival of or misuse of habits and tendencies left over from our animal ancestry, from earlier stages of development, and their sinfulness lies in their anachronism. The remaining animal nature is shared by all people; sin is universal, but so is moral responsibility and guilt.

This attempt to reconcile Augustine and Pelagius fails at several levels. Apart from the lack of proof for materialistic evolution, the major obstacle is explaining the origin of a free human will in the evolutionary process. To think of the will as somehow outside of human nature and unrelated to it is psychologically inconceivable. In fact, moral freedom not only becomes precarious, moral improvement becomes virtually impossible. Sin's power increases, and explanations for its origin flounder. Thinkers move from attributing it to human nature to cosmic explanations—all matter is evil. From there it was an easy step to locate evil in a tension of potencies within God himself as in the theosophical tradition of Böhme and Schelling. Hegel even considered the fall as the Ur-fact of history when the Absolute realized itself in the world as its own alternative existence. From here it is a small step to Buddhism, which considers existence itself as the greatest sin.

The question of sin's origin, like the question of existence itself, is an enigma. The philosophical tradition provides evidence for the scriptural teaching that this world is inexplicable without a fall but provides no satisfactory explanation. Sin cannot be inferred from the sensual nature of humanity since the "spiritual" sins of those who are older are often more appalling than the "fleshly" sins of youth. Asceticism does not solve the problem of sin; monks take sin with them into the cloister in their hearts. Appealing to the Pauline understanding of "flesh" to defend this view fails. "Flesh" is a sinful direction of the heart in opposition to the Holy Spirit and is not a contrast between material and immaterial or spiritual. From attributing sin to human nature it is a natural move to attribute it to the Creator. Consistent with our experience of life's contradictions, sin is the necessary obstacle to our moral development and perfection. Sin is God's own will; it is his design for creation. While there is a semblance of truth here, sin is made eternal, inferred from physical matter, necessary not accidental, seen not as the antithesis

*of good but as a lower grade of the good; this view makes God the author of
sin. Scripture and human moral consciousness rebel against these conclusions.
Pessimism and libertinism are the natural consequence of this view.*

*The question of God's will in relation to sin is vexing. Those who speak of
God's permission with respect to sin rightly seek to avoid making him the author
of sin. However, because this formulation risks denying God's full sovereignty,
Reformed theology, following Augustine, was never satisfied with the idea of
permission. At the risk of using "hard sayings," Reformed theologians insist that
while God does not sin or cause sin, sin is yet not outside his will. In addition,
God created human beings holy and without sin; sin's origin is in the will of
the rational creature. God most certainly created human beings to be capable
of sin; he willed the possibility of sin. How that possibility became reality is,
however, a mystery. Sin defies explanation; it is a folly that does not have an
origin in the true sense of the word, only a beginning. Attempting to locate the
time of the fall, too, is impossible. Attempts to identify that time in the preformed
chaos of Genesis 1:1 or in notions of preexistent souls are theologically and
philosophically, as well as scripturally, without ground. We must be satisfied
with the straightforward account of Scripture: humanity was created good and
by its own volition, at a given time in the beginning, fell from that state and
plunged into sinful alienation from God, who incorporates sin into his purposes,
even as something that had to be there though it ought not to be there.*

[307] When God had completed the work of creation, he looked down with
delight on the work of his hands, for it was all very good (Gen. 1:31). Granted, at
that moment the world was only at the beginning of its development and hence
enjoyed a perfection, not in degree but in kind. Inasmuch as it was something
that was positively good, it could become something and develop in accordance
with the laws God had set for it. When Scripture has a positively good world
precede this fallen world, it presents to human thought a basis of support that
philosophy simply cannot provide. For when philosophy conceives original being
as insubstantial potency, which *is* nothing, but can *become* anything, it reasons
apart from reality and attempts to satisfy us with an abstraction. From nothing,
nothing can become; apart from any antecedent being, there can be no becoming, and evil only becomes possible if the good has priority, not only in an ideal
sense but in reality. The fallen world in which we live rests on the foundations of a
creation that was very good inasmuch as it came forth from the hands of God. But
that world did not long continue to exist in its original goodness. It had scarcely
been created before sin crept into it. The mystery of existence is made even more
incomprehensible by the mystery of evil. Almost at the same moment creatures
came, pure and splendid, from the hand of their Maker, they were deprived of all
their luster, and stood, corrupted and impure, before his holy face. Sin ruined the
entire creation, converting its righteousness into guilt, its holiness into impurity,

its glory into shame, its blessedness into misery, its harmony into disorder, and its light into darkness. But where does that evil come from? What is the origin of sin? Scripture vindicates God and presents a continuous theodicy when it proclaims and maintains that God is in no way the cause of sin. He, Scripture says, is righteous, holy, far from wickedness (Deut. 32:4; Job 34:10; Ps. 92:15; Isa. 6:3; Hab. 1:13), a light in whom there is no darkness (1 John 1:5); he tempts no one (James 1:13), is an overflowing fountain of all that is good, immaculate, and pure (Ps. 36:9; James 1:17). He prohibits sin in his law (Exod. 20) and in the conscience of every human (Rom. 2:14–15), does not delight in wickedness (Ps. 5:4), but hates it and demonstrates his wrath against it (Ps. 45:7; Rom. 1:18). He judges it and atones for it in Christ (Rom. 3:24–26), cleanses his people from it by forgiveness and sanctification (1 Cor. 1:30) and, in the event of continued disobedience, wills to punish it with both temporal and eternal penalties (Rom. 1:18; 2:8).

THE GENESIS STORY OF THE FALL

When it comes to the origin of sin, Scripture always points us in the direction of the creature. For that reason, however, it is never isolated from God's government nor excluded from his counsel. On the contrary: it is God himself who, according to his special revelation, created the possibility of sin. Not only did he make humanity in such a way that it could fall, but he also planted the tree of the knowledge of good and evil in the garden, confronted Adam with a moral option by means of the probationary command, whose decision had the greatest significance for himself and all his posterity, and, finally, even permitted the temptation of the woman by the serpent. It was God's decision to take humanity on the perilous path of freedom rather than elevating it by a single act of power above the possibility of sin and death.

According to Genesis 2:9, there were two trees in the garden for which God had a special purpose: the tree of the knowledge of good and evil and the tree of life. Since the tree of life does not surface again in the story, except in Genesis 3:22, 24, some scholars believed that it did not belong in the original report and was only inserted later. An argument against this, however, is that it is most natural for the tree of life not to be mentioned again between 2:9 and 3:22, because the entire narrative revolves around the other tree, the tree of knowledge. Furthermore, the tree of life occurs not only in 2:9 and 3:22, 24 but also in Proverbs 3:18; 13:12; Revelation 2:7 and 22:2, and in the sagas of many peoples.[1] Others, accordingly, have voiced the suspicion that the tree of life is original in the Genesis story but that the tree of the knowledge of good and evil was inserted later.[2] And it is in

1. A. Wünsche, *Die Sagen vom Lebensbaum und Lebenswasser* (Leipzig: Pfeiffer, 1905); *B. D. van der Voo, "De boom des levens," *Tijdspiegel* (1909).

2. B. D. Eerdmans, "De beteekenis van het Paradijsverhal," *Theologische Tijdschrift* 39/6 (November 1905): 481–511; cf. C. Clemen, *Die Christliche Lehre von der Sünde* (Göttingen: Vandenhoeck & Ruprecht, 1897), I, 155ff.

fact true that up until now no parallel has been found elsewhere; but this circumstance does not change anything by having it arise later and having it inserted in the paradisal story. The questions still remain and become much harder to solve: Where does the tree of the knowledge of good and evil come from, and why was it included in Genesis 2 and 3? More important is the fact that this tree cannot be taken out of this narrative without completely changing its character and even robbing it of its real content. The probationary command, the temptation, and the punishment all concern the eating of the fruit of that tree. If the original story had only mentioned the tree of life, the reason why eating from that tree was prohibited and threatened with such a heavy penalty makes no sense. Some argue that the intent of Genesis 3 is simply to relate how humans, by eating from the tree of life, became conscious of their vitality, awakened to their sex drive, and passed from a state of childlikeness to that of maturity.

But if that is the heart of the story, why were humans prohibited from eating the fruit of that tree, fruit that would give them this vitality and life? Were they not permitted to outgrow their childlikeness and to become conscious of their sex life? But they had already been given the mandate to multiply, to fill the earth and subdue it (1:28); Adam had already been given a wife with whom he was to become one flesh (2:24); and what evidence is there in the narrative or in its entire context that the life of sex and being sexually awakened was something sinful in itself? Resounding from the entire Old Testament, rather, is that fertility is a great blessing from God. If Genesis 3 were designed to tell us about the awakening of the sex drive, the punishment threatened and applied to the violation of the command would be totally incomprehensible. Why did the punishment consist in death? Why did it strike the woman especially in her becoming a mother? Why, despite all this, is she nevertheless called "the mother of all living"? And, finally, why were both the man and his wife denied the chance to eat from the tree of life and to stay in the garden? Reading the narrative without bias, one gets an impression of profound unity[3] and of its obvious aim to tell us not about the progress and development but about the fall of humankind. The entire context in which the story occurs shows that it seeks to tell us about the origin of sin. Preceding it is the creation of humans by the hand of God and in his image, and following it, in brief outline, comes the story of increasing wickedness in the human race up until the flood.

The Knowledge of Good and Evil

The tree of the knowledge of good and evil is undoubtedly so named because humans, by eating of it, would acquire a knowledge of good and evil such as they had not had until then, one that was forbidden to them and denied to them. The

---

3. Eerdmans, although he acknowledges interpolations, nonetheless is convinced that Genesis 2–3 is a unit. W. B. Kristensen, "Een of twee boomen in het Paradijsverhaal," *Theologische Tijdschrift* 42 (May 1908): 215–33, judges that the *two* trees belongs to a very old tradition. Cf. also J. C. Eykman, "De eenheid en beteekenis van het paradijsverhaal, onderzocht met het oog op de meeningen der jongste critiek," *Theologische Studiën* 25/3–4 (1907): 197–237.

question, however, is what that knowledge of good and evil amounts to. The usual explanation is that, by eating of the tree, humans would gain empirical knowledge of good and evil. But this has rightly prompted the objection that this knowledge of good and evil would make humans like God—as not just the snake (in Gen. 3:5) but also God himself (in 3:22) says—and God certainly has no empirical knowledge of evil, nor can he have it. In addition, by eating of the tree, humans especially lost the empirical knowledge of the good. Finally, [in this view] Genesis 3:22a must then be interpreted as irony, which by itself is already implausible but specifically in conflict with verse 22 as a whole. Others therefore came up with the idea that Genesis 3 relates the development of the human race from an animal state to self-consciousness and reason, and they therefore viewed the fall as the first hazardous undertaking of reason, the genesis of moral life, the origin of culture, the happiest event in the history of humanity. This, in earlier times, was the idea of the Ophites, who held the snake to be an incarnation of the Logos,[4] and later of Kant, Schiller, Hegel, Strauss, and others.[5] This view is so contrary to the intent of the narrative, however, that today it has almost universally been abandoned. For it would assume that God created humanity in a state of childlike, even animal, innocence, and planned to keep it in that state. However, knowledge, also moral knowledge, had already been given to mankind at the time of its creation, as is evident from the creation in God's image, the naming of the animals, and the reception and understanding of the probationary command. The knowledge that humanity acquired by the fall was a very different kind of knowledge, one that was forbidden by God and made humans deserving of various punishments. Genesis 3 does not tell the story of a "giant step of progress" but of a human fall.

Nowadays, though this is again acknowledged by many people, they connect it with the idea that the knowledge of good and evil that was forbidden to humans was a special kind of knowledge.[6] This cannot be the very first intellectual or

---

4. Cf. Luthe, "Ophir," *PRE*[3], XIV, 400–404. Ed. note: The Ophites (also known as Naasseni) were a group of gnostic sects who inverted biblical morality and especially revered the serpent.

5. I. Kant, "Mutmasslicher Anfang der Menschengeschichte," in *Berliner Monatsschrift* 7 (January–June 1786); F. Schiller and W. Scherer, *Über die erste Menschengesellschaft*, in vol. 3 of *Thalia*, 3 vols. (Leipzig: Georg Joachim Göscher, 1787–91); G. W. F. Hegel, *Sämtliche Werke* (Stuttgart: F. Frommann, 1952), VII, 30ff. (*Philosophie des Rechts*, *Werke*, VIII, 14ff.). Ed. note: When possible, references to Hegel's writings will be cited from the modern Stuttgart edition and/or a published English translation. The title of Hegel's work and Bavinck's original citation from Hegel's *Werke* will be given in parentheses. Idem, *Sämtliche Werke*, XI (1949), 390ff. (*Philosophie der Geschichte*, *Werke* IX, 390ff.); idem, *Sämtliche Werke*, XV (1959), 210 (*Vorlesungen über die Philosophie der Religion* [1832], *Werke*, XI, 194); D. F. Strauss, *Die Christliche Glaubenslehre in ihrer Geschichtlichen Entwicklung und im Kampfe mit der modernen Wissenschaft* (Tübingen: C. F. Osiander, 1840–41), II, 29; cf. K. G. Bretschneider, *Systematische Entwickelung*, 4th ed. (Leipzig: J. A. Barth, 1841), 589.

6. J. Wellhausen, *Geschichte Israels*, 2 vols. (Berlin: Reimer, 1878), 344ff.; R. Rütschi, *Geschichte und Kritik der katholischen Lehre von der ursprünglichen Vollkommenheit* (Leiden: E. J. Brill, 1881), 8; R. Smend, *Lehrbuch der Alttestamentlichen Religionsgeschichte* (Freiburg: J. C. B. Mohr, 1893), 120; K. Marti, *Geschichte der Israelitischen Religion*, 3rd ed. (Strassburg: F. Bull, 1897), 197; C. Clemen, *Sünde*, I, 151ff.

moral knowledge, for it is contrary to the tradition of all peoples to imagine the
first humans as a kind of animal that was still bereft of all that knowledge, nor
does the author of the Genesis story take this view. For, according to him, the
first two people were created as adults. They were created as man and woman and
united with each other in marriage; they think and speak and know the things
around them; they also have a moral consciousness and know, from receiving the
probationary command, that obedience to God brings with it blessing and reward,
and that evil consists in the violation of his law and is followed by punishment.
The paradisal story, therefore, absolutely does not describe the human person as
an intellectual or moral tabula rasa on which everything still has to be inscribed
from without. Therefore, it cannot mean by the knowledge of good and evil an
awakening to self-consciousness and reason nor the origination of conscience.
But by the knowledge of good and evil that is prohibited, they say, we must understand the achievement of a mature intellect (3:6), the ability to distinguish
between the useful and the harmful (Deut. 1:39; 2 Sam. 19:35–36; Isa. 7:16;
Jonah 4:11); independent insight enabling persons to help themselves and not
be dependent on others; intellectual knowledge of the world, the metaphysical
knowledge of things in their connectedness, their value or worthlessness, their
utility or inutility for people. In other words, this refers to wisdom, to the skills
of controlling the world, the culture that is said to make humans independent
of God and like God.

This opinion, however, has the same drawbacks as that which speaks of the
progress mankind made in the fall and actually introduces only a slightly different twist in it. According to both views, the paradisal story describes the passage
of humanity from a state of rural simplicity to that of world-dominating culture.
Whereas the proponents of the first opinion, from their point of view regard this
passage as progress, others stress that, from the viewpoint of the author, it was a
decline and a fall. But in saying this, they fail to reproduce the idea of the paradisal
story correctly. Culture as such is absolutely not sinful or wrong. In Genesis 1:28,
the humans, who were created in the image of God, were instructed to exercise
dominion over the earth (cf. 9:1–2), and in Genesis 2:15 and 19, they were instructed to till and keep the Garden of Eden and to name the animals (cf. 3:23).
In Genesis 3:21, the manufacture of clothing for Adam and Eve is attributed to
God himself, while in Genesis 4:17, 21–22, the building of a city, dwelling in tents,
the keeping of cattle, making a range of musical instruments, and the processing
of metal, though attributed in origin to the descendants of Cain, are not in any
way at all condemned. The Old Testament generally accords such high status to
wisdom that there can be no question of condemnation. This is all the more the
case because, also according to the proponents of the above view, the first human
couple even before the fall possessed an intellectual and moral knowledge that
may at best differ from wisdom in degree but not in kind.

Hence the knowledge of good and evil that is prohibited to human beings
has to mean something different. Marti points in the right direction when he

describes it as the ability to stand on one's own feet and to find one's own way and speaks of the desire of humans to emancipate themselves from God by cultivating that ability. In Genesis 3, the issue is not primarily the *content* of the knowledge that humans would appropriate by disobedience but the *manner* in which they would obtain it. The nature of the knowledge of good and evil in view here is characterized by the fact that humans would be like God as a result of it (Gen. 3:5, 22). By violating the command of God and eating of the tree, they would make themselves like God in the sense that they would position themselves outside and above the law and, like God, determine and judge for themselves what good and evil was. The knowledge of good and evil is not the knowledge of the useful and the harmful, of the world and how to control it, but (as in 2 Sam. 19:36; Isa. 7:16) the right and capacity to distinguish good and evil on one's own. The issue in Genesis is indeed whether humanity will want to develop in dependence on God, whether it will want to have dominion over the earth and seek its salvation in submission to God's commandment; or whether, violating that command- ment and withdrawing from God's authority and law, it will want to stand on its own feet, go its own way, and try its own "luck."[7] When humanity fell, it got what it wanted; it made itself like God, "knowing good and evil" by its own insight and judgment. Genesis 3:22 is in dead earnest. This emancipation from God, however, did not lead and cannot lead to true happiness. For that reason, God by the probationary command forbade this drive to freedom, this thirst for independence. But humanity voluntarily and deliberately opted for its own way, thereby failing the test.

The Serpent's Lie

[308] Humanity had probably existed in the state of innocence only for a short while when it was tempted and toppled from without by a serpent that was more crafty (עָרוּם; LXX φρονιμος; *prudens*; cf. Matt. 10:16; 2 Cor. 11:3) than any other wild animal. The serpent addressed not the man but the woman, who had not herself received the probationary command directly from God but through her husband and was therefore more open to argumentation and doubt. The serpent, accordingly, first of all tried to create doubt in the heart of the woman about the commandment of God and to that end presented it as having been given by God out of harshness and selfishness. The woman, by the manner in which she reproduces and expands the command, clearly shows that it had come to her mind as a sharp boundary and restriction. After raising the doubt and bringing home to the woman the inconvenience of the command, the serpent continues by sowing unbelief and pride in the woman's now well-prepared mind. The serpent now firmly denies that violating the command will result in death, indicating that God gave the command out of sheer selfishness. If humans will eat of the tree,

7. J. Köberle, *Sünde und Gnade im religiösen Leben des Volkes Israel bis auf Christum* (Munich: Beck, 1905), 64ff.

they will, instead of dying, become like God and receive perfect, that is, divine, knowledge. The serpent's assurance and the high expectation it raised prompted the woman to look at the tree, and the longer she looked, the more she became enchanted with its fruit. The desire of the eyes, the lust of the flesh, and the pride of life [cf. 1 John 2:16] made the temptation irresistible. Finally she took of the fruit, ate it, and gave some to her husband, and he ate.

The fact of the serpent's speaking has suggested to many people that this story is an allegory, in any case that the serpent was not a real animal but only a name and image for lust,[8] or sexual desire,[9] or errant reason,[10] or Satan.[11] But this explanation is not acceptable. In Genesis 3:1, the serpent is counted among the animals; the punishment (vv. 14–15) presupposes a real snake; and in 2 Corinthians 11:3 Paul is of the same opinion. Also, the mythical view that arose later and was widely accepted is inconsistent with the intent of the narrative, the entire context in which it occurs, and the ongoing teaching of Scripture. The mythical interpretations themselves, moreover, are most divergent.[12] The serpent's speaking, accordingly, has to be explained differently. Not, however, along the lines of Josephus,[13] in terms of the opinion of the narrator that before the fall animals had the gift of language, for he has just informed us that humans are essentially distinct from animals, that they gave names to the animals and could not find a suitable helper among them. It undoubtedly has to be explained in terms of the infiltration of a spiritual superterrestrial power. In the narrative itself there is not a word that describes the nature of that power. Genesis 3 simply sticks to the visible facts; it describes but does not explain. Granted, many scholars have believed that Genesis 3 only tells us of the origin of the hostility existing between humans and animals. But aside from the fact that this explanation is too banal to be persuasive, it is in conflict with what Genesis 2 says about the relation between humans and animals and fails to tell us how and why the serpent acts toward humankind as a seductive power. This is the reason why many exegetes today again return to the ancient exegesis, if for no other reason than that this is the viewpoint held in the apocryphal literature of the Old Testament.[14]

8. Philo, *De opificio mundi*, §56; Clement of Alexandria, *Stromateis*, III, 14, 17; Origen, *On First Principles*, IV, 16; cf. also Augustine, *City of God*, XIII, 21.

9. A. Schopenhauer, *Die Welt als Wille und Vorstellung*, 6th ed. (Leipzig: Brockhaus, 1887), II, 654, 666.

10. C. K. J. Bunsen, in his *Bibelwerk*, 9 vols. (Leipzig: F. A. Brockhaus, 1858–70).

11. Thus Cajetan, Eugubinus, Junius, Rivetus, Amyraut, Vitringa Sr., Vitringa Jr., Venema, and others. Cf. J. Marck, *Historia paradisi* (Amsterdam: Gerardus Borstius, 1705), III, 5, 5; C. Vitringa, *Doctr. christ.*, II, 256; also J. P. Val D'Eremao, *The Serpent of Eden: A Philological and Critical Essay on the Text of Genesis III and Its Various Interpretations* (London: K. Paul, Trench & Co., 1888).

12. E. W. Hengstenberg, *Christologie des Alten Testamentes*, 2nd ed., 3 vols. (Berlin: L. Oehmigke, 1854–56), I, 5 (ed. note: ET: *Christology of the Old Testament* [Grand Rapids: Kregel Publications, 1988]); *L. Köhler, *Biblische Geschichte*, I, 6; F. Delitzsch, *A New Commentary on Genesis*, trans. Sophia Taylor (Edinburgh: T&T Clark, 1899), on Gen. 3:1.

13. F. Josephus, *Antiquities*, I, 1, 4.

14. C. Clemen, *Sünde*, I, 158ff.

It is also understandable, moreover, that Genesis 3 makes no mention of the spiritual background of the events in question. Only gradually, as revelation progressively unfolds, does the depth of the darkness come out. Though seemingly innocent in the beginning, sin in its basic nature and power only becomes known in the course of history. At the start the deviation from the right road is small and scarcely perceptible, but when continued, it leads into entirely the wrong direction and to a completely opposite outcome. This also explains why Scripture, both in the Old and the New Testament, relatively rarely harks back to the story of the fall. The principal verses that have a bearing on it are Job 31:33; Psalm 90:3; Proverbs 3:18; 13:12; Ecclesiastes 12:7; Isaiah 43:27; 51:3; 65:25; Joel 2:3; Hosea 6:7; Ezekiel 28:13–15; John 8:44; Romans 5:12ff.; 8:20; 1 Corinthians 15:21–22, 42–49; 2 Corinthians 11:3; 1 Timothy 2:14; Revelation 2:7; 22:2; and in part these verses are uncertain in their interpretation or contain no more than an allusion.[15]

Yet, this relative silence cannot be explained in terms of the idea that the origin of the story in Genesis 3 is very late, for also according to recent criticism, it is Yahwist and existed prior to the rise of the writing prophets in the eighth century, and almost all peoples possess ancient traditions about a golden age in which humanity lived originally. It should be remembered, however, that the fall, though not mentioned very often, still underlies the entire scriptural teaching on moral perfection as integral to the essence of humankind, on sin and redemption. Old Testament revelation also bears a prophetic character and looked forward, not backward, and thus only the second Adam was able to illumine the full significance of the first Adam.[16] Paul looks back from the second Man to the first. Only gradually, in the course of the history of revelation, does the spiritual power emerge that hid behind the appearance and seductive activity of the serpent. Then we learn that involved in the struggle of evil on earth there is also a contest of spirits and that humanity and the world are the spoils for which the war between God and Satan, between heaven and hell, is waged.

All the power of sin on earth is connected with a kingdom of darkness in the world of spirits. There, too, a fall has occurred. In John 8:44, Jesus himself states that the devil was a murderer from the beginning (ἀπ᾽ ἀρχῆς) of the existence of humankind, that he did not and hence does not stand in the truth (οὐχ ἔστηκεν) because there is no truth in him. When he lies, he speaks according to his own nature. First John 3:8 similarly teaches that the devil has sinned from the beginning. Paul warns the neophyte (1 Tim. 3:6) against being puffed up that he may not fall

15. For references in the apocryphal literature, see Clemen, *Sünde*, I, 169ff., 173.

16. Cf. O. C. Krabbe, *Die Lehre von der Sünde und vom Tod* (Hamburg: Friedrich Perthes, 1836), 83–100; J. C. K. von Hofmann, *Der Schriftbeweis*, 2nd ed., 2 vols. (Nördlingen: Beck, 1857–60), I, 364ff.; J. H. Kurtz, *Geschichte des alten Bundes*, 2nd ed., 2 vols. (Berlin: J. A. Wohlgemuth, 1853–58), I, 69; F. R. Tennant, *The Origin and Propagation of Sin*, 2nd ed. (Cambridge: Cambridge University Press, 1906), 142ff., 227ff.; J. Orr, *God's Image in Man and Its Defacement in the Light of Modern Denials* (London: Hodder & Stoughton, 1906), 199; J. H. Gerretsen, *De Val des Menschen* (Nijmegen: Ten Hoet, 1909), 11, 14ff.

into the condemnation of the devil, that is, fall into the same condemnation that has struck the devil. And Jude (v. 6) speaks of "the angels that did not keep their own position, but left their proper dwelling," that is, of angels who did not hold onto their principle, origin, or even rule, and left the dwelling place assigned to them. Clearly implied here is that many angels were not content with the state in which God had placed them. Pride took possession of them to make them strive for another and higher position. Sin first broke out in the realm of spirits; it arose in the heart of creatures of whom we have but little knowledge, under conditions that are almost completely unknown to us. On the basis of Scripture, however, it is certain that sin did not first start on earth but in heaven, at the feet of God's throne, in his immediate presence and that the fall of angels took place before that of humankind. Scripture is silent on whether there is a connection between that fall of the angels and the creation of humankind, nor does it tell us what drove the fallen angels to seduce humans. But whatever the reason may have been, Satan is the adversary, the tempter, the slanderer of the human race, the murderer of mankind (Matt. 4:3; John 8:44; Eph. 6:11; 1 Thess. 3:5; 2 Tim. 2:26), the "great dragon," the "ancient serpent" (Rev. 12:9, 14–15; 20:2). As such he came to Christ, the second Adam, and as such he also came to the first. That he did not appear to him directly and personally but used a serpent is probably to be explained from the idea that he had better hopes of success if the seduction occurred by means of a being that was known to humans as good. Undoubtedly the serpent's speaking must have seemed strange to the woman, but precisely this strangeness enhanced the seduction: even an animal, rejecting God's command, had achieved a higher level of perfection! For the rest Scripture teaches us that even unclean spirits can do superhuman things and temporarily take possession of bodies and organs of speech (Matt. 8:28ff.; Mark 5:7ff.; Luke 8:28ff.; Acts 19:15). In the case of humanity the temptation by Satan resulted in the fall. Scripture looks for the origin of sin solely in the will of rational creatures.

The Fall as History

[309] The historical character of the paradisal story was maintained in the Christian church throughout the ages. There were different opinions about the location of paradise, the character of the two trees, the serpent, and so on, but the historical truth of the knowledge of good and evil, of the probationary command, of the temptation by the serpent, and of the willful disobedience of Adam and Eve was certain to everyone and rigorously maintained against the allegorical interpretation of Philo and Origen.[17] But in modern times the historicity of the paradisal story was put under serious pressure from the side of historical criticism and even more from the side of evolutionary theory. Geology, paleontology, and all prehistorical studies seem to leave no room whatsoever for an original moral perfection and for a subsequent fall of the first humans. The further we go

17. J. Marck, *Historia paradisi*, 1ff.

back into the past, scholars tell us, the more we find people who lived in a most primitive state and were virtually without any culture. Human beings seem to have gradually evolved from the animal world, so that with reference to the past as well as to the present one can only speak of progress. Paradise lies ahead of, not behind, us. We have emerged from darkness and are progressively moving in the direction of light and life, peace and happiness.[18]

Over against this criticism, many scholars believed they were on firmer ground if they took position not in the paradisal story but in the midst of sinful reality. Bishop Charles Gore, for example, claims that the doctrine of the fall and original sin has certainly not been constructed on the assumption that the early chapters of Genesis are purely historical. This doctrine is not a dogma proclaimed solely on the basis of external authority but finds its substantiation in experience. Granted, there is an inspirational activity of the Holy Spirit present in the Genesis narratives, but if Irenaeus, Clement, Athanasius, and Anselm can interpret them, in whole or in part, as allegorical, then we have the same freedom. In any case, "the Christian doctrine of sin rests on a far broader and far surer foundation than the belief that the early chapters of Genesis belong to one form or stage of inspired literature rather than to another. It rests on the strong foundation of our Lord, accepted and verified by man's moral consciousness."[19] Others, however, go still further and believe they can totally dispense with Genesis 3 and Romans 5. It is incorrect, according to de Hartog, to present the fall of humankind as a truth of *faith* that we accept because Scripture speaks of it. The reverse is the case: because the fall is evident from experience, Genesis 3 witnesses to this reality. The fall of humankind, sin, and death are not articles of faith but the data of experience.[20]

In this connection, we cannot avoid speaking to the misunderstanding present here. If Genesis 3 reports history, then the fall is a fact that occurred at one time at the beginning of the human race and constitutes an indestructible component of the world and of history. As fact the fall is not based on the story of Genesis 3, but, conversely, it is reported in Genesis 3 because it had occurred long before in history. Furthermore, according to Scripture, the fall of humankind was such a serious and appalling fact that the consequences of it continue to have their effect in the history of the human race to the present. Indeed, experience is full of data that point back to the fact of the fall. But it is wrong to infer from all this that the Genesis story is unnecessary and superfluous and can, if necessary, be altogether dispensed with or totally and without loss be deprived of its

18. Cf. H. Bavinck, *Reformed Dogmatics*, II, 511–20 (#279–80) (= *In the Beginning*, 137–47).

19. C. Gore, *Lux mundi*, 13th ed. (London: Murray, 1892), 395; idem, *The New Theology and the Old Religion* (London: J. Murray, 1907), 233; cf. also J. Orr, *God's Image in Man*, 298ff.

20. Dr. A. H. de Hartog, *De Heilsfeiten* (Amersfoort: Veen, 1907), 34–39; cf. Dr. Gerretsen, who writes as follows: "The fall of man is the necessary presupposition underlying the whole of soteriology. Even if it were not mentioned in Genesis 3 and Romans 5, keen dogmatic thinking would still have to make the inference that there has been a first transgression of original man by which the entire development of the human race is controlled."

historical character by criticism. For there is a distinction between a fact and the knowledge of a fact. A fact is a piece of reality that can never be undone, and the weightier it is, the more vast will be its consequences; however, for the knowledge of a fact, especially when it is part not of the present but of the past, we are dependent on a witness, in whatever form it may be given. Based on this, in part, is the distinction between natural science and historical science. Nature remains the same, and its phenomena can be studied independently and anew by every natural scientist; but the practitioners of the science of history, because they are not present at the events themselves, depend for their knowledge on testimonies. Such historians would act very foolishly if they reasoned thus: all the events that have occurred are constituents of reality and still, to the degree that they were important, affect the present. If necessary I can dispense with the testimonies, for from the data in the present I can reason back to this or that event in the past. Essentially, that person would not act any differently from those who would reconstruct the fact of the fall, aside from the historic witness of Scripture, on the basis of the data of experience. There may be a difference in degree because the fall of the human race far surpasses in importance and consequences all other world events, but materially the reasoning remains the same and is absurd in both cases.

Another thing that must not be forgotten in connection with this reasoning is that people have known the witness of Scripture beforehand and learned to read reality in the light of that witness. People may say they can reconstruct the fall from the data of experience without the help of Genesis 3 and Romans 5, but in reality they have already incorporated the witness of Scripture in the data of experience. Thousands, even millions, of people have observed the same reality that still presents itself to us today, but it has never suggested to them the idea of a fall of the first human couple. Instead, they have sought to explain it by means of a precosmic fall or an evil god or blind fate. The fact that we view reality in such a way that it everywhere shows the consequences of a fall in paradise is something we owe exclusively to the light Scripture has shed on it. It is not a noble act, after having first made use of its services, to then bid it farewell and pretend that one has oneself achieved such insight by one's own reasoning.

Finally, if one really seriously believes in a fall of the first humans (even though it is, as one thinks, on the basis of the data of experience), then all reason to question the historical character of Genesis 3 actually collapses. For the main critical objection (of both Old Testament scholars and evolutionists) is not directed against the literary report in Genesis as such but against the event reported there. This event is of such great weight that the whole of Christian doctrine stands or falls with it. "All of faith consists in Jesus Christ and in Adam and all of morality in lust and in grace" (Pascal). The two truths or facts by which all of Christian dogmatics is governed are (1) the fall of Adam and (2) the resurrection of Christ (Gerretsen). If one recognizes this and considers Adam's fall an appalling reality, one will in any case be at odds with present-day criticism in the matter of both of its attacks and will gain nothing by making a few literary concessions. The theory of evolution, as it is usually presented today and applied to the history of the human race and of Israel, leaves no room for a state of integrity and for a fall of the first humans. According to this theory, there never even existed a first human, for the transitions were so minute and stretched out over so many centuries that no one can say where the animal stops and humanity begins. Its beginnings are shrouded in darkness, and its state was originally like that of an animal.

However strongly this theory of evolution claims a factual basis for itself, one should bear in mind the following: (1) While investigations into prehistoric humanity have brought to light that it lived in very primitive conditions, there is no evidence that it gradually evolved from the animal world and is still caught up in a period of transition. Confirmed, rather, is the idea that prehistoric humans were persons of like nature to ourselves and that, living in Europe, they came from Asia. (2) The discoveries that occurred in the past century in the land of Babylon and Assyria reveal to us that the most ancient inhabitants we find there were not a savage, coarse, semibestial race but enjoyed a high level of civilization and *regressed* in their subsequent history rather than *progressed*. (3) The *Ur*-history, which is contained in Genesis 1–10, has received powerful support as a result. On the one hand, it has emerged in its uniqueness—the marvelous purity of its historical, religious, and ethical ideas—and, on the other, it has been relieved of its isolation and connected with all the peoples, traditions, customs, mores, and so on. In this connection a strong light has fallen on the distinction between the antiquity of a story and the time at which it was recorded. Also, if the *Ur*-history of Genesis dates from the time of Moses, it is separated by a series of centuries from the events it narrates. (4) Modern science, although believing in evolution, still as a rule assumes the unity of the human race. When it does this, it accepts in the bargain a series of inferences that are of the greatest importance. For if humankind is one, then it has descended from one ancestral couple; then it has spread out over the whole world from one specific location; then from the beginning it held in common a complex of intellectual, religious, and moral ideas and traditions; then a moral deviation must have occurred at the beginning in the life of the first human couple, for sin is universal.[21] All in all, the science of nature and history to this day lacks the right to make a pronouncement on the truth of the state of integrity and the fall of the first humans. The witness pertaining to these things contained in Genesis, confirmed by the later appeal made to it by prophets and apostles and Christ himself, and intertwined as a necessary constituent in the whole revelation of salvation, continues to maintain itself in people's conscience and meshes perfectly with the reality our daily experience informs us about.

21. For a more thorough treatment, see H. Bavinck, *Philosophy of Revelation* (Grand Rapids: Eerdmans, 1953), 146ff., 172ff., 188ff.

ALTERNATIVE EXPLANATIONS OF SIN

Indirectly this witness of Scripture is also borne out by the traditions, sagas, or myths that among various peoples speak of a fall into sin. A true parallel to the biblical story has so far not been found anywhere. Delitzsch believed he saw one in a representation on a cylindrical seal that depicts two persons stretching out their hands to the fruit of a tree. On the left of this representation, something has been set up that may be a snake, but since both persons are clothed and sitting down, both stretch out their hands toward the tree, and are probably both male figures, there is here no discernible kinship with the story in Genesis 3. Also other stories, cited for the purpose of comparison, upon further inquiry cannot serve this purpose or are too problematic to base anything on them.[22] Nevertheless, it is remarkable that in a Babylonian myth Adapa loses eternal life by not consuming the food and drink set before him. Furthermore, in many religions the serpent was venerated as an embodiment of hostile or beneficent powers. There is also a widespread popular belief forging a connection between different trees, especially the tree of life, and the destiny of humans. In many sagas the memory of a golden age experienced by the human race has been preserved, and according to the Avesta, the holy book of the Persian religion, the first human, Yima, the noble ruler of the golden age, lived for a time in paradise but, having fallen as a result of pride, was driven from it and was finally killed by an evil spirit.[23] All these stories and others like them have no higher meaning other than to show that the human race from ancient times and everywhere wanted to give an account of the horrendous destruction the world exhibited, by seeing in it the result of a fall that took place in the life of humanity. But in that light they are valuable. Underlying the religious and moral convictions of human beings, more or less clearly articulated or unconscious, there is belief in the divine origin and destiny of humanity, in a golden age and subsequent decline, in the battle between good and evil, and in the wrath and appeasement of the deity.[24]

At the same time, they bring out how pagans, though they gropingly searched for God, did not find him [cf. Acts 17:27]. Both the origin and the essence of sin remained unknown to them. Even the Jews, who recognized the fall and the temptation by Satan (Wis. 2:24) and therefore frequently called him the "ancient

---

22. H. H. Kuyper, *Evolutie of Revelatie* (Amsterdam: Höveker & Wormser, 1903), 37, 112–14.

23. Cf. "Fall," *DB*, I, 839.

24. See further H. Bavinck, *Philosophy of Revelation*, 187–88. Ed. note: Bavinck refers here to literature cited at the beginning of *Gereformeerde Dogmatiek*, II, §37, #291 dealing with human nature ("Het Wezen van den Mensch"). Included are the following authors (for full information see bibliography): Oehler; Hofmann (*Schriftbeweis*); Delitzsch (*Psychology*); Laidlaw; Van Leeuwen (*Anthropologie*); John of Damascus; Peter Lombard; Thomas Aquinas (*Summa theol.*, I, qu. 75ff.); Bonaventure; Bellarmine; Petavius; Kleutgen; Möhler (*Symbolik*); Heinrich; Stöckl (*Menschen*); Oswald (*Urgeschichte*) (*Vorzeit*); Köstlin (*Luther*); Oorthuys (*Zwingli*); Talma (*Anthropologie*); Gerhard; Quenstedt; Hollaz; Calvin (*Institutes*); Polanus; Zanchius; Mastricht; Turretin; Marck; Moor; Vitringa; Ch. Hodge; Schleiermacher; Dorner; Philippi; Frank; Kohler; Oettingen; and articles in *PRE*[3] on "Geist," "Herz," "Seele," "Ebenbild Gottes," "(ursprüngliche) Gerechtigkeit des Menschen."

serpent," sometimes taught that Satan was created simultaneously with Eve on the sixth day, that, being sensually titillated, he tried to tempt man, and that even before the fall humans received, along with an impulse toward the good (יצר הטוב), an impulse toward evil (יצר הרע), in order to overcome it and so to make their works truly meritorious.[25] Similarly, in the pagan world, the origin of sin was found, not in the will of rational creatures, but in the essence of things.

The fall is simply unknown. Confucianism is a shallow form of rationalism and moralism that considered humans naturally good and sought the way of salvation in a virtuous life in keeping with the world order.[26] According to Buddhism, the Atman, or Brahman, the divine substance, is the only reality; the world of phenomena is but a dream, is fundamentally maya, illusion, and in a state of perpetual becoming and change. Suffering and sorrow, accordingly, are universal, for all things are subject to transitoriness, to birth, aging, and death. The cause of that suffering is to be found in desires, in the desire for existence, in the will to exist. Salvation therefore consists in extinguishing the consciousness or in the annihilation of existence: nirvana.[27] Parsism traced evil to an original evil spirit, Ahriman, who is opposed to the supreme god, Ahuramazda, has his own kingdom of darkness and corrupts the creation of God, but is subordinate to Ahuramazda and will someday yield to him.[28] The Greeks and the Romans, though in their sagas of a golden age, of Prometheus and Pandora, they possessed something reminiscent of the biblical stories, originally knew nothing of evil spirits that were opposed to the good and attributed to the gods all sorts of evil desires and misdeeds. The human race did not fall all at once but gradually degenerated. And the human will still possesses the power to live a virtuous life, to stay within moral bounds, and thus to conquer sin, which is essentially hubris.[29]

Philosophy, as a rule, took the same position. According to Socrates, the cause and essence of sin consists solely in ignorance. No one is voluntarily evil, that is, unfortunate. Hence the person who knows the good is good and acts according to the good. All that is needed is education to guide humans, who are by nature good, to the practice of virtue.[30] Plato and Aristotle indeed understood the inadequacy of this view. Reason, they said, is certainly far from always being able to control the passions. Sin is too deeply rooted in human nature to be overcome by knowledge alone. Plato even arrived at a totally different theory about the origin of sin, locating it in a fall of preexistent souls. Still, both maintained free will and continued to believe that virtue remains within our power. Our external lot

25. F. W. Weber, *System der altsynagogalen palästinischen Theologie* (Leipzig: Dörffling & Franke, 1880), 210ff., 242ff.

26. P. D. Chantepie de la Saussaye, *Lehrbuch der Religionsgeschichte*, 3rd ed., 2 vols. (Tübingen: J. C. B. Mohr [Paul Siebeck], 1905), I, 249, A. I, 100ff.

27. Ibid., I, 411ff.; II, 89ff.

28. Ibid., II, 34ff., 199ff.

29. Ibid., II, 191, 397.

30. E. Zeller, *Philosophie der Griechen*, 4th ed., 3 vols. (Leipzig: O. R. Reisland, 1879), II, 141ff.

may be determined, but virtue is without a master (ἀδέσποτος) and depends on the human will alone. "Both virtue and evil depend upon us."[31] The Stoics could not, on the basis of its pantheistic and deterministic position, locate the cause of sin in the human will and therefore attempted to fit both physical and moral evil into the order and beauty of the whole. It was not even possible for the deity to keep human nature free from every defect. Sin is as necessary as diseases and disasters and is something good to the degree that it serves and brings out the good.[32] Still also the Stoics knew no way to overcome sin and to practice virtue other than the human will.[33] Finally, in the works of Cicero, Seneca, Plotinus, and others, there was the ever-recurring thought that sin was an act of the will and could also be undone by the will.[34] Outside the area of special revelation, therefore, sin was always either interpreted deistically in terms of the human will and construed purely as an act of the will or derived pantheistically from the essence of things and incorporated as a necessary component in the order of the universe as a whole.

[310] Both views also found their way into Christianity and repeatedly met, in smaller or larger circles, with agreement and had their defenders. The practical Christianity that prevailed in the churches following the death of the apostles and is known to us from the so-called Apostolic Fathers and other writings already contained all kinds of religious and ethical notions that deviated from the New Testament and especially from Paul and were formed under the influence of Jewish piety and popular pagan philosophy, especially that of Cicero. Believers were indeed convinced that in Christ they had received great benefits, especially the forgiveness for all past sins in baptism; but if after that event they saw themselves called to a holy life, they already opened up a large space for free will, for their own power, and for the meritoriousness of good works.[35] When, at the beginning of the fifth century, Pelagius proposed his theories, he could appeal to countless statements made by others before him. Still he isolated them from the context in which they occurred and combined them into a single whole in such a way that they ran fundamentally counter to the Christian doctrine of sin and grace.

To this monk from Britain everything depended on the free will. He saw it as the characteristic feature of human nature, the image of God, the first principle and foundation of the dominion granted him. Human nature has been so created by God that, depending on its free choice, it is able to and able not to sin; and this equal possibility in either direction, as a natural good, as a constituent of human nature, cannot be lost. As a result Pelagius had to reject all notions of original sin. Adam only brought sin into the world as an example or form. There

---

31. E. Zeller, *Philosophie der Griechen*, 3rd ed., 5 vols. (Leipzig: Fues's Verlag. [L. W. Reisland], 1895), II, 852; III, 588.

32. Ibid., IV, 175ff.

33. Ibid., IV, 167ff.

34. Ibid., IV, 667–717, 722; V, 585.

35. F. Loofs, *Leitfaden zum Studium der Dogmengeschichte*, 4th ed. (Halle a.S.: M. Niemeyer, 1906), 85ff.

is indeed a power of evil custom, but this does not so completely control humans that, if they seriously wanted to avoid sin and lead a holy life, they would be prevented from doing so. In any case, sin is not innate; it is always—and cannot be anything but—a free act of the will. The fall, accordingly, did not just occur once, in Adam, and take the whole human race with it, but every human being is still born in the same state in which Adam was, granted that, as a result of the power of custom, conditions are less favorable now. And all humans therefore stand or fall by themselves. Sin originates anew in every person; in every human life there occurs a fall when the power of free will is neglected or applied in a wrong direction.[36]

These ideas of Pelagius were so obviously at odds with the teaching of Scripture and the faith of the church that they could not possibly be accepted by the church. They were, accordingly, modified and toned down in various ways. Specifically, to Adam's transgression was ascribed a stronger influence on the state of human nature, and, correspondingly, grace was credited with more vigorous cooperation at the beginning and in the development of the new Christian life. But, fundamentally, the final decision at all these points was again reserved for the free will. In Roman Catholicism, Adam's transgression did result for him and his descendants in the loss of the superadded gift; and insofar as God had granted this gift to Adam and he therefore should have enjoyed it, the loss of it can be called culpable. But original sin is no more than this privation; it does not consist in the concupiscence that by itself is not sin, nor in an innate evil of the will, for though the will may have been weakened, it is neither lost nor corrupted. Thus fallen nature is actually totally identical with uncorrupted nature; true, the supernatural gifts have been lost, but the natural gifts continue intact. In the abstract, therefore, a person could possibly abstain from all actual sins and, like unbaptized children dying in infancy, acquire a natural state of bliss.[37] In this connection Rome could still maintain the absolute necessity of Christianity, however, inasmuch as humans, although in the most favorable scenario they could also acquire a natural state of bliss, could never by their free will receive supernatural righteousness and salvation. To that end the church with its sacraments is the only proper road. But when this Roman Catholic dualism was cast aside by the Reformation, the modalities that, within the circle of Protestantism, took over the Roman Catholic assumptions about original sin and free will[38] virtually automatically had to relapse into the ancient errors of Pelagius and Coelestis or in any case into those of Hilary of Arles and John Cassian.[39] For if Adam's fall did not, or did only in part, deprive the will of the freedom and power to do good, and original sin did not consist either in

36. Ibid., 418ff.; B. B. Warfield, *Two Studies in the History of Doctrine: Augustine and the Pelagian Controversy* (New York: Christian Literature Co., 1897).

37. Decrees of the Council of Trent, V, 2–5; VI, 1.

38. O. Fock, *Der Socianismus* (Kiel: C. Schröder, 1847), 484ff., 653ff.

39. Episcopius, *Institutes theologicae*, in *Opera* (Amsterdam: Johan Blaeu, 1650), IV, 3 c. 6; IV, 5 c. 1, 2; P. van Limborch, *Theol. Christ.*, II, 24; III, 2ff.; cf. also, Canons of Dort, III/IV: "Rejection of Errors."

a culpable loss of an original supernatural gift, then in that same measure grace
became dispensable and Christianity was robbed of its absolute character.[40]

Sin as an Act of Will

This is actually what happened in Socinianism, Remonstrantism, and rationalism, in which, despite small modifications, the basic idea was always that sin is not
rooted in a nature and is not a disposition or a state, but always an act of the will.
In the case of humans, the image of God then primarily or exclusively consisted in
dominion. To the extent that a state of integrity was assumed, it consisted mainly
in childlike innocence, in the freedom of indifference, in the possibility of opting
for either good or evil. The fall itself, when it is still recognized as a historical
fact, loses its appalling significance and is an event rather like what occurs at every
moment in human life when evil is chosen over the good. And the consequences
of the fall are therefore also of little weight. Children are born in the same state
as that in which Adam lived before his disobedience. Freedom of the will, that
is, the image of God, remains intact. At most a certain tendency toward sin is
transplanted from person to person, but such a tendency is not really the result
of the first sin of Adam but of all the sins of all our ancestors. Nor is it a sin by
itself; it only becomes a sin when the free will gives free rein to that tendency.
Hence there is a distinction between sin (pollution; sinful inclination) and guilt
(an evil deed; deliberate and voluntary transgression). Only the latter needs atonement and forgiveness; the former, the inclination to sin and unconscious and
involuntary compliance with it, is really not a sin. Rather, it is ignorance that is
not culpable. And just as sin and guilt have to be distinguished, so also sin and
suffering. There are many kinds of suffering that exist independently of sin and
would also exist if there were no sin. Death is essentially not a consequence of sin
but integral to the nature of humanity. Spiritual and eternal death was in no way a
punishment for the first sin. At most the punishment consists in the necessity of
dying (*moriendi necessitas*), which, in the case of Adam, had he not fallen, would
have been prevented by a miracle; or in the manner of dying, which, without sin,
would have been less painful and less premature.

Despite the unsatisfactory character of this view, it has again, also in our time,
been revived by many theologians. First to be considered in this connection is
Ritschl and his school. As he does with all the doctrines of dogmatics, so also in
the doctrine of sin Ritschl takes his position in the Christian faith. This is in itself
commendable, of course, for the origin and essence of sin are first known to us
from revelation and hence the object of Christian belief. But from this position
Ritschl drew the false conclusion that sin has become known to us, not from the
story of Adam and his fall, nor from the law and the Old Testament, but solely
from the gospel, which in Ritschl means from the person and teaching of Jesus.

---

40. J. Wegscheider, *Institutiones theologiae Christianae dogmaticae* (Halle: Gebauer, 1819), §§99–112; K. G.
Bretschneider, *Handbuch der Dogmatik* (Leipzig: J. A. Barth, 1838), II, 17ff.

Sin, he says, must be understood from the viewpoint of the reconciled church; the gospel of the forgiveness of sins is the basis for the knowledge of our sinfulness. Although sin exists and is known also outside Christianity, its nature has certainly first been revealed to us by the gospel. To know it for what it is, we must measure it by the good that is opposed to it, namely, the kingdom of God. Christ, who has revealed the destiny of man to us, also informs us about the nature of sin. Now, this position brings with it that Ritschl attaches no value to the doctrine of the state of integrity. Genesis does not say a word about it. At the beginning of history such a high moral state is inconceivable. If it had existed, Christ would have been an irregular phenomenon in history, a Doppelgänger, nothing but the bearer of the divine counteraction against sin. But Christ was much more than that: he brought us the highest ideals for life. Orthodox dogmatics, accordingly, dates these ideals much too early, namely, already in the life of Adam.

Reconciling Augustine and Pelagius

Adam's trespass, therefore, cannot have been the origin of sin in the human race; perhaps it was the first of a series of subsequent trespasses, but it is neither their source nor their first principle. Is sin, then, rooted in human nature? Ritschl denies this in the strongest possible terms. Sin is sin: its cause is not in God; it is not a functional element in his world order. It is, after all, the opposite of the good and experienced by us as guilt. But in the interpretation of the origin of sin, Ritschl can concur neither with Augustine nor with Pelagius. The former made humanity or human nature the subject of sin. But in that case every human already participates in the highest degree of sin in participating in original sin, and actual sins virtually no longer count. As a result of original sin, after all, humanity is already a "lost mass" (*massa perdita*), deserving of eternal punishment. But this cannot be true, for such a doctrine not only leads to untruth and makes all nurture impossible, but actual sins, according to everyone's mind, are something other and more than the mere phenomena and accidents of original sin. Also, Pelagius's view, according to which not human nature but the will of the individual is the subject of sin, is untenable, for sin is in fact something communal. Ritschl, therefore, tries to bridge the difference between the two, thinking he can achieve this by saying that the subject of sin is indeed humanity as a whole but the latter viewed as the sum of all individuals. He therefore agrees with Pelagius insofar as he, like Pelagius, has the sinful deed precede the sinful state, not the sinful state the sinful deed. All sin is grounded in the self-determination of each person's own will. And granted, under the existing circumstances and especially as a result of human ignorance, sin is indeed a "seemingly unavoidable testimony" to his will; still, the possibility of a sinless life cannot a priori be denied. So far Ritschl agrees with Pelagius. But he then tries to approximate Augustine's position by viewing sins as a unity that arises, not in virtue of their origin from a single principle, but as a result of mutual interpenetration and connectedness. Sin begins with an act of the will, but every act retroactively shapes the will, gives it a nature and a character, produces an egoistic tendency in it, and so cooperates in establishing the dominion of the law of sin. But this is not all; sinful human acts and tendencies in turn exert influence on each other. Just as a sinful environment accustoms us to sin and dulls our moral judgment, so our own sinful deeds call those of others into being. In short: there is no original sin, but out of the sinful acts of all people collectively arises a collective unity, a realm of sin.[41]

But also after Ritschl, Pelagius's theory of the origin of sin has been defended and in a unique way connected with the theory of evolution. When this evolution is construed along purely and consistently materialistic-mechanical lines, there is no longer any room for a typically moral life, for sin and virtue. In that case, so-called good and evil acts are chemical products in the same sense as vitriol and sugar, only somewhat further and more finely distilled. But since nature is usually stronger than theory, the proponents of a mechanical evolution also continue to speak of good and evil, of moral law and moral obligation, of a culture of the true, the good, and the beautiful. Materialistic atheism, moreover, has lost credibility in recent years, and since the rebirth of philosophy and the revival of metaphysics, many thinkers do their best to restrict mechanical evolution to the material world and to make it subservient to a teleological ethical idealism. The world, according to Carlyle's saying, is something more than a kitchen and a cow barn; it is also an oracle and a temple. People thus fully accept the animal ancestry of humanity and do not object to construing the first human state in extremely primitive terms. They cannot picture the *Ur*-human as being "dumb, bad, coarse, egoistic, mean, or otherwise reprehensible enough by the standards of contemporary ethics."[42]

In this state one can, of course, not yet speak of good and evil, justice and injustice, religion and morality. Human beings are still like animals, slaves of their lusts and passions. But in view of what we later became, primitive man must have been potentially different in aptitude from animals. It is hard to say in what that aptitude consisted—whether it was originally present in humans or gradually instilled in them from without; whether humans originated from the animal world by a single leap of chance or by a series of slow and small mutations. Let it be enough to say that primitive man *could* become something different and higher than he was at the time, because he in fact *did* become something different and higher.

41. A. Ritschl, *Die christliche Lehre von der Rechtfertigung und Versöhnung,* 2nd ed., 3 vols. (Bonn: A. Marcus, 1880–83), II, 241–46; III, 304–57 (ed. note: The third volume of Ritschl's work is available in English: *The Christian Doctrine of Justification and Reconciliation* [Clifton, NJ: Reference Book Publishers, 1966]; the section on sin is found on pp. 327–84); J. Kaftan, *The Truth of the Christian Religion,* trans. George Ferries, 2 vols. (Edinburgh: T&T Clark, 1894), 246ff.; J. Kaftan, *Dogmatik* (Tübingen: Mohr, 1901), §§34, 38–40; F. Nitzsch, *Lehrbuch der Evangelischen Dogmatik,* prepared by Horst Stephan, 3rd ed. (Tübingen: J. C. B. Mohr, 1902), 319ff.; H. Siebeck, *Lehrbuch der Religionsphilosophie* (Freiburg i.B. and Leipzig: Mohr, 1893), 436ff.; T. Häring, *The Christian Faith,* trans. John Dickie and George Ferries, 2 vols. (London: Hodder & Stoughton, 1913), I, 391–93.

42. W. Ostwald, *Energetische Grundlagen der Kulturwissenschaft* (Leipzig: W. Klinkhardt, 1909), 120.

Once primitive "humans" had been placed on the road toward humanization, they advanced with great strides. In that development they owed an enormous lot to the influence of society. Even an animal lives in the society of others and has consequently acquired a wide range of intellectual and moral attributes. But in the formation of a human person, society plays an even larger and richer role. From birth on, a child lives in the company of its mother and is subject to her authority. The wife is subject to her husband, a man, who for his part is a member of a tribe, owes obedience to the tribe's chief, is subject to the rules that society, labor, war, the hunt, the fishery, and so on prescribe to the individual. In short: whereas primitive "man" originally carries with him nothing but self-centered animal desires, he is tied down from all directions by the environment in which he lives. His egoistic tendencies are balanced by altruistic duties. Initially these are not yet duties, for all law arose from power and violence.[43] But gradually that power that confronted the individual from without is ethicized, and human beings, who first rebelled against that power, became accustomed to living under and adjusting to it. They begin to do on their own and willingly what they first did unwillingly. They gradually even acquire the awareness that they *ought* to do what society demands of them. A moral consciousness is formed in them. Altruistic demands acquire for them the character of moral duties, later even of divine commandments. Then comes the time in which the moral life is born, the contrast and contest between good and evil emerges, and sin as well as a fall become possible.

The self-centered tendencies and desires that humans bring along with them from their animal past are not, of course, as yet sinful as such. For where there is no law, there is no transgression, and humanity in its first period lived without law. But when the law came to his notice, there also arose within society the possibility of submission or nonsubmission to that law. Ideally speaking, it would now have been the will of God that humanity should have developed normally, that is, in keeping with then-current norms of the moral life; some even claim that with the rise of moral consciousness in humans a free will came into being as well by which they could overcome their selfishness and pursue their altruistic tendencies. But whereas this was perhaps a possibility in the abstract, in reality it was very difficult. In any case, humans from the beginning and repeatedly ever since made their self-centeredness triumph over the moral law given them. Their development has been not normal but abnormal. They fell not once but persistently. Their fall did not consist "in a fall from an actual state of original righteousness," but their entire state, after the inauguration of the moral life, implies "a fall from the divine intention, a parody of God's purpose in human history."[44] Also, sin did not arise all at once and suddenly, but its origin, like all the origins,

43. Ibid., 137.

44. Ed. note: The cited passages in this sentence and in the remainder of this paragraph are English-language insertions into Bavinck's Dutch text without attribution. Likely they are from F. R. Tennant (see following note).

was "a gradual process, not an abrupt and inexplicable plunge." The first human sins were like those of a child, not the most horrible but the least culpable of all. If we remember that the aftereffect of their self-centered animal past was still very strong, that the instincts, lusts, and inclinations were natural to them and uncommonly powerful, and that in that early period the moral consciousness was still weak and impersonal, it is not at all hard to understand that in the struggle between egoistic and altruistic tendencies people kept yielding [to their original instincts]. Actually the word "sin" is too strong to describe these weaknesses; it is fitting only when moral evil evolves and finally even rises to the level of hostility against God. But that does not describe the early transgressions of humans; they were of a rather innocent nature and can at most be described by the term "moral evil." They are "the continuance of a primitive society or group of individuals in certain practices or in the satisfying of certain natural impulses, after that things had come to be regarded as conflicting with a recognized 'sanction' of ethical rank as low as that of tribal custom." In other words, from an evolutionary viewpoint, "sin is not an innovation, but is the survival or misuse of habits and tendencies that were incidental to an earlier stage of development and whose sinfulness lies in their anachronism."

In this manner also Augustine and Pelagius can be reconciled. Ritschl did not succeed in doing this, for though he accepted a kind of oneness in sins, it was only oneness that arises as a result of their mutual connectedness and cooperation. There is still another and deeper kind of oneness, however, that underlies sins as a substratum. And it consists in a self-seeking animal nature that belongs to humanity in virtue of its origin and extends to all humans individually. Though this is not inherently sinful, it is nevertheless "the raw material for the production of sins, as soon as these native propensities are brought into relation with any restraining or condemning influence." It explains the universality of sin, the "mistakes" of childhood, the typical moral state of uncivilized peoples, the phenomenon of crime in a civilized society. But that inborn nature is not sinful in itself, for, as Pelagius clearly saw, sin is always an act of the will. Self-seeking lusts and tendencies only become sins when the will maintains and yields to them against better knowledge, and the culpability of sins increases in proportion as the intellect is better informed and the will has become morally more vigorous. Every human is "the Adam [or Eve] of his [or her] own soul." While Augustine rightly stressed the universality of sin, the moral unity and solidarity of the human race, Pelagius with no less warrant upheld personal responsibility and guilt.[45]

45. F. R. Tennant, *Origin and Propagation of Sin*; cf. the declaration of Clemen (*Theologische Literaturzeitung* [January 23, 1904]), who argues with Tennant but repudiates his doctrine of human free will. Others, too, attempt to reconcile a more or less Christian-tinted doctrine of sin with theories of evolution. Thus, e.g., Illingworth, *Personality Human and Divine* (London: Macmillan, 1908), ch. 6; R. J. Campbell, *The New Theology,* popular edition (New York: Macmillan, 1907), 38ff.; Sir Oliver Lodge, *The Substance of Faith Allied with Science: A Catechism for Parents and Teachers,* 3rd ed. (London: Methuen, 1907), 6ff.; Orchard, *Modern Theories of Sin* (London: Clark, 1909), 114ff. Sin is then regarded as a necessary element in the development process of

EVOLVING OUT OF A SINFUL NATURE?

[311] Although this theory was presented as one that reconciled Augustine and Pelagius and as the solution to an age-old problem, upon reflection it absolutely cannot be used for that purpose. In the first place, it has obviously been constructed under the influence of the theory of evolution, specifically that of the descent of humanity, and already assumes it as certain and proven,[46] while in fact all solid ground for it is lacking.

In the second place, it does not account for the contrast in the view of humanity that exists between the evolutionary hypothesis and the teaching of Scripture and therefore oscillates between the two. If it accepts the former and wishes to remain faithful to it to the end, it cannot maintain the essential distinction between humans and animals, the absolute character of the moral law, the origin and abnormal character of sin. If, however, it does not wish to abandon all this, it must to the same extent relinquish the evolutionary theory accepted earlier. In the case of Tennant, this is very clearly evidenced in the fact that, in a most deterministic sense, he again attributes to the human being, who slowly evolved from the animal world, a free will[47] that has the power to make a choice between egoistic and altruistic tendencies. But he fails to explain with a single word how in the process of evolution there is room for such a free will. In the third place, he wraps himself in even greater difficulty when answering the question how that will relates to the innate animal tendencies. According to Tennant, the free will already evolved in primitive "man" *before* the awakening of a moral consciousness. Hence, for a considerable period of time primitive "man" was already an intellectual and volitional being before becoming a moral being and in that period lived without law, without sin, and without virtue:[48] a conception of humanity that is completely impossible and that in its inscrutability ranks with that of *homo naturalis*. Gradually, however, there arises in primitive "man" a moral consciousness, a sense of responsibility, an accusing or excusing conscience, and in connection with all this a moral will as well. So far we have ignored the question—as yet never adequately answered—how this higher rational and moral life could emerge, by evolution, in primitive humanity from without. What is the nature and power that characterizes the will that is thus formed in humans? Innate animal tendencies and lusts, according to Tennant, are not sinful. They are only the "raw material for the production of sin," but equally the "raw material" for doing good. They are simply "non-moral, natural, necessary, neutral, indifferent material waiting to be moralized; they may be turned to bad or they may be turned to good; our

---

humanity that will gradually be overcome by the awakened and strengthened moral consciousness. Orchard denies any objective guilt to sin and regards the consciousness of guilt (sorrow, contrition) as an instrument used by God to morally instruct human beings and lead them to perfection.

46. F. R. Tennant, *Origin and Propagation of Sin*, 10, 27, 142.

47. Ibid., 121ff.

48. Ibid., xxii.

virtues and vices, in fact, have common roots." The will, accordingly, seems to be unrelated or opposed to the innate animal tendencies and does so without "any bias to evil."[49]

Such a will, which is in no way rooted in human nature but exists outside it and hangs in the air far above it, however, is psychologically inconceivable and open to many more objections than the creation of humans in an adult state and possessing original righteousness. Such a conception of the will, accordingly, cannot be practically maintained and soon becomes its precise opposite. For one who ponders the power of inborn animal tendencies and contrasts it with the vagueness of the original moral consciousness, the weakness of the moral will, senses that the theory of freedom in this argument will soon have to make way for a theory of necessity. This is clearly evident in Tennant. Not only does he assume the absolute universality of sin, but he recognizes that our nature and our surroundings are such that they make "the realization of our better self" into "a stupendously difficult task." Indeed, the internal conflict between "nature and nurture, natural desire and moral end" is the inevitable condition of human life and the expression of God's intent.[50] As a result, sin, in its rise and further development, in the child and in the people of nature, has been precariously weakened,[51] and the definition of it is really restricted to those transgressions of the moral law that occur with full awareness and intention.[52] Let me say briefly, finally, that this theory of the origin of sin is diametrically opposed to the witness of Scripture and entails the modernization of the entire Christian confession concerning revelation, atonement, infant baptism, and so on.[53]

It is not surprising, therefore, that this new theory about the origin of sin has evoked a wide range of criticism.[54] In fact, it again comes down to the ancient view of Pelagius that was repudiated by the entire Christian church. But whereas Pelagius remained true to his starting point and attempted to maintain the freedom of the will to the end, the new theory, though it begins by giving prominence to free will, in fact allows it again to be bested in the struggle against the power of inborn animal nature. The more deeply people penetrate the phenomenon of sin, the less it becomes something accidental and arbitrary, and the more it gains in power and importance, not only for the religious and ethical life but also for the intellectual, the aesthetic, the psychological, and all of cosmic life. If, in this connection, one asks about the origin of sin, however, one again receives a variety of answers. Not all people go equally far. Some explain it in terms of human nature, others in terms of the cosmos as a whole, still others in terms of God himself.

49. Ibid., xvii, xxii, 84, 95, 101, 102.

50. Ibid., 86, 92, 113, 118, 119.

51. Ibid., 82ff., 89ff., 93ff., 100, 105ff.; cf. Brown, "The Over-emphasis of Sin," *Hibbert Journal* 8 (April 1909): 614–22.

52. Tennant, *Origin and Propagation of Sin*, xxiii, 163ff.

53. Cf. ibid., xii, xxviii, 113, 119, 123ff., 144, 446.

54. Cf. ibid., preface, xi–xxx.

In the first category are those who locate the origin of sin in the domination of humans by matter. Greek philosophy was generally committed to the view that the role of reason was to curb one's sensual urges and passions. Jews assumed the existence in humans of an "impulse toward evil" (יֵצֶר הָרַע) that in the course of one's physical development steadily gained in strength, reached its peak in sexual desire, and while not evil in itself nonetheless seduced humans into a variety of sins.[55] This notion regularly returns in ascetic movements. Catholic theology even recognized its relative validity when in the case of humans devoid of the controls of the superadded gift they spoke of a natural conflict between flesh and spirit and of a "sickness" and "faintness" (*morbus* and *languor*) of human nature.[56] In modern philosophy and theology, sin is often similarly derived from an original opposition between nature and reason, sensuality and intellect, a lower and a higher self, flesh and spirit, egoistic and social tendencies. Sensuality in this view, though not itself considered sinful, is nevertheless regarded as the occasion and stimulus to sin. All sin, therefore, essentially consists in a person's mind serving his or her sensuality and permitting it to control it; and all virtue consists in humans ruling over nature by their reason and thus developing into free and independent personalities.[57] For this view people even eagerly appeal to the Pauline doctrine of the flesh (σάρξ) and delight in this scriptural support.

But this interpretation of sin is marked by halfheartedness. One has to make a choice: either the sensual nature of humans is not as such sinful, sin arising only if reason and will comply with its demands—and then the theory relapses into Pelagianism; or one's sensual nature is inherently sinful and then sin is inherent in matter as such—and the anthropological interpretation has to proceed to the cosmic. This, accordingly, is precisely what happened in the thinking of many. Plato assumed the existence of eternal matter (ὕλη) alongside of and over against God. Though the cosmos was a work of reason, from the beginning there was also at work in it another factor, a blind force that could not be completely controlled by the demiurge. Therefore, God could not make the world as good as he wanted it to be: he was bound to finiteness, to matter. The cause of sin, suffering, and death, therefore, lies in the corporeal; matter (ὕλη) holds back the invasive and pervasive power of the idea. The body is a prison house of the soul, the source of

55. F. W. Weber, *Syst. der altsyn. pal. Theol.*, §§49–50.

56. R. Bellarmine, *De gratia primi hominis* (Heidelberg: J. Lancellot, 1612), c. 5.

57. Cf. Descartes, Wolff, Fichte, Hegel, in F. Jodl, *Geschichte der Ethik in der neuern Philosophie*, 2 vols. (Stuttgart: Cotta, 1882–89), I (1882), II (1889); and E. von Hartmann, *Das sittliche Bewusstsein*, 2nd ed. (Leipzig: W. Friedrich, 1886), 265ff., in F. Schleiermacher, *The Christian Faith* (Edinburgh: T&T Clark, 1989), §66; R. Rothe, *Theologische Ethik*, 2nd rev. ed., 5 vols. (Wittenberg: Zimmerman, 1867–71), §§459ff.; A. E. Biedermann, *Christliche Dogmatik* (Zürich: Füssli, 1869), §§763ff.; O. Pfleiderer, *Grundriss der christlichen Glaubens- und Sittenlehre* (Berlin: G. Reimer, 1888), §§100ff.; R. A. Lipsius, *Lehrbuch der evangelisch-protestantischen Dogmatik* (Braunschweig: C. A. Schwetschke, 1893), §§468ff., 477ff.; Schultz, *Grundriss der evangelischen Dogmatik*, 2nd ed. (Göttingen: Vandenhoeck & Ruprecht, 1892), 61; J. H. Scholten, *De Vrije Wil, Kritisch Onderzoek* (Leiden: P. Engels, 1859), 177; idem, *De Leer der Hervormde Kerk in Hare Grondbeginselen*, 2nd ed., 2 vols. (Leiden: P. Engels, 1850–51), II, 422ff., 574ff.

fear and unrest, of desire and passion.[58] Matter (ὕλη) has the same significance in Neoplatonism and Gnosticism and in numerous ascetic and theosophical schools of thought.[59] Related to this doctrine of Plato are all the theories that derive sin from matter, which, though created by God, is opposed to him;[60] or from the finiteness, "the original imperfection," of creatures;[61] or, generally speaking, from the realization of the "cosmic idea."

This interpretation of sin in terms of creaturely existence, however, cannot consistently avoid somehow having to go back to God to locate the origin of sin in *his* nature or work. In the thought of Plato, matter (ὕλη) itself had eternal and independent status alongside God. In Parsism and Manicheism, two personal divine entities stood eternally over against each other as the creators of light and darkness and gave to the existing world its dual character. Neoplatonism and Gnosticism made the creation, fall, redemption, and so on into aspects of an emanation that as the "unknown deep" (βυθος ἀγνωστος), the absolute pleroma, issued from God in ever-descending formations, finally giving existence to the material world with its ignorance, darkness, sin, suffering, and death, but then, by a process of redemption, led that divinely emanated but now fallen world back to God.[62]

Theosophy, in the case of Böhme and Schelling, fed on these ideas when it attempted to interpret the personality of God, the Trinity, creation, fall, and redemption in terms of the being of God.[63] The three potencies assumed in God—to ensure his becoming person, mind, spirit—are at the same time the basic elements of another existence, namely, that of the world. As person, God has the freedom and the power also to project outside himself and to set in polar tension the potencies that are present in him and that he eternally controls.[64] In that tension lies the possibility of sin. In the original creation, the first either ideally or also in reality, these potencies were at rest. Sin, misery, darkness, death, and so on existed only potentially; they slumbered in the womb of creation. But humans, who bore these potencies within themselves, broke their oneness and unleashed

58. E. Zeller, *Philos. der Griechen.*, II, 765ff., 855ff.

59. Ibid., v, 125, 171, 236, 297, 386, 547.

60. C. H. Weisse, *Philosophische Dogmatik oder Philosophie des Christentums*, 2nd ed. (Freiburg: Mohr, 1890), §§541ff., 561ff.; R. Rothe, *Theol. Ethik*, §55.

61. G. W. Leibniz and J. C. Gottsched, *Theodicee* (Leipzig: Forester, 1744), §156.

62. A. Stöckl, *Die spekulative Lehre vom Menschen und ihre Geschichte* (Würzburg: Stahel, 1858), II, 52ff.

63. Cf. H. Bavinck, *Reformed Dogmatics*, II, 322–29, 412–15 (##230–31, 252).

64. F. W. J. Schelling, *Ausgewählte Werke*, IV, 275–360. ("Philosophische Untersuchungen über das Wesen der menschlichen Freiheit und die damit zusammenhängenden Gegenstände," [1809]), *Werke*, 1/7, 331–416. Ed. note: Bavinck's references to Schelling that are to works incorporated into the new, unrevised, but abridged and repaginated *Ausgewälte Werke* (Darmstadt: Wissenschaftliche Buchgesellschaft, 1968) will be cited with the full title of the work as well as Bavinck's original reference. Since this is not a complete edition of Schelling's original *Ausgewählte Werke* (Stuttgart and Augsburg: Cotta, 1856–61), writings not included in the new edition will be cited as *Werke*, using Bavinck's original reference. Cf. E. von Hartmann, *Schellings philosophisches System* (Leipzig: H. Haacke, 1897), 118ff.

the evil forces that were potentially present in the creation. A world like the present one, with so much savagery and misery, can only be explained in terms of a fall. This fall is the *Ur*-fact of history.[65] Hegel, even more strongly, viewed it as a fall that the idea of the Absolute realized itself in the world as its own alternative existence. However much he regarded nature as a product of reason, he could not deny that it was powerless to fully realize the Idea; he therefore stated that the Idea, in giving existence to such a world, had become unfaithful to itself, had in fact apostatized from itself.[66] Thus he paved the way for the pessimism that, in the manner of Buddhism, considers existence itself the greatest sin, a sin committed by the blind irrational will, which is the ultimate guilty party.[67]

THE ENIGMA OF SIN'S ORIGIN

[312] The question of the origin of evil, second to that of existence itself, is the greatest enigma of life and the heaviest cross for the intellect to bear. The question, Whence is evil? has occupied the minds of humans in every century and still waits in vain for an answer that is more satisfactory than that of Scripture. Insofar as philosophy has taught us anything significant in this matter, it is, broadly speaking, a strong proof for the scriptural truth that *this world is inexplicable without a fall*. All the great thinkers, even if they were ignorant of Genesis 3 or rejected it as myth, have, despite themselves, given tacit or explicit support to this simple story. And insofar as philosophy looked for a solution to the problem in another direction, it has gotten off the track and sadly gone astray. This applies first of all to the Pelagian explanation of sin, the many objections to which have been touched on above and will come up at length in our discussion of the essence and propagation of sin. But it applies further to all the systems that trace evil not to a creaturely act of will but to the nature of humanity, the world, or God.

In the first place, sin cannot be inferred from the sensual nature of the human race. If that were the explanation, sin certainly would always have a sensual or carnal character. But this is far from being always the case. There are also spiritual sins, sins of a demonic nature, such as pride, envy, hatred, enmity against God, which, though less visible, are absolutely no less serious than the sins of carnality; and these cannot be explained by sensuality, any more than the existence of fallen angels can be explained on this basis. If sins originated from humanity's sensual nature, one would certainly expect that they would be most vigorous and numerous in the early years of life, and that to the degree that the mind became more developed it would also exert firmer control over it and finally overcome it altogether. But experience tells a very different story. To the degree that people

---

65. Cf. J. Claassen, *Jakob Böhme, sein Leben und seine theosophischen Werke*, 3 vols. (Stuttgart: J. F. Steinkopf, 1885), II, 185ff.; F. W. J. Schelling, *Werke*, I/7, 336–416; I/8, 331ff.; II/3, 344ff., 358ff.

66. G. F. Hegel, *Werke*, VI, 413; VII, 1, 23ff., 15ff.

67. A. Schopenhauer, *Die Welt als Wille*, I, 193ff.; II, 398ff.; E. von Hartmann, *Philosophie des Unbewussten*, 9th ed., 2 vols. (Berlin: C. Duncker, 1882), II, 198ff., 273ff., 295ff.

grow up, sin—also sensual sin—has a stronger grip on them. It is not the child but the young man and the adult male who are frequently enslaved by their lusts and passions; and mental development is often so little able to curb sin that it tends rather to make available the means of seeking the satisfaction of one's desire on a larger scale and in more refined ways. And even when at a later stage in life the sensual sins have lost their dominance, they still secretly stay on in people's hearts as desires or make way for others that, though more spiritual in nature, are no less appalling. Accordingly, if this explanation of sin in terms of sensuality is meant in earnest, it should result in seeking release by suppressing the flesh; but it is precisely the history of asceticism that is best calculated to cure us of the error that sin can be overcome in that fashion. People take their hearts with them when they enter a monastery, and from the heart arise all sorts of sins and iniquities.

The Sinful "Flesh"

This theory erroneously tries to keep itself afloat with an appeal to the idea of flesh (בשׂר and σαρξ) in Scripture, especially in Paul. This word first of all denotes the material substance of the human body (1 Cor. 15:39); second, the body itself that is composed of matter in contrast to spirit (πνευμα), mind (νους), and heart (καρδια) (Rom. 2:28; 2 Cor. 7:5; Col. 2:5); further, in the Old Testament sense of humans as earthly, weak, fragile, and transient beings (Gen. 6:3; 18:27; Job 4:17–19; 15:14–15; 25:4–6; Pss. 78:39; 103:14; Isa. 40:6; Jer. 17:5; Rom. 3:20; 1 Cor. 1:29; Gal. 2:16); and finally in Paul the sinful life-orientation of humans. Thus he speaks of "carnal," "in the flesh," of "being, living, walking according to the flesh," of "the body of sin," "the mind of the flesh" (Rom. 3:7; 7:14; 8:3f.; 1 Cor. 3:3; 2 Cor. 10:2–3; etc.). In this sense "flesh" is contrasted with "spirit," though not with the human πνευμα, which, after all, is also sinful and needs sanctification (Rom. 12:1–2; 1 Cor. 7:34; 2 Cor. 7:1; Eph. 4:23; 1 Thess. 5:23), but with the "Holy Spirit" (πνευμα άγιον) of God (Rom. 8:2, 9, 11), which renews the human spirit (Rom. 7:6; 8:14; Gal. 5:18) and also consecrates the body and puts it at the disposal of righteousness (Rom. 6:13, 19; 12:1; 1 Cor. 6:13, 15, 19–20), thus putting in people a "new person" (καινος άνθρωπος) in opposition to the old sinful life-orientation, the "flesh" (σαρξ) of the "old person" (παλαιος άνθρωπος) (Rom. 7:5f.; 8:1ff.; Gal. 5:13–25; Eph. 2:3, 11; Col. 3:9). Some now have the idea that in this view the "flesh" is not only the seat and organ of sin but also its source and origin.[68]

But this cannot be maintained against or squared with the undeniable fact that Paul clearly traces sin to the temptation of the serpent and the transgression by Adam (Rom. 5:12; 2 Cor. 11:3). Paul also speaks of the defilement of the body and of the spirit and desires the cleansing of both (2 Cor. 7:1) and lists, among

68. F. C. Baur, Holsten, Lüdemann, Zeller; O. Pfleiderer, *Der Paulinismus*, 2nd ed. (Leipzig: O. R. Reisland, 1890), 60ff.; H. J. Holtzmann, *Lehrbuch der neutestamentlichen Theologie*, 2 vols. (Freiburg and Leipzig: Mohr, 1897), II, 13ff.; C. Clemen, *Sünde*, I, 188ff.; J. C. Matthes, "De Inrichting van den Eeredienst door Jerobeam," *Theologische Tijdschrift* 24 (1890): 225–39; W. Wrede, *Paulus* (Halle a.S.: Gebauer-Schwetschke, 1904), 59ff.

the works of the flesh, a range of spiritual sins such as idolatry, strife, anger, and even heresy (Gal. 5:19f.). Paul describes hostility against God as the "mind of the flesh" (φρονημα της σαρκος; Rom. 8:7) and accepts the existence of evil spirits, which, after all, have no σαρξ (Eph. 6:12). [Positively] Paul recognizes Christ, though born of a woman (Gal. 4:4) and of Jewish stock "according to the flesh" (το κατα σαρκα; Rom. 9:5), as being without any sin (2 Cor. 5:21) and calls the body a temple of God, claiming all its members for the service of righteousness (Rom. 6:13, 19; 12:1; 1 Cor. 6:13–20). Finally, Paul teaches a resurrection of dead bodies (1 Cor. 15), and in principle opposes asceticism (Col. 2:16; 1 Thess. 4:4). The proponents of the view that Paul considers the "flesh" to be the principle of sin, accordingly, often turn around halfway by saying that human flesh is not itself sinful and does not automatically bring sin with it but does incite and tempt people to sin.[69]

Other scholars have therefore expressed the view that Paul, when he uses the word σαρξ in an ethical sense, completely ignores the original meaning.[70] This in itself is not too likely, however, and fails to do justice to the connection Scripture repeatedly makes between the earthly, weak, and transient nature of humans and their sin. There is undoubtedly a close connection between the two; while the sensual nature of humans is not itself sin, nor the source or principle of sin, it is its dwelling place (Rom. 7:17–18) and the instrument of its dominion over us (Rom. 6:12). Human beings are not pure spirit but from the earth, people of "dust," and become living souls (1 Cor. 15:45ff.), and are therefore connected with the cosmos and always have bodies as their instrument and as organs of their activity (Rom. 6:13; 8:13). This sensual nature gives to sin, as it characterizes our humanity, a character distinct from that of the angels, both in origin and in essence. Temptations come to us from without via "the desire of the flesh, the desire of the eyes, and the pride in riches" (1 John 2:16). It is the sensual nature of human beings that makes their sin such that they make a god of their belly, that they think the things that are below, that they are self-seeking and live for themselves, and honor the creature more than the Creator (Rom. 1:21ff.; Phil. 2:4, 21; 3:19; Col. 3:2; etc.).

Σαρξ denotes the sinful life-orientation of humans who in soul and body turn away from God and toward the creature. The Pauline use of the word "flesh" becomes clear to us when we abandon the familiar Greek contrast between the material and the immaterial and replace it with the biblical contrast between the earthly and the heavenly, the divine and the creaturely, between what is below and what is above. Thus Jesus spoke of the flesh in John 3:6. Flesh became "the

69. C. Clemen, *Sünde*, I, 204; H. J. Holtzmann, *Lehrbuch*, II, 38.

70. A. Neander, *Geschichte der Pflanzung und Leitung der christlichen Kirche durch die Apostel*, 5th ed., 2 vols. (Gotha: F. A. Perthes, 1890), 508ff.; Tholuck, "Erneute Untersuchung über σαρξ als Quelle der Sünde," *Studien und Kritiken* 28 (1855): 477ff.; B. Weiss, *Biblical Theology of the New Testament*, trans. David Eaton and James E. Duguid, 2 vols. (Edinburgh: T&T Clark, 1883), §68; H. H. Wendt, *Die Begriffe Fleisch und Geist im biblischen Sprachgebrauch untersucht* (Gotha: F. A. Perthes, 1878); F. Nitzsch, *Ev. Dogm.*, 315ff.

proper designation of the race as self-evolved and self-continued. Human nature as now constituted can produce nothing but its like, and that like is now sinful. Flesh therefore may be appropriately used for the principle of corrupt nature in the individual, for the obvious reason that it is in the course of the flesh, or of the ordinary production of human nature, that the evil principle invariably originates."[71]

Sin as God's Design?

The explanation of sin from the sensual nature of humans cannot, however, as noted above, stop here but has to move on to locating its cause in the material nature or the finiteness of the creature, and so in an eternal and independent power alongside God, or in the dark nature or blind will in the divine being itself. This view of the origin of sin commends itself over the preceding one by its profounder insight into the power and dominion of sin. It has a keen eye not only for its ethical and anthropological but also for its cosmic and theological meaning. It takes seriously the undeniable truth that a power as appalling as sin cannot have originated accidentally, outside God's will and counsel. It finds support in the whole present state of the world, both the physical world and the world of ethics. Everywhere in nature and history there are stark and deep contrasts that seem to be necessary for life and development. Heaven and earth, light and darkness, day and night, summer and winter, storm and quiet, war and peace, labor and rest, prosperity and adversity, love and hate, joy and sorrow, health and sickness, life and death, truth and falsehood, sin and virtue: these are the contradictory factors of which the whole of our existence is composed and without which there can apparently be no continuation and progress. What storms are in nature, wars and revolutions in society, peasants and slaves in a drama, solecisms and barbarisms in a language, antitheses in a public address, false notes in music, dark shadows on a painting: that sin is in the world.[72] All activity seems also to presuppose some hindrance. A pigeon might imagine it could fly better in a vacuum, but precisely the resistance of the air is what enables it to fly. Similarly, human beings may think they could live better without sin, but in fact sin is necessary for their moral perfection (Kant). The law of contradiction is the fundamental law of all that is, the "source of eternal life. What prompts, even compels, us to act is contradiction alone. Without it there would be no movement, no life, no progress, but everlasting repose, the

---

71. Laidlaw, "Psychology," *DB*, IV, 166; cf. also Hofmann, *Schriftbeweis*, I, 559; J. Müller, *The Christian Doctrine of Sin*, trans. Rev. Wm. Urwick, 5th ed., 2 vols. (Edinburgh: T&T Clark, 1868), I, 326ff.; G. Lechler, *Das apostolische und das nachapostolische Zeitalter*, 3rd ed. (Karlsruhe und Leipzig: H. Ruether, 1885), 289ff.; H. Ernesti, *Die Ethik des Apostels Paulus*, 3rd ed. (Göttingen: Vandenhoeck & Ruprecht, 1880), 32ff.; H. Cremer, "Fleisch," *PRE*[3], VI, 98–105; J. Gloël, *Der heiligen Geist in der Heilsverkündigung des Paulus* (Halle: M. Niemeyer, 1888), 14–61, 246; P. Feine, "Der Ursprung der Sünde nach Paulus," *Neue kirchliche Zeitschrift* (October 1899): 771–95.

72. These and similar images were already used by Plato, the Stoics, and Plotinus; see E. Zeller, *Philosophie der Griechen*, II, 765, 929; IV, 173; V, 548–62. Later they were taken over by Augustine, Erigena, Leibniz, and others.

death slumber of all forces."[73] What would be a life without sin? It would be an existence without content, an empty abstraction without opportunity for struggle and victory or conflict and reconciliation; without material for drama and song, for science and art. That was the reason why Dante could paint his inferno with colors derived from this earth, but for the portrayal of heaven this earth offers no materials (Schopenhauer). The proponents of this view of the origin of sin delight in appealing to many verses in Scripture that speak of a necessity of sins and disasters (Matt. 18:7; Luke 24:26; John 9:3; 1 Cor. 11:19; 2 Tim. 2:20); to the teaching of Augustine and Calvin, who include sin in God's counsel and providence; to the well-known words in the Easter vigil of the Roman missal: "O truly necessary sin of Adam that is wiped out by the death of Christ! O happy fault that was worthy to have such and so great a Savior!" There is so much truth in this conception that it need not surprise us that it has at all times fascinated people. Sin is not accidental or arbitrary but incorporated in the counsel of God. It is so intertwined with our whole existence that we cannot even picture a holy life or a sinless history. It is, against its will, made subservient by God Almighty to the revelation of his attributes and the honor of his name.

Still, despite all the truth that is concealed in this idea and will come out even more clearly later on, it cannot and may not be accepted. In the first place, it robs sin of its ethical character. Sin is certainly not only and not always an act of the will, as Pelagianism teaches, and certainly also a state of the will, but it never completely occurs apart from the will. Augustine said: "All sin is voluntary." This sentiment is undoubtedly true when understood in the sense in which Augustine understood it. In the view being considered, however, sin is made analogous to and—in Gnostic and theosophic fashion—equated with the physical phenomena of darkness, sickness, death, and so on. Moreover, it is inferred from the flesh, from matter, from the essence of creatures, from the nature of God, and thus made into a substance or a necessary quality of the existence of things. In the process, sin is deprived of its ethical character and degraded to a physical phenomenon.

Second, in this view sin is made eternal and invincible. Inasmuch as it is not ethical but physical in nature, it is necessarily a feature of what exists, God as well as the universe, and indispensable to the existence of everything. Not only is the good necessary to evil, but, conversely, evil is necessary to the good. Evil, here, is not a quality of the good and of existence but is itself a kind of existence and good, without which even the good cannot exist. Human beings who strove to be freed from sin would entertain a wicked wish and work for their own ruin. A world without sin could not be, and a state of glory would be nothing but a dream.

In the third place, in this view sin ceases to be antithetical; it simply becomes a lower or lesser degree of the good, in its place as good as the good itself. It becomes

73. F. W. J. Schelling, *Ausgewählte Werke*, V, 25, 127 ("Die Weltalter Erstes Buch" [1813]); *Werke*, I/8, 219, 321; cf. also John Fiske, *Through Nature to God* (Boston and New York: Houghton Mifflin and Co., 1899), first essay on "The Mystery of Evil."

a component in life and history that is always destined to disappear but never does: a not-yet being what a creature ought to be, yet never becomes or can become, a pure negation that has no reality and exists only in thought. "As far as good and evil are concerned, they also indicate nothing positive in things, considered in themselves, nor are they anything other than modes of thinking, or notions we form because we compare things to one another."[74]

In the fourth place, in this view God has to become the author of sin. Parsism and Manicheism still shrank from this conclusion, set the kingdom of light and the kingdom of darkness in direct opposition to each other, and placed an eternal divine being at the head of each. The god of nature is very different from the god of the good, the moral power, which asserts itself in the human conscience.[75] But Gnostic philosophy and theosophy incorporated the opposites into a single Absolute. God himself, in order to become a person or spirit, had to carry within himself and to perpetually overcome a dark nature as well. By a conflictual process, before and from without or in and through the world, he himself arrives at divine existence. In himself he is an "unknown abyss" (βυθος ἀγνωστος), a dark nature, a blind will, and as such the creator of matter. "In order for there to be no evil, God himself would have to not be."[76]

Not only does Scripture testify against this view, but the moral consciousness of all humans rises up in protest against it. Sin may be whatever it is, but one thing is certain: God is the Righteous and Holy One who prohibits it in his law, witnesses against it in the human conscience, and visits it with punishments and judgments. Sin is not rational, nor is it lawful; it is lawlessness (ἀνομια); it is not necessary to the existence of creatures, much less to the existence of God. The good is necessary even for evil to exist, but the good does not need evil, nor does holiness need sin, nor truth falsehood, nor God Satan. If sin, nevertheless, frequently serves to bring the good to fuller disclosure and to glorify God's attributes, this occurs—against sin's intent, not with its consent and cooperation—by the wisdom and omnipotence of God. Against its own genius, sin is forced to serve the honor of God and the coming of his kingdom. Thus evil frequently pays tribute to the good, the lie is overtaken by the truth, and Satan, to accomplish his deceptions, often has to appear as an angel of light. But all this is attributable, not to sin, but to the almighty power of God, who is able to bring good out of evil, light out of darkness, and life out of death.

---

74. B. Spinoza, *Ethics*, ed. and trans. James Gutman (New York: Hafner, 1949), preface; cf. idem, *The Letters*, trans. Samuel Shirley (Indianapolis: Hackett Publication Company, 1995), 32, 34; idem, *Cogitata metaphysics*, I, 6, 7; G. W. F. Hegel, *Sämtliche Werke*, VII, 9, 196 (*Philosophie des Rechts, Werke,* VIII, 180); D. F. Strauss, *Glaubenslehre*, II, 365–84; F. Schleiermacher, *Christian Faith*, §81; F. Paulsen, *System der Ethik mit einem Umriss der Staats- und Gesellschaftslehre,* 2 vols. (Berlin: Hertz, 1889), I, 551ff.; J. H. Scholten, *Leer der Hervormde Kerk*, II, 34ff., 422, 580.

75. This thought recurs frequently in more recent theology and philosophy. Cf. H. Bavinck, *Reformed Dogmatics,* I, 555–56 (#146); II, 173–77 (#197); and also H. Bavinck, *Philosophy of Revelation*, 209–11.

76. F. W. J. Schelling, *Ausgewählte Werke*, IV, 347. ("Philosophische Untersuchungen über das Wesen der menschlichen Freiheit und die damit zusammenhängenden Gegenstände" [1809]; *Werke*, I/7, 403).

Finally, this entire false conception has a horrible effect on the practice of life. If philosophy announces in so many words "God is to blame for everything; humans are blameless," then in practice libertinism and pessimism are not far behind. This is the libertinism that considers sin an illusion, and this illusion, as the only sin, erases all boundaries between good and evil, falsifies or, with Nietzsche, transvalues all moral concepts, and, under the rallying cry of the emancipation of the flesh, glorifies bestiality as geniality. This is the pessimism that, blind to sin, has eyes only for suffering, projects the blame for all that suffering upon the irrational act of an absolute will, and seeks deliverance from suffering in the destruction of the existing world. Judging by the outcome, so-called independent philosophy is also guided by the native tendency of all humans to justify themselves and to charge God with injustice.[77]

SIN AND THE WILL OF GOD

[313] Still, in saying that God is not the cause of sin, we have not said everything. Scripture, which strongly distances God from all wickedness, firmly announces, on the other hand, that his counsel and government also extend to sin.[78] God is not the author of sin, yet it does not lie outside his knowledge, his will, and his power. Then how are we to conceive God's relation to sin? Some, to exempt God from all responsibility for sin, have even deprived him of omniscience and omnipotence.[79] Others were of the opinion that, though sin does not lie outside God's knowledge, it does lie outside his will, and contented themselves with the concept of "permission." Though he knew of sin before it occurred, God did not will it. He only permitted it and did not prevent it. Thus spoke the church fathers[80] and were followed in this respect by

77. John H. Edwards, in "The Vanishing Sense of Sin," *Presbyterian and Reformed Review* 10 (October 1899): 606–16, points out how positivism, pantheism, Buddhism, and others are accompanied with a weakened consciousness of sin. One can add to this list the new religion of Christian Science, according to which matter, illness, sin, and death exist only in the mind; they can be nothing except the results of material consciousness, but material consciousness can have no real existence, because it is not a living reality (Mary Baker G. Eddy, *Unity of Good*, [Boston: J. Armstrong, 1898], 53). Cf. also J. Müller, *Christian Doctrine of Sin*, I, 276ff.; K. H. von Weizsäcker, "Zu der Lehre v. Wesen der Sünde," *Jahrbuch für deutsche Theologie* (1856): 131–95; K. F. A. Kahnis, *Die lutherische Dogmatik, historisch-genetisch dargestellt*, 3 vols. (Leipzig: Dörffling & Francke, 1861–68), I, 478ff.; A. F. C. Vilmar, *Theologische Moral: Akademische Vorlesungen* (Gütersloh: C. Bertelsmann, 1871), I, 143ff.; I. A. Dorner, *A System of Christian Doctrine*, trans. Rev. Alfred Cave and Rev. J. S. Banks, rev. ed., 4 vols. (Edinburgh: T&T Clark, 1888), III, 9ff.; J. Orr, *The Christian View of God and the World as Centering in the Incarnation* (New York: Randolph, 1893), 193; A. M. Fairbairn, *The Philosophy of the Christian Religion* (London: Hodder & Stoughton, 1905), 94ff.

78. Cf. H. Bavinck, *Reformed Dogmatics*, II, 345–47, 393–95, 615–19 (##233, 246, 306).

79. Cf. ibid., II, 196–203 (#201). More recently many proponents of Personal Idealism either deny God omnipotence and omniscience or ascribe to God a self-limitation [of power and knowledge]; cf. J. McTaggart, *Some Dogmas of Religion* (London: E. Arnold, 1906), 186ff., 221ff.; F. R. Tennant, *Origin and Propogation of Sin*, 141ff.

80. Clement of Alexandria, *Stromateis*, ch. 12; Origen, *On First Principles*, III, 2, 7; John of Damascus, *Exposition of the Orthodox Faith*, II, 29; cf. J. C. Suicerus, *Thesaurus ecclesiasticus*, 2 vols. (Amsterdam: J. H. Wetstein, 1682), s.v. προνοια and συγχωρησις.

Pelagians,[81] Roman Catholics,[82] Remonstrants,[83] Lutherans,[84] and many modern theologians.[85] Indeed, people in this camp acknowledged that "permission" did not mean a lack of divine knowledge and power, nor did it make God an idle spectator of sin. Still, "permission" was always described as a "negative act," as a "withholding of obstacles" (*suspensio impedimenti*), as neither a positive willing nor a positive non-willing of sin, but as an unwillingness to prevent it (*non velle impedire*).

It is clear that this view not only fails to provide a solution but also is ambiguous and avoids the real issue. The question at issue is this: Suppose that in a certain case a more or less negative act of divine permission precedes. Then does sin or does sin not follow, is it still a matter of the free will of humans or not, and can they still equally well commit as not commit the sin? If the decision then still depends on the free will of humans, Pelagius is right, and the control of sin has in fact been totally taken away from God and he is at most an "idle spectator of sins." If, on the other hand, the divine permission is such that humans, situated in those circumstances, have to commit the sin, not by compulsion but in virtue of the ordinances that pertain especially to the moral life, then Augustine is right, regardless of what one thinks of the word "permission." In posing this issue, Augustine already saw that "permission" could not be merely negative but had to be an act of God's will. "Nothing, therefore, happens unless the Omnipotent wills it to happen: he either permits it to happen or he brings it about himself." God does everything he wills; he does not will anything without doing it, but what he wills he does, and what happens does not ever happen apart from his will. "In a wondrous, indescribable way even that which is done against His will is not done without His will. It simply could not be done if He did not permit it, and of course He permits it not against His will, but with it; nor would He in His goodness permit evil unless in His omnipotence He could bring good even out of evil."[86] Many scholastic and Augustinian theologians still spoke along the same lines. Even when they used the word "permit," it was still understood as a "willing to permit" or a "willing to permit evil to happen."[87]

---

81. Augustine, *Against Julian*, trans. M. A. Schumacher, vol. 16 of *Writings of Saint Augustine* (Washington, DC: Catholic University of America Press, 1984), V, ch. 3.

82. Decrees of Council of Trent, VI, ch. 6; R. Bellarmine, "De amiss. gr. et stat. pecc.," *Controversiis*, II, 16; D. Petavius, *De Deo* (in *De theologicis dogmatibus*, 8 vols. [Paris: Vives, 1865–67]), VI, c. 6, 5.

83. J. Arminius, *Opera theologica* (Lugduni Batavorum [Leiden]: Godefridum Basson, 1629), 644ff., 694ff.; S. Episcopius, *Inst. theol.*, IV, sect. 4, c. 10; P. van Limborch, *Theol. christ.*, II, 29.

84. J. Gerhard, *Loci theol.*, VI, c. 9; J. A. Quenstedt, *Theologia.*, I, 533; D. Hollaz, *Examen theologicum acroamaticum* (Rostock and Leipzig: Russworm, 1718), 449; J. F. Buddeus, *Institutiones theologiae moralis* (Leipzig: T. Fritsch, 1715), 560; K. G. Bretschneider, *Dogmatik*, I, 506.

85. J. H. A. Ebrard, *Christliche Dogmatik*, 2nd ed., 2 vols. (Königsberg: A. W. Unzer, 1862–63), §265; A. von Oettingen, *Lutherische Dogmatik*, 2 vols. (Munich: C. H. Beck, 1897–1902), II, 339ff.; W. G. T. Shedd, *Dogmatic Theology*, 3rd ed., 3 vols. (New York: Scribner, 1891–94), I, 419, 444ff.

86. Augustine, *Enchiridion*, III, 95–100; idem, *The Trinity*, III, 4ff.; idem, *City of God*, XIV, 11; idem, *On Free Will*, 20, 21.

87. P. Lombard, *Sent.*, I, 46; T. Aquinas, *Summa theol.*, I, 19, art. 9; idem, *Summa contra gentiles*, I, 95; II, 25.

Essentially, the Reformed had no other conviction. For that reason a certain Livinus de Meyer correctly said: "One egg is no more like another egg than the Calvinian doctrine is to the Thomistic one."[88] Only, they had found that the word "permission" was used in a most ambiguous sense to conceal Pelagianism. For that reason they did not like the word. But they had so little objection to it per se that in fact they all again used it.[89] In their view, however, "permission" was no pure negation, no mere cessation of volition, proceeding from ignorance or impotence or negligence, but a positive act of God, an efficacious will, not efficient or productive, but deficient, an act upon which, in keeping with the nature of the moral life, sin has to follow.[90] It is true that sometimes in the heat of battle, the Reformed used "hard sayings" (*dicta duriora*).[91] Catholics,[92] Socinians,[93] Remonstrants,[94] and Lutherans,[95] consequently, referring to these sayings, did not lose any opportunity to charge the Reformed with making God the author of sin. But, first of all, these "hard sayings" are all less hard than those that sometimes occur in Holy Scriptures (e.g., Exod. 7:3; 2 Sam. 16:10; 24:1; Mal. 1:3; Luke 2:34; Rom. 9:17–18; 2 Thess. 2:11; etc.). Further, all such hard sayings have been held against Paul by Judaizers, against Augustine by the Pelagians, against Gottschalk by Hincmar, and against the Jansenists by the Jesuits. Third, the Reformed have always avoided using them in their confessions. Maccovius was challenged in this connection at the Synod of Dort.[96] Subsequently, they were either avoided or explained by most Reformed theologians.[97] And finally, their meaning and intent are perfectly transparent from

88. In C. G. Daelman, *Theologia seu observationes theologicae in summam D. Thomae*, 9 vols. in 8 (Antwerp: Jacob Bernard Jouret, 1734), II, 308.

89. In J. H. A. Ebrard, *Christliche Dogmatik*, §265.

90. U. Zwingli, *Opera*, ed. M. Schuler and J. Schulthess (Turici [Zürich]: Officina Schulthessiana, 1842), III, 170; IV; idem, *On Providence and Other Essays*, ed. William John Hinks, trans. Samuel Macauley Jackson (Durham: Labyrinth Press, 1983), c. 5; J. Calvin, *Institutes,* I.xvii.11; xviii.1–2; II.iv.2–4; II.xxiii.4, 8–9; T. Beza, *Tractationum theologicarum* (Geneva: Jean Crispin, 1570), I, 315, 387, 399; II, 347; III, 426; J. Zanchi, *Operum theologicorum*, 8 vols. (Geneva: Samuelis Crispini, 1617), II, 279; P. Martyr Vermigli, *Loci communes* (London: Kyngston, 1576), 206; F. Gomarus, *De provid. Dei* (in *Opera theologica omnia* [Amsterdam: J. Jansson, 1664]), c. 11; W. Twisse, *de permissione* (in *Opera theologica polemico-anti-arminiana* [Amsterdam, 1699]), I, 544–688; J. Maccovius, *Loci communes theologici* (Amsterdam: n.p., 1658), 206; H. Alting, *Theologia elenctica nova* (Amsterdam: J. Jansson, 1654), 316; A. Comrie and N. Holtius, *Examen van het Ontwerp van Tolerantie*, 10 vols. (Amsterdam: Nicolaas Byl, 1753), VI, 277; C. Vitringa, *Doctr. christ.*, II, 96.

91. E.g., J. Calvin, *Institutes*, III.xxiii.7; T. Beza, *Tract. theol.*, I, 319, 360, 401; J. Zanchi, *Opera*, V, 2; cf. also II, 328.

92. R. Bellarmine, *Controversiis*, II, c. 3ff.; D. Petavius, *De Deo*, VI, ch. 5; X, ch. 8; J. A. Möhler, *Symbolik* (Mainz: F. Kupferberg, 1838), 2–4.

93. Racovian Catechism, X, 16.

94. *Apologia Confessionis Augustanae*, ch. 2, 6; S. Episcopius, *Op. theol.*, I, 375ff.

95. J. Gerhard, *Loci theol.*, VI, ch. 10; J. A. Quenstedt, *Theologia*, II, 97.

96. Cf. H. Bavinck, *Reformed Dogmatics*, II, 361–68 (#238).

97. G. Voetius, *Select. disp.*, I, 1119–37; S. Maresius, *Syst. theol.*, IV, 18; F. Turretin, *Institutes of Elenctic Theology*, VI, qu. 7–8; J. Trigland, *Kerckelycke geschiedenissen* (Leyden: Andriae Wyngaerden, 1650), IV, 673ff.; V, 694; idem, *Antapologia* (Amsterdam: Joannam Janssonium [et al.], 1664), chs. 8–10; D. Chamier, *Panstratiae Catholicae, sive controversiarum de religione adversus pontificios corpus*, 4 vols. (Geneva: Rouer, 1626), II, lib. 3;

their connection with the whole of Reformed theology to everyone who wants
to understand them. The issue is simply that the word "permission" conceived
in a negative sense offers no solution whatever to the problem of God's relation
to sin, fails utterly to answer the objection that God is the author of sin, and in
fact withdraws the whole reality of sin from the context of God's providential
government. After all, one who can prevent an evil but, while quietly looking on,
lets it happen is as guilty as one who commits that evil.[98] Furthermore, even if
God merely allowed sin to occur, there has to be a reason why he did not want to
prevent it. That reason cannot be a lack of knowledge or power; hence it has to
lie in his will. So "permission" proves to be an act of his will after all. He *willed*
to permit it; and this willing can only be construed to mean that sin now also
actually occurs not by divine but by creaturely agency.

Not Mere "Permission"

Christian theology, for that matter, when speaking of God's government over
sin, never stopped with the idea of permission. For if both Scripture and Christian
thought forbade placing sin completely or partly outside the will and providence
of God, a solution could only be attempted by making a distinction in the *manner*
of God's government over the good and over the evil. And indeed, though in a
sense it can be said that God willed sin, that is, he willed that there would be sin,
he willed evil in a totally different sense than good. He takes delight in the good
but hates evil with divine hatred. In order that this difference in God's government
may stand out, we need first of all to point out that God and humanity, though
never separate, are nevertheless always distinct. Faith is a gift. God causes people to
believe; still, formally speaking, it is not God who believes, but the human being.
This applies even more intensely to the sinful deed. Materially, certainly, this must
be attributed to God, but formally it remains the responsibility of human beings.
When a murderer kills somebody, all the planning ability and the power he needs
for that purpose come from God, but the act, from a formal point of view, is his,
not God's. Indeed, the fact of homicide taken by itself is not yet a sin, for the same
thing frequently occurs in war and on the scaffold. What makes homicide a sin is
not the matter, the substrate, but the form, that is, the depravity, the lawlessness
(ἀνομία) of the deed; not the substance but the accident in the act.[99]

Lodged against this view is the objection that this distinction, even though
correct, actually makes no difference because it places the formal aspect of the

---

B. de Moor, *Commentarius perpetuus in Joh. Marckii compendium theologiae christianae didactico-elencticum*, 6
vols. (Leiden: J. Hasebroek, 1761–71), II, 487.

98. T. Beza, *Tract. theol.*, I, 315.

99. "Take the vilest crime, and Christianity assures you, that throughout the transaction, as you observe
it, there is nothing evil in the natural material which is employed, there is only the lawless misuse of material
which is in itself good. The worst passions are but the disorderly exercise of feelings and faculties in themselves
good and capable of redemption. Lust is only love uncontrolled by the will, and therefore lawless." C. Gore,
Lux mundi, 13th ed. (London: Murray, 1892), 388.

deed, the sinfulness in the sin, outside God's government.[100] This comment is only partly correct: it contains truth, not in general but in this particular case as it pertains to sin. In respect of faith, no one will infer from the fact that humans are the formal subject of it that it therefore lies outside God's providence. But it is true that, in the case of faith, things are very different than in the case of sin. Faith, after all, is an absolute gift and excludes all merit; sin, by contrast, is a human deed and carries guilt with it. Consequently, sin here must be opposed not to faith, which is given by God out of grace, but to the good that humans would have done had they not fallen. That good, materially speaking, would have been totally the work of God; formally, however, human beings would be the subject of it, and for them it would have carried with it—not of itself but in virtue of the covenant of works—a claim to reward. Now, sin is no more situated outside God's providence than the good, on the ground that it formally has humanity, not God, as subject.

Yet there is more. In the case of the good, God's providence must be understood as God himself by his Spirit working in the subject and positively enabling this subject to do good. In the case of sin, it may not be pictured that way. Sin is lawlessness, deformity, and does not have God as its efficient cause, but at most as its deficient cause. Light cannot of itself produce darkness; the darkness only arises when the light is withdrawn. God, therefore, is at most the negative or incidental cause of sin; its real and positive cause is located in human beings. However, because sin is merely a form and not a substance, it is in no way placed outside God's providence by being formally a human act. He impacts it in a way that completely corresponds to the nature of sin. Just as in his providence he governs all things in keeping with their nature, so in the domain of morality God also upholds the ordinances he has established specifically for that domain. Sin also arises and develops in accordance with a fixed law, not the laws of nature or of logic but those that are increated in the ethical life and are still operative in its destruction. Sickness, decomposition, and death are the antipodes of health, development, and life, but are no less than these controlled from beginning to end by fixed laws. In the same way, there is a law of sin that determines its entire history both in individuals and in humanity as a whole. And precisely this normativity in sin proves that God's kingdom governs in and over it as well. People who sin do not make themselves free and independent of God; on the contrary, though they were sons and daughters before, they are now slaves. Those who commit sin become the slaves of sin.[101]

100. S. Episcopius, *Op. theol.*, I, 180; J. A. Quenstedt, *Theologia*, II, 101.

101. On God's relation to sin, see the church fathers Origen, Athanasius, Basil, and others in W. Münscher, *Lehrbuch der christlichen Dogmengeschichte*, 3rd ed. (Cassel: J. C. Krieger, 1832–38), I, 157; and also T. Aquinas, *Summa theol.*, I, qu. 49, art. 2; II, 1, qu. 79, art. 2; idem, *Summa contra gentiles*, III, 3, 71; idem, *Sent.*, I, dist. 46–48; II, dist. 37; R. Bellarmine, "De amiss. gr. et statu pecc.," *Controversiis*, II, 18; D. Petavius, *De Deo*, VI, ch. 6; J. A. Quenstedt, *Theologia*, I, 535; D. Hollaz, *Examen*, 448; J. Calvin, *Institutes*, I.xviii. 18; II.iv; idem, *Concerning the Eternal Predestination of God*, trans. J. K. S. Reid (London: James Clarke & Co., 1961), 162–82

Possibility of Sin as God's Will

[314] By the distinction of the material and the formal aspect of sin, however, we have not yet [in any way] answered the question why God included sin in his decree and its execution. The answer is implied in the providence of God as it also pertains to sin. Scripture repeatedly states that God uses sin as punishment of the wicked (Deut. 2:30; Josh. 11:20; Judg. 9:23–24; John 12:40; Rom. 1:21–28; 2 Thess. 2:11–12), as a means of saving his people (Gen. 45:5; 50:20), to test and chastise believers (Job 1:11–12; 2 Sam. 24:1; 1 Cor. 10:13; 11:19; 2 Cor. 12:7), and to glorify his name (Exod. 7:3; Prov. 16:4; Rom. 9:17; 11:33; etc.). Precisely because God is the absolutely Holy and Almighty One, he can use sin as a means in his hand. Creatures cannot do that; with the least contact, they themselves become polluted and impure. But God is so infinitely far removed from wickedness that he can make sin, as an unresisting instrument, subservient to his glorification. There are countless examples that prove that also in this connection "when two parties do the same thing, it is not the same." It was God's will that Shimei cursed David, that Satan tested Job, that Jews and Gentiles wanted to give up God's holy servant Jesus to death—still in all these iniquities, human creatures are guilty and God is innocent. For even when he wants there to be evil, he only wants it in a way that is holy: though using it, he never commits it. And for that reason, he has also allowed sin in his creation. He would not have tolerated it had he not been able to govern it in an absolute holy and sovereign manner. He would not have put up with it if he were not God, the Holy and Omnipotent One. But being God, he did not fear its existence and its power. He willed it so that in it and against it he might bring to light his divine attributes. If he had not allowed it to exist, there would always have been a rationale for the idea that he was not in all his attributes superior to a power whose possibility was inherent in creation itself. For all rational creatures as creatures, as finite, limited, changeable beings, have the possibility of apostatizing. But God, because he is God, never feared the way of freedom, the reality of sin, the eruption of wickedness, or the power of Satan. So, both in its origin and its development, God always exercises his rule over sin. He does not force it, nor does he block it with violence but rather allows it to reach its full dynamic potential. He remains king yet still gives it free rein in his kingdom. He allows it to have everything—his world, his creatures, even his Anointed—for evils cannot exist without goods. He allows it to use all that is his; he gives it opportunity to show what it can do in order, in the end, as King of kings, to leave the theater of battle. For sin is of such a nature that it destroys itself by the very freedom granted it; it dies of its own diseases; it dooms itself to

(*Corpus reformatorum*, 36:347–66 and 37:262–318); T. Beza, *Tract. theol.*, I, 312ff., 337ff.; J. Zanchi, *Opera*, II, 259; D. Chamier, *Panstratiae catholicae*, II, lib. 3; W. Twisse, *Vindiciae gratiae, potestatis ac providentiae Dei*, 3 vols. (Amsterdam: Guilielmum Blaeu, 1632), I, 317ff., 544ff.; J. Trigland, *Antapologia*, ch. 9, 10; F. Gomarus, *Opera*, 136; Peter van Mastricht, *Theologia*, III, 10, 19ff.; F. Turretin, *Institutes of Elenctic Theology*, VI, qu. 8; B. de Moor, *Comm. theol.*, II, 492; C. Vitringa, *Doctr. Christ.*, II, 196.

death. At the apex of its power, it is, by the cross alone, publicly shown up in its powerlessness (Col. 2:15).[102]

For that reason God willed there to be sin. "Although, therefore, what is evil, insofar as it is evil is not a good, nevertheless it is well that not only good but also evil should exist. For, were it not a good that evil things should also exist, the Omnipotent Good would most certainly not allow evil to be, since beyond doubt it is just as easy for Him not to allow what He does not will, as it is for Him to do what He wills. Unless we believe this, the very first sentence of our profession of faith is endangered, wherein we profess to believe in God the Father Almighty."[103] Because he knew he was absolutely able to control sin, "he deemed it better to bring good out of evil than not to permit any evil to exist at all."[104] He thinks and guides evil for good and makes it subservient to his glory. Augustine even employs an array of images to assign to sin a place in the order of the whole. There it has the same function as the shadows in a painting, the solecisms and barbarisms in the language, the contrasts in a song.[105] God composed the order of history, like a beautiful poem, of antithetical elements to heighten the beauty and harmony of the whole.[106] Though these images contain some truth, they easily occasion misunderstanding. They tend to make sin appear necessary and entirely fitting in the whole of things. They sacrifice the particular to the universal and as a result offer no reconciliation or solace to those who wrestle with sin or experience suffering. But it *is* true that also and even especially in God's government over sin his attributes are splendidly displayed. The riches of God's grace, the depth of his compassion, the unchanging nature of his faithfulness, the inviolable character of his justice, the glory of his wisdom and power have shone out all the more brilliantly as a result of sin. When humans broke the covenant of works, God replaced it with the greatly improved covenant of grace. When Adam fell, God gave Christ as Lord from heaven. It is precisely God's greatness to so rule and overrule sin that against its own genius and intent it becomes serviceable to the honor of his name. And therefore the sin that is in the world, so far from being able to rob us of our faith in God, his love, and his power, rather confirms and strengthens us in that faith. "*If there is evil, there is a God.* For there would be no evil, if the order of good were removed, the privation of which is evil; and there would be no such order, if there were no God."[107]

102. A. von Oettingen, *Lutherische Dogmatik* (Munich: C. H. Beck, 1897), II, 469ff.

103. Augustine, *Enchiridion*, 96.

104. Ibid., 112, 27; idem, *City of God*, XXII, 1; idem, *The Literal Meaning of Genesis*, trans. John Hammond Taylor, Ancient Christian Writers 41 (New York: Newman, 1982), II, 9; idem, *On Genesis, Against the Manichees*, II, 28.

105. Augustine, *City of God*, XI, 18, 23; idem, *On Order*, II, 11.

106. Augustine, *City of God*, XI, 18; idem, *On Genesis, Against the Manichees*, I, 16; J. S. Erigena, *The Division of Nature* (1681), trans. Myra L. Uhlfelder (Indianapolis: Bobbs-Merrill, 1976), V, 35; T. Aquinas, *Summa theol.*, I, qu. 48, art. 2; idem, *Summa contra gentiles*, III, 61; A. Pichler, *Die Theologie des Leibniz aus sämmtlichen gedruckten und vielen noch ungedruckten Quellen*, 2 vols. (Munich: J. G. Cotta, 1869–70), I, 264ff.

107. T. Aquinas, *Summa contra gentiles*, III, 71.

[315] Although sin has thus been subject to God's government from the beginning, its origin is in the will of the rational creature, not in God. At this point, however, there immediately arises another problem. How can sin ever be explained in terms of the will of a being created after God's image in true knowledge, righteousness, and holiness? The Pelagian notion that the first human existed in a state of childlike innocence, of moral indifference, already proved unacceptable to us earlier;[108] it does not explain the fall but changes it into a minor misfortune and renders unintelligible the fact that from it such appalling consequences and horrendous miseries for the entire human race should result. If a spring can produce such a stream of polluted water, it must itself be inwardly polluted. It is impermissible, therefore, to so minimalize the distance between the state of integrity and the state of corruption that the transition becomes easy and gradual. Humans were not created morally indifferent by God, but positively holy. Still we have to bear in mind the following as well. In the first place, God most certainly willed the *possibility* of sin. The possibility of sinning is from God. The idea of sin was first conceived in his mind.[109] God eternally conceived sin as his absolute polar opposite and thus, in that sense, included it in his decree, or else it would never have been able to arise and exist in reality. It was not Satan, nor Adam and Eve, who first conceived the idea of sin: God himself as it were made it visible to their eyes. By means of the tree of the knowledge of good and evil and the probationary command, he clearly showed human beings the two roads they could take. And before the fall he even permitted an evil power from without to insinuate itself into Paradise, using the snake as its medium, and to discuss with Eve the meaning of the probationary command. There is therefore no doubt that God willed the possibility of sin.

In the second place, in keeping with this objective possibility, God so created angels and humans that they could sin and fall. They did not yet possess the highest [gift];[110] they were placed at the beginning of the road, not the end. The gift of perseverance, which is and always remains a gift and can never really be merited and be part of the nature of a creature, was still denied to them. Otherwise it would have seemed as if God feared the power of sin and wanted to prevent it by force. Angels and humans, accordingly, received the grace by which they *could* stand,

---

108. H. Bavinck, *Reformed Dogmatics*, II, 536–39 (#286).

109. Cf. ibid., 207–10 (#203).

110. Cf. ibid., 572–76 (#297). In describing Adam's state, the Reformed consistently used sober language. Though they held onto original righteousness, they avoided the exaggerated notions that occurred in the work of the church fathers and others (*Reformed Dogmatics*, II, 564–65 [#294]). Still, one cannot say with certainty why the words in article 14 of the Belgic Confession ("entirely perfect in all things"; *Reformed Dogmatics*, II, 565–68 [#295]) were omitted by the Synod of 1566 at Antwerp. Van Toorenenbergen (*De Symbol. Geschriften*, 24–25) suspects that people found the expression exaggerated, but this suspicion lacks adequate grounding. However this may be, the doctrine of the covenant of works gave Reformed theology the opportunity to say that Adam did not yet have the highest [gift]. An expression like that of Bishop South ("An Aristotle was but the rubbish of an Adam, and Athens but the rudiments of Paradise," in F. R. Tennant, *Origin and Propagation of Sin*, 25) was therefore rightly rejected. Culture, in a sense, only began after the fall, Gen. 4:17ff.

not the grace by which they *would* stand in perpetuity.[111] They did not yet possess the highest, inadmissible freedom, that is, the freedom of no longer being able to want to sin. The image of God in humanity was therefore still limited; it had not developed in all its fullness; it still had its limit in the possibility of sinning. Humanity was positioned in the good, but the possibility of evil still lay right alongside it. Human beings, though they walked on the right road, could stray onto a side road. They were good, but changeably so. God alone is fully existent in all his attributes and therefore immutable. Creatures, however, *become* and can therefore also *de*generate. All that has been created can change (παν κτιστον τρεπτον). If matter and form are distinct, as is always the case in creatures, there is always a possibility that the matter can change its form. What has been formed can be *de*formed and hence again be *re*formed; what has been created can become a *mis*creant and hence also be *re*-created. Moral freedom, however vigorous, is inherently distinct from logical necessity and physical force. A creature naturally incapable of sin, therefore, is a contradiction.[112]

In the third place, in the question concerning the origin of sin the faculty and activity of the imagination must be considered. In earlier times dogmaticians paid little attention to this subject, even though they were aware that in the case of humans temptation is first of all and primarily directed toward the imagination and thereby seeks to affect desire and the will.[113] In mysticism, however, the imagination played a large role. According to Böhme, it was by fantasy that Lucifer imagined himself into the abyss of sin; he dipped deeply into fantasy, so it took hold of him and surrendered itself to him in his life.[114] And in fact this is how things always go in the origination of the sinful act, as Thomas à Kempis describes it: "At first it is a mere thought confronting the mind; then imagination paints it in stronger colours; only after that do we take pleasure in it, and the will makes a false move, and we give our assent."[115] The mind entertains the idea of sin, the imagination beautifies and converts it into a fascinating ideal, desire reaches out to it, and the will goes ahead and does it. Thus, in the case of both angels and humans, the imagination was the faculty that made the violation of the commandment appear as the road to equality with God.[116]

111. H. Heppe, *Dogmatik der evangelischen reformierten Kirche* (Elberseld: R. L. Friedrich, 1861), 178, 179.

112. T. Aquinas, *Summa theol.*, I, qu. 63, art. 1; idem, *Summa contra gentiles*, III, 109.

113. G. Voetius, *Select. disp.*, I, 943; F. Burman, *Synopsis theologiae* (Ienae [Jena]: Joan. Felic. Bielckium, 1717), I, 46, 54; J. Edwards, *Works*, III, 122.

114. J. Claassen, *Jakob Böhme*, II, 95.

115. Thomas à Kempis, *The Imitation of Christ*, trans. William C. Creasy (Macon, GA: Mercer University Press, 1989), I, 13, 5; Augustine (*On Genesis, Against the Manichees*, II, 21) therefore already pointed out that in the experience of everyone who falls into sin the same process occurs that is described for us in Gen. 3. See also James 1:13–15.

116. C. H. Weisse, *Philos. Dogm.*, II, 422ff.; F. H. R. Frank, *System der christlichen Wahrheit*, 2nd ed., 2 vols. (Erlangen: A. Deichert, 1884), 433ff.; Kuyper, "Van de engelen," *De Heraut* 906 (May 5, 1895): 1–2.

Finally, we must note that Paul speaks in 1 Corinthians 15:45ff. of the first
man as "from the earth, a man of dust," who by creation became a living soul, thus
contrasting him with Christ, the Lord from heaven who became a life-giving
Spirit. This comparison and contrast between Adam and Christ is also deeply
significant for the fall of the first human. Adam was from the earth, a man of dust,
even before the violation of God's commandment. By his creation he became a
living soul. The natural comes first, then the spiritual. Articulated here is that in
the case of angels and humans the origin and nature of sin is very different. True,
we know little about the fall of angels, but in view of 1 Timothy 3:6 and 2 Peter
2:4, it must be considered highly probable that *pride,* the will to be equal to
God in power and dominion, was the beginning and principle of their fall. The
angels were not, like humans, led astray. Temptation did not come to them from
without. They fell by their own agency. Jesus says that the devil speaks "according
to his own nature" [John 8:44] when he lies. He became discontented with his
status and power on his own, that is, by his own thinking; he produced the lie
from within himself and projected it as a realm, a system, over against the truth
of God. But in the case of the first human, it was not so. He was not a pure spirit;
he was not as highly positioned, although, being created after God's image, he was
closer to God than the angels. He could not think as loftily and elevate himself
as boldly: he was from the earth, a man of dust, a living soul, a being more finely
and delicately organized but for that reason also weaker and more fragile. As such
a being, a being created in God's image, yet earthly and sensual, he presented to
Satan a suitable target for temptation. Satan came to him from without, adapted
himself to his nature as it were, aroused in him the lust of the eyes, the craving
of the flesh, and the pride of life, and so brought about his fall. The origin and
essence of sin has a very different character in the case of humanity than in that
of the angels. In both it is evident that we sin as human beings, not as devils, but
as beings who are from the earth, made of dust, and who by the act of creation
were made into living souls.

For this reason Scripture, and Paul in particular, so closely links the sensual
nature of a human being and sin. We must not for a minute think that underlying this connection there is a dichotomy between sensuality and reason, or the
idea that matter is of a lower order and the principle of sin. The origin of this
contrast and this idea is not Hebraic but Greek. Scripture knows nothing of
such a dualism, but it does know something else, namely, that, in virtue of their
origin, humans are sensual, "psychic," or earthly beings. From the very start the
first person was created a living soul, from the earth, a man of dust. He was that,
accordingly, in the state of integrity; and for that reason, despite the knowledge
and righteousness he possessed, was susceptible to seduction and temptation.
Already from the first sin it was evident that human beings are σαρξ ("flesh").
All subsequent sins have only and consistently highlighted our human nature as
temptable, weak, and unreliable beings. All human sin, also that of an intellectual
or spiritual kind, bears a character that corresponds to our "psychic" (earthly)

nature and thus differs from the sin of angels. The pre-fall human was not the image of God despite but *in* his or her peculiar "psychic" (earthly) nature; and it is from this nature that his or her sin receives its stamp.

With all this we have established nothing other and nothing more than the possibility of sin. How that possibility became a reality is and will presumably remain a mystery. We can show that the idea of sin was eternally present in God's mind; that it was made visible to humans in the probationary command; that they, therefore, aside from the good, also had knowledge of a forbidden evil; and that the imagination is the faculty by which humans transform ideas into ideals. But this is by no means to explain the passage from possibility to reality, from the bare notion to the sinful deed. This explanation eludes us, not only in connection with the origin of the first sin but over and over with respect to all sorts of human deeds and actions. In psychology and biography we indeed content ourselves with a few scant data. If we know something of people's ancestry, parents, upbringing, and so on, we think we have explained their personality, life, and conduct. But certainly this is rather superficial: every human being is a mystery, and every action is grounded in something other and deeper than the environment. To a much greater degree, the same applies to sin. Here we enter the mysterious area of moral freedom and face a phenomenon that in the nature of the case, as it concerns its origin, escapes explanation. A moral act, after all, is never equivalent to a conclusion from premises nor to a physical or chemical result. It essentially differs from both and has a character of its own. The moral life is utterly unique; it is always a life of freedom and that, in the nature of the case, is a riddle. But this is even much more the case with a sinful act, specifically with the first sinful act. Sin cannot be physically or logically deduced from antecedent circumstances, reasonings, or considerations. Above all, it cannot be inferred from a holy nature created in God's image. One who understood and explained sin, that is, could demonstrate that it necessarily followed from antecedent factors, would fail to do justice to its nature, erase the boundaries between good and evil, and trace something evil to something good. The sinful act is caused by the sinful will, but who will indicate to us the cause of this sinful will? "Trying to discover the causes of such deficiencies—causes which, as I have said, are not efficient but deficient—is like trying to see the darkness or hear the silence."[117] Sin started with lying (John 8:44); it is based on illusion, an untrue picture, an imagined good that was not good. In its origin, therefore, it was a folly and an absurdity. It does not have an origin in the true sense of the word, only a beginning. Satan has, therefore, not incorrectly been called an "irony of all logic."[118] The impossibility

---

117. Augustine, *City of God*, XII, 7.

118. A. Tholuck, *Die Lehre von der Sünde und vom Versöhner* (Gotha: F. A. Perthes, 1862), 15; J. Müller, *Christian Doctrine of Sin*, II, 159ff.; F. A. Philippi, *Kirchliche Glaubenslehre*, 3rd ed., 7 vols. in 10 (Gütersloh: Bertelsmann, 1870–90), III, 256; A. F. C. Vilmar, *Theol. Moral*, I, 37; A. von Oettingen, *Luth. Dogm.*, II, 26ff.; W. G. T. Shedd, *Dogmatic Theology*, II, 156; J. Laidlaw, *The Bible Doctrine of Man* (Edinburgh: T&T Clark, 1895), 209. When Kant explained that the origin of sin was to be found in an intelligible act of the will, that

of explaining the origin of sin, therefore, must not be understood as an excuse, a refuge for ignorance. Rather, it should be said openly and clearly: we are here at the boundaries of our knowledge. Sin *exists*, but it will never be able to justify its existence. It is unlawful and irrational.

TIME OF THE FALL

[316] As to the time of the fall, we cannot possibly pinpoint it precisely. For Manicheism and pantheism the very question is meaningless. Sin, in these systems, is eternal. It is rooted in an evil being or in God himself and coincides with the existence of the finite. There is no distinction between the creation and the fall; creation itself is an "apostasy" of God from himself as pure being. According to theosophists, the fall of the angels occurred in the period that lay between Genesis 1:1 and 1:2. The formlessness, emptiness, and darkness of the earth, in their opinion, cannot have been created by God, who is the God of life and light; they presuppose a fall and a subsequent curse. The angels first lived on this earth, which was their proper dwelling (Jude 6). This is also evidenced by the fact that Satan is even now called the prince of this world; that he wants to wrest it out of the hands of humanity that later received it from God as an inheritance; that in the temptation [in the wilderness] he was prepared to relinquish it to Christ in exchange for being worshiped; that he now still lives in the air; and that the world lies in the Evil One. The heaven and earth that were created in Genesis 1:1 and assigned to the angels, however, were of a very different nature than those that were later formed in the six days of Genesis 1:3ff. They were a spiritual, that is, immaterial, realm of light. The material earth that came into being in the six days, like the formlessness, emptiness, and darkness of Genesis 1:2, already presupposes the fall of angels. Matter itself is impure, self-seeking, and *cannot* have been directly created by God. "Only an enormous transgression, less a fall than an uprising, could occasion this material manifestation as a crisis—a movement of contradiction and restoration—and only the continuation of this transgression makes the continued existence or the continued generation of this matter intelligible" (Baader).[119]

But this theory, however attractive, lacks sufficient grounding in Holy Scripture. In Genesis 1:2 we read, not that the earth *became* formless and void, but that it *was*. Not a word suggests that this formless and empty state consisted in a destruction that followed an ordered state. Much less is there mention of the idea that the

was simply another way of acknowledging that the problem is unsolvable. Tennant (*Origin and Propogation of Sin*, 187), by contrast, insists that the origin of sin is foolish but not inexplicable.

119. J. Claassen, *Jakob Böhme*, II, 127ff.; *idem, *Franz von Baader* (1887), II, 157; P. F. Keerl, *Der Gottmensch, das Ebenbild des unsichtbaren Gottes*, vol. 2 of *Der Mensch, das Ebenbild Gottes* (Basel: Bahnmeier, 1866), I, 166ff.; and many others, for example, Hamberger, Schubert, K. von Raumer, R. Wagner, Kurtz, Delitzsch, and others; F. H. Reusch, *Bibel und Natur: Vorlesungen über die mosaische Urgeschichte und ihr Verhältnis zu den Ergebnissen der Naturforschung* (Freiburg i.B.: Herder, 1862), 88 (ed. note: ET: *Nature and the Bible*, trans. Kathleen Lyttleton from 4th ed. [Edinburgh: T&T Clark, 1886]); see also J. H. Gerretsen, *De Val des Menschen*, 45ff.

fall of the angels took place before that time and was the cause of the desolation. It is impossible to see, moreover, what connection there can be between the fall of the angels—supposing it took place before Genesis 1:2—and the desolation of the earth. To make such a connection, one has to resort to all sorts of gnostic ideas. One then has to teach that in some sense angels are corporeal beings and were assigned the original earth as their dwelling, just as according to some they still inhabit the fixed stars. Also, then the first earth, which was created in Genesis 1:1, has to be essentially different from what was prepared in the six days and consisted of more refined material. The coarse matter of which it now consists, though created by God, nevertheless presupposes the fall, is something unspiritual and essentially impure and self-seeking. All these opinions are derived, not from Scripture, but from Gnosticism.

Nor is there any ground for the opinion that the fall of humans occurred already before Genesis 3, either in the preexistent state of the souls or in Genesis 2 at and before the creation of the woman. The former notion was widely dispersed in antiquity. We find it in India, Persia, and Egypt; in various Greek philosophers such as Empedocles, Pythagoras, and Plato; in Rome; and in the Jewish Kabbalah. The rise of such a notion is not hard to explain. The wretchedness of life—outside the light of revelation—drove people toward such a hypothesis. According to the witness of the moral consciousness of humankind, virtue and happiness, as well as guilt and misery, are most intimately connected. When this life frequently seems to be pure misery, when that misery does not just begin at a later age but already at the time of conception and birth, it points to a moral debt that humans brought down upon their own heads before their earthly existence. The present life with its distress and sorrow is a penalty for the evil they have done in a previous existence, and if they fail to fully pay that penalty in this life or even increase the debt, they will in the hereafter be accorded a lot that corresponds to their conduct in this life. The ideas of the preexistence of souls and of the transmigration of souls, therefore, are correlative: both are controlled by the idea of retribution, of karma.[120]

Also, later this idea of retribution repeatedly helped win acceptance for the notion of preexistence. Origen adopted the theory of the preexistence and fall of souls in order thereby to explain the inequality of rational creatures in their lot in life[121] and was later followed in this also by Synesius and Nemesius. Theosophy was similarly attracted to it, frequently combining with it the idea that human beings were first created androgynous and that the creation of the woman was in fact proof of an antecedent fall.[122] In modern philosophy the idea of a preexistence and the fall of souls surfaced again as well. It has even been attributed to Kant, because he tried to explain the radical tendency toward evil and inborn guilt from

---

120. P. Gennrich, *Die Lehre von der Wiedergeburt: Die christliche Zentrallehre in dogmengeschichtlicher und religionsgeschichtlicher Beleuchtung* (Leipzig: Deichert, 1907), 275ff.

121. Cf. H. Bavinck, *Reformed Dogmatics*, II, 460–63, 557–61 (#265, #292); J. Müller, *Christian Doctrine of Sin*, II, 76, 155.

122. Cf. H. Bavinck, *Reformed Dogmatics*, II, 565–68 (#295); C. Vitringa, *Doctr. christ.*, II, 265.

an "intelligible" act of freedom. Over against the superficial rationalistic optimism of his day, Kant in fact again upheld the absolute character of the moral law and elucidated the universal and radical corruption of human nature. But, in addition, he was committed to the view that in the core of their being, humans were nevertheless good and could—in line with the inference "you must, therefore you can"—also again opt for and do good. Further, though one can speak of a tendency (*Hang*) but not of an inherent predisposition (*Anlage*) toward evil in humans, Kant believed that the tendency to sin, therefore, cannot be acquired by heredity nor be innate. Finally, he also believed that every human was personally responsible for his or her own acts, but only for them, and therefore there could be no fall involving the whole human race in Adam or original sin. If the tendency toward evil was nevertheless a characteristic feature of every human from conception and birth on, this can only be explained from the fact that the fundamental decision of all humans with respect to their good or evil character is an "intelligible" act. This is not a pretemporal, but an atemporal and extratemporal act, not a temporal, but a logical act. This was not an explanation, of course, but only an acknowledgment that we are here confronted by a mystery and can only maintain human responsibility and guilt by affirming the inexplicability of the origin of sin.[123]

By this theory of intelligible freedom, Kant not only collided with his own criticism but also paved the way for all sorts of confusion and misunderstanding. If the act of intelligible freedom were to mean anything, it could not be merely atemporal and extratemporal but had to be conceived as pretemporal. From being an idea, it had to be transferred into reality, even if as a preexistent reality. This was done in particular by Julius Müller in his famous work on the Christian doctrine of sin. He considered the church's confession that the whole human race had fallen and was guilty in Adam inadequate, since it failed to do justice to personal responsibility. If, however, humans are responsible—as appears from the witness of their conscience—for their entire moral state, that is, in this case, sinful state; if then this state has to be rooted in an antecedent act of the free will; if (since the sinful state is inborn) no room can be found in this life for such an all-determining decision, then the first sinful act must in fact have occurred in a time that preceded this life: inborn personal guilt makes the preexistence of souls necessary.[124]

Although the preexistence of humans in this sense found little acceptance, in another form it was adopted by many scholars and linked to the theory of evolution. If there are no leaps in nature but all higher forms of life have developed from lower forms, then also humans, or the human soul, cannot at one time have sprung into life all of a sudden. It must, then, have its preformation in the animal

---

123. J. Müller, *Christian Doctrine of Sin*, II, 77ff.; T. Hoekstra, *Immanente Kritik zur kantischen Religionsphilosophie* (Kampen: J. H. Kok, 1909), 26–41.

124. J. Müller, *Christian Doctrine of Sin*, II, 66–72, 137ff.

world, continuously develop in humans, and at death pass over into a higher form of existence. This modification in the theory of preexistence, which already started with Helmont, Leibniz, Bonnet, Lessing, and others,[125] was combined in the nineteenth century with the theory of human descent and currently enjoys widespread acceptance. Darwinism and Spiritism are on the same wavelength. The preformation of humans downward is supplemented by their metamorphosis upward: the animal becomes a human and "man" becomes "Superman."[126]

But all these assertions lack sufficient grounding, philosophically as well as theologically. In the first place, they imply the preexistence of souls—something that is unacceptable for various reasons[127]—or proceed, in the modern form, from the essential identity of animals, humans, and angels, an assumption that rests on false philosophical postulates, not on the facts of reality.[128] In the second place, the fall, the story of which is told in Genesis 3, is robbed of its character and meaning. It ceases to be a fall and becomes the mere appearance of something that occurred long before. In this connection the temporal empirical freedom given to humanity loses all its value. The soul already abused its freedom beforehand in its preexistent state and was lodged in a body as punishment, and this body is thus from the start dualistically opposed to the soul and cannot be said to belong to the essence of humans. In the third place, this theory is also in conflict with the organic connectedness of the human race. Every human individually is the creator of his or her own destiny. "The essence of a man is essentially his own deed" (Schelling), in which connection it makes one wonder why all people individually, without exception, choose to do evil and why only the first human, though fallen, was still tested to see if perhaps he wanted to remain "upright" and correct his fall. It is clear, finally, that humanity, thus dissolved into an aggregate of individuals, can neither have a common head in Adam nor in Christ. There is no common fall; neither, therefore, is there a common restoration. Everyone falls by himself; everyone must therefore also rise up by himself. Despite the "tendency to radical evil," Kant, accordingly, drew the inference "you can" from the imperative "you must."

We must therefore confine ourselves to the scriptural data, however scanty they may be. The time of the fall of the angels is nowhere reported. With a view to the phrase "from the beginning" (ἀπ᾽ ἀρχῆς, John 8:44), many theologians judged that the angels—certainly not at the very moment of their creation but then surely immediately after—by their first act of volition were either confirmed in the good or had fallen into sin.[129] Others assumed that a short period elapsed after their creation and that their fall occurred either still before the creation of

---

125. P. Gennrich, *Die Lehre v. d. Wiedergeburt*, 338ff.

126. Cf. H. Bavinck, *Philosophy of Revelation*, 293.

127. Cf. H. Bavinck, *Reformed Dogmatics*, II, 579–84 (#299).

128. Ibid., II, 485–88 (#272).

129. Augustine, *City of God*, XI, 13; T. Aquinas, *Summa theol.*, I, qu. 62, art. 5; qu. 63, art. 5–6.

heaven and earth (Gen. 1:1),[130] or within the period of the six creation days,[131] or (with a view to Gen. 1:31) only after the completion of the work of creation as a whole.[132]

Equally little can be said with certainty about [the time of] the fall of humanity. Some theologians speak of years after creation; others—because Genesis proceeds immediately after the creation narrative to that of the fall and also on the basis of Genesis 4:1—think that the fall of humanity occurred only a few days after, or even on the same day as, its creation.[133] These time stipulations, for that matter, are of little importance. What *is* important is that, according to Scripture, the fall is essentially distinct from the creation itself. Sin is a phenomenon whose possibility was indeed given in the creation of finite, mutable beings, but whose reality could only be called into being by the will of the creature. It is a power that does not belong to the essential being of the creation, a power that originally did not exist, but that came by way of disobedience and transgression, that is, entered the creation unlawfully, and did not belong there. It is there, and its existence is no accident. With a view to the counsel of God that incorporated it and assigned a place to it, it may up to a point and in a sense even be said that it had to be there. But then certainly it always *had to* be there as something that *ought not* to be and has no right to exist.

130. S. Episcopius, *Inst. theol.*, IV, 3, 1.

131. J. Coccceius on John 8:44.

132. G. Voetius, *Select. disp.*, I, 919–20; F. Turretin, *Institutes of Elenctic Theology*, IX, 5; C. Vitringa, *Doctr. Christ.*, II, 261.

133. J. Marck, *Hist. parad.*, III, 7; B. de Moor, *Comm. theol.*, IV, 166; C. Vitringa, *Doctr. chr.*, II, 261; O. Zöckler, *Die Lehre vom Urstand des Menschen* (Gütersloh: C. Bertelsmann, 1879), 35ff.

2

THE SPREAD OF SIN

*Since the first sin of our original ancestors, the entire human race bears
the guilt, pollution, and consequence of sin. That sin is a universal reality is
universally acknowledged, but it is most articulately voiced in Holy Scripture.
Creation itself, as corrupted by sin, now becomes the evil "world" that will one
day pass away. Human beings are sinful from conception on; they are "flesh,"
impure and corrupt through and through. The universality of sin and human
depravity is a simple assumption of Scripture as a whole. Even the saints in
Scripture have their sins, and Romans 7:10–25 is not a counterargument, since
it too speaks of the struggle of the regenerate person.*

*According to Scripture, the universality of sin derives from the fall of our
first parents, Adam and Eve. Though it is clearly implied in Genesis 3 and in
the rest of the Old Testament, it is especially the apostle Paul who spells this out
in Romans 5 and 1 Corinthians 15. What must never be overlooked is Paul's
concern that the gift of life in Christ is so much greater than the result of Adam's
fall. While we are also judged because of our own sin, according to Paul our
sinful condition is God's antecedent judgment on the entire human race thanks to
the sin of the representative man, Adam. This is the doctrine of original sin.*

*Original sin was not a new teaching of Augustine, though earlier theologians
did tend to stress free will and actual sin more than the sin inherited from Adam.
Still, when Pelagius appealed to earlier writers, he disguised the radical novelty
of his own anthropology. According to Pelagius, all persons were born with pure
souls; sin and evil come into being only through imitation. On our own, without
grace, we can will and do the good. Even Roman Catholic thought sounds a semi-
Pelagian note in its supernaturalist anthropology, where only the superadded gift
of grace is lost in the fall and nature remains unblemished. Similarly, Rousseau
became the apostle of a "back to nature movement" that repudiated human
culture as the source of all evil. Utopians continue to manufacture ideal "natural"
societies on paper that inevitably fail in practice. Even Ritschl reduced sin to
actual sins; "the law of sin" is only a sum of individual sins. But history and
experience suggest that the scriptural portrait is true. Even "innocent" children
display that seeds of sin are sown in the soil of their hearts from the beginning. A*

claim of sinlessness is universally repudiated, and imitation cannot explain the universal power of sin. A people without sin has never existed.

Pelagianism was condemned by the Christian church. Nonetheless, a semi-Pelagianism that taught a weakened but not totally corrupt will gained much headway in the church. This view holds that while Adam's fall had consequences also for his descendants, our moral condition is only sick and weak, prone to the desires of the flesh. The Council of Trent taught that the will's freedom had not been destroyed and that concupiscence as such was not sin. Anabaptists, Remonstrants, and many modern theologians agree. Adam's sin affects us all but only weakens our will and does not plunge us into the total corruption of original sin. This semi-Pelagianism ignores the character and seriousness of sin as willful lawlessness, separates sin and guilt, and fails to resolve the question of human freedom. An intact but weakened will is no real improvement on a will bound by original sin. While imitation is a superficial explanation for the universality of sin, the semi-Pelagian rejection of imitation leaves it with no explanation at all.

The apostle Paul and after him Augustine were instructed by the contrasting model of Christ as the second Adam and placed the blame for universal and original sin at the feet of the first Adam. The only way to understand the crushing yoke of sin's miseries on all people is to believe that all share Adam's guilt. Augustine did not, however, adequately describe the transmission of guilt and pollution to Adam's posterity, and his understanding of concupiscence is too closely linked to spontaneous sexual desire. Roman Catholic scholastic theology modified this view to understand original sin as the loss of a superadded gift of grace (original righteousness) to which was added the active element of concupiscence. In Roman Catholic theology, the center of gravity shifted from concupiscence to loss of original righteousness. When concupiscence is not itself seen as sinful, it is hard to see what concrete effects still remain of original sin except for the imputation of Adam's trespass. The state of man after Adam's fall differs little from the pre-fallen Adam. We are left in only a state of "naked naturalness," not a state of depravity.

The Reformation opposed this Roman Catholic weakening of original sin. It is not just a loss of something but a total corruption of our nature. If we call this "concupiscence," we must define it in terms of the totality of human appetites. In this sense, contrary to Augustine, concupiscence is itself sin. Opposition to this doctrine within the Reformed community arose in the school of Saumur (France) in the form of mediate imputation of sin. Instead of teaching that we are corrupt because of imputed guilt, this school reversed the order, claiming that we have guilt imputed to us because we are born corrupt. This view was also championed by Jonathan Edwards and the New England Theology. Modern thought, however, especially in historical and sociological studies, has given support to the doctrine and breathed new life into it. After theology rejected it, philosophy again took it up.

The doctrine of original sin is one of the weightiest and most difficult subjects in Christian theology. Without it we cannot comprehend ourselves, and yet it remains finally an incomprehensible mystery to us. Adam's disobedience is the originating sin; that is the clear teaching of Scripture. How can that not be seen as arbitrary? Only by recognizing the organic unity and solidarity of the human race. This unity is first of all physical and organic, but, more importantly, also representative. Here too we must begin with Christ, who is our representative mediator in redemption. Physical unity and a realistic understanding of the transmission of sin is inadequate. For one thing, the strict parallel between Adam and Christ breaks down. How could Christ then, being truly human, Adam's son, be without sin? Among human beings there is a moral solidarity that is greater than the physical. Reformed theology tries to explain this through the doctrine of the covenant—the covenant of works with Adam and the covenant of grace in Christ. The covenant of works and the covenant of grace are the forms by which the organism of humanity is maintained, also in a religious and ethical sense. This is God's ordinance.

Sin gives birth to sin. In the case of Adam and all his descendants, a sinful state followed a sinful deed. It is exactly this consequence that is denied by Pelagians. According to Pelagians, the will that sins is then fully free to sin or not to sin. This is not true to Scripture or to experience, where we discover that every act of the will, arising from antecedent impulses and desires, has a retroactive impact on it and reinforces it. It is in this way that sin becomes a habit. Those who commit sins become servants of sin. Guilt and pollution go together. In virtue of God's judgment, Adam's disobedience plunged all his posterity into guilt, pollution, and death. That is the condition into which we are all born. There is an antecedent judgment of God, and in virtue of that judgment all people are born of Adam, guilty, impure, and in the process of dying. This Christian view has some interesting parallels with, but is not to be identified with, the notion of hereditary transmission of traits. Too often an evolutionary mind-set that focuses on inherited traits sees human persons as nothing more than products of nature and risks becoming deterministic and fatalistic. The notion of inherited traits is too complex to be summed up in a few laws; along with inherited continuities, there are also variations. Human beings are spiritual and moral beings who have the ability to rise above even strong negative inherited tendencies and traits. Physical heredity cannot explain original sin.

There is no exception to the universal rule of sin except for our Lord Jesus Christ. Scripture gives no warrant to the Roman Catholic dogmas of Mary's immaculate conception and bodily assumption. If there are not individual human exceptions to the universality of sin, no aspect of human existence is free from the stain of sin either. Sin holds sway over the whole person, body and soul, mind and spirit, over all our human capacities and powers. The doctrine of total human moral depravity is a hard one and naturally evokes aversion and even incomprehension. Yet it is the clear teaching of Scripture, which is confirmed by daily experience. This means neither that people all maximize their evil inclinations nor that they are incapable of accomplishing many "natural goods." The doctrine of the incapacity for good is a religious confession—before God we can do no good; we need to be renewed by God's Spirit. We must never forget that as we are judged and condemned by God's standard, he at the same time offers us his full love, mercy, and forgiveness in Christ. A lesser judgment on us would require a lesser grace and thus diminish the love of God to us.

SIN IS UNIVERSAL

[317] The first sin, the sin for which our original human ancestors are responsible, has had calamitous consequences for them as well as all their descendants and unleashed a flood of misery on the human race. In consequence, humanity as a whole, and every person in particular, is burdened with guilt, defiled, and subject to ruin and death. These facts are so potent and so obvious that they have also frequently been noted and acknowledged outside the circle of special revelation. Frivolous people may think of life as a game; but all those who respect moral ideals, seriously contend with their own sins, and have the courage to look at reality as it is have acknowledged the deep depravity of human nature. The different religions with their priests and altars, sacrifices and penances, are all based on the presupposition of sin. Dogma and worship, prayer and song, religion and philosophy have everywhere—and sometimes in poignant ways—given expression to humanity's sense of sin. "To sin is common to all people." "No one is born without defects." "There will be faults as long as there are human beings." "[Moral] failure is common to all."[1] This universality of sin is even more articulately voiced in Holy Scripture. After telling the story of the fall in the third chapter of Genesis, it traces in the following chapters how sin spread and expanded in the human race, finally reaching such a pitch that it necessitated the judgment of the flood. Of the generation before the flood, it is said that human wickedness was great in the earth and that "every inclination of the thoughts of their hearts was only evil continually," and that "the earth was corrupt in God's sight" and "filled with violence" (Gen. 6:5, 11–12). But the flood did not bring about any

1. T. Pfanner, *Systema theologiae gentilis purioris* (Basel: Joh. Hermann Widerhold, 1679), IX, 7; K. G. Bretschneider, *Systematische Entwickelung,* 4th ed. (Leipzig: J. A. Barth, 1841), II, 16; R. Schneider, *Christliche Klänge aus den griechischen und römischen Klassikern,* 2nd ed. (Leipzig: Siegismund & Volkening, 1877), 121ff.; F. R. de Lamennais, *Essay on Indifference in Matters of Religion,* trans. Henry Edward John Stanley (London: John Macqueen, 1895), III, 393–408; F. Hettinger, *Apologie des Christentums,* ed. Eugen Müller, 9th ed., 5 vols. (Freiburg i.B. and St. Louis: Herder, 1906–8), III, 30, 412; A. M. Weiss, *Apologie des Christentums,* 5 vols. in 7 (Freiburg i.B.: Herder, 1904–8), I, 487ff.; II, 38ff.

change. Also after the flood, speaking about the new humanity that was to spring from Noah's family, God pronounced the judgment that "the inclination of the human heart is evil from youth" (Gen. 8:21). All the devout members of the old covenant agree with this divine witness. No one, laments Job, can bring a clean thing out of an unclean (14:4). There is not a human being—Solomon confesses in his prayer at the dedication of the temple—who does not sin (1 Kings 8:46). When "the Lord looks down from heaven on humankind," we read in Psalms 14 and 53, "to see if there are any who are wise, who seek God," he sees nothing but decline and iniquity: "They have all gone astray, they are all alike perverse; there is no one who does good, no, not one." No one, accordingly, can stand before the face of the Lord, for no human living is righteous before him (Pss. 130:3; 143:2). "Who can say: 'I have made my heart clean; I am pure from my sin'"? (Prov. 20:9). "Surely there is no one on earth so righteous as to do good without ever sinning" (Eccles. 7:20). The apocryphal books teach the same (Sir. 8:5; 25:24; Wis. 9:6, 13–18; 12:10–11; etc.).

The new covenant also leaves us in no doubt whatsoever about the sinful condition of the human race. The whole gospel is based on this assumption. When John the Baptist announces the proximity of the kingdom of heaven, he demands from the Jews that they repent and be baptized, inasmuch as circumcision, sacrifices, and observance of the law have not given the people of Israel the righteousness needed to enter the kingdom. Christ came on the scene preaching the same message of the kingdom of God; he, too, testifies that only rebirth, faith, and repentance can unlock the door to that kingdom (Mark 1:15; 6:12; John 3:3, 5). He does speak of the "well" and the "righteous" (Matt. 9:12–13; Mark 2:17; Luke 5:31–32), but he does so—without pronouncing an opinion on the nature of that health and righteousness—objectively, in accordance with the opinion of those whom he describes. What he himself thinks about that righteousness is sufficiently clear from other passages. Where he called to himself those who are weary and heavy-laden, tax collectors and sinners, and promises them rest, he says of the Pharisees that their righteousness is insufficient (Matt. 5:20; Luke 18:14), that prostitutes and tax collectors will enter the kingdom of heaven ahead of them (Matt. 8:11; 21:31). Similarly, the apostles taught that all people are sinners and that all need the forgiving love of the Father, redemption by Christ, the renewal of the Holy Spirit (Acts 2:38; 5:31; 10:43; etc.). The apostle Paul even begins his letter to the Romans with a lengthy argument showing that the whole world is damnable before God and therefore that no flesh will be justified by the works of the law (Rom. 3:19–20; cf. 5:12; 11:32; 2 Cor. 5:19; Gal. 3:22; 1 John 1:8; 5:19). As a result of this universal sinfulness, even the word "world" acquires an unfavorable meaning in Scripture. Although originally created by God (John 1:3; Col. 1:16; Heb. 1:2), it is nevertheless so corrupted by sin that it now faces God as a hostile power. It does not know the Logos to whom it owes its existence (John 1:10), lies altogether under the power of the evil one (1 John

5:19), is subject to Satan as its ruler (John 14:30; 16:11), and will, with all its lusts, one day pass away (1 John 2:17).

Furthermore, according to Scripture sin characterizes human beings from their youth, their birth, even from their conception (Gen. 6:5; 8:21; Job 13:26; 14:4; Pss. 25:7; 51:5; 58:3; 103:14; Isa. 43:27; 48:8; 57:3; Ezek. 16:3; Hosea 5:7; John 3:6; Rom. 7:7ff.; Eph. 2:3). David, in his confession of guilt, goes back to the very root of his sinfulness, locates it in the sins of his parents, and thus explains how he himself is impure before God and has been from his conception and birth on (Ps. 51:5). In John 3:6, Jesus says that the "flesh," that is, humans as earthly sensual beings, is from below (3:31; 8:23) and can only produce "flesh." A person of "flesh" cannot enter into the kingdom of God and to that end needs rebirth by the Spirit. Sensual beings as such, as σαρξ, humans are impure and corrupt from birth. And in Ephesians 2:3, Paul declares that Jews and Gentiles are "by nature children of wrath." Certainly he does not here oppose "by nature" (φυσει) to actual sins about which he has just been speaking (vv. 1–3) but says that they *were*, by nature, children of God's wrath whereas now, having been made alive and saved by grace, they *are* objects of his love, and so indicates that their earlier state—being dead through trespasses and sins—was a natural state, a φυσις, that rested in their very existence (cf. Rom. 2:14–15; 1 Cor. 2:14).

For the rest it is true that Holy Scripture *assumes* and manifests in reality the universality of sin and the human depravity that has its beginning in conception rather than describing it at length in words. People themselves are everywhere depicted as sinners, not only the generation before the flood and all the Gentiles and the ungodly but also the people of Israel. And among that people, one also hears of the sins of the pious, of the patriarchs, Moses, Job, David, Solomon, and others. Indeed, it is especially the pious who, even when they are convinced of the righteousness of their cause, nevertheless fall down before God, humbly confessing their sin and begging for compassion and forgiveness (Pss. 6; 25; 32; 38; 51; 130; 143; Neh. 9:33; Isa. 6:5; 53:4–6; 64:6; Jer. 3:15; Dan. 9:5ff.). It is the human heart that is corrupt (Gen. 6:5; 8:21; Ps. 14:1; Jer. 17:9; Ezek. 36:26; Matt. 15:19); from it flow the springs of life (Prov. 4:23). It is from within the human heart that all iniquities and all sorts of incomprehension flow (Mark 7:21). The mind of humans is darkened (Job 21:14; Isa. 1:3; Jer. 4:22; John 1:5; Rom. 1:21–22; 1 Cor. 1:18–23; 2:14; Eph. 4:18; 5:8). The human soul is guilty and impure and needs atonement and repentance (Lev. 17:11; Pss. 19:7; 41:4; Prov. 19:3, 16; Matt. 16:26; 1 Pet. 1:22). The human spirit is proud, errant, and polluted and therefore has to be broken, illumined, and cleansed (Ps. 51:19; Prov. 16:18, 32; Eccles. 7:9; Isa. 57:15; 66:2; 1 Cor. 7:34; 2 Cor. 7:1; 1 Thess. 5:23). The human conscience is stained and needs cleansing (Titus 1:15; Heb. 9:9, 14; 10:22). The human desire, inclination, and will reach out to what is forbidden and is powerless to do good (Jer. 13:23; John 8:34, 36; Rom. 6:17; 8:7; 2 Cor. 3:5). And the body, with all its members—the eyes (Deut. 29:4; Ps. 18:27; Isa. 35:5; 42:7;

2 Pet. 2:14; 1 John 2:16), the ears (Deut. 29:4; Pss. 115:6; 135:17; Isa. 6:10; Jer. 5:21; Zech. 7:11), the feet (Ps. 38:16; Prov. 1:16; 4:27; 6:18; Isa. 59:7; Rom. 3:15), the mouth and the tongue (Job 27:4; Pss. 17:10; 12:3f.; 15:3; Jer. 9:3, 5; Rom. 3:14; James 3:5–8)—is in the service of unrighteousness. In a word: sin is not located on and around humans but within them and extends to the whole person and the whole of humankind.[2]

Of the texts cited for the contrary view, only Romans 7:7–25 requires some further discussion. Pelagians have at all times appealed to this pericope to prove that the mind (νους) or the spirit (πνευμα) in humans has remained free from sin, and the latter only resides in the flesh (σαρξ); in modern times this exegesis has been adopted almost universally. But Augustine in his later period and all his followers, both in the Catholic Church and in Protestant churches, have consistently rejected this interpretation and understood verses 14–25 as having been said by Paul as regenerate and with reference to the present, an explanation that is still advocated by Delitzsch, Philippi, Luthardt, Harless, Thomasius, Umbreit, Kohlbrugge, and others.[3] The latter exegesis deserves preference for various reasons: (1) Paul argues, in Romans 7:7–25, that the law from which the believer, by having died with Christ, has been released, is itself not sinful. And he does this by showing that the law has first brought the believer to the knowledge of his sin and his death (vv. 7–13) and that even now it still has the consent of his inner self, although his flesh is still opposed to it (vv. 14–25). In this connection the argument that the law still has the consent of the believer, though the believer is released from it, is necessary. For the thesis that the law itself is holy, it is not enough that the unregenerate should approve of it but necessary that the regenerate approve of it. Paul, accordingly, speaks from verse 14 on in the present tense, not to make the description more vivid, but because as a regenerate person he loves and approves of the law. Since the law served mediately to give him the painful experience of his sin and death, since in communion with Christ (v. 4; Gal. 2:19–20) Paul died to the law by the law and was freed from its curse (Gal. 3:13), he thereby learned to know it as holy, just, and good and testifies to and confirms the law by faith (Rom. 3:30). (2) Because Paul, following the course of his argument, wants to honor the holy character of the law, he throws all the blame on sin. First, it was an objective power that initially, as long as he lived without the law (v. 9), did not exist for Paul and was not known by him. Then sin, working by means of the law, produced covetousness in him (v. 8) and was able to do this because

2. H. Schultz, *Alttestamentliche Theologie*, 4th ed., 2 vols. (Göttingen: Vandenhoeck & Ruprecht, 1889), 670ff.

3. A. Tholuck, *Commentar zum Brief an die Römer* (Halle: E. Anton, 1856), 333–69; M. R. Engel, *Der Kampf um Römer Kapitel 7* (Gotha: Verlagsbureau, 1902); *J. van Lonkhuijzen, *H. F. Kohlbrügge en zijn Prediking* (Wageningen: Vada, 1905), 363ff.

that covetousness resided in him by nature and he was carnal (v. 14).[4] Finally sin, thus revived and revealed as sin, made him die (vv. 9ff.), that is, made him despair of himself and his own righteousness.

But since this death was a death in communion with Christ (Gal. 2:19), Paul also rose again by that death, was inwardly reborn in his will and inner disposition, so that he can now make a sharp distinction between the center and the periphery of his being. Inwardly, in terms of his will, his inner self, he loves God's law, but in his members there lives another power and another law, namely, sin. Such a deep distinction is nowhere in Scripture assumed in the case of the unregenerate. In the case of the latter, there is indeed a knowledge of God and of the law and a doing by nature of the things of the law (Rom. 1:19; 2:14–15), that is, a struggle between reason and sensuality, conscience and covetousness, intellect and heart. However, a struggle between "flesh" and "spirit," as Paul pictures it here, occurs only in the life of the regenerate (Gal. 5:17): only they can say they love the law of God, approve of it, and want to keep it with all their heart. (3) Although as a regenerate person Paul still calls himself "of the flesh," "sold into slavery under sin" (Rom. 7:14), he does not mean by it that he is "in the flesh" (8:8–9) or walks "according to the flesh" (8:4). He only describes himself in those words because, on account of the sin "dwelling in his members," he cannot do what he wants to do and is held captive by "that law of sin in his members." Although he is wretched, because with the flesh he serves the law of sin, still he thanks God through Jesus Christ and with his mind (νοῦς) serves the law of God (v. 25); and it is above all this latter thing that is further developed in Romans 8. In Christ he is righteous and walks according to the Spirit. (4) Add to this that, if Romans 7:14ff. were to be understood of the unregenerate, rebirth itself would be unnecessary, a helping grace would be sufficient, and the entire teaching of Scripture on sin and grace, justification and sanctification, faith and repentance would be toppled. Romans 7:7–25 is rather a strong proof for the total depravity of human nature. For if the regenerate person still has to complain so intensely about the power of sin that resides in him or her, then the unregenerate person is totally—without knowing it—a servant of sin, being in the flesh and walking according to the flesh; and the mind of the flesh is hostility to God.

4. J. H. Gerretsen, in his *Rechtvaardigmaking bij Paulus in verband met de prediking van Christus in de synopticien de beginselen der Reformatie* (Nijmegen: H. ten Hoet, 1905), 78–92, rightly says about Rom. 7:7–13 that this pericope is the individual parallel of Rom. 5:12ff. and describes the origin of sin in the individual person. But this must not be understood in the sense that sin originally is not to be found in a person but stands completely outside him as long as he lives without any awareness of the law, before the awakening of a moral consciousness. On the contrary, the objective power of sin is able, by means of the law, to awaken the sinful desires of individual persons and in that way become sin, precisely because a person is "fleshly" by nature and his desire is from the outset present in him, albeit in a slumbering and unself-conscious manner. For that reason it is not correct to speak of still a second "fall" for every human person after the original fall of Adam.

IN ADAM'S FALL

[318] This universality of sin is derived in Genesis 3 from the fall of the first human beings. Granted, this is not said in so many words. Genesis 3 focuses more on the change in circumstances that is ushered in as a result of the fall (the pangs of childbirth, the curse on the earth, the expulsion from the garden) than on the moral reversal that took place in the life of Adam and his descendants.

Still it tells us that, immediately after the evil that was done, shame and fear took possession of them, that a sense of guilt awakened in them, and that they fled from the presence of God. The punishments pronounced in Genesis 3:16ff. have bearing not only on Adam and Eve but undoubtedly also on their descendants and, according to the whole Old Testament view, also presuppose communal guilt. The first event reported after the fall is Cain's fratricide. History itself changes, though this is not expressly stated; it becomes a history of sin, misery, and death. Humanity is now by nature evil (Gen. 6:5; 8:21). Similarly, the remaining Old Testament writings do not expressly connect the universality of sin with the fall of the first human. They confine themselves to reporting the fact of the universality of sin or trace it to the perishable sensual nature of humanity (Job 4:17f.; 14:4; 15:14f.; 25:4f.; Pss. 78:38f.; 103:13f.; Mark 14:38; John 3:6; Rom. 6:7ff.; etc.).

Not until Paul did anyone explain the universality of sin in terms of Adam's disobedience (1 Cor. 15:21f.; Rom. 5:12ff.).[5] In 1 Corinthians 15:21f., he states that just as the death of all humanity has its cause in the person of Adam, so the resurrection from the dead has its cause in the person of Christ. Clearly implied here is that just as the death of all people was not first caused by their personal sins but already pronounced upon all humanity and passed on to all solely because of Adam's disobedience, so the resurrection has not been won by the personal good works and faith and so on of the believers but exclusively by the obedience of Christ. They die, not in and by themselves, but in Adam; and they rise again, not in and by themselves, but only in Christ. How and why death spread to all is further explained in Romans 5:12f. Since, while we were enemies, we were reconciled by the death of Christ, we are certain that we will also live eternally with him. We are so certain in fact that now already we boast [in God] through [our Lord Jesus] Christ through whom we have received reconciliation (vv. 10–11). The grace and life of Christ, therefore (διὰ τοῦτο, v. 12), far exceed the sin and death of Adam. The idea of the abundance of God's grace is in the foreground here:[6] it is the theme of the pericope from verse 12 to verse 21 and is developed and proven in this manner. By one human being, sin, as a powerful and all-controlling principle, came into the world; in the same way also death spread to all humans, because all sinned. The words ἐφ' ᾧ are not, with Origen, the Vulgate, Augustine,

---

5. Similar ideas already appear in the apocryphal literature: Wis. 1:13–14; 2:23–24; Sir. 25:24; 40:1; 2 Bar. 17:3; 23:4; 54:19; 56:5, 9; 4 Ezra [2 Esd.] 3:7, 21–22; 4:11, 30; 7:68, 118; cf. *DB*, I, 840; C. Clemen, *Die Christliche Lehre von der Sünde* (Göttingen: Vandenhoeck & Ruprecht, 1897), I, passim.

6. J. H. Gerretsen, *Rechtvaardigmaking*, 73.

and others to be translated by *in quo,* for they are too far removed from ἀνθρωπος to connect with it, nor do they mean "in which," although this idea as such is not unscriptural (Heb. 7:10; 1 Cor. 15:22); but they are a conjunction: ἐπι τουτῳ ὁτι, "because," "on account of which," as Calvin, Peter Martyr, and most modern exegetes render it; or also with the meaning "on the basis of which," as some other scholars interpret it.[7] Furthermore, ἡμαρτον refers not to a sinful state but to an act. Accordingly, Paul says in verse 12: Adam sinned; consequently sin and death entered the world and held sway over all.

The clause "inasmuch as all sinned" does not mean that Paul locates the cause of every person's death in his or her actual personal sins, for in 1 Corinthians 15:22, he expressly states that all die in Adam. Here in verse 14, he writes that death also reigned over those whose sins were not like the transgression of Adam and—we may add—over the children; and in verses 15 and 17, he states with all the vigor he can muster that through the trespass of the one the many died. On the other hand, certainly, we must not tacitly add to the causal clause the idea that all have sinned *in Adam.* This is already unlikely as such, but it is here made impossible because verses 13 and 14 expressly concern the sin that people committed, not in Adam but personally on their own, even though then, too, their sin was not like the transgression of Adam. But Paul's point is that as a result of Adam's trespass both sin and death, in their interconnectedness, achieved dominion over humankind, that as a result of Adam's trespass all humans personally became sinners and all die individually. He argues this position in the succeeding verses as follows: sin, which entered the world as a result of Adam's trespass, was also present and dominant in the time from Adam to Moses, when God had not yet announced his law; then, too, people sinned. But—argues Paul, as it were, against himself—sin is not reckoned when there is no law; the law of Moses did not yet exist, hence no sin could be charged against anyone. To that objection he responds by saying: yet death reigned from Adam to Moses, even though at the time people did not transgress any concrete, explicitly announced divine law and could therefore not sin in the likeness of Adam's trespass. Still they sinned because they too had a law then that was known to them "by nature" (Rom. 1:18ff.; 2:12–15). After all, if death reigned then, sin must also have reigned then. And it reigned then, not because everyone personally broke a concrete commandment as Adam did and thus everyone became a sinner for and by himself or herself; no, but because as a result of Adam's trespass sin entered the world and reigned over everyone and, in its wake, also death reigned. Adam, therefore, is an exact type of Christ.

The way things go in the case of the sin and death that accrue to us from Adam is identical with the way the righteousness and life that Christ acquired accrue to us. There is a difference in intensity: grace is more abundant and life is more

---

7. Ibid., 68ff. The objection to this translation is that the spread of death to all humanity has to be regarded as the *cause* of all human sin (p. 72), and that death in Rom. 5:12ff. has to be seen as spiritual death, as human alienation from God (p. 70). Both interpretations are untenable.

powerful, but the manner in which both are imparted to us is the same. Just as the trespass of one was the cause of the guilt, the sin, and the death of all humans, so the obedience of one is the cause of the righteousness, acquittal, and life of all. In the one [Adam] all are condemned and have died; in the one [Christ] all are justified and saved. In both cases there is an antecedent judgment of God; and from that judgment (κρίμα) our sin and death are derived, on the one hand, and our righteousness and life, on the other. Accordingly, the idea that Paul develops in this pericope comes down to this: (1) upon the one trespass of Adam, God pronounced a judgment consisting in a guilty verdict and a death sentence; (2) that judgment was pronounced over all humans because, in some fashion that Paul does not further explain here but that can be surmised from the context, they are included in Adam; all were declared guilty and condemned to death in Adam; (3) in virtue of this antecedent judgment of God, all humans personally became sinners and all in fact die as well. God apprehends and regards, judges and condemns all humans in one [representative man], and so also they all descend from him as sinners and are all subject to death.[8]

THE PELAGIAN OBJECTION TO ORIGINAL SIN

[319] In the Christian church, the doctrine of original sin was based on the above scriptural data. From the beginning, people discerned a certain connectedness between Adam's sin and that of his descendants.[9] In that respect the assertion that the doctrine of original sin is an invention of Augustine is totally incorrect, and he himself could write: "I did not dream up original sin, which the catholic faith believes from of old."[10] Yet it is true that theology in the early centuries, especially in the East in its struggle with Gnosticism, tended much more to stress free will and actual, personal sin than the sin inherited from Adam. Where it is recognized that "an evil of the soul proceeds from an original fault,"[11] the essence of that original sin is not necessarily further defined and the manner of its

---

8. B. de Moor, *Comm. theol.*, III, 255; F. Turretin, *Institutes of Elenctic Theology*, trans. George Musgrove Giger, ed. James T. Dennison, 3 vols. (Phillipsburg, NJ: Presbyterian & Reformed, 1992), IX, 9; A. Comrie and N. Holtius, *Examen van het Ontwerp van Tolerantie*, 10 vols. (Amsterdam: Nicolaas Byl, 1753), X, 373; A. Dietzsch, *Adam und Christus* (Bonn: Adolph Marcus, 1871); E. Hünefeld, *Römer 5,12–21: Von neuem erklärt* (Leipzig: G. Strübig, 1895); J. C. K. von Hofmann, *Der Schriftbeweis*, 2nd ed., 2 vols. (Nördlingen: Beck, 1857–60), I, 524ff.; O. Pfleiderer, *Der Paulinismus*, 2nd ed. (Leipzig: O. R. Reisland, 1890), 53; C. Clemen, *Die christliche Lehre von der Sünde*, 52ff.; J. H. Gerretsen, *Rechtvaardigmaking*, 68, 78.

9. See numerous citations by Vossius, *Historia Pelagianismi* (1655), 134ff.; and, in addition, G. F. Wiggers, *Versuch einer pragmatischen Darstellung des Augustinismus und Pelagianismus*, 2 vols. (Hamburg: F. A. Perthes, 1830–31), I, 403ff.; W. Münscher, *Lehrbuch der christlichen Dogmengeschichte*, ed. Daniel von Coelln, 3rd ed. (Cassel: J. C. Krieger, 1832–38), I, 343, 353; J. Schwane, *Dogmengeschichte der neuern Zeit*, 2nd ed., 4 vols. (Freiburg i.B.: Herder, 1892–), II, 439; A. von Harnack, *History of Dogma*, trans. N. Buchanan, J. Millar, E. B. Speirs, W. McGilchrist, ed. A. B. Bruce, 7 vols. (London: Williams & Norgate, 1896–99), II, 274, 365n5; III, 265–85.

10. Augustine, *On Marriage and Concupiscence*, II, 42.

11. Tertullian, *A Treatise on the Soul*, 41.

propagation more deeply thought through. Pelagius, therefore, could with some semblance of justice appeal to many predecessors; yet he went much farther than they, taught something essentially different, and denied original sin. According to Pelagius, the image of God consisted solely in a free personality, not in positive holiness, immortality, and so on. Adam's trespass, according to him, did not deprive humans of the image of God and in fact had no adverse consequences whatsoever. There is no such thing as original sin. Adam's trespass negatively affected his descendants only in that it left them a bad example, which, followed by others, made sin a power among humankind. Hereditary transmission of sin is a Manichean error; sin is not a state but an act and always bears a personal stamp. It would be contrary to God's justice to charge us with the sins of others. Also, procreation in marriage would be impermissible if the hereditary transmission of sin took place by that channel. Furthermore, baptized parents can no longer propagate sin since it is eradicated by baptism. Sin, accordingly, is propagated not by generation but by imitation. Humans, whose souls were created pure by God, are still today born in the same state as Adam was before the fall: sickness, suffering, death, and so on are not punishments visited upon sin. Human beings are still completely free and can of themselves know and do the good: they have no need of grace. It is indeed possible for them to abstain from all sins, and a few have in fact attained this ideal.[12]

In voicing these ideas, Pelagius did little more than take over the views that had been promulgated long before by Greek and Roman philosophers and had found acceptance in popular philosophy. Even according to the Jews, souls were still always created pure by God and enabled to counter and conquer the covetousness that dwells in the flesh. It is true that poets and thinkers in the classical world frequently spoke in poignant lament of the universal power of sin, but because they knew of no redemption, they could not remain true to this view and, alongside it, always again taught that humans had the power to liberate themselves from sin and to practice virtue. They were caught up in an antinomy and oscillated from one extreme to another. Sometimes they depicted the depravity of their time in such dark colors that even the most somber pessimism could not make it seem worse; then again they idealized the world, considering nature perfect and not capable of improvement. Among them already the antithesis between culture and nature emerges; the former may be corrupt, but the latter is good, both within humanity and outside it. Evil is not born along with us but is later voluntarily committed by us; by contrast, the seeds of virtue have been planted in our heart, and virtue itself is within our power. "Existing in our minds are inborn seeds of the virtues which, if permitted to mature, nature itself will lead to a life marked by happiness."[13]

12. Cf. the anti-Pelagian writings of Augustine, e.g., as listed and summarized by B. B. Warfield, *Two Studies in the History of Doctrine: Augustine and the Pelagian Controversy* (New York: Christian Literature Co., 1897), 3–139.

13. M. T. Cicero, *Tusculan Disputations*, trans. John Edward King (London: W. Heinemann; New York: G. P. Putnam's Sons, 1927), II, 1.

"You err if you think that vices are inborn in us; no, they come upon us, they are imposed."[14] Virtue is not given and received; it is acquired only by practice and effort; we thank not God for them but ourselves. However widespread sin may be, there are exceptions. Truly solid, virtuous people exist. However, "no one is almost without defect. The majority are bad."[15]

In Pelagianism this doctrine of the natural goodness of humanity was renewed. Although it was condemned under the name of Pelagius, it continued to assert itself in the Christian church under other names. The Roman Catholic Church, by its supernaturalistic and mechanical conception of the image of God, arrived at the confession that the "natural man" (*homo naturalis*), after losing the super-added gifts, can still do truly good works, not, to be sure, in a supernatural sense, but certainly in the natural sense.[16] One needed only to remove the supernatural addition to suddenly come face to face with unblemished nature. This occurred in humanism; and Coornhert, who remained Catholic and humanist till his death, articulated this sentiment when he was greatly scandalized by the fifth and eighth questions [and answers] of the Heidelberg Catechism. Socinians,[17] Anabaptists,[18] and Rationalists[19] returned to this identical Roman Catholic viewpoint. Especially in the eighteenth century, the glorification of nature was fashionable, with Rousseau as its eloquent interpreter. Everything that comes to us from the hands of nature is good, but everything turns rotten in the hands of human beings. Nature is always and everywhere good, but culture is the source of all deficiency and misery. Take away the work of human beings, and everything is good. An animal in its natural state is happy, but, as a result of society, people have become miserable. Accordingly, in education, in religion, in morality, in society and the state let us return to nature, to the idyllic circumstances of shepherds and farmers, the innocent and carefree lifestyle of Hottentots and natives. Then, for humanity, virtue and happiness will instantly be restored.[20] The revolution attempted to realize that ideal practically. Numerous utopians designed a political "state of happiness" on paper. A few attempted to establish a colony based on these principles in foreign parts of the world. But in the face of all sorts of disappointments, and despite the fact that the theory of evolution suggested a very different view of the state of nature, thousands upon thousands of people exist who believe

14. L. A. Seneca, *Letters from a Stoic*, trans. Robin Campbell (Harmondsworth: Penguin, 1969), #96.

15. R. Schneider, *Christliche Klänge*, 141ff.

16. Decrees of the Council of Trent, VI, can. 5, 7.

17. O. Fock, *Der Socinianismus nach seiner Stellung in der Gesammtentwicklung des christlichen Geistes, nach seinem historischen Verlauf und nach seinem Lehrbegriff* (Kiel: C. Schröder, 1847), 654ff.

18. J. Cloppenburg, *Theologica opera omnia*, 2 vols. (Amsterdam: Borstius, 1684), II, 151ff.

19. J. A. L. Wegscheider, *Institutiones theologiae christianae dogmaticae* (Halle: Gebauer, 1819), §117.

20. Rousseau in his *Profession of Faith of the Vicar* (New York: P. Eckler, 1889). In the same way that he was taken in by the goodness of his own heart, so Lamartine testified that his soul breathed nothing but goodness, according to A. M. Weiss, *Apol. des Christ.*, II, 38. A. Pierson also claimed that he was not fully inclined to all evil but rather to much good: "Over Ethika," *De Gids* (November 1895): 259.

in the total natural goodness of humanity, who proceed from it in the upbringing of children, and who build their optimistic future expectations upon it.[21]

In theology this outlook was even advocated by Ritschl. In his view, we may not assume a universal concept of sin behind the phenomena of particular and actual sins, for such a notion is completely unintelligible. A passively inherited state cannot be construed as sin. Scripture does not teach it; Psalm 51:5 is but a personal confession; Ephesians 2:3 refers to the actual sins committed earlier by people who are now Christians; and Romans 5:12 is too unclear to base any conclusions on it. Original sin, moreover, would take away all personal responsibility, make child upbringing impossible, and wipe out any difference in gradation between sins. Given original sin, every individual human would already have reached the highest level of sin, and actual, personal sins would hardly be worth considering by comparison. No: sin is not a unity arising from one principle, but a collective unity resulting from all individual actions and inclinations. The subject of sin is not humanity as a race—which is an abstraction and merely a mental picture—but humanity as the sum of all individuals. Not the sinful state is first and then the deed, but, conversely, the self-determination of the will is the basis of all sins. Granted, the will that consistently does what is wrong will gradually acquire a tendency or habitual predisposition, and this in turn impacts the actions of the will. Not only that, but the sinful deeds and inclinations of humans exert mutual influence as well and promote and confirm each other. In human society, consequently, there arises "a law of sin," a realm of sin, a common sinfulness, but that is something very different from original sin and was wrongfully so called by Schleiermacher. A sinless unfolding of life can therefore not be a priori ruled out; the will of children is not aimed at evil; rather, there is in them a general tendency toward the good.[22]

This Pelagian explanation of the universality of sin, however, encounters too many serious objections to be accepted for long and by many people. In the eighteenth century, with its rationalism, individualism, and optimism, there was room for it. But the sense of history that awakened after the Revolution including insight into the incalculable value of community, society, and state, the organic understanding that has penetrated everywhere and above all the theory of heredity, whose meaning, also in the domains of religion and morality, has been highlighted more than in the past—all these factors have collectively put an end to the individualistic and atomistic view of humanity and of the sin dominant in it. If anything is certain, it is that sin is not an accidental phenomenon in the life of individuals, but a state and manner of life involving the whole human race, a property of human nature. The sinful deeds, which occur not just now and then but characterize all persons of all ages and circumstances, point back to a sinful

---

21. Cf. H. Bavinck, *Paedagogische Beginselen* (Kampen: Kok, 1904), 82; idem, *Philosophy of Revelation* (Grand Rapids: Eerdmans, 1957), 279.

22. Cf. see above, 42–45 (#310); and also Ritschl, *Unterricht in der christlichen Religion*, 3rd ed. (Bonn: A. Marcus, 1886), 25; C. Clemen, *Die christliche Lehre von der Sünde*, I, 256.

inner disposition, just as bad fruit presupposes a bad tree and muddied water an impure spring.

This alone, after all, explains why all children from their infancy on display delight in doing the forbidden and a tendency to all sorts of wrong. True, Pelagians, appealing to Jonah 4:11; Psalm 106:38; Matthew 18:3; 19:14; Luke 18:17; John 9:3; 1 Corinthians 7:14, have often spoken of the innocence of children. And in a relative sense, this is correct. Between sins there are differences in degree. Depending on a child's age and level of maturity, sin among children has not yet come to its full development and cannot yet manifest the hideous forms that occur at a later age. But the experience of all parents and teachers also tells us that the seeds of all sorts of sins have already been sown in the soil of the child's heart. It is certainly not the sensual sins that most vigorously come out in early youth; it is especially the defects and vices of a spiritual nature that are most prominent. Self-seeking, vanity, jealousy, lovelessness, pride, craftiness, deception, untruth, disobedience, stubbornness, and so on: these are the flaws that at an early stage already surface in children and that, if they are not checked by a wise upbringing, increase with the years. And when we look at our own life, we find sin as far back as our memory reaches. The more deeply our sense of guilt descends, the farther it goes back to the sins of youth, even to our birth and conception (Pss. 25:7; 51:5). The Scripture passages cited above, therefore, do not support the Pelagians; at most they speak of a relative innocence but fail to teach the sinlessness of children.

The assertion, moreover, that there have been people who have lived, or can live, without sin is devoid of all probability and without ground. Xenophon's witness to Socrates[23] is certainly not understood by anybody in an absolute sense. About the pious in the Old as well as the New Testament we are told countless sinful acts. Those most advanced on the road of sanctification have to the same degree felt their guilt and imperfection. So strong and so universal is the conviction of the sinfulness of the entire human race that if anyone were to make the claim of being sinless, we would all immediately attribute it to a lack of self-knowledge, to pride or mental illness.[24] This total universality of sin cannot be explained in terms of imitation. It is anterior to every conscious and intentional act of the will and is in every one of us a state long before it turns into deeds. That Ritschl does not recognize this is due in his case to nominalism. He regards humanity as the sum of all individuals, not an organism. Sin is not a state but consists only in acts of the will. Things in general exist in their effects or are in any case only knowable in their effects. Yet Ritschl does not remain true to his starting point. For though he denies innate sin and teaches the integrity of human nature, he, like Pelagius, attributes to the bad example and influence of society such a power that in conse-

23. Xenophon, *Memorabilia and Oeconomicus*, trans. E. C. Marchant, 7 vols., Loeb Classical Library (New York: G. P. Putnam's Sons, 1918–68), I, 1, 11; IV, 8, 11.

24. J. Müller, *The Christian Doctrine of Sin*, trans. Rev. Wm. Urwick, 5th ed., 2 vols., (Edinburgh: T&T Clark, 1868), II, 261.

quence the universality of sin still becomes a fact and there even arises a common sin. Now one has to make a choice: either these influences from without have only incidental impact, and then they explain nothing, and the universality of sin is an enigma; or they do in fact cause this universal sinfulness, but in that case they are even much worse than the scriptural doctrine of original sin. Furthermore, though Ritschl fights this doctrine by saying that it destroys all gradations in sin, this is a misunderstanding. He himself knows only two categories of sins, those of ignorance and those of a final and definitive evil, categories that certainly do not capture the many-sidedness of the sinful life. And his attempts to remove this doctrine from Scripture, for all their sophistication, are too violent for them to be considered successful.[25]

SEMI-PELAGIANISM

[320] Pelagianism was condemned by the Christian church. From the outset the church fathers assumed a certain connection between Adam's sin and that of his descendants. Although this connection was not yet examined in detail, Adam's trespass did bring about a great moral upheaval in his own life and that of his descendants. The nature of that moral change, however, was viewed in very diverse ways. According to semi-Pelagianism, the consequences of Adam's fall consisted for him and his descendants, aside from death, primarily in the weakening of moral strength. Though there is actually no real original sin in the sense of guilt, there is a hereditary malady: as a result of Adam's fall, humanity has become morally sick; the human will has been weakened and is inclined to evil. There has originated in humans a conflict between "flesh" and "spirit" that makes it impossible for a person to live without sin; but humans can will the good, and when they do, grace comes to their assistance in accomplishing it.[26] This is the position adopted by the Greek church;[27] and although in the West Augustine exerted strong influence, the [Western] church increasingly strayed toward semi-Pelagianism. The Council of Trent taught that though the freedom of the will had diminished, it had not been destroyed, and that concupiscence as such is not a sin.[28] Totally in agreement with this is the opinion of Anabaptists,[29] Zwingli,[30]

25. Cf. O. Pfleiderer, "Die Theologie der Ritschl'schen Schule, nach ihrer religionsphilosophischen Grundlage kritisch beleuchtet," *Jahrbuch für Protestantische Theologie* 17, no. 3 (1889): 321–83; I. A. Dorner, *A System of Christian Doctrine*, trans. Rev. Alfred Cave and Rev. J. S. Banks, rev. ed., 4 vols. (Edinburgh: T&T Clark, 1888), III, 44ff.; J. Orr, *The Ritschlian Theology and the Evangelical Faith* (London: Hodder & Stoughton, 1897), 145.

26. G. F. Wiggers, *Augustinismus und Pelagianismus*, II, 54–82.

27. John of Damascus, *Exposition of the Orthodox Faith*, II, 29, 30; *The Orthodox Confession of Faith*, trans. Ronald Peter Popivchak (Washington, DC: n.p., 1975), qu. 26–30; cf. H. Bavinck, *Reformed Dogmatics*, II, 347–51 (#234).

28. Cf. H. Bavinck, *Reformed Dogmatics*, II, 351–55 (#235); see also 93–97 (#321), below.

29. B. de Moor, *Comm. theol.*, III, 205.

30. H. Bavinck, *De Ethiek van Ulrich Zwingli* (Kampen: G. P. Zalsman, 1880), 17–18.

the Remonstrants,[31] the Moravian Brethren,[32] the Supernaturalists,[33] and many modern theologians.[34] All agree in believing that Adam's fall had consequences also for his descendants, because they are physically connected with him. But the moral state that came into being in the human race as a result of Adam's trespass is not one of sin and guilt but of weakness, lack, sickness. Original sin as such cannot damn humans and at most results in a punishment of the damned [*poena damni*—the pain of eternal separation from God][35] without a punishment of the senses (*poena sensus*). It is an occasion for sin, not sin itself in the true sense of the word. Since the will is in a weakened state, however, it easily yields to the temptations of the flesh; then, when the will agrees and consents to concupiscence, original sin turns into personal sin, which renders a person guilty and deserving of punishment. Materially this theory of original sin completely corresponds to the theory that sin is the product of sensuality and a remnant of humanity's earlier animal state.[36]

This semi-Pelagian view of original sin, however, is basically not much better than that of Pelagius and is open to the same objections. (1) It denies the character and seriousness of sin. Sin, after all, is lawlessness (ἀνομία). The state in which humans are born either corresponds to God's law or deviates from it; it is good or evil, sinful or not sinful. There is no third category. That that state is good and agrees in all parts with God's law, semi-Pelagians dare not assert either. Yet they do not call it sinful in the true sense of the word. So they create an intermediate state and speak of original sin as a disease, a deficiency, an illness that is not a real sin but can only be an occasion for sin. Or they separate sin and guilt and say, like Rothe and Kaftan, that though original sin is sin, it is not guilt.[37] (2) This is

---

31. *Confessio sev declaratio sententiae pastorum... remonstrantes* (1622), and *Apologie pro confessione* (1629), ch. 7; S. Episcopius, *Institutiones theologicae*, in *Opera*, vol 1. (Amsterdam: Johan Blaeu, 1650), IV, sect. 5, ch. 2; P. van Limborch, *Theologia christiana ad praxin pietatis ac promotionem pacis christianae unice directa* (Amsterdam: Wetstein, 1735), III, c. 2.

32. H. Plitt, *Zinzendorfs Theologie*, 3 vols. in 1 (Gotha: F. A. Perthes, 1869–74), II, 213ff.

33. F. V. Reinhard, *Grundriss der Dogmatik* (Munich: Seidel, 1802), §§81–84; O. Krabbe, *Die Lehre von der Sünde und vom Tode in ihrer Beziehung zu einander und zu der Auferstehung Christi* (Hamburg: Friedrich Perthes, 1836), 148ff.

34. R. Rothe, *Theologische Ethik*, 2nd rev. ed., 5 vols. (Wittenberg: Zimmerman, 1867–71), §§485ff.; J. Kaftan, *The Truth of the Christian Religion*, trans. George Ferries, 2 vols. (Edinburgh: T&T Clark, 1894), II, 219ff.; F. Nitzsch, *Lehrbuch der Evangelischen Dogmatik*, 3rd ed. prepared by Horst Stephan (Tübingen: J. C. B. Mohr, 1902), 325; W. Schmidt, *Christliche Dogmatik*, 4 vols. (Bonn: E. Weber, 1895–98), II, 297; J. J. van Oosterzee, *Christian Dogmatics*, trans. J. Watson and M. Evans, 2 vols. (New York: Scribner, Armstrong, 1874), II, 594ff.; J. I. Doedes, *De Leer der Zaligheid Volgens het Evangelie in de Schriften des Nieuwen Verbonds Voorgesteld* (Utrecht: Kemink, 1876), 27.

35. Cf. Richard A. Muller, *Dictionary of Latin and Greek Theological Terms* (Grand Rapids: Baker, 1985), 229, s.v. *poena*.

36. Cf. above, the discussion on the doctrine of sin in Tennant and others, 46–53 (##310–11).

37. F. R. Tennant restricts the word "sin" strictly to actual sins and refuses to speak of a sinful nature, sinful inclinations, and so on, *The Origin and Propagation of Sin*, 2nd ed. (Cambridge: Cambridge University Press, 1902), 163–76. Our impulses and passions can no more be called sinful in the strict sense than alcohol or dynamite (ibid., 167). Where Paul speaks of sin as a power that has come into the world and rules, Tennant

impossible both ways. Sin and guilt are inseparable (Gal. 3:10; James 2:10; 1 John 5:17). If sin is lawlessness, it is punishable; and, conversely, where there is guilt and punishment, there has to be sin. Original sin, however, is such that death is its consequence (Rom. 5:14), that it makes us unworthy of the fellowship of God and his heaven (Doedes), that it is inherently impure, the occasion and source of many sins, and is presumably therefore itself sin. Otherwise God would be unjust for punishing with death, the wages of sin (Rom. 6:23), that which *is* no sin and does not deserve death. The law would lose its absolute validity, for there would be deviation that did not deserve punishment, fellowship with God would be withheld where there was no guilt. Between heaven and hell, good and evil, light and darkness there would come a state that was neither, a "punishment of the damned" without a "punishment of the senses." That which engenders all sorts of sins would not itself be sinful. The tree, though good, would still bear bad fruit. The spring, though pure, would produce impure water. (3) The notion that innate sinfulness only becomes sin and guilt when the will consents to it, so far from improving the theory, makes it worse. We have to choose: either the will, as it were, stands above and outside that innate tendency, and then original sin consists in nothing but the innate sensual nature, and the entire [moral] character of sin is lost; or the will is itself more or less affected and weakened by original sin. It is rooted in the sinful nature and arises from it, and then one loses—to precisely the same degree as that to which one allows the will to be weakened—that which the theory was designed to maintain: that there is no sin without a decision of the free will.

Furthermore, even if one could conceive a will such that it existed in part or in whole outside the inborn sinful nature, it would still not in fact yield what it is intended to yield. The first decisions of the will that consent to innate concupiscence all occur in the early years when the will is still weak and powerless. No persons are aware that with those first decisions of the will, they are incurring such a guilt, that they actually did not fall and become children of wrath until then. Over against those who say this, everyone could excuse himself by saying he did not know better and could not act otherwise, that for such a weighty decision about his eternal weal or woe, he was positioned in most unfavorable circumstances. Indeed, if original sin is not sin, all other later sins, which so readily and so necessarily spring from it, cannot be sin either. Also Schleiermacher, therefore, rejected the notion that original sin cannot be guilt until it breaks out in actual sins, "for the mere circumstance that there has been no opportunity for and no outward incentive to sin cannot enhance the spiritual status of man."[38] (4) The semi-Pelagian theory not only does not solve the problem present here, but it does not even begin to touch it and even deliberately shuts its eyes to it.

---

uses the language of figure: abstract nouns are but conceptual, short, and useful for economy of words and thought (ibid., 173).

38. F. Schleiermacher, *The Christian Faith* (Edinburgh: T&T Clark, 1989), §71, 1.

The universality of sin is a fact that also semi-Pelagians acknowledge. They reject its explanation in terms of imitation. They accept that an impure, effective, sick, sinful (though nonculpable and nonpunishable) state is anterior to sinful acts. They acknowledge that that impure, sick state, in the lives of all without distinction, leads to culpable, punishable deeds, so that the weakened free will actually means very little. Now then, how must we explain that appalling phenomenon? How can it be squared with God's justice that, aside now from the covenant of grace, he permits all humans to be born in such a state, a state that, in any case, for children dying in infancy entails death and exclusion from his fellowship, and for all others eternal ruin? The semi-Pelagian theory fails totally to enter into the problem and contents itself with a superficial and inconsequential doctrine of free will.[39]

ORIGINAL SIN AND CONCUPISCENCE

[321] Paul, however, having been instructed by the contrasting model of Christ, responded to this problem by saying that by the trespass of one sin death came into the world and so spread to all humans. Very gradually, in Christian theology, people opened their minds to this deep doctrine.[40] Irenaeus said: "We offend (against God) in the first Adam, not doing his commandments; but we are reconciled in the second Adam, being made obedient even unto death."[41] Tertullian spoke of "an evil of the soul" that came to us from "an original defect" and is to be inferred from Adam's fall. "Therefore every soul, as long it is stained, is judged in Adam, until it is re-judged in Christ."[42] Most vigorous is the language of Ambrose, who more than others before him stressed the guilt character of all sin and the sinful state in which we are born and traced it to Adam's fall: "Adam lived and we all lived in him; Adam died and we all die in him."[43] Still, more than anyone else, it was Augustine who took hold of Paul's thought and developed it further. Over and over, especially in his writings against Julian, he appeals to Romans 5:12; 1 Corinthians 15:22; Ephesians 2:3. Also, he cites Cyprian, Hilary, Ambrose, Gregory of Nazianzus, Chrysostom, and others in support of his sentiments. In the practice of infant baptism as well, he sees a compelling argument for his doctrine of original sin. Finally, he points out that the appalling misery of the human race can only be explained as a punishment upon sin. How can God, who certainly is good and just, subject all humans from their conception on to sin and death if they are completely innocent? An original moral debt must rest upon all; there is no other way to understand the crushing yoke that weighs upon all the children of Adam. One who examines the miseries of human life, from the

39. J. Müller, *Christian Doctrine of Sin*, II, 388ff.
40. Cf. J. Schwane, *Dogmengeschichte*, II, 439ff., 480ff.
41. Irenaeus, *Against Heresies*, V, 16, 3.
42. Tertullian, *A Treatise on the Soul*, 40, 41; Cyprian, *On Works and Alms*, I, ep. 64, 5.
43. A. von Harnack, *History of Dogma*, V, 49ff.

first cries of infants to the final groans of the dying, has to come, with Paul, to the acknowledgment of original sin. "Inasmuch as God is not an unfair judge, we must acknowledge original sin in the misery of the human race, which begins with the tears of the little ones."[44]

Adam's sin must therefore be viewed as an act committed by him and all his followers. Adam was not a private person, not one individual alongside other such individuals, but all humans were included in him. The manner of it does not become completely clear in Augustine. As in the question concerning the origin of the soul, he abstained from making a choice between traducianism and creationism, so here also he does not definitely say whether the inclusion of the human race in Adam is to be conceived just realistically or also federally. On the one hand, he repeatedly states that all were in Adam's loins like the Israelites in those of Abraham; that Adam could not procreate people who are morally better than he himself was; that Adam's sin is transmitted by propagation not by imitation; that by birth we are the heirs of Adam's sin in the same manner as by rebirth we become heirs of the righteousness and life of Christ.[45] On the other hand, it is significant that he does not accept the traducianism of Tertullian and that he repeatedly states in the strongest possible way that all were in Adam and sinned in him. "All were that one man; we all were in that one."[46] Original sin differs from actual sins in that it was not personally committed by us; but it is still sin, since in a sense it was our deed. It is both: another's and our own sin. "Original sins are alien because each individual person does not commit them in his or her own life; truly it is ours, too, because Adam lived and all lived in him";[47] "it is even a voluntary sin because, contracted by an evil will from the first man, it was done in some hereditary fashion."[48] The sinful state in which we are conceived and born is a consequence and punishment of our trespass in Adam. God frequently punishes sin with sin.[49] This original sin in fact consists in "concupiscence." Sometimes Augustine takes this word in a broad sense and says that inherited sinfulness is not just located in the sex drive but is to be learned, in a certain sense, from the body. Carnal concupiscence thus also has its seat in the soul, and original sin is not a substance but a quality of the affections, a defect, weakness, disease, an accident

44. Augustine, *Against Julian, an Unfinished Book*, in *The Works of St. Augustine: A Translation for the 21st Century*, ed. J. E. Rotelle (New York: New City Press, 1999), II, 77 and passim; I, 25, 49; II, 107; III, 44, 202; VI, 17, 28.

45. Augustine, *City of God*, XIII, 3; idem, *Against Julian, Unfinished*, I, 48.

46. Idem, *On the Merits and Remission of Sins*, I, 10; idem, *City of God*, XIII, 14.

47. Idem, *Against Julian, Unfinished*, III, 25; I, 48–57.

48. Idem, *The Retractions*, trans. Mary Inez Bogan, Fathers of the Church 60 (Washington, DC: Catholic University of America Press, 1968), I, 13; idem, *Against Julian*, III, 5; idem, *On Marriage and Concupiscence*, II, 28.

49. Idem, *Against Julian, Unfinished*, I, 47; VI, 17; idem, *Against Julian*, V, 3; idem, *On Nature and Grace*, 22; cf. B. B. Warfield, *Two Studies in the History of Doctrine*, 128.

of our nature.[50] Still, in referring to concupiscence, he thinks first of all of the sex drive; the depravity of nature comes out especially in the spontaneous motion of the genitals, which occurs independently of the will, and shame is there to prove it. By the sex drive, accordingly, sin propagates itself and turns all of humankind into a corrupt mass, subject to the wretched necessity of not being able not to sin.[51] This concupiscence can better be called "original" than "natural" sin, since it is not of divine but of human origin. It is sin "because by sin it has been created and also seeks to sin" and makes humans the "originally guilty party."[52] Children who die unbaptized are lost on account of it; and when their guilt is removed in baptism, it nevertheless remains as a stimulus to the struggle: "The defendant is absolved by his regeneration; the torment remains for the ongoing battle."[53]

Scholasticism and Roman Catholic theology, while continuing to build on this foundation, nevertheless introduced a significant modification. What remained was the idea that Adam's trespass was the cause of the sin and death of all humans. Original sin consists first of all in the imputation to all humans of the trespass committed by Adam, since they were all included in him. It is, in the first place, guilt, then punishment. Scripture, accordingly, clearly states this, and the church made it part of its confession.[54] Pighius and Catharinus even went so far as to totally equate original sin with this imputation of Adam's trespass and wanted to consider everything that followed—the loss of original righteousness, the corruption of nature—only as punishment, not as sin.[55] But these theologians, in doing so, undoubtedly expressed an idea that had its roots in the development of the doctrine of original sin in Roman Catholic theology. Soon, in fact, there arose a difference about the character of the moral state that, following Adam's disobedience, set in both in his life and in that of his descendants. In Augustine it consisted in the concupiscence that, according to him, had its primary seat and organ in the sex drive. Lombard still stuck with this view.[56] But slowly gaining ground was the doctrine of the superadded gift that had been given to Adam but was lost by his fall. Hence for him and all humans, the first consequence of Adam's trespass was the loss of supernatural grace (original righteousness); this was the first and negative element in original sin, to which was added a second and positive element, viz., concupiscence. Anselm already described original sin

50. Augustine, *Against Julian, Unfinished,* IV, 28; V, 7; VI, 7; idem, *On Marriage and Concupiscence,* I, 24, 25; II, 34; idem, *Confessions,* I, 27–207; VII, 12.

51. Thus, repeatedly in his *On Marriage and Concupiscence;* cf. A. von Harnack, *History of Dogma,* V, 194ff.; G. F. Wiggers, *Augustinismus und Pelagianismus,* I, 107ff.

52. Augustine, *Against Julian, Unfinished,* I, 71; V, 9; idem, *Against Julian,* VI, 5.

53. Idem, *Against Julian, Unfinished,* I, 71, 101; idem, *Against Julian,* VI, 5; idem, *On the Merits and Remission of Sins,* II, 4; cf. T. Gangauf, *Metaphysische Psychologie des heiligen Augustinus* (Augsburg: K. Kollman, 1852), 420ff.

54. Council of Milev, 2; Council of Araus, c. 2; Decrees of the Council of Trent, V, 2; Roman Catechism, I, 3, 2.

55. R. Bellarmine, "De amiss.," *Controversiis,* V, 16.

56. P. Lombard, *Sent.,* II, dist. 30, 31.

in this way[57] and was followed in this respect by Hales, Bonaventure, Albert, and Aquinas. Original sin, accordingly, consisted in two things: the loss of original righteousness and a certain inordinate disposition of nature (concupiscence).[58] But on further reflection, disagreement about the latter was inevitable.

The image of God, as we recall, was gradually conceived as a supernatural gift. Consequently, one could also conceive as existing a human without that image, yet without sin: a natural human (*homo naturalis*). In such a human, flesh and spirit would in the nature of the case be at odds with each other; that is, concupiscence, the desire of the flesh against the spirit, naturally and necessarily belongs to being human in virtue of creation and can therefore not as such be sinful. Granted, the image of God had been given to Adam as a remedy and a bridle, but when he lost it, the war between flesh and spirit automatically broke out again. This inner conflict in his nature, though it had been suppressed, was now again free to assert itself. Concupiscence is "a disease and faintness of human nature that arises from a material condition."[59] It cannot per se be sinful nor therefore be part of original sin. Here the Catholic doctrine of the superadded gift causes serious difficulty in connection with original sin. It can be historically demonstrated, therefore, that in Catholic theology the center of gravity in the doctrine of original sin gradually shifted from concupiscence to the loss of original righteousness, from the positive to the negative. Augustine described original sin totally in terms of concupiscence. The scholastics included in it the loss of original righteousness but still maintained original sin in a positive sense as an inordinate disposition, a "languor" of nature, a corrupt habit.[60] Trent expressed itself very cautiously. It says that Adam not only lost righteousness but was also changed for the worse in soul and body. After being defiled, he not only transfused death and the punishments of the body but above all sin into his descendants, and the sin of Adam is in each one as his own, not by imitation but by propagation, and can be removed only by Christ's merit in baptism.[61] But the council deliberately refrained from laying down more specific determinations.[62] The nature of sin was not further defined; the words "for the worse" do not say much. Concupiscence, which remains in the baptized, is not itself seen as sin but only arises from sin and inclines to sin. The free will is not lost but weakened and can also do good works before sin. All in all, it is hard to see in what, besides the imputation of Adam's trespass and the loss of original righteousness, original sin could still further consist. There is nothing left for it.

57. Anselm, *The Fall of the Devil*, in *Anselm of Canterbury*, trans. and ed. Jasper Hopkins and Herbert Richardson, 4 vols. (Toronto and New York: Edwin Mellen Press, 1975), II, 27.

58. T. Aquinas, *Summa theol.*, II, 1, qu. 82, art. 1; cf. also J. Schwane, *Dogmengeschichte*, III, 393–413.

59. H. Bavinck, *Reformed Dogmatics*, II, 548–50 (#289); cf. Schwane, *Dogmengeschichte*, I, 508.

60. T. Aquinas, *Summa theol.*, II, 1, qu. 82, art. 1.

61. Decrees of the Council of Trent, sessions V–VI.

62. J. A. Möhler, *Symbolik: Oder Darstellung der Dogmatischen Gegensätze der Katholiken und Protestanten nach ihren öffentlichen Bekenntnisschriften* (Mainz: F. Kupferberg, 1838), 57.

After Trent, accordingly, there is express opposition to the view of Lombard—later still embraced by Henric, Gregory Arim, and Driedo—that, formally or materially, original sin consists in concupiscence, a positive quality.[63] With an appeal to Aquinas, Bonaventure, Duns Scotus, and others, original sin was defined as only the loss of original righteousness. Bellarmine openly and clearly stated this point: "The state of man after Adam's fall does not differ much from his state in its natural purity, any more than a man stripped of his clothes differs from a nude; nor is human nature worse if you subtract original sin; neither does it labor more under infirmity and ignorance than it would have while established in its purely natural state. In like manner the corruption of nature did not flow from the lack of some natural gift nor from the accession of some bad quality but only from a loss of the supernatural gift occasioned by Adam's sin."[64]

The state in which humans are born after the fall is completely identical to that of Adam before the fall but without the supernatural gift. One can speak of a corruption or wounding of nature only in the sense that this state ought not to be, since, after receiving the superadded gift, Adam lost it; the loss of it is culpable. But materially that state is not wrong: it is "naked naturalness." Original sin consists in nothing but reduction to a merely natural state; the supernatural things having been lost, the natural [nevertheless] remains intact. In baptism this loss is made up with infused grace; after death original sin is punished only with the "punishment of the damned." Although some theologians still attempted to maintain a "corruption of nature," the supernaturalistic view of Christianity made this impossible.[65] The only remaining difference pertains to whether the imputation of Adam's sin, which resulted in the loss of the superadded gift for all his descendants, is based on a physical or on a moral (federal) connection. Some say that all humans are—not formally but causally, materially, and seminally—included in Adam; others think they can only explain the imputation by assuming that Adam was not only our original ancestor but also our head and our representative. Still others combine the two views.[66]

---

63. R. Bellarmine, "De amiss. gr. et statu pecc.," *Controversiis*, V, 15; M. Becanus, *Summa theologiae scholasticae* (Rothmagi: I. Behovrt, 1651), qu. 3–4; *Theologia Wirceburgensi*, 3rd ed., 10 vols. in 5 (Paris: Berche & Tralin, 1880), VII, 84–94; cf. also J. H. Busch, *Das Wese der Erbsünde nach Bellarmin und Suarez* (Paderborn: Ferdinand Schöningh, 1909).

64. R. Bellarmine, "De gratia primi hominis," *Controversiis*, 5.

65. Baius and Jansen did try to find acceptance for a more rigorous view of original sin, but their theses were rejected by Rome. H. Denzinger, *Enchiridion symbolorum*, ##881, 966; ed. note: ET: *The Sources of Catholic Dogma*, translated from the 30th ed. by Roy J. Deferrari (London and St. Louis: Herder, 1955).

66. Cf., in addition to those mentioned above, J. Schwane, *Dogmengeschichte*, 166–98; P. Dens, *Theologia moralis et dogmatica*, 8 vols. (Dublin: Richard Coyne, 1832), I, 356ff.; J. Schwetz, *Theologia dogmatic catholica*, 3 vols. (Vienna: Congregatio Mechitharistica, 1851–54), II, 163–77; H. T. Simar, *Lehrbuch der Dogmatik*, 3rd ed. (Freiburg i.B.: Herder, 1893), 351–67; C. Pesch, *Praelectiones dogmaticae*, 9 vols. (Freiburg: Herder, 1902–10), II, 111–52; G. M. Jansen, *Theologia dogmatica specialis* (Utrecht, 1877–79), II, 495ff.; P. Mannens, *Theologiae dogmaticae institutiones*, 3 vols. (Roermand: Romen, 1910–15), II, 336ff.; *Bensdorp, *De Katholiek*, CX, 39ff.

TOTAL CORRUPTION

[322] The Reformation opposed this Roman Catholic weakening of original sin. By itself the scholastic definition of original sin as "the loss of original righteousness which ought to be in humans" was not found objectionable, provided it was not understood in purely negative terms. In Roman Catholic theology, however, this increasingly became the case, and so the Reformation in turn stressed that original sin is not just a loss of something but simultaneously a total corruption of human nature. In the early years this corruption was still called by the name of "concupiscence," but this term was construed, not one-sidedly with Augustine and Lombard, as the sex drive, but as the "disordered state of all the appetites," seated in the higher as well as the lower faculties of humans.[67] Calvin very clearly puts it this way: those who define original sin as the loss of original righteousness, while they do describe it in its totality, do not adequately give expression to its power and energy. For our nature is not only destitute of good but "fertile and fruitful of every evil." If then original sin is described as "concupiscence," this is fine provided there be added "that whatever is in man, from the understanding to the will, from the soul even to the flesh, has been defiled and crammed with this concupiscence. Or, to put it more briefly, the whole man is of himself nothing but concupiscence."[68] The Reformers further taught that from its very first motion this concupiscence was also sin: it does not first become sin when the will has consented to it, but it is sin in itself, not only as formed, therefore, but already as unformed. Calvin again states that on this point he disagrees with Augustine, who describes concupiscence, after its guilt has been removed from it in baptism, by the word "weakness." "We, on the other hand, deem it sin."[69] Finally, this corruption of human nature is so total that humans are by nature incapable of any spiritual good, inclined to all evil, and on account of it alone deserving of eternal punishment.

It cannot be denied that, out of reaction against Rome, especially among Lutherans, people sometimes expressed themselves too strongly. Though it was meant well, it was certainly open to serious misunderstanding when Luther called original sin "essential sin" and "the essence of humans."[70] Even more strongly, Flacius spoke of original sin as "the substance of humans." And also the Formula of Concord stated, in Luther's own words, that in spiritual matters the mind, heart, and will were "altogether corrupt and dead," no more capable [of good] than "a stone, a trunk, or mud."[71] Catholics for that reason accused the Lutherans

---

67. W. Braun, *Die Bedeutung der Koncupiscenz in Luthers Leben und Lehre* (Berlin: Trowitsch, 1908).

68. J. Calvin, *Institutes*, II.i.8.

69. Ibid., III.iii.10.

70. According to J. Köstlin, *Luthers Theologie in ihrer geschichtlichen Entwicklung und ihrem inneren Zusammenhange*, II, 366ff. Ed. note: ET: *Theology of Luther in Its Historical Development and Inner Harmony*, trans. Charles E. Hay, 2 vols. (Philadelphia: Lutheran Publication Society, 1897).

71. J. T. Müller, *Die symbolischen Bücher der evangelisch-lutherischen Kirche*, 8th ed. (Gütersloh: Bertelsmann, 1898), 589, 594; cf. F. H. R. Frank, *Theologie der Concordienformel*, 4 vols. in 2 (Erlangen: T. Blaesing, 1858–65), I, 138.

of Manicheism.[72] But in the Formula of Concord, they nevertheless expressly confessed that sin was not a substance, and all the theologians agreed. Although Lutherans as a rule even held to traducianism and were therefore inclined to regard original sin as being propagated by carnal concupiscence,[73] Melanchthon also states there that he has no objection to saying that humans are "born guilty on account of Adam's fall." The Formula of Concord declares that original sin is "a fault or an indictment as a result of which, on account of the disobedience of Adam and Eve, we are all at enmity with God and by nature children of wrath,"[74] and several Lutheran theologians later say that Adam must not only be viewed as the "physical head" but also as the "moral or federal head of the human race" and that therefore his trespass is imputed to all.[75]

From the beginning the Reformed were on their guard against the strong expressions the Lutherans sometimes used. Calvin, for example, absolutely refused to approve of the above-mentioned images.[76] Still they too taught that original sin consisted, negatively, in the loss of original righteousness and, positively, in the corruption of nature, and that it was rooted in the imputed trespass of Adam.[77] There was a high degree of consensus on this point. Rivetus compiled a long list of pronouncements from church confessions and theological works, all of which taught the same thing.[78] Opposition to this doctrine, however, arose in the school of Saumur [France]. In his theses "concerning the state of fallen man before grace,"[79] Placaeus taught that Adam's disobedience was only imputed to his descendants mediately, that is, only insofar as, and on the basis of the fact that, they were already born of him in a state of impurity. In the past theologians had unanimously taught that "we are born corrupt because original sin is imputed to us"; Placaeus, turning

72. R. Bellarmine, "De amiss. gr. et statu pecc.," *Controversiis*, V, 4ff.; M. Becanus, *Summa theologiae scholasticae*, 2ff.; J. A. Möhler, *Symbolik*, 66ff.

73. Luther, according to J. Köstlin, *Theology of Luther*, II, 367; P. Melanchthon, *Loci communes* (Berolini: G. Schlawitz, 1856), XXI, 668ff.; cf. F. H. R. Frank, *Theologie der Concordienformel*, I, 50ff.

74. J. T. Müller, *Die symbolischen Bücher*, 576.

75. J. A. Quenstedt, *Theologia*, II, 53, 118; D. Hollaz, *Examen theologicum acroamaticum* (Rostock and Leipzig: Russworm, 1718), 515; H. F. F. Schmid, *The Doctrinal Theology of the Evangelical Lutheran Church*, trans. Charles A. Hay and Henry Jacobs, 5th ed. (Philadelphia: United Lutheran Publication House, 1899), 172ff.

76. Cf. A. Schweizer, *Die protestantischen Centraldogmen in ihrer Entwicklung innerhalb der reformierten Kirche*, 2 vols. (Zürich: Orell Fussli, 1854–56), I, 385, 394.

77. J. Calvin, *Institutes*, II.1; idem, *Commentary on the Book of Psalms*, trans. James Anderson (Grand Rapids: Eerdmans, 1949), Ps. 51:7; idem, *Commentary on the Epistle of Saint Paul to the Romans*, ed. and trans. John Owen (Grand Rapids: Eerdmans, 1948), Rom. 5:12; T. Beza, *Tractationum theologicarum* (Geneva: Jean Crispin, 1570), I, 344; P. Vermigli, *Loci comm.*, 68ff.; Z. Ursinus, *Volumen tractationum theologicarum* (Neustadii, 1584), 202; idem, *The Commentary of Dr. Zacharius Ursinus on the Heidelberg Catechism*, trans. G. W. Willard (Grand Rapids: Eerdmans, 1954), qu. 7; J. Zanchi, *Op. theol.*, IV, 30; F. Junius, *Op. theologica select.*, 19–20; H. Heppe, *Dogmatik der evangelischen reformierten Kirche* (Elberseld: R. L. Friedrich, 1861), 245ff.

78. A. Rivetus, "Testimonia de imputatione primi peccati omnibus Adami posteris," in *Operum theologicorum*, 3 vols. (Rotterdam: Leers, 1651–60), III, 798–826. Translated into English in *Princeton Theol. Essays* (1846), 195–217.

79. L. Cappel, M. Amyraut, and J. de la Place, *Syntagma thesium theologicarum in academia salmuriensi variis temporibus disputatarum* (Salmurii: Prostant exemplaria apud Ioannem Lesnerium, 1665), 205.

this around, said: "Original sin is imputed to us because we are born corrupt," and further elucidated his position in his "Two-Part Disputation Concerning Adam's First Sin" (1655). The Synod of Charenton condemned his views in 1645. Rivetus, on instruction from the synod, collected the testimonies referred to above; and several theologians launched attacks on Placaeus's teachings, namely, Heidegger, Turretin, Maresius, Driessen, Leydekker, Marck, Comrie, Holtius, and others. But the Reformed doctrine of original sin seemed to have had its time. Placaeus found acceptance everywhere—in France, Switzerland, England, America—among theologians like Wyttenbach, Endemann, Stopfer, Whitby, John Taylor, Roell, Vitringa, Venema, and others,[80] as well as among Lutherans.[81] In America, Jonathan Edwards, though in 1757 he wrote his famous treatise *Original Sin Defended*[82] against Whitby, himself already in its pages championed the mediate imputation of Adam's sin and completely aligned the New England Theology of Hopkins, Edwards Jr., Dwight, Emmons, and others with Placaeus. Pelagianism found acceptance everywhere; Protestantism, to the degree that it broke with its past, fell back into Romanism: humans are by nature good but easily succumb in the struggle against sensuality. Even modern theologians, who assume an influence of Adam's sin on his descendants, have by that token only partially returned to the doctrine of the Reformation.[83] Yet, as a result of various factors, the deep meaning of the doctrine of original sin has again become clear to many. In 1845, Gervinus wrote: "We have lost the fear of hereditary sins which, like the fear of ghosts, was only the fear of a superstitious religious doctrine."[84] There are probably not many people who would still endorse that shallow view today. The philosophy of Kant, Schelling, Schopenhauer, and others; the theory of [human] heredity and [human] solidarity; a spectrum of historical and sociological studies—all have offered unexpected but significant support for the dogma of original sin. After theology rejected it, philosophy again took it up.

EXPLAINING ORIGINAL SIN: HUMAN SOLIDARITY

[323] The doctrine of original sin is one of the weightiest but also one of the most difficult subjects in the field of dogmatics. "Nothing is better known than

---

80. C. Vitringa, *Doctr. christ.*, II, 349.

81. J. G. Walch, *Bibliotheca theologica selecta, litterariis adnotationibus instructa*, 4 vols. (Jenae: vid. Croeckerianal, 1757–65), I, 85.

82. J. Edwards, *Original Sin*, ed. Clyde A Holbrook, in *The Works of Jonathan Edwards*, vol. 3 (New Haven: Yale University Press, 1970), II, 305–10; cf. J. Ridderbos, *De Theologie van Jonathan Edwards* ('s Gravenhage: J. A. Nederbragt, 1907), 150ff., 319ff.

83. A. F. C. Vilmar, *Dogmatik*, 2 vols. (Gütersloh: C. Bertelsmann, 1874), I, 270; F. A. Philippi, *Kirchliche Glaubenslehre*, 3rd ed., 7 vols. in 10 (Gütersloh: Bertelsmann, 1870–90), III, 40; J. H. A. Ebrard, *Christliche Dogmatik*, 2nd ed., 2 vols. (Königsberg: A. W. Unzer, 1862–63), §§340–44; I. A. Dorner, *System of Christian Doctrine*, §§82–83; F. H. R. Frank, *System der christlichen Wahrheit*, 2nd ed., 2 vols. (Erlangen: A. Deichert, 1884), I, 460–682; J. Müller, *Christian Doctrine of Sin*, II, 300–347.

84. F. Delitzsch, *System der christlichen Apologetik* (Leipzig: Dörffling & Franke, 1870), 119.

original sin for preaching; for understanding, nothing is more mysterious."[85] "It is astonishing, however, that the mystery furthest from our understanding is the transmission of sin, the one thing without which we can have no understanding of ourselves! Because there can be no doubt that nothing shocks our reason more than to say that the sin of the first man made guilty those who, so far from that source, seem incapable of having taken part in it.... Nevertheless without this most incomprehensible of all mysteries we are incomprehensible to ourselves. Within this gnarled chasm lie the twists and turns of our condition. So, humanity is more inconceivable without this mystery than this mystery is conceivable to humanity."[86] "Original sin explains everything and without it one cannot explain anything" (de Maistre), and yet the doctrine itself needs explanation more than anything.[87] From ancient times it was described in theology as original sin (*peccatum originale*), not because it was peculiar to humans from their origin by virtue of creation, but because in all humans it is the origin and source of all other sins. Much misunderstanding could be avoided if in original sin we differentiated between an originating sin (*peccatum originans*; imputed, guilt) and the sin originated (*peccatum originatum*; inherent, punishment). Actually by original or hereditary sin, one should only understand the moral depravity that people carry with them from the time of their conception and birth from their sinful parents.

But this moral depravity, which is characteristic of all people by nature and does not just arise later as a result of their own misguided deeds, certainly must have a cause. According to Scripture and for Christian thought, this cause can be no other than the first trespass of the first human, by which sin and death entered the world. Adam's disobedience is the originating sin. Scripture plainly says it (Rom. 5:12; 1 Cor. 15:22), and experience confirms it every minute: all people are conceived in sin and born in iniquity. This is conceivable only if we adopt the idea that this trespass of Adam in some way concerns us all. If there were absolutely no connection between Adam and us, it would be impossible for us to be born in sin because he broke God's commandment. Scripture and history, accordingly, together point us to an original common moral debt incurred by the human race. The hypothesis of Plato and others that every soul before its advent into the human body had already existed for a long time and fallen during its preexistence earlier proved, for good reason, to be totally untenable to us. Underlying it, however, is the undeniable truth that every human is born under a moral debt. That debt is not something each one of us has—personally, individually, actually—brought down on ourselves. It rests on each one of us on account of Adam. "By one man's disobedience the many were made sinners" (Rom. 5:19). Regardless of whether we can make some sense out of the fact that God—immediately, by and on account of Adam's disobedience—makes us all

---

85. Augustine, *On the Catholic and Manichaean Ways of Life*, I, 22.

86. Pascal, *Pensees and Other Writings* (Oxford: Oxford University Press, 1995), 42–43.

87. Even Rousseau acknowledges that original sin explained everything except itself.

sinners, that fact itself is certain, based on Scripture and experience. Still, some things can be said, if not to explain this action of God, then certainly to strip from it the appearance of arbitrariness.

In the first place, remember, humanity is not an aggregate of individuals but an organic unity, one race, one family. Angels, on the other hand, all stand side-by-side, independently of one another. They were all created at the same time and are not the products of procreation. Among them a divine judgment such as was pronounced upon all humanity in Adam would not have been possible: everyone stood or fell on his own. But that is not how it is among us. God created all of us from one man (Acts 17:26); we are not a heap of souls piled on a piece of ground, but all blood relatives of one another, connected to one another by a host of ties, therefore conditioning one another and being conditioned by one another. And among us the first human again occupies an utterly unique and incomparable place. Like branches in a trunk, a mass at its beginning, members in a head, so all of us were germinally present in Adam's loins, and all proceeded from that source. He was not a private person, not a loose individual alongside other such loose individuals, but a root-source, the base, the seminal beginning of the whole human race, our common natural head. In a sense it can be said that "we all were that one human," that what he did was done by us all in him. The choice he made and the action he undertook were those of all his descendants. Certainly this physical oneness of the whole of humanity in Adam as such is of great importance for the explanation of original sin. It is its necessary presupposition and prerequisite. If Christ was to be able to bear our sins and to share with us his righteousness, he first of all had to assume our human nature. Still, realism by itself is insufficient as an explanation of original sin.[88] In a certain sense it can indeed be said that all humans were comprehended in Adam, but then only in a certain specific sense: it is *representatively* but not *physically* true. In connection with the covenant of grace, no one talks that way. We can and may indeed say that God so imputes to us the righteousness of Christ as if we ourselves had accomplished the obedience that Christ accomplished for us,[89] but we are not, by that token, the people who personally and physically satisfied God's righteousness. Christ satisfied God's righteous requirement for us and in our place. So it is also with Adam: virtually, potentially, and seminally, we may have been comprehended in him; personally and actually, however, it was he who broke the probationary command, and not we. If realism were to reject this distinction and be totally consistent, all imputation, both in the case of Adam and in that of Christ, would be unnecessary. In both cases it would be each individual himself or herself who had personally committed the sinful deed and personally made satisfaction by his or her suffering and death.

88. Realism was promoted in America by Shedd and found in the Netherlands an able and convinced defender in Dr. Greydanus. Cf. also the identity doctrine of Jonathan Edwards in J. Ridderbos, *Jonathan Edwards*, 162; and that of Bilderdijk, in H. Bavinck, *Bilderdyk als Denker en Dichter* (Kampen: Kok, 1906), 82ff.

89. Heidelberg Catechism, Q. 60.

Further, if Adam's trespass had been ours in this realistic sense, we would also be responsible for all the other sins of Adam, all the sins of Eve, even all the sins of all our ancestors, for we were included in them as much as in Adam when he violated the probationary command. It is impossible to see, therefore, how Christ, who physically descended from the fathers and from Adam and Eve, could be free from original sin. On this view, certainly, physical unity necessarily entails also moral unity. Furthermore, realism gets itself in considerable trouble when it comes to the covenant of grace. For if there was no covenant of works, neither would there be a covenant of grace: the one stands and falls with the other. Now if the righteousness of Christ is acquired and applied not in the way of a covenant but realistically, then in the case of Christ it consists in the fact that he assumed our nature, and in that case the satisfaction and salvation accrues to all humans, for Christ assumed the nature of them all. Or it consists in the fact that everyone first acquires this physical and realistic unity with Christ only by regeneration or faith, and then it is impossible to see how Christ could make satisfaction in advance for those with whom he does not become one until they believe in him; then regeneration and faith run the risk of losing their ethical character, the focus is shifted from Christ to the Christian, and the benefits of the covenant are realized only after and by faith. Finally, while realism does represent an excellent interest, namely, the unity of the human race, in the process it loses sight of another interest that is no less weighty, namely, the independence of the human personality. A human is a member of the race as a whole, certainly, but in that whole he or she occupies a unique place of his or her own. Individuals are more than ripples in the ocean, more than passing manifestations of human nature in general. Earlier already we remarked that the relations in which people stand to one another are distinct from those that are found among angels and animals.[90] While related to both, humans are also different from both. They are creatures with a character of their own. For that reason, physical unity in their case is not enough; an ethical, a federal unity is added as well.[91]

As soon as theologians in the Christian church began to reflect on the link between Adam's sin and our sin, physical unity proved to be insufficient. Shedd admittedly asserts that Augustine, the scholastics, as well as the earliest Reformed theologians were all realists.[92] But that is incorrect. Whereas the doctrine of the covenant had not yet been developed, the idea already occurs in the church fathers and the medieval theologians.[93] The mere fact that almost all of them adhered to

---

90. H. Bavinck, *Reformed Dogmatics*, II, 568–72 (#296).

91. Cf. against realism, A. A. Hodge, *The Atonement* (Philadelphia: Presbyterian Board of Publication, 1867), 99ff.

92. W. G. T. Shedd, *Dogmatic Theology*, 3rd ed., 3 vols. (New York: Scribner, 1891–94), II, 37.

93. Cf. H. Bavinck, *Reformed Dogmatics*, II, 565–68 (#295); J. Schwane, *Dogmengeschichte*, III, 393ff.; IV, 166ff.; J. Kleutgen, *Theologie der Vorzeit vertheidigt*, 2nd ed., 5 vols. (Münster: Theissing, 1867–74), II, 711; J. H. Oswald, *Religiöse Urgeschichte der Menschheit* (Paderborn: Ferdinand Schöningh, 1887), 165, 167; M. J. Scheeben, *Handbuch der katholischen Dogmatik*, 4 vols. (1874–98; repr., Freiburg i.B.: Herder, 1933), I, 500.

creationism says enough, for a creationist cannot be a realist. Federalism certainly does not rule out the truth contained in realism; on the contrary, it fully accepts it. It proceeds from it but does not confine itself to it. It recognizes a unity of nature on which the federal unity depends. In the human race, we encounter a variety of forms of community that are absolutely not based only, nor even principally, on physical descent but on another, a higher, moral unity. There are "moral communities"—the nuclear and extended family, society, the nation, the state and the church, associations and federations of all kinds and for a variety of purposes—that have a life of their own, are subject to particular laws, especially to the law that Paul formulates when he says: "If one member suffers, all suffer together; if one member is honored, all rejoice together" (1 Cor. 12:26). All the members of such a body can be either a blessing or a curse to one another, and increasingly so to the degree that they themselves are more outstanding and occupy a more pivotal place in the organism. Fathers, mothers, guardians, caretakers, teachers, professors, patrons, guides, princes, kings, and so on have the greatest influence on those under their jurisdiction. Their life and conduct decides the fortunes of their subordinates, elevates them and brings them to honor, or drags them down and pulls them along to destruction. The family of the drunkard is ruined and disgraced because of the father's sin. The family of a criminal is widely and for a long time identified and condemned along with him. A congregation languishes under the faithless conduct of a pastor. A people decline and are eventually destroyed as a result of the foolish policies of a king. "In whatever thing the kings go crazy, the Achaeans [Homer's Greeks] are punished." Among people there is solidarity for good or ill: community in blessing and in judgment. We stand on the shoulders of earlier generations and inherit the things they have accumulated in the way of material and spiritual wealth.

We enter into their labors, rest on their laurels, enjoy the things they have frequently acquired at great cost. We receive all this undeservedly, without having asked for it. It is waiting for us at our birth; it is bequeathed to us by grace. There is no one who objects to this and opposes this law. But if the same law begins to exert its effects in things that are bad and makes us partakers in the sins and sufferings of others, the human mind revolts and charges this law with being unjust. The same son who [blithely] accepts his father's inheritance refuses to pay his father's debts.

In Israel the same lament was heard in the days of Ezekiel.[94] In the Old Testament there existed a law of solidarity (Gen. 9:25; Exod. 20:5; Num. 14:33; 16:32; Josh. 7:24–25; 1 Sam. 15:2–3; 2 Sam. 12:10; 21:1f.; 1 Kings 21:21, 23; Isa. 6:5; Jer. 32:18; Lam. 3:40f.; 5:7; Ezra 9:6; Matt. 23:35; 27:25). But when Israel in its sup-

---

Ed. note: ET: *A Manual of Catholic Theology: Based on Scheeben's "Dogmatic,"* trans. and ed. Joseph Wilhelm and Thomas Bartholomew Seannell, 4th ed., 2 vols. (London: Kegan Paul, Trench, Trubner and Co.; New York: Benziger Brothers, 1909); C. Pesch, *Prael. Dogm.,* III, 136.

94. A. B. Davidson, *The Theology of the Old Testament,* ed. from the author's manuscripts by S. D. F. Salmond (New York: Charles Scribner's, 1904), 219ff., 283.

posed righteousness complains about this, the Lord has the prophet announce, not what he can rightfully do, but what he will do if Israel repents and stops walking in the ways of the ancestors. There is indeed a solidarity in sin and suffering, but God permits it and frequently gives people the power to break with that moral community and themselves to become the forerunners of a generation that walks in the fear of the Lord and enjoys his favor. But so far from suspending the law of solidarity, it rather confirms it. Christ demonstrated the truth of the solidarity of the human race in another and better way than Adam. If this solidarity also could be broken, not only all compassion but all love, friendship, intercession, and so on would cease to exist. Humankind would fall apart in lifeless atoms; there would be no mystery, no mysticism, no human life left.

Still, Shedd is correct in saying that the solidarity of suffering does not yet explain the imputation of Adam's sin to all his descendants.[95] To suffer for the sin of another is not the same as to be punished for the sin of another and hence to be viewed as the perpetrator of that sin oneself. There is suffering without personal transgression (Luke 13:1–5; John 9:3). But this solidarity, which we witness every day, deprives us of a reason for charging God with injustice when he causes all of humankind to share in Adam's punishment. For thus he acts every moment, both in blessings and in judgments. If such conduct is consistent with his justice, then this is and has to be the case also with respect to Adam's trespass. There is, moreover, a special reason why in the case of Adam the above law of solidarity does not and even cannot completely hold true. The law of solidarity does not explain the covenant (of works or grace) but is based on it and harks back to it. It always holds sway within circles that are more circumscribed than that formed by humankind itself. However great the blessing or curse of parents and guardians, philosophers and artists, founders of religion and reformers, kings and conquerors, and so on may have been, there were always "circumstances" of place, time, country, people, language, and so on that set limits to it. The circle within which their influence was exerted was always enclosed within other and larger circles. Only two persons have existed whose life and works extended to the boundaries of humanity itself, whose influence and dominion had effects to the ends of the earth and into eternity.

We are referring to Adam and Christ. The former brought sin and death into the world, the latter righteousness and life. It follows from the totally exceptional position occupied by Adam and by Christ that they alone can be compared to each other, and that all other relations, which are derived from circles within humankind, though they can serve as illustrations and are of great value, merely offer analogies, not identity. That is to say that both Adam and Christ were placed under an utterly special ordinance of God, precisely with a view to the special position they occupy in humankind. When a father plunges his family into misery along with himself, or a king his people, or a philosopher his followers, or a boss

---

95. W. G. T. Shedd, *Dogmatic Theology*, II, 187.

his workers, we can go back behind these persons and to some extent find some explanation and satisfaction in the solidarity that prevails in humankind as a whole and in its various circles. But in the case of Adam and Christ, we cannot do this. They have the human race not behind them but before them; they do not spring from it but give rise to it; they are not sustained by it but themselves sustain it; they are not the product of humankind, but are, each in his own way, the beginning and root of it, the heads of all humanity. They are not explained by the law of solidarity but explain this law by their own existence. They do not presuppose but constitute the organism of humanity. If humanity, both in a physical and an ethical sense, were to remain a unity, as it was intended to be; hence, if in that human race there were to exist, not just community of blood, as in the case of the animals, but on that basis also community of all material, moral, and spiritual goods, then that could be brought about and maintained only by judging all in one person. As things went with that person, so they would go with the whole human race. If Adam fell, humanity would fall; if Christ remained standing, humanity would be raised up in him. The covenant of works and the covenant of grace are the forms by which the organism of humanity is maintained also in a religious and an ethical sense. Because God is interested, not in a handful of individuals, but in humanity as his image and likeness, it had to fall and be raised up again in one person. So reads God's ordinance, so reads his judgment. In one person he declares all guilty, and so humankind is born—unclean and in the process of dying—from Adam; in one person he declares all righteous and consecrated to eternal life. "For God has imprisoned all in disobedience so that he may be merciful to all" [Rom. 11:32].[96]

SIN AS SIN'S CONSEQUENCE

[324] The consequence of "originating sin" (*peccatum originans*) is the "sin originated" (*peccatum originatum*). Because all are considered sinners in Adam, they are all also born of him in a sinful state. Original pollution is a punishment for original guilt. From this perspective original sin was first viewed by Augustine, a view that elicited a strong protest from the side of the Pelagians,[97] as later from the Remonstrants.[98] But Scripture frequently speaks along those lines and regards consequent sins as punishment for previous sins (2 Sam. 12:11–12; 1 Kings 11:11–31; 22:30ff.; Isa. 6:9–10; 7:17; 10:5–7; 14:3; Jer. 50:6–8; Rom. 1:24–28; 2 Thess. 2:11–12; etc.). Also human sins are subject to God's govern-

---

96. In recent years, over against the individualism of Adam Smith c.s., the idea of solidarity has become very popular in social ethics. See, inter alia, *E. Bersier, *La Solidarité* (Paris, 1870); *Vercueil, *Étude sur la solidarité dans le Christianisme l'après St. Paul* (Mantauban, 1894); H. Pesch, *Lehrbuch der Nationalökonomie* (Freiburg: Herder, 1905), 351ff. The Seventh Congress on Sociology, held in Bern during July 1909, was dedicated entirely to discussing the idea of solidarity in its various forms and applications.

97. Augustine, *Against Julian*, V, 3.

98. In their *Apologia pro Confessione* (1629), VII, 4.

ment; the laws and ordinances that apply to the life of sin have been laid down and are being maintained by him. And to that category of laws belongs also this one: "The curse of an evil deed is above all that it must continually give birth to evil." The nature of sin is such that it progressively renders sinners more foolish and hard, entangles them ever more firmly in its snares, and propels them ever more rapidly down a slippery slope toward the abyss. It is true that sin, viewed by itself, can never be a punishment for sin, for the two are essentially different and opposed to each other. Sin arises from the will, and people undergo punishment against their will. Sin is a violation of the law; punishment an act of upholding the law. God is the author of punishment, not of sin. Still, a subsequent sin may be called a punishment for a prior sin, since it distances the sinner even further away from God, makes him more wretched, and abandons him to all sorts of covetousness and passion, dread and remorse.[99]

According to this law, in the case of Adam and all his descendants, a sinful state followed the sinful deed. The picture Pelagians have of this is that an act of the will, whatever it is, has absolutely no consequences. The will that did wrong the one moment can, a moment later, if it so pleases, again do good. In this view, the will never has a fixed nature, a determinate character, and never attains one; it is and remains neutral, indifferent, without any inner bias, always situated between opposites and focusing, with incalculable caprice, now in one and now in another direction. But such a view is contradicted from all directions. In the case of Adam and Eve, when they violated God's command, an enormous moral change occurred. Shame and dread before God took possession of them. Serenity, peace, and innocence were gone; they hid from God in the trees of the garden and blamed each other. Cain committed fratricide. And soon the Lord saw that the wickedness of humans was great on the earth, and all the imaginations of the thoughts of their heart were evil from their youth. In Adam's trespass an appalling degeneration of the human race had its inception. We are here confronting a horrible reality whose explanation escapes us. How can it be that one single sin had such dreadful consequences and brought about such a radical reversal in the nature of humans?

Generally speaking, we can begin by saying that frequently in life the relation between an act and its consequences seems to us to be totally disproportionate. One hour of thoughtlessness can produce a lifetime of tears. A small error, a single misstep can radically change the direction of the lives of numerous people. Seemingly insignificant incidents have an aftermath that lasts for generations. Our happiness or unhappiness often hangs by the thread of a single "chance" event.

99. P. Lombard, *Sent.*, II, dist. 36; T. Aquinas, *Summa theol.*, I, 2, qu. 87, art. 2; qu. 75, art. 4; qu. 84, art. 1–4; J. Gerhard, *Loci theologici*, ed. E. Preuss, 9 vols. (Berlin: G. Schlawitz, 1863–75), VI, c. 10, n. 140; F. Turretin, *Institutes of Elenctic Theology*, IX, 15; F. Spanheim, *Opera*, 3 vols. (Lugduni Batavorum [Leiden]: Cornelium Boutestein [etc.], 1701–3), III, 1268–70; B. de Moor, *Comm. theol.*, III, 332–35; F. Schleiermacher, *The Christian Faith* (Edinburgh: T&T Clark, 1989), §71, 2; J. Müller, *Christian Doctrine of Sin*, II, 589ff.; F. H. R. Frank, *System der christlichen Wahrheit*, I, 489; P. Christ, *Die sittliche Weltordnung* (Leiden: E. J. Brill, 1894), 59.

Adam's one trespass brought about an overall change in the thoughts, attitudes, and inclinations of his whole nature. Experience teaches us, after all, that no matter what people do, the act to some degree boomerangs on them and leaves tracks on their character. At bottom nothing is indifferent, and nothing passes us by without a trace. Every act of the will, arising as it does from antecedent impulses and desires, has a retroactive impact on it and reinforces it. In that way every sin can become a habit, a tendentious pattern, a passion that controls a person like a tyrant. Humans are changeable, extraordinarily moldable, and pliable. They adapt themselves to all occasions; they accommodate themselves to every kind of environment; they get used to everything and orient themselves to all fashions. Those who commit sins become the servants of sin. A crime, a lie, a theft, a murder never vanishes with the moment in which it has been committed. In a similar way but on a much larger scale, the disobedience of Adam changed his entire nature.

His trespass, moreover, had not only an exterior but also an interior side. The situation was not that the sinful deed done by Adam, consisting in eating of the forbidden fruit, happened all at once without any preparation and only afterward resulted in an assortment of moral changes in his nature. In that way there is no connection between Adam's guilt and moral pollution. The very act of eating was itself already a revelation of a sweeping moral change that had occurred in his inner self. Strictly speaking, it was not the first sin, but the first fully matured sin in the sense of James 1:15. Anterior to the sinful deed, there were sinful considerations of the mind (doubt, unbelief) and sinful tendencies of the heart (covetousness, pride), which had been prompted by the temptation of the serpent and were fostered by the will of man. Both before, during, and after the act of eating from the forbidden tree, the relation of humans to God and his law was changed. They did not first become one thing and then another, but all at once and interconnectedly they became both guilty and impure before the face of their Maker. Guilt and pollution are two simultaneous consequences of one and the same sin, two aspects of the same occurrence. Finally, the change initiated in Adam did not consist in that now some sinful principle was implanted in him or some component of his being, his soul or body, his abilities or powers was removed from him. It consisted in that, by his doubt and unbelief, his pride and covetousness, and finally by the sinful deed itself, the person himself progressively detached himself further from God and his law, positioned himself outside the circle of his favor and fellowship and began to use all his gifts and powers above all against God and his commandments. And when this happens, when a human being positions himself or herself outside God's fellowship and God's law, the sinful state automatically follows, just as the darkness sets in when the light goes out. "It is impossible for a creature that the love of God has not saturated fully to love itself" (Melanchthon). A human being who withdraws himself from the communion with God in which he was created can only be conceived as a sinner, guilty and depraved before the face of God.

The same religious and ethical change that occurred in Adam at the time of his fall befalls all his descendants as well. These are all born in the same moral state as that into which Adam fell by his trespass. This fact can hardly be in any way denied. Not only Scripture teaches it, but experience and history prove it daily. If anything is certain, it is certainly that humans are conceived and born not as saints but as sinners. This indicates that they have one and the same guilt in common with Adam, for in sin, guilt and pollution always go together.

At this point we must avoid two extremes. On the one hand, some theologians argue that in the case of Adam, before the act of eating of the forbidden fruit, there could not have been any sinful considerations and desire, for desiring it was not sinful but merely the natural operation of his bodily appetites. If he had resisted that desire, he would have remained free from all sin. The sin of Adam, accordingly, lay solely in the act of eating, "not in the inward state but in the outward act."[100] Against this view, however, is the fact that Genesis 3 clearly shows how the serpent managed gradually to arouse doubt, unbelief, and covetousness in the heart of the woman. In Christian theology, therefore, it was consistently pointed out that the first sin originated in the consciousness and, as a result of various considerations and inclinations, was completed in the act.[101] When this act is viewed totally as something external and is detached from everything that occurred internally, consistency seems to demand as well that justification by faith not only precedes but is also separated from regeneration. Jones, at least, declares that an unregenerate man can believe and that Scripture for that reason also says that God justifies the ungodly. "Sinless man can sin—that is the mystery of the fall; an ungodly man can believe—that is the mystery of the rise."[102]

On the other hand, it is equally incorrect for us to draw from the fact that guilt and pollution always go together in sin the conclusion that the pollution is actually anterior to guilt. Jonathan Edwards in part arrived at this position because he tried to deduce the sinful deed from the sinful inclination that originated earlier and sought to explain the latter in terms of the natural principles inherent in humanity's lower nature.[103] But this position was advocated decisively and candidly in the school of Saumur (France) by Placaeus and all the proponents of a mediate imputation of Adam's sin.[104] To this view, however, there are serious objections: (1) in that case, there is no reason why Adam's descendants should be born impure; (2) there then could exist a moral impurity that is not at the same time guilt; and (3) humans would only become sinners personally by consenting to that moral impurity by an act of the will. Over against this position, the Reformed have always maintained that there had to be an objective reason why all

100. J. C. Jones, *Primeval Revelation: Studies in Genesis I–VIII* (London: Hodder & Stoughton, 1897), 253ff.
101. See, e.g., J. Marck, *Historia paradisi*, 526ff.
102. J. C. Jones, *Primeval Revelation*, 256, 257.
103. J. Ridderbos, *Jonathan Edwards*, 171ff.
104. See above, 99–100 (#322); cf. also, Shedd, *Dogmatic Theology*, II, 170.

of Adam's descendants are born guilty and impure, and that the reason cannot be other than that in some way they themselves were guilty in Adam. Some tried to explain this more realistically, others more federalistically, but either way Adam's trespass is the sin of all his descendants. On the ground that they were comprehended in Adam, either as the natural or the federal head, they were declared guilty by God. There is an antecedent judgment (κριμα) of God as Judge on one human and one trespass, and this (κριμα) contains the κατακριμα (the sentence) that not only Adam but all his descendants were guilty, impure, and worthy of death (Rom. 5:16). Being born in this state of guilt, impurity, and depravity is the execution of the sentence passed by God on Adam's trespass. Just as, as a result of his trespass, he himself was immediately burdened with guilt, defiled by pollution, and subjected to death, so this also takes place, in virtue of God's judgment, in the life of all his descendants. Guilt, pollution, and death in the case of Adam's descendants are interconnected in the same way as in Adam himself and have thus, in that mutual connectedness, passed to all.

INHERITED SIN?

[325] The way in which this "originated sin" becomes the experience of all of us is not through imitation but through generation based on imputation. There is an antecedent judgment (κριμα) of God, and in virtue of that judgment all people are born of Adam guilty, impure, and in the process of dying. They do not become all this only at a later age as a result of actual sins but are this from conception and birth on. Proof of this is death, for death holds sway not only over adults but in even greater measure over infants, even the unborn, and according to Scripture death is not a natural process but "the wages of sin." Rationalism condemned the doctrine of original sin as irrational, but in the nineteenth century it was again gradually recognized as containing truth. Whereas the eighteenth century raved over the natural goodness of humans and held society responsible for all sin and imperfection, nowadays people often adopt the opposite position: since humans originate from the animal world, they remain animals at heart. Concealed in every person is "the human beast" (*la bête humaine*). "Its [inherited] animal nature is humanity's defect."

Now, [so it is believed] however, we fortunately have a "holy" society and a "holy" state that curb the instincts of these coarse, animalistic humans and compel them in the direction of virtue. All vice is inborn, and all virtue is acquired.[105] In connection with this change in viewpoint with regard to humanity's origin and nature, the theory of hereditary transmission also emerged. For if there were no transmission of traits acquired in the struggle for survival, there could, of course, not be anything like development and progress, especially no human descent from the animal world. In Darwin's theory of descent, hereditary transmission,

105. F. Brunetière, *La moralité de la doctrine évolutive* (Paris: Firmin-Didot et Cie, 1896).

accordingly, plays a key role, and on the position of evolution it has with good warrant been called the primary cause of all the progress made by the human race, even "the most splendid of all natural phenomena." Yet the facts on which the theory of hereditary transmission is based were in large part also known earlier. For the fact that every species reproduces its kind, that children take after their parents, that not only physical but also mental characteristics pass from parents to children and grandchildren—that, as is evident from the theory of traducianism, was known also in the past. And that nonetheless not all traits are biologically transmitted, that every individual is still something other and more than the sum of the product of his or her parents—that too, as the theory of creationism testifies, was not unknown to previous generations. But at that time people didn't yet read all these facts in the light of a materialistic or pantheistic worldview or make them subservient to a preconceived doctrine of evolution. Above all, these facts were not yet misused in literature and drama to picture humans as the passive products of their origin and environment at the mercy of chance or fate, thus robbing them of all moral energy, all courage-to-be, and all zest for living. All this did not occur until the nineteenth century. When the people of science proclaimed hereditary transmission as an immutable law and an inescapable fact, numerous moralists, writers, and criminologists stood ready to draw the conclusion that humans were products of nature in the same sense as plants and animals, that their independence and freedom are an illusion, that they must by necessity be what they are.

Against these false and dangerous conclusions, fortunately, there has been a reaction. Always, when science continues its research, it corrects itself again. This has also happened in the present cases, and that on good grounds.

1. The facts on which the theory of hereditary transmission is based all consist in the reality that many traits that distinguish the parents also return in children and grandchildren. Among them are such physical traits as the body build, posture, and manners, hair color, shape of the limbs, the strength or weakness of the senses, deformities (polydactyly, albinism). But also countless mental traits pass from parents to children: a strong or weak memory, intellect and capacity for judgment, emotion and will, characteristic moods, temperament, character, aptitudes, instincts, inclinations, talents. Among all these traits, there are good ones that are a blessing to the children: gifts of intellect and heart, gentleness, compassion, sensitivity, cheerfulness, a feeling for order, craftsmanlike skills. But often there are also bad impulses and passions, such as a tendency toward mendacity, miserliness, greed, gluttony, addiction to gambling or alcohol, lechery, kleptomania, murder; or a disposition to certain diseases such as tuberculosis, gout, epilepsy, hypochondria, mental illness, and so on. All these traits often pass from parents to children and grandchildren to the third and fourth generation or leap over one or more generations and return in later descendants. These facts have been observed so precisely and frequently that their truth cannot be doubted. Everybody, for that matter, knows examples of it from his or her own

environment. Even proverbial sayings refer to it: "like father like son"; "the apple never falls far from the tree."

2. The moment one tries to classify or group these facts, however, one immediately runs into great difficulties. That generic traits are transmitted—for example, that parents always produce children of the same species—is certain, but this does not help us get much further in this case. Admittedly, it is a fact of great importance, for it proves most definitely that species are constant and bound to a law, the law of their own kind. But this law of generation—like seeks like and produces like—is actually the underlying assumption of heredity in the restricted sense, which consists in the transmission of all kinds of traits, traits that as such do not belong to the species. Which of these traits are transmissible and which are not is something no one can tell; one cannot classify them by this criterion. That racial and variant traits are propagated constantly is subject to legitimate doubt; undoubtedly races exist—also among humans—that persist century after century (the Indo-Germanic, the Semitic race, and others), but these races originally stemmed from the one human race. We do not know how, nor can we say with certainty that they will continue to exist in the future under very different circumstances. We *do* know that strains and breeds, say of plants and animals, can be changed and improved by selection. This improvement, however, is limited, temporary, and dependent on human culture. As a rule, the peak of development is reached after four or five generations. The moment one stops the process of selection, the descendants return to the old type. Acquired traits are not incorporated into the species, but rather the species shows a tendency to return to its original form. That individually acquired traits pass from parents to children, though asserted by Darwin and others, has been rejected in the strongest possible terms by A. Weismann, professor at Freiburg, and his theory is finding increasing acceptance nowadays.

3. Even much less successful has been the attempt to reduce the phenomena that occur in this area to a few laws. They are much too numerous and complex for that purpose. Our knowledge of life is still very deficient. Countless influences that control the structure and traits of an organism are still unknown. At all times the danger threatens that we seek to explain a given phenomenon from a cause that has nothing to do with it and completely overlook the true cause. So long as the research has not advanced any further, it is premature to speak of fixed laws. Ribot, admittedly, formulated four laws for the heredity of psychic traits, but he mistakenly used the word "laws" to describe certain regularities that he thought he observed in the phenomena in question. This is clearly evident in his third "law," that of atavism, which seems only to have been invented to give a semblance of regularity to the many cases in which favorable traits are not passed on and the "law" of heredity is therefore not operative. "Facts that are not understood seem to be at last familiar the moment one describes them with a familiar word."[106]

---

106. J. H. F. Kohlbrugge, *Der Atavismus* (Utrecht: G. J. C. Scrinerius, 1897), 3.

Lombroso's hypothesis on the criminal type is today a thing of the past.[107] And though statistics may show a certain regularity in births, marriages, crimes, and so on, this by no means warrants the conclusion that every person is forced to do what he does, any more than the fact that the average longevity of a population amounts to thirty years forces every thirty-year-old to die.[108]

4. The difficulty of speaking about the phenomena of heredity increases significantly as a result of the fact that they are consistently coupled with the phenomena of variation. Heredity exists, but so does variation. There is unity *and* diversity, memory but also imagination. It is usually said that heredity is the "law" and the rule, and variation the exception. But this is done without sufficient basis in fact, for variation plays as big a role as heredity. No two leaves on the same tree and branch are the same, and this is the case in all of organic creation. The children of the same parents sometimes differ a great deal, both physically and mentally, from each other. And the reasons for this are as hard to establish as those for the unity and similarity. Heredity and variation are continually connected; they work together and intersect each other, but up until now no one can say how that happens and what the causes are. This is all the more impossible since among all the higher creatures procreation occurs by the union of two individuals (amphimixis: the union of germ cells), each of which has its own peculiarities and exerts its own special effect. Then the fruit of that union, before and after birth, gets to live in an environment in which the many operative factors and influences are incalculable. An intense battle is waged, accordingly, between those who want to explain everything from the inside out, from the disposition of the individual, and those who want to explain everything from without, from the social environment. Extreme caution is needed not to err here. Countless phenomena, such as diseases and aberrant tendencies, initially explained in terms of heredity, later proved to be the result of environment and upbringing. People may bring with them a certain disposition, but this disposition only develops in a corresponding environment.

5. Up until now all the differing theories submitted to explain heredity and variation have proved inadequate. The great number of them itself is evidence that not a single one of them is satisfactory. All natural philosophers and biologists have tested their powers on this problem, without having unveiled this mystery of life. In his learned work *La structure du protoplasma et les théories sur l'hérédité*

---

107. *Schermers, *De leer van Lombroso* (Heusden, 1896).

108. W. M. Wundt, *Grundzüge der physiologischen Psychologie*, 3 vols. (Leipzig: W. Engelmann, 1908–11), II, 397; W. Windelband, *Über Willensfreiheit: Zwölf Vorlesungen* (Tübingen: J. C. B. Mohr, 1904), 134; A. von Oettingen, *Die Moralstatistik in ihrer Bedeutung für eine Socialethik* (Erlangen: A. Deichert, 1882), 24ff.; ed. note: Bavinck's footnote simply reads A. von Oettingen, *Die Moralstatistik*, 1882, pp. 24ff. This could refer to either *Die Moralstatistik in ihrer Bedeutung*, etc. (as already in note) or to *Die Moralstatistik und die christliche Sittenlehre* (Erlangen: A. Deichert, 1882).

et les grands problèmes de la biologie générale,[109] Yves Delage, professor at the Sorbonne, discussed all the theories at length and then concluded: "After having studied and discussed the numerous theories proposed for the resolution of the problems of heredity and evolution, we are obliged to acknowledge that not one presents an acceptable solution. All err on some points, not just incidentally but fundamentally, and the majority, moreover, are based on gratuitous and completely improbable hypotheses." He himself, accordingly, refrains from offering the reader a complete theory: "Our knowledge is not sufficiently advanced for that to be possible."[110] That was a wise thing to say, for as of now we have not progressed much beyond the insight that both heredity and variability exist. The riddle of how, in virtue of what causes, according to which laws, and to what extent they cooperate and take turns, however, is still unsolved. It even seems to be the case that the continued pursuit of scientific research, instead of solving the existing problems, increases them in number and importance.

6. The blame for this uncertainty, however, may not be lodged against science, for no one is obligated to go beyond the possible, and science may be able to tell us tomorrow what it doesn't know today. Yet attention may be called to this lack of certain results in order to warn others against premature and dangerous conclusions and to warn us to be on our guard ourselves. Fortunately, the voices warning us to be cautious are also coming from the circles of the experts themselves. They point out that disturbances and deviations absolutely do not always and in all cases pass from the parents to the children. Insanity, for example, though in many cases hereditary, is not in many other instances. In a family, one of whose members became mentally ill as a result of heredity factors, still other members were not infrequently struck by the same fate as well, but it is absolutely not the case that all or most members of such a family were affected. Further, in the higher organisms procreation is bound to amphimixis, and this circumstance often, especially in the case of wise choices, introduces new blood and regenerative power. Finally, there certainly is something like what is called a hereditary defect and hereditary degeneracy. At any rate, many children at birth already carry with them a susceptibility to some disease. Yet one must not for that reason close one's eyes to the healing power inherent in nature. There is in heredity not only a conservative and progressive side but also a regressive side. In the construction of any living being, heredity not only seeks to maintain inviolate the type of genus to which it belongs but also has a tendency to return to the original type. If that were not the case, the population of Europe would—on account of the vices and illnesses that in previous centuries sometimes expanded on an enormous scale—already be totally defective and degenerate.

109. Yves Delage, *La structure du protoplasma et les théories sur l'hérédité et les grands problèmes de la biologie générale* (Paris: C. Reinwald, 1895).

110. Ibid., 743, 747.

7. On these grounds we are also warned against letting heredity lead us into fatalism and pessimism. Heredity is only one side of the matter; alongside it there is also variability; degeneration is operative, but so is regeneration. Put more generally and in other words: on the one hand, human beings are the product of their parents and ancestors, of their environment and upbringing; on the other, they are something else and something more: egos in their own right, personalities. People will never succeed in explaining the human person—traducianistically—totally from the perspective of the past, for we are more than products of preexistent and external factors; we have an existence and life of our own; we are beings that know, and will, and can.[111] By these attributes of higher cognitive and conative capacities, human beings transcend the physical domain and enter another, a higher, a moral world. That, too, is a world where law, rule, and order prevail. The difference between the physical and the psychic (mental, intellectual, ethical) world is certainly not that in the one everything is governed by the law of cause and effect and that in the other chance, arbitrariness, and Pelagian free will are in control. On the contrary, also in the psychic world one finds cause and effect, ordinances and laws, but they are of a different order than those of nature. As a result there is as much diversity in the psychic world as in the physical. All people are dissimilar, also in the degree of their self-reliance, freedom, responsibility, accountability, and guilt. We cannot and may not lump everything together. To whom much is given, from him much will be required; and one to whom little has been given much less will be required. But all this does not change the fact that human persons are different and higher beings than plants and animals; they rise above the power of nature and over against it postulate their "I know, I will, I can." They act and can act as humans, as persons; they are and remain the cause of their own actions. They act, not without reasons, but without compulsion. They are free and in proportion to their freedom remain responsible for their actions. Besides a physical, there is a psychic causality; besides a mechanical, an energetic causality; besides a causal, a teleological causality. Today this is again increasingly recognized; and, by implication, the independence, the generic uniqueness, the special nomothetic regularity of the moral world order continues to be maintained.[112]

---

111. The individual is not a mere manifestation of the race. God applies to the origination of every single man a special creative thought and act of will. J. C. Jones, *Primeval Revelation*, 263.

112. From the abundance of literature we mention only the following: Hugo de Vries, "Eenheid in Veranderlijkheid," *Album der Natuur* (1898): 65–80; T. Ribot, *L'hérédité psychologique* (Paris: F. Alcan, 1894); J. F. Van Bemmelen, *De erfelijkheid von verworven eigenschappen* ('s Gravenhage: Nijhoff, 1890); R. Schäfer, *Die Vererbung: Ein Kapitel aus einer zukünftigen psycho-physiologischen Einleitung in die Pädagogik* (Berlin: Reuther & Reichard, 1897); A. J. Th. Jonker, "De Beteekenis van de Nieuwste Beschouwingen over Erfelijkheid en Toerekenbaarheid voor de dienaar van het Evangelie," *Theologische Studiën* 12 (1894): 291–322; W. H. Gispen Jr., "De Leer der Erfelijkheid en de Leer der Erfzonde," *Tijdschrift voor Gereformeerde Theologie* 9 (1902): 289–311; C. H. Kuhn, "Herediteit en pessimisme," *De Gids* 18/3 (July 1900): 114–34; G. von Rohden, *Erbliche Belastung und ethische Verantwortung* (Tübingen: Mohr, 1907); L. Büchner, *Die Macht der Vererbung und ihr Einfluss auf*

8. Inasmuch as in the moral world not chance or fate but holy order prevails, we deny neither the facts of heredity nor its extensive rule. Christian theology does not have the least interest in detracting from it in any way. On the contrary, Christian theology fully recognizes and respects the laws God has laid down in this domain. The more we track down in heredity the fixed laws that govern it, the greater will be the glory of him who is the Creator of all ordinances, not a God of confusion but the God of order. It is also completely true that we can never with complete accuracy indicate the boundaries that separate personal guilt from communal guilt. What Schleiermacher says of original sin is something very different from what Scripture and the church say concerning it, but by itself it is completely true of sin in general that it is the collective deed and collective guilt of the human race as a whole. In other words, the sinful state and sinful deeds of each individual are, on the one hand, conditioned by those of the previous generation, and, on the other, they in turn condition the sinful state and acts of later descendants. Sin is "in each the work of all and in all the work of each."[113] However true all this may be, so long as biology has to acknowledge variation as well as heredity, we have no right whatsoever to rob human beings of their independence and freedom and to picture them as passive instruments of evil powers. Such a picture is not based on sound science but is a product of a sick imagination and, by destroying all will power, wreaks incalculable devastation in the lives of people.

9. Finally, although to a certain extent we may gratefully acknowledge the support offered by the science of the day to the ecclesiastical doctrine of original sin, that doctrine itself is not strengthened by it any more than it would be weakened if tomorrow that same science might delight in pillorying it as foolish and nonsensical. Original sin cannot be equated with what is known today as heredity. It is not, after all, a generic trait that belongs to the human essence, inasmuch as it entered human nature by a violation of God's command and can be again removed from it by regeneration and sanctification. Neither, on the other hand, is it an individually acquired trait, for it characterizes all people without exception and is so much a part of human nature that even the regenerate still produce children who are "by nature children of wrath." "The righteous do not generate from the source from which they themselves were *re*generated but from that from which they were generated" (Augustine).

Original sin, therefore, occupies a special place. The current theory of heredity, while it may have relieved it of its seeming absurdity because it has again shown humanity to be a physical and ethical organism, does not explain original sin. This was attempted in earlier centuries by traducianism or creationism. But whatever position one adopts with respect to the origin of souls, the propagation of original sin remains equally difficult. Original sin, after all, is not a substance that inheres

den moralischen und geistigen Fortschritt der Menschheit (Leipzig: A. Kröner, 1909); L. Bouman, "Degeneratie," *Orgaan van de Christelijke Vereeniging van Natuur- en Geneeskunde* (1908–9).

113. F. Schleiermacher, *Christian Faith*, §71, 1, 2.

in the body and can be transmitted by procreation. On the contrary, it is a moral quality of the person who lacks the communion with God that one should and does possess by virtue of one's original nature. Adam's depravity automatically began the moment he—in doubt and unbelief, pride and covetousness—tore himself away from God. In the same way, moral depravity starts in his descendants from the first moment of their existence. Just as God withdrew his communion from Adam on account of his trespass, so he withdraws it from all his descendants. Nor does he become the cause of the depravity of Adam's descendants—whether one views the origin of souls along traducianistic or creationist lines—any more than he was when he, still upholding Adam after his trespass, withdrew his communion from him. Every human person, in virtue of the physical and ethical relation in which he or she stands to Adam, is born culpable and stained. "Each person, accordingly, is the proximate principle and subject and author of his or her own original sin."[114]

No Exceptions

[326] Original sin is a characteristic of human nature and therefore peculiar to all creatures possessing this nature. "In Adam the person corrupts the [human] nature; in other humans the [human] nature corrupts the person."[115] The Pelagian claim that there are, or at least can be, people without any sin is contradicted by Scripture, by experience, and by the testimony of all religions and peoples. To the rule that all humans are sinners, there is only one exception: Christ, but he, accordingly, was the only-begotten Son of God, the second Adam, the head of another and better covenant and conceived by the Holy Spirit in a special way. Catholics, however, also except Mary, the mother of Jesus. The three privileges incrementally accorded in Catholic theology to Mary (freedom from original sin—the immaculate conception; freedom from actual sin—the perfection of justice; and exemption from death—assumption into heaven) are simply inferences from the high rank of mediatrix to which she was elevated by the church on the basis of her virginity and divine motherhood. With respect to the immaculate conception, Pius IX declared in the bull Ineffabilis of December 10, 1854, "that the most Blessed Virgin Mary was preserved from all stain of original sin in the first instant of her Conception, by a singular grace and privilege of Almighty God, in consideration of the merits of Jesus Christ, Savior of the human race." Not implied here is that Mary was not comprehended and fallen in Adam, for Mary was only preserved from all stain of original sin by a special grace of God in

---

114. G. Voetius, *Selectae disputationes theologicae*, 5 vols. (Utrecht, 1648–49), I, 1104; P. Martyr Vermigli, *Loci comm.*, 70; A. Polanus, *Synt. theol.*, VI, ch. 3; J. Zanchi, *Op. theol.*, IV, 50; G. Voetius, *Select. disp.*, I, 1078ff.; F. Turretin, *Institutes of Elenctic Theology*, IX, 12; B. de Moor, *Comm. theol.*, III, 289; C. Vitringa, *Doctr. christ.*, II, 358; J. Edwards, *The Works of Jonathan Edwards*, ed. Paul Ramsey (New Haven: Yale University Press, 1989), II, 478.

115. T. Aquinas, *Summa theol.*, III, qu. 8, art. 5; qu. 69, art. 3.

consideration of the merits of Christ. Nor is it said that Mary was first conceived in sin and sanctified immediately thereafter, for it is expressly stated that she was preserved from original sin in the very first instant of her conception.

In Scripture, however, there is not the slightest ground for this dogma. Aquinas frankly stated that "nothing is handed down in the canonical Scriptures concerning the sanctification of the Blessed Mary as to her being sanctified in the womb."[116] Catholic theologians, accordingly, find themselves in no little embarrassment with respect to this doctrine. They therefore search out all sorts of reasons to explain "this mystery of Mary" in Scripture and force the strangest texts to bring about a semblance of proof. Thus they appeal to Genesis 3:15; Psalm 45:11f.; Song of Solomon 1:8–16; 2:2; 3:6; 4:1f.; 6:9; Wisdom 1:4; Luke 1:28, 41, 48; Revelation 12, and to typologies such as Noah's ark, the dove with the olive branch, the burning bush, and so on.[117] But all these references and reasonings only serve to cover up their dearth of arguments and require no refutation. Scripture decisively teaches, rather, that all humans, Christ alone excepted, are sinners. No exception is ever made for Mary. Although no specific sinful words or deeds are recorded of her (not in Mark 3:21; John 2:3–4 either), still she rejoices in God her *Savior* (Luke 1:47), is called blessed because of her motherhood of Christ but never on account of her sinlessness (Luke 1:28, 48), and even in her motherhood per se she is made secondary to those who are mother and brothers and sisters to Jesus in a spiritual sense (Matt. 12:46f.; Mark 3:31f., Luke 8:21), and along with the apostles devoted herself to prayer (Acts 1:14). Neither do the church fathers ever teach either the immaculate conception or the sinlessness of Mary. Irenaeus, Tertullian, Origen, and others speak in connection with her of daily transgressions.[118] Even Catholic theologians cannot deny these facts. Dr. von Lehner says that this was the dominant opinion at the time.[119] Schwane acknowledges that the tradition dating from that time no more furnishes us with stringent proofs than does Holy Scripture.[120] And Scheeben agrees that the person of Mary remains in the background and in relative obscurity during the first four centuries.[121] People at most believed that for the sake of the Lord's honor, Mary had by a special grace remained free from actual sins.[122] Even when, after the fifth century, the veneration

116. Ibid., III, qu. 27, art. 1.

117. Cf., e.g., Spencer Northcote, *Mary in the Gospels* (London: Burns & Oates, 1906); A. Schaefer, *The Mother of Jesus in Holy Scripture* (Ratisbon [Regensburg]: F. Pustet, 1913); M. Scheeben, *Handbuch der katholischen Dogmatik*, III, 455–72.

118. Irenaeus, *Against Heresies*, III, 16, 7; Tertullian, *On the Flesh of Christ*, 7; *Origen, *Homilies in Luke*, 17; Ernst Lucius, *Die Anfänge des Heiligenkults in der christlichen Kirche*, released posthumously by Gustav Anrich (Tübingen: Mohr, 1904), 420–504, presents a comprehensive overview of the ways in which the veneration of Mary became included.

119. F. A. von Lehner, *Die Marienverehrung in der ersten Jahrhunderten* (Stuttgart: J. G. Cotta, 1881), 151.

120. J. Schwane, *Dogmengeschichte*, I, 382.

121. M. Scheeben, *Handbuch der katholischen Dogmatik*, III, 474, 476.

122. Augustine, *On Nature and Grace*, 36; John of Damascus, *Orthodox Faith*, IV, 14.

of Mary progressively increased and later also the feast of Mary's conception arose, the top theologians—as Canus, Scheeben, and others admit[123]—though teaching "a sanctification of the Blessed Virgin after the quickening and the contraction of sin in the soul," opposed a preservation that kept Mary a priori free from all stain of original sin.[124] But Duns Scotus introduced a change in this picture: he argued that, though Mary was also comprehended in Adam, God could certainly, in the very first moment of her conception, grant her the grace that kept her free from all sin. And since this was more worthy of God, Christ, and Mary, and not inconsistent with the authority of Scripture and the church, he deemed it "probable that it was better to attribute this [grace] to Mary."[125] And with that we have been given the ground on which this dogma rests in the Catholic Church. It has no support in Scripture or in the tradition of the ancient church but is simply, like Mary's assumption, an inference from the mediatorship gradually attributed to her. It is not fitting (*conveniens*) that Mary should be conceived in sin, should have committed sin, and died. She has to be sinless; therefore she *is* sinless, even though neither Scripture nor tradition teaches this.[126]

TOTAL DEPRAVITY

[327] As extensive as original sin is in humanity as a whole, so it is also in the individual person. It holds sway over the whole person, over mind and will, heart and conscience, soul and body, over all one's capacities and powers. A person's heart is evil from his or her youth and a source of all sorts of evils (Gen. 6:5; 8:21; Ps. 51:5; Jer. 17:9; Ezek. 36:26; Mark 7:21). One cannot renew one's self (Jer. 13:23; Ezek. 16:6), understand the things of God (1 Cor. 2:14), or submit to the law of God (John 8:34, 36; Rom. 6:17, 20; 8:7), and one is dead through trespasses and sins (Eph. 2:1). Rebirth, accordingly, is a prerequisite to entrance into the kingdom of God (John 3:3). The whole of salvation is objectively and subjectively a work of divine grace (John 6:44; 15:5; 1 Cor. 4:7; 15:10; Phil. 2:13; etc.). Upon these firm pronouncements of Holy Scripture, Augustine and his followers, and later the Reformers, built the doctrine of humanity's incapacity for good. Inasmuch

123. M. Canus, *Melchioris Cani episcopi canariensis, ex Ordine Praedicatorum opera: In hac primum editione clarius divisa, et praefatione instar prologi Galeati illustrata* (Bassani: Remondini, 1746), VII, ch. 1; M. Scheeben, *Handbuch der katholischen Dogmatik*, III, 541ff.

124. Anselm, *Why God Became Man, and The Virgin Conception, and Original Sin*, trans. Joseph M.Colleran (Albany: Magi Books, 1969), II, 16; Lombard, T. Aquinas, Bonaventure, *Sent.*, III, 3; T. Aquinas, *Summa theol.*, II, 1, qu. 81, art. 3; III, qu. 27, art. 1, 2; idem, *Compendium of Theology*, trans. Cyril O. Vollert (St. Louis: B. Herder Book Co., 1947), 224.

125. Duns Scotus, *Quaestiones in libros sententiarum* (Frankfurt: Minerva, 1967), III, dist. 3, qu. 1.

126. Cf. E. Preuss, *The Romish Doctrine of the Immaculate Conception, Traced from Its Source*, trans. George Gladstone (Edinburgh: T&T Clark, 1867); Benrath, "Zur Geschichte der Mariaverehrung," *Theologische Studien und Kritiken* 59 (1886): 197–267; K. A. von Hase, *Protestantische Polemik*, 5th ed. (Leipzig: Breitkopf & Härtel, 1891), 379ff.; P. Tschackert, *Evangelische Polemik gegen die römische Kirche* (Gotha: F. A. Perthes, 1885), 118ff.; O. Zöckler, "Maria," *PRE*³, XIII, 309–36; J. B. Mayor, "Mary," *DB*, III, 286–93; G. J. P. J. Bolland, *Rome en de geschiedenis* (Leiden: A. H. Adriani, 1897), 1–53.

as in Adam all of human nature has been corrupted, nothing truly good can any longer proceed from it, any more than a bad tree can produce good fruit. Human persons are now under the hard necessity of not being able not to sin. Their virtues are vices rather than virtues; they are by nature inclined to all evil, inclined even to hate God and their neighbor. This reasoning is undoubtedly hard, and it is not surprising that it has at all times encountered strong contradiction.[127] Besides the natural aversion that spontaneously arises in the human heart against the doctrine of the total moral depravity of humans, there is undoubtedly also much incomprehension on the part of its opponents. Certainly, if this doctrine is clearly elucidated, it is daily confirmed by everyone's experience and vindicated by the witness of its opponents themselves.

1. The teaching of Scripture, after all, is not that every human lives at all times in all possible actual sins and is in fact guilty of violating all God's commandments. It only refers to the deepest inclination, the innermost disposition, the fundamental directedness of human nature and confesses that it is not turned toward God but away from him. If a human being is an organic unity, then one of these two things has to be true. Many people brush this aside by saying that humans are by nature neither or both at the same time,[128] but this betrays a lack of reflection, is contrary to the nature of the good, and was therefore very seriously opposed even by Kant.[129] A person who commits one sin is in principle guilty of violating all the commandments; and a person who truly possesses one virtue in principle possesses them all. The human being is at the center of his or her being either good or evil—there is no third option.

2. Sin, however, is not a substance. It does indeed inhabit and infect all of us, but it is not and cannot be the essence of our humanity. Also, after the fall, we human beings remained humans. We have retained our reason, conscience, and will, can therefore control our lower sensual drives and inclinations, and thus force them in the direction of virtue. Augustine, who called the virtues of Gentiles "splendid vices," candidly acknowledged this truth. Many of their actions not only do not deserve to be reprimanded but are worthy of our praise and emulation.[130] While Lutherans spoke of the "natural man" as stocks and blocks in matters spiritual, in the so-called lower hemisphere of civic life they still credited "him" with all sorts of powers for good.[131] And more than them all, Calvin and the Reformed have honored the virtues of unbelievers and frequently held them up as examples to

---

127. See above, 85–90 (#319).

128. G. W. F. Hegel, *Philosophie der Religion* (2), in *Sämtliche Werke*, 16 (Stuttgart: Frommanns, 1959), 209ff. (*Werke*, XII, 209). Ed. note: ET: G. W. F. Hegel, *Lectures on the Philosophy of Religion*, ed. Peter E. Hodgson, vol. III, *The Consummate Religion* (Berkeley: University of California Press, 1998), 173ff. ("The Metaphysical Concept of God").

129. I. Kant, *Religion within the Limits of Reason Alone*, trans. Theodore M. Greene and Hoyt H. Hudson (New York: Harper & Row, 1960 [1934], 23–27).

130. G. F. Wiggers, *Augustinismus und Pelagianismus*, I, 119–23.

131. F. H. R. Frank, *Theologie der Concordienformel*, I, 144ff.

Christians themselves.[132] The doctrine of the total corruption of human nature by no means implies, therefore, that the sinful disposition that lies at the bottom of the human heart always erupts in the kind of deeds that betray clear hostility and hatred toward God and one's neighbor. There are various circumstances that intervene and keep the disposition from fully expressing itself. Not only are many sinful deeds restrained by the sword of the government, common civil decency, public opinion, the fear of disgrace and punishment, and so on, but a variety of factors—such as the natural love still inherent in every person; the moral character fostered by upbringing and struggle; favorable circumstances of constitution, environment, or job; and so on—all these frequently lead people to practice beautiful and praiseworthy virtues. Note, however, that while these factors may subdue the sinful disposition of the heart, they do not eradicate it. In all kinds of nasty considerations, thoughts, and desires, it keeps rising to the surface. When conditions are favorable and the need arises, it often breaks through the dams and dikes that restrained it. And those who show by their appalling words and deeds that they hate God and their neighbor have no other nature than the one all people share.

3. When we are taught that as a result of sin humans are incapable of any good and this inability is called "natural," this does not refer to physical necessity or fatalistic coercion. Humans have not, as a result of sin, lost their will and their increated freedom: the will, in virtue of its nature, rules out all coercion and can only will freely. What humans have lost is the free inclination of the will toward the good. They now no longer want to do good; they now voluntarily, by a natural inclination, do evil. The inclination, the direction, of the will has changed. "The will in us is always free but it is not always good."[133] In this sense the incapacity for good is not physical but ethical in nature: it is a kind of impotence of the will. Some theologians therefore preferred to speak of a moral rather than a natural impotence—Amyraut, Testard, Venema,[134] and especially Jonathan Edwards among them. Edwards in his day, one must remember, had to defend the moral impotence of humans against Whitby and Taylor, who denied original sin and deemed humans able to keep God's law. They argued, against Edwards, that if humans *could* not keep God's law, they did not have to, and if they *did* not keep it, they were not guilty. To defend himself, Edwards made a distinction between natural and moral impotence, saying that fallen humans did have the natural but not the moral power to do good. And he added that only natural impotence was real impotence, but moral impotence could only be figuratively so called. For sin is not a physical defect in nature or in the powers of the will; but it is an ethical

132. Cf. H. Bavinck, "Common Grace," trans. Raymond C. Van Leeuwen, *Calvin Theological Journal* 24 (1989): 50ff.

133. Augustine, *On Grace and Free Will*, 15; for the Reformed view, see H. Heppe, *Dogmatik*, 237, 264; W. Cunningham, *The Reformers and the Theology of the Reformation*, ed. James Buchanan and James Bannerman (Edinburgh: T&T Clark, 1862), 471ff.; idem, *Historical Theology*, I, 568ff.

134. B. de Moor, *Comm. theol.*, III, 231–33.

defect, a lack of inclination toward or love for the good.[135] Now Edwards did say that human beings could not give themselves this inclination toward the good nor change their will. In this respect he was completely on the side of Augustine and Calvin. But by his refusal to call this disinclination toward the good "natural impotence," he fostered a lot of misunderstanding and actually aided the cause of Pelagianism.

The Reformed, therefore, consistently spoke of natural impotence. This word "natural," however, can have different meanings.[136] One may use it to refer to the original human nature, created by God in Adam according to his image, in the sense used by Protestants when they said that the image of God is natural. In that case, the incapacity for good is not natural, but rather contrary to nature, unnatural, and subnatural.[137] One can mean by it the physical substance or power of any creature, and in that case, too, this incapacity—since all substance and power is created by God—cannot be called natural. Incapacity for good is not a physical impossibility, like the inability of human beings to put their hands on the stars. But, speaking of natural impotence, one can also have in mind the characteristics of fallen human nature and mean by it that the incapacity for good in this fallen state is "by nature" characteristic for all human beings, congenital and not first introduced in them from without by custom, upbringing, or imitation. In this sense the term "natural impotence" is absolutely correct, and the term "moral impotence" open to misunderstanding. "Morally impossible," after all, is the phrase often used to describe what is considered impossible for a given person on the basis of that person's character, custom, or upbringing. It is morally impossible for a virtuous person all at once to become a thief, for a mother to hate her child, or a murderer to strangle an innocent child. Such a moral "impossibility" nonetheless definitely does occur under certain circumstances. This kind of moral impotence is not what describes the incapacity for good. Though ethical in nature, and an incapacity of the will, natural impotence belongs to humans by nature; it is innate, and a property of the volition itself. And precisely because the will, in its present fallen state, in virtue of its nature cannot do other than to will freely, it cannot do other than what it wills, than that to which it is by nature inclined.[138]

4. Finally, one must bear in mind that Scripture and the church, in teaching the total depravity of humanity, apply the highest standard, namely, the law of God. The doctrine of the incapacity for good is a religious confession. In light

135. J. Edwards, *Freedom of the Will*, in *The Works of Jonathan Edwards*, II, 1–190; cf. J. Ridderbos, *De Theol. van J. Edwards*, 77ff.

136. On the notion of "nature," see W. Geesink, *Van 's Heeren Ordinantiën*, 1st ed., 3 vols. (Amsterdam: W. Kirchener, 1907), I, 1.

137. Thus Augustine in A. M. Weiss, *Apol. des Christ.*, II, 71ff.

138. Cf. T. Aquinas, *Summa contra gentiles*, IV, 52; *Formula of Concord*, I, 12; J. Calvin, *Commentary*, on Eph. 2:3; Z. Ursinus, *The Commentary of Dr. Zacharius Ursinus on the Heidelberg Catechism*, trans. G. W. Willard (Grand Rapids: Eerdmans, 1954), qu. 5, 8; Helvetic Confession, §§21, 22; F. Turretin, *Institutes of Elenctic Theology*, X, 4, 39; B. de Moor, *Comm. theol.*, III, 232; C. Vitringa, *Doctr. christ*, II, 362ff.; C. Hodge, *Syst. Theol.*, II, 257–72; W. G. T. Shedd, *Dogm. Theol.*, II, 219–57; III, 364–74.

of the standard people usually follow in their daily life or in philosophical ethics, one can wholeheartedly admit that much of what people do is good and beautiful. The follower of Augustine, using this standard in the assessment of human virtues, can be even more generous and broad-minded than the most confirmed Pelagian. But there is still another, higher, ideal for us humans. There is a divine law with which we must comply. Virtues and good works are distinct. Good, true good—good in the eyes of a holy God—is only what is done out of faith, according to God's law, and to God's glory. And measured by this standard, who would dare to say that any work performed by humans is completely pure and does not need forgiveness and renewal? To divide persons in two—like Rome and in part like the Lutherans—and to say that in the realm of the supernatural and spiritual they are incapable of any good but in the natural realm they can do things that are totally good is contrary to the unity of human nature, to the unity of the moral law, and to the teaching of Scriptures that humans must always be images of God, do everything they do to the glory of God, and always and everywhere love God with all their heart, mind, and strength. Now if that is true, if the human essence consists in being the image and likeness of God, then nothing in them, as they now live and work, can stand before the face of God. Weighed in the scales of God's sanctuary, all their works are found to be wanting.

One can disagree about this standard and, to reach a more favorable conclusion, bring down the law of God and tailor it to human behaviors. But given this standard, the only possible judgment is that of Scripture: "There is no one who does good, no, not one" (Pss. 14:3; 53:3). And this judgment of Scripture is confirmed by a variety of testimonies. Let those who do not believe Scripture listen to the voices of the greatest people of our race! As soon as one, both in one's own life or that of others, goes beyond words and deeds and inquires into the hidden motives and secret intentions, the sinful nature of all human striving comes to light. "Our virtues are often no more than vices in disguise" (Rochefoucauld). "Man is only a disguise, a lie and hypocrisy, both within himself and with respect to others" (Pascal). "Man to man is a wolf." Without the state, human society would degenerate into "a war of all against all" (Hobbes). According to Kant, humans are by nature evil. There is in them a natural tendency toward evil, a radical inborn evil. The appalling facts evidenced to us by the history of humankind are sufficient proof of this. "Every man has his price, for which he will sell himself." What the apostle says is a universal truth; there is no one who does good, not one.[139] "Those who maintain the bondage of the will and characterize humans as stocks and blocks are completely correct."[140] "The natural heart in which a human is caught up is the enemy one must fight."[141] "Humans have from eternity entangled themselves

139. I. Kant, *Religion within the Limits of Reason*, 34ff.

140. J. G. Fichte, *Das System der Sittenlehre nach den Prinzipien der Wissenschaftslehre* (Hamburg: Meiner, 1798), 265. Ed. note: ET: *The Science of Ethics as Based on the Science of Knowledge*, trans. William Torrey Harris (London: K. Paul, Trench, Trübner, 1897).

141. G. W. F. Hegel, *Sämtliche Werke*, 16, 270 (*Werke*, XII, 270).

in themselves and in self-seeking, and all who have been born were born with the attached dark principle of evil. This original evil in humans, which only those can dispute who have only a superficial acquaintance with people as they are in themselves and in their relation to others, in its origin is their own deed."[142] "The main and fundamental motive in people as in animals is egoism, that is, the drive to exist and to prosper. This egoism, in animals as it is in humans, is most intimately connected, yes, identical with their inner core and essence." This egoism is restrained by the bonds of decency, fear, punishment, government, and so on, but when these restraints are removed, "insatiable greed, despicable money-hunger, deeply concealed falseness, and spiteful evil again spring to the surface. One must read the histories of criminals and accounts of anarchic states to recognize what humans really are from a moral perspective. Thousands of people who before our eyes are peacefully commingling in public must be viewed as just so many tigers and wolves whose mouth has been secured by a strong muzzle." Even the composition of the human conscience is one-fifth fear of other humans, one-fifth superstition, one-fifth prejudice, one-fifth vanity, and one-fifth custom.[143] The adherents of the theory of evolution have returned to the teaching of Mandeville, Helvetius, Diderst, d'Alembert, and others that egoism is the basis of morality and the norm of all human conduct. Humans are descended from animals and fundamentally remain animals guided by egoistic instincts. Civilization can tame humans but can never make of them something other than what they originally and temperamentally are. What we call moral life is an accidental product of circumstances of the life of people in a specific society. Under different circumstances and in another society, good and evil would have a very different content.[144] In his *Ethisch Idealisme*, De Bussy makes a sharp distinction between the moral person whose self-centered nature has been curbed in its capriciousness by the community but not annihilated, whose virtues are often splendid vices, and the moral person in whom a new principle has been implanted.[145]

It is truly not Scripture alone that judges humans harshly. It is human beings who have pronounced the harshest and most severe judgment on themselves. And it is always better to fall into the hands of the Lord than into those of people, for his mercy is great. For when God condemns us, he at the same time offers his forgiving love in Christ, but when people condemn people, they frequently cast them out and make them the object of scorn. When God condemns us, he has this

---

142. F. W. J. Schelling, "Philosophische Untersuchungen über das Wesen der menschlichen Freiheit," in *Ausgewählte Werke* (Darmstadt: Wissenschaftliche Buchgesellschaft, 1968), IV, 332 (*Werke*, I/7, 388).

143. A. Schopenhauer, *Die Beiden Grundprobleme der Ethik*, 3rd ed. (Leipzig: F. A. Brockhaus, 1881), 186ff.; idem, *Die Welt als Wille und Vorstellung*, 6th ed. (Leipzig: Brockhaus, 1887), I, 391ff.; idem, *Parerga and Paralipomena*, trans. E. F. J. Payne, 2 vols. (Oxford: Clarendon Press, 1974), II, 229ff.

144. C. Darwin, *The Descent of Man*, rev. ed. (New York: D. Appleton, 1896), chs. 3–5; L. Büchner, *Kraft und Stoff* (Leipzig: Thomas, 1902), 478–92; ed. note: ET: *Force and Matter*, trans. from 15th German ed., 4th ed. (New York: P. Eckler, 1891); W. Wachter, *Bestia sum: Einige Kapitel über die Kehrseite des Menschentums* (Berlin: E. Felber, 1898).

145. I. J. le Cosquino de Bussy, *Ethisch Idealisme* (Amsterdam: J. H. de Bussy, 1875), 22ff.

judgment brought to us by people—prophets and apostles and ministers—who do not elevate themselves to a level high above us but include themselves with us in a common confession of guilt. By contrast, philosophers and moralists, in despising people, usually forget that they themselves are human. When God condemns, he speaks of sin and guilt that, though great and heavy, can be removed because they do not belong to the essence of humanity. But moralists frequently speak of egoistic animal tendencies that belong to humans by virtue of their origin and are part of their essence. They put people down but do not lift them up. If by origin we are animals, why then should we live as children of God?

3

THE NATURE OF SIN

Original sin is not mere heredity; it is a universal reality in all people, everywhere. The original sin should not be reduced to one kind of trespass; it was a conscious, willful disobedience that in principle transgressed all of God's commandments. Adam's sin was a reversal of all created relationships and a rebellion against God decisive for the whole world.

Though sin is appallingly many-sided, with untold moral dimensions, at its heart it is a religious revolt against God and thus appropriately summarized as lawlessness. Contrary to some interpretations of the Old Testament, going back to the early church, sin is never an arbitrary matter, merely a whimsical displeasure of a jealous God. Sin is knowingly breaking God's command and flows from a heart that rebels against God. God's law may incorporate human customs but is always more than custom. Especially the second table of the law is reflected in the laws of the nations, but for Israel all moral and ceremonial commands are framed by the command to serve the Lord God of Israel, the Creator and Redeemer of his people. Jesus does not repudiate Old Testament law but fulfills it and with his Spirit writes God's law on our hearts.

On the basis of this biblical teaching, Christian theology has always rejected all substantive notions of sin. Sin as a no-thing can only be a privation or corruption of the good. The idea of sin as privation, however, is incomplete; sin is also an active, corrupting, destructive power. Christian theology also rejects all pantheistic notions of sin as pure negation, as a state of "not yet," as a necessary component in the development of being, or as an illusion of thought. Sin is a privation of the moral perfection human persons ought to possess and includes active transgression. Having no existence on its own, sin is ethical-spiritual in nature, though it always comes to expression in concrete terms. It is a deformity, a departure from God's perfect law by rational creatures who can know God's will. Because in its existence it has no real right to exist, sin is a riddle, a mystery.

There is variety and degree in sin, beginning with the distinction between human and diabolical sin. The Bible speaks of a kingdom of evil, a host of darkness ultimately opposed to Christ and his kingdom, the deceivers and accusers of God's children. Though Satan is the archenemy of God and his people and irredeemable, there is no Supreme Evil corresponding to God as the Supreme Good. Even among devils, sin is form and not substance. Sin is not; it wants to be.

There is also diversity in human sin. Human intention is very important in assessing degrees of culpability. Inadvertent sins done out of ignorance are not the same as those done "high-handedly." Sins against the first table of the law are more serious than those against the second. Circumstances and degree always need to be taken into account.

Sin also develops in an order dynamic; there is a law of sin that proceeds from suggestion to enjoyment to consent to execution and involves both our sensuality and our self-seeking. Neither sensuality nor self-seeking can be explained one from the other; both are involved in our sins as embodied spiritual persons. In all the variety of forms that sin can take, we need to consider the traditional Roman Catholic distinction between mortal and venial sins. Rooted in the practice of penance, the distinction was intended to honor the diversity and degree of sin discussed above. However, the Reformers rejected the distinction. While not denying the variety and degree of sin, the Reformers insisted that sins must never be individualistically and atomistically abstracted from the person who commits the sin. It is the sinful person who needs forgiveness and liberation from all sin. Thus, only the so-called sin against the Holy Spirit is considered by Reformed thought to be a "mortal" sin. This biblical category applies only to the case where someone denies the conviction of his own heart and consciously and willfully blasphemes the Holy Spirit by putting God in Satan's place and Satan in God's place. This is a demonic posture; it is pure conscious hatred of God and his work. For this there can be no forgiveness.

[328] Among other things original sin is distinguished from heredity by the fact that, aside from Christ, it is common to and the same in all humans. The disposition to crimes and certain diseases that children sometimes inherit from their parents does not spread to all their descendants and all generations nor is everyone affected to the same degree. While the Lord punishes the iniquity of parents to the third and fourth generation of those who reject him, he shows his steadfast love to the thousandth generation of those who love him and keep his commandments (Exod. 20:5–6). Original sin, by contrast, has passed to all humans and characterizes all of them to the same extent. It is, after all, nothing other than the sin of Adam himself, imputed to all his descendants; it regards every one of them as born with the same guilt, the same impurity, and the same perverseness as, in the case of Adam, made their appearance immediately after his violation of God's commandment. Neither is the question concerning the essential character of sin identical, therefore, with that concerning its origin and hereditary transmission, for only upon a period of development does what is hidden in the germ become fully manifest. Yet in the first sin the nature of sin

itself as principle and power is already at work and can, accordingly, be known from it to some degree.

About the character and nature of the first sin, both in the case of the angels and in that of humans, there is, however, disagreement. The opinion that the sin of the angels began with sensuality has already been refuted earlier.[1] It is much more likely—in view of the nature of temptation in Genesis 3:5 and Matthew 4:3; 6:9, and the admonition in 1 Timothy 3:6 not "to be puffed up with conceit and fall into the condemnation of the devil"—that the first sin of the angels consisted in pride. But about their fall too little has been revealed for us to be able to speak about it with complete certainty. Others think in this connection of lying (John 8:44), or of envy (Wis. 2:24), or some other sin.[2]

According to Roman Catholics, the first sin of humans also consisted in pride; Bellarmine, for example, based this view on Sirach 10:13; Tobit 4:13; and Romans 5:19 and on the testimony of Augustine, Aquinas, and others.[3] But these proofs are not compelling. Sirach and Tobit only speak of pride in general; Paul denominates the first sin "disobedience"; and the church fathers and scholastics, when they call the first sin "pride," are especially combating the view that equates it with sensuous lust. Protestants, however, in considering the sin of Eve, usually have it start already with doubt and unbelief, which were later followed by pride and covetousness.[4] But Tertullian and others were correct in saying that the first sin already contains within itself a variety of sins and was in principle a transgression of all God's commandments. It was, after all, disobedience to God, doubt, unbelief, self-elevation, pride, homicide, theft, covetousness, and so on. Accordingly, various different thoughts, feelings, lusts, and movements were triggered by it in humans; the intellect and the will, the soul and the body, all took part in it.[5] It was a conscious and voluntary act—ἁμαρτια (sin), παραβασις (transgression), παραπτωμα (misstep), παρακοη (unwillingness to hear; disobedience), in the true sense of these words (Rom. 5:12ff.).

Although the first humans were tempted, they were not brought down as innocent children who did not know better. They deliberately and freely broke God's commandment; they knew what they were doing and wanted to do it. There is no room here for excuses. The circumstances under which the first sin was committed by angels and humans, rather than extenuating the guilt, tend

1. H. Bavinck, *Reformed Dogmatics*, II, 454–58 (#263).

2. H. Heppe, *Dogmatik der evangelischen reformierten Kirche* (Elberseld: R. L. Friedrich, 1861), 157.

3. R. Bellarmine, "De gratia primi hominis," *Controversiis*, III, 4; Augustine, *The Literal Meaning of Genesis*, trans. John Hammond Taylor (New York: Newman, 1982), XI, 30; idem, *Enchiridion*, 45; idem, *City of God*, XIV, 13; T. Aquinas, *Summa theol.*, II, 2, qu. 163ff.

4. M. Luther, *Lectures on Genesis 1–3*, in vol. 1 of *Luther's Works* (St. Louis: Concordia, 1958); J. Gerhard, *Loci theol.*, IX, 2; J. Calvin, *Institutes of the Christian Religion*, II.i.iv; J. Zanchi, *Op. theol.*, IV, 30; H. Bavinck, ed., *Synopsis purioris theologiae* (Leiden: D. Donner, 1881), XIV, 9ff.; J. Marck, *Historia paradisi* (Amsterdam: Gerardus Borstius, 1705), III, 2; C. Vitringa, *Doctr. christ.*, II, 27.

5. Tertullian, *An Answer to the Jews*, 2 (*ANF*, III, 151–74); Augustine, *Enchiridion*, 45; J. Marck, *Historia paradisi*, III, c. 2.

rather to aggravate it. It was done against God's express and clear command, by a person created in God's image, in a matter of little consequence that hardly required any self-denial, and very likely soon after the command had been received. It has become the source of all the iniquities and horrors, all the calamities and misfortunes, all the sickness and death suffered and committed in the world since. From this source have sprung all those tears (*Hinc illae lacrimae*)! The sin of Adam cannot be a minor thing. It must have been a fundamental reversal of all relationships, a revolution by which the creature detached himself from and positioned himself against God, an uprising, a fall in the true sense, which was decisive for the whole world and took it in a direction and on a road away from God, toward wickedness and corruption—an unspeakably great sin.[6] That is how seriously the first sin has been regarded in the Christian church and Christian theology. It was a fall in the true sense, not a half-conscious, virtually innocent aberration, much less an instance of development and progress.[7]

SIN AS RELIGIOUS, NOT MORAL

[329] The wide assortment of names that Scripture uses for sin describe its appalling character and many-sided development. חַטָּאת is the word for sin as an act that misses its mark and consists in a departure from the right way; עָוֶל or עָוֹן describes it as injustice, twistedness, wrongness, as a deviation from the right direction; פֶּשַׁע indicates a crossing of set boundaries, as an act of breaking the covenant relation to God, as apostasy and rebellion; שְׁגָגָה as a wrong act that occurred unintentionally, by mistake; רֶשַׁע as godless, deviant, guilty conduct. It is further described by אָשָׁם as guilt or offense; by מַעַל as unfaithfulness, infidelity, betrayal; by אָוֶל as nothingness; by שָׁוְא as falseness; by נְבָלָה as folly; by רַע as an evil; and so on. The main Greek words are ἁμαρτια, ἁμαρτημα, ἀδικια, ἀπειθεια, ἀποστασια, παραβασις, παρακοη, παραπτωμα, ὀφειλημα, ἀνομια, παρανομια. They speak for themselves and describe sin as deviation, injustice, disobedience, violation, apostasy, lawlessness, guilt. The power of sin at work in humans is further denoted by such words as σαρξ, ψυχικος, and παλαιος ἀνθρωπος and at work in the world as κοσμος. The Latin word *peccatum* is of uncertain derivation; the Dutch word *zonde* (sin), which is probably related to the Latin *sons,* that is, *no-*

6. Augustine, *Against Julian*, trans. M. A. Schumacher, vol. 16 of *The Writings of Saint Augustine* (Washington, DC: Catholic University of America Press, 1984), I, 165.

7. Augustine, *City of God*, XIV, 11–15; XXI, 12; idem, *Enchiridion*, 26–27, 45; T. Aquinas, *Summa theol.*, II, 2, qu. 163, art. 3; Decrees of the Council of Trent, V, 1; R. Bellarmine, "De gratia primi hominis," *Controversiis*, III, 8–10; M. J. Scheeben, *Handbuch der katholischen Dogmatik*, 4 vols. (Freiburg i.B.: Herder, 1933), II, 594; ed. note: ET: *A Manual of Catholic Theology: Based on Scheeben's "Dogmatik,"* trans. and ed. Joseph Wilhelm and Thomas Bartholomew Scannell, 4th ed., 2 vols. (London: Kegan Paul, Trench, Trubner and Co.; New York: Benziger Brothers, 1909); Belgic Confession, art. 14; Heidelberg Catechism, qu. 7, 9; P. van Mastricht, *Theologia*, IV, 1, 15; J. Marck, *Historia paradisi*, III, c. 2, 10.

cens,[8] in its Christian usage has become a religious concept through and through. It denotes a violation not of a human but of a divine law. It situates humans, not in relation to their fellow humans, society, and the state, but in relation to God, the heavenly Judge. In many circles, therefore, it is not popular and is preferably replaced by "moral evil" and so on. By far the majority of these names describe sin as "deviation, a violation of the law." Scripture consistently views sin as lawlessness (ἀνομία, 1 John 3:4); its norm is the law of God.

In different periods this law appeared in different forms. Adam's case was utterly unique; no one coming after him can commit sin in the way he did (Rom. 5:14). From Adam to Moses there was no positive, divinely proclaimed law. The objection could therefore be advanced that where there is no law, there can be no transgression, sin, and death either (Rom. 5:13; 4:15). In Romans 5:12f., Paul offers no other response to this than that by the one trespass of Adam sin came into the world as a power and holds sway over all and so death spread to all people. Adam's trespass has made all of us sinners and subjected all to death. This influence of Adam's trespass does not exclude but rather includes the fact that all people are all personally sinners as well. Precisely because by the one trespass of Adam, sin became the dominant power in the human world and in consequence all human beings themselves are sinners, therefore also death spread to all. That is all Paul says in Romans 5:12f. In *that* context that statement was sufficient. But this answer can be illumined and augmented from other texts. If sin and death existed from Adam to Moses (Rom. 5:13–14), there must also have been a law—perhaps not a positive law that was audibly proclaimed by God as in paradise and on Mount Sinai, but still a law that then obligated people personally and rendered them guilty. That is also clearly stated by Paul in Romans 2:12–26. The Gentiles, who did not have the Mosaic law, nonetheless sinned and are lost apart from the law (ἀνόμως) because they are a law to themselves and their own conscience accuses them. There is a revelation of God in nature, a revelation both religious and intellectual in content, which is sufficient to strip them of all innocence (Rom. 2:18f.; 1 Cor. 1:21). But whereas God permitted the Gentiles to follow their own ways, he clearly made known his laws and claims to Israel. And for Israel this law is now the standard for all moral conduct.

In recent times this view has been sharply contested. Naturally the concept of sin occurred from ancient times in Israel, as it did among all other peoples.[9] But, say these scholars, sin still did not yet have anything to do with morality. Not only was it utterly unknown that sin could consist in disposition, in an inner tendency and direction of the heart, but by sinful acts they understood something totally different from what we usually understand by them. The sense of sin was almost totally lacking. Generally prevalent in ancient Israel, however, was the idea that

---

8. J. Müller, *The Christian Doctrine of Sin*, trans. Rev. Wm. Urwick, 5th ed., 2 vols. (Edinburgh: T&T Clark, 1868), I, 88ff.

9. Westcott, "Religious Thought in the West," *DB,* IV, 534.

the misery in which people were caught up, the sickness they experienced, the defeat they suffered in war were all proofs of Yahweh's wrath and that in some way they were therefore in the wrong (Gen. 42:21–22; Josh. 7:11f.; 1 Sam. 4:3; 14:37–44; 2 Sam. 21:1). Originally the word חטא meant nothing other than to be or to be put in the wrong over against a superior (Exod. 5:16; 1 Kings 1:21; 2 Kings 18:14). Only later did it mean an action that was contrary to custom (Gen. 19:7f.; 34:7; Josh. 7:15; Judg. 19:23; 20:6; 2 Sam. 13:12; 21:1–14), and again later, especially after the prophets had proclaimed ethical monotheism, it meant a violation of God's law. The word therefore only gradually acquired ethical significance.

In the earliest period, however, [so it is said], this was not yet the case. In disasters people only read Yahweh's displeasure. But that displeasure was absolutely manifested not against what we call sin but against all kinds of random things. Inasmuch as Yahweh as yet had no ethical character, he often expressed his wrath randomly without any reason. He was still solely and totally a God of caprice and himself the Author not only of the good but also of the bad. He gave orders to rob the Egyptians (Exod. 3:22) and to destroy the Canaanites (Deut. 9:3). He sent an evil spirit (Judg. 9:23; 1 Sam. 16:14, 23; 18:10; 19:9), incited Saul against David (1 Sam. 26:19), incited David (2 Sam. 24:1), caused a lying spirit to speak in the mouth of the prophets (1 Kings 22:21f.), arranged that Samson look for a wife among the Philistines (Judg. 14:3), brought about the division of the kingdom (1 Kings 12:16–24), used sin as a means of punishment (2 Sam. 12:4; 16:21), and was the cause of all evil in the city (Amos 3:6). And as arbitrary as he was in the expression of his wrath, so he was also in the infliction of punishment. He punished the guilty and the innocent alike; because of Achan's sin, he destroyed Achan's entire family (Josh. 7:24); because of Saul's apostasy, he wiped out seven of his sons (2 Sam. 21:1ff.); and he visited the iniquities of the fathers to the third and fourth generation (Exod. 20:5; 34:7; Deut. 5:9f.).[10]

In the past all these charges against the morality of the Old Testament were already made by the Gnostics and the Manicheans, who for that reason distinguished the God of the Old Testament from the Father of Christ.[11] A feature of these charges is that they are a mixture of truth and falsehood. It is false to say that in ancient Israel the true concept of sin as an offense against God was lacking. In Genesis 13:13, the men of Sodom were already called "great sinners against the Lord." In Genesis 38:9–10, the sin of Onan was evil in the sight of the Lord. Of Joseph it is said that he feared God (Gen. 42:18) and refused to sin against God (39:9). David did not want to raise his hand against the Lord's anointed (1 Sam. 24:6; 2 Sam. 1:14), praised the Lord who kept him from avenging himself on Nabal (1 Sam. 25:39), and in the matter of Uriah and Bathsheba confessed that

10. B. Stade, *Geschichte des Volkes Israel*, 2 vols. (Berlin: Baumgärtel, 1887), 507ff.; C. Clemen, *Die christliche Lehre von der Sünde* (Göttingen: Vandenhoeck & Ruprecht, 1897), I, 21ff.; B. D. Eerdmans, "De gedachtezonde in het O.T.," *Theolgische Tijdschrift* 39 (1905): 307–24.

11. L. Diestel, *Geschichte des Alten Testament in der christlichen Kirche* (Jena: Mauka, 1869), 64ff., 114ff.

he sinned against the Lord (2 Sam. 12:13 etc.). All these testimonies together make abundantly plain that also ancient Israel already knew very well that sin is an evil in the sight of God. And not only the sinful act but also the sinful disposition fell into the category of evil. What else would we expect in a view of human beings where the "heart" occupies such a large place? In Genesis 6:5 and 8:21, already God says that every inclination of the thoughts of human hearts is evil from youth on; and elsewhere it is repeatedly stated that God tests the minds and hearts (Pss. 7:9; 17:3; 26:2; 139:23; Jer. 11:20; 17:10; 20:12); that he looks at the heart (1 Sam. 16:7); that he demands the heart of a person (1 Kings 11:4; 15:13; Isa. 29:13; Ezek. 33:31; Prov. 23:26), since from it flow the springs of life (Prov. 4:23); that he will give people a pure heart, a new heart, a heart of flesh (Ps. 51:12; Jer. 24:7; 31:33; 32:39; Ezek. 11:19; 36:26; etc.).[12] Add to this the consideration that in the Yahwistic narrative of Genesis 3, the first sin consists in a violation of God's command; that in Genesis 4:10f., the Lord severely condemns fratricide; that the evil committed by human beings is not only discerned by the Lord in deeds but also in the inclinations of their heart (Gen. 6:5) and that it made the flood necessary; that God prohibits homicide (Gen. 9:6) and in Babel punished human arrogance (Gen. 11:5 etc.).

Compatible with this, certainly, is that folk customs frequently serve as a standard for moral conduct, for Joshua 7:15 clearly shows that both the violation of God's covenant and doing an "outrageous thing" in Israel can very well go together. Custom as such is no more opposed to God's law than conscience, which is also a subordinate subjective norm of the moral life and for that reason always remains, even in the best societies, a secondary norm (*norma normata*). This is why, when God gave his law to Israel, he did not abolish such folk customs but instead recognized, incorporated, and modified them in keeping with his purpose for his people. This applies to circumcision, the sacrificial cult, the priesthood, the feast days, blood revenge, hospitality, and so on, which from ancient times had existed among the nations and also in Israel and were not abolished but modified and incorporated in a higher order of things (i.e., in the covenant of grace) and made serviceable to it. There is even more: with respect to divorce Jesus says that Moses allowed it on account of the hardness of people's hearts (Matt. 19:8), and this is true of many rules in God's laws (polygamy, slavery, blood revenge, corporate responsibility, and others). One must not judge it by the legislation in force in a Christian nation nor even by that of Hammurabi, which was written for another people and in other circumstances, but must take account of the peculiar circumstances in which Israel found itself when it was led out of Egypt and of the purpose God had in mind for his people when he made a covenant with them. One must bear in mind the harshness of the times if one wishes to judge fairly the cases of cruel treatment sometimes reported (Judg. 1:6; 4:21; 2 Sam.

---

12. G. Wildeboer, "De Dekaloog," *Theologische Studiën* 21 (1903): 109–18; idem, "Nog Eens de Dekaloog," *Theologische Studiën* 24 (1906): 94–110.

8:2; 12:31; etc.). One must view the destruction of the Canaanites in the light of God's judgment that sometimes extends to generations and peoples and that at the time had already been begun by God himself—by way of warning—with the destruction of Sodom and Gomorrah (Gen. 18:20f.; cf. Lev. 18:24–25; 20:23; Deut. 9:4–5; 12:29f.; 1 Kings 21:26; Ezra 9:11). And in general one must put oneself in the position of the apostle Paul, who testified that the law came after the promise and was added to the promise "because of transgressions" and to lead Israel in its nonadult state to the freedom that is in Christ Jesus (Rom. 4:15; 5:20; 7:4; Gal. 3:19, 23–24; 4:1f.).

SIN AS LAWLESSNESS

Further, while popular custom need not be incompatible with God's law, it does not follow that it is always in agreement with it. Frequently the conscience of Christians is only in part conformed to God's law, and among them, from generation to generation, any number of habits and practices persist that cannot stand the test of that law. This was even more strongly the case in ancient times in Israel. At all times there was an enormous difference between the ideas and conduct of the people and the revelation that God gave them through Moses and the prophets. The people again and again lapsed into idolatry, image worship, and all sorts of pagan horrors. Even when Israel remained outwardly faithful to the Lord, it prided itself in its election, its possession of the temple, and its sacrifices and burnt offerings and believed itself to be pleasing to the Lord on that account. Even the devout remained sinners who daily stumbled in many ways. Many acts told of the saints in the Old Testament—of Noah, Abraham, Isaac, Jacob, Rachel, David, and others—are to be strictly condemned, therefore, and not to be excused because they were believers, as did the rabbis. The essential character of sin, after all, is determined not by what was customary or sometimes done in Israel, but by the divine law.

This law, embedded as it was in the entire economy of salvation, contained not only moral but also civil and ceremonial commandments. In a sense, therefore, sin was a much broader concept than it is for us today, inasmuch as it also included everything that was contrary to civil legislation and Levitical purity. Consequently, [the idea of] sin was expanded and broadened, its essential character brought home to the consciousness of the people, as it were, by external means, which also implied the danger of taking the moral commandments lightly and of looking for righteousness in external Levitical purity. Prophecy, therefore, at all times insisted on the Lord's assessment that obedience and mercy are better than sacrifices. In addition, in Israel all commandments were one code of law and placed under the guardianship of the civil government. All sin therefore acquired the character of crime. It was a violation not only of God's law but at the same time of the law of the state. It was a breach of the covenant with God but also of the bond with the people. Therefore, those who deliberately sinned and had intentionally broken the covenant had to be removed from the fellowship of God and his people. Finally, in Israel sin and punishment were most intimately connected. Every Israelite was and viewed himself as a part of the whole, a member of the national community. This community of the immediate and the extended family, of lineage and people, was much stronger and more deeply felt than it is among us today, though this does not warrant the conclusion that the individual in those days counted for virtually nothing.[13] People regarded themselves as a part of that community and therefore naturally shared in its lot, its blessings, but also in its judgments and punishment. The law itself gave expression to this and incorporated it into its commandments (Exod. 20:5–6, 12); children were blessed *and* punished with their parents. For this reason the word הַטָּאת can denote sin as well as punishment and sin offering.[14] The two ideas were closely related: if sin was not expiated it had to be punished. By this means the consciousness of the culpability and damnableness of sin was aroused in Israel. When the status quo did not correspond to this demand, when life over and over presented the spectacle of the prosperity of the wicked and the oppression of the pious, the expectation arose of the innocent suffering of one party for the guilt of another, of the suffering servant of the Lord, "who was bruised for our iniquities" and "by whose stripes we are healed" (Isa. 53:5). The law came after the promise but from that point on also became subservient to its fulfillment.

It must be noted, finally, that with respect to the moral commandments of the second table of the law there is always much agreement among the nations, inasmuch as the work of the law continues to be written in their hearts (Rom. 2:15). But the new and unusual feature in the legislation of Israel is that preceding the second table there is the first, and that in it the service of the Lord as the God of Israel alone is prescribed in unmistakable terms. Whereas all other nations pay tribute to polytheism and as a result become entangled in superstition and magic, in Israel all idolatry and image worship, all fortunetelling and sorcery, all abuse of the name of the Lord and desecration of the Sabbath—the sign of the covenant (Exod. 31:17; Isa. 56:6)—are strictly forbidden. In this feature lies what distinguishes Israel's religion: the Lord, who has chosen Israel, is the only God,

13. *M. Löhr, *Socialismus und Individualismus im A.T.* (Giessen, 1906), has conclusively demonstrated that this conclusion of Stade and Smend et al. is incorrect.

14. The idea that the verb חטא in Exod. 5:16; 1 Kings 1:21; and 2 Kings 18:14 has the meaning of "being or being put in the wrong over against someone more powerful" apart from any association with guilt has absolutely not been demonstrated. The word actually means "to miss (the mark)" (Judg. 20:16) and would therefore allow for that broader meaning. But the above texts do not prove it. In Exod. 5:16, the Israelites simply say to Pharaoh: "Your servants are given no straw, yet we are told, 'Make bricks!' Your servants are being beaten, but the fault is with your own people" (NIV). In 1 Kings 1:21, Bathsheba says to David: "If you do not decide and Adonijah becomes king, then we, Bathsheba and Solomon, will be counted the offenders, who will be killed by Adonijah because we do not recognize him, whereas actually, based on your oath [v. 17], we are in the right" (paraphrase). And in 2 Kings 18:14, Hezekiah makes confession of wrongdoing, a confession that was extorted from him under duress and that he himself does not recognize later on. In all these places, accordingly, the word retains its ordinary meaning.

the God of justice but also the God of grace and redemption; his law is a covenant law; because Israel is the people of the Lord by grace, it has to walk in his way.

In the Old Testament this is always what gets all the emphasis: the sin may be great or small; it is sin only because it is contrary to God and his law (Gen. 13:13; 20:6; 39:9; Exod. 10:16; 32:33; 1 Sam. 7:6; 14:33; 2 Sam. 12:13; Ps. 51:4; Isa. 42:14; Jer. 14:7, 20; etc.). In the future, when God pours out his Spirit, the intent is that the children of Israel will walk in his statutes and observe his ordinances (Ezek. 36:27). And the prayer of the pious is that their ways may be steadfast in keeping his statutes (Ps. 119:5).

The New Testament fundamentally takes the same position. As the model, Jesus holds up God himself (Matt. 5:48) and judges all things by his law (Matt. 19:17–19; Mark 10:17–19; Luke 18:18–20). This constitutes for him the content of the law and the prophets. He maintains it fully, not detracting from it in any way (Matt. 5:17–19, 23f.; 6:16f.; 12:12f.; 23:3, 23; 24:20), and from this position he judges all human ordinances (Matt. 5:20ff.; 15:2f.; Mark 2:23f.; 7:8, 13; etc.). In Matthew 7:12, accordingly, he does not propose any new ethical principle, but only offers a practical interpretation of the command to love one's neighbor. Nonetheless, the concept of sin and the sense of sin is sharpened and deepened by Jesus. Precisely by moving away from human ordinances and going back to the law of God in the Old Testament, he again makes that law known to us in its spiritual character (Matt. 5), reducing it to one spiritual principle, namely, love (Matt. 22:37–40) and communicates it to us as a single whole (cf. James 2:10). Judging by that law, he unmasks hypocrisy (Matt. 23), breaks the bond between the ethical and the physical (Mark 7:15), goes back to the heart as the source of all sin (Matt. 15:18–19), and even makes suffering independent of personal guilt (Luke 13:2–3; John 9:3).

Against the backdrop of the revelation of God's grace in the gospel, sin stands out all the more darkly. The law remains the source of our knowledge of sin (Rom. 3:20; 7:7), but when that law is read in light of the gospel, sin becomes manifest in all its hideousness. Then it becomes evident that it is a power that makes its servants into slaves (John 8:34; Rom. 6:20), a power that finds its strength in the law (1 Cor. 15:56), is rooted in the flesh with its desires (Rom. 7:18; James 1:14), and can only be broken and overcome by Christ (John 8:36; Rom. 8:2). Because God's grace has fully appeared in Christ, unbelief is such a great sin (John 15:22, 24; 16:9), being offended at Christ is so serious (Matt. 11:6), falling away from grace is so frightful (Heb. 2:3; 4:1; 6:4–5; 10:26), and blaspheming the Holy Spirit an unpardonable sin (Matt. 12:31). Accordingly, the Mosaic law may—as concerns its demands and curse, its civil and ceremonial commandments—have reached its goal and end in Christ (Rom. 10:4; Gal. 3:24): the believer may be exempt from its yoke of servitude and stand in freedom (Rom. 6:14; 7:4; 10:4; Gal. 2:19; 3:13; 5:18); still, that freedom does not cancel out the ethical content of that law but rather confirms it (Rom. 3:31). The just requirement of the law is above all fulfilled in those who walk according to the Spirit (Rom. 8:4). That Spirit, after all, renews the heart and teaches us to search out, know, and fulfill what God's will is (Rom. 12:2; Eph. 5:10; Phil. 1:10). This will can be known and remains knowable from the Old Testament (Rom. 13:8–10; 15:4; 1 Cor. 1:31; 10:11; 14:34; 2 Cor. 9:9; 10:17; Gal. 5:14), has been explained to us in Christ's words and life (1 Cor. 11:1; 2 Cor. 3:18; 8:9; 10:1; Phil. 2:5; 1 Thess. 1:6; 4:2), and also resonates in our own conscience (1 Cor. 8:7; 10:25; 2 Cor. 1:12). It is indeed written in the heart of believers (Heb. 8:10; 10:16). Throughout Scripture, therefore, the essential character of sin consists in lawlessness (ἀνομια, 1 John 3:4), in violating the law that God has revealed in his Word.

ESSENTIALS OF SIN

[330] It was this teaching of Scripture that shaped the view of sin in Christian theology. This resulted, on the one hand, in the rejection of the view that finds the essential character of sin in any substance and traces it to a principle of wrath in God (Böhme) or to an evil power beside God (Mani), to some kind of "stuff" such as matter (ὑλη) or flesh (σαρξ) (Plato, the Jews, Flacius, and others). It resulted, on the other hand, in the rejection of the theory that sin consists in a not-yet-being, that it belongs to the necessary contrasts in life and is by nature inherent in the finite, evolving human being striving toward perfection (Spinoza, Hegel). Christian theology, by contrast, from the beginning maintained that sin was not a substance. On this point there has never been disagreement or controversy. Petavius cites any number of church fathers who in this respect all teach the same thing. For that matter, no doubt or hesitation was possible in this connection. If sin were a substance, there would exist an entity that either was not created by God or was not caused by God. Sin, accordingly, has to be understood and described neither as an existing thing nor as being in things that exist but rather as a defect, a deprivation, an absence of the good, or as weakness, imbalance, just as blindness is a deprivation of sight.[15] In the West especially Augustine brought out and upheld this privative character of sin in his opposition to the Manicheans. All being is per se good. All that is natural, to the degree that it is natural, is good. Evil can therefore only be something about the good. There cannot be any evil at all except in something good, because it cannot be except in something natural. It is itself not nature, but a lack, privation, or corruption of the good, a vice or defect of nature; for good to be diminished is evil.[16] It therefore has no efficient but only a deficient cause.[17] Scholastics and Catholic, Lutheran, and Reformed theologians similarly reduced the concept of sin in a metaphysical sense to that of privation.[18]

15. Athanasius, *Against the Heathens*, 3ff.; Gregory of Nyssa, *The Catechetical Oration*, ch. 5; Pseudo-Dionysius, *The Divine Names,* ch. 5; John of Damascus, *Exposition of the Orthodox Faith*, 30.

16. Augustine, *City of God*, XI, 9, 17, 22; idem, *Enchiridion*, 11–13; idem, *Against Julian*, 3.

17. Augustine, *City of God*, XII, 7, 9.

18. In addition to the literature already mentioned, see, e.g., also M. Becanus, *Summa theologiae scholasticae*, II, 1, tract. 1, ch. 5, qu. 1; J. F. Buddeus, *Institutiones theologiae moralis* (1715), 546; Z. Ursinus, *Volumen tractationum theologicarum*, 199; F. Turretin, *Institutes of Elenctic Theology*, IX.

On the other hand, it is also clear that sin cannot be adequately described with the concept of privation. Certainly it is not a mere lack, pure nonbeing, but an active and corrupting principle, a dissolving, destructive power. Scripture usually speaks of it in a very positive sense as an act of transgression, wrongness, disobedience, lawlessness, and so on and ascribes to it the activity of witnessing, ruling, moving, thinking, fighting, and so on. Various theologians have therefore rejected the distinction between matter and form in their definition of sin. They based their views on the premise that blasphemy, idolatry, hatred against God, and so on are sinful actions and can never assume a good form, and so they described sin rather as a "certain real and positive something," as a "real something."[19]

To understand this correctly, however, we must note the following: (1) When the majority of Christian theologians conceive sin as privation, they first of all have opposition to Manicheism in view. To that extent their opinion is completely correct and to be accepted without reservation. Sin is not a substance, neither spiritual nor material, for then it would either have God as its cause or else God would not be the creator of all things. (2) Also the nature of sin itself keeps us from viewing it as a substance, for sin is not a physical but an ethical phenomenon. It is a state and act of the will and is rooted in the will; it is not given with creation but originated after the creation as a result of disobedience. Accordingly, it cannot be a material thing that existed eternally or was created in time by God but only exists as a deformation of existence; in that sense it can even be called something that does not exist, a "nothing."[20] (3) This is not to be understood as meaning that sin is a nonnegative. The case is rather that Christian theology has at all times very firmly opposed the pantheistic view of sin as pure negation, as a state of not yet being, as a necessary component in the development of a finite being, as an illusion of thought. Sin was no "mere negation" but a "privation," the difference between them being that "negation" is only a matter of "being without" (*carere*), while "privation" is lacking something essential to life (*egere*). The fact that a stone does not see is a negation, but that a human should not see is a privation, since sight belongs to the essential functions of a human being. Sin is a privation of the moral perfection a human ought to possess. (4) The characterization of sin as privation, accordingly, by no means excludes its being also—viewed from a different angle—an action. It is not a "substance" or thing, but in its being deprived of the good, it is an activity (ἐνεργεια), just as the limp of

19. Cajetan in M. Becanus, *Summa theologiae scholasticae*, II, 1, tract. 1, ch. 5, qu. 1; *Theol. Wirceb.*, VII, 15; C. Vitringa, *Observationum sacrarum*, VI, ch. 15, 16; C. Vitringa, *Doctr. Christ.*, II, 288–90; J. Arminius, *Opera theologica* (Lugduni Batavorum [Leiden]: Godefridum Basson, 1629), 730; P. van Limborch, *Theologia christiana*, V, 4; D. F. Strauss, *Die christliche Glaubenslehre in ihrer geschichtlichen Entwicklung und im Kampfe mit der modernen Wissenschaft*, 2 vols. (Tübingen: C. F. Osiander, 1840–41), II, 360ff.; J. Müller, *Christian Doctrine of Sin*, I, 290–99; W. G. T. Shedd, *Dogmatic Theology*, 3rd ed., 3 vols. (New York: Scribner, 1891–94), I, 371.

20. Dr. R. P. Mees, *Wetenschappelijke Karakterkennis* ('s Gravenhage: Nijhoff, 1907), is therefore in error when he states (pp. 63ff.) that in previous times sin was regarded as an *ens positivum* (in the same manner that sickness was considered something material).

a cripple is not the absence of walking but a defective kind of walking. Augustine, who over and over describes sin as "privation," therefore calls it a transgression of the law (*transgressio legis*),[21] the will to hang on to or pursue something that justice forbids,[22] a defect that includes a tendency, a defect that is not altogether nothing but tends toward nothingness,[23] a leaning away from what is more to what is less.[24] He then gives this definition: "Sin is something done, or said, or desired contrary to eternal law; the law that is truly eternal is the divine reason or will of God, which demands the preservation of the natural order and forbids its disturbance."[25] Later this definition was universally accepted: sin is not mere or pure privation but an action deprived of due order,[26] a privation having a positive quality and action, that is, an *active privation*.[27]

[331] On the basis of Holy Scripture, and in keeping with the confession of the Christian faith, therefore, the essential character of sin can be defined and explained as follows.

As Ethical-Spiritual

1. Inasmuch as sin is not a physical or metaphysical but an ethical antithesis of the good, it has no self-existent, independent being of its own. Those who consider sin a substance may seem to be deeply convinced of its power and importance but in fact weaken it by transferring it from the ethical to the physical domain and turn the conflict between good and evil into a struggle between light and darkness, spirit and matter, a good and an evil God, a struggle that is never-ending and makes all redemption from sin impossible. For that reason it is of supreme importance always to view sin as an ethical phenomenon. Certainly the punishments and consequences of sin extend also to the physical domain, but sin itself is and remains ethical in character. That being the case, sin cannot have its own principle and its own independent existence; it only originated *after* and exists only *by* and in connection *with* the good. While evil does depend on the good, the reverse is not true. "It is possible for the good (noble) to become bad."[28] "The better and more honorable seems to be prior by nature."[29] "The good (true) is its

---

21. Augustine, *The Consensus of the Evangelists*, II, ch. 4 (*NPNF* [1], IV).

22. Augustine, *On the Two Souls, Against the Manicheans*, I, ch. 11 (*NPNF* [1], IV, 95–107); idem, *Retractions*, 11.

23. Augustine, *Against Secundus the Manichee*, 11 (*NPNF* [1], VI).

24. Ibid., 12; cf. *De libero arbitrio libri tres: The Free Choice of the Will*, trans. Francis Edward Tourscher, 3 vols. (Philadelphia: Peter Reilly Co., 1937), I, 16; II, 19.

25. Idem, *Against Faustus the Manichee*, XXII, 27 (*NPNF* [1], IV).

26. P. Lombard, *Sent.*, II, dist. 35; T. Aquinas, *Summa theol.*, II, 1, qu. 71; 6, qu. 72; 1, ad. 2, qu. 75; 1, ad. 1.

27. J. Zanchi, *Op. theol.*, IV, 1ff.; A. Polanus, *Syn. theol.*, 3; J. H. Heidegger, *Corpus theologiae*, X, 8; G. Bucanus, *Inst. theol.*, XV, 7; *Synopsis purioris theologiae*, XVI, 4–9.

28. Plato, *Protagoras*, trans. C. C. W. Taylor (Oxford: Clarendon Press, 1976), 344.

29. Aristotle, *Categories, and De Interpretatione*, trans. J. L. Ackrill (Oxford: Clarendon Press, 1963), ch. 9.

own standard as well as that of evil (falsehood)." The good, by a free choice, was the cause of evil and remains its substratum. Fallen angels and humans as creatures are and remain good and exist from moment to moment only by, and in, and for God. And just as sin is dependent on the good in its origin and existence, so it is in its operation and struggle. It has power to do anything only with and by means of the powers and gifts that are God-given. Satan has therefore correctly been called the ape of God. When God builds a church, Satan adds a chapel; over against the true prophet, he raises up a false prophet; over against the Christ, he poses the Antichrist. Even a band of robbers can only exist if within its own organization it respects the rules. A liar always garbs himself or herself in the guise of truth. A sinner pursues evil under pretense of the good. Satan himself appears as an angel of light. In its operation and appearance, sin is always doomed to borrow, despite itself, from the treasury of virtue. It is subject to the unalterable fate—while striving for the destruction of all good—of working simultaneously on its own demise. It is a parasite of the good.

2. Thus, although sin in virtue of its own nature strives toward nonbeing, it nonetheless has no power over being itself. It cannot create; neither can it destroy. Accordingly, neither the essential character of the angels, nor that of humans, nor that of nature, has been changed as a result of sin. Essentially they are the same creatures before and after the fall, with the same substance, the same capacities, the same powers. Both before and after the fall, humans have a soul and a body, intellect and will, feelings and passions. What has changed is not the substance, the matter, but the form in which these show themselves, the direction in which they function. With the same power of love with which human beings originally loved God, they now love the creature. The same intellect with which in the past they sought the things above now frequently, with admirable acuteness and profundity, makes them hold falsehood to be truth. With the same freedom with which they formerly served God, they now serve the world. Substantially, sin has neither removed anything from humanity nor introduced anything into it. It is the same human person, but now walking, not toward God but away from him, to destruction. "Sin is not some positive essence but a defect, a corruptive tendency; that is, a force that contaminates mode, species, and order in the created will."[30]

3. Nor is the loss of the image of God and the breaking of the covenant of works inconsistent with this view of sin. For the image of God, though no superadded gift but integral to human nature, was not a substance but an accident; that is, human beings, as they were created, were so designed that their nature automatically—without supernatural grace, but not without God's good providence—carried with it and displayed the knowledge, holiness, and righteousness that were the primary components of the image of God. When humanity fell, it lost nothing substantial, no faculty even and no power. What happened was that

30. Bonaventure, *The Breviloquium,* vol. 2 of *The Works of Bonaventure,* trans. Jose De Vinck (Paterson, NJ: St. Anthony Guild Press, 1963), 109.

since sin violated the form of the entire human nature, these faculties and powers now function so as to produce, no longer the knowledge and righteousness of God, but their very opposites. As a result of the fall, accordingly, human beings have not just lost an inessential addition to their nature (a superadded gift), while for the rest their nature remained intact; nor did they become devils who, incapable of being re-created, can never again display the features of the image of God. Instead, while they remained essentially and substantially the same, that is, human, and kept all their human components, capacities, and powers, the form, the character and nature, the set and direction of all these capacities and powers were so changed that now, instead of fulfilling the will of God, they fulfill the "law of the flesh." The image has changed into a caricature. Similarly, the covenant of works has been broken, inasmuch as by the works of the law no human flesh can any longer be justified (Rom. 3:20; Gal. 3:2). However, it has been so little destroyed and abolished that the law of the covenant of works still obligates every human to absolute obedience; it has been incorporated by Christ into the covenant of grace and has been completely fulfilled and now still remains as a rule of gratitude for believers.

As Privation

4. Aside from the good substratum by which sin is sustained and to which it clings, it can therefore never be defined in any way other than as "privation of the good." One must remember, however, that in using this language we are speaking abstractly and metaphysically about sin. And from that viewpoint, it has no existence, is no substance, but a nothingness, nothing positive, but only something privative. Anyone who wanted to conceive it differently would thereby make evil independent and eternal in a Manichean sense and posit a supreme evil over against a supreme good. The above objection raised against defining sin as privation, accordingly, actually rests on misunderstanding. Abstractly and metaphysically, sin is privation and may not, nor can from a Christian position, be viewed in any other way. But concretely, sin only occurs as the wrong "form" of a certain state or act and makes that state or act itself sinful, just as an illness, without being a substance, still makes a body sick. Concretely, therefore, sin is always in and attached to something that is substantially good. It may be hard in certain cases to make a distinction between "matter" and "form" and even more difficult to separate them, just as at any given time the heat of a stove cannot be separated from the stove. Yet, just as on that account the stove is not identical with its heat, so the being or act to which sin is attached cannot be identified with sin. Even in the case of blasphemy, the power needed to express it and the language in which it is couched are themselves good; what makes it and all things wrong and sinful is the *deformity,* the departure from divine law.

5. For the standard of sin is God's law alone. What sin is is finally determined not by the church (Rome), nor by the state (Hobbes), nor by an autonomous moral law (Grotius), nor by the autonomous Self (Kant), nor by humanity as a

whole (Comte), nor by social instincts (Darwin), but solely and exclusively by the law of God. This is clearly expressed in the concept of sin, a concept that is therefore avoided by everyone who knows no higher standard for moral evil than a human one. God is also the only Agent who has absolute authority over us and can bind and obligate us in our conscience. He laid down numerous laws for the various distinct creatures: laws for sun and moon, heaven and earth, plants and animals, humans and angels; and as it concerns humans, distinct laws again for their physical, spiritual, intellectual, and aesthetic life; and distinct laws for their moral life as well. Now, precisely speaking, it is this moral law that is the standard of all sin. The violation of all other laws—aesthetic, social, political, ecclesiastical, and so on—is sinful only insofar as it directly or indirectly includes a violation of the moral law. It is this moral law—which was implanted in humans at their creation, had its post-fall effect in their conscience, was announced on Mount Sinai, and remains a binding rule of life for Christian believers as well—that is the source of the knowledge of sin (Rom. 3:20; 4:14; 5:20; 7:7). Schleiermacher, Ritschl, and others correctly stressed that sin only comes to its most appalling manifestation vis-à-vis the gospel of the grace of God in Christ and hence within the boundaries of Christianity.[31] Scripture itself testifies to this when especially in the New Testament it repeatedly discusses at length the sins of unbelief, offense, apostasy, and particularly the blasphemy of the Holy Spirit and brings to light its great culpability and punishability.

However, from this it does not follow that all sins committed before or outside the knowledge of the gospel are only sins of ignorance and weakness, nor that not the law but the gospel is the source of our knowledge of sin. Christian faith is needed to rightly know sin, but that faith also looks back toward the law, discovers its spiritual character, and thus receives insight into the true nature of sin. The gospel would not be gospel if it did not include forgiveness of all those transgressions we have committed against the law of God. Just as grace presupposes sin, forgiveness, and guilt, so the gospel presupposes law. In that moral law, God comes to us not only as Father with fatherly admonitions and chastisements but, as the categorical imperative testifies to every human being, also as Lawgiver and Judge with commandments and punishments. Although it is not coercive like the laws of logic nor unbreakable as the laws of nature, the moral law surpasses all others in majesty. It addresses the will, breathes freedom, and desires fulfillment out of love. At the same time, it speaks to all humans without distinction, confronts them in all circumstances, extends not only to their words and acts but also to their moral condition, sticks relentlessly to its guns, speaks inexorably and categorically with sovereign authority, and avenges its violations

---

31. F. Schleiermacher, *The Christian Faith* (T&T Clark, 1989), §112, 5; A. Ritschl, *The Christian Doctrine of Justification and Reconciliation* (Clifton, NJ: Reference Book Publishers, 1966), 407ff.; J. Kaftan, *The Truth of the Christian Religion,* trans. George Ferries, 2 vols. (Edinburgh: T&T Clark, 1894), 250; J. H. Gerretsen, *De val des menschen: Dogmatisch fragment* (Nijmegen: Ten Hoet, 1909), 57.

with severe punishment. It is a divine decree, a revelation of the will of God, the expression of his being.

By Rational Creatures

6. From the character of moral law it follows that sin can only reside in a rational creature. Irrational nature can suffer the consequences of sin, but sin itself can only occur in a being endowed with intellect and will. More specifically, the will is the true subject, sin's showplace. The moral law is, above all, the law for the will of the creature; what is morally good is of such a kind that it can only be realized by the will. What absolutely and definitively passes by all influence of the will cannot be sin. In that sense Augustine was correct when he said: "In fact sin is so much a voluntary evil that it is not sin at all unless it is voluntary."[32] But this statement is open to misunderstanding. And when the Pelagians used it as proof that sin cannot consist in anything but an act of the will, Augustine later offered an explanation of it such that sins of ignorance and concupiscence and original sin were not excluded from it,[33] and he elsewhere expressly states that the law also prohibits "the involuntary motions of concupiscence."[34] In keeping with this view, many scholastics taught that though sin indeed had its final cause in the will and therefore was always rooted in the will but then not "in the will as subject but as a cause,"[35] sin can therefore also be rooted in "sensuality," even if it is only a "venial sin."[36]

But various factors gradually produced a change in this teaching. "Concupiscence" was a vague concept; it could be used equally well in a good and in a bad sense, inasmuch as natural, instinctively emerging desires, those, for example, of the hungry person for food, were, of course, not sinful. Augustine therefore sometimes spoke of concupiscence in a nonsinful sense, desire that could not do harm if only it was not met illegitimately.[37] Scholasticism, furthermore, began gradually to distinguish between *primo-primi*, *secundo-primi*, and *plane deliberati* desires, that is, those thoughts and desires that arise in us spontaneously before any consent of the will and are not at all sinful; those against which the will has offered resistance but by which it has been overpowered and which are venial sins; and those to which the will has consciously and fully consented and which are mortal sins. Added to this was the fact that the conception of original sin was becoming

---

32. Augustine, *On True Religion*, 24.

33. Augustine, *Retractions*, I, 13.

34. Augustine, *On the Spirit and the Letter*, 36; idem, *On Marriage and Concupiscence*, I, 17, 23; idem, *Against Julian*, IV, ch. 2; VI, ch. 8; idem, *City of God*, XIV, 10.

35. T. Aquinas, *Sent.*, II, dist. 24, qu. 3, art. 2, ad. 2; idem, *Summa theol.*, II, 1, qu. 74, art. 2, ad. 2, qu. 10; art. 2.

36. P. Lombard, *Sent.*, II, dist. 24, 8; T. Aquinas, *Summa theol.*, II, 1, qu. 74, art. 3; Bonaventure, *Brevil.*, III, ch. 8; idem, *Sent.*, II, dist. 24, pars 2, art. 2, qu. 2.

37. Augustine, *Against Julian*, VI, 5; idem, *On Genesis: Against the Manichees*, II, 14; ed. note: available in *On Genesis*, vol. I/13 of *The Works of Saint Augustine: A Translation for the 21st Century*, trans. Edmund Hill, O. P. (Hyde Park, NY: New City Press, 2004).

ever weaker and original sin itself viewed as wholly eradicated by baptism. What remained, concupiscence, was itself not sinful but only a "possible incentive to sin." Rome, accordingly, decreed that the guilt and pollution of original sin was totally removed by baptism, that though concupiscence remained, it does not injure those who do not consent to it and can only be called sin "because it is of sin, and inclines to sin."[38]

The Reformation spoke out against that position, asserting that also the impure thoughts and desires that arose in us prior to and apart from our will are sin. By this it meant to say, not that all desiring was sin in a psychological and philosophical sense, but that in a scriptural and theological sense concupiscence made us guilty before God. And in this it was undoubtedly correct. For sin certainly began with a conscious and voluntary act of the will. But that first sinful act did not pass us by without leaving a trace; it in fact corrupted human nature and left a condition that in all respects is contrary to the law of God. So although sin originated by the will, it does now exist outside of the will and is also rooted in all the other faculties and powers of human beings, in soul and body, in the lower and the higher cognitive and conative capacities (Gen. 6:3; 8:21; Exod. 20:17; Pss. 19:13; 51:5; Jer. 17:9; Matt. 5:28; Mark 7:21; Rom. 7:7, 15–17; 8:7; Gal. 5:7; etc.). "Sin cannot exist without the will because without the will it cannot exist as it is; without the will, however, it cannot be, because without the will, what exists cannot remain."[39]

Lutheran and Reformed theologians, therefore, usually fought against the position that all sin was voluntary. By taking that stance, they did not at all mean, however, that there could also be sin that totally and absolutely passed by the faculty of the will. The point is to gain a correct view of the nature and operation of the will. The will, after all, is absolutely not the whole of our capacity for desire but only a special power and expression of it.[40] In this restricted sense, the will is antecedent only to our actual sins, as James 1:15 speaks of it, but absolutely not to the sins of our state and to our involuntary sins. If the condition of being voluntary in this sense were a necessary element of sin, not only all impure thoughts and desires would cease to be sin, but almost all actual sins could be excused with the motto "To understand all is, in a way, to forgive all." In order to maintain the innocence of concupiscence, Bellarmine, accordingly, already arrived at the state-

---

38. *The Catechism of the Council of Trent,* trans. J. Donovan (New York: Catholic Publ. Society, 1829), V, 5; *The Racovian Catechism,* trans. Thomas Rees (London, 1609; repr., London, 1818), II, 2, 7; M. Becanus, *Summa theologiae scholasticae,* II, 145–50; F. Sylvius, *Commentarii in totam primam partem S. Thomae Aquinatis,* 4th ed., 4 vols. (Venetiis: Typographia Balleoniana, 1726), II, 336ff.; C. G. Daelman, *Theologia seu observationes theologicae in summam D. Thomae,* 9 vols. (Antwerp: Jacob Bernard Jouret, 1734), II, 174ff.; P. Dens, *Theologia moralis et dogmatica,* 8 vols. (Dublin: Richard Coyne, 1832), I, 314ff.; J. Kleutgen, *Die Theologie der Vorzeit vertheidigt,* 2nd ed., 5 vols. (Münster: Theissing, 1867–74), II, 644.

39. Augustine, in I. A. Dorner, *A System of Christian Doctrine,* trans. Rev. Alfred Cave and Rev. J. S. Banks, rev. ed., 4 vols. (Edinburgh: T&T Clark, 1888), 129.

40. Cf. H. Bavinck, *Beginselen der Psychologie* (Kampen: Bos, 1897), 166ff.

ment "Not everything that is contrary to the law is sin"; the involuntary motions, though in conflict with the law, are nonetheless not sins.[41]

However, though it is true that the voluntary element in this restricted sense is not always a constituent in the concept of sin, the sins of the human state and involuntary sins still do not totally occur apart from the will. There is not only an antecedent but also a concomitant, a consequent, and an approving will. Later, to a greater or lesser degree, the will approves of the sinfulness of our nature and takes delight in it. And also when later the will, illumined by reason, fights against it, or the born-again person can testify with Paul that he does not will the evil that he does [cf. Rom. 7:7–25], then this certainly decreases the degree of sin but does not define the nature of the sin. For sin has its standard only in God's law. Paul definitely denominates as sin the evil he does not will but nevertheless commits and so agrees that the law is good. But even then the sin that is done without having been willed does not occur totally apart from the will. For, certainly, Paul can say: "It is no longer I that do it but sin that dwells within me" [Rom. 7:17], thus drawing a contrast between his regenerate "I" and unregenerate flesh, but Augustine already rightly explained these words as follows: "Even though I do not consent to lust (concupiscence) and even if I do not pursue my desires, nevertheless, I still feel desire and am personally present in that very part of me. For I am not one person in my mind and another in my flesh. But then what *am* I? For I exist both in my mind and in my flesh. For the two natures are not contrary but the one human being is composed of both, inasmuch as God, the God by whom the person was made, is one."[42] Certainly, it is not one person who does this sin in the flesh and another who does not want this sin. In both instances it is the same person who, on the one hand, impurely pursues what is forbidden (concupiscence) and who nevertheless in the deepest part of his will turns away from it and fights it. And since a human being, also the born-again person for as long as he or she is in the flesh, always to some degree desires what is forbidden, even though he or she fights it in the restricted sense, it can be said that at the most fundamental level all sin is voluntary. There is nobody or nothing that compels the sinner to serve sin. Sin is enthroned not outside the sinner but in the sinner and guides the sinner's thinking and desiring in its own direction. It is the sinner's sin insofar as the sinner has made it his or her own by means of his or her various faculties and powers.[43]

41. R. Bellarmine, "De gratia primi hominis," *Controversiis* V, 10.

42. Augustine, *De verbis apost. Serm.*, 5.

43. P. Melanchthon, *Apology of the Augsburg Confession*, art. 2; idem, "De peccato," *Loci communes* (Berolini: G. Schlawitz, 1856); *Formula of Concord*, II, 1; J. Gerhard, *Loci theol.*, X, ch. 6 and 11; J. A. Quenstedt, *Theologia*, II, 60, 92, 139; D. Hollaz, *Examen theologicum acroamaticum* (Rostock and Leipzig: Russworm, 1718), 501, 525; J. Calvin, *Institutes*, II.i; III.iii; IV.xv.10–11; J. Zanchi, *Op. theol.*, IV, 56ff.; T. Beza, *Tractationum theologicarum* (Geneva: Jean Crispin, 1570), II, 345; A. Polanus, *Syn. theol.*, 336; P. Martyr Vermigli, *Loci communes* (London: Kyngston, 1576), 70; F. Turretin, *Institutes of Elenctic Theology*, IX, 2; XI, 21; P. van Mastricht, *Theologia*, IV, 2, 22; idem, *Commentaries*, on Exod. 20:17, Rom. 7:7, and Gal. 5:16; Heidelberg Catechism, Q. 113; J. Müller, *Christian Doctrine of Sin*, I, 185ff.

As Mystery in Variety

7. When all is said and done, sin proves to be an incomprehensible mystery. We know neither whence it is nor what it is. It exists, but has no right to existence. It exists, but no one can explain its origin. Sin itself came into the world without motivation, yet it is the motivation for all human thought and action. From an abstract point of view, it is nothing but a privation, yet concretely it is a power that controls everyone and everything. It has no independent principle of its own, yet it is a principle that devastates the whole creation. It lives off the good, yet fights it to the point of destruction. It is nothing, has nothing, and cannot do anything without the entities and forces God has created, yet organizes them all into rebellion against him. With everything that belongs to God, it opposes everything that belongs to God. It is the will of a weak, finite creature in its revolt against the Creator. It is dependence at war with the Independent One and striving for its own independence. It is impermanent becoming in a struggle with him who exists eternally. It is the greatest contradiction tolerated by God in his creation, yet used by him in the way of justice and righteousness as an instrument for his glory.

[332] Although sin is always singular in principle and essential character and always consists in lawlessness (ἀνομία), in its manifestations and operations there are very different degrees. In the first place, there is a big distinction between diabolical and human sin. In the Old Testament we do not yet find a developed demonology. That in Genesis 3 an evil spiritual power appears on the scene is something we only know from the New Testament. Goat demons (Lev. 17:7; 2 Chron. 11:15; Isa. 13:21; 34:14), demons (Deut. 32:17; Ps. 106:37), Lilith (Isa. 34:14), and the leech [poss. a vampire-like demon] (Prov. 30:15) are certainly not to be viewed as elements of revelation.[44] Furthermore, that in the case of Azazel (Lev. 16) we must think of an evil spirit is not demonstrable.[45] Evil spirits are mentioned only in 1 Samuel 16:14–23 and 1 Kings 22:19f., and Satan occurs only in Job 1; 1 Chronicles 21:1; Zechariah 3. The split between good and bad angels has not yet been effected; the evil spirit still comes from God; Satan is still among the sons of God. Only gradually do we see a sharper contrast between them. The word "satan" means "adversary" and can by itself have a positive meaning. It is used with reference to human adversaries (1 Sam. 29:4; 1 Kings 5:4; 11:14, 23, 25), adversaries on the road (2 Sam. 19:22), human accusers (Ps. 109:6, 20, 29),

---

44. Belief in evil spirits is found among all peoples. Just as, generally speaking, all natural phenomena are personified (animism), so especially disasters and accidents, earthquakes, storms, lightning, fire, misfortunes, and illnesses are attributed to evil spirits. This superstition in turn always led to magic, i.e., to the art of persuading supernatural personal spirits, by special words or actions, to effect something good or to avert some evil. Especially in Babylon this superstition flourished, which is then further traceable to ancient Sumerian culture (O. Weber). Although superstition and sorcery played a large role in Israel as well, the law and the prophets over and over again took a strong stand against them (Lev. 19:31; 20:6, 27; Deut. 18:10–11; Isa. 8:19–20; Jer. 27:9; 29:8–9; etc.).

45. On "Azazel," see S. R. Driver, *DB*, I, 207, s.v. "Azazel."

even to the angel of Yahweh who blocks Balaam's path (Num. 22:22, 32). Still, even in the Old Testament already Satan is conceived as a being who is hostile to God and his people. And when revelation has been complete and Christ comes to destroy the works of the devil, then also the "deep things of Satan" become manifest.

THE KINGDOM OF EVIL

The New Testament reveals to us a kingdom (βασιλεια; Matt. 12:26; Mark 3:24; Luke 11:17–18) of evil spirits, a kingdom that is the antithesis of Christ and his kingdom. At the head of it is Satan, a being called by various names: "devil," "Satan," "the enemy" (Matt. 13:39; Luke 10:19), "the accuser" (Rev. 12:10), βελιαρ (Syriac for Belial; worthlessness), "the evil one" (Matt. 13:19; Eph. 6:16; 2 Thess. 3:3; 1 John 2:13–14; 3:12; 5:18), "Beelzebul" (lit. lord of the dwelling, but probably derived from Beelzebub, god of the flies[46]) (Matt. 10:25), "prince of demons" (Matt. 9:34), "the ruler of the kingdom of the air" (Eph. 2:2 NIV), "the ruler of this world" (John 12:31), "the god of this world" (2 Cor. 4:4), "the great dragon," "the ancient serpent" (Rev. 12:9; 20:2; etc.). Subordinate to him are numerous demons, evil spirits, unclean spirits, and spiritual hosts of wickedness, which are in turn subdivided into various classes and ranks (1 Cor. 15:24; Eph. 6:12; Col. 2:15; Jude 6), surpass each other in wickedness (Matt. 12:45; Luke 11:26), and together form Satan's messengers (Matt. 25:41; 2 Cor. 12:7; Rev. 12:7, 9).[47] Although there is among them some difference in strength and evil, altogether they are nevertheless pictured as thoroughly corrupt. Always and everywhere they are the adversaries of God, the disturbers of his kingdom, the opponents of Christ, the deceivers of humans, the accusers of God's children. They live in sin as their natural element. They never appear as the object of God's love, though they are his creatures. Christ has not assumed their nature. They may never be the object of our love or intercession. For them there is no hope of restoration and salvation.

---

46. Other interpretations in W. Baudissin, "Beelzebub," *PRE*[3], II, 514–16; Owen C. Whitehouse, "Satan," *DB*, IV, 409.

47. J. C. K. von Hofmann, *Der Schriftbeweis*, 2nd ed., 2 vols. (Nördlingen: Beck, 1857–60), 418ff.; *I. F. E. Sander, ed., *Die Lehre der Heiligen Schrift vom Teufel* (Schönebeck: Berger, 1858); G. F. Oehler, *Theology of the Old Testament*, trans. Ellen D. Smith and Sophia Taylor (Edinburgh: T&T Clark, 1892–93), §200; G. L. Hahn, *Die Theologie des Neuen Testaments*, 8 vols. (Leipzig, 1854–), §§128ff.; P. Schwartzkopff, "Der Teufels- und Dämonenglaube Jesu," *Zeitschrift für Theologie und Kirche* (1897): 289–330; H. J. Holtzmann, *Lehrbuch der neutestamentlichen Theologie*, 2 vols. (Freiburg and Leipzig: Mohr, 1897), I, 53ff., 167; II, 238ff.; H. Weser, "Die verschiedenen Auffassungen vom Teufel im Neuen Testament," *Studien und Kritik* 55/2 (1882): 284ff.; O. Everling, *Die paulinische Angelologie und Dämonologie* (Göttingen: Vandenhoeck & Ruprecht, 1888); J. Weiss, "Dämonen," *PRE*[3], IV, 408–10; idem, "Dämonische," *PRE*[3], IV, 410–19; A. Wünsche, "Teufel," *PRE*[3], XIX, 564–74; H. Duhm, *Die bösen Geister im A.T.* (Tübingen: Mohr, 1904); Owen C. Whitehouse, "Demon, Devil," *DB*, I, 590–94, and "Satan," *DB*, IV, 407–12.

In the essential character and concept of the devils, there is something completely incomprehensible. "We can only conceive of an absolutely evil being on condition that we either omit something from their absolute wickedness or from their true existence."[48] They cannot be absolutely evil, for they are God's creatures and therefore good as such; yet they are only an object of God's hatred and eternal wrath. On account of the incomprehensibility of the nature of devils, many [authors] have denied their existence and held them to be the souls of dead persons, or the personifications of our wicked sins, or the impersonal first principles of evil.[49] Scripture, however, has raised the reality of Satan and his angels beyond doubt; we can in no way posit the possibility of accommodation here. Either Jesus was completely wrong about a most important point of religion, or things are as he says they are.[50] And for the teaching of Christianity as a whole, the doctrine of Satan is far from immaterial. It is of value against Manicheism, for Satan is not an original being but a fallen angel; against Pelagianism, for by one decision of his will Satan was totally corrupted; against the theory of sin as weakness and sensuality, for Satan is an elevated, majestic, and richly endowed spirit; against the opinion that sin is a passing phase in the evolutionary process, for Satan remains Satan and will never be restored. It is also of value against the degradation of humans to devils, for whereas Satan fell of his own accord, humans were seduced by him and, though not innocent, are not "protologically" guilty either;[51] against the view of atonement as an ethical process, for Christ came to destroy the works of the devil. Belief in Satan is not an element of saving faith in Christ, but it is closely connected with it. There is truth in the saying "No devil, no redeemer!" If there were no sin, there would be no savior, and the seriousness of sin stands out most vividly in the doctrine of Satan.[52]

From everything Scripture tells us of the angels, it is obvious that with them the moral life differs in character from that of human beings. In every domain of

48. C. E. Nitzsch, *System of Christian Doctrines* (Edinburgh: T&T Clark, 1849), §116; ed. note: Bavinck erroneously cites this as C. J. Nitzsch; F. A. B. Nitzsch, *Lehrbuch der Evangelischen Dogmatik,* prepared by Horst Stephan, 3rd ed. (Tübingen: J. C. B. Mohr, 1902), 337.

49. B. Bekker, *De Betoverde Weereld,* 4 vols. (Amsterdam: D. van den Dalen, 1691–93), II, ch. 20ff.; *J. S. Semler and Christian Edzard Betke, *De daemoniacis quorum in Evangeliis fit mentio* (Halle: n.p., 1760); F. Schleiermacher, *Christian Faith,* §§44–45; F. W. J. Schelling, *Ausgewählte Werke,* 4 vols. (Darmstadt: Wissenschaftliche Buchgesellschaft, 1968), II/4, 241ff.; R. Rothe, *Theologische Ethik,* 2nd rev. ed., 5 vols. (Wittenberg: Zimmerman, 1867–71), §503; H. L. Martensen, *Christian Dogmatics: A Compendium of the Doctrines of Christianity,* trans. William Urwick (Edinburgh: T&T Clark, 1871), §§99ff.; D. F. Strauss, *Die christliche Glaubenslehre,* II, 1ff.; A. E. Biedermann, *Christliche Dogmatik* (Zürich: Füssli, 1869), 614ff.; R. A. Lipsius, *Lehrbuch der evangelisch-protestantischen Dogmatik* (Braunschweig: C. A. Schwetschke, 1893), §§521–24; W. Beyschlag, *Neutestamentliche Theologie, oder, geschichtliche Darstellung der Lehren Jesu und des Urchristenthums nach den neutestamentlichen Quellen,* 2 vols. (Halle: Strien, 1891–92), I, 93ff.; J. Kaftan, *Dogmatik* (Tübingen: Mohr, 1901), §38.

50. J. H. Gerretsen, *De val des menschen,* 43.

51. Ed. note: Bavinck's distinction here is between human beings who are not un*schuldig* but also not ur*schuldig.*

52. A. von Oettingen, *Lutherische Dogmatik,* 2 vols. (Munich: C. H. Beck, 1897–1902), II, 459.

life and therefore also in the moral, human persons are subject to development. They are born very small—in knowledge, strength, virtue, or vice—and gradually mature in all these respects. But that is not how it is with angels. They have all been created at the same time and fully mature. Those who remained upright were all at once confirmed in the good, and those who fell were immediately hardened and became consummately evil. Satan was not led astray, but he produced sin—the lie—from within himself (John 8:44) and became all at once confirmed in it. The nature of his sin is such that he is no longer capable of remorse. In his case, there is no moral consciousness, no conscience; he lives off hatred. "The real Satanic character consists in a hatred of everything that is above him and solely because it is above him" (Baader). Also, in devils sin is not substance (*materia*) but form (*forma*). There is no supreme evil as there is a supreme good. But the "form" of sin is so fused with the [fallen] angelic nature that there is no longer any possibility of separation.

Certainly it is presumptuous to say that fallen angels are irredeemable even by God's omnipotence; and it is better at this point to rest in God's good pleasure.[53] Still, it is sufficiently clear that "good pleasure" is not identical with arbitrariness. Even among us humans here on earth there is a sin that cannot be forgiven: the blasphemy against the Holy Spirit. With death, that is, with the peculiar dispensation in which we live here on earth, the forgiveness of the sins of all human beings ends. In the case of the angels, however, the nature of sin rules out the way of salvation. Added to this is the fact that the angels are not constituted as a single race. Humans could and did fall in one person; and they can be and are saved in one person. But the devils did not fall "in" another, but everyone fell by himself individually. Among them there was no covenant of works, and so there is no room for a covenant of grace either. Satanic sin, therefore, for all its similarity to human sin, is nonetheless totally different in origin, character, and consequences. It bears an absolute character: Satan is the supreme revelation of evil. For that reason, Scripture gives him such splendid names as "ruler of this world," "the god of this age," and so on. But for that reason, too, Satan's victory is the complete triumph of sin. In Satan, God gave sin every opportunity to show what it is and what it can do. And sin has made the highest and best, the most noble and greatest creature in God's creation subservient to itself. Yet it finally becomes apparent that in the conflict between power and right sin proves powerless. "It is the nature of evil that it always starts out energetically and ends in weakness" (Baader). Sin *is* not: it *wants to be*; it neither has nor ever achieves true reality. It is falsehood in its origin and falsehood in its ending. And therefore, for all his power, Satan is finally subservient to God's glorification. "Lucifer—one can say—has learned from experience that nothing is true but God. Therefore Satan is as good a proof

53. G. Voetius, *Select. disp.*, I, 920; F. Turretin, *Institutes of Elenctic Theology*, IX, 5, 8; J. H. Heidegger, *Corpus theologiae*, VIII, 49; B. de Moor, *Comm. theol.*, II, 414.

for God as an angel. Whereas goodness proves that God exists, evil proves that only God exists" (Baader).[54]

DIVERSITY AND DEVELOPMENT OF SIN

[333] Aside from the difference between diabolical and human sins, there is also a great deal of difference among the latter. The Stoics, Novatian, Sebastian Franck, Deurhof, and others have denied this, but they are wrong.[55] Granted, in principle sin and virtue are indivisible: those who have one have them all, and those who lack one lack them all. Between good and evil there is no gradual transition. A person consents or does not consent to the law of God. The law of God is an organism that, when violated in one of its commandments, is violated in its totality, for God, who gave the commandment that was violated, is the author of all the other commandments as well (James 2:10).[56] But not all sins are for that reason equal. The different names used for sin already bear this out. In Genesis 4, in connection with the sacrifice of Cain and Abel, we learn that the inner disposition is of greater value than the gift. Though the law given to Israel contains a wide range of ceremonial commandments, the entire Old Testament makes clear that the value of ethical conduct far surpasses that of cultic and ceremonial acts. Faith is reckoned as righteousness (Gen. 15:6), obedience is better than sacrifice (1 Sam. 15:22; Amos 2:6ff.; 5:14, 21f.; Hosea 4:1f.; 12:6; Mic. 6:6, 8; Isa. 1:11f.; 5:8f.; Jer. 7:3; 22:3; Ezek. 16:49; 18:5f.; Zech. 7:5f.; Mal. 3:5; etc.).[57] When, after the exile, Pharisaism comes into vogue and reverses this relation, Jesus and his apostles again go back to the law and the prophets (Matt. 5–7; 19:18f.; Mark 7:21f.; Rom. 1:29f.; 1 Cor. 5:10f.; 6:9f.; 2 Cor. 12:20f.; Gal. 5:19f.; etc.). The law itself, moreover, makes a distinction between sins that are committed inadvertently, out of ignorance or weakness, do not break the covenant, and can be expiated within the covenant (בִּשְׁגָגָה) and sins that are committed consciously and intentionally (בְּיָד רָמָה—"with a high hand"), place the perpetrator outside the covenant, and

---

54. Augustine, *City of God*, XI, XII; Anselm, *The Fall of the Devil*, in *Anselm of Canterbury*, trans. and ed. Jasper Hopkins and Herbert Richardson, 4 vols. (Toronto and New York: Edwin Mellen Press, 1975), II, 127–77; P. Lombard, *Sent.*, II, dist. 2–7; T. Aquinas, *Summa theol.*, I, qu. 63–64; D. Petavius, *De angelis*, 1, III; M. J. Scheeben, *Dogmatik*, II, 670; H. T. Simar, *Lehrbuch der Dogmatik*, 3rd ed. (Freiburg i.B.: Herder, 1893), 294; J. Gerhard, *Loci theol.*, V, ch. 4, sect. 10ff.; J. A. Quenstedt, *Theologia*, I, 450ff.; J. Zanchi, *Op. theol.*, III, 167–216; G. Voetius, *Select. disp.*, I, 906ff.; C. Daub, *Judas Ischariot: Oder das Böse in Verhältnis zum Guten* (Heidelberg: Mohr & Winter, 1816); F. A. Philippi, *Kirchliche Glaubenslehre*, 3rd ed., 7 vols. in 10 (Gütersloh: Bertelsmann, 1870–90), III, 251ff.; J. P. Lange, *Christliche Dogmatik*, 3 vols. (Heidelberg: K. Winter, 1852), II, 559ff.; I. A. Dorner, *System of Christian Doctrine*, III, 85ff.; F. H. R. Frank, *System der christlichen Wahrheit*, 2nd ed., 2 vols. (Erlangen: A. Deichert, 1884), I, 428; A. von Oettingen, *Lutherische Dogmatik*, II, 459ff.; J. J. van Oosterzee, *Christian Dogmatics*, trans. J. Watson and M. Evans, 2 vols. (New York: Scribner, Armstrong, 1874), §76; A. Kuyper, *De Engelen Gods* (Amsterdam: Höveker & Wormser, 1900), 197ff.; W. Geesink, *Van 's Heeren Ordinantiën*, 1st ed., 3 vols. (Amsterdam: W. Kirchener, 1907), I, 261ff.

55. C. Vitringa, *Doctr. christ.*, II, 377.

56. *Vinet, *L'unité de la loi* (Nouv. Et. Evang.); R. Rothe, *Theologische Ethik*, §§730–31.

57. C. Clemen, *Die christliche Lehre von der Sünde*, I, 70.

make him worthy of death (Lev. 4; 5; 22:14; Num. 15:22f.; 35:11f.; Josh. 20:3, 9). Scripture never abandons the objective position that locates the standard of sin solely in the law of God.

Yet the guilt of violation is greater or less to the degree the commandment was violated more or less intentionally. On the one hand, Stade[58] is mistaken when he infers from Genesis 12:17; 20:3; 26:10; Numbers 22:34; and 1 Samuel 14:24f., 36f. that the distinction between conscious and unconscious violations of the law was unknown to ancient Israel and that one could therefore become culpable entirely apart from one's knowledge and will, for all these texts either hold ignorance to be the responsibility of the perpetrator or do not speak of guilt. On the other hand, it is also untrue "that in general sin only exists insofar as there also exists an awareness of it."[59] Sin does indeed presuppose some knowledge of the law. A person without any moral sense would not be responsible but would also cease to be human (Rom. 2:14–15), and in fact sin is usually accompanied by some sense of guilt. Nonetheless, the standard of sin is not the consciousness of guilt but the law of God. There are sins that are concealed not only from others but also from ourselves (Job 11:4f.; Pss. 19:13; 90:8) or are only later recognized and confessed as guilt (Pss. 25:7; 51:5). Often ignorance itself is sin, and the consciousness of sin weakness to the degree that sin has been pursued for a shorter or longer period (Amos 2:11f.; Hosea 4:6; Mic. 3:1; 6:8; Prov. 24:12; Eccles. 5:1). For that reason the subjective consciousness of guilt cannot define the character of sin. So, though ignorance can never make up for sin itself, it does frequently, when unintentional, conduce to exoneration. Paul writes that he was formerly a blasphemer, a persecutor, and an oppressor, but adds that he received mercy because he acted in ignorance (1 Tim. 1:13). In the same way, Scripture repeatedly speaks of the sins of Jews and Gentiles as having been done in ignorance (Luke 23:34; Acts 3:17–19; 13:27; 17:30; Eph. 4:18; Heb. 5:2; 1 Pet. 1:14; 2:25). Those sins are not thereby stripped of their culpable character, as Ritschl seems to think,[60] for in Romans 1–3; 5:12f.; Ephesians 4:17–19; Colossians 3:5–7; 1 Corinthians 15:9; 1 Timothy 1:13, 15; and other places, we are taught otherwise. Still, sins

58. B. Stade, *Geschichte des Volkes Israel*, I, 512ff.

59. F. Schleiermacher, *Christian Faith*, §68, 2.

60. A. Ritschl, *Die Christliche Lehre von der Rechtfertigung und Versöhnung*, II, 38, 241–46; III, 350–54 (ed. note: The second reference [III, 350–54] is found in *The Christian Doctrine of Justification and Reconciliation*, 370–74). E. Bernard is correct when he writes: "There is no trace of the Ritschlian view that till He (Jesus Christ) came all sin was practically ignorance, and that sinners only needed to lay aside their sense of guilt. That ignorance, even where it exists, is but a partial and not a sufficient excuse, appears in Luke 12:47, and the explanation of that passage is that moral ignorance is never total and only comes near totality by man's own fault. The sharp distinction between sins of ignorance, which are forgivable, and sins without ignorance, which are not, is untrue to life. The man who sins from ignorance has still some spark of knowledge which is enough to condemn him, and the man who sins against light has still some ignorance, for how can a man in his present limitations realize the gravity of the issues which are presented to him here? For the first point see Luk. 23:34; the soldiers in their ignorance nevertheless need forgiveness; and for the second see the lament over Jerusalem, Luk. 19:42" ("Sin," *DB*, IV, 532). Cf. also C. Clemen, *Die christliche Lehre von der Sünde*, 82.

committed in ignorance are distinct from sins that arise from hardness of heart. Ignorance does constitute a ground for the plea for forgiveness.

And just as sins differ in degree and extent depending on whether they were committed out of ignorance and weakness or intentionally out of wickedness, so they also differ in terms of the *object* against which they are directed. Sins committed against the first table of the law are more grave than those against the second (Matt. 22:37–38). Or they differ in terms of the *subject* who commits them: the more richly gifted a person is, the more the guilt of his or her sin increases (Matt. 11:21; Luke 12:47–48; John 9:41; 15:22, 24). Or they differ in terms of the *circumstances* under which they are committed: the person who steals because he is poor is less guilty than the person who steals out of avarice (Prov. 6:30; Isa. 26:10). Or they differ in terms of the *degree* to which people give in to sin: those who commit adultery in thought and word are culpable but increase their judgment when they proceed to complete the sin by action (cf. Matt. 5:28).

In sin, too, there is a dynamic of development: there is a law of sin. A given sin originates step-by-step by suggestion, enjoyment, consent, and execution. In the suggestion is the seed of sin; in enjoyment the nourishment; in consent the completion.[61] In that way sin also develops gradually in a person, a nuclear or extended family, a society and nation, and humanity as a whole as well. Not that sin in itself is so resourceful that it can assume so many forms, for it is not an independent principle and is, metaphysically speaking, nothing but the privation of the good. As in its origin, however, so in its development, it exists solely in connection with and by means of the good. It unites with the boundless resources of the created world, destroys everything that exists, with the entire world as its instrument wars against God and his holy law, and as a result assumes all those diverse forms and appearances that in their totality give it the character of a well-administered kingdom, an organism animated by a single principle, a cosmos subject to the rule of the "prince of this world," the "god of this age."

Inasmuch as sin is essentially privation, one can derive from it neither a principle of differentiation nor a division. "Privation takes its species from the form to which it is opposed" [Aristotle]. The earlier dogmatics and ethics, while they spoke about the character of the first sin, made very little effort to discover a so-called *principle* of sin and to trace all violations of the moral law to that first principle. Only in later times did theologians make an attempt to identify such a principle, finding it in turn in sensuality,[62] or in self-seeking,[63] or in both.[64] And in fact human sins do usually display the character of sensuality or self-seeking,

---

61. Gregory the Great and others; P. Lombard, *Sent.*, II, dist. 24, 8; Bonaventure, *Brevil.*, III, 8.

62. F. Schleiermacher, *Christian Faith,* §66.

63. J. Müller, *Christian Doctrine of Sin*, I, 135; A. Tholuck, *Die Lehre von der Sünde und vom Versöhner* (Gotha: F. A. Perthes, 1862), 18, 98; A. F. C. Vilmar, *Theologische Moral: Akademische Vorlesungen* (Gütersloh: C. Bertelsmann, 1871), I, 136; F. A. Philippi, *Kirchliche Glaubenslehre*, III, 3; K. Burger, "Selbstsucht," *PRE*³, XVII, 172–74.

64. R. Rothe, *Theologische Ethik*, §461; R. A. Lipsius, *Dogmatik*, §480.

of carnal covetousness or spiritual pride, of weakness or wickedness. Sometimes sin seems to consist in the rule of matter over mind, sometimes also in the abuse of freedom in rebellion against God's ordinances. Yet Rothe failed to explain self-seeking from sensuality, and J. Müller, with his preexistentialism, failed to explain self-seeking from sensuality.[65] Nor is it hard to understand why.

Metaphysically and abstractly sin cannot be described in a way other and more precisely than as privation of the good. As such it has no principle of its own, no real existence: it exists solely in relation to the good. It derives the forms it assumes from the good it inhabits and corrupts. It will therefore differ in appearance depending on the creatures in which it lodges and the organs and powers it utilizes. Although it is always privation of the good, in angels and humans and again in each of these individually it bears a particular character. Since human beings are originally not just sensual but also spiritual beings and always both in conjunction, all sin in their case will display this character. No single human sin is exclusively either sensual or self-seeking. As in the first sin in the case of Adam, so in every subsequent sin various aspects can be discerned, even though one of these aspects is usually more prominent than the others. In humans every sin is a turning away from God, disobedience, rebellion, anarchy, lawlessness, and at the same time, since sin is never self-sufficient, a turning toward a creature, idolatry, pride, self-seeking, sensuality.[66] And because the creatures to which humans can turn are so numerous, sin in their case can also assume a wide variety of forms. There are as many kinds of sin as there are different commandments, duties, virtues, and moral goods. Aquinas categorized sins in terms of the *objects* to which they were directed,[67] Duns Scotus in terms of the *virtues* of which they were the opposites.[68] In addition there were numerous other arrangements, such as the list of seven deadly sins: pride, avarice, lust, anger, gluttony, envy, and sloth.[69] Or they were arranged in terms of the *norms,* in terms of sins against the various commandments of the law, or sins against God, one's neighbor, and ourselves. Or they were distinguished by the *instrument* with which they are committed, as sins of thought, word, and deed; or as sins of the spirit and of the flesh; or, in keeping with 1 John 2:16, as sins of feeling, knowing, and controlling; or as sins of weakness, ignorance, and wickedness. Sins can also be categorized in terms of the *form,* as sins of omission and commission; or as sins as such and sins incidentally; or, according to the connecting words, as secret and open, controlling and noncontrolling, silent and crying sins, and so on.[70]

65. Cf. I. A. Dorner, *System of Christian Doctrine,* II, 90–98.

66. Bonaventure, *Sent.,* II, dist. 42, art. 3, qu. 2.

67. T. Aquinas, *Summa theol.,* II, 1, qu. 72, art. 1.

68. Duns Scotus, *Sent.,* II, dist. 37, qu. 1, 9; A. M. dé Liguori, *Theologia moralis,* ed. P. Leonardi Gaudé, 4 vols. (Graz: Akademische Druck- und Verlangsanstalt, 1954), II, 32.

69. O. Zöckler, *Das Lehrstück von den sieben Hauptsünden* (Munich: Beck, 1893).

70. P. Lombard, *Sent.,* II, dist. 42; T. Aquinas, *Summa theol.,* I, qu. 72; J. Gerhard, *Loci theol.,* X, 5ff.; Z. Ursinus, *Tract. theol.,* 202; B. de Moor, *Comm. theol.,* III, 313; P. van Mastricht, *Theologia,* IV, 3, 10; J. H. Heidegger, *Corpus theologiae,* X, 61; A. F. C. Vilmar, *Theologische Moral,* I, 221.

MORTAL AND VENIAL SINS

Leaving further elaboration to ethics, we will here discuss additionally only the Catholic distinction between mortal and venial sins. This distinction has its origin in the practice of penance[71] and occurs materially already in Tertullian and Augustine, who spoke of light, superficial, minor, very small, and daily sins that still remain in believers.[72] Elaborated in scholasticism,[73] they were fixed by the church[74] and since then zealously defended by all theologians against all opposition.[75] According to this distinction, there are sins that cause people to lose the grace received and make them deserving of death, and others, such as an idle word, overly boisterous laughter, spontaneously arising desire, outbursts of temper or anger, a very small theft, and so on, that do not entail the loss of grace, are not so much against as outside of the law, and are essentially pardonable. The distinction is based on the fact that Scripture speaks of various sins and punishments (Matt. 5:22; 7:3; 23:23; Luke 6:41; 1 Cor. 3:12–15), sometimes links death to them (Rom. 1:32; 6:23; 1 Cor. 6:9; James 5:20; 1 John 3:14), yet in many cases continues to recognize believers as such, even though they make many mistakes (Prov. 24:16; Matt. 1:19; Luke 1:6; James 3:2); further, on the consideration that there are curable and incurable diseases, and that there are minor insults that do not destroy a friendship.

The Reformers, however, rejected the distinction as incompatible with the Word of God. They did not deny that there are degrees of sin, and while they continued to employ the terms "mortal" and "venial sins," they attached a different meaning to them. Lutherans to some extent had to take over this distinction, inasmuch as believers could commit some sins without losing the grace of God and others that cost them that grace.[76] But the Reformed went further and wanted nothing to do with the whole distinction. If they did at times still use the words, they meant by them that all sins, except the sin of blaspheming the Holy Spirit, can be forgiven and are actually forgiven to believers, but that they are all inherently deserving of death.[77]

71. F. Pijper, *Geschiedenis der boete en biecht in de Christelijke kerk* ('s Gravenhage: Nijhoff, 1891), 306ff.

72. Tertullian, *On Modesty* (*ANF*, IV, 74–101), 2, 3, 19; idem, *Against Marcion*, IV, 9 (*ANF*, III, 269–475); Augustine, *Enchir.*, 44, 71; idem, *City of God*, XXI, 27; idem, *On Nature and Grace*, 39 (*NPNF* [1], V); idem, *On the Spirit and the Letter*, 36 (*NPNF* [1], V, 80–114).

73. P. Lombard, *Sent.*, II, dist. 42; T. Aquinas, *Summa theol.*, II, 1, qu. 88–89.

74. *Council of Trent*, VI, ch. 11, can. 27; XIV, 5; *Cat. Rom.*, II, 5, qu. 40.

75. R. Bellarmine, "De gratia primi hominis," *Controversiis*, I, ch. 3ff.; M. Becanus, *Summa theol. schol.*, II, 117; A. M. dé Liguori, *Theologia moralis*, 51ff.; H. Busenbaum, *Medulla theologia moralis* (Tornaci [Tournai]: J. Casterman, 1848), 31ff.; P. G. Antoine and F. de Carbognano, *Theologia moralis universal,* 2 vols. (Rome: Excudebat Antonius Fulgonius, 1783), ch. 2.

76. J. Köstlin, *Theology of Luther in Its Historical Development and Inner Harmony,* trans. Charles E. Hay, 2 vols. (Philadelphia: Lutheran Publication Society, 1897), II, 465ff.; P. Melanchthon, *Loci comm.*; J. Gerhard, *Loci theol.*, X, ch. 20; cf. R. Bellarmine, "De gratia primi hominis," *Controversiis*, I, ch. 4.

77. J. Calvin, *Institutes*, II.viii.58; III.ii.11; III.iv.28; *The Catechism of the Council of Trent*, VI, 12; Z. Ursinus, *Tract. Theol.*, 209; F. Gomarus, *Opera theologica omnia* (Amsterdam: J. Jansson, 1664), disp. 13; B. de Moor, *Comm. theol.*, III, 308–12; F. Turretin, *Institutes of Elenctic Theology*, IX, 4; P. van Mastricht, *Theologia*, IV, 3,

The Scripture texts on which Roman Catholic scholars base their distinction, accordingly, are all without any value as evidence. Only Matthew 5:22 offers some semblance of proof, but the intent of Jesus' saying is nonetheless very different from wanting to distinguish minor from major sins. Over against the ancients who said that only the sinful deed, the actual homicide, made a person culpable and liable in the local court, Jesus says that not just the deed, but even the first upsurge of illegitimate anger—even if not expressed in a single word—made people liable to judgment; that when that anger vents itself in a brief hostile epithet, the sin is already so great that it has to be adjudicated by the Sanhedrin; and that when the anger is vented in an insult, it is immediately—aside from any legal process—deserving of the fire of hell. The reference here has so little to do with venial sins that Jesus—conversely—deems the slightest sin worthy of the gravest punishment, *as* deserving of punishment as the ancients considered the sinful deed, that is, the act of homicide. Jesus equates the upsurge of illegitimate anger with homicide. He says that the slightest sin is indeed already a very grave sin, one that is as deserving of the most dreadful punishment as homicide was according to the ancients. What punishment this upsurge of anger deserves in the hereafter Jesus does not say, but when that anger is accompanied by an insulting word, this sin is so great that at that very moment it deserves hellish punishment. No court is needed any longer to fix a penalty. Hence, properly understood, this text is an argument *against* rather than *for* the distinction between mortal and venial sins. In the same way, the whole of Scripture is opposed to this division. The law is an organic whole (James 2:10). Whoever violates one commandment is in principle guilty of violating all of it (Matt. 5:17–19). It claims us totally—with heart and mind, soul and body (Matt. 22:37). To the law nothing is immaterial and small: cursed is the person who does not keep all that is written in the book of the law (Deut. 27:26; Gal. 3:10). Even the slightest violations of the law—an upsurge of anger, an impure desire, a redundant confirmation, an idle word (Matt. 5:22, 28, 37; 12:36; Eph. 5:4)—are sins equal, in principle, to sinful deeds and therefore to sin as lawlessness, hostility against God. Regarded in terms of principle, there are no peccadilloes. "No sin is to be despised as small, since in truth no act is little when Paul states with respect to every sin in general that sin is 'the sting of death.'"[78]

When a sin, say an idle word, is considered by itself and detached from its connection with the person and circumstances in question, the statement that it is deserving of eternal death seems inordinately severe. But it is precisely that abstract atomistic view that is fundamentally rejected by the Reformed as being contrary both to Scripture and to reality. Sin is not a quantity that, isolated from the perpetrator of it, can be counted on one's fingers and weighed in a scale. The

---

22; B. Pictet, *De christelijke god-geleertheid, en kennis der zaligheid,* trans. Johannes Wesselius ('s Gravenhage: Pieter van Thol, 1728), VI, 11; H. Heppe, *Dogmatik der evangelischen reformierten Kirche,* 257.

78. Basil, in J. Gerhard, *Loci theol.*

Roman Catholic distinction, accordingly, has in fact led to all sorts of bad practices. The theologians do not agree whether a venial sin does or does not insult God, ought or ought not to be confessed; whether real repentance is required for rectification or whether the performance of some meritorious work is sufficient. But all acknowledge that, both in theory and in practice, the distinction is virtually impossible to maintain. People therefore have to resort to all kinds of subtle arguments, arguments that in being pursued undermine the entire character of sin. Where arguments fail, people add up the opinions of the doctors of theology and content themselves with a greater or lesser degree of probability. In that way they end up with an atomistic, casuistic, mechanical, and materialistic assessment of sins and their reparations, while keeping the souls in a perpetual state of fear about whether they have committed a mortal sin, *or* inciting them to frivolousness and indifference, since the sins are usually of a very light kind and very easy to correct.

SIN AGAINST THE HOLY SPIRIT

[334] Holy Scripture mentions only one sin that both in this life and in the life to come is unpardonable: blasphemy against the Holy Spirit. There is no reference to it in the Old Testament, though [it must be recalled that] for the sins committed "high-handedly" [Num. 15:30] no sacrifice was instituted in the law, because it set aside the law itself (cf. Heb. 10:28). Jesus is the first to speak of it (Matt. 12:31; Mark 3:29; Luke 12:10). At one time, when he completely healed a demoniac who was also blind and dumb, the multitudes were so amazed that they recognized Jesus as the son of David, the Christ. But as a result the Pharisees were so enraged that they said not only that he cast out demons by the prince of demons, but that he himself was possessed by the devil (Mark 3:22). This accusation was inspired solely by hatred, springing as it did from pure, conscious, and intentional hostility. In Matthew 12:25–30, Jesus also demonstrates the truth of this: a kingdom divided against itself cannot stand. Satan does not cast himself out, so the ejection of Satan is proof that the kingdom of God has come upon them. Jesus cast out the devil by the Spirit of God. The antithesis between Jesus and the Pharisees, therefore, has here reached its moment of maximum tension. They say that Jesus is possessed, does wonders by the power of the devil, and so establishes the kingdom of the devil. And Jesus declares that he is the Christ, that he casts out the devil by the Spirit of God, and so brings the kingdom of God upon them. In this setting and prompted by this occasion, Jesus speaks of blasphemy against the Holy Spirit as the unpardonable sin. Whether people think that at that moment the Pharisees actually committed that sin or whether they believe they have to deny it (among other things because the Holy Spirit had not yet been poured out, John 7:39), the context makes clear that the sin against the Holy Spirit has to consist in a conscious, deliberate, intentional blasphemy

of the—clearly recognized yet hatefully misattributed to the devil—revelation of God's grace in Christ by the Holy Spirit.

The blasphemy against the Holy Spirit, therefore, does not simply consist in unbelief, nor in resisting and grieving the Holy Spirit in general, nor in denying the personality or deity of the Holy Spirit, nor in sinning against better knowledge and to the very end without qualification. Nor is it a sin solely against the law, but also a sin specifically against the gospel, and that against the gospel in its clearest manifestation. There is much, therefore, that precedes it: objectively, a revelation of God's grace in Christ, the nearness of his kingdom, a powerful working of the Holy Spirit; and subjectively, an illumination and conviction of the mind so intense and powerful that one cannot deny the truth of God and has to acknowledge it as being divine. In this case it does not itself consist in doubt toward or the denial of that truth, but in a denial that contradicts the conviction of the mind, the illumination of the conscience, and the intuitions of the heart. It then consists in a conscious and deliberate attribution of what has been clearly perceived as God's work to the influence and activity of Satan, that is, in a deliberate blaspheming of the Holy Spirit, a defiant declaration that the Holy Spirit is the spirit from the abyss, that the truth is a lie, that Christ is Satan himself. Its motivation, then, is conscious and intentional hatred against God and what is recognized as divine; its essence is sin in its ultimate manifestation, the complete and consummate revolution, putting God in the place of Satan and Satan in the place of God. Its character is no longer human but demonic. Although it is the case that the devils do not commit this sin in this particular form, since God's grace has not appeared to them, Christ has not assumed their nature, the Holy Spirit has not been poured out among them, and the kingdom of God has not come upon them, yet demonic sin bears the same character as the blasphemy against the Holy Spirit. It is also for that reason unpardonable. God's grace, indeed, is not too little and too powerless to pardon it; but also in the realm of sin, there are laws and ordinances that God has implanted in it and maintains. And in connection with this sin, that law consists in the fact that it rules out all remorse, scorches the conscience shut, definitively hardens the sinner, and in this way makes his sins unpardonable.

Aside from in the Gospels, there is nowhere in Scripture any direct mention of this sin. But this act of blaspheming the Holy Spirit can be committed in various circumstances. Thus we read in Hebrews 6:4–8 and 10:25–29 (cf. 2:3; 4:1; 12:15–17) that those "who have once been enlightened, and have tasted the heavenly gift, and have shared in the Holy Spirit," then falling back into Judaism, spurn, crucify, and hold the Son of God up to contempt, profane the blood of the new covenant, and outrage the Spirit of grace, cannot possibly be restored to repentance. In 1 John 5:16, we similarly find a testimony to the effect that there is a sin that in virtue of its very nature necessarily leads to death without conversion and for which John does not say, that is, does not command, that one should pray. Such prayer, if not impermissible, is nonetheless fruitless. In the context of

John's letter as a whole, it is probable he was thinking of a firm and deliberate denial of the Christ as the incarnate Son of God. Thus, in both these passages we are dealing with sins that leave a person completely hardened and are therefore inherently unpardonable. Factually and materially they coincide with the sin of blaspheming the Holy Spirit.[79]

79. On the wealth of literature on this topic, I shall mention only the following: T. Aquinas, *Summa theol.*, II, 2, qu. 14, art. 1; P. Lombard, and others, *Sent.*, II, dist. 43; C. Vitringa, *Doctr. christ.*, II, 378; J. G. Walch, *Bibliotheca theologica selecta*, 4 vols. (Jenae: vid. Croeckerianal, 1757–65), I, 88, 254; P. Schaff, *Die Sünde wider den heiligen Geist und die daraus gezogenen dogmatischen und ethischen Folgerungen* (Halle: Lippert, 1841); J. Müller, *Christian Doctrine of Sin*, II, 596; C. Clemen, *Die christliche Lehre von der Sünde*, I, 89–100; A. von Oettingen, *Luth. Dogm.*, II, 526ff.

4

THE PUNISHMENT OF SIN

The punishment of sin was not administered immediately after the fall; it does not even go into effect fully now but only after the final judgment. God delayed and moderated sin's punishment of death to make the continuation of human life and history possible. Punishment serves the purpose of God's justice. Jesus, recognizing the human propensity to abuse the law of vengeance for self-interest, offered a higher principle: love and patience. When we insist on rights, we must do so out of love for God and our neighbor.

Retribution, however, is the principle and standard of judgment in Scripture. God himself is just and righteous; he never clears the guilty and is merciful to the poor and afflicted. Imposing judgment on another human being is permissible only to those who are legitimately clothed with authority; it is never the prerogative of the strong or the saintly. All authority is subject to God's justice. Efforts to establish justice, right and wrong, apart from God ultimately annihilate justice and morality. To blame society's conditions as the cause of crime, to treat crime as a social disease, is to eliminate human responsibility.

In such cases, it is hard to overlook two glaring contradictions. First, if society is to be blamed for the criminal's acts, then why should society too not be absolved? It too has a past to which it is bound. Second, turning crime into a disease does not solve the problem. Crimes are still punished when criminals are sent away to be "cured." When the boundaries between crime and disease are wiped out and justice declines into mere cultural preference, freedom itself is forfeited and citizens are handed over to an arbitrary and omnipotent state.

While there are positive elements in modern criminology, such as distinctions among crimes and criminals, taking into account persons and circumstances, the state cannot do without retribution and punishment. To reduce crime to disease and punishment to remediation is to enter a labyrinth. No earthly judge can know the human heart or decide a person's capacity for improvement. For modern criminology to eliminate notions of retribution and punishment in favor of moral improvement is to take away the norm of justice from the power of the state. The purpose of punishment is justice; failure to serve that end results

*in mere coercion, an exercise of the will to power. Here the weak have no legal
protection.*

*In part, punishment flows from sin itself. To a degree, the history of the world
is the judgment of the world. This is not the whole story, however, for God also
visits this world with concrete and specific punishments in addition to "natural"
punishments. Concrete punishments are never arbitrary, even when we fail to
see connections between them and our sin. God has his own purposes in visiting
us with guilt, pollution, suffering, death, and Satan's dominion. In God's
providence and by his grace and wisdom, suffering serves not only as punishment
but also as trial, as chastisement, and as nurture.*

*Sin always has guilt as its concomitant. Those who violate the law become
more tightly bound to its demand. God never relinquishes his hold on the sinner;
those who position themselves outside the law are struck with its curse. Divine
wrath is a reality at work throughout the creation; there is a divine curse resting
on the world and humanity. This objective curse finds its reflection in human
consciousness through the guilty conscience by which human beings condemn
themselves as sinners.*

*Sin's punishment is also found in pollution, in the corruption of thought,
desire, and inclination that is contrary to God's holiness. Whereas guilt obligates
us to endure punishment, pollution renders us unclean. Sin is simultaneously a
violation of the covenant of works and the destruction of God's image. Human
beings do not cease to be human, but our whole lives are disturbed and devoted
to the service of sin. We are all part of a single corrupt race though we sin in a
variety of ways.*

*Thanks to the entry of sin into the world, humanity lost dominion and glory,
and suffering is the result. Suffering is not always a consequence of personal
sin, but it is nonetheless still a consequence of sin in general. Reason can neither
explain nor ameliorate suffering. Even if all evil obviously caused by human
sin were eliminated, disasters in nature would still cause suffering. While not
directly traceable to a specific sin, there is a connection with sin; the world is
under a curse. As in the case of human beings, a significant change has taken
place in nature as a result of divine judgment. Lament, not pessimism, is the
scriptural way of acknowledging suffering.*

*Suffering culminates in sin's other penalty, death. Though there is some truth
in the notion that the difference between the righteous and the wicked in the
Old Testament rests not in death itself but in the meaning of suffering and death,
Scripture does not consider death natural or necessary. The New Testament
clearly teaches the bond between sin and death. Science cannot, finally, account
for death on natural terms; it is a mystery in the full sense of the word.*

*The full penalty of sin discussed in this chapter is the dominion of Satan
in this world. Belief in evil spirits must never, for Christians, become similar*

to pagan superstition that attributes all physical evil in the world—disease,
crop failures, famine, plague, death—to Satan and the demonic. Even when
Protestants repudiated elements of Roman Catholic superstition that saw
Christians as threatened by devils everywhere, they were not entirely successful in
eliminating such social evils as witches' trials. The Reformation, however, while
acknowledging the reality of evil spirits, did emphasize the sovereignty of God's
providence and the victory of Christ and his kingdom. The church continues to
struggle against the kingdom of darkness, but Jesus is Lord.

MERCY AND JUSTICE

[335] The punishment of sin cannot be fully treated in this section. Although God threatened in advance to requite sin with the full punishment it deserved, this punishment did not go into effect [immediately] after the sin had been committed. Nor does it fully go into effect in this life, and even at the time of death, it is not yet administered in full. Only after the judgment of the last day does it strike the guilty with all its severity. In Genesis 2:17, God had expressly stated: "In the day that you eat of it you shall die." This emphatic threat, however, was not carried out.[1] An element intervened that moderated and delayed this punishment. Adam and Eve continued to live still many years after the fall. Eve even became the mother of all living. A human race sprang from them that was sustained and nourished by the earth. The beginnings of history, be it in a very modified form, continued after the fall. All this was due, not to God's justice, but, as will appear more clearly later, to his grace. God's grace went into effect immediately after the fall. It was given a presiding role in history, not at the expense of, but in union with, the justice of God. All the consequences and punishments that went into effect after the entry of sin, accordingly, from that moment display a double character. They are not merely the consequences and punishments appointed by God's justice but, from another perspective, also all without exception appointed means of grace, proofs of God's patience and compassion. One cannot object that, given this scenario, God spoke falsehood in Genesis 2:17. For in that verse we are only given the announcement of the true and full punishment that sin deserves: sin breaks up communion with God, both *is* spiritual death and *deserves* death. That this punishment would be moderated, delayed, and even forgiven could in the nature of the case not be communicated before the transgression. In Genesis 2:17, therefore, God speaks only of the one momentous punishment of sin, that is, death. With death, after all, everything—life, joy, development, work, but also the possibility of repentance and forgiveness, the restoration of communion with God—ceases all at once.

---

1. Others give to the expression "in the day" a broader sense (i.e., "when"), or they have death begin on the day of the transgression insofar as humans were then subjected to it and immediately had to endure all sorts of sorrow and suffering. See C. Clemen, *Die Christliche Lehre von der Sünde* (Göttingen: Vandenhoeck & Ruprecht, 1897), 242.

All sin deserves is death—death in its totality and fullness. All other punishments that went into effect and were pronounced after the fall—such as shame, fear, concealment from God, the curse pronounced on the serpent and the earth, and so on—though indeed punishments, nevertheless also presuppose that God did not instantly and fully carry out his threat. God still has another plan for humankind and the world and therefore, in his patience and compassion, allows them to exist. Yet, from a certain point of view, they are very definitely also punishments and to that extent must be discussed here. In them, certainly, God's grace comes to expression but also his justice.

The purpose of punishment, according to the overall belief of Scripture, is to redress the justice of God that has been violated by sin. In Israel its intent was to uphold the laws that God had appointed and to remove evil from the midst of the people (Deut. 13:5; 17:7, 12; 22:21f.; 24:7). Further, punishment sought to prevent such violations and to prompt Israel, in the fear of the Lord, to walk in his ordinances (Deut. 13:11; 17:13; 19:20; 21:21). The goal of punishment, then, was twofold: relating to the past and to the future, it both had to redress past violations and to prevent future ones. The standard of punishment might not be hatred or vengeance, for these motives were forbidden the Israelite in his or her conduct toward the neighbor (Lev. 19:17–18; Prov. 24:29), but had to be derived from the nature of the criminal offense committed (Exod. 21:23–25; Lev. 24:19–20; Deut. 19:21). As among other peoples, especially the Egyptians, the law of retribution (*ius talionis*) was in force also in Israel. But already in antiquity it was understood that this principle, if applied consistently, could lead to gross injustices and be made an instrument of vindictiveness. If for some criminal offense a person was condemned to lose one of his eyes, hands, or feet, it made a vast difference whether up until that time he still had two healthy eyes, hands, or feet, whether he had to lose the left or the right one in each case, and whether in the past he needed it for a special occupation, say, for the practice of the art of writing or painting. For different persons living in different circumstances, the same punishment is most unequal in effect and may therefore be fair in one case and highly unfair in another. For that reason, also in Israelite legislation, the law of retribution was not always applied rigorously and literally. The courts took account of the differences between cases and sometimes prescribed a fine instead (Exod. 21:20–26). If someone made a false accusation and wanted to abuse the law in his own interest, he was to receive the same punishment he had meant for his brother (Deut. 19:19). Still, in practice the law of retribution was often abused, and it was against this abuse that Jesus spoke out in the Sermon on the Mount (Matt. 5:38–42).

To understand this saying correctly, one must note that Jesus does not cite the words "an eye for an eye and a tooth for a tooth" directly from the Old Testament, for in that case he would certainly have introduced it with the formula "it is written." But he cites it in the way it had from ancient times been taught and explained in Jewish schools and opposes the false interpretation that had been given of it.

And that false interpretation did not consist in the fact that people considered the law of retribution as taught in the Old Testament also applicable in private life and mutual interactions, but that publicly as well, before a judge, they made it a tool of self-interest, personal vengeance, and hatred. Jesus, opposing this abuse, offers in its place the principle of love and patience. His disciples must not resist one who is evil, that is, they must not (according to the rule "an eye for an eye and a tooth for a tooth") return evil for evil. They must not counter an unfair demand of their neighbor with an equally unfair demand of their own. They must not attempt to avenge themselves on their neighbor with like conduct but rather seek to win him with love, patience, long-suffering, leniency, and a spirit of accommodation. In saying this, however, Christ is absolutely not condemning every instance of defending one's own rights. For when one of the officers in the high priest's hall of justice struck Jesus, Jesus does not turn the other cheek but defends himself, saying: "If I have spoken wrongly, testify to the wrong. But if I have spoken rightly, why do you strike me?" (John 18:22–23; also cf. Paul, Acts 22:25; 23:3; 25:10). But the rights of others as well as our own must, according to Christ, be esteemed so highly that they may not in any way be subordinated to personal vindictiveness, hatred, self-interest, to the evil tendencies of the human heart. When we fight for them, we must do so out of love for God and our neighbor. Vengeance and recompense, also according to the Old Testament, are the Lord's own cause (Deut. 32:35).

CRIME AND PUNISHMENT

For that very reason, however, retribution is the principle and standard of punishment throughout Scripture. There is no legislation in antiquity that so rigorously and repeatedly maintains the demand of justice as that of Israel. This comes out especially in the following three things: (1) the guilty person may by no means be considered innocent (Deut. 25:1; Prov. 17:15; 24:24; Isa. 5:23); (2) the righteous may not be condemned (Exod. 23:7; Deut. 25:1; Pss. 31:18; 34:21; 37:12; 94:21; Prov. 17:15; Isa. 5:23); and (3) the rights of the poor, the oppressed, the day laborer, the widow, and the orphan especially may not be perverted but, on the contrary, must be upheld for their protection and support (Exod. 22:21f.; Deut. 23:6; 24:14, 17; Prov. 22:22; Jer. 5:28; 22:3, 16; Ezek. 22:29; Zech. 7:10). In general, justice must be pursued both in and outside the courts (Deut. 16:20). All this is grounded in the fact that God is the God of justice and righteousness, who by no means clears the guilty, yet is merciful, gracious, and slow to anger, and upholds the rights of the poor and the afflicted, the widow and the orphan (Exod. 20:5–6; 34:6–7; Num. 14:18; Ps. 68:5; etc.). He, accordingly, threatens punishment for sin (Gen. 2:17; Deut. 27:15f.; Pss. 5:5; 11:5; 50:21; 94:10; Isa. 10:13–23; Rom. 1:18; 2:3; 6:21, 23; etc.) and determines the measure of the punishment by the nature of the offense. He repays everyone according to his or her deeds (Exod. 20:5–7; Deut. 7:9–10; 32:35; Ps. 62:12; Prov. 24:12; Isa. 35:4; Jer. 51:56; Matt. 16:27; Rom. 2:1–13; Heb. 10:30; Rev. 22:12).

[336] In keeping with the above, Christian theology spoke of a distributive in distinction from a remunerative and vindicatory or punitive justice,[2] and derived from the latter the right and essential character of punishment. In fact, there exists no final principle on which punishment can be based other than the justice of God. All punishment presupposes that the person who pronounces and imposes punishment is clothed with authority over those who have violated the law. This authority cannot have its origin in humanity itself, for what human being can claim any right as such vis-à-vis others who are of the same nature? It cannot rest in a person's physical condition, for that only creates the so-called right of the strongest; neither can it be grounded in one's ethical qualities, for all people are sinners, violators of all the commandments of the divine law, and cannot in a moral sense claim the right to summon, judge, and convict others before their judgment seat. The moment God's justice is denied, and there is no longer any belief in a moral world order that is elevated far above human beings, the right and essential character of punishment immediately collapses as well, even when the word "justice" is still retained. "The doctrine of the divine justice of punishment is among the fundamental articles of the Christian faith. The fact that God punishes evil is the basis of all human punitive justice. Those who carry it out judicially act in the name of God as his servants, perform a sacred office on his orders. Punishment, therefore, is never a matter of expediency but rests in the inviolable ideas of good and evil that are rooted in the holy will of God."[3]

The history of the last [nineteenth] century[4] has most clearly illustrated the correctness of the statement just cited. After the worship of God had yielded in the eighteenth century to the deification of humanity and in the nineteenth century to the glorification of society and the state, all moral and judicial concepts were gradually changed and falsified. For a time Kant's absolute idealistic ethics still held back the flow of things, but after his categorical imperative had also been absorbed into the process of evolution, historicism and relativism achieved an across-the-board victory. The decline of the ancient Christian worldview has also resulted in the modification, indeed the abolition and banishment of the concepts of good and evil, responsibility and accountability, guilt and punishment. Along with belief in the justice of God, belief in justice on earth disappeared as well. Atheism proved to be the annihilation of all justice and morality: no God, no master. The modern, positivist, evolutionistic worldview, after all, though it cannot deny the fact that there is something like good and evil, sin and virtue, guilt and punishment, looks at and attempts to explain these things very differ-

---

2. Cf. H. Bavinck, *Reformed Dogmatics,* II, 221–28 (#206).

3. J. Kaftan, *Dogmatik* (Tübingen: Mohr, 1901), 339–40.

4. Ed. note: What Bavinck observed about the nineteenth century is doubly true of the bloody, barbarous twentieth century. It was not religious conflict but atheism that led to the death camps, the gulags, and the killing fields of the last century.

ently. Sin and crime are not traceable to the evil will of individual persons, are not their responsibility nor imputable to them personally, but are, generally speaking, remnants or aftereffects of the animal ancestry of humans and to be explained in terms of their nature or of their environment.

On this last point opinions differ. The anthropological or biological school of Lombroso, Ferri, Garofalo, and others regarded every criminal case separately and individually and viewed criminals as victims of heredity, people who stayed behind in the evolutionary process. Initially, Lombroso even assumed the existence of a criminal type. But already at the first congress of criminal anthropologists at Rome in 1885, this position encountered criticism from the side of Lacassagne, criticism that increased at subsequent congresses. In opposition to the anthropological arose a sociological school that tried to explain crime, not in terms of the innate nature of individuals, but in terms of their environment and upbringing, the whole surrounding society. It viewed crime as a symptom of social disease, a necessary product of circumstances, a consequence of ignorance, poverty, poor upbringing, and heredity. "Societies have the criminals that they deserve" (Lacassagne).[5] From this position, naturally, it becomes impossible to maintain the justice and essential character of punishment. For if crime can, in fact, be totally traced to the innate animal nature of humans or to the environment in which they grew up, and their own evil nature need not or may not be taken into account, criminals are completely free of blame, and society loses all right to punish them. Rightly considered, the roles are even totally reversed. Criminals have nothing on their conscience vis-à-vis society, but society bears an enormous burden of guilt toward them. "It is not [criminals] who must be nailed to a cross but those who have made them criminals."[6] Society has failed to nurture and educate them into civilized moral beings. Just as nowadays many educationists tell us that the parents are to blame for the badness of their children, so also many criminologists have adopted the opinion that society is to blame for its criminals.

It is difficult, however, to be consistent in this connection. For then we would have to pity criminals and imprison society as the really guilty party. But since this is impracticable, people commit two inconsistencies. The first is that they accuse society of every possible injustice; the criminal is excused, defended, sometimes even praised and glorified, but to modern criminologists, educationists, and sociologists, society is proportionately all the worse. No words are sharp enough to condemn it, no columns of print long or wide enough to properly castigate it.

5. A. E. J. Modderman, *Straf geen kwaad* (Amsterdam: Muller, 1864); J. R. Brandes de Roos, *De strafmiddelen in de nieuwere strafrechtswetenschap* (Amsterdam: Scheltema, 1900); D. Simons, "Nieuwe Richtingen in de strafrechtwetenschap," *De Gids* (April 1900): 48–84; idem, "Nieuew Strafrechtspolitiek," *De Gids* (May 1901): 253–96; ed. note: Bavinck erroneously cites this as May 1900; idem, "Het congres van crimineele anthropolgogie te Amsterdam," *De Gids* (December 1901): 483–519; idem, *Leerboek van het Nederlandse strafrecht* (Groningen: Nordhoff, 1904), 5–18.

6. *Merkel, according to Dr. G. von Rohden, *Das Wesen der Strafe im ethischen und strafrechtlichen Sinne* (Tübingen, 1905), 53.

But if in the case of crime the evil will, personal responsibility, accountability, and culpability may not at all be considered, where do people then derive the right to bring all these ethical factors to bear in the case of society? Criminals can only be the persons they are, but can society be other than it is? Does society not have a past to which it is bound, from which it came into being? Does society have a free will, the very thing that is denied to all its members personally? Clearly, those who throw away ethical standards in the case of the crime of the individual cannot again pick them up when it concerns that of society.

The other inconsistency is no less momentous. There can be no legitimate talk of punishing the criminal: criminals are actually completely innocent, the dupes of society, the victims of wretched circumstances, deserving not its condemnation but its pity. Society, however, can hardly leave criminals free to roam; it tracks them down, summons them before a judge, examines their life and actions, condemns them, isolates them, and locks them up. There are very few people who, like Tolstoy, would abolish the entire government and all judicial power. But from what source then does society nevertheless derive the right to institute judicial proceedings? To this question no answer can be given, for in modern criminology there is actually no longer any room for justice. People try to maintain the ancient institutions of justice, however, by turning crime into a disease and punishment into a means of cure. People undergird this opinion with the following considerations: (1) Just as all that is higher has proceeded from what is lower, so also punishment originally arose from hatred and vengeance; and even when this power to punish was gradually taken away by society from the individual, the family, and the tribe, it still for a long time retained the character of a lust to inflict pain and torment. But that period is now past. Jesus already condemned the right to exact revenge. Justice has to be ethicized. Retribution and punishment no longer belong in a Christian or an ethical society. (2) Statistics show that crimes, especially the repetition of offenses, and also crimes committed at an early age, are on the increase. This proves the inadequacy of the old system. Crime is not deterred by punishment; not even the death penalty is capable of deterring it. Therefore, both in the theory and the practice of punishment, we need another system, that is, a system, not for punishing crime, but for studying the criminal and for dealing with him in accordance with this nature. (3) The fact of the crime committed by a person is, as such, already a proof of his abnormality, of a deficiency in his upbringing, of a defect in his mind or a weakness in his will, of an obsession or hereditary defect, in general of a certain degeneration. Real punishment, therefore, does not benefit him; he should much rather be treated as a patient, nursed in an institution. In many cases he should be put on probation, given an indefinite sentence, be released conditionally, and also after his release be put under surveillance. In this way there is a chance that society will gradually be relieved of its criminal population and itself be raised to a higher moral position.

Even if all these considerations were correct, they would still not prove the right of a society to deal with criminals as it does and will have to continue to do in the future. For whether one inclines to the theory that over against the criminal the state may and must protect itself (the theory of the maintenance of social order, of self-defense, self-preservation, and deterrence), or whether one tends to stress that society is called to bring up and to correct the criminal, the state nevertheless always assumes the position of utility, and utility creates no law but leads inevitably to coercion and introduces no other right than the right of the strongest. If criminals are to be treated as sick people, the downside of this is that the sick must be "nursed" in the manner of criminals. If the state has no other right to act against criminals than thereby to protect itself and to improve them, on what grounds then will it be denied the right to deal with all kinds of sick people on its own authority and by its own methods, to view the religious and moral convictions to which it cannot agree as so many diseases, remnants and aftereffects of an earlier state, and to take charge of the entire upbringing of its citizens and the whole culture of the society in question? Those who wipe out the boundaries between crime and disease let a state grounded in principles of justice decline into a state based on cultural mores, violate freedom in the life of the people, and hand all its citizens over to the arbitrariness and omnipotence of the state.

Nonetheless, far from everything proposed and pursued by modern criminology is wrong. Over against an abstract view of crime and punishment, it correctly focuses attention on the connection between the act and the person of the criminal. Research into the causes, the treatment, and the means of diminishing crime is undoubtedly legitimate. In dealing with crime, we may and must take account of the person by whom and the circumstances under which the crime has been committed. Not only is there a difference between crimes that violate the stipulations of the moral code and offenses that are committed against police measures, but also circumstances and relations can mitigate or aggravate the crime. A soldier who abandons his post in wartime is immediately shot to death without a trial, and a wretch who takes advantage of an earthquake, a fire, or a war to rob dead bodies and to loot often experiences the same fate. It is an abstract and untrue philosophy that treats all criminals alike and judges all cases to be the same. The law of retribution does not demand the same thing from all but demands that to each be given his or her due; it does not demand a precise payment in kind but punishment proportionate to the seriousness of the offense. To the degree that a person is guilty, to that degree he or she deserves punishment. Retribution, therefore, is not inconsistent with the interests of the criminal, the state, or the social order. Retributive penalties and appropriate penalties need not be mutually exclusive, for retribution must occur in accordance with justice, and justice takes into account also the person and the circumstances. The interest of the state, self-defense, deterrence, amelioration are all components that can be incorporated into and be constituents of retributive justice. In Israel's legislation also the prevention and the deterrence of crimes had a niche (Deut. 13:11; 17:13; 19:20; 21:21).

On the other hand, those who want to remove retribution and punishment from the treatment of the criminals themselves undermine justice and involve themselves in endless difficulties. For if the judge is required to make the improvement of the criminal his aim, he enters a labyrinth in which he is bound to lose his way. How, if he loses sight of the crime and only undertakes to study the person of the criminal, will he ever be able to pronounce a just sentence and determine the measure of moral guilt? He would have to know the human heart to pronounce a fair sentence by that standard. Furthermore, how would he ever be able to determine which penalty would be suited for a specific person in a specific case, that is, suited to bring about the criminal's improvement? If utility had to be the principle and standard of punishment, the judge would slip into all sorts of arbitrariness and the criminal in question would forever be in a state of uncertainty. And what are we to understand by improvement? Does this mean that the criminal will later desist from his misdeeds out of fear of punishment or on the basis of moral principle? But how can this ever be determined? Can improvement be inferred from signs of remorse, from a confession of guilt, from a period of good conduct? A great danger exists that the smartest criminals will fare the best. And who is to decide about that improvement? The jail warden, the fellow prisoners, a committee of oversight? Everyone can sense that any one of these choices is burdened by problems. Modern criminology, by calling the notions of retribution and punishment antiquated and adopting as its goal the moral improvement of the criminal, takes from the government's arm the power of justice and assigns to it a task for which it is utterly unqualified and unfit.

[337] For all these reasons, punitive justice cannot do without the element of retribution. Punishment is imposed, in the first place, not because it is useful, but because justice requires it, because the criminal has incurred a moral-judicial debt. Professor Kahl, speaking at the Evangelical Social Congress at Darmstadt, made this point as follows: "The principle aim of punishment is retribution. Not vengeful reprisal, nor coarse retaliation, or external repayment; it is rather the authoritative restoration of the broken judicial order, in accordance with the laws of a higher set of values, by a punishment that fits the measure of indebtedness. Other goals accompany this aim, such as the protection of society, deterrence, and improvement. For the administration of justice and expediency are not mutually exclusive. But these accompanying goals must be dovetailed with and subordinate to the fundamental idea of justice."[7] This justice is of such superlative value that it exacts the goods and life of persons for its maintenance and restoration. But this moral world order is not an idea concocted by humans, not a state of affairs produced by men. Nor is it an independent self-based power of which no one can say what it is. Rather, it is the revelation and operation of the justice of God in this world; it is rooted in the perfect, holy will of him who upholds and governs all things. Those who violate it are violating God himself. It

7. See the Acts of the Congress (ed. Kahl) cited in the following note.

is therefore highly elevated above humanity and of greater value than all creatures together. If it should come to a conflict, it is humans who would be ruined. "Let justice prevail, though the world perish." "If justice should collapse, human life on earth would become worthless" (Kant). Punishment was instituted to maintain it. The purpose of punishment is the restoration of justice, the maintenance of divine justice. Failing to serve that end, it becomes coercion and a mere exercise of superior power.[8]

Punishment always consists in a kind of suffering, in the deprivation of a certain good, be it in property or in freedom, in body or in life. It is an "evil of suffering inflicted on account of an evil of action." Just why the judicial order demands suffering specifically from the person who violates it and is thereby restored and pacified is hard to say. This is certainly not caprice or accident. Behind that judicial order stands the living, true, and holy God, who will by no means clear the guilty, and for him punishment rests not on "an absolute dominion" in the sense of Duns Scotus but on the demands of his justice. If he did not punish sin, he would give to evil the same rights he accords to the good and so deny himself. The punishment of sin is necessary so that God may remain God. The moment the moral or judicial order has been violated, therefore, it rises up and demands restoration. It avenges itself in punishment, internal as well as external punishment, weighs the transgressor down, and so exhibits its incomparable majesty. God cannot bear to let sinners, instead of submitting to his law and obeying it, defy that law, in principle making themselves God's equals. In punishment, accordingly, God maintains his sovereignty; by means of suffering he sets sinners down on the place where they belong and by punishment brings them—where

8. In addition to the older literature cited at the head of this section (ed. note: Bavinck refers to §43 of the Dutch edition, titled "De Straf der Zonde"; these works are listed at the end of the present note), cf. the following more contemporary works: F. J. Stahl, *Die Philosophie des Rechts,* 5th ed, 2 vols. in 3 (Tübingen: Mohr, 1878), II, 1, 160ff.; 2, 681ff.; H. Ulrici, *Gott und der Mensch,* 2 vols. (Leipzig: Weigel, 1866–73), II, 391ff.; J. Kohler, *Das Wesen der Strafe* (Würzburg: Druck & Verlag der Stahel'schen Universitäts-Buch- und Kunsthandlung, 1888); H. Seuffert, *Was will, was wirkt, und was soll die staatliche Strafe?* (Bonn: Cohen, 1897); F. van Calker, *Strafrecht und Ethik* (Leipzig: Dunkert & Humblod, 1897); P. Drews, *Die Reform des Strafrechts und die Ethik des Christentums* (Tübingen: Mohr, 1905); Dr. G. von Rohden, *Das Wesen der Strafe im ethischen und strafrechtlichen Sinne;* *Kahl, "Die Reform des deutschen Strafrechts im Lichte evang. Sozialpolitik," in *Die verhandl. des vierzehnten Evang.-soz. Kongresses in Darmstadt am 3. und 4. Juni 1903* (Göttingen: Vandenhoeck & Ruprecht, 1903), 94–114; V. Cathrein, *Die Grundbegriffe des Strafrechts* (Freiburg i.B.: Herder, 1905); J. Domela Nieuwenhuis, *Het wezen der straf* (Groningen: Wolters, 1899); B. Gewin, *Beginselen der Strafrecht* (Leiden: Brill, 1907); R. van der Meij, *Een Studie over de Gronslagen der zoogenaamde "Nieuwe Richting" in de Strafredchtswetenschap* (Leiden: S. C. van Doesburgh, 1904); R. Koppe, *Eenige Strafrechtelijke Beschouwingen in Verband met het Beginsel van de Wet van 12. Febr. 1901* (Groningen: Jan Haan, 1906); D. P. D. Fabius, *Schuld en Straf* (Leiden: Donner, 1900); idem, *De Dodstraf* (Amsterdam: Van Schaïk, 1906). Ed. note: Bavinck lists the following "older" works at the head of §43: Augustine, *City of God,* XIII; P. Lombard, *Sent.,* II, dist. 30; III, dist. 16; T. Aquinas, *Summa theol.,* II, 2, qu. 164; idem, *Summa contra gentiles,* IV, 51; Bonaventure, *Brevil.,* III, 5, 7; Bellarmine, "De amiss. gr.," *Controversiis,* IV; *Theol. Wirceb.* (1880), VII, 125ff.; Heinrich, *Dogmatik,* VI, 703; Scheeben, *Dogmatik,* II, 596ff., 670ff.; A. M. Weiss, *Apologie des Christentums,* 5 vols. in 7 (Freiburg i.B.: Herder, 1904–8), II³, 414ff.; Luther, according to Köstlin, II, 375; Gerhard, *Loci theol.,* IX, 3 and 8; X, 4; Hollaz, *Ex. theol.,* 502ff.; Polanus, *Syn. theol.,* 340; Mastricht, *Theologia,* IV, 4; B. de Moor, *Comm. theol.,* III, 328ff., C. Vitringa, *Doctr. Christ.,* II, 295.

they do not accept it voluntarily—to the involuntary confession that they are his inferiors, that they are not God but creatures. Those who will not listen must accept the consequences. Punishment is powerful proof that only justice has the right to exist, that only God is good and great.

SIN AND ITS CONSEQUENCES

In part, punishment flows from sin itself. Sin by its very nature produces separation from God and thus carries with it darkness, ignorance, error, deception, fear, disquietude, a sense of guilt, regret, misery, and enslavement. Bondage to sin is unspeakably hard. But in part punishment is also added to the transgression by a qualified authority from without. This is what happens in the family, in school, in society, and in the state; and so it is with the punishments with which God visits sin. Many people have denied this last point and acknowledge only "natural" punishments, and want nothing to do with concrete punishments.[9] On this position there is actually no reward and punishment. Virtue brings its own reward, vice its own punishment. There is neither heaven nor hell except in the mind of people themselves. The history of the world is the judgment of the world. At most there exists a subjective necessity in the guilty person to construe his or her suffering as punishment. In this philosophy the following words of the poet are true: "Life is not the greatest of all goods; the greatest of all evils, however, is guilt." "To be punished is not an evil; but it is an evil to be made worthy of punishment." "Fault has more of the nature of evil than pain has."[10] Guilt turns suffering into punishment; take away the guilt, and the fact of suffering can remain the same yet totally change in character. The fact of death is the same for believers and unbelievers; for the latter, however, it is a punishment, for the former a passing into eternal life. For that reason one may not infer personal sin from the suffering a given person has to endure (Luke 13:4; John 9:1). In God's providence and by his grace and wisdom, suffering serves not only as punishment but also as a trial, as chastisement and nurture. He is so powerful that he can make all things work together for good (Rom. 8:28).

9. B. Spinoza, *Ethics,* trans. and ed. James Gutman (New York: Hafner, 1949), prop. 42. This view was held by many rationalists in the eighteenth century, according to K. G. Bretschneider, *Systematische Entwickelung,* 4th ed. (Leipzig: J. A. Barth, 1841), 391; idem, *Handbuch der Dogmatik,* 4th ed., 2 vols. (Leipzig: J. A. Barth, 1838), I, 527; D. F. Strauss, *Die christliche Glaubenslehre in ihrer Geschichtlichen Entwicklung und im Kampfe mit der modernen Wissenschaft,* 2 vols. (Tübingen: C. F. Osiander, 1840–41), I, 603; J. H. Scholten, *De Leer der Hervormde Kerk in Hare Grondbeginselen,* 2nd ed., 2 vols. (Leyden: P. Engels, 1850–51), II, 108ff., 569ff.; idem, *De vrije wil, kritisch onderzoek* (Leiden: P. Engels, 1859), 236; cf. also F. Schleiermacher, *The Christian Faith* (Edinburgh: T&T Clark, 1989), §84; A. E. Biedermann, *Christliche Dogmatik* (Zürich: Füssli, 1869), II, 575ff.; R. A. Lipsius, *Lehrbuch der evangelisch-protestantischen Dogmatik* (Braunschweig: C. A. Schwetschke, 1893), §393; A. Ritschl, *Die christliche Lehre von der Rechtfertigung und Versöhnung,* 4th ed., 3 vols. (Bonn: A. Marcus, 1895–1903), I², 397; III², 326ff.; ed. note: ET: *The Christian Doctrine of Justification and Reconciliation* (Clifton, NJ: Reference Book Publishers, 1966); J. Kaftan, *Dogmatik,* §36.

10. T. Aquinas, *Summa theol.,* I, qu. 48, art. 6.

But for all this, the objective God-made connection between sin and suffering is not broken. Scripture on almost every page offers proof of this. History, while not *the* judgment of the world, is *a* judgment. It makes known to us facts that make even the most skeptical person confess: this is the finger of God. While suffering may frequently not be caused by personal sin, it does have its cause in the sin of a generation, a people, or humankind. The conscience of every individual testifies that there has to be a connection between holiness and blessedness, between virtue and happiness. Immanuel Kant was so convinced of this connection that from the disharmony existing between the two on earth, he concluded there had to be a hereafter. The pious do not serve God for the sake of reward but neither are they indifferent to it, as the advocates of "disinterested love" say they are. Paul says that believers are of all people most to be pitied if for this life only they have hope in Christ [1 Cor. 15:19]. After the fall God has forged a bond between "ethos" and "nature," between the moral and the natural order, between fallen humans and a ruined earth, a bond such that together they are subservient to the honor of his name and the coming of his kingdom. The concrete punishments with which God often already in this life visits sin, accordingly, are not arbitrary but—even when we have no insight into the connection—occupy a well-ordered place in the history of human sin and guilt. Those who deny their existence or ascribe to them no more than a subjective existence run the danger of regarding sin itself as not much more than a figment of the imagination and an illusion. To such, history becomes a cacophony that is never resolved into a higher chord and the world a mysterious entity whose existence and nature mock all rationality.[11]

Guilty Conscience

[338] The punishments that God has ordained for sin in this life are guilt, pollution, suffering, death, and the dominion of Satan. Guilt is the first and heaviest punishment. The word "guilt" [Old English *gylt*, crime] in the first place means that someone is the author or doer of something, like an αἰτια (Gr.), *causa* (Lat.). Usually it includes the idea that someone is the cause of something that ought not to be or to happen (it is his fault). In this sense guilt presupposes that we are obligated to do or to refrain from doing something. We are obligated to keep the whole law (Luke 17:10; Gal. 5:3). And if we fail to keep it, we are guilty. Inasmuch as we are the active cause of the violation, we are under indictment (αἰτιασθαι, *accusare, reus*); the act is imputed to us. We must account for it[12] and are obligated to satisfy the law; we are liable to punishment. Guilt is an

---

11. J. F. Stapfer, *Onderwys in de gantsche wederleggende godsgeleertheit,* 5 vols. in 6 (Utrecht: Gisb. Tieme van Paddenburg and Abraham van Paddenburg, 1757–63), IV, 448ff.; K. G. Bretschneider, *Dogmatik,* I, 525ff.; *van Voorst, *Over de Goddelijke straffen* (Haagsch Gen., 1798); *van de Wijnpersse, *Over de straffende gerechtigheid* (1798); I. A. Dorner, *A System of Christian Doctrine,* I, 299ff.; III, 120ff.

12. Accountability and imputability, or liability, though closely related concepts, are not identical. Accountability is the moral and judicial state of a free rational being who is obligated to account for his or her actions to others; it always presupposes a relation to other persons such that it gives them the right to call

obligation incurred through a violation of the law to satisfy the law by suffering a proportionate penalty. It binds the sinner, immediately after the violation of the law, to its demand for satisfaction and punishment. People believe that by violating the law they become free from the law, but precisely the opposite occurs: in another way they are now much more tightly bound to its demand. God, who cannot cease to be himself, even though he accords to humans the freedom to oppose him, never relinquishes his hold on them, and the latter never become free from him. At the very moment when they position themselves outside the law (i.e., outside love), it strikes them with its curse and binds them to its punishment. Guilt is an "obligation for the purpose of enduring a fair punishment," "the subjection of a sinner to a penalty."[13] The Roman Catholic Church makes a distinction between "being accused of a fault" (*reatus culpae*) and "judged fit for a punishment" (*reatus poenae*).[14] But this distinction obviously betrays the intent to justify the "satisfactory" punishments for believers here on earth and in purgatory and is directly at variance with the nature of guilt and punishment. It is indeed true that the sins of believers, that is, of those who have received forgiveness in full, *in themselves* always remain sins and therefore culpable. Against the Antinomians, who denied this and therefore deemed prayer for forgiveness unnecessary in the case of believers, the Reformed have always maintained this, making the distinction between "potential" and "actual" guilt.[15] But when the guilt of sins has been removed, all satisfaction and punishment automatically expire as well, for guilt is nothing other than an "obligation to endure punishment." In that case, God is no longer a Judge but a Father, who, though he chastises the son whom he loves (2 Sam. 12:13–14), does not punish him, nor does he

---

someone to account on the basis of certain actions. Accountability always implies a dependence of a person vis-à-vis others. Imputation, by contrast, is the action of others who attribute or charge a certain act to the responsible will of a free, rational being. This imputation may and must take place if and to the extent (for there are degrees) that such a person is legally liable. Liability is a broader concept than accountability. If a person is not obligated to account for his or her actions to others (say a king, who has immunity) or cannot do so (as a result of illness, insanity, death), he or she still remains liable. The act committed remains his or her responsibility, but others lack the authority or power to call such a person to account, to judge, and possibly to punish him or her. Cf. R. Eisler, *Wörterbuch der Philosophischen Begriffe*, 3 vols. (Berlin: E. S. Mittler, 1910), s.v. "Zurechnung"; V. Cathrein, "Die strafrechtliche Zurechnungsfähigkeit," *Stimmen aus Maria-Laach* 24 (1904): 357–73; De Bussy, "Over Verantwoordelijkheid," *Teyler's Theologisch Tijdschrift* 1 (1903).

13. A. Polanus, *Synt. theol.*, 338; B. de Moor, *Comm. theol.*, III, 135; F. Turretin, *Institutes of Elenctic Theology*, trans. George M. Giger, ed. James T. Dennison, 3 vols. (Phillipsburg, NJ: Presbyterian & Reformed, 1992), XI, qu. 3; P. van Mastricht, *Theologia*, IV, 2, 7; J. Müller, *The Christian Doctrine of Sin*, trans. Rev. Wm. Urwick, 5th ed., 2 vols. (Edinburgh: T&T Clark, 1868), I, 195; A. F. C. Vilmar, *Theologische Moral: Akademische Vorlesungen* (Gütersloh: C. Bertelsmann, 1871), I, 195; M. Kähler, "Schuld," *PRE*[3], XVII, 784–89; A. Wuttke, *Christian Ethics*, trans. John P. Lacroix (New York: Nelson & Phillips, 1873), II, 97; J. H. Scholten, *De Vrije Wil*, 217ff.; S. Hoekstra, *Vrijheid in verband met zelfbewustheid, zedelijkheid en zonde* (Amsterdam: P. N. van Kampen, 1858), 303ff.

14. P. Lombard, *Sent.*, II, dist. 42; T. Aquinas, *Summa theol.*, II, 1, qu. 87, art. 6; Council of Trent, c. 14, can. 30, XIV; "De poenit.," c. 8, can. 18–15; R. Bellarmine, "De amiss. gr.," *Controversiis*, V, 19; *Theologia Wirceburgensi*, 3rd ed., 10 vols. in 5 (Paris: Berche at Tralin, 1880), VII, 27.

15. B. de Moor, *Comm. theol.*, III, 135.

demand satisfaction from him for whom the perfect righteousness of Christ has been acquired. In the same way, Augustine says of the baptized person that "he lacks all sin, not all evil, for it is rather plainly stated thus that he is without the guilt of all evils, not without all evils."[16]

The fact that sin truly has guilt as its concomitant is certain both from the witness of God in Scripture and in the human conscience. In Scripture the concepts of sin, guilt, and punishment are so deeply interwoven that the words for sin (like עָוֹן and חַטָּאת) imperceptibly acquire the sense of guilt (Gen. 4:13; Exod. 34:7; Lev. 24:15; Num. 9:13; etc.). The word in the Old Testament that actually denotes sin in the sense of guilt is אָשָׁם (Gen. 26:10; Lev. 4:13; 5:2; Num. 5:7; etc.), and ὀφείλημα (Matt. 6:12; cf. 5:26; Luke 7:41–42; 13:4)[17] in the New Testament. God by no means clears the guilty and pronounces a curse upon all who do not abide by all things written in the book of the law (Deut. 27:26; Gal. 3:10). Curse (אָלָה, ἀνάθεμα, *maledictum*) is the opposite of blessing (בְּרָכָה, εὐλογια, *benedictio*, Deut. 11:26; 30:19). Just as God's blessing bestows all kinds of well-being and life on a person, so a divine curse is the abandonment of a person to corruption, ruin, death, judgment, Satan. Human beings can only wish another person blessing or curses, but God's blessing and cursing is always performative; it accomplishes what it wishes. At first, God's blessing rested on the creation (Gen. 1:22, 28; 2:3), but that blessing changed into a curse (Gen. 3:17). Indeed, the blessing of God was again pronounced upon the earth and humankind later, but this proceeded from God's grace. Pagans, accordingly, do not know the concept of divine blessing. But they are all the more acutely familiar with the idea of a divine curse. Classic antiquity was dominated by dread of the vengeance of the Erinyes (the fates and the furies), the goddesses of the curse. In all pagan religions, fear (δεισιδαιμονια, *religio*) far outweighs trust in the gods. Religion increasingly turns into superstition. People everywhere consider themselves surrounded and dominated by destructive gods whom they seek in vain to appease by sacrifices and [self-inflicted] torments. There really is a divine curse resting on humanity and the world. It is impossible to interpret life and history in light of the love of God alone. At work throughout the creation is a principle of divine wrath that only a superficial person can deny. Not communion but separation prevails between God and humankind; the covenant has been broken; God has a quarrel with his creatures. All stand guilty and punishable before his face (Matt. 5:21–22; Mark 3:29; James 2:10).

16. Augustine, *Against Julian*, trans. M. A. Schumacher, vol. 16 of *The Writings of Saint Augustine* (Washington, DC: Catholic University of America Press, 1984), VI, c. 16; cf. H. Alting, *Theologia elenctica nova* (Amsterdam: J. Jansson, 1654), XVII, 5; F. Turretin, *Institutes of Elenctic Theology*, IX, qu. 3; B. de Moor, *Comm. theol.*, III, 136; W. G. T. Shedd, *Dogmatic Theology*, 3rd ed., 3 vols. (New York: Scribner, 1891–94), II, 414.

17. H. Schultz, *Alttestamentliche Theologie*, 4th ed., 2 vols. (Göttingen: Vandenhoeck & Ruprecht, 1889), 684ff.

The whole world is accountable to God (Rom. 3:19); it is subject to divine judgment and has no defense.[18]

Subjectively this is confirmed by the divine witness in the conscience of every human being. Guilt and the consciousness of guilt are not the same. Those who try to deduce guilt from the consciousness of it block themselves from understanding guilt in its true significance and gravity. Ignorance can to some extent excuse sin (Luke 23:34; Acts 17:30), just as conscious and intentional violation aggravates sin (Luke 12:47; John 15:22; 9:41). But there also exist sins that are hidden from ourselves and others (Ps. 19:12), and also sins of ignorance are culpable (Acts 17:27–30; Rom. 1:19–21, 28; 1 Tim. 1:13–15). Yet objective guilt is more or less firmly reflected in the human consciousness. Immediately after the fall, the eyes of Adam and Eve were opened, and they discovered that they were naked. Implied here is that they knew and recognized that they had done wrong. Shame is the fear of disgrace, an unpleasant and painful sense of being involved in something wrong or improper. Added to the shame was fear before God and the consequent desire to hide from him—that is to say, the human conscience was aroused. Before the fall, strictly speaking, there was no conscience in humans. There was no gap between what they were and what they knew they had to be. Being and self-consciousness were in harmony. But the fall produced separation. By the grace of God, humans still retain the consciousness that they ought to be different, that in all respects they must conform to God's law. But reality witnesses otherwise; they are not who they ought to be. And this witness is the conscience. The conscience, accordingly, is not the consciousness of God's communion with a person, as Schenkel conceived it.[19] The opposite, rather, is true; it is proof that communion with God has been broken, that there is a gap between God and us, between his law and our state. This is clearly evident when our conscience accuses us. But also when in a given case it excuses us, that is, keeps silent, that separation from God underlies it (Rom. 2:14–15). The human conscience is the subjective proof of humanity's fall, a witness to human guilt before the face of God. God is not the only accuser of humankind; in their conscience humans condemn themselves and take God's side against themselves. The more precisely and meticulously the human conscience functions, the more it validates God's idea of humans in Scripture. The best and most noble members of our race, confirming God's truthfulness, have declared the race guilty at their very own expense.[20]

Pollution

[339] Another punishment of sin is pollution. As in the case of the first sin, so also with sins in general, the external violation is a revelation and proof of an

18. R. Kittel, "Segen und Fluch," *PRE*[3], XVIII, 148–54; W. B. Stevenson, "Benediction," *DC*, I, 189–91; James Denney, "Curse," *DB*, I, 534–35; J. Heinrici, "ἀνάθεμα," *PRE*[3], I, 493–95.

19. D. Schenkel, "Gewissen," *PRE*[3], VI, 646–54; idem, *Die christliche Dogmatik vom Standpunkte des Gewissens aus dargestellt,* 2 vols. (Wiesbaden: Kreidel & Niedner, 1858–59).

20. Cf. also H. Bavinck, *Beginselen der Psychologie* (Kampen: Bos, 1897), 111, 303.

internal one. Sin not only consists in an act but also in the thought, the desire, the inclination, and so on. On each of these levels, sin is both guilt and pollution. Adam did not become guilty only when he ate the forbidden fruit but already brought guilt upon himself when he desired the fruit of the tree. Guilt and pollution always go together as the two inseparable sides of sin; where the one is, there the other is as well. Sin is guilt inasmuch as it militates against God's righteousness; it is pollution inasmuch as it is contrary to his holiness. Guilt obligates us to [endure] punishment; pollution renders us unclean. By guilt the objective relation between us and God is disturbed; by pollution our subjective communion with God is vitiated. Sin is simultaneously a violation of the covenant of works *and* the destruction of God's image. The former implies that God is no longer our covenant Partner. God, consequently, cannot turn in favor and love to the guilty party; the second means that the sinner is no longer in the covenant, can no longer love and keep the law, and can therefore no longer secure life in this way. By the works of the law, no flesh can any longer be justified (Ps. 143:2; Rom. 3:20; 2 Cor. 3:6f.; Gal. 3:2, 10). This is true even though it be the case that the law of the covenant of works still continues to obligate us—aside from our having to make restitution for the evil done by undergoing punishment—to across-the-board obedience to its commandments (Matt. 5:48; 22:37) and even though God himself keeps his promise and continues to link life to the observance of the law (Lev. 18:5; Matt. 19:17; Luke 10:28); indeed, though the covenant of works is indissoluble in the sense that in the covenant of grace God has laid the demand for satisfaction and absolute obedience to the law on Christ, yet it is broken in the sense that humanity is unable to enter life by way of this method. Paradise has been sealed shut to us; access to the tree of life has been denied.[21]

At the same time and by the same token the image of God has been destroyed by sin. Rome understands by that statement that, while the supernatural gifts have been lost, the natural gifts have remained intact. Lutheran theologians originally held that humanity had totally lost the image of God inasmuch as that image consisted exclusively in moral attributes and that human beings were now like inanimate blocks. But the Reformed maintained that, while the image of God had been lost in the restricted sense, yet in the broader sense, though completely mutilated and corrupted, it has not been destroyed.[22] The image of God is not an external and mechanical appendage to us but integral to our very being: it is our health. Human beings who violate God's law do not cease to be human; they retain their body, soul, faculties, powers, intellect, will, and so on. But now these faculties are all devoted to the service of sin and function in the wrong direction.

21. B. de Moor, *Comm. theol.*, III, 105–8; J. Marck, *Historia Paradisi* (Amsterdam: Gerardus Borstius, 1705), II, ch. 15; A. von Comrie and N. Holtius, *Examen van het Ontwerp van Tolerantie*, 10 vols. (Amsterdam: Nicolaas Byl, 1753), X, 478–80; H. Witsius, *The Oeconomy of the Covenants between God and Man: Comprehending a Complete Body of Divinity*, 3 vols. (New York: Lee & Stokes, 1789), I, ch. 9; P. van Mastricht, *Theologia*, III, 12, 22.

22. Belgic Confession, art. 14.

As deprivation and disturbance of the image of God, the pollution of sin is characteristic for all humans excepting only Christ. Qualitatively, there is no difference, but this does not rule out a quantitative difference. Though all have turned away from God and are by nature on the road that leads to destruction, not all have progressed equally far down that wrong road and not all are equally far removed from the kingdom of heaven. There is endless diversity and degrees of difference in the sinful life between the start of it and the highest levels of its development. Individuals, families, generations, classes, peoples are utterly divergent also in sin. There are those who are not far from the kingdom of God; there also exist people who drink sin like water, who live lives totally given over to wickedness, who are utterly hardened and impervious to any good impression.

This difference, however, does not originate among people as a result of their personal deeds but is congenital. The original sin that comes to us from Adam is indeed the universal presupposition and source of all the actual sins of individuals, but these sinful deeds then also impact, reinforce, develop, and direct that innate moral depravity. Just as a sinful deed, when repeated over and over, fosters a sinful habitual propensity, say, to drink, sensuality, and lust, so sinful mores and habits can also reinforce an innate depravity in a family, among relatives in a family line, or among a people and develop it in a certain direction. Also, that special modification of innate depravity often passes from parents to children, from one generation to the next. Human beings are not individuals in an absolute sense. "The individual, like the atom, is a fiction."[23] A human being is born from the matrix of a community and from that very first moment lives in a certain circle, situation, and period. The immediate and the larger family, society, nation, climate, lifestyle, culture, the spirit of an age, and so on—all of them together impact the individual person and modify his or her innate moral depravity. Sin, therefore, though it is indeed always essentially the same, manifests itself in differing ways and forms in different persons, families, classes, and nations and in different states and times. Also, as a sinner each person has his or her own physiognomy. Sins in the East differ from those in the West, in tropical zones from temperate zones, in rural areas from cities, in civilized states from uncivilized ones, in the twentieth century from earlier centuries. There are family sins, societal sins, national sins. Statistics show that in certain situations, periods, and circles there is a horrifying regularity in the incidence of certain moral offenses such as homicide, suicide, illegitimate births, and so on.[24] In every area of life, we are all subject to the influence of bad habits and sinful examples, of the zeitgeist and public opinion. Aside from what we call "original sin," there is also "corporate guilt and the corporate action of sin." As people are interconnected, so also are their sinful inclinations and deeds. Penetrating the infinite riches of all creation, sin also forms a realm

23. *P. Natorp, *Archiv für systematische Philosophie*, III, 1, 81.
24. A. von Oettingen, *Die Moralstatistik in ihrer Bedeutung für eine Socialethik* (Erlangen: Deichert, 1882).

that, animated by a single life principle, organizes itself in multiple forms and appearances.[25]

SUFFERING

[340] According to Scripture, in addition to guilt and pollution, suffering also is a punishment for sin. As a result of it, humanity not only lost true knowledge, righteousness, and holiness, but also dominion and glory. This became evident already immediately after the fall and is further confirmed throughout Scripture. God put enmity between the human race and the serpent and thereby in principle took from humanity the dominion over the animal world originally granted to it (Gen. 1:26; 2:19). God further pronounces upon the woman the penalty of painful childbirths and of an ever-gnawing desire for her husband despite the former. The man himself gets his share of suffering from the curse pronounced upon the earth, a curse that obligates him to work arduously for his appointed share of daily bread. With this, a history of suffering is ushered in for all humanity and all the earth. And all the suffering that strikes people here on earth—a short life; a sudden, violent death; famine; plagues; wars; defeats; childlessness; painful losses; deprivation of goods; impoverishment; crop failure; cattle mortality; and so on—all has its root in sin, indeed not always in personal sins (for there is also a sparing of the wicked [Gen. 18:26ff.] and punishment as a testing of the righteous [Job 1; Matt. 13:21;[26] John 9:1; 11:4; 2 Cor. 12:7]), yet still in sin in general. Without sin there would be no suffering (Lev. 26:14f.; Deut. 28:15f.; Ezek. 4:17; Hosea 2:8f.; Rev. 18:8; 21:4). Even the irrational creation has been subjected to futility and decay and now collectively sighs, as though in labor pains, looking forward to the revelation of the glory of the children of God, in hope of being itself set free from bondage to decay (Rom. 8:19–22). Scripture is not pessimistic in the usual sense of the word, but it knows and acknowledges suffering, interpreting it in the most moving laments (Gen. 47:9; Job 3; 6; 7; 9; 14; etc.; Pss. 22; 38; 39; 69; 73; 74; 79; 89; 90; etc.; Ecclesiastes; Lamentations; Matt. 6:34; Rom. 7:24; 8:19ff.; 1 Cor. 15:19; etc.).

Such laments incessantly arise from all of humanity. Teachers of religion, moralists, philosophers, poets, artists, the gifted, and the disadvantaged, all speak in the same spirit. The lighthearted and superficial may not give it a second thought, but all serious-minded persons have always sensed something of the mysterious nexus between life and suffering. Nor was Greek antiquity an exception to this rule. The basic mood there was not as cheerful as people used to think but bitter and melancholy. "To live in sorrow is the lot that the gods have decreed for

25. F. Schleiermacher, *Christian Faith*, §§71–72; A. Ritschl, *The Christian Doctrine of Justification and Reconciliation*, III, 334ff. (#41: "The Kingdom of Sin"); F. H. R. Frank, *System der Christlichen Wahrheit*, 2nd ed., 2 vols. (Erlangen: A. Deichert, 1884), I, 463ff.; I. A. Dorner, *A System of Christian Doctrine*, trans. Rev. Alfred Cave and Rev. J. S. Banks, rev. ed., 4 vols. (Edinburgh: T&T Clark, 1888), III, 54ff.

26. Ed. note: Bavinck cites Luke 13:21 here.

mortals; only they themselves are free from cares" (Homer). "Aside from God, no one is happy" (Euripides). "No mortal remains untouched by misfortune; no one escapes his lot. Humans are transient as a shadow; vain as a dream; their happiness is illusion. The best thing is not to be born; but if one has been born, it is to die as young as possible" (Sophocles). "Death is perhaps the greatest good" (Socrates). "Sudden death is the greatest good fortune; a short life the greatest benefit; the desire for death the deepest wish" (Pliny).[27] In Voltaire, after the earthquake of Lisbon, eighteenth-century optimism turned into pessimism,[28] and Hegel's rationalism made way for Schelling's philosophy that made the will, not reason, the governing principle of the world.[29] Reason may be able to explain what and how things exist; *that* they exist can only be inferred from a will; and this existence of things is the truly positive, the irrational remnant that is ultimately left on the bottom of all existing things.

For, according to the eternal act of self-revelation, everything in the world as we now see it before us is rule, order, and form; but fundamental to it is the chaos, which could at some point break through again, and nowhere does it seem as if order and form were primordial, but rather as if something primordially chaotic had been brought to order. This, as it pertains to things, is the incomprehensible basis of reality, the permanently inscrutable remnant, that which does not even with the greatest effort resolve itself in understanding, but remains eternally fundamental. . . . Without this antecedent darkness, there is no creaturely reality; darkness is its necessary portion . . . all birth is birth out of darkness into light.[30]

For this reason Schelling also had a totally different view of life and the world than Hegel. To the latter everything was rational, but Schelling saw the irrational, the darkness, the chaotic, as fundamental to everything and acknowledges the via dolorosa of the world process.

It is a futile effort to attempt to explain diversity in nature in terms of a peaceful joining of diverse forces. All that becomes can only become in displeasure, and just as dread is the basic sensation of every living creature, so everything that is alive is only conceived and born in vehement conflict. Who could possibly believe that nature could have created such a wide range of marvelous products in this horrendous external confusion and chaotic internal mixture . . . in any way other

27. T. Pfanner, *Systema theologiae gentilis purioris* (Basel: Joh. Hermann Widerhold, 1679), ch. 17; K. F. von Nägelsbach, *Homerische Theologie* (Nürnberg: Geiger, 1861), 310ff.; F. Paulsen, *System der Ethik mit einem Umriss der Staats- und Gesellschaftslehre*, 2 vols. (Berlin: Hertz, 1889), I, 80ff.; A. M. Weiss, *Apol. des Christ.*, I, 475–501; II, 464–517.

28. Voltaire, *Candide*, trans. Robert Martin Adams (New York: Norton, 1966).

29. Cf. H. Bavinck, *Reformed Dogmatics*, II, 228–33 (#207).

30. F. W. J. Schelling, "Philosophische Untersuchungen über das Wesen der menschlichen Freiheit," in *Ausgewählte Werke*, 4 vols. (1809; repr., Darmstadt: Wissenschaftliche Buchgesellschaft, 1968), IV, 303ff. (*Werke*, I/7, 359ff.).

than in the fiercest conflict of forces? Are not most products of inorganic nature obviously the offspring of dread, of fear, indeed of despair?"[31]

Even in God there is "a wellspring of sadness that, however, is never realized but only serves to enhance the eternal joy of victory. Hence the veil of melancholy spread over the whole of nature, the deep undisturbable melancholy of all of life. Joy must have sorrow; sorrow must be expressed in joy."[32] The present world in which we live can only be understood as one that is extra-divine. Humanity by its fall is the cause of it.[33] "This extra-divine world is the world of divine displeasure; all humans, Jews and Gentiles, are the children of wrath, by nature the children of divine displeasure."[34]

All these ideas return in systematic contexts in the philosophers Schopenhauer and Hartmann and in poetic form in Rückert, Lenau, Byron, Shelley, George Sand, Alfred de Musset, Leopardi, and especially in the current fin-de-siècle literature as well. Buddhism, which regards the will to live—in fact being itself—as the cause of all suffering, is acclaimed as the highest wisdom. Life is suffering; it swings back and forth between sorrow and boredom; it is not worth the effort of living. The world with its hospitals, lazarets, surgical tortures, prisons, torture chambers, slave stalls, battlefields, courts, dwellings of wretchedness, and so on offers apt material for a description of hell and is itself a hell in which one denizen is a devil to another. If it were a trifle worse, it would collapse under the weight of its own misery. Accordingly, all that exists deserves to perish.[35]

On the origin and purpose of suffering, there have been many views. Philosophy is almost always intent on casting the blame for it, as well as for that of sin, either directly or indirectly on God. Suffering in that scenario is derived from an independent evil principle (Parsiism, Manicheism), from an original evil being (Daub), from a dark strain in God (Böhme, Schelling), from the blind, irrational will to be (Buddhism, Schopenhauer, Hartmann), from the self-objectivization and self-realization of God (Hegel), from matter (Plato, Aristotle, Philo), from the necessities of nature (Weisse, Rothe), from the finiteness of creatures (Leibniz), from the developmental state of the world (Ulrici), from the sinful human consciousness that construes the inherently necessary imperfections of the world

31. F. W. J. Schelling, "Die Weltalter. Erstes Buch (1813)," *Ausgewählte Werke,* V, 128; cf. 135, 141 (*Werke,* I, 8, 322; cf. 328, 335); idem, *Werke,* II, 1, 582.

32. F. W. J. Schelling, "Freiheit," in *Ausgewählte Werke,* IV, 343 (*Werke,* I/7, 399).

33. F. W. J. Schelling, *Werke,* II, 3, 352ff.

34. Ibid., II, 3, 372; cf. E. von Hartmann, *Gesammelte Studien und Aufsätze* (Berlin: C. Duncker, 1876), 683ff.

35. A. Schopenhauer, *The World as Will and Representation,* trans. E. F. J. Payne, 2 vols. (1896; New York: Dover Publications, 1966), I, 401ff. (section 57); II, 573f., (ch. 46: "On the Vanity and Suffering of Life"); idem, *Parerga and Paralipomena,* trans. E. F. J. Payne, 2 vols. (Oxford: Clarendon Press, 1974), II, 303ff. (chs. 11–12); E. von Hartmann, *Philosophie des Unbewussten,* 9th ed., 2 vols. (Berlin: C. Duncker, 1882), II, 273–390; F. Ueberweg-Heinze, *Geschichte der Philosophie,* 9th ed., 5 vols. (Berlin: E. S. Mittler & Son, 1898–1903), III, 2, 183ff., 481.

as being evil (Schleiermacher, Lipsius, Ritschl), and so on.[36] The fact, however, that suffering cannot be attributed in that sense to God and that it is given with the creation itself is certain on the basis of the doctrine of Scripture, the witness of our conscience, and the essential truth of religion that most intimately unites holiness and blessedness. Yet an existence and development of the world and humankind without suffering seems to be an impossible idea. We cannot even picture a history without sin and misery. The moment we try to do this, the framework of time and space is left empty. Pain and death seem to be integral to a physical organism. Impassibility is an attribute one cannot possibly assign to a sensible creature. This is already true of humans but even more so of plants and animals. Modern science has everywhere made us see, in organic as well as in inorganic nature, an ongoing struggle for life in which all creatures are pitted against one another and aiming at one another's death.

Yet, however natural pain and suffering may seem, one can on good grounds lodge the following objections against the above view.

1. If we could someday remove from the world and humankind all the suffering that has undoubtedly been directly and indirectly caused by sin, then in a flash far and away the most painful suffering would have disappeared, and the problem of suffering would be reduced to very small dimensions. No one can deny that between sin and misery there is a very close link. Many sins, as everyone agrees, bring with them all sorts of frightening consequences, not only mentally, such as fear, regret, shame, disgrace, remorse, and so on, but also materially, such as illness, misery, pain, poverty, degradation, and so on. This is true not only in the case of carnal sins, such as sensual indulgence, drunkenness, lust, and so on, but also in the case of sins that bear a more spiritual character, such as idolatry, superstition, unbelief, deception, greed, vanity, pride, hatred, envy, short-temperedness, and so on. All of them to a greater or lesser degree impact also the body and devastate it. A stream of spiritual and physical misery in individual persons, families, generations, and nations, in state, church, society, science, and art has its origin in sin. Remove it and—as everyone agrees—there is almost no suffering left. "The world is perfect everywhere—where humans have not trod with their troubles" (Schiller). "The primary source of the most serious evils affecting humans is human beings themselves." "Man to man is a wolf" (homo homini lupus).[37]

2. Yet, however much truth there is in Schiller's saying, it is not altogether correct. Even if in our thinking we remove all the suffering that by common consent directly or indirectly has its cause in sin, the world would still not be perfect all at

---

36. Earlier already we have given attention to the fact that, on the grounds of the irrefragable laws of nature and the horror of natural disasters, many thinkers made the world in part independent of God, ascribed to it a principle and power of its own, and to that extent curtailed God's omniscience, omnipotence, and absoluteness. Many of them are returning from monism to dualism and pluralism. Cf. H. Bavinck, *Reformed Dogmatics*, I, 555–59 (#146); idem, *Philosophy of Revelation*, 106–7, 211–13; E. Giran, *A Modern Job: An Essay on the Problem of Evil*, trans. Alfred Leslie Lilley and Fred Rothwell (Chicago: Open Court Publishing Co., 1916).

37. A. Schopenhauer, *World as Will and Representation*, II, 577.

once. Still remaining would be all those disasters that strike humans from without and are not, to everyone's mind, traceable to sin, such as earthquakes, hurricanes, thunderstorms, floods, famines, plagues, train accidents, and so on. Here, too, admittedly, as Scripture testifies, there is a connection with sin; but that is different from the above-mentioned suffering. The Pharisees and the Mutazilites[38] tried to explain these disasters in terms of personal sins, but Jesus judged otherwise (Luke 13:4; John 9:1). The disharmony and enmity of nature is rooted, not in personal sins, but in the sin of the human race. On account of this sin, God struck the earth with a curse and subjected the creation as a whole to futility and decay. Fallen people no longer belong in paradise. Corresponding to their state is the earth, which exists between heaven and hell. Along with knowledge and righteousness, humanity has also lost dominion and glory. The forces and elements of nature are often at war with it. Humanity can no longer subdue these forces and elements except by burdensome and exhausting labor. In its totality humanity no longer deserves a better place than this earth; nor is a better one possible for its development, nurture, and salvation. Of particular disasters we can almost never tell the purpose for which God sent them, although they are certainly never totally "speechless" for those who are struck by them. It is all the more presumptuous, therefore, with Schopenhauer and Hartmann to take scales in hand in order to weigh the weal and woe of the whole world against each other, thus to arrive at the conclusion that the sorrow far outweighs the joy. For every creature and every person, even the most seasoned pessimist, when given a choice between painful existence and painless nonexistence, actually prefers the former and tries to persevere in that existence. In the struggle with nature, humanity as a whole has found a spur for its energy, material for its labor, a stimulus for its development. By God's grace the curse upon the earth has been turned into a blessing for it.

3. The fact that all of nature shares in humanity's fall is not only certain on the basis of Scripture but also follows naturally from the central place that humanity occupies in the creation and is more than probable with a view to modern-day science as well. About the state of the world before the fall and about its change through and after the fall, people have sometimes said strange things, but the Reformed, generally speaking, have observed a prudent sobriety[39] here and followed the golden rule that though, indeed, the form of things was changed by sin, the essence remained the same. Sin, after all, is not a substance and can neither increase nor decrease the substance of things of which God alone is the author. Just as following the fall, human beings essentially remained human, so it is with nature as a whole. No new species were added in the world of plants and animals. Thorns and thistles were not created new by a word of God, like the vegetation, the herbs, and the fruit trees on the third day (Gen. 1:11). Creeping things and wild animals also

---

38. Ed. note: The Mutazilites ("separatists") were an early sect of Islam, emphasizing human free will and the sufficiency of reason as the means for knowing God.

39. Cf. H. Bavinck, *Reformed Dogmatics*, II, 565–68, 572–76 (##295, 297).

existed already prior to the fall (Gen. 1:24). But just as in the case of humanity the same capacities and forces—now corrupted by sin—began to function in another direction, so also with creation as a whole after it was struck by God with a curse. Left to itself, emancipated from the dominion and care of humans, and burdened by a divine curse, nature gradually became degraded and adulterated and brought forth thorns and thistles, all sorts of vermin, and carnivorous animals. The possibility of such adulteration has been raised beyond any doubt by modern science. Paleontology offers very few fossils of carnivorous animals; the large animals of the earliest times—the rhinoceros, the mammoth, and the mastodon—were all herbivorous. Of the so-called *Sauria*, which are considered lizards, this is uncertain; but even whales live in part on plants. Insects are all herbivorous; indeed, there are some who in an undeveloped state, such as caterpillars, larvae, and ichneumon wasps, feed on constituents of animal entities, but beetles, ants, bees, butterflies, and others all live on plant food. Among birds, there are many species that consume animal food, but they can live on plants as well. Among carnivorous animals there are three genera of *Felis* (lion, tiger, cat, panther, leopard, and so on), *Canis* (dog, wolf, fox), and *Ursus* (bear and so on). But of all these animals, it is at least questionable whether eating meat is a part of their nature. Charles Darwin—in his work *The Variation of Animals and Plants under Domestication,* a work that is most instructive for theologians in this respect also—has demonstrated that animals can grow accustomed to a changed diet, citing various examples to this effect.[40] Similarly, as a result of degeneration, branches can change into thorns, and as a result of cultivation, thorns can change into branches.[41]

In many respects nature has now become the antithesis of humanity (2 Kings 17:25; Job 5:22–23; Hosea 2:18; Isa. 11:6ff.; 7:23; 65:20f.; Ezek. 14:15, 21; Rev. 21; Sir. 39:29f.). Plants and animals have become living symbols of sinful human inclinations and passions. Fear of animals and worship of animals demonstrate humanity's abnormal relation to its natural environment. But the amazing power over animals, which is still found at times among humans, the numerous changes that, according to paleontology, have emerged in the plant and animal kingdom, the domestication and gradual variability in plants and animals—all amply prove that a state such as Isaiah depicts in chapters 11 and 65 is by no means impossible. There is nothing absurd in the notion that in nature, as in the case of humans, a significant change has occurred as a result of a divine judgment. Scripture in any case is much more rational than what is sometimes peddled in the name of science: according to Lindenschmit, human beings were at one time predatory animals who had to protect themselves from each other by living in houses built on stilts set in the water, whereas in that period predatory animals were extremely innocent creatures.[42]

---

40. C. Darwin, *The Variation of Animals and Plants under Domestication,* 2 vols. (New York: D. Appleton and Company, 1896).

41. Ibid., 310.

42. A. M. Weiss, *Apologie des Christentums,* II, 497.

4. It must not be overlooked in this connection that, theologically speaking, the creation itself was in a sense infralapsarian.[43] For God the fall was neither a surprise nor a disappointment. He anticipated it, incorporated it into his counsel, and already took account of it in creating the world. Creation, therefore, took place in such a way that, in case Adam as its head fell, the whole world could become as it is now. Prior to the fall, the state of humanity and of the earth as a whole was a provisional one that could not remain as it was. It was such that it could be raised to a higher glory but in the event of human transgression could also be subjected to futility and decay. As a result of sin and the curse of God, there everywhere emerged from under and behind the primordial harmony, the "unruly," the chaotic, and the demonic, which confuses and frightens us. Spread over the whole creation there is now a veil of melancholy. "The whole creation has been groaning in labor pains" [Rom. 8:22].[44]

DEATH

[341] This suffering culminates in that other penalty on sin, which is called death. Many theologians are of the opinion that Scripture—aside from a few places—does not view death as a consequence and penalty of sin. Granted, in Genesis 2:17 sudden, immediate death is threatened as punishment for sin, and this death is always indeed viewed as a disaster and a punishment. But death in itself is much more natural and automatically given with the material organism of a human being (Gen. 3:19; 18:27; Job 4:19; Pss. 89:48f.; 90:3; 103:14f.; 146:4; Eccles. 3:20; 12:7). So, in

43. F. Delitzsch, *A New Commentary on Genesis,* trans. Sophia Taylor (Edinburgh: T&T Clark, 1899), 80.

44. E. Nauville, *Le problème du mal* (Geneva: Librairie Cherbuliez, 1868); F. Delitzsch, *System der christlichen Apologetik* (Leipzig: Dörffling & Franke, 1870), 141ff.; J. H. Ebrard, *Apologetics: The Scientific Vindication of Christianity,* trans. William Stuart and John Macpherson, 2nd ed., 3 vols. (Edinburgh: T&T Clark, 1886–87), I, 275ff.; E. de Pressensè, *Études évangèliques* (Paris: C. Meyrueis, 1867), 1–168; P. W. von Keppler, *Das Problem des Leidens in der Moral* (Freiburg i.B.: Herder, 1894); T. S. Berry, *The Problem of Human Suffering in Light of Christianity* (London: Religious Tract Society, 1893); W. A. Holliday, "The Effect of the Fall of Man on Nature," *Presbyterian and Reformed Review* 7/3 (1896): 611–21; P. Cadène, *Le pessimisme légitime* (Montauban: J. Granié, 1894); J. Orr, *The Christian View of God and the World as Centering on the Incarnation* (New York: Randolph, 1893), 217, 495; F. W. Harnisch, *Das Leiden, beurteilt vom theistischen Standpunkt* (Halle: E. Karras, 1880); *Lamers, "Het probleem des lijdens," *Theologische Studiën* (1896); ed. note: Neither the full bibliography of *Theologische Studiën* nor the table of contents for volume 14 (1896) lists this essay; Illingworth, "The Problem of Pain," 3rd essay in C. Gore, *Lux Mundi,* 13th ed. (London: Murray, 1892), 82–92; H. Hayman, *"Why We Suffer," and Other Essays* (London: W. H. Allen & Co., 1890), 1–109; L. Lemme, "Leiden," *PRE*[3], XI, 360–63; P. Badet, *Le Problème de la souffrance humaine* (Paris: Libraire Bloud, 1915); ed note: Bavinck cites a German translation, *Das Problem des Leidens* (Strassburg, 1905); P. Grünberg, *Das Übel in der Welt und Gott* (Lichterfelde-Berlin: Runge, 1907); D. Vorwerk, "Die Naturkatastrophen und die moderne Literatur," *Beweis des Glaubens* 44 (1908): 104–10; E. W. Mayer, "Über das Leid der Welt," *Glauben und Wissen* 6 (1908): 402–10; *J. Breitenstein, *Le Problème de la souffrance* (Strassburg, 1903); A. M. Fairbairn, *The Philosophy of the Christian Religion* (London: Hodder & Stoughton, 1905), 94ff.; A. Bruining, *Het Geloof aan God en het Kwaad in de Wereld* (Baarn: Hollandia, 1907); *cf. *Teyler's Theologisch Tijdschrift* 6 (1908): 372ff.; H. Bavinck, *Philosophy of Revelation,* 108ff.

earlier times, judged the Pelagians, Socinians, Rationalists, and so judge many theologians today.[45] And there is some truth in this idea. Indeed, what is threatened in Genesis 2:17 is not death in general but specifically the death that takes effect upon sin immediately after the transgression. Genesis 3:19, accordingly, does not convey the full execution of the punishment threatened but modifies and postpones it. In consequence, the Old Testament regards sudden death occurring in the prime of life above all as a punishment for sin (Gen. 6:3; Num. 16:29; 27:3; Ps. 90:7–10), in the same way the death penalty is viewed. This view is bound up with the then-prevailing economy of the covenant and the pedagogical nurture of the people of Israel. To the observance of his commandments in the days of the Old Testament, God linked a long and happy life, and for the violation of these commandments, he laid down all kinds of punishments on this side of the grave. Thus the mind of the righteous was especially focused on their lot in this life and restricted to the circle of their existence on earth; only rarely did it penetrate to the other side of the grave. The difference between the righteous and the wicked, therefore, did not lie primarily in death as such—for it was the same for all—but consisted in the different kind of life that preceded death. And when there was often but little difference there as well, the difference between the righteous and the wicked was sought in the distinct meaning that suffering had for the former and the latter (Deut. 8:2f.; Hosea 2:5f.; Isa. 1:25f.; Jer. 5:3; 9:7; 31:18; Lam. 3:27f.; Ps. 119:67, 71, 75; Prov. 3:11f.; Job 1; etc.). To the pious in Israel, the righteousness of God, which punishes sins, again becomes the principle of redemption and salvation as well.[46]

But from this it does not by any means follow that death itself was considered natural and necessary. For the view that death is a consequence of the material organism of a human being by no means rules out the fact that it is the penalty of sin. The reason why for humans the punishment of sin can consist in death is that humans are made of dust and taken from the earth. Paul similarly teaches that Adam is of the earth, earthly, and yet that death came into the world through sin. And all Christians speak in the same way: humans are dust, flesh, perishable; nevertheless their death is the consequence of sin. Furthermore, there is not a people on earth who felt the horror and unnaturalness of death more deeply than Israel. Human beings are dust and have to return to dust, but this is not natural. Sin has gradually weakened the vitality of people. Enoch and Elijah escaped death. It violates the inner nature of a human being (Job 14:1–12). Righteousness and life are intimately intertwined

45. F. Schleiermacher, *Christian Faith*, §59; R. A. Lipsius, *Dogmatik*, §414; A. Ritschl, *Christian Doctrine of Justification and Reconciliation*, III, 345ff.; J. Kaftan, *Dogmatik*, §29; R. Smend, *Lehrbuch der alttestamentlichen Relgionsgeschichte* (Freiburg i.B.: Mohr, 1893), 504; K. Marti, *Geschichte der israelitischen Religion*, 3rd ed. (Strassburg: F. Bull, 1897), 193; C. Clemen, *Sünde*, I, 233ff.; J. Köberle, *Sünde und Gnade im religiösen Leben des Volkes Israel bis auf Christum: Eine Geschichte des vorchristlichen Heilsbewusstseins* (Munich: Beck, 1905), 54; J. C. Matthes, "De Inrichting van den Eeredienst bij Jerobeam, I Kon. 12:26–33," *Theologische Tijdschrift* 24/6 (1890): 239–54; K. Beth ("Über Ursache und Zweck des Todes," *Glauben und Wissen* [1909]: 285–304, and 335–48) demonstrates that science has not up to this point been able to explain the riddle of death but considers death to be natural to all earthly creatures and subordinates all exegesis of Scripture to this point of view.

46. Cf. H. Bavinck, *Reformed Dogmatics*, II, 221–28 (#206).

(Lev. 18:5; Deut. 4:1; 30:15; Jer. 21:8; Hab. 2:4; Ezek. 33:16; Ps. 36:10; Prov. 3:2, 18; 4:4, 13, 22; 8:35; etc.). In the perishability of life, we see the manifestation of a judgment of God (Ps. 90:7–12).[47] Finally, in Apocryphal and Jewish literature (Sir. 25:24; 39:29; 40:9; 1 Enoch 69:11; Wis. 1:12f.; 2:24; 4 Ezra [2 Esdr.] 3:7; 2 Bar. 23:4) and in the New Testament (John 8:21; Rom. 1:32; 5:12; 6:23; 1 Cor. 15:22, 55–56; Heb. 2:14; 1 Pet. 4:6; James 1:15; 5:20; Rev. 20:14; 21:4; etc.), it is clearly stated that death is the wages of sin. For those who consistently elevate the New Testament over the Old Testament, there is, therefore, absolutely no reason to deny the bond between sin and death. Yet this is frequently done on the basis of the witness of history and the pronouncements of the natural sciences.

The fact is that there are many people who seem to have overcome the fear of death and die very peacefully. Others, committing suicide, even put an end to their own life. Rousseau claimed that the people of nature (*natuurvolken*) all died in peace and without fear. Lessing believed that the ancients held death to be a brother of sleep and saw nothing frightening in it. Romanticism often in sentimental fashion raved over death. Still, though some people in practicing their stoic apathy have gotten to the point where they look on death as their fate with calm, the fear of death is innate in all things living. At bottom we do not believe we have to die. Death plays such a huge role in human life that philosophy is rightly called a "training for death."[48] Death has always been for humans the last and greatest enemy. Finally, all recognize in death an unnatural power and flee from it as long as they can.[49] Natural science, admittedly, has frequently called death natural and necessary. Lauvergne, for example, said: "The death of humans is a logical and natural consequence of their existence. Everything has an end: it is a hard law but it is the law."[50]

But when it talks this way, science is saying more than it can account for. Death is a mystery in the full sense of the word. According to natural science, matter and energy are immortal, and so, say Weismann and others, are unicellular protozoa.[51] Why then is the physical organism that is composed of such materials and forces and cells mortal? According to science, that organism is further renewed in people every seven years. It is nourished and fortified from day to day; why

47. O. Krabbe, *Die Lehre von der Sünde und vom Tode in ihrer Beziehung zu einander und zu der Auferstehung Christi* (Hamburg: Friedrich Perthes, 1836), 68ff.; H. Schultz, *Altt. Theol.*, 690ff.; G. F. Oehler, *Theology of the Old Testament,* trans. Ellen D. Smith and Sophia Taylor (Edinburgh: T&T Clark, 1892–93), §77.

48. A. Schopenhauer, *World as Will and Representation*, I, 353ff. (section 54); II, 463ff. (ch. 41: "On Death and Its Relation to the Indestructability of Our Inner Nature").

49. For the people of nature (*natuurvolken*), cf. W. Schneider, *Die Naturvölker: Missverständnisse, Missdeutungen, und Misshandlung,* 2 vols. (Paderborn: Schöning, 1885–86), II, 397ff.; C. P. Tiele, *Elements of the Science of Religion,* 2 vols. (Edinburgh and London: William Blackwood, 1897–99), II, 237.

50. In F. Delitzsch, *System der christlichen Apologetik* (Leipzig: Dörffling & Franke, 1870), 132; cf. H. Wagner, *De dood toegelicht van het standpunt der natuurwetenschap* (Utrecht, 1856); for additional similar expressions about the naturalness and necessity of death, see R. Eisler, *Wörterbuch der Philosophischen Begriffe,* s.v. "Tod."

51. Cf. W. von Schnehen, "Die Ewigkeit des Lebens?" *Glauben und Wissen* (March 1907): 91–99; Prof. Weismann calls the origin of death one of the most difficult questions in physiology; cf. J. Orr, *God's Image in Man and Its Defacement in the Light of Modern Denials* (London: Hodder & Stoughton, 1906), 253ff.

then cannot this process continue indefinitely, and why does it stop already after a few decades? Let us not speak of aging and the decline of one's faculties, for these are terms that, though they point to the phenomena, do not explain them and themselves need explanation. "Why do the cells wear out and waste away? Why do they succumb in old age to changes from which they remain protected in youth? That, up until now, is still a mystery to us."[52] Many plants and animals, moreover, sometimes exceed the life span of humans by hundreds of years. Why is a human's vitality so quickly spent, and why do humans at most reach the age of seventy or eighty years if they are very strong?[53]

Add to this that death as a result of the decline of one's vital powers almost never happens, neither in the case of humans nor in that of plants or animals. Almost always, death results from illness, a disaster, an accident, or such. Even in the rare instance when a person dies supposedly as a result of a decline in vital powers, the death still bears a pathological character and is caused by a disturbance of certain cells in the body. Then what is the reason death carries off almost all people before their time, often even in the prime of life or in the bloom of youth or even in the first few hours of their existence?[54] Science does not know the cause that makes death a necessity.[55] The fact that human beings die—says Professor Pruys van der Hoeven in his study of Christian anthropology—is a riddle that can only be explained by the degeneracy of their nature.[56] The mystery of death remains as much intact as that of life.[57]

DOMINION OF SATAN

[342] The final penalty of sin to be discussed here consists in that, ethically speaking, the world has fallen into the power of Satan and his angels. Since Satan seduced humanity and brought about its fall (John 8:44; 2 Cor. 11:3; 1 Tim. 2:14; Rev. 12:9,

52. H. de Varigny, *Wie stirbt man? Was ist der Tod?* trans. S. Wiarda (Minden: n.p., n.d.), 52.

53. Some time ago, Paul Ballion wrote a study in which he demonstrated that animals, too, have some sense of death, grieve over the death of one of their own, utter complaints, and sometimes even remove or bury the body (*Handelsblad* [Jan. 25, 1901]). On the age of many plants, trees, and animals, see H. Miehe, *Die Erscheinung des Lebens* (Leipzig: Teubner, 1907), 64–70.

54. E. Metchnikoff; see *Van Loghem, *Mannen en Vrouwen van beteeknis*; K. Girgensohn, *Zwölf Reden über die christliche Religion* (Munich: Beck, 1916), 361.

55. H. de Varigny, *Wie stirbt man? Was ist der Tod?* 18.

56. In F. Delitzsch, *Apologetik*, 126.

57. Y. Delage, *La structure du protoplasma et les théories sur l'hérédité et les grands problèmes de la biologie générale* (Paris: C. Reinwald, 1895), 354, 771; *Sabatier, *La problème de la mort* (1896); L. Bordeau, *La problème de la mort, ses solutions imaginaires et la science positive*, 2nd ed. (Paris: F. Alcan, 1896); idem, *La probléme de la vie* (Lyon: F. Alcan, 1901); N. Smyth, *The Place of Death in Evolution* (London: T. Fisher Unwin, 1897); *Henry Mills Alden, "A Study of Death," *Harper's* (1895); ed. note: This essay cannot be found in *Harper's Magazine* 1894–96; the closest is a short story by Flavel Scott Mines, "The Flower of Death," *Harper's Monthly Magazine* 88 (Feb. 1894): 442–45; P. Grawitz, *Über Leben und Tod* (Greifswald: Julius Abel, 1896); C. T. Müller, *Das Rätsel des Todes* (Barmen: Wuppertaler Traktat-Gesellschaft, 1905); O. Bloch, *Vom Tode*, 2 vols. (Berlin: Juncker, 1909).

14–15; 20:2, 10), the world is in his power, lying as it does in the evil one (1 John 5:19). He is the "prince of this world" and the "god of this age" (John 12:31; 16:11; 2 Cor. 4:4). Although it is true that after their fall the devils have been thrown into hell to be kept there till the judgment (2 Pet. 2:4; Jude 6), they have not yet been struck by that judgment (Matt. 8:29; Luke 8:31; James 2:19). They still appear in the gathering of the angels (Job 1; Luke 10:18; Rev. 12:7), hang around in the air (Eph. 2:2; 6:12), roam around, live and work on this earth, and have great power here. Especially the Gentile world is the sphere of their activity (Acts 16:16; 26:18; Eph. 2:2; 6:12; Col. 1:13; 1 Cor. 10:20; 8:5; Rev. 9:20). But when Christ appeared on earth, they also joined battle with him within the boundaries of the people of God. Satan held sway and worked in the Jews who were hostile to Christ (John 8:44f.), tempted Jesus (Matt. 4:1–11), sent unclean spirits, entered Judas (Luke 22:3; John 6:70; 13:2, 27), and so on. That was Satan's hour (Luke 22:53; John 14:30). But Christ was the stronger antagonist (Luke 11:22), opposed him all his life (Luke 4:13), overcame him and cast him out (Luke 10:18; John 14:30; 12:31; 16:11; Col. 2:15; Heb. 2:14; 1 John 3:8), and in principle withdrew the domain of the church from his rule (Acts 26:18; Col. 1:13; 1 John 2:13; 4:4; Rev. 12:11). Nevertheless he still inwardly impacts the church from without; he goes about on earth (Job 1), tempts believers and works against them (Luke 22:31; 2 Cor. 12:7; 1 Thess. 2:18), attempts to lead them astray and to cause them to stumble (1 Cor. 7:5; 2 Cor. 2:11; 11:3, 13–15; 1 Pet. 5:8; 1 Thess. 3:5; Rev. 12:10), so that the church is called to fight against him always (Matt. 6:13; Eph. 6:12f.; Rom. 16:20; 1 Pet. 5:9; James 4:7; Rev. 12:11). At some point at the end of time, he will once more raise himself up in all his power (Matt. 24; Mark 13; Luke 21; 2 Thess. 2:1–12; Rev. 12f.). But then he will also be overpowered by Christ and hurled with all his angels into the pool of fire (2 Thess. 2:8; 1 Cor. 15:24; Rev. 20:10).

Belief in evil spirits occurs among all peoples and in all religions. Sometimes the fear of evil spirits almost completely crowded out trust in good spirits.[58] And in almost all Gentile religions, evil in nature is attributed to one or more spiritual beings who in character and rank equal the good gods.[59] Scripture, however, teaches otherwise; and Christianity in the early centuries in various ways restrained and opposed Jewish and pagan superstition. Church and state laid down all sorts of regulations against magic, fortune-telling, and so on, and still, up until the thirteenth century, imposed no more than disciplinary penalties on those who practiced them.[60] Even when the authorities later resorted to the death penalty, what they actually had in mind was the eradication of pagan superstition. It is therefore not right simply to hold the Christian religion and church responsible

---

58. G. Roskoff, *Geschichte des Teufels* (Leipzig: F. A. Brockhaus, 1869), I, 20.

59. Ibid., 24–175.

60. Ibid., 287, 293; A. von Harnack, *Die Mission und Ausbreitung des Christentums in den ersten drei Jahrhunderten,* 2 vols. (Leipzig: J. C. Hinrichs, 1905), I, 92; ed. note: ET: *The Expansion of Christianity in the First Three Centuries,* trans. James Moffat, 2 vols. (New York: Williams & Norgate, 1904–5), bk. II, ch. 3: "The Conflict with Demons."

for all the superstition that prevailed also among Christians, especially from the thirteenth to the eighteenth centuries. Various factors contributed to it: wretched conditions in state and society, appalling occurrences of famine and the plague, the gross ignorance of the people, deficient knowledge of nature, magical kabbalistic trends among natural scientists, and so on.[61]

Nevertheless, the church is not exempt from blame in this matter. In many cases, both in theory and practice, the church took over this pagan superstition. This is already evident in the case of the church fathers. Just as every person has his or her guardian angel, they said, so does each have his or her own demon. Outside Christianity the devil holds virtually unlimited sway. Redemption in Christ is, in the first place, liberation from the devil. All physical evil in the world—disease, crop failure, famine, plague, death—is attributable to Satan. He is the invisible cause of all idolatry, magic, astrology, heresy, unbelief. Superstition is based on demonic reality. While the largely shallow conversions of the people of Europe ensured the survival, under a Christian veneer, of all sorts of pagan teachings and practices, there was added, in the Middle Ages, the belief that the devil could appear in all sorts of guises (cats, mice, goats, swine, werewolves), create all sorts of vermin, engage as incubus and succubus in fornication, seduce people into covenants sealed with blood, bewitch them, enter into them, ride with them through the air, change them into animals, and stir up all sorts of misfortune also in the natural environment.

Rome has consistently defended the demonic reality of this superstition, not only in the Middle Ages (the bull of Innocent VIII, 1484; *Malleus maleficarum*, 1487) but also after the Reformation and right up to the present day. In Catholic theology, for example, that of Suárez, Vázquez, Lessius, Liguori, Görres, and others, belief in the power of the devil occupies an extraordinarily large place.[62] And the extent to which superstition among Roman Catholics continues to live on in practice sadly came to light not long ago in the notorious history of Leo Taxil.[63] To Rome, all of existing reality is split between a lower (secular) and a higher (sacred) realm. In the former, Satan reigns with virtually unlimited power; the latter has to be protected from his influence and activity by the sign of the cross, holy water, exorcisms, and so on.[64] Catholic Christians see themselves threatened by the devil everywhere and have to take all sorts of measures to drive him away.[65]

It is also true that Protestantism at the outset almost completely left this Catholic and basically pagan superstition intact. Belief in witches and witches' trails were as vigorously defended by Protestants as by Catholics[66] and were later opposed equally by Catholics (Spina, Molitor, Loos, Tanner, Spee) and Protestants

61. G. Roskoff, *Geschichte des Teufels*, II, 314ff.

62. P. Van Hoensbroech, *Religion oder Aberglaube* (Berlin: Hermann Walther, 1897), 56ff.

63. *H. Gerber, *Leo Taxils Palladsmusroman*, 2 vols. (Berlin, 1897).

64. J. Deharbe, *Verklaring der katholieke Geloofs- en Zedeleer* (Utrecht, 1888), IV, 598ff.

65. T. Kolde, *Die kirchlichen Bruderschaften und das religiöse Leben im modernen Katholizimus* (Erlangen: n.p., 1895), 47.

66. O. Zöckler, "Hexen- und Hexenprozess," *PRE*³, VIII, 30–36.

(Weier [1563], Godelmann [1562], Reginald Scott [1584], van Dale [1685], Bekker [1691], Thomasius [1701]).[67] Following Luther's example, the Lutherans attributed extremely great power to the devil, deduced all evil from him, and maintained the practice of exorcism.[68] Still, the Reformation, especially its Calvinistic branch, brought about a significant change in belief in the devil. Going back to Scripture and not going beyond it, confessing the absolute sovereignty of God, it could not view Satan and his angels, however powerful, as anything other than creatures who without God's will cannot so much as move. The Reformation, let it be said, was not rationalistic. It maintained that there are evil spirits who exert an inward influence on people, especially on their imagination, and can even degrade them into their instruments. This power of Satan over humanity, however, is always subject to God's providence. It is primarily ethical in character and has its origin in sin. It is, moreover, restricted within narrow bounds. God, not Satan, is the Creator of light and darkness, good and evil. Sickness and death are sent to us by him (Isa. 45:7). Hebrews 2:14 only says that Satan possesses the power of death, since through sin he has brought death to dominion in the world and is therefore a murderer from the beginning (John 8:44). Our life, and the end of our life, is not in Satan's hand but in God's. Luke 13:11, 16, and 2 Corinthians 12:7 do not accord us the right to ascribe all sickness and evil to Satan. Moreover, Satan cannot create and produce something out of nothing, nor can he as incubus or succubus bring forth children; he cannot change humans into animals, kill, or bring back to life. He cannot immediately exert influence on the human intellect and will nor alter the substance or quality of things, and so on.[69]

Only by a faith that conscientiously follows Scripture can we overcome the superstition that has struck such deep roots in the human heart and, despite all so-called intellectual development, keeps on reemerging. Rationalism first combated the inward operations of evil spirits in humans and subsequently the existence of such spirits. The result has been that, while belief in Scripture has been abandoned, superstition has not been rooted out. On the contrary, it is presently making its

67. Dr. W. P. C. Knuttel, *Balthasar Bekker, de Bestrijder van het Bijgeloof* ('s Gravenhage: M. Nijhoff, 1906).

68. J. Köstlin, *Theology of Luther in Its Historical Development and Inner Harmony,* trans. Charles E. Hay, 2 vols. (Philadelphia: Lutheran Publication Society, 1897), 410–19; ed note: This reference remains an educated conjecture, since Bavinck cites vol. II, pp. 351ff. in the German edition, which begins the index; vol. I, pp. 351ff. in the German, which includes a couple of indexed references to "Teufel" (pp. 354, 356), is the section on "Christian Liberty" (*De servo arbitrio; Wille und Prädestination*). In the English edition, this section covers pp. 410–19; J. T. Müller, *Die symbolischen Bücher der evangelisch-lutherischen Kirche,* 8th ed. (Gütersloh: Bertelsmann, 1898), 477, 483, 771; G. Roskoff, *Geschichte des Teufels,* II, 364ff.; F. A. Philippi, *Kirchliche Glaubenslehre,* 3rd ed., 7 vols. in 10 (Gütersloh: Bertelsmann, 1870–90), III, 341.

69. G. Voetius, *Select disp.,* I, 906ff.; A. Polanus, *Syn. theol.,* V, ch. 12; J. Zanchi, *De operum theologicorum,* 8 vols. (Geneva: Samuelis Crispini, 1617), III, 167–216; H. Bavinck, ed., *Synopsis purioris theologiae* (Leiden: D. Donner, 1881), XII, 36ff.; F. Turretin, *Institutes of Elenctic Theology,* VII, qu. 5; P. van Mastricht, *Theologia,* III, ch. 8; J. J. Brahe, *Aanmerkingen over de vyf Walchersche Artikelen* (Middleburg: Callenfells, 1758), 195ff.; B. de Moor, *Comm. theol.,* II, 328; C. Vitringa, *Doctr. christ.,* II, 117ff.

debut—in the form of magnetism, hypnotism, telepathy, spiritism, astrology, and so on—especially in the circles of unbelief. Occultism, which throughout the ages has flourished among all peoples,[70] in this [nineteenth] century numbers its adherents in the millions and is even glorified as supreme wisdom in art and science. Also, vis-à-vis this modern superstition the foolishness of God is wiser than human beings. For not only cannot anything rational be said against the existence of fallen spirits, but also the possibility that they can lead people astray cannot be denied on a single solid ground. Just as human beings by their words and deeds, their example and conduct, exert influence on others, so there is nothing absurd in the idea that the fallen world of spirits exerts a deceptive influence on the imagination, intellect, and will of humans. Sometimes people object against this view that in that case people can always blame their faults on the devil, but this is also the case when a person is led astray by a fellow human. Furthermore, temptation always occurs along ethical channels and does not cancel out people's own guilt. And in circles where there is belief in the existence of fallen angels, the sense of guilt is usually not weaker than in places where their existence is denied. Belief in the devil simultaneously upholds both the appalling seriousness of sin and the human capacity for redemption. Our choice here is between "a devil outside of humanity or thousands of devils in human form."[71] Manifest in people, sometimes, there is such fierce, conscious, and intentional hatred against God and all that is divine.[72] There are children of God—and not the weakest or smallest but the most advanced, people who are foremost in the struggle and who live in the closest fellowship with God—who often complain of horrible temptations and inner assaults. They hint at such wicked thoughts suddenly arising in their hearts that it is a privilege to them to be allowed to believe in the existence of devils. There are "depths of Satan" that—in Scripture, in the history of humankind, in the struggle of the church of Christ, and in the experience of believers—sometimes in a flash become real to them.

One must realize in this connection that this sinful power forms a kingdom that, in its opposition to God and his kingdom, operates systematically. If one were able to survey the whole of it, one would undoubtedly discover a plan of attack and defense in the history of its struggle. In the sinful life of the individual but much more in that of families, generations, peoples, and humanity as a whole throughout the ages, there is a deliberate methodical opposition to God and all that is his. And the leadership of this opposition is in the hands of him who is called in Scripture "the prince of this world" and the "god of this age." In that capacity he already made his appearance immediately in the temptation and fall of the first human being. In paganism he organized a power that stands opposed against all true religion, morality, and civilization. When Christ appeared on

---

70. C. Kiesewetter, *Geschichte des neueren Occultismus* (Leipzig: Friedrich, 1891); A. Lehmann, *Aberglaube und Zauberei* (Stuttgart, 1898; 2nd ed., 1908).

71. A. M. Weiss, *Apol. des Christ.*, II, 519.

72. Ibid., II, 574–87.

earth, this "prince" concentrated his power against him, not only by assaulting him personally and persecuting him relentlessly, but also by surrounding him on all sides with demonic forces in order to thus break down and resist this work. The (demon-)possessed in the New Testament were not ordinary sick folk, even though symptoms of illness—deafness, muteness, epilepsy, dementia—also occurred among them. For each time they are clearly distinguished from ordinary sick folk (Matt. 4:24; 8:16; 10:1; Mark 1:32; 3:15; Luke 13:32). The exceptional features of the (demon-)possessed are that out of their mouths speaks a subject other than they themselves, that this subject recognizes Jesus as the Son of God, is totally hostile toward him, and leaves the patient only at Jesus' command (Matt. 8:29, 31; Mark 1:26, 34; 3:11; Luke 4:34, 41; 8:2, 30; Acts 16:17–18; 19:15). Now this obsession, however appalling, is so far from being impossible that in hypnotism—where one person is subjected to the thought and will of another—we see the manifestation of an analogous phenomenon; further, that such cases of possession still occur today and that those who consider it impossible would also have to deny the soul's inner impact on the body and God's inward working on humans and the world. Satan mimics everything: God reveals himself in theophany (incarnation), prophecy, and miracle; the demonic caricature of these three, accordingly, is obsession, mantic, and magic. To this trio, Scripture for that reason repeatedly accords reality (Gen. 41:8; Exod. 7:12, 22; 8:7, 18–19; Num. 22; Josh. 24:10; 1 Sam. 6:2, 7–9; 2 Chron. 33:6; Isa. 47:9–12; Jer. 39:13; Nah. 3:4; Dan. 1:20; 2:10; Acts 8:9; 13:6–10; 16:16; etc.), a reality that it very firmly censures and prohibits (Exod. 22:18; Lev. 20:27; Deut. 18:10; Jer. 27:9; 2 Chron. 33:6; Mic. 5:12; Gal. 5:20), but that toward the end of history will once more be revealed by Satan in all its seductive power (1 Thess. 2:18; 2 Thess. 2:8–11; Rev. 9:1–11; 13:13–15; 19:20).[73]

---

73. In addition to the previously cited literature on demonology, see also F. Delitzsch, *A System of Biblical Psychology,* trans. Robert. E. Wallis (Edinburgh: T&T Clark, 1899), 293; J. C. K. von Hofmann, *Der Schriftbeweis,* 2nd ed., 2 vols. (Nördlingen: Beck, 1857–60), I, 445ff.; F. A. Philippi, *Kirchliche Glaubenslehre,* III, 334ff.; K. F. A. Kahnis, *Die lutherische Dogmatik, historisch-genetisch dargestellt,* 3 vols. (Leipzig: Dörffling & Franke, 1861–68), I, 445ff.; J. T. Beck, *Vorlesungen über christliche Glaubenslehre,* 2 vols. (Gütersloh: Bertelsmann, 1896–97), II, 390ff.; *B. Weiss, *Das Leben Jesu,* 2 vols. (Stuttgart, 1882), I, 454ff.; J. Kerner, *Geschichten Besessener neuerer Zeit: Beobachtungen aus dem Gebiete kakodämonisch-magnetischer Erscheinungen; Nebst Reflexionen von C. A. Eschenmayer über Besessenseyn und Zauber* (Stuttgart: Wachendorf, 1834); *D. F. Strauss, *Charakteristiken und Kritiken* (Leipzig: n.p., 1839); J. L. Nevius, *Demon Possession and Allied Themes: Being an Inductive Study of Phenomena of Our Own Times,* by Rev. John L. Nevius, D.D., for forty years a missionary to the Chinese, with an introduction by Rev. F. F. Ellinwood, D.D., 2nd ed. (New York, Chicago, and Toronto: Fleming H. Revell Company, 1896); G. Hafner, *Die Dämonischen des Neuen Testaments* (Frankfurt a.M.: Brechert, 1894); H. Lachr, *Die Dämonischen des Neuen Testaments* (Leipzig: Richter, 1894); K. F. Zimmer, *Sünde oder Krankheit* (Leipzig, 1894); *J. A. H. van Dale, *Bezetenheid en krankzinnigheid* (Heusden, 1896); F. Chable, *Die Wunder Jesu in ihrem innern Zusammenhange betrachtet* (Freiburg i.B.: Herder, 1897), II, 4, 45ff.; F. von Bodelschwingh, *Die Mitarbeit der Kirche an der Pflege der Geistenkranken* (Bielefeld: Schriftenniederlage der Anstalt Bethel, 1896), 13ff.; W. Menzies Alexander, *Demonic Possession in the New Testament* (Edinburgh: T&T Clark, 1902); W. Ebstein, *Die Medizin im Neuen Testament und im Talmud* (Stuttgart: Enke, 1903); *B. Heyne, *Besessenheitswahn bei geistigen Errankungszuständen* (Paderborn, 1904); *Familler, *Pastoral-Psychiatrie* (Freiburg, 1888), 44.

PART II

CHRIST THE REDEEMER

5

THE COVENANT OF GRACE

The universal reality of misery evokes in all people a need for deliverance, a deliverance from above. Pagans who construe misery as basically physical know neither the essential character of sin nor the deliverance of grace. Scripture, however, sees our misery as sin, as an ethical violation of communion with God, who alone can restore it. This requires grace, which in biblical revelation assumes the form of a covenant.

This covenant begins immediately after the fall as evidenced by Adam and Eve's shame in their nakedness, a sign of lost innocence. Guilt and shame reveal both God's wrath and his grace, but the latter is shown especially when God seeks out Adam and Eve and interrogates them. In his punishment on the serpent and on humanity, God's mercy triumphs over judgment as he annuls the covenant made with evil and puts enmity between the seed of the serpent and the seed of the woman. Now the path of glory must pass through suffering for man and woman. In the promise of Genesis 3, we find the gospel in a nutshell and, in principle, the entire history of the human race.

The word "covenant" is not found in Genesis 3, but the reality is. Modern critics judge that covenant ideas arose late in Israel's history but need circular arguments for their case. A history of Israel is constructed by alleging that certain biblical sources are inauthentic, which history is then used to demonstrate the inauthenticity of documents that witness against it. It is better scholarship to see the latter prophets as standing on the foundation of a real covenant made with the patriarchs.

Covenant (בְּרִית) is characterized by three factors: an oath or promise including stipulations, a curse for violation, and a cultic ceremony that represents the curse symbolically. Covenant making is a religious and social act. The covenant of grace is unilateral, indissolubly grounded in the merciful promises of the sovereign God. God cannot break his promise; he has sworn himself to uphold it. The unilateral divine origin and character attributed to the covenant in Hebrew is likely the reason why the Septuagint translates בְּרִית by διαθήκη, or "testament," rather than συνθήκη.

193

The doctrine of the covenant achieved dogmatic significance in the Christian church because the Christian religion had to understand its relation to and distinction from Judaism. Over against Gnosticism and Marcion, the church had to maintain the unity of and, over against Judaism, the distinction between the two covenants. Law and gospel, Old Testament and New Testament, are to be distinguished but never separated. During the Reformation this issue became crucial as Anabaptists and others (Arminians, Socinians) devalued the Old Testament. Key differences also arose between the Lutheran and Reformed traditions. It is in the latter, beginning with Zwingli and Calvin, that the doctrine of the covenant is most fully developed, notably in the German Reformed theology of Olevianus and Ursinus, English Puritanism, and the Westminster Confession.

Among the Dutch Reformed, Cloppenburg and Cocceius made the covenant the fundamental premise and controlling principle of dogmatics as a whole. Cocceius had an eccentric view of the covenant, notably the notion of successive covenantal abrogations, which in fact undermined the key element of grace, making it uncertain. After Cocceius, a more general disparagement of the Old Testament took place among modern thinkers such as Spinoza, Kant, Hegel, and Schleiermacher. Judaism was then seen as no better than paganism as preparation for Christianity.

In the Reformed church and theology, covenant became a very important practical encouragement for Christian living. Here the basis of all covenants was found in the eternal counsel of God, in a covenant between the very persons of the Trinity, the pactum salutis (counsel of peace). The work of salvation is an undertaking of the one God in three persons in which all cooperate and each one performs a special task. It is the triune God—Father, Son, and Spirit—who together conceive, determine, carry out, and complete the entire work of salvation. The benefit to the believer is in knowing that the covenant of grace executed and revealed in time and history nevertheless rests on an eternal, unchanging foundation, the counsel of the triune God. The Father is the eternal Father, the Son the eternal Mediator, the Holy Spirit the eternal Paraclete.

Care must be taken in considering the execution of the pact of salvation in time and history. Though God elects Abraham and Israel as his chosen people, his salvific purpose is universal, with all peoples. In the fullness of time, humanity as a whole, Jew and Gentile, is reconciled in the one man, Jesus Christ, at the cross. After the fall, grace and judgment alike are extended to the whole human race. In the beginnings of human history, we see great blessing in remarkable longevity and the great judgment of the flood. After the flood, God makes a covenant with nature not to destroy the world with water again, reduces human life span, and spreads humanity across the world, preventing humans from reaching heaven itself with their ambition. Despite letting the Gentiles *walk in their own ways, God providentially grants them significant cultural and social development. He did not leave them without witnesses to himself through the works of his hands. In this way God is present to all people, and they are in some sense "prepared" for the message of salvation.*

The universal scope of God's intention for all peoples—Jew and Gentile— must never obscure the special favor of God to Israel. While Israel is drawn from the nations and there are analogies between Israel's religious practices and those of the nations, the essential difference is that special grace is reserved for Israel and is not known among the pagans. Pagan religion is self-willed and legalistic. The covenant made with Abraham is new and comes from God alone. Through his covenant with Abraham and Israel, the Creator proves himself to also be the Re-creator and Savior. Elohim, Creator of heaven and earth, is Yahweh, the God of the covenant.

The old covenant with Israel is the necessary preparation for the new covenant in Christ. Though the covenant is one, there are two dispensations. In God's own time, the promise of the old covenant was fulfilled in the new. The shadow and particularity of the letter became the substance, universality, and freedom of the Spirit. Nothing of the Old Testament is lost in the New, but everything is fulfilled, matured, has reached its full growth, and now, out of the temporary husk, produces the eternal core.

The covenant of grace, fulfilled in the New Testament, was and is surrounded and sustained by God's covenant with nature, with all creatures. Unlike what Cocceius taught, the covenant of grace is not the successive abolition of the covenant of works but its fulfillment and restoration. "Grace repairs and perfects nature." God's demand of obedience remains as the only way to eternal life. The difference between the covenant of works and grace is that God now approaches us not in Adam but in Christ, who fulfilled all the obedience required of Adam. Christ is the second and last Adam who restores what the first Adam had corrupted; he is the head of a new humanity.

The covenant of grace is also integrally united with the counsel of peace, though it should be distinguished from it. In the counsel of peace, Christ is the guarantor and head; in the covenant of grace, he is the mediator. In this way the doctrine of the covenant maintains God's sovereignty in the entire work of salvation. It is the Father who conceives, plans, and wills the work of salvation; it is the Son who guarantees it and effectively acquires it; it is the Spirit who implements and applies it.

At the same time, the covenant of grace also allows the rational and moral nature of human beings to come into their own. Here it differs from election, in which humans are strictly passive. The covenant of grace describes the road by which elect people attain their destiny; it is the channel by which the stream of election flows toward eternity. Christ sends his Spirit to instruct and enable his own so that they consciously and voluntarily consent to this covenant. The covenant of grace comes with the demand of faith and repentance, which may in some sense be said to be its "conditions." Yet, this must not be misunderstood. God himself supplies what he demands; the covenant of grace is thus truly unilateral—it comes from God, who designed, defines, maintains, and implements it. It is, however, designed to become bilateral, to be consciously and voluntarily accepted by believers in the power of God. In the covenant of grace, God's honor is not at the expense of but for the benefit of human persons by renewing the whole person and restoring personal freedom and dignity.

The covenant of grace, with Christ as the new head of humanity, reminds us of the organic unity of the church. The covenant of grace reminds us that election is about not only individual persons but also organic wholes, including families and generations. Therefore, some who remain inwardly unbelieving will for a time, in the earthly administration and dispensation of the covenant of grace, be part of the covenant people. The final judgment belongs to God alone, and in this life the church must regard such with the judgment of charity.

SIN, GRACE, AND COVENANT

[343] Sin, misery, and death are facts whose existence is undeniable and that therefore to some extent evoke in all people a need for reconciliation and redemption. The desire for salvation, no less than the knowledge of misery, is common to all of us. We are even more or less aware that redemption must come from above. "All humans have need of the gods" (Homer, *Odyssey* III, 48). Just as in time of trouble the people of Israel returned to the Lord, saying "Come and save us!" (Jer. 2:27), so extreme distress at all times prompts people to pray. "Misfortunes summon (people) to religion" (Livius). "The wretched worship the gods more than the happy" (Seneca). But to the degree that the misery is construed differently, to that degree also the salvation people look for changes. When that misery is solely construed as a physical evil, as a disaster and misfortune, sickness and death, then people's idea of salvation does not go beyond rescue from this distress. As long as moral and physical evil, sin and misery, are equated, the distinction between God and the world cannot come into its own. Among pagans, therefore, the sense of holiness faded away. The deity was either confused with nature, divided into many particular spirits and gods that had to be served and venerated, each in his own domain, *or* in pantheistic fashion equated with the world and regarded as the soul of all existing things. Among pagans there is no idea of a covenant of grace freely established with humanity in time by God himself; the relation in which they stand to their gods is not the result of free choice but on both sides a matter of necessity. Grace in its true sense was unknown to them because they did not comprehend the essential character of sin, just as, conversely, the character of iniquity remained a mystery to them because the revelation of grace had not illumined them on this issue. Thus they managed to hope and wish but

never came to a firm belief concerning salvation from all evil. "Homer attributed human properties to the gods; I would prefer to attribute divine properties to us humans" (Cicero).

But in Scripture the grace of God comes out to meet us in all its riches and glory. Special revelation again makes God known to us as a Being who stands, free and omnipotent, above nature and has a character and will of his own. The relation in which human beings stand to him is essentially different from the position in which they have been put with respect to all creatures. Sin, accordingly, is different from misery; its character is ethical, not physical. It is a violation of God's commandment and a severance of his communion. Consequently, that communion can only be reestablished from the side of God and at a certain point in time. From the very first moment of its revelation, grace assumes the form of a covenant, a covenant that arises, not by a natural process, but by a historical act and hence gives rise to a rich history of grace.

This covenant of grace already begins immediately after the fall. When the expression "in the day" in Genesis 2:17 is understood literally, the punishment threatened is obviously not fully carried out, for Adam and Eve did not die the day they sinned but lived on for many years afterward. Had the full punishment of sin been immediately carried out, in that first human couple the whole human race would have been annihilated, the earth laid waste, and the cosmos would have returned to chaos or to nothingness. In that case, however, Satan would have been victorious and God defeated. For that reason another principle went into effect immediately after the fall, a principle that restrains, opposes, and overcomes sin. Not only is the punishment not immediately applied to the full, but the punishment that *is* applied at the same time serves as a blessing. All that occurs at God's first encounter with fallen humanity is both proof of his wrath and a revelation of his grace.

The moment Adam and Eve had violated God's commandment, "the eyes of both were opened, and they knew that they were naked" (Gen. 3:7). The promise of the serpent was fulfilled in that event, but very differently from the way they had anticipated. Their eyes were indeed opened, only to see the evil they had done and the punishment they had brought down on themselves, and they began to be ashamed of their nakedness. Shame is an unpleasant feeling that steals over us after we have done something wrong or improper and consists especially in the fear of disgrace. Noteworthy here is that in the case of Adam and Eve this shame immediately concerns their nakedness and prompts them to conceal it with some fig leaves sewn together. But, certainly, there is a historical and ethical reason for it. Shame does not occur in animals nor yet in small children. It can only originate when we have become aware of the contrast between what is fitting and what is unfitting, between beauty and ugliness, good and evil. In the first human couple, it occurred as a result of violating God's commandment. Their eyes were opened to what they had been moments earlier and were obliged to be and had now in fact become as a result of sin. They no longer felt free in each other's presence; they no longer dared look each other in the eye; they became aware of their nakedness. Innocence was gone, and a sense of guilt first became manifest in their sense of shame.[1] The fact that in Adam and Eve a sense of shame over their nakedness had an ethical cause is further evident in that the sense of guilt in their case also manifested itself in still another way: in fear before God. When they heard the voice of the Lord, they "hid themselves from the presence of the LORD God among the trees of the garden" (Gen. 3:8). While as a result of their transgression they felt unfree in each other's presence, they were much more ashamed vis-à-vis the One who had given them the commandment. Their *conscience* had awakened—the realization that they had sinned and deserved punishment. And that conscience gives them no peace; it drives them away from God, not toward him. It makes them fear, flee, and hide themselves from his presence. Shame over their nakedness and fear of God are both rooted in their violation of the divine law and are proof that both their communion with each other and with God has been broken by sin.

At the same time, they show that the human beings in question had not been hardened, that they had not become devils but remained human. With the angels, we find that when they fell, they fell all at once into hell (Jude 6); they immediately became hardened in evil and, in fact, irredeemable. But human beings are created such that when they fall, they can be raised up again: they remain capable of redemption. In the case of humans, God held back the full effect of the principle and power of sin. Moreover, God did not withdraw himself after the fall, nor does he even for a moment abandon the transgressors. If immediately after the transgression a sense of guilt, shame, and fear arose in humans, then that in itself is already an operation of God's Spirit in them, indeed a revelation of his wrath but also of his grace, a revelation that is the foundation of all the religious and ethical life that still persists in humans after the fall.

But God reveals himself in still another way as well. When the human pair hide themselves from him, God finds them and calls out to them. Granted, God comes to them from afar, and they want to hide from him and distance themselves even further from him. There is no longer any communion between God and them but only estrangement and separation: the covenant is broken. Still, God comes to them and seeks them out. He no longer abandons them to their own folly and fears that prompt them to seek refuge in hiding from him. But of his own accord he himself calls them back to him. In so doing he does not take them by surprise and terrify them; he comes to them, as it were, from a great distance. He does not come to them in a hurricane or a thunderstorm but in the cool of the day, in the solemn rustling of the trees in the evening. And from that they recognize the voice of God and perceive his approach. This drawing near to them

---

1. On the evolutionistic interpretations of shame, the reader may wish to consult C. Darwin, *The Expression of the Emotions in Man and Animal* (London: J. Murray, 1872); Havelock Ellis, *Geschlechtstrieb und Schamgefühl* (Leipzig: Wigand, 1900); *C. Mélinand, *Wetenschappelijke Bladen* (November 1901): 220–34; Cornelis Johannes Wijnaendts Francken, *Ethische Studiën* (Haarlem: Tjeenk Willink, 1903), 110–28.

is grace. God gives people time to come to themselves and to consider how they will answer him.

This revelation of God's grace is even more pronounced in the interrogation and words of punishment that follow (Gen. 3:9–13). The Lord specifically calls Adam, for he is the head and responsible party. The Lord does not immediately pronounce his verdict but makes an inquiry, interrogating the people and giving them every opportunity to defend themselves. When they take advantage of that opportunity and, though not denying all blame, do not fall humbly and penitently before God's feet but instead try to excuse themselves, God does not erupt in anger but to a degree honors their apology. And then, although starting the interrogation with Adam, in pronouncing the verdict, he first turns to the serpent, then to Eve, and subsequently to Adam. And in that verdict mercy triumphs over judgment. The punishment (Gen. 3:14–15) first of all concerns the serpent as an ordinary animal. God humbles the serpent, putting enmity between it and humanity. Henceforth, in place of the earlier subordination of animals to human beings, there will be conflict between the two, a conflict in which human beings will have the upper hand but still have to suffer much from the animals, especially from the serpent. This punishment, further, passes through the serpent to the evil power whose instrument it was. With this power humanity had made a covenant and for its sake broken the covenant with God. God graciously annuls it, puts enmity between the seed of the serpent and the woman's seed, brings the seed of the woman—humanity, that is—back to his side, hence declaring that from Eve will spring a human race and that that race, though it will have to suffer much in the conflict with that evil power, will eventually triumph. From this point on, the road for the human race will pass through suffering to glory, through struggle to victory, through the cross to a crown, through the state of humiliation to that of exaltation. This is the fundamental law that God here proclaims before the entrance into the kingdom of heaven.

The penalty for the woman (Gen. 3:16) strikes her both as mother and as wife. Precisely as wife she will have to bear much pain. Her dearest dream, that is, motherhood, will be attained in no other way than by various kinds of suffering, desire for and submission to her husband, and bringing forth children in pain. But thus in any case she will obtain her dearest wish and reach her destiny. She will be the mother of all living—although by her transgression and self-elevation over her husband she had deserved death—and she will be blessed in bearing children (1 Tim. 2:15).

The penalty for the man (Gen. 3:17–19) consists in the fact that the ground will be cursed because of him, that he will eat bread in the sweat of his face, and after a life of toil and trouble return to the dust. In that connection he is driven from paradise and sent out into the wide world (Gen. 3:22–24). But this punishment, too, is a blessing. There is nobility in labor. It preserves humans from moral and physical degradation, stimulates their energy, and heightens their activity. Though banished from paradise, humans are not consigned to hell. They are sent into the world in order to subdue and control it by burdensome and exhausting labor. Here lies the beginning and first principle of all culture. Human dominion is not totally lost but is expanded by labor (Ps. 8). Also in fallen humanity, the image of God, in which it was created, is still discernible. Even a temporal death is not just a punishment but also a benefit. God instituted death so that sin would not be immortal.[2] After the fall, accordingly, a dual principle immediately takes effect: wrath and grace, justice and mercy. In light of this double principle alone, one can interpret the world as we know it. This is a world full of humor, laughter mixed with tears, existing in the sign of the cross, and given immediately after the fall to Christ, the Man of sorrows, that he might save and subdue it.

Thus, after hearing God pronounce his verdict, Adam and Eve humbly bow their heads. They have nothing left to say; in silence they accept the divine verdict without objection. Though that verdict sounds incredible and the truth of it can only be evident in a remote future, they believe it, blind to the future but seeing in the light of God's Word. Leaning on God's promise, Adam calls his wife Eve: life, source of life, mother of the living. Before the fall, he saw her primarily as the wife who had been given him as helper, and so he called her Woman (*ishshah*). But now he views her primarily as mother and calls her Eve. Though they have deserved death and decay, God's blessing makes the woman fruitful and causes her to bring forth the humanity that, in her greatest son, the Son of Man, will conquer the evil power of sin. In the divine promise, Adam reads the guarantee of the propagation, the existence, the development and salvation of the human race, and accepts it as such in genuinely childlike faith. And this faith was reckoned to him as righteousness. In principle Genesis 3 contains the entire history of humankind, all the ways of God for the salvation of the lost and the victory over sin. In substance the whole gospel, the entire covenant of grace, is present here. All that follows is the development of what has been germinally planted here.

COVENANT IN SCRIPTURE

[344] Nevertheless, in Genesis 3 the word "covenant" has not yet been mentioned. There is no mention of it until Noah, Abraham, and Israel at Mount Sinai make their appearance. Modern critics think that also in these places it is antedated, and that Israel's religion originally did not differ from that of other peoples. Yahweh's relation to Israel, they say, is like that of Chemosh to Moab. The idea of a covenant existing between Yahweh and his people was totally foreign to ancient Israel. They had no idea that God—as the God of heaven and earth—had chosen Israel from among all the peoples, had made it his own possession, and placed it in a covenant with him. These ideas did not arise until much later. Even in Amos the covenant relation does not yet occur. Hosea only states that Israel's unfaithfulness is comparable to a breach of covenant (6:7). The first true covenant

---

2. Irenaeus, *Against Heresies*, III, 23, 6.

book is Deuteronomy. It is introduced and accepted in the manner of a covenant (2 Kings 23:3; Jer. 34:8f.; Ezra 10:3; Neh. 9:38). But at its rise, that covenant was viewed very differently from later. That first time it was interpreted as Israel's obligation to Yahweh to be a holy people and to observe his laws. So if Israel did not keep the covenant, it was canceled and Israel was burdened with a curse (Deut. 27 and 28). But, though in Josiah's reformation Israel formally accepted the covenant, it did not adhere to it, was punished, and was sent into exile. Then, gradually, the idea arose that God's covenant consisted in a law that he had given, that God obligated himself to remain faithful to Israel and not abandon it even if it fell away from him. Though he could punish Israel, he could not abolish the covenant. Upon its return from exile, Israel clung tightly to this covenant idea and retrojected it into its past, into the history of the patriarchs.[3]

True in this conception is that in prophecy the covenant idea did not achieve prominence until later, especially after Jeremiah. But there was a reason for this. For only after the people's apostasy had assumed definitive form and made the exile necessary did the question whether or not God had permanently abandoned his people on account of it become urgent. To this the covenant God had made with Israel answered that the unfaithfulness of God's people would not nullify the faithfulness of God. The free covenant that God in his loving-kindness made with Israel increasingly became the foundation of Israel's faith and the ground for its hope in the future (Isa. 54:10). It became increasingly evident that the expectations Israel cherished were all exclusively grounded in the covenant God in his grace had established with his people. That covenant alone assured Israel of its continued existence, the appearance of the Messiah, and all the blessings of the future kingdom of God. Hence in Isaiah this Messiah acquired the name "covenant of the people" (Isa. 42:6; 49:8), for he would keep and confirm the covenant for the people and establish a new covenant (Jer. 31:31–34), and the blessings he bestowed would be covenant blessings (Isa. 55:3; Jer. 33:20–21; Ps. 89:29).

From this it does not follow, however, that this covenant idea was unknown in earlier times. Modern criticism can only maintain this view by a very arbitrary working procedure. For countless testimonies, which also according to this criticism belong to the older sections of the Pentateuch, make mention of such a covenant. In Genesis 15:18, for example, there is mention of a covenant that God made with Abraham; but without adequate grounds, it is said that this word is only a solemn name for the oath with which God obligated himself to give the land of Canaan to Abraham's descendants. The words in Genesis 28:21 ("then the LORD shall be my God") undoubtedly suggest the idea of a covenant relation, but they are considered a pure addition. Exodus 21–23 is called "the book of the covenant" (Exod. 24:7); the blood of the sacrifice with which it was confirmed

---

3. J. Wellhausen, *Geschichte Israels,* 2 vols. (Berlin: Reimer, 1878), I, 434ff.; R. Smend, *Lehrbuch der alt-testamentlichen Religionsgeschichte* (Freiburg i.B.: Mohr, 1893), 116ff.; R. Kraetzschmar, *Die Bundesvorstellung im Alten Testament in ihrer geschichtlichen Entwicklung* (Marburg: N. G. Elwert, 1896).

is called "the blood of the covenant" (24:8), and in Exodus 34:27 there is reference to covenant words. But [according to the critics] these documents, even if they are pre-Deuteronomic, do not date from Moses' time and in any case do not contain the covenant idea as it was later conceived. A criticism that operates in this manner gets no other result than what it wanted beforehand. First, on the basis of the alleged inauthenticity of the writings, it constructs a history of religious concepts, then it uses this history to demonstrate the inauthenticity of the documents that witness against it.[4]

But even with this arbitrary criticism, the critics do not end up where they want to be. For all the prophets proceed from the idea that there exists a special relationship between Yahweh and the people of Israel. Amos begins his prophecies with an oracle of doom against Damascus, on account of whose crimes the Lord will act on behalf of his people (1:3–5), and he will not spare Israel precisely because it alone he has known of all the families of the earth (3:2). Hosea pictures the relation between God and his people as a marriage and in 6:7 and 8:1 speaks of the covenant that Israel has broken. The prophets are not the founders of a new religion but, jointly with the people, stand on the foundation of the same covenant, therefore calling the people to repentance and conversion. Not only does Israel always trace its history to the patriarchs and the countries of Syria and Egypt (Deut. 26:5; Hosea 12:13), but the covenant established at Sinai is above all the basis on which Israel's whole religion rests. This is the reason why many scholars who otherwise accept the principle of modern criticism still maintain the historical reality of Moses' person and work.[5]

In the study of the meaning of the covenant in Israel, however, the main question is not whether the word used to designate it (ברית) originally meant "covenant" or "statute." Some scholars, such as [Franz] Delitzsch, Gesenius, Dillmann, Schultz, Oehler, Wellhausen, Guthe, Bredenkamp, König, and Cremer, say the first, then assume as a second meaning that of "covenant condition" and so let it pass into the meaning of "statute," "law," inasmuch as a law acquires legal force in the way of a covenant. Others, such as Hofmann, Buhl, Friedrich Delitzsch, Orelli, Strack, Siegfried, Stade, and Nowack, believe that "regulation," "statute," is the most ancient meaning and that it gradually passed into that of covenant because the law governs a reciprocal relation. The scriptural data do not enable us to make a firm choice between these two opinions and to demonstrate historically the transition from the one meaning to the other. Sometimes the one

---

4. Cf. G. Vos, "Recent Criticism of the Early Prophets," *Presbyterian and Reformed Review* 9 (April 1898): 214–18; Herman L. Strack, "Zur alttestamentlichen Theologie," *Theologisches Literaturblatt* 19/5 (February 4, 1898): 49–53.

5. Thus, not only Lotz, Vos, Davidson, also cf. F. Giesebrecht, *Die Geschichtlichkeit des Sinaibundes* (Königsberg: Thomas & Opermann, 1900); E. König, *Geschichte des Reiches Gottes* (Berlin: M. Warneck, 1908), 62ff.; idem, "Die religionsgeschichtliche Bedeutung der Patriarchen," *Glauben und Wissen* (1900): 361–77; M. Löhr, *Alttestamentliche Religions-Geschichte* (Leipzig: Göschen, 1906), 30, 32; G. Wildeboer, *Het Oude Testament van Historisch Standpunt Toegelicht* (Groningen: Wolters, 1908), 59.

meaning predominates, sometimes the other, and in that connection one cannot distinguish the earlier from the later sources.

The concept of covenant (בְּרִית), accordingly, must be defined in another way. The derivation is not very helpful in this connection. According to most linguists, it comes from the verb בָּרָה, "to cut," and so refers to the ancient Eastern custom, followed in the making of a covenant, of passing between the parts of slain animals laid out on opposite sides from each other, to symbolize that the same fate as that of the animals may befall the violator of the covenant in question, hence the expression "to cut a covenant" (כָּרַת בְּרִית, ὅρκια τεμνειν, *foedus ferire*; cf. Gen. 15:8f., Jer. 34:19ff.). According to others, it derives from an Assyrian stem meaning "to bind."[6] However this may be, it is clear from Genesis 21:22f.; 26:26f.; and 31:44f. that a בְּרִית is characterized by three features: an oath or promise that includes the stipulations agreed upon, a curse that invokes divine punishment upon the violator of the covenant, and a cultic ceremony that represents the curse symbolically. The making of a covenant, accordingly, was always a religious act. The word was admittedly first employed in the profane world of everyday for contractual provisions and agreements between people. Long before God established his covenant with Noah and Abraham, covenants had been made between humans. And this *had to be* the case for Noah, Abraham, and Israel to understand and appreciate religion as a covenant. This is also why the word does not yet occur in Genesis 3:15. Only when covenants were needed in a sinful and deceptive human society for the defense or acquisition of any good could the value of a covenant be appreciated and religion be regarded from this point of view. Still, though the word בְּרִית was first used to denote human covenants, it always refers to a religious act. The main issue in the word בְּרִית is not whether it denotes a covenant or a statute. What matters is that it refers in general to the kind of promise, agreement, treaty, covenant, ordinance, grant, and so on that is placed by a solemn ceremony under the protection of God and so achieves a kind of indissolubility.[7]

Whether בְּרִית is a bilateral covenant or a unilateral [royal] grant depends neither on the word nor on the historical development of the concept but simply on the parties involved. To the degree that one of the two parties is inferior and has less "say," the בְּרִית automatically gets the character of a "grant" imposed by one party on the other. In that case, בְּרִית becomes synonymous with חֹק (enactment, decree) (Exod. 34:10; Isa. 59:21; Jer. 33:20 [cf. 31:36]; 34:13); and כָּרַת בְּרִית is not only construed with עִם (with) and בֵּין (between) but also with לְ (for the benefit of) (Josh. 9:6; Isa. 55:3; 61:8; Jer. 32:40). When a conqueror makes a בְּרִית with the conquered, or a king with his subject, the whole emphasis is on the obligations the latter will have to fulfill in the context of that covenant

---

6. R. Kraetzschmar, *Die Bundesvorstellung*, 245; A. B. Davidson, "Covenant," *DB*, I, 509, who also observes that the word appears three hundred times in the Old Testament.

7. R. Kraetzschmar, *Die Bundesvorstellung*, 29, 30, 39–41.

(Josh. 9; 1 Sam. 11; 2 Sam. 5:3; 1 Kings 20:34; Ezek. 17:13). The meaning of grant, ordinance, and statute becomes even stronger when there is metaphorical mention of a ברית with the eyes (Job 31:1), with stones and animals (Job 5:22; 41:4), with death (Isa. 28:15), of God with nature (Gen. 8:22; Jer. 33:20, 25) or with animals (Gen. 9:12; Hosea 2:17–22; Isa. 11:6; etc.). But also when God makes a covenant with humans, this unilateral character comes repeatedly to the fore: the parties, after all, are not equal, but God is the sovereign who imposes his ordinances on his creatures. When in Genesis 15:8f. God makes a covenant with Abraham, it is not really a compact but a pledge. God gives his promise; he obligates himself to fulfill it and passes between the pieces of the sacrificial animal. Elsewhere he swears by himself (Gen. 22:16), by his life (Deut. 32:40), by his "soul" [*nephesh*] (Amos 6:8; Jer. 51:14) to show to people "the unchangeable character of his purpose" (Heb. 6:17).

This unilateral character had to come out with ever-increasing clarity in the course of history. True, the covenant of God imposed obligations also on those with whom it was made—obligations, not as conditions for entering into the covenant (for the covenant was made and based only on God's compassion), but as the way the people who had by grace been incorporated into the covenant henceforth had to conduct themselves (Gen. 17:1–2; Exod. 19:5–6, 8; 24:3, 7; Lev. 26:14f.; Deut. 5:29; 27:10f.; 28:1f.; 30:1f.; etc.). But although Israel repeatedly accepted God's covenant (Exod. 19:8; 24:3, 7; Deut. 29:10–13; Josh. 24:16; 2 Kings 23:3; 2 Chron. 15:12; 23:16; 29:10; 34:31; Neh. 8; etc.), it did not walk in the way of the covenant but consistently desecrated and broke it. Thus the question arose whether this covenant of grace was as unstable as the covenant of works had been before the fall. Replying to this question, revelation answered ever more forcefully and loudly as apostasy increased. No, this covenant does not falter; *people* may become unfaithful, but *God does not* forget his promise. This covenant is anchored solely in his compassion (Lev. 26:40–44; Deut. 4:31; 30:1f.; 32:36f.; Judg. 2:1; 2 Kings 13:23; Pss. 81:8, 11; 89:1–5; 105:8–10; 106:45; 111:5; Isa. 1:3; 5:13; 54:10; Jer. 18:5–10; Ezek. 33:10–16; Hosea 6:1–3; 11:7–9; 14:2–9; Joel 2:12–14). God cannot and may not break his covenant. Voluntarily, of his own accord, he bound himself to its provisions with a solemn oath; his name, his honor, his very being depend on it (Exod. 32–33; Num. 14:16; Deut. 32:26; 1 Sam. 12:22; Isa. 48:8–11; Jer. 14:7, 20–21; Ezek. 20:9, 14, 22, 43–44; Joel 2:17–19; etc.).

In this firmness and steadiness of the covenant of grace lies the glory of the religion we as Christians confess. Earlier already we indicated why true religion has to come in the form of a covenant.[8] If religion is to be a true fellowship between God and humanity, fellowship in which not only God but also the human partner preserves his or her independence as a rational and moral being and along with his or her duties also receives rights, this can only come into being by God's

---

8. Cf. H. Bavinck, *Reformed Dogmatics*, II, 568–72 (#296).

coming down to humans and entering into a covenant with them. In this action God obligates himself with an oath to grant the human partner eternal salvation despite his apostasy and unfaithfulness; but by the same token, the human partner on his or her part is admonished and obligated to a new obedience, yet in such a way that "if we sometimes through weakness fall into sins we must not despair of God's mercy, nor continue in sin," since we have an everlasting covenant of grace with God.[9] The covenant of grace is unalterably grounded, not in our virtues and works, but in God's mercies.

This indissolubility, which was inferred with increasing clarity from the covenant idea by Old Testament prophecy, is probably also the reason why the word is translated in the Septuagint, not by συνθηκη (covenant) but by διαθηκη (testament). According to Deissmann,[10] the latter word always has the meaning of "testament," never that of "covenant." As this concerns the Old Testament and the New Testament, however, this may be questioned on good grounds. The unilateral divine origin and character attributed to the covenant in the Hebrew is sufficient reason why the Septuagint preferred διαθηκη to συνθηκη. Further, between the testamentary disposition made in the time of the Septuagint in accordance with Graeco-Syrian law and that made in accordance with Roman law, there was a notable distinction. According to the former, διαθηκη was a solemn act in which an irrevocable transfer of rights and goods took place, a transfer that, at least in part, went into effect immediately and was therefore not dependent on the death of the testator. By contrast, according to Roman law the execution of a testamentary disposition had to wait till the death of the testator. The Greek word διαθηκη could therefore readily serve as a translation of the Hebrew ברית, for in the covenant God had bequeathed benefits and goods to his people by which it was privileged above all other peoples of the earth.[11] In this sense the word passed into the New Testament. Here, by comparison with the Old Testament, it occurs relatively rarely (only thirty-three times), and in only one place (Heb. 9:15–17) does it definitely have the meaning of testament, for the author alludes here to the Roman law, according to which a testament takes effect only upon the death of the testator. In Galatians 3:17–18, the meaning "testament" is admittedly probable, but despite this the execution of it is not connected with the death of Christ. In all other places, as so often also in the Old Testament, it is hard to tell which meaning—disposition or covenant—the authors had in mind. In the covenant of grace that God established in Christ, both elements are present as well. Noteworthy, finally, is that the authorized Dutch version, as also the [Authorized, or King James] English translation, renders the word as "covenant" when the reference is to the old covenant with Israel (Luke 1:72; Acts 3:25; 7:8; Rom. 9:4; 11:27;

---

9. Ed. note: Much of this sentence is quoted from the Form for Infant Baptism, used from the sixteenth century on in the Reformed Churches of the Netherlands.

10. A. Deissmann, *Licht vom Osten* (Tübingen: Mohr, 1908), 243.

11. G. Vos, "Covenant," *DC*, I, 374; W. M. Ramsay, "A Historical Commentary on the Epistle to the Galatians," *The Expositor* 4/4 (November 1898): 326–39.

Gal. 3:15, 17; 4:24; Eph. 2:12; Heb. 9:4) and as "testament" when the reference is to the new covenant with the church of Christ (Matt. 26:28; Mark 14:24; Luke 22:20; 1 Cor. 11:25; 2 Cor. 3:6[14]; Heb. 12:24; 13:20), although in the latter case, for obvious reasons, the word "covenant" is retained in Hebrews 7:22; 8:6f.; Revelation 11:19. Underlying this difference in translation is the idea that the term "covenant" is more appropriate to the dispensation of the Old Testament and the term "testament" more to that of the New Testament.[12] After the covenant with carnal Israel was broken, there came in its place the spiritual Israel, which according to God's election was gathered from all peoples, receives the goods of salvation from the Son as by a testamentary disposition, stands in a child-Father relation to God, and expects salvation from heaven as an inheritance (Luke 22:29; Rom. 8:16; Gal. 3:15–17; Heb. 9:15–17; 1 John 3:1–2; 1 Pet. 1:4).

COVENANT IN CHRISTIAN THEOLOGY

[345] From Scripture this covenant idea passed automatically into Christian theology. In the church fathers it occurs repeatedly, especially in their commentaries. But the doctrine of the covenant achieved dogmatic significance because the Christian religion had to be understood in its connection with, and simultaneously in distinction from, the religion of Israel. In this matter, from the days of the apostles on, there were two opposing schools of thought. The Judaism that in almost all the churches opposed Paul in person and doctrine, demanded the keeping of the Mosaic law—specifically the law of circumcision—also by Christians from among the Gentiles (Acts 15; Rom. 16:17f.; 1 Cor. 7:18; Gal. 5:3; 6:13; Phil. 1:15f.; 3:2f.; Col. 2:16, 21; Titus 1:10, 14; 3:9; 1 Tim. 1:7f.). After the break between Jews and Christians had become complete, Jerusalem was destroyed, the Christian church had fled to Pella, and a Gentile Christian church had been founded (AD 135) in Jerusalem, [this Judaizing party in the church] had increasingly become a sect (Nazarenes and Ebionites) that became Jewish in its doctrine of God and denied the deity of Christ.[13] On the other side was Gnosticism, which had its origins already in the time of the apostles (Simon Magus, Cerinthus), but spread from East to West especially in the second and third centuries and in the person of Marcion aimed its sharp attacks on the Old Testament. Proceeding from an eternal dualism between God and matter, he believed the transition between the two was mediated by an assortment of aeons and attributed the creation of the world to a lower god, the demiurge, or the god of the Jews. This was not the supreme and true God, but a god of lower rank, the god of law, of righteousness, and of vengeance. The Old Testament was on a level far below that of the New Testament, for the god of the Old Testament was jeal-

---

12. Cf. J. A. Bengel, *Gnomon of the New Testament,* 5 vols. (Edinburgh: T&T Clark, 1877), I, 455–56, on Matt. 26:28.

13. Cf. F. Loofs, *Leitfaden zum Studium der Dogmengeschichte,* 4th ed. (Halle a.S.: M. Niemeyer, 1906), 81ff.

ous, vindictive, the creator of evil; he hardened human hearts, ordered people to commit sins, such as robbing the Egyptians and killing the Canaanites. He gave laws that were bad and entered into covenant with people like Abraham, Isaac, Jacob, David, and others, men who were guilty of a wide range of sins, deception, lies, and so on. It is that god of the Jews who even had Christ nailed to a cross but was himself consigned to hell by Christ. In Christ a totally different god revealed himself, the god of grace and love. Consequently, the entire legalistic position is now passé. A Christian is free from the law and from the whole Old Testament. The only person who from the start understood this correctly is Paul; he is the only real and the only true apostle.[14]

Over against these two parties, the Christian church and theology saw itself commissioned to a double task. Over against Gnosticism it had to maintain the unity of, and over against Judaism the distinction between, the two Testaments.[15] To that end it used Paul's doctrine regarding the old and the new "covenant" (δι-αθηκη, 2 Cor. 3; Latin *testamentum* or *instrumentum*, words first applied to the economies, then to the Scriptures, of the Old Testament and the New Testament). The two are one in origin and content. God, or the Logos, is the author of both, and in both we are presented one faith, one covenant, one way of salvation. There is a difference between the two only in the form, and this had to be so. For, indeed, God is one, but people differ and therefore have to be brought up differently as well. God successively reveals his grace in ever richer and fuller ways. In the days of the Old Testament, there was servanthood, but now there is freedom; then there was the image, now the truth; then there was a kind of shadowy twilight, now there is light; then there was grace for one people, now for all; then fear, now love; then the Messiah was the one who was to come, now the Messiah who has come. This difference, however, does not at all diminish the essential unity between the two, for the law was especially given to Israel and given only because it was stiff-necked (Amos 5:17; Jer. 7:21; Ezek. 20:19). In addition it typically pointed to Christ, educated Israel for the Christ, and therefore also attained its end and goal in Christ.

The church fathers, accordingly, repeatedly said that though law and gospel can be distinguished, they cannot be separated from each other. Just as fruit is separated from seed even though it comes out of seed, so also the gospel is separated from the law, inasmuch as it proceeds from the law; the one comes from the other but is not alien to it, different though not opposed to it.[16] Fear does belong more to the Old Testament and love to the New; yet the New is concealed in the Old Testament, and the Old is revealed in the New Testament.[17] The Old Testament anticipates and interprets the New. The Old Testament is the concealment of

---

14. Cf. F. Loofs, *Dogmengeschichte*, 111ff.

15. Cf. esp. Irenaeus, *Against Heresies*, IV; Tertullian, *Against Marcion*.

16. Tertullian, *Against Marcion*, V, 11.

17. Augustine, *Questionum in heptateuchum*, bk. VII, in *Corpus scriptorum ecclesiasticorum*, vol. XXVII, part 2 (Vienna: F. Tempsky, 1895), 141, "Quaest. de Exodo," 73.

the New and the New the revelation of the Old. The difference is not a matter of essence but a matter of chronological sequence.[18] In the hierarchy, the priesthood, and the idea of sacrifice, the legalistic conception of the gospel, worship, and art, the Old Testament even gained great power over the church, which in many respects wanted to be an Old Testament theocracy and absorbed a strongly Judaistic element into itself.[19] Still, the church in the new dispensation was also elevated high above the old. In scholastic and Roman Catholic theology, the distinction between the two testaments was described by saying that in the Old Testament the promises concerned earthly things but now heavenly things; that then the precepts were external regulations but are now fuller, governing not only the hand but even the mind; that then the sacraments were figurative but now confer grace.[20] In connection with this the believers of the Old Testament went not directly to heaven but to the limbo of the fathers, from which they were only transferred to heaven by Christ.[21]

The Reformation saw emerging alongside itself all kinds of schools of thought, with respect to which it also had to define its position on this point. The Judaistic and Gnostic ideas that had propagated themselves in the Middle Ages also made their influence felt in the sixteenth century. Anabaptism was radical: it sought not only religious-ethical but also social and political reformation. Appealing to Scripture, it demanded the abolition of interest, polygamy, community of goods, and so on. The same dualism of nature and grace that initially prompted the desire for the introduction of all sorts of Old Testament and New Testament rules gradually led the movement to subordinate Scripture to the inner Word. Scripture was a dead letter; especially the Old Testament was devoid of evangelical content. Israel, like a herd of swine, was fed only with temporal goods; the law has lost all value and power for us.[22] Socinianism, pursuing its own rationalistic principles, arrived at a similar result. The value of the Old Testament was far below that of the New Testament. It teaches polygamy, limits the love of neighbor, totally neglects to prescribe a great many virtues, and imposes disproportionate penalties for minor sins. It only knows slavish fear and earthly promises, no full righteousness and forgiveness. It has been abolished, therefore, and Christ came on the scene as a new lawgiver.[23] Arminianism, though less bold in its language, nevertheless viewed the Old

18. J. C. Suicerus, *Thesaurus ecclesiasticus*, 2 vols. (Amsterdam: J. H. Wetstein, 1682), s.v. διαθηκη.

19. L. Diestel, *Geschichte des alten Testaments in der christlichen Kirche* (Jena: Mauke, 1869); A. von Harnack, *History of Dogma*, trans. N. Buchanan, J. Millar, E. B. Seirs, and W. McGilchrist, ed. A. B. Bruce, 7 vols. (London: Williams & Norgate, 1896–99), II, 256.

20. P. Lombard, *Sent.*, III, dist. 40; T. Aquinas, *Summa theol.*, III, qu. 60, art. 6, ad. 3; qu. 61, art. 4, ad. 2.

21. T. Aquinas, *Summa theol.*, qu. 60, art. 4–6; R. Bellarmine, "De Christo," *Controversiis*, IV, 10, 11; Roman Catechism, I, 3, 4; I, 6, 6.

22. L. Diestel, *Geschichte des A.T.*, 307ff.; C. Vitringa, *Doctrina christianae religionis*, 8 vols. (Leiden: Joannis le mair, 1761–86), IV, 238.

23. O. Fock, *Der Socinianismus* (Kiel: C. Schröder, 1847), 325; L. Diestel, *Geschichte. des A.T.*, 535.

Testament as a covenant that promised only temporal goods.[24] Even Luther often opposed the Old Testament and the New Testament to each other as law and gospel, but became more careful later and taught that the Old Testament also contained rich evangelical promises.[25] Still, his view had its aftereffects in Lutheran theology. It does accept that there is but one Messiah, one faith, and one way of salvation in the Old and New Testaments but refuses to say that there is only one testament. In Lutheranism the word "testament" denotes the legalistic covenant established with Israel on Mount Sinai; and in this sense it essentially differs from, is opposed to, and is abolished by the New Testament. In the Old Testament there are indeed many promises given to Israel that still hold true for us today, but as a legalistic covenant of God with Israel, the Old Testament was not a covenant of grace. The gospel promises were given to Adam, Abraham, and others, though they may be summed up in the term "covenant of grace." This covenant differs not only incidentally but also substantially from the New Testament, just as the promise differs from the fulfillment, and the shadow from the body.[26]

The doctrine of the covenant was most fully developed in Reformed theology. Covenant theology is not the brainchild of Cocceius, as Ypey thought, nor a peculiar feature of the German Reformed theology that is supposed to have been begotten by Melanchthon, as Heppe pictured it.[27] The incorrectness of these sentiments has been demonstrated with a forceful array of arguments and is now also recognized by everyone.[28] The doctrine of the covenant does not even originate with Olevianus, Calvin, or Bullinger but is found in principle already in Zwingli, who, in his polemic with the Anabaptists, maintained the essential

24. S. Episcopius, *Opera theologica,* disp. 18–20; IV, disp. 12–14; P. van Limborch, *Theologia christiana ad praxin pietatis ac promotionem pacis christianae unice directa* (Amsterdam: Wetstein, 1735), III, c. 9; cf. C. Vitringa, *Doctr. christ.,* IV, 242.

25. Luther, in J. Köstlin, *Theology of Luther in Its Historical Development and Inner Harmony,* trans. Charles E. Hay, 2 vols. (Philadelphia: Lutheran Publication Society, 1897), I, 110ff.; II, 538ff.; ed. note: Bavinck's point is clearer in the original German edition (II, 258), which cites Old Testament passages such as Isa. 55:10; F. Loofs, *Dogmengeschichte,* 770ff.

26. J. Gerhard, *Loci theol.,* XIV, 119ff.; J. A. Quenstedt, *Theologia,* IV, 255–80; D. Hollaz, *Examen theologicum acroamaticum* (Rotstock and Leipzig: Russworm, 1718), 1043–53; H. Heppe, *Dogmatik des deutschen Protestantismus im sechachnten Jahrhundert,* 3 vols., (Gotha: F. A. Perthes, 1857), II, 258.

27. A. Ypey, *Beknopte Letterkundige Geschiedenis der Sijststematische Godgeleerdheid,* 3 vols. (Haarlem: Platt, 1793–98), II, 70ff.; H. Heppe, *Geschichte des Pietismus und der Mystik in der reformierten Kirche* (Leiden: Brill, 1879); idem, *Dogmatik des deutschen Protestantismus.*

28. C. Sepp, *Het Godgeleerd Onderwijs in Nederland, Gedurende de 16e en 17e Eeuw,* 2 vols. (Leiden: De Breuk & Smits, 1873–74), II, 220; A. Schweizer, *Die Glaubenslehre der evangelisch-reformierten Kirche,* 2 vols. (Zürich: Orell & Füssli, 1844–47), I, 103; W. Gass, *Geschichte der protestantischen Dogmatik,* 4 vols. (Berlin: G. Reimer, 1854–67), II, 265; M. Schneckenburger and E. Güder, *Vergleichende Darstellung des Lutherischen und Reformierten Lehrbegriffs,* 2 vols. (Stuttgart: J. B. Metzler, 1855), II, 146; L. Diestel, "Studien zur Foederealtheologie," *Jahrbücher für deutsche Theologie* 10 (1865): 209–76; Willem van den Bergh, *Calvijn over het Genadeverbond* ('s Gravenhage: Beschoor, 1879), 7ff.; H. Heppe, *Geschichte des Pietismus;* E. Korff, *Die Anfänge der Foederaltheologie und ihre Ausgestaltung in Zürich und in Holland* (Bonn: E. Eisele, 1908).

unity of the Old and New Testaments.[29] From Zwingli it passed to Bullinger and Calvin[30] and from there found acceptance in the German Reformed theology of Olevianus, Ursinus, Sohnius, Eglin, Boquinus, Hyperius,[31] and others; in the English theology of Rollock, Howie, Cartwright, Preston, Thomas Blake, Perkins, Ames, John Ball, James Ussher, the Westminster Confession (ch. 7), Francis Roberts, Thomas Boston, and others;[32] in the Netherlands in the work of Snecanus, Junius, Gomarus, Trelcatius Sr. and Jr., Nerdenus, Ravensperger, and others. Long before Cloppenburg and Cocceius, therefore, the doctrine of the covenants was native to Reformed theology. But these latter figures made the covenant idea the fundamental premise and controlling principle of dogmatics as a whole and, by doing so, produced a basic change.[33]

The polemic against Cocceius did not at all directly concern the doctrine of the covenant, which was recognized by everyone, but the Sabbath (in the case of Essenius and Hoornbeek, 1655–59), the state of the church in the two economies (in Maresius, 1662), forgiveness (πάρεσις, a casting aside) in the Old Testament (in Voetius, 1665). The thing to which his critics objected in Cocceius was not his concept of the covenant but his biblical theology and historical method. Like Descartes in philosophy, so Cocceius in theology protested against scholasticism and traditionalism, insisted on the study of the Scriptures, and wanted a "comprehensive survey of theology grounded in the Scriptures" (*summa theologiae ex Scripturis repetita*), as the title of his dogmatics reads. In order to obtain this, he did not, in his survey of the doctrine of the covenant, proceed from God and his eternal counsel but took his stance in history and the covenant of God with humans. His dogmatics, accordingly, became a history of redemption, a biblical theology in historical form, of which Scripture was the object and content but not its first principle and norm. He explored that covenant, that is, true religion, historically from its earliest beginnings to the present and especially pointed out the development and progress of that covenant in the various successive dispensations. There was therefore not just a difference in the clarity of the revelation,

29. U. Zwingli, "Elenchus contra Anabaptistas," in *Opera*, ed. M. Schuler and J. Schulthess (Turici [Zürich]: Officina Schulthessiana, 1842), III, 412ff., 418ff., 421ff.; V, 45.

30. H. Bullinger, *De Testamento seu Foedere Dei unico et aeterno* (Zürich: Christoph Froschauer, 1527); idem, *Compedium Cristianae Religionis* (Zürich: Christoph Froschauer, 1556); idem, *The Decades of Henry Bullinger*, trans. Thomas Harding, 4 vols. (Cambridge: Cambridge University Press, 1849–52); J. Calvin, *Institutes*, II.x.–xi; cf. W. van den Bergh, *Calvijn over het Genadeverbond*.

31. Cf. H. Heppe, *Dogmatik der deutschen Protestantismus*, I, 150ff.

32. G. Vos, "The Covenant in Reformed Theology," in *Redemptive History and Biblical Interpretation: The Shorter Writings of Geerhardus Vos*, ed. R. Gaffin (Phillipsburg, NJ: Presbyterian & Reformed, 1980), 234–71.

33. J. Cloppenburg, *Disp. de foedere Dei, theologica opera omnia,* 2 vols. (Amsterdam: Borstius, 1684), I, 487–570; J. Cocceius, *Summa doctrinae de foedere et testamento Dei*, 2nd ed. (Leiden: Elsevier, 1654); F. Burman, *Synopsis theologiae,* 2 vols. (Amsterdam: Joannem Wolters, 1699); J. Braun, *Doctrina foederum* (Amsterdam: A. Van Sommeren, 1668); H. Witsius, *The Oeconomy of the Covenants between God and Man,* 3 vols. (New York: Lee & Stokes, 1798).

that is, in the lucidity of insight and clarity of consciousness, as the Reformed said. No, under the different dispensations of the covenant of grace, there was a difference in the objective benefits themselves. Salvation in the Old Testament was objectively more limited in scope than in the New Testament. In the Old Testament the Sabbath consisted in the cessation of work; Israel did not yet have true and permanent salvific goods but was a people of hope, yearning for a long life on earth and still caught up in the fear of death. It had no full forgiveness (ἄφεσις) but only "a casting aside" (πάρεσις). Justification was incomplete inasmuch as an animal sacrifice could not effect atonement. The comfort of believers was still tenuous, their consciences not yet being at peace. Though in the Old Testament the circumcision of the heart was promised, in the New Testament it was actually granted. The law was administered by angels. In a word, though in the Old Testament all the benefits of the covenant were present, they were present only in the form of types and shadows; the reality of the thing itself was largely, if not totally, lacking. Not just subjectively but also objectively, not just in the incidentals but in the substance, the Old Testament differed from the New. Indeed, Cocceius even undermined the whole doctrine of the covenant when he construed the covenant of grace exclusively in negative terms, as a gradual, historical, and successively unfolding abolition of the covenant of works. In the end there was nothing left of the covenant; it was merely a temporary, human, and ever-changing form of religion.[34]

In writing as he did, Cocceius undoubtedly departed from the basic starting point of Reformed theology and broke with its continuity. This was immediately felt by many of his contemporaries and therefore more or less opposed by them. But it was rather an attack on subordinate points than a polemic on the level of principle. Cocceianism, soon allied with Cartesianism, found increasing acceptance and not only led to resistance against various dogmas but also contributed to a degradation of the Old Testament. Everywhere, though unintentionally, the opinion gained ground that the Old Testament still retained only historical value and no longer had any dogmatic importance. In time, out of this changed dogmatic outlook, the historical criticism of the Old Testament spontaneously sprang up, especially after B. Spinoza [1632–77] and R. Simon [1638–1712]. Rationalism and supernaturalism had no sense whatever of the significance and value of the Old Testament. According to Kant, Judaism was merely "the embodiment of purely statutory laws on which a state constitution was grounded"; the moral ordinances were a mere appendix and not essentially a part of it. Judaism desired to be not a church but only a state and consequently demanded only an outward observance of the commandments, no inner disposition. Christianity did not

---

34. Cf. H. Bavinck, *Reformed Dogmatics*, I, 603–7 (#156); and further W. Gass, *Geschichte der protestantischen Dogmatik*, II, 266ff.; G. F. Karl Muller, "Coccejus," *PRE*[3], IV, 186–94; H. Heppe, *Geschichte des Pietismus*, 217ff.; A. van der Flier, *Specimen historico-theologicum de Johanne Coccejo, anti-scholastico* (Utrecht: Kemink et Filius, 1859); W. Geesink, *De Ethiek in de Gereformeerde Theologie* (Amsterdam: Kirchner, 1897), 49ff.

arise out of Judaism but constitutes the full abolition of it.[35] On account of its particularism, says Schleiermacher, Judaism still has an affinity with fetishism and in its relation to Christianity is on the same level as paganism.[36] Hegel put Judaism, as the religion of the sublime, even below the Greek religion of beauty and the Roman religion of utility.[37] Vatke and Bruno Bauer, both of them pupils of Hegel, attempted to confirm this philosophical estimate of the Old Testament by the historical criticism of the Bible books. The scriptural criticism of the last century has not changed the worldview, but the changed worldview required an often very negative estimate of the great facts of Holy Scripture.[38] In Old Testament biblical criticism today, accordingly, all the opinions have returned that in the past were advocated by the Gnostics, Anabaptists, Socinians, and Rationalists concerning the Old Testament. Yahweh is not the one true God, the Father of our Lord Jesus Christ, but a nationalistic god of Israel, originally a sun god. The people of Israel were not chosen by God but were from ancient times a wild horde of various tribes who were committed to various forms of polytheism. The stories of the creation, the fall, the flood, the patriarchs, the judges, and so on are myths and sagas derived in part from other peoples. The law is on a level far below that of the prophets and often bears an external, sensual, eudaemonistic character. Old Testament saints such as Abraham, Isaac, Jacob, and especially David do not deserve that designation and either never existed at all or were idealized by their descendants. The distinction between true and false prophets is entirely subjective. Paganism has been a preparation for Christianity at least as much as Judaism.

THE PACTUM SALUTIS

[346] For dogmatics as well as for the practice of the Christian life, the doctrine of the covenant is of the greatest importance. The Reformed church and theology have grasped this fact more clearly than the Roman Catholic and Lutheran churches. Basing itself on Scripture, it consistently viewed the true religion of the Old Testament and the New Testament as a covenant between God and humans, whether it was established with unfallen humanity (the covenant of works), or with the creation in general in the person of Noah (the covenant with nature), or with the chosen people (the covenant of grace). But it did not even stop there; instead, it sought and found for these covenants in time a stable, eternal

35. I. Kant, *Religion within the Limits of Reason Alone,* trans. Theodore M. Greene and Hoyt H. Hudson (New York: Harper & Brothers, 1934), 153–55.

36. F. Schleiermacher, *The Christian Faith* (Edinburgh: T&T Clark, 1989), §8, 4; §12; §132.

37. G. W. F. Hegel, *Sämtliche Werke,* 26 vols. (Stuttgart: F. Frommann, 1949–59), XVI, 39ff. (*Werke,* XII, 39ff.: "Vorlesungen uber die Philosophie der Religion," vol. 2). Ed. note: Hegel discusses the relation between Jewish, Greek, and Roman religion in his 1827 *Lectures on the Philosophy of Religion,* ed. Peter C. Hodgson, trans. R. F. Brown, P. C. Hodgson, and J. M. Stewart, with the assistance of H. S. Harris (Berkeley: University of California Press, 1988), 328–87.

38. Van den Bergh van Eysinga, *Levensbeschouwing* (Zutphen: Thieme, 1897), 25; B. D. Eerdmans, "Reactie of Vooruitgang," *Theologische Tijdschrift* 42 (1908).

foundation in the counsel of God, and again regarded this counsel—conceived as aiming at the salvation of the human race—as a covenant between the three persons in the divine being itself (*pactum salutis,* counsel of peace, the covenant of redemption). This last-mentioned covenant occurs, briefly and materially, already in Olevianus, Junius, Gomarus, and others[39] and was then further developed at length by Cloppenburg and Cocceius.[40] It subsequently received a fixed place in dogmatics in Burman, Braun, Witsius, Vitringa, Turretin, Leydekker, Mastricht, Marck, Moor, and Brakel, in order finally to be opposed by Deurhof, Wesselius, and others[41] and gradually to be banished from dogmatics altogether.

The development of the doctrine of the *pactum salutis* [the intratrinitarian pact of salvation] among the Reformed was not free of scholastic subtlety. The classic text (Zech. 6:13) cited in support of this doctrine does not prove anything and only states that the Messiah, who unites in his person both the kingship and the priesthood, will consider and promote the peace of his people (Keil).

From Job 17:3; Isaiah 38:14; and Psalm 119:122 (none of which refer to the Messiah), and from Hebrews 7:22 (where we are told only that Christ, because he lives forever, is the guarantee that the new covenant will continue forever), it was inferred that in the pact of salvation Christ had from all eternity become the guarantor, not of God to us, as Crell and Limborch claimed[42] (for God, being trustworthy, needed no guarantor), but of us before God, as Cocceius, Witsius, and others tried to argue.[43] From the jurists, moreover, the disputants derived the distinction between a *fideiussor* (one who gives bail in advance, a guarantor) and an *expromissor* (one who promises to pay for another), and dealt with the question whether in the "pact of salvation" Christ took the sins of the Old Testament elect upon himself "conditionally" or "absolutely." The former was the position

39. K. Olevianus, *Het wezen van het Genadeverbond,* in *Geschriften* (Den Haag: Het Reformatische Boek, 1963), §1; F. Junius, *Theses theologicae,* in *Opuscula theologica selecta,* ed. Abraham Kuyper (Amsterdam: Muller, 1882), c. 25, th. 21; F. Gomarus, *Opera theologica omnia* (Amsterdam: J. Jansson, 1664), on Matt. 3:13; Luke 2:21; XIX, 1; J. Arminius, *De sacerdotio Christi,* in *The Writings of James Arminius,* trans. James Nichols and W. R. Begnall, 3 vols. (Grand Rapids: Baker, 1952), I, 2–51; W. Ames, *De morte Christi,* in *Medulla theologica,* 12 vols. (Amsterdam: Loannem Lanssonium, 1628), I, 5; G. Voetius, *Selectae disputationes theologicae,* 5 vols. (Utrecht, 1648–69), II, 266; A. Essenius, *Dissertatione de subjectione Christi ad legem divinam* (Utrecht: Antonii Smytegelt, 1666), X, 2.

40. J. Cloppenburg, "De foedere Dei," *Op. theol.,* III, 4–28; J. Cocceius, *De foedere,* ch. 5.

41. W. Deurhof, *Overnatuurkundige en Schriftuurlijke Samenstelling van de H. Godgeleerdheid,* 2 vols. (Amsterdam: Nicolaas ten Hoorn, 1715), I, 12; Wesselius, in B. Pictet, *De christelijke God-geleertheid, en Kennis der Zaligheid,* trans. Johannes Wesselius ('s Gravenhage: Pieter van Thol, 1728).

42. J. Crell, *The Expiation of a Sinner: In a Commentary upon the Epistle to the Hebrews,* trans. Thomas Lushington (London: Thomas Harper, 1646), on Heb. 7:22; P. van Limborch, *Theol. Christ.,* III, 21, 7.

43. J. Cocceius, *De foedere,* V, §§150–62; H. Witsius, *Oeconomy of the Covenants,* ch. 5; T. H. van den Honert, *Het Hoogepriesterschap van Christus* (Amsterdam: Wetstein, 1712), 403; J. H. Heidegger, *Corpus theoliae Christianae,* 2 vols. (Zürich: J. H. Bodmer, 1700), XI, 23; J. Owen, *A Continuation of the Exposition of the Epistle of Paul to the Hebrews* (London: Nathaniel Ponder, 1680), on Heb. 7:22; T. Boston, *Eene Beschouwing van het Verbond der Genade,* trans. Alexander Comrie (Leiden: J. Hasebroek, 1741), 68ff.; ed. note: English original version: *A View of the Covenant of Grace from the Sacred Records* (Glasgow: Chapman & Duncan, 1784).

of Cocceius, Wittichius, Allinga, van Til, d'Outrein, Perizonius, and others;[44] the latter that of Leydekker, Turretin, Mastricht, Voetius, and others.[45] Finally, they discussed whether this pact of salvation was more like a "testament" (with an appeal to Luke 22:19; John 17:24; Heb. 6:17; 8:6; 9:15; 13:20) as Cocceius, Burman, Heidegger, and Schiere[46] claimed, or more like a "covenant" as Leydekker, Wesselius, and others maintained.[47]

Nevertheless, this doctrine of the pact of salvation, despite its defective form, is rooted in a scriptural idea. For as Mediator, the Son is subordinate to the Father, calls him his God (Ps. 22:2; John 20:17), is his servant (Isa. 49f.) who has been assigned a task (Isa. 53:10; John 6:38–40; 10:18; 12:49; 14:31; 17:4) and who receives a reward (Ps. 2:8; Isa. 53:10; John 17:4, 11, 17, 24; Eph. 1:20f.; Phil. 2:9f.) for the obedience accomplished (Matt. 26:42; John 4:34; 15:10; 17:4–5; 19:30). Still, this relation between Father and Son, though most clearly manifest during Christ's sojourn on earth, was not first initiated at the time of the incarnation, for the incarnation itself is already included in the execution of the work assigned to the Son, but occurs in eternity and therefore also existed already during the time of the Old Testament. Scripture also clearly attests this fact when it attributes the leadership of Israel to the Angel of Yahweh (Exod. 3:2f.; 13:21; 14:19; 23:20–23; 32:34; 33:2; Num. 20:16; Isa. 63:8–9), and sees Christ also functioning officially already in the days of the Old Testament (John 8:56; 1 Cor. 10:4, 9; 1 Pet. 1:11; 3:19). For there is but one mediator between God and humankind (John 14:6; Acts 4:12; 1 Tim. 2:5), who is the same yesterday and today and forever (Heb. 13:8), who was chosen as Mediator from eternity (Isa. 42:1; 43:10; Matt. 12:18; Luke 24:26; Acts 2:23; 4:28; 1 Pet. 1:20; Rev. 13:8), and as Logos existed from eternity as well (John 1:1, 3; 8:58; Rom. 8:3; 2 Cor. 8:9; Gal. 4:4; Phil. 2:6; etc.). As a result of all this, Scripture offers us a multifaceted and glorious picture of the work of redemption. The pact of salvation makes known to us the relationships and life of the three persons in the Divine Being as a covenantal life, a life of consummate self-consciousness and freedom. Here, within the Divine Being, the covenant flourishes to the full. Whereas the covenant between God and humankind—on account of the infinite distance between them—always more or less has the character of a sovereign grant (διαθηκη) here, among the three persons,

---

44. J. Cocceius, *De foedere*, V, §§150–62; C. Wittichius, *Theologia pacifica* (Leiden: Boutesteyn, 1671), §290.

45. M. Leydekker, *Fax veritatis* (Leiden: Daniel Gaesbeeck & Felicem Lopez, 1677), V, 7; idem, *Vis veritatis* (Utrecht: Franciscum Halma, 1679), II, 1; idem, *Filius Dei sponsor* (Amsterdam: Jacobus van Hardenberg, 1674); F. Turretin, *Institutes of Elenctic Theology*, trans. G. M. Giger, ed. J. T. Dennison, 3 vols. (Phillipsburg, NJ: Presbyterian & Reformed, 1992), XII, 9; P. van Mastricht, *Theoretico-practica theologia*, (Utrecht: Appels, 1714), V, 1, 34; G. Voetius, *Selectae disputationes theologicae*, 5 vols. (Utrecht, 1648–69), V, 346; B. de Moor, *Commentarius perpetuus in Johannis Marckii compendium theologiae christianae didactico-elencticum*, 7 vols. in 6 (Leiden: T. Hasebroek, 1761–71), IV, 569–80; C. Vitringa, *Doctr. Christ.*, III, 12.

46. N. Schiere, *Doctrina testamentorum et foederum divinorum omnium* (Leovardiaw: M. Ingema, 1718), I, ch. 10.

47. M. Leydekker, *Fax veritatis*, V, 6; Wesselius, in B. Pictet, *De christelijke God-geleertheid*.

it is a pact (συνθηκη) in the full sense of the word. The greatest freedom and the most perfect agreement coincide. The work of salvation is an undertaking of three persons in which all cooperate and each performs a special task. In the decrees, also in those of predestination, the one will of God occupied the foreground, and their trinitarian character was still blurred. But here, in the pact of salvation, the work of redemption stands out in its full divine splendor. It is *the* divine work par excellence. Just as at the time of the creation of humanity, God intentionally consults with himself in advance (Gen. 1:26), so, in the work of re-creation, each of the three persons even more clearly acts in his own distinct character, is a work of God alone: of, through, and unto him are all things. No human offered him advice or gave him a gift that he might be repaid [cf. Rom. 11:34–36]. It is the triune God alone, Father, Son, and Spirit, who together conceive, determine, carry out, and complete the entire work of salvation.

This pact of salvation, however, further forms the link between the eternal work of God toward salvation and what he does to that end in time. The covenant of grace revealed in time does not hang in the air but rests on an eternal, unchanging foundation. It is firmly grounded in the counsel and covenant of the triune God and is the application and execution of it that infallibly follows. Indeed, in the covenant of grace established by God with humanity in time, human beings are not the active and acting initiators, but it is again the triune God who, having designed the work of re-creation, now brings it about. It is a false perception that God first made his covenant with Adam and Noah, with Abraham and Israel, and only finally with Christ; the covenant of grace was ready-made from all eternity in the pact of salvation of the three persons and was realized by Christ from the moment the fall occurred. Christ does not begin to work only with and after his incarnation, and the Holy Spirit does not first begin his work with the outpouring on the day of Pentecost. But just as the creation is a trinitarian work, so also the re-creation was from the start a project of the three persons. All the grace that is extended to the creation after the fall comes to it from the Father, through the Son, in the Holy Spirit. The Son appeared immediately after the fall, as Mediator, as the second and final Adam who occupies the place of the first, restores what the latter corrupted, and accomplishes what he failed to do. And the Holy Spirit immediately acted as the Paraclete, the one applying the salvation acquired by Christ. All the change that occurs, all the development and progress in insight and knowledge, accordingly, occurs on the side of the creature. In God there is no variation or shadow due to change [James 1:17]. The Father is the eternal Father, the Son the eternal Mediator, the Holy Spirit the eternal Paraclete. For that reason the Old Testament is also to be viewed as one in essence and substance with the New Testament. For though God communicates his revelation successively and historically and makes it progressively richer and fuller, and humankind therefore advances in the knowledge, possession, and enjoyment of revelation, God is and remains the same. The sun only gradually illumines the earth, but itself remains the same, morning and evening, during the day and at night. Although Christ completed his work on earth only in the midst of history and although the Holy Spirit was not poured out till the day of Pentecost, God nevertheless was able, already in the days of the Old Testament, to fully distribute the benefits to be acquired and applied by the Son and the Spirit. Old Testament believers were saved in no other way than we. There is one faith, one Mediator, one way of salvation, and one covenant of grace.[48]

THE COVENANT WITH NATURE

[347] In regard to the execution of the pact of salvation in time, however, we must be careful to distinguish between the covenant of grace in a broader and in a more restricted sense. The universal idea of the revelation of salvation does not get its due when, in the discussion of the covenant of grace in time, we immediately proceed to Israel and the church of the New Testament. Scripture, after all, does not move all at once from Adam to Abraham either; it does not abandon humanity as a whole but in broad strokes describes its development up to the time of Abraham. Then, when out of the whole human race, Abraham and Israel are chosen, the bond with that mass of humanity is not severed. Israel does not float, like a drop of oil, on the sea of peoples but remains connected by numerous ties to those peoples and to the end keeps expectation alive also for them. In the fullness of time, Jew and Gentile were reconciled in the one Man: humanity as a whole gathers around the cross; and the church, chosen from that humanity, is closely united with it. Nature and grace, creation and re-creation, must be related to each other in the way Scripture relates them. And when we do, we note that the first promises of grace that are addressed by God to Adam and Eve after the fall are totally universal and concern the whole human race. Earlier we pointed out that all punishment pronounced on sin in Genesis 3 can be simultaneously recognized as a revelation of God's grace. And that grace is there extended without any restriction to the whole of humanity. Common grace and special grace still flow in a single channel. In the punishment that God pronounced after the transgression on the serpent, the woman, and the man, we hear the voice of God's mercy more than that of his wrath. It is both punishment and promise; it is a "gracious and joy-filled punishment" (Luther). In it, accordingly, lies the origin and guarantee of continued existence, the expansion and development, the struggle and victory of humankind as a whole. Religion and morality, cult and culture have their beginnings there. In the long period from Adam to Noah, all of them develop under the influence of God's common and special grace. The original powers, instilled by God at the creation in the various creatures, though broken, continue to be effective even after the fall for a long time.

This comes to expression especially in the strength and the strikingly greater life expectancy of the people before the flood (Gen. 5:5f.) and in the dramatically

---

48. M. Schneckenburger and E. Güder, *Vergleichende Darstellung*, II, 135ff.; G. Vos, "Covenant in Reformed Theology."

more powerful operation of the natural elements, which was only curbed after that time (Gen. 8:22). This history in Scripture is confirmed by the tradition of peoples that refers, in their golden, silver, bronze, and iron age, to a gradual decline of humankind, as well as by geology, according to which, preceding our period, there was another in which a higher temperature prevailed throughout the earth, the seasons were not yet defined, and fire and water played a much more sensational role than today. In the transition from the Mesozoic to the Cenozoic era, a number of weighty changes took place, we are told: a vast expansion of continents by the elevation of extensive sections of the sea floor above the water; the formation of mountains such as the Alps, the Pyrenees, the Carpathians, the Himalayas, the Cordilleras, and others; a marked changed in climate; the extinction of the large prehistoric animals and plants, and so on.[49] In connection with all this, the greater strength and longer life expectancy of humans in the period from Adam to Noah is not at all improbable. The simpler lifestyle, the less exhausting labor, the smaller number of malignant diseases, the continued operation of the situation before the fall offer sufficient explanation for this fact. Even today, by way of exceptions, we still hear of life spans from 120 to 150 years. We cannot conceive of any physical necessity as a reason why human vitality should be exhausted after 70 or 80 years.[50] Religion, too, survived the fall and acquired fixed forms in sacrifice (Gen. 4:3), prayer, and preaching (Gen. 4:26). Culture got started with agriculture, cattle breeding, and the construction of cities (Gen. 4:17); the arts and sciences began to flourish (Gen. 4:20ff.).

But this first period in the history of humankind also soon became marked by the most fearsome wickedness. The corruption of the best proved the worst; the extraordinary powers and gifts were abused in the service of sin. This period was ushered in with fratricide. The Cainites, separating themselves from the Semites, concentrated on dominating the earth (Gen. 4:20ff.) and found their strength in the sword (Gen. 4:24). But only when the two, the Sethites and the Cainites, intermingled did wickedness explode: the imagination of the thoughts of their hearts were continually only evil (Gen. 6:5). It was a period so full of iniquity as would never come again until its return in the days of the Son of Man (Matt. 24:37). In a calamitous flood this whole generation disappears, except for Noah's family, which then becomes the nucleus of a second humanity. The period after the flood is essentially different from that before the flood. In the time from Adam to Noah, nature—the world of plants and animals—as well as humankind bore a

49. F. Pfaff, *Schöpfungsgeschichte* (Frankfurt a.M.: Heyder & Zimmer, 1877), chs. 11–15; E. Haeckel, *Natürliche Schöpfungsgeschichte*, 5th ed., 2 vols. (Berlin: G. Reimer, 1874), 520ff.; P. Wossidlo, *Leitfaden der Mineralogie und Geologie für höhere Lehranstalten* (Berlin: Weidmann, 1889), 196ff. And see further on the geological significance of the Noahic flood, H. Bavinck, *Reformed Dogmatics*, II, 505–7 (#278).

50. *Fürer, "Das Lebensalter des Menschen usw.," *Der Beweis des Glaubens* (1868): 97ff., 184ff.; O. Zöckler, *Die Lehre vom Urstand des Menschen* (Gütersloh: C. Bertelsmann, 1879), 244–88; P. Schanz, *Das Alter des Menschengeschlechts nach der Heiligen Schrift der Profangeschichte und der Vorgeschichte* (Freiburg i.B.: Herder, 1896); L. Büchner, *'s Menschen Levensduur*, trans. J. J. Schwecke (Amsterdam: N. J. Boon, 1892).

very different character from that of the time following. Powerful and copiously supplied with gifts, the world was, as it were, left to itself for a time; but it soon became evident that if God did not forcefully intervene, the world would perish in its own wickedness. With Noah, therefore, a new period begins. The grace that manifested itself immediately after the fall now exerted itself more forcefully in the restraint of evil. God made a formal covenant with all his creatures. This covenant with Noah (Gen. 8:21–22; 9:1–17), though it is rooted in God's grace and is most intimately bound up with the actual covenant of grace because it sustains and prepares for it, is not identical with it.[51] It is rather a "covenant of long-suffering" made by God with all humans and even with all creatures. It limits the curse on the earth; it checks nature and curbs its destructive power; the awesome violence of water is reined in; a regular alternation of seasons is introduced. The whole of the irrational world of nature is subjected to ordinances that are anchored in God's covenant. And the rainbow is set in the clouds as a sign and pledge (Gen. 8:21–22; 9:9–17).

A humanity now appears that, by comparison with the preceding one, is much gentler in nature, diminished in power, and of a much shorter life span. The blessing of multiplication is again expressly stated (Gen. 9:1); the fear and the dread of humans is laid on every animal (v. 2); green plants and meat are given to humans for food (v. 3). Human life is safeguarded by the requirement of the death penalty for murder and by implication, in principle, by the institution of government (vv. 5–6). And later when humanity in building the tower of Babel conceives a plan to continue to live together in one location and to start a world empire, God frustrates the plan, disperses it in peoples and languages, and in that way, too, counters the development and explosion of wickedness. The grace of God, accordingly, manifests itself much more forcefully after the flood than before. To it is due the existence and life of the human race; the expansion and development of peoples; states and societies, which gradually came into existence; religion and morality, which were not completely lost even among the most degenerate peoples; and the arts and sciences, which achieved a high level of development. Everything that after the fall is still good even in sinful humans in all areas of life, the whole structure of civil justice, is the fruit of God's common grace.[52] Granted, God did allow the Gentiles to walk in their own ways (Acts 14:16), but he did not leave them; he did not leave himself without witnesses to them but revealed himself to them through the works of his hands (Acts 14:16–17; 17:27–28; Rom. 1:19; James 1:17). The Logos illumines every human coming into the world (John 1:9). The Holy Spirit is the author of all life, power, and virtue, also among the Gentiles (Gen. 6:17; 7:15; Pss. 33:6; 104:30; 139:2; Job 32:8; Eccles. 3:19). Humankind was led by

51. Older literature on the Noahic covenant can be found in C. Vitringa, *Doct. christ.*, IV, 286.

52. Cf. previous discussion on general revelation, in H. Bavinck, *Reformed Dogmatics*, I, 302–22 (##85–89).

this grace and under the dispensation of this covenant of nature before Christ and prepared for his coming.[53] One can indeed speak in a positive sense of mankind's education by God.[54] A susceptibility for salvation was maintained and the need for it aroused.[55]

THE COVENANT IN OLD TESTAMENT SALVATION HISTORY

[348] Of an essentially different character was the preparation of salvation in Israel. In this connection we must not lose sight of the connection between the covenant of grace and the covenant of nature, between Israel and the peoples of the earth. Israel was taken from among the nations. It was neither different from nor better than other peoples. It even surpassed them in stubbornness and refractoriness and was chosen solely out of grace (Deut. 7:7; 9:13; 32:5f.; Jer. 5:23; Ezek. 16:3ff.; Amos 9:7; Matt. 11:21ff.). Neither is it the peculiar feature of Israel's religion that all sorts of elements occur in it that do not occur in other religions. On the contrary, there is nothing in Israel for which analogies cannot be found elsewhere as well: circumcision, sacrifice, prayer, priesthood, temple, altar, ceremonies, feast days, mores, customs, political and social codes, and so on occur among other peoples as well, and, conversely, institutions that appeared only after the fall, such as polygamy, slavery, and so on, are found also in Israel. Even theophany, prophecy, and miracle have their analogy and caricature in paganism.[56] It is not

53. On the late date of Jesus' coming, see, among others, Bonaventure, *The Breviloquium*, trans. J. De Vinck, vol. 2 of *The Works of Bonaventure* (Paterson, NJ: St. Anthony Guild Press, 1963), IV, 4; D. Petavius, "De incarn.," in *De theologicis dogmatibus*, 8 vols. (Paris: Vives, 1865–67), II, ch. 17; G. M. Jansen, *Praelectiones theologiae dogmaticae*, 3 vols. in 2 (Utrecht: Van Rossum, 1875–79), II, 561.

54. On the topic of divine education of the human race, see the works of Lessing, Herder, Van Heusde, Hofstede de Groot, and H. Lotze, *Microcosmus,* trans. Elizabeth Hamilton and E. E. Constance Jones (New York: Scribner & Welford, 1866), II, 144, bk. VII, ch. 2: "The Meaning of History"; A. Ritschl, *The Christian Doctrine of Justification and Reconciliation* (Clifton, NJ: Reference Book Publishers, 1966), §37.

55. In this regard, the doctrine of common grace, the development and significance of paganism, the preparation of Christ's coming, and the fullness of times also need to be considered here. See F. W. J. Schelling, *Ausgewählte Werke,* 4 vols. (Darmstadt: Wissenschaftliche Buchgesellschaft, 1968), II/ 4, 74–118; A. Wuttke, *Geschichte des Heidenthums in Beziehung auf Religion, Wissen, Kunst, Sittlichkeit, und Staatsleben,* 2 vols. (Breslau: Max, 1852–53); A. Tholuck, *Der sittlicher Charakter des Heidenthums* (Gotha: Perthes, 1867), VII, 1–91; G. Uhlhorn, *Der Kampf des Christenthums mit dem Heidenthum* (Stuttgart: Gundert, 1899), chs. 1–2; D. Zahn, *Die natürliche Moral christlich beurteilt und angewandt auf die Gegenwart in Kirche, Schule, und innerer Mission* (Gotha: G. Schloeszmann, 1881); F. Hettinger, *Apologie des Christentums,* ed. Eugen Müller, 9th ed., 5 vols. (Freiburg i.B. and St. Louis: Herder, 1906–8), II, 52ff.; P. Schanz, *A Christian Apology,* trans. Michael F. Glancey and Victor J. Schobel, 4th rev. ed. (Ratisbon: F. Pustet, 1891), II, 1ff.; O. Pfleiderer, *Vorbereitung des Christentums in der griechischen Philosophie* (Halle: Gebauer & Schwetschke, 1904); *Schucklebier, "Ein Streifzug durch die antike Philosophie, als die Zeit erfüllt war," *Neue kirchliche Zeitschrift* (1908): 935–72; P. Wendland, *Die hellenistisch-römische Kultur in ihrer Beziehungen zu Judentum und Christentum* (Tübingen: Mohr, 1907); A. Deissmann, *Licht vom Osten*; J. Boehmer, *Reichsgottesspuren in der Völkerwelt* (Gütersloh: Bertelsmann, 1906); Talbot, "The Preparation in History for Christ," in *Lux Mundi,* ed. C. Gore, 13th ed. (London: Murray, 1892), 93–131; H. M. van Nes, *De Adventstijd der wereld* (Rotterdam: Wenk & Birkhoff, 1896).

56. F. W. J. Schelling, *Werke,* II, 119–51.

only the right but also the duty of Old Testament science to bring all these things into the light of day.

Yet we must not—for the sake of the kinship and connection between them—overlook the essential difference. This is the special grace that was unknown to the pagans. All pagan religions are self-willed and legalistic. They are all the aftereffects and adulterations of the covenant of works. Human beings here consistently try to bring about their own salvation by purifications, ascesis, penance, sacrifice, law observance, ceremony, and so on.

All this, however, is different in Israel.[57] This is immediately evident from the fact that for Israel Yahweh was from the start also Elohim, the Creator of heaven and earth. Even the most ancient parts [of the Old Testament], according to modern criticism, clearly voice this belief (Gen. 2:4; Exod. 20:11). In Israel the God-world relation is never conceived other than as that between the Creator and the creature.[58] With this one dogma alone, all paganism is in principle rejected; it is the foundation of true and pure religion. This Creator of heaven and earth, moreover, is also he who maintains and governs the world and who freely and graciously entered into a special relationship with Israel. Israel was taken from among the peoples; Abraham was a descendant of Shem, in whose lineage the knowledge and worship of God had been preserved most purely and for the longest period. The covenant with Abraham was prepared in history from the time of Adam. Israel's religion was built on the broad foundation of the original religion of humankind. Yet the covenant with Abraham is a new and higher revelation that again totally proceeds from God alone. In this covenant it is he who takes the initiative; he establishes it and chooses Abraham. By the miraculous birth of Isaac, he proves himself both the Creator and the Re-creator of Israel. In the religion of Israel it is not humans who search for God but God who seeks out humans.

This covenant with the ancestors continues, even when later at Sinai it assumes another form. It is the foundation and core also of the Sinaitic covenant (Exod. 2:24; Deut. 7:8). The promise was not nullified by the law that came later (Gal. 3:17). The covenant with Israel was essentially no other than that with Abraham. Just as God first freely and graciously gave himself as shield and reward to Abraham, apart from any merits of his, to be a God to him and his descendants after him, and on that basis called Abraham to a blameless walk before his face, so also it is God who chose the people of Israel, saved it out of Egypt, united himself with that people, and obligated it to be holy and his own people. The covenant on Mount Sinai is and remains a covenant of grace. "I am the LORD your God, who brought you out of the land of Egypt, out of the house of slavery" (Exod. 20:2) is the opening statement and foundation of the law, the essence of the covenant of grace. Yahweh is and perpetually remains Israel's God before and aside from any

57. Also cf. H. Bavinck, *Philosophy of Revelation* (Grand Rapids: Eerdmans, 1953), 187ff.
58. H. Schultz, *Alttestamentliche Theologie,* 4th ed., 2 vols. (Göttingen: Vandenhoeck & Ruprecht, 1889), 565.

dignity or worth that Israel may have. It is an everlasting covenant that cannot be broken even by any sins and iniquities on the part of Israel (Deut. 4:31; 32:26f.; Judg. 2:1; Pss. 89:1–5; 105:8; 111:5; Isa. 54:10; Rom. 11:1–2; 2 Cor. 1:20).

The benefits granted to Israel by God in this covenant are the same as those granted to Abraham, but more detailed and specialized. Genesis 3:15 already contains the entire covenant in a nutshell and all the benefits of grace. God breaks the covenant made by the first humans with Satan, puts enmity between them, brings the first humans over to his side, and promises them victory over the power of the enemy. The one great promise to Abraham is "I will be your God, and you and your descendants will be my people" (Gen. 17:8 paraphrase). And this is the principal content of God's covenant with Israel as well. God is Israel's God, and Israel is his people (Exod. 19:6; 29:46; etc.). Israel, accordingly, receives a wide assortment of blessings, not only temporal blessings, such as the land of Canaan, fruitfulness in marriage, a long life, prosperity, plus victory over its enemies, but also spiritual and eternal blessings, such as God's dwelling among them (Exod. 29:45; Lev. 26:12), the forgiveness of sins (Exod. 20:6; 34:7; Num. 14:18; Deut. 4:31; Pss. 32; 103; etc.), sonship (Exod. 4:22; 19:5–6; 20:2; Deut. 14:1; Isa. 63:16; Amos 3:1–2; etc.), sanctification (Exod. 19:6; Lev. 11:44; 19:2), and so on. All these blessings, however, are not as plainly and clearly pictured in the Old Testament as in the New Testament. At that time they would not have been grasped and understood in their spiritual import. The natural is first, then the spiritual. All spiritual and eternal benefits are therefore clothed, in Israel, in sensory forms. The forgiveness of sins is bound to animal sacrifices. God's dwelling in Israel is symbolized in the temple built on Zion. Israel's sonship is primarily a theocratic one, and the expression "people of God" has not only a religious but also a national meaning. Sanctification in an ethical sense is symbolized in Levitical ceremonial purity. Eternal life, to the Israelite consciousness, is concealed in the form of a long life on earth. It would be foolish to think that the benefits of forgiveness and sanctification, of regeneration and eternal life, were therefore objectively nonexistent in the days of the Old Testament. They were definitely granted then as well by Christ, who is eternally the same. But the consciousness and enjoyment of those benefits were far from being as rich in the Old Testament as in the time of the New Testament. The reason why the covenant of grace in Israel assumed such a unique symbolic form is that this consciousness of the pious might gradually over the centuries open up to the riches of God's benefits. Israel's religion aligned itself with the religious forms—forms that occur among all peoples—of sacrifice, altar, temple, priesthood, ceremonies, and so on. The spiritual and eternal clothed itself in the form of the natural and temporal. God himself, Elohim, Creator of heaven and earth, as Yahweh, the God of the covenant, came down to the level of the creature, entered into history, assumed human language, emotions, and forms, in order to communicate himself with all his spiritual blessings to humans and so to prepare for his incarnation, his permanent and eternal indwelling in humanity. We would not even have at our disposal words with which to name the spiritual had not the spiritual first revealed itself in the form of the natural. Sensory creatures that we are, we can only express spiritual things analogically. If the eternal had not come within our reach in time, if God had not become a human, then neither could his thoughts have been conveyed to us in our language in Holy Scripture. God would have remained perpetually unknowable to us, and we would always have had to remain silent about him.

Just as Abraham, when God allied himself with him, was obligated to "walk before his face," so Israel as a people was similarly admonished by God's covenant to a new obedience. The entire law, which the covenant of grace at Mount Sinai took into its service, is intended to prompt Israel as a people to "walk" in the way of the covenant. It is but an explication of the one statement to Abraham: "Walk before me, and be blameless" [Gen. 17:1], and therefore no more a cancellation of the covenant of grace and the foundation of a covenant of works than this word spoken to Abraham. The law of Moses, accordingly, is not antithetical to grace but subservient to it and was also thus understood and praised in every age by Israel's pious men and women. But detached from the covenant of grace, it indeed became a letter that kills, a ministry of condemnation. Another reason why in the time of the Old Testament the covenant of grace took the law into its service was that it might arouse the consciousness of sin, increase the felt need for salvation, and reinforce the expectation of an even richer revelation of God's grace. It is from that perspective that Paul views especially the Old Testament dispensation of the covenant of grace. He writes that Israel as a minor, placed under the care of the law, had to be led to Christ (Rom. 10:4; Gal. 3:23f.; 4:1f.) and that in that connection sin would be increased and the uselessness of works for justification and the necessity of faith would be understood (Rom. 4:15; 5:20; 7:7f.; 8:3; Gal. 3:19). On the one hand, therefore, the law was subservient to the covenant of grace; it was not a covenant of works in disguise and did not intend that humans would obtain justification by their own works. On the other hand, its purpose was to lay the groundwork for a higher and better dispensation of that same covenant of grace to come in the fullness of time. The impossibility of keeping the Sinaitic covenant and of meeting the demands of the law made another and better dispensation of the covenant of grace necessary. The eternal covenant of grace was provoked to a higher revelation of itself by the imperfection of the temporary form it had assumed in Israel. Sin increased that grace might abound. Christ could not immediately become human after the fall, and grace could not immediately reveal itself in all its riches. There was a need for preparation and nurture. "It was not fitting for God to become incarnate at the beginning of the human race before sin. For medicine is given only to the sick. Nor was it fitting that God should become incarnate immediately after sin that man, having been humbled by sin, might see his own need of a deliverer. But what had been decreed from eternity occurred in the fullness of time."[59]

59. T. Aquinas, *Summa theol.*, III, qu. 1, art. 5.

THE NEW COVENANT

The necessity of this upbringing and preparation does not arise, objectively, in God as though he were variable; nor in Christ as though he were not the same yesterday and today and forever; nor in the spiritual benefits as though they did not exist and could not be communicated by God. But it arises, subjectively, in the state of the human race, which, precisely as a race, had to be saved and hence had to be gradually prepared and educated for salvation in Christ.[60] Christ, accordingly, is the turning point of the times, the cross the focal point of world history. First, everything was led in the direction of the cross; subsequently, everything was inferred from the cross.

So when the fullness of time had come and Christ had completed his work on earth, the covenant of grace moved into a higher dispensation. Believers in Israel indeed knew that the Sinaitic dispensation was merely temporary and therefore anticipated the day of the new covenant with longing. And Jesus with the apostles who read the Old Testament in that way saw in it the same covenant of grace with the same benefits that now became fully manifest. The Old and the New Testaments are in essence one covenant (Luke 1:68–79; Acts 2:39; 3:25). They have one gospel (Rom. 1:2; Gal. 3:8; Heb. 4:2, 6; 2 Tim. 3:15); one mediator, namely, Christ, who existed also in the days of the Old Testament (John 1:1, 14; 8:58; Rom. 8:3; 2 Cor. 8:9; Gal. 4:4; Phil. 2:6; etc.), exercised his office of mediator (John 8:56; 1 Cor. 10:4; 1 Pet. 1:11; 3:19; Heb. 13:8), and is the only mediator for all humans and in all times (John 14:6; Acts 4:12; 1 Tim. 2:5). It included one faith as the way of salvation (Matt. 13:17; Acts 10:43; 15:11; Rom. 4:11; Gal. 3:6–7; Heb. 11); the same promises and benefits of God's communion (2 Cor. 6:16; Rev. 21:3), forgiveness, justification (Acts 10:43; Rom. 4:22), and eternal life (Matt. 22:32; Gal. 3:18; Heb. 9:15; 11:10; etc.). The road was the same on which believers in the Old and the New Testaments walked, but the light in which they walked was different.[61]

For all the unity between them, therefore, there is also difference. The Old and the New Testaments as different dispensations of the same covenant of grace are related as promise and fulfillment (Acts 13:32; Rom. 1:2), as shadow and substance (Col. 2:17), as the letter that kills and the Spirit that makes alive (2 Cor. 3:6ff.), as servitude and freedom (Rom. 8:15; Gal. 4:1ff., 22ff.; Col. 2:20; Heb. 12:18f.), as particular and universal (John 4:21; Acts 10:35; 14:16; Gal. 4:4–5; 6:15; Eph. 2:14; 3:6).

The new thing in the New Testament, therefore, is the shedding of the non-arbitrary but still temporary sensory national forms under which one and the same grace was revealed in the old day. The new dispensation already starts in a sense when, with the births of John the Baptist and Jesus, the promises of the Old

---

60. J. Calvin, *Institutes*, II.xi, xiii, xiv.

61. J. Calvin, *Commentary on the Epistles of Paul the Apostle to the Galatians, Ephesians, Philippians and Colossians,* trans. T. H. L. Parker (Grand Rapids: Eerdmans, 1965), on Gal. 3:23.

Testament begin to be fulfilled. Yet the old dispensation still remained in effect up until the death of Christ.[62] Jesus himself was an Israelite, fulfilled all righteousness, and still concerned himself only with the lost sheep of the house of Israel. But at his death, the curtain in the temple tore in two (Matt. 27:51), the testator himself died (Heb. 9:15–17), the New Testament was founded in his blood (Matt. 26:28), the bond that stood against us was canceled (Col. 2:14), the dividing wall was broken down (Eph. 2:14), and so on. Factually the old dispensation may long linger, but legally it has been abolished. Better still, nothing was abolished, but the fruit was ripe and broke through the husk. The church, carried like a fetus in Israel's womb, was born to an independent life of its own and in the Holy Spirit received an immanent life principle of its own. The sun of righteousness rose to its zenith in the heavens and shone out over all peoples. The law and the prophets have been fulfilled and in Christ as their end and goal reached their destiny. The law was given through Moses; grace and truth came through Jesus Christ (John 1:14). He is the truth (John 14:6), the substance (Col. 2:17) in whom all the promises and shadows have been realized. In him all things have been fulfilled. He is the true prophet, priest, and king; the true servant of the Lord, the true expiation (Rom. 3:25), the true sacrifice (Eph. 5:2), the true circumcision (Col. 2:11), the true Passover (1 Cor. 5:7), and therefore his church is the true seed of Abraham, the true Israel, the true people of God (Matt. 1:21; Luke 1:17; Rom. 9:25–26; 2 Cor. 6:16–18; Gal. 3:29; Titus 2:14; Heb. 8:8–10; 1 Pet. 2:9; Rev. 21:3), the true temple of God (1 Cor. 3:16; 2 Cor. 6:16; Eph. 2:21; 2 Thess. 2:4; Heb. 8:2, 5), the true Zion and Jerusalem (Gal. 4:26; Heb. 12:22), its spiritual offering, the true religion (John 4:24; Rom. 12:1; Phil. 3:3; 4:18; etc.). Nothing of the Old Testament is lost in the New, but everything is fulfilled, matured, has reached its full growth, and now, out of the temporary husk, produces the eternal core. It is not the case that in Israel there was a true temple and sacrifice and priesthood and so on and that all these have now vanished. The converse, rather, is true: of all this Israel only possessed a shadow, but now the substance itself has emerged. The things we see are temporal, but the invisible things are eternal.[63]

RELATION TO THE COVENANT OF NATURE

[349] This covenant of grace, which through various dispensations has now been fully realized in the New Testament, was from the first moment of its reve-

---

62. Cf. C. Vitringa, *Doctr. christ.*, VI, 292–300: de initio Novi Testamenti.

63. We cannot possibly enter a discussion and refutation of the new views on Israel's religion here. Yet the reader must be briefly reminded that these views, so far from being unanimous, diverge in three directions. Many scholars believe that Israel's religion developed evolutionistically out of polydaemonism through henotheism into ethical monotheism (Wellhausen, Kuenen, Graf, Stade, Guthe, Marti, and others). Others try to trace the monotheism of Israel, as well as numerous stories and customs, to Babylonia (Winckler, F. Delitzsch, Jeremias, Erbt, and others). Yet a considerable group of scholars still maintain that the religion of Israel was from the start one of a kind and the result of a special revelation in the life of the patriarchs or at least in the life of Moses. For the sake of brevity, cf. E. König, *Geschichte des Reiches Gottes*, 33; G. Wildeboer, *Het Oude Testament*, 34ff.

lation and is still today surrounded and sustained on all sides by the covenant of nature God established with all creatures. Although special grace is essentially distinct from common grace, it is intimately bound up with it. After all, though the covenant with Noah is called—for the purpose of differentiation—the "covenant of nature," it did not flow from God's nature and was not given with the nature of things; it, too, rests on grace, proceeds from God's patience, and grants all natural benefits and blessings out of God's general goodness. It is a covenant of grace in the broad sense. Further, it is the Father who—not apart from the Son but specifically through the Logos and the Spirit—produces all the forces and gifts present in nature and unregenerate humankind (John 1:4–5, 9–10; Col. 1:17; Pss. 104:30; 139:7). And this Logos and Spirit who dwell and work in all creatures and humans are the same agents who as Christ and the Spirit of Christ acquire and apply all the benefits pertaining to the covenant of grace. Father, Son, and Spirit, then, prepare for the covenant of grace in the covenant of nature and reach back from it, as it were, into the covenant of nature.

The essential character of the covenant of grace, accordingly, consists in the fact that it proceeds from God's special grace and has for its content nothing other than grace—undeserved and forfeited blessings. To that extent it is essentially distinct from the covenant of works, which was established before, and broken by, the fall. Granted, it is also true of the covenant of works that God was not obligated to introduce it. It was his condescending goodness, and thus also grace in a general sense, that prompted him to grant this covenant to human beings. He, accordingly, established it and determined every part of it: it is his ordinance and institution. Yet in that covenant of works God came to humanity with the demand of obedience and—only in that way and upon the accomplishment of it—promised to grant them the blessedness of heaven, eternal life, and the enjoyment of the beatific vision. The covenant of works, accordingly, factored in the free will of the first human pair; in part it depended on them and was therefore insecure and unstable. In fact, therefore, it was broken, not by God, but by [the first] human pair. God stands by the rule that those who keep the law will receive eternal life. He posits this in his law, attests it in everyone's conscience, and validates the statement in Christ. But human beings broke the covenant of works; now they are no longer able to acquire life by keeping it. By the works of the law no human can be justified. In distinction from and contrast to the covenant of works, God therefore established another, a better, covenant, not a legalistic but an evangelical covenant. But he made it, not with one who was solely a human, but with the man Christ Jesus, who was his own only begotten, much-beloved Son. And in him, who shares the divine nature and attributes, this covenant has an unwaveringly firm foundation. It can no longer be broken: it is an everlasting covenant. It rests not in any work of humans but solely in the good pleasure of God, in the work of the Mediator, in the Holy Spirit, who remains forever. It is not dependent on any human condition; it does not confer any benefit based on merit; it does not wait for any law keeping on the part of humans. It is of, through, and for grace. God himself is the sole and eternal being, the faithful and true being, in whom it rests and who establishes, maintains, executes, and completes it. The covenant of grace is the divine work par excellence—his work alone and his work totally. All boasting is excluded here for humans; all glory is due to the Father, Son, and Holy Spirit.

Yet this still does not describe the full implications of the covenant of grace. To that end it must be elucidated, not only in distinction from but also in its connection with the covenant of works. After the covenant of works had been broken, God did not immediately conceive a totally different covenant unrelated to the preceding one and that has a different character. That simply could not be the case, for God is unchangeable; the demand posed to humans in the covenant of works is not arbitrary and capricious. The image of God, the law, and religion can by their very nature only be one; grace, nature, and faith cannot or may not nullify the law. Nor is it so. The covenant of grace is not, as Cocceius taught, the successive abolition of the covenant of works but its fulfillment and restoration. "Grace repairs and perfects nature." God stands by the demand that eternal life can be obtained only in the way of obedience; and when a person violates his law, it is expanded with another: the law that the violation must be paid for by punishment. After the fall, therefore, God lays a double claim on humans: that of the payment of a penalty for the evil done and that of perfect obedience to his law (satisfaction and obedience). In a letter to Uytenbogaert, Arminius expresses the view that before the fall humans were indeed obligated to obedience but after the fall only to payment of the penalty, because the contract was now broken and the [human] party relieved of its obligation. But though in the covenant of works, obedience to God's law had been cast in a special form and was directed to a special end (i.e., the securing of eternal life), it is, as such, grounded in the nature of humans and hence an obligation from which they can never be released. Otherwise, they could by one violation free themselves for all time from keeping all God's commandments and so from all sins and penalties. Scripture, accordingly, not only pronounces God's judgment on sinners (Deut. 27:26; Gal. 3:10; Rom. 6:23; Heb. 10:27), but also after the fall maintains for humankind the demand of perfect obedience as the way to eternal life (Lev. 18:5; Matt. 19:17; Luke 10:28).

The difference between the covenant of works and the covenant of grace therefore consists in the fact that in the latter God asserts not one but a double demand, and that with this double demand he approaches not humanity in Adam but humanity in Christ. The covenant of works and the covenant of grace primarily differ in that Adam is exchanged for and replaced by Christ. In Galatians 3:16–18, Paul states that the covenant with Abraham was not nullified by the law that came later but actually related to and essentially rested in Christ, who fulfilled the whole promise and bequeathed the inheritance. He goes back even further in Romans 5:12–21 and 1 Corinthians 15:22, 45–49. Sin and death accrue to humanity from Adam; righteousness and life from Christ. Christ is the second and last Adam who restores what the first Adam had corrupted and takes over what he had neglected. He is the mediator of the covenant of grace, the head of the new humanity. To this idea of Scripture, Reformed theology in its doctrine of the covenant has done more justice than any other.

The course of development in this connection, briefly, was this. The doctrine of the covenant of grace first emerged for the purpose of maintaining the essential unity of the Old and the New Testaments. In keeping with this, also the relation between God and humans *before* the fall was portrayed as a covenant, specifically a covenant of works. Reflection on the similarity and difference between the covenant of works and the covenant of grace then led to the insight that the covenant of grace, insofar as it was made with Christ, was essentially a covenant of works. It was then discovered that in the covenant of grace a further distinction had to be made between the covenant as it was made with Christ from eternity (the pact of salvation, the counsel of peace) and the covenant as it is made with the elect or believers in time as the implementation of that counsel of peace. Finally, this distinction was voided; the covenant of grace and the counsel of peace were now viewed as being essentially identical; the covenant of grace itself was shifted to eternity as being made there with Christ and in him with all his own. This last point, the identification of the counsel of peace with the covenant of grace, was first developed in England in the work of Rollock, Preston, Blake, and the Longer Westminster Catechism,[64] and was later taken over from the English by Comrie, Brahe, and others.[65] Many Reformed theologians, however, continued to object to this identification and to insist on the difference between the two.[66]

Indeed, there is a difference between the pact of salvation and the covenant of grace. In the former, Christ is the guarantor and head; in the latter, he is the mediator. The first remains restricted to Christ and demands from him that he bear the punishment and fulfill the law in the place of the elect; the second is extended to and through Christ to humans and demands from them the faith and repentance that Christ has not, and could not, accomplish in their place. The first concerns the acquisition of salvation, is eternal, and knows no history; the second deals with the application of salvation, begins in time, and passes through several dispensations.

Still, given this distinction, we must not overlook the connection between them and their unity. In Scripture there are only two covenants, two ways to heaven for

64. Cf. G. Vos, "Covenant in Reformed Theology"; T. Boston, *Eene Beschouwing van het Verbond der Genade.*

65. Cf., e.g., J. J. Brahe's explanation of Psalm 89, *Ethans onderwyzinge in den negenentachtigsten Psalm* (Amsterdam: Nicolaas Byl, 1765), v–xxxvi; W. G. T. Shedd, *Dogmatic Theology,* 3rd ed., 3 vols. (New York: Scribner, 1891–94), II, 360.

66. F. Turretin, *Institutes of Elenctic Theology,* XII, 2, 12; H. Witsius, *Oeconomy of the Covenants,* II, 2, 1; idem, *Miscellaneorum sacrorum,* 3rd ed., 2 vols. (Herborn, Germany: Iohannis Nicolai Andreae, 1712), II, 820–24; R. Schutte, *Tweetal verhandelingen behelzende de eerste eene verklaring van Gods Testament* (Amsterdam: de Bruyn & van Toll, 1785), 143ff.; C. Hodge, *Systematic Theology,* 3 vols. (New York: Charles Scribner's Sons, 1888), II, 358.

human beings, the covenant of works and the covenant of grace. The covenant of works is the way to heaven for the unfallen, the covenant of grace that for fallen humans. The covenant of works was made with humankind in Adam; the covenant of grace was made with humankind in Christ. He, and he alone, is the substitutionary and representative head of humankind. So then, when it is said in Scripture that the covenant of grace was made with Adam, Noah, Abraham, Israel, and others, this must not be understood to mean that they were the actual parties and heads in this covenant. On the contrary, then and now, in the Old and the New Testaments, Christ was and is the head and the key party in the covenant of grace, and through his administration it came to the patriarchs and to Israel. He who existed from eternity and had made himself the surety, also immediately after the fall acted as prophet, priest, and king, as the second Adam, as head and representative of fallen humankind. In the covenant with Adam, Noah, Abraham, David, and others, he is the mediator, the guarantor who takes responsibility for the implementation of the covenant, realizes it in the hearts of humans by his Spirit, administers it to sinners, bestows its benefits, and incorporates his own in the covenant. From start to finish, the whole covenant is entrusted to him. In him alone it is secure and firm. Just as the Father had ordained the kingdom for him, so he ordains it for those who have been given to him. He distributes the benefits he has acquired as an inheritance. The covenant is certain as a testament; it is a covenant of testaments and a covenantal testament. It involves no principle and is relatively immaterial whether one highlights the duality or the unity of the pact of salvation and the covenant of grace, provided it is clear that in the pact of salvation Christ can never even for a second be conceived apart from his own, and that in the covenant of grace believers can never even for one second be regarded outside Christ. In both cases it is the mystical Christ,[67] Christ as the second Adam, who acts as the negotiating party. Adam, Abraham, David, and others may be types, but the antitype is Christ. And since (as is evident from 1 Cor. 15:45ff.) Adam was a type of Christ even before the fall, so the covenant of grace was prepared, not first by Noah and Abraham nor first by the covenant of grace with Adam, but already in and by the covenant of works. God, who knows and determines all things and included also the breach of the covenant of works in his counsel when creating Adam and instituting the covenant of works, already counted on the Christ and his covenant of grace.[68]

COVENANT AND ELECTION

[350] Thus in a marvelous way the doctrine of the covenant maintains God's sovereignty in the entire work of salvation. It far surpasses the covenant of works to the degree that Christ exceeds Adam. God's threefold being is manifest much

---

67. J. Zanchi, *De operum theologicorum*, 8 vols. (Geneva: Sumptibus Samuelis Crispini, 1617), II, 400ff.; P. van Mastricht, *Theologia*, V, 1, 4.

68. Cf. H. Bavinck, *Reformed Dogmatics*, II, 561–62 (#293).

more clearly in the re-creation than in the creation. It is the Father who conceives, plans, and wills the work of salvation; it is the Son who guarantees it and effectively acquires it; it is the Spirit who implements and applies it. And into that entire work of salvation, from beginning to end, nothing is introduced that derives from humans. It is God's work totally and exclusively; it is pure grace and undeserved salvation. Despite, or rather because of, the fact that this doctrine of the covenant so purely and fully maintains God's sovereignty in the work of salvation, however, it is all the more important to note that it at the same time beautifully allows the rational and moral nature of humans to come into their own. In the covenant of works, this point has already been explained in detail.[69] But in the covenant of grace, it comes to even more striking expression. In this respect it is very different from election.[70] Admittedly, the two are not so different that election is particular while the covenant of grace is universal, that the former denies free will and the latter teaches or assumes it, that the latter takes back what the former teaches. But the two do differ in that in election humans are strictly passive but in the covenant of grace they also play an active role. Election only and without qualification states who are elect and will infallibly obtain salvation; the covenant of grace describes the road by which these elect people will attain their destiny. The covenant of grace is the channel by which the stream of election flows toward eternity. In this covenant Christ indeed acts as the head and representative of his own, but he does not efface and destroy them. He vouches for them but does so in such a way that they themselves, instructed and enabled by the Spirit, also consciously and voluntarily consent to this covenant. Although the covenant of grace has been made with Christ, through him it nevertheless reaches out also to his own, completely embraces and incorporates them body and soul. The pact of salvation expands to become a covenant of grace. The head of the covenant of grace is at the same time its mediator. For that reason, from the moment of its public announcement, it comes with the demand of faith and repentance (Mark 1:15). In the beginning Reformed theologians spoke freely of "the conditions" of the covenant.[71] But after the nature of the covenant of grace had been more carefully considered and had to be defended against Catholics, Lutherans, and Remonstrants, many of them took exception to the term and avoided it.[72]

69. Ibid., 568–72 (#296).

70. Cf. H. H. Kuyper, *Hamabdil: Van de heiligheid van het Genadeverbond* (Amsterdam: Bottenburg, 1907), 18ff.

71. J. Calvin, *Inst.*, IV, 15, 17; idem, *Commentary on Genesis,* trans. John King (Grand Rapids: Baker, 1979), on Gen 15:6; 17:4; idem, *Commentary on a Harmony of the Gospels Matthew, Mark, and Luke* (Grand Rapids: Eerdmans, 1949), on Matt. 3:7, 9; F. Gomarus, *De foedere*; S. Maresius, *Systema Theologicum* (Groningen: Aemilium Spinneker, 1673), VII, 5; J. Trigland, *Antapologia* (Amsterdam: Joannam Janssonium [et al.], 1664), ch. 18.; foreword to the Dutch Authorized Version (*Statenvertaling*) of the New Testament; G. Voetius, *Select. disp.*, V, 272–73.

72. K. Olevianus, *Het wezen van het Genadeverbond*, I, 13–14; F. Junius, *Op. theol. select.*, XXV, 12, 13, 19; J. Cocceius, *De foedere*, §87; idem, *Summa theologiae ex scripturis repetita* (Amsterdam: J. Ravensteinium, 1665), 41, 5, 12, 13; J. Cloppenburg, *De foedere*, §29; H. Witsius, *Oeconomy of Faith*, III, 1, 8–16; A. Francken,

In the covenant of grace, that is, in the gospel, which is the proclamation of the covenant of grace, there are actually no demands and no conditions. For God supplies what he demands. Christ has accomplished everything, and though he did not accomplish rebirth, faith, and repentance in our place, he did acquire them for us, and the Holy Spirit therefore applies them. Still, in its administration by Christ, the covenant of grace does assume this demanding conditional form. The purpose is to acknowledge humans in their capacity as rational and moral beings; still, though they are fallen, to treat them as having been created in God's image; and also on this supremely important level, where it concerns their eternal weal and eternal woe, to hold them responsible and inexcusable; and, finally, to cause them to enter consciously and freely into this covenant and to break their covenant with sin. The covenant of grace, accordingly, is indeed unilateral: it proceeds from God; he has designed and defined it. He maintains and implements it. It is a work of the triune God and is totally completed among the three Persons themselves. But it is destined to become bilateral, to be consciously and voluntarily accepted and kept by humans in the power of God. This is the will of God, which so clearly and beautifully manifests itself in the covenant in order that the work of grace may be clearly reflected in the human consciousness and arouse the human will to exert itself energetically and forcefully. The covenant of grace does not deaden human beings or treat them as inanimate objects. On the contrary, it totally includes them with all their faculties and powers, in soul and body, for time and eternity. It embraces them totally, does not destroy their power, but deprives them of their impotence. It does not kill their will but frees them from sin; it does not numb their consciousness but delivers it from darkness. It re-creates the whole person and, having renewed it by grace, prompts it, freely and independently, with soul, mind, and body, to love God and to dedicate itself to him. The covenant of grace declares that God's honor and acclaim is not won at the expense but for the benefit of human persons and celebrates its triumphs in the re-creation of the whole person, in his or her enlightened consciousness and restored freedom.

This at the same time implies still another idea, one that stands out in the covenant of grace in distinction from election. In election the elect appear as so many persons known to God by name. Granted, they are elect in Christ, and constitute an organism with him as their head. Still, in election this reality does not stand out. In the covenant of grace, however, this is very different. Here Christ appears on the scene as the replacement of Adam, as the second head of the human race. Here Christ with his church manifestly stands connected with humanity under Adam. Election calls attention especially to individuals; by itself it leaves

---

Kern der Christelyke leere (Rotterdam: Losel, 1756), ch. 23; W. Brakel, *The Christian's Reasonable Service*, trans. B. Elshout, 4 vols. (Ligonier, PA: Soli Deo Gloria Publications, 1992–95), XVI, 17; A. von Comrie, *Stellige en praktikale verklaring van den Heidelbergschen Catechismus* (Minnertsga: J. Bloemsma, 1844), I, 352; C. Vitringa, *Doctr. Christ.*, VI, 224. In England the Antinomians, such as Tobias Crisp, criticized it but were in turn opposed by others such as R. Baxter, D. Williams.

open the possibility that each of the elect would individualistically and by leaps be taken out of the human race, born again, and transferred to heaven. But the covenant of grace says that that election is realized in a very different manner. It pronounces the deep and beautiful truth that Adam has been replaced by Christ, that the humanity that fell in the person of the first is restored in the second; that not just a few separate individuals are saved but that in the elect-under-Christ the organism of humanity and of the world itself is saved; that not only the persons of the elect but also the "structure of the organism" that they form in Christ is derived from the original creation in Adam. For that reason the covenant of grace does not leap from individual to individual but perpetuates itself organically and historically. It passes through a history and through different dispensations. It accommodates itself to times and occasions appointed by the Father as Creator and Sustainer. It is never made with a solitary individual but always also with his or her descendants. It is a covenant from generations to generations. Nor does it ever encompass just the person of the believer in the abstract but that person concretely as he or she exists and lives in history, hence including everything that is his or hers. It includes him or her not just as a person but him or her also as father and mother, as parent or child, with all that is his or hers, with his or her family, money, possessions, influence, and power, with his or her office and job, intellect and heart, science and art, with his or her life in society and the state. The covenant of grace is the organization of the new humanity under Christ as its head, as it links up with the creation order, and, reaching back to it, qualitatively and intensively incorporates the whole of creation into itself.

It is self-evident, therefore, that the covenant of grace will temporarily—in its earthly administration and dispensation—also include those who remain inwardly unbelieving and do not share in the covenant's benefits. With a view to this reality, Reformed scholars made a distinction between an internal and an external covenant,[73] or between "covenant" and "covenant administration,"[74] or between an absolute and a conditional covenant.[75] Some[76] even went so far as to assume the existence of two covenants, one with the elect and true believers, the other with external, not genuinely believing members of the church, and thereby tried to justify the [church] membership of the latter and their access to the Lord's

73. Marginal comment in the Authorized Version of the Dutch Bible on 1 Cor. 7:14, 1 Pet. 2:9; H. Witsius, *Oeconomy of Faith*, III, 1, 5; P. van Mastricht, *Theologia*, V, 1, 28.

74. K. Olevianus, *Het wezen van het Genadeverbond*, I, 2; H. Alting, *Scriptorum Theologicorum Heidelbergensium*, 2 vols (Freistadii [Amsterdam?]: Typographorum Belgicae Foederatae, 1646), 33; F. Turretin, *Institutes of Elenctic Theology*, XII, 6, 5.

75. S. Maresius, *Syst. theol.*, VIII, 7; J. Koelman, *Historisch verhael nopende der Labadisten* (Amsterdam: Johannes Boeckholt, 1683), 566.

76. Blake, in G. Vos, "Covenant in Reformed Theology"; Stoddard in Northampton, in J. Edwards, *Works*, I, 34 (ed. note: it is not clear to which work Bavinck is referring here and in note 77 below); J. Schuts, *Verhandeling over des heeren H. Avondmaal* (Utrecht: Johannes van Schoonhoven, 1765); R. Schutte, *Tweetal Verhandelingen* (Amsterdam: de Bruyne & van Toll, 1785).

Supper. But others[77] rightly opposed this scheme. The covenant of grace is one, and the external and internal sides of it, though on earth they never fully coincide, may not be split apart and placed side by side. Certainly, there are bad branches on the vine, and there is chaff among the wheat; and in a large house, there are vessels of gold as well as vessels of earthenware (Matt. 3:12; 13:29; John 15:2; 2 Tim. 2:20). But we do not have the right and the power to separate the two: in the day of the harvest, God himself will do this. As long as—in the judgment of love—they walk in the way of the covenant, they are to be regarded and treated as allies. Though not *of* the covenant, they are *in* the covenant and will someday be judged accordingly. Here on earth they are connected with the elect in all sorts of ways; and the elect themselves, since they are members of the Adamic race, can as an organism only be gathered into one under Christ as their head in the way of the covenant.

77. J. Edwards, *Works*, I, 185–295; J. Koelman, *Historisch Verhael Nopende der Labadisten*, 95ff.; J. C. Appelius, *De hervormde leer van den geestelyken staat der mensen* (Groningen: Wed. J. Spandaw, 1769); C. Vitringa, *Observationum sacrarum libri sex* (Franeker: Wibii Bleck, 1712), II, ch. 6; W. Brakel, *Christian's Reasonable Service*, ch. 16; B. de Moor, *Comm. theol.*, V, 470; also, *Ds. De Herder, *De Heraut* 937; cf. H. H. Kuyper, *Hamabdil*, 141ff.

6

The Person of Christ

The necessity of a mediator between humanity and the divine is universally found in all religions. This phenomenon is not accidental but rooted in human nature and religion itself. The ideas of incarnation and apotheosis occur in virtually all religions. This had led many to treat Israel's messianic expectations as simply borrowed from the nations surrounding it.

The history-of-religions school, however, mistakes analogy for identity and overlooks key differences. Prophecy in Israel includes divine judgment on God's own people, and the Savior delivers them from sin and death rather than provide social and political deliverance. Prophecy, charting a new course in Israel's history, includes divine promise and typological messianic fulfillment. King David's great Son will found a kingdom that includes the Gentiles; he will be prophet and priest as well as king. He will be the Lord's anointed; the Spirit of God will be upon him.

In the fullness of time, Jesus the Christ appears, proclaiming the presently coming kingdom of God. He introduces a new understanding of the kingdom: it is religious-ethical and not political; it is present in repentance, faith, rebirth, and it is yet to come as a full eschatological reality. The one idea of the kingdom of God is realized in two sweeping moments. Jesus knows himself to be both the apocalyptic Son of Man from Daniel 7 and the royal Son of God, the one whom the Father loved and sent as his emissary. It is as the Son who alone knows the Father and is known by the Father that Jesus exercises his special authority to forgive sins, to reveal the Father's will.

All the things that the apostles and the Christian church later taught about the person of Christ are already contained in principle in the Synoptic Gospels. The resurrection illumined, clarified, and confirmed what the Synoptics teach: Jesus is the unique Son of God, God himself in the flesh. This glorious truth was too rich and too deep to be immediately absorbed into the Christian consciousness and reproduced in a clear formula to provide proof against all error. Ebionitism regarded Jesus as only a superior man; Gnosticism sharply divided the material from the divine. In neither case did the full union of the human and divine receive proper treatment. Not until Chalcedon did the Nestorian tendency to

233

separate the divine and the human and the Eutychian tendency to commingle them get definite formulation: "One person in two natures, without confusion, without change, without division, without separation." The formula did not, however, prevent the East from tending toward Monophysitism, nor was the West free from mysticism and deification of the human.

The two natures of Christ, according to Roman and scholastic theology, remained distinct though there was communication of properties from the divine to the human nature. This led to the idea that Jesus was never really a child; in him, from the beginning, the human nature was divinized and therefore to be worshiped. Lutheran theology, though it regarded the communication of properties as taking place from the divine nature to the person rather than the human nature, also mingled the divine and the human, elevating the human nature above the boundaries set for it.

In contrast, Reformed theology, insisting that "the finite is not capable of [containing] the infinite," clearly distinguished without separation the human and divine natures, making room for genuine human development on the part of Jesus and also a real change from the state of his humiliation to his exaltation. Reformed theologians insisted that it was the person of the Son who became flesh, not the divine nature itself.

Many modern thinkers are no longer satisfied with Chalcedon's boundaries. They consider Chalcedon a fruit of Greek rationalism and seek to redefine the person of Christ in a new religious-ethical direction. For Immanuel Kant, since the moral imperative "you shall" necessarily implies "you can," Jesus can only be a moral model, a teacher of virtue. The historical Jesus and his ministry, death, and resurrection are unimportant; it is the ideal Christ that counts. In different ways, the same basic approach is taken by Fichte, Schelling, and Hegel. Schleiermacher, on the other hand, rejected this speculative philosophical approach and sought Jesus' significance for the church in his powerfully developed God-consciousness, which he passed on to his followers. The person of Jesus and his religious life are the key to Christianity.

While theology after Schleiermacher did place a great deal of emphasis on the historical personality of Jesus and stimulated a great deal of creative christological reflection in the nineteenth century, the results did not satisfy many, and, following the lead of Albrecht Ritschl, theologians turned back to ethical concerns. For Ritschl, Jesus was an ordinary man whose will was completely in tune with God's will. This enabled him to found the kingdom of God on earth. In this approach, Ritschl was followed by others such as Herrmann and Harnack. The Jesus of history, especially of the Synoptics and the Sermon on the Mount, had to be recovered from the additions and distortions of Paul, John, and the early church.

New Testament scholarship, however, including among the radical critics themselves, did not permit theologians to assert the simple, ethical Jesus portrayed by the Ritschlians. Johannine and Pauline ideas are found in nuce in the Synoptics themselves with Jesus highly self-conscious of his messianic role, speaking as an apocalyptic figure, doing miracles, and taking on divine prerogatives such as forgiving sins. The real historical Jesus proved to be elusive and the church's confession not unreasonable. Furthermore, it became clearer that the revisionist portraits of Jesus were woefully inadequate in explaining the rise of the Christian church and the strength of its confession about Jesus the Christ, the Son of God. To suggest all this as the fantastic creation of the church itself stretched credulity. The conclusion of the matter: the historical Jesus of the Gospels is one and the same as the confessed Christ of Paul, John, and the early church.

The doctrine of Christ is the central point of the whole system of dogmatics. Here, too, pulses the whole of the religious-ethical life of Christianity. Christ, the incarnate Word, is thus the central fact of the entire history of the world. The incarnation has its presupposition and foundation in the trinitarian being of God. The Trinity makes possible the existence of a mediator who himself participates both in the divine and human nature and thus unites God and humanity. The incarnation, however, is the work of the entire Trinity. Christ was sent by the Father and conceived by the Holy Spirit. Incarnation is also related to creation. The incarnation was not necessary, but the creation of human beings in God's image is a supposition and preparation for the incarnation of God. Given with and in creation is the possibility of revelation and also incarnation. In fact, creation itself must be conceived in infralapsarian fashion and Adam seen as a type of Christ. The world was so created that when it fell, it could again be restored. While the notion that the incarnation could have taken place apart from sin's entry has much about it that is attractive—sin cannot be accidental; true religion needs a mediator; Christ precedes the church— there is no need for the hypothesis. The scriptural teaching of God's decree and counsel is sufficient.

The incarnation did not take place immediately after the fall but was prepared for by a long history of divine revelation. Revelation, like the eternal generation of the Son and the creation of man, is another presupposition and preparation for the incarnation. The Logos, who was with God and by whom all things were made, is the One who became flesh. Revelation and incarnation are both based on the communicability of God. The history of revelation as preparation for the incarnation is concentrated and comes to completion in the election and favoring of Mary the mother of Jesus, the blessed one among women. Mary is thus held in high esteem by all Christians, though the veneration paid to her by Rome is excessive and unscriptural, tied more to tradition and the Roman hierarchical system.

Opposition to the doctrine of the incarnation usually begins with an appeal to Scripture, but such an illusory ground cannot last long. The seeds of later church doctrine are truly present in the New Testament. Finally, the Christian religion itself, that is, true communion between God and humans, can be maintained in no way other than by confessing the deity of Christ. Modern attempts to permit the name "God" for Jesus while denying the incarnation are in the final analysis a pantheistic mixing of Creator and creature and a return to pagan idolatry. The irony here is that, like Roman notions of divinization, modern theology denies the deity of Christ while positing the possibility of human apotheosis as a reasonable conclusion to the process of evolution.

According to the Scriptures, the incarnation takes place through a virgin birth. This doctrine, too, has been attacked throughout the history of the church and again in the late nineteenth century by textual critics who claim, from the evidence of a Syrian text, that the reference to virgin birth in Matthew 1 was not original. The textual evidence does not warrant this conclusion, and though it is found in only the two Gospels of Matthew and Luke, we can be certain that Jesus' supernatural conception was part of the original message of the gospel. The doctrine has been part of Christian confession from the time of the earliest symbols of the faith. All Gospels consistently portray Jesus as the eternal Son of God who is also the Son of David. For this to be possible, that the eternal Son of God could simultaneously be human, descended from other human beings, it was necessary for him to be supernaturally conceived by the Holy Spirit. Our Lord was not born by the will of man.

It needs to be said that the importance of the virgin birth does not depend on the theological construct that Mary in and after the birth remained a virgin. This is a later notion, and debates about whether Mary had more children, though interesting and contentious, are dogmatically of secondary importance. The supernatural conception by the Holy Spirit is crucial, however, and it does not stand alone. The power of the Holy Spirit in Christ continued throughout his entire life, even into the state of exaltation. As Scripture prophesied, the Messiah would be anointed in a special way with the Holy Spirit, and the New Testament teaches us that Christ received that Spirit without measure (John 3:34). The exclusion of the man from his conception meant that Jesus was not included in the covenant of works and thus, in the judgment of God, remained exempt from human sin. By the Holy Spirit's power, he remained free from sin.

In this way the Son of God became a true and complete human person. In the history of the church, there have been any number of strange and bizarre attempts to deny the full and true humanity of Jesus. Scripture, however, clearly portrays his full humanity, growing up and developing, experiencing hunger and thirst, anger and grief, and then suffering and dying. Denials of Christ's humanity were rightly opposed by the early church for pastoral and soteriological reasons with the formula "What is not assumed is not saved." Objections are for the most part rooted in a dualism that is antithetical to the Christian religion. Whether it is found in ancient or modern Gnosticism, in Reformation-era Anabaptism, or in nineteenth-century speculative philosophy, the dualist conviction that the finite and the infinite are mutually exclusive must be repudiated. There is one mediator between God and humanity, the true God-man Jesus Christ. This is the heart of the gospel.

The scriptural teaching was drawn together in the church's language of the "two natures." In Scripture both divine and human predicates are attributed to the same personal subject, the one person, Jesus Christ. Modern attempts to reduce the divinity to a mere moral unity with God utterly fail to do justice to biblical givens. Thus, Chalcedon correctly pronounced that the union of the two natures was without division or separation and without confusion or change. Both Monophysitism and Kenoticism in all their varieties are unacceptable because they are at odds with the immutability of God and with the nature of a finite being. A deity or divine attribute that is purely a "potentiality" is inconceivable, and a human being who by development appropriates the divine nature ceases to be a creature. Such a being cannot be the mediator between God and man since he is neither.

The language of Chalcedon is not sacrosanct and is open to reformulation. However, up to now all efforts to improve on it have failed, and the church can do no better at this time than to maintain the two-natures doctrine. Since the essence of religion is communion with God, the two-natures doctrine is integrally connected to the heart of religion. If the incarnation is impossible, then religion cannot consist in communion between God and human creatures. Because sin ruptured that communion, the Son's union is with an impersonal human nature. Christ is the second Adam, the head of a new humanity, not just another individual person. That is why the distinction between "nature" and "person" is so important. Ancient and modern thinkers—from Nestorius and Eutyches to Hegel and Dorner—fail to grasp this. Yet, we too can never fully understand this most profound mystery of godliness, which exceeds all our thinking and speaking of it.

The objection that a union of two-natures doctrine fails to do justice to the full humanity of Jesus does carry some credibility in some versions of Roman Catholic and Lutheran theology where the communication of properties of the divine to the human nature seems to overwhelm the latter. Here the doctrine of communication of properties is itself destroyed; why should such gifts be needed when they are already shared? Here we clearly find elements of Docetism. Reformed theology, however, insisted that Christ as the second Adam was nonetheless different from Adam, particularly here in the fact that Adam was an adult while Christ came as an infant, not to a paradise but to a sinful world where he faced its temptation and evil in every way. Unlike Adam, Christ came in the form of sinful flesh, susceptible to suffering and death.

It is for that reason alone that the incarnation was an act of humiliation. Christ grew in wisdom and knowledge; on earth he too was a pilgrim. He too lived in faith and hope by the promises of God. His divine and human consciousness were united in that he knew the Father's will perfectly but not exhaustively. Jesus also grew morally. Though he was not able to sin, his sinlessness had become manifest through response to temptation and struggle. His power, too, was limited in his human nature. It is by his resurrection that he becomes Lord over all and is given a name above all other names. It is as Lord of all, as the mediator who is God with us and for us, that Christ is worshiped.

UNIVERSAL NEED FOR A MEDIATOR

[351] The covenant of grace also differs from the covenant of works in that it has a mediator who not only unites God and humanity but prior to this reconciles the two, so restoring the broken fellowship between them. Also with respect to this doctrine of a mediatorship, Holy Scripture does not stand alone but is supported and confirmed on all sides by ideas concerning such a mediatorship in the religions of all peoples. Generally speaking, the words and deeds of great men, as such, already have extraordinary significance for the life and development of the nations. Granted, among historians there is vast disagreement over the role to be attributed to these great men. Whereas some view them merely as conduits for ideas or as exponents of the people's soul, others ascribe to them great creative power and all-controlling influence. The truth undoubtedly is that there is interactivity here: on the one hand, heroic figures in history are the products of their own time, and on the other, they transcend their own time and change its direction.

Every exaggeration, therefore, results in a reaction. After Hegel, Max Stirner made his appearance; after Marx, Nietzsche became prominent; after Bentham and Mill, we heard from Carlyle.[1] Particularly in religion the person of the founder and mediator plays a large role. Mediators between humanity and the deity, messengers of God who convey his blessings and revelations to humans and, conversely, lay their prayers and gifts before his throne, occur in all religions. Sometimes it is subordinate deities or lower spirits, at other times people who—dedicated to God and animated by his spirit—are favored with special revelations and endowed with supernatural powers. But between humanity and the deity there

1. Cf. H. Bavinck, *Philosophy of Revelation* (Grand Rapids: Eerdmans, 1953), 44ff.

is always another who effects and maintains fellowship between the two. Belief in mediators is universal.[2]

In the religions of the races who have strayed the farthest, such as, for example, the aborigines of Australia, the American Indians, and others, medicine men perform this service. In the religions of more highly developed peoples, soothsayers, priests, and kings take their place. Soothsayers made the will of the deity known by interpreting external signs (the constellation of the stars, the flight of birds, sacrifices, and so on), or, like the Pythian oracles in ancient Greece, by internal inspiration (Deut. 18:10–14).[3] Priests, who frequently form a very distinct class or caste of their own, delivered the people's sacrifices and prayers and distributed God's blessing to them.[4] Kings were often regarded as the sons or emissaries of the gods, who in turn were themselves represented as kings, the bearers of their wisdom and power, the founders and protectors of righteousness.[5] History does not tell us how all these sacred persons acquired their rank and status; but their universal presence serves to show that we are here dealing with a phenomenon that is not accidental but rooted in the characteristic essence of religion itself and corresponds to a profound need in human nature. Many historic religions, moreover, are linked to the names of certain founders who were later elevated above the rank of ordinary people and to some extent deified. The ideas of incarnation and apotheosis occur in virtually all religions. The distinction Tiele makes between theocratic and theanthropic religions, accordingly, cannot be strictly maintained. In the final analysis, the difference is one of degree.

In many religions there is even not merely a general expectation that one day good will overcome evil, but that expectation is connected with a specific person: in Indian religion, for example, to Krishna; in Persian religion, to Saoshyant; in Egyptian religion, to Osiris; in Norse religion, to Balder. In recent years documents and inscriptions have come to light that indicate that, first in the East but later also in the West, the expectation of a kingdom of peace was especially based on the figure of a king. Of Cyrus (cf. Isa. 45:1), and the Assyrian kings Ashurbanipal I, Merodach-baladan, Ashurbanipal II, and so on, it is stated that with their rule years of righteousness and prosperity began. Like the gods, so kings were addressed and greeted as σωτηρ (savior). In Thucydides this name is applied to Brasidas; in Polybius to Philip of Macedon; it was applied to the

---

2. C. P. Tiele, *Elements of the Science of Religon*, 2 vols. (Edinburgh and London: William Blackwood and Sons, 1897), I, 130, 167; II, 119ff.; O. Pfleiderer, *Religionsphilosophie auf geschichtlicher Grundlage*, 3rd ed. (Berlin: G. Reimer, 1896), 679–727; E. von Hartmann, *Religionsphilosophie*, 2nd ed., 2 vols. (Bad Sachsa i.H.: Hermann Haacke, 1907), I, 122ff.

3. K. Köhler, *Der Prophetismus der Hebräer und die Mantik der Griechen in ihrem gegenseitigen Verhältniss* (Darmstadt: Eduard Zernin, 1860); G. F. Oehler, "Abhandlung über das Verhältniss der alttestamentlichen Prophetie zur heidnischen Mantik," in *Glückwunschschreiben an die Universität Breslau* (Tübingen: Fues, 1861); E. König, *Das alttestamentliche Prophetentum und die moderne Geschichtsforschung* (Gütersloh: Bertelsmann, 1910), and additional works on prophetism.

4. J. Lippert, *Allgemeine Geschichte des Priesterthums*, 2 vols. (Berlin: T. Hoffman, 1883–84).

5. J. Boehmer, *Reichsgottesspuren in der Völkerwelt* (Gütersloh: Bertelsmann, 1906), 67–124.

Ptolemies and the Seleucids and especially to Roman emperors such as Caesar, Augustus, Claudius, Vespasian, Hadrian, and so on. In this connection also the myth of Hercules, Plato's familiar statement about the just man in book VII of his *Republic,* and especially the fourth eclogue of Virgil and the Sibylline books acquire a new meaning.[6] One can with some reason speak of an "unconscious prophetic tendency" in paganism. In its most beautiful and noble expressions, it points to Christianity.[7] Jesus Christ is not only the Messiah of Israel but also, as the Authorized Version puts it in Haggai 2:7, "the desire of all nations." Though this translation may be incorrect—for the meaning of the original is that the Gentiles, as a result of the Lord's disturbing them, will bring their treasures to the temple in order that the Lord may fill it with glory—the idea expressed in the name "desire of all the Gentiles" is completely scriptural. The Gentiles hope for the arm of the Lord, and the coastlands await the instruction of his Servant (Isa. 42:4; 51:5; 60:9).

ISRAEL'S MESSIANIC HOPE

[352] Surprised by the discovery that such striking expectations for the future occur also among the peoples around Israel, many [scholars] have related all the messianic prophecies in the Old Testament to these expectations and attempted to explain them completely in light of those expectations. In this attempt there is an element that brings us cheer and confirms the credibility of Scripture. For it offers proof that the purely literary criticism of the Old Testament has had its day. As long as it was in the saddle, scholars were inclined to view all messianic prophecies as *vaticinia ex eventu* [prophecies made *after* and *on the basis of* the event] and to remove them as later interpolations wherever they occurred in preexilic writings. Hope for the restoration of the Davidic dynasty, it was thought, could only arise in the time after the exile, and when this hope was repeatedly dashed, it gradually became concentrated in the expectation of a future Messiah

---

6. G. Anrich, *Das antike Mysterienwesen in seinem Einfluss auf das Christentum* (Göttingen: Vandenhoeck & Ruprecht, 1894), 47; G. Wobbermin, *Religionsgeschichtliche Studien zur Frage der Beeinflussung des Urchristentums durch das antike Mysterienwesen* (Berlin: E. Eberling, 1896), 105ff.; A. von Harnack, *Reden und Aufsätze,* 2nd ed., 2 vols. (Gieszen: A. Töpelmann, 1906), I, 301ff.; P. Wendland, "Σωτηρ: Eine religionsgeschichtliche Untersuchung," *Zeitschrift für neutestamentliche Wissenschaft* 5 (1904): 335ff.; A. Jeremias, *Babylonisches im Neuen Testament* (Leipzig: J. C. Hinrichs, 1905), 27ff.; K. Breysig, *Die Entstehung des Gottesgedankens und der Heilbringer* (Berlin: G. Bondi, 1905); H. Gressmann, *Die Ursprung der israelitisch-jüdischen Eschatologie* (Göttingen: Vandenhoeck & Ruprecht, 1905); H. Lietzmann, *Der Weltheiland* (Bonn: Marcus & Weber, 1907); A. Deissmann, *Licht vom Osten* (Tübingen: Mohr, 1908), 265; W. O. E. Oesterley, *The Evolution of the Messianic Idea* (London: Pitman, 1908).

7. Cf. H. Bavinck, *Reformed Dogmatics,* I, 318 (#88); F. R. de Lamennais, *Essai sur l'indifférence en matiéfe de religion,* 4 vols. (Paris: Tournachon-Molin & H. Seguin, 1818–23), III, 408ff. (ed. note: ET: *Essay on Indifference in Matters of Religion,* trans. Henry Edward John Stanley [London: John Macqueen, 1895]); A. Tholuck, *Die Lehre von der Sünde und vom Versöhner* (Gotha: Perthes, 1862); R. C. Trench, *The Hulsean Lectures for 1845 and 1846,* 4th rev. ed. (London: Parke, 1859), 153ff.: "Christ the desire of all nations or the unconscious prophecies of Heathendom."

born of David's lineage.[8] This construal was already highly improbable as such and led to extraordinarily arbitrary criticism,[9] but has now been almost completely abandoned as a result of the above-mentioned discoveries. In the place of it, it is now recognized that the preexilic prophets themselves not only cherished such messianic expectations but also assumed their existence among their people. Nor did they dream them up and proclaim them to the people for the first time but derived them from the past and continued to build on expectations that had already existed from ancient times and were widely popular in Israel. This new trend among Old Testament scholars, consequently, has almost completely given up the earlier interpolation hypothesis. It now attributes great antiquity to all eschatological ideas concerning the day of the Lord, the destruction of Israel's enemies, the salvation of the people, the appearance of the Messiah, the completion of the kingdom of God, and so on, and in the image of the Messiah, as the Old Testament pictures it, again allows to come into their own such supernatural traits as the miraculous birth (Isa. 7:14; Mic. 5:2), the divine names (Isa. 9:6), and so on. Countless texts and pericopes viewed by earlier critics as postexilic are now again regarded as authentic, and the so-called Christology of the Old Testament has again been more or less vindicated in its validity and value.

The followers of the history-of-religions school, however, are now swinging to another extreme. The messianic expectations did not first arise after the exile, they claim, but date back to the dim past and have their origin in Babylonia, Assyria, Persia, and Egypt. This position too contains an element of truth, which Scripture fully recognizes. God did not let the human race start its history without instilling in its heart the hope that some day the offspring of the woman would achieve victory over the seed of the serpent (Gen. 3:15). As Eve did at the birth of Cain (Gen. 4:1), so Lamech saw in Noah a man whom the Lord had given him and would give him relief from the work and toil of his hands (Gen. 5:29). After the flood Canaan was indeed cursed, but Shem was blessed, and this blessing was also extended to Japheth (Gen. 9:25–27). According to the Old Testament itself, the messianic promises given to the people of Israel are broadly based in the promises that God gave to humanity as a whole and after the flood specifically to the Semitic peoples. But then, with the election of Abraham, the human race is split up, and Israel is separated from the other nations. This is what the history-of-religions school overlooks: from the analogy it finds between messianic expectations outside Israel and those within Israel, it immediately infers identity; for the sake of the external similarity between them, it denies the deep internal difference.

After all, when in the expectations we encounter in Egypt and elsewhere there is mention of a great disaster that precedes the ultimate rescue, it is never un-

8. Cf., e.g., Paul Volz, *Jüdische Eschatologie von Daniel bis Akiba* (Tübingen: J. C. B. Mohr, 1903).

9. This is clearly pointed out by W. Möller, *Die messianische Erwartung der vorexilischen Propheten: Zugleich ein Protest gegen moderne Textsplitterung* (Gütersloh: C. Bertelsmann, 1906).

derstood as a judgment that God conducts over the people's sins, but only as a political or social catastrophe that strikes the nation. The king who effects the rescue, though he is given a series of splendid attributes, remains a ruler like all his predecessors, limited in his dominion to the boundaries of his own people and country as well as in duration. And the salvation he brings is not primarily religious and ethical in character but mainly consists in—or is any case consistently accompanied by—a number of cultic, magical, and political changes. It is true that the name σωτηρ (savior) may also frequently have been accorded to kings and emperors; but when in the New Testament it is given to Christ, it has a totally different meaning and becomes the term for a savior who delivers people from sin and death and grants them righteousness and life. It is indeed possible, therefore, that in the New Testament, say in the Pastoral Letters, the name is applied to Christ with an additional antithetical and apologetic twist. Just as Paul can say in 1 Corinthians 8:5–6 that "even though there may be so-called gods in heaven or on earth—as in fact there are many gods and many lords—yet for us there is one God, the Father, . . . and one Lord, Jesus Christ," so the apostles may on occasion have attributed the name σωτηρ to Christ to bring out that, although others may call a king or emperor their σωτηρ, Christ alone in truth is the Savior for believers. From this it does not by any means follow, however, that the New Testament authors derived this name from the speech of pagans and transferred it from there to Christ. For in the circle of the disciples, this name evidently arose in connection with Jesus' Hebrew name (Matt. 1:21; cf. Luke 1:47, 2:11; Acts 5:31; 13:23). Much less was the Hebrew name for the king expected from the house of David taken over from Gentile peoples, for whereas there the name σωτηρ is customary for the king, the Messiah is only rarely designated with the name מוֹשִׁיעַ and usually with very different names. In all this, we have still left unchallenged that the documents that have come to light in fact say the things people read in them, but one must not forget, finally, that many of these pronouncements stand by themselves and often, in the environment in which they originated, contain a meaning very different from what is now read in them; further, that there is a great temptation to look at them and to explain them in the light that the Old Testament itself has furnished us; and that in many cases one cannot determine whether the Israelite prophecy in earlier or later times perhaps exerted influence on Gentile expectations for the future.[10]

[353] Subject to this provision, one cannot doubt, however, that prophecy in Israel is linked with the promises that, according to Scripture's own witness (Gen. 3:15; 8:21; 9:9f., 25–27), were already given to the human race beforehand and preserved there in a more or less pure form. Perhaps this connection is even much

---

10. W. Wagner, "Ueber σωζειν und seine Derivata im N.T.," *Zeitschrift für neut. Wiss.* (1905): 205ff.; Giesebrecht's review of Gressmann, *Die Ursprung der israelitisch-jüdischen Eschatologie,* in *Theologische Studien und Kritiken* (1907): 619ff.; Gressmann's response to Guisebrecht's review in *Theologische Studien und Kritiken* (1908): 307–17; E. Sellin, *Die israelitisch-jüdische Heilandserwartung* (Lichterfelde-Berlin: E. Runge, 1909), 44ff.; G. Vos, "Saviour," *DC,* II, 573. Cf. also *Stimmen aus Maria-Laach* (1906): 588–92.

closer than we can establish at this time. Indeed, the idea advanced in recent years by numerous scholars that the Israelite prophets, in their description of the Messiah and his kingdom and in their eschatological expectations in general, employed notions and expressions, similes and imagery that had already existed for a long time and date back to a remote past is far from improbable. It occurred in the giving of the law, for temples, altars, priesthood, sacrifices, circumcision, and so on occur among many peoples, and prophecy is similarly rooted in the history of Israel and that of the surrounding nations.

On the other hand, it is equally certain that prophecy in Israel went far beyond that history and developed in a manner and direction of its own. This uniqueness is proven by the fact that, while the prophets shared with all of Israel a common basis of law and promise, when the people abused their covenant with the Lord in order to elevate themselves above all other peoples on earth and to assure themselves of a happy future, these prophets radically opposed such abuse and portrayed the day of the Lord as a day of darkness and judgment (Amos 5:18; Mic. 3:5; Joel 2:2; Isa. 5:19; Jer. 5:12; etc.). And this independent character belonged to prophecy in Israel from the beginning. The patriarchs were already promised that in their descendants all the families of the earth would be blessed (Gen. 12:2–3; 18:18; 22:18; 26:4; 27:29; 28:14), and from the patriarch Jacob this promise passed to Judah, from whom the scepter would not depart until Shiloh came, whom the peoples would obey (Gen. 49:10).[11] Prophecy does not limit its field of vision to the people of Israel and the land of Canaan but extends it to the whole earth and promises the blessing of Abraham to all of humankind; and the central content of that blessing is that God will be his God and the God of his children. It is a universal spiritual kingdom that God promises to his people at the end of human history.

This promise was not nullified by the law that was later added when the covenant was made with the people of Israel, but further unfolded and guided to its fulfillment. The Old Testament does not contain just a few isolated messianic texts; on the contrary, the entire Old Testament dispensation with its leading persons and events, its offices and institutions, its laws and ceremonies, is a pointer to and movement toward the fulfillment in the New Testament. There is a "symbolism in creation," a typology in nature that, as is evident from Jesus' parables, finds its realization in him and his kingdom. There is an unconscious expectation and hope in the religion and history of the nations, which is realized in Christianity. There exists a direct and intentional preparation and adumbration of the λογικη λατρεια ["spiritual worship," RSV, NIV] in the institutions and events of the Old

---

11. There are many interpretations of the word "Shiloh," but none is certain. Cf. E. Sellin, "Die Schiloh-Weissagung in 1 Mos. 49:10," *Theologische Studien und Kritiken* (October 10, 1908): 369–90; J. Hastings, "Shiloh," *DB*, IV, 500; A. Posnanski, *Schiloh: Ein Beitrag zur Geschichte der Messiaslehre*, vol. 1, *Die Auslegung von Gen 49:10 im Altertum bis zum Ende des Mittelalters* (Leipzig: Hinrichs, 1904). Ed. note: Bavinck misspelled Posnanski (Poswanski) and cites 1909 as the date of publication. The messianic character of the text, however, is not subject to doubt.

Testament. Temple and altar, priest and sacrifice, Zion and Jerusalem, prophet and king—they are all models and shadows of a higher spiritual and genuine reality. Especially the office of king achieved such typical significance in Israel. The theocratic king, embodied especially in David with his humble beginnings, many-sided experience of life, deep emotions, poetic disposition, unflinching courage, and brilliant victories,[12] was a son of God (2 Sam. 7:14; Pss. 2:6–7; 89:27), the anointed one par excellence (Pss. 2:2; 18:50). People wished for him all kinds of physical and spiritual blessings (Pss. 2:8f.; 21, 45, 72), and he was even addressed as "Elohim" (Ps. 45:6). The king is the bearer of the highest—of divine—dignity on earth. Theocratic kingship, as suggested above, found its purest embodiment in David; for that reason the kingship will remain in his house (2 Sam. 7:8–16). This promise of God to David, accordingly, is the foundation and center of all subsequent expectation and prophecy. Prophecy, which is added to interpret the typology, looks out from the past and present to the future and ever more clearly portrays the—to be expected—son of David in his person and work. To the degree that kingship in Israel and Judah answered less to the idea of it, to that degree prophecy took up the promise of 2 Samuel 7 and clung to it (Amos 9:11; Hosea 1:11; 3:5; Mic. 5:1–2; Isa. 9:6–7; 11:1–2, 10; Jer. 23:5; 30:9; 33:17, 20–22, 26; Ezek. 34:23–24; 37:22–24). This anointed king will arise from the dynasty of David when—in utter decay and thrust from the throne—it will resemble a hewn trunk (Isa. 11:1–2; Mic. 5:1–2; Ezek. 17:22). God will cause him to grow as a branch from David's house (Jer. 23:5–6; 33:14–17), so that he himself will bear the name "Branch" (Zech. 3:8; 6:12). Despite his humble birth, he will be the true and authentic theocratic king. Coming from despised little Bethlehem, where the royal house of David originated and to which, driven from the throne, it withdrew (Mic. 5:2; cf. 3:12; 4:8, 13), the Messiah will nevertheless be a ruler over Israel; his origins as ruler—proceeding from God—go back to the distant past, to the days of old. He is God-given, an eternal king, bears the name Wonderful, Counselor, mighty God (cf. Isa. 10:21; Deut. 10:17; Jer. 32:18), everlasting Father (for his people), Prince of Peace (Isa. 9:6–7).[13] He is anointed with the Spirit of wisdom and understanding, of counsel and courage, of knowledge and the fear of the Lord (Isa. 11:2) and laid as a tested, precious foundation stone in Zion (Isa. 28:16). He is just, victorious, meek, a king riding on a donkey; as king he is not proud of his power but sustained by God (Jer. 33:17, 20, 22, 26; Zech. 9:9f.), a king whom the people call and acknowledge as "the Lord our righteousness" (Jer. 23:6—cf. 33:16, where Jerusalem is called the city in which Yahweh causes his righteousness to dwell). He will be a warrior like David, and his house will be like God, like the angel of the Lord who at the time of the exodus led Israel's army (Zech. 12:8; cf. Mal. 3:1). He will reign forever; found a kingdom of righteousness,

---

12. R. Smend, *Lehrbuch der alttestamentlichen Religionsgeschichte* (Freiburg i.B.: Mohr, 1893), 58.

13. W. Caspari, *Echtheit, Hauptbegriff und Gedankengang der Messianischen Weissagung Jes. 9:1–6* (Gütersloh: C. Bertelsmann, 1908).

peace, and prosperity; and also extend his domain over the Gentiles to the ends of the earth (Pss. 2, 45, 72; Ezek. 37:25; Zech. 6:13; 9:10; etc.).

The splendid profile of the Messiah is then further augmented by the portrayal of the future king as prophet and priest. Granted, these features are not highlighted, for in the kingdom of God the Spirit of God will be poured out upon all (Joel 2:28; Zech. 12:10; 13:2f.; Jer. 31:34), and all the people will be priestly and "holy to the Lord" (Isa. 35:8; Joel 3:17; Zech. 14:20–21). Still, the Messiah is also represented as a prophet on whom the Spirit of the Lord rests to an unusual degree and who will bring good news to Israel and the Gentiles (Deut. 18:15; Isa. 11:2; Isa. 40–60; Mal. 4:5), who will unite in himself both priestly and royal dignity (Jer. 30:21; Zech. 3; 6:13; Ps. 110). In Isaiah all three offices come to light in the servant of the Lord: he is the priest who by his suffering atones for the sins of his people; he is a prophet who, anointed with the Spirit of God, announces the acceptable year of the Lord; and he is the king who is glorified and enjoys the fruit of his labor. The deep-rootedness of this messianic expectation in Israel is evident from the psalms. Many of them are based on the kingship of David and are messianic in a restricted sense (Pss. 2, 18, 20, 21, 45, 61, 72, 89, 132). Others only speak of God or Yahweh as king (Pss. 10, 24, 29, 44, 47, 48, 66, 68, 87, 93, 95–100, 145–150). All of them, nevertheless, point to a future in which the Lord himself will establish his kingdom in Israel and from that base expand it to the nations.[14]

[354] Messianic expectation lived on in the heart of the people of Israel also after the demise of prophecy. In [Jewish] apocryphal literature, we indeed encounter the expectation of Israel's future deliverance and rule but without more than a few references to the Messiah (1 Macc. 2:57; 4:46; 9:27; 14:41). Nor does Philo say anything about the Messiah. Generally speaking, the self-righteousness of Judaism was not favorable to messianic expectation. Israel, after all, had the law; it was righteous by its observance of the law and needed no Savior. At most there was room for an earthly king who rewarded the Jews in accordance with their merits and led them to a position of dominance over the peoples of the world. The Messiah became solely a political person. But among the people, messianic expectation lived on and kept resurfacing, especially in times of stress. This current of expectation was maintained and fed by the reading of the Old Testament. Any number of texts, as the Septuagint proves, were interpreted messianically. In the Scriptures, the Jews found as many as 456 messianic promises: 75 in the Pentateuch, 243 in the prophets, and 138 in the Hagiographa. Especially the apocalyptic literature of *1 Enoch*, the *Psalms of Solomon*, *2 Apocalypse of Baruch*, the *Sibylline Oracles*,

---

14. On the messianic prophecies, see also A. Kuenen, *De profeten en de profetie onder Israël*, 2 vols in 1 (Leiden: P. Engels, 1875); B. Duhm, *Die Theologie der Propheten als Grundlage für die innere Entwicklung der israelitischen Religion* (Bonn: Marcus, 1875); J. König, *Die Theologie der Psalmen* (Freiburg i.B.: Herder, 1857); J. Boehmer, "Das Reich Gottes in den Psalmen," *Neue kirchliche Zeitschrift* (1897): 8–10; H. Weiss, *Die messianischen Vorbilder im Alten Testament* (Freiburg i.B.: Herder, 1905); A. Schulte, *Die messianischen Weissagungen des Alten Testaments nebst dessen Typen* (Paderborn: Ferdinand Schöningh, 1908).

and *4 Ezra* [2 Esdras] again took up the messianic expectation and elaborated it. Generally it was expected that the Messiah would appear at the end of the present age, following anxious times, the so-called messianic woes; this would occur after Elijah or another prophet like Moses or Jeremiah had heralded his coming. He was usually described as the Messiah, the Son of Man, the Chosen One, or the Son of David and a few times also as the Son of God. He was viewed as a human being who already existed beforehand and was hidden with God, as a person who would come forth from Bethlehem; was righteous, holy, and endowed by God with many gifts; and would establish God's kingdom on earth. This, in the main, corresponds to the expectation that, according to the New Testament witness (Luke 1:48, 74; 2:25; etc.), was found in lower-class circles.[15]

THE PRESENT AND COMING KINGDOM

In the context of these expectations, Christ himself appeared, preaching the gospel of the kingdom of God and saying: "The time is fulfilled, and the kingdom of God has come near; repent and believe in the gospel" (Mark 1:15). The kingdom of God, which was foretold and expected by the prophets, in which God would be king and his will the delight of everyone, which in origin and character is a heavenly kingdom and already present in heaven now (Matt. 6:10)—that kingdom is now coming on earth and is near (Mark 1:15). But tying in with those expectations, Jesus immediately introduced a big change. From the Jewish tradition he went back to Scripture and interpreted that kingdom, not first of all as a political but as a religious-ethical dominion. The God of Abraham, Isaac, and Jacob (Mark 12:26), the God of Israel (Matt. 15:31) whom Jesus recognizes and confesses as his God, is also and before all else king (Matt. 5:35; 18:23; 22:2), the Lord of heaven and earth (Matt. 11:25). At the same time, he is the Father in heaven, who in his kingdom wants to rule as a Father over his children. His kingdom is simultaneously a family, a community (Matt. 6:4, 6, 9; 7:11; Mark 3:34–35); and these two ideas, that of the kingship and the fatherhood of God, do not compete with but reinforce each other. Further, entrance into that kingdom occurs, not by Pharisaic observance of the law, but by repentance, faith, rebirth (Matt. 18:3; Mark 1:15; John 3:3), and for that reason is open above all to the poor, the lost, publicans, and sinners (Matt. 5:3; 9:11–12; 11:5, 28–30; Luke 19:10). That kingdom is, on the one hand, something that must be sought, is far greater than

---

15. Ludwig Paul, *Die Vorstellung vom Messias und vom Gottesreich bei den Synoptikern* (Bonn, 1895); W. Baldensperger, *Das Selbstbewusstsein Jesu im Lichte der messianischen Hoffnungen seiner Zeit*, vol. I, *Die messianisch-apokalypt. Hoffnungen des Judentums* (Strassburg: Heitz & Mündel, 1903); P. Volz, *Jüdische Eschatologie von Daniel bis Akiba*; W. Bousset, *Die Religion des Judentums im neutestamentlichen Zeitalter*, 2nd ed. (Berlin: Reuther & Reichard, 1906); L. Couard, "Die messianische Erwartung in den alttestamentlichen Apokryphen," *Neue kirchliche Zeitschrift* (1901): 958–73; J. Klausner, *Die messianischen Vorstellungen des jüdischen Volkes im Zeitalter der Tannaiten* (Berlin: M. Poppelauer, 1904); M. Rabinsohn, *Le Messianisme dans la Talmud et les Midraschim* (Paris: A. Reiff, 1907); M. J. Lagrange, *Le Messianisme chez les juifs (150 av. J.-C. à 200 ap. J.-C.)* (Paris: J. Gabalda, 1909).

the righteousness taught by the Pharisees (Matt. 5:20; 6:33; 13:44–46), and is presented as a reward stored in heaven (Matt. 5:12; 6:20; 19:21; 20:1–7; 24:45). On the other hand, it is a gift that far exceeds all human work and merit (Matt. 19:29; 23:12; 24:47; 25:21, 34; Luke 6:32f.; 12:32, 37; 17:10; 22:29) and has as its content the forgiveness of sins (Matt. 9:2; 26:28; Luke 1:77; 24:47), righteousness (Matt. 6:33), and eternal life (Matt. 19:16; 25:46; Mark 9:43). Accordingly, to the extent that the rule of God is not immediately fully realized in believers here on earth, and they on their part do not yet fully receive and enjoy the goods of that kingdom—eternal life, the vision of God, complete salvation—the kingdom is indeed still in the future (Matt. 5:3f., 20; 6:10, 33; 7:21; 18:3; 19:23–24; 25:34; 26:29; etc.). But insofar as it is established here on earth by the person and works of Christ and is planted in human hearts by rebirth, faith, and repentance, that kingdom is present (Matt. 11:11–12; 12:28; 13:11, 19, 24, 31, 52; Mark 4:26–29; 9:1; Luke 10:9; 17:21), and believers are already citizens of and participants in it (Matt. 7:13–14; 13:23, 30; 28:18, 20; Mark 10:15; Luke 7:28). In Paul, in the same way, the kingdom of God is at one time a description of a presently existing dominion (Rom. 14:17; 1 Cor. 4:20; 15:24–25; Col. 1:13; 4:11) and then again a name for God's government in the future (1 Cor. 6:9; 15:50; Gal. 5:21; Eph. 5:5; 1 Thess. 2:12; 2 Thess. 1:5). Christ is king now and makes his own into kings and priests as well (Rev. 1:6, 18; 3:21; 5:10). Yet the kingdom of God is only made complete at the time of his return (Rev. 19–21).

Schmoller, Johannes Weiss, and others were therefore mistaken when they attributed to the kingdom of God an exclusively eschatological meaning.[16] In the words of Jesus and the apostles, it is not merely a future good, preserved in heaven and granted as a reward for a righteous life; it is also provisionally realized on earth in the benefits of repentance, faith, rebirth, renewal. It is something that gradually grows and permeates the whole of life. At the same time, it is a religious-ethical concept; that is, Jesus takes over the idea of the kingdom of God as it was developed in Scripture, and especially later in apocalyptic literature, in an eschatological sense. But with it he unites the thought—later neglected by Judaism—that, though the kingdom of God in an eschatological sense will only be realized at the end of time by an act of divine intervention, it must be preceded and prepared for by a religious-ethical renewal: the kingdom of God in that sense. In the prophets of the Old Testament, these two ideas coincide and are interwoven. They know only of *one* coming of the Messiah. The kingdom of God is the sum of all spiritual and natural benefits. It simultaneously brings repentance and return (the restoration of Israel as a people and a kingdom). But Jesus makes a distinction between the two. According to him, it is *present* in a religious-ethical sense; it is *coming* in an eschatological sense. The one idea of the kingdom of

16. O. Schmoller, *Die Lehre vom Reiche Gottes in den Schriften des Neuen Testaments* (Leiden: E. J. Brill, 1891); J. Weiss, *Die Predigt Jesu vom Reiche Gottes* (Göttingen: Vandenhoeck & Ruprecht, 1892); in the second, revised edition (1900), the eschatological perspective is maintained though slightly softened; W. Bousset, "Das Reich Gottes in der Predigt Jesu," *Theologische Rundschau* 5 (1902): 397–436.

God is realized in two sweeping moments. The single coming of the Messiah divides into two: one for the purpose of salvation, the other for judgment; one for preparation, the other for completion. "The work of the Messiah becomes the work of redemption: it extricates itself from eschatology and becomes part of soteriology."[17] Regardless of how long a period would pass—to Jesus' mind and that of the apostles—between his present and his future kingdom, it is a fact that the two are temporally distinct as well.[18]

[355] Jesus did not arrive at this distinction because his work, begun with hope in Galilee, later remained without effect and he could therefore only remain faithful to his calling by simultaneously revealing his messiahship and his program of suffering.[19] For from the very beginning, Jesus was completely clear about his role in that kingdom whose gospel he preached. Aside from John's designation of Jesus in his baptism (Matt. 3:11ff.; John 1:26ff.), this is evident from the fact that Jesus from the start presented himself as the "Son of Man" and the "Son of God." Jesus consciously derived the first designation—as is now almost universally recognized, especially after Baldensperger's important study on *Das Selbstbewusstsein Jesu*[20]—from Daniel 7:13. He did this in order to make clear *both* that he was the Messiah without whom the kingdom of God could not come *and* that he was the Messiah in a sense quite different from the way his contemporaries, in their earthbound expectations, pictured it. In Daniel 7:13, the designation "one like a son of man" is a description of the Messiah. Many exegetes, certainly, relate this term to the "saints of the Most High" because verses 18, 22, and 27 say that the kingdom would be given to the people of "the saints of the Most High" in the same way as this kingdom was given to the son of man in verse 14. But this view is untenable. For the "son of man" came with the clouds of heaven and positioned himself before the Ancient of Days, but the people of the saints are on earth, suffer, and look longingly for redemption. Moreover, while in verse 17 it is indeed said that the four beasts are four kings, concerning the "son of man," who receives the kingdom already in verse 14, there is no further explanation. Finally, in verse 21

17. W. Baldensperger, *Das Selbstwusstsein Jesu im Lichte der messianischen Hoffnungen seiner Zeit* (Strassburg: J. H. E. Heitz, 1888), 114.

18. H. J. Holtzmann, *Lehrbuch der neutestamentlichen Theologie*, 2 vols. (Freiburg and Leipzig: Mohr, 1897), I, 215–25; F. Krop, *La pensée de Jésus sur Royaume de Dieu, d' après les évangiles synoptiques avec un appendice sur la question du "Fils de l'homme"* (Paris: Fischbacher, 1897), who cites literature on p. 7; P. Wernle, *Die Reichsgotteshoffnung in den ältesten christlichen Dokumenten und bei Jesus* (Tübingen: J. C. B. Mohr, 1903); F. Traub, "Die Gegenwart des Gottesreiches in den Parabeln vom Senfkorn und Sauerteig, von der selbst wachsenden Saat, dem Unkraut und dem Fischnetz," *Zeitschrift für Theologie und Kirche* 15 (1905): 58–75; J. Gottschick, "Reich Gottes," *PRE*[3], XVI, 783–806; J. Orr, "Kingdom of God," *DB*, II, 834–56; B. Bartmann, *Das Himmelreich und sein König* (Paderborn: Ferdinand Schöningh, 1906); J. Boehmer, *Der religionsgeschichtliche Rahmen des Reiches Gottes* (Leipzig: Dieterich, 1909); cf. also R. Wegener, *A. Ritschl's Idee des Reiches Gottes im Licht der Geschichte* (Leipzig: Deichert, 1898); J. Weiss, *Die Idee des Reiches Gottes in der Theologie* (Giessen: J. Ricker, 1901).

19. H. J. Holtzmann, *Lehrbuch der neutestamentlichen Theologie*, I, 284.

20. W. Baldensperger, *Das Selbstbewusstsein Jesu* (Strassburg: J. H. E. Heitz, 1888; 2nd ed., 1892; 3rd ed., 1903).

there is mention of a war waged against the saints, but nothing is said of the "son of man." Evidently, the "son of man" is the Messiah who receives the kingdom of God (v. 14), and the future Ruler of the people of the saints. Thus, accordingly, the text of Daniel 7:13 was understood in the apocryphal literature of *1 Enoch* and 4 Ezra [2 Esdr.].[21]

If the name "son of man" was derived by Jesus from the Old Testament, it is self-evident that it cannot be a symbol for the future kingdom (Hoekstra) or a designation of Jesus as the true ideal human (Herder, Schleiermacher, Neander, Lange, Ebrard, Thomasius, Godet, Beyschlag, and others), or as the fragile, humble human (Grotius, De Wette, Ewald, Baur, Strauss, Kuenen, Schenkel, Stier, Nösgen, and others). On the contrary, it has to be a designation of his surpassing messianic dignity as he himself understood it. Now, just as earlier the rationalist Paulus (*Commentary on the New Testament,* on Matt. 8:20) and Uloth (*Theol. Essays,* 1862), so in recent times Lagarde, Wellhausen, Brandt, Oort, and especially Lietzmann indeed claimed that Jesus never called himself בר נוש (in Aramaic) or made exclusive use of that name, in order to describe himself in the third person as "the human," that the Aramaic words were later mistakenly translated as "son of man" (υἱος του ἀνθρωπου) and understood in Christian apocalyptic literature, in connection with Daniel 7:13, of the Messiah and then put on Jesus' lips in that sense.[22] But on further inquiry this opinion proved highly improbable. For, in the first place, the ordinary Aramaic word for "man" (generic) was אנש and never, at least in Jesus' time, בר נוש. In the New Testament, the term "sons of men" occurs only once in the plural (Mark 3:28), but otherwise a human is always referred to with the single word ἀνθρωπος. The term "son of man" was therefore unusual; it was reminiscent of Daniel 7:13, and understood in the apocalyptic literature of that time as a reference to the Messiah. In the second place, the above opinion fails to explain why the Aramaic expression was rendered in Greek not simply by ἀνθρωπος but by υἱος του ἀνθρωπος, understood in a messianic sense, and put on Jesus' lips.[23]

Although research into the meaning of the term "son of man" is still far from finished,[24] it may be considered highly probable at this point that Jesus derived it from Daniel 7:13 and used it for a specific reason. To understand this reason, we need to note that though Jesus repeatedly used the term with reference to himself, others—with the exception of Stephen (Acts 7:56)—never referred to

21. E. Sellin, *Die israelitisch-jüdische Heilandserwartung,* 70ff.; Gould, "Son of Man," *DC,* II, 660.

22. J. Wellhausen, *Israelitische und jüdische Geschichte,* 1st ed. (Berlin: Reimer, 1894), 312; idem, *Skizzen und Vorarbeiten* (Berlin: Reimer, 1899), 187–215; H. Lietzmann, *Der Menschensohn: Ein Beitrag zur neutestamentlichen Theologie* (Freiburg i.B.: J. C. B. Mohr, 1896); H. L. Oort, *De Uitdrukking ὁ υἱος του ἀνθρωπου in het Nieuwe Testament* (Leiden: Brill, 1893); A. Meyer, *Jesu Muttersprache* (Freiburg: Mohr, 1896).

23. G. Dalman, *Die Worte Jesu* (Leipzig, 1898); *Schmiedel, *Protestäntische Monatshefte* (1899): 252–67, 291–308; S. Driver, "Son of Man," *DB,* IV, 581; Gould, "Son of Man," *DC,* II, 661; W. Baldensperger, "Die neueste Forschung über den Menschensohn," *Theologische Rundschau* 3 (1900): 201–10, 243–55.

24. J. G. Boehmer, "Zum Verständnis des Menschensohnes," *Die Studierstube* (1905): 411–18.

him by that name. The term never occurs in the letters, although expressions in 1 Corinthians 15:47 and Hebrews 2:6 are closely related to it. Furthermore, Jesus called himself by that name, not just after Peter's confession in Caesarea Philippi (Matt. 16:13f.), but already long before that time. In the Gospel of Matthew, the name is found nine times before this weighty event, in Mark twice, and in Luke four times; and when Jesus began to apply this name to himself, no one expressed surprise at it and no one inquired about its meaning. Finally, the name occurs in connection with Jesus' descent from heaven (John 3:13) and communion with heaven (John 1:51); with the authority and power that is his in the kingdom of heaven (Matt. 9:6; 10:32; 12:8, 32; John 6:27, 53f.); in connection with his humble state (Matt. 8:20; 11:19), his suffering and death (Matt. 16:21; 17:12, 22; 20:18, 28; 26:2, 24, 45; John 3:14; 12:23; 13:31), but also with his resurrection, ascension, seating at the right hand of God, and coming again to judge (Matt. 10:23; 13:41; 16:27–28; 24:27, 30, 37; 25:31; 26:64; John 3:13; 6:62).

Taking all this into consideration, we realize that with this name Jesus intends to distinguish himself from and position himself above all other humans. The name also undoubtedly implies that he was truly human, akin not only to Israel but to all humans; yet it simultaneously expresses the fact that he occupies an utterly unique place among all humans. He was conscious from the start that he came from above, from heaven, and had a most special calling to fulfill on earth. He is the Christ, the Son of the living God, as Peter later confesses. But he does not thus identify himself or let others thus identify him in public, lest people mistake his person and work. He therefore chose the name "Son of Man," a name that in Daniel 7:13 refers to the Messiah and is so understood in apocryphal literature as well. But it does not follow that the people in general, or that even the disciples, on hearing the name, immediately thought of the Messiah. The opposite is likely the case, because he was never attacked on account of this title. People perhaps understood by it only that he was special, that he was an extraordinary human being, a fact that was immediately substantiated by his words and works. But for that very reason this name afforded Jesus an opportunity to cut off in advance all misunderstanding about his person and work, and to gradually inject into that name and unite with it the peculiar meaning of the messiahship that, in accordance with the Scriptures, was inherent in it to his mind. And this meaning comes down to the fact that the Christ, who came from above, had to suffer many things and after that enter his glory. So then Jesus chose this name for himself to make known: (1) that he was not just the Son of David and King of Israel but the Son of Man, connected with all humans and giving his life as a ransom for many; (2) that he nonetheless occupied an utterly unique place among all humans, because he had descended from above, from heaven, lived in constant communion with the Father during his stay on earth, and had power to forgive sins, to bestow eternal life, to distribute to his own all the goods of the kingdom; (3) that he could not grasp this power by violence, as the Jews expected their Messiah to do, but that as the Servant of the Lord, he had to suffer and die for

his people; and (4) that precisely by taking this road he would attain to the glory
of the resurrection and the ascension, the elevation to God's right hand, and the
coming again for judgment.[25]

As stated above, Jesus did not just identify himself as the Son of Man toward
the end of his life but was conscious of his messiahship from the first moment of
his public activities and began to do so by virtue of that consciousness. Already
at the age of twelve, he knew he had to be in the things of his Father (Luke 2:49).
In his baptism by John, he received the divine sign and seal of his calling (Luke
3:21). And he immediately acted under the name "Son of Man," long before
the incident in Caesarea Philippi (Mark 2:10, 28). From the beginning he gave
himself an utterly unique place in the kingdom of God, performed works that
presuppose his messiahship, and demanded a status that was his due only if he
was the Messiah (Matt. 5:11; 10:18, 32, 37; 12:6, 41; 19:29). It is true that in the
early period he used the name sparingly and that he used it more frequently when
after the incident in Caesarea he could link his messiahship with his program of
suffering. Jesus had to train his disciples in such a way that, while recognizing him
as the Messiah, they did not project on him all those earthly, political expectations
that were associated at the time with the idea of the Messiah. Also implied in this
is that Jesus' self-consciousness as Messiah cannot be explained in historical or
psychological terms. It is present from the moment of Jesus' public appearances
and cannot be inferred from the influence of the apocalyptic literature. Its importance is undoubtedly overestimated by Baldensperger in general as well as in
relation to Jesus. The latter therefore sees himself compelled to go back further,
that is, to Jesus' God-consciousness, and to say that at the baptism, along with
his God-consciousness, he immediately became aware of his messiahship. At that
moment, he perceived God's nearness as never before and heard within himself
the voice that said: "You are my Son."[26] To a certain extent, this is true. Jesus'
realization that he was the Messiah flowed from the knowledge that he enjoyed
an utterly unique relationship to God. He, accordingly, called himself the Son of
Man but also "the Son of God."

25. Cf. H. Appel, *Die Selbstbezeichnung Jesu, der Sohn des Menschen* (Stavenhagen: Beholtz, 1896); H. J.
Holtzmann, *Lehrbuch der neutestamentliche Theologie*, I, 246ff.; idem, *Das messianische Bewusstsein Jesu*
(Tübingen: Mohr, 1907), 50ff.; M. Kähler, *Zur Lehre der Versöhnung* (1898), 75ff.; P. Fiebig, *Der Menschensohn:
Jesu Selbstbezeichnung mit besonderer Berücksichtigung des aramäischen Sprachgebrauches für "Mensch"* (Tübingen:
Mohr, 1901); F. Tillmann, *Der Menschensohn: Jesu Selbstbezeugnis für seine messianische Würde* (Freiburg i.B.:
Herder, 1907); B. B. Warfield, *The Lord of Glory* (New York: American Tract Society, 1907).

26. W. Baldensperger, *Das Selbstbewusstsein Jesu*, 160; Harnack says the following about Jesus as the Son
of God: "How he came to this consciousness of the unique character of his relation to God as a Son, how he
came to the consciousness of his power and the mission which this power carries with it, is his secret and no
psychology will ever fathom it" (A. von Harnack, *What Is Christianity?* trans. Thomas Bailey Saunders [New
York: Harper, 1957], 128). Cf. also R. F. Grau, *Das Selbstbewusstsein Jesu* (Nordlingen: C. H. Beck, 1887); C. F.
D'Arcy, "Consciousness," *DC*, I, 361ff.; J. Steinbeck, *Das göttliche Selbstbewusstsein Jesu nach dem Zeugnis der
Synoptiker* (Leipzig: Deichert, 1908).

In the Old Testament it was first the people of Israel who were described by that name, then the king, and especially the Messiah.[27] The name "Son of God" perhaps still has this theocratic meaning when it was used by the demoniacs (Matt. 8:29), the Jews (Matt. 27:40), the high priest (Matt. 26:63), and even the disciples in the early period (John 1:49; 11:27; Matt. 16:16). But Jesus invests it with another and deeper meaning. He is the Son of God not because he is Messiah and king, but he is king because he is the Messiah, because he is the Son of the Father. God is his Father (Luke 2:49); he is the only Son, whom the Father loved and whom he sent as his last emissary (Mark 12:6). At the baptism (Matt. 3:17) and later at the transfiguration (Matt. 17:5), God calls him his "beloved son with whom he is well pleased." In Matthew 11:27, he states that all things needed for the realization of God's gracious will (εὐδοκια) have been delivered to him and that only the Father knows the Son and only the Son knows the Father. This sonship is the source of his whole life, all his thinking and acting. In that consciousness he puts himself on a level above the elders (Matt. 5:18ff.), above Jonah and Solomon (Luke 11:31–32), above the angels even (Mark 13:32). Knowing that he stood in a totally unique relationship to the Father and was king of the divine kingdom, he pronounced people blessed (Matt. 5:3ff.; Luke 10:23), forgave sins (Mark 2:10ff.), demanded that his disciples leave everything for his sake (Matt. 5:11; 10:18, 22; etc.), and linked with it entrance into eternal life.

The Synoptics already contain in principle all the things that the apostles and the Christian church later taught about the person of Christ. True, before Jesus' resurrection, the disciples did not yet have the right insight into his person and work. The Gospels themselves tell us that. It is for this reason that Jesus in his teaching also took account of the disciples' capacity to understand, gradually introduced them to the knowledge of his sonship and messiahship, and left a great deal to the instruction of the Spirit (John 16:12). But the resurrection already marvelously illumined the person and work of Christ. From that time on, he was to all the disciples "a heavenly being"; the teaching of Paul and John concerning the essential character of Christ was in no way opposed by any of the other disciples.[28]

What they added to it is not anything new but only expansion and development. Jesus became human—"flesh"; he came into the flesh (John 1:14; 1 John 4:2–3) from the loins of the patriarchs according to the flesh (Rom. 9:5); he is Abraham's offspring (Gal. 3:16), from the tribe of Judah (Heb. 7:14), a descendant of David (Rom. 1:3), born of a woman (Gal. 4:4; Heb. 2:14), a human in the full and true sense of the word (Rom. 5:15; 1 Cor. 15:45; 1 Tim. 2:15) who was tired, thirsty, sad, happy as we are (John 4:6ff.; 11:33, 38; 12:27; 13:21; Heb. 4:15); he

27. Cf. H. Bavinck, *Reformed Dogmatics*, II, 264–68 (#214); G. Dalman, *Die Worte Jesu*; H. J. Holtzmann, *Lehrbuch der neutestamentlichen Theologie*, I, 265ff.; W. Sanday, "Son of God," *DB*, IV, 568ff.; J. Stalker, "Son of God," *DC*, II, 654ff.

28. K. H. von Weizsäcker, *Das apostolische Zeitalter der christlichen Kirche*, 2nd ed. (Freiburg: Mohr, 1890), 16, 110.

was under the law (Gal. 4:4), learned obedience unto death (Phil. 2:8; Heb. 5:8; 10:7, 9), suffered, died, was buried, and so on.

This same person, however, was simultaneously free from all sin (Matt. 7:11; 11:29; John 4:34; 8:29, 46; 15:10; Acts 3:14; 2 Cor. 5:21; Heb. 4:15; 7:26; 1 Pet. 1:19; 2:22; 1 John 2:1; 3:5); he also rose again, was glorified, and is seated at God's right hand (Acts 2:34; 5:31; 7:55; etc.). He already existed before his incarnation (John 1:1; 17:5; 1 Cor. 10:4, 9; Heb. 11:26) and was then "in the form of God" (Phil. 2:6), the firstborn of all creation (Col. 1:15), superior to angels (Heb. 1:4), the one by whom God created all things and in whom all things hold together (John 1:3; 1 Cor. 8:6; Col. 1:16; Eph. 3:9), the Son of God in an utterly unique sense (John 1:14; 5:18; Rom. 8:3, 32; Gal. 4:4), and himself God (John 1:1; 20:28; Rom. 9:5; 1 Thess. 1:1; Titus 2:13; Heb. 1:8–9 [1 John 5:20], 2 Pet. 1:1).

CHRISTOLOGICAL CONFLICTS

[356] This apostolic witness concerning Jesus the Christ was too rich and too deep for it to be immediately absorbed into the Christian consciousness and reproduced in a clear formula such that it would be proof against all error. In the case of the Apostolic Fathers, accordingly, though they assign to Christ an utterly unique place and call him by an array of glorious and sublime names, this does not happen.[29] First, the errors of Ebionitism and Gnosticism on the left and the right made it obligatory for the church to think through the content of the apostolic witness and to give a clear account both of Christ's relation to God and of his relation to humankind. Ebionitism, though it did hold Jesus to be the Messiah and sometimes also believed that he was supernaturally conceived and endowed at his baptism with divine power, saw in Jesus nothing more than a human being, a descendant of David, anointed with the Spirit of God and appointed king over an earthly realm to be established at his return.[30] Gnosticism, despising matter and ascribing the creation of the world to a demiurge, drew a sharp line of separation, also in the case of Christ, between the divine and the human. The highest aeon, namely, Christ, descended from heaven and for a time united himself with the earthly man Jesus, or brought a psychic body with him from heaven, or for a time assumed a seeming body with a view to liberating humankind from the bonds of matter.[31] Whereas Harnack thinks that the recognition of Jesus as a divinely chosen and Spirit-endowed human was not Ebionite but Christian and also states that the doctrine of the two natures of Christ was originally Gnostic,[32] he nevertheless

29. Cf. H. Bavinck, *Reformed Dogmatics,* II, 279–85 (#218).

30. G. Uhlhorn, "Ebioniten," *PRE*[3], V, 125–28; F. A. Loofs, *Leitfaden zum Studium der Dogmengeschichte,* 4th ed. (Halle a.S.: M. Niemeyer, 1906), 83.

31. F. A. Loofs, *Dogmengeschichte,* 105–11; G. Krüger, "Doketen," *PRE*[3], IV, 764–65; idem, "Gnosis, Gnosticismus," *PRE*[3], VI, 728–38.

32. A. von Harnack, *History of Dogma,* trans. N. Buchanan, J. Millar, E. B. Speirs, and W. McGilchrist, ed. A. B. Bruce, 7 vols. (London: Williams & Norgate, 1896–99), I, 256, 231; II, 239.

has to admit that in the most ancient tradition Jesus was also confessed as Son of God and never considered a "bare human being" (ψιλος ἀνθρωπος).[33]

Though there may have been different conceptions as to how one and the same subject could be simultaneously Son of God and a human being, this nevertheless was how all Christians from the beginning saw Christ. This confession had to lead and—under Justin, Irenaeus, and Tertullian[34]—did lead to the doctrine of the two natures. The expression "the two essences of Christ" (δυο οὐσιαι χριστου) first occurs in a fragment of Melito, the genuineness of which, however, is called into question.[35] Irenaeus, though he does not yet have the two-natures formula, clearly teaches that Christ is truly the Son, the Logos, and himself God; that as such he became a human; and that this incarnate Logos constitutes an unbreakable unity. He is truly man and truly God (*Adv. haer.,* IV, 6, 7); it is one and the same Christ who created the world and who was born and died (*Adv. haer.,* III, 9, 3, 16, 6, 19, 1, etc.). Tertullian teaches the same thing but speaks even more forcefully of two substances in Christ, a fleshly and a spiritual substance; of two conditions, a divine and a human (*De carne chr.,* 5); and assumed there was in him a double state, not confused but conjoined in one person, truly God and truly human (*Adv. Pr.,* 27). Soon afterward, in the West, the formula used for this doctrine of Christ is that he was one person with two natures. Augustine regularly expresses himself as follows: "Thus there appeared a mediator between God and humans that, combining the two natures in the unity of the person, he might elevate what is earthly to the heavenly and temper the heavenly with the earthly" (*Ep. ad Volus,* 3). In the East, however, the terminology—like the doctrine of the Trinity—for a long time remained unstable and therefore susceptible to all kinds of misunderstanding. The words οὐσια, φυσις, ὑποστασις, προσωπον, still lacked strict definition and were therefore used interchangeably. Even Cyril still frequently describes the human nature of Christ as ὑποστασις instead of as φυσις and then still speaks of one nature in Christ: μια σεσαρκωμενη φυσις (one enfleshed nature). The union of the two natures was described by Gregory of Nazianzus and Gregory of Nyssa as a "mixture" or a "mingling" and by Cyril as a "natural union" or a "uniting according to nature"; and what came about as a result of the hypostatic union was repeatedly called not εἰς (one [masculine]) but ἐν (one [neuter]).[36] Pope Leo the Great's "dogmatic epistle," however, helped a great deal to bring about also in the East clear insight and precise word usage in

---

33. A. von Harnack, *History of Dogma,* I, 162–79; cf. F. A. Loofs, "Christologie, Kirchenlehre," *PRE*[3], IV, 18; idem, *Dogmengeschichte,* 83.

34. Cf. H. Bavinck, *Reformed Dogmatics,* II, 279–85 (#218); A. L. Feder, *Justin des Märtyrers Lehre von Jesus Christus dem Messias und dem menschgewordenen Sohn Gottes* (Freiburg i.B.: Herder, 1906); on Irenaeus and Tertullian, see F. A. Loofs, *Dogmengeschichte,* §§21, 22.

35. A. von Harnack, *History of Dogma,* I, 175; cf. F. A. Loofs, "Christologie, Kirchenlehre," 31; idem, *Dogmengeschichte,* 151.

36. J. Schwane, *Dogmengeschichte,* 2nd ed., 4 vols. (Freiburg i.B.: Herder, 1892–1985), II, 294ff., 341ff.

the doctrine of Christ.[37] And at Chalcedon, after the rejection of Nestorianism, patripassianism, Eutychianism, and others, the confession of Christ was defined as being about one and the same Son and Lord, "the same perfect in Godhead, the same perfect in humanhood, truly God and truly man . . . one and the same Christ, Son, Lord, Only-begotten, made known *in* two natures [according to the original reading; not *out* of two natures], without confusion [ἀσυγχυτως], without change [ἀτρεπτως], without division [ἀδιαιρετως], without separation [ἀχωριστως]."[38]

With Chalcedon, clear-cut boundaries had been drawn within which the church's doctrine of Christ would be further developed. It was far from being the case, however, that with it, in earlier and later times, unanimity had been achieved. The question, What do you think of the Christ? has evoked a wide assortment of answers in the Christian life as well as in theology. All through history it has divided the heads and hearts of people. Even within the churches that accept the Chalcedonian symbol, for all their agreement, there is also still substantial difference.

In the theology of the East, the basic idea remained that God himself had to become a human so that human beings might become partakers in the divine nature, immortality, eternal life, divinization (θεωσις).[39] The consequences of sin are much more physical than ethical in nature; consequently, a current of mysticism always flows alongside rationalism in the Greek church. The result of this mysticism had to be that, though the human nature of Christ was recognized as well, the major emphasis fell on his deity, on the penetration of the divine into the human nature, on the union of the two, on Christ's essential being more than on his historical appearance, on his incarnation rather than on his satisfaction. Hence, with respect to the person of Christ, what mattered most was his divine essence, which was communicated in human form and thus received and enjoyed by human beings. No particular need was felt, therefore, for a sharp distinction between the two natures. It is lacking in Athanasius, the Cappadocians, even in part in Cyril. The Greek reading of the Chalcedon decree is a correction of the original text: the expression "in two natures" has been replaced by "out of two natures." Monophysitism was a power in the East. However condemned and suppressed, it kept surfacing in the teaching of the Theopaschites, the Aphthartodocetists, the Aktistetai, and the Monothelites. It tended to erase the boundary line between the divine and the human and increasingly to make the churches in the East ready for their dissolution into paganism.[40]

By contrast, the West made a sharp distinction between the divine and the human nature of Christ. Already since Tertullian, the terminology of the one

37. A. Hahn, *Bibliothek der Symbole und Glaubensregeln der alten Kirche,* 3rd ed. (Breslau: E. Morgenstern, 1897), 321–30.

38. A. Hahn, *Bibliothek,* 166.

39. Cf. H. Bavinck, *Reformed Dogmatics,* I, 134n51 (#42).

40. Cf. G. Krüger, "Monophysiten," *PRE*[3], XIII, 372–401; idem, "Monotheleten," *PRE*[3], XIII, 401–13.

person and the two natures had been fixed. The emphasis was more on the ethical than on the physical; on Christ's satisfaction, his suffering and death, than on his incarnation. Yet not all danger of deifying the human nature of Christ was averted here either. The East hardly took any notice of the West and—to be specific—in no way even underwent the influence of Augustine. Conversely, the West did take over the theology and particularly the mysticism of the East. As a result the idea of a deification of the human also penetrated the Latin church and Latin theology. Mystical contemplation, the doctrine of the superadded gifts, the theory of transubstantiation, all rest on the idea that the finite is capable of participating in the infinite. This idea could not but have an impact on Christology, for in Christology human nature is more tightly united with the deity than any other creature. If Adam already participated in the divine nature by the superadded gift, if believers participated in it by infused grace, if mystics participated in it by contemplation and were in a sense divinized,[41] then this had to be true in much greater measure of the human being Christ, in whom the fullness of God dwelt bodily.

THE TWO NATURES OF CHRIST

[357] Entirely in accordance with John of Damascus,[42] scholastic and Roman theology therefore taught that, though each nature in Christ remains itself and the communication of the divine attributes to the human nature must not be conceived realistically, yet the divine nature completely permeates and sets aglow the human nature, as heat does iron, and makes it participatory in the divine glory, wisdom, and power (περιχωρησις, θεωσις). From this premise it was then inferred that Christ as a human being on earth already possessed the blessed knowledge, the beatific vision of God. Even on earth Christ was already both a pilgrim and one who fully understood (*comprehensor ac viator*), walking not by faith but by sight. In his case, therefore, we cannot and may not speak of faith and hope. Moreover, all the gifts of which the human nature of Christ was capable were given him, not gradually but all at once, at his incarnation. As a human he remained indeed finite and limited; in the state of his humiliation, he also had a variety of defects (susceptibility to suffering and death) and affects (sensations of grief, hunger, cold, and so on). Still, at his incarnation he all at once received all the wisdom of which his human nature was capable. His increase in wisdom (Luke 2:52) must be understood not objectively but subjectively. It seemed so to others; also, when he prayed he did not pray out of need, but only for our sake, to give us an example. Actually Jesus was never a child; he was a man from the start. And because his human nature was thus glorified and divinized by God, it

41. Cf. H. Bavinck, *Reformed Dogmatics,* I, 359–62 (#99); II, 188–91 (#199); 539–42 (#287).
42. John of Damascus, *Exposition of the Orthodox Faith*, III, 3, 7, 17, 19; cf. I. A. Dorner, *History of the Development of the Doctrine of the Person of Christ*, trans. William Lindsay Alexander, 5 vols. (Edinburgh: T&T Clark, 1863–78), III, 215ff.; F. A. Loofs, *Dogmengeschichte*, 324.

too is entitled to be worshiped. Indeed, every part of the human nature of Christ, his holy heart in particular, is deserving of divine veneration.[43]

In Lutheran theology we encounter the same basic idea. Its development and application, however, is different. Greek and Roman theology indeed taught a communication of divine gifts, but not of divine attributes, to human nature. They also taught a true and real communication of divine attributes, not to human nature as such, but to the hypostasis (the person) of the two natures. Luther, however, taught that even already in the state of humiliation, the humanity of Christ was where his deity was, and that the two natures were "united and commingled" with their attributes, not only in the person but also mutually.[44] Consequently, Roman theologians could unanimously oppose Lutheran Christology and especially the doctrine of ubiquity.[45] Still, here as well as in the doctrine of the Lord's Supper, there is kinship. Lutherans, after all, expressly teach that the two natures of Christ are never mixed or transmuted into each other, but that each remains itself in perpetuity and preserves its essential attributes and never receives the attributes of the other nature as its own.[46] Nor do they say that all the divine attributes are imparted to the human nature in the same sense and the same measure. The quiescent attributes of infinity and so on were never given to it directly but only through the mediation of the other attributes. The operative attributes, however, such as omnipresence, omnipotence, and omniscience, were immediately and directly a possession of the human nature. People even frequently attributed to it not just the multivolipresence [presence in as many places as he wished] or ubiquity, as Chemnitz spoke of it, but specifically omnipresence.[47] Materially, Roman and Lutheran theology agree in the sense that both elevate the human nature above the boundaries set for it and dissolve into mere appearance both the human development of Jesus and the state of his humiliation.

---

43. Cf. J. Kleutgen, *Die Theologie der Vorzeit verthedigt,* 2nd ed., 5 vols. (Münster: Theissing, 1867–74), III, 3–333; H. Pesch, *Lehrbuch der Nationalökonomie* (Freiburg: Herder, 1905), IV, 1–174; H. T. Simar, *Lehrbuch der Dogmatik,* 3rd ed. (Freiburg i.B: Herder 1893), §§94ff.; G. M. Jansen, *Praelectiones Theologiae Dogmaticae,* 3 vols. in 2 (Utrecht: Van Rossum, 1875–79), II, 567ff.; P. Mannens, *Theologiae Dogmaticae Institutiones,* 3 vols. (Roermand: Romen, 1910–15), II, 349ff. Ed. note: Bavinck also refers here to the literature cited in the Dutch edition at the head of this chapter (= §45 of the Dutch edition). The items listed there are referenced in the notes and will not be repeated here. The noteworthy addition is Bavinck's final reference to *DC,* II, appendix, "which contains articles about Christ in the early church, in the Middle Ages, in Reformation theology, in the seventeenth century, in modern thought, in Jewish literature, in Muslim literature, and finally an article about Paul."

44. J. Köstlin, *Theology of Luther in Its Historical Development and Inner Harmony,* trans. Charles E. Hay, 2 vols. (Philadelphia: Lutheran Publication Society, 1897), II, 415ff.

45. R. Bellarmine, "De Christo," *Controversiis,* III, 9; D. Petavius, "De incarnation," *Op. theol.,* X, 7–10.

46. "Formula of Concord," in *Die symbolischen Bücher der evangelisch-lutherischen Kirche,* ed. J. T. Muller, 8th ed. (Gutersloh: Bertelsmann, 1898), 675–76. Ed. note: English version can be found in *Formula of Concord,* in vol. 3 of *Creeds of Christendom,* ed. Philip Schaff, rev. David S. Schaff, 6th ed. (New York: Harper & Row, 1931; reprinted, Grand Rapids: Baker, 1983).

47. "Formula of Concord," in *Die symbolischen Bücher der evangelisch-lutherischen Kirche,* 685.

In the course of the development of Lutheran theology, this became all too apparent. In the case of Christ's becoming a man, a distinction was made—not temporally but logically—between the incarnation (the assumption of flesh) and the exinanition (self-emptying: conception in the womb). Of the former, only the Logos is the subject; it consists in making the human nature, which is inherently finite, fit for the indwelling of the fullness of the deity and imparting to it the above-mentioned divine attributes. But in this way not only the distinction between the divine and the human nature was in danger of being lost but also that between the state of humiliation and that of exaltation. For that reason it was assumed that in the second moment, in the self-emptying (exinanition), of which not the Logos but the "God-man" was the subject, the latter had in a sense again divested himself of the attributes first imparted to him. But concerning the nature of this "exinanition," there was much disagreement. Between the Giessen and the Tübinger theologians a lengthy controversy (1607–24) was even conducted over this issue. According to the Tübingers, Christ only refrained from the *public* use of these attributes. He retained them, mind you, and also used them (for the distinction between potentiality and act does not apply to the divine attributes; a potential omnipresence, omniscience, and so on is an absurdity), but in the state of his humiliation, Christ used the attributes imparted only in a latent or hidden manner; the state of exaltation is nothing other than a visible display of what existed invisibly already from the hour of his conception. In this fashion, however, Jesus' whole human development, his growth in knowledge and wisdom, his hungering and thirsting, suffering and dying, became mere appearance. For that reason the Giessen theologians, as well as the later Lutherans, preferred to say that in the moment of exinanition Christ totally ceased to use the attributes communicated to him. Though he retained them, he retained them only as a capacity but did not use them. Only after his exaltation did he also exercise them.[48]

Reformed theologians were, from the very beginning, in a much more favorable position. They had fundamentally overcome the Greek-Roman and Lutheran commingling of the divine and the human, also in Christology. While rigorously maintaining the unity of the person, they applied the rule "the finite is not capable of [containing] the infinite" also to the human nature of Christ and maintained this rule not only in the state of humiliation but even in that of Christ's exaltation.

---

48. In addition to Chemnitz, *De duabus naturis Christi* (1570), see also I. A. Dorner, *Person of Christ*, IV, 266–315; idem, *Geschichte der protestantischen Theologie*, 2 vols. (Munich: J. G. Cotta, 1867), 569ff.; F. H. R. Frank, *Theologie der Concordienformel*, 4 vols. in 2 (Erlangen: T. Blaesing, 1858–65), III, 165–396; M. Schneckenburger, *Vergleichende Darstellung des Lutherischen und Reformierten Lehrbegriffs*, 2 vols. (Stuttgart: J. B. Metzler, 1855), §26; idem, *Zur kirchlichen Christologie: Die orthodoxe Lehre vom doppelten Stande Christi nach lutherischer und reformirter Fassung* (Pforzheim: Flammer & Hoffmann, 1848); E. W. C. Sartorius, *Die Lehre von Christi Person und Werk,* 3rd ed. (Hamburg: F. Perthes, 1837), I, 520ff.; F. A. Philippi, *Kirchliche Glaubenslehre*, 3rd ed., 7 vols. in 10 (Gütersloh: Bertelsmann, 1870–90), IV, 1, 243ff.; E. Güder, "Stand Christi, Doppelter," *PRE*[1], XV, 784–99; J. Wagenmann, "Kenotiker und Kryptiker," *PRE*[2], VII, 640–46; R. Seeberg, "Communicatio idiomatum," in *PRE*[3], IV, 254–61; H. E. Weber, *Der Einfluss der protestantischen Schulphilosophie auf die orthodox-lutherische Dogmatik* (Leipzig: Deichert, 1908), 96ff.; 153ff.

In that way Reformed theology secured space for a purely human development of Christ, for a successive communication of gifts, and for a real distinction between humiliation and exaltation. Still, in the process, it seriously avoided the Nestorianism of which it was always accused. The reason for this is that in Greek, Roman, and Lutheran theology the emphasis always fell on the incarnation of the divine being, the divine *nature*. If that nature does not become flesh, the work of salvation, communion with God, seems to be at risk. But Reformed theology stressed that it was the *person* of the Son who became flesh—not the *substance* [the underlying reality] but the *subsistence* [the particular being] of the Son assumed our nature. The unity of the two natures, despite the sharp distinction between them, is unalterably anchored in the person. As it does in the doctrine of the Trinity, of humanity in the image of God, and of the covenants, so here in the doctrine of Christ as well, the Reformed idea of conscious personal life as the fullest and highest life comes dramatically to the fore.[49]

MODERN CHRISTOLOGY: KANT, SCHLEIERMACHER, RITSCHL

[358] All these developments in the doctrine of Christ are based on and occur within the boundaries of the Chalcedon symbol. But—to put it mildly—not all Christians were comfortable with this confession. At all times there were those who deviated from it either to the right or to the left and again pursued the tracks of the old Ebionitism or Gnosticism. Gathered on the one side are Arianism, Nestorianism, Socinianism, Deism, rationalism, and others; and presenting themselves on the other are patripassianism, Sabellianism, Monophysitism, Anabaptism, and pantheism in all its different forms.[50] Particularly in modern theology, the dominant view is that, though the doctrine of the two natures fits Greek theology and the Greek church, for us it has lost all religious value; that it has irrevocably succumbed under the criticism of Socinianism and rationalism, and should therefore now be redefined in a totally new, religious-ethical direction.[51] The most significant representatives of this new Christology are Kant, Schleiermacher, and Ritschl.

49. See also J. Owen, "Declaration of the Glorious Mystery of the Person of Christ, God and Man," in vol. I of *The Works of John Owen*, ed. William H. Goold (Edinburgh: T&T Clark, 1862); J. G. Walch, *Bibliotheca theologica selecta, litterariis adnotationibus instructa*, 4 vols. (Jenae: vid. Croeckerianal, 1757–65), I, 259; C. Vitringa, *Doctr. christ.*, V, 45, 202.

50. On these deviations, cf. H. Bavinck, *Reformed Dogmatics*, II, 288–322 (##220–29); D. Petavius, "De incarnatione," *Op. theol.*, I, ch. 1: "Synopsis haeresium omnium, quae cath. incarnationis fidem oppugnarunt"; J. Forbes, *Instructiones historico-theologicae de doctrina Christiana* (Amsterdam: Ludovicum Elzevirium, 1645), 2–3, 5–6; C. Vitringa, *Doctr. christ.*, V, 46ff.

51. D. F. Strauss, *Die christliche Glaubenslehre in ihrer Geschichtlichen Entwicklung*, 2 vols. (Tübingen: C. F. Osiander, 1840–41), II, 153ff.; A. von Harnack, *History of Dogma*, I, 1ff.; VII, 118ff.; 168ff.; F. A. Loofs, *Dogmengeschichte*, 942ff.; G. Krüger, *Das Dogma von der Dreieinigkeit und Gottmenschheit in seiner geschichtlichen Entwicklung* (Tübingen: Mohr, 1905), 267ff.

Kant, for one, could not accept the biblical and ecclesiastical doctrine of Christ because he denied the knowability of the supernatural and, reasoning from the imperative "you shall" to the "you can," had no need of a Redeemer. To Kant, Christ could therefore function only as a model of morality and a teacher of virtue. All that Scripture and the church said about Christ beyond this had a merely symbolic value. The Christ of the church is the symbol of a humanity pleasing to God: it is the true, only-begotten, much-beloved Son for whom God created the world. The incarnation of Christ symbolizes the origination of a truly moral life in humans. His substitutionary suffering signifies that the moral person in us has to pay for the evil done by the sensual person. Faith in Christ means that for their salvation people must believe in the idea of a humanity that is pleasing to God. In short, the historical person called Jesus is neither a mediator nor a savior. All the church confesses about that person fully applies to the idea of humankind as a whole.[52] In the new philosophy, Kant began—like the ancient Gnostics—to separate the historical Christ from the ideal Christ, and others have since followed him in this regard. Fichte proceeded from the idea that God and humanity are absolutely one. Christ, however, was the first to recognize and clearly articulate this oneness in himself: that is his great historical significance. Thousands of people have come to this recognition, this communion with God, through him. But though this has been historically the case, it is not to say that humans cannot arrive at this communion by themselves, cannot achieve this in any way other than through Christ. If Jesus were to come back, he would be completely content to find that Christianity ruled in people's hearts even though his person had been completely forgotten. Only the eternal metaphysical truth, the recognition of our oneness with God, saves us. The historical dimension is an independent passing reality.[53]

For in Schelling, in his first period, the absolute is no unchanging existent but an eternal becoming that, accordingly, comes to manifestation in the world as its logos and son. Theology believes that Christ is the only begotten incarnate Son of God. But that is a mistake. God is eternal and cannot have assumed human nature in a specific moment of time. As historical fact, Christianity is of passing significance. The idea, however, endures forever: the world is the son of God. The incarnation of God consists in the fact that the absolute, in order to be itself, becomes manifest in a world, a multiplicity of individuals, an enormously rich history, and a historical process. The world, accordingly, is God himself in the process of becoming. The incarnation of God is the first principle of all life and history. The finite is the necessary form for God's self-manifestation. All things

---

52. I. Kant, *Religion within the Limits of Reason Alone*, trans. Theodore M. Greene and Hoyt H. Hudson (New York: Harper & Brothers, 1934), 115ff. Cf. I. A. Dorner, *Person of Christ*, V, 35; J. W. Chapman, *Die Teleologie Kant's* (Halle: C. A. Kaemmerer, 1905). Ed. note: Bavinck erroneously cites this title as *Die Theologie Kants*.

53. J. G. Fichte, *Die Anweisung um seligen Leben oder auch die Religionslehre* (Berlin: Verlag der Realschulbuchhandlung, 1806); cf. I. A. Dorner, *Person of Christ*, V, 95ff.

must be understood in terms of the idea of incarnation. This is the esoteric truth of Christianity as well: the outward historical expression is but the form for this eternal idea.[54]

Hegel, too, said that what theology conveys symbolically in graphic representation, philosophy converts into concepts. Christ is not the only divine-human figure; humans are basically one with God and, at the apex of their development, also become conscious of this fact.[55] On the basis of these philosophical premises, Marheineke, Rosenkranz, Göschel, Daub, Conradi, and others still tried to maintain the incarnation of God in Christ, but Strauss, taking the logical next step, said in his *Life of Jesus*[56] that the idea does not empty its fullness in a single exemplar but only in a plethora of individuals. Humanity itself is the incarnate God who was conceived by the Holy Spirit, lives a sinless life, rises from the dead, ascends to heaven, and so on. In the modern systematic theology that is based on this philosophical idea, there is therefore no room left for Christ other than as a religious genius, a teacher of virtue, a prophet who had a deeper understanding of religion than anyone else, disclosed the love of God most vividly, and expressed the unity and community of God and humankind most clearly. The person of Christ himself, however, is actually not a part of basic Christianity.[57] With a view to this modern theology, therefore, Hartmann spoke with good reason of a crisis and the "self-replacement" of Christianity.[58]

54. F. W. J. Schelling, "Vorlesungen über die Methode des akad. Studiums [1803]," in *Ausgewählte Werke*, 4 vols. (Darmstadt: Wissenschaftliche Buchgesellschaft, 1968), II, 520ff. (*Werke*, I/5, 286ff.); ed. note: Bavinck is referencing the eighth lecture, "Über die historische Construktion des Christenthums." Cf. I. A. Dorner, *Person of Christ*, V, 100.

55. G. W. F. Hegel, "Religionsphilosophie," in *Sämtliche Werke*, 26 vols. (Stuttgart: F. Frommann, 1949–59), XVI, 235ff. (*Werke* XII, 235ff.); ed. note: Bavinck is referring to the third part of Hegel's philosophy of religion (1831 lectures), "The Consummate (Absolute) Religion," specifically the section "The Kingdom of the Father." An abbreviated form of this can be found in *Hegel Lectures on the Philosophy of Religion*, vol. III, *The Consummate Religion*, ed. Peter C. Hodgson (Berkeley: University of California Press, 1985), 363–64. Cf. I. A. Dorner, *Person of Christ*, V, 131ff.

56. D. F. Strauss, *Das Leben Jesu*, 2 vols. (Tübingen: C. F. Osiander, 1835–36), II, 716ff., 734ff.; ed. note: ET: *The Life of Jesus: Critically Examined*, trans. Marian Evans, 2 vols. (New York: Calvin Blanchard, 1860; reprinted, St. Clair Shores, MI: Scholarly Press, 1970). The passage Bavinck cites is taken from the "Concluding Dissertation: The Dogmatic Import of the Life of Jesus," sect. 144–52, pp. 867–901; idem, *Christliche Glaubenslehre*, II, 193; cf. concerning Strauss, A. Hein, "Die Christologie von D. Fr. Strauss," *Zeitschrift für Theologie und Kirche* 16 (1906): 321–46.

57. D. F. Strauss, *Christliche Glaubenslehre*, II, 214ff.; idem, *The Old Faith and the New*, trans. Mathilde Blind (New York: Hold, 1873), 26ff.; A. Schweizer, *Christliche Glaubenslehre* (Leipzig: S. Hirzel, 1863–72), §§116ff.; O. Pfleiderer, *Grundriss der christlichen Glaubens-und Sittenlehre* (Berlin: G. Reimer, 1888), §128; A. E. Biedermann, *Christliche Dogmatik* (Zürich: Füssli, 1869), II, 580ff.; R. A. Lipsius, *Lehrbuch der evangelisch-protestantischen Dogmatik* (Braunschweig; C. A. Schwetschke, 1893), §588; J. H. Scholten, *Dogmatices christianae initia*, 2nd ed. (Leiden: P. Engels, 1858), ch. 4, 171.

58. E. von Hartmann, *Die Krisis des Christentums in der modernen Theologie* (Berlin: C. Duncker, 1880); ed. note: Bavinck erroneously cites the title as "Die Krisis der Theologie in der modernen Theologie"; idem, *Die Selbstzersetzung des Christentums und die Relgion der Zukunft*, 3rd ed. (Leipzig: Friedrich, 1888); idem, *Das Christentum des Neuen Testaments*, 2nd ed. (Sachsa i.H.: Haacke, 1905).

Another road was taken by Schleiermacher. Although he too rejected the church's doctrine of Christ, he nevertheless sought to avoid the mistake of speculative philosophy, the mistake of looking for the essence of Christianity in an abstract idea and detaching it from the historical person of Christ. To that end, he based his view on the experience of the church, on the Christian consciousness, whose content is reconciliation and fellowship with God. The ultimate cause of it can be found nowhere but in the founder of the Christian church, in whom, accordingly, God-consciousness must have been present with absolute power. And this power of God-consciousness was God's being in him, so that he is the religious archetype of humankind, sinless, the supreme product of the human race, simultaneously brought forth by an act of divine creation as the perfect subject of religion. What is above all important is not his doctrine but his person, not what he did but what he was, not his ethical example but his religious life.[59] By thus locating the realization of the religious idea not in Christ's humanity but in his person, Schleiermacher exerted enormous influence and again secured for Christology a place in dogmatics.

Schleiermacher's influence became perceptible, first, in that, in contrast to Kant, Fichte, and Hegel, theologians tried to maintain that Christ was a most extraordinary and wholly unique revelation of God. If God-consciousness in Christ was absolute and never disturbed by any sin, God must also have dwelt in him in an entirely unique way. These theologians could, of course, construe this in various ways, depending on their view of the Trinity. Those who rejected the ontological Trinity assumed that in Christ we have a special manifestation of God, a perfect indwelling of God, the realization of God's eternal idea of the world or of humanity.[60] Others, though acknowledging an ontological Trinity, construed the relation of the Son to the Father in more or less subordinationist fashion and so arrived at an Arian Christology.[61] Still others made the Son coordinate with the Father and in so doing approximated the doctrine of the church.[62]

Second, as a result of Schleiermacher's work, an unaccustomed interest in the historical human development of the person of Christ occurred in the newer Christology. Hence the doctrine of the *communicatio idiomatum* [the commu-

59. F. Schleiermacher, *The Christian Faith* (Edinburgh: T&T Clark, 1989), §§91ff.; D. F. Strauss, *Christliche Glaubenslehre*, II, 175: Schleiermacher's Christology; I. A. Dorner, *Person of Christ*, V, 98ff.

60. R. Rothe, *Theologische Ethik*, 2nd rev. ed., 5 vols. (Wittenberg: Zimmerman, 1867–71), §§533ff.; C. H. Weisse, *Philosophische Dogmatik oder Philosophie des Christentums*, 2nd ed., 3 vols. (Leipzig: Hirzel, 1855–62), I, 437–556; D. Schenkel, *Die christliche Dogmatik vom Standpunkte des Gewissens aus dargestellt*, 2 vols. (Wiesbaden: Kreidel & Niedner, 1858–59), II, 2, 717, 724.

61. W. F. Gess, *Die Lehre von der Person Christi* (Basel: Bahnmaiers Buchhandlung, 1856), 157ff.; Hofstede de Groot, *De Groninger Godgeleerdheid in Hunne Eigenaardigheid* (Groningen: Scholtens, 1855), 157ff.

62. C. E. Nitzsch, *System of Christian Doctrines* (Edinburgh: T&T Clark, 1849); K. F. A. Kahnis, *Die lutherische Dogmatik, historisch-genetisch dargestellt*, 3 vols. (Leipzig: Dörffling & Franke, 1861–68), II, 3, 69ff.; G. Thomasius, *Christi Person und Werk*, 3rd ed., 2 vols. (Erlangen: A. Deichert, 1886–88), I, 447ff.; J. P. Lange, *Christliche Dogmatik*, 3 vols. (Heidelberg: K. Winter, 1852), II, 594ff.; also see bibliographic references to Sartorius, Liebner, Ebrard, Philippi, and Vilmar.

nication of proper qualities] was virtually abandoned, and the human nature of Christ moved to the fore; the doctrine of the two states became a life of Jesus, and that life was traced in its preparation, development, and influence. A favorite object of study became the history of Israel, of the classic world of antiquity, and especially of Jesus' own time.[63] Furthermore, the incarnation had to be viewed, not as incidentally necessary on account of sin, but as flowing from the idea of God and given with the creation itself.[64] And Jesus' development as a human being then had to be traced in its development until he became the second Adam, the head of humanity, the central individual.[65]

Finally, in the recent Christology that still held to the confession of Christ as the "God-man," there came a trend to maintain the unity of these two in another, better way than was done in the Chalcedon Confession and the dogmatics of the church. To that end, the idea of *becoming* was applied in part to God himself but especially to the God-man. Schelling started this trend in his second period.[66] Granted, in a sense the Son existed eternally in the Father; but as generated by the Father, as Son existing outside (*praeter*) the Father, he first made his appearance in the creation. Even then, however, the Son does not exist as a real person but as a potency that can and must realize itself. But as a result of human sin, the world becomes "extra-divine," something existing outside God, and the Son, who was generated for the sake of that world and remains united with it, acquires an existence that is externally (not internally) independent of the Father.[67]

He was in an intermediate state, "in the form of God"; he becomes the Christ, remains attached to the fallen world that the Father leaves in his hands, leads it back—in the way of self-annihilation and obedience—to the Father, and thereby himself becomes Son in a perfect sense at the end of the world.[68] This idea of the "God-man's" becoming exerted great influence in theosophic circles, for example, on Baader, Steffens, and others. And even Rothe and Dorner adopted the notion that God or the Logos began to indwell the historical person of Jesus to the degree that Jesus himself developed into a religious personality, into "spirit"; the humanization of God here increases in proportion to the divinizing of the human. In another yet related manner, the explanation of the God-man was attempted by means of the *kenosis* doctrine, that is, by the assumption that at the incarnation the Logos emptied himself of all or some of his properties down to the level of

---

63. M. Schneckenburger, *Vorlesungen über neutestamentliche Zeitgeschichte* (Frankfurt a.M.: Brönner, 1862); see also bibliographic references to Hausrath, Schürer, O. Holtzmann, and W. Staerk.

64. C. E. Nitzsch, *System of Christian Doctrines*, 258; H. L. Martensen, *Christian Dogmatics*, trans. William Urwick (Edinburgh: T&T Clark, 1871), 237ff.; L. Schöberlein, *Prinzip und System der Dogmatik* (Heidelberg: C. Winter, 1881), 627ff.; and many others; cf. I. A. Dorner, *Person of Christ*, V, 236–48.

65. R. Rothe, *Theologische Ethik*, §541; J. P. Lange, *Christliche Dogmatik.*, II, §60, and others; cf. I. A. Dorner, *Person of Christ*, V, 232ff.

66. Cf. H. Bavinck, *Reformed Dogmatics*, II, 322–29 (#230).

67. F. W. J. Schelling, *Werke*, II, 3, 317ff.

68. Ibid., II, 4, 35ff.

the human development attained and then gradually won them back in the way of development.[69]

Corresponding to Schleiermacher's Christology is that of Ritschl. Only Ritschl's Christology, adhering, as it does, more closely to the philosophy of Kant, stresses the work of Christ more than the person and, in describing the nature of Christianity, assigns a larger role to the ethical dimension. In the doctrine of Christ, Ritschl, too, rejects all metaphysics and everything that is condemned by natural science and historical criticism, such as the preexistence of Christ, his supernatural conception, resurrection, ascension, and second coming. In that respect Christ is an ordinary human being. But his uniqueness lay in his calling, the work he did, that is, the founding of a kingdom of God. As an ethical person, Christ is on a level far above all [other] humans. His will was completely one with the will of God, with the plan and purpose God had in mind for the world and humanity. For that reason, however, enormous religious significance is due to Christ. In him God himself, his grace and faithfulness, his will and purpose for humankind have become manifest. Christ has shown us and confirmed by his death that the kingdom of God is the destiny of all humans, that his will must become the will of all humankind. Therein consists his royal power, his world dominion, and therein consists his deity as well. Christ is not God in a metaphysical sense; rather, in his case the name "God" denotes his rank and status in the kingdom of God. It is not a reference to his being, but to his office.

---

69. W. F. Gess, *Lehre von der Person Christi*, 281ff., 309ff.; G. Thomasius, *Christi Person und Werk* I, 409–45; E. W. C. Sartorius, *Die Lehre von der heiligen Liebe* (Stuttgart: S. G. Liesching, 1861), II, 21; L. Schöberlein, *Prinzip und System der Dogmatik*, 167ff.; H. L. Martensen, *Christian Dogmatics*, §133; J. C. K. von Hofmann, *Der Schriftbeweis*, 2nd ed., 2 vols. (Nördlingen: Beck, 1857–60), II, 1, 20ff.; F. Delitzsch, *A System of Biblical Psychology*, trans. Robert E. Wallis (Edinburgh: T&T Clark, 1899), 384ff.; K. F. A. Kahnis, *Die lutherische Dogmatik*, II, 83; F. H. R. Frank, *System der christlichen Wahrheit*, 2nd ed., 2 vols. (Erlangen: A. Deichert, 1884), II, 137ff.; R. B. Kübel, *Über den Unterschied zwischen der postitiven und der liberalen Richtung in der modernen Theologie*, 2nd ed. (Munich: C. H. Beck, 1893), 124; A. von Oettingen, *Lutherische Dogmatik*, 2 vols. (Munich: C. H. Beck, 1897), II, 107ff. (teaches setting aside the use but not the possession of divine attributes); H. Schmidt, "Zur Lehre von der Person Christi," *Neue kirchliche Zeitschrift* (1896): 972–1005, esp. 982ff.; *Steinbeck, on O. Bensow, "Die Lehre von der Kenose," *Theologisches Literaturblatt* 25/4 (January 22, 1904): 44–46; F. L. Godet, *Commentary on John's Gospel* (Grand Rapids: Kregel Publications, 1978), on John 1:14; A. Grétillat, *Exposé de Théologie Systématique*, 4 vols. (Paris: Fischbacher, 1885–92), IV, 180ff.; *Recolin, *La personne de Jesus-Christ et la théorie de kenosis* (Paris, 1890); J. J. van Oosterzee, *Christian Dogmatics*, trans. J. Watson and M. Evans, 2 vols. (New York: Scribner, Armstrong, 1874), II, 752; P. D. Chantepie de la Saussaye, in H. Bavinck, *De theologie van Prof. Dr. Daniel Chantepie de la Saussaye*, 2nd ed. (Leiden: D. Donner, 1903), 44. This hypothesis was also received favorably by many English and American theologians; e.g., Dr. Lewis Edwards of Bala (ca. 1850); O'Brien in Ireland; H. W. Beecher (1871); H. M. Goodwin (1874); Howard Crosby in America, and especially after 1890, with the goal of bringing Jesus' understanding of the Old Testament in line with that of historical criticism, by W. S. Swayne, *An Inquiry into Our Lord's Knowledge as Man* (London and New York: Longmans, Green, 1891); A. Plummer, "The Advance of Christ in Σοφία," *The Expositor* (1891); C. Gore, *The Incarnation of the Son of God* (London: Murray, 1891); idem, *Dissertations on Subjects Connected with the Incarnation* (London: Murray, 1895); A. J. Mason, *Conditions of Our Lord's Life on Earth* (London and New York: Longmans, Green, 1896); B. B. Warfield, "Recent Theological Literature," *Presbyterian and Reformed Review* 10 (1899): 701–25; W. Lock, "Kenosis," *DB*, II, 835; Alfred E. Garvie, "Kenosis," *DC*, I, 927–28.

Christ may be called "God" because in his relation to us he occupies the place and value of God.[70]

RETURN TO THE HISTORICAL JESUS

[359] The Christology of the nineteenth century, as it took shape under the influence of Schelling and Hegel, Schleiermacher and Ritschl, was generally characterized by the fact that, in reaction to rationalism and moralism, it returned to the person of Christ and attempted to assign to his appearance in history permanent significance for the religious life. This purpose was also characteristic of Ritschl's followers. Herrmann, for example, made a distinction between the ground and the content of faith and counted as the first only what even the most rigorous historical criticism has to recognize and respect in Jesus, namely, his "inner life," his moral grandeur and goodness. However little this may be, in Hermann the Christian faith still remains somewhat tied to the historical person of Jesus and regards his moral goodness as proof of the indwelling and revelation of God in him.[71] Kaftan, adopting a much more conservative position, does not at all consider himself bound by "science" to restrict the historical image of Jesus to his inner life. On the contrary, the exalted Lord whom the church confesses is none other than the historical Savior who walked about on earth. But because God was with him in a totally unique manner, because the perfect revelation of God came to us in him, and God communicates his spirit and life to us in him, the church rightly speaks of his deity and confesses him as its Lord and God.[72] Häring does not consider it particularly necessary to speak of Jesus' deity because this term creates all sorts of misunderstanding and division, but he does maintain the [church's] right to use it because Christ is the full self-revelation of God; and he sees this revelation in the historical Jesus as the Gospels describe him, a revelation that among other things also includes his resurrection.[73] Among the followers of Ritschl, there-

---

70. A. Ritschl, *The Christian Doctrine of Justification and Reconciliation* (Clifton, NJ: Reference Book Publishers, 1966), III, 379ff.; idem, *Unterricht in der christlichen Religion,* 3rd ed. (Bonn: A. Marcus, 1886), 17ff.; cf. J. Wendland, *Albrecht Ritschl und seine Schüler im Verhältnis zur Theologie* (Berlin: George Reimer, 1899), 84ff.

71. W. Herrmann, *Der Verkehr des Christen mit Gott,* 4th ed. (Stuttgart: Cotta, 1903), 18ff., 92ff.; idem, *Warum bedarf unser Glaube geschichtlicher Thatsachen?* (Halle a.S.: Niemeyer, 1893); R. Favre, "Le Christ historique d'après W. Herrmann," *Revue de Théologie et de Philosophie* 33 (1900): 454–76. Cf. H. Bavinck, *Reformed Dogmatics,* I, 168–70 (#52), 541–44 (#142).

72. J. Kaftan, *Das Wesen der christlichen Religion* (Basel: C. Detloff, 1888), 295ff.; idem, *Brauchen wir ein neues Dogma?* 2nd ed. (Bielefeld: Velhagen & Klasing, 1890), 49–72; idem, *Dogmatik* (Tübingen: Mohr, 1901), §§45–47; H. Schultz, on Rom. 9: 5, *Jahrbuch für deutsche Theologie* (1868): 463–507; idem, *Die Lehre von der Gottheit Christi: Communicatio idiomatum* (Gotha: Perthes, 1881); idem, *Grundriss der evangelischen Dogmatik zum Gebrauche bei akademischen Vorlesungen* (Göttingen: Vandenhoeck & Ruprecht, 1892), 72ff.; J. Gottschick, *Die Kirchlichkeit der sogenannten kirchlichen Theologie* (Freiburg i.B.: J. C. B. Mohr, 1890), 207.

73. T. Häring, *The Christian Faith,* trans. John Dickie and George Ferries, 2 vols. (London: Hodder & Stoughton, 1913), II, 549; idem, "Gehört die Auferstehung Jesu zum Glaubensgrund?" *Zeitschrift für Theologie und Kirche* 7 (1897): 332–51; also F. Nitzsch, *Lehrbuch der evangelischen Dogmatik,* prepared by Horst Stephan,

fore, there is all sorts of disagreement about what may be deemed certain in the historical Jesus. Some allow the image of Christ to impact people straight from the Gospels (Herrmann, Haupt); others think more in terms of a mediation by the Word and the church, by the example of Christians and the working of the Holy Spirit (Joh. Weiss, O. Ritschl, Max Reischle, Gottschick); some (O. Ritschl, Max Reischle, Häring) are more averse to philosophy and metaphysics; some less (Kaftan, Wobbermin, Wendt).[74] All nevertheless assume a special revelation of God in the historical person of Christ, and all exert themselves to preserve a place for Christology in dogmatics.

These features distinguish them from the modern theologians who, like Biedermann, separate the principle of Christianity from its founder and therefore have to eliminate Christology from dogmatics. At the same time, however, they also separate themselves from the theological schools that find in the confessions or at least in the New Testament a faithful reproduction of the historical person of Christ. For all of them consider themselves compelled by the natural and historical sciences of modern times to make a distinction between the historical Jesus and the Christ of dogmatics. Greek philosophy and eastern metaphysics, they say, have corrupted and falsified the original gospel of Jesus. There is disagreement about the time when this harmful synthesis began. Some years ago Lagarde already claimed that Paul had corrupted the religion of Jesus by making Christ into its content and object. This falsification consisted specifically in the following four points. First of all, he introduced "the deification of the man Jesus" and made of the historical Jesus a preexistent being who appeared for a time on earth and then again returned to heaven. Second, he incorporated into the original gospel a "supernatural redemption" consisting in the idea that the redemption of humanity was effected objectively, apart from these human beings themselves. Third, he attributed to the sacrificial death of Jesus an "atoning significance" and thereby laid the groundwork for the Catholic sacrifice of the Mass. Fourth, he added to all this a doctrine of the sacraments as objective, self-operative mysteries.[75] Not

---

3rd ed. (Tübingen: J. C. B. Mohr, 1902), 514, who prefers to speak of Christ as God's Son rather than as God.

74. E. Haupt, *Die Bedeutung der Heiligen Schrift für den evangelischen Christen* (Bielefeld and Leipzig: Velhagen & Klasing, 1891); J. Weiss, *Die Nachfolge Christi und die Predigt der Gegenwart* (Göttingen: Vandenhoeck & Ruprecht, 1895), 134ff.; O. Ritschl, "Der geschichtliche Christus, der christliche Glaube und die theologische Wissenschaft," *Zeitschrift für Theologie und Kirche* 3 (1893): 384ff.; O. Kirn, *Glaube und Geschichte* (Leipzig: Edelmann, 1901); idem, *Grundriss der evangelischen Dogmatik* (Leipzig: Deichert, 1905), 91ff.; F. Traub, "Die religionsgeschichtliche Methode und die systematische Theologie: Eine Auseinandersetzung mit Tröltschs theologischem Reformprogramm," *Zeitschrift für Theologie und Kirche* 11 (1901): 323; M. Reischle, "Der Streit über die Begründung des Glaubens auf dem geschichtlichen Christus," *Zeitschrift für Theologie und Kirche* 7 (1897): 171–264; idem, *Leitsätze für eine akademische Vorlesung über die christliche Glaubenslehre* (Halle a.S.: Niemeyer, 1899), 89ff.; H. H. Wendt, *System der christlichen Lehre*, 2 vols. in 1 (Göttingen: Vandenhoeck & Ruprecht, 1907); cf. O. Kirn, "Aus der dogmatischen Arbeit der Gegenwart," *Zeitschrift für Theologie und Kirche* 18 (1908): 337–88.

75. P. de Lagarde, *Deutsche Schriften*, 4th ed. (Göttingen: Horstmann, 1903).

all of them, however, go this far, and especially Harnack and Kaftan still try to appreciate Paul as a person who understood Jesus correctly.[76] In virtue of their starting point, however, they feel forced to admit that Paul "shifted" the original gospel of Jesus. For Jesus the gospel was a matter between God and the soul, and redemption was a subjective experience, but in Paul's thinking Christ comes to stand between God and humans and brings about our salvation apart from us. For that reason all followers of Ritschl have in common the motto "From Paul and John we have to go back to the Jesus of the Synoptics, especially to the Jesus of the Sermon on the Mount."

[360] This view, however, totally contrary to what these people expected, led to great uncertainty concerning the person and work of Christ. In the winter of 1899–1900, Harnack, speaking in Berlin, gave his lectures about the essence of Christianity, which, though tremendously successful and given high praise by his theological friends,[77] aroused great unrest among others and highlighted the vast distance between the confession of Christ according to the Scriptures and the modern theory of Jesus. For, according to Harnack, the essence of Christianity consists in the assurance that, by the appearance, the doctrine, and the life of Jesus, people can incur the experience that God is their Father and that they are his children. For the moral person, he says, there is a deep chasm between the visible and the invisible world, between the external and the internal, between flesh and spirit, between the here-and-now and the beyond, between God and the world. But the Christian religion raises people up and above this painful dichotomy. It puts

---

76. A. von Harnack, *What Is Christianity?* 148; idem, *History of Dogma*, I, 17; J. Kaftan, *Jesus und Paulus: Eine freundschaftliche Streitschrift gegen die religionsgeschichtlichen Volksbücher von D. Bousset und D. Wrede* (Tübingen: Mohr, 1906); cf. H. Bavinck, *Reformed Dogmatics*, I, 117 (#36).

77. Cf., e.g., E. Foerster, "Harnacks Wesen des Christentums: Eine Bestreitung oder eine Verteidigung des christlichen Glaubens?" *Zeitschrift für Theologie und Kirche* 12 (1902): 179–201; E. Rolffs, *Harnacks Wesen des Christentums und die religiösen Strömungen der Gegenwart* (Leipzig: Hinrichs, 1902). In agreement with Harnack on the essence of Christianity are A. Sabatier, *Esquisse d'une philosophie de la religion d'après la psychologie et l'historie,* 7th ed. (Paris: Fischbacher, 1903), 139–215; and to a large extent, A. F. Loisy, *Evangelium und Kirche* (Munich: Kirchheim, 1904) (ed. note: ET: *The Gospel and the Church* [Philadelphia: Fortress Press, 1976]); cf. G. Wobbermin, "Loisy contra Harnack," *Zeitschrift für Theologie und Kirche* 15 (1905): 76–102. It is also noteworthy that Harnack's lectures were acclaimed by Jewish writers, who produced numerous responses of their own, such as: J. Eschelbacher, *Das Judentum und des Wesen des Christentums* (Berlin: Poppelauer, 1905); M. Joseph, *Zur Sittenlehre des Judenthums* (Berlin: Poppelauer, 1902); L. Bäck, *Das Wesen des Judentums* (Berlin: Nathansen & Lamm, 1905); F. Perles, *Was lehrt uns Harnack?* (Frankfurt a.M.: Kauffman, 1902); A. Ackermann, *Judentum und Christentum* (Leipzig: Kauffman, 1903). These raised objections against Harnack's continued acceptance of Christianity's originality and independence [from Judaism], insisting that there was nothing original about his teaching. However, they were glad that the doctrines of the Trinity, the deity of Christ, original sin, satisfaction, and sacraments had been set outside the essence of the Christian faith. This represented the breach of the foremost wall of separation between Judaism and Christianity. According to Rabbi Levy ("Actes du IIIme Congrès International du christianisme libéral et progressif" [Geneva, 1905] [Geneva, 1906], 121), if the previously noted Jewish authors were to shed themselves of their Talmudic orthodoxy and come to the side of liberal [Reform] Judaism, there would be nothing to stand in the way of full unity between the two. This is also the conclusion of Fiebeg in *Die Christliche Welt*, 1907, No. 40; cf. Strack and Bieling in *Jahrbuch der evangelischen Judenmission* (Leipzig: Hinrichs, 1906), I, 20ff., 47ff.

human beings on the side of God, furnishes them eternal life in the midst of time, and brings God and the soul together in union and communion. And it does this by consistently preaching the fatherhood of God and the nobility of the human soul and exhaustively pouring itself out in these two great truths. In the original gospel as Jesus himself proclaimed it, accordingly, not the Son but the Father is central. Jesus did not preach himself; he did not demand faith in his own person. He did not have a Christology: the wretched publican, the woman by the treasury, the prodigal son all conspire to make this very plain.

This does not alter the fact, however, that Jesus by his unique knowledge of God, by his person, his word, and his deeds, is nevertheless in truth the guide to God and the way to the Father. Thousands of people have come to God by him. He was and still remains today the personal realization and power of the gospel. The personal life that exists in us derives its existence solely from his personal powers. How Jesus obtained this totally unique knowledge of God, the knowledge by which he achieved his eminence, is not explained by Harnack. For this claim he appeals exclusively to the mystery of personality. But we attain to communion with God, to peace of soul, to victory over the world, only in the way of faith in the gospel of Jesus. This faith, however, does not consist in accepting a doctrine, for the gospel is not a doctrine but good news and consists in a moral experience, in doing the will of the Father, in a life in keeping with the gospel of Jesus, in a personal "experience" of the soul, which Jesus effects in us by his appearance, word, and life.

As everyone can immediately tell, the description that Harnack offered in his lectures on the nature of Christianity differed appreciably from what had been given throughout the ages in the church confessions. And it was no small sign of arrogance when the Ritschl school counterposed this Jesus image as a purely historical portrait of him to the Jesus image of the churches and cried out through Wernle: "Christianity had for thousands of years forgotten who its Master was," as if over against all sorts of sects the churches had not done their utmost to confess no other Christ than the Christ depicted before their eyes in the Scriptures. But the slogan "back to Jesus" led to still a very different set of conclusions than people had initially suspected. Once a dichotomy has been created between the so-called historical Jesus and the apostolic Christ, one instantaneously faces the double question of who, then, that historical Jesus had actually been and how in the hands of the apostles he had been malformed into the Christ. Though Kähler had warned against this position and clearly stated that such a dichotomy was not possible and that, for example, also Christ's atoning death and the resurrection were included in the story of the historical Jesus,[78] people nevertheless went further down this path, ending up in the greatest difficulty with respect to these two questions.

78. M. Kähler, *The So-Called Historical Jesus and the Historic Biblical Christ,* trans. Carl E. Braaten (Philadelphia: Fortress Press, 1988).

For to the degree that the study of the "historical" Jesus continued, it became all the more clear that the Christ figure does not first occur in Paul and John but is already present in the Synoptics. The glory of the Christ may not be as brilliantly highlighted in the first three Gospels as in the fourth, but it is fundamentally the same Christ who is being described in all four. Also attributed to the Synoptic Jesus is a lofty, self-consciousness, messianic dignity, divine sonship, the power to do miracles and forgive sins, an unparalleled position in the kingdom of God, the atoning power of his suffering and dying, the resurrection and glorification with the Father, and the coming again unto judgment.[79] And all this is not said of him by others but, from his first public appearances on, he himself is borne up by this high self-consciousness and he himself continually speaks and acts in accordance with this royal power. It is the same Christ who comes out to meet us throughout the New Testament. What else can we expect? The Synoptic Gospels are no less apostolic than the letters of Paul and were written down even later than the letters. Of controversy concerning the person of Christ, there was never any sign among the apostles. They all confessed their faith and found their salvation in the same Christ, even though it is true that—depending on their character and experiences—they picture him from various perspectives. By shoving Paul and John aside, therefore, these theologians absolutely failed to find the original "historical" Jesus. Instead, in the Synoptic Gospels they again had to distinguish between the features that had originally belonged to Jesus and those his disciples had later added. They had to penetrate deep into the strata of the tradition until they reached the nethermost and oldest layer; the reduction had to continue until only the human being called Jesus remained.

But this process proved endless and led to boundless caprice. Everyone fashioned a Jesus on his own and in the end found the Jesus whose image he had concocted earlier in his own mind. To Carlyle he was a hero, to Strauss a religious genius, to Renan a liberal reformer and preacher of humanity, to Schopenhauer a herald of the negation of the will to live, to Proudhon a social reformer.[80] Kalthoff was not altogether mistaken when he scoffed at the Christ of the professors, who looks

---

79. Cf., e.g., M. Kähler, *So-Called Historical Jesus*; and also E. Schaeder, *Über das Wesen des Christentums und seine modernen Darstellungen* (Gütersloh: Bertelsmann, 1904); W. Walther, *Ad. Harnacks Wesen des Christentums: Für die christliche Gemeinde geprüft,* 5th ed. (Leipzig: Deichert, 1904); L. Ihmels, *Wie war Jesus? Was wollte Jesus?* (Leipzig: Deichert, 1905).

80. H. Weinel, *Jesus in the Nineteenth Century and After,* trans. Alban Gregory Widgery (Edinburgh: T&T Clark, 1914); A. Schweitzer, *The Quest for the Historical Jesus: A Critical Study from Reimarus to Wrede,* trans. W. Montgomery (New York: Macmillan, 1968); G. Pfannmüller, *Jesus im Urteil der Jahrhunderte* (Leipzig: Tübner, 1908); G. W. Hollmann, "Leben und Lehre Jesu," *Theologische Rundschau* 7 (1904): 197–211; idem, "Das Leere Grab und die gegenwärtigen Verhandlungen über die Auferstehung Jesu," *Theologische Rundschau* 9 (1906): 119–58; idem, "Die Berliner Kirchenväterausgabe," *Theologische Rundschau* 9 (1906): 239–86; S. Faut, *Die Christologie seit Schleiermacher, ihre Geschichte und ihre Begründung* (Tübingen: Mohr, 1907); A. Rau, *Harnack, Goethe, D. Strauss, und L. Feuerbach über das Wesen des Christentums* (Delitzsch: C. A. Walter, 1903); A. Hein, "Die Christologie von D. F. Strauss," 321–45; Hollensteiner, "Harnack and Bousset," *Neue kirchliche Zeitschrift* (1906): 517–33; W. Sanday, *The Life of Christ in Recent Research* (Oxford: Clarendon Press, 1907).

very different from one university to the next and was nevertheless still held up to the common people as the way, the truth, and the life.[81] On the character and work of Jesus, on his relation to the Jewish people and the law, to culture and humanity, there is maximal disagreement; even on the question whether he considered himself the Messiah, opinions are highly divergent. Many scholars still favor an affirmative answer to that question but then frequently view messiahship as the temporary national form in which Jesus had to clothe his special calling vis-à-vis the kingdom of God but which in fact has lost its value for us (Harnack, Schürer, Jülicher, Holtzmann, and others), and others are inclined to answer that question more or less decisively in the negative (Lagarde, Wrede, Merx, and others).[82] Given such a wide range of disagreement, one is not surprised at the conclusion—drawn by some—that on account of the faulty and tendentious character of the sources, we will probably never get to know anything with certainty concerning Jesus and that even his existence is subject to serious doubt.

[361] This radicalism, however, does not clear away the objections but entails even graver difficulties. For in that case the second of the two questions mentioned above arises with even greater intensity, namely, to what does the Christ figure in the New Testament writings owe its existence? On this point the ideas are even farther apart—if that is possible—than in the inquiry into the existence and character of the "historical" Jesus. Some believe that even before the Christian era there existed a sect of Nazoreans that venerated a certain deity under the name of Jesus, that is, Savior or Liberator, and gradually began to link this cult with the Messiah, the anointed King expected by the Jews as their Messiah.[83] Others picture the situation differently. As a result of oppressive social conditions in Jerusalem, a church had formed there that was constructed along communistic lines and that, under the influence of the ideas of the time, attributed to Jesus—a person they venerated, who had died a martyr's death—all sorts of noble predicates such as a supernatural conception, miraculous powers, resurrection, elevation to the right hand of God, and a speedy return for judgment.[84] As to the ideas that formed

81. A. Kalthoff, *Was wissen wir von Jesus?* (Schmargendorf-Berlin: Renaissance-Otto Lehrmann, 1904), 40.

82. Cf. H. J. Holtzmann, *Das messianische Bewusstsein Jesu*, and the literature cited there; cf. also W. Brandt, "Jezus en de Messiaansche verwachting," *Teyler's Theologisch Tijdschrift* 5 (1907): 461–568; J. A. Bruins Sr., *Hoe onstond de overtuiging dat Jezus de Christus is?* (Leeuwarden: Eekhof, 1909); and the critical reviews of Bruins by W. Brandt, in *Teyler's Theologisch Tijdschrift* 7 (1909): 583–92; and also by H. de Graaf, in *Teyler's Theologisch Tijdschrift* 7 (1909): 413–34.

83. H. U. Meyboom, "Jezus de Nazoraeer," *Theologische Tijdschrift* 39 (1905): 512–36; W. B. Smith, *Der vorchristliche Jesus nebst weiteren Vorstudien zur Entstehungsgeschichte des Urchristentums* (Giessen: Alfred Töpelmann, 1906); and the reviews of Smith by P. Wernle, *Theologische Lit. Zeitung* 31 (August 1907); and also by H. Meyboom, "Loman Redivivus," *Theologische Tijdschrift* 41 (1907): 1–17.

84. A. Kalthoff, *Das Christusproblem: Grundlinien zu einer Sozialtheologie*, 2nd ed. (Leipzig: Diederichs, 1903); idem, *Die Entstehung des Christentums: Neue Beiträge zum Christusproblem* (Leipzig: Diederichs 1904); idem, *Was wissen wir von Jesus? Eine Abrechnung mit Prof. D. Bousset von Göttingen* (Berlin, 1904); K. Kautsky, *Foundations of Christianity* (New York: Monthly Review Press, 1972); and the review of Kautzky's book by M. Maurenbrecher, in *Sozial. Monatshefte* (1909): 36ff., 94ff.; cf. also the lecture of Dr. G. A. van den Bergh van

the Christ figure, some favor Old Testament prophecies[85] or the apocalyptic expectations of the Jews then living;[86] others the Buddhist teachings that then gradually began to penetrate the West[87] or, more generally, the syncretistic blend of a variety of Eastern and Western, Jewish and Greek ideas that characterized the first centuries of the Christian era.[88]

All these attempts are most unsatisfactory if for no other reason than that they eliminate the personality and replace it with the creative fantasy of the church. In addition, however, they have led to a horrifying conclusion. For if the features of the Christ figure—divine sonship, his supernatural birth, messiahship, the resurrection, and so on—are the products of the church's fantasy and must be explained from an assortment of alien ideas then current, then, though one can for a while construe them symbolically and so smooth them over, the reality is that they were basically false notions and pernicious errors. The moment one has taken this position, reverence for the person of Jesus is lost. Attempts to hold Paul, John, or the church in general responsible for the creation of the dogmatic Christ all still proceed from a certain piety toward the person of Jesus. Scholars still try to safeguard him from the errors the disciples formed concerning his person and

Eysinga on Kautzky's book at the Conference of Modern Theologians (April 1909) (ed. note: the Conference of Modern Theologians [*Vergadering vand Moderne Theologen*] began as a student fellowship at the University of Leiden in 1866 and then became a general gathering for all interested, theologically progressive-minded members of the Dutch Reformed Church); M. Maurenbrecher, *Von Nazareth nach Golgotha: Untersuchung über die weltgeschichtlichen Zusammenhänge des Urchristentums* (Berlin-Schöneberg: Buchverlag der "Hilfe," 1909); K. C. Anderson, "The Collapse of Liberal Christianity," *Hibbert Journal* 8/2 (January 1910): 301–20.

85. Thus, already, Schelling and after him, especially Strauss; cf. K. Weidel, "Studien über den Einfluss des Weissagungsbeweises auf die evangelische Geschichte," *Theologische Studien und Kritiken* (1910): 83ff.

86. W. Bousset, *Die Religion des Judentums*; P. Wernle, *Die Anfänge unserer Religion*, 2nd ed. (Tübingen: Mohr, 1904).

87. R. Seydel, *Die Buddha-Legende und das Leben Jesu nach den Evangelien*, 2nd ed. (Weimar: Felber, 1897); G. A. van den Bergh van Eysinga, *Indische Einflüsse auf evangelische Erzählungen*, 2nd ed. (Göttingen: Vandenhoeck & Ruprecht, 1909); O. Pfleiderer, *Das Christusbild des urchristlichen Glaubens und Sittenlehre* (Berlin: G. Reimer, 1903). Anti-Semitism and the glorification of the Aryan race along with Buddhism led Duhring, Chamberlain, and others to deny Jesus' Jewish descent and to posit for him an Asian lineage. Cf. A. Müller, *Jesus ein Arier: Ein Beitrag zur völkischen Erziehung* (Leipzig: Mar Sängeward, 1904); T. J. Plange, *Christus–ein Inder? Versuch einer Entstehungsgeschichte des Christentums unter Benutzung der indischen Studien Louis Jacolliots* (Stuttgart: Schmidt, 1907).

88. J. M. Robertson, *Pagan Christs: Studies in Comparative Hierology* (London: Watts, 1903); *K. Breysig, Die Entstehung des Gottesgedankens*; W. B. Smith, *Der vorchristliche Jesus*; P. C. A. Jensen, *Das Gilgamesch-Epos in der Weltliteratur* (Strassburg: Trübner, 1906); A. Drews, *The Christ Myth* (Amherst, NY: Prometheus Books, 1910 & 1998); H. Gunkel, *Zum religionsgeschichtlichen Verständnis des Neuen Testaments* (Göttingen: Vandenhoeck & Ruprecht, 1903); C. Clemen, *Primitive Christianity and Its Non-Jewish Sources*, trans. Robert George Nisbet (Edinburgh: T&T Clark, 1912); M. Brückner, *Die sterbende und auferstehende Gottheiland in den orientalischen Religionen und ihr Verhältnis zum Christentum* (Tübingen: Mohr, 1908); G. J. P. J. Bolland, *De evangelische Jozua: Eene Poging tot Aanwijzing van de oorsprong des Christendoms* (Leiden: A. H. Adriani, 1907); idem, *Het Evangelie: Eene "vernieuwde" poging tot aanwijzing van de Oorsprong des Christendoms* (Leiden: A. H. Adriani, 1910); cf. in opposition to this Christ myth, K. Dunkmann, *Der historische Jesus, der mythologische Christus und Jesus der Christ* (Leipzig: Deichert, 1910); H. Weinel, "Ist unsere Verkündigung von Jesus unhaltbar geworden?" *Zeitschrift für Theologie und Kirche* 20 (1910): 1–88.

thereby to excuse even those errors somewhat. But, as things evolve, also that need disappears. Reverence toward the person of Jesus no longer holds people back. Jesus himself was already complicit in the errors of his church. The so-called historical explanation leads to the mythological and symbolic explanation, and these in turn lead to the psychological and pathological explanation. So it happens that in recent times there have arisen men who regard Jesus as a victim of heredity who suffered from epilepsy, paranoia, and hallucinations, who fostered megalomaniacal ideas about himself, and when he became disillusioned in his expectations with respect to people, he sought to get back on top by a tour-de-force.[89]

But this coarse and even violent treatment of the "Christ problem" has again opened the eyes of others and triggered a remarkable reaction. It has clarified the insight that the historical Jesus and the apostolic Christ cannot be separated in the manner the Bible critics had initially pictured to themselves. The Christ of Paul and John is no other than the Christ of the early church and corresponds in all respects to the Son of Man drawn for us in the Synoptic Gospels.[90] One cannot

89. Thus, earlier already, A. F. B. Dulk, *Der Irrgang des Lebens Jesu,* 2 vols. (Stuttgart: Dietz, 1884–85); J. Soury, *The Religion of Israel,* trans. Annie Wood Besant (London: Bradlaugh Bonner, 1895); E. Rasmussen, *Jesus: Eine vergleichende psychopathologische Studie* (Leipzig: Zeitler, 1905) (ed. note: Bavinck erroneously cites this author as F. Rasmussen); G. Lomer, *Jesus Christus vom Standpunkt des Psychiaters* (Bamberg: Handels-Druckerei, 1905); *Binet-Sanglé, *La folie de Jésus,* 2 vols. (Paris, 1908–10); A. Heulhard, *La mensonge Chrétien (Jésus Christ n'a pas existé)* (Paris: A. Heulhard, 1908); cf. also O. Holtzmann, *War Jesus Ekstatiker?* (Tübingen: Mohr, 1903); J. Baumann, *Die Gemütsart Jesu nach jetziger wissenschaftlicher, insbesondere jetziger psychologischer Methode erkennbar gemacht* (Leipzig: Kröner, 1908). Among those rising in opposition are E. G. Steude, "Wie ein moderner Seelenarzt über Jesus urteilt," *Der Beweis des Glaubens* (1906): 325–30; P. Knieb, *Moderne Leben-Jesu-Forschung unter dem Einflusse der Psychiatrie* (Mainz: Kirchheim & Co., 1908).

90. On the relation between Jesus and Paul, a large body of literature has appeared in recent years: W. Bousset, *What Is Religion?* trans. Florence B. Low (New York: Putnam, 1907); M. Brückner, *Die Entstehung der paulinischen Christologie* (Strassburg: Heitz & Mündel, 1903); P. Wernle, *Die Anfänge unserer Religion*; M. Goguel, *L'apôtre Paul et Jésus-Christ* (Paris: Fischbacher, 1904); O. Michel, *Vorwärts zu Christus! Fort mit Paulus! Deutsche Religion!* (Berlin: Seeman, 1906) (ed note: Bavinck erroneously cites the date of publication as 1905); A. Meyer, *Wer hat das Christentum begründet, Jesus oder Paulus?* (Tübingen: Mohr, 1907); J. Weiss, *Paul and Jesus,* trans. H. J. Chaytor (New York: Harper, 1909); cf. critical reviews of a number of works on the relation between Jesus and Paul: E. Vischer, "Jesus und Paulus," *Theologische Rundschau* 8 (1905): 129–43; idem, "Wernles Einführung in das theologische Studium," *Theologische Rundschau* 11 (1908): 301–12. On the other hand, there are those who hold fast to the conviction that the doctrine of Paul (and John) is a true development of Jesus' preaching as well as the work that he established: W. Götz, *Paulus, der wahrhaftige Zeuge Jesu Christi* (Hannover: Feesche, 1903); P. Feine, *Jesus Christus und Paulus* (Leipzig: Hinrichs, 1902); L. Ihmels, "Jesus und Paulus," *Neue kirchliche Zeitschrift* 17 (1906): 453–83, 485–516; E. Schaeder, *Über das Wesen des Christentums*; idem, *Das Evangelium Jesu und das Evangelium Gottes* (Gütersloh: Bertelsmann, 1904); G. Wustmann, *Jesus und Paulus: Die Abhängigkeit des Apostels von seinem Herrn* (Gütersloh: Bertelsmann, 1907); H. Bachmann, "Stehen der Jesus der synoptischen Evangelien und der Christus des Paulus in Widerspruch?" *Der Beweis des Glaubens* 44 (1908): 278–88; A. Scholz, "Besteht ein wesentlicher Unterschied zwischen dem Johann. Christusbilde und dem der Synoptiker?" *Glauben und Wissen* (1908): 243ff. The exaggerations of Wrede, *Paul,* trans. Edward Lummis (Boston: American Unitarian Association, 1908), were also opposed by P. Kölbing, *Die geistige Einwirkung der Person Jesu auf Paulus* (Göttingen: Vandenhoeck & Ruprecht, 1906); J. Kaftan, *Jesus und Paulus*; A. Jülicher, *Paulus und Jesus* (Tübingen: Mohr, 1907); cf. also G. A. Deissmann, *Die Christl. Religion* (in *Die Kultur der Gegenwart*), 77–138.

honor Jesus without accepting him as the Christ, the Son of the living God. In modernist circles of recent years, there has even arisen a need for a Christology, not just in a subjective symbolic sense,[91] but one that is related to the historical Jesus and the apostolic witness.[92] Among others, people who have been influenced by Schleiermacher and Ritschl, one senses an endeavor to maintain Jesus not just as a prophet, teacher, and example but specifically also as a revelation of God, as a person who lived in communion with God in an entirely unique sense, in whom God dwelt as in no one else, and through whom God therefore revealed himself in a particular and absolute way.[93] But if Christ is to be maintained in this role and rank, if he is going to be not the subject but the object and center of the Christian religion, and if this Christian religion is to preserve its uniqueness and not degenerate into an idolatrous Jesus cult,[94] it is not enough for Christ to be in God (ἐνθεος), but he must himself be God (θεος), the only begotten of the Father. Thus the truth and value of the deity of Christ has again been rightly placed in the foreground by others.[95] With that, finally, the connectedness of dogmatics

91. Following Kant, Hegel, E. von Hartmann, A. Drews, A. D. Loman, and G. J. P. Bolland (ed. note: G. J. P. Bolland [1854–1922] was professor of philosophy at the University of Leiden and a Hegelian), the following scholars defend a symbolic Christology: J. G. Boekenoogen, "Christologische Beschouwingen," *Theologische Tijdschrift* 26 (1892); Eldering, "De plaats en de beteekenis der Christusgestalte in ons geloofsleven," a lecture given at the Conference of Modern Theologians on April 8–9, 1909 (ed. note: see note 84 above for further information on this conference); G. A. van den Bergh van Eysinga, *Christusbeschouwingen onder modernen* (Baarn: Hollandia, 1909), 223–71.

92. H. T. de Graaf, "De waarde der moderne Christologische beweging," a lecture given at the Conference of Modern Theologians on April 8–9, 1909 (see note 84 above). Such a revision of Christology was already disputed by R. Hugenholtz, "De Christologie en de huidige godsdienstwetenschap," *Theologisch Tijdschrift* 15 (1881): 30–52; and echoed by A. Bruining, "Over de methode van onze Dogmatiek," *Tylers Theologisch Tijdschrift* 1 (1903): 426–58; G. A. van den Bergh van Eysinga, "Jezus van Nazaret en ons geloofsleven," in *Christusbeschouwingen onder modernen*, 3–41.

93. J. Kaftan, *Dogmatik*, 411ff.; idem, *Zur Dogmatik* (Tübingen: Mohr, 1904), 211ff.; T. Häring, *Christian Faith*, II, 500ff., 548ff.; idem, "Einfachste Worte für eine grosse Sache, die Stellung Jesu im christlichen Glauben," *Zeitschrift für Theologie und Kirche* 19 (1909): 177–203; F. A. Loofs, "Christologie, Kirchenlehre," *PRE*³, IV, 16–56; K. Thieme, "Die neuesten Christologien im Verhältniss zum Selbstbewustsein Jesu," *Zeitschrift für Theologie und Kirche* 18 (1908): 401–72; R. Seeberg, *The Fundamental Truths of the Christian Religion*, trans. Rev. George E. Thomson and Clara Wallentin (New York: G. P. Putman's Sons, 1908), 71ff., 109ff.; idem, *Die Persönlichkeit Christi, der feste Punkt im fliessenden Strome der Gegenwart* (Berlin: Berliner Stadtmission, 1903); T. Kaftan, *Moderne Theologie des alten Glaubens* (Schleswig: J. Bergas, 1905); idem, *Der Mensch Jesus: Der einige Mittler zwischen Gott und den Menschen* (Berlin: Edwin Runge, 1908); R. J. Campbell, *The New Theology* (New York: Macmillan, 1907), 66ff.; O. Lodge, *The Substance of Faith Allied with Science: A Catechism for Parents and Teachers*, 6th ed. (London: Meuthen, 1907), 86ff.

94. Cf. the warning against the Jesus cult given by A. Drews, cited in F. Meffert, *Die geschichtliche Existenz Christi*, 2nd ed. (Mönchengladbach: Verlag der Zentralstelle des Volksvereins für das katholische Deutschland, 1904), 94; R. Eucken, *Der Wahrheitsgehalt der Religion* (Leipzig: Veit & Co., 1905), 428; W. von Schnehen, *Der moderne Jesuskultus* (Frankfurt a.M.: Neuer Frankfurter Verlag, 1906); A. M. Weiss, *Die religiöse Gefahr* (Freiburg i.B.: Herder, 1904), 168.

95. J. Kunze, *Die ewige Gottheit Jesu Christi* (Leipzig: Dörfling & Franke, 1904); Steinbeck, *Das göttliche Selbstbewusstsein Jesu*; K. Braig et al., *Jesus Christus* (Freiburg i.B.: Herder, 1908); A. Arnal, *Personne du Christ et le rationalisme allemand contemporain* (Paris: Fischbacker, 1904); A. M. Fairbairn, *The Place of Christ in Modern*

with the confession of the church has again been restored, for throughout all the centuries the latter has confessed the crucified and risen Christ as its Lord and its God.

THE CENTRALITY OF THE INCARNATION

[362] The doctrine of Christ is not the starting point, but it certainly is the central point of the whole system of dogmatics. All other dogmas either prepare for it or are inferred from it. In it, as the heart of dogmatics, pulses the whole of the religious-ethical life of Christianity. It is "the mystery of godliness" (1 Tim. 3:16). From this mystery all Christology has to proceed. If, however, Christ is the incarnate Word, then the incarnation is the central fact of the entire history of the world; then, too, it must have been prepared from before the ages and have its effects throughout eternity. Schelling rightly says that it has to be hard for a person "to ascribe to a personality whom he did not know prior to the moment when that person appeared in human form—which to him is a purely historical one—it must be exceptionally hard for him *afterward* to ascribe to such a personality a prehuman, indeed even a precosmic, existence. He will, of course, be inclined to view this only as an idea with which, as history advanced, the person of the great founder of a religion was surrounded and glorified."[96] All this changes, like any other fact of revelation, when also the person of Christ is viewed theologically in accordance with the Scriptures as the one who is ordained by God to display his attributes in this world of sin, particularly the attributes of righteousness and grace and, against all opposition, to maintain his honor as God.

Incarnation and Trinity

In that case, first of all, the incarnation has its presupposition and foundation in the trinitarian being of God. In Deism and pantheism there is no room for an incarnation of God. In the former, God is abstracted and separated from the world and humanity; in the latter, God loses himself in his creatures and has no being and life of his own. It is quite natural, therefore, when on this position the incarnation is rejected as absurd. The Socinians were quite candid about this and made their exegesis serviceable to this dictate of reason.[97] They called the incarnation a human fantasy and a monstrous dogma and deemed it easier for a human to become a donkey than for God to become a human.[98] Spinoza similarly commented that the incarnation of God is as absurd as saying that "a circle

Theology (London: Hodder & Stoughton, 1905); P. T. Forsyth, *The Person and Place of Jesus Christ* (Boston: Pilgrim Press, 1909); J. M. S. Baljon et al., *Jezus Christus voor onzen tijd* (Baarn: Hollandia Drukkerij, 1908).

96. F. W. J. Schelling, *Werke*, II, 4, 35.

97. *The Racovian Catechism,* trans. Thomas Rees (London, 1609; reprinted, London, 1818), qu. 98, 111.

98. O. Fock, *Der Socinianismus* (Kiel: C. Schröder, 1847), 525.

assumes the nature of a square."[99] Only the theistic and trinitarian confession of God's characteristic essence opens the possibility for the fact of the incarnation. For here God remains who he is and can yet communicate himself to others. If, as Vinet says, one must first possess oneself to be able to give oneself, then absolute love is only conceivable as the perfection of a triune divine being. In that case alone there is a distinction between "being" and "person" and therefore communion of a human being through the person with the being of God, without this being being identified with the human or flowing over into that human. In a word, the Trinity makes possible the existence of a mediator who himself participates both in the divine and human nature and thus unites God and humans. However aberrant the theosophy of Böhme and Schelling may be when it attempts to infer the incarnation from the essence of God, yet God's trinitarian essence is the presupposition and condition of the incarnation of God.[100]

It is also important, therefore, to maintain that not the divine nature as such but specifically the person of the Son became a human. The patripassianism of Praxeas, Hermogenes, Noetus, Beron, Beryll, and Sabellius[101] has at all times been condemned by the church (at the Synod of Aquileia, for example) and no longer occurs in this form. But in terms of its basic idea, it is inherent in all pantheistic systems, especially that of Hegel, Schelling, Hartmann, and others, who conceive the absolute not as *being* but as *becoming* and who allow the divine to pour itself out in the world and to finitize itself. In that case the world and humanity with all its sorrow and misery is a moment in the life of God, and the history of revelation is the history of God's suffering.[102] Even though one can acknowledge an element of truth in this account—as will be shown in a moment—still Holy Scripture also ascribes the incarnation to the Son (John 1:14; Phil. 2:6; Heb. 2:14–15). The Reformed even preferred to say that the *person* of the Son, rather than that the *divine nature* in the Son, as the Lutherans said, had become human. In putting it this way, they did not wish to deny that the fullness of deity dwelt bodily in Christ (Col. 2:9), that the Son shared in the same essence with the Father and the Spirit, and that to that degree also the divine nature had assumed our flesh. Yet—against every tendency to mix the two natures—they emphasized that the person of the Son, in whom the divine nature existed in a manner of its own, had assumed human nature.

---

99. B. Spinoza, *The Letters,* trans. Samuel Shirley (Indianapolis and Cambridge: Hackett Publication Company, 1995), epist. 21; cf. also, K. G. Bretschneider, *Handbuch der Dogmatik,* 4th ed., 2 vols. (Leipzig: J. A. Barth, 1838), II, 195; J. A. L. Wegscheider, *Institutiones theologiae christianae dogmaticae* (Halle: Gebauer, 1819), §128; F. Schleiermacher, *The Christian Faith,* §96; D. F. Strauss, *Die christliche Glaubenslehre,* II, 153.

100. I. A. Dorner, *A System of Christian Doctrine,* trans. Alfred Cave and Rev. J. S. Banks, 4 vols. (Edinburgh: T&T Clark, 1888), III, 291.

101. C. Vitringa, *Doctr. chr. relig.,* V, 52; I. A. Dorner, *Person of Christ,* IV, 60; F. A. Loofs, *Dogmengeschichte,* 184.

102. Also cf. A. von Oettingen, *Das göttliche "Noch nicht!" Ein Beitrag zur Lehre vom Heiligen Geist* (Erlangen: Deichert, 1895).

The difference is certainly not very important, as Mastricht and Moor commented;[103] yet it is remarkable that many Lutherans preferred to say that the divine nature in the person of the Son became human, a formulation that is undoubtedly connected with their basic idea. But the Reformed favored the formulation that the person of the Son was immediately united with the human nature, and the divine nature was [therefore] mediately united with it.[104] This is how the church fathers had taught earlier and how the church confessed it. The sixth Synod of Toledo (AD 638) declared that although the entire Trinity cooperates in the incarnation, inasmuch as all the works of the Trinity are inseparable, nevertheless "only (the Son) assumes human nature in the singularity of the person, not in the unity of the divine nature: in what is peculiar to the Son, not what is common to the Trinity."[105] Questions such as those were treated in scholasticism;[106] whether the Father and the Holy Spirit could have become a human, therefore, need not detain us. The Father could not be sent, for he is the first in order and is self-existent; the Spirit proceeds from the Son, succeeds him, and is sent by him. But the Son was the one suited for the incarnation. In the divine being he occupies the place between the Father and the Spirit, is by nature the Son and image of God, was mediator already in the first creation, and as Son could restore us to our position as children of God.[107] Yet though subjectively and as it pertains to its end, the incarnation is peculiar only to the Son, still with respect to its origin, beginning, and effectiveness, it is a work of the whole Trinity. Christ was sent by the Father and conceived by the Holy Spirit. Reformed theology already expressed this truth in its doctrine of the pact of redemption (*pactum salutis*). The entire work of re-creation is not just a decree of God; it is rooted in the free and conscious consultation of the three persons. It is a personal, not a natural, work. In the Son, the Father is from all eternity the Father of his children; the Son is eternally their guarantor and mediator; the Holy Spirit is eternally their Comforter. Not just after the fall, not even first at the creation, but in eternity the foundations of the covenant of grace were laid. And the incarnation is not an incidental decree that emerged later: it was decided and determined from eternity. There was no time when the Son did not exist; there was also no time when the Son did not know he

---

103. P. van Mastricht, *Theologia*, V, 4, 15; B. de Moor, *Comm. theol.*, III, 480.

104. J. Zanchi, *Op. theol.*, VIII, 47; A. Polanus, *Syn. theol.*, VI, ch. 13; H. Bavinck, ed., *Synopsis purioris theologiae*, XXV, 8; H. Alting, *Loci communes*, in *Scriptorum theologicorum Heidelbergensium*, 2 vols. (Freistadii [Amsterdam?]: Typographorum Belgicae Foederatae, 1646), 74; S. Maresius, *Systema theologicum* (Groningen: Aemilium Spinneker, 1673), IX, 12; C. Vitringa, *Doctr. christ.*, V, 51, 63.

105. A. Hahn, *Bibliothek der Symbole und Glaubensregeln*, 237; cf. also, I. A. Dorner, *Person of Christ*, III, 312; P. Lombard, *Sent.*, III, dist. 5; T. Aquinas, *Summa theol.*, III, qu. 3, art. 4; R. Bellarmine, *Controversiis*, I, lib. 3, c. 8; M. Becanus, *Summa theologiae scholasticae* (Rothmagi: I. Behovrt, 1651), III, 1, ch. 4, qu. 1.

106. P. Lombard, *Sent.*, III, dist. 1.

107. P. Lombard, *Sent.*, III, dist. 1; T. Aquinas, *Summa theol.*, III, qu. 3, art. 8; D. Petavius, "De incarn.," *Op. theol.*, II, 15; J. Kleutgen, *Theologie der Vorzeit*, III, 180ff.; F. Turretin, *Institutes of Elenctic Theology*, XIII, qu. 4; W. G. T. Shedd, *Dogmatic Theology*, 3rd ed., 3 vols. (New York: Scribner, 1891–94), II, 266; I. A. Dorner, *System of Christian Doctrine*, III, 290.

would assume and when he was not prepared to assume the human nature from the fallen race of Adam. The incarnation was prepared from eternity; it does not rest in the essence of God but in the person. It is not a necessity as in pantheism, but neither is it arbitrary or accidental as in Pelagianism.

Incarnation and Creation

[363] The incarnation, aside from its rootedness in the Trinity, also has its presupposition and preparation in the creation. Creation gives existence to finite, limited beings; it is absolutely impossible for God to create something that would be identical with himself in essence and itself God. God, accordingly, from all eternity, conceived finite creatures and gave them existence within the necessary boundaries of space and time. In those creatures, therefore, he has, as it were, limited his eternal thoughts and infinite power. Specifically, the creation of humans in God's image is a supposition and preparation for the incarnation of God. Under the influence of a pantheistic doctrine of identity as well as in connection with the Lutheran [idea of the] "communication of proper qualities," modern theology has greatly abused this reality. For the old rule "the finite is not capable of the infinite," it substituted "humans are capable of the divine nature." This new rule, though pointing to the kinship between God and humans, wiped out the distinction between the two and proceeded from the idea that the incarnation (humanization) was necessary for the perfecting of both.[108] This line of thought is prohibited by Christian theism. Still, man [generis] *is* akin to God; man is his image, his son, his offspring. Thus the incarnation of God is a possibility,[109] and the question whether God can take on the nature of a stone, a plant, or an animal—which Occam answered in the affirmative[110]—is out of order. When God creates humans in his image and dwells and works with his Spirit in them, exerts influence on their heart and head, speaks to them, and makes himself known to them and understood by them, that is an act of condescension and accommodation to his creature, an anthropomorphizing of God and so, in a sense and to that extent, a humanization of God. Given with and in creation is the possibility of revelation and also of incarnation. Those who consider the incarnation impossible must, on further reflection, also at some point deny creation. Those who accept the latter have fundamentally lost the right to combat the former.[111] Earlier we saw that the possibility of creation is given with the generation of the Son:[112] if God were incommunicable, he would not have been able to give life either

---

108. I. A. Dorner, *Person of Christ*, V, 232.

109. T. Aquinas, Bonaventure, and others in *Sent.*, III, dist. 1.

110. In A. Stöckl, *Geschichte der Philosophie des Mittelalters*, 3 vols. in 4 (Mainz: Kirchheim, 1864), II, 1620.

111. The pantheistic assertion that God cannot pour out his fullness in an individual person but can in humankind or the world as a whole is therefore self-contradictory. Even a multiplicity of finite creatures remains finite.

112. H. Bavinck, *Reformed Dogmatics*, II, 329–34 (#231), 420–23 (#255).

to the Son or to any creature. Now we must add that if God was able to create (and could reveal himself to) beings essentially distinct from him, then he must also be able to become human. For while the incarnation is certainly different from all other revelation, it is also akin to it: it is its climax, crown, and completion.[113] All revelation tends toward and groups itself around the incarnation as the highest, richest, and most perfect act of self-revelation. Generation, creation, and incarnation are closely related, even if the latter ones do not necessarily flow from the preceding.

But there is more. Creation itself already must be conceived in infralapsarian fashion, and Adam was already a type of Christ. This view is unacceptable from the standpoint of those who think that God proceeded to the work of creation without a plan or decree and at the creation passively awaited to see what humans would do. But Scripture teaches us otherwise. In the act of creation, God already had the Christ in mind. In that sense the creation itself already served as preparation for the incarnation. The world was so created that when it fell, it could again be restored; humanity was organized under a single head in such a way that, sinning, it could again be gathered together under another head. Adam was so appointed as head that Christ could immediately take his place; and the covenant of works was so set up that, broken, it could be restored in the covenant of grace. People were therefore wrong in thinking that the incarnation of the Son of God would also have taken place without sin. This sentiment does not yet clearly occur in the church fathers,[114] but in scholasticism the question was actively discussed! In addition to the Trinity, the incarnation was an article of faith also before the fall and necessary to bring humans to their supernatural goal.[115] The question was therefore answered in the affirmative by Rupert von Deutz, Duns Scotus, Alexander of Hales, Albert the Great, John Wessel, Catharinus, Pighius, Suárez,[116] further by Osiander and Socinus,[117] and later by many modern theologians such as Steffens, Göschel, Baader, Nitzsch, Martensen, Liebner, Lange, Rothe, Schöberlein, Ebrard, and others.[118]

One can understand how these theologians, taking one deductive step after another, arrived at this opinion. A fact like the incarnation of God cannot be

---

113. Athanasius and Gregory of Nyssa, in A. von Harnack, *History of Dogma*, III, 300.

114. Cf. only Tertullian, *On the Resurrection of the Body*, 5; idem, *Against Praxeas*, 12.

115. Cf. H. Bavinck, *Reformed Dogmatics*, I, 609 (#158); II, 542–48 (#288).

116. See, e.g., Duns Scotus, *Sent.*, III, dist. 7, qu. 3; R. Bellarmine, "De Christo," *Controversiis*, V, ch. 10, takes no stance on this question.

117. Socinus, *Prael. theol.*, ch. 10.

118. Cf. I. A. Dorner, *Person of Christ*, V, 236–48; idem, *System of Christian Doctrine*, II, 205ff. In England many theologians came to the same conclusion, such as B. F. Westcott, *Christus Consummator: Some Aspects of the Work and Person of Christ in Relation to Modern Thought* (London and New York: Macmillan & Co., 1886), 99ff.; Illingworth, "The Incarnation in Relation to Development," 5th essay in C. Gore, *Lux Mundi*, 13th ed. (London: Murray, 1892). In the Netherlands, also, J. J. van Oosterzee, *Christologie: Onderzoek naar den persoon en het werk des verlossers*, 3 vols. (Rotterdam: Van der Meer & Verbruggen, 1855–61), III, 85ff.; idem, *Christian Dogmatics*, II, 464, 753.

accidental and cannot be grounded in sin as an accidental and arbitrary act of humans; sin may be able to modify the plan of God, but it cannot destroy it; the incarnation, accordingly, has to be certain apart from sin. What sin brought about is only that the incarnation has to occur for the redemption of the sinner. Add to this that religion before the fall cannot differ in essence from religion after the fall. If a mediator is needed now, then such a mediator was also needed in religion before the fall. Christ's person and work, accordingly, is absolutely not exhausted in the atonement of sin, in the acquisition of salvation. He is not only the mediator but also the head, not a means but also an end, an end in himself (1 Cor. 15:45–47; Eph. 1:10, 21–23; 5:31–32; Col. 1:15–17). He does not just exist for the church; the church also exists for him: the predestination of Christ to glory has precedence over that of humans. These considerations contain so much truth that the agreement elicited by the hypothesis of the incarnation of God apart from sin is not surprising. If one assumes a Pelagian freedom of the will, and sin, therefore, is something accidental and a disappointment to God, there is no better way to harmonize free will with the plan of God than by saying that the incarnation was in any case determined and only modified on a subordinate point.

On the basis of Augustine's standpoint and more specifically on that of Reformed theology, however, there is no need for this entire hypothesis. There is but one plan and decree of God; with a view to the counsel of God, there is no room for any reality other than the existing one. Accordingly, however much sin entered the world by the will of the creature, it was nevertheless included in God's counsel from eternity and to him was not contingent or unforeseen. In that eternal counsel the incarnation on account of sin also has a place; it depends only on God's good pleasure, not on human beings. What is more, the Son was also the mediator of union for humanity apart from sin, as many Reformed scholars recognized with Calvin.[119] Inasmuch as Quenstedt[120] did not correctly understand this point, he could count Zanchius, Bucanus, and Polanus among the proponents of the incarnation apart from sin. The idea was only that religion is essentially identical in the covenant of works and that of grace, and that salvation, accordingly, always has to consist in communion with the triune God. Only Comrie—as a result of his rigorous supralapsarianism—arrived at the theory that the predestination of the human Christ was antecedent to that of the fall.[121] For the rest, most theologians stuck to Scripture, which always and exclusively connects the incarnation of Christ with sin and regards it as the most magnificent proof of God's compassion (Matt. 1:21; 9:13; 20:28; Luke 1:68; 2:30; John 1:29; 3:16; Rom. 8:3; Gal. 4:4–5; 1 Tim. 3:16; Heb. 2:14; 1 John 3:8; etc.). The opposite view also very readily leads to the idea that the incarnation as such was

119. J. Calvin, *Institutes*, II.xii.4, 6.

120. J. A. Quenstedt, *Theologia didactico-polemica sive systema theologicum* (1685), I, 110; cf. M. Schneckenburger, *Vergleichende Darstellung*, II, 190.

121. Cf. H. Bavinck, *Reformed Dogmatics*, II, 361–68 (#238), 382–88 (#244).

appropriate and necessary for God, that is, to the pantheistic teaching of the eternal self-revelation of God in the world.[122]

Incarnation and the History of Revelation

[364] A third and final preparation for the incarnation is the history of revelation from the time of paradise. The incarnation did not take place immediately after the fall; in fact many centuries passed between the first sin and the coming of Christ in the flesh. Scripture, in speaking of the fullness of time (Eph. 1:10; Gal. 4:4), shows that this delay was not an accident or an arbitrary thing, but thus determined by God in his wisdom. By all sorts of means and ways, the groundwork for the incarnation first had to be laid in the preceding history. Just as the incarnation presupposes the generation [of the Son] and the creation [of humans in the image of God], so now there is added still another presupposition and preparation: revelation. It is especially John in his prologue who brings out for us this preparation for the incarnation in a preceding history. Not only was the Logos in the beginning with God and himself God and not only were all things made by him, but from the moment of creation this Logos also communicated his life and light to creatures. For in him was life, and the life was the light of all people. Even after the fall, this revelation did not stop. On the contrary, the light of that Logos shone in the darkness and enlightened everyone coming into the world. He revealed himself particularly in Israel, which he had chosen for his own inheritance and led and blessed as Angel of the covenant. He came continually to his own in theophany, prophecy, and miracle. In that manner the Son prepared the whole world, including Jews as well as Gentiles, for his coming in the flesh. The world and humanity, land and people, cradle and stable, Bethlehem and Nazareth, parents and relatives, nature and environment, society and civilization—these are all components in the fullness of the times in which God sent his Son into the flesh. It was the Son himself who thus immediately after the fall, as Logos and as Angel of the covenant, made the world of Gentiles and Jews ready for his coming. He was in the process of coming from the beginning of time and in the end came for good, by his incarnation making his home in humankind.[123] The incarnation links up with the preceding revelation, both the general and the special. It stands and falls with them. For if God was able to reveal himself in the

122. Irenaeus, *Against Heresies*, V, 14; Gregory of Nazianzus, *Theological Orations*, 36; *Augustine, *De verbis Apost.*, 8, 2, 7; T. Aquinas, *Summa theol.*, III, qu. 1, art. 3; but otherwise in *Sent.*, III, 1, qu. 1, art. 3; Bonaventure, *Sent.*, III, dist. 1, art. 2, qu. 2; D. Petavius, "De incarn.," *Op. theol.*, II, ch. 17; C. von Schäzler, *Das Dogma von der Menschwerdung Gottes: Im Geiste des heiligen Thomas* (Freiburg i.B.: Herder, 1870), 307; J. Kleutgen, *Theologie der Vorzeit*, III, 400; J. A. Quenstedt, *Theologia*, II, 108–16; A. Calovius, *Isagoge ad summa theologia* (Wittenberg: A. Hartmann; typis J. S. Fincelli, 1652), 59–99; J. Calvin, *Institutes*, II.xii.4–7; P. van Mastricht, *Theologia*, V, 4, 17; F. Turretin, *Institutes of Elenctic Theology*, XIII, 3; B. de Moor, *Comm. theol.*, III, 759; C. Vitringa, *Doctr. christ.*, V, 47; J. Müller, *Dogmatische Abhandlungen* (Bremen: C. E. Müller, 1870), 66–126; F. A. Philippi, *Kirchliche Glaubenslehre*, IV, 376; F. H. R. Frank, *System der christlichen Wahrheit*, II, 80; J. Orr, *The Christian View of God and the World as Centering in the Incarnation* (New York: Randolph, 1893), 319–27.

123. W. Baldensperger, *Der Prolog des vierten Evangeliums* (Freiburg i.B.: Mohr, 1898).

way Scripture testifies with respect both to the Gentile world and to Israel, then the possibility of the incarnation is inherently included in that revelation; and if the incarnation were not possible, then neither could the revelation be maintained. Revelation, after all, is based on the same idea as the incarnation: on the communicability of God, both in his being to the Son (generation) and outside his being to creatures (creation).

Now this entire preparation of the incarnation in the preceding centuries is concentrated, as it were, and completed in the election and favoring of Mary as mother of Jesus. Mary is the blessed one among women. She received an honor bestowed on no other creature. In the undeserved favor granted her, she far exceeds all other people and all angels. Rome was right in maintaining this; those who deny it are not taking the incarnation of God seriously. However, from this acknowledgment alone Rome proceeded without any ground to the doctrine of the immaculate conception of the Blessed Virgin. What led it in this process and brought it to this point was not the authority of Scripture or of tradition; nor was it the attempt thereby to explain and guarantee the sinlessness of Jesus, for this sinlessness rests causally in his divine nature and instrumentally in his conception by the Holy Spirit. But the driving force behind this dogma is again to be found, for Rome, in the idea of hierarchy. The closer a creature is to God, to that degree that creature must also participate in his nature and attributes, share in the process of deification. Now no creature is greater than Mary; she is most intimately united with God, the God bearer (θεοτοκος), who bore God's own Son beneath her heart, and was indwelt by God himself. Whether or not Scripture or tradition affords us evidence for this is not the point. The Catholic Christian can only conceive the mother of the Savior as being exalted above all the members of the human race and above all the angels in heaven, pleasing to God, pure and immaculate. Was she not united with the "God-man," hence with the divine Person of the Word, with holiness itself, by means of the closest and most tender ties? Has not God, by the very fact of her election to so high a dignity and so intimate a familiarity, demonstrated most clearly that he loved this pure virgin above all creatures? And for that reason, aside from any proof from Scripture and tradition, is it not most plausible that God should endow the holy virgin with his charismata above all other creatures? The honor of the Savior required that his elect mother should remain exempt even from any hint or shadow of sin. It is *fitting* that a creature who had to have such intimate dealings with God and enjoyed such a tender relationship with him should be safeguarded from the least taint of sin. It is *fitting* for the house of the Lord to be holy.[124]

The doctrine of the immaculate conception and sinlessness of Mary fits into the hierarchical system of the Roman church and theology and was therefore gradually incorporated into it. Even the doctrine of Mary's ascension to heaven is only a matter of time. For that reason, the predicates attributed to Mary keep

124. Thus Bensdorp, in *Die Katholiek* 112 (1897): 429, 445, 447.

increasing in number and rank: she is the daughter of the Father, the bride of the Son, the temple and organ of the Holy Spirit, the completion of the Trinity. She is the instrumental and, in part, the meritorious cause of our eternal election, the chief reason for the natural and supernatural creation, coredemptrix. She is the wise, all-wonder-working governess of the church, equipped with unlimited dominion, all-powerful, like God who governs the world, and so on.[125] In Rome, Mariolatry increasingly crowds out the true Christian worship of God. Professor Schoeler sees this superstition characteristically expressed in a Vatican mural that features the Madonna, placed high in the middle, while the Father and the Son are seated to the right and to the left as instruments of her almighty will.[126] It is against this idolization of the human that the Reformation rose up in protest. It would not have been surprising if out of fear of such idolatry it had not always paid to Mary the honor due to her. But even that is not the case, though it was, of course, cautious in its praise. Among all Protestants who confess the incarnation of the Word, Mary is held in high esteem. She was chosen and prepared by God to be the mother of his Son. She was the favored one among women. Christ himself desired her to be his mother, who conceived him by the Holy Spirit, who carried him beneath her heart, who nursed him at her breast, who instructed him in the Scriptures, in whom, in a word, the preparation of the incarnation was completed.

Incarnation and Testimony of Scripture

[365] Nevertheless, though in his incarnation Christ connected with preceding revelation and prepared his own coming by way of nature and history, he is not a product of the past nor the fruit of Israel or humanity. To some extent it is true of all human beings that they cannot be explained in terms of their parents and environment. For that reason also Kuenen,[127] after he had described the conditions and building materials for the emergence of Christianity, had to admit that this did not yet explain the person of Christ. But it is true of Christ in still another and higher sense than Kuenen had in mind. For, according to Scripture, in Christ that Word became flesh who was in the beginning with God and himself God. At all times and from all sorts of directions, this deity of Christ has been denied and opposed. But Scripture teaches no other doctrine. As Chantepie de la Saussaye

125. Cf. above in the doctrine of original sin, 117–19 (#326); and also L. M. Wörnhart, *Maria, die wunderbare Mutter Gottes und der Menschen* (Innsbrück: F. Rauch, 1890), 13, 19, 244, 289; D. Petavius, "De incarnatione," *Op. theol.*, XIV; M. J. Scheeben, *Handbook der katholischen Dogmatik*, 4 vols. (1874–98; reprinted, Freiburg i.B.: Herder, 1933), III, 69ff. (ed. note: ET: *A Manual of Catholic Theology: Based on Scheeben's "Dogmatik,"* ed. Joseph Wilhelm and Thomas Bartholomew Scannel, 4th ed., 2 vols. [London: Kegan Paul, Trench, Trubner & Co.; New York: Benziger Brothers, 1909]); J. B. Heinrich and C. Gutberlet, *Dogmatische Theologie*, 2nd ed., 10 vols. (Mainz: Kirchheim, 1881–1900), VII, 363–495; B. Bartmann, *Christus ein Gegner des Marienkultus?* (Freiburg i.B.: Herder, 1909).

126. Schoeler, *Das vatikanische Bild* (Gütersloh, 1898).

127. A. Kuenen, *De godsdienst van Israël tot den ondergang van den Joodschen staat,* 2 vols. (Haarlem: Kruseman, 1869–70), 158, 193; cf. A. von Harnack, *What Is Christianity?* 126.

once remarked, we are used to the superlatives of Scripture and frequently no longer understand the force of its expressions. But if a person spoke of himself in the way Jesus regularly did; if others venerated a person the way prophets and apostles do Christ, then everyone would consider it insane fanaticism or horrendous blasphemy. Scripture attributes to Christ—not in few rare instances but repeatedly—personal eternal preexistence (John 1:1; 8:58; 17:5; Rom. 8:3; 2 Cor. 8:9; Gal. 4:4; Phil. 2:6), divine sonship in a supernatural sense (Matt. 3:17; 11:27; 28:19; John 1:14; 5:18; Rom. 8:32), the creation and sustaining of all things (John 1:3, 1 Cor. 8:6; Eph. 3:9; Col. 1:16–17; Heb. 1:3; Rev. 3:14), the acquisition for all and everyone of all weal and salvation (Matt. 1:21; 18:11; John 1:4, 16; 14:6; Acts 4:12; 1 Cor. 1:30), kingship in the church (Matt. 3:2; 5:11; 10:32, 37; John 18:37; 1 Cor. 11:3; Eph. 1:22; Col. 1:18), dominion over all things (Matt. 11:27; 28:18; John 3:35; 17:2; Acts 2:33; 1 Cor. 15:27; Eph. 1:20–22; Phil. 2:9; Col. 2:10; Heb. 2:8), and judgment upon the living and dead (John 5:27; Acts 10:42; 17:31; Rom. 14:10; 2 Cor. 5:10); it calls him directly and unambiguously by the name "God" (John 1:1; 20:28; Rom. 9:5; 2 Thess. 1:12; Titus 2:13; 2 Pet. 1:1; Heb. 1:8–9).[128]

Granted, all opposition to the deity of Christ begins with an appeal to Scripture against the confessions. But this illusion only lasts a very short time. Impartial exegesis soon shows that the doctrine of the church is more firmly grounded in Scripture than one had originally expected. So then the critics find themselves forced to go back from the Christ of apostolic proclamation to the Jesus of the Synoptics and to criticize the latter as long as it takes to strip him of all that is supernatural. The deity of Christ can then be explained as a fruit of profound theological or philosophical speculation that was originally totally foreign to the church.[129] This always lasts only as long, however, as one sets store by and has an interest in presenting one's own faith as Christianity in its original purity. The moment that standpoint has been abandoned, impartiality again recovers its voice and agrees with the church confession. "It cannot be denied that in the words of Holy Scripture there are really present some seeds of the doctrines of the church."[130] "It is undeniable that also what the doctrine of the church teaches

128. All this is more fully discussed in H. Bavinck, *Our Reasonable Faith,* trans. H. Zylstra (Grand Rapids: Eerdmans, 1951), chs. 15–16; cf. H. Cremer, *Wörterbuch,* s.v. θεος, κυριος; B. B. Warfield, *Lord of Glory*; Bröse, "Wird Christus Rom. 9:5 θεος gennant?" *Neue kirchliche Zeitschrift* (1899): 645–57; J. Kunze, *Die ewige Gottheit Jesu Christi*; J. Steinbeck, *Das göttliche Selbstbewusstsein Jesu*; K. K. Grass, *Zur Lehre von der Gottheit Jesu Christi* (Gütersloh: Bertelsmann, 1900); A. von Schlatter, *Jesu Gottheit und das Kreuz* (Gütersloh: Bertelsmann, 1901); H. Cremer, *Die Bedeutung des Artikels von der Gottheit Christi für die Ethik* (Leipzig: Dörffling & Franke, 1901); M. Kähler, *Angewandte Dogmen,* 2nd ed. (Leipzig: Deichert, 1908), 132–55; T. Simon, *Der Logos: Ein Versuch erneuter Würdigung einer alten Wahrheit* (Leipzig: Deichert, 1902); E. F. K. Müller, *Our Lord: Belief in the Deity of Christ* (New York: Eaton & Mainz, 1908); A. Seitz, *Das Evangelium vom Gottessohn* (Freiburg i.B.: Herder, 1908).

129. F. Nitzsch, *Lehrbuch der Evangelischen Dogmatik,* 522; H. Schultz, *Die Lehre von der Gottheit Christi,* 417ff., 438, 468.

130. J. A. L. Wegscheider, *Inst. theol.,* §128.

about the divine nature of Christ has points of support in the New Testament."[131] With that, then, the explanation of this dogma in terms of later theological or philosophical speculation again collapses.

As does the study of Scripture, so also does dogma-historical research always again set the seal of truth on the church's confession of the deity of Christ. The development of christological dogma exhibits a logical progression that in the end is noted and recognized by all research scholars.[132] The faith with which the church appeared in the world was a simple one, but of one thing it was sure: in Christ, God himself had come to it and taken it into his fellowship. That was certain; that was something it would not let itself be deprived of and that it defended against a wide range of attacks and formulated plainly and clearly in its confession. In the doctrine of the deity of Christ, it maintained the character of the Christian religion, the reality of its fellowship with God. In Christianity, Christ occupies a very different place than Buddha, Zarathustra, and Muhammad do in their respective religions. Christ is not the teacher, not the founder, but the content of Christianity.[133] For that reason, judged by the doctrine of Scripture and the faith of the church, men like Irenaeus, Athanasius, and Augustine are finally always vindicated again over against their opponents. People count it an honor to be in agreement with them; no one is eager to be named after Arius, Pelagius, or Socinus. It is also clear that the Christian religion, that is, the true fellowship between God and humans, can be maintained in no other way than by the confession of the deity of Christ. For if Christ is not truly God, he is only a human being. And however highly he may be placed, he can neither in his person nor in his work be the content and object of the Christian faith. Then whether with respect to himself Christ stood in unbroken fellowship with God (Schleiermacher), was the first to have voiced the unity of God with humans (Hegel), had fully realized within himself the sonship of God (Lipsius), had revealed the love of God and founded the kingdom of God (Ritschl), Christianity, now that it exists, is certainly not dependent on him. Yes, he is its founder. Historically his significance remains great and his example still influences people, but he himself exists outside the essence of Christianity. Arian Christology, the moral Christology of rationalism, the symbolic Christology of Kant, the ideal Christology of Hegel, the aesthetic Christology of De Wette, the anthropological Christology of Feuerbach—none of them leave a place for Christ in dogmatics. "If one retains the personality of Christ as a human one, however idealized it may be, it cannot as personality itself be the redeeming power for believers."[134]

131. F. Nitzsch, *Lehrbuch der Evangelischen Dogmatik*, 518, 521; H. J. Holtzmann, *Lehrbuch der neutestamentlichen Theologie*, I, 353, 418; W. Baldensperger, *Der Prolog des vierten Evang.*, 4ff.; J. Weiss, *Paul and Jesus*, 9.
    132. E. von Hartmann, *Die Krisis des Christ.*, 6; idem, *Das Christ. des Neuen Test.*, VIIIff.
    133. F. W. J. Schelling, *Werke*, II, 4, 35; E. von Hartmann, *Die Krisis des Christ.*, 1.
    134. E. von Hartmann, *Die Krisis des Christ.*, 15.

Ritschl and some of his followers, like Schultz and Kaftan, still tried to maintain the title of God for Jesus, though [they considered him] merely human, because to the church he occupies the place of God and has the value of God. Earlier this had been tried in the same way by the Socinians. They opposed the deity of Christ as strongly as possible and said that Christ, in the few passages where he is called God (such as John 1:1; 20:28; Rom. 9:5), was so named on account of his rank, dignity, and rule, to which he had been elevated especially after his resurrection.[135] Christ by divine power works the same things "that God himself does, just as God himself does.[136] This name 'God' is not the name proper to any substance or to a person, but is the name proper to an authority, a power," just as the angels and authorities in Scripture, according to Jesus' own saying (John 10:34), are sometimes called gods.[137] This same view is currently propagated by Ritschl and his school. The name "God," though used in Scripture and in the church for Christ, is in that case a reference to his office, not to his characteristic essence. This view, however, is altogether untenable. While angels and authorities in Scripture are sometimes called "gods," the metaphorical, office-related sense in these cases is obvious. With Christ the case is very different. To him a personal eternal preexistence is attributed; of him it is said that he was God, existed in the "form" of God, was the effulgence of God's glory, the only-begotten Son of God, the image of the invisible God, indeed, God above all, to be praised forever. How can anyone possibly understand this of a human being who acquired the honorary title "God" only in virtue of the office he discharged and the work he did?

Furthermore, the Christian church, in calling Jesus "God," meant it to be a reference never to his office but always to his characteristic essence. When people begin to use the same word and the same name in a totally different sense, they deliberately sow misunderstanding and confusion and act unfairly toward the church. Further, if Christ is not God in any essential sense, then neither may he be called "God" or venerated as God. To say that he perfectly manifested the love of God, that he completely incorporated within himself God's plan for the world and for humanity, that he fully made the will of God his own is no warrant—from a scriptural and Christian viewpoint or on logical and philosophical grounds—for conferring on the human person Jesus the name "God." To be one with God in a religious and ethical sense is something totally different from being one with God in a metaphysical sense. A value judgment is false unless it is grounded in a factual judgment.

Finally, naming Jesus "God" and venerating him as God, if he is in fact only a human, is a pantheistic mixing of the Creator with the creature, a return to pagan idolatry and Roman Catholic creature deification, both of them things that are diametrically opposed to the principle of Protestantism. If Jesus, though he is

135. *The Racovian Catechism*, qu. 94–190.
136. Ibid., qu. 120, 164.
137. F. Socinus on John 1:1.

[considered] only a human, may be called upon and venerated as God, then by that token we have in principle justified also the Catholic veneration of Mary, the saints, and the angels, and all pagan idolatry. While they deny that God can become a human, people simultaneously teach that humans can elevate themselves to the rank and dignity of God.[138] Incarnation is said to be impossible, but apotheosis is considered perfectly possible. The incarnation of God is [said to be] absurd, but the process of humans becoming God is supposed to be reasonable—as though the product of evolution can ever be God. "For what is evolving is not God."[139]

THE VIRGIN BIRTH

[366] This Son of God became human, according to Scripture, as a result of being conceived by the Holy Spirit and born of the Virgin Mary. This supernatural conception was already denied in ancient times by the Jews;[140] by Ebionites; by Cerinthus, Carpocrates, and Celsus;[141] by Deists and rationalists in the eighteenth century such as Morgan and Chubb;[142] by later critics such as Strauss, Bruno Bauer, Renan, and others; and, most recently, by Harnack.[143] His opinion that the words "conceived by the Holy Spirit and born of the Virgin Mary" were not part of the original gospel message triggered a serious controversy in which many sided with him[144] but others took a firm stand against him.[145] This controversy became even more important after the discovery in the summer of 1892 of a Syrian translation of the Gospels, a discovery made by Mrs. Lewis and her sister Mrs. Gibson, in a

138. H. Schultz, *Die Lehre von der Gottheit Christi*, 386, 389, 407, 411, 454, 463.

139. Gregory of Nazianzus, cited in C. von Schäzler, *Das Dogma von der Menschwerdung Gottes*, 56; cf. further, O. Fock, *Der Socinianismus*, 538ff.; *R. A. Lipsius, *Theologisches Jahresbericht*, X, 378; *O. Pfleiderer, *Jahrbuch für Protestantische Theologie* (1889): 168ff.; A. Dieckhoff, *Die Menschwerdung des Sohnes Gottes* (Leipzig: Naumann, 1882); L. Stählin, *Kant, Lotze, Albrecht Ritschl: Eine kritische Studie* (Leipzig: Dörffling & Franke, 1888), 165ff.; ed. note: ET: *Kant, Lotze, and Ritschl: A Critical Examination*, trans. D. W. Simon (Edinburgh: T&T Clark, 1889); **Hoensbroech, *Christ und Widerchrist: Ein Beitrag zur Vertheidigung der Gottheit Christi und zur Char. des Unglaubens in der prot. Theol.* (Freiburg, 1892); J. Wendland, *Albrecht Ritschl und seine Schüler*, 114ff.; C. Stange, *Der dogmatische Ertrag der Ritschlschen Theologie nach Julius Kaftan* (Leipzig: Dieterich, 1906), 110ff.

140. J. A. Eisenmenger and F. X. Schieferl, *Entdecktes Judenthum*, 2 vols. (Königsberg in Preussen: n.p., 1711), I, 105.

141. B. de Moor, *Comm. theol.*, III, 722.

142. K. G. Bretschneider, *Systematische Entwickelung*, 4th ed. (Leipzig: J. A. Barth, 1841), 567.

143. A. von Harnack, *Das apostolische Glaubensbekenntnis* (Berlin: Haack, 1892).

144. E. C. Achelis, *Zur Symbolfrage: Zwei Abhandlungen* (Berlin: Reuther, 1892); W. Herrmann, *Worum handelt es sich in dem Streit um das Apostolikum?* (Leipzig: F. W. Grunow, 1893); A. Hering, "Die dogmatische Bedeutung und der religiöse Werth der übernatürlichen Geburt Christi," *Zeitschrift für Theologie und Kirche* 5 (1895): 58–91; P. Lobstein, *The Virgin Birth of Christ*, trans. Victor Leuliette (London: Williams & Norgate, 1903).

145. G. Wohlenberg, *Empfangen vom Heiligen Geist, geboren von der Jungfrau Maria* (Leipzig: Deichert, 1893); H. Cremer, *Zum Kampf um das Apostolikum* (Berlin: Wiegandt & Grieben, 1893); T. Zahn, *Das apostolische Symbolum* (Erlangen and Leipzig: Deichert, 1893).

palimpsest belonging to the St. Catherine monastery on Mt. Sinai.[146] The text that this translation offered as a reading of Matthew 1:16 produced a lively discussion in which Conybeare, Sanday, Charles, and others took part and which was mainly conducted in *The Academy* of November 1894 to February 1895. Many of the participants took the Syrian reading to be older than the text found in our Gospel of Matthew and deduced from this that Jesus' supernatural birth from the Virgin Mary was something that had emerged later and that Jesus was originally viewed as the natural son of Joseph and Mary.[147] In America, interest in this question significantly increased when Dr. Crapsey, minister in the Episcopal Church, rejected the confession of Jesus' supernatural conception and was condemned by his church on that ground. When in November 1906 the Protestant Episcopal Diocese of New York held its 123rd annual convention, Bishop Potter defended this verdict and said that a minister who contradicted the confession of his own church was obligated to resign from office. This circumstance explains why the virgin birth emerged again and was discussed by various scholars.[148]

The Syrian translation of Matthew 1:16 reads: "Jacob begot Joseph; Joseph, to whom the Virgin Mary was betrothed, begot Jesus who was called Christ." Now if this Syrian translation had been meant to deny Jesus' supernatural conception, this fact would have stood by itself in the history of the Gospel among the Syrians and remained without influence. For the Syrian Diatesseron of Tatian, the Syrian Gospel fragments published by Cureton in 1858, plus all later Syrian editions, clearly teach this doctrine. Furthermore, the newfound translation of this same verse, Matthew 1:16, clearly calls Mary a virgin and describes her as being betrothed to Joseph, has the same text in verse 18 as our Gospel, and therefore definitely teaches the conception of the Holy Spirit, as it does also in verse 20 and in Luke 3:23. Hence there is not the slightest evidence that the Syrian translator with his text of Matthew 1:16 sought to deny the supernatural conception [of Christ].[149]

Further, there is here no support for the opinion that the reading in the Syrian version represents a text other than that found in our Gospel of Matthew. Indeed,

146. *The Four Gospels in Syriac*, transcribed from the Sinaitic palimpsest by the late Robert L. Bensley and by J. Rendel Harris and F. Crawford Burkitt, with an introduction by Agnes Smith Lewis (Cambridge: Cambridge University Press, 1894).

147. *Also cf. *Theol. Tijdschr.* (May 1895): 258ff.; W. C. Van Manen, "Een ouodsyrische Vertaling," *De Gids* 13 (July 1895): 88–104.

148. W. M. Ramsay, *Was Christ Born at Bethlehem?* (London: Hodder & Stoughton, 1898); B. W. Randolph, *The Virgin-Birth of Our Lord* (London and New York: Longmans Green, 1903); J. Gresham Machen, "The New Testament Account of the Birth of Jesus," *Princeton Theological Review* 3 (1905): 641–70; 4 (1906): 37–81; C. A. Briggs, "Criticism and the Dogma of the Virgin Birth," *North American Review* 182/6 (June 1906): 861–74; idem, "The Virgin Birth of Our Lord," *American Journal of Theology* 12 (1908): 189–210; R. Knowling, "Birth of Christ," *DC*, I, 202ff.; G. H. Box, "The Virgin Birth," *DC*, II, 804ff.; J. Orr, *The Virgin Birth of Christ* (London: Hodder & Stoughton, 1908).

149. T. Zahn, "Die syrische Evangelienübersetzung vom Sinai," *Theologisches Literaturblatt* 16/3 (January 18, 1895): 25–30.

of Matthew 1:16 there are a number of readings that differ from those found in our own and the Syrian translation. Some minuscules read: "Jacob begot Joseph, to whom being betrothed, a virgin [named] Mary, begot Jesus, who was called Christ." The Syrian Gospel published by Cureton here reads: "Jacob begot Joseph, to whom was betrothed Mary the virgin, who gave birth to Jesus Christ." The Armenian translation has the text: "Jacob begot Joseph, husband of Mary, to whom was betrothed Mary the virgin, to whom was born Jesus, who was called Christ," and this text is also found (with the omission of the words "the virgin") in the dialogue, published by Conybeare, between the Christian Timothy and the Jew Aquila. Comparison of these different texts makes very clear that most of the changes in the original text have been introduced with the intent to highlight the virginity of Mary. For that reason the expression "Mary's husband" is sometimes omitted, and the word "virgin" is sometimes added to Mary. The newfound Syrian translation betrays the same intent when it omits the addition of "Joseph, Mary's husband," and replaces it with the words "to whom the virgin Mary was betrothed." But this change prompted the translator to repeat the name "Joseph" and to make it the subject of the predicate clause "begot Jesus." This could be done in all innocence because in Matthew 1:1, Jesus was called "the son of David," and he is repeatedly mentioned elsewhere as "the son of Joseph" (Matt. 13:55; Luke 2:27, 41, 48; 4:22; John 1:45; 6:42). Legally and in the civil domain, he had to be called that as well.[150]

It may, moreover, be considered certain that Jesus' supernatural conception was part of the original message of the gospel. The two accounts left to us in Matthew and Luke bear their Palestinian character on their face and doubtlessly have their origin in the circle of Jewish Christians and further on the lips of Joseph and Mary. It is natural that they first kept the secret of Jesus' conception to themselves and only later disclosed it to a small circle of friends after Jesus had been resurrected and was confessed as the Christ in the church. From there it may readily be inferred that this supernatural birth did not have prominence in the apostolic message and does not explicitly occur in most New Testament writings. Still, this is something very different from saying that this truth was denied or was put aside as worthless. For that thesis there is not even one shred of evidence. On the contrary, the reports in Matthew and Luke—the former derived perhaps from Joseph and the second from Mary—assume that Jesus' supernatural birth was known in the Jewish-Christian church around the middle of the first century, and they were never subject to any contradiction or opposition by believers in general. The ancient Roman symbol, which certainly existed before the middle of the second century and was probably already extant toward the end of the first, contains the words "who was born of the Holy Spirit and the Virgin Mary," words later somewhat modified in the interest of greater clarity. Critics of the

150. T. Zahn, *Einleitung in das Neue Testament,* 2nd ed., 2 vols. (Leipzig: Deichert, 1900), II, 298–300; W. Sanday, "Jesus Christ," *DB,* II, 644.

supernatural conception, also Cerinthus, a contemporary of John, never claimed that this doctrine was of later origin. In their time it must therefore have been a part of the universal Christian faith. It is groundless and also very strange to regard, with Harnack, the heretics Cerinthus and others as the pure transmitters and custodians of the faith of the primitive Christian church. Further back the doctrine can already be found in the letters of Ignatius, who died a martyr's death around the year 117,[151] as well as in the Apology—found some time ago—of the philosopher Aristides of Athens, who handed it to Emperor Hadrian in the year 125. It must all the more certainly have been a part of the apostolic message because pagan fables about the sons of the gods would certainly have frightened Christians away from a teaching that seemed so closely akin to them. There is nowhere any trace of the influence of these pagan fables on the genesis of the evangelical story of the supernatural conception, as Usener, Hillmann, Hilgenfeld, Soltau, van den Bergh van Eysinga, and others assume there is.[152] For that matter, while there is some superficial external similarity, there is profound essential difference. The shameless glorification of sensual lust attributed to the gods in the teaching of the fables is a million miles removed from the simplicity, the delicacy, and the sanctity one marvels at in the Gospel stories.[153] Harnack,[154] accordingly, sought to explain them from Jewish data, specifically from an incorrect exegesis of Isaiah 7:14. However, there is no evidence that Isaiah 7:14 was applied by the Jews to the Messiah and understood to refer to his birth from a virgin.[155]

Finally, while it is true that the conception by the Holy Spirit is related in the New Testament only by Matthew and Luke, that which is pivotal in the narratives of Matthew and Luke is the doctrine of all evangelists and apostles. Jesus, that is, is first of all genealogically a son of David. This is what he is universally regarded to be by the multitudes that kept crowding around him and by all his disciples (Matt. 1:1, 20; 9:27; 12:23; 15:22; 20:30–31; 21:9, 15; 22:42–45; Mark 10:47; 11:10; 12:35–37; Luke 1:27, 32, 69; 18:38–39; 20:41–44; John 7:42; Acts 2:30; 13:23; Rom. 1:3; 9:5; 2 Tim. 2:8; Heb. 7:14; Rev. 3:7; 5:5; 22:16). Further, he is the Holy One who never committed or knew sin (Matt. 7:11; 11:29; 12:50;

---

151. Ignatius, *Epistle to the Smyrnaeans*, I, 1–3; idem, *Epistle to the Ephesians*, VII, 1–2.

152. H. Usener, *Religionsgeschichtliche Untersuchungen*, 3 vols. (Bonn: Cohen, 1889–1911), 69ff.; J. Hillmann, "Die Kindesheitsgeschichte Jesu nach Lukas," *Jahrbuch für protestantische Theologie* 27 (1891): 192ff.; A. Hilgenfeld, "Die Geburts- und Kindheitsgeschichte Jesu," *Zeitschrift für wissenschaftliche Theologie* (1901): 204–15; W. Soltau, *The Birth of Jesus Christ*, trans. Maurice A. Canney (London: Adam & Charles Black, 1903); E. Petersen, *Die wunderbare Geburt des Heilandes* (Tübingen: Mohr, 1909); G. A. van den Bergh van Eysinga, *Indische Einflüsse*, 22ff.; P. Saintyves, *Les vierges mères et les naissances miraculeuses* (Paris: Nourry, 1908).

153. G. H. Box, "The Gospel Narratives," *Zeitschrift für neutestamentliche Wissenschaft* (1905): 80ff.; L. M. Sweet, "Heathen Wonderbirths and the Birth of Christ," *Princeton Theological Review* 6 (1908): 83–117.

154. *A. von Harnack, *Theologische Literaturzeitung* (1889): n. 8; idem, *History of Dogma*, I, 100; cf. B. Weiss, *Das Leben Jesu*, 2 vols. (Stuttgart: 1882), I, 217ff.

155. G. H. Box, "Virgin Birth," *DC*, II, 806ff.; J. Orr, *Virgin Birth of Christ*, 124ff.; W. Schmidt, *Christliche Dogmatik*, 4 vols. (Bonn: E. Weber, 1895–98), II, 346.

Mark 1:24; Luke 1:35; John 4:34; 6:38; 8:29, 46; 15:10; 17:4; Acts 3:14; 22:14; Rom. 5:12f.; 1 Cor. 15:45; 2 Cor. 5:21; Heb. 4:15; 7:26; 1 Pet. 1:19; 2:21; 3:18; 1 John 2:1; 3:5). Finally, he is the One born of Mary, the Son of God in a wholly unique sense, who did not just begin to exist at his coming in the flesh, but who was with the Father from eternity (John 1:1; 8:58; 17:5; Rom. 8:3; 2 Cor. 8:9; Gal. 4:4; Phil. 2:6; Col. 1:15; Heb. 1:3). To obtain the result that the eternal Son of God would simultaneously be the Son of David, a human being descended from human beings, like us in all things, sin excepted, it was necessary for him to be supernaturally conceived by the Holy Spirit in Mary. It was the Son of God himself who in this way prepared for himself a human nature in Mary's womb. Though sent by the Father, he at the same time came by his own will and deed (John 3:13; 6:38). The supernatural conception, therefore, is not a matter of indifference and without value. It is most intimately tied to the deity of Christ, to his eternal preexistence, his absolute sinlessness, and is therefore of great importance for the faith of the church.[156]

Before we expand our discussion of this point, let us briefly indicate that such a religious interest does not depend on the theological construct that in and after the birth, Mary remained a virgin. We do not yet find this idea of Mary's continuing virginity during and after the birth of Jesus in the church fathers before Nicea.

Tertullian, Origen, and Irenaeus do not yet attest a virginity in childbirth,[157] and Tertullian also rejects the virginity after the birth.[158] The virginity in childbirth surfaces for the first time in the Protevangelium of James (not before AD 150), and was also known to Clement of Alexandria as the opinion of some.[159] But after Nicea, Mary's virginity both in and after childbirth was ever more clearly taught in connection with her motherhood of God (θεοτοκος, *deipara*) by Epiphanius, Jerome, Gregory of Nyssa, Ephraem, Ambrose, Augustine, and others and defended against the Apollinarians, Helvidius, Jovinian, and Bonosus.[160] The fifth ecumenical council (can. 6) took over from Epiphanius the title "perpetual virgin" (ἀειπαρθενος) for Mary, and the Lateran synod of 649 also established (can. 3) her

156. In addition to the literature cited above, cf. also A. Nebe, *Die Kindheitsgeschichte unseres Herrn Jesu Christi nach Matthäus und Lukas* (Stuttgart: Greiner & Pfeiffer, 1893); T. Zahn, *Das Evangelium des Matthäus,* 3rd ed. (Leipzig: Deichert, 1910); F. L. Godet, *A Commentary on the Gospel of St. Luke,* trans. E. W. Shalders and M. D. Cusin, 2nd ed. (New York: I. K. Funk, 1887); *K. F. Nösgen, "Die Geburtsgeschichte Christi in Lukas," *Die Studierstube* (1903); *Steudel, "Die Wahrheit von der Präexistenz Christi in ihrer Bedeutung für christliche Glauben und Leben," *Neue kirchliche Zeitschrift* (December 1900); J. Kreyher, *Die jungfräuliche Geburt des Herrn* (Gütersloh: Bertelsmann, 1904); R. H. Grützmacher, *Is Jezus bovennatuurlijke wijze geboren?* trans. from German by W. Back (Baarn: Hollandia Drukkerij, 1909); A. Thraen, *Conférences apologétiques et dogm.* (Paris, 1900), 51–161.

157. Tertullian, *On the Flesh of Christ*, 23; Origen, *Homilies in Luke,* trans. Joseph T. Leinhard (Washington, DC: Catholic University of America Press, 1996), homily 14; Irenaeus, *Against Heresies*, IV, 66.

158. Tertullian, *On the Flesh of Christ*, 7; idem, *Against Marcion*, IV, 19.

159. Clement of Alexandria, *Stromateis*, VII, ch. 16; cf. F. Loofs, *Dogmengeschichte*, 170, 315.

160. R. Bellarmine, "De sacr. euch.," *Controversiis*, III, ch. 6; D. Petavius, "De incarn.," *Op. theol.*, XIV, ch. 3ff.; F. A. von Lehner, *Die Marienverehrung in den ersten Jahrhunderten,* 2nd ed. (Stuttgart: Cotta, 1886), 120ff.

virginity during and after the birth of Jesus.[161] The term "perpetual virgin" (*semper virgo*) was also included in the Smalcald Articles, yet Lutheran and Reformed theologians still taught that the birth of Jesus had taken place in the usual way and that Mary's virginity after childbirth, though acceptable by reason of piety, was no article of faith and in any case had not been assumed by Mary by way of a vow. For the idea that Mary had given birth to Jesus while her womb remained shut (*utero clauso*), there is not a single word of evidence in Scripture. That she committed herself to virginity by a vow cannot be inferred from Genesis 3:15; Isaiah 7:14; Luke 1:34, and from certain so-called types (Judg. 6:36; 11:29; Dan. 2:34; Ezek. 44:2). Opinions are divided even today on the question whether Mary had still more children. Lightfoot[162] divided these opinions in three categories, calling them after Jerome, Epiphanius, and Helvidius. According to the first sentiment, the brothers of Jesus must be regarded as the sons of Clopas or Alphaeus, who was married to the sister of Jesus' mother, and were therefore his cousins. But this view seems hard to maintain against the strong statements of Scripture in Matthew 1:18, 25; 12:46–47; 13:55; Mark 3:21, 31; 6:3–4; Luke 2:7; 8:19; John 2:12; 7:3, 5; Acts 1:14; 1 Corinthians 9:5; and Galatians 1:19. According to the second sentiment, the brothers of Jesus were the sons of Joseph from a previous marriage and therefore his stepbrothers. According to the third sentiment, that of Helvidius, the brothers of Jesus were born after him from the marriage of Joseph and Mary. The issue is too complex to be treated here and dogmatically of secondary importance. Remarkable, however, is that while Catholics generally follow Jerome's opinion, numerous Protestants still today either lean to the same opinion or favor that of Epiphanius over that of Helvidius.[163]

[367] Things stand very differently with respect to the supernatural conception. It is of supreme importance for the person of Christ and therefore also of religious importance. Scripture attributes the conception of Jesus to the Holy Spirit or to "the power of the Most High" [Luke 1:35]. The Holy Spirit, the author of all physical, psychic, and pneumatic life,[164] is deemed—in Matthew 1:18, 20, as

---

161. Cf. Roman Catechism, I, 4, 8.

162. In a special essay on the brothers of Jesus in his commentary on the Epistle to the Galatians, J. B. Lightfoot himself opts for the second view, that of Epiphanius (*St. Paul's Epistle to the Galatians,* 10th ed. [London: Macmillan & Co., 1890]), 252–91.

163. J. Calvin on Luke 1:34; A. Polanus, *Syn. theol.,* VI, ch. 17; A. Rivetus, "Apol. pro S. Virgine Maria," *Op. theol.,* 601–744; D. Chamier, *Panstratiae catholicae* 4 vols. (Geneva: Rouer, 1626), II, 4, ch. 3; F. Turretin, *Institutes of Elenctic Theology,* XIII, 10; P. van Mastricht, *Theologia,* V, 10, 12; B. de Moor, *Comm. theol.,* III, 563, 716; J. Quenstedt, *Theologia,* III, 401; T. Zahn, *Forschungen zur Geschichte des neutestamentlichen Kanons und der altkirchlichen Literatur,* 10 vols. (Erlangen: Deichert, 1881–1929), VI, 328–63; idem, *Einleitung in das Neue Testament,* I, 73ff.; II, 74ff., considers the brothers of Jesus as sons of Mary and Joseph; Endemann, "Zur Frage über die Brüder des Herrn," *Neue kirchliche Zeitschrift* (1900): 833–62, considers them as sons of Clopas; J. B. Mayor, "Brethren of the Lord," *DB,* I, 320–26, also takes the position of Helvidius; C. Harris, "Brethren of Christ," *DC,* I, 232–36, takes that of Epiphanius. Cf. O. Zöckler, "Maria," *PRE*[3], XI, 309–36; A. Kuyper, *De vleeschwording des Woords* (Amsterdam: Wormser, 1887), 141ff.; Kohlbrugge denies that Mary remained a virgin; J. van Lonkhuijzen, *Hermann Friedrich Kohlbrügge en zijn Prediking* (Wageningen: Vada, 1905), 425.

164. Cf. H. Bavinck, *Reformed Dogmatics,* II, 261–64 (#213).

is evident from the preposition ἐκ—to be the efficient cause of that conception, while it is attributed in Luke 1:35 to the power that will proceed from God the Most High and come over Mary. From this it is evident that the activity of the Holy Spirit with respect to this conception did not consist in the infusion of any heavenly or divine substance in Mary but in a demonstration of power that made her womb fertile in the act of overshadowing her as with a cloud (cf. Exod. 40:34; Num. 9:15; Luke 9:34; Acts 1:8). When the ancient argument between "spermatists" and "ovists" is settled in favor of the latter—which, however, is as yet far from being the case[165]—then this activity of the Holy Spirit would also be physiologically more transparent. But however this may be, what is begotten in Mary is of the Holy Spirit as efficient cause, has its cause in the activity of the Holy Spirit, and not in the will of a man or of the flesh. Aside from Mary's impregnation, the Holy Spirit also brought about the sanctification of the child that would be born of her. It is something holy that is born of her and will be called Son of God, Son of the Most High (Luke 1:35).

At this point it is important to note that this activity of the Holy Spirit with respect to Christ's human nature absolutely does not stand by itself. Though it began with the conception, it did not stop there. It continued throughout his entire life, even right into the state of exaltation. Generally speaking, the necessity of this activity can be inferred already from the fact that the Holy Spirit is the author of all creaturely life and specifically of the religious-ethical life in humans. The true human who bears God's image is inconceivable even for a moment without the indwelling of the Holy Spirit.[166] In addition, in Christ the human nature had to be prepared for union with the person of the Son, that is, to a union and communion with God as that to which no other creature had ever been dignified. If humans in general cannot have communion with God except by the Holy Spirit, then this applies even more powerfully to Christ's human nature, which had to be unified with the Son in an entirely unique manner. This special union, which far exceeds and differs essentially from the immanence of God in his creatures, the manifestation of God in his people, makes a priori probable and even necessary a very special activity on the part of the Holy Spirit. But Scripture also expressly teaches it. Prophecy already announced that the Messiah would be anointed in a

165. R. Schäfer, *Die Vererbung* (Berlin: Reuther & Reichard, 1897). In recent years, some have attempted to defend the supernatural birth of Christ by applying the idea of so-called parthenogenesis (the development of eggs [into zygotes] without fertilization). Among others, E. Griffith-Jones, *The Ascent through Christ* (New York: Edwin S. Gorham, 1901; reprint, 1978), 262, cited by J. Orr, *Virgin Birth of Christ*, 221. The appropriateness of this application is questionable, but the asexual reproduction of many plants and animals has led to a remarkable conclusion: "The union of two sex cells is not the necessary condition for the establishment of a new individual" (E. G. G. Teichmann, *Der Befruchtungsvorgang, sein Wesen und seine Bedeutung* [Leipzig: Teubner, 1905], 67). In any case, Huxley's comment rings true: "The mysteries of the church are child's play compared with the mysteries of nature. The doctrine of the Trinity is not more puzzling than the necessary antinomies of physical speculation; virgin procreation and resuscitation from apparent death are ordinary phenomena for the naturalist" (cited by Orr, *Virgin Birth of Christ*, 221).

166. Cf. H. Bavinck, *Reformed Dogmatics*, II, 557–61 (#292).

special sense with the Holy Spirit (Isa. 61:1), and the New Testament tells us that Christ received that Spirit without measure (John 3:34). Not only did he receive the Spirit, but the Spirit descended on him at the baptism (Matt. 3:16), completely filled him (Luke 4:1, 18), led him into the wilderness and to Galilee (Matt. 4:1; Luke 4:14), gave him power to cast out demons (Matt. 12:18), to offer himself up to God without blemish (Heb. 9:14), to be designated Son of God in power by his resurrection as Lord with a glorified body (Rom. 1:4), just as he had become Son of David in the way of the flesh, thus to vindicate himself as such before the eyes of all (1 Tim. 3:16), to leave the earth and to ascend to heaven (1 Pet. 3:19, 22), and to manifest himself to his own as life-giving Spirit who is the Spirit and who works by the Spirit (1 Cor. 15:45; 2 Cor. 3:17–18).[167]

Put in this context, the conception by the Holy Spirit becomes abundantly meaningful. In terms of his human nature, from the very first moment, throughout his entire life right into the state of exaltation, Jesus had to be shaped into the Messiah, the Christ, Son of God Most High. He could not become this except κατα σαρκα, in the way of the flesh, by being born of a woman (Rom. 1:3; 9:5; Gal. 4:4), and precisely to this end, he could not be the product of the will of a human or of the flesh. What is born of flesh is flesh. Given that scenario, Jesus would perhaps have been David's son and heir of David's earthly kingdom, but not David's Lord, the Messiah, Son of God, designated to be king in the kingdom of God. And that he had been, hadn't he, from all eternity. Paul says that by the resurrection he had been designated Son of God and Lord (Rom. 1:4), but this does not rule out that already at and before his conception, he was the Son of God (Rom. 1:3), any more than that the sonship to which believers aspire in the future (Rom. 8:23) rules out that they already possess it now (Rom. 8:15). Christ was Son of God from eternity. He was in the beginning with God: he is the firstborn of all creatures. In that way, accordingly, he could not be procreated and brought forth by the will of a man. He was himself the acting subject who by the Holy Spirit prepared a body for himself in Mary's body. In the Old Testament, for that reason, he is therefore promised especially as the seed of the woman (Gen. 3:15), as the one given by God (Isa. 9:6), as the one raised up by the Lord (Jer. 23:5–6; 33:14–17), as a shoot from the trunk of Jesse (Isa. 11:1), as the son of an עַלְמָה (a young woman in general, specifically an unmarried one, Gen. 24:43; Exod. 2:8; Ps. 68:25; Song of Sol. 1:3; 6:8; Prov. 30:19) who will be called Immanuel (Isa. 7:14).[168] In that connection nothing further is said in the Old Testament about the manner of his conception—only that he will be the son of a woman and at the same time a gift and revelation of God. This is thus fulfilled in Christ. We will leave aside the difficult question whether Luke presents the genealogy of

---

167. J. Gloël, *Der heilige Geist* (Halle: M. Niemeyer, 1888), 113ff.

168. The story of Jesus' supernatural birth cannot, as Keim, Beyschlag, Harnack, and Lobstein believe, have originated from Isa. 7:14 (cf. above, 288–89 [#366]), but it is true that in the fact of that birth, people saw a fulfillment of Old Testament prophecy recorded in Isa. 7:14. Cf. Orr, *Virgin Birth*, 127–36.

Mary and whether Mary herself was of Davidic descent;[169] Jesus was counted a son of David by the reckoning of Joseph's lineage, not by that of Mary's. All the emphasis is on Joseph's Davidic descent, not only in Matthew (1:16, 20) but also in Luke (1:27; 2:4). Although Jesus was not the natural son of Joseph, through Mary, who was engaged to Joseph, he was civilly and legally the son of Joseph (Luke 2:27, 41, 48) and inherited from him the rights to David's throne. Also for that reason Joseph was warned by God to take Mary as his lawful wife, to act as head and father of the family, and in that capacity to give the child the name "Jesus" (Matt. 1:18–21). Thus Christ became David's son and simultaneously remained David's Lord.

The exclusion of the man from his conception at the same time had the effect that Christ, as one not included in the covenant of works, remained exempt from original sin and could therefore also be preserved in terms of his human nature, both before and after his birth, from all pollution of sin.[170] As subject, as "I," he did not descend from Adam but was the Son of the Father, chosen from eternity to be the head of a new covenant. Not Adam but God was his father. As a person he was not the product of humankind but himself came to humankind from without and entered into its ranks. And since he thus, in God's righteous judgment, remained exempt from all original sin, he could be conceived by the Holy Spirit and by that Spirit remain free from all pollution of sin. Conception by the Holy Spirit was not the deepest ground and final cause of Jesus' sinlessness, as many theologians say,[171] but it was the only way in which he who already

169. The church fathers were generally of the opinion that both Matthew and Luke presented the genealogy of Joseph, but to escape the difficulties inherent in this position, Anias of Viterbo (approx. 1490) put forth the idea that the first evangelist gave us the genealogy of Joseph and the third that of Mary (B. Weiss, *Das Leben Jesu*, I, 221, and others [see G. W. Bacon, "Genealogy of Jesus Christ," *DB*, II, 139]; cf. esp. P. Vogt, *Der Stammbaum Christi bei den heiligen Evangelisten Matthäus und Lukas* [Freiburg i.B.: Herder, 1907]). The words "from the house of David" in Luke 1:27 are then applied to the Virgin Mary, and Luke 3:23 is then understood as if it said "Jesus . . . being a son (as it was supposed, of Joseph, but in fact, through his mother Mary) of Eli." This explanation does not seem likely, though there are good grounds, on the basis of Luke 1:32, 69; 2:4–5, to posit a Davidic ancestry for Mary. Cf. G. W. Bacon, "Genealogy of Jesus Christ," *DB*, II, 137–41; and P. M. Barnard, "Genealogies of Jesus Christ," *DC*, I, 636–39; J. M. Heer, *Die Stammbäume Jesu nach Matthäus und Lukas* (Freiburg: Herder, 1910).

170. Peculiar is the view held by Kohlbrugge that the conception by the Spirit consisted not in the Spirit's making Mary pregnant or sanctifying something in her but in uniting himself with Mary's spirit so that she obediently accepted the angel's message, completely submitted to the divine will, and by this faith became pregnant and brought her child to term. Thus Jesus was conceived by Mary's faith and is therefore "the pure fruit of faith." This peculiar view is linked in Kohlbrugge to his doctrine of the image of God as an element in which Adam lived, as a state in which he was placed by God; to his doctrine of the incarnation, which consisted in the assumption of a sinful human nature; and to his doctrine of satisfaction, whose main feature is that, despite all temptation and opposition, Christ by faith maintained himself to the end in the state he occupied as the Son of God. Cf. Dr. J. van Lonkhuijzen, *Kohlbrügge*, 423ff.

171. R. Rothe, *Theologische Ethik*, 2nd rev. ed., 5 vols. (Wittenberg: Zimmerman, 1867–71), §§533ff.; J. Müller, *The Christian Doctrine of Sin*, trans. Rev. Wm. Urwick, 5th ed., 2 vols. (Edinburgh: T&T Clark, 1868), II, 535; J. H. A. Ebrard, *Apologetics*, trans. William Stuart and John Macpherson, 2nd ed., 3 vols. (Edinburgh: T&T Clark, 1886–87), I, 4–10.

existed as a person and was appointed head of a new covenant could now also in a human way—in the flesh—be and remain who he was: the Christ, Son of God the Most High.[172]

CHRIST'S TRUE HUMANITY

[368] As a result of this conception by the Holy Spirit and birth from Mary, the Son of God became a true and complete human person. His humanity, however, was no less vigorously contested than his deity. The Gnostics, in virtue of their dualism, could not recognize it and therefore stated that the aeon Christ had only assumed a phantom body (Saturninus, Marcion). Or that he had brought with him from heaven a glorious spiritual body and had only passed through Mary like water through a conduit (Valentinus, Bardesanes). Or that at his descent he had indeed formed a body for himself from the elements of the earth and suffered therein, but that upon his return to heaven, he had dissolved and abandoned it (Apelles). Or that he had only temporarily at his baptism descended on the man Jesus and before his suffering again abandoned the latter (Cerinthus). Or that he had exchanged himself with Simon of Cyrene before the suffering and abandoned the latter to death by crucifixion (Basilides). Or that Christ, the impassible Jesus who had already descended from the realm of light to Adam and only appeared on earth in a phantom body, must be clearly distinguished from the passible Jesus, who was the son of a poor widow and an emissary of the devil and, since he opposed Christ, was nailed by the latter to the cross (Mani).

All these ideas were propagated in medieval sects and, under the influence of pantheistic mysticism, kabbalistic theosophy, and modern nature philosophy, in the age of the Reformation came to new and extensive dominance among the Anabaptists. They, too, taught that Christ could not assume his human nature from Mary, from Adamitic humanity, because he would then necessarily have to be a sinner. But he assumed it from eternity out of himself, hence brought his body with him from heaven, and passed through Mary as through a channel (Hoffmann, Menno Simons; cf. the related idea of an eternal divine corporeality in the Kabbalah with its Adam Cadmon in Swedenborg, Dippel, Detinger, Petersen). Or he formed for himself this heavenly invisible corporeality from eternity out of the eternal maiden, the Divine Eve, the wisdom of God, and in that way already immediately after the fall dwelt in Adam, Abel, and others and then made it visible and mortal through conception and birth from Mary (Weigel). Or he assumed that glorious human nature immediately at the creation

---

172. A. Polanus, *Syn. theol.*, XI, 13; F. H. R. Frank, *System der Christlichen Wahrheit*, II, 109ff.; J. Orr properly argues: "It is objected that birth from a Virgin does not itself secure sinlessness. But turn the matter round, and ask: Does not perfect sinlessness, on the other hand, imply a miracle in the birth?" Indeed, in the words of A. B. Bruce: "A sinless man is as much a miracle in the moral world as a Virgin birth is a miracle in the physical world." Those who deny the supernatural conception of Jesus generally tend to deny his divinity and sinlessness as well (J. Orr, *The Virgin Birth*, 189ff.).

from Adam before the fall, who at that point still possessed a refined heavenly corporeality, in order later to clothe it from Mary with a weak and mortal humanity (Antoinette Bourignon, Poiret, Barclay). Or he formed his human nature from Mary, not from the carnal but from the regenerate Mary, who by her union with divine wisdom had received a holy divine element within herself and had recovered the maidenly essence from Adam before the fall (Schwenckfeld and others).[173] To us these ideas seem bizarre. Yet in other forms they express nothing but what modern philosophy since Kant and Hegel, with their split between the ideal Christ and the historical Christ, has proposed. The ideal Christ is the eternal Logos, absolute reason, the *one* substance, which eternally realizes itself in the world and cannot pour out its fullness in a single individual, but assumes human nature in humankind as the Son of God. The historical Jesus, however, is not the true essential Christ; in the process of incarnation, he forms an admittedly important, yet a merely passing, moment. He was a weak, mortal, sinful human who, though he revealed the idea of the true Christ, absolutely did not coincide with him and is not one with him.[174]

It requires no long argument to demonstrate that Scripture is diametrically opposed to the above views. Promised under the Old Testament as the Messiah who is to come as a descendant of a woman of Abraham, Judah, and David, he is conceived in the fullness of time by the Holy Spirit in Mary (Matt. 1:20) and born of her, of a woman (Gal. 4:4). He is her son (Luke 2:7), the fruit of her womb (Luke 1:42), a descendant of David and Israel according to the flesh (Acts 2:30; Rom. 1:3; 9:5), sharing in our flesh and blood, like us in all things, sin excepted (Heb. 2:14, 17–18; 4:15; 5:1); a true human, the Son of Man (Rom. 5:15; 1 Cor. 15:21; 1 Tim. 2:5), growing up as an infant (Luke 2:40, 52), experiencing hunger (Matt. 4:2), thirst (John 19:28), weeping (Luke 19:41; John 11:35), being moved (John 12:27), feeling grief (Matt. 26:38), being furious (John 2:17), suffering, dying. For Scripture it is so much an established fact that Christ came in the flesh that it calls the denial of it anti-Christian (1 John 2:22). And it teaches that Christ assumed not only a true but also a complete human nature. Arius, denying this, said that the Logos, itself a creature after all, could not become human but merely appeared in human form and to that end assumed a body but not a soul.[175] Apollinaris, on the other hand, wanted above all to maintain that Christ was not merely a Logos-illuminated human but that he was himself God and his work divine. So he arrived at the doctrine that the Logos had assumed an animated human body without a spirit (pneuma) and that he himself took the place of that spirit (pneuma).[176] But Scripture clearly states that Jesus was completely human

173. For all these opinions on the human nature of Christ, cf. I. A. Dorner, *The Person of Christ*; also see the dogma-historical volumes of Harnack, Seeberg, Loofs, and Schwane.

174. G. Runze, *Katechismus der Dogmatik* (Leipzig: J. J. Weber, 1898), §78.

175. According to his opponents, Arius viewed Christ's body as a σῶμα ἄψυχον, F. Loofs, *Dogmengeschichte*, 236.

176. F. Loofs, *Dogmengeschichte*, 226ff.; G. Krüger, "Apollinaris," *PRE*³, I, 671–76.

and ascribes to him all the constituents of human nature, not only a body (Matt. 26:26; John 20:12; Phil. 3:21; 1 Pet. 2:24), flesh and blood (Heb. 2:14), bones and a side (John 19:33–34), head, hands, and feet (Matt. 8:20; Luke 24:39) but also a soul (Matt. 26:38), spirit (Matt. 27:50; Luke 23:46; John 13:21), consciousness (Mark 13:32), and a will (Matt. 26:39; John 5:30; 6:38; etc.). Apollinarianism, accordingly, has at all times been condemned by the Christian church and Christian theology. They understood the important issue involved in the matter: "For the whole Christ assumed the whole me that he might grant salvation to the whole me, for what is unassumable is incurable."[177]

The denial of the true and complete human nature always results from a certain dualism. The σαρξ, "matter," is then by nature sinful and cannot be a constituent of the true Christ. Christ, accordingly, derived his substance not from the sensible, material world but from the invisible heavenly essential being that is in God, in himself, in the divine wisdom, in the unfallen Adam or the regenerate Mary. The connection between this ideal Christ and the historical Jesus, therefore, can only be accidental and mechanical. No true unity is achieved; neither, therefore, is there true communion between God and humanity, God and the world, creation and re-creation, nature and grace, the eternal and the temporal. The heavenly and the earthly remain forever caught up in a dualistic relationship.

Among the Gnostics and the Anabaptists all this is clear. But however strange it may sound, this same dualism is also integral to the modern pantheistic philosophy, which loves to trick itself out with the name monism. It is an axiom of this philosophy, after all, that the idea cannot fully pour itself out in a single individual; that is, no oneness, no communion between God and a human is possible. To attain to communion with God, the individual must lose himself, must erase his personality, must dissolve like a wave in the ocean of the All. God and humans, eternity and time, especially holiness and finiteness, are at odds with each other. The finite is by its very nature deficient, imperfect: sin is a necessity. It is for that reason that Hegel, Strauss, Baur, and others cannot maintain the sinlessness of Jesus.[178] A finite individual cannot be perfect and enjoy full communion with God. This pantheism believes, however, that it can make up in another way for what it took away earlier. It attributes to the whole what it took away from the parts: not one single human being but humankind is the true Christ, the Son of God. Humankind enjoys supreme union and communion with God; in it God assumes human nature. This compensation, however, is merely apparent and actually futile. Not only does the human race consist solely of individuals and is the All no different than the sum of its parts, but neither is it true that the All, that humanity as a whole, is closer to God than the individual person. Though Goethe

177. John of Damascus, *The Orthodox Faith*, III, 6; P. Lombard, *Sent.*, III, 2; D. Petavius, "De incarn.," V, ch.11.

178. Hegel in I. A. Dorner, *Person of Christ*, V, 146ff.; D. F. Strauss, *Die Christliche Glaubenslehre*, II, 164; B. Weiss, *Das Leben Jesu*, II, 716–18; F. C. Baur, *Die christliche Lehre von der Dreieinigkeit und Menschwerdung*, III, 963ff.

wrote: "If you want to familiarize yourself with the infinite, immerse yourself in all the dimensions of the finite," the endless is something very different from the infinite; eternity is something totally different from the inexpressible sum of all the moments of time, and perfection something totally different from the totality of all imperfections. Even if pantheism trades off the individual for humanity, and the part for the whole, it has not gained a thing. It leaves completely unexplained the transition from the infinite to the finite, from eternity to time, from God to the world, and for explanation offers nothing but words and images.[179] If God cannot become man in one person, neither can he do so in all persons. Against this dualistic and atomistic viewpoint, Scripture posits the organic one. In the one, God comes to all, not in appearance but in reality. There is one mediator between God and humankind, Christ Jesus, himself human [1 Tim. 2:5]. But for that very reason his true and complete humanity is as important as his deity. If even one essential constituent in the human nature of Christ is excluded from true union and communion with God, there is an element in creation that remains dualistically alongside and opposed to God. Then there is an eternal ὕλη—"matter." Then God is not the Almighty, Creator of heaven and earth. Then the Christian religion is not truly catholic. For what is unassumable is incurable.

DIVINE AND HUMAN UNITED

[369] Thus God and man are united in Christ. While Scripture does not speak the language of the later theology, materially it contains what the Christian church confesses in its doctrine of the two natures. "Pauline Christology," says Holtzmann, "is of course a first approach to the church doctrine of the two natures."[180] For according to Scripture, the Word that was with God and was himself God became flesh (John 1:14). He who was the reflection of God's glory and the exact imprint of God's very being has become partaker in our flesh and blood and like us in all things (Heb. 1:3; 2:14). God sent his own Son into the world, who was born of a woman (Gal. 4:4). Though existing in "the form of God," he "emptied himself, taking the form of a slave" (Phil. 2:7). From the fathers, according to the flesh (κατα σαρκα), comes the Messiah, who is over all, God blessed forever (Rom. 9:5). Though the image of the invisible God, the firstborn of all creation, he is nevertheless also the firstborn from the dead (Col. 1:13–18); though son of David, he is simultaneously David's Lord (Matt. 22:43); even though walking about on earth, he still continues to be "in the bosom of the Father" (John 1:18), "the one who is in heaven" (John 3:13),[181] and existed before Abraham was (John 8:58); in a word, the fullness of deity dwells in him bodily (σωματικως, Col. 2:9). Every moment in Scripture, divine as well as human predicates are attributed to

179. Cf. H. Bavinck, *Reformed Dogmatics*, II, 412–15 (#252).

180. H. J. Holtzmann, *Lehrbuch der neutestamentlichen Theologie*, II, 75; A. Drews, *Christ Myth*, 103.

181. Ed note: Cf. E. Nestle, *Novum Testamentum Graece*, 27th ed., note at John 3:13 for the alternate reading, ὁ ὢν ἐν τῷ οὐρανῷ.

the same personal subject: divine and human existence, omnipresence and [geographical] limitation, eternity and time, creative omnipotence and creaturely weakness. What else is this but the church's doctrine of the two natures united in one person?

Modern theology, however, has a profound aversion to a part of this doctrine of the two natures, considers it the height of absurdity, and replaces it with "two-sidedness,"[182] with a "duality of perspectives,"[183] with the doctrine of two successive states before and after the resurrection,[184] with that of idea and appearance,[185] and especially with the doctrine of immanence, according to which God dwells in Christ in a special manner and reveals himself to us through him. This view can in turn be developed in either a more theistic or a more pantheistic direction. In the former, all the emphasis falls on the uniqueness of Jesus' person, sometimes so strongly that the revelation that comes to us in nature and history is denied and religion is rigorously divorced from all metaphysics. In the other, the person of Christ is put in the context of evolution, which offers a view of the whole world and sees him as the flower and crown of humankind. The first trend can be observed in Ritschl and his school and is under Kantian influence. The other trend found its voice especially in *The New Theology* of R. J. Campbell and underwent the influence of Hegel and Darwin. These two schools are both interested in making Jesus known not only as teacher and example but specifically as a special revelation of God. They try to maintain, not his deity, except as a value judgment, but his divinity: although Christ was not God in the sense of the church's doctrine, he was *in God,* full of God, and God dwelt in him as in no other creature. Hence this divinity of Christ did not consist in that he was the Logos, the Son of God in a metaphysical sense, who was with the Father from eternity, nor that in his person he shared in the metaphysical attributes of omnipresence, omnipotence, omniscience, and so on. Rather, his divinity consisted in the fact that he was one with the Father in a *moral* sense, fulfilled God's will, founded his kingdom on earth, and manifested to us God's love in his person and work.[186] In that sense, as they put it, prototypical humanity and ectypical divinity are one.[187] "Humanity is divinity viewed from below; divinity is humanity viewed from above."[188] "Every son of man is potentially also a son of God, but the union was deepest and completest in the Galilean. The humanity of God, the divinity of man is the essence of the Christian revelation. It was truly a manifestation of Immanuel."[189]

---

182. H. J. Holtzmann, *Lehrbuch der neutestamentlichen Theologie*, II, 65, 94.

183. O. Pfleiderer, *Grundriss*, §129; F. Nitzsch, *Lehrbuch der evangelischen Dogmatik*, 513.

184. H. Schultz, *Die Lehre von der Gottheit Christi*, 417.

185. A. Schweizer, *Christliche Glaubenslehre*, II, 12.

186. So also Kaftan, though he does want to retain the name "God" for Christ, *Dogmatik*, 427, 430–31; cf. C. Stange, *Der dogmatische Ertrag der Ritschlschen Theol.*, 110ff.

187. H. J. Holtzmann, *Lehrbuch der neutestamentlichen Theologie*, II, 94.

188. R. J. Campbell, *New Theology*, 67.

189. O. Lodge, *The Substance of Faith Allied with Science* (London: Meuthen, 1907), 87, 89.

But all these views seriously diverge from what Scripture teaches about the person of Christ. One may feel some sympathy for the attempt to do justice to the person of Christ—more than occurred in eighteenth-century rationalism—but one cannot for that reason close one's eyes to the profound difference that exists between this doctrine of the divine human being Jesus and the scriptural confession of Christ as the only begotten Son of God. Although it is true, especially in Paul, that only through his resurrection did Christ enter into full sonship (Rom. 1:4; cf. Acts 2:36; 5:30), become Lord from heaven and life-giving Spirit (1 Cor. 15:45; 2 Cor. 3:17), and receive a name above every name (Phil. 2:9), Paul does not for that reason in any way deny that also before his incarnation Christ already possessed a personal divine existence (2 Cor. 8:9; Phil. 2:6; Col. 1:15–17) and was God's own Son (Rom. 1:3; 8:32; Gal. 4:4). The doctrine of the two natures is something very different from the doctrine of two dimensions or two states in the life of Christ. In Scripture Jesus does not bear all those glorious attributes because, on the one hand, as a human being he devoted himself completely to God and thus proved himself a true human and, on the other hand, as that same human being he perfectly revealed the love of God,[190] but because he really was God and human in one person. Human beings, however elevated they may be in a religious and ethical sense, cannot and may not—surely according to the rigorous monotheism of Holy Scripture—bear the divine attributes that Scripture ascribes to Christ. It is telling, therefore, that those who replace the doctrine of the two natures with that of the two dimensions or that of the two states cannot and dare not in any way speak of Christ as Scripture does. The names "God," "God's Son," "Logos," "image of God," "firstborn of all creatures," and so on are therefore all robbed of their scriptural meaning and either construed very differently or completely abandoned.[191] When modern theology assumes Jesus to have only a human nature, it can honor him neither on his religious side as the revelation of the love of God, nor in the state of exaltation in which he is said to have been made Lord, with the names that Scripture attributes to him. Its exegesis, supposing it were correct, would not be of the least benefit to its own Christology. For the subject no longer exists if Jesus is only a human being and not the eternal and only Son of God as well.[192]

190. H. Schultz, *Die Lehre von der Gottheit Christi*, 338.

191. Some followers of Ritschl indeed did try to maintain Jesus' deity. But since this was no more than an office-related and honorary title, it seemed to others to be close to an untrue and inappropriate use of language. Häring, though he believes this language to be still somewhat "justified," finds it unnecessary and more calculated to produce division than unity (*Christian Faith*, II, 592).

192. Prof. Bruining grants Jesus important historical significance but arrives at a position in conflict with the modern Christology in *Teyler's Theologisch Tijdschrift* 1 (1903): 426–58. All who, in some sense or other, want to maintain a similar Christology can choose from the following options (references that follow are taken from G. A. van den Bergh van Eysinga, *Christusbeschouwingen onder Modernen*): (a) distance it completely from the historical Jesus, and create of him their own religious, ethical, and social ideal (R. Hugenholtz, "De Christologie en de huidige godsdienstwetenschap," 45–78); (b) extrapolate from the centuries of Jesus' influence on the religious and moral life of his followers to his historical existence and see in his life the embodiment and

In order to do justice to all the scriptural data concerning the person of Christ, [Christian] theology arrived gradually at the two-natures doctrine. It did not put this doctrine forward as a hypothesis, nor did it intend it as an explanation of the mystery of Christ's person. In it, it only summed up, without mutilation and diminution, the whole scriptural doctrine of Christ and thereby maintained it against the errors that cropped up both to the left and to the right: in Ebionitism and Gnosticism, Arianism and Apollinarianism, Nestorianism and Eutychianism, Adoptionism and Monotheletism, and in modern times in the doctrine of Rothe and Dorner on the becoming "God-man" and in the kenosis doctrine of Gess and others. Nestorianism was a product of the Antiochian school. It had its start in the thinking of Diodore of Tarsus and Theodore of Mopsuestia, and was later developed by Nestorius so that the eternal and natural Son of God was distinct from and other than the son of David who was born of Mary. For, as Nestorius argued, there is a difference between the temple and he who lives in it; between him who was in the form of God and him who went about in the form of a servant; between God and man in Christ, both of whom exist personally. Mary, therefore, cannot be called "mother of God" (θεοτοκος), and the human being born of her is not the eternal Son of God but his adopted Son (Adoptionism). The union between God and man in Christ is not a natural but a moral union, like that between a man and a woman in marriage, not a union (ενωσις) but a conjunction (συναφεια) of two natures. The indwelling of God in Christ does not differ in kind but only in degree from that in believers; it increased to the degree that the man Jesus advances in virtue and increasingly becomes an organ and instrument, a temple for and garment of deity to the extent that it is God-

---

revelation of God's love and power (A. W. van Wijk, 81–32); (c) emphasize that Jesus' existence and life can be known in its major outline, notwithstanding historical criticism, and that he can be called the "Christ" by us because he is the founder of a spiritual kingdom of God; in other words, he believed in the progress of the human race, a progress that cannot be imagined in any way other than through the message he proclaimed (C. J. Niemeyer, 135–83); (d) honor Jesus as the Christ because he was not only a religious redeemer but also the one who delivers from social and political distress, the one who renewed our earthly (human) relationships (J. A. Bruins, 187–222); (e) treat Christian doctrine in Hegelian fashion by representing a speculative interpretation in which the Father represents the Divine *above* nature as Creator; Christ without any connection to the historical Jesus becomes the revealed God, the Divine *in* nature as the soul and essence of things; and the Holy Spirit is the Divine that elevates itself *above* the natural *in* nature, and re-creates nature to become the kingdom of God (G. A. van den Bergh van Eysinga, 225–71).

All these perspectives oscillate between the historical Jesus and the philosophical (ideal) Christ, depending on the degree to which their proponents are inclined to be more critical or more mystical. For the historically inclined, Jesus is primarily a teacher and example who has no claim on the name "Christ"; for the others, Christ is primarily a religious, or rather, philosophic, idea that has only accidental connection to the historical Jesus. Scripture, by contrast, distinctively insists that the historical Jesus of Nazereth *is* the very same Christ, the Son of the living God. Hugenholtz (65) acknowledges that according to Paul it is most clear how the Christ ideal is dependent on the historical Jesus. However, this conviction [he believes] is singularly wrong and has been thoroughly discredited by, among others, J. Weiss (*Paulus und Jesus* [Berlin, 1909]; ET: *Paul and Jesus*, trans. H. J. Chaytor [New York: Harper, 1909]) even though Hugenholtz does not agree with Weiss that Paul knew Jesus personally.

possessed (θεοφορος).[193] Related to this view in recent times is Dorner's teaching that the Logos gradually and increasingly communicates himself to the man Jesus and enters into a more organic union with him to the degree the latter develops morally under the former's influence.[194]

This entire view is condemned by Scripture. Scripture ascribes all kinds of and very different predicates to Christ but always to one and the same subject, the one undivided "I" who dwells in him and speaks out of him. It also specifically says, not that the Logos dwelt in a human being, but that the Logos became flesh (John 1:14). A person is what he or she has become. If the Son of God became a human being, he is himself human. Many things can be predicated of a person but never another person. In one respect or another, one can say of a multiplicity of humans that they are one, but one can never say of one person that he or she is the other. A husband and a wife are one flesh, but the husband is never the wife or vice-versa. Therefore, if the human subject in Christ was another than the Logos, Scripture could never have said that the Logos became, and therefore is, flesh. In Nestorius, accordingly, the union between God and man in Christ is not a personal and a natural one but a moral union; however increasingly the two become morally one, they perpetually remain two distinct subjects. And even this moral union is not a starting point but an ultimate goal and result. It is not even, as in Origen, the fruit of the merits of the preexistent soul (one that did not fall but in its preexistence achieved union with the Logos),[195] but gradually comes about in the earthly life of Jesus and depends on a variety of conditions. It only differs in degree from God's union with other people; that is, Christ loses his wholly unique place: he is only a person in whom God manifests himself more than in others. The idea of the "God-man" is lost, and the work of redemption is undermined. Nestorianism is akin to Deism and Pelagianism.

Chalcedon, accordingly, correctly pronounced that the union of the divine and the human nature in Christ was without division (ἀδιαιρετος) and without separation (ἀχωριστος). But over against the opposing school, it maintained with equal firmness that the union was without change (ἀτρεπτος) and without confusion (ἀσυγχυτος). Over against Nestorius, Cyril maintained that the union in Christ was not a moral one, but a union in "nature" or in "substance," a "natural union." But since he did not yet distinguish the words προσωπον (person), ὑποστασις (substance), and φυσις (nature) as clearly as later theologians did, he did not hesitate to speak of "two natures" in Christ while also occasionally saying that "out of two natures" Christ had become one, that in fact he is one nature (μια φυσις), and that the divine and the human natures have united in him "into one thing,"

193. J. Schwane, *Dogmengeschichte*, II, 317ff. In recent years, with new discoveries, Nestorius's own views have become much better known; cf. F. Loofs, *Nestoriana: Die Fragmente des Nestorius* (Halle a.S.: M. Niemeyer, 1905); idem, "Nestorius," *PRE*³, XIII, 736–49; idem, *Dogmengeschichte*, 289ff.; J. F. Bethune-Baker, *Nestorius and His Teaching: A Fresh Examination of the Evidence* (Cambridge: Cambridge University Press, 1908).

194. I. A. Dorner, *System of Christian Doctrine*, §§102ff.

195. Origen, *On First Principles*, II, 6, 3; idem, *Against Celsus*, VI, 47.

"into one being." This was open to misunderstanding and in fact misunderstood by Eutyches, according to whom, after and through the union, each of the two natures lost its own peculiar properties, and they were changed and transformed into one new divine-human nature.[196]

Related to this Monophysitism, in modern times, is the kenosis doctrine. It had its origin in the Lutheran doctrine of the communication of proper qualities (*communicatio idiomatum*), was further developed by Count von Zinzendorf,[197] and then, in the nineteenth century, under the influence of the philosophy of Schelling and Hegel (who adopted the idea of "becoming" in God), defended with ardor by many theologians as the only possible explanation of the person of Christ. It means that at his incarnation the Logos divested himself of all his divine attributes, including the immanent ones, or at least the transcendent ones, descended to the level of pure potentiality, and from there again gradually in union with the human nature developed into a divine-human person.[198] But this theory as well is as unacceptable as that of Dorner. Scripture knows only one person, one subject, one Christ, yet ascribes to him two kinds of attributes, divine and human. He is Logos and became flesh; according to the flesh, he is stock of Israel, yet God overall, forever praised [Rom. 9:5]. Now whether, as was done in the past, one lets the human nature change into the divine, or, as is done today, one lets the divine nature empty itself down to the level of the human, or lets the two natures merge in whole or in part into a third, a mixed something—always, in pantheistic fashion, the boundary between God and humanity is erased and the idea of the "God-man" falsified. The Monophysite and kenotic doctrine is at odds with the immutability of God, with all the attributes and the essence of God, and similarly with the nature of the creature, of the finite human being. A deity or a divine attribute that is purely a "potentiality" and not "actual" is inconceivable; and a human being who by development can appropriate the divine nature ceases to be a creature and passes out of time into eternity, the finite into the infinite. Even the very idea of a "God-man" in whom the union of two natures has been replaced by the mingling of the two is an anomaly, with which no one can make any association whatever. Such a being cannot be the mediator between God and humankind, since he is neither. He cannot truly bring about union, reconciliation, and communion between the two, since by the mixing of the two natures, he himself is different from both and a "third kind" of being (*tertium genus*).[199]

196. J. Schwane, *Dogmengeschichte*, II, 351ff.; F. Loofs, "Eutyches," *PRE*[3], V, 635–47; idem, *Dogmengeschichte*, 291ff., 297ff.

197. H. Plitt, *Zinzendorfs Theologie*, 3 vols. in 1 (Gotha: F. A. Perthes, 1869–74), II, 166ff.

198. See above, 262–64 (#358).

199. Cf. *Formula of Concord*, in J. T. Müller, *Die symbolischen Bücher der evangelisch-lutherischen Kirche*, 8th ed. (Gütersloh: Bertelsmann, 1898), 550, where kenosis is repudiated; I. A. Dorner, *Person of Christ*, V, 249–56; idem, *System of Christian Doctrine*, III, 332; idem, *Gesammelte Schriften aus dem Gebiet der systematischen Theologie* (Berlin: Hertz, 1883), 207–41; A. F. C. Vilmar, *Dogmatik*, 2 vols. (Gütersloh: C. Bertelsmann, 1874), II, 54; F. A. Philippi, *Kirchliche Glaubenslehre*, IV, 386; M. Kähler, *Die Wissenschaft der christlichen Lehre*, 3rd ed. (Leipzig: A. Deichert, 1905), 340; A. Ritschl, *Die christliche Lehre von der Rechtfertigung und Versöhnung*,

"NATURE" AND "PERSON"

[370] Theology, if it truly wants to be scriptural and Christian, cannot do better for now than to maintain the two-natures doctrine. In the process it may thoroughly convince itself of the inadequate character of its language, specifically also in its doctrine of Christ. But all other attempts undertaken up until now to formulate christological dogma and to bring it home to us fail to do justice to the riches of Scripture and the honor of Christ. Yet to be on its guard for these riches and that honor is theology's primary task. Whatever the objections that have been advanced in earlier and later times against the two-natures doctrine, it has the advantage that it does not neglect any of the scriptural data, maintains the name of Christ as the only mediator between God and humankind, and in addition still offers the plainest and clearest understanding of the mystery of the incarnation. This incarnation, after all, does not stand by itself in history. Granted, it is essentially different from all [other] facts and occupies a place uniquely its own, yet it is intimately connected with everything that took place before, alongside, and after itself. As we found earlier, its preparation and presupposition is the generation [by the Father], creation [in the image of God], revelation, and inspiration. Now it must be added, finally, that it is also integrally connected with the essence of religion. Religion is communion with God. Without it humans cannot be truly and completely human. The image of God is not a superadded gift but belongs to human nature. That communion with God is a mystical union. It far exceeds our understanding. It is a most intimate union with God by the Holy Spirit, a union of persons, an unbreakable and eternal covenant between God and ourselves, which cannot be at all adequately described by the word "ethical" and is therefore called "mystical." It is so close that it transforms humans in the divine image and makes them participants in the divine nature (2 Cor. 3:18; Gal. 2:20; 2 Pet. 1:4).

When this communion with God and humankind is truly—not as a fiction but as true reality—understood, its kinship with and analogy to the incarnation leap out at us. Those who truly confess generation, creation, immanence, revelation, inspiration, religion—that is, the communicability of God—have fundamentally also recognized the incarnation, not in the sense that the incarnation is a natural

4th ed., 3 vols. (Bonn: A. Marcus, 1895–1903), III, 377–81; H. Schultz, *Die Lehre von der Gottheit Christi,* 277ff.; R. A. Lipsius, *Dogmatik.,* §579; F. Loofs, "Kenosis," *PRE*[3], X, 246–63; P. Lobstein, "Études critiques de dogmatique protestante," *Revue de théologie et de philosophie* 24/2 (March 1891): 186ff.; idem, *Études christologiques* (Paris: Fischbacher, 1891); P. Chapuis, "La transformation du dogme christologique au sein de la théologie moderne," *Revue de théologie et de philosophie* 24/5 (September 1891): 426ff.; A. B. Bruce, *The Humiliation of Christ: Its Physical, Ethical, and Official Aspects,* 3rd ed. (Edinburgh: T&T Clark, 1889); E. H. Gifford, *The Incarnation: A Study of Philippians 2:5–11* (New York: Dodd, Mead & Co., 1897); W. Bright, *Waymarks in Church History* (London: Longmans Green, 1894); H. C. Powell, *The Principle of the Incarnation* (London: Longmans Green 1896); F. J. Hall, *The Kenotic Theory* (New York: Longmans Green, 1898); B. B. Warfield, "Recent Theological Literature," *Presbyterian and Reformed Review* 10 (1899): 701–25; J. H. Scholten, *De Leer der Hervormde Kerk,* 2nd ed., 2 vols. (Leyden: P. Engels, 1850–51), II, 385ff.

implication of the essence of religion but in the sense that the recognition of the one takes away all right to deny the other. For if the incarnation is impossible either from the side of God or from the side of humankind, then neither can religion truly consist in communion between God and human creatures.

But since religion in this sense has been disturbed by sin, there is no true, blessed communion between God and humanity. For that reason the union forged in Christ between the divine and the human nature had to be of a very special kind. It could not be identical with the religious relation between God and humanity, for its specific nature had to be the beginning, the first principle, the objective realization of true religion. A covenant is not something that can be improvised; it has to be made with a people in the person of its king or representative. Similarly, God, to make his communion with humankind a reality, united himself with it in Christ as its head. Christ, accordingly, is not an individual beside other individuals, but the head and representative of humanity, the second and last Adam, the mediator between God and humanity. Hence the union of the divine and the human nature in Christ also differs essentially from God's indwelling in his creatures and in believers. It is not a union of persons; it is a personal and substantial union; it is not a moral union like a marriage, not a matter of agreement in disposition and will, no communion of love alone. It is, however, a natural union (ἕνωσις φυσικη), as Athanasius and Cyril called it.[200] This is not to say that that union was necessary and automatically resulted from one of the two or from both natures; rather, it is so called because it is not moral in nature, but a union of natures in the person of the Son, not a natural but a personal union.[201] And the result of that union is not a new nature, nor even a new personality, but only the person of Christ as Christ. He who existed in the form of God from that time on existed also in the form of a man.

In virtue of its wholly unique nature, this union can only be conceived as a union of the person of the Son with an impersonal human nature. For if the human nature in Christ had its own personal existence, no union other than a moral one would have been possible. Then, too, Christ would be not personally divine but only a human living in close fellowship with God. Then Christ would also have been a specific human being with an individuality of his own, not the second Adam, head of the human race. He, however, could not be an individual beside others. His work did not consist in bringing back to communion with God the one individual person with whom he united himself; on the contrary, his assignment was to assume the seed of Abraham, to be head of a new humanity and the firstborn of many brothers. To that end he had to assume an impersonal human nature. This is not to be construed, with Athanasius and others, in the sense that Christ assumed human nature in its generality, in the sense of a Platonic idea, for this nature, though existing in humankind as a whole, does not exist by

---

200. Athanasius, *Against Apollinaris*, I, 8; Cyril, *The Anathemas*, 3.
201. D. Petavius, "De incarn.," *Op. theol.*, III, 4; F. Turretin, *Institutes of Elenctic Theology*, XIII, 6, 3.

itself in numerical oneness.[202] On the contrary, the human nature in Christ is very definitely an individual one to the degree that by it, though sharing in the same nature, he was distinguished from all other humans by certain characteristics. Yet this does not make Christ an individual alongside others, for the human nature had no personal existence in him alongside the Logos but was from the very beginning so prepared by the Holy Spirit for union with the Logos and for his work that in that Logos it could represent the entire human race and be the mediator of God for all humans of all the races and classes and age groups of all times and places.[203]

It is precisely this distinction between "nature" and "person," however, that encounters most resistance in both the doctrine of the Trinity and the doctrine of Christ and is therefore also the curse of most errors in both of these doctrines. Neither Nestorius nor Eutyches was able to appreciate this distinction and consequently reasoned either from the two natures to two persons or from the one person to one nature.[204] Christian theology, however, was led to this weighty distinction in both the doctrine of God and that of Christ. In God, they said, there is one nature and three persons; in Christ there is one person and two natures. The unity of the three persons in the divine being is in the full sense natural, consubstantial, coessential; the unity of the two natures in Christ is personal. This distinction is philosophically justified as well. "Nature" and "person" are not related, as in Hegel's philosophy, as essence and appearance, as potency and act, so that "nature," which is essentially one in all creatures, by an immanent force develops into "persons" in humans. But "nature" is the substratum, the presupposition, that by which a thing is what it is, the "principle by which"; and "person" is the subject not of a given nature in general but of a rational nature, the individual substance of a rational nature, the "principle which." "Person" is what exists in and for itself, the owner, possessor, and master of the nature, a completion of existence, sustaining and determining the existence of a nature, the subject that lives, thinks, wills, and acts through nature with all its abundant content, by which nature becomes self-existent and is not an accident of another entity.[205] This, now, is how Christ's human nature is united with the person of

202. J. Schwane, *Dogmengeschichte*, II, 369.

203. Gregory of Nyssa, Hilary, Basil, Ephraem, Apollinaris, and others; I. A. Dorner, *Person of Christ*, V, 23ff.; John of Damascus, *The Orthodox Faith*, III, 3, 6, 11; T. Aquinas, *Summa theol.*, III, qu. 4, art. 4; D. Petavius, "De incarn.," *Op. theol.*, V, 5; B. de Moor, *Comm. theol*, III, 776; B. Pictet, *Christian Theology*, trans. Frederick Reyroux (Philadelphia: Presbyterian Board of Publication, 1845), I, 552; M. Schneckenburger, *Zur kirchlichen Christologie*, 74ff.; A. Ritschl, *Rechtfertigung und Versöhnung*, III, 405; W. G. T. Shedd, *Dogmatic Theology*, II, 295.

204. Leontius of Byzantium already demonstrated that Nestorians and Eutychians proceeded from the same incorrect presuppositions but drew opposing conclusions from them. O. Bardenhewer, *Patrologie* (Freiburg i.B.: Herder, 1909), 507.

205. Schwane, *Dogmengeschichte*, II, 369ff.; J. Kleutgen, *Theologie der Vorzeit*, III, 71ff.; C. von Schäzler, *Das Dogma*, 3ff. In recent years there has been a significant amount of study devoted to the idea of personality; e.g., E. Pfennigsdorf, *Persönlichkeit* (Schwerin: Bahn, 1907); A. Richter, *Geschichtsphilosophische Untersuchungen*

the Son. The Son does not just become a person in and through human nature, for he was that from eternity. He needed neither the creation nor the incarnation to arrive at himself, to become a personality, a spirit, or a mind. The incarnation does mean, however, that the human nature that was formed in and from Mary did not for an instant exist by and for itself, but from the very first moment of conception was united with and incorporated in the person of the Son. The Son increated it within himself and, by creating, assumed it in himself.

Yet that human nature is not for that reason incomplete, as Nestorius and nowadays still Dorner assert.[206] For though it did not complete itself with a personality and selfhood of its own, it was nevertheless from the start personal in the Logos, who as subject lived, thought, willed, acted, suffered, died, and so on in and through it with all its constituents, capacities, and energies. The fact that it did not receive a distinct completion of existence of its own in an independent self was not the result of a deficiency but resulted from its purpose of being the human form of existence belonging to the Logos. "The assumed nature does not have its own proper personality, not because some perfection of human nature is wanting, but because something surpassing human nature is added, i.e., union to a divine person."[207]

Accordingly, the human nature in Christ is not coordinated with the Logos by a personality of its own but subordinated to the Logos. The two natures, indeed, are and remain "one thing and [then] another" (ἄλλο καὶ ἄλλο), but not "one person and [then] another" (ἄλλος καὶ ἄλλος). It is always the same person, the same subject, the same "I," who lives and thinks, speaks and acts through the divine and the human nature. The human nature is the tent in which the Son assumes residence; the garment that he himself prepared and put on; the form (μορφή) in which he has appeared to us; the instrument and organ that he has consecrated for himself and that, with divine wisdom, he employs for his office and work. "The human nature in Christ must be considered as though it were a kind of organ of the divine nature."[208] There is nothing here to which we need to take exception. Without in any way failing thereby to do justice to the self-activity of creatures, we confess that the whole world is an instrument of the revelation of God in which he simultaneously reveals himself to us and conceals himself from us. The church and all believers have no higher goal than to be at the service of God with their whole soul, their whole body, and all their strengths and to be an instrument in his hand. Then what objection would there be to the idea that in an even much greater measure—in an absolute sense—the human nature in

über den Begriff der Persönlichkeit (Lagansalza: H. Beyer & Söhne, 1907). This study, however, is of greater importance for ethics than for dogmatics and more for anthropology than for Christology.

206. I. A. Dorner, *Person of Christ*, V, 230.

207. T. Aquinas, *Summa theol.*, III, qu. 4, art. 2, ad 2.

208. T. Aquinas, *Compendium of Theology*, trans. Cyril O. Vollert (St. Louis: B. Herder Book Co., 1947), c. 212; idem, *Summa theol.*, III, qu. 19, art. 1; D. Petavius, "De incarn.," *Op. theol.*, IV, 8, 6; F. Turretin, *Institutes of Elenctic Theology*, XIII, 6–7.

Christ is the splendid, willing organ of his deity? How utterly the mystery of the union of the divine and human nature in Christ exceeds all our speaking and thinking of it. All comparison breaks down, for it is without equal. But it is, accordingly, the mystery of godliness, which angels desire to look into and the church worshipfully adores.

COMMUNICATION OF PROPERTIES

[371] Yet, as a serious objection to the two-natures doctrine, it is forever being advanced that it fails to do justice to the human nature of Christ and makes any human development in him an impossibility. Both Catholic and Lutheran Christology, in fact, give some ground for this objection. In the earlier dogmatics, the union of the two natures in Christ carried with it three consequences: the communication of proper qualities (*communicatio idiomatum*), the completion of a work (*apotelesmatum*), and the charismata. The first implied that in the incarnation the two natures along with all their attributes were communicated to the one person and the one subject who can therefore be described with divine and human natures. Accordingly, one can say that the Son of God was born, suffered, and died (Acts 20:28; 1 John 1:7) but also that the man Jesus Christ exists from eternity and descended from heaven (John 3:13). The second meant that the true works of the mediator or of redemption all bore a divine human character, that is, they all have as their efficient cause the one undivided personal subject in Christ; they were all performed by Christ with the cooperation of his two natures and with a double working (ἐνέργεια), and in the result nevertheless again form an undivided unity inasmuch as they are the work of one person. The third indicated that from the first moment of its existence the human nature of Christ was adorned with all kinds of splendid and copious gifts of the Holy Spirit.

These three effects of the union (*effecta unionis*) prompted significant disagreement.[209] The Lutherans took the communication of proper qualities to mean that not only the attributes of the two natures were communicated to the one [divine] person but those of the divine nature were also communicated to the human nature. By its union with the divine nature, the human nature was elevated to a position of divine omnipotence and omnipresence;[210] it received "singular, most excellent, super-great, supernatural, untraceable, unutterable, and heavenly prerogatives of majesty, glory, virtue, and power, which were not just created, finite gifts but divine and infinite endowments, such as the ability to make alive, omnipotence, omniscience, and discretionary omnipresence."[211] It is plain that this view of the communication of proper qualities completely robs the communication of gifts of its meaning: why should gifts be needed when

209. Cf. above, 256–59 (#357).
210. J. T. Müller, *Die symbolischen Bücher*, 679–80.
211. Müller, *Die symbolischen Bücher*, 685–86, 689, 691–92.

divine attributes are shared! While Lutheran Christology still speaks of gifts,[212] it actually does not know what to do with them[213] and no longer has room even for Christ's anointing with the Holy Spirit.[214]

Catholic scholars, on the other hand, while indeed teaching a communication of gifts and opposing the Lutheran doctrine of the communication of proper qualities, say that in virtue of the hypostatic union, the human nature of Christ, at the first moment of its conception, received a "copious supply of the Spirit of God and an abundance of spiritual gifts."[215]

The union of the two natures in Christ, after all, is so intimate that they interpenetrate and inwardly impact each other. The communication of proper qualities, accordingly, does not at all mean only that the attributes of the two natures may be ascribed as predicates to one and the same subject; it is not exclusively grammatical and logical in nature, but true and real. The concomitance of the two natures and their proper qualities is intrinsic and substantial, so that they do not run parallel to each other but as it were coinhere. As a result, God is humanized in Christ, and, conversely, the human nature in Christ is deified. It is indeed not the case that the attributes of the divine nature formally become the properties of the human nature, as is the position of Rome according to the Lutherans. These attributes do, however, inwardly impact human nature; flow over into human nature as a result of their excess energy; take that human nature to its apex; equip it with a plenitude of grace and truth, with all spiritual gifts and virtues; and thus make it a participant in the divine dignity, glory, and power and worthy of divine worship and veneration.[216] Both Lutheran and Catholic Christology, consequently, contain within them a docetic element. The purely human development does not come into its own in them. In reaction, theologians in the nineteenth century swung over to the other extreme and denied the deity of the Lord.

Reformed theologians, however, have so construed the communication of the gifts as to make possible a human development in Jesus. Although he was the second Adam, Christ was nevertheless another person. Adam was created as an adult, was given paradise as place of residence, and was not subject to suffering and death; Christ, however, was conceived by the Holy Spirit and born as a helpless baby. He was not placed in a paradise but came into a world that lies in the evil one; he was vulnerable to temptation on every side. He bore a nature that was susceptible to suffering and death. His was not the human nature of Adam before

212. Müller, *Die symbolischen Bücher*, 686.

213. I. A. Dorner, *Person of Christ*, IV, 368–71.

214. M. Schneckenburger, *Zur kirchlichen Christologie*, 30.

215. Roman Catechism, I, 4, 4.

216. P. Lombard, *Sent.*, III, 12–16; T. Aquinas, *Summa theol.*, III, qu. 7–26; D. Petavius, "De incarn.," *Op. theol.*, IX–XII, 1; *Theol. Wirceb.*, IV, 233–95; J. Kleutgen, *Theologie der Vorzeit*, III, 193–333; J. Heinrich, *Dogmatische Theol.*, VII, 689–775; M. J. Scheeben, *Handbuch der katholischen Dogmatik*, 4 vols. (1874–98; repr., Freiburg i.B.: Herder, 1933), III, 20ff., 157–261; H. T. Simar, *Lehrbuch der Dogmatik*, 420–28; C. Pesch, *Praelectiones dogmaticae*, 9 vols. (Freiburg: Herder, 1902–10), IV, 86–175; G. M. Jansen, *Theologia dogmatica specialis* (Utrecht, 1877–79), II, 640ff.; P. Mannens, *Theologiae dogmaticae institutiones*, II, 397–432.

the fall; rather, God sent his Son in the likeness of sinful flesh, that is, in flesh that was the same in form and appearance as sinful flesh (Rom. 8:3).

In virtue of this splendid doctrine of the communication of proper qualities, Reformed theology was able, better than any other, to maintain in addition to Christ's deity also his true and genuine humanity. In this regard it renders excellent service.

But among the Reformed there was lingering disagreement over the question whether the incarnation as such, aside from the condition of sin in which it occurred, was already an act of humiliation. On the one hand, one could appeal to the idea that the distance between God and humankind is so enormous that the assumption of human nature as such is already humiliating. But on the other, one could advance that in that case Christ would even now, glorified at the Father's right hand, be in a state of humiliation.[217] The controversy can best be settled by saying that the incarnation as such, without any further qualification, always was and remains an act of condescending goodness but not, strictly speaking, a step in the state of humiliation. It became this as a result of the fact that it was an *incarn*ation, the assumption of a weak human nature. There was no disagreement, after all, over the fact that Christ assumed a weak human nature, a nature that was subject to suffering and death, and that for the Son of God this was an act of humiliation. Scripture certainly establishes this point beyond the shadow of a doubt (Isa. 53:2–3; John 1:14; 17:5; 1 Cor. 2:8; 2 Cor. 8:9; Phil. 2:7–8; etc.). However, the moment we try to add up the things that are included in that weak human nature, the question becomes more difficult. Jesus most certainly needed a great variety of things: food, drink, rest, sleep, and so on, but these needs also characterized Adam before the fall. Conversely, it is hard to think that in his human nature Jesus was of himself susceptible to illness and death. He himself, after all, had the power to lay down his life (John 10:17) and was not automatically—aside from his will—subject to death. From ancient times, therefore, opinions on this issue were divided.

There was disagreement even over Jesus' external appearance. Some, like Origen, Chrysostom, Jerome, Ambrose, Augustine, and others, appealing to Psalm 45:2 ["You are the most handsome of men"], ascribed to him very good looks; others, such as Justin, Clement, Tertullian, and Basil, thought that he was physically without form or comeliness (Ps. 22:7; Isa. 53:2–3). Still others took an intermediate position or abstained from judgment.[218] Similarly, with respect to Jesus'

---

217. A. Kuyper, *De vleeschwording des Woords*, 38ff., 180ff.

218. Obviously, we have no true portrait of Christ. In the early centuries no likeness was made of him, but he was always represented by symbols, types, and monograms. The most ancient depictions, accordingly, differ greatly in the form they ascribe to Christ, but they are all idealistic. The ascetic trend that later emerged in the church often led artists to deny Christ all beauty of form and depict him accordingly. Still, idealism won the day and undoubtedly was more congruent with Holy Scripture, which ascribes to Jesus' appearance, words, and deeds an impressive majesty. Cf. C. Vitringa, *Doctr. Christ.*, V, 501; J. G. Walch, *Bibliotheca theologica selecta*, III, 439; W. Menzel, *Christliche Symbolik*, 2nd ed., 2 vols. (Regensburg: Manz, 1855), I, 177ff.; E. Riehm,

susceptibility to suffering and death, the Aphthartodocetae and the Phthartolatrae took opposing positions.[219] Now in this connection there was no doubt that the Son of God assumed a human nature that was susceptible to suffering and death. Otherwise his suffering and death would have been mere appearance, not real. Even Catholics and Lutherans have to acknowledge this. On the other hand, it is also true that Christ assumed this human nature altogether voluntarily and, abstractly speaking, always retained the right to lay this weak human nature down again or change it into a glorious nature that was above all suffering and death. To that degree, suffering and dying always remained a matter of his own free choice. He had and kept the power to take up or lay down his life. No one could cause him any sorrow or deprive him of his life unless he himself gave that person power to do this. He decided the hour and the power of darkness. But presupposing this will, we have to say that suffering and death for him were a natural given of the human nature he assumed. Hilary and others, however, frequently pictured the situation in reverse, seeing the unnatural in Christ's sorrow and suffering, and the natural in Christ's miracles.[220]

Although this can be construed in a positive sense, it does not take sufficient account of the fact that Jesus assumed a weak human nature and in that respect differed from Adam. But one may not infer from this that Christ was also susceptible to all kinds of illness, for though he did take upon himself the general consequences of sin—suffering and death—that now belong to human nature, he did not assume every particular illness, which is the consequence of special circumstances, a weak constitution, an irregular or imprudent lifestyle.[221] Also, the human nature in Christ was much more highly developed than was Adam's, for in the state of integrity there was simply no occasion for many emotions, such as anger, sadness, pity, compassion, and so on. But Christ did not just visit us with the inner movements of God's mercy; rather, in his human nature he opened for us the abounding world of the mind and the heart that did not and could not yet exist in Adam.

[372] In addition, there was in Christ a human faculty of knowing, intellectual development, an increase in wisdom and knowledge. Arians and Apollinarians, according to whom the Logos occupies the place of the spirit ($\pi\nu\epsilon\upsilon\mu\alpha$) in Christ, could not accept the presence of human knowledge in Christ. Monophysites, too,

---

Handwörterbuch des biblischen Altertums, I, 724; N. Müller, "Christusbilder," *PRE*[3], IV, 63–82; E. von Dobschütz, *Christusbilder: Untersuchungen zur christlichen Legende* (Leipzig: Hinrichs, 1909); G. A. Müller, *Die leibliche Gestalt Jesu Christi nach der schriftlichen und monumentalen Urtradition* (Graz: Verlagsbuchhandlung Styria, 1909); Höhne, "Wandlungen des Christusbildes bei seiner Wanderung durch die Geschichte," *Der Beweis des Glaubens* 40 (1904): 33–49; P. Dearmer, "Christ," *DC*, I, 308–16; J. Burns, *The Christ Face in Art* (New York: Dutton & Company, 1907); K. L. R. Jenner, *Christ in Art* (London: Meuthen & Co., 1906); G. D. J. Schotel, *Iets over de uitwendige gedaante van Jezus Christus* ('s Hertogenbosch: Gebroeders Muller, 1852).

219. F. Loofs, *Dogmengeschichte*, 303.

220. Hilary, in J. Schwane, *Dogmengeschichte*, II, 260.

221. T. Aquinas, *Summa theol.*, III, qu. 14; B. de Moor, *Comm. theol.*, III, 591; IV, 26; J. H. A. Ebrard, *Dogmatik*, §417; A. Kuyper, *De vleeschwording des Woords*, 116ff.

had to reject this presence but could equally well teach a kind of omniscience in Christ (that is, when Christ's human nature had been absorbed into the divine) as (in the opposite case) a kind of ignorance (Themistius, leader of the Agnoetae)[222] with an appeal to texts such as Matthew 20:32; 21:19; Mark 5:9; 13:32; Luke 2:52; 8:30; John 11:34. Over against these parties, the church fathers tended increasingly to present the human knowledge of Christ as perfect from the first moment on and insusceptible to increase. From them this sentiment passed over into Scholastic, Catholic, as well as Lutheran Christology. In consequence, they came into conflict with the clear pronouncements of Scripture cited above and had to resort to a docetic explanation. The true ground for this doctrine, accordingly, is only the "fittingness" that requires that God in fact had to give the human nature, which was so closely united with him, this gift of knowledge.[223] The Scripture passages to which they appeal (such as John 1:14; 2:24–25; 6:64; 13:3; Col. 2:3, 9) do not prove the contrary, inasmuch as they speak of the whole Christ, not specifically of his human nature, much less of the latter in its historical development.

The reaction of Reformed theologians was, first of all, that Christ's infused and acquired knowledge was not immediately complete but gradually increased; and, second, that Christ on earth was a pilgrim, not a comprehensive knower, that he walked by faith and hope, not by sight, that he did not yet share the "beatific knowledge" (*scientia beata*) here on earth. Naturally faith for Christ was not, as it is for us, trust in the grace and mercy of God, for this feature is something faith only obtained as a result of the state of sin in which we find ourselves. By nature, faith for Adam and Christ was nothing other than the act of clinging to the word and promises of God, a holding on to the Invisible One. And that is what Jesus did as well (Matt. 27:46; Heb. 2:17–18; 3:2). In the case of Christ, that faith and that hope were not wavering and hesitant but firm and strong. They kept him, the pioneer and perfecter of our faith, standing in the midst of temptation, enabling him, for the joy awaiting him as the reward for this labor, to endure the cross and to despise the shame (Heb. 12:2). Thus, there was an increase in wisdom and knowledge in Christ, as Scripture also clearly teaches, not only in Luke 2:40, 52 but in all situations in which Jesus asks about or investigates something (Mark 5:30; 6:38; 9:21; 11:13; etc.). The human consciousness in him, though having the same subject as the divine consciousness, only to a small degree knew that subject, that "I," indeed knew it as a whole but not exhaustively. Just as behind our limited consciousness there also lies within us a world of being, so behind the human consciousness of Christ there lay the depths of God, which could only very gradually and to a limited degree shine through that human consciousness.[224] From this, one may not infer, however, that in various domains Jesus

222. J. Schwane, *Dogmengeschichte*, II, 366; F. Loofs, *Dogmengeschichte*, 303.
223. J. Kleutgen, *Theologie der Vorzeit*, III, 251.
224. F. Gomarus, *Opera theologica omnia* (Amsterdam: J. Jansson, 1664), I, 196; G. Voetius, *Select. disp.*, II, 155ff.; F. Turretin, *Institutes of Elenctic Theology*, XIII, 12–13; B. de Moor, *Comm. theol.*, III, 804; C. Vitringa,

could err. This, admittedly, is currently being taught in broad circles to escape Jesus' authority in the matter of his view on demon possession, his eschatological predictions, and especially in relation to the Old Testament. But in so doing one violates the Christ himself. Granted, Jesus did not give instruction in any human science, nor did he come on earth for that purpose. He came to make known to us the Father and to carry out his work. But to that end he also needed to know that Father in his revelation and works and hence whether the Old Testament was, or was not, the Word of God. This was knowledge not of a purely scientific but of a religious nature, one that was of the greatest importance for the faith of the church. One who in this respect charges Jesus with error comes into conflict not only with his divine nature but also with his prophetic office and with all the testimonies in which he ascribes his teaching to the Father (John 7:16; 8:26, 28, 38; 12:49–50).[225]

In Christ, moreover, there is also moral development. Theodore of Mopsuestia, Nestorius, and all who take their point of departure in the human nature of Christ assume that through all kinds of struggle and temptation he perfected himself. Jesus was not positively holy. He did not bring with him the inability to sin (*non posse peccare*); on the contrary, they said, such an innate holiness is impossible and without ethical value. Instead, Jesus was a human being who brought with him the possibility of sinning, but by moral exertion and struggle actually kept himself free from all sins, developed himself ethically to the highest level, and made himself worthy of union with God.[226]

Doctr. christ., V, 246; H. Heppe, *Dogmatik der evangelischen reformierten Kirche* (Elberseld: R. L. Friedrich, 1861), 315; W. G. T. Shedd, *Dogmatic Theology,* II, 281, 307, 329; A. Kuyper, *De vleeschwording des Woords,* 152; idem, *Het Werk van den Heiligen Geest,* II, 281ff.; ed. note: ET: *The Work of the Holy Spirit,* trans. Henri de Vries, 3 vols. (New York: Funk & Wagnalls, 1900); C. Lucassen, "Der Glaube Jesu Christi," *Neue kirchliche Zeitschrift* (1895): 337–47; A. Meyer, "Der Glaube Jesu und der Glaube an Jesum," *Neue kirchliche Zeitschrift* (1900): 621–44.

225. Cf. H. Bavinck, *Reformed Dogmatics,* I, 394–402 (#107); H. Voigt, *Fundamentaldogmatik* (Gotha: F. A. Perthes, 1874), 527ff.; A. Tholuck, *Das Alte Testament im Neuen Testament,* 4th ed. (Gotha: F. A. Perthes, 1854); W. Caven, "The Testimony of Christ to the Old Testament," *Presbyterian and Reformed Review* 3 (1892): 401–20; P. Schwartzkopff, *Konnte Jesus irren?* (Giessen: J. Ricker, 1896); idem, *Die Irrtumslosigkeit Jesu Christi und der christliche Glaube* (Giessen: J. Ricker, 1897); L. Lemme, *Jesu Irrtumslosigkeit* (Berlin: Runge, 1907); J. Denney, "Authority of Christ," *DC,* I, 146–53; D. W. Forrest, *The Authority of Christ* (Edinburgh: T&T Clark, 1906).

226. J. Schwane, *Dogmengeschichte,* II, 319, 325; these same objections to Jesus' sinlessness return later in the rationalism of Kant, Fichte, Strauss, and others. Additional arguments are advanced, such as the claim that Jesus' temptations necessarily imply fallibility; that certain givens from his life present him as less than perfect, such as his baptism by John (Matt. 3:13), his relationship to his parents (Luke 2:49; John 2:4; Mark 3:33), his appearance in the temple (John 2:15; Matt. 21:12), his sharp rebukes of the Pharisees (Matt. 23:13), his sending demons into the swine (Matt. 8:31), his curse of the fig tree (Matt. 21:19)—especially noted by F. Pécaut, *La Christ et la conscience* (Paris: Cherbuliez, 1859), and E. Renan, *The Life of Jesus* (Buffalo: Prometheus Books, 1991)—and, finally, arguments that seek to prove that Christ, in order to be our mediator, had to be born under the curse of original sin and take on sinful flesh. This argument is made by, among others, Irving and especially Bula, whose views are discussed and criticized by A. Kuyper, *De vleeschwording des Woords.*

This conception is rooted, however, in a failure to take account of the deity of Christ. It proceeds from the mistaken idea that there is no virtue other than what is acquired by struggle, and at most achieves a factual, historical sinlessness, which is insufficient for Jesus as Mediator. Attempts to prove Jesus' sinlessness solely on historical grounds,[227] though not without value, are inadequate.[228] Historical certainty, which is before long again made uncertain by others, is not enough for us. However much we appreciate that so many scholars, such as Daub, Marheineke, Rosenkranz, Vatke, Schleiermacher, Beyschlag, Hase, Schenkel, Lipsius, and others—from whom in terms of their first principles one would expect otherwise—still have a profound sense of Jesus' moral perfection, yet faith that is not based on the witness of Scripture is unstable and therefore always burdened and threatened by an assortment of philosophical and historical objections. Scripture, however, prompts us to recognize in Christ, not just an empirical sinlessness, but a necessary sinlessness as well. He is the Son of God, the Logos, who was in the beginning with God and himself God. He is one with the Father and always carries out his Father's will and work.[229] For those who confess this of Christ, the possibility of him sinning and falling is unthinkable.[230] For that reason Christian theology maintained, against Arians, Pelagians, and nominalists such as Duns Scotus, Biel, Durandus, Molina, and others that Christ could not sin. For in that case either God himself would have to be able to sin—which is blasphemy—or the union between the divine and the human nature is considered breakable and in fact denied.[231]

Still, this is not to cancel the essential distinction between the holiness of God and the holiness of Christ as a human being. With reference to this distinction, Jesus could say that no one is good, no one is goodness itself but God alone (Matt. 19:16–17; Mark 10:17–18; Luke 18:18–19).[232] The goodness or holiness of

227. Like those of C. Ullmann, *The Sinlessness of Jesus*, trans. Sophia Taylor (Edinburgh: T&T Clark, 1882); I. A. Dorner, "Über Jesu sündlose Vollkommenheit," *Jahrbücher für deutsche Theologie* 7 (1862): 49–107; ***"Sündlosigkeit Jesu," *Herzog*; P. J. Gouda Quint, *De zondeloosheid van Jezus Christus* (Utrecht: n.p., 1862); P. Schaff, *The Person of Christ, the Miracle of History* (New York: C. Scribner & Co., 1866); J. J. van Oosterzee, *Het Leven van Jezus*, 3 vols. (Utrecht: Keminck, 1846–51), I, 569ff.; idem, *Christian Dogmatics*, §93; P. Chapuis, "La Sainteté de Jésus," *Revue de théologie et de philosophie* 30 (1897): 297–321, 409–27, 539–69; M. Meyer, *The Sinlessness of Jesus* (New York: Eaton & Mains, 1897); J. Stalker, "Sinlessness," *DC*, II, 636–39; E. A. Rumball, "The Sinlessness of Jesus," *Hibbert Journal* 5/3 (April 1907): 600–605.

228. F. A. Philippi, *Kirchliche Glaubenslehre*, IV, 161.

229. Cf. above, 248–53 (#355).

230. H. J. Holtzmann, *Lehrbuch der neutestamentlichen Theologie*, II, 446; F. H. R. Frank, *System der christlichen Wahrheit*, II, 178.

231. Augustine, *Enchiridion*, 36, 40–41; P. Lombard, *Sent.*, III, dist. 12 (as well as the commentaries of Aquinas and Bonaventure in this same place); B. de Moor, *Comm. theol.*, III, 692; W. G. T. Shedd, *Dogmatic Theology*, II, 330; F. A. Philippi, *Kirchliche Glaubenslehre*, IV, 161ff.; K. F. Nösgen, *Der einzige Reine unter den Unreinen* (Gütersloh: Bertelsmann, 1908).

232. Others take this passage to mean that Jesus here condemns the frivolous practice of calling someone good. Or else they take "goodness" to mean not moral perfection but the generosity of God according to which he alone is the giver of all good and perfect gifts.

Christ according to his human nature is not a divine and original goodness but one that has been given, infused, and for that reason it must also—in the way of struggle and temptation—reveal, maintain, and confirm itself. Infused goodness does not rule out acquired goodness. The latter presupposes the former; good fruit grows only on a good tree, but the soundness of the tree still has to be shown in the soundness of the fruit. Similarly, Christ had to manifest his innate holiness through temptation and struggle; this struggle is not made redundant or vain by virtue of the inability to sin (*non posse peccare*). For although real temptation could not come to Jesus from within but only from without, he nevertheless possessed a human nature, which dreaded suffering and death. Thus, throughout his life, he was tempted in all sorts of ways—by Satan, his enemies, and even by his disciples (Matt. 4:1–11; Mark 1:13; Luke 4:1–13; Matt. 12:29; Luke 11:22; Matt. 16:23; Mark 8:33).[233] And in those temptations he was bound, fighting as he went, to remain faithful; the inability to sin (*non posse peccare*) was not a matter of coercion but ethical in nature and therefore had to be manifested in an ethical manner.

The same is true of Christ's power. Although as the Son of God he was omnipotent, he was nevertheless limited as it concerns the power of his human nature. The Monophysites do not distinguish the two and permit the two natures, the two wills, and the distinct powers to dissolve into each other. But Scripture and the church made a distinction between the two and view the two natures as being united in such a way that in the one divine-human work each nature does the thing that belongs to it. And for that reason the performance of miracles, the forgiving of sins, the granting of eternal life, and all that belongs to the work of the mediator is attributable not only to his deity but also to his humanity. Christ as Son of Man, as Messiah, therefore, ascribes to himself this power to forgive and to come in judgment (Matt. 9:2–8; John 5:27). Upon his being touched, power comes forth from him (Luke 6:19). His flesh is the bread that gives life to the world (John 6:51). The Father has given all things into his hand (John 3:35; 13:3; 17:2). No one can snatch the sheep out of his hand or his Father's hand (John 10:28–30). Like the Father, he answers prayer (John 14:13; cf. 16:23), sends the Spirit (John 15:26; cf. 14:26), and gives eternal life (John 10:28; 17:2). Still, all this does not rule out that his power, as human power, is susceptible to increase. He was born as a tiny child, weak and helpless; he needed food and drink; he was exhausted by travel and sat down by the well (John 4:6). Even in the performance of miracles, he was dependent on the faith of people (Matt. 13:58). In the garden he was strengthened by an angel (Luke 22:43). Only after the resurrection does he

---

233. The temptation to which Jesus was exposed according to the Letter to the Hebrews (2:18; 4:15) did not lie, strictly speaking, in the realm of morality and was not a temptation to sin, but consisted in the fact that the manifold and heavy suffering he had to endure tested him on the point of whether he would persevere to the end in his messiahship, in his calling as Redeemer, in his office of Savior. But Jesus was and remained Christ. He *learned* obedience, not in the sense that he gradually changed from disobedience to obedience but in the sense that, in and through suffering, he increasingly proved his perfect obedience by his deeds. Cf. Karl Bornhauser, *Die Versuchung Jesu nach dem Hebräerbrief* (Leipzig: Deichert, 1905).

say that all power in heaven and on earth has been given him (Matt. 28:8; Mark 16:20; Luke 24:19). Then as Mediator he receives the glory he had beforehand with the Father as the Son (John 17:5) and causes his human nature to share in it. By his resurrection Christ—also as a human being—became Lord over the living and the dead, received a name that is above every name and power over all creatures (Matt. 28:18; Col. 2:3, 9; Phil. 2:9; Heb. 2:7–8).

WORSHIP OF THE CHRIST

[373] The confession concerning Christ has its practical application in the veneration extended to him, in the honor of adoration. For those who with Arius deny the deity of Christ, or with Nestorius separate it from his human nature, or with Socinus see in Jesus only a human being, all ground for the worship of the mediator vanishes. Still, in all sorts of ways, people try to maintain it. Nestorius stated that also the human Jesus as confessor and defender of the honor of God might be worshiped: "Though I separate the two natures, I bring them together in worship."[234] Socinus defended it by saying that Christ had been elevated to the status of Lord and had received all power and could therefore help us in distress. Many members of his faction, however, such as Davidis, Francken, and others, opposed the idea because God alone should be worshiped and the power of Christ was in any case limited. Socinus, accordingly, saw himself compelled to make a distinction between the worship of God as the primary cause of our salvation and that of Christ as the secondary cause.[235] Also, the Remonstrants derived the ground for the worship of Christ from the fact that he was Mediator, King, and Lord and as such had received from the Father an "honor of adoration" that, though "true" and "divine," was not supreme.[236] Ritschl and his school's defense of the worship of Christ materially agrees with that of Socinus: Christ, as a human in relation to God, though he may be honored, may not be worshiped; but Christ, viewed religiously, as a revelation of God, as the person in whom the church possesses God, should be worshiped, for in that case we do not worship him alongside God but worship God in him. This worship of Christ, moreover, though it is appropriate in public worship, does not belong in the private prayer of individuals. The latter is unhealthy, makes Christ a subject distinct from God, fosters sentimentalism, and leads to creature deification.[237] Just as among the Socinians, so also among the followers of Ritschl, there are those who totally reject the worship of Christ. They call him an object of faith and an example to be fol-

234. J. Schwane, *Dogmengeschichte*, II, 349.

235. O. Fock, *Der Socinianismus*, 538ff.; C. Vitringa, *Doctr. christ.*, V, 252.

236. *Apol. Conf.*, c. 2, p. 39; c. 3, p. 50; c. 16, p. 153; J. Arminius, *Opera theologica* (Lugduni Batavorum [Leiden]: Godefridum Basson, 1629), 436; P. van Limborch, *Theologia christiana* (Amsterdam: Wetstein, 1735), V, 18; S. Episcopius, *Institutiones theologicae*, in vol. 1 of *Opera* (Amsterdam: Johan Blaeu, 1650), IV, 35; VII, 27, 6; cf. *Censura in conf. rem.*, c. 2, 3, 12; J. Trigland, *Antapologia* (Amsterdam: Joannum Janssonium [et al.], 1664), c. 44; A. Heidanus, *Causa Dei*, V, 12; C. Vitringa, *Doctr. christ.*, 268.

237. H. Schultz, *Die Lehre von der Gottheit Christi*, 706ff.

lowed but not an object of religious veneration.[238] In that way both Socinianism and Ritschlianism culminate in Unitarianism, which robs Christ of all religious veneration. To the degree they still want to maintain a kind of worship of the human being named Christ, however, they are akin, and offer support to those who, though recognizing Christ's deity, also derive from his human nature a ground for worship.

Among these, in the first place, are the Monophysites, against whom the fifth ecumenical council (ch. 9) decreed[239] that the worship of Christ does not rest on a "commingling of the deity and the humanity" but must be directed toward God, the incarnate Logos with his flesh. But also Scholastic and Roman Catholic theologians gradually decided to offer religious worship to Christ's human nature as such. The basis, in this connection, was the universal teaching of the church fathers that the person of Christ had to be honored, in the undivided unity of the two natures, as the Incarnate Word, as God and man in conjunction, with one and the same kind of worship. From this it was inferred that the human nature of Christ himself, by itself, could and must also be the object of divine worship (λατρεια); not, however, for its own sake, but on account of its hypostatic union with the Son of God. To this it was further added that, though the human nature is to be worshiped by itself and hence is a material object of adoration, it is nevertheless always a partial and not the total object; that is, those who worship it always worship along with it him who united himself with that human nature. In that manner it was considered permissible and possible to make not only the human nature of Christ as such but even a part of that nature, as, for example, the holy heart of Jesus, an object of worship. Such worship, after all, does not just concern the heart only but the whole Christ, who indwelled that heart with his love. And, finally, many theologians added that the human nature of Christ could be not only the object of worship (λατρεια) on the ground of its hypostatic union with the Logos but also, on the basis of the numerous and abundant gifts given to it, the object of veneration (δουλεια), and then further the object of high veneration (ὑπερδουλεια) according to the hierarchical rule: "Worship is diverse in proportion to the diversity of the excellence that is its formal object."[240] In virtue of their doctrine of the communication of the divine attributes to the human nature, the Lutherans also taught that the human nature of Christ is to be worshiped.[241] And finally among the Herrnhuter, the human Christ almost

---

238. P. Chapuis, "L'adoration du Christ," *Revue de théologie et de philosophie* 28/6 (November 1895): 560–86; idem, "Die Anbetung Christi," *Zeitschrift für Theologie und Kirche* 7 (1897): 28–79.

239. In H. Denzinger, *Enchiridion*, #180.

240. John of Damascus, *The Orthodox Faith*, III, c. 8; P. Lombard, *Sent.*, III, dist. 9; T. Aquinas, *Summa theol.*, III, qu. 25; R. Bellarmine, "De imag. sanct.," in *Opera omnia*, II, c. 12ff.; J. B. Heinrich and C. Gutberlet, *Dogmatische Theologie*, VII, 656ff.; M. J. Scheeben, *Dogmatik*, III, 51ff.; C. Pesch, *Prael. theol.*, IV, 97ff.; H. T. Simar, *Dogmatik*, 411.

241. J. Gerhard, *Loci theologici*, 9 vols. (Berlin: G. Schlawitz, 1863–75), IV, §23; J. A. Quenstedt, *Theol.*, III, 190–208; V, 353; J. F. Buddeus, *Institutiones theologiae dogmaticae* (Leipzig: T. Fritsch, 1723), 771ff.

completely took the place of God. He is not the mediator but the vicar of God and virtually the only object of religious worship.[242]

By contrast, entirely in keeping with their doctrine of Christ, the Reformed said that the Mediator was indeed the proper object of worship but that the ground for that worship lay solely in his divine nature. Yet among them there was still some disagreement. All were agreed that Christ had to be worshiped and venerated also as Mediator, but some believed that the ground for that worship lay solely in the deity of Christ,[243] whereas others judged that the formal object was not only Christ's deity but also his mediatorship.[244] Now, Scripture leaves no doubt about whether Christ, as he may be the object of our faith and trust (John 14:1; 17:3; Rom. 14:9; 2 Cor. 5:15; Eph. 3:12; 5:23; Col. 1:27; 1 Tim. 1:1; etc.), so he may also be the object of our religious veneration and worship (John 5:23; 14:13; Acts 7:59; 9:13; 22:16; Rom. 10:12–13; 1 Cor. 1:2; 2 Cor. 12:8; Phil. 2:9–11; Heb. 1:6; Rev. 5:12; 12[:10–11]; 22:17, 20).[245] Still, the ground for the worship of Christ can, according to the Scriptures, be derived only from his deity. The word of Scripture is firm: "Worship the Lord your God, and serve only him." That is the word that in principle condemns all pagan and Roman Catholic creature deification. If the royal power of Christ or his mediatorship is also advanced as ground for religious worship, then this divine command is weakened and violated. As mediator, king, priest, and prophet, Christ is not absolutely supreme but subordinated to God. In that capacity he has another glory and power than what he has as the Son with the Father and the Spirit. In that capacity he is not the efficient cause of our salvation, which God alone is, but the instrumental cause. If, then, the ground for worshiping the Mediator consists, aside from his deity, also in his mediatorship, then that ground also in fact lies in his human nature, for as the mediator Christ cannot be conceived without it. Then the Father and the Spirit, who are not mediators, have one ground less for being worshiped than the Son, and so the Son achieves a position higher than the Father and the Holy Spirit.

242. H. Plitt, *Zinzendorfs Theologie*, III, 20ff.; C. J. Römheld, *Theologia sacrosancta,* 2 vols. (Gotha: Schloeßmann, 1888–89).

243. G. Voetius, *Select. disp.*, I, 520ff.; II, 304ff.; J. Maccovius, *Collegia theologica,* 3rd ed. (Franeker: Joannis Fabiani Deuring, 1641), I, 369; idem, *Redivivus* (Franeker: Idzardus Albertus et Johannes Arcerius, 1654), c. 91; J. Hoornbeek, *Socinianismus confutatus,* 3 vols. (Utrecht, 1650–54), I, 36ff.; P. van Mastricht, *Theologia,* V, 2, 261.

244. W. Ames, "De adoratione Christi," *Medulla theologica,* 12 vols. (Amsterdam: Loannem Lanssonium, 1628); A. Walaeus, *Loci communes s. theologiae* (Leiden: F. Hackius, 1640), I, 389; J. Trigland, *Antapologia,* c. 46; H. Alting, *Theol. problem.*, in *Scriptorum theologicorum,* XII, 20; J. Cloppenburg, *Theologica opera omnia,* 2 vols. (Amsterdam: Borstius, 1684), I, 461; G. Bucanus, *Institutiones theologicae* (Bern: Johannes & Isaias La Preux, 1605), XXXV, qu. 9; F. Turretin, *Institutes of Elenctic Theology,* XIV, qu. 18; Hottinger, Heidanus, Burman, Heidegger, B. de Moor, *Comm. theol.*, III, 829; C. Vitringa, *Doctr. christ.*, V, 247.

245. F. A. Loofs, "Christologie, Kirchenlehre," *PRE*[3], IV, 21; T. Zahn, *Die Anbetung Jesu im Zeitalter der Apostel* (Stuttgart: Buchhandlung der evangelischen Gesellschaft, 1885); idem, *Das apostolische Symbolum,* 271–308; W. Lütgert, *Die Anbetung Jesu* (Gütersloh: Bertelsmann, 1904); F. Barth, *Die Anrufung Jesu in der christlichen Gemeinde* (Gütersloh: Bertelsmann, 1904).

Then there are two grounds for adoration: one derived from the deity [of Christ], the other from something else, something creaturely; in principle the Catholic distinction between worship (λατρεια) and veneration (δουλεια) has been introduced, and creature deification has been legitimated. Christ, accordingly, is most certainly to be worshiped as our mediator, just as God is also venerated and invoked as Creator and so on, but the ground for it lies solely in his deity. He is not God because he is the mediator, but he is the mediator because he is God, with the Father and the Spirit the one and only God, to be praised over all forever. The dignity and the works of the mediator can and may be motives for worship and adoration, just as all sorts of benefits prompt us to worship God. They may also be called "grounds" for worship insofar as the divine being works and reveals himself in them. But the foundation of worship is the [mediator's] being God alone.

PART III

THE WORK OF CHRIST

7

CHRIST'S HUMILIATION

*The universal sense of sin and misery among the peoples of the world is
accompanied by the felt need and hope for redemption and reconciliation.
Culture, satisfying many needs, creates others and is inadequate for quenching
the thirst for eternity, for redemption. This longing can only be met by religion,
the basis of all culture. People take various roads toward redemption, but the
virtual universality of sacrifice requires explanation. The Vedic religion, for
example, speaks of sacrifice as the navel of the world.*

*There is no one single explanation of sacrifice. Likely, a notion of sacrifice
as a gift of communion to God existed before the fall; sin changed its character
and linked sacrifice to reconciliation and expiation. A special class of priests to
offer sacrifices and serve as mediators also gradually arose in all religions. Israel's
priests instructed the people in God's law, performed the sacrifices, and blessed
Israel on Yahweh's behalf. The key to Old Testament sacrifice is atonement,
covering for sin by means of shed blood. These were, however, incomplete, needed
to be endlessly repeated, and anticipated the coming Suffering Servant, who
would make himself an offering for the sins of the people.*

*According to the New Testament, Christ fulfills the Old Testament law and
prophets with its sacrificial system. He is the true covenant sacrifice, the Lamb
of God who takes away the sins of the world. By his sacrifice he acquired his own
exaltation and, for his own, the blessings of salvation, notably the forgiveness and
removal of our sins, peace with God.*

*The history of the doctrine of Christ's work lacks the sharp controversy and
clear-cut formulation that characterizes the trinitarian and christological
dogmas. The rich diversity of Scripture's teaching yields an array of views, all
of which contain a core of truth. Christ is prophet, priest, and king; his death
is ransom, sacrifice, satisfaction, payment, healing, reconciliation. Nonetheless,
some views, such as those that consider Christ's work as primarily exemplary
or as a mystical reality in believers, are inadequate and to be rejected. Others
include Stancarus's teaching that Christ is our mediator only in his human
nature and Johannes Piscator's denial of Christ's actual obedience.*

The most serious challenge came from the rationalist Socinians, who denied the doctrine of satisfaction as well as that of the Trinity and the deity of Christ. In their view satisfaction is unbiblical, unnecessary, and impossible—an innocent cannot die for the guilty. Though orthodox theologians raised serious objections against them, the Socinians greatly influenced modern theology. For Schleiermacher, a mystical reconciliation is effected by Christ in us, while Ritschl made of Christ the perfect man who brings the moral kingdom of God to humanity. Where dissatisfaction with modern theology arose, notably in the English-speaking world, and the atonement was reemphasized, the vicarious substitutionary understanding of Christ's death was still rejected.

In the biblical view, Jesus is the Christ, the anointed mediator who fulfills the office of prophet, priest, and king. He is the perfect mediator between God and man because he is himself true God and true man. All who are in communion with Christ are named "Christian" and anointed to be prophets, priests, and kings in him. Even within this framework, Reformation theologians debated questions such as whether Christ was the mediator in both natures or only in his human nature (Stancarus). Others rejected the distinction between the three offices or acknowledged only one at the expense of the others. For example, rationalists acknowledge only Christ's prophetic office; mystics only his priestly; millennialists only his royal office.

In the entirety of Christ's person and work, this Christ is a revelation of God's love. This means, on the one hand, that it is a mistake to regard Christ's work solely as a revelation of God's punitive justice. This would turn God the Father of our Lord Jesus Christ into a pagan deity whose wrath must be averted by sacrifice. Yet Christ's death is also an act of God's justice. Was Christ's death thus necessary? Was it arbitrary (Duns Scotus)? The incarnation as well as the satisfaction of Christ's death are not necessary in any absolute sense; they are not a necessity imposed on God from without or from which he cannot except, but they are necessary as actions that are in agreement with his attributes and display them most splendidly to his glory.

A long-standing position in broader Christian circles sets justice and love, gospel and law, Old Testament and New Testament, over against each other. God, in this view, is only a loving Father, never a judge who punishes sin. The Christian religion has nothing to do with law and satisfaction or justice; it is a spiritual-moral program of salvation. Only the state is the sphere of law and punishment, and this is separated entirely from the gospel of grace. This Marcionite juxtaposition of opposites has always been rejected by Christianity. If sin does not deserve punishment, there is no grace either. In fact, there is no need for forgiveness at all. God wills that we love him and his law, even apart from sin, as the norm for our lives.

It is Christ whose active work of complete obedience accomplished his own exaltation and the salvation of his own. His entire life and work, from his conception to his death, was substitutionary in nature. In its entirety, Christ's life was an act of self-denial, an offering presented to the Father as head of the new humanity. The redemption he obtained for us is also complete redemption of the whole person, body and soul. The whole renewal of all things is the fruit of his obedience though we now experience it only in part, particularly as deliverance from sin's guilt and power.

Modern theology also misjudges or denies Christ's passive obedience by repudiating all notions of satisfying God's righteousness and seeing his life merely as an exemplary instance of holy, moral obedience. Others, such as Hegel, see the incarnation and God becoming human so that humans might become divine as the real redemptive act. Schleiermacher stressed the perfect God-consciousness of Christ and his holy life as the means by which we too achieve communion with God. Still others reduce the death of Christ to an exemplary instance of solidarity with all humanity.

This variety of views on Christ's death is sometimes justified by the claim that Scripture itself has no one definitive understanding and thus legitimates different theories of the atonement. It is better to acknowledge that while there is indeed a rich variety of images in the New Testament to explain Christ's death and no one single formula suffices, there is a consistent explanation. Christ Jesus was sent by the Father, entered our existence, took on himself the guilt of our sins, gave his life as the Lamb of God for the sins of the world, as a ransom, and having completed his priestly work continues to intercede for us. The many diverse theories are thus not untrue as such; only when they become exclusive and particularly when they are used to deny the propitiatory character of Christ's death are they incomplete and in error.

It is in this connection that some theologians refuse to speak about an "office" for Christ and speak only of a "vocation" or calling. There is a vast difference between these terms. The latter does not acknowledge the divinely appointed character of Christ's mission and reduces him to a mere human person of great gift or genius who senses a duty to God and humanity. He does not then have a special revelation and unique mission from God himself. This view, however, does not adequately explain the death of Christ or do justice to the biblical givens concerning our Lord's own consciousness of his office. According to the Apostle Peter at Pentecost, Jesus was handed over to those who killed him "by God's set purpose and foreknowledge" (Acts 2:23). Jesus' death was not an accident; it had to happen. *At the same time, seeing the death of Christ as satisfaction for sin, as divine punishment, does not mean that there is a rift in the Godhead between an angry Father and the loving Son he punishes. Through Christ's death, expiation of sins, righteousness, and eternal life are secured for believers. God's grace does* not nullify the satisfaction and merit of Christ but is the ultimate ground for that merit. It is the love of God that sent the Son into the world (John 3:16), and on the cross Jesus remained the beloved Son. Mystical and moral theories of the atonement, though they contain elements of scriptural truth, cannot stand detached from this foundation.

The full scriptural teaching concerning the connection between Christ's death and our salvation comes into its own only when his full and complete obedience is viewed as vicarious satisfaction. Christ came not only to bear our punishment but also to obtain for us the righteousness and life Adam had to secure by his obedience. Christ's obedience returns us not to the beginning but to the end of the road Adam had to walk. Christ's active and passive obedience stand side by side. His activity was suffering and his suffering an act. It was not only a satisfaction but a vicarious satisfaction.

Serious objections have been raised against the doctrine of vicarious substitution. This substitution must not be understood in a pantheistic-physical or mystical sense; it bears a legal character. The understanding of Christ's paying for human sin must never be taken in a purely quantitative sense; the sin for which Christ atones is not something that can be weighed and measured. Vicariousness concerns Christ as our representative; his obedience and death are in our place. The moral objection that one cannot suffer and die for another is contradicted by the human reality of loving sympathy and "suffering with." All human analogies, however, pale in significance before the great love of Christ for us in his obedience and death. Christ took on himself the unimaginable burden of all human sin and guilt under God's punishment.

In order to link the teaching about Christ's human and divine nature with his humiliation, theologians began to speak of the two states—humiliation and exaltation. These must always be seen together; Christ's whole life was in the service of his office as mediator. The life of Jesus, beginning with the incarnation, begins his suffering, which culminates on the cross. The creedal statements about his burial and descent into hell have elicited much discussion. Does this refer to a stay in the abode of the dead? This idea surfaced rather early in the Christian church as a comfort to believers concerning those who had already died, including Old Testament saints. However, since the biblical passages adduced as warrant for this view are not very convincing, Reformation theologians, even when they disagreed with Rome, also disagreed among themselves. It is best understood as referring to the state of death in which Christ existed between his dying and rising again to bear the punishment of sin to the end and to redeem us from it. "Christ descended into hell so that we would not have to go there."

RELIGION, CULTURE, AND REDEMPTION

[374] Among all peoples of the world, we encounter a sense of sin and misery, and all feel the need and a hope for redemption. Optimism is powerless to override the first fact and to completely reconcile human beings to themselves and the world. Pessimism, however, never succeeds in undoing the second fact and in eradicating hope for the future from the human heart. We saw earlier, moreover, that expectation of a coming redemption is bound up in many religions with a coming person and specifically built on the appearance of a king.[1] Here we may add that the idea of redemption is almost always coupled with that of reconciliation.[2] Redemption, we must say, is primarily a religious concept and, accordingly, occurs in all religions. Granted, human beings have at their disposal many means to maintain themselves in the struggle of existence and to protect themselves against the forces of violence. They are not alone but live in communities. They can combine forces with others and seek strength in union. They have brains to think with, hands to work with, and can by labor and struggle conquer, establish, and expand a place for themselves in the world. It is noteworthy, however, that all theses aids and supports are not enough for them. However much people may have achieved culturally, they are never satisfied with it and do not attain the redemption for which they are thirsting. For while all culture satisfies needs, it also creates and arouses needs. While, on the one hand, culture prompts them to take pride in the great progress they have made, on the other, it gives them a progressively clearer sense of the long road they still have to travel. To the degree people subdue the world under their feet, to that degree they feel more and more dependent on those heavenly forces against which, with their limited power and puny means, they avail nothing. To the extent they solve problems, to that extent they see the riddles of the world and of life multiply and increase in complexity. As they dream of progress and civilization, they at the same time see opening up before them the instability and futility of the existing world. Culture has great, even incalculable, advantages but also brings with it its own peculiar drawbacks and dangers. "The more abundantly the benefits of civilization come streaming our way, the emptier our life becomes."[3]

This is why, in addition to culture, there has always been religion. Rather, religion preceded culture, and culture everywhere came to birth and maturity under the influence of religion. If the ills of humanity were caused by culture, they could certainly be cured in no way other than by culture.[4] But the ills we have in mind are native to the human heart, which always remains the same, and

---

1. Cf. above, 238–40 (#351).

2. Ed. note: In this chapter, the Dutch word *verlossing* will be translated as "redemption"; *verzoening* will be translated as "reconciliation" when used in a general sense, and as "atonement" when used in a more specific sense as the doctrine of Christ's saving work on the cross.

3. G. Heymans, *Der Toekomstige Eeuw der Psychologie* (Groningen: Wolters, 1909), 9.

4. Ibid., 15.

culture only brings them out. With all its wealth and power, it only shows that
the human heart, in which God has put eternity [Eccles. 3:11], is so huge that
all the world is too small to satisfy it. Human beings are in search of another and
better redemption than culture can give them. They are looking for lasting happiness, an enduring eternal good. They are thirsting for a redemption that saves
them physically as well as spiritually, for time but also for eternity. And this only
religion, and nothing else, can give them. God alone can give it to them, not
science or art, civilization or culture. For that reason redemption is a religious
concept, is found in all religions, and is almost always coupled with the idea of
reconciliation. For the redemption that humans seek and need is one in which
they are lifted up above the whole world into communion with God.

To the degree that the evil from which human beings want to be redeemed
and the deity with whose help they hope to obtain redemption are construed
differently, they naturally also take another road to redemption. If they take
physical evil (diseases, disasters, and so on) to be the greatest evil and equate the
deity with the power of nature, they will have recourse—not only among crude
and uncivilized peoples but also in the centers of culture and among the most
civilized classes—to the practices of theurgy and magic. If the deity is equated
with the unity of the All and evil is found above all in finiteness and particularity,
there arises in religion the mystical trend that seeks to deliver humans from their
finiteness by asceticism and to bring them to communion with the deity by ecstasy
(meditation, contemplation). And if the deity is conceived as distant from the
world, and nature and the moral order are viewed as independent, humans seek
their redemption in a way that involves imitating nature or keeping the commandments. Polytheism (in its different forms: animism, spiritism, polydaemonism,
pluralism, and so on), pantheism, and Deism, each in its way, give to the idea of
redemption a peculiar modification of their own.

There is one phenomenon in religions, however, that, in respect to redemption,
particularly deserves our attention, and that is sacrifice. If one does not want—in
a confusing way—to expand its meaning to every act in which a person devotes
something of his or her person, services, or possessions to the deity, one should
understand by sacrifice the religious act in which a person offers a material gift
to the deity and destroys it in the service of that deity in order to secure that
deity's favor. Almost all the names customarily used for it point to the voluntary
gift that in sacrifice is offered to the deity or to the destruction that takes place
with it (מִנְחָה, עֹלָה, זֶבַח, אִשֶּׁה; δωρον, ἱερειον, προσφορα, θυσια, τελετη; *oblatio,
sacrificium*) but shed little light on the origin and nature of sacrifices.

SACRIFICE

For that reason a wide range of hypotheses have been framed to somewhat
explain them. In earlier times scholars especially stressed the destructive element
in sacrifice and hence attributed to all sacrifices a conciliatory character (the ex-

piatory theory),[5] or regarded the sacrifice as a gift that people offer to the deity in token of their reverence and submission, self-denial and devotion (the symbolic theory).[6] These two theories proceed tacitly from the assumption that human beings from the beginning had some knowledge of God and were prompted, either by a sense of guilt or by feelings of gratitude, to bring sacrifices. But the theory of evolution does not give us liberty to equip the first humans with such knowledge and has therefore given rise to the formulation of a very different set of hypotheses. Some scholars explain sacrifice in terms of the disposition of people to propitiate a leader, a ruler, and hence also the deity by some gift or other and thus to secure their assistance (the *do-ut-des,* the "I give that you may give" theory).[7] In addition many also believe that originally humans thought the gods to be totally like themselves and therefore in their sacrifices offered them especially foodstuffs (the food theory).[8] Others favored the mystical or sacramental theory, thinking that the essence of a sacrifice does not consist in a gift but in the exercise of communion with the gods, with whom one sits down at the same table and partakes of the same food and drink.[9] This last theory is then developed still further by relating it to the primitive belief—present among many peoples—that eating the meat (kidneys, fat, and so on) and drinking the blood of an animal or, in the case of cannibalism, of another person is the means by which one appropriated the psychic, intellectual, or moral properties of that other being. Since in the case of many tribes there was also the practice of totemism, that is, the veneration of animals as sacred beings who participated in the divine nature, people gradually came to believe that eating the flesh and drinking the blood of an animal (or a human) was a means of fortifying oneself with the divine powers present in the animal and simultaneously, by offering the best parts of the sacrifice to the gods and letting them take part in the meal, to placate them and win their favor. "The person who believes that by eating the flesh of other humans or of animals he can gain their powers seeks in the sacrifice to propitiate the demons or gods or to win favors from them by letting them share in the enjoyment of the sacrifice.

5. Thus Bellarmine, Vázquez, and many other Roman Catholic theologians; cf. V. Thalhofer, *Das Opfer des alten und des neuen Bundes* (Regensburg: G. A. Manz, 1870); idem, *Handbuch der katholischen Liturgik,* 2nd ed., 2 vols. (Freiburg i.B.: Herder, 1912), I, 197ff.

6. A. Wuttke, *Geschichte des Heidentums in Beziehung auf Religion*, 2 vols. (Breslau: Max, 1852–53), I, 127ff.

7. P. D. Chantepie de la Saussaye, *Lehrbuch der Religionsgeschichte,* 3rd ed., 2 vols. (Tübingen: J. C. B. Mohr [Paul Siebeck], 1905), I, 101ff.; E. von Hartmann, *Religionsphilosophie,* 2nd ed., 2 vols. (Bad Sachsa i.H.: Hermann Haacke, 1907), I, 35; H. Spencer, *Principles of Sociology* (New York: Appelton, 1897), §§139ff., according to whom the offerings are closely related to the gifts of food and drink provided to accompany the dead.

8. E. von Hartmann, *Religionsphilosophie*; H. Siebeck, *Lehrbuch der Religionsgeschichte* (Freiburg i.B. and Leipzig: Mohr, 1893), 279.

9. W. R. Smith, *Die Religion der Semiten* (Freiburg i.B.: Mohr, 1899), 206ff.; R. Smend, *Lehrbuch der alttestamentlichen Religionsgeschichte* (Freiburg i.B.: Mohr, 1893), 24; K. Marti, *Geschichte der Israelitischen Religion*, 3rd ed. (Strassburg: F. Bull, 1897), 36; O. Pfleiderer, *Religionsphilosophie auf geschichtlicher Grundlage*, 3rd ed. (Berlin: G. Reimer, 1896), 648.

Accordingly, a bloody sacrifice originally always combined both sides: the offering of a sacrificial animal or a sacrificed human as food for the god and the
enjoyment of the sacrificial meat on the part of the sacrificer."[10] After the idea
of a propitiatory sacrifice had emerged in this fashion, it in turn retroactively affected the character of the sacrifices: it became the reason why people gradually
began to prefer a bloody sacrifice, why the blood became increasingly important
in connection with the sacrifices, why in many special cases animal sacrifice began
to replace human sacrifice.[11]

About the origin, nature, and purpose of sacrifices, therefore, opinions vary
widely. One scholar considers the bloody, another the unbloody sacrifices the most
ancient. According to some, the sacrifices were originally completely consumed
by fire; according to others, only in part. In the opinion of one group, sacrifices
originated from the sacrificial meals; in the opinion of others, the reverse is true.
Some consider the substitutionary character as integral to the sacrifice, but others
believe it is a later addition. In light of this state of affairs, it is not hard to understand that Lagrange refrains from making a firm choice[12] and that Tiele makes
the comment that in the study of this subject one must not proceed from one
specific category of sacrifice, for there have always and everywhere been widely
different sacrifices existing side by side.[13] This comment is undoubtedly correct:
human beings sacrifice a variety of objects (grains, fruits, animals, humans, and
so on), are guided by a variety of motives (reverence, gratitude, feelings of guilt,
fear, and so on), and in each case seek to reach different goals (propitiating the
wrath of the deity, the aversion of some evil, the acquisition of some specific
favor). Just as this is true in the case of religion, so in respect to sacrifices it will
be extremely hard to find a theory that embraces them all and explains them all
in terms of a single principle. But however this may be, remarkable in any case
is the universal, profound, and powerful urge that at all times and places drives
people to offer sacrifices. That urge arises from the ineradicable sense that human
beings are related in some fashion to an invisible divine power, whether reconciled
or unreconciled, and that by their sacrifice they can exert some influence on the
deity. Sacrifice is so central and prominent in worship that the Vedic religion can
speak of it as the navel of the world.[14]

Scripture, accordingly, tells us that sacrifice existed from the earliest history of
humanity. Before the fall it makes no mention of it. Yet there is nothing absurd
in the notion that then too sacrifice in a broad sense, like prayer, belonged to
the elements of worship. Sacrifice in a broad sense, as Augustine describes it, is

10. W. M. Wundt, *Mythus und Religion*, 2 vols. (Leipzig: Engelmann, 1905), II, 336.
11. W. R. Smith, *Die Religion der Semiten*, 271ff.; J. G. Frazer, *The Golden Bough* (London and New York:
Macmillan, 1900); cf. W. Paterson, "Sacrifice," *DB*, IV, 331–32.
12. M. J. Lagrange, *Études sur les religions sémitiques* (Paris: Victor Lecoffre, 1903), 244–56.
13. C. P. Tiele, *Elements of the Science of Religion*, 2 vols. (Edinburgh and London: William Blackwood,
1899), II, 127–38.
14. P.D. Ch. de la Saussaye, *Religionsgeschichte*, I, 33.

"every work that unites us in a holy communion with God."[15] As such it also befits humans in the state of integrity. They were created, after all, after God's image in true knowledge, righteousness, and holiness. Adam was prophet, priest, and king, and as such was called to glorify God's name, to consecrate himself with all he had to God, and to govern and direct all things in accordance with the will of God. In the Sabbath he was given a special day for the service of God and to that end needed certain forms of worship. There is nothing strange in the idea that, in addition to prayer, sacrifice also belonged to it. Granted, humans cannot really give anything to God, for the earth is the Lord's and the fullness thereof (Ps. 24:1). Yet God gave the earth to humanity and appointed it to be its ruler. And, therefore, in a symbolic sense, humans can offer something to God in token of reverence and dependence. If sacrifice originally belonged to the religion of humanity—religion that cannot in essence be different before and after the fall—then it is also easy to explain why soon after the fall there is mention of Cain's and Abel's sacrifices without any reference to God expressly instituting sacrificial worship.

Protestants and Catholics used to debate the question whether sacrifice was rooted in a divine command or in an inward religious impulse of humans.[16] But if sacrifice already existed before the fall, that settles the argument. Sin admittedly introduced a great change in sacrifice, not only in the sense that expiatory sacrifice was mechanically added to the existing sacrifice but especially in the sense that the nature of sacrifice itself was changed. Fallen humans experience fear before God and hide themselves before his face. They live much more under the impression of his wrath than of the sense of having his goodness. Not reverence and gratitude alone but especially fear and dread impel them to bring sacrifices as they also impel them to pray. The idea of redemption is therefore wedded to that of reconciliation, and the two are so closely coupled to each other that we cannot draw a sharp distinction between ordinary and expiatory sacrifices. In all sacrifices there is a certain acknowledged expiatory power.[17] To the degree that a sense of guilt and misery increases, the actual expiatory sacrifice increasingly becomes the center of the liturgy. And it is true that sacrifices are then frequently followed by sacrificial meals at which humans are, as it were, the guests of the deity, sit down with the deity at the same table, and are full of delight;[18] but those sacrificial meals are always based on the preceding sacrifices. As further development occurred, the expiatory sacrifices tended increasingly to make use of animal sacrifice. Animals were the most precious things humans could give of their possessions, for the blood was the seat of the soul. Pursued by fear and desiring to

---

15. Augustine, *City of God,* X, 6.

16. C. Vitringa, *Doctrina christianae religionis,* 8 vols. (Leiden: Joannis le Mair, 1761–86), IV, 275–80; C. Orelli, "Opferkultus des Alten Testaments," *PRE*[3], XIV, 387ff.; W. P. Paterson, "Sacrifice," *DB,* IV, 330. The question had practical implications since Roman Catholic, Lutheran, and Anglican ceremonies seemed warranted if sacrifices, instituted by human beings, were nevertheless pleasing to God.

17. W. R. Smith, *Die Religion der Semiten,* 305, 309.

18. Ibid., 196ff., 200ff.

obtain the favor and peace of the deity, they even resorted to offering up human lives.[19] This gruesome error was further strengthened by the physiological idea that eating the flesh and drinking the blood of the one sacrificed imparted the latter's physical and mental power to the person who partook of it. And this, on the one hand, again led to the idea of the sacrifice as a meal for the anthropomorphically conceived gods and, on the other, to anthropophagy, which has its origin not in the animal nature of humanity but in degenerate religion.[20]

Finally, in all religions, there gradually arose a special class of priests. Holy persons who effect and maintain communion with God for others occur among all peoples and tribes; magicians and fortune-tellers are found everywhere. Especially kings, prophets, and priests act as such mediators in religion as well. The word "priest" comes from "presbyter" (elder) and originally, therefore, had no hieratic meaning at all. The names in other languages (such as כֹּהֵן, ἱερεύς, sacerdos) describe the priests as persons who stand before God, are active in his service, and are specifically charged to perform the sacrifices. Though such a priesthood occurs in almost all religions,[21] its origin is unknown to us. In the earliest times, according to Scripture, there was not yet a special class of priests. Abel, Cain, Noah, and the patriarchs still bring their sacrifices themselves (Gen. 4:3–4; 8:20; 12:7; etc.). It is only as the sense of sin among peoples grows stronger and the consciousness of separation from God deepens that everywhere the idea of a mediatorship arises. Human beings, who themselves lost the image of God and could no longer act as prophets, priests, and kings, felt a need for special persons, who, invested with these offices, could take their place, plead God's cause with them and their cause with God. In that way, all human priesthood and sacrifice points—directly in Israel, indirectly also among other peoples—to the one perfect sacrifice that was brought in the fullness of time by Christ, the mediator between God and humankind, on Golgotha.[22]

[375] The change that sin introduced in sacrifice only gradually manifested itself. First, the offering was simply called מִנְחָה, "gift" (Gen. 4:3); and the of-

---

19. W. Schneider, *Die Naturvölker: Missverständnisse, Missdeutungen, Misshandlung,* 2 vols. (Paderborn: Schöning, 1885–86), I, 186ff.

20. Ibid.; cf. W. R. Smith, *Die Religion der Semiten,* 279, according to whom, human sacrifices began to take place after animal sacrifices.

21. J. Lippert, *Allgemeine Geschichte des Priesterthums,* 2 vols. (Berlin: T. Hoffman, 1883–84).

22. Further cf. T. Pfanner, *Systema Theologiae Gentilis Purioris* (Basel: Joh. Hermann Widerhold, 1679), c. 15; E. von Lasaulx, *Die Sühnopfer der Griechen und Römer und ihr Verhältnis zu dem einen auf Golgotha* (Würzburg: Voigt & Mocker, 1841); K. F. Nägelsbach, *Die nachhomerische Theologie des griechischen Volksglaubens bis auf Alexander* (Nürnberg: Conrad Gieger, 1857), 315ff.; K. C. W. F. Bähr, *Symbolik des mosaischen Cultus,* 2 vols. (Heidelberg: Mohr, 1837–39), II, 217ff., 269ff.; J. H. Oswald, *Die dogmatische Lehre von den heiligen Sakramenten der katholischen Kirche,* 2nd ed., 2 vols. (Münster: Aschendorff, 1864), I, 503ff.; N. Gihr, *Die heilige Messopfer, dogmatisch, liturgisch, und aszetisch erklärt,* 6th ed. (Freiburg i.B.: Herder, 1897), 10ff. (ed. note: ET: *The Holy Sacrifice of the Mass: Dogmatically, Liturgically, and Ascetically Explained,* translated from the German [St. Louis: Herder, 1902]); M. Scheeben, *Dogmatik,* III, 387ff. (ed. note: ET: *A Manual of Catholic Theology: Based on Scheeben's "Dogmatik,"* ed. Joseph Wilhelm and Thomas Bartholomew Scannell, 4th ed., 2 vols [London: Kegan Paul, Trench, Trubner & Co.; New York: Benzinger Brothers, 1909]).

ferings were made by the offerers themselves. But from very early times there nevertheless were already different sacrifices: covenant sacrifices (Gen. 15:9), burnt offerings (22:13), libations (28:18), peace offerings (31:54). The offerings consisted of the fruits of the soil (4:3), sheep (4:4), cattle and birds (8:20; 15:9), but human sacrifices were prohibited (22:12). When the sacrificial cult and the priesthood had already become developed among other peoples, they were regulated for Israel as well. Like the prophetic and kingly, so also the priestly office was based, according to the law, on election by Yahweh (Num. 16:7; Heb. 5:4). The task assigned to the priests was a dual one: it was to instruct the people of Israel, in part by the Urim and Thummim, concerning the rights and the laws of the Lord (Exod. 28:30; Deut. 17:9; 33:8–10; Jer. 18:8; Ezek. 7:26; 44:23–24; Hag. 2:12; Mal. 2:7), further to approach Yahweh with the sacrifices of the people (Lev. 21:8; Num. 16:5; etc.) and then to bless the people on Yahweh's behalf (Lev. 9:23; Num. 6:23).

The offerings Israel had to bring were of different kinds. The paschal offering (Exod. 12) occupies a place of its own, is simultaneously a peace offering and a burnt offering, a sacrifice and a sacrament. The covenant offering (Exod. 24:3–11) served, as in the case of Abraham (Gen. 15:9; Jer. 34:18ff.), to confirm the covenant; it therefore consisted of burnt offerings of bulls, whose blood was sprinkled, in part on the altar and in part on the people, as a covering of sin and for sanctification by Moses as mediator of the covenant, and was concluded with thank offerings. The burnt offering and thank offering (Lev. 1; 3) served to maintain covenant-based communion with God. The sin and guilt offering (Lev. 4–6) presupposed that communion with God had been disturbed by a sin of weakness [committed unwittingly] and, by the sprinkling of the blood of the slain animal, offered a cover for sin and restoration of communion with God. Atonement occurred when by the laying on of hands, the offerer transferred his sin to the animal. Admittedly, this is often denied, but wrongly so: in Scripture the laying on of hands always implies some kind of transmission: of a blessing (Gen. 48:13; Matt. 19:13), of a curse (Lev. 24:14), of an office (Num. 27:18; Deut. 34:9), of the Holy Spirit (Acts 8:17), and so on, and similarly in the case of bloody sacrifices as well as burnt and thank offerings (Lev. 1:4; 3:2) for sin that has been acknowledged and confessed (Lev. 4:4, 15; 16:21; 2 Chron. 29:23). The sacrifice itself was called חַטָּאת [sin offering] or אָשָׁם [guilt offering]. Consequently, the sacrificial animal was now worthy of death. But since the sacrifice was not only a way of undergoing the punishment for the offerer, but above all a way to make atonement for his sin, the killing of the animal was always called a slaying. The idea was not a death for the sake of death but to obtain by it the blood that had to effect atonement. God had intentionally given the blood of the animal on the altar to bring about atonement and this because the blood is the bearer of the soul, the carrier of a life that had again been made free from sin after and by the slaying (Lev. 17:11). Now when this blood on the altar or on the mercy seat came into God's presence, the offerer or his sin was thereby covered before the holy face of

God; or rather, it was God himself (Deut. 21:8; Jer. 18:23; Mic. 7:19) and the priest as his deputy (Lev. 5:13; 10:17; 15:15) who by the sacrifice—conceived as a ransom (כֹּפֶר, λυτρον)—covered the persons of the offerers from their sins or even covered those sins themselves before his face (כִּפֶּר with the preposition בְעַד or עַל).[23]

It needs to be said, however, that the sacrifices for atonement absolutely atone not for all but only for a few specific unintentional sins. The penalty for sins committed "high handedly" (sins of defiance) was death (Num. 15:30). Even though the sins of aberration were taken very broadly (Lev. 5; 6), the atonement effected by the sacrifices for atonement remained highly restricted. For that matter, the covenant of grace that God made with Israel was not based on the sacrifices for atonement but preceded them and had its basis exclusively in the promise: "I am the Lord your God." The sin and guilt offerings served only to atone for inadvertent violations that did not entail a breach of the covenant, and to restore the communion with God, which had been disturbed by them. This is also evident from the fact that they were enacted for cases of Levitical impurity but not of subjective guilt (Lev. 5:2; 12:6–7; 15:14). Countless sins remained, therefore, for which the law did not indicate any atonement by sacrifices: not only a few sins committed "high handedly" (sins of defiance), which were punished with death, but also a wide range of spiritual and carnal sins, sins by thoughts and words, sins of pride and self-seeking. For all these sins, no prescribed sacrifices existed.

Admittedly, certainly not only sin and guilt offerings but also burnt and thank offerings bore an atoning character (Lev. 1:3–4; 9:7), and on the great Day of Atonement all the sins of the people were atoned for (Lev. 16:16; 23:26–32; Num. 29:7–11). It remains remarkable, nonetheless, that in that connection no mention is made of all the above sins and that the real sin and guilt offering made provision only in certain cases. On special occasions when the people had sinned grievously and broken the covenant, atonement was obtained by extraordinary means: by Moses' intercession (Exod. 32:30–35; Num. 14; Ps. 106:23) or by extraordinary sacrifices (Num. 16:45–50; 2 Sam. 24:25; 2 Chron. 29:8–11). This was something the pious in Israel knew; they knew that sacrifice for atonement opened a way of atonement in only a very few cases; and for that reason they repeatedly reached behind those sacrifices and appealed to the mercy of God. And that, too, is what the Old Testament sacrificial cult was designed to teach Israel. The few sacrifices prescribed in the law did not cover the whole of life; they did not

23. The symbolic and sacramental theories that in the past were sometimes framed to explain Old Testament sacrifices have again fallen into discredit; and also Ritschl's peculiar view, according to which the *kopher* [covering, ransom] served to cover and protect the weak mortal human being from God's sublimity, no longer has many advocates. By contrast, the old idea that the blood of the slain animal was a "cover," an atonement for the sin of the offerer, and thus as a kind of ransom purchased his freedom from guilt is again recognized by many scholars as correct. Cf., e.g., H. J. Holtzmann, *Lehrbuch der neutestamentlichen Theologie*, 2 vols. (Freiburg and Leipzig: Mohr, 1897), I, 67–68; J. Köberle, *Sünde und Gnade im religiösen Leben des Volkes Israel bis auf Christum* (Munich: Beck, 1905), 306ff.

bring about true atonement; they served only to arouse a sense of sin and were types that pointed to another and better sacrifice. The sacrificial cult of the Old Testament was incomplete. The priests themselves were sinners. The blood of bulls and goats could not take away sins. The sacrifices had to be endlessly repeated. Everything indicated that the ceremonial dispensation of the Old Testament merely had passing, symbolic, and typological significance. And therefore, according to prophecy, there is on its way another covenant, a covenant that will be not broken but kept by everyone (Jer. 31:31); another prophet, who will be anointed in extraordinary measure with the Spirit of God and bring good news to Israel and to the Gentiles (Deut. 18:15; Isa. 11:2; Mal. 4:5). There will come another priest who will not be appointed in the manner of Aaron but according to the order of Melchizedek and therefore unite in himself both priestly and royal dignity and bear the two forever (Ps. 110; Jer. 30:21; Zech. 6:13); another king who will come out of the house of David and be a ruler in Israel (Mic. 5:1–2). And in that way another and better sacrifice will come as well. Animal sacrifices are not the true sacrifices (Pss. 40:6; 50:8; 51:17; Amos 4:4; 5:21; Hosea 6:6; 8:11; Isa. 1:11; Jer. 6:20; 7:21; etc.).[24] The true sacrifices to God are obedience (1 Sam. 15:22), mercy (Hosea 6:6), a broken spirit (Ps. 51:19), listening to the voice of God (Jer. 7:23). And that sacrifice will be brought by the Servant of the Lord who will take Israel's place, do its work, be a covenant to the people and a light to the Gentiles (Isa. 42:6; 49:6), and make himself an offering for the sins of his people (Isa. 53:10).

In the Old Testament this promise of the Suffering Servant and that of the anointed king still in part run parallel. Both promises are rooted in the firmness of God's covenant. Despite Israel's unfaithfulness and apostasy, God cannot forget his covenant. He cannot forget it for his name's sake. It is an everlasting covenant that cannot be shaken. Israel, therefore, however fallen into misery on account of its sin, still again gets a king out of David's house. That king will be of humble birth (Isa. 11:1–2; Micah 5:1–2; Ezek. 17:22). He will not only be a king but also a priest (Jer. 30:21; Zech. 3:1; 6:13; Ps. 110) and execute righteousness for his people (Jer. 23:6), make the sacrifices superfluous (Isa. 60:21; Jer. 24:7; 31:34; Ezek. 36:25, 27), and make all of them priests (Isa. 61:6). Parallel to this runs the other promise, namely, that this righteousness will only be obtained in the way of suffering. The sacrificial cult symbolized the necessity of the sacrifice of atonement. In so many examples, in Moses, David, Job, the prophets, and in the small group of the faithful who did not bow their knees before Baal, history has shown that the best suffer most, that they who represent God's cause and are

---

24. That the prophets, by saying this, did not condemn all sacrifices is clear from places like Amos 3:14; 9:1f.; Isa. 19:21; Jer. 33:18; 17:26; cf. F. J. Krop, "Nog eens: Welke beteekenis heeft de dood van Jezus Christus, volgens Zijn eigen verklaringen in de evangeliën voor mensch en menschheid," *Theologisch Studiën* 24 (1906): 153–75; and the texts Amos 5:25 and Jer. 7:21–22 cannot in any case be used in support of this assertion, cf. E. König, "Der Jeremiasspruch Jer. 7:21–23 nach seinen Sinn, seiner kulturgeschichtlichen Stellung und seinem geistesgeschichtlichen Anlass untersucht," *Theologische Studien und Kritiken* 69 (April 1906): 327–93.

to that extent righteous must pass through suffering to glory. In the exile and thereafter as a religious community, Israel became the servant of the Lord who in distress and misery, and oppressed on every side, would still be redeemed by the Holy One of Israel (Isa. 41:8f.).

Yet Israel is not the true servant of the Lord either. Israel itself needs redemption (Isa. 41:14; 42:19f.) Where in the past or present could the prophet find a collective or individual person, a prophet, a martyr, who was so marvelously equipped by Yahweh, who remained so unfalteringly faithful, who in proclaiming the truth to the Gentiles experienced the most severe suffering and the most disgraceful death? Modern exegesis exerts itself in vain when in the few pious persons in Israel, in the prophets, in Jeremiah, Zerubbabel, Jehoiachin, or some other sufferer, it tries to find the model for Isaiah's portrait of the servant of the Lord and itself offers the proof for this when it ascribes the Ebed-Yahweh songs to different authors or explains the figure of the servant of the Lord in terms of Oriental ideas. The truth is, the servant of the Lord receives a message particularly for the Gentiles, while Israel itself with all its pious people and prophets ranges itself in Isaiah 53 against the servant of the Lord, acknowledges that it despised him on account of his suffering, and confesses that he was wounded especially for their transgressions and bruised for their iniquities. Although it is not expressly stated, the servant of the Lord cannot be any other than the Messiah, who, remember, will also be a priest and execute righteousness for his people.[25] It is doubtful, however, whether Jewish theology before Jesus' coming saw these two lines in prophecy as coincident and thus expected a suffering Messiah.[26] Though in some circles this was certainly the case, the expectation of a suffering Messiah was not

25. F. Delitzsch, *The Prophecies of Isaiah* (London: Hodder & Stoughton, 1891), II , 42ff.; C. Orelli, "Messias," *PRE*[3], XIII, 723–39; G. Füllkrug, *Der Gottesknecht des Deuterojesaja* (Göttingen: Vandenhoeck & Ruprecht, 1899); K. Budde, *Die sogenannten Ebed-Jahwe-Lieder und die Bedeutung des Knechtes Jahwes in Jes. 40–55* (Giessen: J. Ricker, 1900); E. Sellin, *Der Knecht Gottes bei Deuterojesaja* (Leipzig: Deichert, 1901); idem, *Das Rätsel des deuterojesajanischen Buches* (Leipzig: Deichert, 1908); F. Giesebrecht, *Der Knecht Jahves des Deuterojesaja* (Königsberg in Preußen: Thomas & Oppermann, 1902); H. Gressmann, *Die Ursprung der israelitisch-jüdischen Eschatologie* (Göttingen: Vandenhoeck & Ruprecht, 1905); cf. also, A. van der Flier, "Drieërlei verklaring van den Ebed-Jahwe bij Deuterojesaja," *Theologische Studiën* 22 (1904): 345–76.

26. A. Wünsche, *Yisure ha-Mashiah, oder die Leiden des Messias* (Leipzig: Fues, 1870); G. Dalman, *Der leidende und der sterbende Messias der Synagoge im ersten nachchristlichen Jahrtausend* (Berlin: H. Reuther, 1888); F. W. Weber, *System der altsynagogalen palästinischen Theologie: Aus Targum, Midrasch und Talmud* (Leipzig: Dörffling & Franke, 1880), 344ff.; E. Schürer, *Geschichte des judischen Volkes im Zeitalter Jesu Christi*, 4th ed., 3 vols. (Leipzig: J. C. Hinrichs, 1901–9), II, 553ff.; W. Baldensperger, *Das Selbstbewusstsein Jesu im Lichte der messianischen Hoffnungen seiner Zeit* (Strassburg: J. H. E. Heitz, 1888), 121ff.; C. Orelli, "Messias," *PRE*[3], XIII, 723–39; H. J. Holtzmann, *Lehrbuch der neutestamentlichen Theologie*, I, 65ff. For the atonement of sins in a biblical sense, there was no longer any room in the teaching of Judaism. Sins were atoned by penitence (also again conceived as a work), confession, fasting, enduring punishment, almsgiving, study of the Torah, and so on. The sins that for all this remained unatoned were made good on the great Day of Atonement. Beyond this, people themselves had to acquire righteousness by keeping the law. When they did this, they deserved a reward from God. And the expectation of a messiah was limited to the hope that in the end he would vindicate the people of Israel and raise it above all the peoples of the earth. See F. W. Weber, *System*, c. 19ff.

the content of popular belief. Jesus' disciples show themselves to be completely unreceptive to it (Matt. 16:22; Luke 18:34; 24:21; John 12:34).

THE SACRIFICE OF CHRIST

[376] According to the New Testament, all these different testimonies of the law and the prophets culminate in Christ. The whole Old Testament is basically fulfilled in him. In him all the promises of God are yes and amen (Rom. 15:8; 2 Cor. 1:20). He is the true Messiah, the king of David's house (Matt. 2:2; 21:5; 27:11, 37; Luke 1:32; etc.); the prophet who proclaims good news to the poor (Luke 4:17f.); the priest who, according to the Letter to the Hebrews, in his person, office, appointment, sacrifice, and sanctuary far exceeds the priesthood of the Old Testament. He is the Servant of the Lord who as a slave (δουλος, Phil. 2:7–8) came to serve (Mark 10:45), submitted to the law (Gal. 4:4), fulfilled all righteousness (Matt. 3:15), and was obedient to the death on the cross (Rom. 5:19; Phil. 2:8; Heb. 5:8). As such Jesus made a distinction between the kingdom of God as it was now being founded by him in a spiritual sense and as it would one day be revealed in glory; between his first and his second coming, events that in Old Testament prophecy still coincided; between his work in the state of humiliation and that in the state of exaltation. The Christ had to enter glory through suffering (Luke 24:26).

The work that Christ now accomplishes in the state of humiliation is described in the New Testament from many different angles. It is a work that the Father gave him to do (John 4:34; 5:36; 17:4); generally speaking, it consisted in doing God's will (Matt. 26:42; John 4:34; 5:30; 6:38) and specifically included the "exegesis" of God (John 1:18), the revelation and glorification of his name (17:4, 6, 26), the communication of God's words (17:8, 14), and so on. Christ is a prophet, mighty in words and deeds (Luke 24:19); he is not a new legislator but interprets the law (Matt. 5–7; 22:40; Luke 9:23; 10:28; John 13:34; 1 John 2:7–8), proclaims the gospel (Matt. 12:16–21; Luke 4:17–21), and in both preaches himself as the fulfiller of the former and the content of the latter. He is the law and the gospel in his own person. He is not a prophet only by the words he speaks but primarily by what he is. He is the Logos (John 1:1), full of grace and truth (John 1:17–18), anointed without measure with the Spirit (John 3:34), the revelation of the Father (John 14:9; Col. 2:9). The source of his message is himself, not inspiration but incarnation. God did not even speak with him as he did with Moses, face to face, but was in him and spoke through him (Heb. 1:3). He is not one prophet among many, but the supreme, the only prophet. He is the source and center of all prophecy; and all knowledge of God, both in the Old Testament before his incarnation and in the New Testament after his resurrection and ascension, is from him (1 Pet. 1:11; 3:19; Matt. 11:27). The will of God that Jesus came to do further included the miracles he performed. The one work (ἐργον) is differentiated in many works (ἐργα, John 5:36), which are the works of his Father (5:20;

9:3; 10:32, 37; 14:10). They prove that the Father loves him and dwells in him (5:20; 10:38; 14:10), bear witness that the Father sent him (5:36; 10:25), and manifest his divine glory (2:11; 11:4, 40). He not only performs miracles but in his person is himself the absolute miracle. As the incarnate Spirit-conceived, risen and glorified Son of God, he is himself the greatest miracle, the center of all miracles, the author of the re-creation of all things, the firstborn of the dead, preeminent in everything (Col. 1:18).

The will of God further and especially includes that the only Son of the Father should lay down his life for his own (John 10:18). The New Testament views Christ's death as a sacrifice and the fulfillment of the Old Testament sacrificial cult.[27] He is the true covenant sacrifice; just as the old covenant was confirmed by the covenant sacrifice (Exod. 24:3–11), so the blood of Christ is the blood of the new covenant (Matt. 26:28; Mark 14:24; Heb. 9:13f.). Christ is a sacrifice (θυσια, זֶבַח), the sacrificial victim for our sins (Eph. 5:2; Heb. 9:26; 10:12), an offering (προσφορα, δωρον; מִנְחָה קָרְבָּן; Eph. 5:2; Heb. 10:10, 14, 18); a ransom (λυτρον, ἀντιλυτρον; Matt. 20:28; Mark 10:45; 1 Tim. 2:6; a translation of the Hebrew words כֹּפֶר, פְּדוּיִם, גְּאֻלָּה) and therefore denoting the price of release, a ransom to purchase someone's freedom from prison, and hence a means of atonement, a sacrifice by which to cover other people's sin and so to save them from death. He is a payment (τιμη, 1 Cor. 6:20; 7:23; 1 Pet. 1:18–19), the price paid for the purchase of someone's freedom; a sin offering that was made to be sin for us (2 Cor. 5:21; 1 John 2:2; 4:10); the paschal lamb that was slain for us (John 19:36; 1 Cor. 5:7), the Lamb of God[28] who takes away the sin of the world and is slain to that end (John 1:29, 36; Acts 8:32; 1 Pet. 1:19; Rev. 5:6; etc.). He is an expiation (ἱλαστηριον, Rom. 3:25, not the mercy seat, but that which serves as a means of expiation),[29] a sacrifice of atonement (θυμα),[30] a curse (καταρα, Gal.

---

27. "Every species of offering has its peculiar fundamental idea. That of the עוֹלָה is the *oblatio* or the gift of devotion; that of the שְׁלָמִים the *conciliatio* or formation of fellowship; that of the מִנְחָה the *donatio* or hallowing dedication; that of the חַטָּאת the *expiatio* or atonement; that of the אָשָׁם the *mulcta* (*satisfactio*) or compensatory payment. The self-sacrifice of the servant of Jahve may be viewed in all these lights" (Franz Delitzsch, *Biblical Commentary on the Prophecies of Isaiah*, trans. James Martin, 2 vols. [Grand Rapids: Eerdmans, 1949], II, 299).

28. F. Spitta, in his *Streitfragen der Geschichte Jesu* (Göttingen: Vandenhoeck & Ruprecht, 1907), translated ὁ ἀμνος του θεου in John 1:29 not as "lamb" but as "ram" (so that the text referred to Jesus not as a sacrificial animal but as a leader [bellwether]). Cf. H. L. Oort, "Iets over het Lam Gods," *Theologisch Tijdschrift* 42 (1908): 1–10, in which he correctly refutes Spitta's interpretation; A. Drews, *The Christ Myth* (Chicago: Open Court, 1910; reprinted, Amherst, NY: Prometheus Books, 1998).

29. A. Deissmann, "Ἱλαστριος und Ἱλαστηριον: Eine lexikalische Studie," *Zeitschrift für die neutestamentliche Wissenschaft* 4 (1903): 193–212. Ritschl and others translate ἱλαστηριον as "cover of atonement" [*verzoendeksel*], but against this, see T. Zahn, *Der Brief des Paulus an die Römer* (Leipzig: Deichert, 1910), on Rom. 3:25; W. Sanday and A. C. Headlam, *A Critical and Exegetical Commentary on the Epistle to the Romans*, 3rd ed. (New York: C. Scribner's Sons, 1897), on Rom. 3:25.

30. Also, the idea of substitution has been remarkably illuminated by the study of the Greek papyri: Leopold Wenger, *Die Stellvertretung im Rechte der Papyri* (Leipzig: B. B. Teubner, 1906); G. A. Deissmann, *Licht vom Osten* (Tübingen: Mohr, 1908), 241.

3:13) who took over from us the curse of the law, like the serpent in the wilderness lifted high on the cross (John 3:14; 8:28; 12:33) and like a grain of wheat dying in the earth in order thus to bear much fruit (John 12:24).

The relation in which Christ's sacrifice stands to us and our sin is likewise expressed in very different ways. He gives or lays down his life (Mark 10:45; John 10:15), consecrates himself (John 17:19), was made sin and a curse (2 Cor. 5:21; Gal. 3:13), was delivered up (Rom. 4:25), gave himself (Gal. 2:20), suffered (1 Pet. 3:18), was crucified and died (John 11:50–51; Rom. 5:6; 2 Cor. 5:15; 1 Thess. 5:10). All of this is a ransom for many (Matt. 20:28; Mark 10:45), in the place of many (with gen. of the person; John 10:15; 11:50–51; Rom. 5:6, 8; 2 Cor. 5:15, 21; Gal. 3:13; Eph. 5:2; Heb. 2:9), on our behalf, on behalf of his people (cf. Philem. 13, ὑπέρ σου, on your behalf, so that you don't have to do it). Or ὑπέρ with the genitive of the thing (John 6:51; 1 Cor. 15:3; Heb. 10:12), for the sake of the sins to remove them, or for the life of the world in order that by Christ's death it might gain life. Or περί with the genitive of the person (Matt. 26:28; 1 John 2:2), for the sake of many or of the whole world; or περί with the genitive of the thing (Rom. 8:3; Heb. 10:6, 18; 1 Pet. 3:18; 1 John 2:2; 4:10), for or on account of sin; or διά with the accusative of the thing (Rom. 4:25), on account of sin, for sin.[31]

What Christ acquired by this sacrifice is beyond description. For himself he acquired by it his entire exaltation, his resurrection (Eph. 1:20), his ascension to heaven (1 Pet. 3:22), his seating at the right hand of God (Eph. 1:20; Heb. 12:2), his elevation as head of the church (Eph. 1:22), the name that is above every name (Phil. 2:9–11), the glory of the mediator (John 17:5; Heb. 2:9), power over all things in heaven and on earth (Matt. 28:18; Eph. 1:22; 1 Cor. 15:24f.), the final judgment (John 5:22, 27). In addition he acquired for his own, for humanity, for the world, an interminable series of blessings. In his person he is himself the sum of all those blessings: the light of the world (John 8:12), the true bread (6:35), the true vine (15:1), the way, the truth, the resurrection, and the life (11:25; 14:6), our wisdom, our righteousness, holiness, and redemption (1 Cor. 1:30), our peace (Eph. 2:14), the firstborn and the firstfruits who is followed by many others (Rom. 8:29; 1 Cor. 15:23), the second and last Adam (1 Cor. 15:45), the head of the church (Eph. 1:22), the cornerstone of the temple of God (Eph. 2:20); and for that reason there is no participation in his benefits except by communion with his person.

Yet from him flow all the benefits, the whole of salvation (σωτηρία,[32] Matt. 1:21; Luke 2:11; John 3:17; 12:47), and more specifically the forgiveness of sins (Matt. 26:28; Eph. 1:7); the removal of our sins (John 1:29; 1 John 3:5); the cleansing or deliverance of a bad conscience (Heb. 10:22); justification (Rom. 4:25); righ-

---

31. The idea contained in ἀπολύτρωσις is illumined by the practice in which a slave on occasion was released after a sacrificial gift of money was brought to the temple; A. Deissmann, *Licht vom Osten*, 232ff.

32. On σωτήρ, see above, 238–40 (#351); and further also W. Wagner, "Über σῴζειν und seine Derivata im Neuen Testament," *Zeitschrift für die neutestamentliche Wissenschaft* 6 (1905): 201–35.

teousness (1 Cor. 1:30); sonship (Gal. 3:26; 4:5–6; Eph. 1:5); confident access to God (Eph. 2:18; 3:12); God's laying aside his wrath in virtue of Christ's sacrifice, that is, the sacrifice of atonement (Rom. 3:25; 1 John 2:2; 4:10; Heb. 2:17); the disposition in God that replaced it, the new reconciled—no longer hostile but favorable—disposition of peace toward the world (καταλλαγη, Rom. 5:10f.; 2 Cor. 5:18–20); the disposition of people vis-à-vis God (Rom. 5:1); further, the gift of the Holy Spirit (John 15:26; Acts 2; Gal. 4:6); the second birth and the power to become children of God (John 1:12–13); sanctification (1 Cor. 1:30); participation in Christ's death (Rom. 6:3f.); the dying to sin (Rom. 6:6f.; Gal. 2:20); the being crucified to the world (Gal. 6:14); the cleansing (Eph. 5:26; 1 John 1:7, 9) and the washing away of sins (1 Cor. 6:11; Rev. 1:5; 7:14) by being sprinkled with the blood of Christ (Heb. 9:22; 12:24; 1 Pet. 1:2); walking in the Spirit and in the newness of life (Rom. 6:4); participation in the resurrection and ascension of Christ (Rom. 6:5; Eph. 2:6; Phil. 3:20); the imitation of Christ (Matt. 10:38; 1 Pet. 2:21f.); increased freedom from the curse of the law (Rom. 6:14; 7:1–6; Gal. 3:13; Col. 2:14); the fulfillment of the old and the inauguration of a new covenant (Mark 14:24; Heb. 7:22; 9:15; 12:24); redemption from the power of Satan (Luke 11:22; John 14:30; Col. 2:15; 1 John 3:8; Col. 1:13); victory over the world (John 16:33; 1 John 4:4, 5:4); deliverance from death and from the fear of death (Rom. 5:12f.; 1 Cor. 15:55f.; Heb. 2:15); escape from judgment (Heb. 10:27–28); and, finally, the resurrection of the last day (John 11:25; 1 Cor. 15:21); ascension (Eph. 2:6); glorification (John 17:24); the heavenly inheritance (John 14:2; 1 Pet. 1:4); eternal life already beginning here with the inception of faith (John 3:15, 36) and one day fully manifesting itself in glory (Mark 10:30; Rom. 6:22); the new heaven and new earth (2 Pet. 3:13; Rev. 21:1, 5); and the restoration of all things (Acts 3:21; 1 Cor. 15:24–28).

THE DOCTRINE OF CHRIST'S WORK

[377] The history of the doctrine of Christ's work is markedly different from that of the dogmas of the Trinity and Christ's person. No particular controversy concerning it has led to a clear-cut formulation. The truth is Scripture is so many-sided in its description of that work that in the history of theology there has emerged an array of views on the work of Christ, all of which contain a core of truth. The Apostolic Fathers, following the language of Scripture, say only that Christ suffered and sacrificed himself for us out of love.[33] Soon, however, people attempted to gain a clearer picture of the work of Christ. As a result a number of different views immediately surfaced side by side. From the

---

33. *Epistle of Barnabas,* 7; Ignatius, *Epistle to the Ephesians,* 1; Polycarp, *Epistle to the Philippians,* 1; *Epistle to Diognetus,* 9; cf. G. Wustmann, *Die Heilsbedeutung Christi bei den apostolischen Vätern* (Gütersloh: Bertelsmann, 1905).

beginning Christ was viewed not only as prophet but also as king and priest.[34] Sometimes these three offices are also expressly listed side by side. Eusebius speaks of Christ as being "of the world the only High Priest, of all creation the only king, of the prophets the only archprophet of the Father,"[35] and similar statements occur also in Lactantius, Gregory of Nyssa, Augustine, and others.[36] This is not to deny that sometimes one or another view comes one-sidedly to the fore. At one time it is stressed that Christ is the Logos who appeared on earth to reveal to people the full truth and to give them an example of virtue.[37] Or sin is perceived more as power than as guilt, and, correspondingly, Christ's work is viewed more as redemption than as reconciliation. God became human in order that he might redeem humans from sensuality, mortality, and demon-control and make them like God, participants in eternal life and immortality.[38] Another familiar and—despite Gregory of Nazianzus's objections[39]—widely held view was that Christ had delivered himself up to Satan as a ransom, bait, or snare (Job 40:24) and thus conquered him by cunning and snatched people from his control.[40] Finally, there was the idea—also in circulation from the beginning—that in his suffering and dying he had offered himself up to God on our behalf and in our place to secure atonement, forgiveness, sanctification, and salvation as a whole. This thought is most beautifully expressed already in the *Epistle to Diognetus*.[41] According to Justin Martyr, Christ did not become man only to share in our suffering and to bring healing, to put a stop to the disobedience that had come into the world, to overcome the power of Satan and death, but his death is also a sacrifice for all sinners who want to repent, the Passover [lamb] slain for all, the cause of the forgiveness of sins.[42] Irenaeus, in much clearer language, states that Christ, who by his incarnation is in com-

34. In a note attached to his article, J. Boehmer ("Zum Verständnis des Reiches Gottes," *Die Studierstube* [1905]: 661ff.) states that Philo in his *Life of Moses* already describes the latter as high priest, king, and lawgiver; that Josephus repeatedly extols his hero Hyrcanus as king, high priest, and prophet; and that the *Testament of Levi* (chs. 8 and 18) bears witness to the future Messiah, saying that he will simultaneously be king, priest, and prophet.

35. Eusebius, *Ecclesiastical History*, I, 3.

36. Augustine, *City of God*, X, 6; cf. Krauss, "Über das Mittlerwerk nach dem Schema des munus triplex," *Jahrbuch für deutsche Theologie* (1872): 595–655; G. F. K. Müller, "Jesu dreifaches Amt," *PRE*[3], VIII, 733–41.

37. Justin Martyr, *First Apology*, 10; Irenaeus, *Against Heresies*, V, 1; Tertullian, *De orat.*, 4; Clement of Alexandria, *Stromateis*, V, 12; Origen, *On First Principles*, III, 5–6; idem, *Against Celsus*, I, 67–68.

38. Irenaeus, *Against Heresies*, III, 16, 6, 20, 2; IV, 2; V, 1; Athanasius, *De incarn.*, 7; Gregory of Nyssa, *Greater Catechism*, 17–26.

39. Gregory of Nazianzus, *Theological Orations*, 45, 22; ed. note: In the original, Bavinck has 42, 48.

40. Origen, on Matt. 20:28; Gregory of Nyssa, *The Catechetical Oration*, trans. J. H. Srawley (Cambridge: Cambridge University Press, 1903), orat. 22–26; John of Damascus, *The Orthodox Faith*, III, 1, 27; cf. J. Wirtz, *Die Lehre von der Apolytrosis* (Trier, 1906).

41. *Epistle to Diognetus*, c. 9; cf. also, Clement of Rome, *First Epistle of Clement to the Corinthians*, 7; *Epistle of Barnabas*, c. 5–7.

42. Justin Martyr, *Dialogue with Trypho*, ch. 40, 111; cf. K. G. Semisch, *Justin der Märtyrer*, 2 vols. (Breslau: August Schulz, 1840–42), II, 416ff.

munion with us and entered our entire condition,[43] by his suffering and death reconciled us to God,[44] restored us in the favor of God, against whom we had sinned, reconciled the Father on our behalf, made good our disobedience by his obedience, and granted us the forgiveness of sins in the [fellowship of] faith.[45] A similar view of Christ's suffering as a sacrifice for our sins that secured for us righteousness and life occurs also in Origen, Athanasius, Cyril, Gregory of Nyssa, and John of Damascus.[46]

In the West, too, these ideas were taken over and further developed. Tertullian regarded religion as a juridical relationship in which humans are subject to God's law and have to make up for transgressions by penance to God. As in the doctrine of the Trinity, so in that of penance, Tertullian introduced a number of terms ("to satisfy an offended God," "to placate an angry God," "to reconcile," "to win God's favor," and so on) that were already applied, though not yet by himself, by Cyprian, Hilary, Ambrose, and others to Christ and his sacrifice.[47] Augustine enumerated the different fruits of Christ's sacrifice, all of which come down to two things: on the one hand, they deliver us from guilt, pollution, death, and the devil; on the other, they confer on us illumination, life, and blessedness. Besides the ethical, the mystical, and the ransom function, also the juridical or satisfaction function occurs in him. Christ is the mediator, reconciler, redeemer, savior, healer, pastor, and so on. He is both priest and sacrifice. He is the true and only sacrifice for sins;[48] being himself without guilt, he took upon himself our punishment in order thereby to pay our debt and end our punishment.[49] "He made our faults his faults, so that he might make his righteousness our righteousness." His curse is our blessing. "Christ was taking to himself flesh from you, and from himself gave salvation to you; was taking death to himself from you, and from himself gave life to you; was taking to himself insults from you and from himself conferred honors on you."[50]

43. Irenaeus, *Against Heresies*, V; praef. III, 18, 7; V, 16, 2.

44. Ibid., III.

45. Ibid., V.

46. G. Thomasius, *Christi Person und Werk,* 3rd ed., 2 vols. (Erlangen: A. Deichert, 1886–88), II, 125ff.; E. Weigl, *Die Heilslehre des hl. Cyril von Alexandrien* (Mainz: Kirchheim, 1905); J. B. Aufhauser, *Die Heilslehre des hl. Gregor von Nyssa* (Munich: Lentner, 1910).

47. A. von Harnack, *History of Dogma,* trans. N. Buchanan, J. Millar, E. B. Speirs, and W. McGilchrist, ed. A. B. Bruce, 7 vols. (London: Williams & Norgate, 1896–99), V, 17ff.; cf. II, 177.

48. Augustine, *City of God*, X, 6; idem, *Enchiridion*, 33, 41.

49. Augustine, *Against Faustus the Manichee*, XIV, 4.

50. Augustine, *Enarrations on the Psalms,* 61.3; cf. K. Kühner, *Augustin's Anschauung von der Erlösungsbedeutung Christi* (Heidelberg: K. Groos, 1890); O. Scheel, *Die Anschauung Augustins über Christi Person und Werk* (Tübingen: Mohr, 1901); J. Gottschick, "Augustins Anschauung von der Erlöserwirkungen," *Zeitschrift für Theologie und Kirche* 11 (1901): 97–213; Scheel reviewed this treatise of Gottschick (*Theologische Studien und Kritiken* (1904): 401–33, 491–553) and leveled serious objections against it. Whereas Gottschick attempts to demonstrate that in fact there is unity in Augustine's doctrine concerning Christ's redemption and that for him it mainly consists in the acquisition of the forgiveness of sins and the gift of the Holy Spirit because as head of the human race Christ bore its punishment, Scheel maintains that Augustine was unable to

The ideas about Christ's suffering that we encounter in the church fathers re-emerge in [medieval] scholasticism.[51] But it is especially Anselm's work *Cur Deus homo* [why God became man] that gave the "satisfaction" view predominance over all others. Anselm's innovation was not that he viewed Christ's death as a sacrifice for our sins. It was that, whereas earlier the predominant emphasis had been that incarnation and satisfaction were not absolutely necessary but only "fitting,"[52] Anselm looked for a ground with which to prove the opposite. He found it in the position that sin always has to result either in punishment or in satisfaction and that if God wants to forgive and save humanity, no other than a "God-man" can give God that satisfaction and restore his honor. Because Christ was that "God-man," his totally voluntary death was of such immense value that he not only delivered people from punishment but in addition earned merit; and since he himself did not need that merit, he relinquished it for the benefit of humankind, in whose place he had restored God's honor.[53] No one took over Anselm's view unaltered. As a rule the absolute necessity of Christ's incarnation and satisfaction was denied. Duns Scotus, who was diametrically opposed to it, rejected the infinity of the guilt and the infinity of Christ's merit, denied that Christ's sacrifice as such was sufficient, taught that God counted it as sufficient, and traced the incarnation and satisfaction to pure arbitrariness, to "absolute dominion" in God.[54] But also Aquinas did not believe it was absolutely necessary, calling it "fitting."[55] Moreover, the odd person, specifically Abelard, one-sidedly stressed that Christ's incarnation and suffering were a revelation not of God's justice but only of his grace and love, that from the beginning to the end of his life, Christ taught us by his word and example and thereby excites in us a love that liberates us from sin and makes us into God's children, and that the redeeming and reconciling power of Christ's person consists in these things.[56]

---

free himself from Neoplatonic influence, that beside the ethical, he also consistently held to the physical view of redemption and, therefore, that he did much less to lay the groundwork for the view of Anselm and the Reformation than Gottschick pictures it. Cf. F. Loofs, *Leitfaden zum Studium der Dogmengeschichte*, 4th ed. (Halle a.S.: M. Niemeyer, 1906), 356ff., 399ff.

51. J. Gottschick, "Studien zur Versöhnungslehre des Mittelalters," *Zeitschrift für Kirchengeschichte* 22 (1901): 371–438; 23 (1902): 35–67, 191–222, 321–75; 24 (1903): 15–45, 198–231.

52. So also Augustine, J. Gottschick, "Augustins Anschauung," *Zeitschrift für Theologie und Kirche* 11 (1901): 158–66.

53. E. von Moeller ("Die anselmsche Satisfactio und die Busse des germ. Strafrechts," *Theologische Studien und Kritiken* [1899]: 627–34) contends against H. Cremer (*Theologische Studien und Kritiken* [1880] and [1893]) as well as J. W. Kunze ("Anselm," *PRE*³, I, 569) that the former [Anselm's satisfaction doctrine, ed.] is not derived from the latter [Germanic notions of punishment, ed.]. Cf. F. Loofs, *Dogmengeschichte*, 505ff.; B. Funke, *Grundlagen und Voraussetzung der Satisfaktionstheorie des hl. Anselm von Canterbury* (Münster: Schöningh, 1903); J. Leipoldt, "Der Begriff meritum in Anselms von Canterbury Versöhnungslehre," *Theologische Studien und Kritiken* (1904): 300–308; L. Heinrichs, *Die Genugtuungstheorie des hl. Anselmus von Canterbury* (Paderborn: Schöningh, 1909).

54. Cf. H. Bavinck, *Reformed Dogmatics*, II, 233–40 (#208).

55. T. Aquinas, *Summa theol.*, III, qu. 1, art. 1; II, qu. 46, art. 1–3; F. Loofs, *Dogmengeschichte*, 513.

56. F. Loofs, *Dogmengeschichte*, 514ff.

A number of elements in Anselm's conception were later rejected by all. Included in this are the private-law character he assigns to Christ's satisfaction, the notion of sin as insult and of satisfaction as the restoration of honor; the one-sided emphasis he puts on Christ's death at the expense of his life; the dichotomy he construes between punishment and satisfaction; the mechanical connection he assumes between satisfaction and merit, between Christ's merit and the reason why it helps the human race. All this does not alter the fact, however, that in its essential constituents—such as Christ's satisfaction of God's justice for the guilt of humanity's sins in order thereby to gain righteousness and life—Anselm's teaching nonetheless achieved permanent significance in later theology. Anselm was the first to understand, and to understand most clearly, that the redemption accomplished by Christ was a deliverance, not primarily from the consequences of sin, from death and Satan's power, but above all from sin itself and sin's guilt. Christ's redemption, according to Anselm, consists mainly in reconciliation between God and humanity.

Yet in scholastic and Roman Catholic theology this truth has come into its own much less than in Protestant theology. Aquinas does not, with Anselm, restrict the satisfaction mainly to Christ's death but extends it to all his suffering and his entire obedience.[57] He also explains—better than Anselm—the transmission of Christ's merit to his own from the fact that Christ is the head and his church his body.[58] But in Christ's suffering Aquinas fails to see its unity, views it successively as merit, satisfaction, sacrifice, and redemption,[59] and then lists as its fruits deliverance from sin, from the power of the devil, from the punishment of sin; reconciliation; and entrance into paradise.[60] Reconciliation here does not yet stand out in the foreground, and it is also fully realized only when Christ as a model of virtue and humility spurs us to imitate him, moves us by his love and grace to love, and, in faith, delivers us from sin. The objective and subjective sides of reconciliation, as also forgiveness and renewal, are not kept sufficiently distinct.[61] Many Catholic theologians later follow suit along these lines,[62] but others subsume the entire work of Christ under the concept of redemption or of satisfaction (and merit) or deal with it under the rubric of the three offices.[63]

57. T. Aquinas, *Summa theol.*, III, qu. 46.

58. Ibid., III, qu. 8.

59. Ibid., III, qu. 48.

60. Ibid., III, qu. 49.

61. Ibid., III, qu. 48, art. 1.; qu. 49, art. 1; P. Lombard, *Sent.*, III, dist. 18–19; Bonaventure, *Breviloquium*, IV, 7, 9.

62. E.g., D. Petavius, "De incarn.," *Op. theol.*, XII–XIII; *Theologia Wirceburgensi*, 3rd ed., 10 vols. (Paris: Berche et Tralin, 1880), IV, 295ff.; J. Deharbe, *Verklaring der Katholieke Geloofs- en Zedeleer*, 3rd ed., 4 vols. (Utrecht: J. R. Van Rossum, 1880–88), II, 267ff.

63. In addition to the literature listed above, cf. also the Roman Catechism, I, c. 3, qu. 7; G. Perrone, *Praelectiones theologicae,* 9 vols. (Louvain: Vanlinthout & Vandezande, 1838–43), IV, 309; F. B. Liebermann, *Institutiones theologicae,* 8th ed., 2 vols. (Mainz: Kirchheim, 1857), II, 264; F. Dieringer, *Lehrbuch der katholischen Dogmatik,* 4th ed. (Mainz: Kirchheim, 1858).

The Reformation originally had no doctrine concerning the work of Christ other than Rome's and so defended Christ's satisfaction tooth and nail against the Socinian attacks. Yet, in virtue of its own principle, it placed this doctrine in a new perspective and within another context. Inasmuch as the Reformation had learned to know sin primarily as guilt, atonement became central in the work of Christ. Sin was of such a nature that it aroused God's wrath. Needed above all to still that wrath, to satisfy God's justice, was the satisfaction accomplished by the "God-man." He achieved it by putting himself in our place as the guarantor of the covenant, taking upon himself the full guilt and punishment of sin, and submitting to the total demand of the law of God. Hence the work of Christ consists not so much in his humility, nor only in his death, but in his total—active as well as passive—obedience. He accomplished this work in his threefold office, not only as prophet by teaching us and giving us an example and exhorting us to love but also as priest and king. Calvin already spoke of this threefold office in his Genevan Catechism, subsequently treated the work of Christ under the rubric of the three offices in the 1539 edition of the *Institutes*,[64] and was in time followed in this approach by numerous Reformed, Lutheran, and Roman Catholic theologians. The objective and subjective sides of reconciliation, accordingly, are clearly distinguished. Christ accomplished everything. All the benefits are objectively contained in his person. Since by his sacrifice Christ met the requirements of God's justice, he objectively changed the relation between God and humankind and, consequently, all other relations between humankind to sin, death, Satan, and the world as well. The primary benefit, therefore, is the forgiveness of sins and consequently also deliverance from pollution, death, law, and Satan. Christ is the only mediator between God and humankind, the all-sufficient Savior, the highest prophet, the only priest, the true king.[65]

[378] The work of Christ, like his person, was very differently understood, however, by others. The Ebionites regarded Christ only as a prophet who by his teaching and example gives people power for the struggle against sin. To Gnostics, Christ was an aeon of divine wisdom who had appeared on earth in phantom human form in order, by enlightenment and knowledge, to free humans from the bonds of matter and to make them into πνευματικοι (spirituals). Over against this speculative rationalism the Montanists maintained the supernatural, transcendent character of Christianity, not only in the person of Christ but also in the continued Spirit-mediated revelation that still comes to believers now and advances the Christian religion from the stage of childhood into that of adulthood. Similarly, in the dualistic, pantheistic, apocalyptic, and libertinistic sects of the Middle Ages, there remained for Christ no other significance than that in his time he had revealed to people their true nature and destiny, thereby enabling

64. J. Calvin, *Institutes*, II.xv–xvii.
65. See, in addition to the works already cited, also F. Turretin, *De satisfactione Christi* (1691); J. Owen, *The Works of John Owen*, ed. William H. Goold (Edinburgh: T&T Clark, 1862), X; P. van Mastricht, *Theoretico-practica theologia* (Utrecht: Appels, 1714), V, c. 5ff.

people in the age of the Spirit to become what Christ was. What Scripture tells us of Christ is realized in every Christian. The true death and resurrection of Christ takes place in the rebirth of every human.

All these ideas were still fermenting in the age of the Reformation and triggered strong opposition to the teaching of Luther and Calvin. Not the Christ for us but the Christ in us, not the Word but the Spirit, was [considered] the essence of religion. Osiander taught that in his human nature Christ brings with him his eternal and essential divine righteousness, infuses this righteousness into his own people by faith, and thus justifies them.[66] Carlstadt, Franck, Schwenckfeld, Weigel, and others regarded trust in Christ's imputed righteousness a dangerous error; our salvation, they said, lies not in what Christ does outside of and for us but in what he does in and through us, in mystical communion with God.[67] This mystical view of redemption by Christ was also accepted by many people later. Böhme viewed the wrath of God and death as real, physical powers that Christ overcame with his death and in whose place he now infuses a new divine life in humankind.[68] Among Quakers, while redemption has its cause in Christ, Christ himself is nothing other than the sum of the grace and light existing in humankind: the real and true redemption is that which occurs in us.[69] Antoinette Bourignon and Poiret called Christ's substitutionary suffering impossible and improper. Christ came on earth not to make satisfaction for us but to preach God's forgiving love and, by his teaching and example, to purify us from sin.[70] Similarly, J. C. Dippel viewed Christ's suffering and death as an example of his spiritual mediatorship by which he kills the old "man" in us and brings about the resurrection of the "new." Redemption is something that happens in us; no objective atonement is needed, for there is no wrath in God.[71] According to Zinzendorf, Christ is the creator and maintainer of all things, the Yahweh of the Old Testament who especially revealed God's love in his becoming so very small, poor, and humble and in suffering so much. His suffering is not so much punishment and satisfaction to God as voluntary and loving martyrdom. This is how his blood and his death became the source of life for humankind. The martyr's wounds in Christ's side are the matrix of the human race, the origin of the Spirit, who, deriving from Christ, pours himself out in everyone.[72] Swedenborg

66. Cf. W. Müller (P. Tschackert), "Osiander," *PRE*[3], XIV, 501–9.

67. H. W. Erbkam, *Geschichte der protestantischen Sekten im Zeitalter der Reformation* (Hamburg and Gotha: Perthes, 1848), 247ff., 340ff., 441ff.

68. Joh. Claassen und J. Böhme, *Jakob Böhme: Sein Leben und seine theosophischen Werke*, 3 vols. (Stuttgart: J. F. Steinkopf, 1885), III, 31–76.

69. *R. Barclay, *Verantwoording van de ware Christ. Godgel.* (Amsterdam, 1757), 154; ed. note: ET: *Barclay's Apology in Modern English*, ed. Dean Freiday (Alburtis, PA: Hemlock Press, 1967).

70. C. Vitringa, *Doctr. christ.*, VI, 51.

71. C. Vitringa, *Doctr. christ.*, VI, 56; I. A. Dorner, *History of the Development of the Doctrine of the Person of Christ*, trans. William Lindsay Alexander, 5 vols. (Edinburgh: T&T Clark, 1863–78), IV, 376.

72. H. Plitt, *Zinzendorfs Theologie*, 3 vols. in 1 (Gotha: F. A. Perthes, 1869–74), I, 291; II, 194ff.; M. Schneckenburger, *Vorlesungen über neutestamentliche Zeitgeschichte* (Frankfurt a.M.: Brönner, 1862), 195ff.

Swedenborg considered the belief that Christ's suffering on the cross is redemption as a fundamental error that, along with the doctrine of the Trinity, ruined the church. Christ's suffering on the cross was not redemption but Jesus' last temptation and, since he remained firm, the means of his glorification. Then the human in him was united with the divine of his Father, God became truly human, and he could approach and overcome the hostile sensual powers of hell. Redemption is an ongoing subjugation of hell and ordering of heaven effected by God in human form.[73]

The church's doctrine concerning the work of Christ came under attack not only from the side of mysticism but also from that of rationalism. As belonging in this category, we may count the teaching of Stancarus that Christ is our mediator and our righteousness only in his human nature,[74] as also the denial of Christ's active obedience by Karg (Parsimonius) and by Johannes Piscator, who first set forth his ideas in a letter in 1604.[75] Karg retracted his sentiments in 1570, but Piscator, getting support from Martinius, Crocius, Pierius, Pareus, Wendelin, H. Alting, and others, later, through Cameron, Placaeus, Cappellus, and others, had a harmful influence on Reformed theology.

THE SOCINIAN CHALLENGE

But the most serious and substantial opposition to the doctrine of vicarious satisfaction came from the side of the Socinians. Though they still refer to Christ as prophet, priest, and king,[76] they in fact make his priestly office a mere appendix to his kingly office. When Christ was on earth, he was only a prophet who, before the start of his public ministry, was taken up into heaven by God (John 3:13, 31; 6:36, 62; 8:28; 10:18),[77] was there instructed in the truth by God himself, and thus enabled to perfect the law with new commandments and to promise to the keepers of those commandments eternal life and the sanctifying power of the Spirit.[78] Christ confirmed his teaching by his sinless life, by his miracles, and especially by his death and resurrection.[79] His death was necessary to prompt his followers to persevere to the end in their piety and holy manner of life and to confirm God's love to us with unmistakable clarity;[80] the purpose of his resurrection was to show by his example that those who obey God are freed from all death and to give to Christ himself the power to bestow eternal life on all who obey him.[81] Here the

---

73. E. Swedenborg, *The True Christian Religion*, 2 vols. (Philadelphia: J. B. Lippencott Co., 1896), 126–38.

74. D. H. Benroth (Schmidt), "Stancarus," *PRE*[3], XVIII, 752–54.

75. This letter was included in the *Epist. praest. virorum*, 156; cf. also, Piscator, *Theses theol.*, XV, 18–19.

76. *Racovian Catechism*, trans. Thomas Rees (London, 1818), qu. 101.

77. Ibid., qu. 195.

78. Ibid., qu. 209ff., 352, 361.

79. Ibid., qu. 374.

80. Ibid., qu. 380, 383.

81. Ibid., qu. 384.

death of Christ, accordingly, has a totally different meaning from what it has in the doctrine of the church. It did not constitute an independent component in the work of Christ but served only, on the one hand, to confirm his teaching and, on the other, to bring him to the resurrection, without which he could not become king and Lord in heaven.[82] And this he actually only became as a result of his ascension. The resurrection was still a part of the state of humiliation, for even afterward he still had a mortal body.[83] But at the ascension he received a glorified body and was exalted to being king, Lord, and God. As such he received from God the power to sustain in all kinds of distress those who follow his example and, in the end, to reward them with immortality. That he is *able* to do this is his royal office; that he *wills* to do this is his high priestly office.[84] Hence on earth he was not yet a priest;[85] his death was not the actual sacrifice but the introduction to and preparation for it. He now offers the true sacrifice in heaven just as the high priest in the Old Testament finally only brings about atonement in the holy of holies.[86] And that sacrifice consists in effecting reconciliation, that is, delivering us from the service and punishment of sin.

Based on this standpoint, the Socinians had to oppose the doctrine of satisfaction just as vigorously as that of the Trinity and the deity of Christ.[87] First of all, in their judgment this doctrine is contrary to Scripture. Those who advocate it cannot advance a single text that unmistakably supports their opinion. Scripture clearly says that God forgives sin out of grace, and forgiveness rules out satisfaction. The statement that Christ suffered for us has no substitutionary significance but only says that Christ suffered for us, not to satisfy God but to free us from sin. The words "redemption," "reconciliation," and so on only indicate that Christ has shown us the way in which we may be freed from the service and punishment of sin, but definitely not that God had to be reconciled by a sacrifice, for God was graciously disposed toward us and has made this known to us by Christ.

Second, satisfaction is not necessary. God's righteousness and mercy are not opposed to each other, and these attributes are not characteristic of God's nature but the effects of his will and dependent on his will. Whether or not God wants to punish or forgive sins is determined not in any way by his nature but by his will. God can just as well—and better than a human being—forgive sins without satisfaction. In fact, his justice is nullified by satisfaction, because it punishes the innocent and acquits the guilty; and his mercy loses its value if it can only manifest itself after satisfaction. God, accordingly, has always promised forgiveness to the penitent and wants us to follow him in that respect.

82. Ibid., qu. 386.
83. Ibid., qu. 465.
84. Ibid., qu. 476.
85. Ibid., qu. 483.
86. Ibid., qu. 413.
87. Cf. esp. ibid., qu. 388–414; and F. Socinus, *Praelectiones theologicae* (Racoviae: Sebastiani Sternacii, 1627), c. 15; idem, *De Jesu Christo Salvatore*, *Bibl. Fr. Polon.*, II, 121–252.

Third, satisfaction is also impossible. Passive obedience is impossible because, unlike money debts, personal moral debts cannot be transferred from one to another. To punish an innocent for the sin of another is unjust and cruel. Even if it were possible, that other would at most be able to undergo the punishment of sin (i.e., eternal death) for one individual, but never for many or for all people. As for active obedience, this is even much less possible, for each individual is personally responsible for keeping God's law, something a person can never do for someone else. Moreover, passive and active obedience are in conflict with each other. Those who carry out the one are free from the other. Christ, accordingly, did not fulfill them. He did not suffer eternal death but was raised from the dead on the third day. However severe, his suffering was finite; his divine nature could not make it of infinite value because it could not suffer and die, or it would make every moment in that suffering infinite and thereby make all the other suffering superfluous. In any case, how could that benefit us, since it is humanity that sinned, and how could God (the Son) offer satisfaction to God himself (the Father)?

Finally, the doctrine of satisfaction is also harmful because it elevates Christ with his mercy above God with his demand for satisfaction. It obligates us to be more grateful to Christ than to God and opens the door to carelessness and ungodliness. All sins, after all, have been atoned for: now we can sin as much as we please. After all, the death of Christ was especially intended to free us from sin and to prompt us to pursue a new and God-fearing life!

The criticism by Faustus Socinus was so sharp and complete that later dissenters could do little other than repeat his arguments. The Remonstrants still tried to maintain the doctrine of Christ's satisfaction but in fact adopted all the objections lodged against it. They not only taught, with Catholics and Lutherans, that Christ had made satisfaction for all humanity but also denied that Christ suffered all the penalties that God had placed on sin, that he suffered eternal death, that his active obedience was vicarious. Even his suffering and death were not a full satisfaction for sins, not a payment of debts, which, after all, would make forgiveness on God's part and faith on our part superfluous, but a sacrifice, a total consecration of Christ to God maintained into death, considered by God as sufficient for all sins. Now on the basis of that sacrifice, God causes the forgiveness of sins to be offered to all by means of the gospel, so that everyone who believes may be saved. But Christ secured not actual salvation for his own but only the possibility of being saved. Whether or not a person is actually saved depends on himself or herself.[88] Hugo Grotius also made an attempt to justify the doctrine of Christ's satisfaction.[89] To that end he derived it not from the will of God, nor from his punitive justice, but from his "governmental" justice, that is, from the necessity for God, in a world of law and order, to uphold justice and law and to take account of the common good.

---

88. *Apology of the Augsburg Confession*, ch. 8; P. van Limborch, *Theologia christiana* (Amsterdam: Wetstein, 1735), III, c. 18–23.

89. In his *Defensio fidei catholicae de satisfactione Christi* (1617).

By viewing that juridical order as a world order existing outside God, however, he made God's justice subordinate and serviceable to it, changed Christ's satisfaction into undeserved suffering, exemplary punishment designed to deter others, a measure of governmental wisdom. In addition he left unexplained why Christ had to be God for this and how God could thus make an innocent person suffer and regard his suffering as a satisfaction for others.

Still, however many objections the Socinian and Remonstrant teaching could provoke, it gradually gained the upper hand. Supernaturalists such as Michaelis, Storr, Morus, Knapp, Steudel, Reinhard, Muntinghe, Vinke, Egeling, and others—sometimes even in the belief they were defending the doctrine of the church—materially presented no other teaching than that of the Remonstrants or Hugo Grotius.[90] The same was true in New England theology. The older Jonathan Edwards still defended the orthodox doctrine,[91] but Edwards Jr., Smalley, Maxcy, Burge, Dwight, Emmons, and Spring promoted the governmental theory of Grotius.[92] Many went further and rejected the entire doctrine of satisfaction. Ernesti fought the doctrine of the three offices by saying that the names of prophet, priest, and king were vague Old Testament notions and that each office already included the two others.[93] Töllner revived all the Socinian objections, not only against Christ's active obedience but against the entire doctrine of satisfaction.[94] And along with him, Bahrdt, Steinhart, Eberhard, Löffler, Henke, Wegscheider, Hobbes, Locke, Chubb, Coleridge, John Taylor, Priestley, and others all argued that Christ was a revelation, not of God's justice, but of his love and mercy; that God only punishes sin with such natural penalties as arise automatically from the sin itself and have a pedagogical character. They regarded the doctrine of substitution as an absurd idea going back to Augustine and Anselm and claimed that it either does not occur in Scripture at all or occurs, by way of accommodation, in Old Testament symbols, and that the active obedience of Christ, if it were vicarious, would make unnecessary all faith, repentance, and moral improvement on

90. Cf., e.g., G. C. Knapp, *Vorlesungen über die christliche Glaubenslehre nach dem Lehrbegriff der evangelischen Kirche*, ed. Carl Thilo, 2 vols. (Halle: Buchhandlung des Waisenhauses, 1827), II, 222ff.; K. G. Bretschneider, *Handbuch der Dogmatik der evangelisch-lutherischen Kirche*, II, 239ff.; F. V. Reinhard, *Grundriss der Dogmatik* (Munich: Seidel, 1802), §107; H. E. Vinke, *Theologiae Christianae Dogmaticae* (Utrecht: Kemink, 1853–54), 1490; L. Egeling, *De weg der zaligheid naar het beloop des Bijbels,* 2 vols. (Amsterdam: Mortier Covens en Zoon, 1844), II, 175.

91. J. Edwards, *The Works of Jonathan Edwards,* 22 vols. (New Haven: Yale University Press, 1957–2003), I, 582; cf. J. Ridderbos, *De Theologie van Jonathan Edwards* ('s Gravenhage: J. A. Nederbragt, 1907), 294ff. Ed note: It is not clear to which of Edwards's writings Bavinck is referring. Perhaps the reference here is to *A Treatise on Grace,* ed. P. Helm (Cambridge and London: James Clarke, 1971), 69, where Edwards makes a clear statement on Christ's satisfaction. For a thorough treatment of Edwards's doctrine of the atonement, see John H. Gerstner, *The Rational Biblical Theology of Jonathan Edwards,* 3 vols. (Powhattan, VA: Berea Publications; Orlando, FL: Ligonier Ministries, 1992), II, 424–73.

92. Cf. E. Park, *The Atonement: Discourses and Treatises* (Boston: Congregational Board of Publication, 1860); A. A. Hodge, *The Atonement* (Philadelphia: Presbyterian Board of Publication, 1867), 328.

93. J. A. Ernesti, "De officio Christi triplici," *Opuscula theologica* (Leipzig: Fritsch, 1773), 413.

94. J. G. Töllner, *Der thätige Gehorsam Jesu Christi untersucht* (Breslau: Johann Ernst Meyern, 1768).

our part. Finally, above all, they objected that the forgiveness of sins, being made children of God, and justification cannot precede moral renewal or sanctification, but must follow them and are all dependent on them.[95] Religion was constructed on the basis of morality; the focus shifted from the objective to the subjective. Atonement became dependent on redemption. God became the servant of man. The death of Christ could only still be an example of virtue and confirmation of the truth (Eberhard, Löffler), or an act of self-offering for the benefit of humanity and a demonstration of God's love (Schwarze), or a factual declaration from God that he wills to forgive the sins of those who repent (Morus, Köppen, Klaiber, Stäudlin). Alternatively, it could be a means of eliciting trust in God and of deterring sin (Töllner, Egeling), or of delivering us from the mistaken idea that God is angry and punishes people (Steinhart), or a symbolic representation of the voluntary assumption by moral persons of the punishment they have deserved in their sinful state (Kant).[96]

[379] In modern theology there has been no lack of attempts to modify the doctrine of Christ's office and work in line with the many objections lodged against it and to maintain it in a new form. Generally speaking, this theology was guided by the endeavor to replace the juridical doctrine of satisfaction, in which Christ fulfilled the demand of God's righteousness in our place, by that of a personal religious ethical activity of Christ by which he effected a moral change, not in God, who is always love, but in us—be it more in our mind, or in our heart, or in our will. Schelling and Hegel attributed only a passing value to Christianity as a historical phenomenon. The idea that God becomes man in a specific person and subsequently suffers and dies for the sin of others is unthinkable. But interpreted symbolically, said these thinkers, the Christian doctrine of atonement contains profound truth. The person and work of Christ are the historical embodiment of the idea that the world as son of God, proceeding from him and returning to him, necessarily has to suffer and thus enter its glory. The world and humanity, subject as they are to time and finiteness, are the suffering and dying God.[97] The reconciliation of God is a necessary objective moment in the cosmic process: God reconciles himself to himself and returns to himself from a state of estrangement.[98] Further pursuing this line of thought, Hartmann said: God cannot save me, but I

95. Cf., e. g., J. A. L.Wegscheider, *Institutiones theologiae christianae dogmaticae* (Halle: Gebauer, 1819), §§140–42; T. Hobbes, *Leviathan* (London: J. M. Dent, 1924), ch. 41.

96. A. van der Willigen, "Oordeelk. Overzigt over de versch. wijzen, op welke men zich heeft voorgesteld het verband tusschen den dood van Jezus Christus en de zaligheid der menschen," *Godgeleerde Bijdragen* 2 (1828): 485–603; K. G. Bretschneider, *Systematische Entwickelung*, 4th ed. (Leipzig: J. A. Barth, 1841), 608ff.; F. C. Baur, *Die christliche Lehre von der Dreieinigkeit und Menschwerdung Gottes in ihrer geschichtlichen Entwicklung*, 3 vols. (Tübingen: Osiander, 1841–43), 478ff.; A. Ritschl, *Die christliche Lehre von der Rechtfertigung und Versöhnung*, 4th ed., 3 vols. (Bonn: A. Marcus, 1895–1903), I, chs. 7–8.

97. F. W. J. Schelling, *Ausgewählte Werke*, 4 vols. (Darmstadt: Wissenschaftliche Buchgesellschaft, 1968), I/5, 386–400.

98. G. W. F. Hegel, *Philosophie der Religion* (2), in *Sämtliche Werke*, 26 vols. (Zürich: J. H. Bodmer, 1700), XVI, 249–56 (*Werke*, XII, 249–56); ed. note: The section Bavinck cites here is from "The Absolute Religion,"

can save God. God can only be saved through me. Actual existence is the incarnation of the deity; the cosmic process is the story of God's passion and at the same time the way to the redemption of the One crucified in the flesh.[99] According to A. Drews, a mediator of redemption is not even a possibility, for all redemption is self-redemption by God in us, for God is the essence of a human being, and in humans he himself achieves self-consciousness and spiritual freedom.[100]

Liberal theology, though it still attempts to reserve a place in its dogmatics for the historical Jesus (inasmuch as it allows itself to be controlled in its philosophical assumptions by Hegel or Kant), does not get beyond saying that it views Jesus as the liberator from legalistic religion and the founder of a free Christian religion; that it sees in him the archetypal realization of the sonship of God; or that it honors him primarily as the preacher of the fatherly love of God and a model for his disciples.[101] In the case of men like Hartmann and Drews, this liberal theology is as hard put to justify itself as orthodoxy is. The latter, in their opinion, is in a strong position because it views the redemptive principle in Christianity as divine and eternal, makes Jesus into God, and ascribes the whole renewal of humankind to the Holy Spirit. But it is mistaken in that it equates this divine redemptive principle with the historical Jesus. The weakness of liberal theology, on the other hand, is that it wants to return to the (untraceable) historical Jesus, has no eye for the metaphysical principle of redemption, and only ascribes—which is all it *can* do—a historical and psychological significance to the personality of Jesus as it exists in its imagination.[102] The philosophers cited above, for their part, insist that theologians should stop trying to unite what cannot be united and make a radical split between the man Jesus, who perhaps never existed and is in any case unknowable, and the eternal Christ-idea, between the divine redemptive principle and the so-called historical facts. We are saved not by Jesus but by Christ, that is, the immanent deity who indwells all humans and brings them to salvation through suffering and death. The life of the world as the life of God; the painful development of humanity as the divine passion story; the cosmic process as the process of a God who suffers, struggles, and dies in each individual creature in order, in

and the section referred to can be found in P. Hodgson, ed., *Hegel: Lectures on the Philosophy of Religion,* vol. III, "The Consummate Religion" (Berkeley: University of California Press, 1988), 201–11.

99. E. von Hartmann, *Das sittliche Bewusstsein* (Leipzig: W. Friedrich, 1886), 688.

100. A. Drews, *Die Religion als Selbst-Bewusstsein Gottes* (Jena & Leipzig: E. Diederichs, 1906), 238ff.

101. O. Pfleiderer, *Grundriss der christlichen Glaubens- und Sittenlehre* (Berlin: G. Reimer, 1888), §§128, 133; A. Schweizer, *Christliche Glaubenslehre* (Leipzig: S. Hirzel, 1863–72), §§115, 125ff.; R. A. Lipsius, *Lehrbuch der evangelisch-protestantischen Dogmatik* (Braunschweig: C. A. Schwetschke, 1893), §§619ff.; A. E. Biedermann, *Christliche Dogmatik* (Zürich: Füssli, 1869), §§802, 815ff.

102. E. von Hartmann, *Die Krisis des Christentums in der modernen Theologie* (Berlin: C. Duncker, 1880); idem, *Die Selbstzersetzung des Christentums und die Religion der Zukunft,* 3rd ed. (Leipzig: Friedrich, 1888); A. Drews, *Die Religion des Selbst-Bewusstsein Gottes,* 239; idem, *Die Christusmythe,* 176ff.; ed. note: ET: *The Christ Myth* (Chicago: Open Court, 1910; reprinted, Amherst, NY: Prometheus Books, 1998); cf. also, F. Overbeck, *Ueber die Christlichkeit unserer heutigen Theologie,* 2nd ed. (Leipzig: Naumann, 1903), 72ff.; ed. note: ET: *On the Christianity of Theology,* trans. John Elbert Wilson (San Jose, CA: Pickwick Publications, 2002).

the religious consciousness of humans, to overcome the limits of finiteness and to anticipate their future triumph over all the suffering of the world: that is the truth of the Christian doctrine of redemption.[103]

MODERN VIEWS OF THE ATONEMENT

Nonetheless, both before and after the publication of Drews's work, there has been no lack of attempts to secure a permanent place in religion for the person and work of Christ. In Germany this was first attempted by Schleiermacher, subsequently by Ritschl. The former tries to effectuate redemption in the way of a mystical union between humans and Christ. Christ participated in communion with God at all times and was consequently holy and blessed. As such he came to us and entered into communion with us. He partook of our suffering, suffered with us in priestly compassion, and upheld his holiness and blessedness down into the deepest sorrow, even to death on the cross. But after thus entering first into communion with us, he then—not only by his word and example but by the mystical effect that emanates from his whole person—takes us up into communion with him and causes us to share by his redemptive activity in his holiness and by his reconciling activity in his blessedness. Hence in Schleiermacher, as it does in Rome, redemption, consisting in regeneration and sanctification, precedes reconciliation, the forgiveness of sins, and both occur not so much outside us, in Christ, as within us.[104] This mystical theory became the fundamental idea of the doctrine of reconciliation in mediation theology,[105] and also exerted strong influence outside it on, among others, Hofmann.[106] But, though Schleiermacher

103. A. Drews, *Die Christusmythe*, 188.

104. F. Schleiermacher, *The Christian Faith* (Edinburgh: T&T Clark, 1989), §§101–4; cf. H. Stephan, *Die Lehre Schleiermachers von der Erlösung* (Tübingen: Mohr, 1901).

105. C. E. Nitzsch, *System of Christian Doctrines* (Edinburgh: T&T Clark, 1849), §§80, 134–36; R. Rothe, *Theologische Ethik*, 2nd rev. ed., 5 vols. (Wittenburg: Zimmerman, 1867–71), §§541–48; L. Schöberlein, "Versöhnung," *PRE*[1], XVII, 87–143; idem, *Prinzip und System der Dogmatik* (Heidelberg: C. Winter, 1881), 182ff., 647ff.; H. L. Martensen, *Christian Dogmatics*, trans. William Urwick (Edinburgh: T&T Clark, 1871), §§156–69; J. P. Lange, *Christliche Dogmatik*, 3 vols. (Heidelberg: K. Winter, 1852), II, 813–908.

106. J. C. K. Hofmann (*Der Schriftbeweis*, 2nd ed., 2 vols. [Nördlingen: Beck, 1841], I, 47ff.; II, 1, 318ff., 455ff.) denies that Jesus' suffering and death were a judgment of God, a punishment for our sins, a vicarious satisfaction. Though Christ did not die in our place, he did die for our benefit. For God permitted his Son, the holy and righteous one, to be handed over into the hands of sinners and to experience the enmity of sin, in order that, proving his faithfulness in that suffering and remaining obedient to the end, he would fulfill his calling as Savior. And this consisted in that, by his perfect obedience, he became the beginning of a new relation between God and humans—a relation qualified no longer by sin but by his righteousness—the head of a new humanity that started with him. This replacement of objective reconciliation with God by the subjective redemption of humans encountered strong contradiction from Philippi, Thomasius, and others; cf. K. H. von Weizsäcker, "Um was handelt es sich in dem Streit über die Versöhnungslehre?" *Jahrbuch für deutsche Theologie* (1858): 155–88; F. A. Philippi, *Kirchliche Glaubenslehre*, 3rd ed., 7 vols. in 10 (Gütersloh: Bertelsmann, 1870–90), IV, 2, 201ff. Closely akin to this is also the view of Kohlbrugge. Through sin, human beings lost the image of God (i.e., the holy element in which they formerly lived) and became flesh through and through. But Christ, the Son of God, assumed this same sinful flesh we now have, yet in that state, despite all temptation and conflict,

adopted the terminology of the church's theology and also took over the doctrine of the three offices, it soon became clear that at many points he deviated from the teaching of Scripture and the church, did not do sufficient justice to sin and the sense of guilt, and viewed redemption too one-sidedly from the aesthetic perspective as harmony with the world.

Ritschl, therefore, took another tack. Averse to theological and philosophical speculation, he returned from the Christ of the church to the person of Jesus and substituted for the mystical unity between Christ and the church the ethical view of his person and work. According to Ritschl, reconciliation too must not be related to God as judge, his retributive justice or wrath, a legal order of reward and punishment, for that is a juridical and pharisaic construal of the God-humanity relation, one that does not belong in religion. God is essentially love, and his justice consists in his constant will to bring humans to salvation and to realize a divine kingdom in them. On account of sin, however, humanity is now far from God. It is weighed down by the consciousness of guilt. It has the feeling that it exists in a state of punishment. It fears God and does not dare approach him. It does not live in communion with God. Christ has come, therefore, to reveal to us the love of God. The doctrine of the three offices triggers resistance in Ritschl. According to him, the word "office" belongs only in a juridical community. In a moral community of love, it is better to speak of a calling. In the case of Christ, moreover, the three offices cannot be kept distinct; they blend into one another. If one wants to keep this terminology, however, one has to give preeminence to the royal office. Christ was appointed king to found a believing community, a realm of God, on earth, and to that end, as a prophet, he revealed God to us, and as a priest he consecrated himself to God on behalf of his own. Christ, says Ritschl, stood in a very special relation to God. He made God's purpose to unite humankind into a realm of God his life's calling. His entire life, his suffering and death, must be viewed from this perspective: as a moral calling that he fulfilled, not as a surety or mediatorship, as a way of substituting for us. Jesus was totally absorbed in the pursuit of that moral life task; to it he devoted himself completely—remaining faithful to death. By thus living his life, he fulfilled the will of God, realized God's purpose for humanity, revealed God's love, grace, and faithfulness, and at the same time, in pursuing this life task even to the point of death, he offered himself up and consecrated himself to God for the benefit of his own. What Jesus achieved by his moral obedience was not some effect in God—a change of God from being angry to being gracious—nor did he bring about the redemption of believers from Satan's power or from death. On the contrary, what he obtained was that all who, like Christ, make God's will their own may in communion with

---

clung by faith to God and his word, maintained himself in the state in which he was, and to the end attested: I am who I am; I and the Father are one. Thereby he made God our God, his Father our Father. He restored God's credit, received honor and glory in exchange, and now causes his people, whom he bore in his body, to share in that glory. See J. van Lonkhuijzen, *Hermann Friedrich Kohlbrügge en zijn Prediking* (Wageningen: Vada, 1905), 418ff.

him lay aside the sense of guilt, unbelief, distrust—the mistaken idea that God was angry and wanted to punish them—and may, despite their sins, believe in God's love and faithfulness, boast of the forgiveness of sins (justification), and afterward also themselves enter positively into the new relation in which God stands to them and so be able to put aside all hostility to God.[107]

No long argument is needed to see that in the theology of Ritschl the person and work of Christ came even less into their own than in that of Schleiermacher. For his whole soteriology comes down to the thesis that Christ—who had a unique knowledge of the Father, lived continually in communion with him, and made the Father's moral purpose with humanity his own—in his life and especially in his death made known, confirmed, and guaranteed to us this purpose of God. There cannot be and need not be any question of a punishment of sin borne by him or of an atonement effected by him, for God is love. The only thing needed was that by his perfect obedience and vocational faithfulness to the point of death, Christ should take away from us all distrust, fear, sense of guilt, and estrangement from God, thus giving us free access to God (justification) and directing our will to the purpose God had in mind with humankind (reconciliation).[108]

The school of Ritschl did not advance beyond this religious-ethical assessment of the work of Christ.[109] Kaftan, for example, though sticking even more closely to the orthodox terminology than Ritschl, completely agrees with him in his fundamental approach.[110] The work of Christ was a divine work, that is, a work qualified by his deity or by his union with God. At the same time, it was from start to finish the personal active work of the man Jesus. Salvation, therefore, is simultaneously the gift of God and the fruit of Christ's obedience. It was not that Christ, by bearing the punishment for our sins, satisfied God's justice and obtained his forgiveness for us; on the contrary, it bore the character of a faithfulness and obedience to God, maintained to the very end. In this sinful world, holy love could not manifest itself in any way other than in an obedience that was true to death. If God indeed wanted to reveal the will of his holy love in Christ, this

---

107. A. Ritschl, *Rechtfertigung und Versöhnung*, II, 34ff.; III, ch. 6–8; idem, *Unterricht in der christlichen Religion*, 3 vols. (Bonn: A. Marcus, 1886), §§40ff.

108. J. Wendland, *Albrecht Ritschl und seine Schüler* (Berlin: George Reimer, 1899), 116ff.; J. Orr, *The Ritschlian Theology and the Evangelical Faith* (London: Hodder & Stoughton, 1897), 149ff.

109. Cf. J. Herrmann, *Die Idee der Sühne im A.T.* (Leipzig: Hinrichs, 1905); H. Schultz, *Grundriss der evangelischen Dogmatik zum Gebrauche bei akademischen Vorlesungen* (Göttingen: Vandenhoeck & Ruprecht, 1892), §§44–46; T. Häring, *Zu Ritschls Versöhnungslehre* (Zürich: Hohr, 1888); idem, *Zu Versöhnungslehre: Eine dogmatische Untersuchung* (Göttingen: Vandenhoeck & Ruprecht, 1893); idem, *The Christian Faith*, trans. John Dickie and George Ferries, 2 vols. (London: Hodder & Stoughton, 1913), II, 690–91; F. Nitzsch, *Lehrbuch der evangelischen Dogmatik*, prepared by Horst Stephan, 3rd ed. (Tübingen: J. C. B. Mohr, 1902), 504–13; K. Ziegler, "Die ethische Versöhnungslehre im kirchlichen Unterricht," *Zeitschrift für Theologie und Kirche* 5 (1895): 1–57, 169–243; J. Gottschick, "Propter Christum: Ein Beitrag zum Verständnis der Versöhnungslehre Luthers," *Zeitschrift für Theologie und Kirche* 7 (1897): 352–84; J. Niebergall, "Die Heilsnotwendigkeit des Kreuztodes Jesu Christi," *Zeitschrift für Theologie und Kirche* 7 (1897): 461–512.

110. J. Kaftan, *Das Wesen der christlichen Religion* (Basel: C. Detloff, 1888), 246ff.; idem, *Dogmatik* (Tübingen: Mohr, 1901), §§58–60.

had to arouse—in the Jews, in the humanity represented by them, in us all—all the hatred and hostility that fills the human heart. In that sense, it is really true: we nailed him to the cross; our sin was the cause of his death. But when Kaftan comes to the question how that death of Christ, which was caused by our sin, is a means of our justification and rebirth and, as such, necessary, he can only say that in fact the knowledge of God's holy love has developed, the church has sprung into being, repentance and faith have been engendered, the benefits of justification and rebirth have been received thanks to the death and resurrection of Christ. In a word, the death of Christ was necessary not as punishment but only as a pedagogical means.[111] But *how* it could serve and had to serve as such remains totally in the dark. An appeal to the facts of the church's origin, of conversion and faith, justification and rebirth, is not sufficient, for from the beginning these have all been based on an assessment of Christ's death that is totally different from that which Kaftan offers.[112] Even more bluntly than in Kaftan, it was later said by Harnack that for the salvation of the church the death of Christ has no meaning higher than a historical and psychological one. For the gospel that Jesus proclaimed did not say a word about his own person; its only content was the fatherly love of God and the infinite value of the human soul. Granted, for others he is a guide to the Father, the personal realization and power of the gospel, but he himself is not a constituent of the gospel.[113]

[380] Similar attempts at mystically or ethically reconstructing the doctrine of the atonement were made in other countries as well. In the Netherlands, the theologians of the Groningen school opposed the theory of satisfaction as a blood theology that is inconsistent with the nature of God. They viewed the death of Jesus—a death inflicted on him by humans, undergone by Jesus himself, not willed but permitted by God—as a revelation of God's love, a proof of Jesus' perfection and of human sin. It worked as a means of salvation in that it startled people into an awareness of their own wickedness and so led them to remorse and amendment of life.[114] Sometimes Chantepie de la Saussaye still spoke of the doctrine of the atonement in an orthodox sense, but soon, under the influence of Schleiermacher and the theology of mediation, he came to the conclusion that it had to be divested of its juridical-scholastic form and ethically reconstructed. Certainly, Christ could not be regarded as a mediator who underwent the punishment of sin in our place and thereby satisfied God's justice. On the contrary, he was a mediator because in his person he united God and humanity. To that union he remained faithful even to death. In communion with God and humankind,

111. J. Kaftan, *Dogmatik*, 565–69.

112. Cf. C. Stange, *Der dogmatische Ertrag der Ritschlschen Theologie nach Julius Kaftan* (Leipzig: Dieterich, 1906), 129ff.; J. Orr, *Ritschlian Theology*, 215.

113. A. von Harnack, *What Is Christianity?* trans. Thomas Bailey Saunders (New York: Harper, 1957), 51–56, 63–70, 77, 125ff.

114. P. Hofstede de Groot, *De Groninger Godgeleerdheid in Hunne Eigenaardigheid* (Groningen: Scholtens, 1855), 181.

a communion he maintained to the end, he did not so much "satisfy"—that expression is far too weak—as fully glorify the justice of God and thereby secured also resurrection and life for all who enter into fellowship with him. It is not so much *by* Christ as *in* Christ that we enjoy forgiveness and peace, resurrection and life. In the thought of Chantepie de la Saussaye, substitution is not—to put it in Ritschl's words—exclusive but inclusive.[115]

At first modern theology had little interest in the doctrine of the atonement (*verzoening*).[116] In terms of its origin, this theology was much more a scientific than a religious phenomenon, having been birthed under the impact of the new science of nature and the historical criticism of Scripture. With respect to sin and atonement it was marked by great sobriety, for it had a high view of the moral disposition of humans and was content with Jesus as prophet, example, and moral ideal.[117] Sin, it claimed, is not the result of a fall and does not pass down from parents to children, but is a necessary defect that will gradually be surmounted. It is a phase in human development, a "not-yet-being" what humans should and will become in line with their true nature. No need was felt, therefore, for atonement: God himself had willed sin as an element in his program of bringing up human beings and would therefore as Father automatically forgive them in the life of every person who with seriousness and perseverance pursued the moral ideal. And this, actually, is true of all people. They are all traveling the same road, one being just a little ahead of another on that road.

Given this moralism, no justice was done to religion, and soon this shallow optimism saw itself sadly disappointed. The power of sin, both in one's own heart and in the human race, proved to be much greater than people initially imagined. With the progress of culture, wickedness and human wretchedness increased as well. The common people proved to have no stomach for the preaching of morality and turned their back on the church or gathered around the proclamation of the gospel of Scripture. Consequently, there emerged from modernist circles a large number of malcontents who, dissatisfied with a frigid preaching of law, again yearned for the language of orthodoxy, ecclesiastical organization, the confession and dogmatics, and who in view of the guilt and power of sin began to feel a need for atonement and redemption.[118] But there is no modernist way of meeting that need. For if the person of Jesus is no more than a human

115. H. Bavinck, *De theologie van Prof. Dr. Daniel Chantepie de la Saussaye*, 2nd ed. (Leiden: D. Donner, 1903), 48.

116. See note 2 above.

117. J. H. Scholten, *De Leer der Hervormde Kerk in Hare Grondbeginselen*, 2nd ed., 2 vols. (Leyden: P. Engels, 1850–51), I, 410ff.; II, 26ff.; *S. Hoekstra, *Godgeleerde Bijdragen* (1866), 273ff.; idem, *Grondslag, wezen, en openbaring van het godsdienstig geloof volgens de Heilige Schrift* (Rotterdam: Altmann & Roosenburg, 1861), 201ff.

118. Cf., e.g., Hylkema, "Hoe te oordeelen over het streven der malcontenten, het besef van zonde te verdiepen," a lecture given at the conference of modern theologians in May 1905; Agnotus (Prof. Eerdmans), "Reactie of Vooruitgang," *Theologische Tijdschrift* 43/1–2 (1908); and the more or less negative response by A. Bruining, "Godsdienst en Verlossingsbehoefte," *Teyler's Theologisch Tijdschrift* 8/1–2 (1910).

being, be it a completely holy one, he can have no other or higher significance for the religious life than is essentially due—though there may be a difference in degree—to all prophets, apostles, and pious people.[119] If, nevertheless, one still continues to honor him as the Christ, the Son of God, the Lord of the church, and so on, one becomes guilty of the sentimental Jesus cult that has been rightly condemned by Hartmann, Drews, Kalthoff, Schnehen, Naumann, and others.[120] For that reason many among the young moderns, led by Hegel and Bolland, go back from the unknown Jesus figure to the never-aging Christ idea, which under other names occurs in virtually all religions, to which also Christianity owes its existence, and which gives expression to the eternal idea that in the world and in humanity, God is gradually freeing himself, by suffering and dying, from sin and misery and thus enters into his glory.[121]

Much more than in Germany and the Netherlands, however, the doctrine of the atonement is a favorite topic in the English-speaking world. Not a year passes without new studies on it seeing the light of day. Right into the beginning of the nineteenth century, the old Protestant view of a covenant made in eternity among the three persons of the Trinity generally continued to hold sway. Especially in Scottish theology the work of Christ was connected with and regarded as the implementation of that covenant.[122] But little by little this doctrine of satisfaction had to yield to newer views. The hypothetical universalism of Amyraut, according to which Christ died for all humans on condition of faith and repentance on their part, also found acceptance among many Presbyterians in England and Scotland. It paved the way for Grotius's theory that forgiveness is not really based on Christ's satisfaction; rather, Christ's exemplary suffering creates the possibility of its application. This theory was embraced as scriptural and orthodox not only by Wesleyan Arminians but also by many Reformed theologians. Even R. W. Dale, who otherwise very strongly opposed the moral theory, stated that Christ did not really satisfy God's justice with his suffering and death, inasmuch as in Christ God himself paid the ransom, which therefore cannot be paid to him. But he made a distinction between abstract eternal justice and the will of God and attempted to argue that that eternal justice, which strongly resembles the governmental justice of Grotius, made Christ's suffering necessary for the violation of the law.[123]

Others, however, traveling much farther down this road, increasingly shifted the point of gravity from the objective work of Christ to the subjective change

119. A. Bruining, article in *Christusbeschouwingen onder modernen,* ed. G. A. van den Bergh van Eysinga (Baarn: Hollandia, 1909), 3–41; see also the articles by Hugenholtz, van Wijk, Niemeyer, and Bruins in the same volume.

120. A. Drews, *Die Christusmythe*, 183.

121. Van den Bergh van Eysinga, *Christusbeschouwingen*, 225–71.

122. J. Walker, *The Theology and Theologians of Scotland, Chiefly of the Seventeenth and Eighteenth Centuries,* 2nd ed. (Edinburgh: T&T Clark, 1888), 67ff.

123. R. W. Dale, *The Atonement,* 18th ed. (London: Congregational Union of England and Wales, 1896).

that takes place in humans through faith and repentance. Horace Bushnell tried to explain Christ's suffering entirely in light of the substitutionary character of all love and further attributed to the love that Christ in his life and suffering exhibited to us an effect that changes and renews persons.[124] Dr. John McLeod Campbell likewise inferred Christ's suffering from God's love, not from his justice. Christ did not secure God's love but was himself a gift, a demonstration, a manifestation of that love. He, accordingly, was our representative with God inasmuch as, entering into fellowship with us, he experienced the deepest sorrow over sin as guilt before God and as the source of all our misery. His suffering was not a punishment laid on him by God; he suffered because he saw sin with the eyes of God, condemned sin in full agreement with the Father, and showed us in his life and death what human sin means to the fatherly heart of God. While on the one hand, in virtue of his union with God, he condemned sin and pronounced his amen on God's judgments, on the other hand, in his acceptance of suffering and in virtue of his oneness with humankind, he confessed our sins before the face of God and in so doing offered to God perfect vicarious repentance, although, of course, the subjective element of a sense of guilt was not present in it. By this vicarious repentance, Christ acquired for us atonement, an atonement that is moral and spiritual, not legal, in nature and not imputed to us juridically but communicated to us mystically and ethically.[125]

Closely related to this view is the doctrine of atonement later proposed by Moberly. He first examines the concepts of punishment, repentance, and forgiveness. In the process he explains that all three are perfect and fulfill their intent only when the sinner himself accepts the punishment as punishment, remorsefully breaks with his sinful past, and by his forgivableness makes the forgiveness of his sins possible and real; in other words, when the new "man" arises from the old. But the natural "man" is incapable of doing this by his own power. Therefore, Christ appeared on earth in order, by his "penitential holiness" and his "sacrifice of supreme penitence," to completely accept the punishment of sin and [thus] to change it into atonement, to make a perfect confession of sin and break with it completely, and to acquire the forgiveness that God can only grant in the way of a perfect confession. Being one with God, he could assess sin in that way and take it upon himself; but by his union with humankind, he could also in that way atone for them on our behalf, and by his Spirit, by means of church and sacrament, communicate to his people the acquired benefits of atonement, repentance, and forgiveness.[126]

---

124. Horace Bushnell, *The Vicarious Sacrifice, Grounded in Principles of Universal Obligation* (New York: C. Scribner's Sons, 1866).

125. John McLeod Campbell, *The Nature of the Atonement and Its Relation to Remission of Sins and Eternal Life*, 6th ed. (London: Macmillan, 1886); cf. H. F. Henderson, *The Religious Controversies of Scotland* (Edinburgh: T&T Clark, 1905), 147–81: "The Row Heresy."

126. R. C. Moberly, *Atonement and Personality*, 6th ed. (London: Murray, 1907).

The point of gravity was even more emphatically shifted from the objective to the subjective side of atonement by Thomas Erskine, Maurice, Kingsley, F. W. Robertson, and others. They in fact viewed the life and death of Christ especially from the vantage point that he, the true and holy human being, immersed himself in our sorrows, took all our diseases upon himself, became sin for us, and identified himself with sinners. In this entire process he completely surrendered himself to the holy will of God but also gave a demonstration of love such that it had to induce people to love God in return and to consecrate themselves to him.[127] Similarly—but with much less warmth and depth—for R. J. Campbell, the value of Jesus' life and death is that he, the holy and divine human, to the end remained faithful to his calling and gave himself completely to his Father. The essence of atonement consists "in the assertion of the fundamental unity of all existence, the unity of the individual with the race and the race with God." All sacrifices and all acts of self-denial give expression to this idea. But Jesus' life and death is the focal point and crown of the age-long process of humankind's atonement in which human selfishness is overcome and the human race is lifted toward God. Now this process of atonement must also be repeated in us. The same spirit that resided in Jesus is [potentially] the spirit of the human race as a whole. The Christ nature, that is, the ideal of the holy and divine human, is potentially present in every human and must—under the influence of Jesus' example and the operation of his Spirit—be aroused in us all and generate a life of love and self-sacrifice.[128]

Similarly, in France and Switzerland the doctrine of vicarious satisfaction gradually made way for the mystical, ethical, or moral view of the work of Christ.[129] According to Ménégoz, for example, the death of Christ was a necessary consequence of his faithfulness to his messianic calling and at the same time a revelation of the seriousness of sin and of the solidarity of the human race. But the idea that that death was demanded by God and necessary for the atonement of sins is not a part of the original gospel of Jesus—which proclaims the gracious forgiveness of sins—but was only added later by Paul. Yet, says Ménégoz, the death of Christ is a source of blessings for the human race, and we may share in it when we unite

127. Thomas Erskine, *The Unconditional Freeness of the Gospel: In Three Essays* (Boston: Crocker & Brewster, 1828); F. D. Maurice, *The Doctrine of Sacrifice Deduced from Scriptures* (Cambridge: Macmillan, 1854).

128. R. J. Campbell, *The New Theology* (New York: Macmillan, 1907); cf. further F. L. Godet, *The Atonement in Modern Religious Thought: A Theological Symposium* (London: Clarke, 1900); A. C. Lyttelton, "The Atonement," in *Lux Mundi*, ed. C. Gore (London: J. Murray, 1892), 201–29; G. B. Stevens, *The Christian Doctrine of Salvation* (Edinburgh: T&T Clark, 1905); W. Porcher Dubose, *The Soteriology of the New Testament* (New York: Longmans, Green, 1906); H. C. Beeching and A. Nairne, *The Bible Doctrine of Atonement* (London: Murray, 1906).

129. Cf. F. Godet, "L'expiation," *Bulletin théologique* (1860); E. De Pressensé, "Essai sur le dogme de la rédemption," *Bulletin théologique* (1867); L. Durand, "Étude sur la rédemption," *Revue de Théologie et de Philosophie* 22 (1889): 337–70; C. Secrétan, *Théologie et religion* (Lausanne: Arthur Immer, 1883), 45; J. Bovon, *Étude sur l'oeuvre de la rédemption*, 6 vols. (Lausanne: Bridel, 1893–96); A. Sabatier, *The Doctrine of the Atonement and Its Historical Evolution*, trans. Victor Leulitte (New York: Putnam, 1904); *G. Frommel, *La psychologie du pardon dans ses rapports avec la croix de Jésus Christ* (1905).

ourselves with him and become one organism with him by faith.[130] Despite all these modern reconstructions, the confession of Jesus' vicarious suffering and death remains alive in the church and is still frequently and more or less decisively advocated in theology as well.[131]

JESUS THE MEDIATOR

[381] From the beginning the belief that Jesus is the Christ was the heart and core of the Christian confession. Jesus himself publicly asserted the claim that he was the Christ. As a result of this belief, Christians came to be a particular sect over against Jews and Gentiles. On account of the name "Christ," believers in Antioch were first called "Christians" (Acts 11:26). In the apostolic writings, accordingly, the names "Jesus" and "Christ" were very soon linked in the closest possible way and were mutually explanatory, just as the person of Christ is known from his work and the work of Christ is known from his person. The name, which is reproduced in Greek by Ἰησοῦς and in Latin by *Jesus, Jhesus,* or *Hiesus,* was a common name among Israelites and occurs in the Old Testament in no fewer than four forms. Sometimes the name is spelled out as יְהוֹשׁוּעַ (Deut. 3:21; Judg. 2:7) or written as יְהוֹשֻׁעַ (Exod. 17:9; Num. 13:16; Josh. 1:1; Judg. 2:6; 1 Sam. 6:14, 18; 2 Kings 23:8; Hag. 1:1; Zech. 3:1); and sometimes it also occurs in the abbreviated form of הוֹשֵׁעַ (Num. 13:8; 2 Kings 15:30; Hosea 1:1; Neh. 10:23) or of יֵשׁוּעַ (Ezra 2:2, 6; Neh. 7:7, 11, 39; etc.).

---

130. E. Ménégoz, *La mort de Jésus et le dogme de l'expiation* (Paris: Fischbacher, 1905).

131. In addition to the works already cited, cf. also A. Tholuck, *Die Lehre von der Sünde und vom Versöhner* (Gotha: F. A. Perthes, 1862); A. F. C. Vilmar, *Dogmatik,* 2 vols. (Gütersloh: C. Bertelsmann, 1874), §48; E. Böhl, *Dogmatik* (Amsterdam: Scheffer, 1887), 361ff.; J. F. Bula, *Die Versöhnung des Menschen mit Gott durch Christum, oder, die Genugthuung* (Basel: F. Schneider, 1874); W. Kölling, *Die satisfactio vicaria: Das ist der Lehre von der stellvertretenden Genugthuung des Herrn Jesu,* 2 vols. (Gütersloh: Bertelsmann, 1897–99); J. H. A. Ebrard, *Christliche Dogmatik,* 2nd ed., 2 vols. (Königsberg: A. W. Unzer, 1862–63), §§396ff.; idem, *Die Lehre von der stellvertredenden Genugthuung in der heiligen Schrift begründet* (Königsberg: A. W. Unzer, 1857); O. Bensow, *Die Lehre von der Versöhnung* (Gütersloh: Bertelsmann, 1904); C. Hodge, *Systematic Theology,* 3 vols. (New York: Charles Scribner's Sons, 1888), II, 480ff.; W. G. T. Shedd, *Dogmatic Theology,* 3rd ed., 3 vols. (New York: Scribner, 1891–94), II, 378ff.; A. A. Hodge, *The Atonement* (1907; reprinted, Grand Rapids: Baker, 1974); B. B. Warfield, "Modern Theories of the Atonement," *Princeton Theological Review* 1 (1903): 81–92; R. S. Candlish, *The Atonement: Its Reality, Completeness, and Extent* (London: T. Nelson & Sons, 1861); H. Martin, *The Atonement in Its Relations to the Covenant, the Priesthood, the Intercession of Our Lord* (London: James Nisbet, 1870; Edinburgh: Knox Press, 1976); J. S. Lidgett, *The Spiritual Principle of the Atonement as a Satisfaction Made to God for the Sins of the World,* 2nd ed. (London: Charles H. Kelley, 1898); J. Denney, *The Death of Christ: Its Place and Interpretation in the New Testament* (London: Hodder & Stoughton, 1909); idem, *The Atonement and the Modern Mind,* 2nd ed. (London: Hodder & Stoughton, 1908); J. Stalker, *The Atonement* (London: Hodder & Stoughton, 1908); M. d'Aubigné, *L'expiation de la croix* (Paris, 1867); H. Bois, "La nécessité de l'expiation," *Revue de théologie de Montauban* (1888); idem, "Expiation et solidarité," *Revue de théologie de Montauban* (1889); A. Gretillat, *Exposé de Théologie Systématique,* 4 vols. (Paris: Fischbacher, 1885–92), IV, 300ff.; J. J. van Oosterzee, *Christian Dogmatics,* trans. J. Watson and M. Evans, 2 vols. (New York: Scribner, Armstrong, 1874), §§108ff.; J. A. C. Van Leeuwen, *Verzoening* (Utrecht, 1903); G. Vellenga, "De voldoening, I, II," *Theologische Studiën* 24 (1906): 269–89, 377–97.

It has not yet been fully explained how the longer form "Jehoshua" can be abbreviated to "Jeshua," nor how the *yod* could drop out completely in the name Hosea. Nor as yet has the derivation of the name been scientifically established. In the past scholars usually read the name "Jehoshua" as the third-person imperfect hiphil (alongside the form יְהוֹשִׁיעַ, Ps. 116:6) of the verb יָשַׁע, so that the meaning would be "he (i.e., Yahweh) will help or save." Nowadays many scholars view the name as composed of יְהוֹ and שׁוּעַ, so that its meaning is "Yahweh is help or salvation" (cf. approx. the same combination, in the reverse order, in the name יְשַׁעְיָהוּ, Isa. 1:1).[132] However this may be, from ancient times the name was related to the verb יָשַׁע, "to help, to save." Moses intentionally gave to Hoshea the son of Nun the name Joshua (Num. 13:8, 16), and in Matthew 1:21, Joseph, at the express command of the angel, gave to his son the name Jesus, because he would save his people from their sins. Although occasionally the name was later also borne by other persons (Acts 7:45; Heb. 4:8 KJV; Col. 4:11), it belongs to Jesus in an utterly unique sense. Granted, the Jesuits later also called themselves by that name but in so doing assumed a title no one has a right to claim, inasmuch as Christ alone is the Savior. Furthermore, by their system and conduct they have on many occasions seriously disgraced their own name. Believers, therefore, all call themselves by the name of Christ, since this is not the personal and historical name but the official one, and in communion with this Christ they are themselves anointed as prophets, priests, and kings. In addition to this historical and official name, Christ is given many other names in Scripture. He is called the Son of God, the only-begotten, beloved Son of God, the Word, the image of God, the reflection of God's glory and the exact imprint of God's very being, the firstborn of all creation, the true God and eternal life, God to be praised above all (or perhaps more correctly: God overall, to be praised forever [Rom. 9:5]), Immanuel. In addition, he is called the Son of Man, the son of Joseph and David, the Nazarene [Matt. 2:23], the Galilean, the holy and righteous one, the second Adam, the Lord from heaven, the firstborn of all creatures, and the firstborn of the dead. Finally, in terms of his office and work, he is called Prophet, Master, Teacher, Priest, the Great Priest, the High Priest, the Servant of the Lord, the Lamb of God, the King, the King of the Jews, the King of Israel, the King of kings, the Lord, the Lord of glory, the Lord of lords, the head of the church, the bridegroom of the church, the shepherd and guardian of souls, the pioneer and perfecter of the faith, the pioneer of salvation, the way, the truth, and the life, the bread of life, the prince of life, the resurrection and the life, the shepherd of the sheep, the door of the sheepfold, the light of the world, the shining morning star, the lion of the tribe of Judah, the Amen, the faithful and true witness, the Alpha and the Omega, the first and the last, the beginning and the end, the judge of the living and the dead, the heir of all things by whom, in whom, and for whom all things have been created. All these names sufficiently prove the incomparable

---

132. Cf. E. Nestle, "Jesus," *DC,* I, 860.

dignity and entirely unique place that belong to Christ.[133] He is the mediator of both creation and re-creation.

The word μεσιτης occurs in the Septuagint, Job 9:33. It denotes the rescuer or helper (umpire, arbitrator) whom Job wished would stand between God and himself. In the New Testament the name is given only to Moses (Gal. 3:19–20) and to Christ (1 Tim. 2:5; Heb. 8:6; 9:15; 12:24) while the verb μεσιτευειν [act as go-between, intervene] is once used of God (Heb. 6:17). In general, the word denotes a person who takes a position between two parties with a view to bringing them together or to reconciling them (Deut. 5:5) and is therefore eminently suited to describe the place of Jesus' person and the character of his work. The idea of a mediatorship, as we found earlier already, is integral to all religions but does not—in the soothsayers and magicians, the priests and the kings—achieve realization. Even Moses only bears that name provisionally, in a temporary and exemplary sense, for, though he was faithful in the house of God, he was there only as a servant to testify to the things that God would tell his people later (Heb. 3:5); though he received the law, he received it not even directly from God but by means of angels (Gal. 3:19). Though a mediator, he actually stood with the people and over against God and received the law, not for Israel alone, but also for himself (John 1:17). Christ, however, is over God's house as the Son (Heb. 3:6), because he is the Son by whom God himself speaks to us, whom he appointed heir of all things, through whom he also created the world (Heb. 1:1–2). He is not a third party who, coming from without, intervenes between God and us but is himself the Son of God, the reflection of his glory and the exact imprint of his very being, a partaker in God's essence, in the attributes of his nature, and at the same time the Son of Man, head of all humanity, Lord of the church. He does not stand between two parties: he *is* those two parties in his own person.

About this mediatorship of Christ a not insignificant dispute arose in the century of the Reformation. Over against Osiander, who held the ontological righteousness of God in Christ to be the "matter" of justification, Stancarus, professor at Königsberg, defended the proposition that Christ was the mediator only according to his human nature and could therefore justify us only on the ground of his humanly acquired righteousness.[134] For this position he could appeal to Augustine, Lombard, Aquinas, and others, who all said that Christ was the mediator only "insofar as he is human, for insofar as he is God he is not a mediator but the equal of the Father,"[135] and these theologians were much more highly esteemed by Stancarus than were the Reformers. "One Peter Lombard," he said, "is worth more than a hundred Luthers, two hundred Melanchthons, three hundred Bullingers, four hundred Peter Martyrs, and five hundred Calvins—who, if they

---

133. For the meaning of all these names, cf. B. B. Warfield, *The Lord of Glory* (New York: American Tract Society, 1907).

134. K. Benrath (Schmidt), "Stancarus," *PRE*³, XVIII, 752–54.

135. Augustine, *City of God*, XI, 2; idem, *Confessions*, X, 40; P. Lombard, *Sent.*, III, dist. 19; T. Aquinas, *Summa theol.*, III, qu. 26, art. 2.

were all crushed together in a mortar, would not yield one ounce of true theology." Lutherans and Reformed theologians, opposing this view with the utmost vigor, asserted that Christ was a mediator in both natures, that he had been appointed as such from eternity, and that he had also fulfilled the office of mediator already in the days of the Old Testament.[136] Catholic scholars, on the other hand, though they maintained that Christ was only a mediator in his human nature, nevertheless had to admit that for Christ to be a mediator, he had to be both God and man, that both natures together constituted the presupposition and basis of the mediator. They could only still say, therefore, that Christ accomplished his mediatorial works—his self-offering, suffering, and death—in his human nature and hence that this nature was only the "principle by which," the "formal principle" of the mediator's works.[137] This split between the person and the work of the mediator, however, cannot be maintained. The peculiar feature of the mediatorial works is precisely that they are performed by one person possessing both natures. That is not to say—as Petavius charges the Lutherans and Calvinists with doing[138]—that they ascribe the work of the mediator to the divine nature of Christ by itself and in isolation from the human. The Son is a mediator, not according to his divine nature as such, as being one with and equal to the Father and the Spirit, but according to that divine nature *by dispensation,* "to the extent that by a voluntary dispensation of grace it submits to it."[139] Scripture, accordingly, repeatedly calls Christ in his divine nature the subject of humiliation (John 1:14; 2 Cor. 8:9; Phil. 2:6), and the church fathers expressed themselves in a similar spirit.[140] Augustine, Lombard, and Aquinas believed nothing other than that Christ was and could be a mediator, not by his divine nature as such (in isolation from his human nature), but only as the incarnate Son of God. In the end Catholic theologians themselves again had to defend this view against Stancarus.

CHRIST'S THREEFOLD OFFICE

Concealed, here, is still another difference. For if Christ is only a mediator in his human nature, as Bellarmine and Petavius claimed, he could not have been a mediator before his incarnation, but only began to be this in the moment of his conception. In effect, therefore, the Old Testament [period] was without a

136. J. T. Müller, *Die symbolischen Bücher der evangelisch-lutherischen Kirche,* 8th ed. (Gütersloh: Bertelsmann, 1898), 622, 684; J. Gerhard, *Loci theologici,* ed. E. Preuss, 9 vols. (Berlin: G. Schlawitz, 1863–75), IV, 325; J. A. Quenstedt, *Theologia,* III, 273; J. Calvin, in two letters, *Corpus ref.,* XXXVII, 337–58; the ministers of Zürich, in two letters, see K. Benrath, "Stancarus," *PRE*[3], XVIII, 753; A. Polanus, *Synt. theol.,* 430; F. Turretin, *Institutes of Elenctic Theology,* XIV, qu. 2.

137. R. Bellarmine, "De Christo," *Controversiis,* V, chs. 1–8; D. Petavius, "De incarn.," *Op. theol.,* VII, c. 1–4.

138. D. Petavius, "De incarn.," *Op. theol.,* XII, 4, 9.

139. In A. Polanus, *Synt. theol.,* 430.

140. D. Petavius, "De incarn.," *Op. theol.,* XII, 1.

mediator.[141] But though it is true that Christ became flesh only in the fullness of time, he was chosen and appointed as the mediator from eternity. One cannot object to this by saying that also David, Solomon, and others were chosen and in that sense anointed from eternity. For the big difference here is that before their conception David, Solomon, and all elect persons existed only in the mind and decree of God, while the Son was in the beginning with God and himself God. His election as the mediator did not occur apart from him but bears the character of a "pact of salvation" (*pactum salutis*). The work of redemption is a joint work of the Father, Son, and Spirit and began to be implemented immediately after the fall by all three persons. In the same sense in which the Father was the Father of his children from eternity and the Holy Spirit was the comforter of believers from eternity, the Son was appointed the mediator from eternity and began his work as mediator immediately after the fall. Already under the Old Testament [dispensation], he was active as prophet, priest, and king.[142] The fallen world was immediately handed over to the Son as the mediator for the purpose of atonement and redemption. And in the fullness of time, he who was already the mediator, was made manifest in the flesh (1 John 1:2; 3:5, 8). This explains why Christ's royal office stands out: in the Old Testament, he is especially sketched and predicted in his kingship, and with that title especially he acts among his people. But that kingship of Christ is very different from that of earthly rulers. It is prefigured in the theocratic Davidic kingship, which is essentially different from that of other kings. It is a kingship in God's name, subject to God's will, designed to direct all things to God's honor. It is not a kingship of violence and weapons; it is exercised and governs in a very different and superior way. It rules by Word and Spirit, by grace and truth, by justice and righteousness. This king, accordingly, is at the same time a prophet and priest. His power is designed to be used in the service of truth and righteousness.

Because Christ's kingship is utterly unique, however, many theologians object to speaking of his kingly office or, in the case of Christ, use the royal title metaphorically.[143] In fact, many deem it better, in the case of Christ, to speak not of office but of a personal calling, for [the idea of] office belongs in a juridical community, whereas Christ's kingdom is a realm of love, not of justice.[144] "Office" is indeed distinguished from profession, trade, or position by the fact that it presupposes a government, is based on an appointment by that government, and involves someone serving that government personally, not for pay. Precisely for this reason, however, "office" is the word that must be used with respect to Christ. For he did not assume the dignity of the mediator himself: God chose, called, and appointed him (Pss. 2:7; 89:19–21; 110:1–4; 132:17; Isa. 42:1; Heb. 5:4–6). The name "Christ" is not a professional name but the name of an office, a title, a

141. D. Petavius, "De incarn.," *Op. theol.*, XII, 4, 10.
142. Augustine, in H. Reuter, *Augustinische Studien* (Gotha: Perthes, 1887), 93.
143. J. A. L. Wegscheider, *Inst. theol.*, §144; J. H. Scholten, *De Leer der Hervormde Kerk*, I, 369ff.
144. A. Ritschl, *Justification and Reconciliation*, III, 425.

dignity Jesus can claim because he has been chosen by God himself. Under the old covenant especially kings were anointed (Judg. 9:8, 15; 1 Sam. 9:16; 10:1; 16:13; 2 Sam. 2:4; 5:3; 19:10; 1 Kings 1:34, 39; 2 Kings 9:1–3; 11:12; 23:30), probably with holy oil (1 Kings 1:39; Ps. 89:20). "Anointed one" was the title of the theocratic king (Pss. 20:6; 28:8; 84:9; 89:38; etc.). The anointing with oil was a symbol of divine consecration, of being equipped with the Spirit of God (1 Sam. 10:1, 9–10). And this was the anointing—not in an external and symbolic sense, but in a truly spiritual sense—that Christ received (Isa. 11:2; 42:1; 61:1; Pss. 2:6; 45:7; 89:20; Luke 4:18; John 3:34; Acts 4:27; 10:38; Heb. 1:9) on the occasion of his conception by the Holy Spirit (Luke 1:35) and at his baptism by John (Matt. 3:16; Mark 1:10; Luke 3:22; John 1:32). His kingship was also as real as his anointing, of which that of the Old Testament was only a shadow. The theocratic Davidic kingship was only a weak prefiguration of it and received its true fulfillment in the kingship of Christ. Christ is king in a greater, much truer sense than David and Solomon. For integral to the idea of a theocratic king was that he had to be a man after God's heart and might not lift himself up like a despot above his brothers (Deut. 17:14–20). Inasmuch as Israel's kings did not conform themselves to this royal law, prophecy expected another and better king who, himself the anointed of the Lord and servant of God, would govern his people by truth and righteousness and conquer his enemies. As such a king, Christ assumes his public ministry. He founds a kingdom of God that, though now it only still exists spiritually and morally, is destined one day to manifest itself also externally and bodily in the city of God, from which all the ungodly are banished and in which God will be all in all. And because he is such a king, a king in the true and full sense, his kingship also includes the prophetic and priestly offices.

[382] Many theologians, however, object to the threefold office of Christ on the ground that one office cannot be distinguished from the others.[145] True, no single activity of Christ can be exclusively restricted to one office. His words are a proclamation of law and gospel and thus point to the prophetic office; but he speaks as one having authority, and all things obey his command (Mark 1:22; 4:41; Luke 4:32; etc.); he calls himself king, comes into the world to bear witness to the truth (John 18:37). His miracles are signs of his teaching (John 2:11; 10:37; etc.) but also a revelation of his priestly compassion (Matt. 8:17) and his royal power (Matt. 9:6, 8; 21:23). In his intercessory prayer not only his high priestly but also his prophetic and royal offices are evidenced (John 17:2, 9–10, 24). His death is a confession and an example (1 Tim. 6:13; 1 Pet. 2:21; Rev. 1:5), but also a sacrifice (Eph. 5:2) and a demonstration of his power (John 10:18). Dogmatics has been perplexed, therefore, as to what things from Jesus' life and

---

145. In the past already among Socinians, Ernesti, Doederlein, and others, and in modern times in A. Ritschl, *Rechtfertigung und Versöhnung*, I, 520ff.; idem, *Justification and Reconciliation*, III, 408ff.; P. Lobstein, "Études critiques de dogmatique protestante," *Revue de théologie et de philosophie* 24/2 (March 1891): 171–212; F. H. R. Frank, *System der christlichen Wahrheit*, 2nd ed., 2 vols. (Erlangen: A. Deichert, 1884), II, 158; J. Kaftan, *Dogmatik*, 486, 531; Th. Häring, *Christian Faith*, II, 493ff.

works had to be assigned to each office in particular. Usually treated under [the heading of] Christ's prophetic office were his teaching, predictions, and miracles; under [the heading of] his priestly office, his acts of sacrifice, intercession, and blessing. Remaining, then, for his royal office in the state of humiliation there was no more than the tribute offered by the magi, the entry into Jerusalem, the appointment of the apostles, the institution of the sacraments—isolated facts that can in part just as well be assigned to the other offices. Even more difficult became the description of the difference in the state of exaltation. For though Jesus' prophetic activity is continued in teaching his church by Word and Spirit, he rules and protects his church by these two as a king also, and his high priestly intercession is not an entreaty but an expression of royal will (John 17:24). It is, accordingly, an atomistic approach, which detaches certain specific activities from the life of Jesus and assigns some to his prophetic and others to his priestly or royal office. Christ is the same yesterday, today, and forever. He does not just perform prophetic, priestly, and kingly activities but is himself, in his whole person, prophet, priest, and king. And everything he is, says, and does manifests that threefold dignity. Granted, in the one activity it is more his prophetic office that is evident to us, and in another it is his priestly or his kingly office that stands out; and it is also true that his prophetic office comes to the fore more in the days of the Old Testament and during his days of traveling around on earth, his priestly office more in his suffering and death, his kingly office more in his state of exaltation. But actually he bears all three offices at the same time and consistently exercises all three at once both before and after his incarnation, in both the state of humiliation and that of exaltation.

However, speaking of Christ's three offices is not for that reason arbitrary, nor is it Oriental imagery that can be abandoned without scruple, nor can the one office be reduced to one of the other two. While it is not possible to separate them, the distinction between them is most certainly there. To be a mediator, to be a complete savior, he had to be appointed by the Father to all three and equipped by the Spirit for all three offices. The truth is that the idea of humanness already encompasses within itself this threefold dignity and activity. Human beings have a head to know, a heart to give themselves, a hand to govern and to lead; correspondingly, they were in the beginning equipped by God with knowledge and understanding, with righteousness and holiness, with dominion and glory (blessedness). The sin that corrupted human beings infected all their capacities and consisted not only in ignorance, folly, error, lies, blindness, darkness but also in unrighteousness, guilt, moral degradation, and further in misery, death, and ruin. Therefore Christ, both as the Son and as the image of God, for himself and also as our mediator and savior, had to bear all three offices. He had to be a prophet to know and to disclose the truth of God; a priest, to devote himself to God and, in our place, to offer himself up to God; a king, to govern and protect us according to God's will. To teach, to reconcile, and to lead; to instruct, to acquire, and to apply salvation; wisdom, righteousness, and redemption; truth, love, and power—all three are essential to the completeness of our salvation. In Christ's God-to-humanity relation, he is a prophet; in his humanity-to-God relation he is a priest; in his headship over all humanity he is a king. Rationalism acknowledges only his prophetic office; mysticism only his priestly office; millennialism only his royal office. But Scripture, consistently and simultaneously attributing all three offices to him, describes him as our chief prophet, our only [high] priest, and our eternal king. Though a king, he rules not by the sword but by his Word and spirit. He is a prophet, but his word is power and [really] happens. He is a priest but lives by dying, conquers by suffering, and is all-powerful by his love. He is always all these things in conjunction, never the one without the other: mighty in speech and action as a king and full of grace and truth in his royal rule.[146]

GOD'S JUSTICE OR LOVE?

[383] In the entirety of his person and work, this Christ is a revelation of God's love. The Gnostics and especially Marcion drew a sharp contrast between the God of wrath, of vengeance and justice, who revealed himself in the Old Testament, and the God of love and grace, who in the New Testament made himself known in Christ.[147] But such a contrast is unknown to Scripture. Yahweh Elohim in the Old Testament, though just, holy, zealous for his honor, and full of ire against sin, is also gracious, merciful, eager to forgive, and abounding in steadfast love (Exod. 20:5–6; 34:6–7; Deut. 4:31; Ps. 86:15; etc.). In the New Testament God, the Father of our Lord Jesus Christ, is the God of all grace and mercy (Luke 6:36; 2 Cor. 1:3; 1 Peter 5:10). There is no antithesis between the Father and Christ. As full of love, merciful, and ready to forgive as Christ is, so is the Father. It is his words that Christ speaks, his works he does. The Father is himself the Savior (σωτηρ; Luke 1:47; 1 Tim. 1:1; Titus 3:4–5), the One who in Christ reconciles the world to himself, not counting its trespasses against it (2 Cor. 5:18–19). Christ, therefore, did not first by his work move the Father to love and grace, for the love of the Father is antecedent and comes to manifestation in Christ, who is himself a gift of God's love (John 3:16; Rom. 5:8; 8:32; 1 John 4:9–10).

In Romans 3:25–26, Paul does say that God put Christ Jesus forward, for all to see, as an expiation, by faith, in his blood, as a demonstration of God's righ-

---

146. H. Witsius, *Hermanni Witsii excercitationes sacrae in symbolum quod apostolorum dicitur* (Amsterdam: Johannem Wolters, 1697), exerc. 10; W. Ames, *The Marrow of Theology*, trans. and ed. John D. Eusden (Grand Rapids: Baker, 1983), I, 19, 11; M. Leydekker, *De veritate religionis reformatae* (Utrecht: Rudolph à Zyl, 1688), IV, 9, 13; F. Schleiermacher, *Christian Faith*, §102; A. E. Biedermann, *Christliche Dogmatik*, II, 235ff.; I. A. Dorner, *A System of Christian Doctrine,* trans. Alfred Cave and Rev. J. S. Banks, rev. ed., 4 vols. (Edinburgh: T&T Clark, 1888), III, 381ff.; F. A. Philippi, *Kirchliche Glaubenslehre*, IV, 2, 5ff.; J. H. A. Ebrard, *Christliche Dogmatik*, §399; M. Kähler, *Die Wissenschaft der christlichen Lehre*, 3rd ed. (Leipzig: A. Deichert, 1905), 347; A. von Oettingen, *Lutherische Dogmatik*, 2 vols. (Munich: C. H. Beck, 1897), III, 177ff.; G. F. K. Müller, "Jesu dreifaches Amt," *PRE*[3], VIII, 733–41; C. Hodge, *Systematic Theology*, II, 459ff.; W. G. T. Shedd, *Dogmatic Theology*, II, 353ff.; A. Kuyper, *De Heraut*, 509.

147. Cf. H. Bavinck, *Reformed Dogmatics*, II, 221–28 (#206).

teousness. In this connection we must undoubtedly think of righteousness as an attribute of God that—because of his passing over, without expiation, of the sins committed in the past by Jews and Gentiles under the regime of God's forbearance—seemed not to come to manifestation and therefore to be nonexistent. In the present time, in the fullness of time, it was necessary, accordingly, for God to put Christ forward as an expiation by his blood to prove that he himself is righteous and could justify those who believe in Jesus. But here, too, the righteousness of God is not viewed as being in conflict with his grace and love. After all, the righteousness of God was demonstrated not in that by it sinners were punished for their transgressions but in that by it Christ was put forward as an expiation by his blood, so that in the forgiveness of sins God himself nevertheless proved righteous and at the same time could justify the believer. The righteousness of God in Scripture consists, first of all, in the fact that he judges justly, does not hold the guilty to be innocent and the innocent guilty; and further, in that he helps, saves, and recognizes the just cause of the poor, the wretched, those who, though personally guilty, materially have the right on their side. In the latter sense, righteousness is akin to mercy, faithfulness, and truth, but is nevertheless always distinct from these qualities in that it focuses on the anomaly that exists between a person's rights and the state in which that person finds herself or himself.[148] Here, too, in Paul, God's righteousness, though not identical with his goodness, mercy, faithfulness, or truth, is even much less opposed to it. In fact it is precisely the attribute of God that gave Christ as an expiation, so that God could forgive sins out of grace while preserving justice. Hence there is no such thing as a conflict between God's justice and his love. In our sinful state it may appear to us that way, but in God all attributes are one and fully consistent with one another.

So, on the one hand, we must reject the notion that Christ was solely a revelation of God's punitive justice. The God of revelation, the Father of our Lord Jesus Christ, is not a pagan God whose spite and hatred against people must be averted by an array of sacrifices. Sacrifice in Scripture, also in the Old Testament, bears a very different character: it presupposes the covenant of grace. If the God of revelation were a pagan God, there would inevitably arise a Gnostic contrast between the Father and the Son that would elevate the Son as the God of grace far above the Father as the God of vengeance and rip apart the Old and the New Testament, creation and re-creation, nature and grace. On the other hand, Christ must not be viewed as solely a demonstration of God's love, at least not love as we frequently conceive it and which is totally different from the love of God in Scripture.[149] In that case, after all, not only the suffering and death of Christ,

---

148. Ibid.

149. P. Schwartzkopff ("Gottes Liebe und Heiligkeit," *Theologische Studien und Kritiken* [1910]: 300–313) recognizes that the love of God must be a holy love that reacts against sin and that righteousness, wrath, vengeance, and so on cannot simply be denied to God as anthropomorphisms, for then, and for the same reason, there could be no love in God either. But he tries, further, to combine love and holiness so that the latter is subordinate and serviceable to the former. God is the Father and attempts to lead all his children to salvation.

which Scripture undoubtedly portrays as a punishment for our sin, would remain completely unexplained, but the word of Paul—that God put Christ forward as an expiation that he might prove himself righteous and could justify those who believe in Jesus—would be directly contradicted. For in Romans 3:21–26, the core idea is that in the gospel God has now manifested his righteousness *apart from the law,* independently of the law. According to the law, God can only manifest his righteousness by condemning all people, for they are all guilty and objects of his wrath. For no human being can be justified by works of the law (3:19–20, 23). But the miracle of the gospel consists in that God manifests his righteousness *apart from the law* in a way that enables him to remain righteous and in virtue of (not in spite of) that righteousness justifies those who believe in Jesus and who in themselves, judged according to the law, are ungodly (4:5). And that has now been made possible by God's putting Christ forward as an expiation, by faith, in his blood. In this connection, therefore, in speaking of God's righteousness we must not think of the attribute of God according to which God condemns and punishes the sinner according to the law (although in dogmatics God's vindictive justice is usually also counted as his righteousness) but, on the contrary, of that property of God according to which, in the gospel, he acquits and justifies those who believe in Jesus. God's righteousness shines out most brilliantly in that in the gospel, apart from the law, he righteously forgives [sinners]. It is not opposed to grace but in a sense includes it; in the expiatory sacrifice of Christ, by faith, it opened a way to justify the ungodly out of grace; and the grace by which we are justified realized itself in the way of justice and righteousness. "Hidden behind the wrath, as final agent, is love, just as the sun is hidden behind thunder clouds" (Delitzsch).[150]

[384] This automatically leads to the often-discussed question whether this way of justice was necessary for God to reveal his grace or whether he could also forgive without satisfaction. Duns Scotus proceeded from the "absolute dominion of God" and held that incarnation and satisfaction were solely determined by God's arbitrary will. Athanasius, Augustine, Aquinas, Calvin, Musculus, Zanchius, Twisse, and others deemed them not absolutely necessary but, in keeping with God's wisdom, as highly fitting and appropriate. Irenaeus, Basil, Ambrose, Anselm, Beza, Piscator, Voetius, Turretin, Owen, Moor, and others inclined to view them

---

But if these children resist it to the end, God's holy love drives them away and abandons them to ruin. Wrath, judgment, and punishment, accordingly, are the expression and consequence of love. In that way, however, God's righteousness retains only an eschatological character, is dependent in its manifestation on the human will, and no justice is done to the Pauline idea that God, by openly putting Christ forward as an expiation by faith in blood, revealed his righteousness in that he could justify those who believed in Jesus.

150. On Romans 3:21–26, cf. the commentaries by Philippi, Tholuck, Meyer, Zahn, and Sanday and Headlam; see also O. Pfleiderer, *Der Paulinismus: Ein Beitrag zur Geschichte der urchristlichen Theologie* (Leipzig: O. R. Reisland, 1890), 143ff.; H. J. Holtzmann, *Lehrbuch der neutestamentlichen Theologie,* II, 100; G. A. Fricke, *Der paulinische Grundbegriff der δικαιοσυνη θεου erörtert auf Grund von Röm. 3:21–26* (Leipzig: Böhme, 1888).

as strictly necessary.[151] One can understand that many theologians prefer to take a middle road rather than enthrone arbitrariness in God or limit his omnipotence by an absolute necessity. Still, there is no objection in this connection to speaking of necessity, provided this concept is properly understood. The will in God is neither a formal arbitrariness divorced from all his attributes and from his being as a whole nor a capacity for choice that is bound by all those attributes and that being as a whole and therefore unfree. For us the will of God is often the final ground of things, and we have to acquiesce in it, even though we do not know why God acts thus and not otherwise. But in God that will always has those wise and holy reasons for his acting thus and not otherwise, for he never acts except in harmony with all his attributes, his love, wisdom, righteousness, and so on. And this agreement of the will of God with all his attributes is not coercive, not a restriction for that will, but precisely the true and highest freedom. To will and to act as his holy, wise, almighty, and loving nature itself wants is for God both the highest freedom and the highest necessity. This, also, is how it is with the incarnation and satisfaction: they may be called "necessary," not as a necessity that is imposed on God from without and from which he cannot escape, but as actions that are in agreement with his attributes and display them most splendidly.

For, in the first place, Scripture teaches that God does all things for his own sake (Prov. 16:4; Rom. 11:36). The final ground and ultimate purpose, also of Christ's incarnation and satisfaction, cannot lie in a creature, in the salvation of the sinner, but has to lie in God himself. For his own sake, he sent his Son into the world as an expiation for our sins that his attributes and perfections might thus be manifested. And indeed, there is no fact that so powerfully brings those perfections of God to the fore as Christ's incarnation and satisfaction. Not just one attribute is brilliantly illumined by these events but all of them together: his wisdom, grace, love, mercy, long-suffering, righteousness, holiness, power, and so on. Although as a rule we hear mention only of God's grace and justice, the other attributes may not be forgotten either. Christ in his own person, word, and work is the supremely perfect, comprehensive revelation of God: his servant, his image, his Son. He has made known to us the Father. If God wanted to reveal himself in his consummate glory, then the creation and re-creation, Christ's incarnation and satisfaction, were necessary. His perfections were already made manifest in creation, but they are much more richly and superbly displayed in the re-creation. In his omnipotence he knows how to utilize [even] sin as a means of self-glorification.

Second, it is the teaching of Scripture that God as the absolutely righteous and holy one hates sin with divine hatred (Gen. 18:25; Exod. 20:5; 23:7; Ps. 5:6–7; Nah. 1:2; Rom. 1:18, 32). There is an absolute antithesis between God and sin that necessarily comes to expression in the fact that God reacts against it with all his perfections. He does not want sin; he takes no pleasure in it; he hates and fulminates against it. Sin cannot exist without eliciting God's hatred

---

151. Cf. H. Bavinck, *Reformed Dogmatics*, II, 233–40 (#208); G. Voetius, *Select. disp.*, II, 238.

and punishment. God cannot deny himself. He cannot recognize the validity of sin. He cannot accord to Satan equal rights with himself. Precisely because he is the absolutely holy one, he has to hate sin. Actually, everyone assents to that truth. Even when people say that God can forgive sin without atonement and, as perfect love, also has to forgive sin, everyone still admits that God *forgives* it, that is, that motivated by grace, he does not punish it, though he has the right and the power to inflict that punishment. Even Mr. Chavannes, speaking to a gathering of modern theologians, incurred little agreement with his proposition that the expression "forgiving love" is a meaningless oxymoron. [152]

Third, God is most certainly the Father of humankind, but this name is far from describing the entire relationship in which God stands to his creatures. He is also Creator, Maintainer, Ruler, Sovereign, Lawgiver, Judge, and so on, and it is one-sided and conducive to error if one takes one of these names—disregarding all the others—to be the full revelation of God. Thus, in relation to sin, God is not just a creator or injured party who can cancel the debt and forgive as well as forget the insult but is himself the giver, protector, and avenger of the law, righteousness in person, and as such he cannot forgive sin without atonement (Heb. 9:22). In that capacity he cannot nullify the just demands of the law, for we are not speaking here about personal or private rights, which one can relinquish, but about the righteousness, that is, the perfections and honor of God himself. Against this idea one could appeal to the prerogative of pardon that an earthly government frequently exercises, but this prerogative of pardon is only given to it because it is fallible and in many cases inflicts a penalty that is too severe or even

---

152. Supplement of the *Hervorming*, June 28, 1895. The freedom to forgive is limited in still another way by Gaston Frommel, *La psychologie de pardon dans ses rapports avec la croix de Jesus Christ*. On the side of the recipient, forgiveness is bound to repentance (the acknowledgment and confession of guilt, contrition, and hence, in a sense, reparation). Without repentance, forgiveness would not be accepted and, granted without repentance, would not be a moral act. True repentance does not earn forgiveness ("pardon is not due to repentance but is only accessible to repentance"), but repentance must still correspond to the gravity of the sin in question and is always to some extent an act of satisfying righteousness. Perfect repentance would be complete expiation. The reality of repentance is expiation, and repentance as such attracts and elicits forgiveness. Moberly (*Atonement and Personality*, 48–73) puts it even more emphatically. Forgiveness is never unconditional but always assumes repentance in the guilty person, i.e., a new human being who has broken with his past and now himself stands outside, and over against, his sin. In other words, forgiveness presupposes "forgiveableness" (which, says Moberly, does not arise from the person himself but is effected in him by the Spirit of Christ), and this "forgiveableness" then makes forgiveness on the part of the injured party necessary. Whether or not God forgives "depends wholly and only upon whether the person is or is not forgiveable." If he is not, he cannot and may not be forgiven. If he is, he may and must be forgiven (pp. 56, 57).

The error of this reasoning is (1) that the sin is one-sidedly viewed as a private insult and is misjudged in its character as a crime, a transgression of the law, and a violation of righteousness; and (2) that repentance is more or less equated with atonement. Regret that might arise in the criminal after the crime—though it may indicate that he was not as bad as the judge perhaps initially thought he was and hence diminish in his mind the gravity of the guilt and the punishment—is, in the nature of the case, powerless to amend the past and to erase the guilt. We will discuss this matter later at greater length, as also the other point broached by Frommel, namely, that forgiveness is also bound to certain conditions on the part of the person who bestows it.

undeserved.[153] In God something like that cannot happen. He is righteousness in person, does not need to restore justice or nullify it by grace, but lets both justice and grace come to expression in the cross of Christ.

Fourth, the moral law as such is not an arbitrary positive law but law grounded in the nature of God himself. Nor is it a self-existent impersonal power independent of God—so that Christ satisfied not God but its demand[154]—but the expression of his being. In maintaining the law, God maintains himself and vice versa. It is therefore unbreakable and inviolable. It bears this character throughout the Scriptures; our own conscience bears witness to it; and the entire so-called moral world order, with its phenomena of responsibility, sense of duty, guilt, repentance, dread, remorse, punishment, and so on, is based on this inviolability. Christ, accordingly, came not to abolish the law but to fulfill it (Matt. 5:17–18; Rom. 10:4). He upheld its majesty and glory; and faith, accordingly, does not nullify the law but upholds it (Rom. 3:31).

Fifth, sin in Scripture bears a diverse character: it is incomprehension, folly, guilt, pollution, impurity, shame, and so on; it is likened to a money debt and, from another viewpoint, is an affront to God. But, additionally, it occurs in Scripture as a crime, an offense against righteousness, a violation of the divine majesty, which brings us under his judgment (Rom 3:19), and it makes us worthy of death (Rom. 1:32). In this capacity it demands punishment, and there is no forgiveness without satisfaction (atonement); it can be completely overcome, as it concerns its guilt and pollution as well as its power and control, only in the way of justice.

To be added, in the sixth place, is that sin is so enormous "that God, rather than ... leave it unpunished, punished it in his beloved Son, Jesus Christ, with the bitter and shameful death on the cross."[155] If righteousness could have been obtained in any other way, Christ would have died to no purpose (Gal. 2:21; 3:21; Heb. 2:10). In sum, Christ's incarnation and satisfaction occurred to the end that God would again be recognized and honored as God by his creatures. Sin was the rejection of God and all his perfections, a turning toward and adoration of creatures. But in Christ, God again revealed himself, restored his sovereignty, vindicated all his perfections, glorified his name, and maintained his deity. God was primarily concerned, also in the work of redemption, to establish himself, his own glory.[156]

153. A. de Jong, *Geschiedenis en Begrip van Gratie* (Rotterdam: De Vries, 1902). Aside from the limitations and deficiencies of positive law, he mentions, as a second legal ground for pardon, the interest of the state or of society (108ff.). This legal ground, however, is not so much a ground for granting a pardon as the necessity forced on a government by circumstances not to impose or to apply fully a deserved punishment and is, moreover, rejected by others (120).

154. As Dale (*Atonement*, 363ff. and elsewhere) imagines it.

155. Ed. note: Quoted by Bavinck, without reference, from the Form for Communion used for centuries in Reformed Churches.

156. G. Voetius, *Select. disp.*, I, 372; II, 238; P. van Mastricht, *Theologia*, V, 18, 34; F. Turretin, *Institutes of Elenctic Theology*, XIV, 1ff.; idem, "De satisf. Christi," disp. 1 and 2; J. H. Heidegger, *Corpus theologiae christianae*, 2 vols. (Zürich: J. H. Bodmer, 1700), XIX, 80ff.; H. Heppe, *Dogmatik*, 341; J. H. A. Ebrard, *Dogm.*, §427; H. L.

[385] Socinians and their spiritual kin, however, have fiercely opposed the necessity of satisfaction (atonement). All their arguments come down to saying that justice and grace, satisfaction and forgiveness, and hence also law and gospel, Old and New Testaments, creation and re-creation, are inconsistent with each other, are in fact mutually exclusive. According to them, the Christian religion is the absolutely spiritual and moral religion, stripped of all natural and sensual elements. God is not to be conceived as a judge but as a father. Punitive justice, holiness, hatred, wrath against sin are not perfections of God; only love describes his being. The religion of the Old Testament was still based on law and viewed the relation of humans to God as a legal relation. Pharisaism carried the viewpoint to the limit and Paul, still employing this Pharisaic terminology, maintained the Pharisaic combination of law-keeping, righteousness, and reward in his thinking. Still, Paul does not derive the "unfulfillability" of the law from human sinfulness but from the law's own nature, which serves not to give life but to increase sin. He therefore still conceives the Christian religion purely as a religion of redemption, as grace, forgiveness, faith. And that, in fact, it is. It is solely a religious-ethical religion and no longer has any cosmic juridical or metaphysical components. It is a doctrine of salvation and nothing more; and all the other things, the doctrine of God, of humanity, of sin, of the world, and so on, must be reviewed and revised, christologically and soteriologically, from this perspective. The state is the sphere of law; but religion and law are diametrically opposed to each other.[157]

This entire set of opposites, however, is false and has always been rejected in Christian theology as Marcionite. In the first place, after all, it is not true that justice and grace (love) are a contrast in God. Not only does the whole Bible ascribe to God the attributes of righteousness, holiness, wrath and hatred against sin,[158] but grace even presupposes righteousness in God and cannot be maintained without it. Remember: grace is that perfection in God by which, for some reason or other, he relinquishes his rights. Hence, if as the righteous and holy one he did not have the right to punish, we cannot speak of grace in relation to him either. Similarly, the highest love in God, that is, the forgiving love that is revealed in Christ, is no longer love if in God's righteous judgment sin did not deserve to be punished. Those who deny justice thereby also deny grace.

In the second place, justice and religion (morality) absolutely do not constitute an antithesis. Religion and morality are themselves a claim that God has on

---

Martensen, *Christian Ethics* (Edinburgh: T&T Clark, 1842), II, 155ff.; I. A. Dorner, *System of Chr. Doctr.*, IV, 82; C. Hodge, *Systematic Theology*, II, 487; A. A. Hodge, *Atonement*, 48; W. G. T. Shedd, *Dogmatic Theology*, I, 378; H. Martin, *Atonement*, 172.

157. For the Socinians, see above, 347–51 (#378); and further, J. Wegscheider, *Inst. theol.*, §142; P. Hofstede de Groot, *De Groninger Godgeleerdheid*, 181; J. H. Scholten, *De Leer der Hervormde Kerk*, II, 46ff., 57ff.; A. Schweizer, *Die Glaubenslehre der evangelisch-reformierten Kirche*, 2 vols (Zürich: Orell & Fussli, 1844–47), §§63ff.; idem, *Christliche Glaubenslehre*, §§94ff.; O. Pfleiderer, *Der Paulinismus*, 86–110, 150–59; H. J. Holtzmann, *Lehrbuch der neutestamentliche Theologie*, II, 108ff.; A. Ritschl, *Justification and Reconciliation*, III, 8–14, 234–80; J. Kaftan, *Dogmatik*, 544ff.; E. von Hartmann, *Religionsphilosophie*, I, 546ff.

158. Cf. H. Bavinck, *Reformed Dogmatics*, II, 221–28 (#206).

us. In his law he demands that we humans shall love him above all else and our neighbor as ourselves. Now, religion and morality are not degraded or externalized by this demand but, on the contrary, *maintained* in their true significance. God wills that humans shall love him with all their heart, mind, and powers. He claims the whole person for this service of love. Religion and morality could not exist were they not rooted in God's just claim on his creatures. In this sense the moral order is upheld by the juridical order. The feeling for justice is even much more deeply grounded in humans than their religious and ethical consciousness. Even in the case of the people who have shaken off all religion and all morality, this sense of justice is frequently still remarkably vital. And though it is true that a perfect human loves God and neighbor spontaneously and in response to the voice of his or her holy nature, this in no way alters the fact that precisely such service out of love agrees with God's law and is prescribed in it. The moral law is very definitely a requirement and a divine right, even when it claims the whole person and desires a service in spirit and truth. For just as religion and morality are rooted in divine right, so conversely, that right of God, so far from being an abstract and formal matter of the will, is above all grounded in God's nature. The juridical order itself has an ethical character and finds confirmation and support in the moral order.

Third, the assertion that the moral world order only became a legal world order as a result of sin is therefore incorrect.[159] Granted, it has become legal for humans as a result of sin in the sense that now the love for God and neighbor comes to them as a command confrontatively from without, a command that they cannot fulfill, that they have violated, and whose penalty they deserve. But it did not become legal as a result of sin as though it were not grounded in a right and law of God. Though Lutheran theology indeed taught this,[160] the judgment of Reformed theology was otherwise and better. Even apart from sin, the law is very definitely the norm for the entire moral world order, for it is a norm grounded in God's being. This order is not even conceivable apart from a law. All religion and morality presuppose a law. Where there is no law, there is no transgression. Those who separate the moral world order from the law turn it both objectively and subjectively into something capricious and undermine its foundation.

Fourth, those who dualistically oppose justice and grace to each other run afoul of Scripture at all points. The state of integrity, as life lived in conformity with the moral law on the part of humans created after God's image, can no longer be maintained. Sin is not culpable, they claim, and deserves no punishment other than in the consciousness of the sinner. The law has no eternal significance but only a temporary, passing, pedagogical function. The Old Testament as the religion of law no longer concerns us. The doctrines of the righteousness of God and of Christ's atonement are Pharisaic Jewish intrusions into the theology of the

159. J. Kaftan, *Dogmatik*, 370, 545.
160. Cf. H. Bavinck, *Reformed Dogmatics,* II, 572–76 (#297).

New Testament. The forgiveness of sins is a matter of arriving at the subjective insight that sins are not culpable and do not deserve punishment. Sanctification is autonomous moral self-development. The church is only a religious-ethical community that has nothing to do with "right" and law. Under the appearance of gaining a purer view of the Christian religion, the promoters of this dualism have robbed it of its core.

Fifth, and finally, if grace, love, and forgiveness are totally undeserved and all presuppose a voluntary relinquishment of a "right," one may most certainly—with Socinus[161]—ask the question whether God cannot relinquish that right without demanding satisfaction. God, after all, is slow to anger, long-suffering, and merciful and, in Scripture, frequently forgives people without there being any satisfaction, provided there is genuine repentance (Deut. 30:1–3; Jer. 3:13–14; 18:8; Matt. 18:24f.; Luke 15:11f.). In this question, if it is really meant seriously, the difference is no longer one de jure (by right) but only one de facto (in fact). God had a right to demand satisfaction. Grace and forgiveness presuppose that right. The difference concerns only whether God in fact demanded that satisfaction. Later we will find that in reality the suffering and death of Christ had a "satisfactory" (atoning) character. In the face of this reality, the question concerning the issue of whether God could not have relinquished his right to satisfaction is of very minor significance. In any case, however, it is not proper to use forgiveness to oppose satisfaction as though the two were mutually exclusive. For in Scripture they are not only connected (Lev. 4:31; Rom. 3:24–26; Heb. 9:22), but they are related in such a way that it is exactly satisfaction that opens the way to forgiveness. In the case of financial debts, satisfaction indeed cancels out forgiveness, since here what matters is not the person who pays but only the sum of money that is paid. But in the case of moral debts, this is very different. They are personal and must be punished in the guilty person himself or herself. If a substitute is admitted in this situation, the admission of such a substitute and the crediting of his merits in exchange for those of the guilty person is certainly always an act of grace. Satisfaction is something Christ gives to God, but forgiveness is something God gives to us. Forgiveness amounts to grace, not vis-à-vis Christ, but vis-à-vis *us*. For God, Christ's satisfaction opens the way—without violating his rights—to forgive sins out of grace and so to justify the ungodly. If sin is of such a nature that "right" and righteousness, law and truth, do not suffer the least damage even when sin is not punished, then neither does the grace of forgiveness amount to much. But if sin is so enormous "that God, rather than . . . leave it unpunished, punished it in his beloved son, Jesus Christ, with the bitter and shameful death of the cross," then the riches of God's grace, the power of his forgiving love, come splendidly to the fore. Then, too, in the face of their accusing conscience, humans find rest and consolation in that satisfaction and can rejoice without any fear in the forgiveness

161. F. Socinus, *De Christo servatore*, I, 1.

of their sins. For a perfect satisfaction (atonement) is the guarantee of absolute, irrevocable, and eternal forgiveness.[162]

THE OBEDIENCE OF CHRIST FOR US

[386] The work Christ accomplished for his own consisted in general in his absolute and total obedience to the will of God (Matt. 3:15; 20:28; 26:42; John 4:34; 5:30; 6:38; Rom. 5:19; Gal. 4:4; Phil. 2:7–8; Heb. 5:8; 10:5–10; etc.). In theology this rich idea has frequently not come into its own. Often Christ's suffering has been separated from the act of obedience expressed in it and thus made into an object of pious reflection. In the Christian church, the martyrs, the monks, the beggars, the flagellants, were successively viewed as the true disciples of Jesus. Asceticism and self-torture were the preeminent Christian virtues. Following Christ consisted in copying and imitating deeds and conditions from his life, specifically from his suffering. Christ was the great sufferer, the sublime martyr, whose suffering had to be the object of contemplation and imitation.[163] In Anselm, Christ's satisfaction—since Christ was obligated to obey God's law first of all for himself—consisted only in his suffering and death, which as a work of supererogation was added to his life by him and offered to the Father as a voluntary gift. Catholic theology does not express itself unanimously and unambiguously about the active obedience of Christ. Though the Council of Trent makes mention of Christ's "most holy Passion,"[164] the theologians either completely reject it or construe it to mean that Christ did not fulfill the law of God in our place.[165]

Also among Protestants—in the case of mystics, Anabaptists, Herrnhuter, and others—occur views of the suffering of Christ as "something objective," views that fail to do justice to his active obedience. Even Parsimonius and Piscator denied it,[166] inasmuch as Christ was already obligated to this obedience for himself, and this obedience, therefore, though for him personally a necessary requirement and for our benefit (*nostro bono*), was not a constituent in his satisfaction accomplished in our place (*nostro loco*); further, because Holy Scripture consistently links our entire salvation, both the forgiveness of sins and eternal life, to Christ's suffering and death alone; and because believers, even though they have the forgiveness of sins and eternal life, are still obligated to keep the law. Lutherans, regarding

---

162. J. Maccovius, *Collegia theologica,* 3rd ed. (Franecker: Joannis Fabiani Deuring, 1641), I, 274; P. van Mastricht, *Theologia*, V, 18, 35; F. Turretin, *Institutes of Elenctic Theology*, XIV, qu. 10, 8; idem, *De satisf.*, 44; J. Hoornbeek, *Socinismus confutatus,* 3 vols. (Utrecht, 1650–54), II, 629; Petrus de Witte, *Wederlegginge der sociniaensche dwalingen,* 3 vols. (Amsterdam: Boeckholt & van den Heuvel, 1662), II, 90ff.; M. Leydekker, *Vis veritatis*, 82; B. de Moor, *Comm. theol.*, III, 1031; W. G. T. Shedd, *Dogmatic Theology*, II, 382; H. Martin, *Atonement*, 183.

163. O. Zöckler, *Askese und Mönchtum*, 2nd ed., 2 vols. (Frankfurt a.M.: Heyder & Zimmer, 1897), I, 145ff.

164. Council of Trent, sess. VI, can. 7.

165. R. Bellarmine, "De justif.," *Controversiis,* I, 2; idem, "De Christo," *Controversiis,* V, 9.

166. See above, 345–47 (#378).

this as Nestorianism, said that the person of Christ was Lord of the law in both his natures and therefore not subject to the law for himself simply as a human being.[167]

Reformed theologians, however, could not speak along those lines since Christ as a true human being was certainly obligated to keep the law, to love God above all, and to love his neighbor as himself. Yet they rightly rejected the sentiments of Piscator. For, in the first place, Scripture views the entire life and work of Christ as a single whole and never makes a dichotomy between an obedience of life (*obedientia vitae*), which he accomplished for himself, and an obedience of death (*obedientia mortis*), which he accomplished for us. It is one single work that the Father assigned to him and that he finished in his death (John 4:34; 17:4; 19:30). His ministry was completed in the giving of his life as a ransom for many (Matt. 20:28). Even Paul, who powerfully emphasizes the cross of Christ, regards his death, not as the whole, but as the consummation of his obedience. He was born under the law (Gal. 4:4), in the likeness of sinful flesh (Rom. 8:3), did not live to please himself (Rom. 15:3); at his incarnation he already emptied himself and assumed the form of a servant; he continually humbled himself and became obedient even to death (Phil. 2:7–8; 2 Cor. 8:9). So it is one single ministry and one obedience, which gives "life-giving justification" (δικαιωσις ζωης) to many (Rom. 5:18–19). It is totally contrary to Scripture, therefore, to restrict the "satisfactory" (atoning) work of Christ to his suffering or even, as Jacob Alting did,[168] to his suffering only during the three hours of darkness on the cross. The appeal to places like Zechariah 3:9; John 19:30; Romans 6:10; Hebrews 7:27; 1 Peter 3:18, where we read that Christ suffered on the cross once for all and cried out "It is finished!" do not in any way serve as an argument against this position because, in his suffering and death, the whole of Christ's preceding life was incorporated, summed up, and completed.[169] The case is rather that Christ's entire life and work, from his conception to his death, was substitutionary in nature. The assumption of human nature itself and by itself does not yet have this character because all Christ's mediatorial works presuppose the two natures; but his holy conception and birth and all his holy works are included in the one work of Christ.[170]

167. J. Gerhard, *Loci theol.*, XVI, 57, 59; J. A. Quenstedt, *Theologia*, III, 284; M. Schneckenburger, *Zur kirchlichen Christologie: Die orthodoxe Lehre vom doppelten Stande Christi nach lutherischer und reformirter Fassung* (Pforzheim: Flammer & Hoffmann, 1848), 58–73; A. Ritschl, *Rechtfertigung und Versöhnung*, I, 274.

168. Jacob Alting, *Opera*, V, 393–95; cf. especially 478–80.

169. B. de Moor, *Comm. theol.*, III, 985ff.; C. Vitringa, *Doctr. christ.*, VI, 102ff.; P. van Mastricht, *Theologia*, V, 11, 34; V, 18, 29; Witsius, *Oeconomy of the Covenants*, II, 6; idem, *Misc. sacra*, II, 771; Maresius, *Syst. theol.*, IX, 46; A. Comrie and N. Holtius, *Examen van het Ontwerp*, X, 467–71.

170. P. Lombard, *Sent.*, III, dist. 18, 2; Heidelberg Catechism, Q. & A. 36; Belgic Confession, art. 22. Concerning the words of this article—"Imputing to us all his merits, and so many holy works, which he has done for us and in our stead"—there was a difference at the Synod of Dort (sessions 172–73). In addition to others, Bogerman and Lubbertus also inclined to the convictions of Piscator; see H. H. Kuyper, *De Postacta of Nahandelingen van de Nationale Synode van Dordrecht* (Amsterdam: Hoveker & Wormser, 1899), 338ff.;

Second, while it is certainly true that as a human and with reference to himself Christ was subject to the law, it must be emphasized that his incarnation and being human occurred not for himself but for us. Christ never was, and may never be regarded as, a private person, an individual alongside and on the same level as other individuals. He was from the very beginning a public person, the second Adam, the guarantor and head of the elect. As Adam sinned for himself and by this act imposed guilt and death on all those he represented, so Christ, by his righteousness and obedience, acquired forgiveness and life for all his own. Even more, as a human being Christ was certainly subject to the law of God as the rule of life; even believers are never exempted from the law in that sense. But Christ related himself to the law in still a very different way, namely, as the law of the covenant of works. Adam was not only obligated to keep the law but was confronted in the covenant of works with that law as the way to eternal life, a life he did not yet possess. But Christ, in virtue of his union with the divine nature, already had this eternal and blessed life. This life he voluntarily relinquished. He submitted himself to the law of the covenant of works as the way to eternal life for himself and his own.

The obedience that Christ accorded to the law, therefore, was totally voluntary. Not his death alone, as Anselm said, but his entire life was an act of self-denial, a self-offering presented by him as head in the place of his own.

Third, that believers are still always obligated to keep the law as the rule of life is no argument against this. If this proved anything, all the "satisfactory" value of Jesus' life and suffering would vanish. For believers must still bear all sorts of suffering as a result of sin(s); they are still tempted by Satan and seduced by the world; they still sin time after time and must still die and so on, and therefore—it is argued—Christ has not delivered them from anything, neither from sin nor from its consequences. This is how Jacob Alting argued and stated, accordingly, that by his hellish bouts of fear during the three hours of darkness on the cross, Christ had delivered his own only from eternal death. But his view of the work of redemption is definitely wrong. Redemption is complete: a redemption of the whole person, in soul and body, from all sins and all consequences of sin. And this has been accomplished by Christ's life and death. But just as his kingdom was differentiated by him into an invisible spiritual realm and a visible realm that would one day be founded on earth; just as he himself came once to suffer, and will in the future return to judge the living and the dead, so the redemption wrought by Christ is gradually worked out and applied, first spiritually, then bodily. In this dispensation believers are delivered from all guilt and the power of sin and all its consequences, from the world, Satan, and death. They have the forgiveness of sins and eternal life. The law, Satan, and death can no longer take these things

---

G. Voetius, *Select. disp.,* II, 282; M. Schneckenburger and E. Güder, *Vergleichende Darstellung des lutherischen und reformierten Lehrbegriffs,* 2 vols. (Stuttgart: J. B. Metzler, 1855), I, 91, 122ff.; A. Ritschl, *Rechtfertigung und Versöhnung,* I, 287.

away. And some day they will also be delivered externally—physically—from all sin and the dominion of sin. The whole re-creation, as it will be completed in the new heaven and the new earth, is the fruit of the work of Christ. Just as it is one-sided, with Alting, to see the fruit of Christ's work only in the redemption from eternal death, so it is equally one-sided, with Ritschl, to limit that fruit to the spiritual-ethical dominion of Christ over sin and the world this side of heaven. The whole person of Christ, in both his active and his passive obedience, is the complete guarantee for the entire redemption that God in his grace grants to individual persons, to humanity, and to the world.[171]

[387] Whereas in earlier centuries Piscator and many others excluded Christ's active obedience from his mediatorial work, in modern theology his passive obedience is very frequently misjudged or totally denied and opposed. After Socinianism and rationalism had subjected the doctrine of Christ's satisfaction to sharp criticism, many theologians in modern times transmuted it into something mystical or ethical and, in so doing, robbed it of its true character. The idea, in the main, is that Christ's suffering and death were not necessary for the purpose of satisfying God's righteousness nor demanded by God as a sacrifice for our sins. Instead, they were the consequence of a life lived in obedience to God's will, proof that in his religious-ethical vocation he remained faithful to God and clung to his fellowship even into death, the historically necessary result of his holy life in the midst of a sinful world. In the elaboration of this main idea, however, the emphasis varies. Among the church fathers, we frequently encounter the statement that God had to become human in order that humans might become his children. Under the influence of Hegel's philosophy, this idea again surfaces in many modern theologians who, for that reason, locate the redemptive deed in the incarnation and regard the reconciliation by his suffering and death as its completion. Christ saves us not so much by what he does as by what he is.[172] Though Schleiermacher's doctrine of redemption shows affinity to that view, he especially stresses the perfect and undisturbed God-consciousness of Christ and the holy life he led from beginning to end. As the Holy One, he entered into our fellowship, acquired profound "sympathy with human guilt and liability to

---

171. On Christ's active obedience, see further: J. Calvin, *Institutes*, II.xvi.5; III.xiv.12; idem, *Commentaries*, on Romans 5:19 and Galatians 4:4; F. Gomarus, *Theses theol. disp.*, 19, 9; F. Junius, *Theses theol.*, 36, 8; *Synopsis purioris theologiae*, 29, 35; F. Turretin, *Institutes of Elenctic Theology*, XI, 22; Cloppenburg, *Opera*, 1, 504; H. Witsius, *Oeconomy of the Covenants*, II, 3, 18ff.; J. Cocceius, *De foedere*, V, 93; J. A. Quenstedt, *Theologia*, III, 281; J. Gerhard, *Loci theol.*, XVI, 57ff.; C. W. F. Walch, *Comm. de obed. Christi activa* (1755); F. C. Baur, *Die christliche Lehre von der Versöhnung in ihrer geschichtlichen Entwicklung von der ältesten Zeit auf die neueste* (Tübingen: Osiander, 1838), 478ff.; F. A. Philippi, *Der thätige Gehorsam Jesu Christi* (1841); idem, *Kirchliche Glaubenslehre*, IV/2, 142ff.; F. H. R. Frank, *Christliche Wahrheit*, II, 172; idem, *Neue kirchliche Zeitschrift* (1892): 856; A. Ritschl, *Rechtfertigung und Versöhnung*, I, 271ff.; A. A. Hodge, *Atonement*, 248–71; J. Scott Lidgett, *Spiritual Principle of the Atonement*, 139ff.

172. Cf., e.g., B. F. Westcott, *Christus Consummator: Some Aspects of the Work and Person of Christ in Relation to Modern Thought* (London and New York: Macmillan, 1886), 99ff.

punishment," and accepted his death as the result of "his zeal for his vocation."[173] Hofmann, too, proceeded from the unity of God and humanity that was accomplished in the person of Christ and further defined atonement by saying that Christ, consecrating himself to God in all his suffering and to the point of death, became the head of a new humanity born from him.[174]

Other theologians tend to take their position in the *work* of Christ and attempt from that vantage point to arrive at a view and appraisal of his person. The work he was to accomplish on earth is then frequently described as the founding of the kingdom of heaven and bringing this about despite all opposition. It was fidelity to his vocation that marks his death as a sacrifice. Still, that death was no true sacrifice, no demand of God's righteousness, and no punishment for sins, but the unintended consequence of the conflict between him, the Holy One, and sinful humankind, "an accident of his positive faithfulness in the pursuit of his vocation."[175] Sometimes the work of Christ is also said to consist in bringing to light, by his death, the severity of the moral law and the appalling character of sin, thus producing in humankind that "state of repentance" in which alone the forgiveness of sins can be received and enjoyed. For there is no atonement for sins other than the repentance that, after all, is itself the "destruction of sin" in us.[176] Others tend to approach the person of Christ more from the side of his solidarity with humankind. Although the Son of God, he was certainly also the Son of Man. By his incarnation he became the head and representative of humankind. He entered into the fellowship of its suffering and death, took on himself its sorrows and diseases, and in his life and death showed what love is and is capable of doing.[177] Some theologians develop this solidarity of Christ with humankind even further into the theory that Christ, taking this suffering on himself as the consequence of sins and in so doing pronouncing his "Amen" to God's righteous judgment on sin, himself thereby made a complete confession of sins, displayed complete repentance over sins, and in that way disclosed a path to atonement for sin—all on behalf of humankind.[178]

173. F. Schleiermacher, *Christian Faith* (1928), §104, 4.

174. See above, 353 (#379).

175. A. Ritschl, *Justification and Reconciliation*, III, 556; J. Kaftan, *Dogmatik,* 565–69; G. A. F. Ecklin, *Der Heilswert des Todes Jesus* (Basel: Reinhardt, 1888); E. Kühl, *Die Heilsbedeutung des Todes Christi* (Berlin: Hertz, 1890), 190ff.

176. Cf. in addition to Grotius, Dale, and others, discussed above, A. Sabatier, "La doctrine de l'expiation et son évolution historique," in *Études de théologie et d'histoire: Publiées par MM. les professeurs de la Faculté de théologie protestante de Paris* (Paris: Fischbacher, 1901), 6–76.

177. In addition to Bushnell, Maurice, and others, cf. C. Secrétan, *La philosophie de la liberté,* 3rd ed., 2 vols. in 1 (Paris: L. Hachette, 1849), II, 285–345; E. de Pressensé, *Le rédempteur* (1859) (ed. note: ET: *The Redeemer: A Sketch of the History of Redemption,* trans. J. H. Myers [Boston: American Tract Society, 1867]); E. Bersier, *La solidarité* (1869).

178. One already encounters this idea in Jonathan Edwards and John Henry Newman (cf. Scott Lidgett, *Spiritual Principle of the Atonement,* 174, 177); but it gets developed in greater detail by Campbell, Moberly, and Frommel; cf. above, 358–61 (#380).

DIMENSIONS OF CHRIST'S DEATH

All these different appraisals of the death of Christ are frequently labeled "theories" that have been constructed by human thought in an attempt to explain the facts. The picture presented is that Scripture does not contain a clear, authoritative, and decisive doctrine of the suffering and death of Christ. If there were such a doctrine, then certainly the matter would not have been debated for centuries and there would not be such an array of theories surviving side by side in the church and in theology. But the New Testament no more affords us a doctrine of redemption than "nature gives us science. It gives us the facts but not the theory, the matter of all Christian doctrine, but no finished doctrine or doctrines of the whole of Christianity." And that is a good thing too. For this makes possible a Christianity in which all agree, although in their views and interpretation of it, there is wide divergence. No two theologians are perhaps agreed on *how* Christ is our salvation and in *what* it actually consists, yet both confess that Christ is our salvation. Especially in our day many people are very dissatisfied with the theories presented in the past concerning the suffering and death of Christ but still continue to believe in the fact of salvation in Christ. The situation is like that of two people who both recognize the fact of gravity but, when they begin to talk about it, find themselves far apart.[179]

This picture of the situation is very unbalanced. The power of the death of Christ is independent of the more or less clear interpretation we can give of it. It is also enjoyed by those who have but very little knowledge of the doctrine of truth. It is indeed not the doctrine concerning the death of Christ but this death itself that atones for our sins and gives peace to our consciences.[180] But some knowledge of the significance and value of that death is nevertheless always needed to distinguish it from that of other people—also that of martyrs and heroes—and to link our salvation to that death. Undoubtedly, a correct insight into its characteristic essence and value is also conducive to the development of the spiritual life of people. The comparison of believers who accept the fact of the death of Christ but differ in theory with the people who accept gravity but differ in their views about it is faulty. For that matter Dubose himself recognizes that it is only partially applicable "because to be practically saved in Christ is not so independent of some knowledge of what and how salvation is in him as living under the law of gravitation is of any theoretical knowledge of it." Much more mistaken, however, is the comparison of the New Testament with nature as if both only supply facts and no theory. For though this may be true of nature, it is absolutely not applicable to the New Testament. Holy Scripture does not relate to us the bare fact of the death of Christ in order then to base the interpretation and appraisal of it to everyone's own taste but from all angles puts that fact in the light of the Word. As elsewhere in revelation, word and fact here are very closely

179. W. Porcher Dubose, *Soteriology of the New Testament*, 16–20.
180. Dale, *Atonement*, 4.

intertwined. Christ is a priest but also a prophet. He explained his own person and work. In his teaching and later through the mouth of his apostles, he himself interpreted his suffering and death, and Christian theology is bound to that word. Accordingly, there are not many theories—moral, governmental, mystical, private and public law-oriented—which are framed by theology in the form of hypotheses in an attempt to explain the facts and phenomena, and, as different attempts at a solution, all have an equal right to exist. The question is what in all these ideas agrees with Scripture and what Scripture itself teaches concerning the significance and power of the death of Christ. That death is not a subject for philosophical speculation, at least not independently of and apart from Scripture, but can only be understood to a degree in theology if it allows itself to be guided by the study of the Scriptures.

The first thing this study teaches, we may say, is that the Scriptures continually view the suffering and death of Christ from a different perspective and in each case illumine another aspect of it. Like the person, the work of Christ is so multifaceted that it cannot be captured in a single word nor summarized in a single formula. In the different books of the New Testament, therefore, different meanings of the death of Christ are highlighted, and all of them together help to give us a deep impression and a clear sense of the riches and many-sidedness of the mediator's work. In the Synoptics, Christ appears on the scene as a preacher and founder of the kingdom of God. That kingdom includes within itself the love of the Father, the forgiveness of sins, righteousness, and eternal life; and Jesus, in his capacity as Messiah, ascribes to himself the power to grant all these benefits to his disciples. Just as he has power to heal the sick, so he also has the authority to forgive sins. By this combination of powers, he proves that he is the complete Savior of his people. For that reason, too, there is no way of gaining admission into that kingdom and no participation in those benefits except by faith in his name. For it is he himself who gives his life as a ransom for many and who, in his death, breaks his body and sheds his blood to inaugurate and confirm the new covenant with all its blessings (Matt. 20:28; 26:28). In the Acts of the Apostles, the death of Christ is especially presented as an appalling crime that was inflicted on Christ by the hands of lawless men but was nevertheless from eternity included in the counsel of God (Acts 2:23; 4:28; 5:30). Therefore, God also raised him from the dead and exalted him as Lord and Christ, Ruler and Savior, in order, in his name, to give repentance to Israel and forgiveness of sins (Acts 2:36; 4:12; 5:31).

For Paul, Christ's death on the cross was originally the great offense, but when it pleased God to reveal his Son in it, that cross became for him the crown of Jesus' messiahship and the only means of salvation. For on that cross God made him to be sin and a curse for us in order that in him we would have wisdom and righteousness, sanctification and redemption, salvation and eternal life (Rom. 3:24; 1 Cor. 1:30; 2 Cor. 5:21; Gal. 3:13). The Letter to the Hebrews describes Christ especially as the perfect and eternal high priest who was not only himself sanctified (perfected) through suffering (2:10; 5:9) but by his one perfect sacrifice put away the sins of his people (7:27; 9:26; 10:12) and is still continually at work as high priest in heaven, continuing and completing the purification, sanctification, and perfecting of his own (7:3, 25; 8:1; 9:14; 10:12ff.). Peter pictures Christ's suffering as that of a lamb without blemish or spot; and in that suffering he not only bore our sins and redeemed us from our futile way of life but left us an example that we might follow in his steps (1 Pet. 1:18f.; 2:21f.). And John makes Christ known to us both as the lamb and the lion, as the life and the light, as the bread and the water of life, as the grain of wheat that, dying, bears fruit, and as the good Shepherd who gives his life for the sheep, as the Savior who gives life to the world, and as the alpha and the omega, the beginning and the end, the first and the last, and so on.

So, indeed, one can find in the New Testament different appraisals of the person and work of Christ, which, however, do not exclude but rather supplement one another and enrich our knowledge. Just as in the old covenant there were diverse sacrifices and the promised Messiah was repeatedly presented under different names, so this many-sidedness in the description carries over into the New Testament and even markedly increases. The death of Christ is a paschal offering, a covenant offering, a praise offering as well as a sacrifice; a ransom and an example; suffering and action; a work and a ministry; a means of justification and sanctification, atonement and consecration, redemption and glorification; in a word, the cause of our whole redemption. Similarly, in theology various "theories" occur side by side, and in the preaching of the church, now one and now another aspect of the work of Christ is in the limelight. None of the above-mentioned mystical and ethical views, accordingly, are untrue as such; on the contrary, they are all based on data contained in Holy Scripture. Christ, by his incarnation, in his person indeed brought about the union of God and humanity and is, as such, God's representative to us and our representative to God: the Immanuel who as prophet makes God known to us and as priest consecrates himself on our behalf to the Father. He is the Son, the Word, the Image of God who shares with the Father in the same essence and attributes, and at the same time the Son of Man, the true human, the head of humankind, the second Adam who became like us in all respects, entered into our community of sin and death and bore our sorrows and diseases. He came on earth to fulfill a vocation, to found the kingdom of heaven, to confirm the new covenant in his blood; and in order to do that, he submitted to the will of the Father, became obedient unto death, and pronounced the "Amen" on the righteous judgment that God executed upon death in his suffering and dying. He became the faithful witness (Rev. 1:5), made the good confession before Pilate (1 Tim. 6:13), and became the high priest of our confession (Heb. 3:1). His suffering, therefore, was not only an atonement for our sins and a ransom for our redemption, but in his death the believing community was crucified with him, and in his resurrection this community itself arose from the grave. Christ was never alone; always he stood in fellowship with the humanity whose nature he had assumed. Just as all die in Adam, so they are again made alive in Christ and called to follow in his footsteps. All these elements, which come one-sidedly to the fore in the above-mentioned conceptions of Christ's death, can be found in Scripture. What matters above all, now, is not to neglect any of them but to unite them into a single whole and to trace the unity that underlies them in Scripture. We can even say they are all inspired by the commendable ambition to link the suffering and death of Christ as closely as possible with his person. For this suffering and death were in fact not "something objective" that can be separated from his person and life and put in a category by itself. Christ's suffering and death were not his "lot" but his deed. He had power to lay down his life as he did to take it up again (John 10:18). His death was the consummation of his obedience (Phil. 2:8).

[388] Still, though the mystical and ethical ideas concerning the death of Christ are not incorrect as such, by themselves they are incomplete and insufficient. In the long run they cannot even be maintained unless they are linked with another thought that is consistently tied in with the death of Christ in Scripture but that is systematically removed and opposed by these theories. The truth is that despite the great diversity they display among themselves, they all have in common that they attempt to transmute the objective satisfaction into a subjective reconcili-ation and to replace the substitutionary-expiatory view of Christ's suffering by a solidaristic-reparatory one. Christ, they say, did not take over the guilt of sin from us, nor did he bear its punishment in our place. His death was not required by the righteousness of God and did not in a real sense secure those benefits that are now, for Christ's sake, bestowed on us out of grace. Instead, in his suffering and death—which was the necessary historical consequence of the life he, the Holy One, lived amid a sinful world—he remained faithful to God to the end, and by his word, example, Spirit, in general by the influence he exerted as a person, created a new religious moral situation in the world in which people are deterred from sin, attracted by the love of God, arrive at remorse, faith, and conversion, and in that way obtain the forgiveness of their sins and a new life. Christ secured those benefits not actually but potentially. He created not the reality but only the possibility of our redemption. By the spiritual and moral power he exerts, he may lead us to conversion and thus to salvation, but he is not our only, complete, and all-sufficient Savior. This picture does not correspond to the profoundly rich thought that Scripture consistently associates with the death of Christ.

Remarkable at first blush already is that, based on these mystical and ethical theories, the theologians in question prefer to speak in the case of Jesus of a "calling" and avoid the word "office." There is a big difference between these two words. If Jesus pursued a vocation or in his public appearances and activity only listened to an internal call, then, certainly, one can still speak of God's providential guid-ance but not of an entirely unique revelation from God. In a religious and ethical sense, he may be far above and ahead of us, yet, in principle, he is not above us at all but beside us. He is our captain and leader, but we nevertheless have the duty and the power to conform to his example and to follow in his footsteps. On the other hand, if Christ has been anointed as prophet, priest, and king, he has been appointed by God, been given a work to do, and is above us in a position of authority, to teach us, to represent us before the face of God, and to govern us according to his will.[181] "Office," with reference to Christ, is not a metaphor, for he did not make himself a high priest but was called and appointed to this position by God (Heb. 5:4–5). Nor was he a prophet, priest, and king only in appearance or name but really, in actual fact. Moses, Aaron, David, and as many prophets, priests, and kings as appeared on the scene under the old covenant were shadows and examples of what Christ is and was and will forever remain in a true sense (Heb. 3:6; 5:5; 10:12; etc.).

Of greater importance is that in the position sketched above, the suffering and death of Christ remain completely unexplained. The Groningen theologians in the Netherlands expressed themselves very strongly when they said that the death of Christ was something perpetrated by humans, endured by Jesus, and permitted by God and that, therefore, the necessity of it, which is mentioned in Matthew 16:21; Mark 8:31; and Luke 9:22, must be understood in a moral sense.[182] But at bottom this is actually what modern theologians think. There may have been a psychological and historical necessity for Christ's suffering and death; for a metaphysical necessity there is no longer any room. They are all united in opposing as vigorously as they can [the idea] that the death of Christ was demanded by the righteousness of God. But such a view, according to which the suffering and death of Christ becomes accidental in a higher sense, is fully condemned by Scripture, for Scripture states expressly that Christ's suffering was determined in advance, predicted for centuries, and necessary to the revelation of God's righteousness (Luke 24:26; Rom. 3:25–26; 1 Pet. 1:11).

MESSIANIC CONSCIOUSNESS

Against this, many theologians have indeed tried to show that in the beginning of his public ministry, Jesus acted with great and joyful expectations and only saw the necessity of his death from the day when, in the district of Caesarea Philippi, Peter confessed that he was the Christ (Matt. 16:20ff.).[183] But Kähler rightly calls this a myth. The messianic consciousness that—as was evident at his baptism by John—Jesus possessed from the beginning of his public ministry; the name "Son of Man," which he assigned to himself with a clear mind and a specific intent; the application to himself of Isaiah's prophecy (Luke 4:21); the prediction that as the bridegroom he would be taken away from his disciples (Mark 2:20); the comparison of himself to Jonah (Matt. 12:40) and to the serpent in the wilderness (John 3:14); the proclamation of the kingdom of heaven in a very different

181. Hugh Martin, *Atonement,* 104ff.
182. L. G. Pareau and P. Hofstede de Groot, *Lineam theologiae Christianae universae,* 3rd ed. (Groningen: C. M. van Bolhuis Hoitsema, 1848), 153; P. Hofstede de Groot, *De Groninger Godgeleerden,* 181.
183. H. J. Holtzmann, *Lehrbuch der neutestamentlichen Theologie,* I, 284–85.

sense from that expected by the Jews, and the consciousness that citizenship in that kingdom required faith and repentance, self-denial and cross bearing, and would provoke the hatred, hostility, and persecution of the world (Matt. 5:10ff.; 10:16f.; 12:25)—all this proves that Jesus was certain from the beginning that suffering and death would describe the end of his life. Prophecy, especially the prophecy of Isaiah (ch. 53), was always present to his mind (Luke 4:21; 18:31; 22:37; 24:26, 46) and instructed him concerning his departure.[184] The day in Caesarea Philippi only effected the change that Jesus, now that the apostles had gradually come to the certain conviction of his messiahship, also openly told them that he was the Christ but would for that reason also be delivered into the hands of sinners, to be raised again on the third day (Matt. 16:21ff.). And he expressly adds that this *had to* take place, not because he was morally obligated to die or could only remain faithful to his calling that way—for a moral obligation to be delivered up, killed, and even raised is nonexistent—but because it was so determined in God's counsel and predicted in Scripture (Matt. 16:21; 26:54; Luke 22:22; 24:26, 44–46; John 3:14; 7:30; 8:20; 10:18; 11:7–15; 12:23; 13:1; 17:1; 20:9; 1 Pet. 1:20). The *necessity* of it is grounded in that counsel; an hour has been set for his suffering and death, his resurrection and glorification.[185] From the beginning, therefore, it was a fixed given in the message of the apostles that Christ had died, was buried, and was raised according to the Scriptures (1 Cor. 15:3). They saw the death of Christ as a great crime on the part of the Jews who thereby sought to destroy and exterminate him. But God frustrated their efforts, raised him from the dead, and made him Lord and Christ, Ruler and Savior (Acts 2:22–36; 3:13–15; 5:30–31). And not only that, but that death was itself a constituent of the work of the Messiah, determined beforehand in God's counsel (Acts 2:23; 3:18; 4:28). This Christ who died and was raised, therefore, is the only name given under heaven by which we must be saved (Acts 4:12).

This necessity of Jesus' dying is not contradicted by the texts of Matthew 26:39, 42 and Hebrews 5:7.[186] According to the latter, Christ did not pray for deliverance from death, as though he did not recognize it as being necessary, for it is clearly stated that, despite his death, God heard his prayer. He, therefore, did not pray to be spared death but to be saved from the jaws of death, to be raised and glorified through death.

In another passage of this letter, therefore, we read that Christ came above all to do God's will in his suffering and death and to sanctify us by that will (Heb. 10:5–10). This in turn sheds light on the words of Matthew 26:39–42,

---

184. K. F. Nösgen, *Geschichte der neutestamentlichen Offenbarung*, 2 vols. (Munich: Beck, 1891–93), I, 395; M. Kähler, *Zur Lehre von der Versöhnung* (1898), 159ff.

185. J. Scholten, *De Leer der Hervormde Kerk*, II, 45.

186. As E. Ménégoz claims (*La mort de Jésus et le dogme de l'expiation* [Paris: Fischbacher, 1905], 26); he even says: "Jesus hardly thought that his death was absolutely necessary for the salvation of humanity but, even at the last minute, hoped to escape it. It requires a whole layer of traditional prejudice not to see this with sparkling clarity."

for in 5:7, the Letter to the Hebrews thinks primarily, if not exclusively, of Jesus' prayer in Gethsemane. Christ there does not pray in line with his will—which he single-mindedly subjects to the will of his Father—but in terms of the tendency, increated in human nature, to flee from one's own doom.[187] As a human being, he dreads death as death and prays that this cup may pass from him, but at the same time, he surrenders himself to the counsel and will of the Father. Just as in that same hour he exhorts his disciples to be watchful and to pray in order not to fall into temptation, for the spirit is willing but the flesh is weak (Matt. 26:40), so he himself, tasting the bitterness of death, prays that God may strengthen him so that, in his death, he may do the will of God, that God's will may not just be done in regard to him but also, in full surrender and devotion, by him. He prayed "to die in the active service of His office, and not as the down-borne victim of death; to die as a Priest in death itself; His priestly action uninterrupted in death, yea, triumphing in death, an offerer as well as a sufferer, an obedient official agent in the article of death itself."[188] And in this act his prayer was heard. Though he was the Son, from what he suffered he learned the obedience required for the fulfillment of the Father's will. The disposition and the will to obey were integral to Christ's nature, but now, in the hour of trial, he must turn them into acts of obedience. Then he learned that obedience and was perfected by it (Heb. 5:8–9), so consecrating himself on our behalf (John 17:19).[189]

In addition, the suffering and death of Christ occupy such a special place in Scripture that they cannot be construed as an "accident" of vocational fidelity. Proportionately, by far the greatest part of the Gospels is devoted to it. And it is described not as a martyrdom but as a judgment of God, as the will of the Father, as the sacrifice of a priest. He did not die for his faith but was judicially condemned for saying he was the Son of God, the Messiah. He did not go rejoicing to his death but was disturbed, sad, astonished, fearful unto death, and intensely conflicted, so that his sweat became like drops of blood (Matt. 26:37–38; Mark 14:33; Luke 22:44; John 12:27). That is not the attitude of a sage who calmly looks death in the eye, nor that of a sufferer who rejoices in his suffering (Rom. 5:3), nor that

187. Marginal note in the Authorized Version of the Dutch Bible. Also cf. P. Lombard, *Sent.*, III, dist. 17; T. Aquinas, *Summa theol.*, III, qu. 21, art. 4; B. de Moor, *Comm. theol.*, IV, 840–70.

188. H. Martin, *Atonement*, 93.

189. Jesus' prayer in Gethsemane does not stand by itself. A. Deissmann, in *Beiträge zur Weiterentwicklung der christlichen Religion* (Munich: Lehmann, 1905), has rightly called attention to Christ's prayer life. It was treated in the past as well (e.g., T. Aquinas, *Summa theol.*, III, qu. 21), but too little use has been made of it for our knowledge of Jesus as a human being. The Gospels repeatedly report that Jesus isolated himself for the purpose of prayer, altogether no fewer than fourteen times from the beginning to the end and especially on the occasion of important events in his life. For example, at his baptism (Luke 3:21), before his first clash with the Pharisees (5:16), on the occasion of his choice of the Twelve (6:12), before the first clear announcement of his messiahship (9:18), at the transfiguration on the mount (9:28), before instructing his disciples on how to pray (11:1), before and after the feeding of the five thousand (Mark 6:41, 46), at the raising of Lazarus (John 11:41), in the high priestly prayer (John 17), in Gethsemane (Matt. 26:39), and on the cross (Luke 23:34). Cf. A. Plummer, "Prayer," *DC*, II, 391.

of a martyr who shouts with joy as he mounts the scaffolding or sings psalms at the stake. The suffering and death of Christ bear an exceptional character. "If the life and death of Socrates are those of a sage, the life and death of Jesus are those of a God" (Rousseau). This comes out with special acuteness in Jesus' cry of dereliction on the cross (Matt. 27:46). Some have interpreted this word from the cross as a cry of despair that his cause was lost and God had abandoned him (Wolfenbüttel fragments)[190] or have understood it merely subjectively of his purely human sense of being momentarily overcome by the deepest pain in the extremity of death (Meyer, op. cit.) or compared it, be it from a remote distance, with the cry of a mother whose heart breaks over the shame of her child but in her great love still takes the child's disgrace on herself and bows her head under the judgment of God (Moberly).[191] But none of these interpretations does justice to the words, and all are at variance with the consistent description of Jesus' death in Scripture. In the cry of Jesus we are dealing not with a subjective but with an objective God-forsakenness: He did not feel alone but had in fact been forsaken by God. His feeling was not an illusion, not based on a false view of his situation, but corresponded with reality. On the other hand, this must not be understood in the sense that the Father was personally angry with Christ. Calvin puts it very correctly:

> Yet we do not suggest that God was ever inimical or angry toward him. How could he be angry toward his beloved Son, "in whom his heart reposed" [cf. Matt. 3:17]? How could Christ by his intercession appease the Father toward others, if he were himself hateful to God? This is what we are saying: he bore the weight of divine severity, since he was "stricken and afflicted" [cf. Isa. 53:5] by God's hand, and experienced all the signs of a wrathful and avenging God.[192]

Also on the cross Jesus remained the beloved Son, the Son of his Father's good pleasure (Matt. 3:17; 17:5). Precisely in his suffering and death, Christ offered his greatest, most complete obedience to the will of the Father (Phil. 2:8; Heb. 5:8; 10:5–10; 12:2); and Jesus himself tells us that the hour would come when all his disciples would abandon him, but that he himself would not be alone for the Father was with him (John 16:32). But, according to Scripture, Christ bore our sins in his body on the tree (1 Pet. 2:24); there he became for us sin and a curse (2 Cor. 5:21; Gal. 3:13) and thus took death on himself, the whole of it, in its true essence and character as the wages of sin. We, on the other hand, cannot taste death in that way, and by faith in Christ all bitterness is removed from it. In death God is near to his own, so that it becomes for them a passage to eternal life.

190. Ed. note: This is the title under which philosopher G. E. Lessing published (1774–78) the writings of H. S. Reimarus on the historical Jesus.

191. Cf. R. Moberly on the cry from the cross, *Atonement and Personality*, 131, 134, 392, 407. Also the view of Brooke, in R. Dale, *Atonement*, 470.

192. J. Calvin, *Institutes*, II.xvi.11.

But that is not how Christ experienced it. He, with his holy nature, lived through it as no sinful person can; he took the cup into his hand and—voluntarily—emptied it to the last drop. By the power of love, he laid down life itself and, fully conscious and with a firm will, entered the valley of the shadow of death. There he was, and felt, forsaken by God, so that in precisely that fashion he might be able to taste death for everyone (Heb. 2:9).[193] This death of Christ, along with his resurrection, is a prominent feature in the preaching of the apostles from the beginning. Jesus himself had repeatedly linked his suffering and death to the goods of the kingdom of heaven or the benefits of the covenant of grace (Matt. 16:21; 20:22, 28; 26:28; John 10:11; 12:24; 13:1; etc.). At first, the disciples did not understand this (Matt. 16:22; Luke 18:34) but learned to grasp it later, after the resurrection. And from that time on the crucified and glorified Christ was the content of their gospel. There may be great diversity in the way in which they explain the value of Christ's death, yet in that diversity there is evident a striking unity. The original believing community already united around the confession that Christ died for our sins according to the Scriptures. "Integral to the most certain things we know is that, according to 1 Corinthians 15:3, the primitive church already related the death of Jesus to sin."[194] And all the apostles in some fashion link the death of Christ to our sins and attribute to it the objective meaning—a meaning considered valid by God—that by it Christ secured for us the benefits of the covenant of grace, forgiveness, and eternal life. Whichever epistle we look into, we everywhere encounter the selfsame idea that Christ was made to be a sin and a curse for us, that in him we might become the righteousness of God (2 Cor. 5:21; Gal. 3:13). He is the expiation for our sins; he purchased us for God by his blood and cleansed us from all our sins (1 John 1:7; 2:2; Rev. 5:9; 7:14). He offered himself up once for all for the sins of the people and thereby secured an eternal redemption (Heb. 1:3; 2:17; 7:27; 9:12; 10:12). He bore our sins on the tree and redeemed us by his blood (1 Pet. 1:18; 2:24). In James this idea is in the background, yet also in him faith has as its object Jesus Christ, who is the Lord of glory and will return as Judge (2:1; 5:9). And in Jude, Christ is the Lord, who at his return will show mercy to his own unto eternal life (vv. 4, 21). In the apostolic writings, accordingly, the emphasis is much more on the death than on the life of Christ: the cross is central in their gospel (1 Cor. 2:2; Gal. 6:14). Although Christ's suffering and death may not be separated from his person, they are nevertheless definitely willed by God as such and offered to him as a sacrifice by the Son. In the life of Christ, they are not an accidental constituent made necessary by circumstances but essential and indispensable. Primarily

193. "Had Jesus enjoyed the consciousness that God was with Him in that dread extremity, he would have been exempted from the most awful experience of the children of men, and his sympathy would have failed us precisely where it is most needed. And therefore the sense of the Father's presence was withheld from Him in that awful hour" (David Smith, "Dereliction," *DC,* I, 448).

194. H. J. Holtzmann, *Lehrbuch der neutestamentlichen Theologie,* I, 366; G. B. Stevens, *The Theology of the New Testament* (Edinburgh: T&T Clark, 1906), 471.

by that suffering and death, as the consummation of his obedience, the expiation of sins, righteousness, and eternal blessedness have been secured.

Against the acquisition of the goods of salvation by the death of Christ, however, some have lodged the objection that God grants to us the benefits of grace only through (*per*), not on account of (*non propter*) Christ.[195] Lutherans even took pleasure in leveling the charge against the Reformed that in virtue of their doctrine of predestination they had to deny the satisfaction of Christ and could only view him as an instrumental cause of salvation. The Reformed themselves, they said, recognized that Christ was not the foundation and cause of election,[196] inasmuch as the elect were already the object of God's love before Christ was appointed their mediator and were elect, therefore, in and unto but not on account of Christ.[197] This charge, however, is unfounded. Certainly Christ was the revelation and proof of the Father's love. Logically, indeed, our election to salvation is anterior to his election as mediator. And God was not first moved by Christ to love sinners and to grant them eternal life but was so moved from eternity from within himself. But the love of the Father consists precisely in that he causes the salvation, which he has intended for sinners, to be secured, in time, by his own Son and grants and will grant it to them in accordance with his own righteousness. God's grace, accordingly, does not nullify the satisfaction and merit of Christ but is the ultimate ground for that merit, for "solely of his own good pleasure God appointed him mediator to obtain salvation for us."[198] "Indeed because he first loved us [1 John 4:19], he afterward reconciles us to himself."

And these two things, the love of God and Christ's satisfaction, had to and could go hand in hand because we were simultaneously the object of his love as his creatures and the object of his wrath as sinners.[199] It is, therefore, purely out of grace that God forgives sins. He does it for his own sake, for his great name's sake (Isa. 43:23–25; Ezek. 36:21; Eph. 1:17; 1 John 2:12); but this is in no way inconsistent with the fact that God forgives us our sins for Christ's sake, since the name of God was first revealed to us in Christ. The fact that God forgives sins and bestows life solely out of grace, for his own sake and not because of something in us—that is something Christ has proclaimed to us and obtained for us. Forgiveness out of grace, eternally present in God as disposition and antecedent to the election and mission of Christ (the love of goodwill), was nevertheless first made possible by Christ's sacrifice in time (the love of delight). The benefits

---

195. So already Socinus and others in earlier times, and in our day J. H. Scholten, *Leer van de Hervormde Kerk*, I, 20; II, 426ff.; J. Gottschick, "Propter Christum," *Zeitschrift für Theologie und Kirche* (1897): 352–84; cf. C. Stuckert, "Propter Christum," *Zeitschrift für Theologie und Kirche* (1906): 143–73.

196. Cf. H. Bavinck, *Reformed Dogmatics*, II, 399–402 (#248).

197. J. Gerhard, *Loci theol.*, loc. XVI, "De justif.," §36; M. Schneckenburger, *Zur kirchlichen Christologie*, 45; idem, *Vergl. Darstellung*, II, 264; A. Schweizer, *Die Glaubenslehre der evangelisch-reformierten Kirche*, II, 379, 389; H. Reuter, *Augustinische Studien*, 52.

198. J. Calvin, *Institutes*, II.xvii.1.

199. Ibid., II.xvi.3–4.

themselves were acquired by Christ, though the disposition to grant them to the elect was present in God from eternity. Christ was made to be sin that we might become the righteousness of God in him. He was born of a woman and under the law that he might redeem us from the curse of the law and we should obtain the adoption as children. As Adam is the cause of sin and death, so Christ is the source of righteousness and life (Matt. 20:28; 27:42; John 1:18; 15:13; Rom. 5:12ff.; 1 Cor. 15:21–22; 2 Cor. 5:19–21; Gal. 3:13; 4:4; 1 John 4:9). So understood, the statement that God forgives us our sins and bestows eternal life on account of Christ is scriptural and taught by all Christianity and by the confession of the Reformed religion as well.[200]

Finally, though the mystical and moral theories do contain elements that occur in Scripture and are perfectly correct as such, these elements are detached from the foundation on which they rest in Scripture and are therefore also robbed of their value and power. The mystical theory contends that the essence of religion lies in the mystical union between God and humankind. This union, though disturbed by sin, has been restored by Christ, indeed not so much by what he does as by what he is, by his person more than by his work, by his birth more than by his cross.[201] How that mystical union between God and humankind has been restored is hard to say on this position. Hegel said that that union exists objectively but was first clearly seen and expressed by Christ. Schleiermacher's view is that Christ, first entering into our sinful fellowship, subsequently incorporates us into the fellowship of his holiness and blessedness. The theology of mediation frequently conveys it by saying that Christ infuses a new divine-human life into us. All these ways of putting it stem from pantheism and are simply unintelligible apart from this philosophical system. The moral theory proceeds from the idea that God does not demand satisfaction but in his love gave us Christ that, by his teaching, life, and death, he would assure us of God's love, change our hostile disposition, and deter us from sin. And also the governmental theory of Grotius views God as the ruler of the world (*rector mundi*) who, though he personally could and would forgive sin, in the interest of the world order and by way of example has to punish sin to deter others.

Now in all these theories, though their proponents still continue to speak of Christ as the Son of God, of his priesthood and sacrifice, they are speaking figuratively, employing the words in an unusual sense and occasioning misunder-

---

200. Ibid., II.xvi.17; idem, *Commentaries*, John 15:13; Rom. 5:10; 2 Cor. 5:19; 1 John 4:19; Belgic Confession, art. 21–23; Heidelberg Catechism, Q. & A. 37; Petrus de Witte, *Wederl. der Soc. dwalingen*, II, 170ff.; P. van Mastricht, *Theologia*, V, 18, 20, 41; Maresius, *Syst. theol.*, IV, 40; X, 30; F. Turretin, *De satisf.*, p. 7; Heppe, *Dogmatik des deutschen Protestantismus*, I, 190; A. Ritschl, *Rechtfertigung und Versöhnung*, I², 265ff.

201. Modern Anglo-Saxon theology, therefore, prefers to use the word "atonement" in the sense of "at-one-ment," making "at-one," and pushes other terms (propitiation, expiation, satisfaction, reconciliation) more or less into the background (C. Hodge, *Systematic Theology*, II, 469; J. Orr, *The Christian View of God and the World as Centering in the Incarnation* [New York: Randolph, 1893], 333).

standing.[202] It is clear, after all, that in pantheism and Deism there is no room for the Christ of the Scriptures. In that case the high priesthood of Christ changes into an example, the Christian religion into an exercise in pedagogics, and the church into a school.

Justice or righteousness, then, is not a perfection of God but belongs exclusively in the state. Sin is not culpable and punishment not a redress of justice. Humans are never so evil that they cannot be changed for the better by a moral example, a shock, or an impression.[203] Thus objective satisfaction is transformed into subjective reconciliation. True and genuine reconciliation occurs only when a person follows Jesus' example and changes himself or herself. Believers under the old covenant did not yet have Jesus' example and were therefore either all lost or saved in a different way than we, and Christ is not the only name given under heaven by which one can be saved. Remaining unexplained in the above theories is, above all, the connection Scripture forges between the death of Christ and the forgiveness of our sins and eternal life. It is not clear how the death of Christ as an example of these benefits can be the basis on which God, for Christ's sake, forgives sins and grants life. Actually what everything comes down to is that Christ, by his image, makes a deep impression on the intellect, the will, or also on the emotions of people and so delivers them from the opinion that God is angry with them on account of their sin, or from the selfishness that keeps them tied down, or from the feeling of wretchedness that oppresses them. But in none of these cases do people find peace and rest. The conscience is not thereby cleansed, nor the sense of guilt removed. Peace can be found only in the blood of the cross!

VICARIOUS SATISFACTION

[389] This scriptural doctrine concerning the connection between Christ's death and our salvation comes into its own only when his full and complete obedience is viewed as *vicarious satisfaction*. Anselm was the first theologian who clearly and firmly conceived Christ's death as a "satisfaction," and who probably borrowed this word from the doctrine of penitence, where it had been in use already from the days of Tertullian. But in adopting it he was not teaching anything new, for long before his day the death of Christ was viewed in theology as the divinely ordained means by which salvation was secured for us. His doctrine of satisfaction was not a "new theory constructed with the help of German-legal views" but rather the "systematic conclusion of an ancient history of dogma development which had been ongoing since Augustine and was extremely influential throughout the Middle Ages both before and after Anselm."[204] Nor is it the product of the mar-

---

202. Cf., e.g., K. H. von Weizsäcker, *Das apostolische Zeitalter,* 2nd ed., 138; A. Biedermann, *Christliche Dogmatik,* §829; O. Pfleiderer, *Grundriss,* 156; A. Sabatier, *La doctrine de l'expiation et son évolution historique* (Paris: Fischbacher, 1903), 62.

203. Cf. Charles Hodge, *Systematic Theology,* II, 566; A. A. Hodge, *Atonement,* ch. 21.

204. F. Loofs, *Dogmengeschichte,* 509ff.; A. von Harnack, *History of Dogma,* III, 312ff.

riage between the original gospel and Greek philosophy. For no one today any longer wants to be responsible for the exegesis that the Socinians and rationalists applied to remove it from Scripture. And though Ritschl's interpretation may for a time have fascinated people on account of its cleverness, its untenability is hardly any longer questioned by anyone today.[205] Impartial investigation always leads to the admission that the doctrine of satisfaction is grounded in Holy Scripture. Thus, according to Holtzmann, Romans 3:26 "really speaks of a bearing, by the Son of God, of the punitive consequences of human sin in the interest of divine righteousness."[206] Not even Paul was the first to apply this idea of a vicarious satisfaction to the death of Christ, for the most ancient Christian community already preceded him in doing this.[207] Jesus himself described his death as a ransom and a covenant offering[208] and the idea of a vicarious atonement was so obvious in connection with the sin offerings and the sacrifice of the great Day of Atonement that "to the popular mind it must have seemed almost unavoidable."[209]

In any case, Scripture regards the entire work of Christ as a fulfillment of God's law and a satisfaction of his demand. As prophet, priest, and king, in his birth and in his death, in his words and in his deeds, he always did God's will. He came into the world to do his will. The law of God is within his heart [Ps. 40:8]. His entire life was a life of complete obedience, a perfect sacrifice, a sweet odor to God.[210] That will of God was one, as was the obedience with which Christ submitted to it and the righteousness he accomplished in it. Still, with reference to the obedience he showed, one can distinguish a passive and an active side. For the demand posed by God to fallen humanity was twofold: one, that humans would keep the law perfectly, and two, that they would redress the violation of it by punishment.[211] Twofold also are the benefits that Christ obtained for us, namely, the forgiveness of sins and eternal life. The two are not identical; justification cannot be automatically equated with heavenly blessedness. Though before his disobedience Adam was righteous, he still had to secure eternal life in the way of works. To bear a punishment is absolutely not as such identical with the observance of the law. A criminal who is punished but who in being punished hardens his heart fulfills the demand of the law but by no means meets the entire demand of the law. In addition, Christ was the second Adam. He came not only to bear our punish-

---

205. Cf. contra Ritschl, G. Kreibig, *Die Versöhnungslehre auf Grund des christlichen Bewusstseins* (Berlin: Wiegandt & Grieben, 1878); I. A. Dorner, *System of Christian Doctrine*, IV, 60ff.; O. Pfleiderer, "Die Ritschl'sche Theologie," *Jahrbuch für prot. Theologie* (1889); idem, *Die Entwicklung der protestantischen Theologie in Deutschland seit Kant und in Grossbritannien seit 1825* (Freiburg i.B.: Mohr, 1891), 228ff.; J. Wendland, *Albrecht Ritschl und seine Schüler*, 116ff.; J. Orr, *Ritschlian Theology* (London, 1897).

206. H. J. Holtzmann, *Lehrbuch der neutestamentlichen Theologie*, II, 100; cf. Wegscheider, *Inst. theol.*, §136; O. Pfleiderer, *Der Paulinismus*, 136.

207. H. J. Holtzmann, *Lehrbuch der neutestamentlichen Theologie*, II, 97.

208. Ibid., I, 292ff.

209. Schmiedel, in H. J. Holtzmann, *Lehrbuch der neutestamentlichen Theologie*, I, 67.

210. Cf. above, 337–40 (#376).

211. Cf. above, 348–49, 377–80 (##378, 386).

ment for us but also to obtain for us the righteousness and life that Adam had to secure by his obedience. He delivered us from guilt and punishment and placed us at the end of the road that Adam had to walk, not at the beginning. He gives us much more than we lost in Adam, not only the forgiveness of sins and release from punishment but also and immediately—in faith—the not-being-able to sin and not-being-able to die.[212] Those who believe in him are not condemned and have eternal life (John 3:16, 18). The two kinds of benefits, though *in concreto* they can never be separated, are still often mentioned separately side by side (Dan. 9:24; John 3:36; Acts 26:18; Rom. 5:17–18; Gal. 4:5; Rev. 1:5–6).

And this is how it is also with Christ's active and passive obedience. Though distinguishable, concretely they always coincide in the life and death of Christ. Christ's active obedience is not an external appendage to his passive obedience, nor vice versa. Not a single act nor any single incident in the life or suffering of Christ is exclusively reducible to one or the other. Just as Christ is always and in everything simultaneously prophet, priest, and king, so he is also consistently active in the interest of atoning for the guilt of sin and securing eternal life. It is not even accurate to say that the forgiveness of sins is secured only by his passive obedience and that eternal life is obtained only by his active obedience. For his suffering was not just a matter of bearing the punishment but also an act of fulfilling the law; and his work was not only a matter of fulfilling the law but also an act of bearing its punishment. His activity was suffering and his suffering an action. It was one single work that Christ accomplished, but one so rich, so valuable in the eyes of God, that the righteousness of God was completely satisfied by it, all the demands of the law were fully met by it, and the whole of [our] eternal salvation was secured by it. The satisfactory nature of Christ's obedience, accordingly, does not consist in that Christ by his blood satisfied a vengeful deity and stilled his hatred and spite by a quantity of suffering; it consists in that, from the beginning to the end of his life, he submitted his will to the complete, perfect, holy, and loving will of God and consecrated himself, with body and soul and all his powers, to being a perfect offering to God. But, according to the teaching of Scripture, that will of God encompassed not only the life but also the suffering of Christ; and that offering consisted not only in his "moral vocation" but also in his death on the cross. Dying, he completed his obedience and consummated his sanctification.[213]

The obedience of Christ, however, is not only a satisfaction: it is a vicarious satisfaction. On this point also Scripture makes itself clear. Actually the idea of substitution is implied in all expiatory offerings. In the place of the offerer, who is deserving of the wrath of God, it puts something else, something that can placate

212. Cf. H. Bavinck, *Reformed Dogmatics*, II, 572–76 (#297).

213. F. Turretin, *Institutes of Elenctic Theology*, XIV, 13, 11ff.; P. van Mastricht, *Theologia*, V, 18, 14; B. de Moor, *Comm. theol.*, III, 960ff.; H. Heppe, *Dogmatik der evangelischen reformierten Kirchen*, 326; F. Schleiermacher, *Christian Faith*, §104, 2; A. Ritschl, *Rechtfertigung und Versöhnung*, I, 279ff.; idem, *Justification and Reconciliation*, III, 62.

him. In the history of Israel, we encounter the idea of substitution already in the life of Abraham when he, at the command of the angel of the Lord, refrains from laying his hand on his son [Isaac] and offers a ram as a burnt offering in the place of his son (Gen. 22:12–13). In the Old Testament cult, when expiatory sacrifices were made, the sins of the offerer were transferred to the sacrificial animals by the laying on of hands (Lev. 16:21). The expiation itself was brought about not in one but in three acts: butchering, sprinkling the blood, and burning. Though burdened with the sins of the offerer and therefore worthy of death, the animal was not simply killed but butchered. Death as such was not the thing in view, for the sacrificial animal was destined to make expiation and to restore the offerer to God's favor. That favor cannot be secured by the death of the sacrificial animal as such; it is won by the fact that the blood—the soul, the life—of a completely innocent animal, bearing the sins of the offerer and therefore killed, is offered and consecrated to God. Thus that blood, as the self-offering of a living being—which is therefore not killed but slain—makes expiation for the sins of the offerer; it is the blood that causes the entire animal, in being burnt, to become a well-pleasing odor to God. At that moment the offerer himself completely shares in his favor. From beginning to end, the animal has taken his place and thus made atonement for him and restored him to communion with God. It is from this cult that Isaiah borrowed the features for his portrayal of the Servant of the Lord. Vicarious punishment cannot be expressed more powerfully than it is in Isaiah 53. The Servant of the Lord has borne our diseases and carried our sorrows. He was wounded for our transgressions and bruised for our iniquities. Upon him was the chastisement that made us whole, and with his stripes we are healed. The Lord has laid on him the iniquity of us all. He was stricken for the transgression of the people. He made himself an offering for sin. Himself righteous, without wrongdoing or deceit, he bears the iniquities of his people, making them righteous. The suffering of the Servant of the Lord is not "merely a confessor's or martyr's suffering, like that of the persecuted church, but a representative and atoning suffering, a sacrifice for sin. . . . Chapter 53 returns perpetually to this mediatorial suffering; it is never weary of repeating it."[214]

All this comes to light with still greater clarity in the New Testament. To be considered here, in the first place, is the word λυτρον (Matt. 20:28; Mark 10:45; 1 Tim. 2:6). In line with its derivation from λυειν, "to release," it denotes the means by which a person is released from bonds or prison and hence in general a ransom or sum of money paid to have someone discharged. In the Septuagint it is the translation of גְּאֻלָּה (Lev. 25:51–52) or of פִּדְיוֹם (Num. 3:46) or of כֹּפֶר (Exod. 21:30, 30:12; Num. 35:31–32; Prov. 6:35; 13:8), but this last word is also rendered elsewhere by ἐξιλασμα (1 Sam. 12:3; Ps. 49:8) or by ἀλλαγμα (Amos 5:12; Isa. 43:3) or by δωρον (Job 36:18). Hence we are not sure which word Jesus used in the Aramaic and cannot yet derive the substitutionary and equivalent character

---

214. F. Delitzsch, *Prophecies of Isaiah*, II, 307.

of his death from the word λυτρον. Still it is incorrect, with Ritschl, to construe Mark 10:45 to mean that Jesus' voluntary death is a gift, a cover, a protective means, from which many are saved—not from death as the fate of all creatures, but from a death experience such as Jesus underwent and hence to be delivered from death in that sense and to be made the heirs of eternal life by his death. For, in the first place, Ritschl already in advance interpreted the Old Testament sacrificial cult so arbitrarily that everything that had to do with substitution and atonement had totally disappeared from it. Second, he so equates λυτρον with the incorrectly construed כֹּפֶר that the possibility of Jesus perhaps using another word is completely overlooked. Third, he does violence to the word λυτρον, a word that simply and naturally has the meaning of a ransom and in that sense finds support in related concepts—to be mentioned in a moment—in the New Testament. Now by itself this word may not yet express the idea that the ransom matches in value that which is purchased by it, yet it is natural to think that someone who has a right to something will not give it up except in exchange for appropriate compensation. In Isaiah 43:3 and Proverbs 21:18, the word כֹּפֶר therefore alternates in the parallelism with תַּחַת, "in the place of," "in exchange for"; and in other places (such as Exod. 21:30; 30:12; Num. 18:15–16; 35:31–32; 2 Sam. 21:3–7; Job 33:24; Ps. 49:7–8), the word clearly denotes a price paid for something else with a view to giving it freedom.

The word λυτρον (Mark 10:45) is further illumined by all those places in the New Testament where the suffering and death of Christ is presented as a τιμη, a costly price (1 Cor. 6:20; 7:23; 1 Pet. 1:18–19), by which believers have been redeemed or ransomed (ἀντιλυτρον, 1 Tim. 2:6; λυτρουσθαι, Luke 24:21; Titus 2:14; 1 Pet. 1:18; ἀπολυτρωσις, Rom. 3:24; 1 Cor. 1:30; etc.; ἀγοραζεσθαι, 1 Cor. 6:20; 7:23; etc.; or ἐξαγοραζεσθαι, Gal. 3:13; 4:5). Underlying all these expressions is the idea that by nature humans find themselves in the bondage or slavery of sin and that they are only released from it by the costly ransom of the blood of Christ. Christ's sacrifice, therefore, is at the same time a ransom. In the Old Testament, the noun כֹּפֶר is never as yet directly applied to the expiatory sacrifices, but the connection between the two concepts is nevertheless close, for the sacrifice was in fact a ransom for the life of the offerer, and the noun כֹּפֶר belongs to the same stem as the verb כִּפֶּר, which was regularly used in the sacrificial cult for expiation.[215] So when Jesus speaks to his disciples of his death as a ransom, this could produce in them no other idea, and, as is evident from their letters, in fact produced no idea other than that that death would ransom them from the bondage of sin and death. This is all the more so because Jesus himself had taught them that the soul (life) of a human is of such great value that, losing it, he or she cannot give any ἀνταλλαγμα (ransom, equivalent compensation) for it (Matt. 16:26; Mark 8:37; cf. Ps. 49:8). Now, however, Jesus himself by his death gives a ransom for or in the place of many (ἀντι πολλων) who are themselves unable to do this and

---

215. H. J. Holtzmann, *Lehrbuch der neutestamentlichen Theologie*, I, 67ff.; J. Orr, "Ransom," *DC*, II, 469.

therefore owe the ransoming of their soul, the salvation of their life, solely to the death of Jesus. Since, then, the word λυτρον denotes a ransom, the words ἀντι πολλων are to be linked not, as Ritschl wishes, with the subject ἠλθεν δουναι but with the object λυτρον, for otherwise the person or thing for whom or for which the ransom was paid would be completely lacking. And by the "many" we are to understand the members of that covenant of grace that, according to Jesus' own testimony, he has confirmed in his own blood and that therefore has as its content the supreme good, namely, the forgiveness of sins (Matt. 26:28).[216]

Finally, as proof for Christ's vicarious satisfaction, the New Testament's entire teaching concerning the sacrifice of Christ must be considered. The prepositions that describe the connection of that sacrifice to us and our sins (ὑπερ, περι, δια)[217] by themselves mean not "in the place of" but "for the benefit of," "for the sake of," "on account of," "by reason of." Between Christ's sacrifice and our sins, however, they forge a link such that the idea of substitution cannot be dispensed with or removed from it. Scripture also teaches that believers have been crucified, have died, and have been buried in and with Christ, that Christ suffered and died as an example to us, but this does not exhaust the meaning of these events and actions. The mystical and moral interpretation of Jesus' suffering and death cannot even be maintained if it is not acknowledged beforehand that in a legal sense he suffered and died *in our place*. Now this is what Scripture teaches in the clearest terms, even though it does not use the expression "vicarious satisfaction" any more than the words "Trinity," "incarnation," "God-man," and so on. For when it says that Christ, though personally without sin, has been put forward as an expiation to show God's righteousness [Rom. 3:25], has been made to be sin for us [2 Cor. 5:21], became a curse for us [Gal. 3:13], bore our sins in his body on the tree [1 Pet. 2:24]; that God condemned sin in his flesh [Rom. 8:3] and punished him with the accursed death on the cross and that through him we now receive reconciliation and forgiveness, righteousness and life, indeed total and complete salvation—then we can construe the interconnection between all these scriptural pronouncements in no other way than that Christ put himself in our place, has borne the punishment of our sin, satisfied God's justice, and so secured salvation for us.[218]

216. On Mark 10:45, see A. Ritschl, *Rechtfertigung und Versöhnung,* II, 68ff.; H. J. Holtzmann, *Lehrbuch der neutestamentlichen Theologie,* I, 292ff.; H. Cremer, *Wörterbuch,* s.v. λυτρον; J. Orr, "Ransom," *DC,* II, 468.

217. Cf. above, 339 (#376). On ὑπερ, see Holwerda, *Jaarbuch van wetenschapelijke Theologie* (1862): 521ff.; on δια, see A. Schettler, *Die paulinische Formel "Durch Christus" untersucht* (Tübingen: Mohr, 1907). Schettler consistently understands this expression ("through Christ") as referring to "mystical influence" originating with the pneumatic Christ. But this view is certainly incorrect. The combination with δια is not a formula (as, e.g., the one with "in" or "in the name of") but simply denotes Christ as mediator, and by itself it says nothing about the way in which he is the mediator. When Paul speaks of Christ as the mediator of creation and providence, that mystical view is also automatically ruled out. And even when he speaks of Christ as mediator, he absolutely has in mind not only the exalted but also and simultaneously the historical crucified Christ. Cf. Heitmüller, *Theologische Literaturzeitung* (1909): cols. 408–10.

218. B. Weiss, *Lehrbuch der biblischen Theologie des Neuen Testaments,* 3rd ed. (Berlin: W. Hertz, 1880), §§49ff.; H. J. Holtzmann, *Lehrbuch der neutestamentlichen Theologie,* I, 64ff.; II, 97ff.; Plantz, "Vicarious

OBJECTIONS TO VICARIOUS SATISFACTION

[390] From ancient times, however, very serious objections have been leveled against this doctrine of vicarious satisfaction. Especially the Socinians attacked it with strong arguments. Money debts, they reasoned, are debts that one person can take over for another and pay on his or her behalf. But sins are moral debts and adhere to the person. They cannot, in the nature of the case, be taken over by another. It is contrary to God's righteousness, which does not hold the guilty to be innocent nor the innocent guilty. It is contrary to the nature of sin, for those who would want to bear it for another could never take over the most horrible features of sin, that is, the self-incrimination and remorse, but only the external suffering and death; and this would be for them not a punishment of sin but a chastisement, a trial, a martyrdom. It is contrary to reality, for Christ did not bear the wrath of God but continued to be the object of his love and favor. Nor did he bear the entire punishment of sin, for he died neither a spiritual death nor eternal death; and even if he had borne it, it would only be on behalf of one single person, never for many, for he bore that punishment only one time. Even if he were God, this could not increase the value of his sacrifice, since in any case his deity could not suffer.[219]

Many of these objections arise from misunderstanding, which therefore has to be cleared up before we can go on. First, then, it is completely true that Christ was never personally—on account of his own self—the object of God's wrath. The reason, of course, is that he was never in his own person a sinner, a violator of God's law. Granted, Gnostics and Anabaptists often made a distinction between a divine, heavenly, immortal, holy corporeality and a human, earthly, impure, and mortal corporeality in Christ.[220] And the Antinomians understood substitution to mean that not only the guilt and punishment but also the stain and impurity of sin were transferred to Christ. The exchange between Christ and the elect was so absolute, in their opinion, that he himself was sin and they were righteousness. In Christ they grieved over their sins, were justified and reborn. The sins they themselves commit are no longer sins, do not torment them in their conscience, no longer require forgiveness, and are only acts of the flesh, the old "human."[221] In later times these sentiments were occasionally renewed by Methodists,[222] by Irvingians,[223] and by some followers of Kohlbrugge.[224] But Scripture teaches with the utmost firmness and

---

Sacrifice," *DC*, II, 793–800; A. A. Hodge, *Atonement*, 161ff.; H. Martin, *Atonement*, 198ff.; Scott Lidgett, *Spiritual Principle of the Atonement*, 286ff.

219. Cf. above, 347–51 (#378).

220. Cf. above, 295–97 (#368).

221. J. Hulsius, *De Hedendaagsche Antinomianerij*, 2nd ed. (Rotterdam: Vermeulen, 1738), 377ff.; J. Hoornbeek, *Summa Controv.* (1653), 704; H. Witsius, *Misc. sacra.*, II, 758–80.

222. M. Schneckenburger, *Vorlesungen über die Lehrbegriffe der kleineren protestantischen Kirchenparteien* (Frankfurt: Brönner, 1863), 146.

223. J. Köstlin, "Irving," *PRE*², VII, 154; cf. T. Kolde, *PRE*³, IX, 424–27.

224. J. F. Bula, *Die Versöhnung des Menschen mit Gott durch Christum* (Basel: F. Schneider, 1874); E. Böhl, *Von der Incarnation des göttlichen Wortes* (Vienna: Faesy, 1884); idem, *Dogmatik*, 299ff.; A. Kuyper, *De vleesch-*

clarity that Christ was personally free from all sins;[225] and the few places to which people appeal for the contrary view (John 1:14; Rom. 8:3; Heb. 2:14) say only that the Son of God assumed a weak nature subject to suffering and death but not that he himself was a sinner in a subjective sense. Some theologians, such as Chrysostom, Oecumenios, Luther, Marlorat, and also Calvin (commenting on Gal. 3:13), have indeed called Christ a sinner but only meant it in the objective sense, as Paul puts it, that Christ was made to be sin and became a curse (2 Cor. 5:21; Gal. 3:13; cf. Isa. 53:12). In saying these things, the apostle was not asserting that Christ was a sinner and an accursed person in himself but that he was regarded and treated by God as a person who was guilty of violating the law and had called the curse down upon himself. Self-accusation, regret, remorse, and confessing one's personal sins could therefore not occur in Christ's case;[226] nor was he subject to spiritual death, to the inability to do any good and the inclination to all evil. Precisely to be able to bear the sins of others and to make satisfaction for them, he could and might not be a sinner himself. The "substitution of persons," which took place between Christ and his own, must not be understood in a pantheistic-physical or mystical sense but bears a legal character: Christ voluntarily entered into the same relation to the law and its demands in which we stood as a result of our transgression.

Second, the substitutionary character of Christ's obedience automatically also involves equivalency inasmuch as it corresponds completely to the demand of the law. This equivalency, however, was understood differently by the Reformation than by Rome. Duns Scotus believed that some holy human being or an angel could also have made satisfaction for our sins if God had approved of this substitution, for "every created offering has as much value as God agrees to and no more."[227] Similarly, the Remonstrants later taught that not the justice of God but only fairness (*aequitas*) demanded any satisfaction and that "the merit that Christ paid was paid off in accordance with the estimation of God the Father."[228]

---

wording des Woords, "Inleiding," and pp. 155ff.; on Kohlbrugge, see J. van Lonkhuijzen's dissertation (*H. F. Kohlbrügge en zijn Prediking*), pp. 406ff., and above, 353–54 (#379).

225. See above, 389–92 (#388).

226. It is therefore also incorrect, with Campbell and Moberly, to view Christ's suffering and death as "vicarious repentance," "as a sacrifice of supreme penitence." Present in that view, of course, was the truth that in his suffering and death Christ recognized the hideousness of sin and confessed the righteousness of God's judgment on it, but that can hardly be described with the word "repentance." For repentance always presupposes personal transgression and guilt. Further, though repentance (conversion, faith) is the only way in which forgiveness can be received and enjoyed by us, it is not the reason why, not the ground on which, it can be granted to us. The theory finally came down to saying that Christ, "repenting" of our sins, by his example, influence, or Spirit arouses repentance in us and so opens the way in which we can receive forgiveness. Objective satisfaction thereby changed into subjective reconciliation, cf. above, 357–61, 370–73, 380–84 (##380, 384, 387).

227. Duns Scotus, *Sent. dist.,* III, dist. 20, qu. un. n. 9; cf. dist. 19, qu. un. n. 7; also see, Biel, Durandus, and, more generally, the nominalists.

228. P. van Limborch, *Theol. christ.,* III, 21, 6, 8, 9; 22, 1; S. Episcopius, *Inst. theol.,* IV, sect. 5, ch. 3.

Squarely in opposition to this view, Aquinas called Christ's passion not only a sufficient "but a superabundant satisfaction for the sins of the human race."[229] The question was even considered whether one drop of Christ's blood would not have been sufficient for the purpose of atonement.[230] This whole way of looking at the subject, both in Aquinas and in Duns Scotus, is based on an external quantitative estimate of the suffering of Christ.

In principle, the Reformation broke with this system of calculation. This is evident from the fact that it rejected both the "acceptation" of Scotus and the "superabundance" of Aquinas;[231] that beside the passive obedience, it also included the active obedience in the work of Christ; that, while it did call Christ's sacrifice equivalent to, it did not consider it identical with what we were obligated to suffer and to do; that it considered it completely sufficient, so that no augmentation by our faith and good works was needed, either along Catholic or Remonstrant lines. The Reformed said that Christ's work by itself was completely sufficient for the atonement of the sins of the whole world so that, if he had wanted to save a smaller number, it could not have been less, and if he had wanted to save a higher number, it would not have had to be greater.

Sins indeed are not money debts, and satisfaction is not a problem of arithmetic. The transfer of our sins to Christ was not so mechanical a process that the sins of all the elect first had to be carefully counted, then laid on Christ, and separately expiated by Christ. Nor did Christ pass through all the phases of human life and make separate satisfaction for the sins of every phase or age, as Irenaeus[232] and others pictured it. Neither did he suffer precisely the same (*idem*)[233] things we do, nor in the same way, for consciousness of guilt and so on could not occur in

---

229. T. Aquinas, *Summa theol.*, III, qu. 48, art. 2; cf. Roman Catechism, I/4, qu. 13, 2; *Theol. Wirceb.*, IV, 317; C. R. Billuart, *Summa S. Thomae*, pars. III, tom. 2, 206–26; M. J. Scheeben, *Dogmatik*, III, 206ff., 343ff.; C. Pesch, *Prael. dogm.*, IV, 208ff.

230. The church fathers sometimes expressed the value of Christ's sacrifice in strong language. Chrysostom, for example, said that Christ gave more than we owed, "by so much more as the measureless expanse of sea exceeds in size a small drop of water." Cyril of Jerusalem wrote: "The iniquity of sinners is not as great as the righteousness of him who died for our sake; we have not sinned to the extent that he excelled who gave his life for us." Proclus, patriarch of Constantinople, taught that Christ "not only possessed a worth and value equal to those of the multitude of the accused but a greater value in the judgments and opinions of everyone." In the same way Anselm, speaking of Christ's death, refers to a "price greater than all debts," and Clement VI, in his bull *Unigenitus*, declared that if Christ had shed only one small drop of blood, "it would have been sufficient for the redemption of the whole human race on account of its union with the Word"; cf. *Theol. Wirceb.*, IV, 318; M. J. Scheeben, *Dogmatik*, III, 344; C. Pesch, *Prael. dogm.*, IV, 211; G. M. Jansen, *Theol. dogm.*, II, 739ff.; cf. J. A. Quenstedt, *Theologia*, III, 327; I. A. Dorner, *Person of Christ*, IV, 313–14.

231. G. Voetius, *Select. disp.*, II, 247; P. van Mastricht, *Theologia*, V, 18, 38; B. de Moor, *Comm. theol.*, III, 1084; H. Alting, *Theol. probl.*, pr. 41.

232. Irenaeus, *Against Heresies*, II, 22, 4.

233. A few theologians clung to the *idem* and found the *tantundem* ("as great as") too weak. Owen, for example, said that "the punishment which our Savior underwent was the same that the law required of us; God relaxing his law as to the persons suffering but not as to the penalty suffered" (W. Cunningham, *Historical Theology*, 3rd ed., 2 vols. [Edinburgh: T&T Clark, 1870], II, 306).

him, nor did he know spiritual death as the inclination to do evil, and he did not suffer eternal death in form and duration, but only intensively and qualitatively as God-forsakenness.[234]

There is even some truth in "acceptation," for the strict justice of God required that every human should personally make satisfaction for himself or herself; and it was his grace that gave Christ as the mediator of a covenant and imputed his righteousness to the members of that covenant. A quantitative calculation, therefore, does not fit in the case of vicarious satisfaction. In the doctrine of satisfaction, we are dealing with factors other than those that can be measured and weighed. Sin is a principle that controls and corrupts the whole creation, a power and a realm that expands and organizes itself in numerous actual sins. The wrath of God is a fury directed against the sin of the whole human race.[235] His righteousness is the perfection by which he cannot tolerate being denied or dishonored as God by his creatures. Vicarious satisfaction, accordingly, means that as the guarantor and head, Christ entered the relationship to God—his wrath, his righteousness, his law—in which the human race stood. For that humankind, which was given to him to reconcile, he was made to be sin, became a curse, and took its guilt and punishment on himself. When the Socinians say that in any case Christ could make satisfaction only for one person and not for many, inasmuch as he only bore the punishment of sin once, this reasoning is based on the same quantitative calculation as the "acceptation" of Duns Scotus and the "superabundance" of Aquinas. For though the sin that entered the world through Adam manifests itself in an incalculable series of sinful thoughts, words, and deeds, and though the wrath of God is felt individually by every guilty member of the human race, it is and remains the one indivisible law that has been violated, the one indivisible wrath of God that has been ignited against the sin of the whole human race, the one indivisible righteousness of God that has been offended by sin, the one unchangeable eternal God who has been affronted by sin. The punishment of Christ, therefore, is also one: one that balances in intensity and quality the sin and guilt of the whole human race, appeases the wrath of God against that whole human race, fulfills the whole law, fully satisfies the righteousness of God, and again makes God known and recognized in all his perfections of truth and righteousness, of love and grace, throughout the human race. That punishment, after all, was laid on him who was not an individual on a level with other individuals but the second Adam, head of the human race, both Son of Man and Son of God.

[391] The doctrine of satisfaction, so understood, now still has to be defended only against the objection that in the moral sphere such a substitution is impos-

234. T. Aquinas, *Summa theol.*, III, qu. 46, art. 4; qu. 48, art. 2; J. Calvin, *Institutes*, II.xvi.12; P. van Mastricht, *Theologia*, V, 12, 9; 21; B. de Moor, *Comm. theol.*, IV, 122–33; H. Witsius, *Misc. sacra*, II, 770; W. G. T. Shedd, *Dogmatic Theology*, II, 454; M. Schneckenburger and E. Güder, *Vergleichende Darstellung*, II, 239; F. A. Philippi, *Kirchliche Glaubenslehre*, IV/2, 29; E. W. C. Sartorius, *Lehre von der heiligen Liebe* (Stuttgart: S. G. Lieschling, 1861), II, 75; J. J. van Oosterzee, *Christian Dogmatics*, II, 586.

235. Heidelberg Catechism, Q. & A. 37.

sible. The first thing to be remarked against this is that the idea of substitution is deeply grounded, also morally, in human nature. Among all peoples it has been embodied in priesthood and sacrifices and expressed in various ways in poetry and mythology. Origen already compared Christ in his death to those who, according to classical traditions, died for their mother country to liberate it from a plague or other disasters, for, conforming to hidden laws, it seems to lie in the nature of things that the voluntary death of a righteous person in the public interest breaks the power of evil spirits.[236] Christian theology, accordingly, frequently cited the examples of Codrus, Curtius, Cratinus, Zaleucus, Damon, Phintias, and the hostages to illustrate the vicarious suffering of Christ. These examples have no other value, of course, than to show that the idea of substitution occupied an important place in the intellectual world of the Greeks and the Romans.[237]

The same is true of tragedy, whose basic idea can certainly be conveyed not always by "guilt and atonement" but often only by "passion and suffering." In many tragedies the death of the hero is not a true atonement for sins committed but yet is always a deliverance made necessary by some mistake or error, hence finally reconciling us and giving us satisfaction. But even viewed that way, tragedy proclaims a great truth: all human greatness walks past abysses of guilt, and satisfaction occurs only when what is noble and great, which for some reason has gone astray, perishes in death. The downfall of Orestes, Oedipus, Antigone, Romeo and Juliet, Max and Thekla, Iphigenia, and others reconciles us with them and their generation. "Pure humanity atones for all human weaknesses" (Goethe).[238]

It is often the same way in history. The final noble Constantine, fighting and dying for his people and country, atones for the horrors of the Byzantine emperors, and Louis XVI, who is innocent by comparison with his predecessors, pays in death for the sins of his dynasty. If the history of whole families and generations were known to us, it would furnish us no end of examples. In the saying "Say nothing of the dead but what is good," we all honor the atoning power of suffering and death. Indeed, all life and joy on earth is the fruit of sorrow and death. All things

---

236. Origen, *Contra Celsum*, I, 31.

237. Substitution in Roman law has been repeatedly studied and is usually understood to exclude direct and immediate substitution. It seems that this thesis, given its absolute form, can no longer be maintained. In any case, in recent years the idea of substitution has become better known from Greek papyri found in Egypt. It is evident from these papyri that substitution, the direct as well as the indirect, played a large role in Egyptian law; it occurred frequently, in public as well as private law, in legal trials and the collection or payment of taxes. The substitute was called κυριος, φροντιστης, ἐπιτροπος (*procurator*). He acted on behalf of (ὑπερ or ἀντι) the person who appointed (συνισταναι, *instituere, mandare*) him, gave him the power to act (συστασις, *mandatum*; the document in question is called συστατικον), and the person who gave this mandate was thus represented by and acted through (δια, *per*) the person so authorized (συνισταμενος or συσταθεις). L Wenger, *Die Stellvertretung im Rechte der Papyri* (Leipzig: Teubner, 1906), 1ff., 7ff.; A. Deissmann, *Licht vom Osten* (Tübingen: Mohr, 1908), 241.

238. W. Wundt, *Völkerpsychologie: Eine Untersuchung der Entwicklungsgesetze von Sprache, Mythus, und Sitte*, 2 vols. (Leipzig: Engelmann, 1900–1909), II; idem, *Mythus und Religion*, 2 vols. (Leipzig: Engelmann, 1905), I, 517ff.

live from the death of others. The grain of wheat has to die to bear fruit. What one person sows, another reaps. In the pangs of childbirth, and sometimes at the cost of her own life, a mother gives life to a child. All birth, also in the field of thought and art, moves from darkness into light. A few work, struggle, and suffer; others enjoy the fruit of their labor. We all live from the hard-won treasures of our ancestors. By struggle and through suffering, a few have conquered the most outstanding goods of humankind for all. Particularly love has a substitutionary character. On earth it can hardly be conceived in any way other than as "fellow suffering," sym-pathy. Those who love most suffer most. A mother suffers on account of, in, and with her child; a father grieves in his heart over the son who has gone astray. Nature and the human race teach that there are "representative, vicarious powers at work."[239]

All these examples and reasonings are undoubtedly somewhat suited as illustrations of the substitutionary suffering of Christ. Against the individualism and atomizing tendencies that tear humankind apart and know nothing of the mysticism of love, they are of great value. Still, they cannot explain the suffering of Christ. Many people do indeed stop to consider these examples and try to understand Christ's suffering as a natural consequence of his entrance into our sinful community.[240] But the sacrifice of Christ does not come into its own by that route. For Christ, and especially for him as the holy and merciful high priest, human sympathy was undoubtedly a cause of deep and painful suffering (Matt. 8:17; 9:36; 14:14; etc.), but it is not the only and most important cause, any more than hunger and thirst, persecution, the temptation of Satan, and abandonment by his disciples. In that case Christ's suffering would be just that, suffering, but not punishment, and he himself would be no more than a witness, a martyr, a sufferer, differing from others only in degree. But Christ himself considered his suffering a punishment laid on him by God on account of our sins (Matt. 20:28; 26:28; 27:46), and Scripture testifies that he was made to be sin for us and became a curse (2 Cor. 5:21; Gal. 3:13).

A further step is taken by those who in a realistic way explain Christ's suffering from the place he occupies in the human race: he, after all, is not an individual on a level with other individuals, but the central individual. He assumed not a human person but human nature. That nature was the bearer of sin and lay under a curse; hence with that nature Christ also took the guilt and punishment

239. Cf. above, 356–61, 380–85 (##380, 387); S. Maresius, *Syst. theol.*, X, 24; F. Turretin, "De satisf.," 51; P. de Witte, *Wederl. der Socin. dwalingen*, II, 221ff.; H. Bushnell, *Vicarious Sacrifice*; J. Cooper, "Vicarious Suffering in the Order of Nature," *Princeton Theological Review* (October 1903): 554–78; I. A. Dorner, *System of Christian Doctrine*, IV, 89; E. Riggenbach, "Jesus trug die Sünde der Welt," *Neue kirchliche Zeitschrift* (1907): 295–307; J. M. comte de Maistre, *Soirées de St. Petersbourg . . . sur les sacrifices*, 5th ed. (Lyon: J. B. Pélagaud, 1845).

240. E.g., F. Schleiermacher, *Christian Faith*, §104; C. H. Weisse, *Philosophische Dogmatik oder Philosophie des Christentums*, 2nd ed., 3 vols. (Leipzig: Hirzel, 1855–62), §876; J. P. Lange, *Dogmatik*, II, 840; H. Schultz, *Der Begriff des stellvertretenden Leidens* (Basel: Bahnmaier Verlag, 1864).

on himself. As Adam could be our representative because he was the ancestor of the entire human race, so Christ is the substitute and representative of the believing community that, as his body, was born from him and is one with him as its head. And as we, for instance, are punished on our back because of what we have misdone with our hand, so Christ was punished for our sins, inasmuch as he is one with us.[241] This realistic-mystical view of Christ's substitution is as such completely correct and is also clearly taught by Scripture; for believers have been crucified with Christ, have died, been buried, raised with him, and been made to sit with him in heavenly places (Rom. 6–8; Gal. 2:20; Eph. 2:6; Col. 2:11; 3:3; etc.).[242] Inasmuch as Christ is not only the atoner but also the redeemer, that is, not only, objectively, had to take away the guilt of sin but also, subjectively, had to break the power of sin, this mystical union between Christ and believers is an essential and indispensable constituent in the work of salvation. Yet it is not the only and the first relation that exists between Christ and his own. In Scripture this relation is built on the federal relation: Romans 6–8 follows Romans 3–5. When it is separated from that federal relation, it loses the foundation on which it has to rest, looks for support in pantheism, which changes re-creation into a process, and increasingly alters objective atonement into subjective redemption. Shedd, for example, already makes the imputation of Christ's righteousness depend on regeneration and faith.[243] This mystical union in the scriptural sense can only be maintained in conjunction with the objective atonement of Christ's sacrifice, when Christ is first of all viewed as the head of the covenant, who took the place of his own in a federalistic legal sense.

The covenant of grace, in fact, is anterior to the person and sacrifice of Christ. That covenant, after all, does not come into effect after Christ has accomplished his work, nor start with the Holy Spirit or with the benefits of regeneration and faith; but Christ himself is *in* that covenant. He is the guarantor and mediator of it (Heb. 7:22; 8:6; 12:24); his blood is blood of the covenant and therefore atoning (Matt. 26:28). Even more, the covenant of grace was not first established in time, but has its foundation in eternity, is grounded in the pact of salvation (*pactum salutis*), and is in the first place a covenant among the three persons of the divine being itself. Father and Son and Spirit are all three active in that covenant; it is so far from beginning in time with the activity of the Holy Spirit that it has its existence and certainty rather from eternity in the counsel of the Triune God. And this covenant, thus grounded, explains also the vicarious satisfaction of Christ. It is based on an ordinance, a free, omnipotent, gracious disposition of God. That is absolutely not to say that it is arbitrary and irrational. All kinds of

241. T. Aquinas, *Summa theol.*, III, qu. 48, art. 1, 2; suppl. qu. 13, art. 2; W. G. T. Shedd, *Dogmatic Theology*, II, 57, 533; R. W. Dale, *Atonement*, lecture X; Scott Lidgett, *Spiritual Principle of the Atonement*, ch. VII; E. W. C. Sartorius, *Die Lehre von der heiligen Liebe*, II, 67; W. Bilderdijk, *Opstellen van Godgeleerden en Zedekundigen Inhoud*, 2 vols. (Amsterdam: Immerzeel, 1883), I, 1–15.

242. H. J. Holtzmann, *Lehrbuch der neutestamentlichen Theologie*, II, 114–21.

243. Shedd, *Dogmatic Theology*, II, 534; cf. Dale, *Atonement*, 422.

relations in nature and humankind offer analogies to Christ's substitution. But analogy here is not and cannot be identity any more than in the case of Adam.[244] Both Christ and Adam occupy a special place in humankind. They alone are heads of the entire human race; their influence and impact is extended to all times and places. And Christ, in turn, is superior to Adam. For while Adam was the representative of humankind, Christ is its substitute. Adam acted in our name but did not take anything over from us; Christ came to us, put himself in our place, bore our guilt and punishment, and secured our righteousness. Adam was head of a covenant of works that was unstable; Christ is head of a better covenant that cannot be shaken. Adam was a human, though without sin, of the earth; Christ is the incarnate Word, the only Begotten of the Father, full of grace and truth, the Lord from heaven. Adam corrupted what was good; Christ restored and perfected what was corrupt. To the extent the covenant of grace surpasses the covenant of works, and the gospel the law, to that extent Christ surpasses Adam. His vicarious satisfaction cannot even be grasped on the basis of the covenant of works. While it is not against the law (for it established the law), it is nevertheless above the law and far exceeds all our thoughts and ideas. It is not reducible to a universal rule, nor can it be explained by reference to a universal law, for it is not one phenomenon among others. On the contrary, it is a concrete fact, wholly unique in the annals of humankind, explained by nothing, but itself explaining everything, rooted in a special ordinance of God. And this ordinance is not an isolated decree but bears a covenantal character. Vicarious satisfaction has its foundation in the counsel of the Triune God, in the life of supreme, perfect, and eternal love, in the unshakable covenant of redemption. Based on the ordinances of that covenant, Christ takes the place of his own and exchanges their sin for his righteousness, their death for his life. "Oh, the sweet exchange! Oh, the unfathomable accomplishment! Oh, the unexpected benefits!—that the wickedness of the many should be hidden in the One who is just; and that the righteousness of the One should justify the wicked many!"[245]

DOCTRINE OF THE TWO STATES

[392] Christ accomplished this obedience throughout the entire state of his humiliation. The formal treatment of the doctrine of the two states arose among the Lutherans to bring the communication of proper qualities (*communicatio idiomatum*) into harmony with Jesus' humiliation but was soon taken over by the Reformed.[246] Since Schleiermacher's critique,[247] however, it was either entirely

---

244. Cf. above, 100–106 (#323); also A. A. Hodge, *Atonement*, 198ff.; Hugh Martin, *Atonement*, 9ff.

245. *Epistle to Diognetus*, 9. Cited from *The Faith of the Early Fathers* (Collegeville, MN: Liturgical Press, 1970), 42.

246. Olevianus, "De subst. foed.," II, 5; A. Polanus, *Synt. theol.*, VI, ch. 13; F. Junius, *Theses theol.*, ch. 29; *Synopsis purioris theologiae*, ch. 27, 28; Westminster Catechism, qu. 46ff.

247. F. Schleiermacher, *Christian Faith*, §105.

abandoned by many theologians or significantly modified. Those who deny the preexistence and resurrection of Christ no longer have any interest in this doctrine.[248] Others, who accept the pertinent testimonies of Scripture, have often converted them into a description of the gradually self-perfecting humanization of the Logos or of the divine-human development and perfection of Christ. In that case his humiliation is conceived as a "steady elevation of his inner life," which automatically resulted in his resurrection and ascension to heaven.[249] In the process the doctrine of the two states gradually turned into a biography of Jesus,[250] but the sources from which we draw our knowledge of the life of Jesus are much too incomplete for them to enable us to write such a biography. Furthermore, the attempt to write a life of Jesus also always leads to a denial of the essence of his person because such attempts either take no account, or do so as little as possible, of his divine nature. No split is possible between a life of Christ and an office of Christ, as Ebrard proposes.[251] His whole life was lived in the service of the office to which the Father had appointed him and for whose fulfillment he was sent into the world. The apostolic message of the Christ is the only explanation that can possibly be given of the evangelical tradition concerning Jesus' life and works and the only means by which we can provide ourselves with a faithful and vital image of the Savior of the world.[252] Christ never for a moment lived for himself (Rom. 15:3), but always for his church to leave it an example (Matt. 11:29; John 13:14–16; etc.), to serve it and to give his life as a ransom for many (Matt. 20:28), and to communicate to it his grace and truth, his light and his life (John 1:16; 6:33f.; Col. 3:4).

The incarnation itself was already a self-emptying (κενωσις) that consisted in Christ—who existed in the form of God, that is, in the same way as God existed, and did not consider this as something stolen or wrongfully assumed—relinquishing this divine mode of existence and assuming the form of a servant, so that he was truly born in human likeness and found in human form (Phil. 2:7–8; 2 Cor. 8:9; Rom. 8:3; Gal. 4:4; John 1:14).[253] His self-emptying (κενωσις) con-

248. A. E. Biedermann, *Christl. Dogmatik*, §§824ff.; R. A. Lipsius, *Dogmatik*, §567.

249. H. L. Martensen, *Christian Dogmatics*, §§139ff.; I. A. Dorner, *System of Christian Doctrine*, §104; J. P. Lange, *Dogmatik*, II, 635; R. Rothe, *Theologische Ethik*, §533.

250. D. F. Strauss, *Life of Jesus* (1846), §1; B. Weiss, *Das Leben Jesu*, 2 vols. (Stuttgart: 1882, 1888, 1902), I, 180; A. Ritschl, *Christian Doctrine of Justification and Reconciliation*, III, 3, 63; M. Kähler, *The So-Called Historical Jesus and the Historic Biblical Christ*, trans. Carl E. Braaten (Philadelphia: Fortress Press, 1988); idem, *Zur Lehre von der Versöhnung*, 68ff.; A. Kuyper, *Encyclopedie der Heilige Godgeleerdheid*, 2nd ed., 3 vols. (Kampen: Kok, 1908–9), III², 158ff.

251. J. H. A. Ebrard, *Christliche Dogmatik*, §408.

252. M. Kähler, *Zur Lehre von der Versöhnung*, 69; idem, *Angewandte Dogmen*, 2nd ed. (Leipzig: Deichert, 1908), 79–131, where Jesus' glory is distinguished from that of heroes and geniuses and described in terms of what is unique to and distinct from it.

253. Cf. W. Weiffenbach, *Zur Auslegung der Stelle Phil. 2:5–11* (Karlsruhe: Ruether, 1884). Earlier (cf. above, 259–65, 298–303 [##358, 369]) we discussed the mistaken view that the so-called Kenotics have of this passage.

sisted, in short, in exchanging the divine mode of existence (μορφη θεου) for the human (μορφη δουλου). And the moment this had taken place, his humiliation (ταπεινωσις) began and consisted in being and remaining obedient to God until death. Christ's whole life from his conception to his death, accordingly, was a humiliation resulting from his obedience, an ever-deeper entering into the communion of our sin and an ever-advancing self-removal from the joys of heaven. His circumcision (Luke 2:21) served as proof that he was truly human and the offspring of Abraham, that as such he was a member of the community of our sin and had to receive the sign signifying the cutting off of our sin; and at the same time, that God was his God and that he was the Son of God. His circumcision pointed to and was completed in his death (Col. 2:11–12).[254] His baptism, which as the Holy One he needed for himself no more than he did circumcision (Matt. 3:14), took place (1) because it was fitting for him as the mediator "to fulfill our righteousness," to satisfy all the claims of the law, and to accomplish all the righteousness required of him by the law; (2) because as such—standing in the community of sinners—he had to receive the sign and seal of his communion with God, as the Son with whom the Father was exceedingly well-pleased; and (3) because he had to be anointed with the Holy Spirit, enabled by him, and thus consecrated to his public ministry as the Christ, who alone can baptize (people) with the Holy Spirit and with fire (Matt. 3:11–17; cf. parallel, Acts 10:38).[255] The purpose of the temptation, which occurred immediately after the baptism and was repeated several times right up and into Gethsemane (cf. "until an opportune time," Luke 4:13; John 12:27; Matt. 26:39; Heb. 4:15; 5:7; 1 Pet. 2:23), was (1) that Christ, having just received the sign and seal of his communion with God and the gifts of the Holy Spirit, would maintain this communion also in the face of temptation from Satan and the world; (2) that as the second Adam, he would not break the covenant with God but uphold and confirm it for himself and his own; and (3) that, as the merciful high priest, tempted in all things like us, he would come to our assistance in all our weaknesses and temptations.[256] All the words Christ uttered and the works he did during his life on earth are an implementation of God's will (John 5:19f.; 6:38) and aim at making known the name, the perfections, the counsel, and good pleasure of God both in law and gospel (Matt. 11:27; John 1:18); at showing his priestly mercy to the poor, the sick, and the lost (Matt. 8:17; 11:5); and at demonstrating his royal power

254. See the older literature on Christ's circumcision, like that of Gerhard, Witsius, Gerdes, and others, in B. de Moor, *Comm. theol.*, V, 276; C. Vitringa, *Doctr. christ.*, V, 531. The feast of the circumcision on Jan. 1 is first mentioned in canon 17 of the Synod of Tours, 567.

255. F. Gomarus, *Opera*, I, 19; B. de Moor, *Comm. theol.*, V, 510; C. Vitringa, *Doctr. christ.*, V, 539; J. Bornemann, *Die Taufe Christi durch Johannes in der dogmatischen Beurteilung der christlichen Theologen der vier ersten Jahrhunderte* (Leipzig: Hinrichs, 1896).

256. F. Gomarus, *Opera*, I, 23; B. de Moor, *Comm. theol.*, IV, 36; C. Vitringa, *Doctr. christ.*, V, 540.

over Satan, the world, sin, and all their operations (Luke 10:18; John 12:31; 14:30; 16:33; 18:37).[257]

The suffering of Christ, which begins with his incarnation and is completed in his "great passion," is the will and command of the Father (Matt. 26:39, 42; John 10:17–18), proof of his absolute obedience (Phil. 2:8; Heb. 5:8), an example to be followed by his disciples (1 Pet. 2:21), a ransom for their sins (Matt. 20:28; 26:28), a victory over the world (John 16:33; Col. 2:15).[258] The purpose of his condemnation, not only by the [Jewish] Sanhedrin but also by the secular Roman judge Pontius Pilate, was that he would not die in secret as a result of an assassination or in an insurrection but that he would be publicly and legally killed, after being properly examined, in accordance with a verdict from the then best and most thorough system of justice, and that in the process his personal innocence (Matt. 27:18–24) as well as the basis for his condemnation, namely, his confession that he was the Son of God and Israel's Messiah (Matt. 26:63; 27:11), as well as the will of God (Acts 2:23; 4:27–28) and the character of his death as a dying for others (Matt. 20:28) would be clearly and incontrovertibly made manifest before the eyes of all.[259] The death by crucifixion, "a most savage and monstrous punishment," and usually inflicted only on slaves and dangerous criminals, meant that Christ, having been condemned in the name of the law to the most terrible and disgraceful punishment, satisfied the most rigorous demand of the law, and as one hanged, became a curse to God but thereby also removed the curse of the law from us (Deut. 21:23; Gal. 3:13), and completely delivered us from all the evil to which the law condemns us on account of our sins. The cross, therefore, stands at the center of the gospel (1 Cor. 1:23; 2:2; Gal. 6:14).[260] The blood that Christ shed demonstrates that he voluntarily consecrated his life to God,[261] that he gave it as an offering, and by it brought about atonement and peace (Matt. 26:27; Acts 20:28; Rom. 3:25; 5:9; Eph. 1:7; Col. 1:20; Heb. 9:12,

257. Concerning the duration of Jesus' public ministry, see B. de Moor, *Comm. theol.*, IV, 40ff.; C. Vitringa, *Doctr. christ.*, V, 543ff. That duration is still today estimated variously, as it was by the church fathers, at more than one year (L. Fendt, *Die Dauer der öffentlichen Wirksamkeit Jesu* [Munich: Lentner, 1906]), at more than two years (J. Zellinger, *Die Dauer der öffentlichen Wirksamkeit Jesu* [Münster: Aschendorff, 1907]), and at more than three years (W. Homanner, *Die Dauer der öffentlichen Wirksamkeit Jesu* [Freiburg i.B. and St. Louis: Herder, 1908]), or even longer (F. Westberg, *Die biblische Chronologie nach Flavius Josephus und das Todesjahr Jesu* [Leipzig: Deichert, 1910]).

258. B. de Moor, *Comm. theol.*, IV, 49ff.; C. Vitringa, *Doctr. christ.*, V, 552ff. See the more recent literature in *DC*, II, 758–59; P. Biesterveld, *Van Bethanië naar Golgotha* (Utrecht: Ruys, 1907).

259. James Moffatt, "Trial of Jesus," *DC*, II, 749–59; James Stalker, *The Trial and Death of Jesus Christ* (London: Hodder & Stoughton, 1908).

260. B. de Moor, *Comm. theol.*, IV, 77; C. Vitringa, *Doctr. christ.*, V, 577; O. Zöckler, *The Cross of Christ: Studies in the History of Religion and the Inner Life of the Church*, trans. Maurice J. Evans (London: Hodder & Stoughton, 1877); M. V. Schultze, "Kreuze und Kreuzigung," *PRE*[3], XI, 90ff.; A. T. Robertson, "Cross," *DC*, II, 394ff.; David Smith, "Crucifixion," *DC*, II, 397ff.

261. "He died, not on account of weakness, but strength," Augustine, *On Nature and Grace*, 26.

22).[262] Finally, Christ's burial has special significance as well. It is mentioned repeatedly (Isa. 53:9; Matt. 12:40; 27:59–60; Luke 11:29; 23:53; John 19:40–42; Acts 13:29; 1 Cor. 15:3–4). It is not only proof that he really died and hence rose again from the dead but particularly means that Christ, though committing his spirit into the hands of his Father, who took him up into paradise (Luke 23:43, 46), nevertheless spent three days in the state of death, belonged to the realm of the dead, and thus fully bore the punishment of sin (Gen. 3:19). To that state of death, Hades, he was not abandoned; his flesh saw no corruption, for he was raised the third day; yet from the time of his death to the moment of his resurrection, he belonged to the dead and therefore spent a period of time in Hades (Matt. 12:40; Acts 2:27, 31).[263]

DESCENT INTO HELL

[393] No other places in Scripture speak of Christ's burial or of his stay in the state of death. Later, when in the Christian church the confession arose of Christ's descent into hell, people indeed looked around for proof texts in Scripture and appealed to numerous places, such as Hosea 13:14; Psalm 16:10; Acts 2:27, 31; Matthew 27:52; Luke 23:43; John 8:56; Romans 10:7; Ephesians 4:9; 1 Peter 3:18–22; Hebrews 11:40; 12:22f. But careful exegesis brings out the unwarranted nature of this appeal. In Hosea 13:14, the Lord promises that he will redeem his people from Sheol and death, but there is no mention of a descent into hell. Acts 2:27, 31, citing Psalm 16:10, teaches that Christ, having died, was in Hades and belonged to the dead but contains no hint of the idea later linked in various church denominations to the article concerning the descent into hell. On the contrary, it is expressly stated that Christ was not abandoned by God in Hades, that his body did not see corruption, and that he was raised the third day. Though as a deceased person belonging to Hades, in terms of his soul, he was in paradise (Luke 23:43). Basic to passages such as John 8:56; Hebrews 11:40; 12:22f., admittedly, is the idea that in many respects Old Testament believers fell behind those of the new covenant, but they say absolutely nothing about their intermediate state. Rather, according to Hebrews 12:23, the devout of the old covenant form the assembly of the firstborn who are enrolled in heaven and have received heavenly citizenship *before* the believers of the New Testament.

In Romans 10:6–8, the apostle argues that Christ's coming on earth and his resurrection from the dead—as a result of which the righteousness of faith is

---

262. P. Cassel, *Die Symbolik des Blutes* (Berlin: Hofmann, 1882); H. C. Trumbull, *The Blood Covenant* (London, 1887); idem, *The Threshold Covenant* (Philadelphia, 1896); W. O. E. Oesterley, "Blood," *DC*, I, 214–16; "Like the heart of Jesus, so also his blood is an object of religious veneration in the Catholic Church; countless societies are especially devoted to its service" (M. Buchberger, *Kirchliches Handlexikon* [Munich, 1907], I, 670).

263. B. de Moor, *Comm. theol.*, IV, 103ff.; C. Vitringa, *Doctr. christ.*, V, 584; G. Milligan, "Burial," *DC*, I, 241–42.

fully present in him—make it unnecessary for them to ascend into heaven or to descend into the abyss, for that would actually be a denial of the fact that Christ had already descended from heaven and been raised from the dead. Now in this picture there may be an allusion to Christ's descent into the abyss, from which, through his resurrection, he returned, yet nothing concrete is further said about that. The word "abyss" is further explained by the addition "from the dead," and the whole sentence contains no other thought than what we also encounter in Acts 2:27, namely, that as a deceased person Christ had been in Hades and belonged to the dead. On the other hand, the descent "into the lower parts of the earth" of which Paul speaks in Ephesians 4:9 seems—by virtue of the contrast with his ascension—to point to Christ's incarnation, in the course of which he descended from heaven to earth. Finally, also 1 Peter 3:18–22 provides no basis for the interpretations given in various church denominations of the descent into hell. Of this pericope there are mainly three explanations. The first, coming from Augustine and taken over especially by the Reformed, is that before his incarnation Christ, speaking in the Spirit through Noah, preached the gospel to his contemporaries and admonished them to repent. The second interprets the text to say that between his death and resurrection, Christ left the grave and went to Hades and preached the gospel to those who were disobedient and died in the days of Noah (so, still today, Luther, Weiss, Lechler, Pfleiderer, Stevens, and others). The third associates "the spirits in prison" with fallen angels to whom judgment was announced by Christ, either in the days of Noah (Spitta), or between his death and resurrection (Baur, Gunkel, Lauterburg, Loofs, and others). Now whichever interpretation one favors, two things are certain. In the first place, Peter is in any case not speaking of what Christ did between his death and resurrection (or vivification) but of what he did either before his incarnation or after having revived his body. Undoubtedly, the words "being made alive in the spirit" indicate that Christ, who was put to death in a "sarkian" body, was raised again in virtue of the spirit (*pneuma*) that was his, so that his life after the resurrection was not "sarkian" but "pneumatic." It is equally beyond dispute, in the second place, that no mention whatever is made in this pericope of a descent of Christ into hell for the purpose of conducting Old Testament believers from Hades to heaven, or in general [of preaching judgment] to all who died in disobedience or ignorance (except, perhaps, the contemporaries of Noah). Therefore, the Greek [Orthodox], Roman Catholic, and later Lutheran view—aside now from the question whether it is true or not—has no basis in Peter's text.

However, the idea that between his death and resurrection, Christ descended into Hades surfaced in the Christian church very early. It is doubtful whether pagan notions concerning the Hades descent of gods and heroes lie behind the rise of this idea in Christian circles. Admittedly, belief in a Hades descent was widespread in the religions of that day. One such descent was attributed to Gilgamesh, Orpheus, Dionysus, Aeneas, and others and was considered proof of their power to slay the monsters and dragons of the underworld and to liberate the dead from their control. Moreover, in the mysteries of that time, the dramatic notions of Demeter-Kora, Attis-Adonis, Isis-Osiris, and others, as symbols of the conflict between death and life in nature and human experience, had become extraordinarily widespread. But among Christians—despite some resemblance between their views and the aforementioned—the view of Hades was from the beginning different from that held by Gentiles and the idea that was associated with Christ's descent into Hades differed greatly from what was thus expressed in the Hades descent of gods and heroes. For in the most ancient Christian documents, Christ's descent into Hades is consistently linked with the state of believers after their death. The Gospel of Peter (discovered in 1886 in a tomb at Akhmim) relates that when Christ arose from the dead, two men who had descended from heaven accompanied him and that the cross followed him. And, according to verses 41–42, these men heard a voice from heaven ask Jesus: "Have you preached to those who sleep?" and the answer that was heard coming from the cross was, "Yes!"

Stated here, generally speaking, is that in the state of death Christ preached to the dead, and these dead are not described in any further details. Many others, however, specifically identify these dead as Old Testament believers. Ignatius, for example, says that Christ, when he was there, raised from the dead the Old Testament believers who expected him.[264] As Hermas pictures it, the apostles and first ministers, after their death, preached the gospel and administered baptism to the devout who died before Christ's appearance.[265] Irenaeus tells of a presbyter who, defending the differing economies of the Old and the New Testament against Marcion, said: "It was for this reason, too, that the Lord descended into the regions beneath the earth, preaching his advent there also and [declaring] the remission of sins received by those who believe in him."[266] Marcion himself was of the opinion that Christ by his preaching in Hades redeemed all the dead who believed him more than they did the demiurge.[267] In the same way also Justin Martyr, Tertullian, and Irenaeus picture Christ's descent into Hades as being for the benefit of the devout of the Old Testament.[268] Clement of Alexandria, then, becomes the first author who associates this teaching with 1 Peter 3:18–22 and, in identifying the dead to whom Christ preaches the gospel, thinks not only of Old Testament believers but also of the righteous Gentiles.[269] Perhaps we may infer from this idea one that repeatedly occurs in the most ancient church authors, that the doctrine of the descent into hell originated in response to the question of where the believers of the Old Testament and also those who died in Christ

---

264. Ignatius, *Magnesians,* IX, 2; cf. F. Loofs, *Dogmengeschichte,* 100.

265. Shepherd of Hermas, *Similitudes,* IX, 16, 5–7.

266. Irenaeus, *Against Heresies,* IV, 27, 2; cited from *The Apostolic Fathers with Justin Martyr and Irenaeus,* vol. 1 of *ANF,* 499. Cf. F. Loofs, *Dogmengeschichte,* 104.

267. F. Loofs, *Dogmengeschichte,* 113.

268. Justin Martyr, *Dialogue with Trypho,* ch. 72; Tertullian, *De anima,* ch. 55; Irenaeus, *Against Heresies,* III, 20, 4; 22, 4; IV, 22, 1; 27, 2; V, 31, 1–2.

269. Clement of Alexandria, *Stromateis,* VI, 6.

stayed as they awaited the day of Jesus' return. The longer this return was delayed, the more urgent this question became, and people found comfort in the thought "for this reason Christ entered hell so that we would not have to go there." Christ preserved his own from Hades by himself descending into it during his own state of death.[270]

Add to this that the word "Hades" gradually changed its meaning. The statement that Christ had descended into Hades could emerge only at a time when this word still denoted the "world after death" in general and had not yet acquired the meaning of "hell." For the idea that Christ had descended to the place of torment, the actual hell, is nowhere to be found in Scripture, nor does it occur in the most ancient Christian writers. This change of meaning that the word "Hades" underwent, however, and that had been prepared here and there in the Old and the New Testament (e.g., in Isa. 14:11; Luke 10:15; 16:23), continued in the later church literature and increasingly led to the identification of Hades with Gehenna (hell, place of torment). This, in turn, prompted the rise of the conception that believers at the time of their death went to paradise, not to Hades;[271] that though the idea of Christ's descent into Hades was retained, it was understood in the sense that he went to a specific division of Hades, the later so-called limbo of the fathers, and had moved the devout of the Old Testament from there to paradise or heaven;[272] and, moreover, that Augustine, who wanted nothing to do with a preaching of the gospel to the ungodly dead, again completely separated this descent into Hades from 1 Peter 3:18–22 and understood this passage to refer to the message that Christ, before his incarnation and in the Spirit, had inspired Noah to bring to his contemporaries.[273]

[394] Where and when the words "descended into hell" (*descendit ad inferna*) were first included in the church's confession cannot be said with certainty. According to Rufinus (d. 410), the Apostolic Symbol [creed] of the church at Aquileia, where he was born, also contained the article "crucified under Pontius Pilate and buried, *he descended into hell.*" In his commentary on that symbol, he says that these last words do not occur in the confession of the church of Rome nor in that of the East and tries to demonstrate that in those confessions the descent into hell is included in the word "buried." However, in that same period these words already occurred in the confession of the synods of Sirmium (359), Nice (359), and Constantinople (360) and gradually passed from there into all the readings of the Apostles' Creed.[274] But large differences of opinion remained in the interpretation of it. The Greek church interpreted it to mean that Christ,

---

270. F. Kattenbusch, "Der geschichtliche Sinn des apostolischen Symbols," *Zeitschrift für Theologie und Kirche* 11 (October 1901): 407–28.

271. Origen, *Reg. hom.*, 2; cf. idem, *Contra Celsum*, II, 43.

272. A. E. Burn, "Descent into Hell," *DC*, I, 714.

273. Augustine, *Epistle 104* (Ad Evodium).

274. A. Hahn, *Bibliothek der Symbole und Glaubensregeln der alten Kirche*, 3rd ed. (Breslau: E. Morgenstern, 1897), 42ff.; F. Kattenbusch, *Das apostolische Symbol*, 2 vols. (Leipzig: Hinrichs, 1894–1900), I, 103ff.; idem,

with his divine nature and his soul, went to Hades to liberate from it the souls of the holy ancestors and conducted them, along with the soul of the murderer on the cross, to paradise.[275] In the West the reality of the descent into hell was maintained, first against Abelard and later against Durandus and Mirandola.[276] Subsequently, at the Fourth Lateran Council (1215), it was determined that after his death Christ truly descended to hell in his soul but not in his body.[277] The meaning of this article was so described in the Roman Catechism as well. Immediately after Christ's death his soul descended into hell and remained there while his body lay in the grave. He went there, not to suffer, but, as victor, to subdue the demons and to deprive them of their spoils. Specifically he despoiled them of those holy fathers of the old covenant who, though suffering no other pains, missed the beatific vision of God and were tormented by the longing for that glory, and were now liberated by him from the limbo of the fathers and (later, at his own ascension) conducted to heaven. Finally, he also made known his power and authority in purgatory in order to grant redemption to all who were there from the days of Adam or would dwell there later and for whom, before his suffering and death, the gates of heaven were closed.[278] The theologians limited themselves to this fruit of the descent into hell or, following the example of Clement, Origen, and others, added that the benefits of that descent accrued to those who "at their death were in some way disposed to the reception of the grace of redemption."[279]

The Reformation could not adopt this interpretation of the article in question because it had a different view of the meaning of the old covenant and the salvation of those who in that dispensation died in the faith, but it found no explanation that was satisfactory to everyone. Luther put forward various interpretations and ended by saying: "The matter is not clear."[280] But the Lutheran Church in its confession finally agreed to the statement that Christ, following his burial, went to hell in both his natures, with soul and body, subdued the devil, and broke the power of hell. Some theologians then expanded this statement by writing that on the morning of the third day, after the vivification, or internal resurrection, but before the external resurrection, Christ, with soul and

---

articles in *Christliche Welt*, nos. 27–28; idem, "Zur Würdigung des Apostolikums," *Heft zur christlichen Welt*, no. 2 (Leipzig, 1892), 29; T. Zahn, *Das apostolische Symbol* (Erlangen: Deichert, 1893).

275. Orthodox Confession, qu. 49.

276. The Council of Sens (1140) condemned Abelard's proposition that "Christ's soul did not as such (per se) descend to hell but only by its power," and Innocent II confirmed this verdict (H. Denzinger, *Enchiridion*, #327).

277. H. Denzinger, *Enchiridion*, #356.

278. Roman Catechism, I, c. 6.

279. W. Koch, in *Kirchliches Handlexikon*, ed. M. Buchberger, I, 2006; cf. R. Bellarmine, "De Christo," *Controversiis*, IV, 6–16; D. Petavius, "De incarn.," XII, 19–20; XIII, 15–18; M. Scheeben, *Dogmatik*, III, 298ff.; C. Pesch, *Prael. dogm.*, IV, 242ff.; H. T. Simar, *Lehrbuch der Dogmatik*, 3rd ed. (Freiburg i.B.: Herder, 1893), 467ff.; J. Pohle, *Lehrbuch der Dogmatik*, 4th ed. (Paderborn: Schöningh, 1912–14), II⁴, 201ff.

280. In F. Loofs, *Dogmengeschichte*, 229ff.

body, went down to hell and there made known to Satan and all the damned spirits—by a proclamation that was not evangelical but legal, refutative, and terrible—his victory over death and hell.[281] Also the Reformed disagreed with one another in their interpretation of this article. Even if we except the Repetitio Anhaltina, the Lipsian Colloquium, and a few theologians such as Zanchius and Aretius who still held to a local descent into hell,[282] the confessions and theological opinions among the Reformed are most divergent. Some (Sohnius, Parker, Martinius, Chamier) read the article to cover the entire state of humiliation. Others (Bucer, Beza, Whitaker, Drusius, Wittichius, Braun) did not see in it much more than a further description of the burial as the last and lowest step of Christ's humiliation. Calvin explained the article as speaking of the hellish pains suffered by Christ on the cross and was followed in that interpretation by many others as well (Ursinus, Polanus, Trelcatius, Bucanus, Cloppenburg, Wendelin) and especially by the Heidelberg Catechism. Zwingli understood it to say that during his death Christ belonged to the dead [the *inferi*: the inhabitants of the lower regions] and made the power of his redemption felt also in the lower regions (*ad inferos*). This view resonated with many people, among them Olevianus, Bullinger, Peter Martyr, Perkins, Ames, Molinaeus, Broughton, Vossius, Bochartus, Pearson, Schultens, Vriemoet, and others, and particularly in the catechism and confession of Westminster. Finally, there were many theologians who tried to combine the different interpretations and associated the descent into hell both with the hellish agony Christ suffered on the cross and with the state of death in which he existed from the moment of dying to the moment of his resurrection (*Synopsis pur. theol.,* Burman, Turretin, Witsius, Heidegger, Mastricht, Gerdes, Pictet, and others).[283]

This great diversity of opinions explains that many theologians were unable to make good sense of this article and totally rejected it[284] or used this article to give a historical and ecclesiastical character to their doctrine of ongoing preaching of the gospel and a permanent mission station in the intermediate state.[285]

The case with this article, briefly put, is as follows:

281. J. T. Müller, *Die symbolischen Bücher,* 550, 556; F. H. R. Frank, *Theologie der Concordienformel,* 4 vols. in 2 (Erlangen: A. Deichert, 1884), III, 397–454; H. F. F. Schmid, *Dogmatik der evangelisch-lutherischen Kirche,* 7th ed. (Gütersloh: Bertelsmann, 1893), 277, 288ff.

282. Repetitio Anhaltina, 9; *Coll. Lips.,* 9; Anglican Articles of 1552 (cited by E. F. K. Müller, *Die Bekenntnisschriften der reformierten Kirche* [Leipzig: Deichert, 1903], 506), noted in the edition of 1563.

283. U. Zwingli, *Exposition of the Christian Faith;* J. Calvin, *Institutes,* I.xvi.8–12; Genevan Catechism, 1; Heidelberg Catechism, Q. & A. 44; Westminster Catechism, Q. & A. 50. Cf. on these and still more interpretations of the descent into hell, B. de Moor, *Comm. theol.,* IV, 331ff.; C. Vitringa, *Doctr. christ.,* V, 558ff.

284. F. Schleiermacher, *Christian Faith,* §99, 1; A. Schweizer, *Christliche Glaubenslehre,* §134.

285. E. Güder, *Die Lehre von der Erscheinung Jesu Christi unter den Todten in ihrem Zusammenhang mit der Lehre von den letzten Dingen* (Bern: Jent & Reinert, 1853); A. von Oettingen, *Lutherische Dogmatik,* III, 135ff.

1. The phrase "descended into hell," to the extent that it may have been derived from texts such as Acts 2:27; Rom. 10:7; Eph. 4:9, has historically acquired a very different meaning from what is contained in these texts.

2. The Greek (Orthodox) and Roman Catholic explanation of this article, to the effect that Christ went to Hades to conduct the devout of the Old Testament from the limbo of the fathers to heaven, lacks all support in Scripture, even in John 8:56; Hebrews 10:20; 11:40; 12:22f.

3. The Lutheran view, according to which Christ went down into Hades to make his victory and power known to Satan, even though, as we will see later, they were based on firm pronouncements in Scripture, cannot be considered a correct explanation of the words "descended into hell," since these words do not—scripturally and historically—permit such an explanation and can evidently not describe a step in the state of exaltation but only a step in the state of humiliation.

4. For the same reason the modern idea that Christ descended into hell to preach the gospel to everyone who did not hear it here on earth cannot be viewed as a correct explanation of this article of the faith either.

5. First Peter 3:19–22 at most says (though it will be shown later that this is not the correct understanding) that Christ preached the gospel to Noah's contemporaries *after* his resurrection, but there is absolutely no ground in this passage for an expansion of this preaching to all or many of the lost.

6. The exegesis that associates "the spirits in prison" (1 Pet. 3:19) with fallen angels is refuted by the further description and the contrast with the eight souls in verse 20.

7. The article concerning the descent into hell is interpreted most congruently with related expressions in Scripture (Acts 2:27, 31; Rom. 10:7; Eph. 4:9), with the probable origin and sense of the words, and with its place between the other articles, when it is understood as referring to the state of death in which Christ existed between his dying and rising again to bear the punishment of sin to the end and to redeem us from it. "Christ descended into hell so that we would not have to go there."

This interpretation, as has consistently been recognized by all Reformed theologians, is not a contradiction or antithesis, but rather an augmentation and extension of the idea expressed in their explanation of this article by Calvin and the Heidelberg Catechism. For Christ in truth bore unspeakable distress, sorrows, horror, and hellish torment on the cross in order that he might redeem us from them. Catholics indeed oppose this view because they put, and have to put, all the emphasis on Christ's physical suffering and death. They, after all, deny Christ's human nature and development in the sense that they make him one who has full comprehension and ascribe to him the beatific vision of God already during his stay on earth.[286] If this is so, one cannot

---

286. See above, 256–57, 308–9 (##357, 371).

speak of Christ's suffering in his rational soul, and his suffering has to be restricted to the sensitive part [of the soul] and to "sym-pathy" (συμπαθεια) with the body.[287] In addition, a statement by Clement VI in the bull *Unigenitus* (1343) made it church doctrine that, on account of its union with the eternal Word, "one small drop of blood" would have been sufficient for the redemption of the whole human race.[288] In that way the Roman Catholic doctrine of satisfaction was totally concentrated on Christ's physical suffering and death, and no need was felt for a suffering by Christ in his rational soul, for his dying a spiritual death, for his undergoing unspeakable distress and hellish torments in the work of salvation.[289] But Scripture speaks of Christ's "soul-suffering" in language that is much too strong (Matt. 26:37–38; 27:46; Mark 14:33–34; 15:34; Luke 22:44; John 12:27; Heb. 5:7–8) for it to be restricted to his sensitive soul. Many Catholics, accordingly, acknowledge that Christ's rational soul was nevertheless in some indirect fashion—through assistance, management, or sympathy—involved in his suffering.[290] And all the Reformed without exception opposed the opinion of Catholics,[291] confessing that Christ bore the wrath of God and tasted the spiritual death of his abandonment also in his soul, although there was no room there for the most horrid element in the punishment, for self-accusation, remorse, or despair.[292] But all this does not in any way alter the other fact that the state of death in which Christ entered when he died was as essentially a part of his humiliation as his spiritual suffering on the cross. In both together he completed his perfect obedience. He drank the cup of suffering to the last drop and tasted death in all its bitterness in order to completely deliver us from the fear of death and death itself. Thus he destroyed him who had the power of death and by a single offering perfected for all time those who are sanctified (Heb. 10:14).

287. R. Bellarmine, "De Christo," *Controversiis,* IV, c. 8; cf. B. de Moor, *Comm. theol.,* IV, 122ff.; C. Vitringa, *Doctr. christ.,* V, 555ff.

288. Cf. above, 401 (#390).

289. R. Bellarmine, "De Christo," *Controversiis,* IV, c. 8; *Theol. Wirceb.,* IV, 317ff.; C. Pesch, *Prael. dogm.,* IV, 211; M. J. Scheeben, *Dogmatik,* III, 343ff.; J. Pohle, *Dogmatik,* II, 189ff.

290. H. Alting, *Theol. el. nova,* 502ff.; B. de Moor, *Comm. theol.,* IV, 122ff.

291. D. Chamier, *Panstr. cath.,* II, 5, 11ff.; A. Rivetus, "Commentary on Psalm 22," in *Opera,* II, 103ff.; F. Turretin, *Institutes of Elenctic Theology,* XIII, 14, 16; B. de Moor, *Comm. theol.,* IV, 122ff.

292. Calvin, accordingly, expressly states: "Yet we do not suggest that God was ever inimical or angry toward him. How could he be angry toward his beloved Son, 'in whom his heart reposed' [cf. Matt. 3:17]? How could Christ by his intercession appease the Father toward others, if he were himself hateful to God? This is what we are saying: he bore the weight of divine severity, since he was 'stricken and afflicted' [cf. Isa. 53:5] by God's hand, and experienced all the signs of a wrathful and avenging God" (*Institutes,* II.xvi.11). The obedience of Christ in his suffering was voluntary and perfect. "In all his afflictions the moderation which restrains excess was strong," and he so bore temptation that it never conflicted with his faith and trust (ibid., II.xvi.12). Cf. above (388–92 [#388]) and further on the descent into hell, Gotthard Victor Lechler, *Das apostolische und das nachapostolische Zeitalter* (Karlsrube and Leipzig: H. Reuther, 1885), 429ff.; Friedrich Spitta, *Christi Predigt an die Geister* (Göttingen: Vandenhoeck & Ruprecht, 1890); C. Clemen, *Niedergefahren zu den Toten: Ein Beitrag zur Würdigung des Apostolikums* (Giessen: J. Ricker, 1900); M. Lauterburg, "Höllenfart Christi," *PRE*[3], VIII, 199–206; G. B. Stevens, *Theology of the New Testament,* I, 304–8; A. E. Burn, "Descent into Hell," *DC,* I, 713–16; H. H. Kuyper, articles in *De Heraut* from around October 1909 to April 24, 1910.

8

CHRIST'S EXALTATION

For Christ, his death was the end of his humiliation and, at the same time, the road to his exaltation. In all religions, and for Israel too, death is the road to life. The mythology of pagan religions, however, offers no real hope of life, only a general sense of alternation between death and life in endless struggle. Israel's hope, based on prophetic promise, came to rest on the Suffering Servant, whose sacrificial death brought life and who calls his followers to deny themselves so they might live in him. Because he humbled himself unto death, God has exalted him and given him a name above all names (Phil. 2:6–11).

Not only Philippians 2 but the whole New Testament teaches the humiliated and exalted Christ as the core of the gospel. Maintaining both the historical reality of incarnation and humiliation and the glory of the exalted Christ as the God-man has proved difficult for theology. The two successive states, humiliation and exaltation, were sometimes too closely linked with the two-natures doctrine— human and divine—thus creating confusion. This is particularly true in the case of Lutheran Christology, where there is no succession in the degrees of exaltation. In fact, strictly speaking, nothing new is communicated to Christ in the state of exaltation that was not his from the time of conception. In radical Anabaptism and Socinianism, a dualism between eternity and time makes both incarnation and exaltation actually impossible, reducing them to graphic depictions of ideals for humanity.

The Reformed view is that Christ is the mediator in accordance with both natures. The office and work of the mediator could only be accomplished by one who was both true God and true man. The divine and human participate in both states in the one person. Reformed theology had to face the difficult question of kenosis: Did the Son of God set aside his divine attributes in the incarnation? Reformed theology denied this, claiming instead that Christ had voluntarily from all eternity taken on the form of a servant and in his incarnation laid aside or concealed the divine glory of his divinity and never used it during his humiliation to defeat his enemies or please himself. He fought and won the battle with his self-denying sacrificial love, culminating in death on the cross. His exaltation is thus a real change, a state gained as a reward of his obedience. The preposition διο ("therefore") in Philippians 2 as well as the Letter to the Hebrews points to Christ earning his exaltation through obedience.

This does not mean, as the Socinians taught, that Christ only had deity and dignity in the state of exaltation. The state of exaltation refers not to the person of Christ and his nature(s) but to the glory of his mediatorial work. By his resurrection and ascension, Christ enters a new state; as the mediator he is now at the right hand of glory. Though he was truly God in his state of humiliation, the glory was hidden. In the state of exaltation, the divine glory radiates outward for all to see, and all who see must confess Jesus as Lord. Resurrection is the first step in Christ's exaltation. Raised by the power of God, he is the firstborn of all creation, the one who has the keys of death and Hades, the one who has power to give eternal life. The historical reality of the resurrection is clearly attested by Jesus' appearances and the apostolic witness to them. All spiritualizing and subjectivizing interpretations of the resurrection must be rejected. Only the bodily resurrection can explain the empty tomb and the firm faith of the disciples; nothing else does justice to the biblical witness. It should be noted that a visionary explanation of the appearances as a "telegram from heaven" is no less miraculous than the straightforward account of the bodily resurrection but it does add elements of deceit and trickery to the apostolic message of the gospel. The bodily resurrection, after three days, is proof of Christ's divine sonship, his messiahship, the Father's endorsement of his work as mediator, and serves as the ground and pledge of our salvation.

After the important period of forty days when Jesus instructed his disciples, he ascended into heaven and is exalted at the Father's right hand. The ascension was a constituent of the faith of the church from the beginning, as much as the resurrection. This is great comfort to believers: our Priest-King pleads on our behalf and is coming to judge the living and the dead at the time of his great and final exaltation. As our mediator he has obtained the full benefits of our whole salvation, beginning with an objective atonement for our sin. Refusals to acknowledge propitiation as the heart of his death and resurrection result from a misunderstanding of God's love. It is God's love that is the basis for his providing Christ as the means of propitiation. By Christ's sacrifice a new relation of reconciliation and peace has been accomplished between God and humanity. The benefit of this work of Christ is unrestricted; it covers every dimension of experience; it extends to all creation.

Modern notions of reconciliation, such as those of Schleiermacher and Ritschl, begin not with Christ meriting our salvation through his obedient sacrifice of propitiation but rather with mystical and moral influence on human persons. The change is in people who are now conscious of God's love to them; they no longer consider God as wrathful. Here a significant shift takes place from the objective work of Christ on our behalf and in our place to a subjective work in us.

This is a partial view that robs us of the assurance that in Christ all things, all creation will be renewed.

Christ's redemptive work is of infinite value and extends to the whole world. Christ came not to condemn but to save the world. This universal scope has sometimes been misunderstood as a promise of salvation to all discrete individual persons, in short, as universal salvation. Over against those such as Origen, Pelagius, and Arminius, the mainstream of the Christian church has been true to the particularist teaching of Augustine—not all are saved. That did not stop theologians and churchmen from intensely debating the issue with such distinctions as God's antecedent will and consequent will and, above all, "sufficient but not efficacious." The Canons of Dort explicitly teach particular atonement, though they also declare Christ's sacrifice "of infinite worth and value, abundantly sufficient to expiate the sins of the whole world." Thanks to the influential work of certain Scottish theologians such as John McLeod Campbell, the doctrine of limited or particular atonement was almost universally abandoned.

It is important to get the terms of this debate straight. The issue is not about whether the death of Christ has infinite value or worth, nor is it about whether in fact some are not saved. The question is whether it was God's will and intent that Christ made his sacrifice for the sins of all people without exception or only for the sins of the elect. When framed thus, the teaching of Scripture is not really in doubt. The key point here concerns assurance to believers: Did Christ in his death and resurrection really procure the salvation of his own, or was this only a potentiality, mere possibility? The Reformed tradition took a clear stance in favor of the former view—only this truth could maintain the unity of the work of the triune God, Father, Son, and Holy Spirit. The advocates of a universal scope for the atonement, ironically, diminish the value and power of Christ's work. The center of gravity shifts from Christ to the Christian; salvation comes to depend on our faith.

Nonetheless, we must not overlook the fact that this particular atonement still has universal significance. It is here that we must understand the doctrine of common grace; it is subservient to special or particular grace. God providentially permits the world to continue because of his higher purposes for his elect. Though Christ is only head of the church as prophet, priest, and king, all human beings benefit from the light that the gospel shines into the world. All creation, even the angels, are enfolded into the glorious redemption of all things.

Another way of stating this is to say that Christ's threefold office of prophet, priest, and king continues into his state of exaltation. As prophet he teaches his disciples in the forty days, and by the Holy Spirit sent at Pentecost, he makes known to the world all the treasures of wisdom and knowledge hidden in him. In the same manner, as the Epistle to the Hebrews points out, he continues as our

High Priest to intercede for us. And, finally, he is our eternal King who rules us by his Word and Spirit and equips us to be victorious over sin and Satan. Christ's mediatorial office ceases at the consummation though he retains his human nature and remains a prophet, priest, and king as a mediator of union and head of the church.

THROUGH DEATH TO LIFE

[395] The death of Christ, the end of his humiliation, was simultaneously the road to his exaltation. In all religions and philosophical systems, one encounters the idea, expressed more or less consciously, that death is the road to life. People saw this phenomenon in nature, where day follows night and an awakening in the spring occurs after a winter of hibernation or dormancy. The history of ethnic tribes and peoples offers proof of this when it frequently takes them through struggle to victory, through oppression to freedom; and every human soul bore witness to it when by self-denial and abstinence that soul regained its independence. This idea was especially widespread in the time when Christianity made its appearance. Under the influence of Eastern cults, the original nature religions in Greece and Rome underwent a vast change. In the mysteries especially, the natural vegetative process of life was given a spiritual and moral interpretation. In dramatic fashion it was represented as a symbol of the alternation of death and life, of the changeover from the visible world on earth to the invisible world beyond, from the descent into and the liberation from Hades, from the pollution to the purification of the soul.[1] The untrustworthiness of observation and reflection, the uncertainty of arriving at truth, the frequently wretched social conditions, the incessant wars, the pressure of foreign domination promoted this mysticism and sparked a universal longing for redemption, for truth and life. It was felt more deeply than ever that life can only arise from death and exaltation can only come after humiliation. There was a general sense of the truth of what was later called "die-and-become," of the "die-to-live" syndrome. But even though in a symbolic-dramatic way the ancient nature myth was transformed into a process of human life and history, it remained an idea to which no reality corresponded. It did not detach itself from mythology but remained bound up with all sorts of superstition and magic and frequently led to excesses of asceticism, on the one hand, and libertinism, on the other.

We enter a very different world when in antiquity we turn to Israel. Here, too, we encounter the idea that death is the road to life. On its first pages the Old Testament already mentions a conflict in which the offspring of the serpent will crush the heel of the woman's offspring, and conversely, the woman's offspring will crush the head of the serpent's offspring (Gen. 3:15). And this saying is, as it were, inscribed above the history of the whole human race, for that history, so

---

1. W. Staerk, *Neutestamentliche Zeitgeschichte*, 2 vols. (Berlin: G. J. Göschen, 1907), I, 99ff.

far from being a linear development, is a constant struggle between sin and righteousness, darkness and light, death and life, between the things that are above and the things that are below. This saying has been especially confirmed, however, in the history of Israel, from the times of the patriarchs right up to the day of Christ. The patriarchs have to leave everything behind and move to a foreign land, but in that way they inherit the promise of the Lord and through their offspring become a blessing to all nations. Moses gave up the treasures of Egypt and was subsequently called by God to be the savior of the people of Israel and the mediator of the old covenant. Israel itself as a people must not intermingle with the nations round about nor walk in their ways; it must be a holy people whose task it is to keep the word of God and in that way receive an array of spiritual and natural blessings. The devout in Israel are often only a small group, people who are poor and wretched in themselves and oppressed and scorned on all sides, but who trust in the Lord and expect their vindication and salvation from him. The suffering of the innocent is graphically pictured to us in the lives of persons such as Job, David, and Jeremiah. Of all those God-fearing people, it is true that, though abandoned, oppressed, and ill-treated, through faith they conquered kingdoms, practiced righteousness, and received promises. In Israel we encounter a struggle not only between the people and the Gentiles around them, but also among the people themselves between the faithful and the unfaithful, and among the faithful themselves between the righteousness of God, to which, by faith, they cling, and the sins of which they are all personally guilty. This is the historical setting in which prophecy depicts the figure of the Servant of the Lord, who, himself free from all sin, bears the sins of his people, atones for them by his suffering and death, but subsequently prolongs his days, makes many righteous, and by his hand the will of the Lord prospers (Isa. 53:10f.). In him is fulfilled that which was prefigured in the experience of believers, namely, that, delivered from their deepest distress, they proclaim his name and righteousness to the great congregation (Pss. 22:22–23; 40:9–10).

From the beginning Christ applied this prophecy of the Suffering Servant of the Lord to himself. This is evident from his public appearance in the synagogue of Nazareth (Luke 4:16ff.) but also from the content of his teaching. For he proclaimed the coming of the kingdom of heaven and told the people that only faith, repentance, rebirth, self-denial, and another and better righteousness than that of the Pharisees gave them access to it. He, therefore, called blessed the poor in spirit, the pure of heart, the meek, and so on, for, though on earth they would be persecuted for his sake and the sake of righteousness, one day they would inherit the kingdom of heaven with all its benefits (Matt. 5:3–12). The basic law of that kingdom, accordingly, is that one must abandon everything for Jesus' sake. Those who love father or mother, son or daughter more than him are not worthy of him and those who do not take his cross upon them and follow him are not worthy of him (Matt. 10:37–38; 16:24). To lose oneself is to save oneself (Matt. 10:39; 16:25). However, this self-denial must not be equated with self-torture, self-destruction, the stupefaction of one's consciousness, or the extinction of one's personality, but is exactly the way to save oneself, to share in eternal life, and to get back all that was left behind (Matt. 10:39; 16:25; 19:29).

This law applies to Jesus' disciples because it applied in the first place to Jesus himself. The disciple is not above his teacher, nor a servant above his master (Matt. 10:24). From the beginning Jesus voluntarily placed himself under this law. In everything he had to be in the business of his Father (Luke 2:49). He had himself baptized because it was fitting for him to fulfill all righteousness (Matt. 3:15). His food was to do the will of his Father (John 4:34), and to that rule he held himself even into death (Matt. 26:39). Self-denial was "the secret of his life" (M. Arnold). His messianic consciousness, which he immediately expressed in the name "Son of Man," implied the certainty that he had to die. But the moment he made this openly and plainly known to his disciples, he also announced that he would rise again in three days and subsequently be taken up into the glory of his Father, where he would sit at his right hand and be once more manifested for the purpose of judgment (Matt. 16:21, 27; 20:18–19; 25:31; 26:64).

In the Gospel of John, this close connection between humiliation and exaltation is made even clearer than in the Synoptics. For in Christ the Word indeed became flesh, yet in his servant form the glory that he had as the Word with the Father still shone through (1:14; 2:11; 11:4, 40). Especially his suffering and death makes that glory manifest (12:23; 13:31), for unless the grain of wheat falls into the earth and dies it cannot bear fruit (12:24). His exaltation, accordingly, begins not at his resurrection and ascension but already at his crucifixion (3:14; 8:28; 12:32). Although it was the people who lifted him up on that cross (8:28), it is actually he himself who by that event elevates himself above the earth (12:32). Cross and crown, death and resurrection, humiliation and exaltation lie on the same line. As Jesus himself put it after his resurrection: It was *necessary* that the Christ should suffer these things and so enter his glory (Luke 24:26).

The sum and substance of the original gospel, therefore, was the Christ who died and rose again. The cross was an immense offense—also for the disciples (Matt. 26:31). But for them that offense was removed by the resurrection. Then they perceived that Jesus had to die and did die in accordance with the counsel of the Father (Acts 2:23; 3:18; 4:28), and that by his resurrection God had made him a cornerstone (4:11; 1 Peter 2:6), Lord and Christ (Acts 2:36), a Leader and a Savior (5:31), the Lord of all (10:36), the Lord of glory (James 2:1), in order by him to give repentance, forgiveness of sins, the Holy Spirit, and eternal life (Acts 2:38; 3:19; 5:31; 10:43; 1 Peter 1:3ff., 21), outside of whom there is no salvation (Acts 4:12). Now taken up into heaven, he remains there until he comes again for judgment (1:11; 3:21), for he is the one ordained by God to be judge of the living and the dead (10:42; 17:31), and then all things will be restored of which God spoke by the mouth of his holy prophets of old (3:21). Similarly Paul teaches that Christ, though he was the Son of God even before his incarnation (Gal. 4:4; Phil. 2:6; Col. 1:15), was designated Son of God in power by his resurrection from the

dead (Rom. 1:4). Then he received a spiritual, glorified body (1 Cor. 15:45; Phil.
3:21), became a life-giving Spirit (1 Cor. 15:45; 2 Cor. 3:17), the firstborn of the
dead (Col. 1:18), who from then on lives to God forever (Rom. 6:10). Precisely
because of his deep humiliation, God highly exalted him, giving him the name
that is above every other name, that is, the name "Lord" (1 Cor. 12:3; Phil. 2:11),
granting him dominion over the living and the dead (Rom. 14:9), and subjecting
all things under his feet (1 Cor. 15:25, 27). As such he is the Lord of glory (1 Cor.
2:8), seated at God's right hand (Rom. 8:34; 1 Cor. 2:8), in whom the fullness of
the deity dwells bodily (Col. 1:19; 2:9), who is the head of the church, prays for it,
and fills it with all the fullness of God (Rom. 8:34; Eph. 1:23; 3:19; 4:16). The
Letter to the Hebrews further adds to this profile the unique idea that Christ, the
Son, who with the Father was the Creator of all things, was also appointed "the
heir of all things" (Heb. 1:2; 2:8) by the Father and designated eternal high priest
(5:6; 7:17). But for a short time, in order to attain this destiny, he had to become
lower than the angels (2:7, 9), assume our flesh and blood (2:14), become like
us in all respects except sin (2:17; 4:15), and learn obedience from the things he
suffered (5:8). But thereby he also sanctified,[2] that is, perfected himself (2:10;
5:9; 7:28), and was designated by God a high priest according to the order of
Melchizedek (5:10). This, accordingly, is the sum of the things of which the
Letter to the Hebrews says that we have such a high priest, one who is seated at
the right hand of the throne of the Majesty in heaven (1:13; 8:1; 10:12). He who
is the liturgist of the heavenly sanctuary (8:2), a high priest, therefore, who is at
the same time the king whose throne is established forever (1:8), who is crowned
with honor and glory (2:9), subjects all things under him (2:8), and is able for
all time to save those who draw near to God through him since he always lives to
make intercession for them (5:9; 7:25; 10:14). The Apocalypse, finally, loves to
picture Christ as the Lamb who purchased us and washed us by his blood (5:9;
7:14) but also as the firstborn of the dead, the ruler of the kings of the earth (1:5),
the King of kings and the Lord of lords, who with the Father sits on the throne,
has power and honor and glory, even the keys of Hades and death (1:18; 3:21;
5:12–13; 19:16). Clothed with such power, he rules and protects his church (2:1,
18; etc.) and will one day triumph over all his enemies (19:12f.).

THE DOCTRINE OF THE TWO STATES

[396] When Holtzmann, referring to the text of Philippians 2:6–11, admits
that it undoubtedly forms the foundation for the doctrine of the two states and
that this doctrine plays an important role in the theological consciousness of the

2. Cf. J. Kögel, "Der Begriff τελειουν im Hebräerbrief," in *Theologische Studien: Martin Kähler zum 6.
Januar 1905*, ed. Friedrich Giesebrecht and Martin Kähler (Leipzig: Deichert, 1905), 35–68; K. Bornhäuser,
Die Versuchung Jesu nach dem Hebräerbrief (Leipzig: Deichert, 1905), 69–86; J. Kögel, *Der Sohn und die Söhne:
Eine exegetische Studie zu Hebräer 2:5–18* (Gütersloh: Bertelsmann, 1897–99).

apostle Paul,[3] that statement may very well be expanded to include Scripture's entire doctrine concerning Christ. In the Old Testament, we already encounter traces of it in the figure of the Servant of the Lord, and in the New Testament, the humiliated and exalted, crucified and resurrected Christ constitutes the core of the gospel. The resurrection decisively uncovered the meaning of Jesus' suffering and death for the disciples, so that they looked back on his earthly life from the vantage point of belief in his exaltation. The assertion of Drews[4] that the Jesus of whom Paul speaks is not for him a historical personality directly contradicts Paul's many testimonies to Jesus' Davidic origin, his birth from the fathers, his perfect obedience, his institution of the Lord's Supper, his suffering and death on the cross (Rom. 1:3; 9:5; Phil. 2:8; 1 Cor. 11:23; etc.). But for Paul and all the apostles, the object of [their] faith was the exalted and glorified Christ, who, however, is the same as the one who descended. And all this is true in the same sense for the community of believers. Very soon the facts of redemption were briefly summed up in the Apostles' Creed of ancient date. Granted, there is in it no formal division into two states, but Christians, following it, confessed their faith in Christ Jesus, the only-begotten Son of God, who was conceived by the Holy Spirit, born of the Virgin Mary, crucified, died, and was buried; the third day he arose from the dead, ascended to heaven, is seated at the right hand of God, whence he will come to judge the living and the dead. The Apostles' Creed sketched the order in which all through the ages the facts of redemption were treated and explained in confessions, catechisms, sermons, and dogmatic works.[5]

Dogmatic disputes about the person of Christ, however, also brought with them differences of insight with respect to the meaning of the facts of redemption and specifically with respect to the states of Jesus' humiliation and exaltation. Gnosticism made a sharp distinction between the historical Jesus and the heavenly Christ. It regarded the latter as the ideal human who had existed from eternity, revealed himself only for a short while in a phantom body, or united himself with the man Jesus, who was born of Mary but did not himself suffer, and therefore had no room in their system for either Christ's humiliation or his exaltation.[6] According to the Monophysites, one can no longer speak of two natures after Christ's incarnation but only of one divine-human nature. This theory, however, led to disagreement about the capacity of Jesus' human nature for suffering and death. Severus and like-minded thinkers still clung to this possibility (*phthartolatri*), but Julian and his followers, drawing out the implications of their monophysite premise, taught that from the moment of its union with the deity,

3. H. J. Holtzmann, *Lehrbuch der neutestamentlichen Theologie*, 2 vols. (Freiburg and Leipzig: Mohr, 1897), II, 87.

4. A. Drews, *The Christ Myth* (Chicago: Open Court, 1910; reprinted, Amherst, NY: Prometheus Books, 1998), 89.

5. C. Blume, *Das apostolische Glaubensbekenntnis* (Freiburg i.B.: Herder, 1893), 27ff.

6. I. A. Dorner, *A History of the Development of the Doctrine of the Person of Christ*, trans. William Lindsay Alexander, 5 vols. (Edinburgh: T&T Clark, 1863–78), III, 310ff.

Christ's body was incorruptible (ἄφθαρτος) and identical in nature with the body he received at the resurrection. Susceptibility to suffering and death, therefore, was not inherent in Christ's nature but based on his free will. Even stranger was the conclusion to which others came when they said that the human nature of Christ, from the moment of its union with the deity, had become uncreated (*actistetae*).[7] By implication the incarnation was actually shifted to eternity, and the historical appearance of Christ was volatilized into a symbol of an eternal idea.

But the theologians who took their position in the Chalcedonian confession also faced serious difficulties. For, looking at the dignity and honor to which the human nature in Christ was elevated by its intimate union with the Logos, one had to conceive of it as being endowed with various extraordinary gifts and powers. Yet, in order to achieve the work of salvation in union with the Logos, that same human nature had to be conceived as being so weak and lowly that it not only remained purely human but could even suffer and die. At an early stage, therefore, it became customary, in considering the person of Christ after the two natures had been treated, to speak first of the gifts of his human nature and then of its defects.[8] Under the heading of the gifts, it was then explained that Christ possessed the fullness of grace and truth. Indeed, according to his human nature, he was not omniscient and omnipotent, but from the moment of his conception he did possess an extraordinary measure of knowledge and power. All at once he received all the perfections and gifts of the Spirit, so that in a real sense they could not be increased. The increase of which Luke 2:52 speaks relates only to the effects "to the extent, that is, that a person performs wiser and more virtuous works."[9] In a word, on earth Christ was already a person with full understanding (*comprehensor*) who, like the blessed in heaven, enjoyed the vision of God and who therefore did not have to exercise faith and hope. At the same time, in both soul and body, he had a variety of defects.[10] The defects of the body consisted especially in his susceptibility to suffering and death and those of the soul in the emotions of sorrow and grief, fear, and anger. In a sense these defects are inherent in human nature, as they were also characteristic of Adam as a natural human being. But to the extent Christ would also have had the right and power to assume a human nature without these defects, one can say they are based on his free will.[11]

This entire theory of gifts and defects, however, contains an antinomy that is most clearly manifest in the fact that Christ in his human nature is at the same time called a pilgrim (*viator*) *and* a person with full knowledge (*comprehensor*).

7. F. Loofs, *Leitfaden zum Studium der Dogmengeschichte*, 4th ed. (Halle a.S.: M. Niemeyer, 1906), 303.

8. John of Damascus, *Expositions of the Orthodox Faith*, III, 17ff.; P. Lombard, *Sent.*, III, 9–17; T. Aquinas, *Summa theol.*, III, qu. 7–15; Bonaventure, *Breviloquium*, IV, 5–10.

9. T. Aquinas, *Summa theol.*, II, qu. 7

10. Ibid., III, qu. 14, 15.

11. Ibid., III, qu. 14, 2, 3.

In his soul or rather his mind, he was a person with full knowledge, contemplated and delighted in the enjoyment of God, and possessed perfect blessedness. But in terms of his lower soul and body (for his soul was susceptible to suffering and his body was susceptible to suffering and death), he was a pilgrim (*viator*) and strove to achieve perfect, soul-and-body-embracing blessedness.[12] From this it followed that also according to his human nature—on account of its intimate union with the Logos—Christ was worthy of divine worship, a worship that was permitted to extend even to special parts of his body: his heart, flesh, and blood.[13] It also followed that Christ's suffering remained restricted to the "lower" soul and to the body.[14] Implied, finally, was that his exaltation did not extend to the "higher" soul of Christ but was similarly restricted to his "lower" soul and body. For though the "higher" soul of Christ was glorious from the moment of conception, in the state of humiliation this glory did not flow down to his body. But when he rose from the dead, his body immediately began to participate in the glory he already possessed in his soul,[15] though that body forever keeps the marks of the wounds as proofs of his victory.[16] At the exaltation his soul, full of divinity,[17] allowed the body—to the extent that it was capable of it—to share in that fullness. For although this body, according to its material nature, is beneath the spiritual substances, on account of the dignity of its union with the deity, it far surpasses these spiritual substances in dignity. "The more noble a being, the more exalted should be the place assigned to it."[18]

[397] Lutheran theology later entangled itself in even much greater difficulties. For whereas the scholastics still spoke only of a communication of extraordinary divine gifts to the human nature of Christ, the Lutherans, as a result of their doctrine of the Lord's Supper, arrived at the confession that certain divine attributes were also given to it.[19] As a result, they were even less able than the Catholics to do justice to the distinction between Christ's state of humiliation and his state of exaltation. At the same moment, certainly, at which the Logos assumed the human nature, it made that nature capable of the indwelling of the fullness of deity and the communication of the divine attributes. Although a moment later the God-man again put these attributes aside in respect to their use or at least to

12. Ibid., III, qu. 15, 10.

13. Cf. above, 316–19, 407–10 (##373, 392).

14. Cf. above, 416–17 (#394).

15. T. Aquinas, *Summa theol.*, qu. 54, 2; "Third, as stated previously, at the first moment of conception, Christ's soul was glorious in the perfect enjoyment of divinity. It was by way of exception, therefore, that the glory of his soul did not overflow into his body; but this was in order that the mystery of our redemption might be accomplished through the passion of Christ. As soon as the mystery of his passion and death was fulfilled and Christ's body once more united to his soul, from his soul glory immediately overflowed into his body. Thus his was a glorious body."

16. Ibid., III, qu. 54, 4.

17. Ibid., III, qu. 59, 4.

18. Ibid., III, qu. 57, 5.

19. Cf. above, 257–58 (#357).

their public use, he nevertheless kept them. Among the Lutherans, accordingly, the state of exaltation cannot be anything other than a resumption of the use or the public use of the divine attributes laid aside earlier. Hence at his exaltation, Christ received nothing he did not have already. "In his exaltation Christ was not given a new power, virtue, or majesty, which he did not have before, but only the full faculty of administering his kingdom, which he received through that union itself."[20] This resumption of the use of the divine attributes occurred, according to the Lutherans, at the moment of vivification, which, accordingly, is the first step of his exaltation. Gerhard, Quenstedt, and others indeed called the descent into hell the first step; but inasmuch as this descent specifically occurred according to Christ's human nature in both soul and body, the vivification has to precede it; and Buddeus as well as others therefore rightly give it first place in the state of exaltation.[21] Concerning this vivification, the Lutherans further affirm that it took place not only by Christ's divine but also by his human nature. Although the latter did not have the power to do this of itself, from the moment of the incarnation it did possess the divine attributes, which included the power to make alive. And so the soul of Christ, by the power of divinity personally communicated to it, made alive its very own temple, the body.[22] In that same moment of vivification, Christ, according to his human nature, further resumed the use of all the divine attributes that it received in the incarnation but that, in the exinanition (self-emptying), it had put aside, at least as the use or the public use of them is concerned. This means that at that same moment it regained the use of omniscience, omnipotence, omnipresence, and the power to make alive.[23]

From this it follows that in Lutheran theology the degrees of exaltation can really not be distinct consecutive steps. At the moment of vivification the human nature of Christ, by its union with the Logos, was immediately omnipotent, omniscient, and omnipresent. The descent into hell, which Lutherans characterize as belonging to Christ's exaltation, is a manifestation of Christ's divine majesty in hell. The resurrection is merely a manifestation of resurrection to humans.[24] Both, accordingly, took place with the sepulcher closed, just as Jesus' appearance to the disciples took place behind closed doors (John 20:19).[25] The ascension is indeed called "a true and real change of location" insofar as Christ ascended visibly before the eyes of his disciples, but it is nevertheless only a visible and local—by no means an invisible—absence of the body of Christ on earth, for also in his human

---

20. J. A. Quenstedt, *Theologia*, III, 368; cf. J. Gerhard, *Loci theol.*, IV, §§306ff., 329; D. Hollaz, *Examen theologicum acroamaticum* (Rostock and Leipzig: Russworm, 1718), 774; J. Buddeus, *Institutiones theologiae dogmaticae* (Leipzig: T. Fritsch, 1723), 788; M. Schneckenburger, *Zur kirchlichen Christologie* (Pforzheim: Flammer & Hoffmann, 1848), 93–114.

21. J. Buddeus, *Inst. theol.*, 789; cf. C. Vitringa, *Doctr. christ.*, V, 573.

22. J. A. Quenstedt, *Theologia*, III, 435.

23. Ibid., III, 154–98.

24. J. Buddeus, *Inst. theol.*, 789.

25. J. A. Quenstedt, *Theologia*, III, 441.

nature Christ is and remains omnipresent, be it in an invisible manner.[26] The seat at the right hand of God, finally, consists in the fact that Christ, specifically in his human nature, participates in the divine, infinite, and measureless power and majesty of God, especially in his omnipresence, and exercises that power in his kingdom of grace and power.[27] If one now recalls that all these attributes were communicated to Christ's human nature at the moment of his incarnation and that he indeed put aside the use but never the possession of these attributes, it is evident that according to the Lutheran view nothing is communicated to Christ in the state of exaltation that he did not already possess from the moment of his conception. Immediately at the moment of his incarnation, Christ *is* that which he could *become*. All at once, also according to his human nature, he is complete, fully matured (τελειος). In his case no development is possible. The exaltation was already present at his conception and hence cannot be regarded as a reward. At this point Lutheran doctrine is akin to that of Rome, which already has Christ be "one with full knowledge" (*comprehensor*) here on earth and has all the gifts of which human nature is capable communicated to him at his incarnation. And it serves to defend the very same religious interest: the bodily presence of Christ in the Lord's Supper.

Common to Roman Catholic and Lutheran theology, then, is the distinction between an ideal and an empirical human nature, one that Christ already possessed in the state of humiliation. But this distinction in any case occurs in time and after the incarnation. Just as in Gnosticism and Monophysitism in antiquity, so among certain Anabaptists in the age of the Reformation the idea again arose that this ideal human nature could not have originated in time but existed already before time. Hofmann, for example, taught that Christ did not assume his flesh from Mary but had brought it with him from heaven. He, consequently, had to arrive at a Docetic view of the entire state of humiliation. Frank strayed even further in the direction of pantheism when he called the incarnation an eternal one and had God's essence indwell every person and the whole of humankind. And Schwenckfeld, though he rejected both of these errors, as a result of his strong polemic against the duality of Christ's natures came to adopt the view that Christ at his incarnation so filled his human nature with grace and truth that it had been spiritualized already from the beginning and was totally divinized throughout the course of his life, particularly at his resurrection.[28]

A very different position was that taken by the Socinians. Proceeding from the absolute antithesis between the infinite and the finite, they denied the incarna-

26. J. Gerhard, *Loci theol.*, IV, §219; XXVIII, §24; J. A. Quenstedt, *Theologia*, III, 380; J. Buddeus, *Inst. theol.*, 796; F. A. Philippi, *Kirchliche Glaubenslehre*, 3rd ed., 7 vols. in 10 (Gütersloh: Bertelsmann, 1870–90), IV, 185; cf. C. Vitringa, *Doctr. christ.*, V, 601; B. de Moor, *Comm. theol.*, IV, 246.

27. J. A. Quenstedt, *Theologia*, III, 383–88, 443–50; J. Gerhard, *Loci theol.*, IV, §218; J. Buddeus, *Inst. theol.*, 797.

28. H. W. Erbkam, *Geschichte der protestantischen Sekten im Zeitalter der Reformation* (Hamburg and Gotha: Perthes, 1848), 445ff.

tion and essential deity of Christ. Christ was only a human being, but was born in an extraordinary manner (God having created the semen in Mary's womb), granted divine revelations (snatched up into heaven), had received a complete revelation of the will of God, and carried it out to the very end. But by this obedience he had merited the resurrection and even more the ascension as his reward, gained all power in heaven and earth, and received the rank and office of God. On earth he was only a prophet, but in his exaltation he became a king, *able* to confer immortality and dominion on those who follow him, and a priest also *willing* to do this.[29]

The supernatural elements that, contrary to its own principle, Socinianism still retained in the person and work of Christ were removed by rationalism. Consequently, in modern theology, what is left of the two states is only that Christ, faithful to his moral calling to the point of death, is glorified by God in the sense that by his word and spirit he lives on in the church and progressively renews humankind into a kingdom of God. The resurrection and ascension, the seat at the right hand of God, and the coming again for judgment are not facts but merely graphic representations of the idea that the moral ideal that Christ pursued corresponds to the will of God and will be realized by him.[30]

THE REFORMED VIEW: EXALTATION THROUGH OBEDIENCE

[398] With regard to the two states (*status duplex*), Reformed theology was in a favorable position. For, in the first place, it maintained that Christ was a mediator in accordance with both natures. It not only rejected the opinion of Osiander, who taught that Christ was a mediator only according to his divine nature, and the sentiment of Stancarus, who asserted that Christ was a mediator only according to his human nature.[31] Moreover, it opposed the scholastic and Roman Catholic doctrine according to which the two natures in Christ were indeed "the principle that performed the works of the mediator," but only the human nature of Christ was "the principle by which the works were accomplished by the mediator."[32] If the view of Lombard, Aquinas, and others that Christ was a mediator only according to his human nature was denied and qualified that way,

---

29. O. Fock, *Der Socinianismus* (Kiel: C. Schröder, 1847), 509ff., 640ff.

30. J. A. L. Wegscheider, *Institutiones theologiae christianae dogmaticae* (Halle: Gebauer, 1819), §131; F. Schleiermacher, *The Christian Faith* (Edinburgh: T&T Clark, 1989), §99, 105; A. Schweizer, *Christliche Glaubenslehre* (Leipzig: S. Hirzel, 1863–72), §123; A. E. Biedermann, *Christliche Dogmatik* (Zürich: Füssli, 1869), §§826–28; D. F. Strauss, *Die christliche Glaubenslehre,* 2 vols. (Tübingen: C. F. Osiander, 1840–41), §§63–66; R. A. Lipsius, *Lehrbuch der evangelisch-protestantischen Dogmatik* (Braunschweig: C. A. Schwetschke, 1893), §669; F. Nitzsch, *Lehrbuch der evangelischen Dogmatik,* prepared by Horst Stephan, 3rd ed. (Tübingen: J. C. B. Mohr, 1902), 522.

31. C. Vitringa, *Doctr. christ.,* V, 452; cf. S. Curcellaeus, *Opera theologicae* (Amsterdam: Elsevir, 1675), 459.

32. See above, 363–66 (#381).

it seems to differ little from the Reformed position. Yet against the Catholic view, it objected that the two natures were not only necessary with a view to qualifying the person but equally with a view to describing the very function of the office of the mediator. If the office of mediator can only be fulfilled by the human nature, it follows that also persons other than Christ, be it in a lesser degree and on a lower level, can act as mediators. But the works of the mediator, both in the state of exaltation (regeneration, conversion, sanctification, and so on) and in the state of humiliation, are of such a nature that they can only be accomplished by one who is simultaneously truly God and truly human (Acts 20:28 KJV; Heb. 9:11ff.; 1 John 1:7).[33] Reformed theology, accordingly, had the advantage that in the doctrine of the two states, it could maintain to the end not only the duality of and the distinction between the two natures but the unity of the person. In both states it was one and the same subject who was humiliated and exalted. Not only the human but also the divine nature participated in both states.

Lutheran theologians, however, picture this matter differently. In the incarnation they distinguish between two—not temporally but logically distinct—moments: the incarnation (the assumption of flesh) and the exinanition (the conception in the womb). The subject of the former is only the Logos (unfleshed, ἀσαρκος) and consists in the assumption of human nature, a nature that is indeed finite and limited but, due to the personal union, clothed with majesty and equipped with divine attributes. In contrast, the exinanition, which is necessary to the effectuation of our salvation, has as its subject the Logos enfleshed (ἐνσαρκος) and consists in the laying aside (either by concealment [κρυψις] according to the Tübingen position or by self-emptying [κενωσις] according to the Giessen position) of the use of these divine attributes.[34] If this distinction should have any real meaning, it would have to lead to the conclusion (drawn by some Anabaptists) that the incarnation, viewed in isolation, was a transcendent, metaphysical, eternal act. The Lutherans, of course, were violently opposed to this notion, but the distinction of the two moments in the incarnation plunged them into an impasse from which (as is evident from the conflict between the Tübingen and the Giessen theologians) there was no escape. Granted, the Reformed still argued as well over the question whether the incarnation as such was or was not part of the state of humiliation. But this argument was purely academic and had hardly any influence on their view of the actual state of the human nature that Christ assumed. In any case all Reformed theologians rejected the Lutheran doctrine of the communication of the divine attributes to the human nature and always construed the latter as a nature that was weak, susceptible to suffering and death, like us in every respect barring sin, and not glorified until the resurrection. Consequently, in reference to Jesus they could assume a purely human and genuine development, as Luke 2:40, 52 indisputably teaches, and also acknowledge that Christ was the subject

33. P. van Mastricht, *Theoretico-practica theologia* (Utrecht: Appels, 1714), V, 2, 16, 21.
34. Cf. above, 257–58 (#357).

of humiliation and exaltation, in both natures. The assumption of human nature, of course, proceeded only from the Logos. He who existed in the form of God is the subject of the words "emptied himself" (Phil. 2:7); but the moment the Logos had assumed human nature, he became the subject, in both natures, of the humiliation and exaltation that followed.

With respect to the question in what way and to what extent the divine nature could participate in Christ's humiliation and exaltation, Reformed theologians, naturally, had to be extremely cautious. Maintaining that the mediatorial works had been accomplished in both states by the one person with two natures, and with a view to the immutability of God, they could not for a moment grant that the κένωσις (self-emptying) consisted in putting aside some or all of the divine attributes. Christ remained who he was even when he became what he was not. The theologians of the Reformed confession, accordingly, unanimously taught that Christ's humiliation according to his divine nature consisted in the fact that (1) in the pact of salvation he had from all eternity voluntarily taken upon himself to be the acquisitor and administrator of our salvation and thus the Servant of the Lord; that (2) in the fullness of time he assumed the human nature, one that was like ours in all respects, only excepting sin; that (3) he laid aside the divine majesty and glory, the form of God, in which he existed before the incarnation, or rather concealed it behind the form of a servant in which he went about on earth; and that (4) during his humiliation he never for a moment used his divine power and divine attributes to please himself and to defeat his enemies. He fought and won with no other weapon than the cross. Self-denial was the secret of his life.[35] To this the state of exaltation corresponds: it involved both natures and consisted in the fact that now Christ caused also his human nature—to the extent it was capable of it—to share in the glory that he as the Son had with the Father from all eternity.

A second advantage Reformed theology possessed in the doctrine of the two states was that it could fully permit to come into its own the intimate connection that Scripture makes between the state of humiliation and that of exaltation, and conceive the exaltation itself as an exaltation in the true sense of the word. At an early stage already the question was discussed in dogmatics whether Christ by his perfect obedience had also merited something for himself. Anselm said that by his nonobligatory and totally voluntary death, Christ indeed merited a reward but that, since he himself already possessed all things, he had relinquished it to his own.[36] Most scholastics as well as most Roman Catholic theologians, however, responded to the question by saying that Christ in his humiliation had

35. D. Chamier, *Panstratiae catholicae,* 4 vols. (Geneva: Rouer, 1626), II, 7, 3; M. F. Wendelin, *Exercitationes theologiae* (Kassel: Schaedewitz, 1652), ex. 66; P. van Mastricht, *Theologia,* V, 2, 16ff., 22ff., 9, 4; H. Witsius, *The Oeconomy of Covenants between God and Man,* 3 vols. (New York: Lee & Stokes, 1789), II, 3, 7; F. Turretin, *Institutes of Elenctic Theology,* XIV, 2; B. de Moor, *Comm. theol.,* III, 585ff.; IV, 21ff.; C. Vitringa, *Doctr. christ.,* V, 457.

36. Anselm, *Why God Became Man,* II, 19.

very definitely merited something for himself and that he also really obtained it in his exaltation. But because they ascribed the fullness of grace and truth to Christ's human nature already from the moment of conception and still spoke only of defects in the "lower" soul and body of Christ, they could let the reward of exaltation consist only in that the grace that Christ possessed in his spirit now also flowed over into his soul and body and caused these to share in the glory.[37] But even in this restricted sense, the Lutherans could not speak of any reward and exaltation for Christ. For according to them, the human nature of Christ shared in the divine attributes of omnipresence, omniscience, and omnipotence already from the moment of the incarnation. It therefore first received these attributes not as a reward for the mediatorial work done in the state of humiliation but already beforehand, in virtue of its union with the divine nature, and also kept them throughout, be it that in his humiliation Christ did not make use of them, at least no public use. The exaltation, therefore, was not a true and real exaltation, but only a matter of using, or publicly using, that which he already possessed from the beginning. It was not the outcome of an antecedent human development but merely a glorious manifestation of what he already was and possessed in secret.[38] Also among the Reformed there were those who said that Christ acquired nothing for himself but everything for us, citing all those texts in Scripture where the work of Christ is related to his people (Matt. 1:21; John 17:19; 1 Cor. 1:30; 1 Tim. 1:15; etc.).[39]

[399] But a great many Reformed theologians believed otherwise and answered the above question in the affirmative. In their opinion, the answer to Christ's prayer (John 11:42; Heb. 5:7) and especially the entire state of exaltation from the resurrection to his coming again for judgment is a reward for the work that he accomplished as the Servant of the Lord in the days of his humiliation.[40] And,

37. P. Lombard, *Sent.*, III, 18; T. Aquinas, *Summa theol.*, III, qu. 19, art. 3; qu. 48, art. 1; qu. 49, art. 6; Bonaventure, *Breviloquium*, IV, 7; R. Bellarmine, "De Christo," *Controversiis*, V, 9, 10; M. Becanus, *Summa theologiae scholasticae* (Rouen: I. Behovrt, 1651), III, tr. 1, c. 14, qu. 5; idem, *Manuale controversiarum huius temporis* (Wurzburg: Johannes Volmar, 1626), III, 2, qu. 4; C. Pesch, *Praelectiones dogmaticae,* 9 vols. (Freiburg: Herder, 1902–10), IV, 226; G. M. Jansen, *Praelectiones theologiae dogmaticae,* 3 vols. in 2 (Utrecht: Van Rossum, 1875–79), II, 736; cf. above, 427–29 (#397).

38. J. Gerhard, *Loci theologici,* ed. E. Preuss, 9 vols. (Berlin: G. Schlawitz, 1863–75), IV, 329; J. Quenstedt, *Theologia*, III, 324; D. Hollaz, *Examen,* 748; J. F. Buddeus, *Inst. theol.,* 787.

39. J. Calvin, *Institutes,* II.xvii.6; idem, *Commentary,* on Phil. 2:9; A. Polanus, *Syntagma theologiae christianae,* 5th ed. (Hanover: Aubry, 1624), VI, 26; F. Junius, *Theses theologicae,* in *Opuscula* (Amsterdam: F. Muller, 1882), 29, 11; D. Chamier, *Panstr. cath.,* II, 7, 8; S. Maresius, *Systema theologicum* (Groningen: Aemilium Spinneker, 1673), 45; cf. marginal notes of the *Statenvertaling* [Dutch Authorized Version] on Phil. 2:9.

40. J. Zanchi, *De operum theologicorum,* 8 vols. (Geneva: Samuel Crispini, 1617), VI, 121; VIII, 477, 502; J. Piscator, *Commentarii in omnes libros Veteris Testimenti* (Herborn: Christopher Corvinus, 1646), on Phil. 2:9; F. Gomarus, *Opera theologica omnia* (Amsterdam: J. Jansson, 1664), I, 230ff.; J. Cloppenburg, *Theologica opera omnia,* 2 vols. (Amsterdam: Borstius, 1684), I, 305, 888; A. Rivetus, *Operum theologicorum,* 3 vols. (Rotterdam: Leers, 1651–60), II, 836; G. Voetius, *Selectae disputationes theologicae,* 5 vols. (Utrecht, 1648–69), II, 265–67; P. van Mastricht, *Theologia,* V, 14, 7; J. H. Heidegger, *Corpus theologiae christianae,* 2 vols. (Zürich: J. H. Bodmer, 1700), XVIII, 39; B. de Moor, *Comm. theol.,* III, 600; C. Vitringa, *Doctr. christ.,* V, 585ff.

given the teaching of Scripture, no other answer is possible. For over and over it presents the state of humiliation as the way and the means by which alone Christ can attain his exaltation (Isa. 53:10–12; Matt. 23:12; Luke 24:26; John 10:17; 17:4–5; Phil. 2:9; Heb. 2:10; 12:2). The preposition διο (therefore) in Philippians 2:9 refers not to the order and logic but specifically to the meritorious cause of the exaltation. *Because* Christ humbled himself so deeply, *therefore* God has so highly exalted him. Especially the Letter to the Hebrews repeatedly puts a heavy accent on this meritorious connection between Christ's humiliation and exaltation (1:3; 2:9–10; 5:7–10; 10:12; 12:2). Christ himself was "sanctified" by suffering. This does not mean that he was consecrated to God or made morally perfect; it means "perfected, brought to full wisdom and maturity," made τελειος, which consists in his now being crowned with honor and glory (2:9), being seated as high priest at the right hand of Majesty in the highest heaven (8:1), having attained the joy for which he endured the cross and despised the shame (12:2), and becoming the source of eternal salvation to all who obey him (5:9).

The reason why many theologians objected to speaking of merit in reference to Christ lay in their opposition to the Socinians, who were prepared to grant royal dignity and the rank of deity only in Christ's state of exaltation. And we must join these theologians in firmly rejecting that view. For Scripture states repeatedly that in the beginning he was with God and himself God (John 1:1ff.; 17:5; Rom. 8:3; 2 Cor. 8:9; Gal. 4:4; Col. 2:9; Heb. 1:3; etc.), and that from eternity he had been anointed prophet, priest, and king by the Father and was active as such already in the days of the Old Testament and further again during his sojourn on earth (2 Tim. 1:9; Titus 3:4; Heb. 13:8; 1 Peter 1:11, 20). Hence, what Christ obtained for himself in the state of exaltation cannot have consisted in the divine nature or the rank of deity, nor in the office of prophet, priest, and king, an office based on divine election and appointment. Rather, it consisted in the exaltation itself, in the resurrection, ascension, seating at God's right hand, and the return for judgment; in other words, in the mediatorial glory to which he was raised in both natures. He did not possess that glory beforehand but obtained it at his exaltation. And this exaltation, therefore, was not mere appearance, no mere manifestation of what he already was internally before, but the attainment of what he did not yet possess in the state of humiliation: an exaltation in an objective and real sense. On this point all the Reformed were in agreement, knowing that with this position they stood on the firm foundation of Scripture.[41]

After all, according to Romans 1:3, Christ descended from David κατα σαρκα, that is, in the way of the flesh, by being born of a woman (Gal. 4:4); but κατα πνευμα άγιωσυνης, that is, according to the Spirit of holiness, who dwelt in him and guided him throughout his life, he was designated Son of God in power by the resurrection (cf. Acts 17:31). Birth and resurrection are opposed to each other

41. Cf. G. Voetius, *Select. disp.*, II, 277.

here.[42] By his birth Christ became the offspring of David (Rom. 9:5), assumed "the likeness of sinful flesh" (Rom. 8:3), became weak (2 Cor. 13:4); but by the resurrection he was openly designated Son of God. That is not to say and cannot mean that at that moment he first received the divine nature or the rank and name of God, for the opposite is clear from Romans 1:3; 8:3, 32; Galatians 4:4; and others. Rather, whereas at his incarnation he exchanged "the form of God" (μορφη θεου, Phil. 2:6) for the "form of a servant" (μορφη δουλου, Phil. 2:7), at the resurrection he received the glory that according to his Godhead he already had before (John 17:2, 24), became the Lord of glory (1 Cor. 2:8), the power of God (1 Cor. 1:24), obtained a name above every name, that is, the name of "Lord" (κυριος) (John 20:28; Acts 2:36; 1 Cor. 12:3; Phil. 2:9–10), and thereby the κυριοτης, the right, the authority, and the power to exercise lordship over all creatures as mediator, prophet, priest, and king, to subdue his enemies, to gather his people, and to regain the fallen creation for God (Pss. 2, 72, 110; Matt. 28:18; 1 Cor. 15:21ff.; Eph. 1:20–23; Phil. 2:9–11;[43] Heb. 1:3f.; 1 Pet. 3:22; Rev. 1:5; etc.). In the resurrection God openly appointed him Son of God, Lord, King, Mediator, saying to him: "You are my Son; today I have begotten you" (Acts 2:33, 36; 3:15; 5:31; 13:33; 17:31; Heb. 1:5).

By his resurrection Christ in fact entered a new state. As the mediator he has been exalted at God's right hand above all creatures. In that exaltation also his divine nature shares in a sense. Just as not only the human nature of Christ but also the person of the Son was the subject of the humiliation, so that same person is the subject of the exaltation in both his natures. For he had put aside "the form of God" (μορφη θεου) that was his and concealed his divine nature behind the garment of a weak human nature; no one saw in him or could see in him the Only Begotten of the Father, except with the eye of faith (John 1:14). But now, in the state of exaltation, his divine glory radiates outward for all to see. Those who see him now have to confess that Christ is Lord to the glory of God the Father. But also his human nature shares in that exaltation. The spirit of holiness (πνευμα αγιωσυνης) already dwelt in Christ before his resurrection from the time of his conception, for he was conceived by the Holy Spirit (Luke 1:35), he was full of the Holy Spirit (Luke 4:1), received him unstintingly (John 3:34 etc.; cf. Matt. 12:18, 28; Luke 4:14; Acts 1:2; 4:27; 10:38). But this glory, which Christ possessed inwardly, still could not manifest itself outwardly. He was flesh, and by virtue of the weakness of the flesh, he was killed on the cross (2 Cor. 13:4). But in death he put aside that weakness and broke off his connection with sin and death. God, who gave his own Son for us in death and therein executed his judgment on sin, by his Spirit—who as the πνευμα αγιωσυνης dwells in Christ and also in all believers (Rom. 8:11)—raised him from the dead in order that he would no longer live in the weakness of the flesh but in the power of the Spirit. He was indeed put to

---

42. Bröse, "Zur Auslegung von Röm. 1:3," *Neue kirchliche Zeitschrift* (1899): 562–73.

43. J. Kögel, *Christus der Herr: Erläuterungen zu Philipper 2,5–11* (Gütersloh: Bertelsmann, 1908).

death in the flesh, therefore, but made alive in the Spirit (1 Pet. 3:18). Also when he was flesh, the Spirit of God dwelt in Christ as the dominant power of his life, doing so as the πνευμα αγιωσυνης, so that Christ always followed the guidance of that Spirit and remained obedient to the Father unto death. At the resurrection, therefore, that Spirit must also manifest himself in Christ as the Spirit of life (πνευμα ζωης), who completely overcomes death in Christ and one day also in believers (Rom. 8:11). Christ has now been raised so far above all fleshly weakness that, by the resurrection, he has become a life-giving Spirit (πνευμα ζωοποιουν, 1 Cor. 15:45). Granted, even after the resurrection, he still has a body (σωμα); he is the same Jesus (Acts 9:5; Rom. 4:24; 8:11; 1 Cor. 12:4–6; 2 Cor. 4:5f.); the second and last Adam (1 Cor. 15:45).[44] He has the same σωμα with which he was raised, but it is now a σωμα πνευματικον (spiritual body). In the place of the corruption, dishonor, and weakness, which marked his natural body (σωμα ψυχικον), and the flesh (σαρξ), that spiritual body has very different attributes, namely, imperishability, glory, and power (1 Cor. 15:42ff.; Phil. 3:21).

Indeed, in 2 Corinthians 3:17, Paul says "The Lord is the Spirit." It is not that the apostle here wishes to give a description of Christ's substantial being, but he makes this statement in support of his argument that Christians are free from the law. That freedom, after all, has its ground in the fact that the Lord, that is, the exalted Christ, is the Spirit: the Spirit of God dwells in Christ so absolutely and is so intimately united with him that all unfreedom is thereby terminated, for where the Spirit of the Lord is, there is freedom. The phrase "the Spirit of the Lord" (πνευμα κυριου) is proof that in the first part of the verse, Paul is not identifying Christ with the Spirit. The Holy Spirit is the Spirit of Christ because he dwells in Christ himself and because through him Christ communicates himself to his own (v. 18).[45] And thus Christ is now he in whom all the "fullness of deity dwells bodily" (Col. 2:9; 1:19). He is the visible image of the invisible God (Col. 1:15). The divine glory is now manifest in his human nature and radiates from his face (2 Cor. 3:18; 4:4, 6).

RESURRECTION AND APPEARANCES

[400] If, in keeping with the Reformed confession, the descent into hell belongs to the state of humiliation, we may distinguish in the exaltation four so-called steps: the resurrection, the ascension, the seating at God's right hand, and the return for judgment. The resurrection was the event in which Christ by his divine power revived his dead body, united it with his soul, and thus left the tomb. As a rule the word αναστασις is used for this, not only with reference to Christ but

---

44. W. Lütgert, "Der Mensch aus dem Himmel," in *Greifswalder Studien,* ed. Samuel Oettli and Hermann Cremer (Gütersloh: Bertelsmann, 1895), 207–28.

45. J. Glöel, *Der heilige Geist in der Heilsverkündigung des Paulus* (Halle: M. Niemeyer, 1888), 113ff.; cf. U. Holzmeister, *Dominus autem Spiritus est, 2 Cor. 3,17: Eine exegetische Untersuchung mit einer Übersicht über die Geschichte der Erklärung dieser Stelle* (Innsbruck: Rauch, 1908).

also with reference to people in general (Matt. 22:31 etc.). This alone proves the incorrectness of the conjecture that this word originally meant "the appointment of Christ to the just established kingdom of God,"[46] for it was a fixed term for "the resurrection of the dead," although this last addition was often omitted. But frequently it is augmented with the further qualification "from the dead" (των νεκρων or ἐκ των νεκρων). When this phrase is added to [the term for] the resurrection of Jesus, it proves that in his death Jesus belonged among the dead and at his resurrection returned from their domain to the land of the living.

The word implies, however, not at all that those who rise again do so by their own power, but rather that they, who are being raised by God, now also themselves arise. In the case of Jesus, however, this word acquires another and deeper sense. For Jesus not only repeatedly predicted his own resurrection (Matt. 20:19), or his being raised by the Father (Matt. 16:21), but he also said about himself that he would raise up the temple of his body in three days (John 2:19–21), that he had power to lay down his life and to take it up again (John 10:18), that he himself was the resurrection and the life (John 11:25). Although others were raised before him in time, he is certainly "the first to rise from the dead" (Acts 26:23), "the firstfruits of those who have fallen asleep" (1 Cor. 15:20), "the firstborn from the dead" (Col. 1:18; Rev. 1:5). For he was also the firstborn of every creature (Col. 1:18; Rev. 1:5), the head and first principle of all that has been created, and derived from this priority the power to become the firstborn among many brethren (Rom. 8:29). In death his divine nature remained most intimately united with his human soul and body and possessed the omnipotent ability to bring forth life out of death. Also, by his suffering and death, he obtained the right to the resurrection, and hence also in his exaltation he made no use of his power other than in the way of justice. Inasmuch as by one human being death came into the world, so also the resurrection from the dead was made into the principle of eternal life by a human being (1 Cor. 15:21). As the firstborn in this sense, therefore, Christ is also raised up to eternal life. Though crucified in weakness, he now lives by the power of God (2 Cor. 13:4). The death he died, he died to sin, once for all, but the life he lives, he now lives to God. He can never die again because death no longer has dominion over him (Rom. 6:9, 10). He died, but now he lives forevermore and has the keys of death and Hades (Rev. 1:18).

No less frequently is the resurrection of Christ attributed to the power of the Father. Jesus himself speaks of it that way (Matt. 16:21 etc.), and in Acts and the letters of the apostles this is even the usual way of putting it (Acts 2:24, 32; 3:26; 5:30; 13:37; Rom. 4:25; 8:11, 34; 1 Cor. 6:14; 15:13ff.; etc.). The resurrection was necessary not only with a view to Christ's own power, authority, and right, but equally in virtue of God's counsel and will. The "must" in Luke 24:26 refers

46. So W. B. Smith, *Der vorchristliche Jesus nebst weiteren Vorstudien zur Entstehungsgeschichte des Urchristentums* (Giessen: Alfred Töpfelmann, 1906); H. U. Meyboom, "Loman Redivivus," *Theologische Tijdschrift* 41 (1907): 1–17.

not only to Christ's suffering but also to his entering into glory. In the counsel of God, it was not possible for Christ to be held by death, and therefore God raised him up, having freed him from the pangs of death (Acts 2:24). Death, as it were, ensnared Christ with its pangs (ὠδῖνες, following the Septuagint translation of the Hebrew, "bands" or "cords"; Ps. 18:5), but those pangs were the labor pains of the resurrection, which would be undone by God in the moment of resurrection. And thus, in God's good pleasure, Christ became the firstborn from the dead. His resurrection was a birth from death and hence a victory over death and over him who had the power of death, the devil (1 Cor. 15:21f.; Heb. 2:14; 2 Tim. 1:10).

From the beginning the resurrection of Christ was an enormously important constituent of the faith of the church: without that faith it would never have started. For all the disciples had been offended by the cross. When Jesus was taken prisoner and killed, they had fled (Mark 14:50) and gone into hiding. But their faith revived when they learned that Jesus had risen. They now reconsidered the earlier life of Jesus in the light of the resurrection: how he had been anointed by God with the Holy Spirit and with power (Acts 4:27; 10:38), how by his works and wonders, he had borne witness to his messiahship (2:22; 10:38), had to die according to God's counsel (2:23; 4:28), and now they also understood that in his resurrection Jesus had been appointed Lord and Christ, Leader and Judge (2:20, 25, 36; 3:15; 4:26; 5:31; 10:42). No less strong is Paul's witness in his first letter to the church in Corinth (written around AD 53). There he says that he had delivered to the Corinthians what he himself had also received, a message that included that Christ died, was buried, and was raised on the third day in accordance with the Scriptures (1 Cor. 15:3–4). If in thinking about what Paul "received" we may include in it the witness to the resurrection he had heard from others, it is proof that belief in the resurrection belonged to the confession of the very earliest church and was encountered there by Paul after his conversion. Indeed, the resurrection is a fact to which all the apostles bear witness in their letters. An important mark of their apostolic office was that they had been witnesses of Jesus' resurrection (Luke 24:48; Acts 1:22; 2:32; 3:15; etc.); and in all four Gospels, the story of the resurrection occupies a smaller or larger place. The circumstances in which this event took place are described in very different ways, but their witness to the fact itself is unanimous.

Certainty concerning that resurrection rested for the believers on the appearances that they themselves had received or of which others in whom they had complete trust had told them (Luke 24:34; 1 Cor. 15:5ff.). Paul speaks of six appearances and mentions as the last of them the appearance he himself received, but in doing so he certainly did not intend to offer a complete list. Remarkable in this connection is that Paul knows of an appearance to James (probably James the Just, a brother of the Lord) that is mentioned nowhere else and to more than five hundred brothers at one time, most of whom were still alive; and, further, that he puts the appearance he himself received after Jesus' ascension on the same level and ascribes to it the same character as he did to the other appearances. Also noteworthy is that he limits the appearances both in time—for the one he received was the last—and in the persons to whom they were granted. In Paul, too, Christ was manifested, not to the people in general, but to the witnesses who had been chosen beforehand by God (Acts 1:3; 10:40–41; 13:31). The appearances were also limited as to locality and took place in either Jerusalem or Galilee. Nowadays many scholars try to represent the former as unhistorical on the basis of the Gospel of Mark, which originally ended with 16:8, with the undeniable intent the more easily to be able to explain the resurrection as a vision. But if Mark originally ended his Gospel with 16:8, this Gospel does not mention any appearances, and consequently one cannot tell whether it only assumed appearances in Galilee. It is further mistakenly inferred from Mark 14:50 that the disciples upon their flight immediately returned to Galilee and hence were no longer in Jerusalem on the morning of the resurrection. Mark 16:7 expressly states, however, that Jesus would *go before* them to Galilee. Finally, Matthew (28:9), Luke (24:13f.), and John (ch. 20) do speak of appearances in Jerusalem, which, like the appearances Paul mentions (aside from those to the five hundred brothers and to himself), probably also took place there. According to John, the appearances occurred during the first eight days in Jerusalem (20:26), where the disciples remained on account of the Passover, and ended with Jesus giving the Holy Spirit to his disciples and granting them apostolic authority (20:22–23).

The appearances probably took place in Jerusalem because the disciples refused to believe the report of the woman (Luke 24:11, 24–25; Mark 16:11, 13–14) and in this state of mind were certainly not inclined to go to Galilee with the expectation of seeing him there. But then followed the appearances in Galilee, with Jesus himself going there before his disciples (Mark 16:7). The disciples had to go there because they could not spend forty days in Jerusalem in fear and idleness. It was in Galilee that Jesus had spent most of his life and gained most of his disciples. There is nothing strange in the fact, therefore, that after his resurrection Jesus again went to Galilee for a time and appeared there to his disciples from time to time, teaching them about the things pertaining to the kingdom of God (Acts 1:3). And there is no reason to link Galilee with a hill on the Mount of Olives by Jerusalem and not with the familiar landscape [to the north].[47] Matthew (28:16ff.) and John (ch. 21) end their accounts with these appearances in Galilee and do not report the ascension. But according to Luke (24:19; Acts 1:4), the disciples had to remain in Jerusalem until they were clothed with power from on high. Luke makes no reference to the Galilean appearances at all. Jesus—during one of his appearances in Galilee—certainly must have charged his disciples to go back to Jerusalem and wait there "for the promise of the Father" (Acts 1:4). The ascension, in any case, again took place in the vicinity of Jerusalem.

47. On this point, cf. E. W. G. Masterman, "Mount of Olives," *DC*, II, 207, according to whom this entire topographical question is discussed at length by J. Lepsius, *Reden und Abhandlungen,* 4 vols. (Berlin: Reich-Christi Verlag, 1902), n. 7, 8.

Whereas the appearances were thus restricted in time, locality, and the persons to whom they came, the resurrection itself, according to the unanimous witness of all concerned, occurred on the third day. The formula "the third day" (Matt. 16:21; 20:19; etc.) alternates with "after three days" (Mark 8:31; 10:34; etc.) without implying any difference in duration (Gen. 42:17–18). But the expression "three days and three nights" (Matt. 12:40; 16:4) has to be understood figuratively and was chosen in these texts on account of the comparison with Jonah or as a general description of a very short period. How the disciples came unanimously to put the resurrection on the third day if it did not really take place is hard to say. This datum cannot be derived from the Old Testament, at least if the disciples did not already believe in the resurrection. If they derived it from Jesus' own prediction, it implies the belief that the prediction was also fulfilled in the fact of the resurrection. Mythology also fails here and has left not a single trace of having influenced this matter in the New Testament. Kirsopp Lake, accordingly, comes to the conclusion that this given must be considered "a reference to the experience of the women."[48] Something must have happened on that third day for the disciples to situate it so unanimously on that day. Add to this the empty tomb, the truth of which is nowadays recognized by almost everyone. But how can the emptiness of the tomb be explained if Christ did not actually arise with the same body he left behind in death? Certainly, the empty tomb as such is not the ground for belief in the resurrection, for in that case the appearances would be unnecessary. But for the reality of a physical resurrection, it is nevertheless of great significance.

For a time people believed they could explain the resurrection by assuming that Jesus only *appeared* to be dead (numerous rationalists, and later also Herder, Schleiermacher, Hase, Gfrörer) or by having Jesus' body disappear as a result of theft.[49] But these attempts have been virtually completely abandoned. Then, in the place of them, Strauss, Lang, Holsten, Hausrath, Renan, and others proposed the idea of a subjective vision as a way of explaining the faith of the disciples. But here, too, numerous difficulties arose. Such a subjective vision *presupposes* faith rather than produces it, and the disciples' state of mind was far from believing: they were despondent, dejected, in great doubt, and initially totally unwilling to believe the report of the resurrection. Furthermore, such a vision does not in any way imply faith in a resurrection, for then as well as later, many people have had visions of the dead without concluding that they had risen from the dead. In addition, such visions are almost always accompanied by and lead to psychological and physical abnormalities, but in the case of the apostles, we see no sign of such abnormalities. They are lifted out of their despondency and doubt, even though the risen Savior again leaves them after a few days, make courageous public ap-

48. Kirsopp Lake, *The Historical Evidence for the Resurrection of Jesus Christ* (London and New York: Williams & Norgate, 1907), 196.

49. Cf. (even now) Paul Rohrbach, *Die Berichte über die Auferstehung Jesu Christi* (Berlin: Georg Reimer, 1898).

pearances as his witnesses, and generate extraordinary activity. Finally—to say no more—the appearances of which the New Testament speaks all occur at a certain place and time and relate to specific persons: they form a series that begins on the third day and ends with the appearance to Paul and must, therefore—as opposed to possible visions—have had a distinct and identifiable character.[50]

For all these reasons, also the theory of a subjective vision has been gradually abandoned and exchanged for that of an objective vision. By this is meant that the glorified Christ himself gave his disciples the certainty of his continued life. He effected this either by working this certainty in their heart and letting the visions arise from this certainty or by effecting the objective visions in them and letting them draw the certainty concerning his continued existence from these visions. The appearances in these visions can then, to the degree that a greater or lesser value is assigned to the material component of the spirit, be construed more or less spiritually: Christ either appeared to them as a spiritual being without any bodily form or as more or less materialized in a body. But in no case did he appear to them in the same body he had left behind in death and assumed again in the resurrection. This theory, which Keim designated "the telegram from heaven," though it found considerable acceptance,[51] is open to no less serious objections than that of the subjective vision. In the first place, it fails to do justice to the testimonies of Scripture, specifically those concerning the empty tomb and the physical resurrection. Second, for the miracle of the physical resurrection, it substitutes another miracle, one that is much less acceptable and makes the glorified Christ responsible for the error in which the disciples were caught up from the beginning. For they all had the conviction that Christ had risen with the body that had been crucified and buried. Third, they make no mention whatever of the deity of Christ, regard him as an ordinary person, though a morally superior one, and actually say nothing about Jesus' appearances after his death that spiritism today does not consider possible and real for any number of deceased persons. By this process the Christian faith is explained in terms of superstition, pure religion in terms of magic, the grape in terms of the thorn, and the fig in terms of a thistle.

50. Thus, especially, T. Keim, *Geschichte Jesu von Nazara,* 3 vols. (Zürich: Füssli, 1867–72); cf. W. J. Sparrow Simpson, "Resurrection of Christ," *DC,* II, 511.

51. C. H. Weisse, *Die evangelische Geschichte,* 2 vols. (Leipzig: Breitkopf & Hartel, 1838), II, 432; T. Keim, *Geschichte Jesu von Nazara,* III, 605; A. Schweizer, *Christliche Glaubenslehre,* II, 216ff.; H. Lotze, *Microcosmus,* trans. Elizabeth Hamilton and E. E. Constance Jones (New York: Scribner & Welford, 1866), III, 365ff.; K. Ziegler, "Der Glaube an die Auferstehung Jesu Christi," *Zeitschrift für Theologie und Kirche* (1896): 219–64; M. W. T. Reischle, "Zur Frage nach der leiblichen Auferstehung Jesu Christi," *Christliche Welt* (1900): 3ff.; idem, *Leitsätze für eine akademische Vorlesung über die christliche Glaubenslehre* (Halle a.S.: Niemeyer, 1899), 99; A. von Harnack, *What Is Christianity?* 124ff.; *Dobschütz, Ostern und Pfingsten: Eine Studie zu 1 Kor. 15* (Leipzig, 1903); K. Lake, *Historical Evidence for the Resurrection of Jesus Christ,* 265–79; Wallis, "Die Erscheinungen des auferstehenden Christus," *Die Studierstube* (1906): 595–99; cf. L. Ihmels, *Die Auferstehung Jesu Christi* (Leipzig: Deichert, 1906); Horn, "Der Kampf um die leibliche Auferstehung des Herrn," *Neue kirchliche Zeitschrift* (1902): 241–49; T. Korff, *Die Auferstehung Christi und die radikale Theologie* (Halle: Strien, 1908); E. G. Steude, "Die neueren Verhandlungen über die Auferstehung Jesu Christi," *Der Beweis des Glaubens* 42 (1906): 46–58.

Finally, moreover, this theory is still connected with a philosophical and religious dualism between "spirit" and "matter," with a denial of death as the wages of sin, with a failure to appreciate the spiritual significance of the physical resurrection. What can hardly be doubted, however, is that the fact of Christ's physical resurrection sufficiently explains everything that is based on it: the empty tomb, the firm faith of the disciples, the conviction of the physical reality of the resurrection, and so on. If one nevertheless still rejects it, one may seek support for this rejection in divergent reports, but one does this invariably on account of a world-and-life view that is diametrically opposed to that of Scripture. The reasoning, then, is as follows: the *that* is certain, but the *how* of it is immaterial. If only Christ is the living Lord, it hardly matters whether he also arose physically.

Scripture, however, proceeds from a totally different view. It teaches that both heaven and earth, spirit and matter, have been created by God; that the body belongs to the essential being of humans and in its way exhibits the image of God; that death is a consequence of and punishment for sin. For Scripture, then, everything depends on the *physical* resurrection of Christ. The *that* is integral to the *how*: if Christ did not arise physically, then death, then sin, then he who had the power of death has not been defeated. In that case, actually, not Christ but Satan came out the victor. According to Scripture, therefore, the significance of the physical resurrection of Christ is inexhaustibly rich. Briefly summarized, that resurrection is (1) proof of Jesus' messiahship, the coronation of the Servant of the Lord to be Christ and Lord, the Prince of life and Judge (Acts 2:36; 3:13–15; 5:31; 10:42; etc.); (2) a seal of his eternal divine sonship (Acts 13:33; Rom. 1:3); (3) a divine endorsement of his mediatorial work, a declaration of the power and value of his death, the "Amen!" of the Father upon the "It is finished!" of the Son (Acts 2:23–24; 4:11; 5:31; Rom. 6:4, 10; etc.); (4) the inauguration of the exaltation he accomplished by his suffering (Luke 24:26; Acts 2:33; Rom. 6:4; Phil. 2:9; etc.); (5) the guarantee of our forgiveness and justification (Acts 5:31; Rom. 4:25); (6) the fountain of numerous spiritual blessings: the gift of the Spirit (Acts 2:33), repentance (Acts 5:31), spiritual eternal life (Rom. 6:4f.), salvation in its totality (Acts 4:12); (7) the principle and pledge of our blessed and glorious resurrection (Acts 4:2; Rom. 8:11; 1 Cor. 6:14; etc.); (8) the foundation of apostolic Christianity (1 Cor. 15:12ff.).[52]

ASCENSION

[401] Following the resurrection Jesus still spent a period of time on earth. Although in Matthew 28:16ff.; Mark 16:19; Luke 24:50, the resurrection is very

52. On the resurrection of Christ, see further F. Loofs, *Die Auferstehungsberichte und ihr Wert* (Leipzig: Mohr, 1898); G. E. Burkhardt, *Die Auferstehung des Herrn und seine Erscheinungen* (Göttingen: Vandenhoeck & Ruprecht, 1899); E. Riggenbach, *Die Auferstehung Jesu*, 2nd ed. (Berlin: Edwin Runge, 1908); *Disteldorf, Die Auferstehung Jesu Christi* (Trier, 1906); W. P. Armstrong, "The Resurrection and the Origin of the Church in Jerusalem," *Princeton Theological Review* 5 (1907): 1–25; J. Orr, *The Resurrection of Jesus* (London: Hodder & Stoughton, 1908).

closely linked to the ascension, according to Acts 1:3 forty days lay between the two events. This last report is indirectly confirmed by the series of appearances that were vouchsafed to various persons after the resurrection. The first appearances took place in Jerusalem—on the day of resurrection itself to Mary Magdalene (Matt. 28:9; John 20:14); to Peter (Luke 24:34; 1 Cor. 15:5); to the men of Emmaus (Luke 24:13ff.); to the apostles without Thomas (John 20:19ff.; 1 Cor. 15:5); and eight days later to the apostles with Thomas (John 20:26). Then follow the appearances in Galilee (Matt. 28:16ff.; John 21; 1 Cor. 15:6) and then again in and near Jerusalem. Some time must have passed, and Luke, in his second book, further informs us that it lasted forty days.

These forty days constitute a very peculiar period in the life of Jesus. This is apparent already in the descriptions of his body. On the one hand, it is completely identical with the body he had before and left behind at his death. There is reference to his hands and feet (Matt. 28:9; Luke 24:39), to his flesh and bones (Luke 24:39). He shows his hands and his side (John 20:20), allows himself to be touched (John 20:27), eats food (Luke 24:43; John 21:12f.), is visibly taken up at his ascension (Acts 1:9), and will one day return again the same way (Acts 1:11; Rev. 1:7). On the other hand, he may not be touched (John 20:17), is not recognized (Luke 24:16; John 20:14), appears and disappears in a mysterious manner (Luke 24:36; John 20:19), and startles the disciples at his coming (Luke 24:37; John 21:12). It is the same Jesus but now appearing in another form (Mark 16:12). He has a body (σωμα) that has been sown in dishonor and weakness but raised in glory and power, and changed into a spiritual body (σωμα πνευματικος) (1 Cor. 15:42ff.; 2 Cor. 13:4; Phil. 3:21). By the resurrection he has become a life-giving spirit (πνευμα ζωοποιουν, 1 Cor. 15:45; 2 Cor. 3:17). Whether this spiritualization occurred gradually in the forty days is hard to say, but the peculiarity of his body in this period is undoubtedly connected with the transitional state in which he existed at the time. It is not only peculiar to his body, but it comes out in all his conduct. He is still on earth, appears from time to time to his disciples, eats and drinks and talks with them. Still he is not the same as he was before. The close personal contact of earlier days is not restored. Jesus keeps himself at a distance, withdraws, and no longer belongs to this world but is in transition to another way of living and working. When the disciples expect and hope for the old ways, Jesus forbids them, as he did Mary Magdalene, to touch him. He is going away from them, is not going to return to them on earth, but continues to go in the direction of heaven. He continually ascends to his God and Father [cf. John 20:17]. This is not to the detriment but rather to the advantage of his disciples. For his God and Father is also their God and their Father; his ascension is preparatory to their ascension; he goes on ahead, but they will follow. Indeed, his association and contact with them is not weakened by his physical disappearance but confirmed and heightened. Now they are no longer allowed to touch him, but when he has ascended, then communion with him will be confirmed and reinforced by the Holy Spirit. Physically and locally restricted, time-and-space-bound contact [with

Jesus] will then make way for spiritual, inward, deep, unbreakable, and eternal fellowship. The forty days, accordingly, were of the utmost importance for the disciples. In that period they were introduced to the practice of communion with the—indeed—living but at the same time glorified Lord. They were becoming accustomed to the idea that in the future Christ would exist and work in another mode and another form (μορφη).

Also, with every appearance Jesus gave them his word and instruction. After he had suffered, he not only presented himself alive with many compelling proofs for forty days but also spoke to them of the things pertaining to his kingdom (Acts 1:3; 10:40–42; 13:31). All too often this instruction that Christ gave to his disciples between his resurrection and ascension is ignored, but it fully deserves our attention. Those who do not take account of it create a large chasm between what Jesus himself taught before his death and what was later preached by his apostles. These men, certainly, linked up with the instruction given by Jesus to his disciples specifically in that forty-day period. Jesus did not appear to his disciples in order from that point on to leave them to their own reflection and reasoning, but in those forty days impressed upon them much more clearly than he could do earlier the significance of his death and resurrection, of his person and work. For before his death and resurrection, his disciples did not understand him. Over and over they misconstrued his intentions. They would only understand them afterward. But after Jesus died and rose again, appeared to them in another form, and spoke with them about the kingdom of God, they learned more in those forty days than in the three years they had daily associated with him. Only then did they for the first time understand the words he had spoken to them earlier.

Of the greatest significance were the things in which Jesus now further instructed them.[53] They concerned—briefly to mention the most important—the necessity and significance of his suffering (Luke 24:26–27), the explanation of the prophecies of the Old Testament in light of their fulfillment (Luke 24:27; 44–46), the glory and power to which he was now being raised (Matt. 28:18). Additionally, his enduring presence in his church (Matt. 28:20), the equipment of his apostles for the office of their ministry (Mark 16:17–18; Luke 24:48; John 20:21–23), the restoration of Peter (John 21:15–17), the proclamation of the gospel to all peoples (Matt. 28:19; Mark 16:15; Luke 24:47; Acts 1:8), the nature of faith in his name (Mark 16:16; John 20:29), the benefits to be obtained by it (Mark 16:16; Luke 24:27). Finally, the meaning and administration of baptism (Matt. 28:19), the future of the kingdom of God (Acts 1:7), the promise of the Holy Spirit (Luke 24:49; Acts 1:4–5), his own deity (John 20:28), and the full revelation of God as Father, Son, and Spirit (Matt. 28:19).

On the fortieth day, after Jesus had thus instructed and equipped his disciples, he ascended to heaven. Matthew and John do not mention this event at all. Mark does refer to it but very briefly and in a section that, according to many scholars,

---

53. R. Seeberg, "Evangelicum quadraginta dierum," *Neue kirchliche Zeitschrift* (1905): 335–531.

does not belong to the original Gospel (16:19). According to the Gospel of Luke (24:50–51), Jesus led his disciples out as far as Bethany, lifted up his hands, and blessed them. While he blessed them, he parted from them and was taken up into heaven (these last words were wrongfully omitted by Tischendorf). In Acts, Luke offers us a more extensive report (Acts 1:1–12). We then learn that the ascension took place, forty days after the resurrection, from the Mount of Olives, a Sabbath day's journey from Jerusalem; that Jesus was taken up as the disciples were looking on, but a cloud took him out of their sight. The event is expressed in the passive (ἀνεφέρετο, Luke 24:51; ἐπήρθη, Acts 1:9; ἀνελήμφθη, Acts 1:2, 11, 22; 1 Tim. 3:16), but also in the active as "a parting" (Luke 24:51), a "going away" (John 13:3, 33; 14:28; 16:5f.; 1 Pet. 3:22), or an ascension (Eph. 4:8). Hence it is both an act of the Father and the Son's own work. While the reports about the event itself are few, the New Testament is rich in indirect testimonies. Jesus himself predicted it (Matt. 26:64) and repeatedly alluded to it (John 6:62; 13:3, 33; 14:28; 16:5, 10, 17, 28; 17:24). Peter, in his public ministry in Jerusalem, mentions it over and over (Acts 2:33–34; 3:21; 5:31; cf. 1 Pet. 3:21). Stephen saw the heavens opened and the Son of Man standing at the right hand of God (Acts 7:56). Paul refers to it repeatedly (Acts 13:30–37; Eph. 4:8–10; Phil. 1:23; 2:9; 3:20; Col. 3:1; 1 Thess. 1:10; 4:14–16; 1 Tim. 3:16). It occurs time and again in the Letter to the Hebrews (2:9; 4:14; 6:19–20; 7:26; 9:24; 10:12–13; 12:2) and similarly in John's Revelation (1:13; 5:6; 14:14; 19:11–16; 22:1). There can therefore be no doubt that the ascension, as much as the resurrection, was a constituent of the faith of the church from the beginning. For that matter, just as the ascension becomes absurd to those who deny the resurrection, so it is natural and self-evident to those who with the whole church and on the basis of the apostolic witness believe in Jesus' resurrection. That is why the ascension as such, as an event on the fortieth day after the resurrection, is so rarely put in the foreground in the New Testament and so tightly linked to the resurrection.[54] But this is certainly not a reason to equate the two or to explain the report concerning Christ's ascension in light of Old Testament stories about Enoch, Moses, and Elijah, or in light of the apotheoses in Greek-Roman mythology or the legend of Buddha.[55] For the equation of the resurrection and the ascension is prohibited by the nature of Jesus' resurrection body and the limited series of his appearances; and the mythological explanation is negated by the sobriety with which the ascension is referred to in the New Testament. Its meaning consists in the fact that he has been exalted by

54. The *Letter of Barnabas* (ch. 15) puts the resurrection and ascension on the same Sunday (or on a different Sunday?), but from this it does not follow that the two are the same. The *Gospel of Peter* (ch. 5), in Docetic fashion, has the ascension occur already in the moment of death on the cross but seems, in ch. 12, where the manuscript breaks off, to be about to tell of an appearance by Jesus in Galilee.

55. *Dobschütz, *Ostern und Pfingsten*; A. Meyer, *Die Auferstehung Christi* (Tübingen: Mohr, 1905); W. Brandt, *Die evangelische Geschichte und der Ursprung des Christenthums* (Leipzig: O. R. Reisland, 1893); K. Lake, *Historical Evidence for the Resurrection of Jesus Christ*, 230ff.

the Father and received in heaven until the time of the restitution of all things (Acts 3:21).[56]

The ascension is the entry into the state of glory that Christ obtains in heaven and that is described with the term "sitting at the right hand of God." This confession also occupies an important place in the New Testament. It is closely related to, but not identical with, the resurrection and ascension and is clearly distinguished from them (Acts 2:32–34; 1 Pet. 3:21–22; Rom. 8:34). This seat at the right hand of God had already been predicted by Christ (Matt. 19:28; 22:44; 25:31; 26:64), and after the resurrection and ascension had taken place, the disciples immediately knew that he was seated at the right hand of God (Acts 2:34; 7:56). They regularly make mention of it in their letters (Rom. 8:34; Eph. 1:20; Col. 3:1; Heb. 1:3, 13; 8:1; 10:12; 12:2; 1 Pet. 3:22; Rev. 3:21). Sometimes the terminology is slightly varied. Sometimes it is said that the Father made him sit down at his right hand (Acts 2:30; Eph. 1:20) and then that he himself sat down there (Mark 16:19; Heb. 1:3; 8:1; 10:12) and is now seated there (Matt. 26:64; Luke 22:69; Col. 3:1; Heb. 1:13). Being seated there is rendered in Hebrews 12:2 in the perfect tense and hence viewed as an ongoing state. The place where he is seated is designated by the words "at the right hand of God" (in heaven) (Mark 16:19; Col. 3:1; Eph. 1:20); at the right hand of (the) power (of God) (Matt. 26:64; Luke 22:69); "at the right hand of the Majesty on high" (Heb. 1:3); on the throne of God (Acts 2:30); "at the right hand of the throne of God" (Heb. 12:2); "at the right hand of the throne of the Majesty in heaven" (Heb. 8:1). Usually we read that he is there (Rom. 8:34; 1 Pet. 3:22), and also that he stands there (Acts 7:56), that he walks among the seven golden lampstands (Rev. 2:1), and that he is clothed with a long robe and, like an officiating priest, with a golden girdle round his breast (Rev. 1:13).

Whether "the right hand of God" describes a specific place in heaven cannot be said with certainty. Some have thought this because the throne of God is in any case thought of as being in heaven and because Christ as a human being is bound to a specific location.[57] We must bear in mind, however, that in speaking of God's right hand, we are expressing ourselves, not incorrectly, but in a human manner and in imagery (1 Kings 2:19; Pss. 45:9; 110:1; Matt. 20:21). The Christian church has always been aware of this and has refrained from a further specification of the place of Christ's exaltation. Undoubtedly implied in Christ's seat at God's right hand, however, is that he has been exalted to the highest power, dignity, and honor conceivable and possible under that of God himself. Angels stand before God's face and cover their own faces (1 Kings 22:19; Isa. 6:2), and the priests stood daily serving in the tabernacle (Heb. 10:11), but the Son is seated at God's right hand. He has received a power that, though not

56. W. Schmidt, *Christliche Dogmatik*, 4 vols. (Bonn: E. Weber, 1895–98), II, 394ff.; James Denney, "Ascension," *DB*, I, 160; *DC*, I, 124; A. Meyer, *Die Auferstehung Christi*, on Luke 24:51.

57. A. Meyer, *Die Auferstehung Christi*, on Mark 16:19 and Eph. 1:20.

identical with omnipotence, encompasses all power in heaven and earth. He obtained a glory that is not identical with the glory of God but still far surpasses that of all creatures. And he received a dignity that prompts every knee in heaven, on earth, and under the earth to bow itself and every tongue to confess that he is Lord to the glory of God the Father. As it is, we do not yet see that all things are subject to him, but he has nevertheless been crowned with glory and honor and must reign as king "until he has put all his enemies under his feet" (1 Cor. 15:25; Heb. 2:8–9). So then our comfort is that "we have such a high priest, one who is seated at the right hand of the throne of the Majesty in heaven" (Heb. 8:1). A Priest-King is seated on the throne of the universe and is still looking forward to his greatest exaltation when he comes again for judgment. (But this event will be treated later under the heading of the doctrine of the last things.)

RECONCILIATION (ATONEMENT)

[402] When Christ descended to earth, he became poor, though he was rich (2 Cor. 8:9), but when he arose and ascended to heaven, he took with him a treasure of merits that he had acquired by his obedience "to death, even death on the cross" (Phil. 2:8). These benefits cannot be separated from his person but are wrapped up in his person and include no less than the whole of salvation. In Scripture, God is repeatedly called Savior (σωτηρ, Luke 1:47 etc.), but Christ too is often called by that name, "for he will save his people from their sins" (Matt. 1:21; Luke 2:11). He is "the pioneer of their salvation" (Heb. 2:10), "the source of eternal salvation" (Heb. 5:9), and his gospel is "the gospel of your salvation" (Eph. 1:13). This salvation is a deliverance from sin and all its consequences and participation in supreme blessedness. It is therefore the opposite of "death" (2 Cor. 7:10), "destruction" (Phil. 1:28), "wrath" (1 Thess. 5:9), and lasts for all eternity (Heb. 5:9). It therefore includes numerous special benefits, all of which are also mentioned separately in Scripture.

At the top of these benefits is reconciliation, atonement (καταλλαγη). For, according to Scripture, Christ's sacrifice has objective significance, a significance also valid to God. In the Old Testament, the sacrifices were intended to cover the sins of the offerer before the face of God (כפר, LXX ἐξιλασκεσθαι). Now nowhere does this atonement have God as its direct object, but it does take place in relation to him and occurs before his face (Lev. 1:3; 6:7; 10:17; 15:15, 30; 19:22; Num. 15:28; 31:50) and aims, by covering the sin, to avert his wrath (Num. 8:19; 16:46) and to propitiate him (ἱλασκεσθαι). Similarly, in the New Testament Christ is an expiation (ἱλαστηριον, Rom. 3:25), the atonement for our sins (ἱλασμος, 1 John 2:2; 4:10), a merciful and faithful high priest in the service of God "to make atonement for the sins of the people" (Heb. 2:17). As high priest, with the offering of his perfect obedience, he has covered the sins of his people, thus averting God's wrath and securing his grace. Granted, Socinians, Remonstrants, and rationalists as well as most modern theologians[58] have asserted that, since God is love, he does not need to be reconciled and is himself rather the author of reconciliation. But this is based in part on misunderstanding and in any case is contradicted by Scripture. Scripture, after all, clearly teaches—even in the New Testament—that God manifests his wrath against sins (Rom. 1:18; Gal. 3:10; Eph. 2:3) and that, as sinners, we are God's enemies (in Rom. 5:10; 11:28; the word "enemies" [ἐχθροί] has a passive meaning and hence indicates that we are by nature objects of God's wrath; in 11:28 it is contrasted with "beloved" [ἀγαπητοί], and in 5:9 there is mention of our being saved from the wrath of God). Reconciliation, therefore, is not unilateral but bilateral: not only must we be reconciled with God, but God, too, must be reconciled with us in the sense that, by giving Christ as expiation (ἱλασμός, Rom. 3:25; Heb. 2:17; 1 John 2:2; 4:10), he puts aside his wrath and establishes a relation of peace between himself and human beings (Rom. 5:9–10; 2 Cor. 5:18–19; Gal. 3:13).[59]

Nor is this in any way in conflict with the fact that God is love and has himself given Christ as an expiation for our sins. For the wrath of God is no evil passion or malice, and his righteousness is not thirst for vengeance. Rather, both his wrath and his righteousness are consistent with the highest love. Just as a mother suffers greater pain over the aberrance of her son to the degree that she loves him more; just as a judge sometimes has to condemn a blood relative or friend with whom as a person he feels the closest ties, so, in God, wrath against the sin of his creatures can go together with love toward them (Isa. 1:2; Jer. 44:4; Amos 3:2). "In each and every one of us he hated what we had done but loved what he had made," says Bede.[60] In the same spirit, Aquinas declares: "In all men God loves the nature that he has made. What he hates in man is the sins that men commit against him."[61] On account of our sins, we are indeed objects of God's wrath, writes Calvin, "but because the Lord wills not to lose what is his in us, out of his own kindness he still finds something to love."[62] And, again, this is not to be construed as if at the moment of Christ's sacrifice, God all at once changed his disposition and mood. For in God there is no variation or shadow due to change.

58. Cf., e.g., F. Schleiermacher, *Christian Faith*, §104, 4; A. Ritschl, *Die christliche Lehre von der Rechtfertigung und Versöhnung*, 4th ed., 3 vols. (Bonn: A. Marcus, 1895–1903), II, 230ff.; J. Kaftan, *Dogmatik* (Tübingen: Mohr, 1901), 460.

59. F. A. Philippi, *Commentary on St. Paul's Epistle to the Romans*, trans. John Shaw Banks, 2 vols. (Edinburgh: T&T Clark, 1878–79), on Rom. 5:10; W. Sanday and A. C. Headlam, *A Critical and Exegetical Commentary on the Epistle to the Romans*, 5th ed. (Edinburgh: T&T Clark, 1902), 129; G. V. Lechler, *Das apostolische und das nachapostolische Zeitalter* (Karlsruhe and Leipzig: H. Reuther, 1885), 344; B. Weiss, *Lehrbuch der biblischen Theologie des Neuen Testaments*, 3rd ed. (Berlin: W. Hertz, 1880), 309; ed. note: ET: *Biblical Theology of the New Testament*, trans. David Eaton and James E. Duguid, 2 vols. (Edinburgh: T&T Clark, 1883); G. B. Stevens, *The Theology of the New Testament*, 2nd ed. (Edinburgh: T&T Clark, 1906), 414; A. Adamson, "Reconciliation," *DB*, IV, 204–7.

60. Bede in F. Turretin, "De satisf.," in *Institutes of Elenctic Theol.*, 86.

61. T. Aquinas, *Summa theol.*, III, qu. 49, art. 4.

62. J. Calvin, *Institutes*, II.vxi.3.

All his attributes are one with his being; in eternity there is no "before" and "after." When Scripture speaks of God's wrath and of his reconciliation with us, it does not speak untruth, yet it speaks in terms of our human capacity to understand. There is no change in God's being or essence but there is in the relation in which he stands to his creatures. Nor does he put himself in relation to his creatures as though they in any way existed outside him, but he himself puts all things and all humans in those relations to himself that he eternally and unalterably wills and precisely in the manner and moment of time in which they occur in reality.[63]

For that reason it is and can be God himself who brings about reconciliation in Christ (2 Cor. 5:19). He reconciles himself by the sacrifice of the cross, not in a patripassianistic or pantheistic sense as though he reconciles himself with himself and reconciliation were an immanent process in the life of God. For Christ is a person other than the Father. He is moreover not only the Son of God but also the Son of Man, the head and representative of humanity, and could therefore offer God a ransom for the redemption of our souls. For that reason it can also be said, however, that God determined and provided that ransom in Christ and to that extent also brought it to himself in Christ. Dale is therefore mistaken when he says that "if God himself provided the ransom he could not pay it to himself."[64] On the contrary, in the person and work of Christ, God maintained himself as God and brought to expression the attributes of his righteousness as well as his love. Inasmuch as Christ was truly God, one in essence with the Father, one could say that by the cross God himself reconciled all things to himself. But since in person Christ was distinct from the Father as well as the Son of Man, the Father was the more remote, the Son the actual subject of reconciliation. The love of the Father gave us his Son as a demonstration of his righteousness and as an expiation for our sins. "Already loving us he reconciled us to himself. Because he first loved us he afterward reconciled us to himself."[65]

63. Cf. H. Bavinck, *Reformed Dogmatics*, II, 153–59 (#193). Concerning such ways of speaking as occur in Rom. 5:10; Gal. 3:10, 13; Col. 1:21–22 (e.g., "God was men's enemy until they were reconciled to grace by the death of Christ" and so on), Calvin says that "expressions of this sort have been accommodated to our capacity that we may better understand how miserable and ruinous our condition is apart from Christ. For if it had not been clearly stated that the wrath and vengeance of God and eternal death rested on us, we would scarcely have recognized how miserable we would have been without God's mercy, and we would have underestimated the benefit of liberation" (*Institutes*, II.xvi.2). Similar expressions occur in J. H. Scholten, *Leer der Hervormde Kerk*, 2nd ed., 2 vols. (Leyden: P. Engels, 1850–51), I, 413ff.; cf. W. Sanday and A. C. Headlam, *Critical and Exegetical Commentary on the Epistle to the Romans*, 130: "κατα ανθρωπον λεγω must be written large over all such language."

64. R. W. Dale, *The Atonement,* 18th ed. (London: Congregational Union of England and Wales, 1896), 357.

65. Augustine, *On The Trinity*, V, 16; idem, *Enchiridion*, 33; cf. P. Lombard, *Sent.*, III, dist. 19, 6; T. Aquinas, *Summa theol.*, III, qu. 49, art. 4; J. Calvin, *Institutes*, II.xvi.2–4; F. Turretin, "De satisf.," in *Institutes of Elenctic Theology*, 49, 86, 87; B. de Moor, *Comm. theol.*, III, 448–50; F. H. R. Frank, *System der christlichen Wahrheit*, 2nd ed., 2 vols. (Erlangen: A. Deichert, 1884), II, 181ff.; *M. Kähler, *Zur Lehre der Versöhnung* (1898), 362ff.; W. G. T. Shedd, *Dogmatic Theology*, 3rd ed., 3 vols. (New York: Scribner, 1891–94), II, 401; A. A. Hodge, *The Atonement* (Philadelphia: Presbyterian Board of Publication, 1867), ch. 9; J. Scott Lidgett, *The Spiritual*

By the sacrifice of Christ, therefore, a relation of reconciliation (Rom. 5:10; 2 Cor. 5:19), of peace (Acts 10:36; Eph. 2:17), and of nearness (Eph. 2:13) has been established between God and humanity. As ἱλασμος, Christ expiated sin and thereby reconciled God. The distinction between ἱλασμος (offering) and καταλλαγη (reconciliation) is not that the former is objective and the latter subjective. For καταλλαγη (reconciliation) too is an objective relation, established by God himself, between him and the world (2 Cor. 5:18–19). But in the ἱλασκεσθαι, Christ as mediator, in covering the sin by his sacrifice, is the subject who averts God's wrath and acquires his grace. In καταλλασσειν (to reconcile), God himself acts as subject (2 Cor. 5:19); by giving Christ as ἱλαστηριον (offering), he establishes a relation of peace between himself and the world. He is no longer wrathful. What made him our ἀντιδικος (adversary at law), namely, sin, has been covered by Christ's sacrifice. In Christ, he established a relation in which we would no longer have him as our adversary. He "put aside" his enmity inasmuch as its cause, namely, sin, had been removed by the death of Christ and now stands to the world in a relation of friendship and peace. Καταλλαγη, accordingly, is the reconciliation effected by expiation and propitiation. This καταλλαγη is the content of the gospel: everything is done, God is reconciled. On our part there is nothing left to do, and the entire ministry of reconciliation consists in an invitation to people: Be reconciled to God! On your part, too, "put aside" your enmity, enter into the relation of peace in which God, in response to Christ's sacrifice, has put himself toward sinners. Believe the gospel (Rom. 5:9–10; 2 Cor. 5:18–21; cf. Eph. 2:16; Col. 1:20–22).[66] With this alone that whole view stands condemned that separates "satisfaction" from "reconciliation" and sees the latter come into being when people believe and repent. People do not reconcile themselves with God as though along and side-by-side with God they were the subject of reconciliation. But God reconciled the world with himself, without its assistance, apart from it, without that world contributing anything to it or needing to contribute to it. People only receive reconciliation as a gift (Rom. 5:11) and accept it by faith (2 Cor. 5:20).

But from this one benefaction of reconciliation, acquired by Christ, flow a variety of benefits. That also stands to reason. If the relation between God and the world has been righted, then in due time everything is corrected, also the relation between heaven and earth, angels and humans, people among themselves, and the relation of people to sin, death, the world, Satan, and so on. In the sphere of justice, the battle has been won. God is right and sooner or later, therefore, he is vindicated everywhere, in all areas of life and with respect to all creatures. The right is on his side, and someday, willingly or unwillingly, this truth will be acknowledged by all.

Principle of the Atonement as a Satisfaction Made to God for the Sins of the World, 2nd ed. (London: Charles H. Kelley, 1898), ch. 5.

66. H. Cremer, *Biblico-Theological Lexicon of New Testament Greek,* trans. D. W. Simon and W. Urwick (Edinburgh: T&T Clark; New York: C. Scribner's Sons, 1895), s.v. ἱλαστηριον and καταλλαγη; F. A. Philippi, *Commentary on Romans,* on Rom. 5:10; H. J. Holtzmann, *Lehrbuch des neutestamentlichen Theologie,* II, 99ff.; G. B. Stevens, *Theology of the New Testament,* 413ff.; S. R. Driver, "Propitiation," *DB,* IV, 128–32.

Hence in the peace-relation of God-in-Christ to the world (καταλλαγη), all sorts of other benefits are implied. The fruits of Christ's sacrifice are not restricted to any one area of life; they are not limited, as so many people think nowadays, to the religious-ethical life, to the heart, the inner chamber, or the church, but are extended to the entire world. For however powerful sin may be, the free gift is not like the trespass. The grace of God and the free gift through grace are superabundant (Rom. 5:15).

The benefits that accrue to us from the reconciliation of God-in-Christ are too numerous to mention.[67] They can be listed as follows:

the *juridical,* that is, the forgiveness of sins (Mark 14:24; Heb. 9:22); justifi-cation (Rom. 3:24; 4:25; 5:9; 8:34; 1 Cor. 1:30; 2 Cor. 5:21); adoption as children (Gal. 3:26; 4:5–6); the right to eternal life and the heavenly inheri-tance (Rom. 8:17; 1 Pet. 1:4); also redemption (ἀπολυτρωσις,[68] Eph. 1:7; Col. 1:14; Heb. 9:15), which, however, sometimes has a broader meaning as well (Rom. 3:24; 8:21, 23; 1 Cor. 1:30; Eph. 1:14; 4:30; 1 Pet. 1:18–19);

the *mystical,* consisting in being crucified, buried, raised, and seated with Christ in heaven (Rom. 6–8; Gal. 2:20; Col. 3:1–13);

the *ethical,* that is, regeneration (John 1:12–13), being made alive (Eph. 2:1, 5); sanctification (1 Cor. 1:30; 6:11), being washed (1 Cor. 6:11), cleansed (1 John 1:9), and sprinkled (1 Pet. 1:2) in body, soul, and spirit (2 Cor. 5:17; 1 Thess. 5:23);

the *moral,* consisting in the imitation of Christ, who has left us his example (Matt. 10:38; 16:24; Luke 9:23; John 8:12; 12:26; 2 Cor. 8:9; Phil. 2:5; Eph. 2:10; 1 Pet. 2:21; 4:1);

the *economic,* that is, the fulfillment of the Old Testament covenant, the inauguration of a new covenant (Mark 14:24; Heb. 7:22; 9:15; 12:24); the freedom from the law (Rom. 7:1ff.; Gal. 2:19; 3:13, 25; 4:5; 5:1; etc.); the cancellation of the bond with its legal demands, the breaking down of the dividing wall, the reconciliation of Jew and Gentile and all other existing sets of opposites into unity in Christ (Gal. 3:28; Eph. 2:11–22; Col. 2:14);

the *physical,* that is, the victory over the world (John 16:33), over death (2 Tim. 1:10; Heb. 2:15), over hell (1 Cor. 15:15; Rev. 1:18; 20:14), and over Satan (Luke 10:18; 11:22; John 14:30; Heb. 2:14; 1 Cor. 15:55–56; Col. 2:15; 1 Pet. 3:22; 1 John 3:8; Rev. 12:10; 20:2; etc.).

In a word, the whole enterprise of re-creation, the complete restoration of a world and humanity, which, as a result of sin, is burdened with guilt, corrupted,

---

67. Cf. above, 339–40 (#376).

68. The ἀπολυτρωσις of believers by Christ is strikingly illustrated by the then-current custom of ransoming or buying off slaves: G. A. Deissmann, *Licht vom Osten* (Tübingen: Mohr, 1908), 234ff.; E. Schürer, *Geschichte des judischen Volkes im Zeitalter Jesu Christi,* 4th ed., 3 vols. (Leipzig: J. C. Hinrichs, 1901–9), III, 18, 53.

and fragmented, is the fruit of Christ's work. Objectively, in principle, in the sphere of legality, he has accomplished that re-creation by his cross. Then καταλ-λαγη was established between God and the world. And for that reason, Christ will in due time—for everything will be done in a set order—present the church without spot or wrinkle to the Father, deliver the kingdom to God, and God will be all in all (1 Cor. 15:22–28).

MODERN NOTIONS OF RECONCILIATION

[403] In theology this vast store of the benefits of Christ has been consistently recognized. Through Christ, said Clement of Alexandria, the earth has become "a sea of good things." Theologians spoke of Christ as Guarantor, Redeemer, Reconciler, Liberator, Administrator, Savior, Physician, Lord, Pastor, King, and so on; described the work accomplished by him as "making divine" (θεοποιη-σις), "becoming divine" (θειωσις), deification, vivification, salvation, liberation, redemption, restitution, purgation, regeneration, resurrection, and so on; and sometimes also tried to somewhat classify all those benefits. This was done, for example, in the familiar lines of verse: "Propitiating, purging, redeeming, as the sacrifice, our Surety brought salvation, as the laws and truth of God require"; or under the headings of "the ordinance of the covenant of grace," "reconciliation," "liberation," "adoption," "justification," "sanctification," or under those of "expiation," "remission," "consummation," and so on.[69] After Anselm the distinction between "satisfaction" and "merit" became current. But this distinction can scarcely serve to divide the fruits of Christ's work since the two, "satisfaction" and "merit," differ only logically, not materially. The same work of Christ is "satisfaction" insofar as he brought his offering to God and satisfied his requirement, and it is "merit" insofar as by it Christ acquired salvation for us with God.[70] Also, the two concepts place the work of Christ too one-sidedly under the category of work and merit. The question is much more what Christ has "merited" and how this relates to his sacrifice. In modern times, therefore, these terms have been almost completely dropped and in place of them the fruit of Christ's work is described as "redemption" (Erlösung) and "reconciliation" (Versöhnung).

The former term was brought into vogue especially by Schleiermacher. He does, admittedly, also speak of a new creation, one brought into being by Christ,

---

69. Athanasius, On The Incarnation, 54; Gregory of Nazianzus, Theological Orations, 2; Eusebius, Demonstratio evangelium, IV, 21; ed. note: ET: The Proof of the Gospel, trans. W. J. Farrar (Grand Rapids: Baker, 1981); Augustine, On the Merits and Remission of Sins, I, 26; T. Aquinas, Summa theol., III, qu. 48, 49; Bonaventure, Breviloquium, IV, I; D. Petavius, "De incarn.," Op. theol., 8 vols. (Paris: Vives, 1865–67), XII, ch. 6, 7; A. Polanus, Syn. theol., VI, ch. 18; G. Voetius, Select. disp., II, 229ff.; P. van Mastricht, Theologia, V, 18, 22; F. Turretin, "De satisf.," in Institutes of Elenctic Theology, 317; C. Vitringa, Doctr. christ., VI, 121ff.

70. T. Aquinas, Summa theol., III, qu. 48, art. 1–2; D. Petavius, "De incarn.," Op. theol., XII, 9; G. Perrone, Praelectiones theologicae, 9 vols. (Louvain: Vanlinthout & Vandezande, 1838–43), IV, 311; J. Calvin, Institutes, II.xvii.1; G. Voetius, Select. disp., II, 228; P. van Mastricht, Theologia, V, 18, 14, 20; C. Vitringa, Doctr. christ., VI, 59, 62; J. Quenstedt, Theologia, III, 225; A. Ritschl, Rechtfertigung und Versöhnung, I, 283.

but this new creation coincides with redemption.[71] And by it he understands the communication of his sinless perfection, the inclusion of believers in the power of his God-consciousness, which occurs neither magically nor empirically but mystically by God's creative activity, by Christ's self-revelation in his church.[72] Schleiermacher further posits a reconciling activity of Christ that consists in the fact that Christ assumes believers into the fellowship of his undisturbed blessedness and, by means of vital fellowship with him, causes them to share in the forgiveness of sins.[73] Ritschl, by contrast, sums up the working of Christ under the heading of justification and reconciliation. The fruits of Christ's life do not consist in changing the mind of God from that of a wrathful judge to that of a gracious Father, not in actual redemption, neither in deliverance from death,[74] nor in mystically dying and rising with Christ (for Rom. 6 is heavily symbolic and furnishes no material for a dogma).[75] Instead, what happens is that Christ by his whole person and life assures and guarantees us that God is love. Despite our sins he admits us into fellowship with God.[76] The justification that Christ grants us is not an acquittal from guilt and punishment, not the imputation of his righteousness, but the removal of the consciousness of guilt and thereby the separation between us and God, the elimination of the idea that sin blocks fellowship with God.[77] The consequence and effect of this justification is reconciliation. Reconciliation consists in the fact that those who in faith accept justification—which is actually the possession of the church—now also enter subjectively into that new relation to God, set aside their enmity, and position themselves in a relation of peace to God. It is an ethical change in us.[78]

There is a substantial difference between Schleiermacher and Ritschl. In the former, the person of Christ is in the foreground; in the latter, the work of Christ. In the former, the subjective change of humans comes about mystically—by the communication of life; in the latter, the change comes about ethically—by teaching and example. In Schleiermacher the primary benefit is redemption, the communication of Christ's sinless perfection; in Ritschl the primary benefit is the objective synthetic justification, which is first of all a possession of the church.

But for all the difference, the agreement is even greater. In both, Christ is the sinless person who lives in special fellowship with God. Both deny Christ's passive obedience. His suffering and death are merely the necessary consequence of his unbroken fidelity to God. In both, the connection between Christ's work

---

71. Schleiermacher, *Christian Faith*, §89, 1, 2.

72. Ibid., §§88, 100.

73. Ibid., §101.

74. A. Ritschl, *Rechtfertigung und Versöhnung*, II, 86, 208ff., 217ff., 221; idem, *The Christian Doctrine of Justification and Reconciliation* (Clifton, NJ: Reference Book Publishers, 1966), III, 439.

75. A. Ritschl, *Rechtfertigung und Versöhnung*, II, 226ff.

76. A. Ritschl, *Justification and Reconciliation*, III, 506ff.

77. Ibid., III, 51, 60, 61.

78. A. Ritschl, *Rechtfertigung und Versöhnung*, II, 230ff., 342ff.; idem, *Justification and Reconciliation*, III, 74–76; idem, *Unterricht in der christlichen Religion*, 3rd ed. (Bonn: A. Marcus, 1886), §37.

and the fruits of it in the life of believers and the church remains unclear. Both of them shift the center of gravity from the objective work of Christ to the subjective change in the life of believers. And even though Ritschl seems to construe justification, as an objective benefit of the church and as a synthetic judgment, as being anterior to faith, in fact in his thinking as well, not indeed for the church as a whole but for the individual, justification becomes dependent on subjective reconciliation.[79] Above all, however, the two agree in that they restrict the effect of Christ's life and suffering to the sphere of religion and ethics. True, even given this restriction, neither of them makes clear *how* the person and work of Christ are able to bring about this change in the sphere of religion and ethics. On the other hand, we can to some extent understand that if the fruit of Christ's work remains restricted to this sphere, then also his person and work will be understood as it is by Schleiermacher and Ritschl. For what Schleiermacher writes is true: "The peculiar activity and the exclusive dignity of the Redeemer imply each other, and are inseparably one in the self-consciousness of believers."[80] Given this viewpoint, it makes sense that Christ's passive obedience is repudiated, that Christ's deity is merely the fact of God's being in him, that the resurrection, ascension, and so on are unnecessary. In that case, either a pantheistic, mystical, or a deistic-moral operation of Christ's person and work is sufficient for salvation.

This position, however, is certainly not in harmony with the teaching of Holy Scripture. It is a misconstrual of the person of Christ and a diminution of his work. Christ is not just a divinely inspired human being (ἄνθρωπος ἔνθεος) but the eternal and only-begotten Son of God, the reflection of his glory and the exact imprint of God's very being, himself God, to be praised forever. And the fruit of his life and death is not just a certain magical or moral influence that he exerts on the world but no less than "universal restoration" (Acts 3:21), the gathering up of all things in Christ as head, "things in heaven and things on earth" (Eph. 1:10). This work of re-creation has its first principle and origin in the perfect sacrifice of Christ, or, even better, in the καταλλαγή (reconciliation) that God in Christ has brought about between himself and the world. God does not want to win by virtue of his superior strength. It would have been easy for him in his fury to destroy the whole world and to produce another world and a new human race (cf. Num. 14:12). But God exalts himself in justice and shows himself holy in righteousness (Isa. 5:16). Sin is not a physical but an ethical power. In sin Satan possesses his ungodly power over the world, and sin derives its power from the law (1 Cor. 15:56). Therefore, it has pleased God to overcome this power in a moral way, the way of justice and righteousness. Not by might, nor by power, but by the cross, which canceled the bond of ordinances, God triumphed over the

---

79. *Cf. *Jahrbuch für deutsche Theologie* (1888): 21, 22; R. B. Kübel, *Über den Unterschied zwischen der positiven und der liberalen Richtung in der modernen Theologie*, 2nd ed. (Munich: C. H. Beck, 1893), 150; *M. Kähler, *Zur Lehre der Versöhnung*, 32ff.; J. Wendland, *Albrecht Ritschl und seine Schüler im Verhältnis zur Theologie* (Berlin: George Reimer, 1899), 120ff.

80. F. Schleiermacher, *Christian Faith*, §92.

principalities and powers, disarmed them, and "made a public example of them" (Col. 2:15). Accordingly, since God has overcome sin and all its power in the way of justice, he is now free, being even the judge of his enemies, to justify the ungodly (Rom. 4:5). No one can bring a charge against the elect of God (Rom. 8:33). It is God who justifies and who, in justifying those who have faith in Jesus, proves that he himself is righteous (Rom. 3:26). God can do this, subject to, indeed, in praise of, his righteousness, because Christ died and is risen (Rom. 8:34). Based on that sacrifice, God can wrench the world and humanity out of the grip of sin, expand his kingdom, gather up all things under Christ as its head, and one day be all in all. No one, not even Satan, can say a word against this. In the end everyone will have to acknowledge that God is righteous and that Christ is the legitimate and rightful Lord (Phil. 2:11). Between the benefits that Christ has acquired and his person and work, there is, accordingly, neither a physical nor a magical connection, as though some substance of divine-human life, divine nature, or other had been transferred from him into us, as theosophists picture this process. Rather, in Christ God has paved for himself a royal road of justice in order to glorify the riches of his grace in the life of his fallen creatures. From the objective καταλλαγη, established by himself apart from the world, flow to humankind, for Christ's sake, all the above-mentioned benefits: justification, sanctification, complete redemption, the whole enterprise of re-creation. And because this work of re-creation is so enormous, bigger even than that of creation and providence, he to whom this task was assigned had to be not only a true and righteous human being, but also stronger than all creatures, that is, truly God. Only the same being by whom God created the world could be the mediator of re-creation also.[81]

THE EXTENT OF CHRIST'S RECONCILIATION (ATONEMENT)

[404] Intensively the work of Christ is of infinite value but also extensively it encompasses the whole world. As the world was the object of God's love (John 3:16), Christ came, not to condemn the world, but to save it (John 3:17; 4:42; 6:33, 51; 12:47). In him God reconciled the world to himself—all things in heaven and earth (John 1:29; 2 Cor. 5:19; Col. 1:20) and in this dispensation gathers it up into one (Eph. 1:10). The world, created through the Son, is also intended for the Son as its heir (Col. 1:16; Heb. 1:2; Rev. 11:15). Origen inferred from this that Christ, by his suffering and death, redeemed the whole world, not only all human beings but also all other rational beings, namely, the fallen angels and all other creatures.[82] He indeed died once for all at the end of the ages (Heb. 9:26), but the power of his death is sufficient for the redemption not only of the present world but also of that which existed in the past and will exist in the future,

81. Bonaventure, *Breviloquium*, IV, ch. 1.
82. Origen, *On John*, I, 40.

not only of humans but also of the heavenly spirits.[83] This kind of universalism has, however, been unanimously repudiated by all Christian churches, and in fact these churches have always been particularistic insofar as they limited the "all things" in Colossians 1:20 and did not include the fallen angels under this rubric. Nevertheless, there are those who, from this passage as well as others where the "world" or "all" is linked to the sacrifice of Christ (Isa. 53:6; Rom. 5:18; 8:32; 1 Cor. 15:22; 2 Cor. 5:15; Heb. 2:9; 1 Tim. 2:4, 6; 2 Pet. 3:9; 1 John 2:2), have drawn the conclusion that Christ made satisfaction for all people individually and that "vicarious satisfaction" must therefore be understood as being universal.

The church fathers before Augustine usually speak very universalistically about the saving will of God and the atonement of Christ.[84] In that period, however, the actual issue did not yet exist and could not yet inasmuch as people only assumed a "foreknowledge" on the part of God and with respect to human beings put all the emphasis on their free will, even though that will was weakened by sin.[85] In the Pelagian controversy, however, this issue had to arise in discussion, and Augustine was the first to clearly teach a "particular satisfaction." Augustine, echoing Scripture, does repeatedly say that God desires the salvation of all; that, if one died for all, all have died; that those who perish refused to believe and those who believe do so voluntarily;[86] that Christ is an expiation for the whole world and has reconciled all things in heaven and on earth.[87] But all this proves virtually nothing over against this other view—expressed by Augustine with equal clarity—that the saving will of God and reconciliation in Christ are limited to those who are predestined. In the first place, this already follows in general from Augustine's doctrine of predestination and grace.[88] If the number of those who will be saved has been eternally and unalterably fixed by God and if they alone are granted the grace of faith and perseverance, then there is no longer any room between these two positions for the thesis that Christ has made satisfaction for all people individually. Second, Augustine always reads 1 Timothy 2:4 in a restricted sense. Granted, he offers different interpretations of that text, sometimes that "all are saved except those who of their own free will are not saved."[89] And then again that by "all people" we must understand all "the predestined" who are chosen from all peoples and classes of the human race;[90] but whenever he deliberately explains the text, he understands it in a limited sense.[91] Third, he repeatedly links the person

83. Origen, *De princ.*, I, 6; II, 3, 5; idem, *Hom. in Lev.*, I, 3; cf. J. Schwane, *Dogmengeschichte*, 2nd ed., 4 vols. (Freiburg i.B.: Herder, 1882–95), I, 254.

84. Cf. D. Petavius, "De incarn.," *Op. theol.*, XIII, 1.2; C. Vitringa, *Doctr. christ.*, VI, 147.

85. Cf. H. Bavinck, *Reformed Dogmatics*, II, 347–51 (#234).

86. D. Petavius, "De incarn.," *Op. theol.*, XIII, ch. 3.

87. K. Kühner, *Augustins Anschauung von der Erlösungsbedeutung Christi* (Heidelberg: K. Groos, 1890), 62.

88. Cf. H. Bavinck, *Reformed Dogmatics,* II, 347–51 (#234); cf. C. Vitringa, *Doctr. christ.*, VI, 147ff.

89. Augustine, *Epist. 107*; idem, *City of God*, XIII, 23.

90. Augustine, *Enchiridion,* 103; idem, *De corr. et gr.*, 14; idem, *Against Julian*, IV, 8.

91. Cf. D. Petavius, "De Deo," *Op. theol.*, XI, 7, 10; idem, "De incarn.," *Op. theol.*, XII, 4.

and work of Christ only with the elect. God, by Christ, called "a people of believers" to adoption. By his resurrection Christ has called "us who are predestined" to a new life; by his blood he purchased into freedom "sinners who are going to be justified"; "everyone who has been redeemed by the blood of Christ is a human; yet not everyone who is a human has been actually redeemed by the blood of Christ."[92] "Not one person perishes of those for whom Christ died."[93]

Although before long semi-Pelagianism gained the upper hand, many people continued to stick with Augustine also on this point. With an appeal to 1 Timothy 2:4, the semi-Pelagians claimed that God embraces all people alike with the same love and bestows on all an equal measure of grace. To this Prosper answered by saying: "God has concern for all and there is not a single person who is not addressed either by the preaching of the gospel or the testimony of the law or even by nature itself. However, we confess the faith of humans to be a gift of God without which grace no person runs to grace." And as it concerns the particularity of salvation, Christ was indeed "crucified for the redemption of the whole world, on account of his true assumption of human nature and on account of the ruin of all in the first man; it can nevertheless be said that he was crucified only for those who were benefited by his death."[94] However moderate this language may be, all followers of Augustine, Prosper, Lucid, Fulgentius, and others are agreed that, though God cares for all people and bestows all sorts of benefits on them, he does not desire the salvation of all in the same way; that he does not grant to all the same measure of grace; and that Christ, though in a sense he died for all, yet he efficaciously died only for those whom his death actually benefits. But the Synod of Arles (475) forced Lucid to revoke his teaching that Christ died only for those who were really saved. And the Synod of Orange (529) declared only that "all those who are baptized" can fulfill what is necessary for salvation.[95] In the ninth century, when the question arose anew, Gottschalk taught that, though Christ "by the sacrament of baptism washes (the reprobate), he did not undergo the cross, neither suffer death, nor shed his blood for them." Lupus said that Christ did not die for all humans, but he did die for all believers, also for those who again lose their faith. Remigius made a similar distinction. And the Synod of Valence (855) spoke along the same lines when it rejected that Christ had shed his blood "even for all the ungodly who from the beginning of the world right up to the passion of Christ had died in their ungodliness and were punished with eternal damnation" and confessed that that price was paid only for those "concerning whom our Lord himself says: just as Moses lifted up the serpent in the wilderness,

---

92. Augustine, *Confessions*, IX, 1; idem, *On The Trinity*, IV, 13; idem, *Adul. conjug.*, I, 15.

93. Augustine, *Epist. 102*; cf. G. F. Wiggers, *Versuch einer pragmatischen Darstellung des Augustinismus und Pelagianismus*, 2 vols. (Hamburg: F. A. Perthes, 1830–31), I, 313.

94. Prosper of Aquitaine, *Responsiones ad capitula obiectionum Gallorum calumniantium*, 8, 9.

95. Cf. D. Petavius, "De incarn.," *Op. theol.*, XIII, ch. 5–7; J. Schwane, *Dogmengeschichte*, II, 571–82.

so the Son of Man must be lifted up, that everyone who believes in him may not perish but have eternal life."[96]

Scholasticism, too, remained largely faithful to Augustine: 1 Timothy 2:4 must not be understood as if God in fact wanted to happen what does not happen, as though he wanted those to be saved who in fact are not saved. Rather, the text means to say that "no human being is saved unless he himself wants to be saved"; or that all sorts of people from all nations and classes will be saved; or sometimes, in the sense of John of Damascus, that God desires the salvation of all, namely, "by a conditional antecedent will," that is, if they themselves wanted and come to him, but in that case this will again was "more a matter of velleity than of an absolute will."[97] And as it concerns satisfaction, scholasticism did teach that it was "superabundant" and took place "for the sin of the whole human race, for the whole of human nature,"[98] but especially asserted the possibility of satisfaction by saying that Christ was the head of the body and believers the members and therefore linked satisfaction in each instance with believers. Aquinas, for example, says: "The head and members form as it were a single mystical person. Christ's satisfaction therefore extends to all the faithful as to his members."[99] "He is our head and has by his passion [. . .] freed us, his members, from our sins, the passion being as it were the ransom. It is as if, by performing some meritorious work with his hands, a man might redeem himself from a sin he had committed with his feet."[100] Elsewhere he says: "Christ's passion benefits all, being sufficient [for the forgiving of sins and the attaining of grace and glory], though it produces no effect save in those who are united to his Passion through faith and charity."[101] That this efficacy depends not on people's free will but on God's election and Christ's sacrifice itself is generally evident from Aquinas's doctrine of grace and specifically from his express statement that "Christ's passion causes the salvation of men [as an efficient cause],"[102] as also Lombard stated: "Christ only loved the elect as he loved himself and chose their salvation"[103] or in another place: "Christ offered himself to the Trinity, a ransom sufficient for all, but only efficacious for the elect, because he effected salvation only for the predestined."[104] Later the same sentiment was championed within the Catholic Church by Baius, Jansen, Quesnel, and also defended by Tapper, Estius, Sonnius, and others.[105]

96. D. Petavius, "De incarn.," *Op. theol.*, XIII, 8; C. Vitringa, *Doctr. christ.*, VI, 149–51.

97. P. Lombard, *Sent.*, I, dist. 46, 2; Bonaventure, *Brevil.*, art. 1, qu. 1; T. Aquinas, *Summa theol.*, I, 19, 7; 23, 4, 3.

98. T. Aquinas, *Summa theol.*, III, 46, 1.

99. Ibid., III, 48, 2.

100. Ibid., III, 49, 1.

101. Ibid., III, 179, 7.

102. Ibid., III, 48, 6.

103. P. Lombard, *Sent.*, III, 31, 4.

104. Ibid., III, 20, 3.

105. Cf. A. Rivetus, *Op.*, III, 438; C. Vitringa, *Doctr. christ.*, VI, 155–59.

But as semi-Pelagianism gained ground in the Catholic Church and theology, the view that gained the upper hand was that God by an antecedent will desires the salvation of all and had Christ make satisfaction for all but that in his consequent will, he took account of the good or evil use that people made of their freedom and the grace offered [to them].[106] From ancient times, this had already been the confession of the Greek [Orthodox] Church.[107] Although Luther originally taught a very different view and the Formula of Concord juxtaposed God's universal saving will and the bondage of the human will without any attempt to reconcile them, this idea soon found acceptance also in Lutheran theology: by an antecedent will, God wills the salvation of all, but by his consequent will, he wills that salvation only for those whose faith and perseverance he foresaw.[108] These churches still possessed a counterweight, however, in their clear and firm confession of the Trinity, the deity of Christ, and satisfaction, so that the Pelagian principle could not exert its influence unhindered. But this changed in the case of the Socinians, who rejected all these objective dogmas, and later also among the Remonstrants. Arminius himself as well as his theological allies initially sought to maintain these doctrines and believed themselves capable of doing this. It seemed as if they held fast to the great Christian truths and only took a stand against Calvinistic excesses. But this soon proved otherwise.[109] The second of their articles, "On the Blood of Christ," was most intimately linked with the four others, and all five of them together, in their logical import, brought with them a totally different view of Christianity as a whole. For, certainly, when it is said of Christ's sacrifice that it was made for all humans, also for those who on account of their unbelief never obtain the fruit of that sacrifice, then that sacrifice itself acquires a very different character from that ascribed to it in Scripture. In that case it was not a complete satisfaction of the demand of divine righteousness, equal in weight to the punishment that sinners deserved, the acquisition for them of actual and genuine salvation, but no more than an exemplary punishment that God deemed necessary and sufficient for reasons other than his severe justice

---

106. Cf. H. Bavinck, *Reformed Dogmatics,* II, 351–55 (#235); Council of Trent, VI, chs. 2–3; Roman Catechism, I, 3, 7; Innocent X, "In damn. 5 propos. Jans."; R. Bellarmine, "De sacrif. missae," *Controversiis,* I, 25; idem, "De poenit.," *Controversiis,* I, 2; idem, "De amiss. gr.," *Controversiis,* IV, 4; M. Becanus, *Manuale controversiarum,* III, 1, qu. 1; D. Petavius, "De incarn.," *Op. theol.,* XIII, 14; *Theologia Wirceburgensi,* 3rd ed., 10 vols. in 5 (Paris: Berche at Tralin, 1880), IV, 322; M. Scheeben, *Handbuch der katholischen Dogmatik,* 4 vols. (1874–98; reprinted, Freiburg i.B.: Herder, 1933), III, 356; G. Jansen, *Prael. theol.,* II, 784.

107. John of Damascus, *The Orthodox Faith,* II, ch. 29; *Orthodox Confession,* 34, 47.

108. J. T. Müller, *Die symbolischen Bücher der evangelisch-lutherischen Kirche,* 8th ed. (Gütersloh: Bertelsmann, 1898), 781; J. Gerhard, *Loci theol.,* VII, ch. 6; J. Quenstedt, *Theologia,* III, 311–24; D. Hollaz, *Ex. theol.,* 745; J. F. Buddeus, *Inst. theol.,* 824; cf. H. Bavinck, *Reformed Dogmatics,* II, 355–58 (#236).

109. The Reformed, accordingly, made a distinction between the earlier and later, between moderate and consistent Remonstrants. To the question whether Remonstrants are heretics, Ames replied: "The opinion of the Remonstrants, as it is received by the common folks who favor them, is not properly a heresy but a dangerous error in the faith, tending to heresy; but as it is defended by some of them, it is a Pelagian heresy, because they deny the effectual operation of internal grace to be necessary for the ingendering of conversion and faith" (*De Conscientia,* IV, 4, Q4).

(acceptation). In addition, Christ's sacrifice then in fact appropriates nothing for anyone but merited for the Father only the authority and possibility "to deal again with man and to prescribe new conditions, such as he might desire, obedience to which, however, depended on the free will of man."[110] By this view, furthermore, the law was robbed of its absolute character, faith and repentance were construed as a new law, and election was not only placed after the satisfaction but also made dependent on the human will, and even the divine nature of the mediator was made superfluous. For if Christ's sacrifice has its ground and standard only in fairness and fittingness and not in the requirement of righteousness, why then could it not be of such a nature that it could be fully made by a holy and righteous human being? All these and similar implications were in principle inherent in Remonstrantism and were gradually also inferred from it. Though at the Synod of Dort the Arminians were condemned, they were not defeated. Their ideas made inroads into the Lutheran and the Anglican [Episcopal] Church and were taken over by an assortment of religious modalities that in Protestantism separated themselves from the official churches (Baptists, Wesleyan Methodists, Quakers, Deists, Herrnhuter,[111] and others) and also exerted a powerful influence within the Reformed churches.

PARTICULAR (LIMITED) ATONEMENT

[405] The Reformed theologians accordingly, with their doctrine of particular satisfaction, stood virtually alone. Add to this that they were not at all unanimous among themselves and gradually diverged ever further from one another as well. Various confessions speak in moderate and general terms.[112] The Anglican confession is silent on the subject. The Heidelberg Catechism does not directly pronounce on it, although the answer to Question 37 has been mistakenly cited as proof for a universal satisfaction.[113] The French, Dutch (Belgic), and Scottish confessions do not teach it except by logical implication. In the Canons of Dort, it is explicitly and firmly confessed, but at the same time it is stated that Christ's sacrifice is "of infinite worth and value, abundantly sufficient to expiate the sins of the whole world" (chapter II, art. 3). It further also occurs in the Westminster Confession, the Larger and Smaller Catechism, in the Helvetic Consensus,[114] and the Articles of Walcheren (1693).

---

110. Canons of Dort, II; Apol. conf., VIII, 10; J. Arminius, *Opera theologica* (Lugduni Batavorum [Leiden]: Apud Godefridum Basson, 1629), 153; S. Episcopius, *Opera theologica*, 2 vols. (Amsterdam: Johan Blaeu, 1650–65), on 1 John 2:2; P. van Limborch, *Theologia christiana* (Amsterdam: Wetstein, 1735), IV, ch. 3–5.

111. C. Vitringa, *Doctr. christ.*, VI, 174ff.

112. For example, the Repetitio Anhaltina; H. A. Niemeyer, *Collectio confessionum in ecclesiis reformatis publicarum*, 2 vols. (Leipzig: Sumptibis Iulii Klinkhardti, 1840), 635, 639; ibid., (*Conf. sigism.*), 650, 651; ibid., (*Lips.*), 662; ibid., (*Thorun*), 674; E. F. K. Müller, *Die Bekenntnisschriften der reformierten Kirche* (Leipzig: Deichert, 1903), 835ff.

113. C. Vitringa, *Doctr. christ.*, VI, 136.

114. E. F. K. Müller, *Die Bekenntnisschriften*, 560, 562, 563, 619, 644, 865.

Among theologians, too, there was no full agreement. Some believed that, though it was proper to say that Christ's sacrifice would have been sufficient for all if God had wanted to make it efficacious for all, it was less than correct to say that it was sufficient for all, for if Christ had not died for all efficaciously, then he did not do so sufficiently for all either. Thus, if people nevertheless spoke in those terms, they occasioned misunderstanding and gave rise to the dangerous distinction between an "antecedent" and a "consequent will," between "sufficient" and "efficacious grace."[115] But others, echoing Augustine and the scholastics, said that Christ had died and made satisfaction "sufficiently" for all and "efficaciously" only for the elect.[116] At the Synod of Dort, the foreign delegates spoke as broadly as possible about the worth and sufficiency of Christ's sacrifice. The English theologians even stated that Christ, in a sense, had died for all: "Christ so died for all that all people and individuals, with faith mediating, can gain remission of sins and eternal life in virtue of this ransom (ἀντίλυτρον)."[117] In England, over against the rigorously Reformed school of Twisse, Rutherford, Gillespie, Goodwin, and others, there was a moderate group represented by Davenant, Calamy, Arrowsmith, Seaman, and others and especially by Richard Baxter.[118] Their view completely agreed in substance with that of the French theologians Cameron, Testard, Amyraut, and others. There was an antecedent decree by which Christ had conditionally satisfied for all, on condition of faith, and another subsequent particular decree by which he had so made satisfaction for the elect that he would in time also grant them faith and infallibly lead them to salvation.[119]

In the Scottish church, the doctrine of particular satisfaction repeatedly emerged in connection with the universal offer of grace. It was even in part responsible for the secession of the Erskines in 1733. To avoid the neonomian school, which made faith a legalistic condition and hence limited the gospel's address to certain qualified persons, the so-called Marrow Men (James Hog, Thomas Boston, Ralph and Ebenezer Erskine, Alexander Moncrieff, and others) taught[120] that Christ's

115. So Beza, Piscator, Twisse, Voetius, and others; cf. G. Voetius, *Select. disp.*, II, 251ff.; C. Vitringa, *Doctr. christ.*, VII, 31; W. Cunningham, *Historical Theology*, 3rd ed., 2 vols. (Edinburgh: T&T Clark, 1870), II, 332.

116. J. Calvin, *Commentary*, on 1 John 2:2; H. Alting, *Theologia problematica nova* (Amsterdam: J. Jansson, 1662), 174; S. Maresius, *Syst.*, X, 31; F. Turretin, *Institutes of Elenctic Theology*, XIV, qu. 14; P. van Mastricht, *Theologia*, V, 18, 21, 39; B. de Moor, *Comm. theol.*, III, 1035–75.

117. *Acta*, National Synod of Dort (1620), Judicia, 79.

118. Richard Baxter (1615–91) published his *Universal Redemption of Mankind by the Lord Jesus Christ* and thereby contributed substantially to the introduction of Amyraldism in England. His contemporary, Isaac Barrow (1630–77), author of *The Doctrine of Universal Redemption Asserted and Explained*, had committed to Arminianism (see W. Cunningham, *Hist. Theol.*, II, 328). Against their hypothetical universalism it was objected that if Christ died for all on condition of faith, he cannot have died for the children who can never actually believe. Cf. B. B. Warfield, "The Making of the Westminster Confession, and Especially of Its Chapter on the Decree of God," *Presbyterian and Reformed Review* 12 (1901): 226–83.

119. Cf. H. Bavinck, *Reformed Dogmatics*, II, 368–72 (#239); C. Vitringa, *Doctr. christ.*, VI, 138ff.

120. Cf. H. Bavinck, *Reformed Dogmatics*, I, 191 (#57); and, further, an article on the Marrow controversy in *Princeton Theological Review* (1906): 331–35.

sacrifice possessed a "legal, federal sufficiency" for all humans and based the universal offer of grace on this sufficiency. They therefore defended the proposition that every person may believe in Christ, for God gave him to the world in its totality. Everyone may be told that there is good news for them, that "Christ is dead" for them. This expression, mind you, was distinguished from the other, which says that "Christ died for them." One cannot and may not say the latter, because one does not know if it is true. But one may tell everyone that "Christ" is dead "for them," that is, that a Savior has been provided for them; there is a crucified Christ for them. And for this universal offer of grace, they appealed to Matthew 22:14; 28:19; John 3:16; and others. Principal Hadow of St. Andrews vehemently opposed these Marrow Men, but Boston and his followers stood their ground and tried to solve the problem of a definite atonement and a universal call in the above-mentioned manner. Others, however, could not agree with this mediating position and proceeded to make a distinction between a universal and a particular grace in the gospel, between an external and an internal covenant. From James Fraser of Brea, who died in 1698, there appeared in 1722 and 1749 a treatise in two parts titled *On Justifying Faith,* which was Amyraldistic and recommended by Thomas Mair, one of the preachers of the Antiburghers. True, Thomas Mair was deposed in 1757, and Adam Gib wrote a tract that was touted as the best English answer to Amyraldism, but the current of the day took a liberal turn, and sometimes even the entire doctrine of satisfaction was contested.[121]

In the nineteenth century, the scope of the atonement was again the subject of a long-lasting controversy. In 1820 the United Associate Synod of the Secession Church issued a statement in which universal satisfaction was condemned. At the same time it asserted that Christ's sacrifice was sufficient for all and had brought everyone into a "salvable state." Both on the right and on the left there were objections to the statement. Some denied that everyone "had a right" to Christ and rejected universal atonement in every sense, for example, as did Palaemon in his "Letters upon Theron and Aspasio, Symington, and Haldane." Others, such as William Pringle, John McLeod Campbell, James Morison, Robert Morison, A. C. Rutherford, and John Guthrie, came across as firm proponents of universal atonement. In 1831 Campbell, a preacher at Row, was condemned and deposed by the synod on account of his deviant views. He taught, namely, that "God loves every child of Adam with a love, the measure of which is to be seen in the agonies of Christ," and "the person who knows that Christ died for every child of Adam is the person who is in the condition to say to every human being: let there be peace with you, peace between you and your God." He believed that Scripture teaches with total clarity that "Christ died for all men, that the propitiation which he made for sin was for all the sins of all mankind," and advanced a couple of unique arguments for this position. In the first place, he commented that Christ had been perfectly obedient to the whole law of God, therefore also to the commandment to

---

121. *M. Gill, *Practical Essay on the Death of Christ* (1786).

love one's neighbor as one's self. Now Christ himself taught us who our neighbor is, not a particular fellow-citizen but human beings in general, people who need our love; and thus Christ perfectly loved his neighbor, not just with words but also with deeds, in his life and in his death.

Second, the Father has delivered all judgment up to the Son, because he is the Son of Man. His judgeship, therefore, rests on his mediatorship. So if Christ is to be judge over all people, his mediatorial work must also be extended to all. And third, to him the denial of the universality of the atonement seemed a denial of God's love and grace. But in the process he nevertheless again had to inwardly weaken this mediatorial work, for if it consists in the fact that Christ acquired something for all, then this in fact came down to a "salvable state," "a state of pardonableness in which the atoning death of Christ has necessarily and unconditionally placed every sinner of mankind." After his deposition, however, Campbell continued to preach. Later, he was even rehabilitated in a wide circle, became the recipient in 1868 of a D.D. degree from the University of Glasgow, and exerted great influence through his work *The Nature of the Atonement*, cited above. James Morison, minister of the United Secession Church at Kilmarnock in 1841, was condemned and deposed on account of his doctrine of universal atonement, as a result of which the Morisonian Church originated, a church that in 1897 united with the Independents. Finally, the two professors Balmer and Brown also had charges lodged against them by Marshall but were cleared in 1845 by the synod.[122] From that time on, there was much reaction against the Reformed doctrine [of limited atonement] and the situation is now being described as follows: "In point of fact, the Calvinistic limitation is little heard of now in Great Britain, except among some of the Evangelicals in the Church of England and some of the Baptists. And few would now rank it as a burning question. The controversy has gone to sleep."[123] And so it has gradually gone in all countries. First, the doctrine of particular satisfaction [limited atonement] was weakened along the lines of Grotius and Amyraut, then it was totally rejected: in England by Daniel Whitby (against whom Jonathan Edwards took action);[124] in America by the Edwardsian or New England theologians: Bellamy, Hopkins, Emmons, and others;[125] in Germany by P. Volckmann and others;[126] and in the Netherlands by Venema.[127] Presently it has been almost universally abandoned[128]

---

122. See W. Cunningham, *Hist. Theol.*, II, 323ff.; J. Walker, *The Theology and Theologians of Scotland,* 2nd ed. (Edinburgh: T&T Clark, 1888), 79ff.; A. Robertson, *History of the Atonement Controversy in Connexion with the Secession Church from Its Origin to the Present Time* (Edinburgh: Oliphant, 1846); H. F. Henderson, *The Religious Controversies of Scotland* (Edinburgh: T&T Clark, 1905).

123. R. Mackintosh, "Universalism," *DC*, II, 785.

124. J. Ridderbos, *De Theologie van Jonathan Edwards* ('s-Granvenhage: J. A. Nederbragt, 1907), 9, 59ff.

125. Ibid., 321ff.

126. W. Gass, "Barckhausen und die allgemeine Gnade," *PRE*², II, 94–98.

127. C. Vitringa, *Doctr. christ.*, VI, 144; A. Ypey, *Geschiedenis van de Kristlijke Kerk,* 15 vols. (Utrecht: W. van Izerworst, 1797–1815), VII, 133ff.

128. Also by J. J. van Oosterzee, *Christian Dogmatics,* trans. J. Watson and M. Evans, 2 vols. (New York: Scribner, Armstrong, 1874), §111, 6; J. I. Doedes, *De Leer der Zaligheid* (Utrecht: Kemink, 1876), no. 66; idem,

and is still defended by only a very few.[129] In recent years it only again received some support from Ritschl, according to whom the correlative of Christ's sacrifice is not the individual, nor all people individually, but specifically the church as a whole. It alone is in possession of justification and full of the forgiveness of sins; in Scripture it is always presented as the object of the effects and influences that have their origin in Christ.

THE CHALLENGE OF UNIVERSALISM[130]

[406] In this important controversy concerning the value of Christ's sacrifice, there is very substantial agreement. For, on the one hand, all disputants are agreed that in fact not all but only some people—be they few or many—obtain the benefits of Christ. On the other hand, all acknowledge that Christ's sacrifice as such would be completely sufficient to let not only some but all people participate in the forgiveness of sins and eternal life. In practice, therefore, these universalists are all committed to the particularity of grace; and all the particularists without exception confess the universality of the sacrifice of Christ as it pertains to its inner value. Even those who object to the formulation that Christ died "sufficiently" for all and "efficaciously" for the elect still fully recognize that the *substance* of Christ's merit is completely sufficient for the atonement of the sins of all people. What they assert is only that the *form* of Christ's merit, considered not in isolation but with a view to the reprobates, can be called not only "not efficacious" but also "not sufficient."[131] Hence the difference concerns only the question whether it was God's will and *intent* that Christ made his sacrifice for the sins of all people without exception or only for the sins of those whom the Father had given him.[132]

When it is framed in this manner, the question is hardly doubtful. For in the first place, Scripture consistently links the sacrifice of Christ only to the church, whether it is described by the word "many" (Isa. 53:11–12; Matt. 20:28; 26:28; Rom. 5:15, 19; Heb. 2:10; 9:28), by "his people" (Matt. 1:21; Titus 2:14; Heb. 2:17; 7:27; 13:12), by "his sheep" (John 10:11, 15, 26f.; Heb. 13:20), by "his

---

De Nederlandsche Geloofsbelijdenis en de Heidelbergsche Catechismus (Utrecht: Kemink & Zoon, 1880–81), 176; J. H. A. Ebrard, *Christliche Dogmatik,* 2nd ed., 2 vols. (Königsberg: A. W. Unzer, 1862–63), §430.

129. Charles Hodge, *Systematic Theology,* 3 vols. (New York: Charles Scribner's Sons, 1888), II, 544–62; A. A. Hodge, *Atonement,* 347–429; W. G. T. Shedd, *Dogmatic Theology,* II, 464–80; W. Cunningham, *Hist. Theol.,* II, 323–70; R. S. Candlish, *The Atonement: Its Reality, Completeness, and Extent* (London: T. Nelson & Sons, 1861); H. Martin, *The Atonement: In Its Relations to the Covenant, the Priesthood, the Intercession of Our Lord* (London: James Nisbet, 1870; reprinted, Edinburgh: Knox Press, 1976); A. Kuyper, *Dat de Genade Particulier Is* (Kampen: Kok, 1906 [1884]).

130. Ed. note: For clarity's sake it is important to note that Bavinck here uses the term "universalism/universalist" not to refer to universal salvation (ἀποκατάστασις, "restoration"; on which see *Reformed Dogmatics,* IV, #578–79) but only with respect to the scope of the atonement.

131. G. Voetius, *Select. disp.,* II, 254.

132. W. Cunningham, *Hist. Theol.,* II, 334.

brothers" (Heb. 2:11), by "the children of God" (John 11:52; Heb. 2:13–15), by "those whom the Father has given him" (John 6:37, 39, 44; 17:2, 9, 24), by "his church" (Acts 20:28; Eph. 5:25), by "his body" (Eph. 5:23), or also by "us" as believers (Rom. 5:9; 8:32; 1 Cor. 5:7; Eph. 1:7; 2:18; 3:12; Col. 1:14; Titus 2:14; Heb. 4:14–16; 7:26; 8:1; 9:14; 10:15; 1 John 4:10; 1 Pet. 3:18; 2 Pet. 1:3; Rev. 1:5–6; 5:9–10; etc.). Ritschl rightly again called attention to this point. For though it is true that he was moved to do this for very different reasons, the fact itself is certain. In Scripture not all persons individually but the communion of believers is the "correlate of all the operations connected with the sacrificial death of Christ."[133] Ritschl's reasons, however, differ from those of the Reformed. The latter said: "Not all but the church of the elect"; Ritschl says: "Not the individual believers but the church," and thereby attempts to remove from Scripture the "mystical union," the communion individual believers enjoy with Christ. Nevertheless, in the matter itself there is agreement.

Against this clear and consistent teaching of Scripture, the few texts to which the universalists appeal have little weight. The vocable "all" in Isaiah 53:6; Romans 5:18; 1 Corinthians 15:22; 2 Corinthians 5:15; Hebrews 2:9 (cf. 10) either proves nothing or proves much more than the universalists assert and would help support Origen's doctrine concerning the restitution of all things. The universalists themselves, accordingly, are compelled to restrict the word "all" in these passages. Of greater weight are texts like Ezekiel 18:23; 33:11; John 1:29; 3:16; 4:42; 1 Timothy 2:4, 6; Titus 2:11; Hebrews 2:9; 2 Peter 3:9; 1 John 2:2; 4:14, where the will of God or the sacrifice of Christ is linked with the salvation of all or of the world. But none of these texts is incompatible with the statements cited above that limit Christ's benefits to the church. The New Testament, after all, is a very different dispensation from that of the old covenant. The gospel is not restricted to one people but must be preached to all creatures (Matt. 28:19). There is no respect of persons with God and no longer any distinction between Gentile and Jew (Acts 10:34–35; Rom. 3:29; 10:11–13). Indeed, even if in Isaiah 53:11–12; Matthew 20:28; 26:28; Romans 5:15, 19; Hebrews 2:10; 9:28, there is mention of the "many" for whom Christ died, this is not grounded in the contrast that has often been insinuated into the text later, namely, that not all but only many will be saved. The idea from which the reference to "the many" arises, however, is a very different one: Christ did not die for a few but for *many*, for a large multitude. He gives his life as a ransom for many; he sheds his blood for many; he will make many righteous. It is not a handful but many who by one man's obedience will be made righteous [Rom. 5:19]. Scripture is not afraid that *too* many people will be saved. Therefore, based on that same consideration, it says that God has no pleasure in the death of the wicked and that he wants all humans to repent and be saved, that Christ is the expiation of and has given his life for the world, and that the gospel must be preached to all creatures. But when universalists deduce from this that

---

133. A. Ritschl, *Rechtfertigung und Versöhnung*, II², 216.

the atonement is completely universal, they run afoul of both Scripture and reality, for the two seem to vie with each other in teaching that not all but only many learn of the gospel and attain genuine repentance. In all these passages, therefore, we are encountering not "the will of God's good pleasure," which is unknown to us and neither can nor may be the rule for our conduct, nor an "antecedent will," which is anterior to the decision of our will and oriented to it, but the "revealed will," which tells us by what standard we are to conduct ourselves in the new covenant. It gives us the right and lays on us the duty to bring the gospel to all people without exception. For the universal offer of grace we need no other ground than this clearly revealed will of God. We no more need to know specifically for whom Christ died than we need to know specifically who has been ordained to eternal life. The calling indeed rests on a particular basis, for it belongs to and proceeds from the covenant, but it is addressed—in keeping with God's revealed will and with the inherently all-sufficient value of Christ's sacrifice—also to those who are outside the covenant in order that they too may be incorporated into that covenant and in faith itself receive the evidence of their election.[134]

In the second place, Scripture implies that the sacrifice and intercession of Christ, hence also the acquisition and application of salvation, are inseparably connected. The sacrifice is the basis for Christ's intercession; the scope of the latter, accordingly, is as extensive as that of the former. Limborch therefore recognizes that "the intercession is not an act distinct from the sacrifice in and of itself insofar as it [the intercession] is accomplished in heaven."[135] If then the intercession is particular, as it is (John 17:9, 24; Rom. 8:34; Heb. 7:25; 1 John 2:1–2), so is the sacrifice. Limborch, opposing this position, indeed cites Luke 23:34,[136] but Jesus prays here not for the salvation of his enemies but only for the nonimputation of the appalling crime that they, in their ignorance, were committing when they crucified the Messiah. There is similarly an inseparable connection between the acquisition and the application of salvation. All the benefits of the covenant of grace are linked (Rom. 8:28–34) and find their ground in the death of Christ (Rom. 5:8–11). Atonement in Christ carries with it salvation and blessedness. For Christ is the head and believers are his body, a body that receives its growth from him (Eph. 4:16; Col. 2:19). He is the cornerstone, and we are the building (Eph. 2:20–21). He is the firstborn, and we are his brothers (Rom. 8:29). Believers, accordingly, have objectively died, been crucified, buried, raised, and

---

134. Cf. H. Bavinck, *Reformed Dogmatics*, II, 240–45 (#209). Whereas in the past people were intent on making Jesus out to be a universalist who was above all Jewish restrictions, nowadays many attempt to push him back into the particularistic stance of his fellow Jews. Harnack, for example, says that though the mission to the Gentiles later issued naturally from the gospel, it lay totally outside Jesus' horizon. He, therefore, could not have given any instructions to start a Gentile mission. Although the Gospels do contain it, it is not authentic and does not belong to the oldest tradition. Cf. A. von Harnack, *The Expansion of Christianity in the First Three Centuries,* 2 vols. (New York: Williams & Norgate, 1904–5), 36ff.

135. P. van Limborch, *Theol. christ.*, III, 19, 11.

136. Ibid., IV, 4, 7.

seated in the heavens with and in him. That is, the church is not an accidental and arbitrary aggregate of individuals that can just as easily be smaller or larger, but forms with him an organic whole that is included in him as the second Adam, just as the whole of humankind arises from the first Adam.[137] The application of salvation must therefore extend just as far as its acquisition. The application is comprehended in it and is its necessary development.

This, for that matter, is true in the nature of the case. If Jesus is truly the Savior, he must also *really* save his people, not potentially but really and in fact, completely and eternally. And this, actually, constitutes the core of the difference between the proponents and the opponents of particular satisfaction (atonement). This difference is defined incorrectly or at least far from completely when one formulates it exclusively in the question whether Christ died and made satisfaction for all humans or only for the elect. Neither is this how the difference is treated and settled in the second chapter of the Canons of Dort. The real issue concerned the value and power of Christ's sacrifice, the nature of the work of salvation. To save, said the Reformed, is to save truly, wholly, for all eternity. This flows naturally from the love of the Father and the grace of the Son. Those whom God loves and for whom Christ made satisfaction are saved without fail. We have to make a choice: either God loved all people and Christ made satisfaction for all—and then they will all, without fail, be saved—or Scripture and experience testify that this is not the case. In that case, then, neither can and may we say that God loved all people, at least not with that special love with which he leads the elect to salvation, nor that Christ died and made satisfaction for all, even if his death indirectly produces some benefit for all. And so they arrived at the confession: "For this was the sovereign counsel and most gracious will and purpose of God the Father that the quickening and saving efficacy of the most precious death of His Son should extend to all the elect, for bestowing upon them alone the gift of justifying faith, thereby to bring them *infallibly* to salvation; in other words, it was the will of God that Christ by the blood of the cross, whereby he confirmed the new covenant, should *effectually* redeem out of every people, tribe, nation, and language, all those, and those only who were from eternity chosen to salvation and given to Him by the Father."[138]

They therefore took a vigorous stand against the universalists, not in the first place because the latter made the atonement applicable to all, but preeminently because, speaking as they did, they began to develop a very different view of the work of salvation and did less than justice to the name of Jesus. In logic there is the rule: "The greater its extent, the weaker its grasp" (*quo maior extensio, minor comprehensio*), and this rule, which applies in numerous areas, is also applicable here. In the guise of honoring the work of Christ, the proponents of universal

137. R. Rothe, *Theologische Ethik,* 2nd rev. ed., 5 vols. (Wittenberg: Zimmerman, 1867–71), I, 501.

138. Canons of Dort, II, 8. Also, cf. The Westminster Confession, VIII, 8; III, 6; E. F. K. Müller, *Die Bekenntnisschriften,* 552, 563.

atonement began to weaken, diminish, and limit it. For if Christ made satisfaction for all, then the acquisition of salvation does not necessarily imply its application unless one embraces Origen's idea that one day all humans will really be saved.[139] But this is not what the advocates of universal atonement said. Like the Reformed they assumed that many people, both inside and outside the circle in which the gospel was and is proclaimed, were lost. Hence the application of salvation was detached from its acquisition; it was an accidental addition, not a logical and natural implication. God, therefore, had ordained his Son to the death of the cross without a definite plan to save anyone without fail. Christ, by his death, secured no one's salvation with certainty. In the final analysis the application of salvation depended totally on the free will of persons. This will must augment the work of Christ, make it fruitful, and let it become reality. In other words, what alone remains for Christ to accomplish is not the reality but the possibility of salvation, not actual reconciliation but potential reconcilability, "the salvable state." Christ only secured for God the possibility of entering into a covenant of grace with us, that is, of granting us the forgiveness of sins and eternal life, if we believe. The most significant part of the work of salvation, that which really effects salvation, is still left for us to do. Christ did not establish the covenant of grace itself in his blood, he did not actually forgive the sins of his people, but only made known that on the part of God there was no objection to making a covenant with us and to forgiving us our sins *if* and *after* we on our part believe. Actually, therefore, Christ did not secure anything for us; he only secured for God the possibility of forgiving us when we fulfill the commandments of the gospel.[140]

The universalists tend, therefore, to diminish the value and power of Christ's work. What they gain in quantity—and then only seemingly—they lose in quality. Rome teaches that the sins committed before baptism, which as a rule means original sin, are forgiven in baptism. Remaining after baptism, however, is *desire* (concupiscence), which is not itself sin but becomes an occasion for sin. The sins then committed are forgiven in the sacrament of penance, as it concerns guilt and eternal punishment, but temporal punishment remains to be borne by people either in this world or in purgatory.[141] The Remonstrants said that God, by the death of Christ, so reconciled all sinners to himself "that through and on account of this very ransom (λύτρον) and sacrifice he wished to return to them in grace and to open to them a harbor of eternal salvation and a way of immortality."[142] The Quakers have it that Christ's work consists in offering reconciliation to us and making God disposed to forgive.[143] And all who teach a universal atonement have

---

139. Thus Schleiermacher, Scholten, and numerous others. Cf. William Hastie, *The Theology of the Reformed Church in Its Fundamental Principles* (Edinburgh: T&T Clark, 1904), 277ff.

140. Canons of Dort, II, "Rejection of Errors."

141. Council of Trent, VI, 30; XIV, 8, 9, can. 12–14.

142. *Conf. rem.*, VIII, 9.

143. *R. Barclay, *Verantwoording van de ware Christ. Godg.* (1757), 153.

to come to the same conclusions.[144] The center of gravity has been shifted from Christ and located in the Christian. Faith is the true reconciliation with God.[145]

The Reformed, however, were of a different mind. "Vicarious atonement" is not a "ready-made quantity" but an operative principle and fundamentally includes the whole enterprise of re-creation. The work of Christ is finished only when he delivers the kingdom to the Father (1 Cor. 15:24). Rather than opening up the possibility of being saved, he perpetually saves [sinners] on the basis of the sacrifice completed on the cross. He is the Savior because he not only died for our sins but rose from the dead, ascended to heaven, and now, as the exalted Lord, prays for his church. He consecrated himself in order that his own also would be consecrated in truth (John 17:19). He gave himself up for the church that he might sanctify it and present it to himself with splendor (Eph. 5:25–27). Christ and his church are of one origin, which is God (Heb. 2:11), and are, as it were, one Christ (1 Cor. 12:12). In and with Christ, God gives to believers all they need (Rom. 8:32f.; Eph. 1:3–4; 2 Pet. 1:3). Election in Christ carries all blessings with it: adoption as children, redemption by his blood (Eph. 1:3ff.), the gift of the Holy Spirit (1 Cor. 12:3), faith (Phil. 1:29), repentance (Acts 5:31; 11:18; 2 Tim. 2:25), a new heart and a new spirit (Jer. 31:33–34; Ezek. 36:25–27; Heb. 8:8–12; 10:16).[146]

Still to be added to this, in the third place, is that universalism leads to all sorts of false positions. It introduces separation between the three persons of the Divine Being, for the Father wills the salvation of all, Christ makes satisfaction for all, but the Holy Spirit restricts the gift of faith and of salvation to a few. It introduces conflict between the purpose of God, who desires the salvation of all, and the will or power of God, who actually either will not or cannot grant salvation to all. It gives precedence to the person and work of Christ over election and the covenant, so that Christ is isolated from these contexts and cannot vicariously atone for his people, since there is no fellowship between him and us. It denigrates the justice of God by saying that he causes forgiveness and life to

144. This is clearly evident from an article by R. Liebe, "Über die Liebe Gottes," *Zeitschrift für Theologie und Kirche* (1909): 347–405. The universal apprehension of the love of God as though it applied to all humans in the same degree has made of God an all-too-cozy kind of being and robbed his love of its power (a petit-bourgeois love, against which Nietzsche rightly fulminated). It is promoted by the national church but is at variance with Christian experience and all of reality. Liebe, therefore, again wants to distinguish between a universal and a particular (individual) love of God, two loves that he then proceeds to link evolutionistically rather than to juxtapose dualistically. See also the discussions of this article by Herrmann and Pauli in the two following issues.

145. R. B. Kübel, *Über den Unterschied*, 135ff.

146. In addition to the Canons of Dort, cf. also the Leiden professors in Censura; *Conf. rem.*, VIII, 9; J. Trigland, *Antapologia* (Amsterdam: Joannam Janssonium [et al.], 1664), ch. 16; P. van Mastricht, *Theologia*, V, 18, 42; G. Voetius, *Select. disp.*, II, 9, 269; V, 270; H. Witsius, *Oeconomy of the Covenants*, II, 7; idem, *Miscellaneorum sacrorum*, 3rd ed., 2 vols. (Herborn: Iohannis Nicolai Andreae, 1712), II, 781; C. Vitringa, *Doctr. christ.*, 301ff.; B. de Moor, *Comm. theol.*, III, 1086ff.; W. Cunningham, *Hist. Theol.*, II, 301ff.; M. Schneckenburger and E. Güder, *Vergleichende Darstellung des lutherischen und reformierten Lehrbegriffs*, 2 vols. (Stuttgart: J. B. Metzler, 1855), II, 26.

be acquired for all and then fails to distribute them [to all]. It elevates free will to the point where it has the power to believe, to undo or not undo the work of Christ, and to decide—indeed, has the outcome of world history in its hands. It leads to the doctrine, as the Quakers rightly observed,[147] that if Christ died for all, then all must be given the opportunity, in either this world or the next, to accept or reject him, for it would be grossly unjust to condemn and to punish those whose sins had all been atoned for solely because they lacked the opportunity to accept Christ by faith. It further arrives at the position, in clear conflict with all of Scripture, that the only sin that leads to a person's being lost is the sin of unbelief. All other sins, after all, have been atoned for, including even those of the "man of sin," the Antichrist.

THE UNIVERSAL SIGNIFICANCE OF PARTICULAR ATONEMENT

[407] Although vicarious atonement as the acquisition of salvation in its totality cannot therefore be expanded to include all persons individually, this is not to say that it has no significance for those who are lost. Between the church and the world there is, at this point, not just separation and contrast. It is not the case that Christ has acquired everything for the former and nothing for the latter. In rejecting universalism one may not forget that Christ's merit has its limits even for the church and its value and meaning for the world. In the first place, it must be remembered, after all, that though Christ as such is indeed the Re-creator, he is not the Creator of all things. Just as the Son follows the Father, so re-creation presupposes creation, grace presupposes nature, and regeneration presupposes birth. Not included in Christ's merits, strictly speaking, is the fact that the elect are born and live, that they receive food, shelter, clothing, and an assortment of natural benefits. One *can* say that God would no longer have allowed the world and humankind to exist had he not had another and higher purpose for it. Common grace is indeed subservient to special grace, and along with salvation God also grants the elect many other, natural, blessings (Matt. 6:33; Rom. 8:28, 32; 1 Tim. 4:8; 2 Pet. 1:3). Still it is wrong, with the Herrnhuter and Pietists, to erase the boundaries between nature and grace, creation and redemption, and to put Christ in the Father's place on the throne of the universe. Even election and the covenant of grace, presupposing as they do the objects of the one and the participants of the other, were not acquired by Christ but precede his merits. With his creation the Father lays the groundwork for the work of re-creation and leads toward it. With his work, on the other hand, the Son goes back deeply—as far as sin reaches—into the work of creation. Still the two works are distinct and must not be confused.[148]

147. *R. Barclay, *Verantwoording*, 92.
148. G. Voetius, *Select. disp.*, II, 271–73.

In the second place, Christ did not, for each of his own, acquire the same thing. There is diversity among believers before they come to the faith, difference in gender, age, class, rank, character, gifts, and so on, and also in the measure and degree of wickedness and corruption. And when they come to the faith, there is diversity in the grace given them. Grace is given to each according to the measure Christ has bestowed (Rom. 12:3; 1 Cor. 12:11; Eph. 3:7; 4:7). The natural diversity among people, though cleansed by grace, is not erased. By the diversity of spiritual gifts, it is even increased, for the body of Christ consists of many members in order that it may be one organism, God's own creation and masterpiece.

Third, though the church is not of the world it is nevertheless in it. It lives and moves squarely within that world and is connected with it in numerous different ways. Believers are brought in from the [whole] human race, and, conversely, there is much chaff among the wheat; there are branches on the vine that bear no fruit and must be eradicated. When Christ went to stand in the place of his own, therefore, he had to assume the flesh and blood that is common to all people. By his incarnation, he honored the whole human race; according to the flesh, he is the brother of all the members of the human family. And also his work has value for all, even for those who have not believed and will never believe in him. For though it is true that Christ did not, strictly speaking, acquire the natural life by his suffering and death, yet the human race was spared on account of the fact that Christ would come to save it. Christ is not the head of all human beings, not the prophet, priest, and king of everyone, for he is the head of the church and has been anointed king over Zion. Yet all human beings owe a great deal to Christ. The light shines in the darkness and illumines every person coming into the world. The world was made through him and remains so, though it did not recognize him. Also as the Christ, he gives to unbelievers many benefits: the call of the gospel, the warning to repent, historical faith, a virtuous life, a variety of gifts and powers, offices and ministries within the church, such as, for example, even the office of an apostle in the case of Judas. "Without Jesus Christ the world would not exist, for it would necessarily either be destroyed or be a hell" (Pascal). Even hanging from the cross, he still prays for forgiveness for the appalling sin being committed by the Jews at that very moment.[149]

Fourth, Christ's work even extends to the world of irrational creatures. One cannot, with Origen, say that Christ suffered somewhat for them and merited something for them. But when Christ was made to be sin and bore the sin of the world, he also nullified sin with all its consequences. The liberation of the created world from the bondage of decay, the glorification of creation, the renewal of heaven and earth—all this is the fruit of the cross of Christ (Rom. 8:19ff.).[150]

Fifth, also the angels in heaven derive profit and advantage from the work of Christ. There is not sufficient ground for the assertion that Christ won for them

149. Ibid., II, 275, 276.
150. Ibid., II, 264, 265.

perseverance and glory, though many theologians, appealing to Job 4:18; 15:15; Ephesians 1:10; Colossians 1:20; 1 Timothy 5:21; Hebrews 12:22–23, taught as much.[151] Angels, of course, do not need Christ for themselves as Reconciler and Savior; they are essentially different from humans, who alone are made in the image of God. If Christ would have had to acquire "grace" and "glory" for them, this would lead one to think that the Son of God would have had to assume a human nature or, better, an angelic nature even if humanity had not fallen.[152] Still, simply to deny that Christ merited something for the angels does less than justice to Ephesians 1:10 and Colossians 1:20.[153] It is clearly stated, after all, that God reconciled all things (τα παντα), that is, not only people or angels, but all created things, the whole creation, the world, the universe, more fully described as "all things either on earth or in heaven," that God reconciled that whole creation by Christ, not to itself, but to *him*self, bringing all things together and into unity in him. The doctrine of the restitution of all things is not supported in these texts. It is repudiated throughout Scripture and has only now and then found defenders in the Christian church. If this doctrine is ruled out, then these two texts can only be understood to mean that, according to Paul's understanding, the demons and the wicked will someday be sent to hell and that the whole creation will be restored in the new heaven and the new earth with its inhabitants. Now this creation as a whole, conceived organically, was brought by sin into a position of hostility against God and internally torn apart and devastated. Implied here is not that the good angels, personally and individually, needed reconciliation, nor that Christ had to suffer and die for irrational creatures. Basic to these passages, however, is the premise that sin modified and disturbed the relation of all creatures to God and to one another.

And that, as we know, is indeed the case. Sin has made the human world into an object of God's wrath and divided and destroyed it internally. The relation of the angels to God was changed, not only inasmuch as many of them became apostate but also because the good angels formed only a part of the entire number of spirits who had served God. Augustine[154] and others were of the opinion that this breach struck in the world of angels was healed by the elect of the human race, and that this constituted the meaning of Christ's atonement for humankind.

151. Augustine, *Cons. ev.*, 35; and many with him, Cyril, Gregory, Bernard, Diez, Valentia, Suárez; J. Calvin, *Commentary,* on Eph. 1:10 and Col. 1:20; A. Polanus, *Syn. theol.*, VI, 27; J. Zanchi, *Op. theol.*, III, 159–64; G. Bucanus, *Institutiones theologicae* (Bern: Johannes & Isaias La Preux, 1605), VI, qu. 30; **Davenant, on Col. 1:20; A. Walaeus, *Synopsis purioris theologiae* (Leiden: Elzeviriana, 1652), XII, 33; idem, *Opera omnia* (Leiden: Ex officina Francisci Hackii, 1643), I, 195.

152. Cf. H. Bavinck, *Reformed Dogmatics*, II, 460–63 (#265); further P. Lombard, *Sent.*, II, dist. 5; III, dist. 13; T. Aquinas, *Summa theol.*, I, qu. 62; III, qu. 8, art. 4; D. Petavius, "De incarn.," *Op. theol.*, XII, 10; M. Becanus, *Summa theol. schol.*, I, 305; J. A. Quenstedt, *Theologia*, I, 476; J. Gerhard, *Loci theol.*, XXXI, §42; F. Gomarus, on Col. 1:20; G. Voetius, *Select. disp.*, II, 263; H. Alting, *Theol. probl. nova*, XII, 24; F. Turretin, *Institutes of Elenctic Theology*, XIV, qu. 3; B. de Moor, *Comm. theol.*, II, 353; C. Vitringa, *Doctr. christ.*, III, 26; VI, 178ff.

153. A. Kuyper, *De Engelen Gods* (Amsterdam: Höveker & Wormser, 1902–4), 164ff.

154. Augustine, *Enchiridion*, 61–62.

This view is not acceptable. Humans are generically distinct from angels, and there is no ground in Scripture for equating the number of the elect with that of the fallen angels. Still, it is true that the fall of so many angels must have profoundly disturbed the organism of the angelic world. As an army is totally thrown into disarray and rendered incapable of fighting when many officers and men leave the ranks and join the enemy, so also the world of angels as an army of God was shattered and made useless for the service of God. It lost its head, its organization. And now it gets this back in the person of the Son, and the Son not only according to his divine nature but also according to his human nature. For not merely the relation to God but also that to the human world was disturbed by sin. It is Christ, therefore, who as Lord of the angels and as head of the church puts both angels and humans in the right relation to God and so to each other. By his cross he restored the organism of creation, both in heaven and on earth, and these two also again in conjunction. The inanimate and irrational components of creation, in other words, heaven and earth itself, are not excluded from this process. This is already simply impossible inasmuch as the relation of the angels to heaven and that of humans to the earth, so far from being mechanical, is organic. With the fall of angels and humans, heaven and earth themselves sank to a level beneath their original state. The whole creation has been groaning and is experiencing the pains of childbirth. "The whole creation as it were collectively produces a colossal symphony of sighs" (Philippi). All the members of that creation groan and experience pain, collectively, in relation to one another (Rom. 8:22). Accordingly, as in the old covenant, the tabernacle and all its liturgical implements were sprinkled with blood (Exod. 24:3–8; Heb. 9:21), so Christ by his cross reconciled all things and acquired a new heaven and a new earth. The whole creation as one day it will stand perfect—without spot or wrinkle—in God's presence is the work of Christ, the Lord of lords and the King of kings (Heb. 12:22–28).

[408] Now if this is the grand project assigned by the Father to Christ, namely, to be a Savior in the full sense of the word and to carry out the entire work of re-creation, one immediately senses that to this end the state of exaltation is as necessary as the state of humiliation. It must be a poor idea of Christ's person and work that is held by those who believe they can abandon the resurrection, the ascension, and the seating at the right hand of God without injury to faith and life and are content with the historical image of Jesus, which, like that of other great men, lives on and exerts influence in history. On the other hand, it is understandable that those who view Jesus as no more than a particularly pious person and his work as nothing other than a religious-ethical reformation consider the entire state of exaltation worthless for the Christian life and deny and oppose the facts of the resurrection and ascension. Scripture, however, proceeds from a very different idea. It is the crucified but also the resurrected and exalted Christ whom the apostles proclaim. From that vantage point of the exaltation of Christ, they view and describe his earthly life, suffering, and death. For the work he now carries out as the exalted mediator, he laid the foundations in his cross.

In his battle with sin, the world, and Satan, the cross has been his only weapon. By the cross he triumphed in the sphere of justice over all powers that are hostile to God. But in the state of exaltation, consequently, he has also been given the divine right, the divine appointment, the royal power and prerogatives to carry out the work of re-creation in full, to conquer all his enemies, to save all those who have been given him, and to perfect the entire kingdom of God. On the basis of the one, perfect sacrifice made on the cross, he now—in keeping with the will of the Father—distributes all his benefits. Those benefits are not the physical or magical aftereffect of his earthly life and death; the history of the kingdom of God is not an evolutionistic process. It is the living and exalted Christ, seated at the right hand of God, who deliberately and with authority distributes all these benefits, gathers his elect, overcomes his enemies, and directs the history of the world toward the day of his parousia. He is still consistently at work in heaven as the mediator. He not only was but still is our chief prophet, our only high priest, and our eternal king. He is the same yesterday, today, and forever.

There is, of course, an enormous difference between the work Christ did in his humiliation and what he accomplishes in his exaltation. Just as after the resurrection, his person appeared in another form, so also his work assumed another form. He is now no longer a servant but Lord and Ruler, and his work is now no longer a sacrifice of obedience, but the conduct of royal dominion until he has gathered all his own and put all his enemies under his feet. Nevertheless, his mediatorial work is continued in heaven. Christ did not ascend to heaven in order to enjoy a quiet vacation at the right hand of God, for, like the Father, he always works (John 5:17). He went to heaven to prepare a place for his own there and to fill them here on earth with the fullness that he acquired by his perfect obedience. What he received as a reward for his labor for himself and what he received for his own cannot be separated. He is all and in all (Col. 3:11). The pleroma (fullness) that dwells in Christ must also dwell in the church. It is being filled with all the fullness of God (Eph. 3:19; Col. 2:2, 10). It is God whose fullness fills Christ (Col. 1:19), and it is Christ whose fullness in turn fills the church (Eph. 1:23). The church can therefore be described as his pleroma, that which he perfects and gradually, from within himself, fills with himself (Eph. 4:10), and is therefore itself being filled by degrees. As the church does not exist apart from Christ, so Christ does not exist without the church. He is "the head over all things" (Eph. 1:22; Col. 1:18), and the church is the body (σῶμα) formed from him and from him receives its growth (Eph. 4:16; Col. 2:19), thus growing to maturity "to the measure of the full stature of Christ" (Eph. 4:13). The union between Christ and the church is as close as that between the vine and the branches, between bridegroom and bride, husband and wife, cornerstone and building. Together with him it can be called the one Christ (1 Cor. 12:12). It is to perfect the church that he is exalted to the Father's right hand. Just as through his suffering and death Christ was exalted in his resurrection and ascension to be head of the church, so now the church has to be formed into the body of Christ. The work of the Mediator is one grand, mighty, divine work that began in eternity and will only be completed in eternity. But in the moment of the resurrection, it was divided into two parts. Then it was suffering; now it is entering into glory. Then it was a descent to the nethermost parts of the earth; now it is an ascent on high. But the two are equally necessary to the work of salvation. In both states it is the same Christ, the same Mediator, the same Prophet, Priest, and King.

CHRIST'S THREEFOLD OFFICE IN THE STATE OF EXALTATION

[409] That Christ continues his prophetic activity in the state of exaltation becomes immediately apparent from the fact that during the forty days between his resurrection and ascension he spoke to his disciples about the kingdom of God (Acts 1:3).[155] In addition, he fulfilled the promise that he had made to them to the effect that they would receive the Holy Spirit and that the Spirit would teach them all things and lead them into all truth (John 14:26; 16:13). He gave the Spirit in a special sense to the apostles (John 20:22) but further also to all believers (Acts 2). By the extraordinary offices of the apostles, prophets, and evangelists, he communicated both orally and in writing the truth that had been revealed in his person and work. By extraordinary gifts of wisdom and knowledge (1 Cor. 12:8), he made that truth known and understood; and by extraordinary signs (Mark 16:17; Acts 5:15; 8:6–7, 13; Rom. 15:18; etc.) he confirmed that truth, leading both Jews and Gentiles to the obedience of faith. And also after this foundational period of the church passed, Christ continues to be prophetically active in his church, for by the word of the apostles recorded in Scripture, he continually brings people to faith in his name (John 17:20) and into fellowship with him and with the Father (1 John 1:3). By the ordinary office of pastors and teachers (Rom. 12:7; 1 Cor. 12:28; Eph. 4:11; 1 Tim. 5:17), he builds up his church in the grace and knowledge of its Lord and Savior, and by the working of the Holy Spirit, he shines on it the light of the gospel of his glory (2 Cor. 4:4, 6).

All these ministries and workings proceed from the exalted Christ, who is the one Lord of the church (1 Cor. 8:6) in whom all the treasures of wisdom and knowledge are hidden (Col. 2:3; 1 Cor. 1:30). He came into the world to bear witness to the truth over against the lie (John 8:44–45; 18:36). He not only spoke the truth but is himself the truth who has made known the Father, leads us to the Father, and, in the knowledge of God, grants eternal life (John 1:17–18; 14:6; 17:3). In fighting falsehood, he therefore uses no other weapon than that of the word: this word is the sword of his mouth (Eph. 6:17; Rev. 2:12, 16; 19:15). By that word he judges and separates things (John 3:17–18; 9:39; 12:47; Heb. 4:12), but he also makes free and gives life (John 8:31–32, 51; 15:3; 17:3). To remain in his word and make his word remain in them is the calling of his disciples (John 8:31, 51; 15:7; 1 John 2:24). They have no other teacher (Matt. 23:8, 10), nor do

155. Cf. above, 442–44 (#401).

they need one. They have received the anointing of the Holy One, that is, Christ, and know all things (1 John 2:20), so that among them there is no need for pagan divination and sorcery, spiritism or occultism, for hierarchical guardianship or an infallible papacy. Christ himself teaches them by his Word and Spirit, so that, being taught by God, they would all be prophets and proclaim the marvelous works of God (Num. 11:29; Jer. 31:33–34; Matt. 11:25–27; John 6:45; Heb. 8:10; 1 John 2:20). And he continues this instruction until they have all attained to the unity of the faith and the knowledge of the Son of God (Eph. 4:13; 3:18f.).

In the same manner Christ in his exaltation remains active as priest. In the Letter to the Hebrews,[156] this idea is very much in the foreground, and Christ's earthly life is often viewed there as preparation for the high-priestly activity he now carries out in heaven. To be able to fulfill this high-priestly office, he had to be the Son, who, as "the reflection of God's glory and the exact imprint of God's very being," creates, upholds, and inherits all things (Heb. 1:1–3; 4:14; 5:5; 9:14). In his human nature, moreover, he needed through suffering and trials to learn obedience and so be "perfected," be fully prepared, for his high-priestly ministry in heaven (2:10f.; 4:15; 5:7–10; 7:28). After thus bringing his one, perfect sacrifice and so effecting purification for our sins (1:3; 7:27; 9:12; etc.), he as high priest entered the heavenly sanctuary foreshadowed in the holy of holies of the Old Testament tabernacle (6:20; 9:12, 24)—not with the blood of goats and calves but by the power of his own blood (9:12–14), through the tent of his body (9:11), the curtain of his flesh (10:20), in order to appear there on our behalf in the presence of God and to pray for those who through him draw near to God (7:25; 9:24).

From this scenario pictured in the Letter to the Hebrews, the Socinians inferred that Christ was not yet actually a priest on earth, that his sacrifice on the cross was not yet the true sacrifice, that all those things still belonged to his preparation and equipment. In the true and full sense, Christ became a priest only in heaven, when he entered it with his own blood and sat down at God's right hand to live and to pray there forever for his own. For just as under the Old Testament dispensation the atoning act consisted not in slaying the sacrificial animal but in sprinkling its blood on the altar or on the mercy seat (Lev. 16:11–16), so Christ really brings about expiation on earth, not by his death, but by his intercession in heaven.[157] In recent times this view has been revived by others, especially by and since William Milligan. They, too, assert that, according to the Letter to the Hebrews, Christ's priesthood only begins with his ascension and that it consists in the self-offering and consecration of Christ to the Father continued in heaven.[158]

---

156. In addition to the various commentaries on this letter, cf. also the studies cited above in note 2 of this chapter.

157. F. Socinus, *De Jesu Christo servatore* (Rakow: Rodecius, 1594), II, 164; J. Völkel, *De vera religione libri quinque* (Racoviae: Typis Sebastiani Sternacii, 1630), III, 37; O. Fock, *Der Socinianismus*, 635, 646ff.

158. W. Milligan, *The Ascension and Heavenly Priesthood of Our Lord* (London: Macmillian, 1892); G. Milligan, *The Theology of the Epistle to the Hebrews* (Edinburgh: T&T Clark, 1899); *J. I. Doedes, *Jahrbuch*

This view, however, has been rightly opposed by others, for in the case of the Old Testament sacrifices, the different expiatory actions, though temporally distinct, still form a single whole. It is the blood of the slain animal that, by being poured out and sprinkled, freed the offerer from his sin and restored him to God's favor. Correspondingly, in the Letter to the Hebrews, as in all the books of the New Testament, the expiatory power is attributed completely to the sacrifice that Christ made on the cross. That is the utterly unique and perfect sacrifice (7:27; 9:12, 26, 28; 10:10, 12, 14; 13:12) by which the new covenant has been established (8:8f.; 9:15f.). By it the forgiveness of sins (8:12; 10:18) and all other benefits, specifically also the free approach to God (4:16; 10:19) have been secured. Because Christ thus once sacrificed himself on the cross, even he cannot do it again a second time, for just as every human dies only once, so also Christ's sacrifice in death is not susceptible of repetition (9:26–28). This absolutely unique value that the Letter to the Hebrews attaches to the death of Christ by itself already rules out that he would now sacrifice himself a second time in heaven or for the first time truly sacrifice himself there. This letter does place a strong accent on Christ's ascension, on his entrance into the true heavenly sanctuary, just as it does on his sacrifice on the cross. One should note, however, that the author of this letter nowhere says that Christ entered heaven *with* his blood, the way the Old Testament high priest on the great Day of Atonement entered the holy of holies with blood to sprinkle it on and before the mercy seat. He only says that Christ once for all entered the sanctuary through his blood (9:12). He did not take with him the blood that was shed on the cross to sprinkle it in the heavenly sanctuary, thereby to bring about atonement. But by means of his blood, on the basis of the sacrifice made on the cross, he secured for himself the right to enter heaven to appear in God's presence on our behalf.

In the Old Testament, after the sacrifice had been brought, the high priest still had to take some of the blood, enter the holy of holies with it, and offer it for both his own and his people's misdeeds. But that was still a part of the imperfect system of the Old Testament. This showed that the way into the sanctuary had not yet been disclosed so long as the first tabernacle was still standing (9:7–8). This, however, did not apply to Christ. He brought a unique and perfect sacrifice on the cross. He did not take his blood with him to heaven to offer it there, but through the tent of his own body and the curtain of his flesh (9:11; 10:20), he entered once for all into the true sanctuary and to that end received the right and the power by his own blood that he had shed on the cross (9:12). His blood had that power because it was his own, because through the eternal Spirit he offered himself to God without blemish (9:14). That blood, to be sure, had been shed only once, and that sacrifice had taken place only once at a specific moment in time; yet this event was not—like the sacrificial cult of the Old Testament—temporary,

---

v. wetenschaaplijke Theol. (1846): 293–313; A. Seeberg, *Der Tod Christi in seiner Bedeutung für die Erlösung* (Leipzig: Deichert, 1895), 14, 16ff.

passing, transient. On the contrary, the sacrifice on the cross was the sacrifice of One who was the Son, Creator, and Heir of all things, who also became human, perfected himself by his obedience, and proved by the shedding of his blood that the eternal Spirit dwelt in him. It, therefore, has eternal, spiritual significance. Christ was high priest already on earth (7:27; 9:11, 14, 25, 28; 10:10; 13:12), but he was that not in the way of Aaron's high priesthood, but according to the order of Melchizedek, eternal and unchanging.

It is for this reason, however, that the Letter to the Hebrews so strongly stresses Christ's entry into the true sanctuary. He entered it by the power of his own blood, not to sacrifice himself again in a different manner, for he did that once for all, and by that sacrifice acquired all the benefits of the covenant of grace (9:26–28; 10:12, 14; etc.). He entered it now to be, in the full and true sense, the high priest of the good things to come (9:11), a high priest seated at the right hand of the throne of majesty on high (1:3; 3:1; 4:14; 6:20; 8:1). We have a perfect high priest, one who learned obedience, who perfected himself, who became like us, who can have compassion with us, who once for all offered himself through the eternal Spirit, but who in that way also secured the right to sit at the right hand of God. He is a high priest who, like Melchizedek, is at the same time king, king of righteousness and king of peace, an eternal, spiritual, and heavenly king; a high priest who acquired, possesses, and distributes the heavenly goods to come, who can appear in heaven before the face of God for our benefit, pray for us, and save us completely (7:25; 9:24). And this describes the priestly activity that Christ still performs even now. He no longer sacrifices himself there, for he did that once for all and completely on the cross. In heaven there is no repetition, no renewal, no reproduction of the sacrifice of the cross. For in the innermost and true sanctuary, there is no room for an altar.

The sacrifice Christ brought on earth has an eternal character. It remains present in and carries over into Christ's appearance before the face of God and in his intercession on our behalf. It is both historical and transhistorical: because it was the sacrifice of the Son by the power of the Holy Spirit, it is an act of and at the same time the enablement for his eternal, royal high priesthood in heaven. Even more vividly than Paul (e.g., in Phil. 2:6–11), the Letter to the Hebrews views Christ's state of humiliation from the vantage point of his exaltation and regards the former as preparation and practice for the latter. At present, in heaven, Christ is the perfectly groomed high priest, the high priest–king who possesses all that he acquired, who is indescribably rich in spiritual and eternal goods, and who, from his position in heaven, administers them to us. To be truly a priest, he had to be a priest in heaven, not on earth, not in a manmade temple, but in heaven, on the throne of the universe. Inasmuch as he once for all offered himself up without blemish and by a single sacrifice for all time perfected those who are sanctified (10:14), he is able for all time to save all those who draw near to God through him, "since he always lives to make intercession for them" (7:25). In this intercession his sacrifice continues to be operative and effective. Not a sacrifice detached from Christ's person, a sacrifice once for all offered on earth, but the exalted Christ, who is simultaneously the crucified Christ, is and remains the expiation for our sins (1 John 2:2). Christ "is the same yesterday and today and forever" (Heb. 13:8).[159]

So, since Christ is an eternal priest-king, the church on earth no longer needs a priest. All believers are priests (Rom. 12:1; 1 Pet. 2:5; Rev. 1:6). There is no further need for sacrifices made for sin, not even for the unbloody one in the Mass, for from the one sacrifice made on the cross there arises, in Christ's intercession, perpetual witness to God, not for vengeance, as from the blood of Abel, but for grace and forgiveness (Heb. 12:24). Christ's intercession is no longer the pleading of a suppliant as in the days of his flesh[160] but the steadfast gracious will of Christ (John 17:24) to lead all his people to the blessedness of heaven on the basis of his sacrifice. Thus Christ is our only priest, who, according to the order of Melchizedek, remains forever, continually covers our sins with his sacrifice, always acts as our Paraclete with the Father, pleads our cause against all the accusations of Satan, the world, and our own heart, makes our prayers and thanksgivings pleasing to the Father, consistently assures us of free and confident access to the throne of grace, and out of his fullness sends to us all the blessings of grace (Luke 22:32; John 14:16; 17:9f.; Rom. 1:7; 8:32f.; 1 Cor. 1:3; 2 Cor. 1:2; Eph. 1:3; 1 Tim. 4:8; Heb. 7:25; 9:24; 1 John 2:2).

In this way Christ is and always remains our eternal king as well. Although he was also anointed with respect to his human nature, he began to act as king only upon his exaltation. Then he received the name "Lord," was designated Son of God, and received all power in heaven and on earth. Christ is first of all king over his people in the kingdom of grace (Ps. 2:6; Isa. 9:6; 11:1–5; Luke 1:33; 19:21–23; 23:42–43; John 18:33; 19:19; etc.) and demonstrates this kingship in gathering, protecting, and ruling his church, leading it to eternal blessedness (Matt. 16:18; 28:20; John 10:28). But in the New Testament, because his kingship bears a very different character from that of the rulers of the earth, he is much more often called the head of the church (1 Cor. 11:3; Eph. 1:22; 4:15; 5:23; Col. 1:18; 2:19). He rules not by violence but by justice and righteousness, by grace and love, Word and Spirit. In the New Testament he is also specially denominated "king" whenever there is reference to his victory over his enemies. For in order for him truly to gather, protect, and lead his church to eternal

---

159. J. Cloppenburg, *Op. theol.*, II, 889–902; N. Arnoldi, *Religio sociniana* (Franeker: Jansson, 1654), 678–706; P. de Witte, *Wederlegginge der sociniänsche dwalingen*, 3 vols. (Amsterdam: Boeckholt & van den Heuvel, 1662), II, 152ff.; P. van Mastricht, *Theologia*, V, 7, 15ff.; J. Maccovius, *Collegia theologica*, 3rd ed. (Franeker: Joannis Fabiani Deuring, 1641), I, 240ff.; *idem, Jahrbuch v. wetenschaaplijke Theol.*, IV, 18ff.; B. Weiss, *Biblical Theology of the New Testament*, §121; M. Scheeben, *Dogmatik*, III, 443ff.; H. T. Simar, *Lehrbuch der Dogmatik*, 3rd ed. (Freiburg i.B.: Herder, 1893), §112; V. Thalhofer, *Handbuch der katholischen Liturgik*, 2nd ed., 2 vols. (Freiburg i.B.: Herder, 1912), I, 223–36; G. B. Stevens, *Theology of the New Testament*, 506ff.; W. H. G. Thomas, "Priest," *DC*, II, 416ff.; G. Vos, "The Priesthood of Christ in the Epistle to the Hebrews," *Princeton Theological Review* (July 1907): 423–47.

160. J. Calvin, *Institutes*, III.xx.20.

salvation, he must as the mediator have power over all creatures (Pss. 2:8; 72:8; 110:1–3; Matt. 28:18; 1 Cor. 15:24, 27; Eph. 1:22; Phil. 2:9–11; 1 Pet. 3:22; Rev. 1:5; 17:14). This implies not that Christ concretely governs the world but that it is under his control, subject to him, and will one day, be it unwillingly, recognize and honor him as Lord. Specifically belonging in this category is his power over the realm of Satan.

The notion of many of the church fathers that Christ made his sacrifice to Satan and by craftiness deprived him of his spoils is unscriptural. Still by his cross Christ also triumphed over the world of fallen spirits. He came to earth to destroy the works of the devil (1 John 3:8) and battled against him all his life (Luke 4:13), especially toward the end when it was the hour and power of darkness (Luke 22:53). He was the stronger contender (Luke 11:22), and the devil has no power over him (John 14:30). He already saw him fall like lightning from heaven and took his armor from him (Luke 10:18; 11:22). Especially by the cross he triumphed over authorities and powers (Col. 2:15), took from Satan the weapons of sin, death, and the world (John 16:33; 1 John 4:4; 1 Cor. 15:55–56; Heb. 2:14), and cast him out of the territory of his kingship (John 12:31). He triumphed over the evil spirits specifically on the occasion of his ascension. In Ephesians 4:8, the apostle Paul says that Christ, ascending on high, led captives in his train; in other words, he overcame all the hostile powers who resisted and opposed him and, as it were, captured them as prisoners of war (cf. Col. 2:15).[161]

We probably find the same idea expressed in the difficult text 1 Peter 3:19–22. This text certainly does not speak of a descent into hell to proclaim the gospel to the lost. We read, after all, that Christ was first made alive, that is, rose from the dead, and then went out to preach. There are no grounds whatever for making a temporal distinction, as the Lutherans do, between Christ's vivification and resurrection and to situate the descent into hell in the interim. Nor is there any indication in Scripture that after his resurrection and before his ascension, Christ first went to hell. Untenable also, however, is the exegesis that Christ went in the Spirit to the contemporaries of Noah and preached to them there. The phrase "in which" (ἐν ᾧ) clearly refers to the Christ who had been made alive; the words "having gone" (πορευθείς; cf. v. 22) permit no other interpretation. Christ's preaching in the Spirit to Noah's contemporaries in former times is not relevant here. The pericope, accordingly, is about something very different.

The case is this: Peter admonishes believers to suffer while doing good and to follow Christ's example in this regard. He, after all, died doing good, for he suffered for sins, as a righteous person for the unrighteous, and did so for the purpose of bringing us, the unrighteous, to God. That is suffering while doing good! Now Christ indeed was killed in the flesh but made alive and resurrected in

---

161. The link between the victory over his enemies and his ascension, therefore, has been repeatedly noticed and expressed. The Larger Catechism of Westminster, Q. 53, for example, says that Christ, "triumphing over enemies, visibly went up into the highest heaven."

the Spirit, since the Spirit of holiness as Spirit was the governing principle of his whole life. And as such, journeying as the vivified, risen Spirit, as Lord and King, he went, not to hell, but as verse 22 indicates, to heaven, and thereby preached to the spirits in heaven. That is, his going to heaven as the risen Lord (Acts 2:36) was a message to the spirits in prison. It is not stated what the content of this message (κήρυγμα) was, nor does it need to be. The fact of his rising again and ascending to heaven was itself the rich, powerful, and triumphant message to the spirits in prison. That Peter now has this κήρυγμα of Christ brought by his ascension, specifically to those spirits in prison who in the days of Noah, in defiance of God's patience and their seeing Noah building the ark, were disobedient, has two reasons. In the first place, the contemporaries of Noah are always pictured in Scripture as the most ungodly people. And in the second place, they were killed, whereas Noah and his family were saved, by the waters of the same flood. Similarly, as a result of *the resurrection of Christ,* the water of baptism is the ruin of the ungodly and salvation for believers. For Christ, who arose from the dead and instituted baptism and gives power to it, after subduing all angels, authorities, and powers by his ascension, now sits at God's right hand. Christ suffered doing good and overcame; now let believers follow in his footsteps! And just as he has power over all fallen spirits, so, as mediator, Christ also has power (in his kingdom of power) over all his enemies. And he will not rest until he has put all his enemies under his feet.

At the end of the days, when Christ has subdued his church and all his enemies, he will deliver the βασιλεία, the kingship, the royal office, to the Father. Then his mediatorial work is finished. The work the Father instructed him to do will have been completed. God himself will then be king forever. Already at an early stage there was controversy over Christ's submission to the Father. Marcellus of Ancyra wrote a treatise about the submission of Christ, the Lord, and was charged with teaching that the kingdom of Christ and also the union of his human nature with the Logos would end.[162] Marcellus was opposed by Eusebius and later by Basil. To the confession that Christ would come again to judge the living and the dead, the Niceno-Constantinopolitan added the words "of whose kingdom there will be no end."[163] Later the Socinians taught that Christ, whom the Father had temporarily appointed as viceroy, would one day abdicate, like a field general who, having achieved victory in battle, returns his commission and power to the king. From this they inferred that the Son of God, since he would one day be subject

---

162. J. Schwane, *Dogmengeschichte,* II, 136, 148. According to O. Scheel (*Die Anschauung Augustins über Christi Person und Werk* [Tübingen: Mohr, 1901]), it is not impossible that Augustine "was for a while persuaded that the Word was not eternally bound to the human nature." F. Kattenbusch, who cites these words (in *Theologische Literaturzeitung* 28 [March 1903]: 204), agrees: "Whenever Augustine speaks of a necessary coming of Christ, his Neoplatonism influences him." However, from this it does not at all follow that the union of the two natures in Christ is only temporary.

163. A. Hahn, *Bibliothek der Symbole und Glaubensregeln der alten Kirche,* 3rd ed. (Breslau: E. Morgenstern, 1897), 146–66; cf. D. Petavius, "De incarn.," *Op. theol.,* XII, 18; C. Pesch, *Prael. dogm.,* IV, 84.

to the Father, could not be the supreme God.[164] Among the Reformed there was also disagreement on this point. Some said that Christ's kingship was "economic" and temporary.[165] Others were of the opinion that though there will be change in the manner of governing, Christ's kingship itself remains in perpetuity.[166] The difference can be easily resolved by saying that the mediatorship of reconciliation, and to that extent also the prophetic, priestly, and royal office of Christ, ends. God will be king and [thus] all in all. But what remains is the mediatorship of union. Christ remains Prophet, Priest, and King as this triple office is automatically given with his human nature, included in the image of God, and realized supremely and most magnificently in Christ as the Image of God. Christ is and remains the head of the church, from whom all life and blessedness flow to it throughout all eternity.[167] Those who would deny this must also arrive at the doctrine that the Son will at some point in the future shed and destroy his human nature; and for this there is no scriptural ground whatever.

164. Cf., contra this position, D. Petavius, "De trin.," *Op. theol.*, III, 5; J. H. Bisterfeld, *De uno deo, Patre, Filio, ac Spiritu Sancto, mysterium pietatis* (Leiden: Elseviriana, 1639), I, 2, 26; C. Vitringa, *Doctr. christ.*, V, 443–46.

165. J. Calvin, *Institutes*, I.xiv.3; I.xv.5; idem, *Commentary*, on 1 Cor. 15:28; H. Alting, *Theol. problematica nova*, XII, 36; D. Pareus, *Ad Corinthios priorem S. Pauli apostoli epistolam commentarius* (Heidelberg: Jonae Rhodii, 1613), on 1 Cor. 15:28.

166. P. van Mastricht, *Theologia*, V, 8, 9; B. de Moor, *Comm. theol.*, III, 1129; C. Vitringa, *Doctr. christ.*, V, 443.

167. A. Kuyper, *Principles of Sacred Theology*, trans. J. Hendrik de Vries (Grand Rapids: Eerdmans, 1954 [1898]), 372; idem, *De vleeschwording des Woords* (Amsterdam: Wormser, 1887), 31, 195.

PART IV

SALVATION IN CHRIST

9

THE ORDER OF SALVATION

The application of Christ's work to the salvation of his own must be viewed theologically, that is, from God's point of view. All religions seek a way of salvation; all human beings long for happiness because the human heart is created for God. Unique to the Christian religion is the reality of Jesus Christ and the redemption he brings as fully God's initiative; all other religions seek redemption through human action. However the human problem is conceived, it remains human beings who must satisfy the deity and fulfill its demands or law. All religions or philosophies other than the Christian faith are autosoteric.

The biblical viewpoint is radically different; salvation is solely a gift of grace. God elects his people, enters into a covenant with them, a covenant that demands reciprocal duties of love and obedience. Pious Israelites meditated on God's law, found their righteousness not in their own works but in God's grace, sought forgiveness, and abandoned their own cause in hope to a righteous God. Israel, too, lived in faith, resting in the eternal faithfulness of their covenant God. However, after the exile, Judaism drifted into greater and greater nomism and prepared itself for the coming Messiah by scrupulous attention to the law's demands. The result was Pharisaic pride, on the one hand, and despair for the sinner, on the other. In this context, Jesus announced the good news of God's reign: forgiveness of sins by the gift of grace. The kingdom was for all who were poor in spirit, not just for Jews who kept the law.

The apostolic preaching was directed to the accomplished work of Christ as the mediator empowered by the Holy Spirit. In his exaltation Christ becomes the life-giving Spirit equipping his disciples for the work of ministry and convicting the world of sin and judgment. The outpouring of the Holy Spirit on the apostles was accompanied by extraordinary forces and works, including the miracle of languages on Pentecost. Later instances of the different gift of glossolalia were weaker and diminished instances of this Pentecost miracle. On the birthday of the church, the church itself acclaims in many languages the great works of God. These and other extraordinary workings of the Holy Spirit continued throughout the apostolic period, when they were necessary to effect in the world the acceptance and permanence of the confession that Jesus is Lord.

Early church theologians such as Irenaeus intimately linked salvation to the applied work of Christ by the Holy Spirit, but for many others the gospel increasingly became construed as a new law, a work that involved human willing and acting. Repentance degenerated into penance, and salvation was externalized as a copying of Christ's life and especially his suffering. This trend culminated in the teaching of Pelagius, who did not deny grace but understood it as a universal gift to all people enabling them to choose the good and refuse evil. Grace is emptied of its real meaning since our appropriation of grace depends on our own will: God helps those who help themselves. The great gift of Augustine to the church was his definitive repudiation of all forms of Pelagianism. According to Augustine, our wills are bound, from beginning to end being redirected to God's good and persevering in it; it is a matter of gift not of merit, of grace not of works. Objectively and subjectively, from beginning to end, the work of salvation is a work of God's grace and of his grace alone. Augustine's viewpoint became the dogma of the church and remains the teaching of all orthodox, evangelical Christianity.

Pelagianism and semi-Pelagianism are also condemned by official Roman Catholic teaching and by the great Roman theologians such as Aquinas and Bonaventure. However, it is fair to ask whether, in a roundabout way, Rome has not smuggled semi-Pelagianism back in again. Trent taught that it is possible to assent to or to reject prevenient grace. Faith here too is not seen as central to justifying faith; it is only assent to the truth of Christianity. Taken by itself it does not justify; it is only preparatory to the infusion of sacramental grace. By the merit of condignity, this grace enables human beings to do good and to merit heavenly beatitude. By grace the Roman Catholic Church does not, at least not primarily, mean the free favor of God by which he forgives sins. Rather, grace is a quality or supernatural power infused in human beings, lifting them into a supernatural order and enabling them to do good works and to merit heavenly blessedness by the merit of condignity.

It was the Roman Catholic penitential system in general and the sale of indulgences in particular that prompted Luther's reformational activity. Luther reemphasized God's righteousness not as his own attribute but as the righteousness of faith granted by God in grace, through faith alone. This led to conflict with Roman church authorities over the abuse of indulgences, though this practice is itself a direct consequence of Rome's nomist degradation of the gospel. For Luther the most important work of penitence had nothing to do with the Roman institution of confession but involved a change of heart characterized by true sorrow for sin and in the word of absolution proclaimed in the gospel of grace. It is not the sacrament but faith that justifies. The three components in Luther's understanding are contrition, faith, and then good works.

Luther always taught absolute predestination, though in his later period, to offset misuse of the doctrine, he accented the revelation of God in Christ and the universal offer of salvation in the world of the gospel. Melanchthon, however, with increasing firmness, adopted a synergistic position. As a result a covert or overt synergism can be found in Lutheranism. Grace is always resistible and therefore amissible, that is, losable, and can be lost and regained over and over again. In the order of salvation, therefore, the center of gravity lies with the human person. Human resistance can nullify the entire work of God the Father, Son, and Spirit. The center is in faith and justification; calling, contrition, and regeneration have only a preparatory function. Everything depends on faith, specifically on the act of believing. Failing to understand the work of God's grace as proceeding from his eternal decree and covenant, Lutherans also fail to relate it back to nature, the world, and humanity.

The Reformed view shares much with the Lutheran, but the order of salvation presupposes communion with Christ, a bond between the mediator and the elect forged in eternity, in the counsel of peace between Father and Son. Atonement and justification are already objectively, actively, present in Christ as the fruit of his work and are appropriated by the believer by the Spirit of Christ. The application of salvation, too, is Christ's work, not ours. Soteriology, too, must be viewed theologically, as a work of God the Father, Son, and Holy Spirit. The covenant of grace precedes and is the foundation and starting point for the work of salvation. Regeneration, faith, and conversion are not preparations for but the benefits of covenantal fellowship of believers with God in Christ imparted to us by the Holy Spirit. For the Reformed penitence, and even conversion, is more significant as a lifelong path of growth in obedient discipleship, of mortification to self and living to Christ. The advantage of this approach is that justification is now seen more purely as an act of juridical acquittal, and faith gains in surety and assurance. The Christian life now also gains a greater ethical significance and the law a greater role as a rule and motivator of the human will. The Reformed Christian is called actively to fight against sin.

Other prominent understandings of the way of salvation include the diametrically opposed approaches of mysticism and rationalism. The former seeks by extraordinary practices, disciplines, and powers—via negativa, purgativa—to achieve some form of ecstatic communion—illuminatio, contemplatio, unitiva—with the divine. Rationalism, on the other hand, only sees Jesus as a teacher to be followed and imitated as best we can. Related to these two are antinomianism and neonomianism. The former reduces salvation to and equates it with its acquisition, thereby eschewing all works, while the latter reinstitutes law. In the former, sin is an illusion and leads to anarchy; in the latter, keeping the law becomes the unevangelical way of salvation. Neonomianism also took a different shape in Pietism and Methodism, where faith and experience, rather than faith and obedience, became the condition for justification. Though properly reacting to dead orthodoxy in the church, this emphasis on living *faith as a practical reality led to a new form of legalism dividing believers into "weak" and "strong," "carnal" and "spiritual." Though in its revivalist, Methodist form this type of Christianity has borne much fruit for renewing people and society, the weakness remains that the human subject and experience or obedience takes center stage rather than the grace of God and the work of Christ.*

Modern thought similarly turns away from God to the human subject. Descartes found the basis of all certain knowledge to be self-knowledge, and Spinoza reduced good and evil to modes of thinking in our consciousness. Salvation is then seen as freedom from the necessary constraints of nature and the senses; enlightenment of the intellect or moral improvement as the road to betterment. All external authority was rejected; individual reason and will were supreme. Kant, however, retained room for faith in practical reason. After concluding that human nature is not intrinsically good but flawed and evil, requiring rebirth and renewal, Kant still followed the Pelagian route and inferred an ultimate human freedom and moral capacity from the existence of the moral imperative. "Thou shalt" necessarily implies "thou can." Human beings simply suffer from a conflict of two predispositions—one toward evil and the other toward good—and must by an intelligible act of freedom redeem themselves. In that effort we can hope for but never be sure of "cooperation from above." Remarkably, Kant here also teaches a form of assurance of faith in perseverance; those who increase in moral betterment may conclude divine favor and the hope of reaching moral perfection. Other thinkers such as Schopenhauer and especially Eduard von Hartmann use the language of faith to point to the reality of human evil and the need of grace but mean by them something quite different from Christian orthodoxy. Grace still includes human moral effort; faith is a totally human act by which we gain grace. The human subject remains at the center.

In philosophical idealism, too, self-determination, the ego, is the essence of human freedom. The historical work of Christ is slighted; it becomes only a metaphysical and moral ideal to be achieved by human willing. Fichte, Schelling, and Hegel, each in his own way, sought to unify philosophic thought with Christian truth, but they so subordinated faith to intellectual constructs such as the Absolute that historical Christianity with the person and work of Christ at the center became unrecognizable. Though modern thought after Kant attempted to overcome rationalism and develop a "philosophy of redemption," it achieved this only in form and not in substance. It is still human thought that brings about true redemption; Christianity's doctrine of reconciliation is only brought to light by philosophy. Thus not religion but philosophy brings about salvation. Stripped of all the speculative wording and reduced to simple words, idealistic philosophy still advocates salvation by human effort of intellect and will. Conversion, for example, is really a human act of penitence viewed from God's perspective.

Modern theology, beginning with Schleiermacher, took the historical person of Jesus more seriously, though the human subject remains at the center of his Christian understanding. For Ritschl justification is synthetic judgment valid for the community; he is to be praised for placing this once again in the center of the redemptive order. Yet, to be faulted is Ritschl's denial of God's wrath on sin and his seeming indifference to personal justification and assurance in his desire to motivate Christians to action in the world of culture. However, this activism was accompanied by a cultural optimism that could not and did not satisfy; many longed for a more mystical and spiritual Christianity. Ritschl's ethical Christianity gave way to the school of the history of religions and to the psychology of religion.

The psychological study of religion is a relatively new science that takes its departure from subjective religious experience and seeks to infer a law governing all religious development. Parallel to the evolutionary notion that ontogeny recapitulates phylogeny, the development of religious sensibility is seen to move from childlike obedience to rules and dogmas, through the labor pains of adolescent conflict into individuality and capacity for reflection, to adult maturity. Since during the years of puberty the soul is subject to continual unrest and disturbance, adolescent sexual awakening is often seen to parallel religious awakening. In this framework, conversion, however strange it may seem, is only the fruit of natural processes that can be explained scientifically as part of ordinary human development. This occurs in all religions in formally similar patterns. The stages of development observed in individuals also characterize humanity as a whole. Humanity's development is recapitulated in the individual person. Human beings emerged from the animal world into their infancy, evolved into social creatures in their adolescence, and enter the new world of universal humanity.

When we return to the starting point of Scripture for our understanding of the order of salvation, we encounter the difficulty that it tells us two apparently contradictory truths: salvation is God's work, and we must work out our salvation. We run the risk of Pelagian nomism, on the one hand, and antinomianism, on the other. Both fail to do justice to the work of Christ. Nomism blurs the line between Christianity and paganism and is present in pietistic as well as rationalistic forms. Antinomianism correctly stresses the full accomplished work of Christ but ignores the application of the work of salvation and thus in effect denies the personality and work of the Holy Spirit.

The biblical view of salvation must be fully trinitarian, acknowledging the distinct work of the Holy Spirit. What Christ gained for us must be applied to and in us in justification and sanctification, freedom from guilt and pollution alike. The Holy Spirit's work in redemption is thus also linked to creation. Natural life itself is renewed. At the same time, the work of the Holy Spirit does not override human willing and acting; grace opposes not our nature but our sin.

All this is summed up in the word "grace," which denotes the unmerited favor of God and the many benefits flowing from it, the gifts of grace. Rome and the Reformation differ here; Rome sees a supernatural power that illumines the intellect and inspires the will, the Reformation thinks of the gracious invitation and call of the gospel. For Rome it is the infusion of this grace that makes one a partaker of the divine nature. Grace is a supernatural quality added to human beings by which they are taken up into a supernatural order. For the Reformation grace is never a substance and does not elevate us beyond nature but rather frees us from the enslavement of sin within our natural order.

The special benefits of grace are manifold and inexhaustible. Theologians have labored mightily to treat them in an orderly and comprehensive manner. Roman Catholic theology treated them from the point of view of the church and ordered them hierarchically: actual grace, habitual grace, the fruits of grace. The Reformation, however, focused more on believers and on the way they were brought to salvation than on the church and sacraments. Since the Holy Spirit must be in the foreground of all discussion concerning Christ's benefits applied to us, Reformation thinkers initially simply spoke of repentance, faith, and good works. Eventually, over against Anabaptists, who detached Spirit and Word, Reformed theologians assigned the first place in the order to "calling." Over against the Remonstrants and the Amyraldians, the Reformed insisted on regeneration as prior, acknowledging the Holy Spirit as the agent moving the human will before any act of its own. Further nuances were made in response to challenges, especially by the revivalism of Pietism and Methodism.

Whatever difficulties Reformed people have with aspects of revivalism, and though they acknowledge the legitimacy of a psychological study of religion, they also insist that religious phenomena cannot be exhaustively explained in psychological terms. Particularly, this study can say nothing about the truth of a religion. Even William James, who thought pragmatic considerations were applicable to the question of truth, had to admit failure and finally turn to mysticism: "The heart has its reasons which reason does not know." Religion can only be maintained as real or true when it rests on revelation.

We cannot use Scripture alone to create a scientific lexicon of words for salvation; they are used there to describe various aspects of the one work of transformation brought about by the Holy Spirit. This, however, should not prevent theologians from attempting to derive from the variety of terms and images in Scripture an orderly account of the Holy Spirit's work in us. The following is such an order: All the benefits we obtain in Christ are benefits

of the covenant of grace. These are acquired first by Christ in all fullness in
an objectively real way. Then they are applied by the Holy Spirit to believers.
In this order, justification based on Christ's objective atonement precedes
the acts of repentance of believers and their lives of sanctification in which
they grow in grace. For this reason the immediate work of the Holy Spirit in
regeneration precedes faith, and since only those who are holy will gain eternal
life, sanctification precedes perseverance in order. Another way of stating this is to
say that Christ first restores our relationship to God, then renews us after God's
image, and finally preserves for us our heavenly inheritance. Another way is to
say that we are called, justified, sanctified, and glorified. All this is from God, in
Christ, through the power and working of the Holy Spirit.

THE UNIVERSAL SEARCH FOR SALVATION

[410] If Christ continues his prophetic, priestly, and royal activities in heaven, it follows that also the order of salvation, with all its attendant benefits, has to be viewed theologically. Just as God is the creator and governor of all things, asserts and maintains himself in Christ against sin, and in him brings to light all his attributes of righteousness and grace, omnipotence, and wisdom, so it is he who also by the Holy Spirit applies the benefits of Christ, brings about in them his own work, and advances his own honor.

The way of salvation (*via salutis*), accordingly, has a character of its own in Scripture; like redemption, it is fundamentally different from what is recommended in the world's religions or its systems of philosophy. There is not a single religion in which the idea of redemption and of a way to participate in it is entirely lacking. Whereas the arts and sciences may be powerful weapons in the struggle for existence, and culture may serve to make human life more pleasant and to enrich it, they are all powerless to bring human beings lasting happiness and an eternal good. Yet that is what humans consistently and everywhere look for in religion. This desire arises in them from much deeper levels of need than those that can be satisfied by the world around them. The human heart is created for God and is restless until it finds rest in him. Insofar as every human more or less consciously strives for a lasting happiness and an unchanging good, one can say, with Augustine, that every human also seeks God, who alone is the highest good and our eternal salvation (Acts 17:27). One must immediately add, however, that in the darkness of our understanding and the evil thoughts of our heart, we seek him not in the right way and not where he may be found. Pagan religions have no concept of the holiness of God. They lack the correct insight into sin and know of no grace. Inasmuch as they do not know the person of Christ, they all hold the way of works to be the way of salvation.[1]

---

1. From a speech that Max Müller delivered before the British and Foreign [Bible?] Society about the sublime nature of the Bible, the publication *Der Beweis des Glaubens* (April 1901): 159, cites the following

The first principle of paganism, after all, is, negatively, the denial of the one true God and disdain for the gifts of his grace and, positively, the idea and endeavor of humans to gain salvation by their own wisdom and strength. "Come, let us build ourselves a city, and a tower with its top in the heavens, and let us make a name for ourselves" (Gen. 11:4). Of course, the concept of redemption and the way that leads to it differs, depending on the evil from which redemption is sought.[2] It is also characteristic of all religions, in distinction from magic, for example, to seek redemption from a supernatural divine power who can help and desires to help but cannot be forced to do so and has to be propitiated and moved to offer help by sacrifices, prayers, ritual ceremonies, and moral conduct.[3] In all these religions, however, the emphasis almost always falls on human action. It is humans who must satisfy the deity and fulfill its law. Whether the works they must perform are more ceremonial or more ethical in kind, whether they are more positive or more negative, humans are always their own savior: all religions other than the Christian religion are autosoteric. In the most primitive religions, the sense of sin is almost completely lost, and atonement, peace, and happiness are primarily achieved by magical actions and ritual ceremonies, though in all religions moral conduct also plays a role. In the higher religions, the duties of morality are frequently given more prominence, and salvation is made dependent especially on their fulfillment.

To the degree that in this fulfillment of the moral law the earthly calling of humans is rated more highly or less so, either a practical or an ascetic school of thought evolves in these moral religions. In Parsiism, for example, the cult forms only a relatively small component of the great battle that must be fought by every human against impurity, death, and devil. This battle must extend to all of life and consists not only in manifold ablutions, purifications, and adjurations, but also in the practice of all kinds of virtues (honesty, truth, righteousness,

---

remarkable words: "I may say that for 40 years, as at the University of Oxford I carried out my duties as professor of Sanskrit, I devoted as much time to the study of the holy books of the East as any other human being in the world. And I venture to tell this gathering what I have found to be the basic note, the one single chord, of all these holy books—be it the Veda of the Brahmans, the Purana of Siwa and Vishnu, the Qur'an of the Muslims, the Sendavesta of the Parsis, etc.—the one basic note or chord that runs through all of them is salvation by works. They all teach that salvation must be bought and that your own works and merits must be the purchase price. Our own Bible, *our* sacred book from the East, is from start to finish a protest against this doctrine. True, good works are also required in this holy book from the East, and that even more emphatically than in any other holy book from the East, but the works referred to are the outflow of a grateful heart. They are only the thank offerings, only the fruits of our faith. They are never the ransom of the true disciples of Christ. Let us not close our eyes to whatever is noble and true and pleasing in those holy books. But let us teach Hindus, Buddhists, and Muslims that there is but one book from the East that can be their comfort in that solemn hour when they must pass, entirely alone, into the invisible world. It is that holy book which contains the message—a message which is surely true and worthy of full acceptance, and concerns all humans, men, women, and children—that Christ Jesus came into the world to save sinners."

2. Cf. above, 327–28 (#374).

3. Cf. the important article by E. W. Mayer, "Zum Stand der Frage nach dem Wesen der Religion," *Theologische Rundschau* (1910): 1–15, 45–63.

mercy, and so on) and the faithful pursuit of one's earthly calling: "He who sows grain, sows holiness."[4] In Buddhism, on the other hand, since misery consists in life itself, redemption consists solely in mortifying the desire for existence. This desire is gradually numbed and quenched by following the eightfold path and especially by withdrawing from the external world into oneself.[5] Yet no matter how the views of the moral law and its fulfillment may differ, it is nevertheless always humans themselves who must redeem themselves. "Be your own light!" Buddha told his pupils. "Be your own refuge. Do not take refuge in anything else. Hold onto the truth as to a lamp. Do not look for a refuge in anyone other than yourself."[6] Also Islam, which, remember, originated after Christianity, offers no deeper view of sin and grace. It locates redemption especially in liberation from the hellish punishment that strikes unbelievers and ranks redemption from sin, as sin, as much less important. Granted, the Muslim does pray for the forgiveness of sin, but one automatically becomes the recipient of it when one repents, that is, when one believes in the oneness of God and in Muhammad as his prophet and in addition performs the duties of religion (prayer, alms, fasts, pilgrimage). Redemption is not a gift of God but a person's own act.[7]

Basically agreeing with these religions are the philosophical systems: the only way to salvation is the path of virtue, moral self-perfection. One can seek it in practical work, in ascetic self-denial, or in mystical contemplation; always, however, it is humans who by exerting all their powers try to work their way upward and to work out their own salvation. In that spirit Seneca said: "It is the task of the gods to see to it that we live, but ours that we live well." In Cicero's opinion, a person need not be thankful to God for the possession of virtue, for our virtue is a just ground for the praise of others and a proper reason for our own pride. This would not be the case if virtue were a gift of God and if we did not possess it as a result of our own efforts. "Did anyone ever render thanks to the gods because he was a good man?"[8]

THE SCRIPTURAL VIEW OF SALVATION: GRACE

Scripture's view is very different. In the Old Testament already, it is God who immediately after the fall, out of grace, puts enmity between humanity and the serpent and brings humanity to his side (Gen. 3:15). It is he who elects Abraham and the people of Israel born of him to be his possession (Gen. 12:1; Exod. 15:13, 16; 19:4; 20:2; Deut. 7:6f.), who makes a covenant with them and gives his laws

4. P. Chantepie de la Saussaye, *Lehrbuch der Religionsgeschichte,* 3rd ed., 2 vols. (Tübingen: J. C. B. Mohr [Paul Siebeck], 1905), II, 208ff.

5. Ibid., II, 89ff.

6. Oldenberg, cited in H. Bouwman, *Boeddhisme en Christendom* (Kampen: Bos, 1906), 62.

7. W. Knieschke, *Die Erlösungslehre des Qoran* (Berlin: Runge, 1910), 34ff.

8. Cicero, *On the Nature of the Gods,* III, 36. Cf. J. Scholten, *De Leer der Hervormde Kerk in Hare Grondbeginselen,* 2nd ed., 2 vols. (Leiden: P. Engels, 1850–51), II, 54.

to them (Gen. 15:1; 17:2; Exod. 2:24–25; Deut. 4:5–13), who gives the blood on the altar for atonement (Lev. 17:11), and does all that is needed for his vineyard (Isa. 5; Jer. 2:21). But in virtue of that election and on the basis of that covenant, that people is also obligated now, on pain of the law's curse (Deut. 27:26), to walk before God's face with integrity and to keep his commandments (Gen. 17:1; Exod. 20; Deut. 10:15–16; etc.). The covenant relation did not depend on the observance of that law as an antecedent condition; it was not a covenant of works, but rested solely in God's electing love. It must, however, receive its proof and seal in conduct according to the Lord's law. After all, on Israel's part it could not be accepted with a perfect heart and become a genuine reality, except by a faith that also had love for and a desire to walk in the way of the covenant. If the covenant is a reality and not just an idea, it includes the obligation and inclination to live in accordance with the requirement of the covenant. It is therefore also self-evident, however, that vis-à-vis the covenant and its law, the people could adopt a very different attitude. There were among them ungodly antinomian people, forerunners of the Sadducees, who cared neither about God nor about his commandments and who heaped scorn on the pious (Pss. 14:1; 36:2; 42:3, 10; 94:2; Mal. 2:17; 3:14). There were the Pharisaically minded, who stressed the outward observance of the law and based their righteousness and salvation on it (Amos 6:1; Jer. 7:4). Between these two groups were the few faithful, the sincerely pious, who were by no means indifferent to the law of the Lord, but meditated on it all day long and loved it with all their soul, yet did not base their righteousness and salvation on the observance of it. For although it is true that they frequently very strongly appealed to their righteousness and cried out to God to do them justice (Pss. 7:8; 17:1ff.; 18:21; 26:1ff.; 35:24; 41:12; 44:18, 21; 71:2; 119:121; 2 Kings 20:3; Job 16:17; Neh. 5:19; 13:14; etc.), these same persons at the same time humbly confess their sins, call on God to forgive them, and plead with him on the basis of his grace (Pss. 31:9–10; 32:1ff.; 38:1ff.; 40:13; 41:4; 130:2, 4; Isa. 6:5; 53:4; 64:6; Jer. 3:25; Mic. 7:9; Neh. 1:6; 9:33; Dan. 9:5, 7, 18; etc.). The righteousness of these godly people is not a personal quality but a characteristic of the cause they represent. They have right on their side because they abandon themselves to God.[9] This trust in God is essentially what makes the righteous righteous in the Old Testament. They believe in God (הֶאֱמִין, Gen. 15:6; Exod. 14:31; 2 Chron. 20:20; Isa. 28:16; Hab. 2:4), trust in him (בָּטַח, Pss. 4:5; 9:10), take refuge in him (חָסָה, Pss. 7:1; 18:2), fear him (יָרֵא, Pss. 22:23; 25:12), hope in him (יָחַל, הוֹחִיל, Pss. 31:25; 33:18), expect things from him (קָוָה, Ps. 25:21), wait for him (חָכָה, Ps. 33:20), lean on him (סָמַךְ, Ps. 112:8; נָכוֹן, Ps. 57:7), and remain faithful to him (חָשַׁק, דָּבַק, Ps. 91:14; 2 Kings 18:6; etc.). This faith is counted as righteousness (Gen. 15:6), just as elsewhere the keeping of God's commandments is called righteousness (Deut. 6:25; 24:13).

---

9. Cf. H. Bavinck, *Reformed Dogmatics*, II, 221–28 (#206).

The Old Testament: Nomism

The fact that this subjective righteousness, which basically consists in trust in God, is also a fruit of God's grace and a working of his Spirit is the nature of the case in the Old Testament. Yet for this, too, the data are not lacking. In the case of Israel, one can never speak of a righteousness of its own: it has been chosen despite its stubbornness (Deut. 9:4–6). God is the source of all life and light, wisdom, power, blessedness (Deut. 8:17–18; Pss. 36:9; 68:19–20, 35; 73:25–26; Jer. 2:13, 31). "Not to us, O Lord, not to us but to your name give glory" is the prayer of Israel's devout (Ps. 115:1). Humility is the disposition of their soul (Gen. 32:10; Ps. 116:12); a broken and contrite heart is pleasing to God (Ps. 51:18; Isa. 57:15). Not humans but God is always credited for every gift, and he is given thanks above all. All things are summoned to praise him; all things are requested from him in prayer, not only salvation from dangers but also knowledge of his law, the enlightenment of the eyes, and so on. It is God who has mercy on whom he will (Exod. 33:19) and records in his book who will live (Exod. 32:33). He promises unconditionally that he will be their God and they will be his people (Exod. 19:6; Lev. 26:12) and that always, after unfaithfulness and apostasy on the part of Israel, he will have compassion on them and give them repentance and life (Exod. 32:30–35; Num. 14; 16:45–50; Lev. 26:40–44; Deut. 4:31; 8:5; 30:1–7; 32:36–43; Neh. 9:31). He forgives sins for his name's sake (Exod. 34:7 etc.) and sends his Spirit, who is the author of all spiritual life (Num. 11:25, 29; Neh. 9:20; Pss. 51:12; 143:10; Isa. 63:10). And if history then shows that Israel continually desecrates, abandons, or nullifies the covenant (Deut. 31:20; 1 Kings 11:11; 19:10, 14; Jer. 22:9; 32:32; etc.), prophecy proclaims that God on his part will never break that covenant and never abandon his people. He cannot do it for the sake of his name and fame among the Gentiles (Num. 14:16; Deut. 32:26–27; 1 Sam. 12:22; Joel 2:17–19; Isa. 43:21, 25; 48:8–11; Jer. 14:7, 20–21; Ezek. 20:43–44; 36:32). It is an eternal covenant that cannot fail because it is anchored in the grace of God (2 Kings 13:23; 1 Chron. 16:17; Pss. 89:1–5; 105:10; 106:45; 111:5; Isa. 54:10). He is responsible for both parties, as it were, not only for himself but also for his people, and he will therefore establish a new covenant, not let his Word and Spirit depart from them, but forgive their sins for his name's sake, pour out his Spirit on all, give them a heart of flesh, write his law in their inmost being, and cause them to walk in his statutes (Deut. 30:6; Isa. 44:3; 59:21; Jer. 24:7; 31:31f.; Ezek. 11:19; 16:60; 18:31; 36:26; 39:29; Joel 2:28; Mic. 7:19; etc.).

[411] After the exile, however, these prophetic elements receded from Israel's religion, a process that steered it in a one-sided, nomistic direction. In the year 445 BC, Ezra and Nehemiah, confronting the returnees with the law of Moses, obligated them all under oath to observe its commandments (Neh. 8–10). As a result a most remarkable change occurred in the mind and life of Israel's people. Before the exile, it was averse to the law, constantly lapsing into all kinds of idolatry and wickedness and constantly becoming guilty of unfaithfulness and apostasy. But after the exile, it humbly submitted to the law, was profoundly averse to all

idolatry and image worship, and took intense delight in the observance of God's commandments. Very soon, however, and ever increasingly with the passage of time, it swung around to the other extreme. Although the postexilic prophets spoke out against this trend, when the voice of prophecy grew silent, the nomistic movement continued unhindered. The true and living God, who had revealed himself to Israel throughout the centuries, was eclipsed by his law, and that law increasingly became Israel's one great privilege and the center of its life. This view was reinforced by the oppression and persecution it repeatedly had to endure. God, it was said, was keeping his distance. On account of their iniquities, he delivered his people up to the Gentiles. Only in the future would he again have compassion on them and by the agency of the Messiah elevate them above all peoples and place them at the head of the nations. Thus messianic expectation indeed continued to be alive in Israel and in time of oppression frequently awakened again with fanatic strength. But from that Messiah, people did not primarily expect the atonement of sin and the establishment of a new covenant but above all hoped that he would do justice to Israel, deliver it from all oppression, and restore its dominion over all the people of the earth.

Israel, accordingly, had to prepare for the coming of the Davidic king by the rigorous observance of the law. In all sorts of ways, this law was glorified. It was identified with the heavenly and eternal wisdom that proceeded from God as the first of his works and with which, as his beloved daughter, he continually occupied himself. Hence, because it was the perfect expression of salvation, it would also exist for all eternity. The other books of the Old Testament are on a less exalted level and will one day pass away, but the law remains from generation to generation. It is the source of all salvation and the fountain of eternal life. Although humankind after the fall only still continues to live by the mercy of God and although, after the appalling sin that Israel committed in the wilderness (Exod. 32), it owes its survival solely to God's grace, it is now all the more obligated and also has the power to gain righteousness by the observance of the law. All human acts, and especially the deeds of the children of Israel, are weighed by God on the scale of the law. He records them in his book and daily renders his verdict, determining for each of them either the reward or the punishment. The good works performed by human beings are a gift to God and obligate him to make a gift in return. God and humanity are two contracting parties. All things in the world are determined in terms of the relation between works and rewards, not only in the life of the individual but also in the history of families, generations, peoples, humanity. All God's acts, from the beginning to the end of the world, are based on human merit. In this system there is no longer any room for the atonement of sins in the biblical sense of the word; one can only speak of "atonement" insofar as repentance, faith, confession of sin (all of which are viewed as works alongside other works), self-chastisement, fasting, prayer, alms, mercy, study of the Torah, martyrdom, and so on can include a person in or restore a person to the ranks of the righteous. In addition, any deficiency in one's own righteousness can be made good by that of others (the patriarchs, Moses, Joshua, David, or persons still living); even the dead still profit from the good works of the living. Hence there are many ways in which to secure atonement of sin and to acquire righteousness. But they all come down to one thing: observance of the law and all its—often endlessly detailed—commandments.

This consistent nomism fostered two minds among the Jews. When they assumed, sincerely or not, as was the case especially with many Pharisees, that they had fulfilled the whole law, they fell into spiritual pride and made their claims on God for reward (Matt. 19:20; Luke 18:11). But in the case of others, this nomism produced the conviction that righteousness could not be attained in the way of works. To the degree that people at the end of the day were satisfied with themselves or not, they had to count themselves among the righteous or the ungodly. But by this route they never arrived at the assurance of salvation. They did not experience delight in God or comfort and peace in his fellowship. Throughout their lives they were held in slavery by the fear of death (Heb. 2:15). To the degree that the law was understood more deeply and its fulfillment was pursued with greater seriousness, it made itself felt all the more as a yoke that the Jews could not bear (Acts 15:10). The book of 4 Ezra expressed this when it said: "We who have received the law must nevertheless perish on account of our sins."[10]

The New Testament: Consolation of God's Reign

One must know this state of Judaism in Jesus' days to somewhat understand, in the richness of its consolation, his message of the gospel of the kingdom. On the one hand, that kingdom is pictured as a treasure kept in heaven and distributed as a reward to the righteous (Matt. 6:20; 13:43; 19:21; 25:46). Needed—to receive it in the future when it will be fully revealed—is another and better righteousness than that of the Pharisees (Matt. 5:20); it must be pursued before all else (Matt. 6:33) and purchased at all cost (Matt. 13:44–46; 19:21; Mark 9:43–47; 10:28–29). Still it is a very different kingdom from what the Jews envisioned at that time. It is spiritual, not political, in nature, as Jesus from the very beginning accepted it and asserted in the time of temptation (Matt. 4:1–10). It is spiritual qualities such as purity of heart, meekness, mercy, humility, and so on that mark its citizens (Matt. 5:3ff.; 18:4; 20:26–27). It is therefore universal: intended not only for the Jews but for all peoples (Matt. 8:11; 21:43). Also, it does not just make its appearance in the future but is already present now (Matt. 11:12; 12:28; Luke 17:21); it grows and expands like the seed and the leaven (Matt. 13:24ff.). Those who here receive it in faith like a child will in the future enter into it (Mark 10:15).

---

10. In F. Loofs, *Leitfaden zum Studium der Dogmengeschichte*, 4th ed. (Halle a.S.: M. Niemeyer, 1906), 59. On the nomism of the Jewish religion, see also E. Schürer, *Geschichte des judischen Volkes im Zeitalter Jesu Christi*, 4th ed., 3 vols. (Leipzig: J. C. Hinrichs, 1901–9), II, 450ff.; W. Staerk, *Neutestamentliche Zeitgeschichte*, 2 vols. (Berlin: G. J. Göschen, 1907), II, 5ff.; J. Felten, *Neutestamentliche Zeitgeschichte: Oder, Judentum und Heidentum zur Zeit Christi und der Apostel*, 2 vols. (Regensburg: Manz, 1910), II, 463ff. H. Strack discusses the present Jewish understanding of the law in *Das Wesen des Judenthums* (Leipzig: Hinrichs, 1906).

So, in an eschatological sense, that kingdom is indeed called a reward, but the work and the reward are in no way proportionate. The kingdom so far surpasses all else in value that all notions of reward vanish (Matt. 19:29; 20:13–15; 25:21; Mark 10:30; esp. Luke 17:10). The righteousness required to enter the kingdom is itself a good that God grants (Matt. 6:33), as are also the forgiveness of sins (Matt. 26:28; Luke 1:77; 24:47; etc.) and eternal life (Mark 10:30; Luke 18:30). And he gives that kingdom with all its benefits, not to the righteous, but to publicans and sinners (Matt. 9:13), to the lost (Matt. 18:11), to the poor and others (Matt. 5), to the children (Matt. 18:3; Mark 10:15). Theirs is the kingdom of heaven already on earth (Matt. 9:15; 11:11; 13:16–17; 23:13; Mark 10:15; Luke 17:21). Needed to participate in that kingdom, therefore, is not a righteousness of one's own but repentance (μετανοια), a change of mind, and faith (πιστις), the acceptance of and trust in the gospel of the kingdom as God's gift to the lost (Mark 1:15), and therefore trust in God (Mark 11:22), in Jesus' word and power (Matt. 8:10; 9:2; Mark 4:40), in Jesus as the Messiah (Matt. 27:42; Mark 9:42; John 1:12; 2:11; 6:29; 17:8; 20:31; Acts 9:22; 17:3; 18:5; etc.). But even this μετανοια and πιστις themselves are again the gifts of God's grace (Matt. 11:25, 27; 15:13; 16:17; Luke 10:22; John 6:44, 65; 12:32), so that only those come to faith who are of the truth (John 8:43, 47; 12:39; 18:37), who have been given to the Son by the Father (6:37ff.; 17:2, 6, 9; 10:26; 12:32), and who have already been born again (1:12–13; 8:47).

In the preaching of the apostles all this is elaborated at much greater length. The relation between the objective acquisition and subjective application of salvation now becomes much clearer. After Jesus died and was raised, it became much clearer to his disciples that the kingdom he preached—the kingdom with all its benefits of forgiveness, righteousness, and eternal life—was acquired by his suffering and death; and that he has been raised and glorified by the Father precisely to the end that he would apply these benefits to his own. The application is inseparable from the acquisition. It is one work that the mediator has been mandated to accomplish; and he will not rest until he can deliver in toto the whole kingdom to the Father. Yet no matter how inseparably connected the acquisition and application of salvation are, there is a distinction between them. Christ accomplished the former on earth, in the state of humiliation, by his suffering and death; he accomplishes the latter from heaven, in the state of exaltation, by his prophetic, priestly, and royal activity at the right hand of the Father. For that reason he also actualizes this application of salvation by the Holy Spirit. He himself was enabled and equipped by that Spirit to do the work he had to accomplish on earth. By that Spirit he was conceived in Mary's womb (Luke 1:35), anointed at his baptism (Matt. 3:11), guided in the wilderness (Matt. 4:1); and by that Spirit he returned to Galilee (Luke 4:14), spoke his word (Mark 1:22), preached the gospel (Luke 4:18ff.), healed the sick and cast out unclean spirits (Matt. 12:28). Hence the Holy Spirit was at work in the power of his word and works, but also in his patient gentleness (Matt. 12:17–20), holy indignation (Mark

11:14–17), and heavenly joy (Luke 10:21). He was always full of the Holy Spirit (Luke 4:1) and accomplished all his work by the Spirit's power, for God was with him (Acts 10:38). By that Spirit he offered himself up in death (Heb. 9:14) and was declared to be the Son of God with power when he was raised from the dead (Rom. 1:3–4). In the forty days between his resurrection and ascension, he issued instructions to his disciples by the Holy Spirit (Acts 1:3). And at the ascension, in which he made all angels, authorities, and powers subject to himself (Eph. 4:8; 1 Pet. 3:22), he fully received the Holy Spirit along with all his gifts. Ascending on high, he took captivity captive, gave gifts to humans, and ascended far above all the heavens, so that he might fill all things (Eph. 4:8–10).

This appropriation of the Holy Spirit by Christ is so absolute that Paul can say in 2 Corinthians 3:17 that the Lord (i.e., Christ as the exalted Lord) is the Spirit. In saying this Paul is not trying to wipe out the distinction between the two, for in verse 18 he again immediately speaks, as he does in other passages (Rom. 8:9; Gal. 4:6), of the "Spirit of the Lord" and thereby describes him as the Spirit who belongs to Christ and proceeds from him. But on the occasion of the ascension, the Holy Spirit became Christ's possession to such a high degree that he himself can be referred to as the Spirit. In his exaltation he became a life-giving Spirit (1 Cor. 15:45). He now possesses the seven Spirits, the Spirit in all his fullness, just as he has the seven stars (Rev. 3:1). The Spirit of God the Father has become the Spirit of the Son, the Spirit of Christ, who proceeds from both the Father and the Son, not only within the Godhead but, in keeping with this, also in the dispensation of salvation, and is sent forth as much by the Son as by the Father (John 14:26; 15:26; 16:7). The Spirit, who during his stay on earth had been poured out without measure on Christ, has now in his exaltation fully become the first principle of his life. He has laid aside all the life that is merely natural and psychological: now, as the life-giving Spirit, he will lead his church to glory by the same route.

THE OUTPOURING OF THE HOLY SPIRIT

[412] The first activity Christ performs after his exaltation, therefore, consists in the outpouring of the Holy Spirit. Because he himself had been exalted by the right hand of God and had received from the Father the promise of the Holy Spirit (i.e., the Holy Spirit promised by God in the Old Testament), he could now impart that Spirit to his church on earth (Acts 2:33). The Spirit he bestows proceeds from the Father, is received by him from the Father, and is subsequently poured out on his church by Christ himself (Luke 24:49; John 15:26). It is the Father himself who sends the Holy Spirit in Jesus' name (John 14:26). Before the ascension, therefore, there was as yet no Holy Spirit because Jesus was not yet glorified (John 7:39). This cannot mean that the Holy Spirit did not yet exist before Christ's exaltation, for in the Old Testament there is repeated mention of

God's Spirit,[11] and the Gospels tell us that Elizabeth and John the Baptist were filled with the Holy Spirit (Luke 1:15, 41), that Simeon was guided to the temple by the Holy Spirit (Luke 2:26–27), that Jesus had been anointed with him without measure (John 3:34). Nor can this mean that before the day of Pentecost the disciples did not know that a Holy Spirit existed. For they had been very differently schooled by the Old Testament and by Jesus himself. Even the disciples of John who told Paul at Ephesus that at their baptism they not only did not receive the Holy Spirit but also had not heard that there was a Holy Spirit (Acts 19:2) were saying not that the Holy Spirit's existence was unknown to them but only that they had not heard of an extraordinary working of the Holy Spirit, that is, of the marvelous event on the day of Pentecost. After all, they knew very well that John was a prophet sent by God and equipped by his Spirit, but they had remained disciples of John, had not joined the company of Jesus, and therefore lived outside the church, which received the Holy Spirit on the day of Pentecost.

The event that took place on that day can therefore have no other meaning than that the Holy Spirit, who also existed before that day and gave many gifts and did great works, now, after Christ's ascension, began to dwell at Christ's initiative in the church as in his temple. After the creation and the incarnation, the outpouring of the Holy Spirit is the third great work of God. This extraordinary gift of the Holy Spirit had already repeatedly been promised in the Old Testament. Not only would the Spirit of the Lord in all his fullness rest upon the Servant of the Lord (Isa. 11:2), but in the last days he would also be poured out upon all flesh, upon sons and daughters, the aged and the young, male and female slaves (Isa. 44:3; Ezek. 39:29; Joel 2:28ff.). John the Baptist, taking over this promise, said of the Messiah that he would baptize, not like himself with water, but with the Holy Spirit and with fire, the purifying and consuming fire of the Holy Spirit (Matt. 3:11; Luke 3:16; cf. Acts 2:3; 18:25; Rom. 12:11; 1 Thess. 5:19). And Jesus likewise promised his disciples that after his ascension he would send to them from the Father the Holy Spirit, who would lead them in all truth. In this connection he clearly distinguished two kinds of activity arising from the Holy Spirit. The one is that the Holy Spirit, poured out in the hearts of the disciples, will comfort them, lead them into the truth, and stay with them forever (John 14:16; 15:26; 16:7). But this Spirit of consolation and guidance is granted only to the disciples of Jesus; the world cannot receive this Spirit, because it neither sees him nor knows him (John 14:17). On the other hand, in the world the Holy Spirit engages in a very different kind of activity; living in the church and impacting the world from that base, he convicts it of sin and righteousness and judgment, proving it wrong on all three points (John 16:8–11).

Jesus fulfilled this promise vis-à-vis his disciples, that is, his apostles, even before his ascension. When on the evening of the day of his resurrection, he appeared to his apostles for the first time, he solemnly introduced them to their apostolic task,

11. Cf. H. Bavinck, *Reformed Dogmatics*, II, 261–64 (#213), 277–79 (#217).

breathed on them, and said: "Receive the Holy Spirit. If you forgive the sins of any, they are forgiven them; if you retain the sins of any, they are retained" (John 20:22–23). They need a special endowment and power of the Holy Spirit for the apostolic office that they will soon have to perform. This is given them by Christ before his ascension, in distinction from what they will later receive on the day of Pentecost in communion with all believers. For on that day the apostles were not alone but were devoted to prayer together with certain women, including Mary, the mother of Jesus, and with his brothers and many others, about 120 persons in all (Acts 1:14; 2:1). All of them were then filled with the Holy Spirit (Acts 2:4). Although the same expression occurs earlier (Exod. 31:3; Mic. 3:8; Luke 1:41), there is a clear difference in meaning. Whereas earlier the Holy Spirit was given temporarily for a specific purpose to certain isolated individuals, he now descends on all the members of the church and from this time on continues to live and work in them all. Just as in the days of the Old Testament, the Son of God in fact repeatedly appeared but did not choose human nature for his dwelling place until he was conceived in Mary's womb, so also in earlier times various activities as well as the gift of the Holy Spirit were present. But it was only on the day of Pentecost that he made the church into his temple, a temple he perpetually sanctifies, builds up, and never again abandons. The indwelling of the Holy Spirit confers on the church of Christ an independent existence. It is now no longer enclosed within the circle of Israel's existence as a people and within the boundaries of Palestine but lives independently by the Spirit, who lives within it, and expands over the whole earth and reaches out to all peoples. God by his Spirit now moves from the temple on Zion to take up residence in the body of Christ's church, which is, consequently, born on this very day as a mission and world church. The ascension of Christ necessarily results and proves its authenticity in the descent of the Holy Spirit. Just as the Spirit first consecrated and perfected Christ through his suffering and raised him to the supreme summit, so now he must in the same manner and by the same means shape the body of Christ until it achieves its full maturity and becomes the fullness (*pleroma*) of him who fills all in all (Eph. 1:23).

In the early period this outpouring of the Holy Spirit was accompanied in the life of Christ's disciples by a range of extraordinary forces and workings. The moment they were filled with the Holy Spirit on the day of Pentecost, they began to speak in other languages as the Spirit enabled them (Acts 2:4). According to Luke's description, we are dealing here not with a miracle of hearing but with a miracle of speaking or language. Luke was a coworker of Paul and entirely familiar with the phenomenon of glossolalia as this occurred, for example, in the church of Corinth. He himself also speaks of it in Acts 10:46–47 and 19:6. Undoubtedly, the phenomenon that occurred on the day of Pentecost was related to glossolalia, for otherwise Peter could not have said that Cornelius and his household had received the Holy Spirit "just as we have" (Acts 10:47; cf. 11:17; 15:8). Yet there was a difference. For in 1 Corinthians 14, as also in Acts 10:46 and 19:6, there is mention of tongues or languages without the adjective "foreign," which the

Authorized Version [Dutch: *Statenvertaling*] therefore mistakenly added, but Acts 2:4 expressly speaks of "other" languages. When the members of the church of Corinth speak in tongues, they are not understood unless someone interprets (1 Cor. 14:2ff.). But at Jerusalem the disciples already spoke in other languages before the crowd came running and heard them, so that a hearing miracle is excluded (Acts 2:4). And when the crowd heard them, they understood what was said, for everyone heard them speak in his or her native language (Acts 2:6, 8). The other languages of which verse 4 speaks are therefore undoubtedly the same as those that in verse 6 are called the native languages of those who heard them (cf. also v. 8). Accordingly, they were not unintelligible sounds that the disciples uttered, but other languages, "new" languages, as they are called in Mark 16:17, languages that unlearned Galileans were not expected to speak (Acts 2:7). And in those languages they proclaimed God's mighty works, especially those that he had done in the last days in the resurrection and ascension of Christ (Acts 2:4, 14ff.).

Now this report by Luke must not be understood to say that the disciples of Jesus at that moment knew and spoke all possible languages from around the world. Nor does it mean that they all individually spoke in foreign languages. It was not even the intent of the miracles of language to say that the disciples proclaimed the gospel to foreigners in their native language because they could not understand it otherwise. For the fifteen names listed in verses 9–11 refer not to that many languages but to the countries from which the foreigners had come to Jerusalem on the occasion of the feast of Pentecost. And all these foreigners understood Aramaic or Greek, so that there was no need for the apostles to be equipped with the gift of foreign languages. In any case, in the New Testament there is never again any reference to this gift of foreign languages. Paul, the apostle to the Gentiles, who more than anyone else would then have needed and received them, never mentions them. In the world of that time, he could manage everywhere with the ability to speak Aramaic and Greek. Hence this speaking in foreign languages on the day of Pentecost was an isolated occurrence. Though related to glossolalia, it was a special kind and a superior form of it. Whereas glossolalia is to be viewed as a weakening and diminution of it—which Paul for that reason rated as much inferior to prophecy—the speaking of languages in Jerusalem was, as it were, a combination of glossolalia and prophecy, an intelligible proclamation of God's mighty deeds in the native languages of the peoples [represented there]. The working of the Spirit, who had just been poured out in his fullness, was then so powerful that it controlled the whole conscious mind and expressed itself in the utterance of articulated sounds that were recognized by those who heard them as their own native languages. The purpose of this miracle of speech, accordingly, was not to equip the disciples permanently with the knowledge of foreign languages but in an extraordinary way to produce a powerful impression of the great fact that had now taken place. How could this have been done better than by letting this just-established, small world church proclaim in many languages the mighty works of God? At the creation the morning stars sang, and all the children of God shouted with joy. At the birth of Christ a multitude of heavenly hosts raised a song of jubilation to God's good pleasure. On the birthday of the church, the church itself acclaims in many languages the great works of God.[12]

Although this speaking in languages on the day of Pentecost occupies a special place, the outpouring of the Spirit becomes manifest in that early period in numerous extraordinary signs of power. In the nomistic Judaism of that time, we rarely find any references to the Holy Spirit. God has become a God from afar and no longer dwells with his Spirit in the hearts of humans.[13] But with John the Baptist and subsequently especially with the appearance of Christ, a new era was ushered in. The Spirit who descended on him was a Spirit of love and of power, and that is how he also became manifest in the church after the day of Pentecost. As a rule the Spirit was granted after someone had come to faith, sometimes at the time of baptism (Acts 2:38), or at the laying on of hands before the baptism (Acts 9:17), or at the laying on of hands after the baptism (Acts 8:17; 19:6), usually bringing along a special gift as well as power. We read, for example, that by the Spirit the disciples were given "boldness" in speaking the word (Acts 4:8, 31), an unusual measure of faith (6:5; 11:24), comfort and joy (9:31; 13:52), wisdom (6:3, 10), glossolalia (10:46; 15:8; 19:6), prophecy (11:28; 20:23; 21:11), appearances and revelations (7:55; 8:39; 10:19; 13:2; 15:28; 16:6; 20:22), miraculous healings (3:6; 5:12, 15–16; 8:7, 13). As did the works Jesus performed, so also these extraordinary feats of power manifested in the church provoked fear and amazement (2:7, 37, 43; 3:10; 4:13; 5:5, 11, 13, 24). On the one hand, they nettled the opposition and provoked the hearts of the enemies to hatred and persecution, but, on the other, they also prepared the soil for the reception of the seed of the gospel. In that first period they were necessary to effect in the world acceptance and permanence for the confession of Christ.

12. W. van Hengel, *De Gave van Talen: Pinksterstudie* (Leiden: D. Noothoven van Goor, 1864); commentary of H. Meyer et al. on Acts 2 and 1 Cor. 14 in *Critical and Exegetical Hand-Book to the New Testament*, 9 vols. (New York: Funk & Wagnalls, 1884); H. Cremer, "Geistesgaben," *PRE*[3], VI, 460–63. In recent years, glossolalia gained renewed attention through the phenomena that accompanied the revivals in Wales, Los Angeles, Christiania, Hamburg, Kassel, and other places. Compare, among others, P. Fleisch, *Die innere Entwicklung der deutschen Gemeinschaftsbewegung in den Jahren 1906 und 1907* (Leipzig: H. G. Wallmann, 1908); *A. Dallmeyer, *Satan unter den Heiligen: Die Casseler Bewegung im Lichte der Erfahrung* (Neumünster, 1908); Sir Robert Anderson, *Spirit Manifestations and the Gift of Tongues* (London: Evangelical Alliance, 1900). D. Walker (*The Gift of Tongues and Other Essays* [Edinburgh: T&T Clark, 1906]) sees glossolalia as actually speaking in foreign languages and points out several related phenomena among the Montanists, Camisards, Irvingites, and others; for more on the latter, see *Kolde, *Neue kirchliche Zeitschrift* (July 1900); F. Hencke, "The Gift of Tongues and Related Phenomena at the Present Day," *American Journal of Theology* 13 (1909): 193–206; E. Lombard, "Le parler en langues à Corinthe d'après les textes de Paul et les analogies modernes," *Revue de Théologie et de Philosophie* 5 (1909): 5–52; C. Gutberlet, *Der Kampf um die Seele* (Mainz: Kirchheim, 1903), 525ff.; *J. Bessmer, "Das moderne Zungenreden," *Stimmen aus Maria-Laach* (1910): 142–56, 262–73; *Beukenhorst, "Het spreken in 'tongen,'" *Stemmen van Waarheid en Vrede* (March 1908).

13. F. W. Weber, *System der altsynagogalen palästinischen Theologie* (Leipzig: Dörffling & Franke, 1880), 184ff.; H. B. Swete, "Holy Spirit," *DB* II, 404.

THE FULLNESS OF SALVATION AS THE SPIRIT'S GIFT

[413] Accordingly, throughout the apostolic period these extraordinary work-ings of the Spirit continued. We know this especially from the witness of the apostle Paul. He himself, in his own person, was amply gifted with the special gifts of the Spirit. In a special manner, by a revelation of Jesus Christ himself, he was brought to conversion on the road to Damascus and called to be an apostle (Acts 9:3ff.). Also later, he repeatedly became the recipient of revelation (Acts 16:7, 9; 2 Cor. 12:1–7; Gal. 2:2; etc.). He knew he had the gift of knowledge, teaching, glossolalia, and prophecy; he preached the gospel in demonstration of the Spirit and of power (1 Cor. 2:4), and Christ worked through him to bring about obedience among the Gentiles with words and works, by the power of signs and wonders, and by the power of the Holy Spirit (Rom. 15:18–19; 2 Cor. 12:12). Similar gifts were also given to other believers. In 1 Corinthians 12:8–10 and Romans 12:6–8, as he lists several of them, the apostle says that in differing degrees they were all distributed by one and the same Spirit, apportioned to each one individually as he wills (1 Cor. 12:11). They are a fulfillment of the promise made already in the Old Testament (Gal. 3:14), and should be viewed as the first fruits that guarantee a great harvest and serve as an advance on the future heavenly inheritance (Rom. 8:23; 2 Cor. 1:22; 5:5; Eph. 1:14; 4:30).

However highly the apostle may value all these gifts, he nevertheless applies to them all the criterion that they must agree with the confession of Jesus as Lord (1 Cor. 12:3). He challenges their misuse in the interest of self-elevation and con-tempt of others and demands that they be sincerely and readily used for the benefit of one's neighbor, for all believers are members of one body and need one another (1 Cor. 12:12–30). For that reason he distinguishes between the gifts in terms of whether they serve to edify the church (1 Cor. 12:7; 14:12). For that reason he rates glossolalia far below prophecy (1 Cor. 14) and counsels all believers to strive after the best gifts. Among these gifts love is the most excellent, for without it all other gifts are worthless (1 Cor. 12:31–13:13). In saying this, the apostle shifted the center of gravity from the temporary and passing manifestations of the Spirit to those regular activities of a spiritual and moral nature that the Holy Spirit continually brings to bear in the church. Already in the Old Testament, this emphasis sometimes comes through, for although all sorts of extraordinary gifts and powers were attributed to the Spirit of God, he is also and will in the future be above all the author of all true spiritual and moral life (Pss. 51:12; 143:10; Isa. 32:15; Ezek. 36:27). Jesus aligns himself with this viewpoint when in his conversa-tion with Nicodemus, he asserts that there is no access to or participation in the kingdom of heaven except by a new birth and that rebirth can only be effected by the Spirit of God (John 3:3, 5). And in his farewell discourses, he explains at length that soon the Holy Spirit will take his place and that he will then be their comforter, guide, advocate, and representative (John 14–16).

Accordingly, though in that early period many extraordinary signs of power attended the outpouring of the Spirit, signs that were appreciated by all and overrated by some, we must not lose sight of the fact that that same abundant communication of the Spirit became manifest in many religious and moral virtues. The disciples of Christ were all most intimately tied together by them into one independent holy community. They persevered in the apostles' teaching and fellowship, in the breaking of bread and the prayers (Acts 2:42). They were of one heart and soul, and no one said that any of the things he possessed was his own, but they had everything in common (Acts 4:32). By that Spirit they gained the freedom and boldness to speak the word, were strengthened in their faith, comforted, and given joy in oppression (Acts 4:8, 31; 6:5; 9:31; 11:24; 13:52; etc.). And, as is evident from the letters of the apostles, this is even much more clearly manifest in the other churches. It is the Holy Spirit who brings about the most intimate fellowship between Christ and his church and among believers mutually. Granted, he is distinct from the Father and the Son, another Comforter (John 14:16), mentioned separately alongside of the two others (Matt. 28:19; 1 Cor. 12:4; 2 Cor. 13:13; Rev. 1:4). But he is also one with them in essence and able therefore to incorporate believers fully into communion with them and to impart to them all their benefits.

His activity is therefore absolutely not exclusively—not even mainly—restricted to the communication of extraordinary gifts and powers, not even solely to the communication of the benefits of Christ, apart from his person. If Christ by his suffering and death had acquired only the forgiveness of sins, it would be enough for the Holy Spirit to confirm the proclamation of this gospel (John 15:26–27; Acts 5:32; 1 Cor. 2:4; 2 Cor. 4:13; 1 Thess. 1:5–6; 1 Pet. 1:12), to prove the world wrong (John 16:8–11), to work faith in people's hearts (1 Cor. 2:5; 12:3; Eph. 1:19–20; 2:8; Col. 2:12; Phil. 1:29; 1 Thess. 2:13), and to assure believers of their status as children of God (Rom. 8:15–16). But this objective judicial benefit of forgiveness is not the only one; it is followed by the ethical and mystical benefit of sanctification. Christ not only takes away the guilt of sin but also breaks its power. He died, one for all, that those who live might live no longer for themselves but for Christ (2 Cor. 5:15). In the fulfillment of the law (the law that gives sin its power), that is, in forgiveness, the power of sin has in principle also been broken: where there is righteousness, there is also life. Romans 3–5 is followed by Romans 6–8. Christ has not only died, but he also rose and was glorified. He is and remains the Lord from heaven, the life-giving Spirit, who not only died for the church but also lives and works in it. Now this communion between Christ and the church is effected and maintained by the Holy Spirit. The Holy Spirit, accordingly, is not only he who produces the faith and assures us of our status as children of God but also the author of a new life; and faith is not merely the acceptance of a witness from God but also the beginning and principle of a new lifestyle (2 Cor. 5:17; Eph. 2:10; 4:24; Col. 3:9–10). In and by the Spirit, Christ himself comes to his own (John 14:18), lives in them (Rom. 8:9–11; 2 Cor. 13:5; Gal. 2:20; Eph.

3:17; Col. 3:11) as, conversely, believers by that Spirit exist, live, think, and act in Christ (John 17:21; Rom. 8:1, 9–10; 12:5; 1 Cor. 1:30; 2 Cor. 5:17; Gal. 3:28; 5:25; Eph. 1:13; Col. 2:6, 10). Christ is all and in all (Col. 3:11).[14]

And not only Christ but God himself by this Spirit comes to take up residence in them and to fill them with his fullness in order that in the end he may be all in all (John 14:23; 1 Cor. 3:16–17; 6:19; 15:28; 2 Cor. 6:16; Eph. 2:22). By effecting communion with the person of Christ, the Holy Spirit also effects participation in all his benefits, his wisdom (1 Cor. 2:6–10), righteousness (1 Cor. 6:11), holiness (1 Cor. 6:11; Rom. 15:16; 2 Thess. 2:13), redemption (Rom. 8:2, 23). He assures believers of their status as children of God (Rom. 8:14–17; Gal. 4:6) and of the love of God (Rom. 5:5). He makes them free from the law and causes them to act together in the world as one church, living by a principle of their own and under a head of their own (Acts 2; 2 Cor. 3; Gal. 4:21–6:10).[15] He unites believers in one body (1 Cor. 12:13), leads them to the one Father (Rom. 8:15; Gal. 4:6; Eph. 2:18), brings all to the confession of Christ as Lord (1 Cor. 12:3), makes them one in heart and soul (Acts 4:31–32; Gal. 5:22; Phil. 2:1–2), and makes them grow up together to maturity in Christ (1 Cor. 3:10–15; Eph. 4:1–16; Gal. 2:19). He is the author of regeneration (John 3:5–6; Titus 3:5), life (John 6:63; 7:38–39; Rom. 8:2; 2 Cor. 3:6), illumination (John 14:17; 15:26; 16:13; 1 Cor. 2:6–16; 2 Cor. 3:12; 4:6; Eph. 1:17; 1 John 2:20; 4:6; 5:6), various gifts (Rom. 12:3–8; 1 Cor. 12:4ff.), renewal and sanctification (Rom. 8; Gal. 5:16, 22; Eph. 3:16), of their being sealed and glorified (Rom. 8:11, 23; 2 Cor. 1:22; 5:5; Eph. 1:13–14; 4:30).[16]

[414] That faith in Christ was the way to salvation was, of course, a certainty in the church from the beginning. Believers, after all, knew themselves to have been placed in a special relationship to God and continuously preserved in it by his grace. They were the elect of God adopted by Jesus Christ to be his own people. By the agency of Christ they had taken refuge in his mercy and were the new people with whom God had established his covenant.[17] And this Christ not only was the revelation of God by whom they had learned to know God but also gave his blood for their sins. He gave himself up to purify them by the forgiveness

---

14. Cf. A. Deissmann, *Die neutestamentliche Formel "ἐν Χριστου Ἰησου"* (Marburg: Elwert, 1892), who incorrectly understands the formula in a spatial manner.

15. Cf. above, 223–24 (#348).

16. Cf. the bibliographic material listed in H. Bavinck, *Reformed Dogmatics*, II, 277–79n37 (#217); and further in K. Nösgen, *Das Wirken des Heiligen Geistes an den einzelnen Gläubigen und in der Kirche* (Berlin: Trowitzsch, 1907); H. B. Swete, "Holy Spirit," *DB*, II, 402–11; J. Denney, "Holy Spirit," *DC*, I, 731–44; I. F. Wood, *The Spirit of God in Biblical Literature* (New York: A. C. Armstrong, 1904); H. B. Swete, *The Holy Spirit in the New Testament* (London: Macmillan, 1909); A. Downer, *The Mission and Ministration of the Holy Spirit* (Edinburgh: T&T Clark, 1909).

17. Clement of Rome, *First Epistle of Clement to the Corinthians*, 4, 20, 50, 58; *Epistle of Barnabas*, 5, 7, 13.

of sins, to vivify them by his wounds.[18] In that way, then, he is the Lord and high priest of their confession, the object of their faith who also continually preserves them and builds them up in the faith.[19] Those who do not believe in the blood of Christ are condemned.[20] We are not justified by ourselves; not on account of our wisdom or piety or works that we have performed in holiness of heart, but by faith, from the beginning, the Almighty God has justified everyone.[21] We are saved by grace, not by works, in virtue of God's will, by Jesus Christ.[22]

After the Apostolic Fathers, we encounter the same thoughts in the writings of the Apologists. Although, against Gnosticism they stress that the true knowledge and wisdom, the real philosophy, has been revealed in Christ, they do not forget that Christ is also the Savior and Redeemer. This comes out especially in Justin. No one is saved except by the merits of Christ, who took the curse on himself and made satisfaction for all, who redeems all who do penance and believe.[23] He even speaks repeatedly of a grace that is anterior to our works, illumines us, and leads us to faith.[24] Irenaeus much more intimately links salvation to faith in Christ[25] and also says that the Holy Spirit has been sent to work out the will of the Father in humans and to renew them, and that that Spirit is as necessary as the rain and the dew are to make the land fruitful.[26] Origen even testifies that the will of humans is of itself incapable of repenting "unless it is assisted or fortified by divine aid." God is the "first and foremost cause of the work."[27] The moral corruption of humanity and the necessity of the grace of the Holy Spirit have been even more strongly expressed by the Latin fathers (Tertullian, Cyprian, Ambrose), on whose pronouncements Augustine therefore based himself.[28] Tertullian says, "This will be the power of the grace of God, more potent indeed than nature, exercising its sway over the faculty that underlies itself within us—even the freedom of our will."[29] From Cyprian come the words that are repeatedly cited by Augustine: "We must boast in nothing since nothing is our own."[30] Ambrose already knows of an interior grace that works upon the will and softens it: "The will of humans

18. Clement of Rome, *First Epistle of Clement to the Corinthians,* 21; *Epistle of Barnabas,* 5, 7; Ignatius of Antioch, *Epistle to the Smyrnaeans,* 7.

19. Polycarp, *Epistle to the Philippians,* 1–3, 12.

20. Ignatius of Antioch, *Epistle to the Smyrnaeans,* 6.

21. Clement of Rome, *First Epistle of Clement to the Corinthians,* 32.

22. Polycarp, *Epistle to the Philippians,* 1.

23. Justin Martyr, *Dialogue with Trypho,* c. 95, 100.

24. Ibid., c. 119; idem, *Apology,* I, 10.

25. Irenaeus, *Against Heresies,* IV, 2, 7; V, 19, 1.

26. Ibid., III, 17; V, 10, 2.

27. Origen, *On First Principles,* III, 1, 18; III, 2; III, 5.

28. Augustine, *Against Two Epistles of the Pelagians,* IV, 8–10.

29. Tertullian, *A Treatise on the Soul,* 21.

30. Cyprian, *The Testimonies,* III, 4.

is prepared by God." The fact that God is venerated by the saints is due to God's grace.[31]

Yet in those first centuries, the doctrine of the application of salvation was not at all developed and in part already steered in wrong directions early on. Although there are a few "testimonies of evangelical truth" here and there, on the whole the gospel was soon construed as a new law. Faith and repentance were generally regarded as the necessary way to salvation but were ultimately the product of human freedom. Though salvation had objectively been acquired by Christ, to become participants in it the free cooperation of humans was needed. Faith as a rule was no more than the conviction of the truth of Christianity, and repentance soon acquired the character of a penance that satisfied for sins. The sins committed before one's baptism were indeed forgiven in baptism, but those committed after baptism had to be made good by penance. Penitence was frequently still viewed as sincere contrition over sin, but the emphasis shifted increasingly to the external acts in which it had to manifest itself, such as prayer, fasting, almsgiving, and so on, and these good works were viewed as a "satisfaction of work." Soteriology was altogether externalized. Not the application of salvation by the Holy Spirit to the heart of the sinner but the achievement of so-called good—often totally arbitrary—works was regarded as the way of salvation. Christian discipleship consisted in copying the life and suffering of Christ, which was vividly portrayed before people's eyes. Martyrs, ascetics, and monks were the best Christians.[32]

PELAGIUS AND AUGUSTINE

Pelagius strayed much farther from the doctrine of grace than any of his predecessors; he abandoned the Christian foundation on which all of them still based themselves and renewed the self-sufficient principle of pagan philosophy, specifically that of the Stoics. Not only did he sever all connections between Adam's sin and ours, so that neither guilt nor pollution nor even death was a consequence of the first transgression, but Christianity itself lost its absolute significance. Salvation was not bound to Christ but could also be obtained by following the natural law (*lex naturae*) and positive law (*lex positiva*). Hence, in Pelagius's theology there could be no internal grace, no regenerating grace of the Holy Spirit which not only illumined the mind but also bent the will. He admittedly did speak of grace but meant by it only: (a) natural ability, the gift of being able to will, which God grants to every person—*creating* grace; (b) the objective grace of the proclamation of the law or the gospel and of the example of Christ, which was directed to the human intellect and instructed people in the way of

---

31. Ambrose, *Commentary on the Gospel of Luke,* on Luke 1:10.
32. Cf. above, 85–90 (#319). Ed. note: Bavinck also makes reference to works listed in a bibliography at the head of this chapter in the Dutch edition. In addition to standard reference works, also included are references to the following works (listed in full in the bibliography at the end of the present volume): Knopf, Wustmann, Wiggers, Landerer, Wörter.

salvation—*illuminating* grace; and (c) the forgiveness of sins and future salvation, which would be granted to the person who believed and did good works. Grace of the first kind, therefore, was proper to all humans. Grace of the second kind was not strictly necessary but served only to make it easier for people to acquire salvation. It was not efficacious grace (*gratia operans*) but only a form of assistance to people. Nor was it granted to all, but only to those who had made themselves worthy of it by the proper use of their natural powers. It was not a preparatory (or arousing) grace, nor was it irresistible grace, which is more truly "fate under the name of grace." Finally, it was not necessary and was not granted by God or by the performance of every good deed (individual acts) but only of some. Many good works were performed by humans without any grace.[33]

Semi-Pelagianism moderated this system. It taught that though humanity was not spiritually dead as a result of Adam's sin, it was ill; that its freedom of the will had not been lost but was weakened; and that humans therefore—to do the good and to obtain salvation—needed the assistance of divine grace. However, the grace that illumines the mind and supports the will may never be detached from but must always be viewed in connection with the freedom of will still remaining in humans. Grace and will work together and do so in such a way that in God's intent grace is universal and meant for all but in fact only profits those who make the proper use of their freedom of will. It is ours to will [the good], God's to carry it to its conclusion (*Nostrum est velle, Dei perficere*). Sometimes, as in Paul, grace may be antecedent; yet, as a rule, the will is first. The beginning of faith and persevering in it is a matter of the will; grace is needed only for the increase of faith. God helps those who help themselves. An efficacious or irresistible grace does not exist, and even prevenient grace is usually denied.[34]

[415] Proceeding, as he did, from humanity's total moral corruption as a result of Adam's sin and of its total inability to do any spiritual good, Augustine arrived at a completely different doctrine of grace. Frequently he also described the objective benefits—the gospel, baptism, the forgiveness of sins, and so on—with the word "grace." But this grace is not enough. Still another grace is needed, an internal and spiritual kind that illumines the intellect and bends the will. First, Augustine had taught another doctrine, namely, that though God called us, believing was something we had to do.[35] But later, around AD 396, especially as a result of reflection on 1 Corinthians 4:7, he arrived at a different insight.[36] Now he writes that grace not only consists in the external preaching of the law and the gospel, which instructs and admonishes us and in that sense offers help, but is above all "a hidden inspiration of God, an inspiration of faith and the fear of

---

33. G. Wiggers, *Versuch einer pragmatischen Darstellung des Augustinismus und Pelagianismus*, 2 vols. (Hamburg: F. A. Perthes, 1830–31), I, 220ff.; B. Warfield, *Two Studies in the History of Doctrine: Augustine and the Pelagian Controversy* (New York: Christian Literature Co., 1897), 7ff.

34. G. Wiggers, *Augustinismus und Pelegianismus*, II, 359ff.

35. Thus in his work *On Different Questions* from the year 386 and in *On Free Will* from 388 to 395.

36. In *To Simplicianus*, written around the year 397.

God, an aid in doing well, joined to nature and to doctrine by the inspiration of a burning and most dazzling love, a supply of virtue, an inspiration of love through the Holy Spirit."[37] A fruit of election, "the effect of predestination itself," grace is distributed according to the divine mercy, not according to merit.[38]

For that reason it is of course gratuitous. It would not be grace were it not wholly free.[39] The Holy Spirit blows where he wills, "not following merits but producing them."[40] Grace is anterior to all merits; it is prevenient, preparatory, antecedent, and efficacious. It "is prevenient to the unwilling to make him will."[41] It inwardly illumines the intellect and frees it from blindness.[42] It produces faith, which is a gift of God, and creates a good will, love for the good, and the capacity to do good and removes the weakness from it. "Let us acknowledge that it is by a secret, wonderful, and ineffable power operating within that God works in human hearts, not only revelations of the truth, but even good dispositions of the will."[43] This grace, furthermore, is irresistible; it inexorably and insuperably has its way with the human will.[44] It is not rejected by any heart, however hard, for God by grace takes away the heart of stone and puts a heart of flesh in its place.[45] The elect, who receive this grace, are not only enabled to come to Christ by it but actually also come to him.

This does not mean, however, that God by his grace suppresses or destroys the free will of humans, for, to the contrary, grace rather liberates the will from the slavery of sin. "Do we then by grace make void free will? God forbid! No, rather we establish free will. For even as the law is established by faith, so free will is not made void by grace but established, for grace restores the health of the will."[46] For that reason Augustine could also say: "To yield our consent to God's summons or to withhold it is the proper function of our own will,"[47] for both those who believe and those who do not believe do this voluntarily: "No one believes except by the consent of the will." So far was he removed from again putting the decision back into human hands by this statement, however, that he immediately continues by saying: "This word does not invalidate but rather confirms the word of the apostle: 'What have you that you did not receive?' For the soul cannot receive and possess these gifts, which are here referred to, except by yielding its consent.

37. Augustine, *On the Grace of Christ and Original Sin,* 2, 35, 39.

38. Augustine, *On the Predestination of the Saints,* 10; idem, *On the Gift of Perseverance,* 12; idem, *Against Two Epistles of the Pelagians,* I, 24.

39. Augustine, *On the Grace of Christ and Original Sin,* 24.

40. Ibid.

41. Augustine, *Enchiridion,* 32.

42. Augustine, *On the Merits and Remission of Sins,* I, 9.

43. Augustine, *On the Grace of Christ and Original Sin,* 24.

44. Augustine, *On Admonition and Grace,* 12.

45. Augustine, *On the Predestination of the Saints,* 8.

46. Augustine, *On the Spirit and the Letter,* 30, cf. 33, 34; see also Augustine, *On Grace and Free Will*; idem, *City of God,* XIV, 11; idem, *Against Two Epistles of the Pelagians,* I, 2.

47. Augustine, *On the Spirit and the Letter,* 34.

And thus whatever it possesses, and whatever it receives, is from God; and yet the act of receiving and having belongs, of course, to the receiver and possessor. Now, should any man be for constraining us to examine into this profound mystery, why this person is so persuaded as to yield, and that person is not, there are only two things occurring to me, which I should like to advance as my answer: 'O the depth of the riches!' and 'Is there unrighteousness with God?'"[48] Like the beginning, so also the progress of faith and love is due solely to God's grace. Operative grace turns into cooperating, consequent, and subsequent grace. It effects not only the willing but also the working and the fulfilling. Without Christ we can do nothing. Therefore, "as we begin, it is said: 'his mercy shall go before me'; as we finish, it is said: 'his mercy shall follow me.'"[49] It is God "who prepares the will and perfects in us by his cooperation what he initiates by his operation. . . . He therefore operates without us in order that we may will, but when we will, and so will that we may act, he cooperates with us. We can, however, do nothing ourselves to effect good works of piety without him either working that we may will or co-working when we will."[50] God's mercy "follows the willing that he may not will in vain."[51] And that grace is necessary not just for the performance of some good deeds but for all. "The human will must be assisted by the grace of God to every good movement of action, speech, or thought."[52] Objectively and subjectively, from beginning to end, the work of salvation is a work of God's grace and of his grace alone.[53]

Pelagianism was condemned at the Synod of Carthage (418), whose canons were endorsed by Pope Zosimus and later by Celestine I, and again at the Council of Ephesus (431) and the Synod of Orange (529). This last synod also rejected semi-Pelagianism, and its canons were confirmed by Boniface II.[54] Consequently, it became official church doctrine that as a result of Adam's sin, the whole person is corrupted, and that both the beginning and the increase of faith is owing, not to ourselves or our natural powers, but to the grace of God. That grace of God not only teaches us what we must do and not do but also enables us "to know what ought to be done, even to love and to be able to do it." It is due to the infusion, operation, inspiration, and illumination of the Holy Spirit in us, which precedes and prepares our will, reforms (corrigens) our will from infidelity to faith, and causes us to will and to work.[55] Since then, the necessity of internal and prevenient

48. Ibid.
49. Augustine, *Against Two Epistles of the Pelagians*, II, 9.
50. Augustine, *On Grace and Free Will*, ch. 33.
51. Augustine, *Enchiridion*, 32.
52. Augustine, *Against Two Epistles of the Pelagians*, II, 5.
53. Wiggers, *August. und Pelag.*, I, 244ff.; C. Luthardt, *Die Lehre vom freien Willen und seinem Verhältnis zur Gnade in ihrer geschichtlichen Entwicklung* (Leipzig: Dörffling & Franke, 1863), 30ff.; B. Warfield, *Two Studies*, 127–39. Compare earlier H. Bavinck, *Reformed Dogmatics*, II, 347–51 (#234).
54. H. Denzinger, *Enchiridion symbolorum*, #200; ed. note: ET: *The Sources of Catholic Dogma* (London and St. Louis: Herder, 1955). Ed. note: Bavinck cites this as #64.
55. Ibid., ##176–83 (Synod of Orange II [529]); ed. note: Bavinck provides two references here, #68 and ##147ff.

grace has been taught by all. Also the Synod of Quiercy (853), which condemned Gottschalk, confessed: "We have free will for good, preceded and aided by grace . . . freed by grace and by grace healed from corruption,"[56] just as Rabanus said that God "by his Holy Spirit rules within and comforts without by spiritual zeal."[57] The scholastics followed the same track. Lombard says that by sin humans lost the freedom of the will and that now "they do not have the strength to rise up either to actually willing the good or doing it unless they are liberated and assisted by grace: liberated indeed so that they may will, and assisted so that they may actually do it."[58] Hence the difference between operative grace and cooperative grace is, as in Augustine, that the former "precedes the good will: by it the human will is liberated and prepared, so that it may will good things and effectively do the good." But "cooperative grace follows the-now-good will with assistance."[59] According to Aquinas, a person can indeed do a number of naturally good things without grace,[60] but that person needs grace "to be healed and to perform the good of supernatural virtue," to love God, to keep the law, to acquire eternal life, to prepare for the grace of justification, to rise up again from sin, to refrain from sinning, and each time he or she needs new grace to know and do the good and to persevere in it.[61] Similarly, Trent established that adults, to prepare themselves for the grace of justification, needed prevenient grace, so that those who "by sin were turned away from God, through his *stimulating* and *assisting* grace are disposed to convert themselves to their own justification."[62] Rome, therefore, definitely teaches the necessity of prevenient (actual, stimulating, or arousing) grace and hence rejects the Pelagianism and semi-Pelagianism that attributed the beginning and increase of faith to the powers of [unregenerate] human nature.

SEMI-PELAGIANISM?

There is reason to ask, however, whether Rome, in speaking of prevenient grace, has in mind anything more than the external call of the gospel, which exerts moral impact on the intellect and will, and which was also recognized by Pelagius and his followers. Sometimes, in any case, its description of that grace is very weak: Trent identifies it with the calling "whereby they are called without any existing merits on their part."[63] Yet Rome understands by prevenient grace an inward influence of the Holy Spirit on intellect and will. The Synod of Orange spoke of an infusion and operation in us of the Holy Spirit. Trent called it "arousing" or "stimulating" (*excitans*) and described it in the words: "God touches the heart of

56. Ibid., ##316–19; ed. note: Bavinck cites this as #280.
57. In *Karl Heinrich von Weizsäcker, *Jahrbuch für deutsche Theologie* (1859): 545.
58. P. Lombard, *Sent.,* II, dist. 25, 16.
59. Ibid., II, dist. 26, 1; and further in his commentary on Eph. 2:4–10; Rom. 5:1–2; 6:23; etc.
60. T. Aquinas, *Summa theol.,* II, 1, qu. 109, art. 1–2.
61. Ibid., II, 1, qu. 109, art. 2–10.
62. Council of Trent, session VI, canon 5, in H. Denzinger, *Sources of Catholic Dogma*, 250.
63. Ibid.

man through the illumination of the Holy Spirit."[64] Aquinas says that the grace by which an adult prepares himself or herself for justification consists not in "some habitual grace" but in "an operation of God by which the soul is turned toward himself,"[65] some "assistance of God moving the soul within or inspiring a good purpose."[66] Bonaventure sometimes also calls it a "grace freely given" and says that humans need it to prepare for justification and that it "arouses" (*excitat*) their free will.[67] Bellarmine describes it as a "grace of special assistance," as a "motion" or "action by which God moves a human toward activity"[68] and as "special assistance," "grace that arouses and assists extrinsically," contrasting it with "indwelling grace," "infused grace," "the Holy Spirit dwelling in us."[69] Among theologians there was much disagreement also about the characteristic nature of that preparatory grace. Thomists considered it a "physical quality supernaturally infused," "a certain physical entity." Molina, Lessius, Ripalda viewed it as "an illumination of the mind and an inspiration of the will." Suárez, Tanner, and others thought that it was not anything created but that the Holy Spirit himself moved the will immediately. Yet it is generally viewed as "gratuitous assistance," "an internal and supernatural gift of God," "an illumination of the mind," and "an immediate movement of the will," which conveys to humans not only "moral strengths" but also "physical powers" and enables them to prepare for justification.[70]

64. H. Denzinger, *Sources of Catholic Dogma*, cf. can. 3.

65. T. Aquinas, *Summa theol.*, I, qu. 62, art. 2, ad 3.

66. Ibid., II, 1, qu. 109, art. 6; II, 1, qu. 112, art. 2; III, qu. 89, art. 1, ad 2.

67. Bonaventure, *Breviloquium*, V, 3.

68. R. Bellarmine, "De gratia et libero arbitrio," *Controversiis*, I, c. 2.

69. R. Bellarmine, "De justificatio," *Controversiis*, I, c. 13.

70. On this difference in understanding "actual grace" (*gratia actualis*), cf. M. Scheeben, *Dogmatik*, III, 635–734 (ed. note: ET: *A Manual of Catholic Theology*, trans. J. Wilhelm and T. Scannell, 4th ed., 2 vols. [London: Kegan Paul, Trench, Trubner and Co.; New York: Benziger Brothers, 1909]); J. B. Heinrich and C. Gutberlet, *Dogmatische Theologie*, 2nd ed., 10 vols. (Mainz: Kirchheim, 1881–1900), VIII, 250; J. Pohle, *Lehrbuch der Dogmatik*, 4th ed. (Paderborn: Schöningh, 1912–14), II, 343–46; C. Pesch, *Prael. dogm.*, 9 vols. (Freiburg: Herder, 1902–10), V, 22ff.; C. Manzoni, *Compendium theologiae dogmaticae*, 4 vols. (Turin: Berruti, 1909), III, 235; G. M. Jansen, *Prael. theol.*, 3 vols. in 2 (Utrecht: Van Rossum, 1875–79), III, 123–35; P. Mannens, *Theologiae dogmaticae institutiones*, 3 vols. (Roermond: Romen, 1910–15), III, 12–16. Stated somewhat more precisely, the issue was this: on the one hand, these theologians unanimously rejected the opinion of Lombard (*Sentences*, I, dist. 17–18), who equated grace with love and love with the Holy Spirit; on the other hand, there was also little openness to Dechamps's opinion (in Heinrich and Gutberlet, *Dogmatische Theologie*, VIII, 23) that grace consists in the illumination of the mind and not in the inspiration of the will, since the will always follows the intellect. Hence, according to everyone, grace consisted in the illumination of the mind and the inspiration of the will. But is grace totally exhausted in these two operations, and does it totally coincide with them? Were they directly and immediately effected by the Spirit in people? Or was there still something else between them? Did the Holy Spirit perhaps first infuse in them a "physical and supernatural quality," not "habitual but fluid," of which "the illumination of the mind" and "the inspiration of the will" was then the result? The latter is the view of the neo-Thomists and is, for example, accepted by Heinrich and Gutberlet, and Manzoni.

Concerning Rome's views on grace, one may further consult K. Heim, *Das Wesen der Gnade und ihr Verhältnis zu der natürlichen Funktion des Menschen bei Alexander Halesius* (Leipzig: M. Heinsius Nachfolger, 1907); M. Glossner, *Die Lehre des hl. Thomas vom Wesen der göttlichen Gnade* (Mainz: Kirchheim, 1871); M. Notton,

[416] But with that Rome's rejection of semi-Pelagianism was over: in any case, in a roundabout way it was again smuggled back in. For, in the first place, Rome taught that the freedom of the will, though weakened by sin, is not lost;[71] even without grace humans can perform many naturally and civilly good works, which are absolutely not sinful. They can know and love God as creator and lead a decent life. And even though in the long run it is difficult to observe the whole law and to resist all temptations, as such this is not impossible. The "natural man" as such is a complete human.[72] Second, Rome departs from Augustine in that it views "prevenient grace" as a grace that confers the capacity to believe but not the act of believing itself. On the contrary, prevenient (actual) grace is granted to all adults within hearing of the gospel, but it lies in their power to accept or reject it. "According to the Catholic faith," said the Council of Orange II, "we believe this also, that after grace has been received through baptism, all the baptized with the help and cooperation of Christ can and ought to fulfill what pertains to the salvation of the soul, if they will labor faithfully."[73] And Trent declared that humans can consent to prevenient grace and cooperate with it but also reject it.[74] Among theologians, however, there was much disagreement on this point. The Augustinians, among whom Berti is the most notable, teach that prevenient (actual, sufficient) grace confers the capacity (*posse*) but not the will (*velle*) to believe. Needed—in order that people may be not only capable but also desirous of believing and may actually believe, and that sufficient grace may in fact become efficacious—is a "victorious delight" (*delectatio victrix*) that overcomes "carnal delight" (*delectatio carnalis*), which is its opposite, and which transforms "being able" into "being willing." Hence the will must be transformed by "victorious delight," which is stronger than desire (*concupiscentia*). Thomists, [such as] Báñez, Gonet, Lemos, Billuart, and others, similarly say that sufficient grace confers the capacity but not the will to believe; to produce the latter must be augmented by a "physical action of God," that is, a "physical advancement" or "predetermination." Augustinians and Thomists accordingly agree in teaching that efficacious grace depends not on the human will but on grace itself and that the act of believing infallibly follows "victorious delight." They differ, however, in that the latter accept an essential, objective distinction between "sufficient" and "efficacious" grace, whereas the former believe that the two do not basically differ but that there are degrees in grace, so that a grace that is only "sufficient" for one person may—because of a lesser hardening—be efficacious in another. But one cannot say that this idea does justice to the Tridentine "capacity to assent or to reject."

Harnack und Thomas von Aquin (Paderborn: Schöningh, 1906); P. Minges, *Die Gnadenlehre des Duns Scotus auf ihren angeblichen Pelagianismus und Semipelagianismus geprüft* (Münster: Aschendorff, 1906).

71. Synod of Orange (529), in H. Denzinger, *Enchiridion*, #144; Council of Trent, session VI, canon 1 and canon 5.

72. Cf. H. Bavinck, *Reformed Dogmatics*, II, 539–42 (#287).

73. H. Denzinger, *Enchiridion*, #169.

74. Council of Trent, session VI, canon 5 and canon 4.

The Molinists therefore made the efficacy of grace depend on the human will,[75] and Congruists like Bellarmine[76] let it be determined by a "foreseen congruence or incongruence of grace" with the condition or circumstances of those to whom at any given time grace was offered.[77]

Catholic doctrine comes down to the following: in baptism the children born in the church receive regeneration (justification; infused grace) but those who hear the gospel at a later age receive "sufficient grace," which consists in an illumination of the intellect and a reinforcement of the will by the Holy Spirit. A person can reject this grace but also assent to it. If he or she assents to it, this "arousing" grace (*gratia excitans*) passes into aiding or cooperative grace. A person works with it to prepare himself or herself for justification (*gratia infusa; habitualis*). This preparation has the following seven components: that humans, aided by God's grace, begin to believe God's Word, discover that they are sinners, learn to hope for God's mercy, begin to love him, begin to hate sin, resolve to have themselves baptized and to lead a new life.[78] Faith here does not occupy a central place but is coordinate with the other six preparations for the grace of justification. It is, accordingly, no more than an assent to the truth of Christianity, that is, to the doctrine of the church (unformed faith), and only acquires its justifying power by love (faith formed by love), which is imparted by the grace infused. Taken by itself it cannot justify; it is only called justifying faith because it is the beginning of human salvation, the foundation and root of all justification, that is, the first of the above preparations.

Now if a person has thus prepared himself or herself and has done what was in him or her[79]—whether this consists in the proper use of his or her grace-sustained[80] or natural[81] powers—God cannot refuse the infused grace. Admittedly, the person has not merited this grace, for the grace given far surpasses it in value; yet it is fair that God should, by the standard of a merit of congruity, reward those who thus do their very best with infused grace.[82] This is granted in baptism and consists in

75. Cf. H. Bavinck, *Reformed Dogmatics*, I, 151–54 (#48); II, 196–203 (#201).

76. R. Bellarmine, "De gratia et libero arbitrio," *Controversiis*, I, 12; IV, 14–16.

77. On these schools of thought, cf. H. Bavinck, *Reformed Dogmatics,* I, 153 (#48); as well as *Theologia Wirceburgensi,* VII, 375; G. Perrone, *Prael. theol.,* 9 vols. (Louvain: Vanlinthout & Vandezande, 1838–43), V, 138; F. Liebermann, *Institutiones theologicae,* 8th ed., 2 vols. (Mainz: Kirchheim, 1857), II, 338; P. Dens, *Theologia ad usum seminariorum et sacrae theologiae alumnorum* (Mechliniae: P. J. Hanicq, 1828–30), II, 219; C. von Schäzler, *Neue Untersuchungen über das Dogma von der Gnade und das Wesen des christlichen Glaubens* (Mainz: Kirchheim, 1867), 87ff.; J. Pohle, *Dogmatik,* II, 458ff.; C. Manzoni, *Compendium theologiae dogmaticae,* III, 261ff.

78. Council of Trent, VI, 6.

79. Materially in the proposition: "If a person does what is in him, God gives him grace," which already occurs in Jerome; cf. F. Loofs, *Dogmengeschichte,* 545.

80. T. Aquinas, *Summa theol.,* II, 1, qu. 109, art. 6, ad 2; II, 1, qu. 112, art. 3.

81. Ibid., II, 1, qu. 98, art. 6; cf. *Theologia Wirceburgensi,* VII, 288; P. Dens, *Theologia,* II, 209; C. Pesch, *Prael. dogm.,* V, 114–20.

82. According to Ripalda, Vázquez, and others, pre-Tridentine theologians generally taught that people could with their natural powers prepare themselves positively for the reception of grace. There is disagreement

the indwelling of the Holy Spirit, the infusion of supernatural virtues, participation in the divine nature, and is followed by the forgiveness of sins, which jointly with infused grace constitutes the two parts of justification.[83] Hence, in the theology of Rome, the forgiveness of sins is the negative counterpart of a person's positive renewal. Sin is forgiven because and insofar as it has been eradicated.

Now if in baptism a person has become the recipient of this infused grace, he or she can in fact lose it again as a result of mortal sins and also must do penance for venial sins, not only with contrition of the heart but also with oral confession and penance. Nonetheless, in infused grace a person has received the supernatural power to do good works and hence all subsequent grace, indeed even to merit eternal life according to a merit of condignity. For the good works one performs flow from a supernatural principle and are therefore deserving of a supernatural reward. From this perspective, finally, the underlying aim of this Catholic doctrine of grace becomes clear. Grace serves only to make it possible for human beings to again merit heavenly beatitude. That was basically the case even in Augustine. In his work, grace, however granted without merit, consisted primarily not in the forgiveness of sins but in regeneration, in the infusion of love, which renders a person capable of doing good works and thus of obtaining eternal life. "[Humans] therefore receive righteousness that, on account of it, they may deserve to receive blessedness."[84] While merits do not precede grace and faith, they do follow them.[85] "Merit is prepared by believing."[86] "Grace precedes merit: grace does not arise from merit but merit arises from grace; grace precedes all merits in order that the gifts of God may follow my merits."[87] Similarly, Ambrose wrote: "Grace itself deserves to be increased in order that, having been increased, it may also deserve to be perfected, one's will accompanying, not leading [it], following, not preceding [it]."[88]

Later, when the doctrine of the image of God as "superadded gift" arose, this [trend] became even worse. The concept of grace underwent an important modifi-

---

only over Aquinas's opinion and his view of the expression "doing what is in oneself." After Trent, however, theologians usually construed the expression a bit differently. It is true that over against Pelagianism and semi-Pelagianism, Rome tried to retain the absolute unmeritability of the first grace (*gratia prima*). The grace of God is not granted according to our merit, neither according to a merit of condignity nor according to a merit of congruity, as (since Eck) merit was usually differentiated (J. Pohle, *Dogmatik*, II, 401). This is why today the expression "facere quod in se est" is generally interpreted by saying that the person who makes the proper use of his or her natural powers prepares himself or herself *negatively* for grace, in the sense that he or she does not pose an obstacle to grace. And some, like Vázquez, Glossner, and others, even reject this negative preparation. Cf. J. Pohle, *Dogmatik*, II, 400–412; C. Pesch, *Prael. dogm.*, V, 105–20; J. B. Heinrich and C. Gutberlet, *Dogmatische Theologie*, VIII, 264–74; C. Manzoni, *Compendium theologiae dogmaticae*, III, 242; P. Mannens, *Theologiae dogmaticae institutiones*, III, 84–89, etc.

83. T. Aquinas, *Summa theol.*, II, 1, qu. 113.

84. Augustine, *The Trinity*, XIV, 15.

85. Augustine, *To Simplicianus, On Different Questions*, I, 2.

86. Augustine, *Eighty-three Different Questions*, trans. D. L. Mosher, in vol. 1 of *Writings of Saint Augustine*, Fathers of the Church 5 (New York: Cima, 1948), #68.

87. Augustine, in P. Lombard, on Eph. 2:4–10.

88. Ambrose, in P. Lombard, on Rom. 5:1–2.

cation. Grace then became something that was needed not only for fallen humanity; by it, even Adam had to be elevated from being an ordinary "natural" human to being the image of God.

After the fall, therefore, grace played a double role: first, to redeem humans from sin (the grace of healing, medicinal grace) and, second, to raise them up to the supernatural order (elevating grace).[89] For the former, grace is only accidentally necessary—only in a moral sense; for the latter, it is absolutely and "physically" necessary. The latter, accordingly, increasingly forces the former into the background. The ethical antithesis between sin and grace yields to the "physical" difference between natural and supernatural. By grace the Catholic Church does not, at least not primarily, mean the free favor of God by which he forgives sins. Instead, it takes grace to mean a quality infused in human beings by which they become partakers in the divine nature,[90] a supernatural, created, hyperphysical power—magically infused into natural humans through the mediation of priest and sacrament—which lifts them up to the supernatural order and enables them, by the performance of good works, to merit all the following graces as well and in the end heavenly blessedness by the merit of condignity.

LUTHER AND THE REFORMATION

[417] It was the Roman Catholic penitential system that prompted Luther's reformational activity. However, the groundwork for the new understanding of the gospel that fueled his opposition to the sale of indulgences—as recent studies have clearly demonstrated[91]—had been done many years earlier. Inasmuch as Luther's marginal comments on Lombard's *Sentences,* which date from the years 1509–10, already articulate the idea that God's "righteousness" in Romans 1:17 is a reference not to the divine attribute by that name but to the righteousness of faith granted by him, some [historians] have even thought that the hour of the Reformation's birth had already struck in the year 1508–9, when Luther stayed at the monastery in Wittenberg.[92] It has been demonstrated by Denifle, however, that this exegesis of God's righteousness in Romans 1:17 was definitely not freshly discovered by

89. T. Aquinas, *Summa theol.,* II, 1, qu. 109, art. 2.

90. Ibid., III, qu. 62, art. 2: "Grace, considered in itself, perfects the essence of the soul, insofar as it is a certain participated likeness of the Divine Nature"; cf. ibid., II, qu. 110, art. 3–4.

91. H. Boehmer, *Luther im Lichte der neueren Forschung: Ein kritischer Bericht* (Leipzig: B. G. Teubner, 1906) (ed. note: ET: *Luther in Light of Recent Research,* trans. C. F. Huth [New York: Christian Herald, 1916]); *G. Kawerau, "Fünfundzwanzig Jahre Lutherforschung 1883–1908," *Theologische Studien und Kritiken* (1908). Also D. Walther in a discussion, "Neue Lutherschriften," *Theologisches Literaturblatt* (October 27, 1905; November 3, 1905; October 5, 1906); W. Köhler, *Katholizismus und Reformation: Kritisches Referat über die wissenschaftlichen Leistungen der neueren katholischen Theologie auf dem Gebiete der Reformationsgeschichte* (Giessen: Töpelmann, 1905).

92. H. Boehmer, *Luther im Lichte,* 33.

Luther but occurs already in numerous church fathers and scholastics.[93] Luther is evidently mistaken when, construing this differently later, he said he had been taught "by the practice and custom of all the learned teachers" to associate that righteousness with the "formal and active justice that makes God just and causes him to punish sinners and the unjust."[94] By saying this, Luther perhaps meant that the theologians before him understood the righteousness of God almost exclusively in terms of his punitive justice.[95] In any case, Luther's conversion was rooted in a new understanding of the sinner's justification before God by grace and through faith alone. In the manuscript of his commentary on the Psalms (1513–15) this view is already clearly stated. Grace here is understood above all in terms of the forgiveness of sins, and the essential character of faith is defined in terms of trust in God's mercy. But here this new insight is still rather obscure and associated with all sorts of medieval and Roman Catholic elements. It was, however, deepened and clarified by the teaching of Staupitz, by Luther's growing acquaintance with a body of mystical writings, especially the *Deutsche Theologie* (*Theologia germanica*) and by his continued study of Paul and Augustine.[96] Then, in his lectures on the Letter to the Romans (1515), this insight emerged in much clearer form. It was Luther's own religious-moral experience that ignited in him a new and startling insight into the basic concepts of the gospel (righteousness, justification, grace, faith, conversion, good works) and prompted him to understand them in a totally different way than was current in Catholic teaching and piety. That this new insight into the gospel would bring him into conflict with the church and the pope of Rome is something he did not at all realize at the time. He did, however, increasingly note all sorts of abuses and, from as early as 1512 and especially in September 1517 in his disputation against scholastic theology, insisted on the reformation of the study of theology, the rejection of scholasticism, and the study of Holy Scripture.

The conflict did not break out until Tetzel, working for the archbishop of Mainz, appeared with his indulgence trade in the dioceses of Halberstadt and Magdeburg, attracting hordes of people. His message, entirely in keeping with the teaching of the Catholic Church, was that every penitent could redeem some or all of the ecclesiastical penalties imposed on him and acquire certain graces by performing various good works (by making a pilgrimage, by giving a donation to a church building project, by participating in a crusade, by outfitting a crusader, or—much

93. H. Denifle and A. M. Weiss, *Luther und Luthertum in der ersten Entwicklung, quellenmässig dargestellt*, 2 vols. (Mainz: Kirchheim, 1904–9), vol. 2.

94. In F. Loofs, *Dogmengeschichte*, 688.

95. D. Walther, in *Theologisches Literaturblatt* (1904): 411ff.

96. H. Barge wrote a biography of Andreas Bodenstein von Karlstadt (2 vols. [Leipzig: Friedrich Brandstetter, 1905]) representing him as an original and independent thinker on whom Luther was in many respects dependent but who was unfairly treated by him. According to others, however, this picture is exaggerated and one-sided. Cf. *F. Cohrs, *Theologische Literaturzeitung* (1908): n. 14; O. Scheel, "Individualismus und Gemeinschaftsleben in der Auseinandersetzung Luthers mit Karlstadt 1524/25," *Zeitschrift für Theologie und Kirche* 17 (1907): 352–75.

more simply and conveniently—by making a confession and paying a smaller or larger sum of money). Not only could one, by the purchase of an indulgence, obtain relief from ecclesiastical penalties, but by this means one could also come to the aid of relatives and friends in purgatory and shorten or alleviate their punishment. Though Tetzel did not precisely repeat the following words, he was practically committed to the proposition that "as soon as the coin in the coffer rings, the soul from purgatory springs."[97] From his preaching it was clear that indulgences had been degraded by the popes into objects of commerce, which were marketed through bankers like the Fuggers to shake down a credulous public.

Manifest in this trade at the same time was a pernicious tendency in the Roman Catholic system, for the trade in indulgences was not an excess or an abuse but the direct consequence of the nomistic degradation of the gospel.[98] That the Reformation started with Luther's protest against this traffic in indulgences proves its religious origin and evangelical character. At issue here was nothing less than the essential character of the gospel, the core of Christianity, the nature of true piety. And Luther was the man who, guided by experience in the life of his own soul, again made people understand the original and true meaning of the gospel of Christ. Like the "righteousness of God," so the term "penitence" had been for him one of the most bitter words of Holy Scripture. But when from Romans 1:17 he learned to know a "righteousness by faith," he also learned "the true manner of penitence." He then understood that the repentance demanded in Matthew 4:17 (μετανοειν) had nothing to do with the works of satisfaction required in the Roman institution of confession, but consisted in "a change of mind in true interior contrition" and with all its benefits was itself a fruit of grace.[99] In the first seven of his ninety-five theses and further in his sermon on "Indulgences and Grace" (February 1518), the sermon on "Penitence" (March 1518), and the sermon on the "Sacrament of Penance" (1519), he set forth this meaning of repentance or conversion and developed the glorious thought that the most important part of penitence consists not in private confession (which cannot be found in Scripture) nor in satisfaction (for God forgives sins freely) but in true sorrow over sin, in a solemn resolve to bear the cross of Christ, in a new life, and in the word of absolution, that is, the word of the grace of God in Christ. The penitent arrives at forgiveness of sins, not by making amends (satisfaction) and priestly absolution, but by trusting the word of God, by believing in God's grace. It is not the sacrament but faith that justifies. In that way Luther came to again put sin and grace in the center of the Christian doctrine of salvation. The forgiveness of sins, that is, justification, does not depend on repentance, which always remains incomplete, but rests in God's promise and becomes ours by faith alone.

97. H. Boehmer, *Luther im Lichte*, 42ff.

98. Most striking are the points of resemblance between Roman Catholic and the Jewish nomism mentioned above, 495 (#410). Cf. *Fiebig, "Judentum und Katholizismus," *Die Studierstube* (1905): 715–26.

99. F. Loofs, *Dogmengeschichte*, 687–88, 697, 717ff.

[418] About the relation Luther construed between repentance and faith, however, there is much disagreement. According to Ritschl,[100] Luther indeed first thought that true repentance is the fruit of faith in the gospel and of love for God. But later, especially after the publication of Melanchthon's *Instruction to the Church Visitors* (1528), in order not to foster a false sense of security, he is said to have placed law-engendered penitence before faith. This is said to be the precise opposite of what Calvin did. In the first edition of the *Institutes*, Calvin is said to have made repentance precede faith, but later, in the Genevan Catechism of 1538 and in the second and following editions of the *Institutes,* he is said to have faith precede true penitence.[101] The historical research of Lipsius[102] has shown, however, that the idea of such a reversal in Luther's doctrine of penitence is groundless. In his thinking penitence always has two parts: (1) contrition, knowledge of and sorrow over sins effected by the law; and (2) faith in the grace of God revealed in the gospel of Christ. By the preaching of the law, God first breaks the hard heart of sinners and then by faith leads them to the comfort of the gospel. But when sinners thus learn to know the grace of God, they for the first time acquire a true love for the good; out of this love the true penitence is then born that persists throughout life and consists in the mortification of the old and the resurrection of the new "man." Granted, in that first period, when he especially fought Catholic "works righteousness," Luther more heavily stressed that true penitence proceeds from faith and encompasses all of life, and later, over against antinomianism, that true faith is preceded by contrition of heart. But materially Luther's teaching always remained the same: contrition (penitence in the restricted sense), faith, and good works are the three central components of the way of salvation.[103] This is also the view of the Lutheran confessions[104] and of the early dogmaticians, Brenz, Strigel, Chytraeus, and others up until Gerhard. The way of salvation was treated under these three headings (*loci*).

Now, in connection with this order of salvation, Luther in his first period consistently proceeded from the premise of "absolute predestination." Also later,

100. A. Ritschl, *Die christliche Lehre von der Rechtfertigung und Versöhnung,* 4th ed., 3 vols. (Bonn: A. Marcus, 1895–1903), I², 198ff.

101. Also cf. A. von Harnack, *History of Dogma,* trans. N. Buchanan, J. Millar, E. B. Speirs, and W. McGilchrist, ed. A. B. Bruce, 7 vols. (London: Williams & Norgate, 1896–99), VII, 252ff.; W. Herrmann, "Die Busse des evangelischen Christen," *Zeitschrift für Theologie und Kirche* 1 (1891): 28–81.

102. R. Lipsius, "Luthers Lehre von der Busse," *Jahrbuch für protestantische Theologie* (1892): 161–340.

103. Further J. Köstlin, *Luthers Theologie,* 2 vols. (Stuttgart: J. F. Steinkopf, 1863), I, 36, 72, 159, 368; II, 75, 493, 496ff. (ed. note: ET: *Theology of Luther in Its Historical Development and Inner Harmony,* trans. C. Hay, 2 vols. [Philadelphia: Lutheran Publication Society, 1897]); idem, "Busse," *PRE³,* III, 584–91; F. Sieffert, *Die neuesten theologischen Forschungen über Busse und Glaube* (Berlin: Reuther & Reichard, 1896); A. Galley, *Die Busslehre Luthers und ihre Darstellung in neuester Zeit* (Gütersloh: Bertelsmann, 1900); F. Loofs, *Dogmengeschichte,* 719ff., 790, 858.

104. J. T. Müller, *Die symbolischen Bücher der evangelisch-lutherischen Kirche,* 8th ed. (Gütersloh: Bertelsmann, 1898), 41, 167, 312, 534, 634.

he never retracted it,[105] although to offset the misuse that could be made of it he increasingly accentuated the revelation of God in Christ and the universal offer of salvation in the word of the gospel. Melanchthon, however, from 1527 on increasingly took exception to the confession of absolute predestination and with increasing firmness adopted a synergistic position. Already in his commentary on the Letter to the Romans, he rejected all investigation of election, since the promise of God is universal, and God expressly wills all humans to be saved. In the second revised edition of the *Loci Communes,* which came off the press in 1535, he stated that three causes worked together in conversion: the Word of God, the Spirit, and the human will assenting to and not resisting the Word of God. Then, in the edition of 1543, he cited with approval the words of others to the effect that free will in humans consists in the "faculty of applying oneself to grace."[106] Also the Formula of Concord no longer had the courage to adopt the confession of [God's] free and unconditional election but did decisively reject the doctrine that the [human] will can, by its *own natural powers,* conform to grace.[107] It also declared its belief in predestination and the spiritual impotence of [unregenerate] humans so that they are "less than a stone or a stick" and purely passively experience conversion.[108] But in addition it no less firmly maintains the universality and resistibility of grace.[109] It then attempts to reconcile these two positions by saying that [unregenerate] humans have still retained a passive, not an active, capacity, can still go to church and so on, and especially that they still experience (and can experience) God working in them.[110] Later on, Lutheran theology usually worked this out by saying that in baptism and the preaching of the Word, God grants to all who live under the gospel "sufficient grace (indispensable, irresistible good motions)" by which the will is liberated and renewed; further, that they can refrain from resisting and allow God's grace to work in them toward regeneration and conversion and undergo it entirely passively, or also cooperate with it actively.[111]

Under the influence of this covert or overt synergism, the order of salvation, when it was later expanded (and as in Hollaz, with reference to Acts 26:17–18, treated in the loci concerning "calling, illuminating, converting, regenerating,

---

105. Cf. H. Bavinck, *Reformed Dogmatics,* II, 355–58 (#236); and F. Loofs, *Dogmengeschichte,* 755ff., 761ff.

106. Melanchthon, in the locus "De libero arbitrio" (freedom of the will) in *Loci communes.*

107. J. T. Müller, *Die symbolischen,* 607, 608, 713. Ed. note: Bavinck cites this as "*Die Bekenntnisschriften der ev. Luth. K.,*" which appears to be an error, a conflation of the title cited and that of another volume by Ernst Friedrich Karl Müller, *Die Bekenntnisschriften der reformierten Kirche* (Leipzig: Deichert, 1903).

108. Ibid., 589, 594, 705.

109. Ibid., 555, 692.

110. Ibid., 609–10.

111. In addition to the works of Gerhard, Quenstedt, and others cited above, see also H. Schmid, *The Doctrinal Theology of the Evangelical Lutheran Church,* trans. Charles A. Hay and Henry Jacobs, 5th ed. (Philadelphia: United Lutheran Publication House, 1899), 293–407; cf. C. Luthardt, *Compendium der Dogmatik* (Leipzig: Dörffling & Francke, 1865), §§57–60.

justifying, renewing and glorifying grace"), obtained this form among Lutherans. Christian children, inasmuch as they cannot yet offer resistance, are born again in baptism and receive the gift of faith. Others are first called at a later age with a "sufficient call," which is the same for everyone and furnishes to all that enlightenment of the intellect and power of the will that enables them not to resist the working of God's grace. In the event they do not resist, they are led to contrition (penitence, conversion, in the restricted sense), regenerated, and endowed with faith, which is a fruit of regeneration. By faith they are then justified, obtain the forgiveness of sins and then, successively, adoption, mystical union, renewal, and glorification. In reality, however, the Christian life does not unfold in such an orderly fashion. Just as grace initially depends on the will as fortified by God's supernatural power, so it remains dependent both in its progression and to the end. Grace is always resistible and therefore amissible [losable] and again obtainable up to the hour of one's death—not once but even many times. In the order of salvation, accordingly, the center of gravity lies with the human person. However emphatically it is said that it is God alone who regenerates and converts us, nevertheless whether God will do so depends on our resistance or nonresistance. Human beings hold the power of decision: by their resistance they can nullify the whole work of the Father, the Son, and the Spirit. And they have that power till the moment of their death. More precisely, the center of gravity in the order of salvation is located in faith and justification. Calling, contrition, and regeneration only have a preparatory function. Actually they are not yet benefits of the covenant of grace; they, as it were, still operate apart from Christ and serve to lead the sinner to Christ. Only when people believe and by that faith embrace the righteousness of Christ does God accept them in Christ, forgive their sins, make them free from the law, adopt them as his children, incorporate them into fellowship with Christ, and so on. Everything depends on faith, specifically, on the act of believing. If a person exerts this power of faith, that person has everything and has it all at once: peace, comfort, life, and blessedness. But if that person neglects to exert it, everything becomes shaky, uncertain, amissible. The whole focus, therefore, is on keeping that faith. But just as Lutheran believers fail to understand the work of grace as arising from God's eternal election and covenant, so they also fail to relate it to nature, the world, and humanity. They are blessed in the possession of their faith but do not allow it to impact the family, school, society, or state. It is sufficient for them to live in communion with Christ and they feel no urge to fight under Christ as king.[112]

The *Ordo Salutis* in Reformed Theology

[419] For all its agreement [with the Lutheran view], the order of salvation in Reformed theology nevertheless from the beginning bore a very different

---

112. Cf. esp. M. Schneckenburger and E. Güder, *Vergleichende Darstellung des lutherischen und reformierten Lehrbegriffs*, 2 vols. (Stuttgart: J. B. Metzler, 1855), passim.

character. True, Calvin treats justification and election[113] after faith, regeneration, conversion, and the Christian life, but this is by no means intended to convey that this is when they objectively originate. The basic idea underlying Calvin's approach is a very different one: election is an eternal decree, even if humans only become conscious of it by faith; and the forgiveness of sins rests in Christ alone even though it is granted to us only in faith. For what keeps coming back in Calvin is the idea that there is no participation in the benefits of Christ other than by communion with his person.[114] Already implied in this idea, in principle, is the difference that exists in the order of salvation between the Lutherans and the Reformed.[115] Indeed, if it is true that the very first benefit of grace already presupposes communion with the person of Christ, then the imputation and granting of Christ to the church precedes everything else. And this, in fact, is the Reformed teaching. A bond was already forged between the mediator and those who were given him by the Father in eternity, in election, and more precisely in the pact of salvation (*pactum salutis*). Then, in the divine decree, a mystical union was concluded between them, and substitution occurred. Christ became human and acquired salvation for his people in virtue of that pact.

He could do this precisely because he already was in communion with them and was their guarantor and mediator. And the whole church, comprehended in him as its head, has objectively been crucified, has died, been resurrected, and glorified with him. All the benefits of grace therefore lie prepared and ready for the church in the person of Christ. All is finished: God has been reconciled; nothing remains to be added from the side of humans. Atonement, forgiveness, justification, the mystical union, sanctification, glorification, and so on—they do not come into being after and as a result of faith but are objectively, actively present in Christ. They are the fruits solely of his suffering and dying, and they are appropriated on our part by faith. God grants them and imputes them to the church in the decree of election, in the resurrection of Christ, in his calling by the gospel.[116] In God's own time they will also become the subjective possession of believers. For though it is true that we humans need not add anything to the work of Christ, Christ himself, by having acquired salvation, is very far from having completed the work assigned to him. He took on himself the task of really and fully saving his people. He will not abdicate as mediator before he has presented his church—without spot or wrinkle—to the Father. The application of salvation is no less an essential constituent of redemption than the acquisition of it. "Take away its application

113. J. Calvin, *Institutes*, III.xii–xviii (on justification); III.xi–xxiv (on election).

114. Ibid., III.i.1; III.iii.2, 9–11, 24.

115. Cf. H. Heppe, *Dogmatik des deutschen Protestantismus im sechzehnten Jahrhundert*, 3 vols. (Gotha: F. A. Perthes, 1857), II, 311–16; M. Schneckenburger and E. Güder, *Vergleichende Darstellung*, I, 195; II, 22; F. Philippi, *Kirchliche Glaubenslehre,* 3rd ed., 7 vols. in 10 (Gütersloh: Bertelsmann, 1870–90), V, 115.

116. "When the Lord calls, justifies, and glorifies us, he is declaring nothing other than his eternal election," says Calvin in a quotation cited in J. Bohatec, ed., *Calvinstudien: Festschrift zum 400. Geburtstag Johann Calvins* (Leipzig: Rudolf Haupt, 1909), 202.

and redemption is not redemption." In heaven, therefore, Christ continues his prophetic, priestly, and royal activity. The application of salvation is *his* work. He is the active agent. By an irresistible and inamissible grace, he imparts himself and his benefits to his own. Also soteriology must be viewed theologically, that is, as a work of the Father, the Son, and the Spirit. Also at stake in *this* domain is the honor of God, the assertion and revelation of all the perfections of God, which have been violated by sin. It is the will of God, in the church of Christ, to redeem the world and humankind from the power of Satan and to present them forever as a model of his wisdom and power, his holiness and grace. Just as surely as the re-creation took place objectively in Christ, so surely it must also be carried out subjectively by the Holy Spirit in the church.

But just as the acquisition of salvation took place in the way of a covenant, that is, by Christ as the mediator and head of the covenant, so also its application must take place in that manner. In the first place, therefore, the ingathering of the elect must not be conceived individualistically and atomistically. The elect, after all, have all been given eternally to Christ, are included in the covenant, have all been born in due time from Christ as the body with all its members are all born from the head, and made partakers of all his benefits. The church is an organism, not an aggregate; the whole, in its case, precedes the parts. Some Reformed theologians therefore treat the doctrine of the church before that of salvation.[117] This is unnecessary inasmuch as Reformed theology, in its doctrine of the covenant of grace—which was often treated at the beginning of its soteriology or, even earlier, before the doctrine of the person and work of Christ—has the advantage that these theologians have in mind when they give priority to the doctrine of the church. Furthermore, this order of treatment easily prompts one to confuse the church as body of Christ with the church as institution and thereby leads to the practice of attributing to the latter a value for the origin and development of the religious life to which, according to Scripture and the confession, it is not entitled.[118] Interpreted in this practice, however, is the true and genuinely Reformed idea that the covenant of grace does not first arise as a result of the order of salvation but precedes it and is its foundation and starting point. While it is true that the believer first, by faith, becomes aware that he or she belongs to the covenant of grace and to the number of the elect, the epistemological ground is distinct from the ontological ground.

117. J. Wollebius, *Compendium theologiae christianae*, c. 21–27; Keckermann, *Syst. theol.* (1603), 370; W. A. Brakel, *The Christian's Reasonable Service*, trans. Bartel Elshout (Ligonier, PA: Soli Deo Gloria Publications, 1992), I, c. 24–29.

118. A. Ritschl (*Rechtfertigung und Versöhnung*, I², 203ff.) believed that Calvin originally thought of penitence only in negative terms, as that which preceded faith, and later began to understand it of the conversion to God that proceeds from faith and then also gave it a place after one's grafting into Christ and one's incorporation into the church. But the positive view of penitence already occurs in the first edition of the *Institutes*, and the grafting into Christ does not coincide, in Calvin, with incorporation into the church, unless one thinks in this connection of the church as an organism and not as an institution. Compare H. Strahtmann, "Die Entstehung der Lehre Calvins von der Busse," in *Calvinstudien*, ed. J. Bohatec, 187–245, esp. 189ff., 200ff.

In the second place, therefore, regeneration, faith, and conversion are not preparations that occur apart from Christ and the covenant of grace nor conditions that a person has to meet in toto or in part in his or her own strength to be incorporated in that covenant. Rather, they are benefits that already flow from the covenant of grace, the mystical union, the granting of Christ's person. The Holy Spirit, who is the author of these benefits, was acquired by Christ for his own. Hence the imputation of Christ precedes the gift of the Spirit, and regeneration, faith, and conversion do not first lead us to Christ but are taken from Christ by the Holy Spirit and imparted to his own.

Consequently, in the third place, penitence in the Reformed order of salvation had to assume a different character from what it had in the Lutheran order. In part personal experience played a role in this as well. Calvin was brought to Christ differently from Luther. The latter lived for a long time under a heavy sense of guilt and in anguish of conscience. For years he felt the curse of the law and the wrath of God on him and in the end found peace in the gracious forgiveness of sins by faith alone. Calvin, on the other hand, was gradually persuaded of the truth of the Reformation but for a considerable period of time could not—held back by respect for the church—decide to join this movement. Then all at once the "sudden conversion" came when all doubt and hesitation was overcome in him and he surrendered himself unconditionally and completely to the will of God. He became obedient and chose God's way. His move therefore consisted above all in learning obedience to what he had long before learned to know as the will of God. For him the newness consisted not so much in a sudden experience of grace and salvation as in a firm decision and the decisive act of obedience to God's will.

This is why Calvin is not concerned to frame a theory of conversion but rather to answer the question, "On what basis must the regenerate person, knowing himself to be a sinner, ground his validity, his being accepted, before God?"[119] Calvin, therefore, like Luther, is well aware of a penitence that precedes faith and consists in contrition of heart and self-mortification before God. There are many "who are overwhelmed by qualms of conscience or compelled to obedience before they are imbued with the knowledge of grace or even taste it." But this is merely an initial fear, a legalistic penitence, that does not with infallible certainty lead to faith. Nor does Calvin want to describe "how variously Christ draws us to himself, or prepares us for the pursuit of godliness." And he expressly rejects the doctrine of many Anabaptists according to which new converts must first practice penitence for a few days in order thereafter to be admitted into the communion of grace. In Calvin the accent lies on a different kind of penitence, namely, that which proceeds from faith, is possible only in communion with Christ, continues

119. F. Loofs, *Dogmengeschichte*, 885.

throughout life, and consists in mortification and vivification, "both of which happen to us by participation in Christ."[120]

Now Luther also knew this kind of penitence. He, too, knew that true contrition presupposes the love of righteousness and has its origin in the benefits of Christ. Still, alongside this view, he consistently clung to the necessity of a prior preaching of the law and so-called passive contrition and called the "fear of threatening" the first component of conversion.[121] Melanchthon went even further in this direction. In the new version of the visitation articles of 1528, he expressly gave to this "passive contrition" that precedes faith the name of "repentance" (although Luther had seldom done this), appealing to Luke 24:47. He added the following remarkable explanation: "Although some people indeed believe one ought not teach anything antecedently to faith but teach repentance in terms of faith and flowing from faith, yet so that the adversary may not be able to say I'm recanting my earlier teaching, one has to assume that, since repentance and law also belong to the common beliefs (for one must certainly have believed beforehand that it is God who threatens, commands, and frightens), it is for ordinary uneducated persons that one should leave such doctrines under the name of 'repentance,' 'command,' 'law,' 'fear,' and so on in order that they may understand the Christian faith all the more discriminatingly."[122] Hence it was practical, pedagogical considerations that led Luther to hold onto "passive contrition" as the first component of conversion.

Conversion for that reason was consistently differentiated—in the Lutheran confession and Lutheran theology[123]—into two parts: *contrition* and *faith*, corresponding to the contrast between law and gospel. Somewhat loosely attached to these two parts, then, was a third part on "good works" or the "new obedience" with the comment: "Then must follow the good works that are the fruits of repentance."[124] Calvin, on the other hand, increasingly let the penitence that sometimes precedes faith slip into the background and increasingly moved the conversion that follows and proceeds from faith into the foreground. This also derived from the fact that, not only in the case of adults but also in that of the children of the church, he increasingly proceeded from the covenant of grace and from their being grafted into Christ. Conversion, accordingly, became a part of the Christian life. It presupposed regeneration and faith. Its parts were not contrition and faith but mortification and vivification. It continued throughout life and had its place in the doctrine of gratitude.[125]

120. J. Calvin, *Institutes*, III.iii.2, 9.

121. In F. Loofs, *Dogmengeschichte*, 719–20, 790.

122. Ibid., 791.

123. Cf. J. T. Müller, *Die symbolischen Bücher*, 41, 167, 171, 174, 312, 634; H. Schmid, *Doctrinal Theology of the Evangelical Lutheran Church*, 339ff.

124. J. T. Müller, *Die symbolischen Bücher*, 41, 171, 531.

125. Some, like Sohn, still refer to contrition and faith as the two parts of conversion, but the majority follow Calvin; cf. esp. the Heidelberg Catechism, qu. 88–89.

Fourth, this carried with it still another change in the doctrine of conversion. Among the Lutherans, "contrition" and "faith" formed the two parts of it. But Calvin took exception to this division. Though he recognized that repentance and faith were closely connected and that, strictly speaking, the former is not possible without the latter and rather flows from it, he observed that Scripture regularly distinguishes between the two, mentioning them side by side (e.g., Acts 20:21), and that therefore "repentance and faith, although held together by a permanent bond, require to be joined rather than confused."[126] Faith and repentance, therefore, each obtained a more or less independent meaning in the order of salvation. Calvin thereby gained a double advantage. In the first place, faith could now be much more closely related to justification, and justification could now be viewed in a purely juridical sense as an act of acquittal by God. Lutheran theology on this point, as we will see later in the locus on justification, is far from clear, but Reformed theology owed to Calvin its clear insight into the religious character of justification and simultaneously its clear view of faith as a "firm and certain knowledge." Thereby justification was now "fully secured in advance."[127]

A second advantage was that one could now fearlessly attribute to repentance an ethical meaning. Among the Lutherans the first part of repentance, namely, contrition, consists almost exclusively of the "terrors of conscience."[128] Now, though Calvin also includes them in the definition of repentance, it nevertheless consists mainly in mortification, that is, in heartfelt sorrow over sin and in hating and fleeing from it; and, further, in vivification (or quickening), that is, a heartfelt joy in God and love and delight in doing his will.[129] Faith and justification, therefore, are not—after contrition—the sum and substance of the order of salvation. Luther tended to favor stopping there, to view Christian liberty especially as deliverance from the law, and, with reference to good works, to expect that they would automatically be produced by faith, like fruit by a tree and sunrays by the sun.[130] Calvin made a clear distinction between the religious and the ethical life and for the latter carved out a field of its own.

Finally, in the fifth place, since repentance was included in the Christian life, Calvin could do justice also to its active side. This was difficult for the Lutherans, since for them contrition formed the beginning of the new life, and, given the confession of human impotence, repentance had to be conceived in strictly passive terms or, in case of this [passive view] being weakened, synergism had to be accepted. But Calvin was able to avoid this by proceeding from the believer's being grafted into Christ; now, in repentance, he addressed the regenerate person who by the power of God had to repent, fight sin, and fulfill the will of God. That will is contained in the law. Since Luther had almost exclusively learned to know the

126. J. Calvin, *Institutes*, III.iii.5.
127. H. Strahtmann, in J. Bohatec, ed., *Calvinstudien*, 227.
128. J. T. Müller, *Die symbolischen Bücher*, 171, 312, 635.
129. J. Calvin, *Institutes*, III.iii.3, 5ff.; Heidelberg Catechism, qu. 89–90.
130. F. Loofs, *Dogmengeschichte*, 772.

law in its condemning force, he considered the believer as having been completely freed from it and left no room for the third use of the law.[131] But Calvin also ascribed to the law a normative significance for the moral life and derived from the will of God a stimulus for urging people to do good works. Sanctification is as much a benefit of Christ as justification. Inasmuch as the good works in which believers must walk are prepared by God in Christ [Eph. 2:10], faith cannot stop at the forgiveness of sins but reaches out to the perfection that is in Christ, seeks to confirm itself from works as from its own fruits, girds itself with courage and power not only to live in communion with Christ but also to fight under him as king against sin, the world, and the flesh, and to make all things serviceable to the honor of God's name.

Since, however, repentance (conversion), has two parts, mortification and vivification, Reformed theology can highlight now one and now the other. There is even disagreement over which of the two predominates in Calvin.[132] But at issue here is not a principle as such. Depending on the persons, the times, and the circumstances, either the negative or the positive side of the Christian life comes to the fore. The Christians' moral life has faith as its root, the law as its rule, and the honor of God as its goal. Also in Luther, Melanchthon, and the later Lutherans, one encounters the idea that the honor of God is the final goal of all things; still, in Bucer, Calvin, and the later Reformed, this idea acquired a much deeper and broader meaning. Obedience to God's will in the interest of advancing his glory—*that,* in Reformed circles, became the task of the Christian life.[133]

THE *ORDO SALUTIS* IN MYSTICISM AND RATIONALISM

[420] Besides these conceptions of the order of salvation in ecclesiastical theology, several others surfaced as well. They are reducible to two main groups, the mystical and the rationalistic. Mysticism is a phenomenon that appears in all the higher religions and seeks to deepen the religious life, usually out of reaction to faith in external authority. Hence, wherever it occurs, in India or Arabia, among Jews or Greeks, in the case of Catholics or Protestants, it has a number of common traits. Generally speaking, it is characterized by the fact that, by an unusual road and with the aid of extraordinary forces, it strives after a higher knowledge and a more intimate communion with the divine than can be attained by means of the [reigning] orthodoxy. Not infrequently it makes use, in this connection, of the mysterious natural forces made available by magic, manticism, and theurgy,

131. In F. Loofs, *Dogmengeschichte,* 777.

132. Schulze and Troeltsch, for example, are directly opposed to each other in their evaluation of Calvin's ethics: H. Strahtmann, in J. Bohatec, ed., *Calvinstudien,* 188.

133. See also H. Strahtmann, "Calvins Lehre von der Busse in ihrer späteren Gestalt," *Theologische Studien und Kritiken* (1909). Also W. Lüttge, *Die Rechtfertigungslehre Calvins und ihre Bedeutung für seine Frömmigkeit* (Berlin: Reuther & Reichard, 1909); C. Lelièvre, "La doctrine de la justification par la foi dans la théologie de Calvin," *Revue chrétienne* 56 (1909): 699–710.

hypnotism, spiritism, and theosophy (occultism in general). But also where it only makes use of those forces that are implied in revelation and religion, it is often accompanied by ecstasies, visions, and all sorts of strange phenomena (stigmatization, bilocation, and so on) and not infrequently lapses into a pantheistic mingling of the divine and the human (not only in Brahmanism, Neoplatonism, Sufism, and others but also in Christianity, in the case of John Scotus Erigena, the Brothers of the Free Spirit, Böhme, Weigel, and others).[134] If we isolate all this from true mysticism under the name of general mysticism, there still remains for the latter the endeavor, with the aid of an extraordinary working of divine grace, to advance to a higher knowledge and a more intimate communion with God than can be achieved by the ordinary believer. Practical, empirical mysticism seeks to obtain this knowledge and communion by means of various exercises; theoretical and speculative mysticism, which is often coupled to the former, yet distinct from it, examines these exercises and attempts to systematize the experiences and insights obtained by them. In the footsteps of Plato, Philo, and Plotinus, and following Pseudo-Dionysius, mainly three stages are distinguished in the mystical life: κάθαρσις (the *via purgativa,* asceticism), φωτισμος (the *via illuminativa,* meditation), and ἐποπτεια (the *via unitiva, contemplativa,* ecstasy). At the stage of purgation, by prayer, penitence, the use of the sacraments, deprivation, self-chastisement, and so on, the soul cleanses itself from sin and withdraws from all that is earthly. In the second stage, the soul with all of its powers of thought and will concentrates on one specific thing, for example, the suffering of Christ, his wounds, heavenly beatitude, the love or the holiness of God. In the third stage, the soul is most intimately united and, as it were, identified with the object to which it fully surrendered by meditation. It then falls into a state that, according to all mystics, is practically indescribable and is therefore denoted by various terms: seraphic contemplation, the mystical union, a betrothal, the mystical kiss, a passive transformation, a mystical sleep, death, or annihilation, the tomb of the soul, and others.[135]

Diametrically opposed to this mystical trend is the rationalism that was prepared in modern times by Socinianism and Remonstrantism and gained hegemony over the human mind in the eighteenth century. It regards Christ as no more than

---

134. Cf. E. Lehmann, *Mystiek heidensche en christelijke,* translated from the Danish by J. E. van der Waals (Utrecht: Honig, 1908).

135. E. Zeller, *Die Philosophie der Griechen,* 4th ed., 3 vols. (Leipzig: O. R. Reisland, 1879), V, 399; Pseudo-Dionysius the Areopagite, *The Divine Names and Mystical Theology;* cf. Hugo Koch, *Pseudo-Dionysius Areopagita in seinen Beziehungen zum Neuplatonismus und Mysterienwesen* (Mainz: Kirchheim, 1900); T. Aquinas, *Summa theol.,* II, 2, qu. 179ff.; J. von Görres, *Die christliche Mystik* (Regensburg: G. J. Manz, 1836); A. M. Weiss, *Apologie des Christentums* (Freiburg i.B.: Herder, 1904–8), vol. 5; D. Hollaz, *Examen theologicum acroamaticum* (Rostock and Leipzig: Russworm, 1718), 208–796, 821; G. Voetius, *Ta askètika, sive Exercitia pietatis* (Gorichem: Paul Vink, 1664), 56ff.; H. Erbkam, *Geschichte der protestantischen Sekten im Zeitalter der Reformation* (Hamburg and Gotha: Perthes, 1848), 52ff.; idem, articles "Theologie" and "Mystik," in *Kirchliches Handlexikon: Ein Nachschlagbuch über das Gesamtgebiet der Theologie und ihrer Hilfswissenschaften,* ed. Michael Buchberger, 2 vols. (Freiburg i.B.: Herder, 1907–12), II, 1068; see also H. Bavinck, *Reformed Dogmatics,* I, 146–49 (#46).

a prophet and a teacher who proclaimed the truth of God and sealed it with his life and death. By following him, humans—weakened by sin but not powerless—obtain salvation. The call that comes to them from the gospel therefore only exerts a moral influence on their intellect and will. If people by their own free choice listen to that call, assent to the truth, trust God's grace, and fulfill Christ's commandments—for the essence of faith is assent, trust, and obedience—then, on account of this faith, which in principle includes the whole [of Christian] obedience and is counted by God out of grace and for Christ's sake as perfect obedience, they are justified and, if they persevere, will obtain eternal salvation.[136]

Related to mysticism and rationalism are also those one-sided conceptions of the order of salvation that are known under the names antinomianism and neonomianism. Antinomianism, generally speaking, is the trend that reduces the application of salvation to its acquisition and almost completely equates the two. On this view, Christ has accomplished everything. He has taken over from us not only the guilt of sin but even its pollution. He has acquired for us not only righteousness but also regeneration and sanctification. Hence for humans there is nothing left to do. Contrition, conversion, repentance, prayer for forgiveness, doing good works—it is all unnecessary, bears a legalistic character, and fails to do justice to the perfection of Christ's sacrifice. People need only to believe; that is, they need only to arrive at the insight that they are justified, born again, sanctified, that they are perfect in Christ. The sins they still commit are no longer sins; they are the works of the old Adam, which do not concern believers as such, for they are perfect in Christ, freed from the law, and now glory in grace. Usually, however, antinomianism does not stop here, but goes back yet one more step. It first reduces the application of salvation to its acquisition and then the latter to God's decree. Even Christ did not actually acquire salvation, for salvation lay prepared from all eternity in God's decree. Christ only revealed the love of God. Believing, accordingly, is nothing other than putting aside the illusion that God is angry with us. Sin solely consists in that illusion. In ancient times such sentiments were propagated by the Gnostics and Manicheans and in the Middle Ages by numerous libertinistic sects. During and after the Reformation, they revived among the Anabaptists, in the sect of the Libertines, against which Calvin joined battle,[137] in the independentistic disturbances in England around the middle of

---

136. Otto Fock, *Der Socinianismus nach seiner Stellung in der Gesamtentwicklung des christlichen Geistes, nach seinem historischen Verlauf und nach seinem Lehrbegriff* (Kiel: C. Schröder, 1847), 651–89; *Conf. rem.* and *Apol. conf.*, VII; P. van Limborch, *Theol. christ.*, IV, 11ff.; V, 8ff.; VI, 4ff.; J. Wegscheider, *Institutiones theologiae christianae dogmaticae* (Halle: Gebauer, 1819), §146; G. Knapp, *Vorlesungen über die christliche Glaubenslehre nach dem Lehrbegriff der evangelischen Kirche*, ed. Carl Thilo, 2 vols. (Halle: Buchhandlung des Waisenhauses, 1827), II, 323ff., 382ff.; F. Reinhard, *Grundriss der Dogmatik* (Munich: Seidel, 1802), §130.

137. On the linkage between the opposition in Geneva and the sect of the Libertines, see F. Kampschulte and W. Goetz, *Johann Calvin: Seine Kirche und sein Staat in Genf*, 2 vols. (Leipzig: Duncker & Humblot, 1869–99), II, 13; A. Lang, *Johann Calvin: Ein Lebensbild zu seinem 400. Geburtstag am 10. Juli 1909* (Leipzig: R. Haupt, 1909), 128ff.

the seventeenth century,[138] and in the Netherlands among the Hattemists and the sect of the Hebrews.[139] Antinomianism is a phenomenon that occurs not only in religion but also in morality and politics. In modern times it found an interpreter in Friedrich Nietzsche and in the spokesmen for anarchism.

All the Reformers rejected this antinomianism as resolutely as possible. Although Luther, as a result of his one-sided view of the law, often spoke as though for Christians—except insofar as they were still sinners—the law no longer had any meaning, yet he most vigorously opposed Agricola, who utterly rejected the preaching of the law and wanted to derive repentance totally from faith in the gospel.[140] In fact, between the Reformation and antinomianism, there is a fundamental difference. For not only did the Reformation uphold the law in the sense that by it the knowledge of sin and misery is effected in humans; but of even greater significance is that, according to the unanimous view of all the Reformers, the whole of salvation was and could be accomplished solely in the way of justice done according to the law. Certainly, the work of Christ consisted in his perfect obedience to the law of God, and justification only took place on the basis of the perfect righteousness accomplished by Christ.[141]

[421] Just as antinomianism on the right falsified the principles of the Reformation, so on the left even more damage was done by the nomism that under the influence of Socinianism and Remonstrantism also penetrated Protestant churches. This nomism, too, has to be differentiated in terms of a rationalistic as well as a Pietistic school. The rationalistic school is rooted basically in Piscator's teaching, according to which the righteousness we need is accomplished not by the active but solely by the passive obedience of Christ![142] Though this view was

138. H. Weingarten, *Die Revolutionskirchen Englands* (Leipzig: Breitköpf & Hartel, 1868), 72ff.

139. J. Hulsius, *De hedendaagsche Antinomianerye met die der Engelsche en oude wet-bestryders vergeleken, en zoo uit het Woord Gods, als uit de formulieren van eenigheid der Gereformeerde Kerken klaar en grondig wederlegt en dere zelve schadelykheit aangewesen*, 2nd ed. (Rotterdam: David Vermeulen, 1738); *J. Fruytier, *Klaer en kort vertoog van de valsheit en gedeformeertheit van het gevoelen der sogen. Hebreen* (1697); M. Leydekker, *Historische en godgeleerde oeffeningen, over de oorsprong, voortgang, en gevoelens van de oude en nieuwe Antinomianen* ('s Gravenhage: Kitto, 1700); B. de Moor, *Comm. theol.*, II, 665–67; A. Ypey, *Geschiedenis van de Kristlijke Kerk in de achttiende eeuw*, 15 vols. (Utrecht: W. van Ijzerworst, 1797–1815), VII, 290ff.; *J. Van Leeuwen, in *Nederlandse Archief voor Kerkelijke Geschiedenis* 8 (1848): 57–169; W. C. Van Manen, "Pontiaan van Hattem," *De Gids* 49/4 (October 1885): 84–115. Ed. note: The Hattemists were followers of Pontiaan van Hattem (1645–1706), a Reformed preacher who was deposed from his ministry because his one-sided emphasis on God's love led his followers to antinomianism. He was also accused of holding to Spinozian pantheism. The "Hebrews" were a sect led by Jacobus Verschoor (1648–1700), who taught a quietist perfectionism based on a rigorous application of the doctrine of full justification through Christ's work. These two men and their followers are often linked, but Verschoor is distinguished from van Hattem by his clear repudiation of antinomianism and the philosophy of Spinoza.

140. On Agricola: F. Loofs, *Dogmengeschichte*, 858ff.; G. Kawerau, "Antinistische Streitigkeiten," *PRE*[3], I, 585–92; Joh. Werner, "Der erste antinom. Streit," *Neue kirchliche Zeitschrift* (1904): 801–24, 860–78.

141. J. Buchanan, *The Doctrine of Justification: An Outline of Its History in the Church and of Its Exposition from Scripture* (Edinburgh: T&T Clark, 1867).

142. Cf. above, 347–51, 377–80 (##378, 386).

rejected by the Reformed churches in France at their synods of Gap (1603) and Rochelle (1607), it nevertheless found much acceptance, especially in the school of Saumur. Here John Cameron taught that, since the will always follows the intellect, the enlightenment of the intellect is sufficient for conversion. Amyraut, on his part, grounded the doctrine of election in what is called hypothetical universalism. Pajon considered internal grace unnecessary and let the efficacy of the gospel call—as in the theology of Bellarmine—depend on its congruity with the circumstances in which it comes to a person.[143]

The result of all this was that the Reformed doctrine of the covenant of works, of the human incapacity for good, of the immediate imputation of Adam's sin and Christ's righteousness, and so on were denied; faith was joined to works and in this combination was viewed as both the means and the ground of justification. This Saumurian theology did not remain limited to France but also crept into other Reformed churches, among others, those in England and the Netherlands. Originally the Episcopal Church in England was in fact Reformed in its confession and doctrine, yet from the beginning of the sixteenth century, also Roman Catholic and Arminian positions found acceptance in it. The antinomian errors into which many zealots in the time of Cromwell fell drove many people back in the same direction, and the school of Saumur, by its avoidance of the two extremes, seemed to commend itself. But it is common to all those who take the "middle way" to show a greater preference "for that extreme they go halfway *to* than for that from which they go halfway."[144]

And so Amyraldism and Arminianism in England soon allied themselves with each other and shaped the features of that conception of the order of salvation that is known as "neonomianism." This name generally characterizes that sentiment that posits the ground for the believer's justification, not in the imputed righteousness of Christ, but in the believer's own, sincere, though imperfect, righteousness. According to this view, Christ, by his suffering and death, made satisfaction for the sins of all humankind and made salvation possible for all humans, and so brought them all into a "salvable state." This salvable state consists in the fact that whereas the old law, the law of the covenant of works, demanded perfect righteousness from everyone, Christ has now introduced "a new law," a law of grace, which is content with faith and repentance, with sincere, albeit imperfect, obedience of the contrite sinner. The work of Christ, therefore, may also still be called our "legal righteousness" because by it he has satisfied the old law; we may even plead our case on the basis of that work when the old law makes its demands on us. But evangelical righteousness that is the ground of our justification is a different one: it consists in our obedience to

---

143. A. Schweizer, *Die protestantischen Centraldogmen in ihrer Entwicklung innerhalb der reformierten Kirche*, 2 vols. (Zürich: Orell Fussli and Co., 1854–56), II, 235ff.

144. James Buchanan, *Doctrine of Justification*, 173.

the new law, that is, in our faith and repentance.[145] This neonomianism, while finding much acceptance, also encountered strong criticism from those who in time were called "antinomians." But this name was unfairly applied to them by their opponents. They were, if you will, "antineonomians" but definitely did not deserve the label "antinomians" (people opposed to law). On the contrary, they took the law much more seriously than did the neonomians, whom they opposed. Whereas the latter presented the law of the covenant of works as a temporary order, which Christ had not fully—in a substitutionary sense— satisfied, which now no longer applies and has been replaced by a "new law," the antineonomians above all emphasized that the moral law is in essence eternal, grounded in the nature of God, has been completely fulfilled by Christ in our place, and now still consistently applies as the rule of our life.[146] A similar disagreement arose in Scotland on the occasion of the new edition, published in 1718, of Edward Fisher's *Marrow of Modern Divinity* (1647). The dispute was in part of a formal nature insofar as it concerned the question whether some antinomian errors were taught in this book, but it also touched on the deeper issue of the neonomianism that had arisen in England a century earlier and had now also penetrated Scotland. The critics of the "Marrow," like Principal Hadow of St. Andrews, were generally still sound in doctrine but often went too far in their criticism, tilted toward neonomianism, and so laid the groundwork for the Arminian or semi-Socinian school, which in the eighteenth century

145. George Bull, *Harmonia apostolica* (London: Wells & Scott, 1670); W. Cave and J. Taylor, *Antiquitates apostolicae* (London: Norton, 1678); in opposition, see H. Witsius, *Miscellaneorum sacrorum*, II, 668–751. Also B. Hoadley, *Several Discourses concerning the Terms of Acceptance with God* (London: Knapton, 1727); Dan. Williams, *Gospel-Truth Stated and Vindicated* (London: Dunton, 1692); Richard Baxter, *A Treatise of Justifying Righteousness* (London: Simons & Robinson, 1676), and many other works; John Goodwin, *An Exposition of the Ninth Chapter of the Epistle to the Romans with the Banner of Justification Displayed, to Which Is Added Eirēnomachia* (London: Baynes & Son, 1835); B. Woodbridge, *The Method of Grace in the Justification of Sinners* (London: Paxton, 1656).

146. The most prominent antineonomians were John Eaton, *The Honey-Combe of Free Justification by Christ Alone* (London: Robert Lancaster, 1642); William Eyre, *Vindiciae justificationis gratuitae* (London: Edward Forrest, 1654); Tobias Crisp, *Christ Alone Exalted, in the Perfection and Encouragements of the Saints, Notwithstanding Sins and Trials* (London: R. Noble, 1643); John Saltmarsh, *Free Grace, or, The Flowings of Christs Blood Free to Sinners* (London: Giles Calvert, 1647); Samuel Crisp, *Christ Made Sin, Evinced from Scripture (2 Cor. v.21)* (London: J. A., 1691); Thomas Tully, *Justificatio Paulina sine operibus ex mente Ecclesiae Anglicanae, omniumque reliquarum quae reformatae audiunt, asserta & illustrata* (Oxford: Hall, 1674); Isaac Chauncy, *Neonomianism Unmask'd, or, The Ancient Gospel Pleaded against the Other, Called a New Law or Gospel* (London: J. Harris, 1692–93); idem, *Alexipharmacon, or, A Fresh Antidote against Neonomian Bane and Poyson to the Protestant Religion* (London: W. Marshall, 1700). For further information on the neonomian and antineonomian debate, see H. Witsius, *Miscellaneorum sacrorum*, II, 753ff.; J. Hoornbeek, *Summa contr.*, 701ff.; B. de Moor, *Comm. theol.*, IV, 835ff.; C. Vitringa, *Doctr. christ.*, III, 296; C. Pfaff, *Introductio in historiam theologiae literariam notis amplissimis*, 3 vols. (Tübingen: Cottae, 1724–26), 257ff.; J. Walch, *Bibliotheca theologica selecta, litterariis adnotationibus instructa*, 4 vols. (Jena: Croeckerianal, 1757–65), II, 1069; idem, *Historische und theologische Einleitung in die Religionsstreitigkeiten außer der evangelisch-lutherischen Kirchen*, 5 vols. (Jena: J. Meyers Witwe, 1733–36), III, 999; J. Buchanan, *Doctrine of Justification*, lectures 6 and 7.

gained the upper hand also in Scottish theology.[147] In the same way, the denial by Jonathan Edwards of immediate imputation in the case of Adam and Christ had the effect of increasingly leading New England theology along the lines of Placaeus.[148]

In the Netherlands from the middle of the seventeenth century on, one could observe a similar weakening of the principles of the Reformation. The first person who clearly adopted the sentiments of Piscator and the Saumurian school with respect to justification was Johannes Vlak, pastor at Zutphen (1674–90). According to him, one must distinguish two kinds of justification. The first consists exclusively in the forgiveness of sins, is grounded in the death of Christ, and can be called a justification of sinners. But the second is a justification of the godly, is grounded in the personal evangelical righteousness that believers themselves work out in the power of the Holy Spirit when they begin to live according to the commandments of Christ, and consists in the bestowal of eternal life and the reward that is linked to good works.[149] Anthony van der Os, who in 1748 became a pastor in Zwolle, went even further and understood the righteousness of God of which Paul speaks as being no more than God's gracious disposition to save sinners by Christ and described faith as trust in Christ and obedience to his commandments.[150] And in the eighteenth century, all Reformed theology moved in this direction. A small group under the leadership of Holtius, Comrie, Brahe, and others did remain faithful to the confession of the fathers and tried to exclude from justification all of people's own work and righteousness in such a way as to view this justification as an eternal one, equating it with the decree.[151]

147. See H. Bavinck, *Reformed Dogmatics*, I, 191–92 (#57); above, 461–63 (#405); and further J. Buchanan, *Doctrine of Justification*, 182ff. In the eighteenth century, against the increasingly influential neonomianism, there still arose resistance from the side of John Glas, *The Testimony of the King of Martyrs concerning His Kingdom: John xviii.36, 37 Explained and Illustrated in Scripture Light* (Edinburgh: G. Lyon, 1729); and his son-in-law, Robert Sandeman, *Letters on Theron and Aspasio* (Edinburgh: Sands, Murray, Donaldson and Cochran, 1759), after whom the small group of followers were called Sandemanians. But they fell into the other extreme and, to keep the faith pure, excluded from it all trust and certainty and therefore allowed it to shrink into mere intellectual assent; see J. Buchanan, *Doctrine of Justification*, 188ff.

148. Cf. above, 100 (#322).

149. In 1684, *Johannes Vlak published *Eeuwig Evangelium of Leer der zaligheid* (1684); and later also *Trias dissertationum de operibus Dei*. He was vigorously opposed by *Henricus Brink, *De waare leer der rechtvaardigmakinge, benadeelt door D. Joh. Vlak*; Melchior Leydekker, *De veritate religionis reformatae seu evangelicae* (Utrecht: Rudolph à Zyll, 1688), III, 6; and others. Cf. B. de Moor, *Comm. theol.*, IV, 679ff.

150. Cf. A. Ypey, *Geschiedenis van de Kristlijke Kerk*, VII, 376ff.

151. In 1750, Nicolaus Holtius, minister at Koudekerke, published a treatise on justification by faith, *De zondaar gerechtvaerdigt om niet, uit de genade Gods* (Leiden: Johannes Hasebroek; Amsterdam: Nicolaas Byl, 1757). Alexander Comrie, minister at Woubrugge wrote (inter alia) the following: *Stellige en praktikale verklaring van den Heidelbergschen Catechismus, volgens de leer en de gronden der reformatie* (Minnertsga: J. Bloemsma, 1844); *Brief over de regtvaardigmaking des zondaars, door de onmiddelijke toerekening der borg-geregtigheid van Christus* (Utrecht: Fisscher, 1889; reprinted, Ermelo: Snoek, 2003) (ed note: ET: *The ABC of Faith*, trans. J. Marcus Banfield [Ossett: Zoar, 1978]); *Verhandeling van eenige eigenschappen des zaligmakenden geloofs*, 4th ed. (Leiden: Johannes Hasebroek; Amsterdam: Nicolaas Byl, 1753). In 1753 and the following years, Holtius and Comrie jointly published *Examen van het Ontwerp van Tolerantie*, 10 vols. (Amsterdam: Nicolaas Byl,

But the tide could no longer be turned. Even the professors J. van den Honert and J. J. Schultens at Leiden raised their voice against this restoration of the Reformed confession, denied the immediate imputation of the righteousness of Christ, and in the order of salvation had faith precede justification.[152] The minister of Voorburg, David Kleman, was the interpreter of the new mind-set when he assumed a connection—forged by the wisdom and goodness of God—between the moral actions of humans and the supernatural communication of faith such that all who made a proper use of their natural powers (improved by the moral teaching of the gospel) and seriously pursued a path of duty could certainly count on obtaining God's supernatural grace.[153]

PIETISM AND METHODISM

[422] In addition, neonomianism also made its appearance in a pietistic form and made, not faith and obedience, but faith and [pietistic] experience the condition for justification. From the beginning, there was in the Reformed church and Reformed theology a practical school of thought that was averse to all scholasticism and put all emphasis on *life*. It was supported and promoted especially by strongly anti-Aristotelian philosopher Peter Ramus, who wanted more simplicity in philosophy and described theology as the "doctrine of living well" whose purpose is not the "knowledge of things but practice and consistent application."[154] This view gained acceptance with many Reformed theologians: at Strasbourg, with Sturm; at Heidelberg, with Tremellius; at Herborn, with Piscator; in the Netherlands, with Snellius, Scaliger, and Jacob Alting; at Cambridge, with Perkins, whose pupil Ames—later professor in Franeker alongside Maccovius—described theology as "the doctrine of living for God, the pursuit of piety," rooted in the

---

1753) with a view to reconciling the doctrines adopted by the Synod of Dort (1619) with the doctrines of the Remonstrants condemned by the synod. When in 1759 the tenth dialogue was published and in its preface it rendered a most unfavorable verdict on Prof. J. van den Honert (who had died on April 6, 1758), the states of Holland prohibited the continuation of the series. Also belonging to this group was the Vlissinger minister Jan Jacob Brahe, who authored *Godgeleerde stellingen over de leer der rechtvaardigmaking des zondaars voor God* (Amsterdam: Den Houden, 1833), and also *Aanmerkingen over de vyf Walchersche Artikelen, welke beneffens de gewoon formulieren van eenigheid in de E. classis ondertekend worden* (Middelburg: Callenfels, 1758). In opposition, Petrus Boddaert set forth *Wolk van getuigen voor de leere der rechtvaardiginge door en uit het geloove*; see B. de Moor, *Comm. theol.*, IV, 668.

152. J. van den Honert's *Verhandeling van de rechtvaardiging des sondaars uyt en door het geloove* was written in opposition to the previously mentioned works of Holtius. J. J. Schultens wrote *Uitvoerige Waerschuwing op verscheiden stukken der Kategismusverklaaringe van Alex. Comrie* in 1755. Alberti, Venema, Hollebeek, Chevallier, and other so-called Tolerants also belonged to this group.

153. D. Kleman, *De Orde des Heils, of het verband tusschen genade en plicht* (Amsterdam: P. Conradi, 1776).

154. On Ramus, see Tideman, in Willem Moll and J. G. de Hoop Scheffer, *Studiën en bijdragen op 't gebied der historisch theologie*, 4 vols. (Amsterdam: G. L. Funke, 1880), III, 389–429; P. Lobstein, *Petrus Ramus als Theologe: Ein Beitrag zur Geschichte der protestantischen Theologie* (Strassburg: C. F. Schmidt, 1878); F. Cuno, "Ramus," *PRE*³, XVI, 426–28.

will.[155] Thus arose a practical form of Pietism, which was represented in England by R. Baxter (mentioned above), Daniel Williams, B. Woodbridge, and many practical authors and promoted in the Netherlands by many theologians and ministers, such as Witsius, Vitringa, Lampe, Mel, d'Outrein, Brakel, Hellenbroek, Smytegelt, Francken, Groenewegen, Borstius, Van der Groe, Eswijler, Schortinghuis, and others.[156]

To the extent that conditions in the church grew worse and a dead orthodoxy gained the upperhand, all these authors stressed the necessity of a genuine conversion. Being born of believing parents, membership in the church, baptism, communion, an orthodox faith—all these things are not enough. One must have a true, saving faith, which is very different from a temporary, a miraculous, and a historical faith. True faith does not arise except when terror before the law, fear of judgment, and anguish over sin have preceded it. The essence of faith, furthermore, does not consist in the assent or conviction of the intellect; it consists in trust rather than in knowledge. Its seat is more in the heart and the will than in the head. Nor is it immediately certain; on the contrary, as Gomarus had already said,[157] we must distinguish between a refuge-taking and an assured trust, the former characterizing only the "being" (essence) of faith, the latter its "well-being" and can be added at a much later time. That faith as refuge-taking trust consisting in hungering and thirsting after Christ and his righteousness is a condition that precedes justification. It entrusts itself to Christ in order to be justified; once it has accepted the righteousness of Christ, it takes it to God the Father, points him to his promises, and is justified by him. Things therefore are not as simple, nor do they flow as smoothly as many people think. The gospel is not for everyone; the offer of salvation is not universal. The law is for all but the gospel is only for certain "qualified" sinners, for those who have received an initial endowment of grace. No one may believe except those who have first received from the Holy Spirit the boldness to take that step. One should beware of an illusory or stolen faith! For that reason permanent self-examination is necessary. One can so easily deceive oneself. There is only a very fine line of distinction between regenerates at their worst and unregenerates at their best. There is so much similarity between false and true grace.[158] Believers must therefore always reexamine and test themselves by the marks of a truly spiritual life. The way of salvation is a narrow way by which even the righteous can scarcely be saved. It is

---

155. H. Visscher, *Guilielmus Amesius: Zijn leven en werken* (Haarlem: J. M. Stap, 1894).

156. Cf. H. Heppe, *Geschichte des Pietismus und der Mystik in der reformierten Kirche* (Leiden: Brill, 1879); M. Goebel and T. Link, *Geschichte des christlichen Lebens in der rheinisch-westphälischen evangelischen Kirche*, 3 vols. (Koblenz: K. Bädeker, 1849–60); A. Ritschl, *Geschichte des Pietismus in der reformierten Kirche* (Bonn: A. Marcus, 1880).

157. F. Gomarus, *Opera theologica omnia*, I, 654; cf. the Westminster Confession, XVIII, 3.

158. Witsius wrote a tract on the regenerate at his worst and the unregenerate at his best, and Theodorus van der Groe authored *Toetssteen der waare en valsche genade*, 8th ed., 2 vols. (Rotterdam: H. van Pelt & A. Douci Pietersz., 1752–53).

also a long road. There is a great distance between a refuge-taking and an assured trust. Between these two poles one finds many classes and groups of people: the "discovered," the "persuaded," the "concerned," the "hungry for salvation," people of little or weak faith, and others. As a rule, the experience of being "sealed" and "assured" only follows after a long period of inner doubt and conflict and then frequently in an extraordinary manner, by a voice, a vision, a sudden word of comfort from Scripture, and so on.[159]

Akin to this Pietism in the Reformed churches is the Lutheran variety, the foundation for which was laid by Musaeus, Arndt, and others and by Reformed authors such as Baxter, Dyke, Bayly, and others. It then became a mighty movement and experienced enormous expansion as a result of the work of Philipp J. Spener (1635–1705). By means of sermons, discipline, lectures on piety, and numerous writings, Spener took action against dead orthodoxy.[160] He sought a return to the grace of regeneration received in baptism but which was later lost. Historical faith is insufficient. Needed for salvation is a vital active faith. And one does not obtain this faith unless one learns to know one's sins through the preaching of the law and has gone through a long and anxious struggle with the devil, the world, and the flesh, sometimes to the point of despair (*Busskampf*). Out of this struggle, then, the true faith breaks through. This faith, accordingly, consists not just in assent but especially in trust: it is an experience of the heart, a vitality of the soul. As such it is also, initially, a means of justification in order then to manifest itself in a holy life that is distinct from the world and even abstains from the adiaphora.[161] This is the Pietism in which Zinzendorf (1700–1760) was brought up. He continued to agree with it in his aversion to dead orthodoxy but found it too legalistic. Dread of the law and anguish over sin, though not wrong and sometimes even having a kind of preparatory power, are not the real thing. True penitence, though the word is not exactly correct because it makes one think of punishment, arises from the gospel, from the message of the suffering Christ. It consists not so much in fear and struggle, in lamenting and weeping, as in trusting in God's grace. It is a matter of the heart, more precisely, of feeling. For that reason the heart has to be made sensitive, a state best accomplished by graphic depictions of Christ as a figure of suffering, of his blood and wounds. By this kind of communication as by immediate observation, by a deep and lively impression, by the sight of Christ's wounds, faith is born in the human heart without its having experienced a penitential struggle (*Busskampf*) or knowing precisely the hour of one's rebirth. That faith brings about union, a betrothal, a

159. Cf. H. Bavinck, *The Certainty of Faith*, trans. H. der Nederlanden (Jordan Station, ON: Paideia, 1980).

160. Especially to be considered here is his work *Pia desideria*, trans. Theodore G. Tappert (Philadelphia: Fortress Press, 1964).

161. J. Walch, *Religionsstreitigkeiten*, II, 239–436; A. Ritschl, *Geschichte des Pietismus*, II; P. Grünberg, *Philipp Jakob Spener*, 3 vols. (Göttingen: Vandenhoeck & Ruprecht, 1893–1906); idem, "Spener," *PRE*[3], XVIII, 609–22.

marriage between Christ and the soul, causes the heart to swim in grace, that is, in the blood of Jesus as in its own element, and makes the believer live constantly in the "precious closeness of the Savior." It simultaneously justifies and regenerates: faith and love coincide. The dynamic communication of the Spirit, the birth from Jesus' side, is of greater value than objective justification. Born of him, believers live without pietistic scrupulosity in his presence, do all things in his name, place everything, also their life in the home and in society, under his rule, and lead a clean Christian life.[162]

What Pietism was for the Lutheran churches, the Methodism of John Wesley (1703–91) and George Whitefield (1714–71) became for the Reformed churches. Originally it only sought to rouse a sleeping church and to animate orthodox Christianity with new life. To that end, by a gripping proclamation of righteousness, sin, judgment, and damnation, people needed first of all to be suddenly brought to a deep sense of their state of lostness. Next, in the same hour, without delay, they had to be led by faith to Christ and assured of their salvation; and finally, they had to be urged to live a new and sinless life, a life of active service in the kingdom of God, of dedication to mission and philanthropy and of abstinence from a wide range of indifferent things. Methodism, in distinction from Pietism, clearly betrays its English roots and Reformed origin. Admittedly, it is just as much a reaction against a dead orthodoxy. But it wants nothing to do with preparation, with a gradual progression of conversion. It knows nothing of a long-lasting "penitential struggle," of a final "breakthrough," of a still later ensuing "sealing." It concentrates everything into a single point, puts conversion in the full light of one's conscious- ness, and keeps a record of saved souls. And when it has converted people, it does not gather them in quiet, introspective circles, in societies and conventicles for the cultivation of piety. Rather, it immediately thrusts them into active service, insists on sudden total sanctification,[163] and organizes them into an army that goes to work by way of attack under the motto "blood and fire" (redemption and sanctification), marches into the world, and takes it by storm for Christ.

The influence that this Methodism has exerted on Protestant Christianity can hardly be exaggerated. It has not only founded a number of large and flourishing churches or societies but also has penetrated all churches and put its stamp on the entire religious life of modern times. Because of it, England and America have undergone a second reformation, as it were, and owe to it that practical, active, and aggressive view of Christianity by which Methodism so characteristically

162. H. Plitt, *Zinzendorfs Theologie*, 3 vols. in 1 (Gotha: F. A. Perthes, 1869–74); A. Spangenberg, *Idea fidei fratrum, oder, Kurzer Begrif der christlichen Lehre in den evangelischen Brüdergemeinen* (Barby: Christian Friedrich Laux, 1779); B. Becker, *Zinzendorf und sein Christentum im Verhältnis zum kirchlichen und religiösen Leben seiner Zeit*, 2nd ed. (Leipzig: F. Jansa, 1900); J. T. Müller, "Zinzendorf," *PRE*[3], XXI, 679–703; A. Ritschl, *Geschichte des Pietismus*, III, 289; H. M. van Nes, *De Graaf van Zinzendorf* (Nijkerk: Callenbach, 1902).

163. Conversion and sanctification are not two gradually merging phases of spiritual development but two "mutations" in the theory of spiritual evolution. S. L. Veenstra, *Het Leger des Heils* (Baarn: Hollandia-Drukkerij, 1910), 14.

distinguishes itself from the Reformation of the sixteenth century. For whereas this Reformation was primarily aimed at the purification of the confession and the church in line with Scripture, Methodism typically attaches but little value to doctrine, largely turns its back on the old organized churches, and directs its vision outward on the world. Mission work among Jews, pagans, and Muslims received from it a fresh impetus that is still having an effect. In recent years it included in its program "the evangelization of the whole world in this generation." The work of so-called inner mission has actually first been undertaken with seriousness by Methodism. Under its inspiration have emerged all those different activities by which the Christian religion has asserted itself as the religion of love and mercy: evangelism among nominal Christians; Sunday-school education; the distribution of Bibles and tracts; street preaching; work among the "fallen," the neglected, the imprisoned; the care of the hearing- and speech-impaired, the blind, the mentally ill, and others.

Religious life has also been changed by it. While in the past, in pious circles, it occupied itself almost exclusively with itself, examining its own states and spiritual experiences, and only after many years and through many fear-filled struggles arriving at certainty and decisiveness, now it assumes this certainty and manifests its genuineness in its devotion to labor in God's kingdom.

Over and over and in the strongest terms, John Wesley stressed that conversion and sanctification are not promises for the future but are *now,* in this very moment, granted by God to everyone who believes. "Christ stands ready, he is waiting for you; believe in him and it will all be granted to you in this selfsame hour."

> You, therefore, look for it every moment; you can be no worse, if you are no better, for that expectation; for were you to be disappointed of your hope, still you lose nothing. But you shall not be disappointed of your hope; it will come, it will not tarry. Look for it then every day, every hour, every moment. Why not this hour? This moment? Certainly you may look for it now, if you believe it is by faith. And by this token you may surely know whether you seek it by faith or works. If by works, you want something to be done *first, before* you are sanctified. You think I must first *be* or *do* thus or thus. Then you are seeking it by works unto this day. If you seek it by faith, you may expect it *as you are;* then expect it *now.* It is of importance to observe, that there is an inseparable connection between these three points—expect it by *faith,* expect it *as you are,* and expect it *now.* To deny one of them, is to deny them all; to allow one, is to allow them all.[164]

This is the tone in which Methodism continually presents the gospel and insists on conversion and sanctification. That salvation is *present,* that it is not granted just at some future date but in the present, that it does not come into a person's possession gradually, organically, by a historical route, but is fully, totally, and immediately obtainable now for everyone who believes—that is not only the

164. Robert Southey, *The Life of John Wesley* (London: Hutchinson & Co., 1903), 236ff.

emphatic one-sidedness but simultaneously the strength of Methodism. This is the presupposition that spawns the revivals that, since Wesley's public ministry, have periodically returned in the English-speaking world and that, despite all the excesses to which they give rise, have in wide circles again awakened and strengthened the religious life and, in respect of morality, have not infrequently borne abundant fruit.[165]

SUBJECTIVISM IN MODERN THOUGHT: KANT

[423] For all their differences, all the religious movements listed have this feature in common: they allow the objective factors of salvation (Christ, church, word, sacrament) to recede and place the religious subject in the center. Also the philosophy and theology of modern times moved in this direction, whether, like rationalism, Methodism, and Pietism, they placed the heavier accent on the intellect, or on the will, or on the emotions in the order of salvation. Descartes found the foundation and starting point of all knowledge in the certainty of the existence that is locked in thought and further made the clarity and distinctness of knowledge the standard of its truth.[166] What followed for us human beings is the calling to free ourselves from sensible, changing, and unreliable impressions and to strive for clear and distinct concepts that the mind, whose essence is thinking, carries within itself as innate ideas and can therefore produce from within itself.

Spinoza also proceeded from the basic idea that "what is clearly and distinctly perceived is true." Sense perception is not the source of knowledge, but "those ideas are true that are produced from a pure mind and not from accidental bodies in motion."[167] But the natural human is the slave of his affects. The natural human is acted upon to the extent that he or she is a part of nature and forms ideas of good and evil in terms of whether a thing advances or suppresses his or her life. Good and evil, therefore, do not exist objectively but are nothing but "modes of thinking, that is, notions," and "the knowledge of good and evil is nothing but an affect of joy or sadness insofar as we are conscious of it."[168] Objectively, in the whole of things, there is no good or evil; rather everything is good since

165. P. Schaff, *The Creeds of Christendom*, 6th ed., 3 vols. (1931; reprint, Grand Rapids: Baker, 1983), I, 882; III, 807; *William Edward Hartpole Lecky, *Entstehungsgeschichte und Charakter des Methodismus,* trans. Ferdinand Löwe (Leipzig, 1880); F. Loofs, "Methodismus," *PRE*[3], XII, 747–801; John L. Nuelsen, "Methodismus in Amerika," *PRE*[3], XIII, 1–25; M. Schneckenburger, *Vorlesungen über die Lehrbegriffe der kleineren protestantischen Kirchenparteien* (Frankfurt: H. L. Brönner, 1863), 103–51; T. Kolde, *Der Methodismus und seine Bekämpfung* (Erlangen: Deichert, 1886); idem, *Die Heilsarmee: Ihre Geschichte und ihr Wesen* (Erlangen: Deichert, 1885); E. Kalb, *Kirchen und Sekten der Gegenwart* (Stuttgart: Verlag der Buchhandlung der Evangelischen Gesellschaft, 1907), 310ff.; W. J. Townsend, H. B. Workman, and George Eayrs, *A New History of Methodism,* 2 vols. (London: Hodder & Stoughton, 1909).

166. "Consequently I now seem to be able to establish as a general rule that everything that I clearly and distinctively perceive is true," Descartes, *Discourse on Method,* ch. 4.

167. Baruch Spinoza, *The Principles of Descartes' Philosophy* (Chicago: Open Court, 1974), i.

168. Baruch Spinoza, *Ethics,* IV, pref. and prop. 8 (ed. note: see *Spinoza Reader* [Princeton: Princeton University Press, 1994], 199, 204).

everything is necessary and proceeds from God. However, as long as we regard things as a part of nature and have inadequate knowledge, we exist in a state of bondage; we suffer; we are limited in our existence and feel oppressed. To gain true freedom it is therefore necessary for a person to pursue another, a better and higher knowledge, a knowledge that cannot, however, as Descartes thought, be attained in rational knowledge, in the knowledge of adequate concepts, but constitutes a third kind of knowledge, which may be called "intuitive knowledge," and proceeds "from a fully adequate idea of certain attributes of God to a fully adequate knowledge of the essence of things."[169] This knowledge furnishes us a clear and distinct idea of the affects and gives us power over them.[170] It teaches us to know all things as necessary and rescues us from the sadness from which we otherwise suffer.[171] It enables us to see that sadness, hope, fear, pity, humility, repentance, knowledge of evil, and meditation or death oppress life and therefore cannot be good.[172] It teaches us to consider all things under the aspect or form of eternity, gives us peace and undisturbed rest, coincides with love for God, which is intellectual love, and expects no blessedness as a reward for virtue, but enjoys blessedness in the virtue itself.[173]

The rule that clarity is the standard of truth subsequently achieved dominance in the Enlightenment. To the extent that the rationalism of the time still clung to a kind of supernatural revelation, it viewed it as a doctrine that clarified and supplemented the knowledge of reason and whose credentials had to be first examined by reason.[174] Grace was judged in the same way. If grace was still necessary, it was granted only to those who did their best; or it was given in sufficient measure to each individual to then see what use he or she would make of it.[175] But consistent rationalism rejected all special revelation and grace. It made individual persons independent both in intellect and will. People must follow their own insight and, as free rational beings, assert themselves against all external authority. Enlightenment of the intellect and moral improvement were *the* road to blessedness.[176]

This rationalism was torn from its pedestal by Immanuel Kant. To clear a place for faith, he subjected the knowledge of reason to a sharp critique and restricted it to the world of sense perception. Besides a theoretical reason, however, humans

169. B. Spinoza, *Ethics*, prop. 38; V, prop. 25ff. (*Reader*, 257).

170. Ibid., V, prop. 3 (*Reader*, 247).

171. Ibid., V, prop. 6.

172. Ibid., IV, prop. 41, etc.

173. Ibid., V, prop. 1–42.

174. See, e.g., Gottfried Wilhelm Leibniz, *A System of Theology*, trans. Charles William Russell (London: Burns and Lambert, 1850), 13.

175. G. W. Leibniz, *Theodicy*, I, 96; "This maxim: 'the person who does what he can is not denied the grace necessary' appears to me to have eternal truth" (ET: *Theodicy: Essays on the Goodness of God, the Freedom of Man, and the Origin of Evil*, ed. A. Farrer, trans. E. M. Huggard [1951; repr., La Salle, IL: Open Court, 1985], 176).

176. J. Wegscheider, *Institutiones theologiae christianae dogmaticae*, §152.

also have a practical reason, which binds them to a moral world order and unconditionally obligates them to do the good. Given immediately with the moral law, however, is the freedom for which, certainly, there is no room in the world of sense perception but which nevertheless prevails in the noumenal or intelligible world that lies behind and above it. Hence, on the one hand, every human action constitutes a necessary part of the mechanism of nature, yet, on the other hand, it is an act that is freely accomplished by an intelligible cause. To this freedom of the human will, Kant attributes the greatest value. For him it is not a hypothesis, no postulate, but a fact that is automatically and necessarily given with the moral law. It is, for Kant, the cornerstone of morality and religion, the basis for faith in God and immortality, and, simultaneously, the way to redemption. For by that freedom, humans remain able to be governed, not by "the instincts of sensuality," but by the moral law, by respect for duty. Still, even when they do this, they are continually required to fight against evil, make only slow progress in doing good, and never reach absolute perfection. Moral improvement is an endless process, but "those who consistently work at self-improvement, those we can redeem."

In these words of Goethe, we can sum up the fundamental ideas that Kant unfolds about sin and salvation in his *Critique of Practical Reason.* But in his *Religion within the Limits of Reason Alone,* and under the influence of historic Christianity, he introduced a number of modifications. He consequently came to acknowledge that humans cannot be indifferent and so stand between good and evil that they can now do the one and then the other. If humans are of one blood, if they are organic beings, they must in the core of their personality, in their inmost disposition, be *either* good or evil. That they are not good is not only the teaching of Christianity but the testimony of the experience of all humans and all of history. "All persons have their price for which they will sell themselves." "There is no one who does good, no, not one" [cf. Ps. 14:3]. As the result of an extratemporal, inexplicable act of freedom, every human is by nature evil. There is in them a bias toward evil. Evil is not something about them, but *in* them. They are radically evil. Kant is so strongly convinced of the evil inherent in human nature that he resolutely and clearly states that for its salvation what is needed is a "new creation, a kind of rebirth." But when it comes to the question whether and by what process such a rebirth is possible, he does not derive the answer from Christianity as, logically, he should have—for if humans are radically evil, how then can they save themselves? But since the doctrine of grace does not please him, he returns to his doctrine of freedom. The moral law implies freedom. If it unconditionally demands that we must do good and be good, this implies that we are also able. Just as Pelagius argued from the "ought" to the "can," so also Kant infers from the "you shall" of the moral law the "you can" of performance.

That humans are able [to do good] he defends by saying that in them there still remains a capacity for good. While there is in them "a bias toward evil," behind this bias there is also "a predisposition toward the good." This disposition consists not only negatively in susceptibility to the good and the possibility of redemption but also positively in a germ of the good, in the power to redeem oneself. It is the disposition that enables humans to change and renew themselves. Just as by an intelligible act of freedom they made themselves sinners, so by a similar use of freedom they can regenerate themselves. This rebirth takes place not slowly and gradually by way of a long process but suddenly: it is a revolution in the intelligible substratum of the human psyche, a new creation, a fundamental change of heart, an instantaneously accomplished laying aside of the old Adam, and a putting on of the new. Although Kant therefore locates the principle of salvation in the free will, it is definitely not at all his intent here to deny all operation of grace. On the contrary, he exhorts all people to do what is in their capacity to do, moreover, to hope for "cooperation from above." But in Kant's opinion, we can never tell whether something is a product of grace, since the category of cause and effect does not function outside nature, and we cannot accept it practically, for the further reason that then the good would be not our deed but that of another being working within us.

What remains, therefore, is that human beings can and must redeem themselves by their own free will. To that end also the idea of a perfect humanity, as it stands symbolically before us in the person of Christ, serves as a guarantee, at the same time offering support to our faith. For this ideal Christ teaches us how, through combat and temptation, perfection can be attained and the good can be brought to dominion. For once we have been born again by an intelligible act of freedom, the slow process of sanctification starts in the practical life. Those who have been born again remain in that state and never again relapse into the old position. However strangely this may fit in Kant's system of freedom, he assumes the perseverance of the regenerate. It is true that a person cannot be directly and immediately assured of this outcome, but those who increase in moral betterment may from this fact conclude that they will, here or in the hereafter, reach perfection. Feelings of guilt and dread of punishment need no longer torment them. For during and after their conversion, humans continue to atone for the sins they have committed in the past. They voluntarily take upon themselves the punishment of sin, though for them it is no longer a punishment but a chastisement that exercises them in doing good and so makes them worthy of forgiveness. Besides, as new persons, they stand free from punishment and pure before God's face. Perfection may not be attained for a long time—God counts the disposition for the deed and justifies us out of grace.[177]

No less forcefully than in Kant is the corruption of human nature taught by Schopenhauer. Hence he, too, came to acknowledge that for the radical improvement of humans, development or enlightenment is totally insufficient, and that to that end nothing less is needed than a rebirth that changes persons in the core

177. Immanuel Kant, *Religion within the Limits of Reason Alone*, trans. Theodore M. Greene and Hoyt H. Hudson (New York: Harper & Brothers, 1934), 85–115. See especially T. Hoekstra, *Immanente Kritik zur kantischen Religionsphilosophie* (Kampen: J. H. Kok, 1909), chapters 1 and 2.

of their being, for good fruit can only be produced by a good tree. What one does follows from what one is.[178] By taking this stand, Kant and Schopenhauer positioned themselves as firmly as possible against the optimism and rationalism of the eighteenth century. They also agreed, however, in rejecting the solution that can be found in the Christian doctrine of salvation. But whereas Kant continued to believe in a kind of salvation, considered it possible and attainable by the freedom of the will, and thereby returned to the optimism of the Enlightenment, Schopenhauer remained entrenched in his pessimism to the end and could accept no other redemption from suffering than that which, as in Buddhism, consists in the destruction of one's consciousness. Art and philosophy do afford us some consolation, but final salvation can nevertheless consist only, in the light of one's own knowledge, in allowing life in all its wretchedness to get through to oneself as a quietus for the will, to negate the will, and so to enter into nirvana, where one's consciousness is totally numbed and the will to live is fully extinguished.[179]

Eduard von Hartmann also proceeds in his soteriology from the wretchedness of humanity but further includes in it not only elements reminiscent of Kant and Schopenhauer but also an assortment of ideas deriving from pantheistic and evolutionistic philosophy. Humans with their eudaemonistic egoism, which is the product of their animal descent and historical development, are radically evil. "The essential and most characteristic nature of humans" is radically evil. They make "sensuality," which by itself is not wrong, into a tool for their egoism. This ethical as well as physical evil, however, is also willed by God, not as a final end, but as a means. It is necessary to make humans into religious-ethical beings, to make them long for salvation and sanctification, and thus to ensure for religion and morality, not a temporary and accidental, but a permanent and necessary existence. Concealed deep in the heart of people, after all, is a latent fundamental tendency of another kind, an ethical disposition that corresponds to the objective moral world order and affords them the strategic basis of operation from which they can fight evil. They are not merely natural but also moral beings, with a sense of responsibility, of duty, and of guilt, contrition, with a need for and susceptibility to salvation. This ethical disposition cannot be explained by saying that human beings are products of nature, in terms of their egoism, but harks back to an immanent objective reason that works in them and realizes itself through the evil present in themselves and the world. In the language of religion, it can therefore be called "grace" and consists not only in the moral disposition inherited from earlier generations (original grace) but also in the moral power to develop and unfold this disposition (actual grace). In its totality, it must therefore be regarded as the immanent rule of the moral world order, as the Holy Spirit by which God realizes the good in humanity. No human being, accordingly, is totally without it.

---

178. A. Schopenhauer, *The World as Will and Representation,* trans. E. F. J. Payne (New York: Dover Publications, 1966), I, 507ff.; II, 603ff.

179. Ibid., I, 508ff.

There are no absolute reprobates or elect. Every person belongs in greater or lesser measure to the company of the blessed. And to everyone is granted a measure of grace, depending on his or her family background and nurture and so on, in that they may appropriate, increase, and merit it.

Salvation, accordingly, is granted on God's part to humans by grace, but in such a way that they themselves must acquire it by moral effort. That is why grace, viewed from the human perspective, may be called faith. The two are essentially one, just as God and humanity are essentially one. But because "grace" and "faith" are identical, though viewed from different angles, redemption and sanctification are therefore a process that moves forward slowly. Salvation is not realized suddenly and all at once but gradually, in the way of faith. This redemptive process begins with illumination, then arouses a sense of guilt and aversion to evil. These components, however, still have only negative and preparatory significance. Then it gives rise to faith, a faith that actually but unconsciously already precedes the above components, but now begins to function consciously and produces the new person. By this faith humans surrender themselves to grace, overcome the consciousness of guilt, obtain reconciliation, peace, "sonship," and union with God, and apply themselves to the sanctification that continues throughout life. This subjective redemptive process, however, is not the final goal, but subordinate to and a means of the objective redemptive process in humanity, which consists in the triumph of the moral world order (a better formulation than "the kingdom of God"), and, since in any other way there is no true redemption, it ends in "the redemption of the world from itself as the triumph of the idea in the collapse of the universe." Universal redemption coincides with the destruction of the world, with "the recall of its spatial-temporal appearance into the eternal Being," with the return of the absolute will from the state of actuality into that of potentiality. The redemption of the world then proves to be a means for the redemption of God.[180]

MODERN PHILOSOPHY AFTER KANT

[424] By another route philosophy after Kant developed into the idealistic systems of Fichte, Schelling, and Hegel. Along with the philosopher of Königsberg, Fichte shifted the center of gravity from theoretical to practical reason, from the intellect to the will, from knowledge to moral conduct. But he was so consistent in this that he completely got rid of "the thing in itself" and completely subordinated knowledge to action. In the beginning was the deed, not the word. The "I" (or self-consciousness) is its own product even, and the "non-I" (the world as idea) is posited by the "I." Nothing exists but the I: "The I is everything." Self-determination is the essence of humanity, freedom its destiny. Those who let

180. E. von Hartmann, *Religionsphilosophie*, 2nd ed., 2 vols. (Bad Sachsa i.H.: Hermann Haacke, 1907), II, 180ff., 271ff.; see also A. Drews, *Die Religion als Selbst-Bewusstsein Gottes*, 1st ed. (Jena and Leipzig: E. Diederichs, 1906), 237ff., 363ff.

themselves be determined by the world are slaves, but those who define themselves are masters, kings, sovereigns. Thus, also the redemption of humans is their own act; they obtain it in the way of consistent striving for self-improvement. And the only lesson they have to put into practice is "posit yourself, become conscious of yourself, strive to be independent, make yourself free."[181] But this was not Fichte's last word. The charge of atheism lodged against him in 1799 led to his having to leave Jena. He became part of a different circle of men and women in Berlin and took a deeper look at religion than ever before. As a result his philosophy developed in a different direction and assumed a different form. Up until then he had continually opposed so-called "obscurantism"; from this point on he turned against the flat rationalism of the Enlightenment. He distanced himself from Nicolai and moved toward Romanticism and Schleiermacher and Spinoza. Up until then his philosophy had moved from the practical to the theoretical and thence to the moral and religious "I." But having arrived there, it took its stance in religion and from that vantage point tried to design an entire worldview. He first climbed up to God in order now to proceed out from God. From volition he pushed through to being in order now, from that being, to look at the entire world. The theory of science became the doctrine of religion.

Consequently, the vocation and destiny of humankind also changed. Up until now Fichte had situated it in moral action, in freedom; now he declared that our certainty of moral conduct as the task and goal of humanity as well as the task and goal of the world is rooted, and can only be rooted, in religious faith. All conviction of the reality of the moral as well as the sensible world is a matter of faith and arises not from the intellect but from the heart. All truth originates from faith, from conscience, from the orientation of the mind. "We are all born in faith." Once people have arrived at this insight, they recognize that God, whom they found last, is first of all. The goal of the world is the world's ground. God and humanity are eternally one. But that unity, which is the foundation, is temporarily broken up by the self-consciousness (knowledge), which always makes a separation between the subject and the object in order that humans may, through the existing disunity, again seek union. In the end, what was eternally one in essence must, through separation, again return to union. Not activity and action, not independence and freedom, but life in God, resting and delighting in his fellowship, intellectual love (*amor intellectualis*), as Spinoza called it, is the destiny of humankind. That is the supreme, the blessed and eternal life.

Fichte believed he could find this idea in Christianity, more specifically, in the Gospel of John. In his opinion the eternal oneness of the divine and the human was the innermost essence of religion and also visually presented to us as such in the person of Christ. Before him, no one recognized and expressed this truth as he did, and after him all people obtained this truth, this union with God, this state of blessedness, only through him. Granted, what saves us is not

181. K. Fischer, *J. G. Fichte und seine Vorgänger*, 2nd ed. (Munich: Basserman, 1884), 432.

a historical faith, for "only the metaphysical, by no means the historical, saves."
But when Christian doctrine is rightly understood, it is certainly absolutely true
and absolutely new. It makes known to us the kingdom of God as the true world,
which God wills from eternity and realizes in history. When humans make this
will their own, they find eternal life. And they incorporate that will of God into
their own when by an internal rebirth they put their own will to death. There
is but one order of salvation: self-annihilation and self-denial; and but one way
to salvation: the death of selfhood, death with Jesus, rebirth. Jesus was by nature
what we, following his example, have to become in freedom: the born son of
God. His historical appearance, therefore, is an eternally valid historical truth.
Dogma has clothed this truth in a series of metaphysical propositions, but the
Holy Spirit, whom Christ promised to us, leads us into all truth and labors at the
completion of that kingdom, which is simultaneously the kingdom of God and
the realm of reason.[182]

Schelling underwent a similar development. In his early period, he was rather
indifferent toward religion, but by a deeper study of nature, he arrived at a so-called
identity philosophy in which not *doing* but *being* constituted the key concept
and in which the unity of subject and object, of spirit and nature, of God and
the All was expressed. This Absolute, however, cannot be found by thought nor
demonstrated by proofs but is known only by intellectual vision, just as religion,
morality, and art can only have their root in this mysticism of the heart. From this,
religion and philosophy appear to be correlative, but in fact they have the same
content, namely, the unity of the eternal and the finite. While paganism pulls the
eternal into the finite, Christianity elevates the finite into the eternal. Therefore,
whereas nature is the content of mythology, the content of Christianity is history, especially as this is concentrated in the person of Christ, who is the center
of history. All these ideas, which already occur in the time of Schelling's identity
philosophy, are later worked out more extensively in his positive philosophy,
especially in his philosophy of revelation.

This positive philosophy supplements the negative, begins where the latter
ends, and discloses that the entire history of humankind consists in a return of the
finite to the infinite. Actually the fall begins with creation, with the event of the
finite's becoming independent, but it is continued in humankind's misuse of
this finite reality as a means of their egoism. God counteracted this estrangement
of his creature in a historical way in the person of Christ. Christ, who already had
an independent existence of his own, put aside his glory and became the Son of
Man. This did not first occur in the moment of his incarnation but long before
that, from the day of the human fall. Though not under the name of Christ, he
was nevertheless already active in paganism, in mythology; and the entire period
of his activity in paganism right up to his death was the period of his humiliation

---

182. For the preceding sketch, cf. esp. Fichte's *Die Bestimmung des Menschen* and his *Die Anweisung um
seligen Leben oder auch die Religionslehre* (Berlin: Im Verlag der Realschulbuchhandlung, 1806).

and suffering. But with his resurrection came the reversal. In that event the entire old world had come to an end: paganism, mythology, the demons were all deprived of their power and dominion, and humanity was fundamentally justified. This justification in the resurrection of Christ (Rom. 4:25) is antecedent to the new life, to good works. Justification *has to* precede truly good works, or otherwise there is at most a fear of evil but no courage to do the good.

> Only when the entire present condition is justified can there be individual good works. Inasmuch as not our particular activity but our whole existence is reprehensible in the sight of God, our works cannot justify us before God, but only he can justify us before God, who has made our whole existence right and pleasing to God, namely, Christ. By the fact that Christ rose—that is, that he did not at one time become a human and then ceased to be a human, that he is continually and eternally a human—by that fact we have received justification, the free gift of righteousness (Rom. 5:17), and hence also our present condition of separation from God has become a condition accepted by God, a condition in which we can move peacefully, even joyfully, far from that melancholy, self-tormenting Christianity that can only impose on us a total denial of what Christ has done for us.[183]

From this alone it is evident that the person of Christ is the true content of Christianity and that this is a historical religion through and through.[184] But there is more: after Christ rose and ascended to heaven, he continues his work until he will finally have vanquished all his enemies. The most immediate action of Christ, therefore, must be that in his resurrection he again made human nature "pleasing and right" in the sight of God, restoring to humans the freedom, power, and possibility to be the children of God. But, subsequently, he also sent the Holy Spirit, who "realizes the entire deity in us."[185] With that the religion of the Spirit and freedom began in which humans obtain life and blessedness in fellowship with Christ, a religion that develops through the Petrine church of Rome and the Pauline church of the Reformation into the Johannine church of the future.[186] With that movement, then, the cosmic process that is grounded in the three potencies (nature, spirit, personality or love) of the divine Being has reached its conclusion, for all things will then have been restored by Christ to their unity with God. Reconciliation between God and his creature is the content of history.

Like his predecessors, Hegel, in contrast to the Enlightenment, was animated by the desire to secure a place in his philosophical system for Christianity and the redemption that constitutes its core. He therefore laid the foundation for recon-

---

183. F. W. J. Schelling, *Ausgewählte Werke*, 4 vols. (Darmstadt: Wissenschaftlichen Buchgesellschaft, 1968), II, 4.

184. On this topic, Schelling wrote a special work, "Über die historische Construction des Christentums," *Werke*, I/5, 286ff.

185. F. W. J. Schelling, *Werke*, II, 4, 217.

186. Ed note: Bavinck's reference here is unclear (op. cit., 298ff.). Most likely it is a repeat of note 184, *Werke*, I/5, 298ff.

ciliation in the movement of the Absolute itself. This Absolute, remember, is not an unchangeable being but an eternal process of becoming, a self-evolving spirit and idea. At its beginning it is mere potentiality in order to impel itself, through the history of the world, to actuality. So it first "empties" itself in nature, therein posing a counterpart to itself in order from that state to return gradually to itself in the spirit. This process, then, moves from self-evacuation to self-reconciliation. This self-evacuation begins with the existence of the finite world and completes itself in humanity. This humanity first lives in a state of naïve innocence and subsequently awakens to self-consciousness, asserts itself in its particularity, makes finite things subservient to its egoism, and so introduces sin into the world. As a result of this sin, humanity exists in opposition to God, just as, as a result of a wide variety of disasters and misfortunes, it exists in opposition to the world. It is its privilege, however, that humanity realizes this and therefore also begins to feel the need for redemption. In general, this redemption must consist in the reconciliation of the existing opposition and the perception and recognition of the essential oneness of God and humanity. It is a mistake to think, however, that reconciliation could be effected by any human being alone or by all humans together. It can only be accepted by it if beforehand it exists in truth. And thus, indeed, it exists in fact, first of all in the idea of God and further also historically in the person of Christ. In the idea of God, the infinite and the finite, God and humanity, are eternally one. This, however, was not enough. If reconciliation was to be really effected in humankind; if people—not just the learned but also the uneducated and common people—were really to obtain absolute certainty concerning it, that idea also had to be visibly and historically presented to them in a person. And that was accomplished by God in Christ, who is not a teacher or martyr but, as it were, the incorporation of this idea, the Son of God, who remained faithful to his unity with God into death and exalted human nature to the point of being seated at the right hand of God. Christ, therefore, is the "God-man," his death the center of reconciliation, for his death was the death of death, the negation of negations, and so led to resurrection and ascension. In Christ, God assumed finiteness, along with evil as its extremity, in order to kill it by his death. "It is infinite love for God to identify himself with what is foreign to him in order to destroy it." With that death, accordingly, begins the reversal of consciousness. With it begins "a new world, a new religion, a new reality, another cosmic condition."

The church has been built on that foundation. By faith it is certain that God and humanity are one, that the finiteness, the weakness, the defectiveness of human nature is not incompatible with this unity. "The basic qualification in this kingdom of God is the presence of God so that the members of this kingdom are commanded not only to love people but to be conscious that God is love." The individual person arrives at this certainty not by reasoning or the evidence of miracles and so on, nor by morality and decency, but by faith, by "the witness of the Spirit, the indwelling idea of the Spirit per se." This witness, however, does not pertain to external history, which is transient and has to disappear, but to the idea that God and humanity are one and that this truth has been realized and revealed in a historical manner in Christ. Hence, though faith may start on the sensible side, it nevertheless penetrates to the idea and has to become totally "spiritual." "The true content of the Christian faith has to be vindicated by philosophy, not by history." Now to the institutional church—in distinction from the Christian community—has been entrusted the task of nurturing its members and of introducing them to the truth. As is evident from infant baptism, it is also conscious of this task. In that baptism it declares the truth that children are born, not in misery, but in the fellowship of the church, and that, though first receiving the truth on authority, they must gradually appropriate it for themselves. They are born in and for freedom. They do not have to experience regeneration and conversion like others who come to the church from the outside, but may proceed from the thought that God has been reconciled, that evil has been overcome, and that the Spirit of God, who by faith is also their Spirit, fights against sin in and through them. In the Lord's Supper, which is the center of Christian doctrine and therefore viewed so variously, believers see exhibited, in a sensory, graphic way, the reconciliation with God and the indwelling of the Spirit in their hearts.[187]

[425] Most remarkable, in the philosophy that emerged after the Enlightenment and started with Kant, is the fact that it again sought to link itself with Christianity and to incorporate its religious truths in its system. To a flat rationalism, Christianity was obsolete. Human beings needed only an enlightened mind and a free will to obtain salvation; no room was left for a revelation of grace. But philosophy, in all its great interpreters, reconsidered this superficial judgment. It took a longer and deeper look at nature and history, at humanity and the world, and in one form or another articulated the idea that redemption from sin and suffering was possible only by an act of God. According to this philosophy, evil is not an accidental phenomenon, an arbitrary human act, but a necessary element in the cosmic process. Consequently, there could be no redemption from it unless in that same cosmic process, it was gradually overcome and banished by a divine power. In Schelling and Hegel, as in Schopenhauer and Hartmann, the later philosophy acquired the character of a "philosophy of redemption."

But though post-Kantian philosophy seriously strove to again do justice to the great ideas of Christianity,[188] it nevertheless only partially succeeded in this attempt. This is due, to a significant degree, to the fact that it only overcame ra-

187. See esp. G. W. F. Hegel, *Philosophie der Religion*, in *Sämtliche Werke*, XVI, 204–28 (*Werke*, XII, 204–29). Ed. note: Hegel discusses communion as a sacrament in *Lectures on the Philosophy of Religion*, vol. III, *The Consummate Religion*, ed. Hodgson et al. (Berkeley: University of California Press, 1985), 23, 152–56, 235–36, 337–39, 372–73.

188. R. Eucken (*Hauptprobleme der Religionsphilosophie der Gegenwart* [Berlin: Reuther & Reichard, 1907], 109) correctly states: "It was not a matter of mere leniency toward existing structures when nearly all the great thinkers of modernity, despite all the independence of their convictions, somehow sought a positive relation to Christianity and usually found it at the core of their thinking."

tionalism in part, more in form than in substance. Hegel, for example, looks down on the Enlightenment from a great height and mocks its intellectual vanity. Over against it, he champions the right to trace reason in the Christian religion, but at the same time, he subjects the Christian religion to his "thinking consciousness" and finds the standard for its truth in his own reason. He does say that philosophy puts itself not above the Christian religion and its content but only above the form in which it possesses the truth. But this pronouncement does not make up for that other statement, namely, that "thought is the absolute judge before which the content must prove and authenticate itself." Accordingly, Christianity may have presented a doctrine of reconciliation that contains a profound meaning; yet this profound meaning is only brought to light in philosophy. Not religion but philosophy brings about true reconciliation. "Philosophy is theology insofar as it represents the reconciliation of God with himself and with nature; it affirms that nature, that otherness as such, as divine; it affirms that the finite Spirit characteristically elevates itself toward reconciliation and in part comes to it in the history of the world."[189] The attempt to reconcile reason with religion, accordingly, ended with a dichotomy between idea and fact, a process by which ultimately the idea could no longer be maintained. Post-Hegelian history clearly demonstrated that the baby had been thrown out with the bathwater and that with the form also the content itself had gone down the drain. Stripped of its speculative phrasing and reduced to simple words, idealistic philosophy was left only with the idea that humans, existing by nature in the polarity between sensuality and reason, nature and spirit, idea and reality, were gradually, by way of a process, lifted above that polarity and that they themselves had to support and promote this process, either more by their intellect or more by their will.

MODERN THEOLOGY: SCHLEIERMACHER AND RITSCHL

The modern theology that surfaced with the work of Strauss gave the philosophy of Hegel this jolt and thereby immediately revealed its own intellectual nature. While frequently still employing Christian terms, it fills them with a different meaning. In the work of conversion, for example, God and humanity, in other words, the grace of God and the human will, are not antithetical: conversion is simultaneously and totally the work of both. For grace actually coincides with divine providence. It only works ethically and pedagogically and itself fosters as well as strengthens in the religious community the capacity for salvation ("the ability to apply oneself to grace"). In time, therefore, it will lead all people to salvation and overcome all opposition. Actually human beings do not really need regeneration; conversion can be so called only when viewed from the side of God. Conversion itself consists in penitence (that is, regret over past sins, the disposition

---

189. G. W. F. Hegel, *Philosophie der Religion*, in *Sämtliche Werke*, XVI, 287–88 (*Werke*, XII, 287–88); ed. note: this passage is in *The Consummate Religion*, ed. Hodgson et al., 370–73. See also C. Opzoomer, *De wijsbegeerte den mensch met zich zelven verzoenende* (Leiden: n.p., 1846).

willingly to bear the punishment for them and henceforth to amend one's life) and faith (that is, trust in the grace of God in Christ). Thus converted, a person is immediately justified. For justification is not a transcendent act of God but only the removal of the consciousness of guilt, a change in the consciousness of one's relation to God, the cancellation of the split between the natural "I" and its destiny. In conversion, says this theology, people are initially renewed and as such carry within themselves the guarantee of perfection, just as the grown plant is hidden in the seed and the full-grown man is concealed in the boy. What matters above all else, therefore, is the heart, the inner disposition. For a long time the deed lags behind that disposition, but this imperfection is a passing moment and therefore in no way still counts in reconciliation and justification.[190]

Like idealistic philosophy, so also Schleiermacher returned to Christianity and, with even more emphasis than this philosophy, placed the historical person of Christ in the center of his doctrine of faith. According to Schleiermacher, after Christ entered into our communion of sin and misery, he possessed the power and the calling to incorporate us into his communion of holiness and blessedness. This incorporation occurs by regeneration and sanctification. Regeneration consists in conversion and justification, two things that are one and the same, viewed now from our side and then from God's side. In conversion, which is again composed of two parts (penitence and faith), a person is neither cooperative nor totally passive, but receptive (in the sense of Melanchthon's "capacity to apply oneself to grace"), so that then humanity as a whole may also at some point become ripe for grace and obtain salvation. Justification is that act of God by which a person is placed in fellowship with Christ. Negatively, it consists in forgiveness, that is, the condemnation of the past, and positively in adoption, that is, exhortation to a new life; and as the counterpart of forgiveness, justification really lets forgiveness take place because and insofar as a person obtains a new life in communion with Christ.[191] Mediating theologians[192] indeed assigned a broader place in dogmatics to

---

190. D. Strauss, *Die Christliche Glaubenslehre in ihrer geschichtlichen Entwicklung und im Kampf mit der modernen Wissenschaft*, 2 vols. (Tübingen: C. F. Osiander, 1840–41), II, 362ff., 463, 492–97; A. Biedermann, *Christliche Dogmatik* (Zürich: Füssli, 1869), §§847–911; A. Schweizer, *Christliche Glaubenslehre* (Leipzig: S. Hirzel, 1863–72), §§138–64; H. Lang, *Versuch einer christlichen Dogmatik allen denkenden Christen dargeboten*, 2nd ed. (Berlin: G. Reimer, 1868), §§19–25; O. Pfleiderer, *Grundriss der christlichen Glaubens- und Sittenlehre* (Berlin: G. Reimer, 1888), §170; J. Scholten, *De Leer der Hervormde Kerk*, II, 76ff., 109ff., initia c. 5. Without being unfair, one can say that modern theology no longer has a Christology and hence no soteriology either, at least none that has a specifically Christian character. It still has Jesus as a moral ideal but no Christ, a law but no gospel. Cf. *A. Bruining, "Godsdienst en Verlossingsbehoefte," *Teyler's Theologisch Tijdschrift* 8 (1910): 226ff. This explains why the need for salvation is again awakening powerfully in others. Miss E. C. Knappert already defended the good right of this at the Conference of Modern Theologians (April 11–12, 1899): The modernists are always urging us to pursue, and they themselves are always pursuing, amelioration, a *becoming* better, but the need for salvation arises where the soul thirsts for *being* better. The emphasis is always put on what *we* have to do but should be put much more on what God is and does, on *his* love and grace. Cf. also above, 356–61 (#380).

191. F. Schleiermacher, *The Christian Faith* (Edinburgh: T&T Clark, 1989), §§106–12.

192. Ed. note: On "Mediating Theology" (*Vermittlungstheologie*), see H. Bavinck, *Reformed Dogmatics*, I, 49n49 (#9), 127 (#39), 166 (#51), 519–20 (#135), 522–24 (#136).

the person of Christ and the activity of the Holy Spirit; but in the order of salvation, they did not entirely rise above the ideas of Schleiermacher. In the first place, they almost all attribute to humans the power to accept or to reject grace, whether that power derives from the creation or the providence of God, or from the enabling grace granted in baptism or the [gospel] call.[193] On the other hand, while they do correct Schleiermacher insofar as they hold justification to be an objective act of God, they all let it happen on the basis, not of the imputed, but of the infused righteousness of Christ, so that it is not only a judicial but also a communicative and sanctifying act of God and a preview (πρόληψις) of the future.[194]

Over against this subject-based justification, Ritschl again returned to the person of Christ seeking the ground for forgiveness in his work, albeit, not in the sense that it was acquired by Christ and consisted in a change of God's disposition, for God is eternal love and there is no punitive righteousness in him. But Christ, by his perfect fidelity to his vocation, his unbroken communion with God, his complete surrender to God's will, nevertheless proclaimed and proved that God is love, that he is not wrathful or punitive, but forgives. Now this was necessary, not because God is far removed from humankind, but because humankind, by its sin (which is actually ignorance, not objective guilt but subjective consciousness of guilt) is far removed from God. For that reason Christ proclaimed God's love even in his death and, making God's purpose with humankind his own, founded a kingdom of God, a church, into which he transplanted the consciousness that God is love and forgives sin, and that it can live in communion with God without needing to be hindered by sin. In Ritschl, therefore, justification is a synthetic judgment, pronounced not on the basis of good works but prior to good works. First, the fear of God as judge must yield in humans to the consciousness of his communion before they can do good works and fulfill their moral calling. Furthermore, this justification is not a verdict on, or experience of, the individual believer, but a possession of the church, which knows that, despite its sins, it exists in communion with God. It coincides with the founding of the church itself.[195]

---

193. Cf. H. Bavinck, *Reformed Dogmatics,* II, 368–72 (#239).

194. A. Neander, *History of the Planting and the Training of the Christian Church by the Apostles,* trans. J. E. Ryland, 2 vols. (London: Bell & Daly, 1864), 551ff.; C. E. Nitzsch, *System of Christian Doctrines* (Edinburgh: T&T Clark, 1849), §§146–47; H. Martensen, *Christian Dogmatics: A Compendium of the Doctrines of Christianity,* trans. W. Urwick (Edinburgh: T&T Clark, 1871), §§230–31; J. Lange, *Christliche Dogmatik,* 3 vols. (Heidelberg: K. Winter, 1852), II, §95; J. Ebrard, *Christliche Dogmatik,* 2nd ed., 2 vols. (Königsberg: A. W. Unzer, 1862–63), §443; L. Schöberlein, *Prinzip und System der Dogmatik* (Heidelberg: C. Winter, 1881), 652; also J. Beck, *Die christliche Lehrwissenschaft nach den biblischen Urkunden* (Stuttgart: J. F. Steinkopf, 1875), I, 522ff., 533ff.; idem, *Die christliche Glaubenslehre,* II, 595ff.; E. T. Gestrin, *Die Rechtfertigungslehre der Professoren der Theologie Johannes Tobias Beck, O. F. Myrberg und A. W. Ingman, geprüft und beleuchtet von mehreren evangelischen Theologen* (Berlin: Wiegandt & Grieben, 1891); and even Hengstenberg in the *Evangelische Kirchenzeitung* during 1866 and 1867, where he appealed to the Letter of James and to Luke 7:36 for his opinions; cf. *Beweis des Glaubens* (1868): 381ff.; A. Ritschl, *Rechtfertigung und Versöhnung,* I², 644ff.; see also the following subsection (#426) concerning justification.

195. A. Ritschl, *Justification and Reconciliation,* 27–130; J. Kaftan, *Dogmatik* (Tübingen: Mohr, 1901), 493; H. Schultz, *Grundriss der evangelischen Dogmatik zum Gebrauch bei akademischen Vorlesungen* (Göttingen: Vandenhoeck & Ruprecht, 1892), §52.

Particular persons only obtain this benefit of justification by joining the church and appropriating it by faith. That faith is free;[196] not individuals but the church is the object of election.[197] That faith is not effected magically: upbringing is the ordinary form in which a person comes to faith.[198] It essentially consists in truth, is independent of historical investigation and its results, and is based on a deep impression made by Jesus' moral grandeur on the unbiased mind.[199] By that faith humans acquire another view of God, of themselves, and of the world. They learn to know God as love and to know that sin is no longer an obstacle to communion with God. They no longer consider disasters and misfortunes to be punishments but spiritually reign over all things; in a word, their consciousness of sin has been removed and therein consists their justification.[200] The consequence of this justification is reconciliation, the putting aside of hostility toward God on the basis of that justification.[201] And essentially identical with that justification and reconciliation is regeneration, for this occurrence does not consist in a hyperphysical change but in a change of mood and disposition.[202]

[426] It is to Ritschl's credit that, in a time when the Reformation doctrine of justification was misconstrued and confused with that of sanctification, he again called attention to its significance for the religious life and again placed the doctrine itself at the center of the redemptive order. He did this, however, in a way that invited criticism. The primary objections raised against it in time can be summed up as follows: (1) Ritschl, in his doctrine of God, gives one-sided prominence to God's love, ignores his holiness and righteousness, and attempts to deduce reconciliation solely from his love. (2) Reconciliation only consists in the fact that Christ, by his teaching and life, has proclaimed that God is love and that in him there is no room for wrath. (3) Guilt and punishment are only human notions and do not correspond to any objective reality, all the less since sin is essentially ignorance. (4) Justification, contained in Jesus' proclamation of the love of God, is a possession of the church as a whole, so that the individual receives it by joining the church. (5) It is completely independent of the subject, excludes all mysticism, and is in no way connected with sanctification. (6) Its aim

196. A. Ritschl, *Justification and Reconciliation*, 568.

197. Ibid., 118–19.

198. Ibid., 587–88.

199. Cf. H. Bavinck, *Reformed Dogmatics*, I, 67–68 (#16), 544–48 (#143).

200. A. Ritschl, *Justification and Reconciliation*, 38ff.

201. Ibid., 75–78.

202. Ibid., 590–96. See further W. Herrmann, *Der Verkehr des Christen mit Gott*, 4th ed. (Stuttgart: Cotta, 1903); idem, "Christl. protest. Dogmatik," in *Die Kultur der Gegenwart*, 583–632, esp. 615–23; J. Kaftan, *Dogmatik*, §§53ff., 68ff.; M. Reischle, *Leitsätze für eine akademische Vorlesung über die christliche Glaubenslehre* (Halle a.S.: Niemeyer, 1899), §§106ff.; O. Kirn, *Grundriss der evangelischen Dogmatik* (Leipzig: Deichert, 1905), §§42ff.; Theodor Häring, *The Christian Faith*, trans. John Dickie and George Ferries (London: Hodder & Stoughton, 1913), II, 649ff.; W. Bousset, *What Is Religion?* trans. Florence B. Low (New York: Putnam, 1907), 262ff.

is not to furnish assurance of salvation to the subject but to enable Christians, by their trust in God, to maintain and assert themselves over against the world.[203]

This summary is far from exhaustive, constituting as it does only some of the serious objections that were in time raised against Ritschl's theology and specifically against his philosophy. The times changed and with them the intellectual climate. When Ritschl appeared on the scene, people in general expected the greatest benefits from science and culture and girded themselves with confidence and courage to take on the challenge. It was to this situation that the theologian of Göttingen responded. He separated theology from metaphysics, gave free reign to the sciences, and was content to give religion, both objectively and subjectively, a small place. In fact, he made religion subservient to culture and derived from it the confidence to undertake the moral task with courage and to establish the kingdom of God on earth. But this cultural optimism (*Kulturseligkeit*) gradually yielded to the insight that science and technology, intellectual knowledge and material prosperity cannot produce peace of heart. Along with material progress, spiritual poverty increased as well. People again began to see the limitations of culture and, in that connection, the social evils, the defects in education and upbringing, the misery of people's earthly existence. Knowledge of their misery again kindled the need for religion and mysticism. Tired of *doing,* people again thirsted for *being.* Philosophy, metaphysics, and idealism were again restored to a position of honor. People turned back from Kant to Hegel, or at least exchanged the slogan "Back to Kant!" for that of "From Kant forward!" People felt all the more compelled in that direction because Ritschl had simply, without proof, positioned himself in historic Christianity and proceeded from the personality of Jesus, and the latest studies of antiquity seemed especially to show that Christianity was a syncretistic religion. Where, then, in view of the loss of a historical foundation, could one still find sure footing except in metaphysics? Finally, there was still the fact that Ritschl had attached too little value and paid too little attention to the religious life in the subject. The individual was for him a part of the church, assured in its fellowship of the love of God, but not living from it in the mysticism of one's own heart. Yet one only rightly learned to know the essence of religion by the study of the religious personality. All these considerations explain why Ritschl's dogmatic theology gradually became a part of the history of dogma, why after him a new mysticism and a new philosophy emerged, and why his method made way, on the one hand, for the school of the history of religion and, on the other, for that of the psychology of religion.[204]

203. Cf. J. Wendland, *Albrecht Ritschl und seine Schüler im Verhältnis zur Theologie, zur Philosophie und zur Frömmigkeit unsrer Zeit* (Berlin: George Reimer, 1899), 120–35.

204. Cf. H. Bavinck, *Reformed Dogmatics,* I, 70ff. (#17); 170ff. (#53); 542ff. (#142); Theodor Häring, "In welchem Sinn dürfen wir uns immer noch 'Göttinger' heissen? Albrecht Ritschls Bedeutung für die Gegenwart," *Zeitschrift für Theologie und Kirche* 20 (May 1910): 165–96.

PSYCHOLOGICAL STUDY OF RELIGIOUS EXPERIENCE

At this juncture especially the latter is important to us. The psychology of religion is still a young science, but the impetus for it arose from the directions in which the religious life had developed in the preceding centuries. Powerful movements, like those that Pietism had called forth in Germany and Methodism had unleashed in England and America, all had in common that they shifted the center of gravity from the object of religion to the subject. Theology followed this track in the systems produced by Kant, Schleiermacher, and their schools. And later this subjective tendency was promoted by agnosticism, biblical criticism, experimental psychology, and by the study of religions and revivals. The reports that revivalists gave of their meetings and conversion results most immediately triggered the rise of the psychology of religion. The current president of Clark University, G. Stanley Hall, was moved by them to the idea of making a painstaking study of the data contained in them. He soon formed a school that, in accordance with experimental methods including the use of questionnaires, examined religious phenomena, a school that branched out in many countries.[205]

The psychology of religion, however, does not examine *all* religious phenomena but leaves the objective phenomena in religion, such as dogma and worship, to the sciences of history and philosophy. It confines itself to the study of subjective religion, to the religious experience of the subject; more precisely, it focuses not so much on religious conceptions as on the feelings, sensations, and passions that accompany them or are aroused by them. It first tries as carefully as possible to gather these phenomena from biographies, letters, conversations, as well as from replies to questionnaires. It then processes this material by means of analysis, comparison, and classification. And, finally, from this factual material it attempts to infer the law that governs religious development.

[427a][206] Now on the basis of such inquiries, some psychologists, exploring the religious development of individuals, offer us the following sketch:

In the child there is as yet no such thing as an independent religious life of its own. Just as the human embryo in its development passes through the various stages of the kinds of organic beings preceding the human species, so childhood represents the original, the oldest, state of the human race. Ontogeny is the repetition and recapitulation of phylogeny. Just as the first humans, in the course of their evolution from lower animals, for a long time remained half-animals, so also a kind of animal life is characteristic of the child. The child enters life with basically the same instincts as animals. The truth of the doctrine of original sin

---

205. Cf. H. Bavinck, *Reformed Dogmatics,* I, 71–72 (#17); also the dissertation by J. Geelkerken, *De empirische Godsdienstpsychologie* (Amsterdam: Scheltema & Holkema, 1909), which provides a lengthy bibliography on pages 407–12.

206. Ed. note: This section is entirely new in the Dutch second edition and represents Bavinck's serious interest, during the last decade of his life, in the psychology of religion. See H. Bavinck, *Bijbelsche en Religieuze Psychologie* (Kampen: Kok, 1920); cf. note 207 below; also see "Editor's Introduction," 19.

is that in humans, by virtue of their origin, the life of the animal is still pulsating and working. The child, accordingly, is by nature self-seeking, self-willed, and combative. It carries with it the elementary instinct of self-preservation, which manifests itself in anger, touchiness, jealousy, and the like. Associated with this is that, in respect of religion and morality, the child manifests the same self-seeking tendencies. To the child the value of religion consists exclusively in what it can give him or her. And because a child lacks independent insight, it is gullible; it accepts as true everything it hears. For a child religion consists mostly in rules and dogmas imposed by the authority of parents, church, or Bible. It believes in and lives by authority. Religion to the child is still something totally external and objective. "Religion is all external to him; God is a being above and beyond him."

But at the onset of puberty, in the case of girls usually in their fourteenth and in that of boys in their sixteenth year, a great change occurs. The shift that occurs in adolescence in how young people perceive the character of the church and the extent and significance of its influence in their lives has in recent years been the object of diligent and extensive research. Stanley Hall published a work on it of more than thirteen hundred pages. Carefully and at length, he explored all the changes that occur in human development in the years of puberty. These changes extend to the whole of life and existence and are simultaneously physiological and psychological, biological and sociological in nature. Just as the child is reminiscent of the earliest state of humankind, so also the period of adolescence is neo-atavistic. The conquests that the human race accomplished in a later period revive and repeat themselves in adolescence. The development that occurs then is marked in general by the fact that it happens less gradually and more abruptly. It repeats the earlier period of storm and stress when the human race broke earlier ties and raised itself to a higher level of civilization. The length, weight, and stamina of the body increase much more rapidly than in earlier years, and functions that did not exist before emerge and become important. The voice changes; hair growth increases; the dimensions and proportions of the limbs are altered; the cerebral nervous system, the condition for the psychic life of maturity, attains its full magnitude. It is as if nature arms humans for the struggle awaiting them with all the powers at its disposal. It makes the [young] man aggressive and prepares the [young] woman for motherhood.

Psychologically the change that occurs at this age is no less impressive. Since boys and girls begin to assume a different relation to the world and acquire other interests, their senses also change in structure and function. The senses of touch, smell, taste, as well as hearing and eyesight undergo significant changes. Sense perception, in general, recedes; on the other hand, remarkable progress occurs in the development of the capacity to deliberate and reflect. Thinking, reason, and self-awareness of personality blossom and take on altogether new, more general, abstract, and spiritual form. Whereas the child is controlled by heredity and imitation, at this stage one's own individuality takes shape. The universally human begins to differentiate and express itself in special, diverging traits of character and facial features. And along with all these new impressions and ideas, another world of sensations also appears in a person. New feelings of pleasure and displeasure, sympathy and aversion, new promptings and desires, wishes and ideals, often unconscious and not understood, enter the human mind. The human being, the individual and personal human being, with its own personal insight, a self of its own, arises in the young man and the young woman: they want to be themselves and live their own life.

Also biologically and sociologically puberty brings about great changes. Puberty is the awakening of one's sexual life, the reproductive life. The boy becomes capable of reproduction; the girl becomes nubile. This sexual development does not run parallel to physiological and psychological development but is actually at the core of it. It may not cause or explain all the other developments but it does impart color and tone to them; it is the mighty impulse and stimulus behind them. And with this awakening to the reproductive life, humans simultaneously grow into a larger whole, into the society that surrounds them. They begin to realize that, besides having to lead a life of their own, they are also destined to live along with and for others. The new personality, with its much richer world of ideas and sensations, wishes and desires, passes from the tight little circle of a childlike, self-seeking life into an adult society with its numerous complex relations. The focus of activity shifts from interest in the self toward interest in the whole. In a word, puberty is a second birth, a rebirth, the birth of a new personality, one's own and simultaneously a social personality.

Like the first birth, however, this second birth is accompanied by labor pains. Puberty brings with it its own pathologies and risks, its own aberrations and sins. Like the corresponding era in the history of the human race, it is a period of storm and stress. The swift asymmetrical growth of the body and its parts triggers a feeling of incompleteness. The enormous potential energy that accumulates in the nervous system and cannot as yet find an outlet brings with it intense unrest and tension. By the arrival in one's consciousness of a wide range of new perceptions and ideas, the life of the psyche is continually kept in motion and stirred up. It resembles a sea, thrown back and forth and up and down by the wind. The new personality, reaching toward independence and wanting to assert itself, feels enclosed from all directions, held back, hindered by society, which seeks to introduce it to an altruistic lifestyle. The subject and its environment collide. Often it is as if two selves in one person confront each other and fight with each other for dominance. Characteristic for this age, on the one hand, is a feeling of dissatisfaction and discontent that expresses itself in multitudinous forms of doubt, unrest, regret, depression, melancholy, daydreaming, self-preoccupation, obsessive brooding and, on the other hand, in a drive toward freedom and independence, a hunger to investigate, intense enthusiasm for great ideas and great personalities, high-spirited generosity, faith in the future, soaring idealism, a desire to reform everything. Like every other period in life, so also and particularly this one has its peculiar virtues and defects. In this period life zigzags between wisdom and folly, adoration and contempt, interest and indifference, excessive exertion and deep slumps, self-sacrifice and self-seeking, credulity and skepticism, noble inclinations and sinful passions. The young man stands at the crossroads. His whole future depends on the direction he now takes. The boy is father of the man.

But all these states and experiences are the labor pains of the new personality. Driven from the paradisal state of childhood, the young man enters the wide, wide world to carve out a place of his own. As he grows toward personal freedom and self-reliance, he at the same time adapts to his surroundings and conforms to his social milieu. The storm and stress he has to endure are useful and good. They strengthen his personality, enrich its insights, and deepen its life. Leaving their childhood behind them, humans pass through the critical period of puberty to the age of masculine and feminine maturity.

Now in this psychophysical process of the years of adolescence, religious development plays a peculiar role. The discovery of the link between these two processes has so surprised some psychologists that they thought they could explain all of religion out of the sex drive and viewed religion as nothing more than "perverted sexuality." But most psychologists of religion oppose this "medical materialism." Certainly, sexual and religious development may well be interrelated and in part coincide for a time, but those who would explain religion totally in terms of sexuality could, in their opinion, just as well derive it from the activities of respiration and metabolism, since it is also related to them, and could equally well pass off science and art—an interest in which also develops in adolescence—as a perverse sexuality. According to Starbuck, sexual development may very well be the occasion and condition for the religious awakening, but one must bear in mind the big difference between condition and cause. In the case of religious development, not only the physical but also the psychological state exerts influence. All sorts of concepts and ideas, especially of an ethical kind, affect it. The religious process is much too complicated to be explained in terms of a single cause or with the aid of a simple formula. To this must be added that the content of the religious consciousness often differs totally from that of the sexual consciousness and therefore also later retains a place and value of its own. There is a dependence of the soul on the body and vice versa; yet one must acknowledge the independent value of the life of the soul and its religious content, since ultimately not the origin but the rational content and moral fruit determine that value. "By their fruits you shall know them (the mental states), not by their roots."

The rejection of this materialistic theory, however, does not alter the fact that all psychologists of religion recognize the existence of a close (though often not more precisely designated) connection between religion and love and understand adolescent religious development as a natural and necessary developmental process of that period in life. Of course, this religious development does not occur in everyone in the same way and form. Differences exist, depending on upbringing and environment, character and temperament, gender and age. There is a difference in religious development specifically between the "healthy-minded" and "the sick soul." There are people who need no conversion, others who do. There are "once-born" and "twice-born" persons. Some people have enjoyed a religious upbringing in their youth and for the remainder of their life continue to feel at home in the religion of their childhood years. They need not go through a crisis, know of no broken heart nor of a struggle with sin. They are strangers to the fear of punishment, the dread of judgment. They go through life as carefree, cheerful children, rejoice in the good that surrounds them from all directions, believe in the progress of the human race, and are animated by confident hope for the future. These are the happy people who by their good humor and pleasant attitude overcome the world's suffering. They are adopted as examples by the Mind-Cure Movement when it seeks by suggestion to banish fear from the human heart and by the mind to annihilate all sin and sickness.

Still, even among these privileged people there often occurs, not perhaps a decisive conversion, yet a more or less vigorous religious revival. In children religion is still external and objective. If this religion is not to remain a merely memorized lesson but a matter of free, personal conviction, a matter of the heart, then an awakening, a revival, a deepening and internalization of the religious life has to take place. And such a development of the religious life usually falls in the same period in which the independent personality is also born in people. But there are different types of religious experience. There is not one standard equally applicable to all. The universe is much richer than we surmise and does not correspond to any single system. There are also sick souls, people who have a very different view of life, who comprehend the misery of the world and the vanity of all things and who, in their own souls, have to wrestle with sin, its guilt, and its power. These are the deeper natures who need a religion of redemption, people with a low "pain, fear, and misery threshold," who arrive at rest and peace only through a crisis.

Now such a crisis is usually called a "conversion," and Christianity views it as the fruit of a supernatural operation. But according to the psychology of religion, there is no necessity, scientifically speaking, to resort to any supernatural factor for an explanation of this religious crisis. Conversion, however strange and abnormal it may seem, is a completely natural process that can be adequately explained by psychology.

In the first place, the psychological study of religious experience has brought to light the close connection between the psychosomatic development of the years of puberty and the religious awakening and deepening that occurs in the same period. Surveys of this phenomenon and the statistical analysis of the results have shown that this religious awakening usually occurs in the period between a person's tenth and twenty-fifth year. One can roughly say that it already occurs at times in the seventh or eighth year, then increases steeply up to and including the sixteenth year, then drops sharply to the twentieth and subsequently steadily decreases to the thirtieth year, and becomes exceedingly rare after that. In this connection, one must note that, although puberty and conversion do not precisely coincide in time, the religious crisis as a rule occurs somewhat earlier in girls than in boys. Among the former, it tends to take place especially in the thirteenth, the sixteenth, and also still—but much less—in the eighteenth year. Among boys, by contrast, it is rare at the age of twelve but occurs most often around sixteen and also still very frequently at eighteen and nineteen.

Even this degree of coincidence is remarkable and prompts the suspicion that there is a close connection between puberty and conversion, love and religion, sexual emotion and religious awakening. This suspicion is confirmed by the fact that, in the second place, one can observe an intimate connection and striking resemblance between the above-mentioned experiences characteristic of young people and the religious experiences that occur in the same years. In the years of puberty, the life of the soul is subject to continual unrest, disturbance, doubt, twists, and so on. Now then, the religious experiences bear the same character: a sense of sin, feelings of guilt, fear of punishment, dejection, melancholy, repentance, dread, and so on are typical. In the moment of conversion, which can be of longer or shorter duration, it is as if two forces—again pictured differently as the old and the new person, darkness and light, sin and virtue, Satan and Christ—wrestle with each other so that the young person in question is not so much himself or herself one of the contending parties but rather appears to himself or herself as the spoils for which the two forces are fighting. In that struggle, finally, the experiences of sin, misery, and calamity gradually, sometimes suddenly, make way for those of peace and joy, of forgiveness and reconciliation, of the favor of God and communion with him. These religious experiences, accordingly, are qualitatively the same as those that are typical of puberty in general and different only in that, being transferred to the religious sphere, they are naturally religiously colored and interpreted.

In the third place, according to the psychology of religion, we need to bear in mind that the religious experiences that we describe with the words "conversion," "awakening," "realization," and so on are not peculiar to one religion but occur in all religions and peoples. Not only people such as Paul, Augustine, and Luther, but also Buddha, Muhammad, and others experienced religious crises. Not only Christianity but every religion can speak of revivals both in the life of individuals and in that of masses of people. All religious phenomena, objective (dogma, cult, church, and so on) as well as subjective (mysticism, asceticism, ecstasy, revelation, inspiration, and so on), are characteristic of all religions. But that is not all. All religions also agree in the fact that, consciously and unconsciously, they accept a connection between religious development and puberty. In all religions, after all, at this age certain ceremonies of separation, testing, circumcision, tattooing, and so on occur, all of which serve to introduce the young man or young woman into full religious communion. Among us, too, Catholics have their first communion, Lutherans their confirmation, the Reformed their public profession. Puberty is the age of the second birth, the birth of an independently religious and religious-social personality.

Finally, in the fourth place, the new psychology considers itself able to offer a very plausible explanation of the change that occurs religiously in persons in the event of conversion or awakening. In recent years many psychologists have discovered the enormous importance in human life of "unconscious," or better "subconscious" or "subliminal cerebration." The images and ideas that are present at a given moment in the human consciousness are but a slim part of those that it really possesses. Perceptions, impressions, impulses and desires, and so on introduced or aroused in people earlier, do not totally disappear but sink beneath the threshold of consciousness into the subconscious, leave behind their imprints in the paths of the cerebral nervous system, and, as it were, continue their life and activity there. As a result of the ongoing changes in our consciousness, resulting from the entry of new perceptions, the unconscious material of the impressions is continually kept in motion. And on some occasion or other, a certain group of impressions can very readily rise to the surface and modify or even drive out and replace the impressions present in the consciousness at that moment.

Such transformations of consciousness, such "alterations of the personality," occur in human life every moment. One day people are full of enthusiasm for one cause or another, and the next they have lost all feeling for it. Hosannas, in the life of the individual or in that of the crowd, can yield at any moment to the cry: "Crucify him." A number, a name, or an incident, despite all our efforts, refuses to come to mind at a given moment but pops up shortly afterward. A sum, problem, or syllogism seems insoluble to us in the evening, and the following morning the solution is already waiting for us in our mind. President Teddy Roosevelt lives in a very different circle of ideas when he amuses himself on the hunt than when he concentrates on matters of state in the White House. At that moment he is both externally and internally a different human being or personality.

Now then, conversion, or a religious awakening, is nothing but such a transformation of one's consciousness. It implies that "religious ideas, previously peripheral in [one's] consciousness, now take a central place and that religious aims form the habitual center of [one's] energy." Conversions may *seem* sudden, immediate, and unprepared, like the sudden occurrence of an idea or the inspiration of a genius. But actually this is not the case. Converts themselves all speak later of religious impressions received earlier. Such impressions, perceptions, and ideas, sometimes received long before in one's early youth, were not destroyed but only sank down into the unconscious. When from without there comes some stimulus that corresponds to the state of a person's soul—say a striking word in a sermon, a text from Scripture crossing one's mind or leaping up from the biblical page, a stirring revival meeting, or other—suddenly what up until that moment lay in the unconscious now stirs and enters one's consciousness, drives out the prevailing ideas, and itself then establishes the central place there. Consciousness then changes radically, receiving an entirely new content. And with that transformation of consciousness, the second birth, the birth of a new religious personality takes place. "Spontaneous awakenings are the fructification of that which has been ripening within the subliminal consciousness."

The sudden character of a given religious awakening, therefore, is not proof for its miraculous supernatural origin nor does it essentially distinguish it from the slow, steady growth that characterizes the religious development of others. Also, the value of a religious "revival" depends not on its origin but on its essence and fruit. The question is not, How does it happen? but, What is attained? Whether a given religious development does or does not entail a crisis depends on the uniqueness of a person's character and is determined by his or her earlier and present state. Conversion, accordingly, is not a sui generis experience of some but the common experience of all: an expression of the awakening of one's religious personality during the years of puberty, a natural, necessary, and normal psychological process in adolescence.

This psychological explanation of conversion finds support in the religious development that manifests itself at a later age and can in general be described with the term "sanctification." At that time, after all, it proves impossible to distinguish people who have undergone a religious crisis from those who are not conscious of having had such a crisis. "Converted men are indistinguishable from natural men." Not infrequently the latter are even morally superior. A state of order and rest—harmony with, and a good adjustment to, one's environment—is not exclusively characteristic of converts nor only of Christians. One finds feelings of certainty and joy as much in Leo Tolstoy as in John Bunyan. Conversely, neither "twice-born men" nor "once-born" or "healthy-minded men" are later exempt from all doubt and inner conflict, from all temptation and unrest. Total apostasies are rare, but a very common phenomenon is that following a period of enthusiasm and activity comes a slump, a period of dullness. Here, too, the adage holds that a "bow long bent grows weak." "Every flow has its ebb."

It is a remarkable phenomenon, moreover, that as a rule when humans reach maturity, they get past their doubts and begin to reconstruct their faith and life. Relatively small is the number of those who as adults continue to assume a purely negative attitude toward religion. Despite all sorts of aberrations, in almost all cases religious development finally ends in "a positive and active religious attitude." Reconstruction seems to be a law of the religious life in the later years. Once people are established citizens, when a man becomes a husband and a father and a woman a wife and mother; when they assume a place of their own in society and are bound to it by all sorts of ties; when after the period of storm and stress, they begin to listen more calmly and seriously to the voices they hear coming from the realms of science and philosophy, religion and art, from a sense of duty and responsibility; when they become personally familiar with the disappointments and disasters of life, they often change their tune, judge more kindly, and reconstruct their religious faith. Some then return to the religion of their youth; others, by separation and combination, construct for themselves a new faith. Also, there remains great religious diversity among people. To the extent life develops, it becomes more differentiated and complex. The religious life in many cases even frequently displays pathological forms.

Yet, says Starbuck, with the diversity also the unity increases, and does so specifically in three ways. In the first place, there arises in everyone a growing consensus in the belief in a personal God, in the existence and immortality of the soul, and in an appreciation of the person of Christ, either as Redeemer or as example. Second, although many religious ideas are restored, in the eyes of everyone the dogmas lose weight. A greater value is attached to religious feeling than to religious faith and more emphasis is put on the inwardness of the religious life than on its external forms. In the third place, according to a growing conviction, motives and intentions in religion even exceed faith and feeling in importance, for people's conduct is increasingly guided in the direction of altruism. Egocentric tendencies have begun to yield to other tendencies of which society, the world, and God constitute the center.

So then—to sum it all up—there is both idea and law, dynamic and design, in religious development, in humanity as well as in the individual person. The former recapitulates itself in the latter. One must discern in it three components: first, the evolution of the human being into an independent personality of its own, corresponding to the centuries-long birth of humans from the animal world; then, the evolution of the individual person into a social entity, corresponding to the slow genesis of society with its infinite forms and complex relations; finally, the evolution of the social person into a part of humanity, of the world as a whole, of the deity, "the Power that makes for righteousness." According to Stanley Hall, right now we are in the middle of this period. The evolution of humans has an infinite number of centuries behind it, also countless centuries ahead of it. Right now we are not in the era of the world's old age, the gray era, as Christians often think. We are in the world's adolescence. The twilight we observe is not that of the evening but that of the dawn. The soul *is* not, but is still in the process of *becoming*—"the soul is still in the making"; there are forces in it that are now still slumbering like sleepers in the forest but which will one day awaken. More than is now possible, they will then more forcefully promote the coming reign of "the kingdom of man."[207]

BASIC OPTIONS AND ERRORS

[427b] The history of the order of salvation convincingly highlights its importance, not only for the enrichment of our knowledge but above all practically for the conduct of our life. Since God has put eternity in the heart of humans, they can never escape the need to—in some way—formulate the question: How do I find the supreme good and lasting happiness? What is it that reconciles me with

207. The preceding sketch was taken from my lecture on the psychology of religion given at the Royal Academy of the Sciences, in 1907. Published in H. Bavinck, *Verzamelde Opstellen* (Kampen: Kok, 1921), 55–77.

God and incorporates me in his fellowship? Which is the road that leads to the eternal blessed life? Or, as Luther once put it: How do I find a gracious God? It is the order of salvation, the order or way of salvation (*ordo* or *via salutis*) that seeks to answer that question. For by it one must understand the manner and order in which, or the road whereby, the sinner obtains the benefits of grace acquired by Christ. It was late before the subject was first assigned an independent place in dogmatics and given a somewhat orderly treatment. In the scholastics the material for this locus is still scattered. The most important material that is discussed under this heading can be found in the commentaries on the *Sentences* II, dist. 26–29; III, dist. 25–27; and in the *Summa* II, 1 qu. 109–114. The Decree of Trent treats all the topics relating to grace under the title of *Justification* session VI. Catholic theologians usually sum up the material in a locus on grace and discuss in it consecutively: actual grace (its nature, necessity, gratuity, universality, sufficiency, and efficacy); habitual or sanctifying grace (its nature, dispositions, effects, stability, and increase); and the fruits of grace or merit (their nature, condition, and objects).

Initially, Reformed theology usually treated the order of salvation under three headings: repentance, faith, and good works. But soon it saw itself compelled to expand this series and subsequently included a variety of topics: the call, illumination, regeneration, conversion, faith, justification, sanctification, and so on. Soon, of course, theologians felt a need to sum up this mass of rich material under a single heading and to arrange it along certain lines. Calvin, taking the lead, gave to the third book of his *Institutes* the title: "The way in which we receive the grace of Christ: what benefits come to us from it and what effects follow." Others spoke of the "applied grace of the Holy Spirit" (Quenstedt), "the effecting of salvation or the mode of pursuing it" (Calovius), "the application of redemption" (Mastricht), "the order or way of seeking and obtaining salvation" (Reinhard), and so on, while in the order of treatment there was even greater diversity.[208]

In treating this order of salvation, however, theologians do not invent a way of salvation of their own, or take instruction from science, art, or culture, but have to adhere to their starting point that Holy Scripture is the sole and sufficient principle of theological science. As in every other locus, so also in the treatment of the way of salvation they have to be on their guard against self-willed religion. To the question, What is the way to heaven? they may give no other answer than what is contained in Scripture. No human, but God himself, has established and made known that way in Christ. It is a fresh and living way that Christ himself has cleared and walked, which truly leads to eternal life (Heb. 10:20) and on which God's children are led from beginning to end by the Spirit of Christ (Ps. 73:24; Rom. 8:14). But precisely when theology seeks—also in the subject of the way of salvation—to adhere as rigorously as possible to the instruction of Holy Scripture, it is immediately confronted by a peculiar difficulty. On the one hand,

208. Cf. above, 520–22 (#418).

after all, everything has been accomplished by Christ: sin has been atoned for, the law fulfilled, death conquered, Satan subdued, forgiveness obtained, eternal life brought to light. Focusing on this fact alone, one would expect that those for whom Christ died would immediately be completely delivered from sin, suffering, and death and obtain holiness and blessedness. That, however, is not the case. On the contrary, we are exhorted, in time, to faith and repentance; have to be regenerated, justified, sanctified, and glorified; remain subject in this life to sin, suffering, and death; and only enter the kingdom of heaven through much affliction. How can we square the one with the other? On the one hand, everything has been accomplished, so that there is nothing left for us humans to do; on the other hand, the most important things still have to happen in the life of humans if they are to obtain the salvation acquired. The Christian religion seems to hold two irreconcilable positions, the heterosoterical and the autosoterical, when it attributes the acquisition of salvation completely to Christ and still exhorts us to work out our own salvation in fear and trembling.[209] There are, accordingly, two submerged rocks on which the ship of the Christian order of salvation is always in danger of suffering shipwreck: antinomianism, on the one hand, and nomism, on the other.

Nomism (Pelagianism in its various forms and degrees) not only collides with the decrees of God,[210] but also fails to do justice to the person and work of Christ. To the degree that in the acquisition of salvation it expands the activity of humans, it shrinks that of Christ. It is clear, certainly, that if faith, repentance, and perseverance are in whole or in part within the powers of human beings and their work; if the decision concerning one's actual salvation ultimately, when it comes to the crunch, lies in human hands, then Christ can at most have acquired the *possibility* of our being saved. Then he has indeed created the opportunity for us to be saved, but whether a person, or a few, or many, or all persons will take advantage and continue to take advantage of that opportunity ultimately depends on the people themselves. God has left them free and put the decision in their hands. It follows, then, that Christ has in fact fallen far short of accomplishing everything; and that the most important thing, namely, what is decisive in actual salvation, still has to be done by us humans. Christ, accordingly, steps down from the unique position he occupies in the work of salvation. He is reduced to the level of all the prophets and teachers by whom God has taught and nurtured humanity. His work is then akin to and joined into all those preparatory and pedagogical activities that God has expended on the human race. The gospel of grace is only distinguished in degree from the law of nature. And humans themselves, though aided and supported by all that God has done to nurture them, are summoned to

209. E. von Hartmann, *Religionsphilosophie*, I, 569.
210. Cf. H. Bavinck, *Reformed Dogmatics*, II, 347–51 (#234), 377–82 (##242–43).

self-activity.[211] It depends on them whether they will seize the opportunity God offers them and thus obtain salvation.

The Pelagian order of salvation, therefore, wipes out the specific distinction between Christianity and the pagan religions, comprehends them all in a single process, and can at most honor the Christian religion as first among equals. It falls back into paganism and has people gain salvation by their own wisdom and strength. And in so doing it undermines the certainty of faith as well. Of the Gentiles, Paul testifies that they are without Christ and therefore also without God and without hope in the world (Eph. 2:12). By the works of the law, no one is justified nor is there certainty of salvation. To the degree that people examine themselves and their work more carefully, they make the sad discovery that even their best works are imperfect and stained with sin. They must therefore content themselves with an appeal to the love of God, who overlooks what is lacking and accepts the will for the deed, or with the authority of their church and priest and surrender themselves to a false security. But they do not have and will never have certainty for themselves. Indeed, since grace—to the degree it is granted to them and necessary for them—is not only resistible but also always remains amissible, they at all times run the danger of losing what they have and the hope of salvation. On this position no steady course, no development of the Christian life, is even possible. It is even quite uncertain what the outcome of world history will be, whether there will even be a church or a kingdom of God. With respect to the most important point, that is, [the world's] eternal destiny, the management of the world rests in human hands.

The errors of this rationalistic nomism are unmistakably clear. But they are no less present when it dresses itself in Pietistic or Methodistic clothing. Like so many other efforts at reforming life in Protestant churches, Pietism and Methodism were right in their opposition to dead orthodoxy. Originally their intention was only to arouse a sleeping Christianity; they wished not to bring about a change in the confession of the Reformation but only to apply it in life. Yet, out of an understandable reaction, they frequently went too far in this endeavor and swung to another extreme. They, too, gradually shifted the center of gravity from the objective to the subjective work of salvation. In this connection it makes essentially no difference whether one makes salvation dependent on faith and obedience or on faith and experience. In both cases humanity itself steps into the foreground. Even though Pietism and Methodism did not deny the acquisition of salvation by Christ, they did not use this doctrine or relate it in any organic way to the application of salvation. It was, so to speak, dead capital. The official activity of the exalted Christ, the Lord from heaven, was overshadowed by the experiences of the

---

211. From Hebbel's diary, Alfred Bertholet cites the following quote: "There is no road to deity except by way of human activity. Human beings are connected with the Eternal by the most excellent power, the most surpassing talent bestowed on each of them. And insofar as they develop this talent and this power, to that extent they approach their Creator and enter into relationship with him. All other religion is mere fog and false appearance" (*Aesthetische und christliche Lebensauffassung* [Tübingen: Mohr, 1910], 30).

subject. In Pietism, instead of being directed toward Christ, people were directed toward themselves. They had to travel a long road, meet all sorts of demands and conditions, and test themselves by numerous marks of genuineness before they might believe, appropriate Christ, and be assured of their salvation. Methodism indeed tried to bring all this—conversion, faith, assurance—together in one indivisible moment, but it systematized this method, in a most abbreviated way, in the same manner as Pietism. In both there is a failure to appreciate the activity of the Holy Spirit, the preparation of grace, and the connection between creation and re-creation. That is also the reason why in neither of them does the conversion experience lead to a truly developed Christian life. Whether in Pietistic fashion it withdraws from the world or in Methodist style acts aggressively in the world, it is always something separate, something that stands dualistically alongside the natural life, and therefore does not have an organic impact on the family, society, and the state, on science and art. With or without the Salvation Army uniform, Christians are a special sort of people who live not *in* but *outside* the world. The Reformation antithesis between sin and grace has more or less made way for the Catholic antithesis between the natural and the supernatural. Puritanism has been exchanged for asceticism. The essence of sanctification now consists in abstaining from ordinary things.

On the other side of the spectrum stands antinomianism. Over against nomism it stands for an important truth, a truth that—to overcome antinomianism—we must fully acknowledge. It is true that Christ has accomplished everything and that humans have not added, nor can add, a thing to his sacrifice for our salvation. But antinomianism (not to be confused with the antineonomianism of England and the Netherlands) only employs this truth to gain acceptance for a completely different doctrine. Surely, Christ has accomplished everything. Does this mean that not just *we* but Christ too has nothing left to do after he has suffered and died? No, for Christ has also been raised and glorified. By his resurrection he has been appointed Ruler and Savior, the Lord from heaven, the life-giving Spirit. In the state of exaltation there still remains much for Christ to do. He must also apply and distribute to his church the salvation he acquired, and to that end he has sent his Spirit to regenerate the whole church and lead it into all truth. Antinomianism ignores this application of the work of salvation. In principle it denies the personality and activity of the Holy Spirit. Ultimately, in keeping with the law that opposites attract, it agrees with nomism. But precisely because it was inwardly motivated by an interest other than that of the perfect sacrifice of Christ, it proceeds even farther and so arrives at the denial and criticism of the objective atonement (satisfaction).

Christ, says antinomianism, did not acquire eternal salvation by his suffering and death but only made known the love of God. Atonement and justification are eternal. Just as in nomism, Christ here descends to the rank of a prophet and teacher. But whereas nomism is driven to these errors by its Deistic principle, antinomianism fundamentally arises from pantheism. It resembles, like two peas in a pod, the philosophy of Gnosticism, of Spinoza and Hegel. God is essentially one with humankind. From all eternity he has been reconciled. Wrath and righteousness are human notions, except that, as a result of their finiteness and limitations, humans feel far removed from God. They think that he is far removed from them, that he is filled with wrath against sin and demands satisfaction. That is an incorrect idea that humans have formed of God. God is eternal life, eternally reconciled, eternally one with humankind. And the whole of redemption is that humans, through the preaching of the prophets, be better informed and enlightened, that they abandon the illusion of the wrath and the punitive righteousness of God, that they acknowledge God as their Father and themselves as his children. Nothing is needed for this redemption other than this enlightenment. It consists in enlightenment. It embraces nothing other than faith. There is no repentance, no contrition, no regret over sin, no fear of hell, no dread of judgment, no prayer for forgiveness, no sanctification: those are all Pelagian errors, which fail to do justice to the objective facts of God's grace and atonement. On a low and legalistic position, people still feel a need for them, just as they still construe the atonement as coming about by Christ's sacrifice and still speak of God's wrath and his righteousness. But these are religious notions, symbolic phrases, which have their value for the common people but which, on the position of the πνευματικοι (the "spirituals"), the philosophers, make way for the pure idea and the fully adequate concept.[212] Like nomism, so also antinomianism ends with a total rejection of the essence of Christianity, sinks back into paganism, and locates salvation from sin in the rationalistic enlightenment or moralistic improvement of humans. Both, either in an Arian or a Sabellian sense, reject the confession of the Trinity.

THE TRINITARIAN WAY OF SALVATION

[428] There is room for an order of salvation in a scriptural, Christian, and Reformed sense only on the foundation of the trinitarian confession. In the first

212. Related ideas occur in Christian Science (so-called), but they are so linked and mixed with other ideas that in the case of Mrs. Mary Baker G. Eddy, one cannot speak of unity and system. The following four ideas, however, recur regularly: (1) God, spirit, soul, intellect, the good, truth, life, love, and so on are the only reality (*Science and Health with Key to Scriptures*, 155th ed. [Boston: J. Armstrong, 1898], 7, 9, 20). (2) Sin, sickness, death have no reality, but are errors, and error "is a belief without understanding, untrue, an illusion." "Sin, sickness and death are to be classified as effects of error" (ibid., 468–69). "Sickness as well as sin involves weakness, temptation, and fall—a loss of control over the body" (ibid., 405). (3) Sin, therefore, like sickness, can be overcome by the power of the mind. "Sin exists only so long as the material illusion remains" (ibid., 207). "You can master sin through divine Mind" (ibid., 390). "If you say: I am sick, you plead guilty" (ibid.). "The only safe course is to take antagonistic grounds against all that is opposed to the health and harmony of mind and body" (ibid., 390, 391). "Resist evil, error of whatever sort, and it will flee from you" (ibid., 405). "Christian Science is the sovereign panacea, giving strength to the weakness of mortal mind, strength from the immortal and omnipotent Mind" (ibid.). (4) Forgiveness of sins, therefore, does not exist. "Sin is forgiven only as it is destroyed by Christ, Truth and Love" (ibid., 311). "The destruction of sin is the divine method of pardon" (ibid., 234, 345). "Universal salvation rests on progression and probation and is unattainable without them" (ibid., 187).

place, it follows from this confession that the application of salvation is distinct from its acquisition. The Holy Spirit, as we know, though one in essence with the Father and the Son, is distinct from them as a person. He has his own way of existing, his own manner of working. Although it is true that all the external works of God [*opera Dei ad extra*] are undivided and inseparable, in creation and re-creation one can nevertheless observe an economy that gives us the right to speak of the Father and our creation, the Son and our redemption, the Spirit and our sanctification. Why is it that Christ can testify that the Holy Spirit had not as yet been given because he himself had not yet been glorified (John 7:39), and why did the Holy Spirit have to be poured out on the day of Pentecost if sanctification were not a work distinct from creation and redemption, just as the Spirit is distinct from the Father and the Son? Accordingly, the work the mediator was charged to do did not end with his suffering and death. Christ is not a historical person like others in the sense that, after living and working for a time on earth, he now still affects people by his mind and exerts influence on them by his word and example. Although he completed all the work the Father had instructed him to do on earth, in heaven he continues his prophetic, priestly, and royal activity. Precisely to this end he was justified and glorified at God's right hand. He is the living Lord from heaven. That activity is distinct from that which he performed on earth, though it is most intimately connected with it. By his earthly sacrifice he accomplished everything there was to do in the sphere of justice: he satisfied God's demand, fulfilled the law, and acquired all the benefits of grace. That work is complete and incapable of being increased or decreased. Nothing can be added to it, and nothing can be detracted from it: it is complete, perfect. The Father rests in it and sealed it with the resurrection of his Son. All the benefits that God bestows in the covenant of grace he bestows "through and on account of Christ."[213]

But there is a difference between ownership and possession. Just as a child, even before birth, has a claim on all the goods of his or her father but only at a much later age enters into possession of it, so also all those who will later believe have—long before they believe—ownership rights in Christ to all the benefits he has acquired but only enter into the possession of them by faith. The acquisition of salvation therefore calls for their application. The former implies and produces the latter. As Christ's exaltation is linked to his humiliation, as his activity in heaven is connected with that on earth, so the application of salvation is bound up with its acquisition.

And that application is twofold. Redemption by Christ, we know, is redemption from sin and its consequences. He not only took over from us our guilt and punishment but also fulfilled the law in our stead. The application of Christ's benefits, accordingly, has to consist in justification (i.e., the assurance of the forgiveness of sins and the right to eternal life) but also in sanctification (i.e., the

213. Cf. above, 389–92 (#388).

renewal in us of the image of Christ). Not only the guilt but also the pollution and power of sin must be removed. It has to be a complete redemption, a total re-creation. To the end of effecting and bringing about this redemption based on his completed sacrifice, Christ was exalted to the right hand of the Father. To that end he sent the Holy Spirit, who not only "bears witness with our spirit that we are children of God" (Rom. 8:16) but who also regenerates us and refashions us after the image of God. This work of application is, therefore, just as much a divine work as the creation by the Father and the redemption by the Son; and the Holy Spirit who brings it about is therefore, together with the Father and the Son, the one, sole God, to be praised and blessed forever.

Implied in the confession of the Trinity, in the second place, is that the work of sanctification—in an "economic" sense, the task of the Holy Spirit—though distinct, is not for a moment separated from the work of redemption and creation accomplished by the Father and the Son. This is already evident from the fact that in the divine being the Spirit proceeds from the Father and the Son and participates with them in the same essence. And as he is, so he works, both in creation and re-creation. From this it follows, first of all, that the work of the Spirit is connected with and agrees with the work of the Father. Between the two there is neither opposition nor contradiction. It is not the case that the Father wills the salvation of all and the Holy Spirit applies it only to the few, or vice versa, but the two work together because they are one in essence. From this it also follows that nature and grace, however distinct from each other, are not mutually exclusive. The Roman Catholic system is totally dominated by the contrast between nature and supernatural grace; and various Protestant groups and sects have relapsed into that error. Pietism and Methodism misjudge the right and value of nature both before and after conversion. But the Reformation, in principle, knew no other antithesis than that of sin and grace. Also nature was a creation of God and subject to his providence. As such it is of no less value than grace. For that reason the Reformation could accord to nature, that is, to God's guidance in the life of nature, both in that of peoples and that of special persons, a pedagogical role and significance. It is God himself who prepares the gracious working of the Holy Spirit in the line of generations; and the Holy Spirit in his activities links up with the guidance of God in the natural life and attempts by his grace to restore the natural life, to free it from the power of sin and consecrate it to God.

From the essential unity of Father, Son, and Spirit, it also follows that the Holy Spirit is connected with the work of the Son. The Son and the Spirit do not work against each other. An illustration of that would occur if, for example, the Spirit would apply salvation only to a few, whereas the Son had acquired it for all humans, or vice versa. One in essence, the three Persons, in their varying activities, work together. By his humiliation the Son himself, after all, became a life-giving Spirit. He lives totally by the Spirit. "The death he died, he died to sin, once for all; but the life he lives, he lives to God" (Rom. 6:10). He has fully attained immortality, the eternal life of the Spirit. In him there is nothing "natural" or "soulish" left that can suffer and die. Having already been equipped by the Spirit for his work on earth and anointed without measure with him, he has fully acquired that Spirit and received all the gifts of that Spirit and now lives, rules, and governs by that Spirit. The Spirit of the Father and the Son has become *his* Spirit, the Spirit of Christ. Before Christ was glorified, he was not yet that Spirit, but now he is the Spirit of Christ, his rightful property, his possession.

And so, on the day of Pentecost, he sends that Spirit in order by the Spirit to apply all his benefits to his church. The Holy Spirit does not acquire those benefits nor add a single benefit, for Christ has accomplished everything. In no respect is the Spirit the meriting cause of our salvation. That is Christ alone, in whom the fullness of the Godhead dwells bodily and whose work therefore does not need to be augmented or improved. On the contrary, the Holy Spirit takes everything from Christ: as the Son came to glorify the Father, so the Holy Spirit in turn came down to glorify the Son. To that Son he bears witness; out of his fullness, he communicates grace upon grace; he leads people to that Son and through the Son to the Father. He applies all Christ's benefits, to each in his measure, at his time, according to his order. He does not stop his activity before he has made the fullness of Christ to dwell in his church and the church has reached maturity, "the measure of the full stature of Christ" (Eph. 4:13). The activity of the Holy Spirit is therefore nothing but an applicatory one. The order of redemption is the application of salvation (*applicatio salutis*). The relevant question, therefore, is decidedly not, What must a person do to be saved? but only, What is God doing in his grace to make the church participate in the complete salvation acquired by Christ? Also the "application of salvation" is a work of God that must be viewed theologically, not anthropologically, which from beginning to end ("economically" speaking) has the Holy Spirit as its author and may be called his special work. The whole "way of salvation" is the "applicatory grace of the Holy Spirit."

Against this view of the order of salvation and from the side of Pelagianism, however, the objection is always raised that in that way the right of humanity is denied, human self-activity is suppressed, and an ungodly life is fostered. Insofar as this objection is fundamentally calculated to overturn the scriptural testimony that by the works of the law no human being will be justified (Rom. 3:20), it is not, from the Christian position, admissible. Those who would to some extent agree with it would at the same time and to the same extent leave the scriptural basis behind. Insofar as it is really an objection and deserves consideration, it is untrue and based on misunderstanding. For the view of the "application of salvation" as God's work does not exclude but includes the full recognition of all those moral factors that, under the guidance of God's providence, affect the intellect and heart of the unconverted person. They may not suffice for salvation, as Scripture and experience clearly indicate, but on a truly reformational position there can be no failure to appreciate their value, even for the work of grace. It is God himself, after all, who thus leads his human children, witnesses to them, and showers benefits down on them from heaven [cf. Acts 14:17] that they should seek God in hope of finding him [cf. Acts 17:27]. We do not see, moreover, why the Holy Spirit, who calls people to faith and repentance by his Word, should nullify that moral effect of the Word on the human heart and conscience that Pelagianism attributes to it.

Reformed doctrine contains not less but more than what is recognized by Pelagius and his followers. *They* think they can be content with that moral effect. Augustine and his allies, however, while considering it inadequate, still fully included it in the Holy Spirit's working of grace. In addition, the application of salvation is and remains a work of the Spirit, a work of the Holy Spirit, the Spirit of Christ, and is therefore never coercive and violent but always spiritual, lovely, and gentle, treating humans not as blocks of wood but as rational beings, illuminating, persuading, drawing, and bending them. The Spirit causes their darkness to yield to the light and replaces their spiritual powerlessness with spiritual power. Grace and sin are opposites; the latter is overcome only by the power of the former, but as soon as and to the same degree that the power of sin is broken, the opposition between God and humans ceases: It is God's Spirit who "bears witness with our spirit that we are children of God" (cf. Rom. 8:16). "I no longer live, but Christ lives in me; the life I now live in the body, I live by faith in the Son of God" (cf. Gal. 2:20). "It is God who is at work in you, enabling you both to will and to work for his good pleasure" and who himself wants us to work out our salvation "with fear and trembling" (cf. Phil. 2:12–13). This theological view is so far removed from fostering an ungodly life that, instead, it alone guarantees the reality of a new Christian life, assures believers of the certainty of their salvation, infallibly vouches for the victory of the kingdom of God, and causes the work of the Father and of the Son to attain completion in that of the Spirit. Pelagianism, by contrast, makes everything wobbly and uncertain—even the victory of the good and the triumph of the kingdom of God—because it hangs everything on the incalculable arbitrariness of humans. Standing up for the rights of humankind, it tramples on the rights of God and for humans ends up with no more than the right to be fickle. But the Reformation, standing up as it did for the rights of God, has by that very fact again gained recognition for the rights of humankind. For here, too, the word of Scripture applies: "those who honor me I will honor, and those who despise me shall be treated with contempt" [1 Sam. 2:30]. The theological view of the order of salvation gathers up all the good that is concealed in the anthropological view, but the reverse does not happen. Those who start with God can also do justice to humans as his rational and moral creatures; but those who start with humans and first of all seek to secure their rights and liberties always end up limiting the power and grace of God.

WHAT IS "GRACE"?

[429] All the benefits of the covenant that Christ acquired and the Holy Spirit applies can be summed up in the word "grace." But grace means different things

to different people. In the first place, it can denote the undeserved favor that God bestows on his creatures, especially on human beings as sinners. As such it already appeared in the doctrine of God's attributes.[214] Next, it is a term for all sorts of physical and spiritual benefits that God out of his grace granted to his creatures and which are collectively called "gifts of grace" and "grace" itself (Rom. 5:20; Eph. 1:7; 2:5, 8; Phil. 1:2; Col. 1:2; Titus 2:11; 3:7; etc.). In addition, the word denotes the charm or gracefulness that a person displays with the gifts with which he or she has been adorned in soul and body. Finally, the Greek word χάρις and the Latin *gratia* frequently also have the meaning of the gratitude a person shows for favors received (*gratias agere*). Here we are concerned only with grace in the second sense. Even so the concept is still much too broad for the matter we are treating here. For in this locus we do not have in view the objective benefits of grace that God has granted in his law, the gospel, the person and work of Christ, the church and the means of grace, and which are treated separately in dogmatics. Here we discuss only those gifts of grace which the Holy Spirit communicates subjectively—internally—to humans and which are most intimately related to their salvation. Excluded here, on the one hand, are the gifts of God's common grace, which are granted in some measure to all people and all sorts of people (Matt. 5:45; Acts 14:17; James 1:17), and, on the other hand, the extraordinary gifts (charismata; usually designated in Catholic theology, with reference to the giving in Matt. 10:8, with the term *gratia gratis data* [grace freely bestowed] because the recipient must employ these charismata freely—for nothing—in the service of others), which the Holy Spirit "allots to each one individually just as the Spirit chooses" (1 Cor. 12:4, 11). Left to be treated in this chapter are only those gifts of God's special grace which in the preaching of the gospel are offered to all hearers and are effectively granted to the elect.

Concerning this grace, there is an important difference between Rome[215] and the Reformation, particularly in its Reformed development. In Catholic theology, the grace referred to here is called *gratia gratum faciens,* the grace that makes humans pleasing to God, and it is further differentiated in actual and habitual grace. The former is granted humans to enable them to engage in saving activities. For the natural human, the human without the superadded gift, though still capable of performing many naturally and morally good works, cannot perform the works that belong to a higher order and are linked with supernatural, heavenly blessedness.

---

214. Cf. H. Bavinck, *Reformed Dogmatics,* II, 210–16 (#204). In A. Dieckmann's work *Die christliche Lehre von der Gnade* (Berlin: C. A. Schwetschke, 1901), the biblical concept of grace fails totally to come into its own. The author derives the grace of God from his universal goodness (29ff.), omits from it the most important element of divine compassion toward sinners (21ff.), describes as its content not only the gospel but also the law (80ff.), views Gen. 1:26 as the "great letter of mercy that God deposited in the cradle of human history, the protevangel" (81), and then makes it totally dependent on the free will of humanity (63ff.). A much better treatment on this topic can be found in R. Vömel and W. Vollert, *Der Begriff der Gnade im Neuen Testament* (Gütersloh: Bertelsmann, 1903).

215. Cf. above, 509–13 (#415).

Absolutely necessary to humans for the performance of saving works is actual grace (sometimes also called prevenient, antecedent, arousing, and even working grace), so that on this point Rome decisively rejects Pelagianism and semi-Pelagianism. By actual grace, Catholic theology means not merely the external call of the gospel with its moral influence on the human intellect and will, but thinks in this connection of an illumination of the intellect and inspiration of the will that communicates to humans not only moral but even natural (physical) powers.

At this point already we need to note that Rome bases the absolute necessity of habitual grace not so much on the sinful state of humankind as on the thesis that humans, having lost the superadded gift, are now purely natural beings who in the nature of the case cannot perform supernatural good works or saving acts, for "it is fitting that acts leading to an end should be proportioned to that end."[216] In addition, Catholic theologians teach that this actual grace is universal, not only in the sense that it may be offered to all, but specifically also in the sense that it is in fact given to all humans without distinction, hence also to unbaptized children who die in infancy, to unbelievers, to hardened sinners, to non-Christians.[217] However, if this is the case and, on the other hand, salvation does not in fact become the portion of all, this discrepancy can only be harmonized by the thesis that from beginning to end actual grace remains resistible and amissible. By itself, objectively, this grace is sufficient, but whether or not it becomes efficacious depends—say Molinists and Congruists—on the human will. Although Catholic theologians make every effort to interpret Augustine in this sense and sharply attack and condemn the proponents of predestination (Gottschalk, Calvin, Jansen, and others), they themselves nevertheless end with the admission that we are here facing an impenetrable mystery.[218] Indeed, many Catholic theologians, following Augustine and Aquinas, ascribe the efficacy of grace to a special operation of God and teach a "predestination to grace and glory before any foreseen merits."[219]

Equally important is the difference between Rome's view and that of the Reformation with respect to the essence of grace. Catholic theologians expressly state that "actual" as well as "habitual" grace is not a substance but a quality. They reject Lombard's opinion according to which love is identical with the Holy Spirit,[220] for though the Spirit is the efficient cause, he is not the formal cause, the

216. T. Aquinas, *Summa theol.*, II, 1, qu. 109, art. 5.

217. Of the above-mentioned Catholic theologians, see, e.g., J. Heinrich and C. Gutberlet, *Dogmatische Theologie*, VII, 303–28; M. Scheeben and ed. L. Atzberger, *Dogmatik*, IV, 163–87; J. Pohle, *Dogmatik*, II, 414–83.

218. For example, Pohle, *Dogmatik*, II, 483: "Thus, finally, all attempts at reconciling grace and freedom end in an incommensurable residue that remains surrounded by a veil of mystery and cruelly mocks everyone's efforts to totally resolve it."

219. Cf. H. Bavinck, *Reformed Dogmatics*, II, 351–55 (#235); and further also J. Heinrich and C. Gutberlet, *Dogmatische Theologie*, VII, 329–476; M. Scheeben and ed. L. Atzberger, *Dogmatik*, IV, 202–78; J. Pohle, *Dogmatik*, II, 434–83; C. Manzoni, *Compendium theologiae dogmaticae*, III, 248–68.

220. P. Lombard, *Sentences*, I, dist. 17–18. But Aquinas already taught otherwise and held charity to be "something creaturely in the soul" (*Summa theol.*, II, 2, qu. 23, art. 2). So also the decree of Trent, session VI,

essence, of grace. They do not want a Deistic separation between God and human-ity but are equally opposed to a pantheistic mingling of the two. Yet even of actual grace it is said that it not only morally but also "physically" elevates our faculties so that they are capable of acting supernaturally, and it is therefore *entitatively* (essentially) supernatural, "transcending the entire natural order,"[221] forming, with merely natural grace, a contrast that is no less sharp than that between nature and supernature.[222] Of habitual (infused) grace it is stated even more sharply that it is a gift of God by which humanity "is elevated to the supernatural order and in some manner made a participant of the divine nature."[223] It is a "divine quality inhering in the soul; like a kind of brightness and light it removes all stains from our souls and renders these same souls more beautiful and more bright."[224] More precisely, it is a "substantial disposition" that, unlike knowledge, for example, renews and perfects not just a certain faculty but the essence of the soul itself.[225]

This renewal and perfection consists in the fact that by infused grace a person is regenerated, justified, and sanctified; that this person receives the status of a child of God, is taken up into friendship with him, and elevated to be a temple of the Holy Spirit. But it finds its most succinct expression in the fact that by this grace a person is made a partaker of the divine nature (2 Pet. 1:4). Grace creates in humans a kind of being by which, in a totally special way, they are divinized. It elevates them "into the divine order." It cannot make them into God but does put them in a very special relation to the Deity. It does not merely raise persons—with all their capacities—to the highest pinnacle of which they are by nature capable, for in that case they would not exceed their natural perfection. But inasmuch as in the strict sense grace is supernatural, it elevates them to a level above their nature, above the nature of angels, above *all* nature, above actual creation, and also above all *possible* natures. It "lifts us not merely above human nature but above *every* nature, above the highest choirs of heavenly spirits ... not merely above the whole existing creation but also above all *possible* beings, the most perfect beings conceivable not excepted." And since only God stands above all possible beings, "this grace-filled elevation must transpose us to a divine sphere."[226] From this account it is clear what the actual intent of grace is in Catholicism. It has a dual role: it seeks to elevate and to make well. The former, however, forces the

---

canon 24. Further, some—Scotus, Bellarmine, Molina, Lessius, and others—equate grace with love, but others, following Aquinas (*Summa theol.*, II, 1, qu. 110, art. 3), accept a real distinction between the two and call grace a *habitus entitativus* (essential disposition) and love a *habitus operativus* (operative disposition). The former has its seat in the substance, the latter in a special capacity of the soul (J. Pohle, *Dogmatik,* II, 521–22). "The light of grace, which is participation in the divine nature, etc." (T. Aquinas, *Summa theol.*, II, 1, qu. 110, art. 3, with an appeal to Eph. 5:8).

221. C. Pesch, *Prael. dogm.*, V, 19, 21.
222. J. Pohle, *Dogmatik,* II, 333.
223. C. Pesch, *Prael. dogm.*, V, 172, 188.
224. Roman Catechism, II, 2, qu. 38.
225. C. Manzoni, *Compendium theologiae dogmaticae,* III, 310; J. Pohle, *Dogmatik,* II, 522.
226. J. Heinrich and C. Gutberlet, *Dogmatische Theologie,* VIII, 588ff.

latter almost completely into the shadows. "The task of elevating is primary and befits grace in the entire supernatural order. The task of making well, however, is accessory and adds to grace in the fallen natural order." In the first sense, it is absolute; in the second, merely incidentally necessary.[227] Grace, in the thinking of Rome, is, in the first place, a supernatural quality added to human beings by which they are in principle taken up into a supernatural order, become partakers of the divine nature, of the vision of God, and are able to perform supernatural acts such as by a condign merit deserve eternal life. The forgiveness of sins is secondary here. Faith has only preparatory value. The primary thing is the elevation of human beings above their nature: divinization, "both becoming like God and union with him."[228]

The Reformation rejected this Neoplatonic mysticism, returned to the simplicity of Holy Scripture, and consequently gained a very different concept of grace. Grace serves, not to take up humans into a supernatural order, but to free them from sin. Grace is opposed not to nature, only to sin. In its real sense, it was not necessary in the case of Adam before the fall but has only become necessary as a result of sin. It is therefore not absolutely necessary but only incidentally. The "physical" opposition between the natural and the supernatural yields to the ethical opposition between sin and grace. When grace totally removes sin, with its entailment of guilt, pollution, and punishment, it has done its work. Then humans automatically again become the image of God, for the image of God is not a superadded gift but integral to the essence of humanity. Accordingly, besides the grace that delivers us from sin, there needs to be another grace that then elevates humans above their nature. Granted, according to the Reformed, grace has given us back more than we lost through Adam. For Christ not only acquired the "ability not to sin and die," as the Lutherans picture the matter, but immediately gave believers the "inability to sin and die" (*non posse peccari et mori*). He does not bring us back to the point on the road where Adam stood but has covered the whole journey for us to the very end. He not only accomplished the passive but also the active obedience. He acquired an inamissible salvation, eternal life, which for Adam still lay in the future. Precisely because Adam's destiny lay in eternal blessedness, Christ could acquire it for us in his place. Yet grace does not give us any more than what, if Adam had not fallen, would have been acquired by him in the way of obedience. The covenant of grace differs from the covenant of works in method, not in its ultimate goal. It is the same treasure that was promised in the covenant of works and is granted in the covenant of grace. Grace restores nature and takes it to its highest pinnacle, but it does not add to it any new and heterogeneous constituents.

From this it follows that in reformational theology, grace cannot in any respect bear the character of a substance. The Reformation did confess of grace

227. C. Pesch, *Prael. dogm.*, V, 32–33.
228. Dionysius, in J. Heinrich and C. Gutberlet, *Dogmatische Theologie*, VIII, 595.

that it is not only external but also internal, that it bestows not only moral but also "hyperphysical" (supernatural) powers, that it is a quality, a disposition. But even though it sometimes expressed itself in the same terminology as Rome, it put a different meaning in it. In Rome grace is a physical power because it has to elevate nature to the supernatural order. With a view to the Catholic doctrine of sin, if grace only served to free humanity from sin, the moral power of grace would probably be sufficient. But the Reformation had a different idea of sin. Sin was both guilt and the total corruption of human nature. Humans are by nature dead in sins and trespasses. Their powerlessness can in a sense be called "natural."[229] Therefore grace must be such that it illumines the mind and bends the will, hence works not only morally but also "hyperphysically" (supernaturally) and restores [human] powers. In the Catholic view, this physical operation of grace is the opposite of an ethical one, in any case, one that far exceeds the ethical; in the view of the Reformation, the operation of grace is and remains ethical. Natural incapacity, after all, is by its very nature a spiritual and moral kind of incapacity: an inability to do good solely caused by sin. It is only called "natural" because it is "by nature" (i.e., by virtue of their fallen sinful nature) characteristic of humanity—not effected in humans by custom, upbringing, or other influences—and cannot, therefore, be removed from them by such moral powers either. Grace only works "supernaturally" because it takes away the incapacity deriving from fallen nature and restores the capacity to do good deriving from original nature. In the thought of Rome, grace, strictly speaking, communicates a "physical" (natural) power that natural humans without the superadded gift, even if they are completely sinless, do not possess and which has to be separately bestowed on them. It is "physically" (naturally) impossible for those humans to do supernaturally good works, just as it is physically impossible for them to touch the stars. But in the Protestant confession, spiritual-moral incapacity is not of such a nature; and therefore grace is not a "physical" quality in the Catholic sense, even if it restores the original power to do good that has been lost by sin.

Moreover, since sin is not a substance and does not deprive humans of anything substantial, grace can never be conceived as a substance either. It is a restoration of the form (*forma*) originally imprinted at the creation on humans and creatures in general. The re-creation is not a second, new creation. It does not add to existence any new creatures or introduce any new substance into it, but it is truly "re-formation." In this process the working of grace extends as far as the power of sin. Sin has infected everything; it has corrupted the organism of the creation, the very nature of creatures. Grace, accordingly, is the power of God that also frees humankind inwardly, in the core of its being, from sin and presents it before God without spot or wrinkle. A morally operative grace, therefore, is inadequate. Rome seems to honor grace when it calls it absolutely necessary and has it confer "physical" powers that far surpass nature. But in the end it makes all that grace so

229. Cf. above, 119–23 (#327).

powerless that in its effect it depends on the will of humans. It effects nothing if the will resists it. And if the will consents to it, it only serves to give to humans the powers needed to merit each following grace and eternal life. It is an aid to humans in their pursuit of deification. In the Reformation, however, grace is the beginning, the middle, and the end of the entire work of salvation; it is totally devoid of human merit. Like creation and redemption, so also sanctification is a work of God. It is of him, and through him, and therefore also leads to him and serves to glorify him.[230]

THE BENEFITS OF GRACE

[430] Included under the general heading of grace are numerous special benefits. Scripture is inexhaustible in its enumeration of the blessings that were acquired by Christ and communicated to the church by the Holy Spirit. Theology, as a result, was at all times perplexed as to how to treat them comprehensively and in a regular order. In Catholic dogmatics it gradually became a rule to sum up all the benefits to be considered here under the word "grace" and to divide them over three sections (actual, habitual, and the fruits of grace). The order of salvation here bears the character of a "hierarchical-ecclesiastical order," according to which the priest, by means of the sacraments, infuses, restores, and increases grace in the heart of believers. Grace follows the track of the sacraments.[231] The Reformation, which had its inception in the experience of regeneration and repentance, from the very beginning focused its attention much more on believers and on the way by which they were led to salvation than on the institution of the church with its sacraments. It therefore no longer spoke of grace as a good that was administered by the church but dealt with the work of the Holy Spirit by which the benefits of Christ are applied to the members of the body. Although in this connection a few theologians still gave precedence to the church and the means of grace over the treatment of the order of salvation,[232] the majority of them followed the reverse order. The organism, after all, is logically antecedent to the institution. The covenant of grace includes believers and their offspring, and based on the fact that the offspring of the church belong to the covenant of grace, they are incorporated by baptism into the institutional church. When, in the order of salvation, the Reformation thus again placed the work of the Holy Spirit in the foreground, it initially simply discussed it under the three headings

---

230. On the Reformed view of grace, see J. Zanchi, *Opera*, II, 342; VII, 266, 354; A. Polanus, *Syn. theol.,* II, c. 21; P. Vermigli, *Loci comm.*, 248; William Perkins, *Works*, I, 799ff.; William Twisse, *Opera*, I, 685ff.; F. Junius, "De natura et gratia," *Op. theol. sel.*, I, 302–5; Gomarus, "De gratia conversionis," *Opera theol. omnia*, I, 85–126; B. de Moor, *Comm. theol.*, I, 670; C. Vitringa, *Doctr. christ.*, III, 173.

231. H. Schultz, "Der ordo salutis in der Dogmatik," *Theologische Studien und Kritiken* (1899): 356ff.

232. See above, 522–28 (#419). In modern times, this order is followed by A. von Oettingen, *Lutherische Dogmatik*, 2 vols. (Munich: C. H. Beck, 1897), III, 317; M. Kähler, *Die Wissenschaft der christlichen Lehre*, 3rd ed. (Leipzig: A. Deichert, 1905), 384ff.; J. Kaftan, *Dogmatik*, §§61ff.; T. Häring, *Christian Faith*, II, 597ff.; M. Reischle, *Christliche Glaubenslehre*, 109ff.

of repentance, faith, and good works. But soon it saw itself compelled to give it a fuller treatment. Not only was the number of loci expanded but in their content and interrelationships there gradually emerged all kinds of important modifications, especially in Reformed theology.

Earlier we pointed out that in the first period the doctrines of election and the covenant of grace were often treated as part of the order of salvation but were later usually moved forward and included in the locus on God and in that on Christ.[233] As a result of changes in the concepts, a similar shift also occurred in the case of other loci in the order of salvation. Whether or not predestination, covenant, church, and the means of grace preceded the treatment of the order of salvation, in the order of salvation the first place was assigned to "calling." As in creation and providence, so in re-creation God also brought all things into being by means of the Word. Also when this calling was broken up into an external and an internal call, when regeneration was understood in a restricted sense and assigned to a place before faith, calling continued to occupy first place in the order of salvation.[234] This order was maintained over against the Anabaptists, who completely detached the working of the Spirit from the Word, and over against the Remonstrants, who accused the Reformed, with their doctrine of a direct and efficacious operation of the Holy Spirit, of disdain for and neglect of the Word as a means of grace. In the order of salvation, furthermore, there was no disagreement over saying that the principle and inception of the new life in a human being was due solely to an internal, direct, efficacious, and invincible operation of the Holy Spirit. Sometimes this operation was even called an "immediate" one, not to exclude the Word as a means of grace from the operation of the Holy Spirit, but for two reasons: first, to uphold against the Remonstrants that the Holy Spirit, though employing the Word, himself with his grace entered into the heart of humans and there effected regeneration without being dependent on their will and consent; and, second, to assert against the theology of Saumur that in regeneration the Holy Spirit does not merely by the Word illumine the intellect but also directly and immediately infuses new affections into the will.[235]

On the other hand, there were disagreements over the terms with which the very first work of the Holy Spirit in the heart of the sinner was designated. Following Luther's experience, many theologians spoke first of repentance and then about faith and good works. But soon they noted that not everyone went through such an experience, and, further, that such an experience could not be required of all, especially not of the children of the covenant. Furthermore, as Luther and Calvin had already pointed out, there is a great difference between the worldly grief that proceeds from the law, may also occur in the unconverted, and definitely does not necessarily lead to a saving faith, and the godly grief that presupposes the

---

233. See above, 520–22 (#418).

234. See Calvin, Gomarus, Maccovius, Voetius, Mastricht, and the synods of Dort and Westminster, cited in H. Bavinck, *Roeping en wedergeboorte* (Kampen: Zalsman, 1903), 60–92.

235. See H. Bavinck, *Roeping en wedergeboorte*, 47–72.

faith and arises from the new life. Following Calvin,[236] the Reformed therefore included penitence in the Christian life and soon gave it a different name. The word "penitence," like the word "penance," had acquired a Roman Catholic flavor and involuntarily made one think of a punishment imposed by the priest and "paid" by the penitent. It might still be suitable, therefore, as a term for the grief or regret that a sinner sometimes feels arising in his or her heart on account of the consequences of sin but is a most inappropriate term for the sincere sorrow over sin as sin that is found only in the believer. Soon, therefore, another word for this came into vogue, the beautiful word *resipiscentia*[237] [lit. "becoming sane again," "coming to one's senses again"]. This again had a double consequence: (1) the necessity of describing the very first work of grace with a name other than "penitence"; and (2) a change in the meaning and place of *resipiscentia*.

As for the former, Calvin began with faith as the first benefit of grace and viewed regeneration in the broad sense as the renewal of humans after God's image.[238] Others distinguished an "inefficacious" from an "efficacious"[239] or an "external" from an "internal" calling[240] as the beginning of the new life. Still others gave it the name of "conversion," "regeneration," "drawing," or "resuscitation" and usually assigned to these words a more restricted meaning than they had had earlier.[241] Various circumstances led Reformed theology, in considering the application of the benefits of salvation, even to go back behind faith. According to the Anabaptists, the children of believers, so long as they had not yet come to the age of discretion and could not in fact believe in Christ, were deprived of the benefits of the covenant of grace and hence of the privilege of baptism. Over against them, the Reformers had to defend the position that the children of believers, though not actually able to believe, nevertheless shared in the principle and "disposition" of faith and therefore ought to be baptized. Hence, if they died they, as much as adult believers, were not lost but saved. Adult believers, moreover, often fell into states in which they did not, or even could not, exercise actual faith but in which they nevertheless retained the faculty of faith. Furthermore, according to the unanimous confession of the Reformation, humans are of themselves incapable of believing or repenting. Faith and repentance, therefore, had to be the fruits of an omnipotent operation of the Holy Spirit, the fruits of a seed planted in the heart by the Holy Spirit. Thus, for a variety of reasons, theologians saw themselves compelled to distinguish between the working of the Holy Spirit and the fruit of

236. J. Calvin, *Institutes*, III.iii.1–2.

237. T. Beza, *Tractationum theologicarum*, I, 327; W. Musculus, *Loci comm.*, 550; Z. Ursinus, *Commentary on the Heidelberg Catechism*, qu. 88–90; F. Junius, *Theses theologicae*, ed. Kuyper, 209; W. Ames, *Medulla theologica*, c. 26; *Synopsis purioris theologiae*, disp. 32.

238. J. Calvin, *Institutes*, III.ii–iii; T. Beza, *Tractationum theologicarum*, I, 671; F. Junius, *Theses theologicae*, 34, 1; Belgic Confession, art. 22.

239. G. Sohn, *Theol. synopsis*, I, 72; idem, *Methodus theol.*, I, 184ff.; P. Vermigli, *Loci comm.*, 246ff.

240. W. Musculus, *Loci comm.*, 647; Canons of Dort, III–IV, 6–10.

241. J. Wollebius, *Compendium theologiae christianae*, c. 28; S. Maresius, *Systema breve universae theologiae*, loc. XI; Canons of Dort, III–IV, 11–12.

that operation; in other words, between the faculty and the act of faith, between conversion in a passive and in an active sense; or also between regeneration in a restricted sense and faith (with conversion in the active sense). "Regeneration" now became the word for the benefit that consisted in the infusion of the very first principle of the new life and as such preceded faith. "The grace of regeneration occurs in us prior to faith, which is the effect of it."[242] Disagreement continued to exist over the time of regeneration. Whereas Catholics, Lutherans, and many British theologians had it occur in baptism in the case of all children (baptismal regeneration), the Reformed said that the grace of regeneration was granted to the elect children of the covenant *either* before, *or* during, *or* after baptism [that is, they specified one of these] or simply before, during, or after baptism [that is, they maintained that it was one of these but refused to specify which].[243]

With respect to the second consequence mentioned above, the following needs to be said. If *resipiscentia* (conversion) differed essentially from *poenitentia* (repentance), it must naturally be located in a place other than that which was initially assigned to it, especially by Lutheran theologians. The Reformed did not deny that many of those who are saved are only born again and converted at a later age. They assumed that frequently in that case numerous experiences and activities, such as going to church, hearing the preaching of the gospel, knowing the will of God, a sense of sin and misery, a fear of punishment, a felt need for redemption, hope of forgiveness, and so on may precede regeneration; they even dared speak in this connection of a "preparatory grace."[244] Usually, however, regeneration (in the restricted sense) took place in covenant children in their early years, before the years of discretion, and therefore preceded faith and conversion in the active sense. In that case it did not always have to be accompanied, as Pietism and Methodism later demanded, by a "noteworthy impact and strong attraction" but could also occur "in time, in stages, and gracefully." Nor was it necessary that people knew exactly and could give a clear account of the manner and time of their conversions,[245] as John Wesley, for example, knew that for him it occurred at a quarter to nine in the evening on the twenty-fourth of May 1738. It was not concentrated then at a single point in time but extended over the whole of the Christian life. Neither, finally, could it be treated any longer, as penitence used to be, at the beginning of the order of salvation, nor could it have contrition and faith as its components, but had to be given a place later, in the doctrine of gratitude, and there be described as a continuing mortification of the old and an ongoing resurrection of the new person.[246]

242. A. Polanus, *Syn. theol.*, 467.

243. Cf. G. Voetius, *Select. disp.*, II, 408ff.; H. Witsius, *Miscellaneorum sacrorum*, II, 614, 627; C. Vitringa, *Doctr. christ.*, III, 80; Hillenius, cited in H. Bavinck, *Roeping en wedergeboorte*, 122ff.

244. Cf. what will be said later about the calling.

245. G. Voetius, *Select. disp.*, II, 415, 460.

246. Heidelberg Catechism, Lord's Day 23; Z. Ursinus, *Commentary on the Heidelberg Catechism*, qu. 59–61; T. Beza, *Tractationum theologicarum*, I, 327ff.; A. Polanus, *Syn. theol.*, 468.

Also with respect to the doctrine of justification, finally, some Reformed theologians arrived at a somewhat different view than was generally assumed earlier. For when neonomianism made faith a condition that had to be fulfilled before one's sins could be forgiven, the antineonomians registered their disagreement, arguing that in this manner violence was done to the doctrine of free justification. Faith and conversion could not and might not be legalistic conditions that persons had to fulfill on their part to be justified, for they were gifts of the Holy Spirit, benefits of the covenant of grace, fruits of the work of Christ. But in that case no participation in these benefits was possible except after and through communion with the person of Christ. The imputation of the person of Christ along with all his benefits, therefore, preceded the gift of the benefits. Justification, in other words, did not occur as a result of or by faith, but *with a view* to faith. Before the elect receive faith, they have already been justified. Indeed, they receive this faith precisely because they have already been justified beforehand. This objective and active justification was made known in the gospel from Genesis 3:15 on and in the resurrection of Christ (Rom. 4:25), but had actually already occurred in the decree of election when they were given to Christ and Christ was given to them, when their sin was imputed to Christ and his righteousness was imputed to them. Although some began to speak in terms of this view of *eternal* justification, this had little or no influence on the treatment of the order of salvation. Fear of the antinomianism that, on the basis of an eternal justification, opposed the satisfaction of Christ, changed the nature of faith, and rejected the normative use of the law, kept Reformed theology from shifting the doctrine of justification back to that of the decrees. Although people recognized the element of truth in it, the doctrine of justification from eternity was not accepted. Even Maccovius expressly rejected and opposed it. He does accept that justification in an active sense occurred for all the elect in what is called the "maternal promise," Genesis 3:15, and finds proof for this in the phrase "before the ages" (Titus 1:2), which does not refer to eternity but to ages of long ago. He, accordingly, treats the benefits in the following order: active justification, regeneration, faith, passive justification, good works; but he nevertheless continues to distinguish justification from its decree in eternity.[247] Add to this that the conditions gradually beginning to prevail in the church increasingly made the maintenance of the Reformed scheme of the order of salvation difficult. In a comparatively sound church life, it is possible to assume that as a rule the children of the covenant will be born again in their youth and come to faith and conversion "in stages and gracefully." But when the world penetrates the church and many people grow up and live for years without showing any fruits worthy of faith and repentance, then the serious-minded feel called to warn against trusting in one's childhood regeneration and one's historical faith in Christian doctrine and to insist on true conversion, conversion of the heart, an experiential knowledge of the truths of salvation. Against a dead

247. Maccovius, *Loci comm.*, 676. Cf. what will be said later about justification.

orthodoxy, Pietism and Methodism, with their conventicles and revivals, always have a right and reason to exist.

RELIGIOUS EXPERIENCE AND THE TRUTH QUESTION

[431] The revivals, as noted above,[248] triggered the rise of the new science that is called the psychology of religion and that sometimes seeks to replace all philosophy of religion and dogmatics. Now we assume there will probably be no disagreement over the possibility and legitimacy of examining religious phenomena from a psychological perspective, provided this is done with appropriate sensitivity and respect.

For although being (*esse*) and perception (*percipi*) are by no means coextensive, the world exists for us humans solely in and through our consciousness. The content of that consciousness can therefore be considered and studied objectively, in itself and for its own sake, but also subjectively, from a psychological angle. And this psychological study in a remarkable way supplements the former and sheds a striking light on the phenomena that it thus considers, as it were, from below. This is the case in art, science, philosophy, the study of society, and elsewhere and has now become evident in the study of religion as well. The distinctive features in the religious life of a child, a young man or woman, the adult, and the aged; the links between religious development and physical, psychological, and moral development; the connection between religious awakening and puberty; the clarification of conversion through recurring transformations of one's consciousness; the operation of subliminal forces in the religious process—all that and much more broadens one's vision, deepens one's insight into the religious life, and produces valuable results for the theologian, pastor, homilist, missionary, teacher, and nurturer.

But the psychology of religion is still a young science and therefore at times bent on picking fruit before it is ripe. One may extend one's survey ever so far, but it is still always limited to a few dozen or hundreds of persons. And what do these say over against the millions who remain outside the survey and the investigation of whom would totally upset the conclusion that conversion or awakening is a natural and necessary process of the years of puberty? Further, one may select the persons one studies with ever so much care and formulate the questions one puts to them ever so skillfully; the answers given in response—like all autobiographies, diaries, confessions, conversion stories, and descriptions of personal states and experiences of the soul—can only be used and processed for the purpose intended with extreme caution. Intentional insincerity need not be a factor; but in this area there is such a serious lack of self-knowledge, so much danger of self-deception, such a gap between being and consciousness that one can frequently base very little on those accounts. And when these religious experiences, which often attach

248. See above, 556 (#426).

very different meanings to the same word, then have to be statistically analyzed, reduced to a single formula, classified, and generalized into laws, the difficulties become so mountainous that people shy away from drawing any general conclusions. In the history of religions, as in sociology and history in general, the search for fixed laws up until now has not met with success. There exists a well-founded fear, therefore, that the psychology of religion will not see its labors bear fruit as speedily as some think.

For example, there *is* probably a connection between religion and love, between religious awakening and pubescence, but what the nature of that connection is remains obscure. The same is true of the relation between soul and body. Also, it is altogether certain that many religious awakenings occur in the years of puberty, but the number of those that occur before and after that period is not insignificant either. The rule is marked by numerous exceptions. Further, while sudden conversions occur quite frequently in Methodist circles—though certainly not universally—some large Christian churches have never promoted them and have a different view of the way they occur. Finally, it can hardly be denied that many people, when questioned about the religion of their youth, tend to speak more of loss than of gain. And aside from these folks, also Starbuck and Hall recognize that in the period of adolescence not only religious-ethical personalities but also criminals, sex addicts, and drunkards are formed. If in the face of all these facts, one still maintains that conversion is a necessary developmental element in the period of puberty, this can be done only by separating conversion from its entire content and equating it with every transformation of consciousness. For example, there is a kind of conversion without any God concept, as James says somewhere, but also one from virtue to sin as well as from sin to virtue. Detached from its content, hence viewed purely psychologically and as a transformation of consciousness, the two are entirely the same. The psychology of religion can up to a point teach us what conversion often means in the practice of life, under what circumstances it sometimes takes place, what is sometimes passed off as conversion and passes for it; and by the study of persons and testimonies it can still significantly expand our knowledge in this area, but by itself it cannot possibly tell us what the difference is between a true conversion and a pseudoconversion, between worldly grief and godly grief; why conversion takes place in the life of one person and not in the life of another who perhaps lives in much more favorable circumstances, for example, as a member of a pious family; why it occurs in one person's life in this period, and in another person's life in a much earlier or later period. The reason is that it has no criterion of its own, and of itself it does not know what conversion is—and has to be. God, in his revelation, alone tells us what it is, or else no one tells us. Most arrogant, accordingly, is the assertion of some psychologists of religion that only psychological factors are operative in conversion and that there is no room for a supernatural factor. It cannot and may not make any pronouncement on this subject, since it only observes the exterior of religious phenomena, and neither here nor anywhere else does it penetrate to the most basic and final ground of the phenomena. The point where the finite touches the infinite and rests in the infinite is everywhere undemonstrable; and what happens in the depths of a human soul, behind one's consciousness and will, is a mystery even for the person in question, and all the more so for those who are on the outside and have to rely on phenomena. The psychology of religion itself demonstrates this when it links seemingly sudden conversions with impressions and experiences incurred much earlier, and thereby confirms the distinction assumed in Christian churches between regeneration and conversion.

If the psychology of religion nevertheless stands by its preconceived dogma and attempts to explain all religious phenomena in exclusively psychological terms, it will get to the point where, instead, it will destroy the object of its study by robbing it of its true character. Suppose, for example, that it examines the religious phenomenon of prayer. It will, then, immediately discover that prayer consistently and everywhere implies the belief that God exists as a personal God who hears and also answers prayer. Now if the psychology of religion does not wish to stop with the observation of this fact but also wants to, and thinks it can, explain it in psychological terms, then at that very moment it is guilty of denying the nature of prayer. Just as the idealism that is grounded in theoretical knowledge, by removing from observation the implied belief in the reality of the outside world, undermines human knowledge, so the psychology of religion, which denies to metaphysics its right to exist, dissolves religious phenomena into delusions.

From this, moreover, it becomes evident that by the road it has chosen to travel, the psychology of religion can never demonstrate the validity, truth, and value of religion. For as long as in religion, as in law, morality, aesthetics, and so on, we cannot hold everything to be true, good, and beautiful but also acknowledge the existence of abnormal and pathological phenomena, as James and others in fact also do, then, in order to make our judgments, we either have to introduce a norm from another area or attempt to derive such a norm from the religious phenomena themselves. This latter option is the one chosen by pragmatism, a school of philosophy that also counts James as one of its adherents. Not the "roots" but the "fruits" will be the standard for the truth and validity of religious phenomena. Religion, says James, belongs to the "sthenic affections"; it is a vital force, one of "the most important biological functions of mankind." What matters in religion is not so much what God is as how he is used by us. "Not God, but life, more life ... is the end of religion. God is not known, he is used" [James]. By being and exercising such a vital force, religion proves its truth and validity.

This is a remarkable standpoint insofar as James here takes a position directly opposed to that of Kant, with whom he otherwise closely aligns himself. For Kant tried to free virtue completely from all eudaemonism. But here religion and virtue are recommended to us precisely because they foster the general well-being: because of their social utility. Still even with this utilitarian norm, James fails to surmount the difficulty, for if "life force" is the sole criterion for deciding the truth and validity of religion, it remains a question—one that can never be answered by historical research—whether Islam or Buddhism is perhaps in a stronger position than Christianity and whether superstition, which survives in all religions among a large segment of their people, does not come out on top against a purified religion. But aside from that issue, also in the assessment of what "life force" and "the promotion of general well-being" is, one cannot dispense with a firm criterion. For what matters in this connection is not merely vigor, power, brute force, but content. If "value" is proof of "truth," there must first of all be agreement about that "value." Pragmatism, to be consistent, would now have to say that that "value" can only be argued by its "value" and so on ad infinitum. Since this is impossible, pragmatism dead-ends unless it turns around and argues the truth and validity of religion by a route other than "value."

James himself felt this as well when at the end of his work, he poses the question whether and to what degree the psychology of religion proves the existence of a corresponding objective reality and thereby the truth and validity of religion. He answers the question by saying that mysticism with its appeal to immediate revelation and theology and metaphysics with its speculation are powerless to prove it. But humans not only possess an intellect; they also have a heart, feelings, will. By means of the intellect, we reach only the phenomena, "the symbols of reality," but by the heart, we come into contact with true objective reality, the noumenal world, "with realities in the completest sense of the term." The heart, accordingly, must be restored to a place of honor. More vigorously even than the intellect in the sciences does this emotional and volitional side of humanity assert itself in the practice of life. It takes us to another view of the world and life than science alone can furnish us. All evaluations, especially religious and ethical evaluations, depend on personal will and are rooted in the heart. "The heart has reasons that reason does not know."

Actually, in saying this, James is returning to the mysticism he initially rejected. On the foundation of a positivistic science, he attempts to erect the building of an idealistic worldview. To that end he splits the human being into an entity of intellect and one of will, and the world into a phenomenal and a noumenal world, and then says that the two are related to each other as symbol and reality, as menu and dinner. With respect to the unconscious, James, like Myers in his *Human Personality* and many members of the Society for Psychical Research, adopted the mystical theory, despite the fact that it has been opposed on very strong grounds by Pierce, Jastrow, Hall, and others. Admittedly, James does not go so far as to say that he accepts the indwelling and interior working of all sorts of supernatural agents in the unconscious, the heart, or feelings. But he does say that reality reveals itself and is felt there, that hidden ideas and forces are at work there, that God's grace works its way through "the subliminal door." Not without reason, therefore, he calls himself a "supernaturalist," be it in a highly modified sense.

But the knowledge that James obtains of the supersensual by this route, the route of Schleiermacher and Schopenhauer, is minimal. It comes down to the fact that the truth of religion is demonstrated by psychological study only to the extent that there proves to be "something more" than science, which investigates the phenomena, makes known to us. Objectively, this "something more" is the essence of all religions, just as the corresponding feeling in humans constitutes the core of subjective religion. Of course, no one is satisfied with this "something more" in religion; everyone dresses it up differently and interprets it in his or her own way. These descriptions and explanations form the content of the "overbeliefs" that, though "absolutely indispensable," still cannot claim objective validity. Everyone, therefore, has and must have his or her own religion, his or her own God. "All ideals are matters of relation." It is even a question whether religious experience in fact proves or demands the unity of God. For it does not need an absolute power or a being with absolute metaphysical attributes, such as independence, simplicity, personality, and so on. All such attributes are empty titles, stones in place of bread; they offer "a metaphysical monster to our worship." Religion only needs a higher power. There is perhaps an important truth inherent in polytheism. The infinite diversity of the world comes more into its own in a polytheistic worldview.

With these research results, James himself furnishes proof that the psychology of religion, although it can make important contributions to a better understanding of the religious life, can never, not any more than can the history of religions, replace or make up for dogmatics, philosophy, or metaphysics. It does admittedly teach us, at least to some extent, what religion is, how it is rooted in and links up with human nature as a whole, but it does not say anything about its content, its truth, and its validity. It is a good thing, therefore, to understand that in the end James again moved back to metaphysical territory and took refuge in the mystical background of religious phenomena. We have to choose: either religious phenomena are merely psychological and therefore a delusion (Feuerbach), or they are grounded in a reality that lies behind them. Even modern theologians and philosophers (Biedermann, Pfleiderer, Hartmann, Drews, and others) still assume the existence of an ontological base. The infinite indwells humanity, working in and through it. But because there is no true revelation of God in word and deed, strictly speaking, we know nothing about him. We only feel him in our heart and interpret what we feel in our religious concepts, which have a merely symbolic value. Granted, the idea of revelation is a necessary product of religion, but there is no revelation that factually underlies religion. Hence also on this position all religious phenomena (ideas, sensations) have only a psychological value, and the reality of religion is only sought in a vague and undefinable "essence" of religion. Religion, with all its ideas, sensations, and actions, can only be maintained as reality when it rests in revelation; and then that revelation at once provides the criterion by which religious phenomena (conversion, faith, prayer, and so on) can be assessed.[249]

249. This section, somewhat modified and supplemented, was adapted from my paper on the psychology of religion referred to in n. 207 above. For further evaluation of this young science, cf. the work of J. Geelkerken, *De empirische Godsdienstpsychologie*, 273; and also, among others, J. Bessmer, "Die Theologie vom Standpunkte der funktionellen Psychologie," *Stimmen aus Maria-Laach* (1906): 154–64; *Linwurzky, "Die Religionspsychologie

ONLY REVELATION YIELDS REALITY AND TRUTH

[432] In distinction from the psychology of religion, a science that can give only an inadequate account of subjective piety, the task of dogmatics is to set forth what the order of salvation is according to the word and thought of God. Knowledge of the Christian life, in its origin and development, can undoubtedly be helpful in teaching the dogmatician to better understand the meaning of Holy Scripture, just as in general it is a requirement for him or her to be a spiritual person able to discern the things of the Spirit (1 Cor. 2:15). But this by no means relieves dogmaticians from—rather only equips them for—the task of reproducing, not their own ideas, nor of writing a conversion history of the sinner, but of putting on display the treasures of salvation that God has caused Christ to acquire for his church and distributes to it by the Holy Spirit. Now Scripture is very effusive in summing up and in describing those benefits. It frequently mentions the same benefits under other names or represents them under other images. In Matthew 4:17, Jesus appears on the scene with the message: "Repent, for the kingdom of heaven has come near," but in Mark 1:15, he says, "Repent, and believe in the good news," and in John 3:3, 5, he speaks only of being born again as the way into the kingdom of God.

Elsewhere we are told that only the narrow gate and the hard road lead to life (Matt. 7:13), or that one must hate and leave behind everything to be his disciples (Matt. 10:37ff.). What in the Old Testament is called the "circumcision of the heart" agrees in substance with what in the New Testament is called "regeneration"; and this word, which in John is repeatedly found on the lips of Jesus, is mentioned only once in Paul (Titus 3:5). Hence the idea here is not, anymore than elsewhere in dogmatics, simply to put side by side the concepts occurring in Holy Scripture or to think that the words that dogmatics employs have precisely the same content they have in Holy Scripture. "Regeneration," "faith," "conversion," "renewal," and so on, after all, here frequently do not denote consecutive components on the road of salvation but sum up in a single word the whole transformation that takes place in humans. "Its expressions are, so to speak, collective concepts, which do not denote either the individual stages, levels, degrees, or phases of development, but rather the completed fact itself."[250]

For this reason repeated attempts at simplification were made in the order of salvation. Pietism started with this when it placed the "penitential struggle"

ein neuer Zweig der empirischen Psychologie," *Stimmen aus Maria-Laach* (1910): 505–19; C. Gutberlet, *Der Kampf um die Seele*, 387ff.; W. Wundt, *Völkerpsychologie*, 2 vols. (Leipzig: Engelmann, 1900–1909), II/3, 372ff.; O. Scheel, "Die moderne Religionspsychologie," *Zeitschrift für Theologie und Kirche* 18 (1908): 1–38; E. Mayer, "Ueber Religionspsychologie," *Zeitschrift für Theologie und Kirche* 18 (1908): 293–324; W. Schmidt, *Die verschiedenen Typen religiöser Erfahrung und die Psychologie* (Gütersloh: Bertelsmann, 1908); G. Daxer, "Ueber die religiöse Erfahrung und die Erfahrungstheologie," *Theologische Studien und Kritiken* (1910): 138–48; F. Niebergall, "Die Bedeutung der Religionspsychologie für die Praxis in Kirche und Schule," *Zeitschrift für Theologie und Kirche* 19 (1909): 411–74.

250. W. Schmidt, *Christliche Dogmatik*, 4 vols. (Bonn: E. Weber, 1895–98), II, 432.

(*Busskampf*) and "breakthrough" (*Durchbruch*) at the center, and Methodism followed suit when it began to speak almost exclusively of conversion and sanctification. Schleiermacher moved rebirth into the foreground, dividing it into conversion and justification, and Ritschl highlighted justification and reconciliation. To the degree that sin is located more in the head or more in the heart (the will), was experienced more as guilt than as a pollution (power), the emphasis falls on justification (reconciliation, forgiveness, "sonship") or on regeneration (conversion, redemption). The one-sidedness of these two tendencies, therefore, again leads others to combine these benefits and to treat—in the order of salvation—both justification and regeneration. As soon as a people want to avoid one-sidedness, however, the simplification they strive for begins to consist more in name than in substance, for in fact they subsume under a smaller number of categories the same subjects that in the older dogmatics were divided over several chapters. Simplification was frequently also achieved by the mere device of transferring various topics, such as regeneration and conversion, to the domain of ethics[251] or treating justification, regeneration, reconciliation, and election as part of the doctrine of the work of Christ, so that only faith was left for soteriology.[252] Over against all these attempts at real or apparent simplification, it is the calling of the dogmatician to proclaim the full counsel of God and to disclose all the benefits that are included in the one splendid work of salvation. As in the doctrine of the Trinity and the person of Christ, dogmaticians will indeed be compelled to sometimes use words that do not occur in Scripture or to assign to them a broader or narrower meaning than they possess in some places there. But their duty is not to repeat Scripture literally word for word but to discover the ideas that are concealed in the words of Scripture and to explicate the relationships between them. The various words and images that the authors of the books of the Old and the New Testament employ all contribute to the disclosure of the pivotal issue from a variety of perspectives and in all its riches and fullness.

Keeping this in mind, one must in the first place note that all the benefits that Christ acquired and distributes to his church are benefits of the covenant of grace. This covenant, though first revealed in the gospel in time, has its foundation in eternity: it is grounded in the good pleasure of God, the counsel of God. Christ was designated from eternity to be the mediator of that covenant and could therefore vicariously atone for his own in time. Hence already in eternity an imputation of Christ to his own and of the church to Christ took place. Between them an exchange occurred, and a mystical union was formed that underlies their realization in history, indeed produces and leads them. In the controversy with neonomianism, some Reformed theologians therefore began to speak of an "eternal justification" or of a "justification from eternity." The concept that these theologians wanted to express by these terms is recognized by all of them, for Christ indeed from

251. Th. Häring, *Christian Faith*, II, 677ff.
252. J. Kaftan, *Dogmatik*, §§48–60, §§68–69.

eternity offered himself as surety for his people, took their guilt upon himself, and imputed his righteousness to them in the counsel of peace. But the name they chose for this matter always elicited criticism from many. For not only did they accord to justification a very different meaning than that which it had from ancient times, but they also lost sight of the difference between the decree and its execution, between the "immanent" and the "objectivizing" act. Furthermore, even when it is considered in the decree, the satisfaction of Christ for his own is undoubtedly logically anterior to the forgiveness of their sins and the imputation of the right to eternal life. After all, those who reversed this order would in fact make Christ's satisfaction superfluous and go down the road of antinomianism. The Reformed were always on their guard against this error as much as they were against that of nomism. Even those among Reformed theologians who accepted a kind of eternal justification never claimed that the exchange between Christ and his church in the pact of redemption already constituted full justification. But they considered it its first component and expressly stated that this justification had to be repeated, continued, and completed in the resurrection of Christ, in the gospel, in the calling, in the testimony of the Holy Spirit by faith and from its works, and finally in the last judgment. Accordingly, not one of them treated or completed [the doctrine of] justification in the locus of the counsel of God or the covenant of redemption, but they all brought it up in the order of salvation, sometimes as active justification before and as passive justification after faith, or also completely after faith. It is of the greatest importance, nevertheless, to hold onto the Reformed idea that all the benefits of the covenant of grace are firmly established in eternity. It is God's electing love, more specifically, it is the Father's good pleasure, out of which all these benefits flow to the church.

In the second place, on the Christian position there can be no doubt that all the benefits of grace have been completely and solely acquired by Christ; hence, they are included in his person and lie prepared for his church in him. Nothing needs to be added to them from the side of humankind, for all is finished. And since these benefits are all covenant benefits, were acquired in the way of the covenant, and are distributed in the same covenantal way, there is no participation in those benefits except by communion with the person of Christ, who acquired and applies them as the mediator of the covenant. The covenant of grace, the mystical union, the imputation of Christ to his church and of the church to Christ, all of which are rooted in eternity, are first of all objectively realized in time in the person of Christ, who was crucified, buried, raised, and glorified for and with his church. The bestowal of Christ on the church, therefore, also in this sense precedes the church's acceptance of Christ by faith. How else could we receive the Holy Spirit, the grace of regeneration, and the gift of faith, all of which after all were acquired by Christ and are his possession? It is therefore not the case that we first repent or are reborn by the Holy Spirit and receive faith without Christ, in order then to go with them to Christ, to accept his righteousness, and are thus justified by Christ. But just as all the benefits of grace come to us from the good pleasure of the Father, so they now proceed from the fullness of Christ. Yet, just as earlier we made a distinction between the decree and its fulfillment, so here we must distinguish between the acquisition and the application of salvation. Kaftan is admittedly correct when he remarks that the doctrines of objective and subjective salvation may not be split up. But, aside from the fact that distinction is something very different from separation, this comment of Kaftan arises from a peculiar view of the benefits of grace. Justification (here equated with atonement) and regeneration (equated with redemption) are viewed by him not as specific moments in the spiritual life of a Christian but as "the saving act of God in Christ, which brings about the whole of Christianity." The doctrine of the saving work of Christ must first of all be developed as the doctrine of regeneration, justification, and election. What is given in the person of Christ, specifically in his death and resurrection, is not merely an objective presupposition of salvation but is *itself* the saving act of regeneration and justification. This salvation in Christ is now effected wherever the word of Christ produces and finds faith. By that faith we are, according to God's will, justified and saved before him.[253] Consequently, all the benefits of salvation are discussed under the rubric of the work of Christ, and only faith is left for the order of salvation. Kaftan, therefore, equates redemption or regeneration with the resurrection,[254] and justification or atonement with Christ's surrender to death.[255] Neither one is actually acquired by Christ, therefore, but is revealed in his death and resurrection,[256] and now, in the word, becomes our possession by faith. Now, though it is perfectly correct to posit a most intimate connection between the work of Christ and the benefits of salvation and not to separate them even for a moment or at any point, there is definitely a distinction between what Christ did for us with God and what he now does for us with God, between the work he did in the state of humiliation and the work he does in the state of exaltation, between the acquisition and the application of salvation.

In the third place, it is only in this manner that justice can be done to the work of the Holy Spirit in the salvation of humans. It is remarkable and at the same time most understandable that in the work of Kaftan the person and the work of the Holy Spirit have almost completely dropped out of the order of salvation. It is only stated that the Spirit of God or Christ, by his vital presence in history and the Word, thus inwardly impacts us.[257] The Spirit of Christ comes even less into his own in Herrmann and all who, with Ritschl, are averse to mysticism in religion. According to Herrmann, it is the image of Jesus that must directly affect people inwardly to arouse faith in them. Others tend to focus more on historical "mediations" in upbringing, preaching, church, sacraments, and so on and regard

253. J. Kaftan, *Dogmatik* (1897), p. 499.
254. Ibid., §55.
255. Ibid., §56.
256. Ibid., pp. 532, 536, etc.
257. Ibid., pp. 592, 601, 624, 625.

faith more as the fruit of the activity of the Holy Spirit in the church than as the effect that proceeds from the image of the historical Jesus in Scripture.[258] In this connection we further encounter the question whether the Holy Spirit works only historically and mediately through the Word, the sacrament, and so on or also immediately and directly in the human heart.[259] Connected with all this, finally, is the fundamental question whether the Holy Spirit is a force, a mind-set, a principle of the new life that proceeds from God, was manifest in the person of Jesus, and presently continues his work in the church, hence whether he is identical with the communal spirit of the church (Schleiermacher), with love (Lombard), with the new and holy life present in believers,[260] or is, with the Father and the Son, the one true God to be praised in all eternity. If the latter is the case, as the Christian church on the basis of Scripture confesses against all Pneumatomachians, we still face the question whether the Holy Spirit always works in the human heart directly and immediately without the Word (Anabaptists), or only by the Word (Lutherans), or exclusively by the sacrament (Rome), or as a rule in connection with the Word. Depending on the answer given to all these questions and points of difference, the order of salvation acquires another character that manifests itself more or less in all subjects (calling, regeneration, and so on).

Reformed theology delineates itself as follows. Along with the whole Christian church, it accepted the Holy Spirit's consubstantiality with, and personal distinction from, the Father and the Son; but from this position, in keeping with the scriptural data, it deduced that the Holy Spirit is the Spirit of Christ, who, on the one hand, takes everything from Christ and freely binds himself to his Word but who, on the other hand, since the day of Pentecost, dwells personally in the church and in each of its members and fills them with all the fullness of God. All the benefits of salvation that the Father has awarded to the church from eternity and the Son acquired in time are at the same time gifts of the Holy Spirit. Thus Christ by the Spirit, and the Father himself by Christ, incorporates all his children into most intimate fellowship with himself.

In the fourth place, inasmuch as all these benefits of Christ are not an accidental aggregate but organically interconnected, the Holy Spirit distributed them in a certain order. Those who believe will be saved. Regeneration is necessary for us to enter the kingdom of God. Without faith it is impossible to please God. Without holiness no one will see God. Those who persevere to the end will be saved. One cannot obtain the ensuing benefits without having received the preceding ones. Calling, the preaching of the gospel, therefore, precedes all other benefits, for as a rule the Holy Spirit binds himself to the Word. That calling, however, serves not

---

258. Cf. H. Bavinck, *Reformed Dogmatics,* I, 545 (#143).

259. Th. Häring, *Christian Faith,* II, 592, 653.

260. M. Reischle says, for example, "All in all, therefore, the Holy Spirit is the vital orientation and power that raises sinful finite humans [to the level of] participation in God's holy and eternal being. This orientation and power derives from God's eternal being, was manifested in the earthly person of Jesus, and, as a result of the continued activity of the exalted Lord, is unfolded in Christianity" (*Christliche Glaubenslehre,* 108).

only at the start to invite nonbelievers to faith and repentance but also to admonish and warn, to teach and lead believers permanently. The proclamation of the Word continues without ceasing and to the end of life continues to insist on the mortification of the old and the putting on of the new "man." It therefore differs depending on the persons to whom and the circumstances in which it addresses them. Peter spoke differently to his hearers on the day of Pentecost, and Paul spoke differently to the Athenians than either of them wrote in his letters to the churches. There is a distinction between mission preaching and church-oriented preaching. Even the administration of the Word in the midst of the congregation now highlights one truth and then another. Sometimes the staff of consolation has to be used, at other times the rod of chastisement. Sometimes one must build; at other times one must break down. The comfort of the promises of the covenant of grace must sometimes alternate from serious exhortation to self-examination. But it is always the same bountiful Word, which the Spirit employs to make the church grow in the grace and knowledge of Christ. The Spirit even employs that Word not only in its public administration in the church but also in the family, the school, in public address, and in reading, in upbringing and education. And this calling (external and internal), with the corresponding acts of faith and repentance (arising from regeneration in the restricted sense), are, as it were, the initiatory benefits by which one obtains those that follow.

In the fifth place, these following benefits can be divided into three groups. Sin is guilt, pollution, and misery: a breach of the covenant of works, a loss of the image of God, and submission to the domination of corruption. Christ redeemed us from all three: by his suffering, by his fulfillment of the law, and by his conquest of death. Thus Christ's benefits consist in the following: (1) he restores our right relation to God and all creatures (the forgiveness of sins, justification, the purification of our conscience, acceptance as children, peace with God, Christian liberty, and so on); (2) he renews us after God's image (regeneration in the broad sense, renewal, re-creation, sanctification); (3) he preserves us for our heavenly inheritance and will some day free us from all suffering and death and grant us eternal blessedness (preservation, perseverance, glorification). The first group of benefits is given us by the illumination of the Holy Spirit, is accepted on our part by faith, changes our consciousness, and makes our conscience free. The second group of benefits is conferred on us by the regenerative activity of the Holy Spirit, renews our very being, and redeems us from the power of sin. The third group of benefits is communicated to us by the preserving, guiding, and sealing activity of the Holy Spirit as the guarantee of our complete redemption and wrenches us free in soul and body from the domination of misery and death. The first group of benefits is that which again anoints us as prophets, the second as priests, the third as kings. In the first, our eye is especially directed toward the past, to the historic Christ, to the cross of Golgotha, where our sin was atoned. In the second, our gaze is directed upward to the living Lord in heaven, where he is seated as high priest at the right hand of God's majesty. In the third, we look forward to Christ's future, a future in which he will have put all his enemies under his feet and deliver the kingdom to God the Father. These benefits, though distinct, are not separate. Like faith, hope, and love, they form a threefold cord that cannot be broken. It is Christ himself, the crucified and glorified Lord, who by his Word directs our faith to his sacrifice, by his Spirit incorporates us into his fellowship, and by both Word and Spirit prepares and preserves us for heavenly blessedness.

In the sixth place, by way of summary, we must treat four groups of benefits in the order of salvation: calling (with regeneration in a restricted sense, faith, and repentance); justification; sanctification; and glorification. Although the last usually is treated only at the conclusion of dogmatics, in the doctrine of the last things, it nevertheless actually belongs to the way of salvation (*via salutis*) and is inseparably bound up with the preceding ones. The four groups correspond to what Paul says of Christ (1 Cor. 1:30), "who became for us wisdom from God, and righteousness and sanctification and redemption." In Romans 8:30, the apostle lists three benefits in which God's foreknowledge is realized, namely, calling, justification, and glorification. All these benefits are temporal. Similarly, the phrase "he glorified" (ἐδόξασεν) does not refer—at least not exclusively and in the first place—to the glorification that awaits believers after death or after the day of judgment but, as is evident from the aorist, to the glorification that believers, by the renewal of the Holy Spirit (Rom. 8:2, 10; 2 Cor. 3:18; Eph. 3:16), already experience on earth and that is fully unfolded at their resurrection on the last day (1 Cor. 15:53; Phil. 3:21). Hence the phrase ἐδόξασεν includes both sanctification and glorification.[261] And therefore here, too, we encounter four main benefits that Christ acquired for and communicates to his own. Corresponding to these benefits are also the activities of the Holy Spirit and the operations of grace. In calling, the Holy Spirit primarily engages his convicting and teaching role and grants us preparatory, prevenient, and effecting grace. In justification, the comforting role of the Spirit and his illuminating grace are prominent. In sanctification, the Holy Spirit fulfills his sanctifying role and renews us day by day by his cooperating grace. And in the glorification that already begins in this life (2 Cor. 3:18), he fulfills his sealing role and totally restores us by his conserving and perfecting grace to the image of Christ in order that Christ may be the firstborn among many brothers (Rom. 8:29).

261. P. Gennrich, "Studien zur paulinischen Heilsordnung," *Theologische Studien und Kritiken* (1898): 377–431.

BIBLIOGRAPHY

T his bibliography includes the items Bavinck listed at the head of sections 40–48 in volume 3 of the *Gereformeerde Dogmatiek* as well as any additional works cited in his footnotes. Particularly for the footnote references, where Bavinck's own citations were quite incomplete by contemporary standards—titles often appearing significantly abbreviated—this bibliography provides fuller information. In some cases, full bibliographic information was available only for an edition other than the one Bavinck cited. Where English translations of Dutch or German works are available, they have been cited in place of the original. In a few instances where Bavinck cited Dutch translations of English originals, the original work is listed. In cases where multiple versions or editions are available in English (e.g., Calvin's *Institutes*), the most recent, most frequently cited, or most accessible edition was chosen. Despite best efforts to track down each reference and confirm or complete bibliographic information, some of Bavinck's abbreviated and cryptic notations remain unconfirmed or incomplete. Where information is unconfirmed, incomplete, and/or titles have been reconstructed, the work is marked with an asterisk.

The improvement of this bibliography over Bavinck's own citations in the *Gereformeerde Dogmatiek* is largely thanks to a valuable tool he did not have available to him—the Internet—and its diligent perusal by a number of Calvin Theological Seminary students who labored as the editor's student assistants. Graduate students Raymond Blacketer and Claudette Grinnell worked on the eschatology section of *GD IV*, published separately as *The Last Things* (Baker, 1996). Colin Vander Ploeg, Steven Baarda, and Marcia De Haan–Van Drunen worked on the creation section of *GD II*, published as *In the Beginning* (Baker, 1999). Ph.D. students Steven J. Grabill and Rev. J. Mark Beach worked on volume 1 of *Reformed Dogmatics*, and Courtney Hoekstra worked full-time during the summer of 2002 to complete the bibliography of volume 1. She also was the major contributor to the completed bibliography of volume 2. Joel Vande Werken worked for over a year with Courtney Hoekstra in tracking down bibliographic items and prepared the bibliography of the present volume. Dr. Roger Nicole carefully checked the eschatology and creation bibliographies and helped reduce the errors and asterisks. The assistance of all is gratefully acknowledged here.

ABBREVIATIONS

ANF   *The Ante-Nicene Fathers.* Edited by Alexander Roberts and James Donaldson. 10 vols. New York: Christian Literature Co., 1885–96. Reprinted, Grand Rapids: Eerdmans, 1950–51.

DB   *Dictionary of the Bible.* Edited by James Hastings. 5 vols. New York: C. Scribner Sons, 1898–1904.

DC   *A Dictionary of Christ and the Gospels.* Edited by James Hastings. 2 vols. New York: C. Scribner Sons, 1906–8.

NPNF (1)   *A Select Library of Nicene and Post-Nicene Fathers of the Christian Church.* Edited by Philip Schaff. 1st series. 14 vols. New York: Christian Literature Co., 1887–1900. Reprinted, Grand Rapids: Eerdmans, 1956.

NPNF (2)   *A Select Library of Nicene and Post-Nicene Fathers of the Christian Church.* Edited by Philip Schaff and Henry Wace. 2nd series. 14 vols. New York: Christian Literature Co., 1890–1900. Reprinted, Grand Rapids: Eerdmans, 1952.

PG   *Patrologiae cursus completus: Series graeca.* Edited by J.-P. Migne. 161 vols. Paris: Migne, 1857–66.

PL   *Patrologiae cursus completus: Series latina.* Edited by J.-P. Migne. 221 vols. Paris: Migne, 1844–65.

PRE[1]   *Realencyklopädie für protestantische Theologie und Kirche.* Edited by J. J. Herzog. 1st ed. 22 vols. Hamburg: R. Besser, 1854–68.

PRE[2]   *Realencyklopädie für protestantische Theologie und Kirche.* Edited by J. J. Herzog and G. L. Plitt. 2nd rev. ed. 18 vols. Leipzig: J. C. Hinrichs, 1877–88.

PRE[3]   *Realencyklopädie für protestantische Theologie und Kirche.* Edited by Albert Hauck. 3rd rev. ed. 24 vols. Leipzig: J. C. Hinrichs, 1896–1913.

BOOKS

Achelis, E. Christian. *Zur Symbolfrage: Zwei Abhandlungen.* Berlin: Reuther, 1892.

Ackermann, Aaron. *Judentum und Christentum.* Leipzig: Kauffman, 1903.

Alden, Henry Mills. *A Study of Death.* New York: Harper & Brothers, 1895.

Alexander, William Menzies. *Demonic Possession in the New Testament.* Edinburgh: T&T Clark, 1902.

Alting, Heinrich. *Scriptorum theologicorum Heidelbergensium.* 2 vols. Freistadii [Amsterdam?]: Typographorum Belgicae Foederatae, 1646. [Contains: *Loci communes cum didactici, tum elenchtici.* 2: *Problemata theologica, tam theorica, quam practica.*]

———. *Theologia elenctica nova.* Amsterdam: J. Jansson, 1654.

———. *Theologia problematica nova.* Amsterdam: J. Jansson, 1662.

Alting, Jacob. *Opera omnia theologica.* 5 vols. Amsterdam: Borst, 1687.

Ambrose. *Commentary of St. Ambrose on the Gospel of Luke.* Translated by Ide M. Ni Riain. Dublin: Halcyon Press (in association with Elo Publications), 2001.

Ames, William. *Conscience with the Power and Cases thereof, divided into five bookes.* London: Rothwell Slater & Blacklock, 1643.

———. *Guiliel Amesii Medulla theologica.* 12 vols. Amsterdam: Loannem Lanssonium, 1628.

Anderson, Robert. *Spirit Manifestations and the Gift of Tongues.* London: Evangelical Alliance, 1900.

Anrich, Gustav. *Das antike Mysterienwesen in seinem Einfluss auf das Christentum.* Göttingen: Vandenhoeck & Ruprecht, 1894.

Anselm. *The Fall of the Devil* [*De casu diaboli*]. In *Anselm of Canterbury,* edited and translated by Jasper Hopkins and Herbert Richardson, vol. II, 127–77. 4 vols. Toronto and New York: Edwin Mellen Press, 1975.

———. *Why God Became Man, and The Virgin Conception, and Original Sin.* Translated by Joseph M. Colleran. Albany: Magi Books, 1969.

Antoine, Paul Gabriel, and Filippo de Carbognano. *Theologia moralis universa.* 2 vols. Rome: Excudebat Antonius Fulgonius, 1783.

Appel, Heinrich. *Die Selbstbezeichnung Jesu, der Sohn des Menschen.* Stavenhagen: Beholtz, 1896.

Appelius, Johannes Conrad. *De hervormde leer van den geestelyken staat der mensen.* Groningen: Wed. J. Spandaw, 1769.

Aquinas, Thomas. *See* Thomas Aquinas.

Aristotle. *Categories, and De Interpretatione.* Translated by J. L. Ackrill. Oxford: Clarendon Press, 1963.

Arminius, Jacob. *Opera theologica.* Lugduni Batavorum [Leiden]: Godefridum Basson, 1629.

———. *The Writings of James Arminius.* Translated by James Nichols and W. R. Begnall. 3 vols. Grand Rapids: Baker, 1952.

Arnal, André. *Personne du Christ et le rationalisme allemand contemporain.* Paris: Fischbacher, 1904.

Arnoldi, Nicolaus. *Religio sociniana, seu, catechesis racoviana maior.* Franeker: Jansson, 1654.

Athanasius. *Against Apollinaris. PG,* XXVI, 1093–1166.

———. *Against the Arians. NPNF* (2), IV, 303–447.

———. *Against the Heathens.* Edited and Translated by Robert W. Thomson. Oxford: Clarendon Press, 1971.

———. *On the Incarnation. NPNF* (2), IV, 31–67.

Aufhauser, Johann Baptist. *Die Heilslehre des hl. Gregor von Nyssa.* Munich: Lentner, 1910.

Augustine, Aurelius. *Against Faustus the Manichee. NPNF* (1), IV, 155–345.

———. *Against Julian.* Translated by M. A. Schumacher. Vol. 16 of *Writings of Saint Augustine.* Fathers of the Church 35. Washington, DC: Catholic University of America Press, 1984.

———. *Against Secundinus the Manichee. PL,* VIII, 577–602.

———. *Against Two Epistles of the Pelagians. NPNF* (1), V, 374–435.

———. *The City of God. NPNF* (1), II, 1–511.

———. *Confessions. NPNF* (1), I, 27–207.

———. *The Consensus of the Evangelists. NPNF* (1), VI, 65–236.

———. *Eighty-three Different Questions.* Translated by David L. Mosher. Fathers of the Church 70. Washington, DC: Catholic University of America Press, 1982.

———. *Enchiridion. NPNF* (1), III, 229–76.

———. *Expositions on the Book of Psalms. NPNF* (1), VIII.

———. *Incomplete Work against Julian. PL,* XLV, 1049–1608.

———. *Letters of St. Augustine. NPNF* (1), I, 219–593.

———. *The Literal Meaning of Genesis.* Translated and annotated by John Hammond Taylor. Ancient Christian Writers 41. New York: Newman, 1982.

———. *On Admonition and Grace. NPNF* (1), V, 468–92.

———. *On Free Will. NPNF* (1), V, 436–43.

———. *On Genesis: A Refutation of the Manichees; Unfinished Literal Commentary on Genesis.* Edited by Boniface Ramsey, translated by Edmund Hill and John Rotelle. Hyde Park, NY: New City Press, 2002.

————. *On Marriage and Concupiscence.* *NPNF* (1), V, 257–308.

————. *On Nature and Grace.* *NPNF* (1), V, 115–51.

————. *On Order.* Translated by R. P. Russell. In *Writings of Saint Augustine.* New York: CIMA, 1948.

————. *On the Catholic and the Manichaean Ways of Life.* *NPNF* (1), IV, 41–63.

————. *On the Gift of Perseverance.* *NPNF* (1), V, 521–52.

————. *On the Grace of Christ and Original Sin.* Translated by P. Holmes, edited by Whitney Oates. In vol. 1 of *Basic Writings of Saint Augustine.* New York: Random House, 1948.

————. *On the Merits and Remission of Sins.* *NPNF* (1), V, 12–79.

————. *On the Predestination of the Saints.* *NPNF* (1), V, 493–520.

————. *On the Spirit and the Letter.* *NPNF* (1), V, 80–114.

————. *On the Two Souls, Against the Manichees.* *NPNF* (1), IV, 95–107.

————. *On True Religion.* Translated by Louis O. Mink and John H. S. Burleigh. Chicago: Regnery, 1959.

————. *Questionum in Heptateuchum libri VII.* In *Corpus scriptorum ecclesiasticorum Latinorum,* vol. XXVIII, part 2, pp. 1–506. Vienna: F. Tempsky, 1895.

————. *The Retractions.* Translated by Mary Inez Bogan. Fathers of the Church 60. Washington: Catholic University of America Press, 1968.

————. *To Simplicianus, On Different Questions.* *PL,* XL, 101–48.

————. *The Trinity.* Translated by Stephen McKenna. Fathers of the Church 45. Washington: Catholic University of America Press, 1963.

Baeck, Leo. *Das Wesen des Judentums.* Berlin: Nathansen & Lamm, 1905.

Bahr, Hans. *Zum Streit um Bibel und Babel: Die babylonischen Busspsalmen und das alte Testament.* Leipzig, Deichert, 1903.

Bähr, Karl Christian Wilhelm Felix. *Die Lehre der Kirche vom Tode Jesu: In den ersten drei Jahrhunderten vollständig und mit besonderer Berücksichtigung der Lehre von der stellvertretenden Genugthuung.* Sulzbach: Seidel, 1832.

————. *Symbolik des mosaischen Cultus.* 2 vols. Heidelberg: Mohr, 1837–39.

Baldensperger, Wilhelm. *Das Prolog des vierten Evangeliums.* Freiburg i.B.: Mohr, 1898.

————. *Das Selbstbewusstsein Jesu im Lichte der messianischen Hoffnungen seiner Zeit.* 1st ed. Strassburg: J. H. E. Heitz, 1888.

————. *Das Selbstbewusstsein Jesu im Lichte der messianischen Hoffnungen seiner Zeit.* 3rd ed. 3 vols. Strassburg: Heitz & Mündel, 1903.

Baljon, Johannes Marinus Simon, et al. *Jezus Christus voor onzen tijd.* Baarn: Hollandia Drukkerij, 1908.

Baltzer, Otto. *Beiträge zur Geschichte des christologischen Dogmas im 11. und 12. Jahrhundert.* Leipzig: Deichert, 1898.

Barclay, Robert. *Barclay's Apology in Modern English.* Edited by Dean Freiday. Alburtis, PA: Hemlock Press, 1967.

————. *Verantwoording van de ware Christ.* Godgel. Amsterdam, 1757.

Bardenhewer, Otto. *Patrologie.* 1st ed. Freibug i.B.: Herder, 1894.

Barge, Hermann. *Andreas Bodenstein von Karlstadt.* 2 vols. Leipzig: Friedrich Brandstetter, 1905.

Barrow, Isaac. *Sermons Selected from the Works of Rev. Isaac Barrow.* Oxford: Clarendon Press, 1810.

Barth, F. *Die Anrufung Jesu in der christlichen Gemeinde.* Gütersloh: Bertelsmann, 1904.

Bartmann, Bernhard. *Christus ein Gegner des Marienkultus?* Freiburg i.B.: Herder, 1909.

————. *Das Himmelreich und sein König.* Paderborn: Ferdinand Schöningh, 1906.

Baumann, Julius. *Die Gemütsart Jesu nach jetziger wissenschaftlicher, insbesondere jetziger psychologischer Methode erkennbar gemacht.* Leipzig: Kröner, 1908.

Baur, Ferdinand Christian. *Die christliche Lehre von der Dreieinigkeit und Menschwerdung Gottes in ihrer geschichtlichen*

Entwicklung. 3 vols. Tübingen: Osiander, 1841–43.

———. *Die christliche Lehre von der Versöhnung in ihrer geschichtlichen Entwicklung von der ältesten Zeit bis auf die neueste.* Tübingen: Osiander, 1838.

Bavinck, Herman. *De Algemeene Genade.* Kampen: G. Ph. Zalsman, 1894.

———. *Beginselen der Psychologie.* Kampen: Bos, 1897.

———. *Bilderdijk als Denker en Dichter.* Kampen: Kok, 1906.

———. *The Certainty of Faith.* Translated by H. der Nederlanden. Jordan Station, ON: Paideia, 1980.

———. *De Ethiek van Ulrich Zwingli.* Kampen: G. P. Zalsman, 1880.

———. *Magnalia Dei.* Kampen: Kok, 1909.

———. *Paedagogische beginselen.* Kampen: Kok, 1904.

———. *The Philosophy of Revelation.* Grand Rapids: Eerdmans, 1953.

———. *Roeping en wedergeboorte.* Kampen: Zalsman, 1903.

———, ed. *Synopsis purioris theologiae.* Leiden: D. Donner, 1881.

———. *De theologie van Prof. Dr. Daniel Chantepie de la Saussaye.* 2nd ed. Leiden: D. Donner, 1903.

Baxter, Richard. *A Treatise of Justifying Righteousness.* London: Simons & Robinson, 1676.

———. *Universal Redemption of Mankind by the Lord Jesus Christ.* London: J. Salusbury, 1694.

Becanus, Martin. *Analogia Veteris ac Novi Testamenti.* Louvain: Martinum van Overbeke, 1754.

———. *Manuale controversiarum huius temporis.* Wurzburg: Johannes Volmar, 1626.

———. *Summa theologiae scholasticae.* Rouen: I. Behovrt, 1651.

Beck, Johann Tobias. *Die christliche Lehrwissenschaft nach den biblischen Urkunden.* Stuttgart: J. F. Steinkopf, 1875.

———. *Vorlesungen über christliche Glaubenslehre.* 2 vols. Gütersloh: Bertelsmann, 1896–97.

Becker, Bernhard. *Zinzendorf und sein Christentum im Verhältnis zum kirchlichen und religiösen Leben seiner Zeit.* 2nd ed. Leipzig: F. Jansa, 1900.

Beeching, Henry Charles, and Alexander Nairne. *The Bible Doctrine of Atonement.* London: Murray, 1906.

Bekker, Balthasar. *De Betoverde Weereld, Zynde een Grondig Ondersoek van't Gemeen Geloeven Aangaande de Geesten, Deselver Aart en Vermogen, Bewind en Bedrijft: Als Ook't Gene de Menschen door Derselver Kraght en Emeenschap Doen.* 4 vols. Amsterdam: D. van den Dalen, 1691–93.

Bellarmine, Robert. *De gratia primi hominis.* Heidelberg: J. Lancellot, 1612.

———. *Opera omnia.* Edited by J. Fèvre. 12 volumes. Paris: Vivès, 1870–74.

Bemmelen, Johann Frans van. *De erfelijkheid von verworven eigenschappen.* 's Gravenhage: Nijhoff, 1890.

Bengel, Johann Albrecht, et al. *Gnomon of the New Testament.* 5 vols. Edinburgh: T&T Clark, 1877.

Bennewitz, Fritz. *Die Sünde im alten Israel.* Leipzig: Deichert, 1907.

Bensly, Robert Lubbock, et al. *The Four Gospels in Syriac.* Cambridge: Cambridge University Press, 1894.

Bensow, Oscar. *Die Lehre von der Kenose.* Leipzig: Deichert, 1903.

———. *Die Lehre von der Versöhnung.* Gütersloh: Bertelsmann, 1904.

Bergh, Willem van den. *Calvijn over het genadeverbond.* 's Gravenhage: Beschoor, 1879.

Bergh van Eysinga, Gustaaf Adolf van den. *Christusbeschouwingen onder Modernen.* Baarn: Hollandia, 1909.

———. *Indische Einflüsse auf evangelische Erzählungen.* 2nd ed. Göttingen: Vandenhoeck & Ruprecht, 1909.

———. *Levensbeschouwing: Elementen tot de vorming eener religieus filosofische wereldbeschouwing.* Zutphen: Thieme, 1897.

Berry, Thomas Sterling. *The Problem of Human Suffering in Light of Christianity*. London: Religious Tract Society, 1893.

Bersier, Eugène. *La Solidarité*. Paris: Fischbacher, 1870.

Bertholet, Alfred. *Aesthetische und christliche Lebensauffassung*. Tübingen: Mohr, 1910.

Bethune-Baker, James Franklin. *Nestorius and His Teaching: A Fresh Examination of the Evidence*. Cambridge: Cambridge University Press, 1908.

Beyschlag, Willibald. *Neutestamentliche Theologie: Oder, geschichtliche Darstellung der Lehren Jesu und des Urchristenthums nach den neutestamentlichen Quellen*. 2 vols. Halle: Strien, 1891–92.

Beza, Theodore. *Tractationum theologicarum*. Vol. 1. Geneva: Jean Crispin, 1570.

Biedermann, Alois Emanuel. *Christliche Dogmatik*. Zürich: Füssli, 1869.

Biesterveld, Petrus. *Van Bethanië naar Golgotha: Overdenkingen over het lijden en sterven onzes Heeren Jezus Christus*. Utrecht: Ruys, 1907.

Bilderdijk, Willem. *Opstellen van Godgeleerden en Zedekundigen Inhoud*. 2 vols. Amsterdam: Immerzeel, 1883.

Billuart, Charles René. *Summa Sanctae Thomae hodiernis academiarum moribus accommodata*. 10 vols. Paris: Lecoffre, 1878.

Binet-Sanglé, Charles. *La folie de Jésus*. 4 vols. Paris: A. Maloine, 1908–15.

Bisterfeld, Johann Heinrich. *De uno deo, Patre, Filio, ac Spiritu Sancto, mysterium pietatis*. Leiden: Elseviriana, 1639.

Bloch, Oskar. *Vom Tode*. 2 vols. Berlin: Junkker, 1909.

Blume, Clemens. *Das apostolische Glaubensbekenntnis: Eine apologetisch-geschichtliche Studie mit Rücksicht auf den "Kampf um das Apostolicum."* Freiburg i.B.: Herder, 1893.

*Boddaert, Petrus. *Wolk van getuigen voor de leere der rechtvaardiginge door en uit het geloove*.

Bodelschwingh, Friedrich von. *Die Mitarbeit der Kirche an der Pflege der Geistenkran-*

ken. Bielefeld: Schriftenniederlage der Anstalt Bethel, 1896.

Boehmer, Heinrich. *Luther in Light of Recent Research*. Translated by Carl Frederick Huth. New York: Christian Herald, 1916.

Boehmer, Julius. *Reichsgottesspuren in der Völkerwelt*. Gütersloh: Bertelsmann, 1906.

———. *Der religionsgeschichtliche Rahmen des Reiches Gottes*. Leipzig: Dieterich, 1909.

Bohatec, Josef. *Calvinstudien: Festschrift zum 400. Geburtstag Johann Calvins*. Leipzig: Rudolf Haupt, 1909.

Böhl, Eduard. *Dogmatik*. Amsterdam: Scheffer, 1887.

———. *Von der Incarnation des göttlichen Wortes*. Vienna: Georg Paul Faesy, 1884.

Böhme, Jakob. *Jakob Böhme: Sein Leben und seine theosophischen Werke*. Edited by J. Claassen. 3 vols. Stuttgart: J. F. Steinkopf, 1885.

Bolland, Gerardus Johannes Petrus Josephus. *Het Evangelie: Eene "vernieuwde" poging tot aanwijzing van de oorsprong des Christendoms*. Leiden: A. H. Adriani, 1910.

———. *De evangelische Jozua: Eene poging tot anwijzing van de oorsprong des Christendoms*. Leiden: A. H. Adriani, 1907.

———. *Rome en de geschiedenis*. Leiden: A. H. Adriani, 1897.

Bonaventure. *The Breviloquium*. Translated by Jose De Vinck. Vol. 2 of *The Works of Bonaventure*. Paterson, NJ: St. Anthony Guild Press, 1963.

———. *Disputata S. Bonaventurae in libros sententiarum*. Lugduni, 1510.

Bornemann, Johannes. *Die Taufe Christi durch Johannes in der dogmatischen Beurteilung der christlichen Theologen der vier ersten Jahrhunderte*. Leipzig: Hinrichs, 1896.

Bornhäuser, Karl. *Die Versuchung Jesu nach dem Hebräerbrief*. Leipzig: Deichert, 1905.

*Bosswet. *Geschiedenis der veranderingen van d. Prot. kerken*. 1829.

Boston, Thomas. *Eene beschouwing van het verbond der genade, uit de heilige gedenkschriften*. Translated by Alexander Comrie. Leiden: J. Hasebroek, 1741.

———. *A View of the Covenant of Grace from the Sacred Records.* Glasgow: Chapman & Duncan, 1784.

Bourdeau, Louis. *Le problème de la mort: Ses solutions imaginaires et la science positive.* 2nd ed. Paris: F. Alcan, 1896.

———. *Le problème de la vie.* Paris: F. Alcan, 1901.

Bousset, Wilhelm. *Die Religion des Judentums im neutestamentlichen Zeitalter.* 2nd ed. Berlin: Reuther & Reichard, 1906.

———. *What Is Religion?* Translated by Florence B. Low. New York: Putnam, 1907.

Bouwman, Harm. *Boeddhisme en Christendom.* Kampen: Bos, 1906.

Bovon, Jules. *Étude sur l'oeuvre de la rédemption.* 6 vols. Lausanne: Bridel, 1893–96.

Brahe, Jan Jacob. *Aanmerkingen over de vyf Walchersche Artikelen, welke beneffens de gewoon formulieren van eenigheid in de E. classis ondertekend worden.* Middelburg: Callenfels, 1758.

———. *Ethans onderwyzinge in den negenentachtigsten Psalm.* Amsterdam: Nicolaas Byl, 1765.

———. *Godgeleerde stellingen over de leer der rechtvaardigmaking des zondaars voor God.* Amsterdam: Den Houden, 1833.

Braig, Karl, et al. *Jesus Christus.* Freiburg i.B.: Herder, 1908.

Brakel, Wilhelmus. *The Christian's Reasonable Service.* Translated by Bartel Elshout. 4 vols. Ligonier, PA: Soli Deo Gloria Publications, 1992–95.

Brandes de Roos, Jacques Reinhard. *De strafmiddelen in de nieuwere strafrechtswetenschap.* Amsterdam: Scheltema, 1900.

Brandt, Wilhelm. *Die evangelische Geschichte und der Ursprung des Christenthums auf Grund einer Kritik der Berichte über das Leiden und die Auferstehung Jesu.* Leipzig: O. R. Reisland, 1893.

Braun, Johannes. *Doctrina foederum: Sive systema theologiae didacticae et elenchticae.* Amsterdam, A. Van Sommeren, 1668.

Braun, Wilhelm. *Die Bedeutung der Koncupiscenz in Luthers Leben und Lehre.* Berlin: Trowitsch, 1908.

Breitenstein, Jules. *Le problème de la souffrance.* Strassbourg, 1903.

Bretschneider, Karl Gottlieb. *Handbuch der Dogmatik der evangelisch-lutherischen Kirche, oder, Versuch einer beurtheilenden Darstellung der Grundsätze, welche diese Kirche in ihren symbolischen Schriften bei der christlichen Glaubenslehre ausgesprochen hat, mit Vergleichung der Glaubenslehre in den Bekenntnisschriften der reformierten Kirche.* 4th ed. 2 vols. Leipzig: J. A. Barth, 1838.

———. *Systematische Entwickelung aller in der Dogmatik vorkommenden Begriffe: Nach den symbolischen Schriften der evangelisch-lutherischen und reformierten Kirche und den wichtigsten dogmatischen Lehrbüchern ihrer Theologen.* 4th ed. Leipzig: J. A. Barth, 1841.

Breysig, Kurt. *Die Entstehung des Gottesgedankens und der Heilbringer.* Berlin: G. Bondi, 1905.

Bright, William. *Waymarks in Church History.* London: Longmans Green, 1894.

*Brink, Henricus. *De waare leer der rechtvaardigmakinge, benadeelt door D. Joh. Vlak.*

Bruce, Alexander Balmain. *The Humiliation of Christ: Its Physical, Ethical, and Official Aspects.* 3rd ed. Edinburgh: T&T Clark, 1889.

Brückner, Martin. *Die Entstehung der paulinischen Christologie.* Strassburg: Heitz & Mündel, 1903.

———. *Der sterbende und auferstehende Gottheiland in den orientalischen Religionen und ihr Verhältnis zum Christentum.* Tübingen: Mohr, 1908.

Bruining, Albertus. *Het geloof aan God en het kwaad in de wereld.* Baarn: Hollandia, 1907.

Bruins, Jan Antonie, Sr. *Hoe ontstond de overtuiging dat Jezus de Christus is?* Leeuwarden: Eekhof, 1909.

Brunetière, Ferdinand. *La moralité de la doctrine évolutive.* Paris: Firmin-Didot et cie, 1896.

Bucanus, Guillaume. *Institutiones theologicae, seu locorum communium christianae religionis, ex Dei verbo, et praestantissimorum the-*

ologorum orthodoxo consensu expositorum.
Bern: Johannes & Isaias La Preux, 1605.

Buchanan, James. *The Doctrine of Justification: An Outline of Its History in the Church and of Its Exposition from Scripture.* Edinburgh: T&T Clark, 1867.

Buchberger, Michael. *Kirchliches Handlexikon: Ein Nachschlagebuch über das Gesamtgebiet der Theologie und ihrer Hilfswissenschaften.* 2 vols. Freiburg i.B.: Herder, 1907–12.

Büchner, Ludwig. *Force and Matter: Or Principles of the Natural Order of the Universe.* 4th ed. New York: P. Eckler, 1891.

———. *Kraft und Stoff: Oder, Grundzüge der natürlichen Weltordnung, nebst einer darauf gebauten Moral oder Sittenlehre in allgemein verständlicher Darstellung.* 16th ed. Leipzig: T. Thomas, 1888.

———. *Die Macht der Vererbung und ihr Einfluss auf den moralischen und geistigen Fortschritt der Menschheit.* Leipzig: A. Kröner, 1909.

———. *'s Menschen Levensduur.* Translated by J. J. Schwecke. Amsterdam: N. J. Boon, 1892.

Budde, Karl. *Die sogenannten Ebed-Jahwe-Lieder und die Bedeutung des Knechtes Jahwes in Jes. 40–55: Ein Minoritätsvotum.* Giessen: J. Ricker, 1900.

Buddeus, Johann Franz. *Institutiones theologiae dogmaticae variis observationibus illustratae.* Leipzig: T. Fritsch, 1723.

Bula, Johann Friedrich. *Die Versöhnung des Menschen mit Gott durch Christum, oder, die Genugthuung.* Basel: F. Schneider, 1874.

Bull, George. *Harmonia apostolica.* London: Wells & Scott, 1670.

Bullinger, Heinrich. *Compendium Christianae religionis decem libris comprehensum.* Zürich: Christoph Froschauer, 1556.

———. *The Decades of Henry Bullinger.* Translated by Thomas Harding. 4 vols. Cambridge: Cambridge University Press, 1849–52.

———. *De Testamento seu foedere Dei unico et aeterno.* Zürich: Christoph Froschauer, 1534.

Bunsen, Christian Karl Josias, Adolf Kamphausen, and Heinrich Julius Holtzmann. *Völlständiges Bibelwerk für die Gemeinde.* 9 vols. Leipzig: Brockhaus, 1858–70.

Burkhardt, Gustav Emil. *Die Auferstehung des Herrn und seine Erscheinungen.* Göttingen: Vandenhoeck & Ruprecht, 1899.

Burman, Frans. *Synopsis theologiae & speciatim oeconomiae foederum Dei: Ab initio saeculorum usque ad consummationem eorum.* 2 vols. in 1. Amsterdam: Joannem Wolters, 1699.

Burns, James. *The Christ Face in Art.* New York: Dutton & Company, 1907.

Busch, Jos. Hub. *Das Wesen der Erbsünde nach Bellarmin und Suarez.* Paderborn: Ferdinand Schöningh, 1909.

Busenbaum, Hermann. *Medulla theologia moralis.* Tornaci: J. Casterman, 1848.

Bushnell, Horace. *The Vicarious Sacrifice, Grounded in Principles of Universal Obligation.* New York: C. Scribner's Sons, 1866.

Bussy, Izaak Jan le Cosquino de. *Ethische Idealisme.* Amsterdam: J. H. de Bussy, 1875.

Cadène, Paul. *Le pessimisme légitime.* Montauban: J. Granié, 1894.

Calker, Fritz van. *Strafrecht und Ethik.* Leipzig: Dunkert & Humblod, 1897.

Calovius, Abraham. *Isagoge ad summa theologia.* Wittenberg: A. Hartmann; typis J. S. Fincelli, 1652.

Calvin, John. *Commentaries.* Translated by John King et al. 22 vols. Grand Rapids: Baker, 1999.

———. *Institutes of the Christian Religion* (1559). Edited by John T. McNeill, translated by F. L. Battles. 2 vols. Philadelphia: Westminster, 1960.

Campbell, John McLeod. *The Nature of the Atonement and Its Relation to Remission of Sins and Eternal Life.* 2nd ed. London: Macmillan, 1867.

Campbell, Reginald John. *The New Theology.* New York: Macmillan, 1907.

Candlish, Robert Smith. *The Atonement: Its Reality, Completeness, and Extent.* London: T. Nelson & Sons, 1861.

Canus, Melchior. *Melchioris Cani episcopi canariensis, ex Ordine Praedicatorum opera: in hac primum editione clarius divisa, et praefatione instar prologi Galeati illustrata.* Bassani: Remondini, 1746.

Cappel, Louis, Moïse Amyraut, and Josué de La Place. *Syntagma thesium theologicarum in Academia Salmuriensi variis temporibus disputatarum.* Salmurii: Prostant exemplaria apud Ioannem Lesnerium, 1665.

Caspari, Wilhelm. *Echtheit, Hauptbegriff und Gedankengang der messianischen Weissagung Jes. 9,1–6.* Gutersläh: C. Bertelsmann, 1908.

———. *Die Religion in den assyrisch-babylonischen Busspsalmen.* Gutersläh: Bertelsmann, 1903.

Cassel, Paulas Stephanus. *Die Symbolik des Blutes.* Berlin: Hofmann, 1882.

Catechism of the Council of Trent, The. Translated by J. Donovan. New York: Catholic Publication Society, 1829.

Cathrein, Victor. *Die Grundbegriffe des Strafrechts.* Freiburg i.B.: Herder, 1905.

Cave, William, and Jeremy Taylor. *Antiquitates apostolicae; or, the lives, acts, and martyrdoms of the Holy Apostles of Our Savior to which are added the lives of the two evangelists SS. Mark and Luke.* London: Norton, 1678.

Chable, Florenz. *Die Wunder Jesu in ihrem innern Zusammenhange betrachtet.* Freiburg i.B.: Herder, 1897.

Chamier, Daniel. *Panstratiae catholicae: Sive controversiarum de religione adversus pontificios corpus.* 4 vols. Geneva: Rouer, 1626.

Chantepie de la Saussaye, Pierre Daniel. *Lehrbuch der Religionsgeschichte.* 3rd ed. 2 vols. Tübingen: J. C. B. Mohr (Paul Siebeck), 1905.

Chapman, William John. *Die Teleologie Kant's.* Halle: C. A. Kaemmerer, 1905.

Chauncy, Isaac. *Alexipharmacon: Or, A fresh antidote against neonomian bane and poyson to the Protestant religion.* London: W. Marshall, 1700.

———. *Neonomianism unmask'd: Or, The ancient Gospel pleaded against the other,* called a new Law or Gospel. London: J. Harris, 1692–93.

Chemnitz, M. *Loci theologici.* 3 vols. Frankfurt and Wittenberg: T. Merius & E. Schumacher, 1653.

Christ, Paul. *Die sittliche Weltordnung.* Leiden: E. J. Brill, 1894.

Cicero, Marcus Tullius. *On the Nature of the Gods.* Translated by H. Rackham. Loeb Classical Library. New York: G. P. Putnam Sons, 1933.

———. *Tusculan Disputations.* Translated by John Edward King. London: W. Heinemann; New York: G. P. Putnam Sons, 1927.

Claassen, Johannes, ed. *Jakob Böhme: Sein Leben und seine theosophischen Werke in geordnetem Auszuge mit Einleitungen und Erläuterungen.* 3 vols. Stuttgart: J. F. Steinkopf, 1885.

Clemen, Carl. *Die Christliche Lehre von der Sünde.* Göttingen: Vandenhoeck & Ruprecht, 1897.

———. *Niedergefahren zu den Toten: Ein Beitrag zur Würdigung des Apostolikums.* Giessen: J. Ricker, 1900.

———. *Primitive Christianity and Its Non-Jewish Sources.* Translated by Robert George Nisbet. Edinburgh: T&T Clark, 1912. [translation of *Religionsgeschichtliche Erklärung des N.T.*]

Clement of Alexandria. *Stromateis.* Translated by John Ferguson. Fathers of the Church 85. Washington, DC: Catholic University of America Press, 1991.

Clement of Rome. *First Epistle of Clement to the Corinthians.* In *The Apostolic Fathers,* translated by Francis X. Glimm, Joseph M.-F. Marique, and Gerald G. Walsh, 9–60. Fathers of the Church 1. Washington, DC: Catholic University of America Press, 1947.

Cloppenburg, Johannes. *Theologica opera omnia.* 2 vols. Amsterdam: Borstius, 1684.

Cocceius, Johannes. *Opera omnia theologica, exegetica, didactica, polemica, philologica: Divisa in decem volumina.* Amsterdam: P. & J. Blaeu, 1701.

————. *Summa doctrinae de foedere et testamento Dei.* 2nd ed. Leiden: Elsevier, 1654.

————. *Summa theologiae ex scripturis repetita.* Amsterdam: J. Ravensteinium, 1665.

Comrie, Alexander. *The ABC of Faith.* Translated by J. Marcus Banfield. Ossett: Zoar, 1978.

————. *Brief over de regtvaardigmaking des zondaars, door de onmiddelijke toerekening der borg-geregtigheid van Christus.* Utrecht: Fisscher, 1889. Reprinted, Ermelo: Snoek, 2003.

————. *Stellige en praktikale verklaring van den Heidelbergschen Catechismus, volgens de leer en de gronden der reformatie.* Minnertsga: J. Bloemsma, 1844.

————. *Verhandeling van eenige eigenschappen des zaligmakenden geloofs.* 4th ed. Leiden: Johannes Hasebroek; Amsterdam: Nicolaas Byl, 1753.

Comrie, Alexander, and Nicolaus Holtius. *Examen van het Ontwerp van Tolerantie.* 10 vols. Amsterdam: Nicolaas Byl, 1753.

Crell, Johann. *The Expiation of a Sinner: In a commentary upon the Epistle to the Hebrews.* Translated by Thomas Lushington. London: Thomas Harper, 1646.

Cremer, Hermann. *Die Bedeutung des Artikels von der Gottheit Christi für die Ethik.* Leipzig: Dörffling & Franke, 1901.

————. *Biblico-Theological Lexicon of New Testament Greek.* Translated by D. W. Simon and William Urwick. Edinburgh: T&T Clark; New York: Charles Scribner's Sons, 1895.

————. *Zum Kampf um das Apostolikum.* Berlin: Wiegandt & Grieben, 1893.

Crisp, Samuel. *Christ Made Sin: II Cor. V.xxii. Evinc't from Scripture.* London: J. A., 1691.

Crisp, Tobias. *Christ alone exalted, in the perfection and encouragements of the saints, notwithstanding sins and trials.* London: R. Noble, 1643.

Cunningham, William. *Historical Theology.* 3rd ed. 2 vols. Edinburgh: T&T Clark, 1870.

————. *The Reformers and the Theology of the Reformation.* Edited by James Buchanan and James Bannerman. Edinburgh: T&T Clark, 1862.

Curcellaeus, Stephanus. *Opera theologicae.* Amsterdam: Elsevir, 1675.

Curtiss, Samuel Ives, et al. *Ursemitische Religion im Volksleben des heutigen Orients.* Leipzig: Hinrichs, 1903.

Cyprian. *Epistles. ANF,* V, 275–409.

————. *On Works and Alms. ANF,* V, 245–63.

————. *Three Books of Testimonies against the Jews. ANF,* V, 520–45.

Cyril of Alexandria. *Third Letter to Nestorius, with the Twelve Anathemas. PG,* LXXVII, 105–18.

Daelman, Charles Guislin. *Theologia seu observationes theologicae in Summam D. Thomae.* 9 vols. in 8. Antwerp: Jacob Bernard Jouret, 1734.

*Dale, J. A. H. van. *Bezetenheid en krankzinnigheid.* Heusden, 1896.

Dale, Robert William. *The Atonement.* 18th ed. London: Congregational Union of England and Wales, 1896.

Dallmeyer, A. *Satan unter den Heiligen: Die Casseler Bewegung im Lichte der Erfahrung.* Neumünster, 1908.

Dalman, Gustaf. *Der leidende und der sterbende Messias der Synagoge im ersten nachchristlichen Jahrtausend.* Berlin: H. Reuther, 1888.

————. *Die Worte Jesu.* Leipzig: n.p., 1898.

Daloz, Le P. *Le problème de la vie.* Lyon: E. Vitte, 1901.

Dankelman, Bernardus, and Joseph Deharbe. *Deharbe's verklaring der Katholieke geloofs- und zedeleer.* Utrecht: Van Rossum, 1888.

Darwin, Charles. *The Descent of Man.* Rev. ed. New York: D. Appleton, 1896.

————. *The Expression of Emotions in Man and Animal.* London: J. Murray, 1872.

————. *The Variation of Animals and Plants under Domestication.* 2 vols. New York: D. Appleton, 1896.

————. *Het vari ren der huisdieren en cultuurplanten.* 2 vols. Translated by H. Hartogh Heys van Zouteveen. Arnhem and Nijmegen: Cohen, 1880–89.

Daub, Carl. *Judas Ischariot: Oder das Böse in Verhältnis zum Guten*. Heidelberg: Mohr & Winter, 1816.

Davenant, John. *Expositio epistolae D. Pauli ad Colossenses*. Cambridge: T&I Bucke, 1627.

Davidson, Andrew Bruce. *The Theology of the Old Testament*. Edited from the author's manuscripts by S. D. F. Salmond. New York: Charles Scribner's, 1904.

Deharbe, Joseph. *Verklaring der katholieke geloofs- en zedeleer*. 3rd ed. 4 vols. Utretcht: J. R. Van Rossum, 1880–88.

Deissmann, [Gustav] Adolf. *Beiträge zur Weiterentwicklung der christlichen Religion*. Munich: Lehmann, 1905.

———. *Licht vom Osten*. Tübingen: Mohr, 1908.

———. *Die neutestamentliche Formel "in Christo Jesu."* Marburg: Elwert, 1892.

Delage, Yves. *La structure du protoplasma et les théories sur l'hérédité et les grands problèmes de la biologie générale*. Paris: C. Reinwald, 1895.

Delitzsch, Franz. *Biblical Commentary on the Prophecies of Isaiah*. Translated by James Martin. 2 vols. Grand Rapids: Eerdmans, 1949.

———. *A New Commentary on Genesis*. Translated by Sophia Taylor. Edinburgh: T&T Clark, 1899.

———. *System der christlichen Apologetik*. Leipzig: Dörffling & Franke, 1870.

———. *A System of Biblical Psychology*. Translated by Robert E. Wallis. Edinburgh: T&T Clark, 1899.

Denifle, Heinrich, and Albert Maria Weiss. *Luther und Luthertum in der ersten Entwicklung, quellenmässig dargestellt*. 2 vols. Mainz: Kirchheim, 1904-9.

Denney, James. *The Atonement and the Modern Mind*. 2nd ed. London: Hodder & Stoughton, 1908.

———. *The Death of Christ: Its Place and Interpretation in the New Testament*. London: Hodder & Stoughton, 1909.

Dens, Pierre. *Theologia ad usum seminariorum et sacrae theologiae alumnorum*. Mechliniae: P. J. Hanicq, 1828-30.

———. *Theologia moralis et dogmatica*. 8 vols. Dublin: Richard Coyne, 1832.

Denzinger, Heinrich. *The Sources of Catholic Dogma (Enchiridion Symbolorum)*. Translated from the 30th ed. by Roy J. Deferrari. London and St. Louis: Herder, 1955.

Descartes, René. *The Philosophical Works of Descartes*. Translated by Elizabeth S. Haldane and G. R. T. Ross. 2 vols. London: Cambridge University Press, 1931.

Deurhof, Willem. *Overnatuurkundige en schriftuurlijke samenstelling van de H. Godgeleerdheid*. 2 vols. Amsterdam: Nicolaas ten Hoorn, 1715.

Dieckhoff, August Wilhelm. *Die Menschwerdung des Sohnes Gottes*. Leipzig: Naumann, 1882.

Dieckmann, August. *Die christliche Lehre von der Gnade*. Berlin: C. A. Schwetschke, 1901.

Dieringer, Franz. *Lehrbuch der Katholischen Dogmatik*. 4th ed. Mainz: Kirchheim, 1858.

Diestel, Ludwig. *Geschichte des Alten Testaments in der christlichen Kirche*. Jena: Mauke, 1869.

Dietzsch, August. *Adam und Christus*. Bonn: Adolph Marcus, 1871.

Dilger, Wilhelm. *Salvation in Hinduism and Christianity*. Translated by Luise Oehler. Mangalore: Basel Mission Book and Tract Depository, 1908.

Disteldorf. *Die Auferstehung Jesu Christi*. Trier, 1906.

Dobschütz, Ernst von. *Christusbilder: Untersuchungen zur christlichen Legende*. Leipzig: Hinrichs, 1909.

———. *Ostern und Pfingsten: Eine Studie zu I Korinther 15*. Leipzig: Hinrichs, 1903.

Doedes, Jacobus Izaak. *De Leer der Zaligheid Volgens het Evangelie in de Schriften des Nieuwen Verbonds Voorgesteld*. Utrecht: Kemink, 1876.

———. *De Nederlandsche Geloofsbelijdenis en de Heidelbergsche Catechismus*. Utrecht: Kemink & Zoon, 1880-81.

Domela Nieuwenhuis, Jacob. *Het wezen der straf*. Groningen: Wolters, 1899.

Dorner, Isaak August. *Gesammelte Schriften aus dem Gebiet der systematischen Theologie*. Berlin: Hertz, 1883.

———. *Geschichte der protestantischen Theologie besonders in Deutschland, nach ihrer principiellen Bewegung und im Zusammenhang mit dem religiösen sittlichen und intellectuellen Leben*. 2 vols. Munich: J. G. Cotta, 1867.

———. *History of Protestant Theology, Particularly in Germany: Viewed according to Its Fundamental Movement and in Connection with the Religious, Moral, and Intellectual Life*. Translated by George Robson and Sophia Taylor. 2 vols. Edinburgh: T&T Clark, 1871.

———. *History of the Development of the Doctrine of the Person of Christ*. Translated by William Lindsay Alexander. 5 vols. Edinburgh: T&T Clark, 1863–78.

———. *A System of Christian Doctrine*. Translated by Rev. Alfred Cave and Rev. J. S. Banks. Rev. ed. 4 vols. Edinburgh: T&T Clark, 1888.

Downer, Arthur Cleveland. *The Mission and Ministration of the Holy Spirit*. Edinburgh: T&T Clark, 1909.

Drews, Arthur. *The Christ Myth*. Chicago: Open Court, 1910. Reprinted, Amherst, NY: Prometheus Books, 1998.

———. *Die Christusmythe*. Jena: Diederichs, 1909.

———. *Die Religion als Selbst-bewusstsein Gottes*. 1st ed. Jena and Leipzig: E. Diederichs, 1906.

Drews, Paul. *Die Reform des Strafrechts und die Ethik des Christentums*. Tübingen: Mohr, 1905.

Dubose, William Porcher. *The Soteriology of the New Testament*. New York: Longmans, Green, 1906.

Duhm, Bernhard. *Die Theologie der Propheten als Grundlage für die innere Entwicklung der israelitischen Religion*. Bonn: Marcus, 1875.

Duhm, Hans. *Die bösen Geister im Alten Testament*. Tübingen: Mohr, 1904.

Dulk, Albert Friedrich Benno. *Der Irrgang des Lebens Jesu*. 2 vols. Stuttgart: Dietz, 1884–85.

Dunkmann, Karl. *Geschichte des Christentums als Religion der Versöhnung und Erlösung*. 2 vols. Leipzig: Dieterich, 1907.

———. *Der historische Jesus, der mythologische Christus und Jesus der Christ*. Leipzig: Deichert, 1910.

Duns Scotus, John. *Quaestiones in libros sententiarum*. Frankfurt: Minerva, 1967.

Eaton, John. *The Honey-Combe of Free Justification by Christ Alone*. London: Robert Lancaster, 1642.

Ebrard, Johannes Heinrich August. *Apologetics: The Scientific Vindication of Christianity*. Translated by William Stuart and John Macpherson. 2nd ed. 3 vols. Edinburgh: T&T Clark, 1886–87.

———. *Apologetik: Wissenschaftliche Rechtfertigung des Christentums*. 2 vols. Gütersloh: Bertelsmann, 1878–80.

———. *Christliche Dogmatik*. 2nd ed. 2 vols. Königsberg: A. W. Unzer, 1862–63.

———. *Die Lehre von der stellvertretenden Genugthuung in der heiligen Schrift begründet*. Königsberg: A. W. Unzer, 1857.

Ebstein, Wilhelm. *Die Medizin im Neuen Testament und im Talmud*. Stuttgart: Enke, 1903.

Ecklin, G. A. Friedrich. *Die Heilswert des Todes Jesu: Nach der Schrift und begrifflicher Notwendigkeit*. Basel: Reinhardt, 1888.

Eddy, Mary Baker G. *Science and Health with Key to Scriptures*. 155th ed. Boston: J. Armstrong, 1898.

———. *Unity of Good*. Boston: J. Armstrong, 1908.

Edwards, Jonathan. *The Works of Jonathan Edwards*. Vol. 8, *Ethical Writings*. Edited by Paul Ramsey. New Haven: Yale University Press, 1989.

Egeling, Lucas. *De weg der zaligheid naar het beloop des Bijbels*. 2 vols. Amsterdam: Mortier Covens en Zoon, 1844.

Eisenmenger, Johann Andreas, and Franz Xavier Schieferl. *Entdecktes Judenthum.* 2 vols. Königsberg in Preussen: n.p., 1711.

Ellis, Havelock. *Geschlechtstrieb und Schamgefühl.* Leipzig: Wigand, 1900.

Engel, M. R. *Der Kampf um Römer Kapitel 7.* Gotha: Verlagsbureau, 1902.

Episcopius, Simon. *Apologia pro confessione sive declaratione sententiae eorum.* N.p., 1629.

———. *The Confession or Declaration of the Ministers or Pastors Which in the United Provinces are Called Remonstrants, concerning the Chief Points of the Christian Religion.* Translated by Thomas Taylor. London: Francis Smith, 1676.

———. *Institutiones theologicae.* Vol. 1 of *Opera.* Amsterdam: Johan Blaeu, 1650.

———. *Opera theologica.* 2 vols. Amsterdam: Johan Blaeu, 1650–65.

Epistle of Barnabas, The. ANF, I, 133–49.

Erbkam, Heinrich Wilhelm. *Geschichte der protestantischen Sekten im Zeitalter der Reformation.* Hamburg and Gotha: Perthes, 1848.

Erigena, Johannes Scotus. *The Division of Nature* (1681). Translated by Myra L. Uhlfelder. Indianapolis: Bobbs-Merrill, 1976.

Ernesti, Heinrich Friedrich Theodor Ludwig. *Die Ethik des Apostels Paulus in ihren Grundzügen dargestellt.* Göttingen: Vandenhoeck & Ruprecht, 1880.

Ernesti, Johann August. *Opuscula theologica.* Leipzig: Fritsch, 1773.

Erskine, Thomas. *The Unconditional Freeness of the Gospel: In Three Essays.* Boston: Crocker & Brewster, 1828.

Eschelbacher, Joseph. *Das Judentum und des Wesen des Christentums.* Berlin: Poppelauer, 1905.

Eschenmeyer. *See* Kerner, J.

Espenberger, Johannes Nepomuk. *Die Elemente der Erbsünde nach Augustin und der Frühscholastik.* Mainz: Kirchheim & Co., 1905.

Essenius, Andreas. *Dissertatione de subjectione Christi ad legem divinam.* Utrecht: Antonii Smytegelt, 1666.

Eucken, Rudolf. *Hauptprobleme der Religionsphilosophie der Gegenwart.* Berlin: Reuther & Reichard, 1907.

———. *Der Wahrheitsgehalt der Religion.* 2nd ed. Leipzig: Veit & Comp., 1905.

Eusebius of Caesarea. *Ecclesiastical History. NPNF* (2), I, 73–404.

———. *The Proof of the Gospel.* Translated by W. J. Farrar. Grand Rapids: Baker, 1981.

Everling, Otto. *Die paulinische Angelologie und Dämonologie.* Göttingen: Vandenhoeck & Ruprecht, 1888.

Eyre, William. *Vindiciae justificationis gratuitae.* London: Edward Forrest, 1654.

Fabius, Dammes Paulus Dirk. *De doodstraf.* Amsterdam: Van Schaïk, 1906.

———. *Schuld en straf.* Leiden: Donner, 1900.

Fairbairn, Andrew Martin. *The Philosophy of the Christian Religion.* London: Hodder & Stoughton, 1905.

———. *The Place of Christ in Modern Theology.* New York: Scribner, 1913.

Familler, I. *Pastoral-Psychiatrie: Ein Handbuch für die Seelsorge der Geisteskranken.* Freiburg i.B.: Herder, 1888.

Faut, S. *Die Christologie seit Schleiermacher: Ihre Geschichte und ihre Begründung.* Tübingen: Mohr, 1907.

Feder, Alfred Leonhard. *Justins des Märtyrers Lehre von Jesus Christus dem Messias und dem menschgewordenen Sohn Gottes.* Freiburg i.B.: Herder, 1906.

Feine, Paul. *Jesus Christus und Paulus.* Leipzig: Hinrichs, 1902.

Felten, Joseph. *Neutestamentliche Zeitgeschichte: Oder, Judentum und Heidentum zur Zeit Christi und der Apostel.* 2 vols. Regensburg: Manz, 1910.

Fendt, Leonhard. *Die Dauer der öffentlichen Wirksamkeit Jesu.* Munich: Lentner, 1906.

Fichte, Johann Gottlieb. *Die Anweisung zum seligen Leben oder auch die Religionslehre.* Berlin: Verlag der Realschulbuchhandlung, 1806.

———. *Die Bestimmung des Menschen.* Leipzig: Reclam, 1879.

————. *The Science of Ethics as Based on the Science of Knowledge*. Translated by A. E. Kroeger. Edited by William Torrey Harris. London: K. Paul, Trench, Trübner, 1897.

————. *Das System der Sittenlehre nach den Prinzipien der Wissenschaftslehre*. Hamburg: Meiner, 1798.

————. *The Vocation of Man*. Translated by Peter Preuss. Indianapolis: Hackett, 1987.

Fiebig, Paul. *Der Menschensohn: Jesu Selbstbezeichnung mit besonderer Berücksichtigung des aramäischen Sprachgebrauches für "Mensch."* Tübingen: Mohr, 1901.

Fischer, Kuno. *J. G. Fichte und seine Vorgänger*. 2nd ed. Munich: Basserman, 1884.

Fiske, John. *Through Nature to God*. Boston and New York: Houghton, Mifflin, & Company, 1899.

Fleisch, Paul. *Die innere Entwicklung der deutschen Gemeinschaftsbewegung in den Jahren 1906 und 1907*. Leipzig: H. G. Wallmann, 1908.

Flier, Albert van der. *Specimen historico-theologicum de Johanne Coccejo, anti-scholastico*. Utrecht: Kemink et Filius, 1859.

Fock, Otto. *Der Socinianismus nach seiner Stellung in der Gesammtentwicklung des christlichen Geistes, nach seinem historischen Verlauf und nach seinem Lehrbegriff*. Kiel: C. Schröder, 1847.

Forbes, John. *Instructiones historico-theologicae de doctrina Christiana*. Amsterdam: Ludovicum Elzevirium, 1645.

Formula of Concord. In vol. 3 of *Creeds of Christendom*, edited by Philip Schaff and revised by David S. Schaff, 93–180. 6th ed. New York: Harper & Row, 1931. Reprinted, Grand Rapids: Baker, 1983.

Forrest, David W. *The Authority of Christ*. Edinburgh: T&T Clark, 1906.

Forsyth, Peter Taylor. *The Person and Place of Jesus Christ*. Boston: Pilgrim Press, 1909.

Francken, Aegidius. *Kern der Christelyke leere, dat is de waerheden van den hervormde Godsdienst eenvoudig ter nedergestelt, en met de oeffening der waere Godtzaligheyd aengedrongen*. Rotterdam: Losel, 1756.

Frank, Franz Hermann Reinhold. *System der christlichen Wahrheit*. 2nd ed. 4 vols in 2. Erlangen: A. Deichert, 1884.

————. *Theologie der Concordienformel*. 4 vols. in 2. Erlangen: T. Blaesing, 1858–65.

Frazer, James George. *The Golden Bough: Studies in Magic and Religion*. London and New York: Macmillan, 1900.

Fricke, Gustav Adolf. *Der paulinische Grundbegriff der δικαιοσυνη θεου erörtert auf Grund von Röm. 3:21–26*. Leipzig: Böhme, 1888.

*Frommel, Gaston. *La psychologie du pardon dans ses rapports avec la croix de Jésus Christ*. 1905.

*Fruytier, Jacobus. *Klaer en kort vertoog van de valsheit en gedeformeertheit van het gevoelen der sogen. Hebreen*. 1697.

Füllkrug, Gerhard. *Der Gottesknecht des Deuterojesaja*. Göttingen: Vandenhoeck & Ruprecht, 1899.

Funke, Bernhard. *Grundlagen und Voraussetzung der Satisfaktionstheorie des hl. Anselm von Canterbury*. Münster: Schöningh, 1903.

Galley, Alfred. *Die Busslehre Luthers und ihre Darstellung in neuester Zeit*. Gütersloh: Bertelsmann, 1900.

Gangauf, Theodor. *Metaphysische Psychologie des heiligen Augustinus*. Augsburg: K. Kollmann, 1852.

Gass, Wilhelm. *Geschichte der protestantischen Dogmatik*. 4 vols. Berlin: G. Reimer, 1854–67.

Geelkerken, Johannes Gerardus. *De empirische Godsdienstpyschologie*. Amsterdam: Scheltema & Holkema, 1909.

Geesink, Wilhelm. *De Ethiek in de Gereformeerde Theologie*. Amsterdam: Kirchner, 1897.

————. *Van 's Heeren Ordinantiën*. 1st ed. 3 vols. Amsterdam: W. Kirchener, 1907.

Gennrich, Paul. *Die Lehre von der Wiedergeburt: Die christliche Zentrallehre in dogmengeschichtlicher und religionsgeschichtlicher Beleuchtung*. Leipzig: Deichert, 1907.

Gerber, H. *Leo Taxils Palladsmusroman*. Berlin, 1897.

Gerhard, Johann. *Loci theologici.* 9 vols. Edited by E. Preuss. Berlin: G. Schlawitz, 1863–75.

Gerretsen, Jan Hendrik. *Rechtvaardigmaking bij Paulus in verband met de prediking van Christus in de synopticien de beginselen der Reformatie.* Nijmegen: Firma H. ten Hoet, 1905.

———. *De val des menschen: Dogmatisch fragment.* Nijmegen: Ten Hoet, 1909.

Gess, Wolfgang Friedrich. *Die Lehre von der Person Christi entwickelt aus dem Selbstbewusstsein Christi und dem Zeugnisse der Apostel.* Basel: Bahnmaiers Buchhandlung, 1856.

Gestrin, E. T. *Die Rechtfertigungslehre der Professoren der Theologie Johannes Tobias Beck, O. F. Myrberg und A. W. Ingman, geprüft und beleuchtet von mehreren evangelischen Theologen.* Berlin: Wiegandt & Grieben, 1891.

Gewin, Bernard. *Beginselen der strafrecht.* Leiden: Brill, 1907.

Giesebrecht, Friedrich. *Die Geschichtlichkeit des Sinaibundes.* Königsberg: Thomas & Oppermann, 1900.

———. *Der Knecht Jahves des Deuterojesaja.* Königsberg in Preußen: Thomas & Oppermann, 1902.

Giesen, Alexander. *Der Zeugniszwang gegen die Presse: Historische und kritische Beiträge.* Frankfurt a.M.: Neuer Frankfurter Verlag, 1906.

Gifford, Edwin Hamilton. *The Incarnation: A Study of Philippians II:5–11.* New York: Dodd, Mead, & Co., 1897.

Gihr, Nikolaus. *Das heilige Messopfer, dogmatisch, liturgisch, und aszetisch erklärt.* 6th ed. Freiburg i.B.: Herder, 1897.

———. *The Holy Sacrifice of the Mass: Dogmatically, Liturgically, and Ascetically Explained.* Translated from the German. St. Louis: Herder, 1902.

*Gill, M. *Practical Essay on the Death of Christ.* 1786.

Giran, Etienne. *A Modern Job: An Essay on the Problem of Evil.* Translated by Alfred Leslie Lilley and Fred Rothwell. Chicago: Open Court Publishing Co., 1916.

Girgensohn, Karl. *Zwölf Reden über die christliche Religion.* Munich: Beck, 1906.

Glas, John. *The Testimony of the King of Martyrs concerning His Kingdom: John xviii.36, 37 Explained and Illustrated in Scripture Light.* Edinburgh: G. Lyon, 1729.

Glöel, Johannes. *Der heilige Geist in der Heilsverkündigung des Paulus.* Halle: M. Niemeyer, 1888.

Glossner, Michael. *Die Lehre des hl. Thomas vom Wesen der göttlichen Gnade gegenüber der neuesten Deutung derselben durch H. v. Kuhn, aus ihren Principien wieder hergestellt.* Mainz: Kirchheim, 1871.

Godet, Frédéric Louis, ed. *The Atonement in Modern Religious Thought: A Theological Symposium.* London: Clarke, 1900.

———. *Commentary on John's Gospel.* Grand Rapids: Kregel Publications, 1978.

———. *Commentary on Romans.* Translated by Alexander Cusin. Grand Rapids: Kregel Publications, 1977.

———. *A Commentary on the Gospel of St. Luke.* Translated by E. W. Shalders and M. D. Cusin. 2nd ed. New York: I. K. Funk, 1887.

Goebel, Max, and Theodor Link. *Geschichte des christlichen Lebens in der rheinisch-westphälischen evangelischen Kirche.* 3 vols. Koblenz: K. Bädeker, 1849–60.

Goguel, Maurice. *L'apôtre Paul et Jésus-Christ.* Paris: Fischbacher, 1904.

Gomarus, Franciscus. *Opera theologica omnia.* Amsterdam: J. Jansson, 1664.

Goodwin, John. *An Exposition of the Ninth Chapter of the Epistle to the Romans with the Banner of Justification Displayed, to Which Is Added, Eirēnomachia.* London: Baynes & Son, 1835.

Gore, Charles. *Dissertations on Subjects Connected with the Incarnation.* London: Murray, 1895.

———. *The Incarnation of the Son of God.* London: Murray, 1891.

———, ed. *Lux Mundi.* 13th ed. London: Murray, 1892.

———. *The New Theology and the Old Religion.* London: Murray, 1907.

Görres, Joseph von. *Die christliche Mystik*. Regensburg: G. J. Manz, 1836.

Gottschick, Johannes. *Die Kirchlichkeit der sogenannten kirchlichen Theologie*. Freiburg i.B.: J. C. B. Mohr, 1890.

Götz, Walther. *Paulus: Der wahrhaftige Zeuge Jesu Christi*. Hannover: Feesche, 1903.

Gouda Quint, Pieter Jurranian. *De zondeloosheid van Jezus Christus*. Utretcht: n.p., 1862.

Grass, Karl Konrad. *Zur Lehre von der Gottheit Jesu Christi*. Gütersloh: Bertelsmann, 1900.

Grau, Rudolf Friedrich. *Das Selbstbewusstsein Jesu*. Nördlingen: C. H. Beck, 1887.

Grawitz, Paul. *Ueber Leben und Tod*. Greifswald: Julius Abel, 1896.

Gregory of Nazianzus. *Theological Orations*. *NPNF* (2), VII, 309–18.

Gregory of Nyssa. *The Catechetical Oration*. Translated by J. H. Srawley. Cambridge: Cambridge University Press, 1903.

———. *Greater Catechism*. *NPNF* (2), V, 471–512.

Gregory the Great. *Epistles*. *NPNF* (2), XIII, 1–111.

Greijdanus, Seakle. *Toerekeningsgrond van het peccatum originans*. Amsterdam: Bottenburg, 1906.

Gressmann, Hugo. *Der Ursprung der israelitisch-jüdischen Eschatologie*. Göttingen: Vandenhoeck & Ruprecht, 1905.

Gretillat, Augustin. *Exposé de Théologie Systématique*. 4 vols. Paris: Fischbacher, 1885–92.

Griffith-Jones, E. *The Ascent through Christ: A Study of the Doctrine of Redemption in Light of the Theory of Evolution*. New York: Edwin S. Gorham, 1901. Reprinted, 1978.

Groe, Theodorus van der. *Toetssteen der waare en valsche genade*. 8th ed. 2 vols. Rotterdam: H. van Pelt & A. Douci Pietersz., 1752–53.

Grotius, Hugo. *A Defence of the Catholic Faith concerning the Satisfaction of Christ, against Faustus Socinus*. Translated by Frank Hugh Foster. Andover: Draper, 1889.

Grünberg, Paul. *Philipp Jakob Spener*. 3 vols. Göttingen: Vandenhoeck & Ruprecht, 1893–1906.

———. *Das Übel in der Welt und Gott*. Lichterfelde-Berlin: Runge, 1907.

Grützmacher, Richard H. *Is Jezus bovennatuurlijke wijze geboren?* Translated from the German by W. Back. Baarn: Hollandia-Drukkerij, 1909.

Güder, Eduard. *Die Lehre von der Erscheinung Jesu Christi unter den Todten in ihrem Zusammenhang mit der Lehre von den letzten Dingen*. Bern: Jent & Reinert, 1853.

Gunkel, Hermann. *Zum religionsgeschichtlichen Verständnis des Neuen Testaments*. Göttingen: Vandenhoeck & Ruprecht, 1903.

Gutberlet, Constantin. *Der Kampf um die Seele: Vorträge über die brennenden Fragen der modernen Psychologie*. Mainz: Kirchheim, 1903.

Guthe, Hermann. *De foederis notione Jeremiana*. Leipzig: Hinrichs, 1877.

Haeckel, Ernst. *The History of Creation: Or, The Development of the Earth and Its Inhabitants by the Action of Natural Causes*. Translated from the German, revised by E. R. Lankester. 2 vols. New York: D. Appleton, 1883.

———. *Natürliche Schöpfungsgeschichte*. 5th ed. 2 vols. Berlin: G. Reimer, 1874.

Hafner, Georg. *Die Dämonischen des Neuen Testaments*. Frankfurt a.M.: Brechert, 1894.

Hahn, August, et al. *Bibliothek der Symbole und Glaubensregeln der alten Kirche*. 3rd ed. Breslau: E. Morgenstern, 1897.

Hahn, Georg Ludwig. *Die Theologie des Neuen Testaments*. 8 vols. Leipzig: Dörffling & Franke, 1854–.

Hall, Francis J. *The Kenotic Theory Considered with Particular Reference to Its Anglican Forms and Arguments*. New York: Longmans Green, 1898.

Häring, Theodor. *The Christian Faith*. Translated by John Dickie and George Ferries. 2 vols. London: Hodder & Stoughton, 1913.

————. *Zu Ritschls Versöhnungslehre.* Zürich: Hohr, 1888.

————. *Zur Versöhnungslehre: Eine dogmatische Untersuchung.* Göttingen: Vandenhoeck & Ruprecht, 1893.

Harnack, Adolf von. *Das apostolische Glaubensbekenntnis.* Berlin: Haack, 1892.

————. *The Expansion of Christianity in the First Three Centuries.* Translated by James Moffat. 2 vols. New York: Williams & Norgate, 1904–5.

————. *History of Dogma.* Translated by N. Buchanan, J. Millar, E. B. Speirs, and W. McGilchrist. Edited by A. B. Bruce. 7 vols. London: Williams & Norgate, 1896–99.

————. *Die Mission und Ausbreitung des Christentums in den ersten drei Jahrhunderten.* 2 vols. Leipzig: J. C. Hinrichs, 1905.

————. *Reden und Aufsätze.* 2nd ed. 2 vols. Giessen: A. Töpelmann, 1906.

————. *Das Wesen des Christentums.* Leipzig: Hinrichs, 1902.

————. *What Is Christianity?* Translated by Thomas Bailey Saunders. New York: Harper, 1957.

Harnisch, F. Wilhelm. *Das Leiden, beurteilt vom theistischen Standpunkt.* Halle: E. Karras, 1880.

Hartmann, Eduard von. *Das Christentum des Neuen Testaments.* 2nd ed. Sachsa i.H.: Haacke, 1905.

————. *Gesammelte Studien und Aufsätze.* Berlin: C. Duncker, 1876.

————. *Die Krisis des Christentums in der modernen Theologie.* Berlin: C. Duncker, 1880.

————. *Philosophie des Unbewussten.* 9th ed. 2 vols. Berlin: C. Duncker, 1882.

————. *Religionsphilosophie.* 2nd ed. 2 vols. Bad Sachsa i.H.: Hermann Haacke, 1907.

————. *Schellings philosophisches System.* Leipzig: H. Haacke, 1897.

————. *Die Selbstzersetzung des Christentums und die Religion der Zukunft.* 3rd ed. Leipzig: Friedrich, 1888.

————. *Das sittliche Bewusstsein.* Leipzig: W. Friedrich, 1886.

Hartog, Arnold Hendrik de. *De heilsfeiten: Een beschouwing.* Amersfoort: Veen, 1907.

Hase, Karl A. von. *Protestantische Polemik.* 5th ed. Leipzig: Breitkopf & Härtel, 1891.

Hastie, William. *The Theology of the Reformed Church in Its Fundamental Principles.* Edinburgh: T&T Clark, 1904.

Haupt, Erich. *Die Bedeutung der heiligen Schrift für den evangelischen Christen.* Bielefeld and Leipzig: Velhagen & Klasing, 1891.

Hayman, Henry. *"Why We Suffer," and Other Essays.* London: W. H. Allen & Co., 1890.

Heer, Joseph Michael. *Die Stammbäume Jesu nach Matthäus und Lukas: Ihre ursprüngliche Bedeutung und Textgestalt und ihre Quellen.* Freiburg i.B.: Herder, 1910.

Hegel, Georg Wilhelm Friedrich. *Sämtliche Werke.* 26 vols. Stuttgart: F. Frommann, 1949–59.

Hehn, Johannes. *Sünde und Erlösung nach biblischer und babylonischer Anschauung.* Leipzig: J. C. Hinrichs, 1903.

Heidanus, Abraham. *Corpus theologiae christianae in quindecim locos digestum.* 2 vols. Leiden, 1686.

Heidegger, Johann Heinrich. *Corpus theologiae Christianae.* 2 vols. Zürich: J. H. Bodmer, 1700.

Heim, Karl. *Das Wesen der Gnade und ihr Verhältnis zu der natürlichen Funktion des Menschen bei Alexander Halesius.* Leipzig: M. Heinsius Nachfolger, 1907.

Heinrich, Joann Baptist, and Constantin Gutberlet. *Dogmatische Theologie.* 2nd ed. 10 vols. Mainz: Kirchheim, 1881–1900.

Heinrichs, Ludwig. *Die Genugtuungstheorie des hl. Anselmus von Canterbury.* Paderborn: Schöningh, 1909.

Henderson, Henry F. *The Religious Controversies of Scotland.* Edinburgh: T&T Clark, 1905.

Hengel, Wessel Albertus van. *De gave van talen: Pinksterstudie.* Leiden: D. Noothoven van Goor, 1864.

Hengstenberg, Ernst Wilhelm. *Christologie des Alten Testaments und Commentar über die messianischen Weissagungen.* 3 vols. Berlin: L. Oehmigke, 1854–56.

———. *Christology of the Old Testament.* Translated by R. Keith. Edited by T. K. Arnold. Grand Rapids: Kregel Publications, 1988.

Heppe, Heinrich. *Die Dogmatik der evangelisch-reformirten Kirche.* Elberfeld: R. L. Friderichs, 1861.

———. *Dogmatik des deutschen Protestantismus im sechzehnten Jahrhundert.* 3 vols. Gotha: F. A. Perthes, 1857.

———. *Geschichte des Pietismus und der Mystik in der reformirten Kirche: Namentlich der Niederlande.* Leiden: Brill, 1879.

Herrmann, Johannes. *Die Idee der Sühne im Alten Testament.* Leipzig: Hinrichs, 1905.

Herrmann, Wilhelm. *Der Verkehr des Christen mit Gott.* 4th ed. Stuttgart: Cotta, 1903.

———. *Warum bedarf unser Glaube geschichtlicher Thatsachen?* Halle a.S.: Niemeyer, 1886.

———. *Worum handelt es sich in dem Streit um das Apostolikum?* Leipzig: F. W. Grunow, 1893.

Hettinger, Franz. *Apologie des Christentums.* Edited by Eugen Müller. 9th ed. 5 vols. Freiburg i.B. and St. Louis: Herder, 1906–8.

Heulhard, Arthur. *Le mensonge Chrétien (Jésus-Christ n'a pas existé).* . . . Paris: A. Heulhard, 1908.

Heymans, Gerard. *Der toekomstige eeuw der psychologie.* Groningen: Wolters, 1909.

*Heyne, B. *Über Besessenheitswahn bei geistigen Erkrankungszuständen.* Paderborn, 1904.

Hoadly, Benjamin. *Several Discourses concerning the Terms of Acceptance with God.* London: Knapton, 1727.

Hobbes, Thomas. *Leviathan.* London: J. M. Dent, 1924.

Hodge, Archibald Alexander. *The Atonement.* Philadelphia: Presbyterian Board of Publication, 1867.

Hodge, Charles. *Systematic Theology.* 3 vols. New York: Charles Scribner Sons, 1888.

Hoekstra, Sytze. *Grondslag, wezen, en openbaring van het godsdienstig geloof volgens de Heilige Schrift.* Rotterdam: Altmann & Roosenburg, 1861.

———. *Vrijheid in verband met zelfbewustheid, zedelijkheid en zonde.* Amsterdam: P. N. van Kampen, 1858.

Hoekstra, Tjeerd. *Immanente Kritik zur kantischen Religionsphilosophie.* Kampen: J. H. Kok, 1909.

Hoensbroech, Paul van. *Christ und Widerchrist: Ein Beitrag zur Vertheidigung der Gottheit Jesu Christi und zur Charakteristik des Unglaubens in der protestantischen Theologie.* Freiburg i.B.: Herder, 1892.

———. *Religion oder Aberglaube.* Berlin: Hermann Walther, 1897.

Hofmann, Johann Christian Konrad von. *Der Schriftbeweis.* 2nd ed. 2 vols. Nördlingen: Beck, 1857–60.

———. *Weissagung und Erfüllung im Alten und Neuen Testamente.* 2 vols. Nördlingen: Beck, 1841.

Hofstede de Groot, Petrus. *De Groninger Godgeleerdheid in Hunne Eigenaardigheid.* Groningen: Scholtens, 1855.

Hollaz, David. *Examen theologicum acroamaticum.* Rostock and Leipzig: Russworm, 1718.

Holtius, Nicolaus. *De zondaar gerechtvaerdigt om niet, uit de genade Gods.* Leiden: Johannes Hasebroek; Amsterdam: Nicolaas Byl, 1757.

Holtzmann, Heinrich Julius. *Lehrbuch der neutestamentlichen Theologie.* 2 vols. Freiburg and Leipzig: Mohr, 1897.

———. *Das messianische Bewusstsein Jesu.* Tübingen: Mohr, 1907.

Holtzmann, Oskar. *War Jesus Ekstatiker? Eine Untersuchung zum Leben Jesu.* Tübingen: Mohr, 1903.

Holzmeister, Urban. *Dominus autem Spiritus est, 2 Cor. 3,17: Eine exegetische Untersuchung mit einer Übersicht über die Geschichte der Erklärung dieser Stelle.* Innsbruck: Rauch, 1908.

Homanner, Wilhelm. *Die Dauer der öffentlichen Wirksamkeit Jesu.* Freiburg i.B.: Herder, 1908.

*Honert, J. van den. *Verhandeling van de rechtvaerdiging des sondaars uyt en door het geloove.*

Honert, Taco Hajo van den. *Het hoogepriesterschap van Christus naar de ordening van Melchisedek, door eene ontleding en verklaaring van het sevende hoofd-stuk in Paulus Send-briev aan den Hebreen.* Amsterdam: Wetstein, 1712.

Hoornbeek, Johannes. *Disputate theologiae practicae, de theologiae praxi.* Utrecht, 1659–61.

———. *Socianismus confutatus.* 3 vols. Utrecht, 1650–54.

———. *Summa controversiarum religionis, cum infidelibus, haeriticis et schismaticis.* Utrecht: J. à Waersberge, 1658.

Hulsius, Johannes. *De hedendaagsche antinomianery met die der Engelsche en oude wetbestryders vergeleken, en zoo uit het Woord Gods, als uit de formulieren van eenigheid der Gereformeerde Kerken klaar en grondig wederlegt en dere zelve schadelykheit aangewesen.* 2nd ed. Rotterdam: David Vermeulen, 1738.

Hünefeld, E. *Römer 5,12–21: Von neuem erklärt.* Leipzig: G. Strübig, 1895.

Ignatius of Antioch. *Epistle to the Ephesians.* In *The Apostolic Fathers,* translated by Francis X. Glimm, Joseph M.-F. Marique, and Gerald G. Walsh, 87–95. Fathers of the Church 1. Washington, DC: Catholic University of America Press, 1947.

———. *Epistle to the Magnesians.* In *The Apostolic Fathers,* translated by Francis X. Glimm, Joseph M.-F. Marique, and Gerald G. Walsh, 96–101. Fathers of the Church 1. Washington, DC: Catholic University of America Press, 1947.

———. *Epistle to the Smyrnaeans.* In *The Apostolic Fathers,* translated by Francis X. Glimm, Joseph M.-F. Marique, and Gerald G. Walsh, 118–23. Fathers of the Church 1. Washington, DC: Catholic University of America Press, 1947.

Ihmels, Ludwig. *Die Auferstehung Jesu Christi.* Leipzig: Deichert, 1906.

———. *Wer war Jesus? Was wollte Jesus?* Leipzig: Deichert, 1905.

Illingworth, J. R. *Personality, Human and Divine.* London: Macmillan & Co., 1895.

Irenaeus. *Against Heresies. ANF,* I, 309–567.

Jansen, Gerardus Martinus. *Praelectiones theologiae dogmaticae.* 3 vols in 2. Utrecht: Van Rossum, 1875–79.

———. *Theologia dogmatica specialis.* Utrecht, 1877–79.

Jenner, Katherine Lee Rawlings. *Christ in Art.* London: Methuen & Co., 1906.

Jensen, Peter Christian Albrecht. *Das Gilgamesch-Epos in der Weltliteratur.* Strassburg: Trübner, 1906.

Jeremias, Alfred. *Babylonisches im Neuen Testament.* Leipzig: J. C. Hinrichs, 1904.

Jodl, Friedrich. *Geschichte der Ethik in der neueren Philosophie.* 2 vols. Stuttgart: Cotta, 1882–89.

John of Damascus. *Exposition of the Orthodox Faith. NPNF* (2), IX, 259–360.

———. *Writings.* Translated by Frederic H. Chase Jr. Fathers of the Church 37. Washington, DC: Catholic University of America Press, 1958. Reprinted, 1970.

Jones, John Cynddylan. *Primeval Revelation: Studies in Genesis I–VIII.* London: Hodder & Stoughton, 1897.

Jong, Albertus de. *Geschiedenis en begrip van gratie.* Rotterdam: De Vries, 1902.

Joseph, Max. *Zur Sittenlehre des Judenthums.* Berlin: Poppelauer, 1902.

Josephus, Flavius. *The Works of Josephus.* Translated by William Whiston. New updated edition. Peabody, MA: Hendrickson, 1987.

Jülicher, Adolf. *Paulus und Jesus.* Tübingen: Mohr, 1907.

Junius, Franciscus. *Opuscula theologica selecta.* Edited by Abraham Kuyper. Amsterdam: F. Muller, 1882.

———. *Theses theologicae.* In vol. 1 of *Opuscula theologica selecta,* edited by Abraham Kuyper. Amsterdam: F. Muller, 1882.

Jurgens, William A., ed. *The Faith of the Early Fathers.* 3 vols. Collegeville, MN: Liturgical Press, 1970–79.

Justin Martyr. *Dialogue with Trypho. ANF,* I, 194–270.

————. *The First and Second Apologies. ANF*, I, 163–93.

Kaftan, Julius. *Brauchen wir ein neues Dogma?* 2nd ed. Bielefeld: Velhagen & Klasing, 1890.

————. *Dogmatik.* Tübingen: Mohr, 1901.

————. *Jesus und Paulus: Eine freundschaftliche Streitschrift gegen die religionsgeschichtlichen Volksbücher von D. Bousset und D. Wrede.* Tübingen: Mohr, 1906.

————. *The Truth of the Christian Religion.* Translated by George Ferries. 2 vols. Edinburgh: T&T Clark, 1894.

————. *Das Wesen der christlichen Religion.* Basel: C. Detloff, 1888.

————. *Zur Dogmatik: Sieben Abhandlung aus der "Zeitschrift für Theologie und Kirche."* Tübingen: Mohr, 1904.

Kaftan, Theodor. *Der Mensch Jesus: Der einige Mittler zwischen Gott und den Menschen.* Berlin: Edwin Runge, 1908.

————. *Moderne Theologie des alten Glaubens.* Schleswig: J. Bergas, 1905.

Kähler, Martin. *Angewandte Dogmen.* 2nd ed. Leipzig: Deichert, 1908.

————. *The So-Called Historical Jesus and the Historic Biblical Christ.* Translated by Carl E. Braaten. Philadelphia: Fortress Press, 1988.

————. *Die Wissenschaft der christlichen Lehre.* 3rd ed. Leipzig: A. Deichert, 1905.

*————. *Zur Lehre von der Versöhnung.* 1898.

Kahnis, Karl Friedrich August. *Die Erfüllung der Zeiten.* Leipzig: Böhme & Dreschner, 1877.

————. *Die lutherische Dogmatik, historisch-genetisch dargestellt.* 3 vols. Leipzig: Dörffling & Francke, 1861–68.

Kalb, Ernst. *Kirchen und Sekten der Gegenwart.* Stuttgart: Verlag der Buchhandlung der Evangelischen Gesellschaft, 1907.

Kalthoff, Albert. *Das Christusproblem: Grundlinien zu einer Sozialtheologie.* 2nd ed. Leipzig: Diederichs, 1903.

————. *Die Entstehung des Christentums: Neue Beiträge zum Christusproblem.* Leipzig: Diederichs, 1904.

————. *Was wissen wir von Jesus?* Schmargendorf-Berlin: Renaissance-Otto Lehrmann, 1904.

Kampschulte, Franz Wilhelm, and Walter Goetz. *Johann Calvin: Seine Kirche und sein Staat in Genf.* 2 vols. Leipzig: Duncker & Humblot, 1869–99.

Kant, Immanuel. *Religion within the Limits of Reason Alone.* Translated by Theodore M. Greene and Hoyt H. Hudson. New York: Harper & Brothers, 1934.

Karge, Paul. *Geschichte des Bundesgedankens im Alten Testament.* 2 vols. Münster: Aschendorff, 1910.

Kattenbusch, Ferdinand. *Das apostolische Symbol: Seine Entstehung, sein geschichtlicher Sinn, seine ursprüngliche Stellung im Kultus und in der Theologie der Kirche.* 2 vols. Leipzig: Hinrichs, 1894–1900.

————. *Zur Würdigung des Apostolikums.* Leipzig: Grunow, 1892.

Kautsky, Karl. *Foundations of Christianity.* New York: Monthly Review Press, 1972.

Keckermann, Bartholomaeus. *Systema s.s. theologiae.* Hannover, 1603.

Keerl, P. F. *Der Mensch, das Ebenbild Gottes.* 2 vols. Basel: Bahnmeier, 1861–66.

Keim, Theodor. *Geschichte Jesu von Nazara in ihrer Verkettung mit dem Gesamtleben seines Volkes.* 3 vols. Zürich: Orell, Füssli, 1867–72.

Keppler, Paul Wilhelm von. *Das Problem des Leidens in der Moral.* Freiburg i.B.: Herder, 1894.

Kerner, Justinus. *Geschichten Besessener neuerer Zeit: Beobachtungen aus dem Gebiete kakodämonisch-magnetischer Erscheinungen; Nebst Reflexionen von C. A. Eschenmayer über Besessenseyn und Zauber.* Stuttgart: Wachendorf, 1834.

Kiesewetter, Carl. *Geschichte des neueren Occultismus.* Leipzig: Friedrich, 1891.

Kirn, Otto. *Glaube und Geschichte.* Leipzig: Edelmann, 1900.

————. *Grundriss der evangelischen Dogmatik.* Leipzig: Deichert, 1905.

Klausner, Joseph. *Die messianischen Vorstellungen des jüdischen Volkes im Zeitalter der Tannaiten.* Berlin: M. Poppelauer, 1904.

Kleman, David. *De Orde des Heils, of het verband tusschen genade en plicht.* Amsterdam: P. Conradi, 1776.

Kleutgen, Joseph. *Die Theologie der Vorzeit vertheidigt.* 2nd ed. 5 vols. Münster: Theissing, 1867–74.

Knapp, Georg Christian. *Vorlesungen über die christliche Glaubenslehre nach dem Lehrbegriff der evangelischen Kirche.* Edited by Carl Thilo. 2 vols. Halle: Buchhandlung des Waisenhauses, 1827.

Kneib, Philipp. *Moderne Leben-Jesu-Forschung unter dem Einflusse der Psychiatrie.* Mainz: Kirchheim & Co., 1908.

Knieschke, Wilhelm. *Die Erlösungslehre des Qoran.* Berlin: Runge, 1910.

Knopf, Rudolf. *Das nachapostolische Zeitalter: Geschichte der christlichen Gemeinden vom Beginn der Flavierdynastie bis zum Ende Hadrians.* Tübingen: J. C. B. Mohr, 1905.

Knuttel, Willem Pieter Cornelis. *Balthasar Bekker: De bestrijder van het bijgeloof.* 's Gravenhage: M. Nijhoff, 1906.

Köberle, Justus. *Sünde und Gnade im religiösen Leben des Volkes Israel bis auf Christum: Eine Geschichte des vorchristlichen Heilsbewusstseins.* Munich: Beck, 1905.

Koch, Hugo. *Pseudo-Dionysius Areopagita in seinen Beziehungen zum Neuplatonismus und Mysterienwesen.* Mainz: Kirchheim, 1900.

Koch, Max. *Der ordo salutis in der alt-lutherischen Dogmatik.* Berlin: A. Duncker, 1899.

Koelman, Jacobus. *Historisch verhael nopende der Labadisten.* Amsterdam: Johannes Boeckholt, 1683.

Kögel, Julius. *Christus der Herr: Erläuterungen zu Philipper 2,5–11.* Gütersloh: Bertelsmann, 1908.

———. *Der Sohn und die Söhne: Eine exegetische Studie zu Hebräer 2,5–18.* Gütersloh: Bertelsmann, 1904.

Kohlbrugge, J. H. F. *Der Atavismus.* Utrecht: G. J. C. Scrinerius, 1897.

Kohler, Josef. *Das Wesen der Strafe.* Würzburg: Druck & Verlag der Stahel'schen Universitäts-Buch- und Kunsthandlung, 1888.

Köhler, Karl. *Der Prophetismus der Hebräer und die Mantik der Griechen in ihrem gegenseitigen Verhältniss.* Darmstadt: Eduard Zernin, 1860.

*Köhler, L. *Biblische Geschichte.*

Köhler, Walther. *Katholizismus und Reformation: Kritisches Referat über die wissenschaftlichen Leistungen der neueren katholischen Theologie auf dem Gebiete der Reformationsgeschichte.* Giessen: Töpelmann, 1905.

Kölbing, Paul. *Die geistige Einwirkung der Person Jesu auf Paulus.* Göttingen: Vandenhoeck & Ruprecht, 1906.

Kolde, Theodor. *Die Heilsarmee: Ihre Geschichte und ihr Wesen.* Erlangen: Deichert, 1885.

———. *Die kirchlichen Bruderschaften und das religiöse Leben im modernen Katholizismus.* Erlangen: n.p., 1895.

———. *Der Methodismus und seine Bekämpfung.* Erlangen: Deichert, 1886.

Kölling, Wilhelm. *Die satisfactio vicaria: Das ist die Lehre von den stellvertretenden Genugthuung des Herrn Jesu.* 2 vols. Gütersloh: Bertelsmann, 1897–99.

König, Eduard. *Das alttestamentliche Prophetentum und die moderne Geschichtsforschung.* Gütersloh: Bertelsmann, 1910.

———. *Geschichte des Reiches Gottes.* Berlin: M. Warneck, 1908.

König, Joseph. *Die Theologie der Psalmen.* Freiburg i.B.: Herder, 1857.

Koppe, Rensinus. *Eenige strafrechtelijke beschouwingen in verband met het beginsel van de wet van 12. Febr. 1901.* Groningen: Jan Haan, 1906.

Korff, Emmanuel. *Die Anfänge der Foederaltheologie und ihre Ausgestaltung in Zürich und in Holland.* Bonn: E. Eisele, 1908.

Korff, Theodor. *Die Auferstehung Christi und die radikale Theologie: Die Feststellung und Deutung der geschichtlichen Tatsachen der Auferstehung des Herrn durch die fortgeschrittene moderne Theologie.* Halle: Strien, 1908.

Köstlin, Julius. *Theology of Luther in Its Historical Development and Inner Harmony.* Translated by Charles E. Hay. 2 vols. Philadelphia: Lutheran Publication Society, 1897.

Krabbe, Otto. *Die Lehre von der Sünde und vom Tode in ihrer Beziehung zu einander und zu der Auferstehung Christi: Exegetische-dogmatisch entwickelt.* Hamburg: Friedrich Perthes, 1836.

Kraetzschmar, Richard. *Die Bundesvorstellung im Alten Testament in ihrer geschichtlichen Entwicklung.* Marburg: N. G. Elwert, 1896.

Kreibig, Gustav. *Die Versöhnungslehre auf Grund des christlichen Bewusstseins.* Berlin: Wiegandt & Grieben, 1878.

Kreyher, Johannes. *Die jungfräuliche Geburt des Herrn.* Gütersloh: Bertelsmann, 1904.

Krop, Frédéric J. *La pensée de Jésus sur Royaume de Dieu, d'aprés les évangiles synoptiques avec un appendice sur la question du "Fils de l'homme."* Paris: Fischbacher, 1897.

Krüger, Gustav. *Das Dogma von der Dreieinigkeit und Gottmenschheit in seiner geschichtlichen Entwicklung.* Tübingen: Mohr, 1905.

Kübel, Robert Benjamin. *Über den Unterschied zwischen der positiven und der liberalen Richtung in der modernen Theologie.* 2nd ed. Munich: C. H. Beck, 1893.

Kuenen, Abraham. *De godsdienst van Israël tot den ondergang van den Joodschen staat.* 2 vols. Haarlem: Kruseman, 1869–70.

———. *De profeten en de profetie onder Israël.* 2 vols. in 1. Leiden: P. Engels, 1875.

———. *The Prophets and Prophecy in Israel.* Translated by Adam Milroy. London: Longmans, Green, 1877.

———. *Volksgodsdienst en Wereldgodsdienst.* Leiden: S. C. van Doesburgh, 1882.

Kühl, Ernst. *Die Heilsbedeutung des Todes Christi: Biblisch-theologische Untersuchung.* Berlin: Wilhelm Hertz, 1890.

Kühner, Karl. *Augustin's Anschauung von der Erlösungsbedeutung Christi im Verhältnis zur voraugustin'schen Erlösungslehre bei den griechischen und lateinischen Vätern.* Heidelberg: K. Groos, 1890.

Kunze, Johannes W. *Die ewige Gottheit Jesu Christi.* Leipzig: Dörffling & Franke, 1904.

Kurtz, Johann Heinrich. *Geschichte des alten Bundes.* 2nd ed. 2 vols. Berlin: J. A. Wohlgemuth, 1853–58.

Kuyper, Abraham. *Encyclopaedie der Heilige Godgeheerdherd.* 2nd ed. 3 vols. Kampen: Kok, 1908–9.

———. *De engelen Gods.* Amsterdam: Höveker & Wormser, 1900.

———. *De gemeene gratie.* 3 vols. Amsterdam: Höveker & Wormser, 1902–4.

———. *De leer der Verbonden.* Kampen: Kok, 1909.

———. *Particular Grace: A Defense of God's Sovereignty in Salvation.* Grandville, MI: Reformed Free Publishing Association, 2001.

———. *De vleeschwording des Woords.* Amsterdam: Wormser, 1887.

———. *Het werk van den Heiligen Geest.* 3 vols. in 1. Amsterdam: Wormser, 1888–89.

———. *The Work of the Holy Spirit.* 3 vols. Translated by Henri de Vries. New York: Funk & Wagnalls, 1900.

Kuyper, Abraham, Jr. *De band des verbonds.* Amsterdam: Kirchner, 1906.

———. *De vastigheid des verbonds.* Amsterdam: Kirchner, 1908.

Kuyper, Herman Huber. *Evolutie of Revelatie.* Amsterdam: Höveker & Wormser, 1903.

———. *Hamabdil: Van de heiligheid van het Genadeverbond.* Amsterdam: Bottenburg, 1907.

———. *De Post-Acta of Nahandelingen van de Nationale Synode van Dordrecht in 1618 en 1619 gehouden, naar den authentieken tekst in het Latijn en het Nederlandsch uitgegeven. . . .* Amsterdam: Höveker & Wormser, 1899.

Laehr, Hans. *Die Dämonischen des Neuen Testaments.* Leipzig: Richter, 1894.

Lagarde, Paul de. *Deutsche Schriften.* 4th ed. Göttingen: Horstmann, 1903.

Lagrange, Marie-Joseph. *Études sur les religions sémitiques.* Paris: Victor Lecoffre, 1903.

———. *Le Messianisme chez les juifs (150 av. J.-C. 200 ap. J.-C.)*. Paris: J. Gabalda, 1909.

Laidlaw, John. *The Bible Doctrine of Man*. Edinburgh: T&T Clark, 1895.

Lake, Kirsopp. *The Historical Evidence for the Resurrection of Jesus Christ*. London and New York: Williams & Norgate, 1907.

Lamennais, Félicité Robert de. *Essai sur l'indifférence en matière de religion*. 4 vols. Paris: Tournachon-Molin et H. Seguin, 1818–23.

———. *Essay on Indifference in Matters of Religion*. Translated by Henry Edward John Stanley. London: John Macqueen, 1895.

Lang, August. *Johann Calvin: Ein Lebensbild zu seinem 400. Geburtstag am 10. Juli 1909*. Leipzig: R. Haupt, 1909.

Lang, Heinrich. *Versuch einer christlichen Dogmatik allen denkenden Christen dargeboten*. 2nd ed. Berlin: G. Reimer, 1868.

Lange, Johann Peter. *Christliche Dogmatik*. 3 vols. Heidelberg: K. Winter, 1852.

Lasaulx, Ernst von. *Die Sühnopfer der Griechen und Römer und ihr Verhältnis zu dem einen auf Golgotha*. Würzburg: Voigt & Mocker, 1841.

Lechler, Gotthard Victor. *Das apostolische und das nachapostolische Zeitalter*. Karlsruhe and Leipzig: H. Reuther, 1885.

Lecky, William Edward Hartpole. *Entstehungsgeschichte und Charakter des Methodismus*. Translated by Ferdinand Löwe. Leipzig, 1880.

Lehmann, Edvard. *Mystiek heidensche en christelijke*. Translated from the Danish by Jacqueline E. van der Waals. Utrecht: Honig, 1908.

Lehner, Friedrich August von. *Die Marienverehrung in den ersten Jahrhunderten*. 2nd ed. Stuttgart: Cotta, 1886.

Lehre der Heiligen Schrift vom Teufel, Die. Schönebeck: Berger, 1858.

Leibniz, Gottfried Wilhelm. *A System of Theology*. Translated by Charles William Russell. London: Burns & Lambert, 1850.

———. *Theodicy: Essays on the Goodness of God, the Freedom of Man, and the Origin of Evil*. Edited by Austin Farrer. Translated

by E. M. Huggard. 1951. Reprinted, La Salle, IL: Open Court, 1985.

Lemme, Ludwig. *Jesu Irrtumslosigkeit*. Berlin: Runge, 1907.

Lepsius, Johannes. *Reden und Abhandlungen*. 4 vols. Berlin: Reich-Christi Verlag, 1902.

Letter of Barnabas, The. In *The Apostolic Fathers*, translated by Francis X. Glimm, Joseph M.-F. Marique, and Gerald G. Walsh, 191–224. Fathers of the Church 1. Washington, DC: Catholic University of America Press, 1947.

Leydekker, Melchior. *Dissertatio historico-theologica de Antinomis antiquis & novis*. 3 vols. Utrecht: Halma, 1696.

———. *Fax veritatis, seu exercitationes ad nonnullas controversias quae hodie in Belgio potissium moventur, multa ex parte theologico-philosophicae*. Leiden: Daniel Gaesbeeck & Felicem Lopez, 1677.

———. *Filius Dei Sponsor*. Amsterdam: Jacobus van Hardenberg, 1708.

———. *Historische en godgeleerde oeffeningen, over de oorsprong, voortgang, en gevoelens van de oude en nieuwe Antinomianen*. 's Gravenhage: Kitto, 1700.

———. *De veritate religionis reformatae seu evangelicae: libri vii. quibus doctrina christiana de oeconomia s.s. Trinitatis in negotio salutis humanae explicatur, et reformata fides ex certis principiis, in verbo Dei revelatis, congruo nexu demonstratur et defenditur*. Utrecht: Rudolph Zyll, 1688.

———. *Vis Veritatis, seu disquisitionum ad nonnullas controversias, quae hodie in Belgio potissimum moventur*. Utrecht: Franciscum Halma, 1679.

Lidgett, John Scott. *The Spiritual Principle of the Atonement as a Satisfaction Made to God for the Sins of the World*. 2nd ed. London: Charles H. Kelley, 1898.

Liebermann, Franz B. *Institutiones theologicae*. 8th ed. 2 vols. Mainz: Kirchheim, 1857.

Lietzmann, Hans. *Der Menschensohn: Ein Beitrag zur neutestamentlichen Theologie*. Freiburg i.B.: J. C. B. Mohr, 1896.

———. *Der Weltheiland*. Bonn: Marcus & Weber, 1909.

Lightfoot, Joseph Barber. *St. Paul's Epistle to the Galatians*. 10th ed. London: Macmillan & Co., 1890.

Liguori, Alfonso Maria dé. *Theologia moralis*. 4 vols. Edited by P. Leonardi Gaudé. Graz: Akademische Druck- und Verlagsanstalt, 1954.

Limborch, Phillip van. *Theologia christiana ad praxin pietatis ac promotionem pacis christianae unice directa*. Amsterdam: Wetstein, 1735.

Lippert, Julius. *Allgemeine Geschichte des Priesterthums*. 2 vols. Berlin: T. Hoffman, 1883–84.

Lipsius, Richard Adelbert. *Lehrbuch der evangelisch-protestantischen Dogmatik*. Braunschweig: C. A. Schwetschke, 1893.

Lobstein, Paul. *Études christologiques: La doctrine des fonctions médiatrices du Sauveur*. Paris: Fischbacher, 1891.

———. *Petrus Ramus als Theologe: Ein Beitrag zur Geschichte der protestantischen Theologie*. Strassburg: C. F. Schmidt, 1878.

———. *The Virgin Birth of Christ*. Translated by Victor Leuliette. London: Williams & Norgate, 1903.

Lodge, Oliver. *The Substance of Faith Allied with Science: A Catechism for Parents and Teachers*. 6th ed. London: Methuen, 1907.

Löhr, Max. *Alttestamentliche Religions-Geschichte*. Leipzig: Göschen, 1906.

Loisy, Alfred Firmin. *Evangelium und Kirche*. Munich: Kirchheim, 1904.

———. *The Gospel and the Church*. Philadelphia: Fortress Press, 1976.

*Lombard, Peter. *Commentaries on the Psalms and St. Paul.*

———. *Sententiae in IV liberis distinctae*. 3rd ed. 2 vols. Grottaferrata: Colleggi S. Bonaventurae et Claras Aquas, 1971–81.

Lomer, Georg. *Jesus Christus vom Standpunkt des Psychiaters*. Bamberg: Handels-Druckkerei, 1905.

Lonkhuijzen, Jan van. *Hermann Friedrich Kohlbrügge en zijn Prediking*. Wageningen: Vada, 1905.

Loofs, Friedrich. *Die Auferstehungsberichte und ihr Wert*. Leipzig: Mohr, 1898.

———. *Die Auferstehungsberichte und ihr Wert*. 3rd ed. Tübingen: Mohr, 1908.

———. *Leitfaden zum Studium der Dogmengeschichte*. 4th ed. Halle a.S.: M. Niemeyer, 1906.

———. *Nestoriana: Die Fragmente des Nestorius*. Halle a.S.: M. Niemeyer, 1905.

Lotze, Hermann. *Mircrocosmus*. Translated by Elizabeth Hamilton and E. E. Constance Jones. New York: Scribner & Welford, 1866.

Lucius, Ernst. *Die Anfänge des Heiligenkults in der christlichen Kirche*. Tübingen: Mohr, 1904.

Lütgert, Wilhelm. *Die Anbetung Jesu*. Gütersloh: Bertelsmann, 1904.

Luthardt, Christoph Ernst. *Compendium der Dogmatik*. Leipzig: Dörffling & Franke, 1865.

———. *Die Lehre vom freien Willen und seinem Verhältnis zur Gnade in ihrer geschichtlichen Entwicklung*. Leipzig: Dörffling & Franke, 1863.

Luther, Martin. *Commentary on Genesis*. Grand Rapids: Zondervan, 1958.

Lüttge, Willy. *Die Rechtfertigungslehre Calvins und ihre Bedeutung für seine Frömmigkeit*. Berlin: Reuther & Reichard, 1909.

Maccovius, Johannes. *Collegia theologica*. 3rd ed. Franeker: Joannis Fabiani Deuring, 1641.

———. *Loci communes theologici*. Amsterdam: n.p., 1658.

———. *Redivivus*. Franeker: Idzardus Albertus et Johannes Arcerius, 1654.

Macdonald, Donald. *Creation and the Fall: A Defence of the First Three Chapters of Genesis*. Edinburgh: T. Constable, 1856.

Maistre, Joseph Marie comte de. *Les soirées de Saint-Pétersbourg: Ou, entretiens sur le gouvernement temporel de la Providence, suivies d'un traité sur les sacrifices*. 5th ed. Lyon: J. B. Pélagaud, 1845.

Mannens, Paulus. *Theologiae dogmaticae institutiones*. 3 vols. Roermand: Romen, 1910–15.

Manzoni, Cesare. *Compendium theologiae dogmaticae, e praecipusis scholasticis antiquis et modernis redactum.* 4 vols. Turin: Berruti, 1909.

Marck, Johannes. *Historia paradisi.* Amsterdam: Gerardus Borstius, 1705.

Maresius, Samuel. *Collegium theologicum sive systema breve universae theologiae comprehensium octodecim disputationibus.* Groningen: Francisci Bronchorstii, 1659.

———. *Systema theologicum.* Groningen: Aemilium Spinneker, 1673.

Martensen, Hans Lassen. *Christian Dogmatics: A Compendium of the Doctrines of Christianity.* Translated by William Urwick. Edinburgh: T&T Clark, 1871.

———. *Christian Ethics.* Edinburgh: T&T Clark, 1842.

Marti, Karl. *Geschichte der Israelitischen Religion.* 3rd ed. Strassburg: F. Bull, 1897.

Martin, Hugh. *The Atonement: In Its Relations to the Covenant, the Priesthood, the Intercession of Our Lord.* London: James Nisbet, 1870. Reprinted, Edinburgh: Knox Press, 1976.

Martin, Konrad. *Die Harmonie des Alten und des Neuen Testaments.* Mainz: Franz Kirchheim, 1877.

Mason, Arthur James. *Conditions of Our Lord's Life on Earth.* London and New York: Longmans, Green, 1896.

Mastricht, Peter van. *Theoretico-practica theologia.* Utrecht: Appels, 1714.

Maurenbrecher, Max. *Von Nazareth nach Golgotha: Untersuchung über die weltgeschichtlichen Zusammenhänge des Urchristentums.* Berlin-Schöneberg: Buchverlag der Hilfe, 1909.

Maurice, Frederick Denison. *The Doctrine of Sacrifice Deduced from the Scriptures.* Cambridge: Macmillan, 1854.

McTaggart, John McTaggart Ellis. *Some Dogmas of Religion.* London: E. Arnold, 1906.

Mees, R. P. *Wetenschappelijke karakterkennis.* 's Gravenhage: Nijhoff, 1907.

Meffert, Franz. *Die geschichtliche Existenz Christi.* 2nd ed. Mönchengladbach: Verlag der Zentralstelle des Volksvereins für das katholische Deutschland, 1904.

Meij, Reinhart van der. *Een studie over de grondslagen der zoogenaamde "Nieuwe Richting" in de strafrechtswetenschap.* Leiden: S. C. van Doesburgh, 1904.

Melanchthon, Philipp. *Confessyon of the fayth of the Germaynes; The apologie.* Amsterdam: Theatrum Orbis Terrarum, 1576. Reprinted, Norwood, NJ: W. J. Johnson, 1976.

———. *Loci communes.* Berolini: G. Schlawitz, 1856.

Ménégoz, Eugène. *La mort de Jésus et le dogme de l'expiation.* Paris: Fischbacher, 1905.

Menzel, Wolfgang. *Christliche Symbolik.* 2nd ed. 2 vols. Regensburg: Manz, 1855.

Merle d'Aubigné, J. H. *L'expiation de la croix.* Paris, 1867.

Meyer, Arnold. *Die Auferstehung Christi: Die Berichte über Auferstehung, Himmelfahrt, und Pfingsten, ihre Entstehung, ihr geschichtlicher Hintergrund und ihre religiöse Bedeutung.* Tübingen: Mohr, 1905.

———. *Jesu Muttersprache: Das galiläische Aramaisch in seiner Bedeutung für die Erklärung der Reden Jesu und den Evangelien überhaupt.* Freiburg: Mohr, 1896.

———. *Wer hat das Christentum begründet, Jesus oder Paulus?* Tübingen: Mohr, 1907.

Meyer, Heinrich August Wilhelm, et al. *Critical and Exegetical Hand-book to the New Testament.* 9 vols. New York: Funk & Wagnalls, 1884.

Meyer, Max. *The Sinlessness of Jesus.* Translated from the German. New York: Eaton & Mains, 1897.

Michel, Oskar. *Vorwärts zu Christus! Fort mit Paulus! Deutsche Religion!* Berlin: Seeman, 1906.

Miehe, Hugo. *Die Erscheinung des Lebens.* Leipzig: Teubner, 1907.

Milligan, George. *The Theology of the Epistle to the Hebrews.* Edinburgh: T&T Clark, 1899.

Milligan, William. *The Ascension and Heavenly Priesthood of Our Lord.* London: Macmillian, 1892.

Minges, Parthenius. *Die Gnadenlehre des Duns Scotus auf ihren angeblichen Pelagianismus und Semipelagianismus geprüft.* Münster: Aschendorff, 1906.

Moberly, Robert Campbell. *Atonement and Personality.* 6th ed. London: Murray, 1907.

Modderman, Antony Ewoud Jan. *Straf geen kwaad.* Amsterdam: Muller, 1864.

Mohila, Peter. *The Orthodox Confession of Faith.* Translated by Ronald Peter Popivchak. Washington, DC: n.p., 1975.

Möhler, Johann Adam. *Symbolik: Oder Darstellung der dogmatischen Gegensätze der Katholiken und Protestanten nach ihren öffentlichen Bekenntnisschriften.* Mainz: F. Kupferberg, 1838.

Moll, Wilhelm. *Johannes Brugman en het godsdienstig leven onzer vaderen in de vijftiende eeuw.* 2 vols. Amsterdam: G. Portielje, 1854.

Möller, Wilhelm. *Die messianische Erwartung der vorexilischen Propheten: Zugleich ein Protest gegen moderne Textsplitterung.* Gütersloh: C. Bertelsmann, 1906.

Monnier, Henri. *Essai sur la rédemption.* Neuilly: La Cause, 1929.

Moor, Bernhard de. *Commentarius perpetuus in Johannis Marckii compendium theologiae christianae didactico-elencticum.* 7 vols. in 6. Leiden: J. Hasebroek, 1761–71.

Müller, A. *Jesus ein Arier: Ein Beitrag zur völkischen Erziehung.* Leipzig: Mar Sängeward, 1904.

Müller, C. Th. *Die Rätsel des Todes.* Barmen: Wuppertaler Traktat-Gesellschaft, 1905.

Müller, Ernst Friedrich Karl. *Die Bekenntnisschriften der reformierten Kirche.* Leipzig: Deichert, 1903.

———. *Our Lord: Belief in the Deity of Christ.* New York: Eaton & Mains, 1908.

Müller, Gustav Adolf. *Die leibliche Gestalt Jesu Christi nach der schriftlichen und monumentalen Urtradition.* Graz: Verlagsbuchhandlung Styria, 1909.

Müller, Joseph T. *Die symbolischen Bücher der evangelisch-lutherischen Kirche.* 8th ed. Gütersloh: Bertelsmann, 1898.

Müller, Julius. *The Christian Doctrine of Sin.* Translated by Rev. Wm. Urwick. 5th ed. 2 vols. Edinburgh: T&T Clark, 1868.

———. *Dogmatische Abhandlungen.* Bremen: C. E. Müller, 1870.

Münscher, Wilhelm. *Lehrbuch der christlichen Dogmengeschichte.* Edited by Daniel von Coelln. 3rd ed. Cassel: J. C. Krieger, 1832–38.

Musculus, Wolfgang. *Loci communes theologiae sacrae.* Basileae: Ex officina Heruagiana,1567.

Nagel, Ernst. *Das Problem der Erlösung.* Basel: Reich, 1901.

Nägelsbach, Karl Friedrich von. *Homerische Theologie.* Nürnberg: Geiger, 1861.

———. *Der nachhomerische Theologie des griechischen Volksglaubens bis auf Alexander.* Nürnberg: Conrad Gieger, 1857.

Nauville, Ernest. *Le problème du mal.* Geneva: Librairie Cherbuliez, 1868.

Neander, August. *Geschichte der Pflanzung und Leitung der christlichen Kirche durch die Apostel.* 5th ed. 2 vols. Gotha: F. A. Perthes, 1890.

———. *History of the Planting and the Training of the Christian Church by the Apostles.* Translated by J. E. Ryland. 2 vols. London: Bell & Daly, 1864.

Nebe, August. *Die Kindheitsgeschichte unseres Herrn Jesu Christi nach Matthäus und Lukas.* Stuttgart: Greiner & Pfeiffer, 1893.

Nes, Hendrik Marius van. *De Adventstijd der wereld.* Rotterdam: Wenk & Birkhoff, 1896.

———. *De Graaf van Zinzendorf.* Nijkerk: Callenbach, 1902.

Nevius, John Livingston. *Demon Possession and Allied Themes, Being an Inductive Study of Phenomena of Our Own Times.* Chicago: F. H. Revell, 1896.

Niemeyer, H. A. *Collectio confessionum in ecclesiis reformatis publicatarum.* 2 vols. Leipzig: Sumptibis Iulii Klinkhardti, 1840.

Nirschl, Joseph. *Ursprung und Wesen des Bösen nach der Lehre des heiligen Augustinus.* Regensburg: F. Pustet, 1854.

Nitzsch, Carl Emmanuel. *System der christlichen Lehre.* 5th ed. Bonn: Adolph Marcus, 1844.

————. *System of Christian Doctrines.* Edinburgh: T&T Clark, 1849.

Nitzsch, Friedrich A. B. *Lehrbuch der evangelischen Dogmatik.* Prepared by Horst Stephan. 3rd ed. Tübingen: J. C. B. Mohr, 1902.

Northcote, J. Spencer. *Maria in den Evangelien.* Mainz: Kirchheim, 1869.

————. *Mary in the Gospels.* London: Burns, Lambert, & Oates, 1867.

Norton, Frederick Owen. *A Lexicographical and Historical Study of διαθήκη from the Earliest Times to the End of the Classical Period.* Chicago: University of Chicago Press, 1908.

Nösgen, Karl Friedrich. *Der einzige Reine unter den Unreinen.* Gütersloh: Bertelsmann, 1908.

————. *Geschichte der neutestamentlichen Offenbarung.* 2 vols. Munich: Beck, 1891–93.

————. *Das Wesen und Wirken des Heiligen Geistes.* 2 vols. Berlin: Trowitzsch, 1905–7.

Notton, M. *Harnack und Thomas von Aquin.* Paderborn: Schöningh, 1906.

Oehler, Gustav Friedrich. *Theology of the Old Testament.* Translated by Ellen D. Smith and Sophia Taylor. Edinburgh: T&T Clark, 1892–93.

Oesterley, William Oscar Emil. *The Evolution of the Messianic Idea.* London: Pitman, 1908.

Oettingen, Alexander von. *Das göttliche "Noch nicht!" Ein Beitrag zur Lehre vom Heiligen Geist.* Erlangen: Deichert, 1895.

————. *Lutherische Dogmatik.* 2 vols. Munich: C. H. Beck, 1897.

————. *Die Moralstatistik in ihrer Bedeutung für eine Socialethik.* Erlangen: Deichert, 1882.

————. *Die Moralstatistik und die christliche Sittenlehre.* Erlangen: Deichert, 1882.

Olevian, Caspar. *De substantia foederis gratuiti inter Deum et electos: Itemque de mediis, quibus ea ipsa substantia nobis communicatur.* Geneva: Vignon, 1585.

————. *Het wezen van het Genadeverbond, in Geschriften.* Den Haag: Het Reformatische Boek, 1963.

Oort, Henricus Lucas. *De uitdrukking ὁ υἱὸς τοῦ ἀνθρώπου in het Nieuwe Testament.* Leiden: Brill, 1893.

Oorthuys, Gerardus. *De Anthropologie van Zwingli.* Leiden: E. J. Brill, 1905.

Oosterzee, Johannes Jacobus van. *Christelijke dogmatiek.* 2nd ed. 2 vols. Utrecht: Kemink, 1876.

————. *Christian Dogmatics.* Translated by J. Watson and M. Evans. 2 vols. New York: Scribner, Armstrong, 1874.

————. *Christologie: Onderzoek naar den persoon en het werk des verlossers.* 3 vols. Rotterdam: Van der Meer & Verbruggen, 1855–61.

————. *Het leven van Jezus.* 3 vols. Utrecht: Keminck, 1846–51.

Opzoomer, Cornelis. *De wijsbegeerte den mensch met zich zelven verzoenende.* Leiden: n.p., 1846.

Orchard, William Edwin. *Modern Theories of Sin.* London: Clark, 1909.

Orelli, Conrad. *The Old Testament Prophecy of the Consummation of God's Kingdom.* Translated by J. S. Banks. Edinburgh: T&T Clark, 1892.

Origen. *Against Celsus. ANF,* IV, 395–669.

————. *Commentary on the Gospel of John. ANF,* X, 297–410.

————. *Homilies on Leviticus.* Translated by Gary Wayne Barkley. Washington, DC: Catholic University of America Press, 1990.

————. *Homilies on Luke.* Translated by Joseph T. Lienhard. Washington, DC: Catholic University of America Press, 1996.

————. *On First Principles. ANF,* IV, 239–384.

————. *Origen Commentary on the Gospel of Matthew. ANF,* X, 411–512.

Orr, James. *The Christian View of God and the World as Centering in the Incarnation.* New York: Randolph, 1893.

————. *God's Image in Man and Its Deface-ment in the Light of Modern Denials.* London: Hodder & Stoughton, 1906.

————. *The Resurrection of Jesus.* London: Hodder & Stoughton, 1908.

————. *The Ritschlian Theology and the Evangelical Faith.* London: Hodder & Stoughton, 1897.

————. *The Virgin Birth of Christ.* London: Hodder & Stoughton, 1908.

Ostwald, Wilhelm. *Energetische Grundla-gen der Kulturwissenschaft.* Leipzig: W. Klinkhardt, 1909.

Oswald, Johann Heinrich. *Die dogmatische Lehre von den heiligen Sakramenten der katholischen Kirche.* 2nd ed. 2 vols. Münster: Aschendorff, 1864.

————. *Religiöse Urgeschichte der Menschheit.* Paderborn: Ferdinand Schöningh, 1887.

Overbeck, Franz. *On the Christianity of Theology.* Translated by John Elbert Wilson. San Jose, CA: Pickwick Publications, 2003.

————. *Ueber die Christlichkeit unserer heuti-gen Theologie.* 2nd ed. Leipzig: Naumann, 1903.

Owen, John. *A Continuation of the Exposition of the Epistle of Paul to the Hebrews viz, on the sixth, seventh, eighth, ninth, and tenth chapters: wherein together with the explica-tion of the text and context, the priesthood of Christ . . . are declared, explained, and con-firmed.* London: Nathaniel Ponder, 1680.

————. *The Works of John Owen.* Edited by William H. Goold. Edinburgh: T&T Clark, 1862.

Pareau, Lodewijk Garlach, and P. Hofstede de Groot. *Lineamenta theologiae Christianae universae: Ut disquisitionis de religione una verissima et praestantissima, sive brevis conspectus dogmatices et apologetics Chris-tianae.* 3rd ed. Groningen: C. M. van Bol-huis Hoitsema, 1848.

Pareus, David. *Ad Corinthios priorem S. Pauli apostoli epistolam commentarius.* Heidel-berg: Jonae Rhodii, 1613.

Park, Edwards Amasa, ed. *The Atonement: Discourses and Treatises.* Boston: Congre-gational Board of Publication, 1860.

Pastor [Shepherd] of Hermas, The. ANF, II, 1–58.

*Paul, Ludwig. *Die Vorstellung vom Messias und vom Gottesreich bei den Synoptikern.* Bonn, 1895.

Paulsen, Friedrich. *System der Ethik mit einem Umriss der Staats- und Gesellschaftslehre.* 2 vols. Berlin: Hertz, 1889.

Pécaut, Félix. *Le Christ et la conscience.* Paris: Cherbuliez, 1859.

Perkins, William. *The workes of that famous and worthy minister of Christ.* 3 vols. London: John Legatt, 1612–18.

Perles, Felix. *Was lehrt uns Harnack?* Frankfurt a.M.: Kauffman, 1902.

Perrone, Giovanni. *Praelectiones theologicae.* 9 vols. Louvain: Vanlinthout & Vandezande, 1838–43.

Pesch, Christian. *Praelectiones dogmaticae.* 9 vols. Freiburg: Herder, 1902–10.

Pesch, Heinrich. *Lehrbuch der Nationalökono-mie.* 5 vols. Freiburg: Herder, 1905–23.

————. *Teaching Guide to Economics.* Trans-lated by Rupert J. Ederer. 3 vols. Lewiston, NY: Lampeter: Edwin Mellen, 2002–3.

Petavius, Dionysius. *De Theologicis Dogmati-bus.* 8 vols. Paris: Vives, 1865–67.

Petersen, Emil. *Die wunderbare Geburt des Heilandes.* Tübingen: Mohr, 1909.

Pfaff, Christoph Matthäus. *Introductio in his-toriam theologiae literariam notis amplissi-mis.* 3 vols. Tübingen: Cottae, 1724–26.

Pfaff, Friedrich. *Schöpfungsgeschichte.* Frank-furt a.M.: Heyder & Zimmer, 1877.

Pfanner, Tobias. *Systema theologiae gentilis purioris.* Basel: Joh. Hermann Widerhold, 1679.

Pfannmüller, Gustav. *Jesus im Urteil der Jahr-hunderte.* Leipzig: Tuebner, 1908.

Pfennigsdorf, Emil. *Persönlichkeit: Christliche Lebensphilosophie für moderne Menschen.* 5th ed. Schwerin: Bahn, 1908.

Pfleiderer, Otto. *Das Christusbild des urchrist-lichen Glaubens in religionsgeschichtlicher Beleuchtung.* Berlin: Georg Reimer, 1903.

————. *The Development of Theology in Ger-many since Kant, and Its Progress in Great Britain since 1825.* Translated by J. Frederick Smith. 2nd ed. London: Swan Sonnen-schein; New York: Macmillan, 1893.

———. *Die Entwicklung der protestantischen Theologie in Deutschland seit Kant und in Grossbritannien seit 1825*. Freiburg i.B.: Mohr, 1891.

———. *Grundriss der christlichen Glaubens- und Sittenlehre*. Berlin: G. Reimer, 1888.

———. *Der Paulinismus: Ein Beitrag zur Geschichte der urchristlichen Theologie*. Leipzig: O. R. Reisland, 1890.

———. *Religionsphilosophie auf geschichtli-cher Grundlage*. 3rd ed. Berlin: G. Reimer, 1896.

———. *Vorbereitung des Christentums in der griechischen Philosophie*. Halle: Gebauer & Schwetschke, 1904.

Philippi, Friedrich A. *Commentary on St. Paul's Epistle to the Romans*. 2 vols. Trans-lated by John Shaw Banks. Edinburgh: T&T Clark, 1878–79.

———. *Kirchliche Glaubenslehre*. 3rd ed. 7 vols. in 10. Gütersloh: Bertelsmann, 1870–90.

———. *Der thätige Gehorsam Jesu Christi: Ein Beitrag zur Rechtfertigungslehre*. Ber-lin: Ludwig Oehmigke, 1841.

Philo of Alexandria. *On the Creation of the Cosmos*. Translated by David T. Runia. Bos-ton: Brill, 2001.

Pichler, A. *Die Theologie des Leibniz aus sämmtlichen gedruckten und vielen noch ungedruckten Quellen*. 2 vols. Munich: J. G. Cotta, 1869–70.

Pictet, Benedictus. *De christelijke god-geleert-heid, en kennis der zaligheid*. Translated by Johannes Wesselius. 's Gravenhage: Pieter van Thol, 1728.

———. *Christian Theology*. Translated by Frederick Reyroux. Philadelphia: Presbyte-rian Board of Publication, 1845.

Pijper, Fredrik. *Geschiedenis der boete en biecht in de Christelijke kerk*. 's Gravenhage: Nij-hoff, 1891.

Piscator, Johannes. *Commentarii in omnes libros Veteris Testamenti*. Herborn: Chris-topher Corvinus, 1646.

———. *Volumen thesium theologicarum: In illustri schola nassovica, partim Hernornae partim Sigenae disputatarum . . . praeaeside Joh. Piscator*. 2 vols in 1. Herborn: Christo-pher Corvinus, 1596.

Plange, Theodor J. *Christus—ein Inder? Versuch einer Entstehungsgeschichte des Christentums unter Benutzung der indi-schen Studien Louis Jacolliots*. Stuttgart: Schmidt, 1906.

Plato. *Protagorus*. Translated by C. C. W. Tay-lor. Oxford: Clarendon, 1976.

Plitt, Hermann. *Zinzendorfs Theologie*. 3 vols. in 1. Gotha: F. A. Perthes, 1869–74.

Pohle, Joseph. *Lehrbuch der Dogmatik*. 4th ed. Paderborn: Schöningh, 1912–14.

Polanus, Amandus. *Syntagma theologiae Chris-tianae*. 5th ed. Hannover: Aubry, 1624.

Polycarp. *Epistle to the Philippians*. In *The Apostolic Fathers*, translated by Francis X. Glimm, Joseph M.-F. Marique, and Gerald G. Walsh, 131–43. Fathers of the Church 1. Washington, DC: Catholic University of America Press, 1947.

Posnanski, Adolf. *Schiloh: Ein Beitrag zur Geschichte der Messiaslehre*. Leipzig: Hin-richs, 1904.

Powell, Henry Clark. *The Principle of the Incarnation with Especial Reference to the Relation between Our Lord's Divine Omni-science and His Human Consciousness*. Lon-don: Longmans Green, 1896.

Pressensé, Edmond de. *Études évangéliques*. Paris: C. Meyrueis, 1867.

———. *The Redeemer: A Sketch of the History of Redemption*. Translated from the 2nd edition by J. H. Myers. Boston: American Tract Society, 1867.

Preuss, Eduard. *The Romish Doctrine of the Immaculate Conception, Traced from Its Source*. Translated by George Gladstone. Edinburgh: T&T Clark, 1867.

Pseudo-Dionysius the Aereopagite. *The Divine Names and Mystical Theology*. Translated by John D. Jones. Milwaukee: Marquette University Press, 1980.

Pullan, Leighton. *The Atonement*. London: Longmans Green, 1906.

Quenstedt, Johann Andreas. *Theologia di- dactico-polemica sive systema theologicum.* 1685. English translation of chapters 1–3 in *The Nature and Character of Theology,* abridged, edited, and translated by Luther Poellot. St. Louis, MO: Concordia, 1986.

Rabinsohn, Marcus. *Le Messianisme dans la Talmud et les Midraschim.* Paris: A. Reiff, 1907.

Racovian Catechism, The. Translated by Thomas Rees. London, 1609. Reprinted, London, 1818.

Ramsay, William Mitchell. *Was Christ Born at Bethlehem?* London: Hodder & Stoughton, 1898.

Randolph, B. W. *The Virgin-Birth of Our Lord.* London and New York: Longmans Green, 1903.

Rasmussen, Emil. *Jesus: Eine vergleichende psychopathologische Studie.* Leipzig: Zeitler, 1905.

Rau, Albrecht. *Harnack, Goethe, D. Strauss, und L. Feuerbach über das Wesen des Christentums.* Delitzsch: C. A. Walter, 1903.

*Recolin, (Numa?). *La personne de Jésus- Christ et la théorie de kenosis.* Paris, 1890.

Reinhard, Franz Volkmar. *Grundriss der Dogmatik.* Munich: Seidel, 1802.

Reischle, Max Wilhelm Theodor. *Leitsätze für eine akademische Vorlesung über die christliche Glaubenslehre.* Halle a.S.: Niemeyer, 1899.

Renan, Ernest. *The Life of Jesus.* Buffalo: Prometheus Books, 1991.

Reusch, Franz Heinrich. *Bibel und Natur: Vorlesungen über die mosaische Urgeschichte und ihr Verhältnis zu den Ergebnissen der Naturforschung.* Freiburg i.B.: Herder, 1862.

———. *Nature and the Bible: Lectures on the Mosaic History of Creation in Its Relation to Natural Science.* Translated by Kathleen Lyttelton from the 4th German edition. Edinburgh: T&T Clark, 1886.

Reuter, Hermann. *Augustinische Studien.* Gotha: Perthes, 1887.

Ribot, Théodule. *L'hérédité psychologique.* Paris: F. Alcan, 1894.

Richter, August. *Geschichtsphilosophische Untersuchungen über den Begriff der Persönlichkeit.* Langensalza: H. Beyer & Söhne, 1907.

Ridderbos, Jan. *De Theologie van Jonathan Edwards.* 's Gravenhage: J. A. Nederbragt, 1907.

Riehm, Eduard. *Handwörterbuch des biblischen Altertums für gebildete Bibelleser.* 2 vols. Bielefeld and Leipzig: Velhagen & Hasms, 1893–94.

———. *Die messianische Weissagung: Ihre Entstehung, ihr zeitgeschichlicher Charakter und ihr Verhältnis zu der neutestamentlichen Erfüllung.* Gotha: Perthes, 1875.

Riggenbach, Eduard. *Die Auferstehung Jesu.* 2nd ed. Berlin: Edwin Runge, 1908.

———. *Der Begriff διαθηκη im Hebräerbrief.* Leipzig: A. Deichert'sche Verlagsbuchhandlung Nachf., 1908.

Ritschl, Albrecht. *The Christian Doctrine of Justification and Reconciliation.* Clifton, NJ: Reference Book Publishers, 1966.

———. *Die christliche Lehre von der Rechtfertigung und Versöhnung.* 4th ed. 3 vols. Bonn: A. Marcus, 1895–1903.

———. *Geschichte des Pietismus in der reformierten Kirche.* Bonn: A. Marcus, 1880.

———. *Unterricht in der christlichen Religion.* 3rd ed. Bonn: A. Marcus, 1886.

Rivetus, Andreas. *Operum theologicorum.* 3 vols. Rotterdam: Leers, 1651–60.

Robertson, Andrew. *History of the Atonement Controversy: In Connexion with the Secession Church, from Its Origin to the Present Time.* Edinburgh: Oliphant, 1846.

Robertson, John Mackinnon. *Pagan Christs: Studies in Comparative Hierology.* London: Watts, 1903.

Rocholl, Rudolf. *Die Fülle der Zeit.* Hannover: Carl Meyer, 1872.

———. *Die Philosophie der Geschichte.* 2 vols. Göttingen: Vandenhoeck & Ruprecht, 1877–93.

Rohden, Gustav von. *Erbliche Belastung und ethische Verantwortung.* Tübingen: Mohr, 1907.

————. *Das Wesen der Strafe im ethischen und strafrechtlichen Sinne.* Tübingen: Mohr, 1905.

Rohrbach, Paul. *Die Berichte über die Auferstehung Jesu Christi.* Berlin: Georg Reimer, 1898.

Rolffs, Ernst. *Harnacks Wesen des Christentums und die religiösen Strömungen der Gegenwart.* Leipzig: Hinrichs, 1902.

Römheld, Carl Julius. *Theologia sacrosancta: Grundlinien der biblischen Theologie.* 1st ed. 2 vols. Gotha: Schloeßmann, 1888–89.

Roozemeyer, *see* Baljon.

Roskoff, Gustav. *Geschichte des Teufels.* Leipzig: F. A. Brockhaus, 1869.

Rothe, Richard. *Theologische Ethik.* 2nd rev. ed. 5 vols. Wittenberg: Zimmerman, 1867–71.

Rousseau, Jean-Jacques. *Profession de foi du vicaire savoyard.* Paris: Persan et Cie, 1822.

————. *Profession of Faith of the Vicar of Savoy.* New York: P. Eckler, 1889.

Rüetschi, Rudolf. *Geschichte und Kritik der kirchlichen Lehre von der ursprünglichen Vollkommenheit und vom Sündenfall.* Leiden: Brill, 1881.

Runze, Georg. *Katechismus der Dogmatik.* Leipzig: J. J. Weber, 1898.

Sabatier, Auguste. "La doctrine de l'expiation et son évolution historique." In *Études de théologie et d'histoire: Publiées par mm. les professeurs de la Faculté de théologie protestante de Paris,* 6–76. Paris: Fischbacher, 1901.

————. *The Doctrine of the Atonement and Its Historical Evolution.* Translated by Victor Leulitte. New York: Putnam, 1904.

————. *Esquisse d'une philosophie de la religion d'après la psychologie et l'historie.* 7th ed. Paris: Fischbacher, 1903.

————. *La problème de la mort.* 1896.

Saintyves, Pierre. *Les vierges mères et les naissances miraculeuses.* Paris: Nourry, 1908.

Saltmarsh, John. *Free Grace, or, the Flowings of Christs Blood Free to Sinners.* London: Giles Calvert, 1647.

Sanday, William. *The Life of Christ in Recent Research.* Oxford: Clarendon Press, 1907.

Sanday, William, and Arthur C. Headlam. *A Critical and Exegetical Commentary on the Epistle to the Romans.* 5th ed. Edinburgh: T&T Clark, 1902.

Sandeman, Robert. *Letters on Theron and Aspasio.* Edinburgh: Sands, Murray, Donaldson & Cochran, 1759.

Sartorius, Ernst Wilhelm Christian. *The Doctrine of Divine Love.* Translated by Sophia Taylor. Edinburgh: T&T Clark, 1884.

————. *Die Lehre von Christi Person und Werk.* 3rd ed. Hamburg: F. Perthes, 1837.

————. *Die Lehre von der heiligen Liebe.* Stuttgart: S. G. Liesching, 1861.

Schaeder, Erich. *Das Evangelium Jesu und das Evangelium Gottes.* Gütersloh: Bertelsmann, 1906.

————. *Über das Wesen des Christentums und seine modernen Darstellungen.* Gütersloh: Bertelsmann, 1904.

Schaefer, Aloys. *Die Gottesmutter in der heiligen Schrift.* Münster: Aschendorffsche Buchhandlung, 1889.

————. *The Mother of Jesus in Holy Scripture.* Ratisbon: F. Pustet, 1913.

Schäfer, Rudolf. *Die Vererbung: Ein Kapitel aus einer zukünftigen psycho-physiologischen Einleitung in die Pädagogik.* Berlin: Reuther & Reichard, 1897.

Schaff, Philip. *The Creeds of Christendom.* Revised by David S. Schaff. 6th edition. 3 vols. New York: Harper & Row, 1931. Reprinted, Grand Rapids: Baker, 1983.

————. *The Person of Christ, the Miracle of History.* Translated from the German. New York: C. Scribner & Co., 1866.

————. *Die Sünde wider den Heiligen Geist und die daraus gezogenen dogmatischen und ethischen Folgerungen.* Halle: Lippert, 1841.

Schanz, Paul. *Das Alter des Menschengeschlechts nach der heiligen Schrift, der Profangeschichte und der Vorgeschichte.* Freiburg i.B.: Herder, 1896.

————. *A Christian Apology.* Translated by Michael F. Glancey and Victor J. Schobel, 4th rev. ed. Ratisbon: F. Pustet, 1891.

Schäzler, Constantin von. *Das Dogma von der Menschwerdung Gottes: Im Geiste des hl. Thomas.* Freiburg i.B.: Herder, 1870.

———. *Neue Untersuchungen über das Dogma von der Gnade und das Wesen des christlichen Glaubens.* Mainz: Kirchheim, 1867.

Scheeben, Matthias Joseph. *Handbuch der katholischen Dogmatik.* Edited by Leonhard Atzberger. 4 vol. 1874–98. Reprinted, Freiburg i.B.: Herder, 1933.

———. *A Manual of Catholic Theology: Based on Scheeben's "Dogmatik."* Translated and edited by Joseph Wilhelm and Thomas Bartholomew Scannell. 4th ed. 2 vols. London: Kegan Paul, Trench, Trübner & Co.; New York: Benziger Brothers, 1909.

Scheel, Otto. *Die Anschauung Augustins über Christi Person und Werk.* Tübingen: Mohr, 1901.

Schelling, F. W. J. *Ausgewählte Werke.* 4 vols. Darmstadt: Wissenschaftlichle Buchgesellschaft, 1968.

Schenkel, Daniel. *Die christliche Dogmatik vom Standpunkte des Gewissens aus dargestellt.* 2 vols. Wiesbaden: Kreidel & Niedner, 1858–59.

*Schermers. *De leer van Lombroso.* Heusden, 1896.

Schettler, Adolf. *Die paulinische Formel "durch Christus" untersucht.* Tübingen: Mohr, 1907.

Schiere, Nicolaus. *Doctrina testamentorum et foederum divinorum omnium.* Leovardiaw: M. Ingema, 1718.

Schiller, F., and W. Scherer. *Über die erste Menschengesellschaft.* Vol. 3 of *Thalia.* 3 vols. Leipzig: Georg Joachim Göscher, 1787–91.

Schlatter, Adolf von. *Jesu Gottheit und das Kreuz.* 1st ed. Gütersloh: Bertelsmann, 1901.

Schleiermacher, Friedrich. *The Christian Faith.* Edinburgh: T&T Clark, 1989.

Schmid, Heinrich Friedrich Ferdinand. *The Doctrinal Theology of the Evangelical Lutheran Church.* Translated by Charles A. Hay and Henry Jacobs. 5th ed. Philadelphia: United Lutheran Publication House, 1899.

———. *Die Dogmatik der evangelisch-lutherischen Kirche.* 7th ed. Gütersloh: Bertelsmann, 1893.

Schmidt, Wilhelm. *Christliche Dogmatik.* 4 vols. Bonn: E. Weber, 1895–98.

———. *Die verschiedenen Typen religiöser Erfahrung und die Psychologie.* Gütersloh: Bertelsmann, 1908.

Schmoller, Otto. *Die Lehre vom Reiche Gottes in den Schriften des Neuen Testaments.* Leiden: E. J. Brill, 1891.

Schneckenburger, Matthias. *Vorlesungen über die Lehrbegriffe der kleineren protestantischen Kirchenparteien.* Frankfurt: H. L. Brönner, 1863.

———. *Vorlesungen über neutestamentliche Zeitgeschichte.* Frankfurt a.M.: Brönner, 1862.

———. *Zur kirchlichen Christologie: Die orthodoxe Lehre vom doppelten Stande Christi nach lutherischer und reformirter Fassung.* Pforzheim: Flammer & Hoffmann, 1848.

Schneckenburger, Matthias, and Eduard Güder. *Vergleichende Dartstellung des lutherischen und reformierten Lehrbegriffs.* 2 vols. Stuttgart: J. B. Metzler, 1855.

Schnehen, Wilhelm von. *Der moderne Jesuskultus.* Frankfurt am Main: Neuer Frankfurter Verlag, 1906.

Schneider, Richard. *Christliche Klänge aus den Griechischen und Römischen Klassikern.* Leipzig: Siegismund & Volkening, 1877.

Schneider, Wilhelm. *Die Naturvölker: Missverständnisse, Missdeutungen, und Misshandlung.* 2 vols. Paderborn: Schöningh, 1885–86.

Schöberlein, Ludwig. *Prinzip und System der Dogmatik.* Heidelberg: C. Winter, 1881.

*Schoeler. *Das vatikanische Bild.* Gütersloh, 1898.

Scholten, Johannes Henricus. *Dogmatices christianae initia.* 2nd ed. Leiden: P. Engels, 1858.

————. *De Leer der Hervormde Kerk in Hare Grondbeginselen.* 2nd ed. 2 vols. Leiden: P. Engels, 1850–51.

————. *De vrije wil, kritisch onderzoek.* Leiden: P. Engels, 1859.

Schopenhauer, Arthur. *Die beiden Grundprobleme der Ethik.* 3rd ed. Leipzig: F. A. Brockhaus, 1881.

————. *Parerga and Paralipomena.* Translated by E. F. J. Payne. 2 vols. Oxford: Clarendon Press, 1974.

————. *Die Welt als Wille und Vorstellung.* 6th ed. Leipzig: Brockhaus, 1887.

————. *The World as Will and Representation.* Translated by E. F. J. Payne. New York: Dover Publications, 1966.

Schotel, Gilles Dionysius Jacobus. *Iets over de uitwendige gedaante van Jezus Christus.* 's Hertogenbosch: Gebroeders Muller, 1852.

Schulte, Adalbert. *Die messianischen Weissagungen des Alten Testaments nebst dessen Typen.* Paderborn: Ferdinand Schöningh, 1908.

*Schultens, J. J. *Uitvoerige Waerschuwing op verscheiden stukken der Kategismusverklaaringe van Alex. Comrie.* 1755.

Schultz, Hermann. *Alttestamentliche Theologie.* 4th ed. 2 vols. Göttingen: Vandenhoeck & Ruprecht, 1889.

————. *Der Begriff des stellvertretenden Leidens in Rücksicht auf Jes. 52,13 bis 53,12.* Basel: Bahnmaier Verlag, 1864.

————. *Grundriss der evangelischen Dogmatik zum Gebrauche bei akademischen Vorlesungen.* Göttingen: Vandenhoeck & Ruprecht, 1892.

————. *Die Lehre von der Gottheit Christi: Communicatio idiomatum.* Gotha: Perthes, 1881.

————. *Old Testament Theology: The Religion of Revelation in Its Pre-Christian Stage of Development.* Edinburgh: T&T Clark, 1895.

————. *Outlines of Christian Apologetics for Use in Lectures.* Translated by Alfred Bull Nichols. New York: Macmillan, 1905.

Schürer, Emil. *Geschichte des judischen Volkes im Zeitalter Jesu Christi.* 4th ed. 3 vols. Leipzig: J. C. Hinrichs, 1901–9.

Schuts, Jacobus. *Verhandeling over des heeren H. Avondmaal, kostelijk verklaart en toegepast, tot overtuiging van onbekeerden, tot vertroosting van heilbegeringen, tot bevorderingen in de heiligmaking van ware gelovingen, in bijf hoofdzaken hehelzende.* Utrecht: Johannes van Schoonhoven, 1765.

Schutte, Rutger. *Twee-tal verhandelingen behelzende de eerste eene verklaring van Gods Testament en Verbond onder de nieuwe huishoudinge, en derzelver zegelen.* Amsterdam: de Bruyn & van Toll, 1785.

Schwane, Joseph. *Dogmengeschichte.* 2nd ed. 4 vols. Freiburg i.B.: Herder, 1882–95.

Schwartzkopff, Paul. *Die Irrtumslosigkeit Jesu Christi und der christliche Glaube.* Giessen: J. Ricker, 1897.

————. *Konnte Jesus irren? Unter dem geschichtlichen, dogmatischen und psychologischen Gesichtspunkte principiell beantwortet.* Giessen: J. Ricker, 1896.

Schweitzer, Albert. *The Quest for the Historical Jesus: A Critical Study from Reimarus to Wrede.* Translated by W. Montgomery. New York: Macmillan, 1968.

Schweizer, Alexander. *Die Christliche Glaubenslehre nach protestantischen Grundsätzen dargestellt.* Leipzig: S. Hirzel, 1863–72.

————. *Die Glaubenslehre der evangelishreformierten Kirche.* 2 vols. Zürich: Orell & Füssli, 1844–47.

————. *Die protestantischen Centraldogmen in ihrer Entwicklung innerhalb der reformierten Kirche.* 2 vols. Zürich: Orell Fussli & Co., 1854–56.

Schwetz, Johannes. *Theologia dogmatic catholica.* 3 vols. Vienna: Congregatio Mechitharistica, 1851–54.

Secrétan, Charles. *La philosophie de la liberté.* 3rd ed. 2 vols. Paris: Hachette, 1849.

————. *Théologie et religion.* Lausanne: Arthur Immer, 1883.

Seeberg, Alfred. *Der Tod Christi in seiner Bedeutung für die Erlösung.* Leipzig: Deichert, 1895.

Seeberg, Reinhold. *The Fundamental Truths of the Christian Religion.* Translated by Rev. George E. Thomson and Clara Wallentin. New York: G. P. Putnam Sons, 1908.

———. *Grundriss der Dogmengeschichte.* 3rd ed. Leipzig: Deichert, 1910.

———. *Die Persönlichkeit Christi, der feste Punkt im fliessenden Strome der Gegenwart.* Berlin: Buchhandlung der Berliner Stadtmission, 1903.

Seitz, Anton. *Das Evangelium vom Gottessohn: Eine Apologie der wesenhaften Gottessohnschaft Christi gegenüber der Kritik der modernsten deutschen Theologie.* Freiburg i.B.: Herder, 1908.

Sellin, Ernst. *Die israelitisch-jüdische Heilandserwartung.* Lichterfelde-Berlin: E. Runge, 1909.

———. *Der Knecht Gottes bei Deuterojesaja.* Leipzig: Deichert, 1901.

———. *Das Rätsel des deuterojesajanischen Buches.* Leipzig: Deichert, 1908.

Semisch, Karl Gottlieb. *Justin der Märtyrer: Eine kirchen- und dogmengeschichtliche Monographie.* 2 vols. Breslau: August Schulz, 1840–42.

———. *Justin Martyr: His Life, Writings, and Opinions.* Translated by J. E. Ryland. 2 vols. Edinburgh: T&T Clark, 1843.

Semler, Johann Salomo, and Christian Edzard Betke. *De daemoniacis quorum in Evangeliis fit mentio.* Halle: n.p., 1760.

Seneca, Lucius Annaeus. *Letters from a Stoic.* Translated by Robin Campbell. Harmondsworth: Penguin, 1969.

Sepp, Christiaan. *Het godgeleerd onderwijs in Nederland, gedurende de 16e en 17e eeuw.* 2 vols. Leiden: De Breuk en Smits, 1873–74.

Seuffert, Hermann. *Was will, was wirkt, und was soll die staatliche Strafe?* Bonn: Cohen, 1897.

Seydel, Rudolf. *Die Buddha-Legende und das Leben Jesu nach den Evangelien.* 2nd ed. Weimar: Felber, 1897.

Shedd, William Greenough Thayer. *Dogmatic Theology.* 3rd ed. 3 vols. New York: Scribner, 1891–94.

Siebeck, Hermann. *Lehrbuch der Religionsgeschichte.* Freiburg i.B. and Leipzig: Mohr, 1893.

Sieffert, Friedrich. *Die neuesten theologischen Forschungen über Busse und Glaube.* Berlin: Reuther & Reichard, 1896.

Simar, Hubert Theophil. *Lehrbuch der Dogmatik.* 3rd ed. Freiburg i.B.: Herder, 1893.

Simon, Theodor. *Der Logos: Ein Versuch erneuter Würdigung einer alten Wahrheit.* Leipzig: Deichert, 1902.

Simons, David. *Leerboek van het Nederlandse strafrecht.* Groningen: Nordhoff, 1904.

Smalcald Articles. In vol. 3 of *The Creeds of Christendom,* edited by Philip Schaff, revised by David S. Schaff. 6th ed. 3 vols. New York: Harper & Row, 1931. Reprinted, Grand Rapids: Baker, 1983.

Smend, Rudolf. *Lehrbuch der alttestamentlichen Religionsgeschichte.* Freiburg i.B.: Mohr, 1893.

Smith, W. Robertson. *Die Religion der Semiten.* Freiburg i.B.: Mohr, 1899.

———. *The Religion of the Semites.* New York: Schocken Books, 1972.

Smith, William Benjamin. *Der vorchristliche Jesus nebst weiteren Vorstudien zur Entstehungsgeschichte des Urchristentums.* Giessen: Alfred Töpelmann, 1906.

Smyth, Newman. *The Place of Death in Evolution.* London: T. Fisher Unwin, 1897.

Socinus, Faustus. *De Iesu Christo servatore: Hoc est cur & qua ratione Iesus Christus noster servator fit.* Rakow: Rodecius, 1594.

———. *Praelectiones theologicae.* Racoviae: Sebastiani Sternacii, 1627.

Sohn, Georg. *Opera sacrae theologiae.* 2 vols. Herborn: C. Corvin, 1598.

Soltau, Wilhelm. *The Birth of Jesus Christ.* Translated by Maurice A. Canney. London: Adam & Charles Black, 1903.

Soury, Jules. *The Religion of Israel.* Translated by Annie Wood Besant. London: Bradlaugh Bonner, 1895.

Southey, Robert. *The Life of John Wesley.* London: Hutchinson & Co., 1903.

Spangenberg, August Gottlieb. *Idea fidei fratrum, oder, Kurzer Begrif der christlichen*

Lehre in den evangelischen Brüdergemeinen. Barby: Christian Friedrich Laux, 1779.

Spanheim, Friedrich. *Opera.* 3 vols. Lyon: Cornelium Boutestein [etc.], 1701–3.

Spencer, Herbert. *Principles of Sociology.* New York: Appleton, 1897.

Spener, Philipp Jakob. *Pia desideria.* Translated by Theodore G. Tappert. Philadelphia: Fortress Press, 1964.

Spinoza, Baruch. *Earlier Philosophical Writings: The Cartesian Principles and Thoughts on Metaphysics.* Translated by David Bidney. Indianapolis: Bobbs-Merrill, 1963.

———. *Ethics.* Edited and translated by James Gutman. New York: Hafner, 1949.

———. *The Letters.* Translated by Samuel Shirley. Indianapolis: Hackett Publication Company, 1995.

———. *The Principles of Descartes' Philosophy.* Chicago: Open Court, 1974.

Spitta, Friedrich. *Christi predigt an die Geister.* Göttingen: Vandenhoeck & Ruprecht, 1890.

———. *Streitfragen der Geschichte Jesu.* Göttingen: Vandenhoeck & Ruprecht, 1907.

Staab, Karl. *Die Lehre von der stellvertretenden Genugtuung Christi.* Paderborn: Schöningh, 1908.

Stade, Bernhard. *Geschichte des Volkes Israel.* 2 vols. Berlin: Baumgärtel, 1887–88.

Staerk, Willy. *Neutestamentliche Zeitgeschichte.* 2 vols. Berlin: G. J. Göschen, 1907.

———. *Sünde und Gnade nach der Vorstellung des alteren Judentums, besonders der Dichter der sogannanten Busspsalmen.* Tübingen: Mohr, 1905.

Stahl, Friedrich Julius. *Die Philosophie des Rechts.* 5th ed. 2 vols. in 3. Tübingen: Mohr, 1878.

Stählin, Leonhard. *Kant, Lotze, Albrecht Ritschl: Eine kritische Studie.* Leipzig: Dörffling & Franke, 1888.

———. *Kant, Lotze, and Ritschl: A Critical Examination.* Translated by D. W. Simon. Edinburgh: T&T Clark, 1889.

Stalker, James. *The Atonement.* London: Hodder & Stoughton, 1908.

———. *The Trial and Death of Jesus Christ: A Devotional History of Our Lord's Passion.* London: Hodder & Stoughton, 1894.

Stange, Carl. *Der dogmatische Ertrag der Ritschlschen Theologie nach Julius Kaftan.* Leipzig: Dieterich, 1906.

Stapfer, Johann Friedrich. *Onderwys in de gantsche wederleggende godsgeleertheit.* 5 vols. in 6. Utrecht: Gisb. Tieme van Paddenburg & Abraham van Paddenburg, 1757–63.

Steinbeck, Johannes. *Das göttliche Selbstbewusstsein Jesu nach dem Zeugnis der Synoptiker.* Leipzig: Deichert, 1908.

Stephan, Horst. *Die Lehre Schleiermachers von der Erlösung.* Tübingen: Mohr, 1901.

Stevens, George Barker. *The Christian Doctrine of Salvation.* Edinburgh: T&T Clark, 1905.

———. *The Theology of the New Testament.* 2nd ed. Edinburgh: T&T Clark, 1906.

Stöckl, Albert. *Geschichte der Philosophie des Mittelalters.* 3 vols. in 4. Mainz: F. Kirchheim, 1864.

———. *Das Opfer nach seinem Wesen und nach seiner Geschichte.* Mainz: Kirchheim, 1861.

———. *Die Speculative Lehre vom Menschen und ihre Geschichte.* Würzburg: Stahel, 1858.

Strack, Hermann Leberecht. *Das Blut im Glauben und Aberglaube der Menschheit.* 7th ed. Munich: Beck, 1900.

———. *Das Wesen des Judenthums: Vortrag gehalten auf der Internationalen Konferenz für Judenmission zu Amsterdam.* Leipzig: Hinrichs, 1906.

Strauss, David Friedrich. *Charakteristiken und Kritiken.* Leipzig: n.p., 1839.

———. *Die Christliche Glaubenslehre in ihrer geschichtlichen Entwicklung und im Kampf mit der modernen Wissenschaft.* 2 vols. Tübingen: C. F. Osiander, 1840–41.

———. *Das Leben Jesu.* 2 vols. Tübingen: C. F. Osiander, 1835–36.

———. *The Life of Jesus, Critically Examined.* Translated by Marian Evans. 2 vols. New York: Calvin Blanchard, 1860. Reprinted, St. Clair Shores, MI: Scholarly Press, 1970.

———. *The Old Faith and the New.* Translated by Mathilde Blind. New York: Hold, 1873.

Suicerus, J. C. *Thesaurus ecclesiasticus.* 2 vols. Amsterdam: J. H. Wetstein, 1682.

Swayne, William Shuckburgh. *An Inquiry into Our Lord's Knowledge as Man.* London and New York: Longmans, Green, 1891.

Swedenborg, Emanuel. *The True Christian Religion: Containing the Universal Theology of the New Church, Foretold by the Lord in Daniel VII.13, 14 and in Revelation XXI.1, 2.* Philadelphia: J. B. Lippencott Company, 1896.

Swete, Henry Barclay. *The Holy Spirit in the New Testament.* London: Macmillan, 1909.

Sylvius, Franciscus. *Commentarii in totam primam partem S. Thomae Aquinatis.* 4 vols. Venice: Typographica Balleoniana, 1726.

Talma, Aricius Sybrandus Elbertus. *De Anthropologie van Calvijn.* Utrecht: Breijer, 1882.

Teichmann, Ernst Gustav Georg. *Die Befruchtungsvorgang, sein Wesen und seine Bedeutung.* Leipzig: Teubner, 1905.

Tennant, Frederick Robert. *The Origin and Propogation of Sin.* 2nd ed. Cambridge: Cambridge University Press, 1902.

Tertullian. *Against Marcion. ANF,* III, 269–475.

———. *Against Praxeas. ANF,* III, 597–627.

———. *An Answer to the Jews. ANF,* III, 151–74.

———. *On the Flesh of Christ. ANF,* III, 521–42.

———. *On Modesty. ANF,* IV, 74–101.

———. *On Prayer. ANF,* III, 681–91.

———. *On the Resurrection of the Body. ANF,* III, 545–94.

———. *A Treatise On the Soul. ANF,* III, 181–235.

Thalhofer, Valentin. *Handbuch der katholischen Liturgik.* 2nd ed. 2 vols. Freiburg i.B.: Herder, 1912.

———. *Das Opfer des alten und des neuen Bundes, mit besonderer Rücksicht auf den Hebräerbrief und die katholische Messopferlehre.* Regensburg: G. A. Manz, 1870.

Theologia Wirceburgensi. 3rd ed. 10 vols. in 5. Paris: Berche at Tralin, 1880.

Tholuck, August. *Das Alte Testament im Neuen Testament.* 4th ed. Gotha: F. A. Perthes, 1854.

———. *Commentar zum Brief an die Römer.* Halle: E. Anton, 1856.

———. *Die Lehre von der Sünde und vom Versöhner.* Gotha: F. A. Perthes, 1862.

———. *Der sittliche Charakter des Heidenthums.* Gotha: Perthes, 1867.

Thomas à Kempis. *The Imitation of Christ.* Translated by William C. Creasy. Macon, GA: Mercer University Press, 1989.

Thomas Aquinas. *Aquinas on Creation: Writings on the Sentences of Peter Lombard, Book II.* Translated by Steven E. Baldner and William E. Carroll. Toronto: Pontifical Institute of Mediaeval Studies, 1997.

———. *Compendium of Theology.* Translated by Cyril O. Vollert. St. Louis: B. Herder Book Co., 1947.

———. *Scriptum super libros sententiarum magistri Petri Lombardi Episcopi Parisiensis.* 4 vols. Paris: Sumptibus P. Lethielleux, 1929–47.

———. *Summa contra gentiles.* Translated by the English Dominican Fathers. London: Burns, Oates & Washbourne, 1924.

———. *Summa theologiae.* Translated by Thomas Gilby et al. 61 vols. New York: McGraw-Hill, 1964–81.

Thomasius, Gottfried. *Christi Person und Werk.* 3rd ed. 2 vols. Erlangen: A. Deichert, 1886–88.

*Thraen, A. *Conférences apologétiques et dogm.* Paris, 1900.

Tiele, Cornelis Petrus. *Elements of the Science of Religion.* 2 vols. Edinburgh and London: William Blackwood, 1899.

———. *Inleiding tot het godsdienstwetenschap.* 2 vols. Amsterdam: P. N. van Kampen, 1897–99.

Tillmann, Fritz. *Der Menschensohn: Jesu Selbstbezeugnis für seine messianische Würde.* Freiburg i.B.: Herder, 1907.

Titius, Arthur. *Die neutestamentliche Lehre von der Seligkeit und ihre Bedeutung für die Gegenwart.* 4 vols. Freiburg: Mohr, 1895–1900.

Töllner, Johann Gottlieb. *Der Thätige Gehorsam Jesu Christi untersucht.* Breslau: Johann Ernst Meyern, 1768.

Toorenenbergen, Johan Justus van. *De symbolische schriften der Nederlandsche Hervormde Kerk in zuiveren, kritisch bewerkten tekst.* Utrecht: Kemink en Zoon, 1869.

Townsend, William John, Herbert B. Workman, and George Eayrs. *A New History of Methodism.* 2 vols. London: Hodder & Stoughton, 1909.

Trench, Richard Chenevix. *The Hulsean Lectures for 1845 and 1846.* 4th rev. ed. London: Parke, 1859.

Trigland, Jacobus. *Antapologia.* Amsterdam: Joannam Janssonium [et al.], 1664.

———. *Kerckelycke geschiedenissen.* Leyden: Andriae Wyngaerden, 1650.

Trumbull, Henry Clay. *The Blood Covenant: A Primitive Rite and Its Bearing on Scripture.* 2nd ed. Philadelphia: Wattles, 1893.

———. *The Threshold Covenant.* New York: Scribners, 1896.

Tschackert, P. *Evangelische Polemik gegen die römische Kirche.* Gotha: F. A. Perthes, 1885.

Tully, Thomas. *Justificatio Paulina sine operibus ex mente Ecclesiae Anglicanae, omniumque reliquarum quae reformatae audiunt, asserta & illustrata.* Oxford: Hall, 1674.

Turretin, Francis. *Institutes of Elenctic Theology.* Translated by George Musgrove Giger. Edited by James T. Dennison. 3 vols. Phillipsburg, NJ: Presbyterian & Reformed, 1992.

Twisse, William. *Guilielmi Twissi opera theologica polemico-anti-arminiana.* Amsterdam, 1699.

———. *Vindiciae gratiae, potestatis ac providentiae Dei.* 3 vols. Amsterdami: Guilielmum Blaeu, 1632.

Ueberweg-Heinze, Friedrich. *Geschichte der Philosophie.* 9th ed. 5 vols. Berlin: E. S. Mittler & Sohn, 1898–1903.

Uhlhorn, Gerhard. *Der Kampf des Christenthums mit dem Heidenthum.* Stuttgart: Gundert, 1899.

Ullmann, Carl. *The Sinlessness of Jesus.* Translated by Sophia Taylor. Edinburgh: T&T Clark, 1882.

Ulrici, Hermann. *Gott und der Mensch.* 2 vols. Leipzig: Weigel, 1866–73.

Ursinus, Zacharias. *The Commentary of Dr. Zacharius Ursinus on the Heidelberg Catechism.* Translated by G. W. Willard. Grand Rapids: Eerdmans, 1954.

———. *Volumen tractationum theologicarum.* Neustadii, 1584.

Usener, Hermann. *Religionsgeschichtliche Untersuchungen.* 3 vols. Bonn: Cohen, 1889–1911.

Val D'Eremao, José P. *The Serpent of Eden: A Philological and Critical Essay on the Text of Genesis III and Its Various Interpretations.* London: K. Paul, Trench & Co., 1888.

Van Leeuwen, Everardus Henricus. *Bijbelsche Anthropologie.* Utrecht: Ruys, 1906.

*Van Leeuwen, J. A. C. *Verzoening.* Utrecht, 1903.

*Van Voorst. *Over de Goddelijke straffen.* Haagsch Gen. 1798.

Varigny, Henry de. *Wie stirbt man? Was ist der Tod?* Translated by S. Wiarda. Minden: n.p., n.d.

Veenstra, S. L. *Het Leger des Heils.* Baarn: Hollandia-Drukkerij, 1910.

*Vercueil. *Étude sur la solidarité dans le Christianisme l'après St. Paul.* Mantauban, 1894.

Verhandlungen des Vierzehnten Evangelisch-Sozialen Kongresses, abgehalten in Darmstadt am 3. und 4. Juni 1903, Die. Göttingen: Vandenhoeck & Ruprecht, 1903.

Vermigli, Peter Martyr. *Petri Martyris Vermilii . . . Loci communes.* London: Kyngston, 1576.

Vilmar, August Friedrick Christian. *Dogmatik*. 2 vols. Gütersloh: C. Bertelsmann, 1874.

———. *Theologische Moral: Akademische Vorlesungen*. Gütersloh: C. Bertelsmann, 1871.

*Vinet, [Alexandre?]. *L'unité de la loi*. Nouv. Et Evang.

Vinke, Henricus Egbertus. *Theologiae Christianae dogmaticae*. Utrecht: Kemink, 1853–54.

Visscher, Hugo. *Guilielmus Amesius: Zijn leven en werken*. Haarlem: J. M. Stap, 1894.

Vitringa, Campegius. *Observationum sacrarum libri sex, in quibus de rebus varii argumenti, & utilissimae investigationis, critice ac theologice, disseritur; scarorum imprimis librorum loca multa obscuriora nova val clariore luce perfunduntur*. 2 vols. Franeker: Wibii Bleck, 1711–12.

———. *Doctrina christianae religionis*. Edited by Martinus Vitringa. 8 vols. Leiden: Joannis le Mair, 1761–86.

*Vlak, Johannes. *Eeuwig Evangelium of Leer der zaligheid*. 1684.

*———. *Trias dissertationum de operibus Dei*.

Voetius, Gisbert. *Ta askètika, sive Exercitia pietatis in usum juventutis academiae nunc edita*. Gorichem: Paul Vink, 1664.

———. *Selectae disputationes theologicae*. 5 vols. Utrecht, 1648–69.

Vogt, Peter. *Der Stammbaum Christi bei den heiligen Evangelisten Matthäus und Lukas*. Freiburg i.B.: Herder, 1907.

Voigt, Heinrich. *Fundamentaldogmatik*. Gotha: F. A. Perthes, 1874.

Völkel, Johann. *De vera religione libri quinque*. Racoviae: Sebastiani Sternacii, 1630.

Voltaire. *Candide*. Translated by Robert Martin Adams. New York: Norton, 1966.

Volz, Paul. *Jüdische Eschatologie von Daniel bis Akiba*. Tübingen: J. C. B. Mohr, 1903.

———. *Die vorexilische Jahweprophetie und der Messias in ihrem Verhältnis dargestellt*. Göttingen: Vandenhoeck & Ruprecht, 1897.

Vömel, Rudolf, and Wilhelm Vollert. *Der Begriff der Gnade im Neuen Testament*. Gütersloh: Bertelsmann, 1903.

Vos, Geerhardus. *De Verbondsleer in de Gereformeerde theologie*. Grand Rapids: Democrat, 1891.

Vossius, Gerardus Johannes. *Historiae de controversiis, quas Pelagius eiusque reliquiae moverunt, libri septem*. Amsterdam: Ludovicus & Daniel Elzevirii, 1655.

Wachter, Wilhelm. *Bestia sum: Einige Kapitel über die Kehrseite des Menschtums*. Berlin: E. Felber, 1898.

Wacker, Emil. *Die Heilsordnung*. Gütersloh: Bertelsmann, 1898. 2nd ed., 1905.

*Wagner, H. *De dood toegelicht van het standpunt der natuurwetenschap*. Utrecht, 1856.

Walaeus, Antonius. *Loci communes s. theologiae*. Leiden: F. Hackius, 1640.

———. *Opera omnia*. Leiden: Francisci Hackii, 1643.

———. *Synopsis purioris theologiae*. Leiden: Elzeviriana, 1652.

Walch, Christian Wilhelm Franz. *De obedientia Christi activa commentatio*. Göttingen: Bossigelianis, 1755.

Walch, Johann Georg. *Bibliotheca theologica selecta, litterariis adnotationibus instructa*. 4 vols. Jena: vid. Croeckerianal, 1757–65.

———. *Historische und theologische Einleitung in die Religionsstreitigkeiten außer der evangelisch-lutherischen Kirchen*. 5 vols. Jena: J. Meyers Witwe, 1733–36.

Walker, Dawson. *The Gift of Tongues and Other Essays*. Edinburgh: T&T Clark, 1906.

Walker, James. *The Theology and Theologians of Scotland, Chiefly of the Seventeenth and Eighteenth Centuries*. 2nd ed. Edinburgh: T&T Clark, 1888.

Walther, Wilhelm. *Ad. Harnacks Wesen des Christentums: Für die christliche Gemeinde geprüft*. 5th ed. Leipzig: Deichert, 1904.

Warfield, Benjamin Breckenridge. *The Lord of Glory: A Study of the Designations of Our Lord in the New Testament with Especial Reference to His Deity*. New York: American Tract Society, 1907.

———. *Two Studies in the History of Doctrine: Augustine and the Pelagian Controversy*. New York: Christian Literature Co., 1897.

Weber, Ferdinand Wilhelm. *System der altsynagogalen palästinischen Theologie: Aus Targum, Midrasch und Talmud*. Leipzig: Dörffling & Franke, 1880.

Weber, Hans Emil. *Der Einfluss der protestantischen Schulphilosophie auf die orthodoxlutherische Dogmatik*. Leipzig: Deichert, 1908.

Weber, Otto. *Dämonenbeschwörung bei den Babyloniern und Assyrern*. Leipzig: Hinrichs, 1906.

Wegener, Richard. *A. Ritschls Idee des Reiches Gottes im Licht der Geschichte*. Leipzig: Deichert, 1897.

Wegscheider, Julius August Ludwig. *Institutiones theologiae Christianae Dogmaticae*. Halle: Gebauer, 1819.

Weiffenbach, Wilhelm. *Zur Auslegung der Stelle Philipper II,5–11 zugleich ein Beitrag zur paulinischen Christologie*. Karlsruhe: H. Reuther, 1884.

Weigl, Eduard. *Die Heilslehre des hl. Cyrill von Alexandrien*. Mainz: Kirchheim, 1905.

Weinel, Heinrich. *Jesus in the Nineteenth Century and After*. Translated by Alban Gregory Widgery. Edinburgh: T&T Clark, 1914.

Weingarten, Hermann. *Die Revolutionskirchen Englands*. Leipzig: Breitköpf & Hartel, 1868.

Weiss, Albert Maria. *Apologie des Christentums*. 5 vols. in 7. Freiburg i.B.: Herder, 1904–8.

———. *Die religiöse Gefahr*. Freiburg i.B.: Herder, 1904.

Weiss, Bernhard. *Biblical Theology of the New Testament*. Translated by David Eaton and James E. Duguid. 2 vols. Edinburgh: T&T Clark, 1883.

———. *Das Leben Jesu*. 2 vols. Stuttgart, various editions (1882, 1884, 1888, 1902).

———. *Lehrbuch der biblischen Theologie des Neuen Testaments*. 3rd ed. Berlin: W. Hertz, 1880.

Weiss, Hugo. *Die messianischen Vorbilder im Alten Testament*. Freiburg i.B.: Herder, 1905.

Weiss, Johannes. *Die Idee des Reiches Gottes in der Theologie*. Giessen: J. Ricker, 1901.

———. *Jesus' Proclamation of the Kingdom of God*. Translated by Richard Hyde Hiers and David Larrimore Holland. Philadelphia: Fortress Press, 1971.

———. *Die Nachfolge Christi und die Predigt der Gegenwart*. Göttingen: Vandenhoeck & Ruprecht, 1895.

———. *Paul and Jesus*. Translated by H. J. Chaytor. New York: Harper, 1909.

———. *Die Predigt Jesu vom Reiche Gottes*. 2nd ed. Göttingen: Vandenhoeck & Ruprecht, 1900.

Weisse, Christian Herman. *Die evangelische Geschichte, kritisch und philosophisch bearbeitet*. 2 vols. Leipzig: Breitkopf & Härtel, 1838.

———. *Philosophische Dogmatik oder Philosophie des Christentums*. 2nd ed. 3 vols. Leipzig: Hirzel, 1855–62.

Weizsäcker, Karl Heinrich von. *Das apostolische Zeitalter der christlichen Kirche*. 2nd ed. Freiburg: Mohr, 1890.

Wellhausen, Julius. *Geschichte Israels*. 2 vols. Berlin: Reimer, 1878.

———. *Israelitische und jüdische Geschichte*. 1st ed. Berlin: Reimer, 1894.

*———. *Reste arabischen Heidentums*. 1887.

———. *Skizzen und Vorarbeiten*. Berlin: Reimer, 1899.

Wendelin, Marcus Friedrich. *Exercitationes theologiae vindices pro theologia Christiana*. Kassel: Schaedewitz, 1652.

Wendland, Johannes. *Albrecht Ritschl und seine Schüler im Verhältnis zur Theologie, zur Philosophie und zur Frömmigkeit unsrer Zeit*. Berlin: George Reimer, 1899.

Wendland, Paul. *Die hellenistisch-römische Kultur in ihrer Beziehungen zu Judentum und Christentum*. Tübingen: Mohr, 1907.

Wendt, Hans Heinrich. *Die Begriffe Fleisch und Geist im biblischen Sprachgebrauch*. Gotha: F. A. Perthes, 1878.

————. *System der christlichen Lehre.* 2 vols. in 1. Göttingen: Vandenhoeck & Ruprecht, 1907.

Wenger, Leopold. *Die Stellvertretung im Rechte der Papyri.* Leipzig: B. G. Teubner, 1906.

Wernle, Paul. *Die Anfänge unserer Religion.* 2nd ed. Tübingen: Mohr, 1904.

————. *Die Reichsgotteshoffnung in den ältesten christlichen Dokumenten und bei Jesus.* Tübingen: J. C. B. Mohr, 1903.

Westberg, Friedrich. *Die biblische Chronologie nach Flavius Josephus und das Todesjahr Jesu.* Leipzig: Deichert, 1910.

Westcott, Brooke Foss. *Christus Consummator: Some Aspects of the Work and Person of Christ in Relation to Modern Thought.* London and New York: Macmillan & Co., 1886.

Wiedemann, Alfred. *Magie und Zauberei im alten Ägypten.* Leipzig: Hinrichs, 1905.

Wiggers, Gustav Friedrich. *Versuch einer pragmatischen Darstellung des Augustinismus und Pelagianismus.* 2 vols. Hamburg: F. A. Perthes, 1830–31.

Wijnaendts Francken, Cornelis Johannes. *Ethische Studien.* Haarlem: Tjeenk Willink, 1903.

*Wijnpersse, [Samuel Johannes?] van de. *Over de straffende gerechtigheid.* 1798.

Wildeboer, Gerrit. *Het Oude Testament van historisch standpunt toegelicht.* Groningen: Wolters, 1908.

Williams, Daniel. *Gospel-Truth Stated and Vindicated.* London: Dunton, 1692.

Windelband, Wilhelm. *Über Willensfreiheit: Zwölf Vorlesungen.* Tübingen: J. C. B. Mohr, 1904.

*Wirtz, Joseph. *Die Lehre von der Apolytrosis.* Trier, 1906.

Witsius, Herman. *Hermanni Witsii excercitationes sacrae in symbolum quod Apostolorum dicitur.* Amsterdam: Johannem Wolters, 1697.

————. *Miscellaneorum sacrorum.* 3d ed. 2 vol. Herborn, Germany: Iohannis Nicolai Andreae, 1712.

————. *The Oeconomy of the Covenants betwéen God and Man. Comprehending a Complete Body of Divinity.* 3 vols. New York: Lee & Stokes, 1798.

Witte, Petrus de. *Wederlegginge der sociniänsche dwalingen.* 3 vols. Amsterdam: Boeckholt & van den Heuvel, 1662.

Wittichius, Christophorus. *Theologia pacifica.* Leiden: Boutesteyn, 1671.

Wobbermin, Georg. *Religionsgeschichtliche Studien zur Frage der Beeinflussung des Urchristentums durch das antike Mysterienwesen.* Berlin: E. Eberling, 1896.

Wohlenberg, Gustav. *Empfangen vom Heiligen Geist, geboren von der Jungfrau Maria.* Leipzig: Deichert, 1893.

Wollebius, Johannes. *Compendium theologiae Christianae.* Basel, 1626; Oxford, 1657.

Wood, Irving Francis. *The Spirit of God in Biblical Literature.* New York: A. C. Armstrong, 1904.

Woodbridge, Benjamin. *The Method of Grace in the Justification of Sinners.* London: Paxton, 1656.

Wörnhart, Leonard Maria. *Maria, die wunderbare Mutter Gottes und der Menschen.* Innsbrück: F. Rauch, 1890.

Wörter, Friedrich. *Die christliche Lehre über das Verhältniss von Gnade und Freiheit von den apostolischen Zeiten bis auf Augustinus.* Freiburg i.B.: Herder, 1856.

Wossidlo, Paul. *Leitfaden der Mineralogie und Geologie für höhere Lehranstalten.* Berlin: Weidmann, 1889.

Wrede, William. *Paul.* Translated by Edward Lummis. Boston: American Unitarian Association, 1908.

————. *Paulus.* Halle a.S.: Gebauer-Schwetske, 1904.

Wundt, Wilhelm Max. *Grundzüge der physiologischen Psychologie.* 3 vols. Leipzig: W. Engelmann, 1908–11.

————. *Mythus und Religion.* 2 vols. Leipzig: Engelmann, 1905.

————. *Völkerpsychologie: Eine Untersuchung der Entwicklungsgesetze von Sprache, Mythus, und Sitte.* 2 vols. Leipzig: Engelmann, 1900–1909.

Wünsche, August. *Die Sagen vom Lebensbaum und Lebenswasser. Altorientalische Mythen.* Leipzig: Pfeiffer, 1905.

———. *Yisure ha-Mashiah, oder, die Leiden des Messias in ihrer Uebereinstimmung mit der Lehre des Alten Testaments und den Aussprüchen der Rabbinen in den Talmuden, Midraschim und andern alten rabbinischen Schriften.* Leipzig: Fues, 1870.

Wustmann, Georg. *Die Heilsbedeutung Christi bei den apostolischen Vätern.* Gütersloh: Bertelsmann, 1905.

———. *Jesus und Paulus: Die Abhängigkeit des Apostels von seinem Herrn.* Gütersloh: Bertelsmann, 1907.

Wuttke, Adolf. *Christian Ethics.* Translated by John P. Lacroix. New York: Nelson & Phillips, 1873.

———. *Geschichte des Heidenthums in Beziehung auf Religion, Wissen, Kunst, Sittlichkeit, und Staatsleben.* 2 vols. Breslau: Max, 1852–53.

Xenophon. *Memorabilia and Oeconomicus.* Translated by E. C. Marchant. Loeb Classical Library. New York: G. P. Putnam's Sons, 1923.

Ypey [Ijpeij], Annaeus. *Beknopte letterkundige geschiedenis der sijstematische godgeleerdheid.* 3 vols. Haarlem: Platt, 1793–98.

———. *Geschiedenis van de Kristlijke Kerk in de achttiende eeuw.* 15 vols. Utrecht: W. van Ijzerworst, 1797–1815.

Zahn, Detlev. *Die natürliche Moral christlich beurteilt und angewandt auf die Gegenwart in Kirche, Schule, und innerer Mission.* Gotha: G. Schloeszmann, 1881.

Zahn, Theodor. *Die Anbetung Jesu im Zeitalter der Apostel.* Stuttgart: Buchhandlung der evangelischen Gesellschaft, 1885.

———. *Das apostolische Symbolum: Eine Skizze seiner Geschichte und eine Prüfung seines Inhalts.* Erlangen and Leipzig: Deichert, 1893.

———. *Der Brief des Paulus an die Galater.* Leipzig: Deichert, 1907.

———. *Der Brief des Paulus an die Römer.* Leipzig: Deichert, 1910.

———. *Einleitung in das Neue Testament.* 2nd ed. 2 vols. Leipzig: Deichert, 1900.

———. *Das Evangelium des Matthäus.* 3rd ed. Leipzig: Deichert, 1910.

———. *Forschungen zur Geschichte des neutestamentlichen Kanons und der altkirchlichen Literatur.* 10 vols. Erlangen: Deichert, 1881–1929.

———. *Theologischen Studien zum 10. Okt. 1908.* Leipzig: Deichert, 1908.

Zanchi, Jerome. *De operum theologicorum.* 8 vols. [Geneva]: Samuelis Crispini, 1617.

Zeller, Eduard. *Die Philosophie der Griechen.* 4th ed. 3 vols. Leipzig: O. R. Reisland, 1879.

Zellinger, Johannes. *Die Dauer der öffentlichen Wirksamkeit Jesu.* Münster: Aschendorff, 1907.

Zimmer, K. F. *Sünde oder Krankheit.* Leipzig, 1894.

Zöckler, Otto. *Askese und Mönchtum.* 2nd ed. 2 vols. Frankfurt a.M.: Heyder & Zimmer, 1897.

———. *The Cross of Christ: Studies in the History of Religion and the Inner Life of the Church.* Translated by Maurice J. Evans. London: Hodder & Stoughton, 1877.

———. *Die Lehre vom Urstand des Menschen.* Gütersloh: C. Bertelsmann, 1879.

———. *Das Lehrstück von den sieben Hauptsünden.* Munich: Beck, 1893.

Zwingli, Ulrich. *On Providence and Other Essays.* Translated by Samuel Macauley Jackson. Edited by William John Hinks. Durham: Labyrinth Press, 1983.

———. *Opera.* Edited by Melchior Schuler and Johannes Schulthess. Zürich: F. Schulthess, 1828–42.

ARTICLES

Adamson, Alexander. "Reconciliation." *DB*, IV, 204–7.

Aglen, A. S. "Shiloh." *DB*, IV, 500–501.

Anderson, K. C. "The Collapse of Liberal Christianity." *Hibbert Journal* 8/2 (January 1910): 301–20.

Armstrong, William P. "The Resurrection and the Origin of the Church in Jerusalem."

Princeton Theological Review 5 (1907): 1–25.

Bachmann, H. "Stehen der Jesus der synoptischen Evangelien und der Christus des Paulus in Widerspruch?" *Der Beweis des Glaubens* 44 (1908): 278–88.

Bacon, G. W. "Geneology of Jesus Christ." *DB*, II, 137–41.

Baldensperger, Wilhelm. "Die neueste Forschung über den Menschensohn." *Theologische Rundschau* 3 (1900): 201–55.

Barnard, P. M. "Geneologies of Jesus Christ." *DC*, I, 636–39.

Baudissin, Wolf. "Beelzubub." *PRE*³, II, 514–16.

———. "Feldgeister." *PRE*³, VI, 1–23.

Beaton, D. "The Marrow of Modern Divinity and the Marrow Controversy." *Princeton Theological Review* 4 (1906): 317–38.

Benrath, Karl. "Stancarus." *PRE*³, XVIII, 752–54.

Bernard, Edward Russell. "Sin." *DB*, IV, 528–36.

Bernard, John Henry. "Fall." *DB*, I, 839–45.

Bessmer, J. "Das moderne Zungenreden." *Stimmen aus Maria-Laach* 78 [79?] (1910): 142–56.

———. "Die Theologie vom Standpunkte der funktionellen Psychologie." *Stimmen aus Maria-Laach* 70 [71?] (1906): 154–64.

Beth, Karl. "Über Ursache und Zweck des Todes." *Glauben und Wissen* (1909): 285–348.

*Beukenhorst. "Het spreken in 'tongen.'" *Stemmen voor Waarheid en Vrede* (March 1908).

*Boehmer, J. "Das Reich Gottes in den Psalmen." *Neue kirchliche Zeitschrift* (1897).

*———. "Zum Verständnis des Menschensohnes." *Die Studierstube* (1905): 411–18.

*———. "Zum Verständnis des Reiches Gottes." *Die Studierstube* (1905): 661ff.

Boekenoogen, J. G. "Christologische Beschouwingen." *Theologisch Tijdschrift* 26 (1892): 147–69, 275–306, 514–43, 568–95.

*Bois, H. "Expiation et solidarité." *Revue de théologie de Montauban* (1889).

*———. "La nécessité de l'expiation." *Revue de théologie de Montauban* (1888).

Bornhäuser, Karl. "Die Versuchungen Jesu nach dem Hebräerbrief." In *Theologische Studien: Martin Kähler zum 6. Januar 1905*, edited by Friedrich Giesebrecht and Martin Kähler, 69–86. Leipzig: Deichert, 1905.

*Bouman, L[eendert?]. "Degeneratie." *Orgaan van de Christelijke Vereeniging voor Natuur- en Geneeskunde,* 1908–9.

Bousset, Wilhelm. "Das Reich Gottes in der Predigt Jesu." *Theologische Rundschau* 5 (1902): 397–436.

*Box, G. H. "The Gospel Narratives of the Nativity and the Alleged Influence of Heathen Ideas." *Zeitschrift für neutestamentliche Wissenschaft* (1905): 80.

———. "The Virgin Birth." *DC*, II, 804–9.

Brandt, Wilhelm. "Jezus en de Messiansche Verwachting." *Teyler's Theologisch Tijdschrift* 5 (1907): 461–568.

Briggs, Charles Augustus. "Criticism and the Dogma of the Virgin Birth." *American Scholar's Review* 182/6 (June 1906): 861–74.

———. "The Virgin Birth of Our Lord." *American Journal of Theology* 12 (1908): 189–210.

Bröse. "Wird Christus in Rom. 9:5 Θεος genannt?" *Neue kirchliche Zeitschrift* (1899): 645–57.

———. "Zur Auslegung von Röm. 1:3." *Neue kirchliche Zeitschrift* (1899): 562–73.

Brown, Alexander. "The Over-emphasis of Sin." *Hibbert Journal* 7/3 (April 1909): 614–22.

*Bruining, Albertus. "Godsdienst en Verlossingsbehoefte." *Teyler's Theologisch Tijdschrift* 8 (1910).

———. "Over de methode van onze Dogmatiek." *Teyler's Theologisch Tijdschrift* 1 (1903): 153–85, 306–34, 426–58.

Burger, Karl. "Selbstsucht." *PRE*³, XVIII, 172–74.

Burn, A. E. "Hell (Descent into)." *DC,* I, 713–16.

*Bussy, [I. J.?] de. "Over Verantwoordelijkheid." *Teyler's Theologisch Tijdschrift* 1 (1903).

Cathrein, Victor. "Die strafrechtliche Zurechnungsfähigkeit." *Stimmen aus Maria-Laach* 66 [67?] (1904): 357–73.

Caven, William. "The Testimony of Christ to the Old Testament." *Presbyterian and Reformed Review* 3 (1892): 401–20.

Chapuis, Paul. "L'adoration du Christ." *Revue de théologie et de philosophie* 28/6 (November 1895): 560–86.

———. "Die Anbetung Christi." *Zeitschrift für Theologie und Kirche* 7 (1897): 28–79.

———. "La Sainteté de Jésus." *Revue de théologie et de philosophie* 30 (1897): 297–321, 409–27, 539–69.

———. "La transformation du dogme christologique au sein de la théologie moderne." *Revue de théologie et de philosophie* 24/5 (September 1891): 417–55.

Cooper, Jacob. "Vicarious Suffering in the Order of Nature." *Princeton Theological Review* 1 (1903): 554–78.

*Couard, Ludwig. "Die messianische Erwartung in den alttestamentlichen Apokryphen." *Neue kirchliche Zeitschrift* (1901): 958–73.

Cremer, Hermann. "Ebenbild Gottes." *PRE*[3], V, 113–18.

———. "Fleisch." *PRE*[3], VI, 98–105.

———. "Geist." *PRE*[3], VI, 444–50.

———. "Geistesgaben." *PRE*[3], VI, 460–63.

———. "Gerechtigkeit des Menschen." *PRE*[3], VI, 546–53.

———. "Der germanische Satisfaktionsbegriff in der Versöhnungslehre." *Theologische Studien und Kritiken* 66 (1893): 316–45.

———. "Herz." *PRE*[3], VII, 773–76.

———. "Seele." *PRE*[3], XVIII, 128–132; *PRE*[2], XIV, 25–30.

———. "Die Wurzeln des anselmischen Satisfaktionsbegriffes." *Theologische Studien und Kritiken* 53 (1880): 7–24.

Cuno, Friedrich Wilhelm. "Ramus." *PRE*[3], XVI, 426–28.

D'Arcy, Charles F. "Consciousness." *DC,* I, 361–66.

Davidson, Andrew Bruce. "Covenant." *DB,* I, 509–15.

Daxer, G. "Ueber die religiöse Erfahrung und die Erfahrungstheologie." *Theologische Studien und Kritiken* 83 (1910): 138–48.

Dearmer, Percy. "Christ." *DC,* I, 308–16.

Deissmann, Gustav Adolf. "Ἱλαστήριος und Ἱλαστήριον, eine lexikalische Studie." *Zeitschrift für die neutestamentliche Wissenschaft* 4 (1903): 193–212.

Denney, James. "Authority of Christ." *DC,* I, 146–53.

———. "Curse." *DB,* I, 534–35.

———. "Holy Spirit." *DC,* I, 731–44.

Diestel, Ludwig. "Studien zur Foederealtheologie." *Jahrbücher für deutsche Theologie* 10 (1865): 209–76.

Dorner, Isaak August. "Ueber Jesu sündlose Vollkommenheit." *Jahrbücher für deutsche Theologie* 7 (1862): 49–107.

Driver, Samuel Rolles. "Azazel." *DB,* I, 207–8.

———. "Propitiation." *DB,* IV, 128–32.

———. "Son of Man." *DB,* IV, 579–89.

Durand, Louis. "Étude sur la rédemption." *Revue de Theologie et de Philosophie* 22 (1889): 337–70.

Edwards, John H. "The Vanishing Sense of Sin." *Presbyterian and Reformed Review* 10 (October 1899): 606–16.

Eerdmans, Bernardus Dirk. "De beteeknenis van het paradijsverhall." *Theologische Tijdschrift* 39 (1905): 481–511.

———. "De gedachte-zonde in het O.T." *Theologische Tijdschrift* 39 (1905): 307–24.

———. [Agnotus]. "Reactie of Vooruitgang." *Theologische Tijdschrift* 43 (1908).

Eisler, Rudolf. "Tod." In *Wörterbuch der Philosophischen Begriffe,* 3 vols., III: 1511–13. Berlin: E. S. Mittler, 1910.

———. "Zurechnung." In *Wörterbuch der Philosophischen Begriffe,* 3 vols., III: 1907–10. Berlin: E. S. Mittler, 1910.

*Endemann. "Zur Frage über die Brüder des Herrn." *Neue kirchliche Zeitschrift* (1900): 833–62.

Eykman, J. C. "De eenheid en beteekenis van het paradijsverhaal, onderzocht met het oog op de meeningen der jongste critiek." *Theologische Studiën* 25/3–4 (1907): 197–237.

Favre, Robert. "Le Christ historique d'après W. Herrmann." *Revue de Theologie et de Philosophie* 33 (1900): 454–76, 481–90.

*Feine. "Der Ursprung der Sünde nach Paulus." *Neue kirchliche Zeitschrift* (October 1899): 771–95.

*Fiebig, "Judentum und Katholizismus." *Die Studierstube* (1905): 715–26.

Fleming, J. Dick. "Christ in the Seventeenth Century." *DC*, II, 864–67.

Flier, Albert van der. "Drieërlei verklaring van den Ebed-Jahwe bij Deuterojesaja." *Theologische Studiën* 22 (1904): 345–76.

Foerster, Erich. "Harnacks Wesen des Christentums: Eine Bestreitung oder eine Verteidigung des christlichen Glaubens?" *Zeitschrift für Theologie und Kirche* 12 (1902): 179–201.

Fürer, [?]. "Das Lebensalter des Menschen usw." *Der Beweis des Glaubens* (1868): 97–184.

Garvie, Alfred E. "Kenosis." *DC*, I, 927–28.

Gass, Wilhelm. "Barckhausen." *PRE²*, II, 94–98.

Gennrich, Paul. "Studien zur paulinischen Heilsordnung." *Theologische Studien und Kritiken* 71 (1898): 377–431.

Gispen, W. H., Jr. "De leer der erfelijkheid en de leer der erfzonde." *Tijdschrift voor Gereformeerde Theologie* 9 (1902): 289–311.

*Godet, Frédéric Louis. "L'expiation." *Bulliten théologique* (1860).

Gottschick, Johannes. "Augustins Anschauung von den Erlöserwirkungen." *Zeitschrift für Theologie und Kirche* 11 (1901): 97–213.

———. "Propter Christum: Ein Beitrag zum Verständnis der Versöhnungslehre Luthers." *Zeitschrift für Theologie und Kirche* 7 (1897): 352–84.

———. "Reich Gottes." *PRE³*, XVI, 783–806.

———. "Studien zur Versöhnungslehre des Mittelalters." *Zeitschrift für Kirchengeschichte* 22 (1901): 371–438; 23 (1902): 35–67, 191–222, 321–75; 24 (1903): 15–45, 198–231.

Gould, George P. "Son of Man." *DC*, II, 659–65.

Graaf, H. T. de. "Jesus-Messias volgens Dr. Bruins." *Theologische Tijdschrift* 43/5 (1909): 413–34.

Gressmann, Hugo. "Erwiderung auf Prof. F. Giesebrechts Besprechung von H. Gressmanns *Ursprung der israelitisch-jüdischen Eschatologie*." *Theologische Studien und Kritiken* 81 (1908): 307–17.

Grünberg, Paul. "Spener." *PRE³*, XVIII, 609–22.

Güder, Eduard. "Doppelter Stand Christi." *PRE¹*, XV, 784–99.

Guthe, Hermann. "Ophir." *PRE³*, XIV, 400–404.

Hackmann, H[einrich?]. "Der Erlösungsgedanken und seine Voraussetzungen in Buddhismus und Christentum." *Zeitschrift für Theologie und Kirche* 17 (1907): 34–52.

Häring, Theodor. "Einfachste Worte für eine grosse Sache, die Stellung Jesu im christlichen Glauben." *Zeitschrift für Theologie und Kirche* 19 (1909): 177–203.

———. "Gehört die Auferstehung Jesu zum Glaubensgrund?" *Zeitschrift für Theologie und Kirche* 7 (1897): 332–51.

———. "In welchem Sinn dürfen wir uns immer noch 'Göttinger' heissen? Albrecht Ritschls Bedeutung für die Gegenwart." *Zeitschrift für Theologie und Kirche* 20 (1910): 165–96.

Harnack, A. von. "Apostolisches Symbolum." *PRE³*, I, 741–55.

Harris, C. "Brethren of Christ." *DC*, I, 232–36.

Hein, Arnold. "Die Christologie van D. Fr. Strausz." *Zeitschrift für Theologie und Kirche* 16 (1906): 321–46.

Hencke, Frederick G. "The Gift of Tongues and Related Phenomena at the Present

Day." *American Journal of Theology* 13 (1909): 193–206.

Herford, R. Travers. "Christ in Jewish Literature." *DC*, II, 876–82.

Hering, A. "Die dogmatische Bedeutung und der religiöse Werth der übernatürlichen Geburt Christi." *Zeitschrift für Theologie und Kirche* 5 (1895): 58–91.

Herrmann, W. "Die Busse des evangelischen Christen." *Zeitschrift für Theologie und Kirche* 1 (1891): 28–81.

———. "Ueber die Liebe Gottes." *Zeitschrift für Theologie und Kirche* 20 (1910): 78–153.

*Hilgenfeld. "Die Geburts- und Kindheitsgeschichte Jesu." *Zeitschrift für wissenschaftliche Theologie* (1901): 204–15.

*Hillmann. "Die Kindesheitsgeschichte Jesu nach Lukas." *Jahrbuch für protestantische Theologie* 27 (1891): 192.

*Höhne. "Wandlungen des Christusbildes bei seiner Wanderung durch die Geschichte." *Der Beweis des Glaubens* 40 (1904): 33–49.

*Hollensteiner. "Harnack und Bousset." *Neue kirchliche Zeitschrift* (1906): 517–33.

Holliday, William Alexander. "The Effect of the Fall of Man on Nature." *Presbyterian and Reformed Review* 7/3 (October 1896): 611–21.

Hollmann, Georg Wilhelm. "Die Berliner Kirchenväterausgabe." *Theologische Rundschau* 9 (1906): 239–86.

———. "Leben und Lehre Jesu." *Theologische Rundschau* 7 (1904): 197–211.

———. "Das leere Grab und die gegenwärtige Verhandlungen über die Auferstehung Jesu." *Theologische Rundschau* 9 (1906): 119–58.

*Horn. "Der Kampf um die leibliche Auferstehung des Herrn." *Neue kirchliche Zeitschrift* (1902): 241–?

Hugenholtz, R. "De Christologie en de huidige godsdienstwetenschap." *Theologisch Tijdschrift* 15 (1881): 30–52.

Ihmels, Ludwig. "Jesus und Paulus." *Neue kirchliche Zeitschrift* 17 (1906): 453–83, 485–516.

Jonker, A. J. Th. "De beteekenis van de nieuwste beschouwingen over erfelijkheid en toerekenbaarheid voor de dienaaren van het Evangelie." *Theologisch Studiën* 12 (1894): 291–322.

Kähler, Martin. "Christologie, Schriftlehre." *PRE³*, IV, 4–16.

———. "Schuld." *PRE³*, XVII, 784–89.

Kant, I. "Mutmasslicher Anfang der Menschengeschichte." *Berlinische Monatsschrift* 7 (January–June 1786).

Kattenbusch, Ferdinand. "Der geschichtliche Sinn des apostolischen Symbols." *Zeitschrift für Theologie und Kirche* 11 (1901): 407–28.

*———. "Zur Würdigung des Apostolikums." *Hefte zur Christlichen Welt* (1892).

Kawerau, Gustav. "Antinistische Streitigkeiten." *PRE³*, I, 585–92.

———. "Fünfundzwanzig Jahre Lutherforschung 1883–1908." *Theologische Studien und Kritiken* 81 (1908): 334–61, 576–612.

Kirn, O. "Aus der dogmatischen Arbeit der Gegenwart." *Zeitschrift für Theologie und Kirche* 18 (1908): 337–88.

Kittel, Rudolf. "Segen und Fluch." *PRE³*, XVIII, 148–54.

Knowling, R. J. "Birth of Christ." *DC*, I, 202–8.

Kögel, Julius. "Der Begriff Τελειουν im Hebräerbrief." In *Theologische Studien: Martin Kähler zum 6. Januar 1905,* edited by Friedrich Giesebrecht and Martin Kähler, 35–68. Leipzig: Deichert, 1905.

Kolde, Theodor. "Irving." *PRE³*, IX, 424–37.

König, Eduard. "Der Jeremiasspruch Jer. 7:21–23 nach seinen Sinn, seiner kulturgeschichtlichen Stellung und seinem geistesgeschichtlichen Anlass untersucht." *Theologische Studien und Kritiken* 79 (April 1906): 327–93.

———. "Die religionsgeschichtliche Bedeutung der Patriarchen." *Glauben und Wissen* (1900): 361–77.

Köstlin, Julius. "Busse." *PRE³*, III, 584–91.

———. "Irving." *PRE²*, VII, 152–60.

*Krauss. "Ueber das Mittlerwerk nach dem Schema des munus triplex." *Jahrbuch für deutsche Theologie* (1872): 595–655.

Kristensen, W. B. "Een of twee boomen in het Paradijsverhaal." *Theologisch Tijdschrift* 42 (May 1908): 215–33.

Krop, Frédéric J. "Nog eens: Welke beteekenis heeft de dood van Jezus Christus, volgens Zijn eigen verklaringen in de evangeliën voor mensch en menschheid?" *Theologische Studiën* 24 (1906): 153–75.

Krüger, Gustav. "Apollinaris." *PRE³*, I, 671–76.

———. "Doketen." *PRE³*, IV, 764–65.

———. "Gnosis, Gnosticismus." *PRE³*, VI, 728–38.

———. "Monophysiten." *PRE³*, XIII, 372–401.

———. "Monotheleten." *PRE³*, XIII, 401–13.

Kuhn, C. H. "Herediteit en pessimisme." *De Gids* 18/3 (July 1900): 114–34.

Kunze, Johannes W. "Anselm." *PRE³*, I, 562–70.

Kuyper, Abraham. "Van de engelen." *De Heraut* 906 (May 5, 1895): 1–2.

Laidlaw, John. "Psychology." *DB*, IV, 163–69.

Lamers, G. H. "Het probleem des lijdens." *Theologische Studiën* 14 (1896): 393–406.

*Landerer. "Das Verhältnis von Gnade und Freiheit in der Aneignung des Heils." *Jahrbuch für deutsche Theologie* (1857): 500–603.

Lauterberg, Moritz. "Höllenfahrt Christi." *PRE³*, VIII, 193–206.

Leipoldt. Johannes. "Der Begriff meritum in Anselms von Canterbury Versöhnungslehre." *Theologische Studien und Kritike* 67 (1904): 300–308.

Lelièvre, Ch. "La doctrine de la justification par la foi dans la théologie de Calvin." *Revue Chrétienne* 56 (1909): 699–710.

Lemme, Ludwig. "Leiden."*PRE³*, XI, 360–63.

Liebe, R. "Ueber die Liebe Gottes." *Zeitschrift für Theologie und Kirche* 19 (1909): 347–410.

Lindsay, Thomas M. "Christ in Reformation Theology." *DC*, II, 860–64.

*Linwurzky. "Die Religionspsychologie: Ein neuer Zweig der empirischen Psychologie." *Stimmen aus Maria-Laach* (1910): 505–19.

Lipsius, Richard Adelbert. "Luthers Lehre von der Busse." *Jahrbuch für protestantische Theologie* (1892): 161–340.

Lobstein, Paul. "Études critiques de dogmatique protestante." *Revue de théologie et de philosophie* 24/2 (March 1891): 171–212.

Lock, W. "Kenosis." *DB*, II, 835.

Lombard, Emile. "Le parler en langues à Corinthe d'après les textes de Paul et les analogies modernes." *Revue de Théologie et de Philosophie* 5 (1909): 5–52.

Loofs, Friedrich Armin. "Christologie, Kirchenlehre."*PRE³*, IV, 16–56.

———. "Dogmengeschichte." *PRE³*, IV, 752–64.

———. "Eutyches." *PRE³*, V, 635–47.

———. "Kenosis." *PRE³*, X, 246–63.

———. "Methodismus." *PRE³*, XII, 747–801.

———. "Nestorius." *PRE³*, XIII, 736–49.

*Lotz. "Der Bund vom Sinai." *Neue kirchliche Zeitschrift* (1901).

*Lucassen, C. "Der Glaube Jesu Christi." *Neue kirchliche Zeitschrift* (1895): 337–47.

Lütgert, Wilhelm. "Der Mensch aus dem Himmel." In *Greifswalder Studien: Theologische Abhandlungen Hermann Cremer zum 25 jährigen Professorjubiläum,* edited by Samuel Oettli and Hermann Cremer, 207–28. Gütersloh: Bertelsmann, 1895.

Machen, J. Gresham. "The New Testament Account of the Birth of Jesus." *Princeton Theological Review* 3 (1905): 641–70; 4 (1906): 37–81.

Mackintosh, Robert. "Universalism." *DC*, II, 783–86.

Martin, A. Stuart. "Christ in Modern Thought." *DC*, II, 867–76.

Masterman, E. W. Gurney. "Mount of Olives." *DC*, II, 206–8.

Matthes, Jan Carel. "De boom des levens." *Theologisch Tijdschrift* 24 (1890): 365–70.

———. "De inrichting van den Eeredienst door Jerobeam." *Theologisch Tijdschrift* 24 (1890): 225–39.

———. "Oorsprong en gevolgen der zonde volgens het O.T." *Theologisch Tijdschrift* 24 (1890): 225–54.

Mayer, E. W. "Über das Leid der Welt." *Glauben und Wissen* 6 (1908): 104–10.

———. "Ueber Religionspsychologie." *Zeitschrift für Theologie und Kirche* 18 (1908): 293–324.

———. "Zum Stand der Frage nach dem Wesen der Religion." *Theologische Rundschau* (1910): 1–15, 45–63.

Mayor, Joseph Bickersteth. "Brethren of the Lord." *DB*, I, 320–26.

———. "Mary." *DB*, III, 286–93.

Meyboom, H. U. "Jezus de Nazoraeer." *Theologisch Tijdschrift* 39 (1905): 512–36.

———. "Loman Redivivus." *Theologisch Tijdschrift* 41 (1907): 1–17.

*Meyer, A. "Der Glaube Jesu und der Glaube an Jesum." *Neue kirchliche Zeitschrift* (1900): 621–44.

Milligan, George. "Burial." *DC*, I, 241–42.

Moeller, E. von. "Die Anselmsche Satisfactio und die Busse des germ. Strafrechts." *Theologische Studien und Kritiken* (1899): 627–34.

Moffatt, James. "Trial of Jesus." *DC*, II, 749–59.

Müller, G. F. Karl. "Coccejus." *PRE*[3], IV, 186–94.

———. "Jesu dreifaches Amt." *PRE*[3], VIII, 733–41.

Müller, Joseph T. "Zinzendorf." *PRE*[3], XXI, 679–703.

Müller, Nikolaus. "Christusbilder." *PRE*[3], IV, 63–82.

Nestle, Eberhard. "Jesus." *DC*, I, 859–61.

Newman, Albert Henry. "Christ in the Middle Ages." *DC*, II, 853–60.

Niebergall, F. "Die Bedeutung der Religionspsychologie für die Praxis in Kirche und Schule." *Zeitschrift für Theologie und Kirche* 19 (1909): 411–74.

Niebergall, J. "Die Heilsnotwendigkeit des Kreuztodes Jesu Christi." *Zeitschrift für Theologie und Kirche* 7 (1897): 461–512.

*Nösgen, Karl Friedrich. "Die Geburtsgeschichte Christi in Lukas." *Die Studierstube* (1903).

Nuelsen, John L. "Methodismus in Amerika." *PRE*[3], XIII, 1–25.

Oehler, Gustav Friedrich. "Abhandlung über das Verhältniss der alttestamentlichen Prophetie zur heidnischen Mantik." In *Glückwunschschreiben an die Universität Breslau zu der vom 2. bis 5. August 1861 zu begehenden Jubelfeier ihres fünfzigjährigen Bestehens vor Rector und Senat der Universität Tübingen*. Tübingen: Fues, 1861.

Oesterley, W. O. E. "Blood." *DC*, I, 214–16.

Oort, Henricus Lucas. "Iets over het Lam Gods." *Theologisch Tijdschrift* 42 (1908): 1–10.

Orelli, Conrad. "Messias." *PRE*[3], XIII, 723–39.

———. "Opferkultus des Alten Testaments." *PRE*[3], XIV, 386–400.

Orr, James. "Kingdom of God." *DB*, II, 834–56.

———. "Ransom." *DC*, II, 468–69.

Paterson, William P. "Sacrifice." *DB*, IV, 329–49.

*Pauli. "Ueber die Liebe Gottes." *Zeitschrift für Theologie und Kirche* 20 (1910): 154–59.

Pfleiderer, Otto. "Die Theologie der Ritschl'schen Schule, nach ihrer religionsphilosophischen Grundlage kritisch beleuchtet." *Jahrbuch für Protestantische Theologie* 17/3 (1889): 321–83.

Pierson, A. "Over ethika." *De Gids* 13/4 (November 1895): 245–63.

Plantz, Samuel. "Vicarious Sacrifice." *DC*, II, 793–800.

*Plummer, Alfred. "The Advance of Christ as Σοφια." *The Expositor* (1891).

———. "Prayer." *DC*, II, 390–93.

*Pressensé, E. de. "Essai sur le dogme de la rédemption." *Bulliten théologique* (1867).

Ramsay, W. M. "A Historical Commentary on the Epistle to the Galatians." *The Expositor* 4/4 (November 1898): 326–39.

Reischle, Max Wilhelm Theodor. "Der Streit über die Begründung des Glaubens auf dem geschichtlichen Christus." *Zeitschrift für Theologie und Kirche* 7 (1897): 171–264.

*———. "Zur Frage nach der leiblichen Auferstehung Jesu Christi." *Christliche Welt* (1900).

*Riggenbach. "Jesus trug die Sünde der Welt." *Neue kirchliche Zeitschrift* (1907): 295–307.

Ritschl, Otto. "Erlösung." *PRE*³, V, 460–69.

———. "Der geschichtliche Christus, der christliche Glaube und die theologische Wissenschaft." *Zeitschrift für Theologie und Kirche* 3 (1893): 371–426.

———. "Versöhnung." *PRE*³, XX, 552–76.

Robertson, Archibald Thomas. "Cross." *DC*, II, 394–96.

Rumball, Edwin A. "The Sinlessness of Jesus." *Hibbert Journal* 5/3 (April 1907): 600–605.

Sanday, William. "Jesus Christ." *DB*, II, 603–53.

———. "Paul." *DC*, II, 886–92.

———. "Son of God." *DB*, IV, 570–79.

Scheel, Otto. "Individualismus und Gemeinschaftsleben in der Auseinandersetzung Luthers mit Karlstadt 1524/25." *Zeitschrift für Theologie und Kirche* 17 (1907): 352–90.

———. "Die moderne Religionspsychologie." *Zeitschrift für Theologie und Kirche* 18 (1908): 1–38.

———. "Zu Augustinus Anschauung von der Erlösung durch Christus." *Theologische Studien und Kritiken* (1904): 401–33, 491–553.

Schenkel. "Gewissen." *PRE*¹, V, 129–42.

Schmidt, H. "Zur Lehre v. d. Person Christi." *Neue kirchliche Zeitschrift* (1896): 972–1005.

Schnehen, Wilhelm von. "Die Ewigkeit des Glaubens." *Glauben und Wissen* (1907): 91–99.

Schöberlein, Ludwig. "Versöhnung." *PRE*¹, XVII, 87–143.

*Scholz, A. "Besteht ein wesentlicher Unterschied zwischen dem johann. Christusbilde und dem der Synoptiker?" *Glauben und Wissen* (1908): 243.

*Schucklebier, [?]. "Ein Streifzug durch die antike Philosophie, als die Zeit erfüllt war." *Neue kirchliche Zeitschrift* (1908): 935–72.

Schultz, Hermann. "Der ordo salutis in der Dogmatik." *Theologische Studien und Kritiken* 72 (1899): 330–445.

Schultze, Maxim. Victor. "Kreuz und Kreuzigung." *PRE*³, XI, 90–92.

Schwartzkopff, Paul. "Gottes Liebe und Heiligkeit." *Theologische Studien und Kritiken* 73 (1910): 300–313.

———. "Der Teufels- und Dämonenglaube Jesu." *Zeitschrift für Theologie und Kirche* 7 (1897): 289–330.

Seeberg, Reinhold. "Communicatio idiomatum." *PRE*³, IV, 254–61.

———. "Evangelium quadraginta dierum." *Neue kirchliche Zeitschrift* (1905): 335–531.

———. "Heilsordnung." *PRE*³, VII, 593–99.

Sell, Edward, and David Samuel Margoliouth. "Christ in Mohammedan Literature." *DC*, II, 882–86.

Simons, David. "Het congres van crim. anthropologie te Amsterdam." *De Gids* 19/4 (December 1901): 483–519.

———. "Nieuwe Richtingen in de strafrechtwetenschap." *De Gids* 18/2 (April 1900): 48–84.

———. "Nieuwe Strafrechtspolitiek." *De Gids* 19/2 (May 1901): 253–96.

Simpson, W. J. Sparrow. "Resurrection of Christ." *DC*, II, 505–14.

Smith, David. "Crucifixion." *DC*, II, 397–99.

———. "Dereliction." *DC*, I, 447–48.

Stade, B. D. "Die messianische Hoffnung im Psalter." *Zeitschrift für Theologie und Kirche* 3 (1893): 369–413.

Stalker, James. "Sinlessness." *DC*, II, 636–39.

———. "Son of God." *DC*, II, 654–59.

*Steinbeck. "Bensow, *Die Lehre von der Kenose.*" *Theologisches Literaturblatt* 25/4 (January 22, 1904): cols. 44–46.

*Steude, E. G. "Die neueren Verhandlungen über die Auferstehung Jesu Christi." *Der Beweis des Glaubens* 42 (1906).

———. "Wie ein moderner Seelenarzt über Jesus urteilt." *Der Beweis des Glaubens* 42 (1906): 325–32.

*Steudel. "Die Wahrheit von der Präexistenz Christi in ihrer Bedeutung für christliches Glauben und Leben." *Neue kirchliche Zeitschrift* (December 1900).

Stevenson, W. B. "Benediction." *DC*, I, 189–91.

Strack, Herman L. "Zur alttestamentlichen Theologie." *Theologisches Literaturblatt* 19/5 (February 4, 1898): 49–53.

*Strahtmann, Hermann. "Calvins Lehre von der Busse in ihrer späteren Gestalt." *Theologische Studien und Kritiken* 82 (1909): 402–45.

Stuckert, Carl. "Propter Christum." *Zeitschrift für Theologie und Kirche* 16 (1906): 143–74.

Sweet, Louis M. "Heathen Wonderbirths and the Birth of Christ." *Princeton Theological Review* 6 (1908): 83–117.

Swete, Henry Barclay. "Holy Spirit." *DB*, II, 402–11.

Thieme, K. "Die neuesten Christologien im Verhältnis zum Selbstbewusstsein Jesu." *Zeitschrift für Theologie und Kirche* 18 (1908): 401–72.

Tholuck, August. "Erneute Untersuchung über sarx als Quelle der Sünde." *Theologische Studien und Kritiken* 28/3 (March 1855): 477–97.

Thomas, W. H. Griffith. "Priest." *DC*, II, 415–18.

Tideman, Johannes. "Remonstrantisme en Ramisme." In *Studiën en bijdragen op 't gebied der historisch theologie*, edited by W. Moll and J. G. de Hoop Scheffer, vol. III, 389–429. 4 vols. Amsterdam: G. L. Funke, 1870–80.

Traub, Friedrich. "Die Gegenwart des Gottesreiches in den Parabeln vom Senfkorn und Sauerteig, von der selbst wachsenden Saat, dem Unkraut und dem Fischnetz." *Zeitschrift für Theologie und Kirche* 15 (1905): 58–75.

———. "Die religionsgeschichtliche Methode und die systematische Theologie: Eine Auseinandersetzung mit Tröltschs theologischem Reformprogramm." *Zeitschrift für Theologie und Kirche* 11 (1901): 301–40.

Tschackert, Paul. "Osiander." *PRE*[3], XIV, 501–9.

Uhlhorn, Gerhard. "Ebioniten." *PRE*[3], V, 125–28.

*Ullman. "Sündlosigkeit Jesu." *PRE*[1].

Van Loenen Martinet, J. "Een theodicie?" *Teyler's Theologisch Tijdschrift* 6 (1908): 372–96.

Van Manen, W. C. "Een oudsyrische vertaling." *De Gids* 13 (July 1895): 88–104.

———. "Pontiaan van Hattem." *De Gids* 49/4 (October 1885): 84–115.

Vellenga, G. "De Voldoening." *Theologische Studiën* 24 (1906): 269–89, 377–97.

Vischer, Eb. "Jesus und Paulus." *Theologische Rundschau* 8 (1905): 129–43.

———. "Wernles Einführung in das theologische Studium." *Theologische Rundschau* 11 (1908): 291–322.

*Voo, B. D. van der. "De boom des levens." *Tijdspiegel* (1909).

Vorwerk, Dietrich. "Die Naturkatastrophen und die moderne Literatur." *Der Beweis des Glaubens* 44 (1908): 104–10.

Vos, Geerhardus. "Covenant." *DC*, I, 373–80.

———. "The Priesthood of Christ in the Epistle to the Hebrews." *Princeton Theological Review* 5 (1907): 423–47.

———. "Recent Criticism of the Early Prophets." *Presbyterian and Reformed Review* 9 (April 1898): 214–18.

———. "Saviour." *DC*, II, 571–73.

Vries, Hugo de. "Eenheid in Veranderlijkjeid." *Album der Natuur* (1898): 65–80.

Wagenmann, J. "Kenotiker und Kryptiker." *PRE*[2], VII, 640–46.

Wagner, W. "Über σωζειν und seine Derivata im Neuen Testament." *Zeitschrift für die neutestamentliche Wissenschaft* 6 (1905): 201–35.

*Wallis. "Die Erscheinungen des auferstandenen Christus." *Die Studierstube* (1906).

Walther, D. "Lutherana I." *Theologisches Literaturblatt* 27/40 (October 5, 1906): cols. 473–75.

———. "Neue Lutherschriften." *Theologisches Literaturblatt* 26/43 (October 27, 1905): cols. 505–11; 26/44 (November 3, 1905): cols. 521–24.

Walther, Wilhelm. "Luther und die Lüge." *Theologisches Literaturblatt* 25/35 (August 26, 1904): cols. 409–17.

*———. "Das Wesen der Sünde." *Neue kirchliche Zeitschrift* (1898): 284–85.

Warfield, Benjamin Breckenridge. "The Making of the Westminster Confession, and Especially of Its Chapter on the Decree of God." *Presbyterian and Reformed Review* 12 (1901): 226–83.

———. "Modern Theories of the Atonement." *Princeton Theological Review* 1 (1903): 81–92.

———. "Recent Theological Literature." *Presbyterian and Reformed Review* 10 (1899): 701–25.

*Weidel, Karl. "Studien über den Einfluss des Weissagungsbeweises auf die evangelische Geschichte." *Theologische Studien und Kritiken* 83 (1910): 83–?.

Weinel, H. "Ist unsere Verkündigung von Jesus unhaltbar geworden?" *Zeitschrift für Theologie und Kirche* 20 (1910): 1–88.

Weiss, Johannes. "Dämonen." *PRE*[3], IV, 408–10.

———. "Dämonische." *PRE*[3], IV, 410–19.

Weizsäcker, K. H. von. "Um was handelt es sich in dem Streit über die Versöhnungslehre?" *Jahrbuch für deutsche Theologie* (1858): 155–88.

———. "Zu der Lehre v. Wesen der Sünde." *Jahrbuch für deutsche Theologie* (1856): 131–95.

Wendland, Paul. "Σωτηρ: Eine religionsgeschichtliche Untersuchung." *Zeitschrift für*

neutestamentliche Wissenschaft 5 (1904): 335–53.

*Werner, Joh. "Der erste antinom. Streit." *Neue kirchliche Zeitschrift* (1904): 801–24, 860–78.

Weser, Hermann. "Die verschiedenen Auffassungen vom Teufel im Neuen Testament." *Studien und Kritiken* 55/2 (1882): 284–303.

Whitehouse, Owen C. "Demon, Devil." *DB*, I, 590–94.

———. "Satan." *DB*, IV, 407–12.

Wildeboer, G. "De Dekaloog." *Theologische Studiën* 21 (1903): 109–18.

———. "Nog eens de Dekaloog." *Theologische Studiën* 24 (1906): 94–110.

———. "De straf der zonde volgens Gen. III." *Theologische Studiën* 8 (1890): 351–62.

Willigen, Adriaan van der. "Oordelk. Overzigt over de versch. Wijzen, op welke men zich heeft voorgesteld het verband tusschen den dood van Jezus Christus en de zaligheid der menschen." *Godgeleerde Bijdragen* 2 (1828): 485–603.

Witham, A. R. "Christ in the Early Church." *DC*, II, 849–53.

Wobbermin. "Loisy contra Harnack." *Zeitschrift für Theologie und Kirche* 15 (1905): 76–102.

Wünsche, August. "Teufel." *PRE*[3], XIX, 564–74.

Zahn, Theodor. "Die syrische Evangelienübersetzung vom Sinai." *Theologisches Literaturblatt* 16/3 (January 18, 1895): 25–30.

Ziegler, Karl. "Die ethische Versöhnungslehre im kirchlichen Unterricht." *Zeitschrift für Theologie und Kirche* 5 (1895): 1–57, 169–243.

———. "Der Glaube an die Auferstehung Jesu Christi." *Zeitschrift für Theologie und Kirche* 6 (1896): 219–64.

Zöckler, Otto. "Hexen- und Hexenprozess." *PRE*[3], VIII, 30–36.

———. "Jesus Christus." *PRE*[3], IX, 1–43.

———. "Maria." *PRE*[3], XIII, 309–36.

SELECT SCRIPTURE INDEX

Ed. note: The Scripture index follows the pattern of the Dutch original, indicating only those passages that receive more or less detailed attention. The key Scripture texts for all four volumes of the *Gereformeerde Dogmatiek* appear at the conclusion of volume 4.

Name Index

Subject Index